Lecture Notes in Computer Science **16207**

The series Lecture Notes in Computer Science (LNCS), including its subseries Lecture Notes in Artificial Intelligence (LNAI) and Lecture Notes in Bioinformatics (LNBI), has established itself as a medium for the publication of new developments in computer science and information technology research, teaching, and education.

LNCS enjoys close cooperation with the computer science R & D community, the series counts many renowned academics among its volume editors and paper authors, and collaborates with prestigious societies. Its mission is to serve this international community by providing an invaluable service, mainly focused on the publication of conference and workshop proceedings and postproceedings. LNCS commenced publication in 1973.

Christina Boura · Atefeh Mashatan · Ali Miri
Editors

Selected Areas in Cryptography – SAC 2025

32nd International Conference
Toronto, ON, Canada, August 13–15, 2025
Revised Selected Papers

Springer

Editors
Christina Boura
Université Paris Cité
Paris, France

Atefeh Mashatan
Toronto Metropolitan University
Toronto, ON, Canada

Ali Miri
Toronto Metropolitan University
Toronto, ON, Canada

ISSN 0302-9743 ISSN 1611-3349 (electronic)
Lecture Notes in Computer Science
ISBN 978-3-032-10535-6 ISBN 978-3-032-10536-3 (eBook)
https://doi.org/10.1007/978-3-032-10536-3

This Springer imprint is published by the registered company Springer Nature Switzerland AG
The registered company address is: Gewerbestrasse 11, 6330 Cham, Switzerland

Preface

Selected Areas in Cryptography (SAC) is Canada's annual research conference on cryptography, held since 1994. The 32nd edition of SAC took place at Toronto Metropolitan University in Toronto, Ontario, Canada, from August 13–15, 2025, and was preceded by the SAC Summer School on August 11–12, 2025.

Each SAC conference covers four areas of cryptography. Three are permanent:

– Design and analysis of symmetric-key primitives and cryptosystems, including block and stream ciphers, hash functions, MAC algorithms, cryptographic permutations and authenticated encryption schemes;
– Efficient implementations of symmetric and public-key cryptography; and
– Mathematical and algorithmic aspects of applied cryptology.

The fourth area is a special topic that changes with each edition. For SAC 2025, the topic was:

– Machine learning and cryptography: applications of machine learning to cryptography and cryptanalysis, and application of cryptanalytic techniques against machine learning algorithms.

SAC 2025 also welcomed papers in any of the above areas with a particular focus on post-quantum cryptography.

For the second consecutive year, SAC offered two submission deadlines, each with an independent review cycle. As in 2024, and even more successfully this year, this model attracted more submissions and, consequently, more accepted papers. The proceedings therefore appear in two volumes: Volume 1 covers symmetric-key cryptography and implementations (Areas 1–2), while Volume 2 covers public-key cryptography (Area 3) and physical security (related to Area 2).

In total, SAC 2025 received 49 submissions for the first cycle and 60 submissions for the second cycle, 11 of which were revised resubmissions from the first. All submissions were evaluated through a double-blind peer review process and received three or four reviews (depending on whether one of the authors was a Program Committee member). In total, 350 reviews were written by the Program Committee, which consisted of 51 members, with the additional help of 45 external reviewers. After review and discussion, 29 papers were accepted for publication and presentation at the conference.

More specifically, of the submissions in the first cycle, 9 were accepted and 6 were invited to resubmit a revised version in the second cycle. Of the submissions in the second cycle, 20 were accepted, including 4 revised resubmissions from the first cycle.

SAC 2025 featured three invited talks: the Stafford Tavares Invited Lecture by Pierre-Alain Fouque (University of Rennes and Institut Universitaire de France) on "Reducing the Number of Qubits in Quantum Factoring"; a talk by Stjepan Picek (University of Zagreb and Radboud University) entitled "AI to the Rescue: Where AI Meets Cryptography"; and a talk by Adi Shamir (Weizmann Institute of Science) on "Deep Neural Cryptography."

The program also included the two-day SAC Summer School. The first day featured lectures on "Differential Cryptanalysis" by Patrick Derbez (Inria) and on "Post-Quantum Cryptography" by Doug Stinson (University of Waterloo). The second day began with a lecture by Clémence Bouvier (Inria) and continued with a lecture by Stjepan Picek (University of Zagreb and Radboud University) on "Deep Learning-Based Side-Channel Analysis."

We would like to thank all our colleagues who helped to make SAC 2025 a success, including all authors of submitted papers. We especially thank the Program Committee members and the external reviewers for their excellent work under a tight schedule, and the SAC steering committee, particularly Douglas Stebila, for their helpful advice and guidance. We would also like to thank the invited speakers and the summer school lecturers for their interesting contributions to the program and the fruitful discussions that they generated. We are appreciative of the financial support provided by Rogers Cybersecure Catalyst, the Office of the Provost and Office of the President of TMU, the Faculty of Sciences at TMU, the Communications Security Establishment and Springer, and thank all the student volunteers for their assistance and help with the local arrangements and logistics.

September 2025

Christina Boura
Atefeh Mashatan
Ali Miri

Organization

Program Chairs

Christina Boura	Université Paris Cité, France
Atefeh Mashatan	Toronto Metropolitan University, Canada
Ali Miri	Toronto Metropolitan University, Canada

Program Committee

Carlisle Adams	University of Ottawa, Canada
Riham AlTawy	University of Victoria, Canada
Frederik Armknecht	University of Mannheim, Germany
Melissa Azouaoui	NXP Semiconductors, Germany
Zhenzhen Bao	Tsinghua University, China
Xavier Bonnetain	Inria, France
Pierre Briaud	Simula UiB, Norway
Sofia Celi	Brave, Portugal
Liqun Chen	University of Surrey, UK
Ilaria Chillotti	DESILO, South Korea
Thomas Debris-Alazard	Inria, France
Luca De Feo	IBM Research Europe, Switzerland
Patrick Derbez	Inria, France
Itai Dinur	Ben-Gurion University of the Negev, Israel and Georgetown University, USA
Orr Dunkelman	University of Haifa, Israel and Technische Universität Berlin, Germany
Avijit Dutta	TCG CREST and AcSIR, India
Maria Eichlseder	Graz University of Technology, Austria
Aleksander Essex	Western University, Canada
Sébastien Gambs	Université du Québec à Montréal, Canada
David Gérault	Technology Innovation Institute, UAE
Guang Gong	University of Waterloo, Canada
Aurore Guillevic	Inria, France
Arash Habibi Lashkari	York University, Canada
Rachelle Heim Boissier	UCLouvain, Belgium
Kai Hu	Shandong University, China
Tetsu Iwata	Nagoya University, Japan

David Jao	University of Waterloo and evolutionQ, Canada
Philippe Lamontagne	National Research Council of Canada and Université de Montréal, Canada
Kalikinkar Mandal	University of New Brunswick, Canada
Bart Mennink	Radboud University, The Netherlands
Kazuhiko Minematsu	NEC and Yokohama National University, Japan
Ruben Niederhagen	Academia Sinica, Taiwan and University of Southern Denmark, Denmark
Svetla Nikova	KU Leuven, Belgium
Daniel Panario	Carleton University, Canada
Léo Perrin	Inria, France
Thomas Peyrin	Nanyang Technological University, Singapore
Stjepan Picek	University of Zagreb, Croatia and Radboud University, The Netherlands
Elizabeth A. Quaglia	Royal Holloway, University of London, UK
Shahram Rasoolzadeh	Ruhr University Bochum, Germany
Matthieu Rivain	CryptoExperts, France
Rei Safavi-Naini	University of Calgary, Canada
Simona Samardjiska	Radboud University, The Netherlands
André Schrottenloher	Inria, France
Benjamin Smith	Inria and École Polytechnique, France
Douglas Stebila	University of Waterloo, Canada
Emmanuel Thomé	Inria, France
Monika Trimoska	Eindhoven University of Technology, The Netherlands
Serge Vaudenay	EPFL, Switzerland
Huapeng Wu	University of Windsor, Canada
Liang Xue	York University, Canada
Amr Youssef	Concordia University, Canada

Additional Reviewers

Aysajan Abidin
Sofiane Azogagh
Mohammadtaghi Badakhshan
Ward Beullens
Zelma Aubin Birba
Chinmoy Biswas
Wonseok Choi
Kunal Dey
Max Duparc
Nada El Kassem
Tako Boris Fouotsa
Lewis Glabush
Shibam Ghosh
Scott Griffy
ZeZhou Hou
Vahid Jahandideh
Tanmayi Jandhyala
Arthur Lavice
Virginie Lallemand
Laura Madison

Long Meng
Mohamed Mobarak
Amin Mohamadali
Christopher Newton
Ngoc Khanh Nguyen
Somnath Panja
Alice Pellet–Mary
Ahmad Ramazanipour
Vincent Rijmen
Francisco Rodriguez-Henriquez
Lawrence Roy
Susanta Samanta
Bishakha Sarkar
Okan Seker
Amit Singh Bhati
Abdullah Talayhan
Élise Tasso
Adrian Thillard
Yangguang Tian
Michiel Verbauwhede
Linya Wang
Yalan Wang
Yuntao Wang
Bruce Xu
Bo-Yin Yang
Liu Zhang
Zhenda Zhang

Invited Talks

AI to the Rescue: Where AI Meets Cryptography

Stjepan Picek

University of Zagreb, Croatia and Radboud University, The Netherlands
stjepan.picek@ru.nl

Abstract. In recent years, artificial intelligence (AI) has become an emerging technology to assess security and privacy. Despite difficult beginnings, today, AI is also used in cryptography, allowing faster (and sometimes) better results than other techniques. AI is successfully applied in a range of cryptographic contexts, including profiled side-channel attacks using neural networks, modeling and attacking physically unclonable functions, detection and classification of hardware Trojans, and even assisting differential cryptanalysis. However, this convergence of AI and cryptography brings a unique set of challenges. The black-box nature of many AI models, the difficulty of ensuring reproducibility, and concerns around adversarial manipulation all pose significant obstacles. In the first part of the talk, we will highlight success stories where AI improved the state of the art in cryptography. In the second part of the talk, we will examine what cryptography can do for the security of machine learning. We will cover examples like differential cryptanalysis used for model stealing, indistinguishable backdoors, and cryptography enabling privacy for neural networks. Finally, we will conclude the talk by discussing diverse challenges and future research directions.

Reducing the Number of Qubits in Quantum Factoring

Pierre-Alain Fouque

University of Rennes and Institut Universitaire de France, France
Pierre-Alain.Fouque@univ-rennes1.fr

Abstract. In this talk, I will recall Shor's quantum algorithm, then its version by Ekera-Hastad through the computation of short discrete-log, before describing our improvement via the May-Schlieper hashing technique.

Deep Neural Cryptography

Adi Shamir

Weizmann Institute of Science, Israel
adi.shamir@weizmann.ac.il

Abstract. The wide adoption of deep neural networks (DNNs) raises the question of how we can equip them with a desired cryptographic functionality (e.g., to decrypt an encrypted input, to verify that this input is authorized, or to hide a secure watermark in the output). The problem is that cryptographic primitives are typically designed to run on digital computers that use Boolean gates to map sequences of bits to sequences of bits, whereas DNNs are a special type of analog computer that uses linear mappings and ReLUs to map vectors of real numbers to vectors of real numbers. In this talk I will describe a new theory of security when digital cryptographic primitives are implemented as ReLU-based DNNs, show that natural implementation techniques are highly insecure, and finally develop a new and completely practical method for implementing any desired cryptographic functionality as a standard ReLU-based DNN in a provably secure and correct way.

Contents

Cryptanalysis of Symmetric Schemes and Primitives

Preimage-Type Attacks for Reduced Ascon-Hash: Application to Ed25519

Marcel Nageler(✉), Lorenz Schmid, and Maria Eichlseder

Graz University of Technology, Graz, Austria
{marcel.nageler,maria.eichlseder}@tugraz.at, schmid.lorenz@protonmail.com

Abstract. Hash functions and extendable output functions are some of the most fundamental building blocks in cryptography. They are often used to build commitment schemes where a committer *binds* themselves to some value that is also hidden from the verifier until the opening is sent. Such commitment schemes are commonly used to build signature schemes, e.g., Ed25519 via Schnorr signatures, or non-interactive zero-knowledge proofs. We specifically analyze the binding security when Ascon-Hash256 or Ascon-XOF128 is used inside of Ed25519, which is closely related to finding second preimages. While there is ample prior work on Ascon-XOF128 and Ascon-Hash256, none of it applies in this setting either because it analyzes short outputs of 64 or 128 bits or because the complexity is above the security claim and generic attack of 128 bits. We show how to exploit the setting of finding a forgery for Ed25519. We find that this setting is quite challenging due to the large 320-bit internal state combined with the 128-bit security level. We propose a second-preimage attack for 1-round Ascon-Hash256 with a complexity of 2^{64} Gaussian eliminations and a random-prefix-preimage attack (also known as Nostradamus attack) for 1-round Ascon-Hash256, for the Ed25519 setting, with complexity $2^{29.7}$ Gaussian eliminations.

Keywords: Digital Signatures · Hash Functions · Preimage Attacks

1 Introduction

The security of hash functions and eXtendable Output Functions (XOF) is commonly discussed by analyzing the classical security notions of preimage resistance, second-preimage resistance and collision resistance. Preimage resistance means that it is difficult to find a message M for a given hash h, such that $\mathcal{H}(M) = h$. Second-preimage resistance means that it is difficult to find a second message M' for a given M (and thus h) such that $\mathcal{H}(M') = \mathcal{H}(M) = h$. Finally, collision resistance means that it is difficult to find messages M, M' such that $\mathcal{H}(M) = \mathcal{H}(M')$. These security notions cover many use cases but are not always an exact fit.

For example, when building a commitment scheme from a hash function, the above notions are not enough. The standard construction is that the committer

C. Boura et al. (Eds.): SAC 2025, LNCS 16207, pp. 3–25, 2026.
https://doi.org/10.1007/978-3-032-10536-3_1

chooses some fixed-length random value R, and then generates the commitment h for M by hashing $h = \mathcal{H}(R\|M)$ and sending h to the verifier. This construction is commonly used in the Fiat-Shamir transformation [FS86] which, in turn, is used for signature schemes like Schnorr signatures [Sch89] and Ed25519 [Nat23] as well as non-interactive zero-knowledge proofs. Later, the commitment can be opened by sending R, M to the verifier who checks whether $\mathcal{H}(R\|M) = h$. Such a scheme needs to be *binding*, i.e., it must be difficult for the committer to change the message M after sending h, and *hiding*, i.e., it must be difficult for the verifier to learn (information about) the message M. While binding security follows from collision resistance of $\mathcal{H}$, hiding security requires additional properties that ensure that the hash function does not leak some part of the message [HM96].

When a commitment scheme is used in a concrete construction, the security requirements might again change. For example, the above hash-based commitment scheme is used in Ed25519, a NIST-standardized deterministic variant of Schnorr signatures. For this setting Neven et al. [NSW09] define the security requirements for hash functions as random-prefix-preimage (rpp) resistance and random-prefix-second-preimage (rpsp) resistance. When formulated in terms of a commitment scheme, rpp security can be phrased as follows. The attacker picks a commitment h and is assigned a random prefix R. Then, the attacker has to find a message M such that $\mathcal{H}(R\|M) = h$. This attack is also called a *Nostradamus* or *chosen-target-forced-prefix* attack and has been applied generically to Merkle-Damgård hashing via the Herding attack [KK06], and in dedicated analysis to AES-based hashing [ZSWH23, DGL+24]. We analyze exactly this setting as it can be used to create forgeries for Schnorr-based signatures, like Ed25519.

The main motivation for this work is the recent standardization of the Ascon family for lightweight cryptography by NIST [Nat25]. These hashing functions are significantly more lightweight than the SHA-2 family, particularly in terms of their area footprint, which is very relevant for embedded devices and other constrained environments. This raises the question whether the currently used SHA-512 in Ed25519 can be replaced by Ascon-XOF128 without loss of security.

Related Work. The Ascon family has been thoroughly analyzed during the CAESAR and NIST LWC competitions, with the hash functions mainly in focus for the last few years. NIST's standardized versions Ascon-XOF128 and Ascon-Hash256 [Nat25] have some minor differences compared to the submitted versions Ascon-XOF and Ascon-Hash [DEMS19a] that were the main target of the analysis, but the results are essentially directly applicable.

While there is ample work on finding preimages for Ascon-XOF128 and Ascon-Hash256, none of it is applicable to the specific setting of Ed25519. We believe this is due to 2 reasons. First, the security claim for Ascon-XOF128 with L-bit output is $\min(128, L)$-bit preimage resistance. As Ascon's rate is 64 bits, we primarily see preimage attacks on 64-bit outputs with complexity below 2^{64}, which can then often be generically extended to preimage attacks on 128-bit outputs with complexity below 2^{128}. Attacking longer outputs is not appealing, since the attack becomes more difficult but the security claim stays 128 bits. The difficulty is primarily that more permutation calls (i.e., more rounds in total) need to be attacked to gain sufficient degrees of freedom and match longer output. However, in 2022 Lefevre and Mennink [LM22] found that the bound for preimage resistance (but not second preimage resistance) is not tight and can be increased to 192 bits for 256-bit outputs. This leads to some preimage attacks on Ascon-Hash256 (with 256-bit output) targeting a complexity below 2^{192}. These resulting attacks have complexity higher than 2^{128}, above the standard's security claim, and are thus worse than the generic random-prefix/second preimage attack.

We summarize existing results in Table 1. The designers of Ascon provide preliminary analysis, including linear equations obtained from the hash value for preimages on 2 rounds with 64 bit output and degree-based accelerated brute-

Table 1. Comparison of preimage attacks on Ascon-XOF128 or Ascon-Hash256 in related work. rpp denotes random-prefix preimage. GE: Gaussian eliminations.

Output	Setting	#R	Complexity	Strategy	Reference
64 bit	preimage	2	$2^{31.6}$	Linearize & Guess	[LHC+23]
	preimage	2	2^{34}	Guess & Determine	[BKK24]
	preimage	2	2^{39} GE	Linearization	[DEMS19b]
	preimage	3	2^{51} GE	Guess & Determine	[FLYS23]
	preimage	3	2^{56} GE	Guess & Determine	[BKK24]
	preimage	4	2^{63}	Guess & Determine	[BKK24]
	preimage	5	$2^{58.9}$	Degree-Based	[DEMS19b]
	preimage	6	$2^{63.2}$	Degree-Based	[DEMS19b]
128 bit	preimage	2	2^{98}	Guess & Determine	[BKK24]
	preimage	3	2^{112}	Linearize & Guess	[LHC+23]
	preimage	3	2^{120}	Guess & Determine	[BKK24]
	preimage	3	2^{120}	Differential-Linear	[NHS+24]
	preimage	4	2^{124}	Linearize & Guess	[LHC+23]
	preimage	4	2^{125}	Meet-in-the-Middle	[QHD+23]
	preimage	4	2^{125}	Differential-Linear	[NHS+24]
	preimage	4	2^{127}	Guess & Determine	[BKK24]
256 bit	preimage	3	2^{163}	Meet-in-the-Middle	[DZQ+24]
	preimage	3	2^{184}	Differential-Linear	[NHS+24]
	preimage	4	2^{185}	Meet-in-the-Middle	[DZQ+24]
	preimage	4	2^{189}	Differential-Linear	[NHS+24]
	preimage	5	2^{191}	Meet-in-the-Middle	[DZQ+24]
any (n-bit)	2nd preimage	1	2^{64} GE	Linearization	Sect. 3
	preimage	1	2^{64} GE + 2^{n-128}	Linearization	Sect. 3
	rpp preimage	1	$2^{29.7}$ GE $\approx 2^{35.3}$	Linearization	Sect. 4

force for 5- and 6-round Ascon-XOF with 64-bit output. Qin et al. [QHD+23] apply the Meet-in-the-Middle attack to various sponge-based hash functions and find preimage attacks for Ascon-XOF with 128-bit output with complexity 2^{125}.

Several papers build upon the linearization approach, some of them also inspired by related attacks on Keccak [GLS16]. Li et al. [LHC+23] propose a linearize and guess approach, where they first guess some set of bits of the input and then create a linear equation system for the missing bits. Furthermore, they combine multiple ways of choosing the set of guessed bits to increase the effective degrees of freedom in their attack. They find preimage attacks with complexity $2^{31.6}$ and 2^{124} for 2-round Ascon-XOF with 64-bit output and 4-round Ascon-XOF with 128-bit output, respectively. Fu et al. [FLYS23] use MILP modeling to find a good set of guessed bits yielding a preimage attack on 64-bit 3-round Ascon-XOF with complexity 2^{51}. Baek et al. [BKK24] show how to guess bits to be able to linearize 1 output bit after 4 rounds, leading to attacks on 4-round Ascon-XOF with complexity 2^{63} and 2^{127} for 64-bit and 128-bit outputs, respectively.

Based on the improved bound by Lefevre and Mennink on the generic complexity for first preimage attacks of 2^{192}, two papers propose first preimage attacks with complexity below 2^{192}. Niu et al. [NHS+24] analyze the security of Ascon-Hash against preimages using high-probability differential-linear distinguishers and find preimage attacks for 4-round Ascon-Hash with complexity 2^{189}. Dong et al. [DZQ+24] use a Meet-in-the-Middle approach to find preimages for 5-round Ascon-Hash with complexity 2^{191}. Note that these works do not apply to random-prefix/second preimages, where the generic attack has complexity 2^{128}.

Our Contribution. We provide a dedicated analysis of Ascon hashing when used in Ed25519. We present the first preimage-type attacks on round-reduced Ascon-Hash256 and Ascon-XOF128 with output longer than 128 bits and complexity below the claimed 2^{128}. Our contribution can be summarized as follows.

- We propose a second-preimage attack on 1-round Ascon-Hash256 and Ascon-XOF128 with arbitrarily long outputs with complexity 2^{64}. We also extend this to a first-preimage attack on Ascon-XOF128 with n-bit output with complexity $2^{64} + 2^{n-128}$ which is below the 128-bit claim for $n \leq 255$.
- We show that the probability of finding a preimage in a random-prefix-preimage setting can be greatly amplified by choosing the target state according to good linear approximations.
- By combining the amplified probability with a new efficient (≈ 7.9 Gaussian eliminations) method to find an internal state matching 128 conditions, we propose a random-prefix-preimage attack on 1-round Ascon-Hash256 and Ascon-XOF128 with arbitrarily long outputs with complexity $2^{29.7}$.

Outline. In Sect. 2, we discuss background on Ed25519 and the Ascon cipher suite. In Sect. 3, we present our second-preimage attack and how to extend it to a first-preimage attack. In Sect. 4, we show how we can optimize the techniques for a random-prefix-preimage attack. We conclude in Sect. 5.

2 Background

In this section, we discuss background on Ed25519 (Sect. 2.1), background on Ascon (Sect. 2.2) and discuss the combination of the two in Sect. 2.3.

2.1 EdDSA and Ed25519

The Edwards-curve Digital Signature Algorithm (EdDSA) is a digital signature algorithm based on a deterministic variant of Schnorr signatures [Sch89] which operates on twisted Edwards curves. It is standardized by NIST as part of the digital signature standard [Nat23] and also specified in RFC 8032 [JL17]. We show the signature generation and verification routines in Fig. 1.

In contrast to Schnorr signatures, where an ephemeral private key (sometimes also called a nonce) is required, EdDSA generates this key using a hash over a private value and the message. There are two versions of EdDSA standardized by NIST: Ed25519 and Ed448, which provide approximately 128 or 224 bits of security, respectively. In this work, we focus on Ed25519.

The signature generation for Ed25519 proceeds as follows. First, the private key d is expanded using SHA-512: $h_1 \| h_2 = \text{SHA-512}(d)$. Then, the private scalar s is calculated by interpreting h_1 as a little endian integer and clearing bits 0, 1, 2, and 254, and setting bit 255. The ephemeral private key r is formed by hashing $h_2 \| M$ and interpreting the result as a little-endian integer. The signature is formed by $R \| S$. The ephemeral public key R is calculated as $R = r \cdot G$. Then, the signer commits to R, Q, and M by hashing $h = \text{SHA-512}(R \| Q \| M)$. Finally, S is calculated using $S = r + h \cdot s \bmod n$.

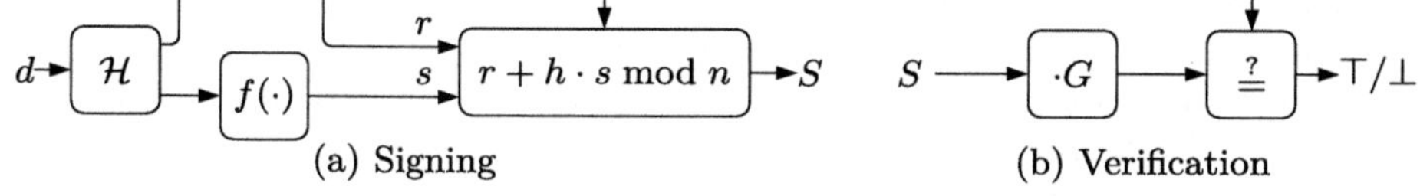

Fig. 1. Ed25519 signing and verification routines. G is the generator of the Elliptic Curve Group. $Q = s \cdot G$ is the public key for the private key d. The inputs of the hash function $\mathcal{H}$ are processed bottom-to-top.

Security Requirements for the Hash Function. The hash function is used in 3 different contexts with different security requirements when signing a message. First, for expanding the private key, the hash function needs to fulfill the requirements of a secure pseudorandom function (PRF). Here, the capabilities of an attacker are rather limited. However, statistical biases in the output could lead to attacks. Next, for generating the ephemeral private key r, again a secure PRF is needed. Here, a statistical bias in the output could be used to recover the private key by solving an instance of the hidden number problem [BV96]. Finally, the hash function is used to commit to R, Q, and M. Here, it is sufficient (but not necessary) for the hash function to serve as a binding commitment scheme. In other words, for a given/chosen commitment h it must be computationally hard to find an opening for a value that was not committed to.

Forgeries Exploiting Non-Binding Commitment schemes. Neven et al. more carefully analyze necessary requirements for hash functions used in Schnorr signatures, and define random-prefix-preimage (rpp) resistance and random-prefix-second-preimage (rpsp) resistance [NSW09] as necessary requirements. Via a non-tight reduction in the generic group model, they also prove them to be sufficient requirements. The two requirements are formulated as follows: For rpp, the adversary picks a target hash H (corresponding to h in Ed25519), then a prefix R is chosen at random, finally, the adversary wins if they find a message M such that $\mathcal{H}(R\|M) = H$. For rpsp, the adversary picks a message M, then a prefix R is chosen at random, finally, the adversary wins if they find a message M' such that $\mathcal{H}(R\|M) = \mathcal{H}(R\|M')$. From Fig. 1a, it is clear that breaking rpp resistance leads to a forgery: An adversary picks h and S to calculate R using the verification equation, then a message M with $\mathcal{H}(R\|Q\|M) = h$ is a forgery. The same idea works when breaking rpsp by requesting a signature for M.

2.2 The Ascon cipher suite and Ascon-XOF128

Ascon is a family of lightweight cryptographic algorithms for authenticated encryption and hashing. Originally proposed as a candidate in the CAESAR competition (2014–2019) [DEMS14] for authenticated encryption (AEAD) and selected as the winning "primary choice" for lightweight authenticated encryption, the family was later extended with various keyed and unkeyed hashing functions [DEMS19a, DEMS24]. The designers' specification was published in the Journal of Cryptology [DEMS21]. In the NIST Lightweight Cryptography (LWC) Project, NIST selected Ascon as the winner of the corresponding LWC competition (2019–2023). Consequently, NIST standardized a selection of the family members in NIST SP 800-232 [Nat25]: the authenticated encryption scheme Ascon-AEAD128 and the unkeyed hashing functions Ascon-Hash256 (with fixed 256-bit output), Ascon-XOF128 (eXtendable Output Function with variable output length), and Ascon-CXOF128 (Customizable XOF with variable output length and supporting a customization string as an additional input). All of these are designed for a security level of 128 bits, or more specifically, $\min(128, L)$-bit preimage resistance and $\min(128, L/2)$-bit collision resistance of the XOF or CXOF with L-bit hash output. Compared to the designers' specification, the NIST version incorporates some tweaks, including a switch from big-endian to little-endian specifications and the addition of the CXOF variant.

Specification of the Ascon-p permutation. All Ascon family members are based on the same lightweight permutation, Ascon-p, with different numbers of rounds. The round function consists of three steps which operate on a 320-bit state divided into 5 words S_0, S_1, S_2, S_3, S_4 of 64 bits each [Nat25]:

- **Round constant addition** p_C: XORS a round constant $\mathcal{RC}$ to word S_2. The constant is simply a concatenation of two 4-bit counters and can be found in the specification. While our attacks take the round constants into account, we do not always mention it explicitly to keep the descriptions simple.
- **Nonlinear substitution layer** p_S: applies the 5-bit S-box $\mathcal{S}$ given in Fig. 2a 64 times in parallel in a bit-sliced fashion (vertically, across words). Here, $\oplus$ denotes XOR and $\odot$ denotes AND.
- **Linear diffusion layer** p_L: XORS different rotated copies of each word (horizontally, within each word) as specified in Fig. 2b.

We denote the state S, at the input to round i and thus to the round constant addition and S-box, as x^i, and the input to the linear layer as y^i. Accordingly, we index the words as $x_0, \ldots, x_4$ in our analysis, similar to the designers' notation [DEMS21]. Since we focus our analysis on single-round permutations, we use i to index permutation calls instead of rounds.

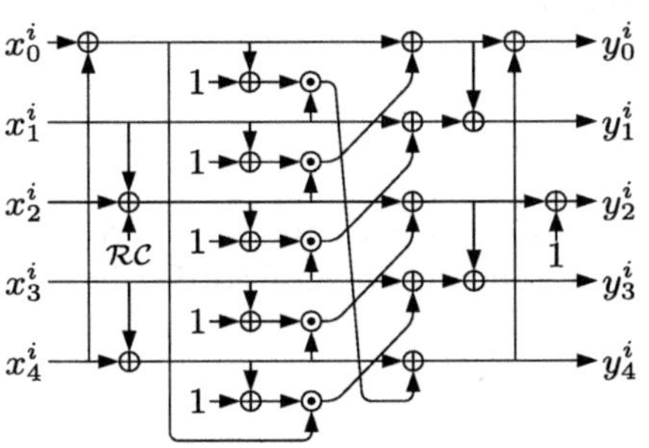

(a) 5-bit S-box $\mathcal{S}(x)$ with constant $\mathcal{RC}$

$$y_0^i \oplus (y_0^i \ggg 19) \oplus (y_0^i \ggg 28) \to x_0^{i+1}$$
$$y_1^i \oplus (y_1^i \ggg 61) \oplus (y_1^i \ggg 39) \to x_1^{i+1}$$
$$y_2^i \oplus (y_2^i \ggg 1) \oplus (y_2^i \ggg 6) \to x_2^{i+1}$$
$$y_3^i \oplus (y_3^i \ggg 10) \oplus (y_3^i \ggg 17) \to x_3^{i+1}$$
$$y_4^i \oplus (y_4^i \ggg 7) \oplus (y_4^i \ggg 41) \to x_4^{i+1}$$

(b) Linear 64-bit functions $\Sigma_j(y_j)$

Fig. 2. Round function of Ascon-p in round i.

Specification of Ascon-XOF128. The eXtendable Output Function Ascon-XOF128 takes a message input M of arbitrary length and produces a hash output H of arbitrary length. Internally, it uses the 12-round permutation Ascon-p[12] in a sponge construction [BDPV07] with a rate of $r = 64$ bits and a capacity of $c = 256$ bits, as illustrated in Fig. 3.

- **Initialization**: The state S is initialized with a fixed initial value, specifically

$$S \leftarrow \text{Ascon-}p[12](\texttt{0x0000080000cc0003} \| 0^{256}) .$$

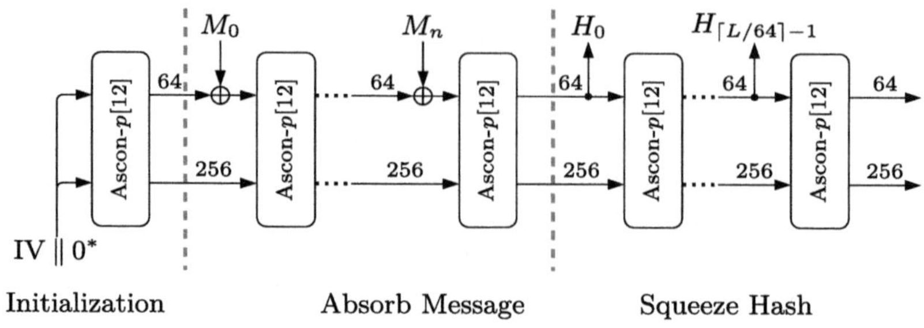

Fig. 3. Mode of operation for Ascon-XOF128.

- **Message Absorption and Padding**: The input message M is padded to a multiple of 64 bits by appending the bitstring $1\|0^*$; in the little-endian encoding of SP 800-232 and when considering byte-level messages, this corresponds to appending the byte `0x01` followed by as many zero bytes as necessary. We remark that this means that when considering bit-level messages, any 64-bit bitstring except the all-zero string corresponds to a valid padded last message block; when considering byte-level messages, an 8-byte byte sequence is a valid padded last message block of it ends in `0x01` (or `0x01 0x00`, or `0x01 0x00 0x00`, etc.).
  The resulting padded message blocks are indexed as $M_0, \ldots, M_n$ when $64n \leq |M| \leq 64n + 63$. For each message block M_i, the state is updated by XORING the message block and applying the permutation:

$$S_0 \leftarrow S_0 \oplus M_i$$
$$S \leftarrow \text{Ascon-}p[12](S)\,.$$

- **Hash Squeezing**: If an L-bit hash output is requested, the XOF produces $\lceil L/64 \rceil$ output blocks H_j, truncating the last output block accordingly:

$$H_j \leftarrow S_0$$
$$S \leftarrow \text{Ascon-}p[12](S)\,.$$

Generic Security of Ascon-XOF128. XOFs aim to provide similar security properties as hash functions, but the specific security levels also depend on the output size. The security level typically increases with the output size according to generic bounds, but is capped at some target security level based on the internal primitive and construction. More specifically, Ascon-XOF128 with L-bit hash output claims $\min(128, L)$-bit (first and second) preimage resistance and $\min(128, L/2)$-bit collision resistance. The limit $128 = \frac{c}{2}$ corresponds to the birthday bound in the inner part of the state. The function also provides some additional properties, such as resistance to length-extension attacks. This follows from the design philosophy of the sponge construction [BDPV07], which is proven to be indifferentiable from a random oracle in the ideal permutation model up to the birthday bound in the capacity.

In fact, it was recently shown that this bound is not completely tight: Lefevre and Mennink [LM22] found that while the collision and second preimage security bounds are tight, the preimage bound is not. For the Ascon hashing functions including Ascon-XOF128, they showed that up to 192-bit preimage resistance can be achieved. More specifically, the claim could be updated from $\min(128, L)$ to $\min(L, \max(L - r, \frac{c}{2}))$ in the ideal permutation model where $L \leq c$, which corresponds to 192 bits for $c = L = 256$ as in Ascon-Hash256. This increase is due to the difficulty of matching multiple squeezed output blocks. However, second preimage resistance remains at $\min(128, L)$. Note that the matching attack was already described by the Keccak team in 2011 [BDPV11].

This discrepancy is interesting in the context of random-prefix (second) preimage resistance (rpp and rpsp). In fact, we can show that both correspond to the second preimage resistance of $\min(128, L)$ bits. For rpsp, the matching attack works as follows. The adversary picks a message M and receives the random prefix R. They can now compute the intermediate state $S^\star$ right before squeezing starts by absorbing R (obtaining S^R) and then M. Then, they can build a 5-block second preimage by constructing an inner collision as illustrated in Fig. 4. Using all $2^{c/2} = 2^{2r} = 2^{128}$ candidates of $M_0\|M_1$ and all of $M_3\|M_4$, they are likely to find a match in the inner part of the state S^M where M_2 is absorbed, while M_2 is chosen to complete the match on the outer part. For an rpp attack of the same complexity, the adversary can directly choose $S^\star$ to determine their chosen target hash H and then proceed as above. These attacks are tight (up to small constants), since an rpp or rpsp adversary can also produce collisions.

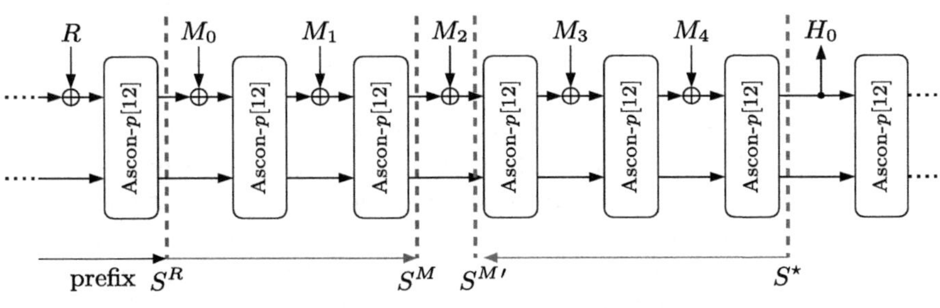

Fig. 4. Generic random-prefix (second) preimage (rpp, rpsp) attacks on Ascon-XOF128 and other sponges.

Dedicated Cryptanalysis of Ascon-XOF128. The analysis of Ascon-XOF128 builds directly on the analysis of the closely related submitted candidate design Ascon-XOF; most results are directly transferable, except if they depend heavily on minor details such as the initial value and round constants, which are slightly different. For an overview of dedicated preimage attacks relevant for Ascon-XOF128, we refer to Table 1 in the introduction.

2.3 Ascon-XOF128 and Ed25519

Ed25519 is currently specified for use with SHA-512 only. However, on constrained platforms and in applications where Ascon is already available, instantiating $\mathcal{H}$ with Ascon-XOF128 instead as a more lightweight alternative has been brought up repeatedly as a discussion point in the NIST Lightweight Cryptography process, including the mailing list and workshops [MSP+23]. This is particularly relevant when the code size and memory requirements are constrained. It is worth noting that SHA-512, which can provide up to 256-bit security, is not chosen here due to its formal security level (Ed25519 aims for 128-bit security overall), but more due to the requirement of hashing the private key to 512-bit outputs to be used for different purposes, as well as the good software performance on 64-bit CPUs. While Ascon-XOF128 clearly satisfies the functional requirements to instantiate $\mathcal{H}$ and brings in the necessary 128-bit security level, the concrete security implications with respect to the specific required security properties warrant further discussion.

One difficult aspect when discussing protocols and composite schemes involving multiple different primitives is how to concretely quantify their security level, specifically, which unit to use. Classically, the security level of symmetric primitives and schemes is quantified with respect to the offline and/or online query complexity of the primitive. For example, the k-bit key recovery security of a block cipher with k-bit key and n-bit block means that we expect that an adversary needs a time complexity of around $T = 2^k$ (offline) cipher evaluations to recover the key with a reasonable success probability ε (e.g., $T = 2^k$ for $\varepsilon = 1$, or $T = 2^{k-1}$ for $\varepsilon = \frac{1}{2}$, etc.), and access to at least $D = 1$ (online) data produced by the target key. However, this is a primitive-dependent metric, and the same bit-level security for two different primitives does not necessarily correspond to equivalent effort for the adversary, as in the notable example of password hashing.

Moreover, for primitives in asymmetric cryptography, the best attacks are typically not generic attacks, but dedicated mathematical algorithms whose complexity is measured in other–more basic–operations, such as arithmetic operations. There are different approaches for handling this discrepancy and assigning bit-level security claims to asymmetric primitives, which relate arithmetic complexities either to the evaluation complexity of the asymmetric primitive or to a symmetric reference primitive such as AES, as in the case of NIST's PQC security levels. A useful intermediate unit is bit operations. On the downside, any step from primitive-dependent metrics (e.g., cipher evaluations) towards more general metrics (e.g., bit operations, arithmetic operations) is typically also a step towards more implementation-specific and platform-specific metrics, which are often more volatile.

In case of Ed25519, the attack complexity based on solving the discrete logarithm problem on Curve25519 has been analyzed by Bernstein [Ber06]. He estimates the complexity to be about 2^{125} elliptic curve point additions, needing around 2^{10} CPU cycles each. If we generously count each CPU cycle as a 64-bit operation, this totals to around 2^{141} bit operations. Other estimates are slightly higher, at around 2^{145} bit operations (for success probability very close to 1).

Comparing this to an rpp/rpsp attack on Ascon-XOF128 as in Fig. 4, the attack complexity is dominated by around 2^{128} permutation calls (absorbing M_1) and around 2^{128} inverse permutation calls (inversely absorbing M_3). One permutation call corresponds to 12 forward rounds of Ascon-p, each of which requires around $22 + 10 = 32$ word operations (XOR, AND, NOT; not counting rotations memory-moving operations, unlike the above estimate), totalling $12 \cdot 32 \cdot 64 \approx 2^{15}$ bit operations. Under the very conservative estimate that an inverse permutation call costs at least as much (while in reality, it is *much* more expensive), and not counting further overheads due to large memories or memoryless cycle-finding, we get an optimistic estimate of around 2^{144} bit operations overall, comparable to the cost to attack Ed25519 via discrete logarithms. Thus, using Ed25519 with Ascon-XOF128 instead of SHA-512 or SHA3-512 is expected to provide the same overall security level, although Ascon-XOF128 is more lightweight.

3 Forgeries via Second Preimages on Ascon-XOF

In this section, we outline our second-preimage attack on Ascon-XOF128 which we use to create forgeries for Ed25519+Ascon-XOF128. In contrast to previous works which focused only on short outputs of 64 or 128 bits, our attack works for arbitrarily long outputs. Instead of targeting the arbitrarily long output in our attack, we instead target the internal Ascon state before the output is generated. This internal Ascon state is directly available to us, since we are performing a second-preimage attack. Alternatively, our attack can be viewed as a first preimage attack on the internal state of Ascon.

Our forgery attack proceeds in 3 steps as depicted in Fig. 5. First, we show how to transform the problem of forging a signature into finding a preimage for an internal Ascon state (Sect. 3.1). Next, we show how to prepare the internal state of Ascon to enable the final part of the attack (Sect. 3.2). Finally, we show how to connect the prepared internal state to the target state (Sect. 3.3).

3.1 Forgeries Based on Second-Preimage Attacks

The more intuitive forgery attack based on a second preimage proceeds by obtaining one signature (R, S) for an arbitrary message M. Since the signature is verified by hashing $\mathcal{H}(R\|Q\|M) = h^\star$, where Q is the public key, we can forge a message by finding an M' such that $\mathcal{H}(R\|Q\|M') = h^\star$. Note that, strictly speaking, this scenario is not covered by a second-preimage attack, because we require a special prefix $R\|Q$. However, for Ascon and many other iterative hash functions, this prefix is equivalent to attacking the function with a modified initial value. Still, we require 1 known signature.

We can formulate a better attack, that requires no known signatures. As discussed in Sect. 2.1, we can create forgeries by breaking the commitment scheme used for generating the signature. Concretely, we choose an arbitrary scalar value

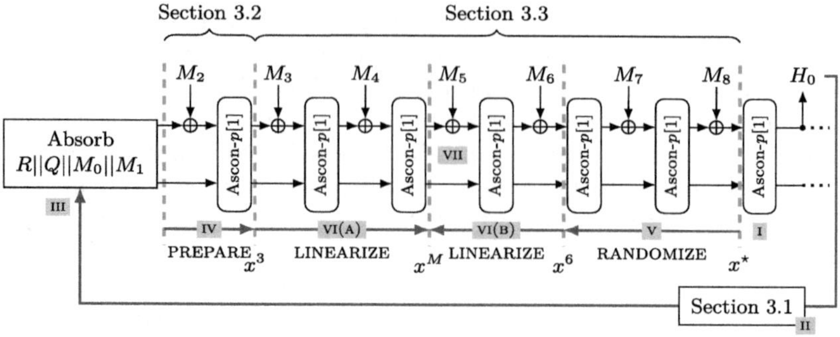

Fig. 5. Finding forgeries with second preimages on Ascon-XOF128.

S and an arbitrary internal Ascon state $x^\star$ that leads to the output $h^\star$. Concretely, we choose a suitable target hash h and an scalar value S. We find the first half of the signature as

$$R = S \cdot G - h^\star \cdot Q\,,$$

where G denotes the elliptic curve generator and Q denotes the public key. Finally, we find a forgery by breaking the random-prefix preimage resistance of the hash function. That is, we find M such that

$$\mathcal{H}(R\|Q\|M) = h^\star\,.$$

Note that we can apply our preimage attack that targets the internal state $x^\star$ and that we do not require any known signatures.

3.2 Preparing the Internal State

As noted in previous works, linearizing the Ascon permutation works best if the diffusion of the message is limited in the first block. The two most effective conditions on the internal state are $x_1 = 0$ and $x_3 \oplus x_4 = 1^{64}$. As depicted in Fig. 6, these two conditions affect the two AND gates that process the message and force the other input to be zero, hence preventing diffusion of the message through the AND gates. Note that after the S-box, the initial conditions lead to $y_4 = 1^{64}$; we will use this fact in Sect. 4. However, satisfying these two conditions simultaneously is not trivial as combined they correspond to 128 single-bit conditions.

Ensuring $x_1^3 = 0$. This step is relatively straight-forward. We start at state x^2 and want to ensure $x_1^3 = 0$. By examining the Ascon S-box (Fig. 2a), we see that the message part (x_0) linearly affects y_1^2 after the S-box. Hence, we can temporarily set $M_2 = 0$ to find what y_1^2 would be: say $y^2_{1|M_2=0} = \alpha$. Then we can set $M_2 = \alpha$, to ensure $y_1^2 = 0$ and $x_1^3 = \Sigma_1(y_1^2) = 0$.

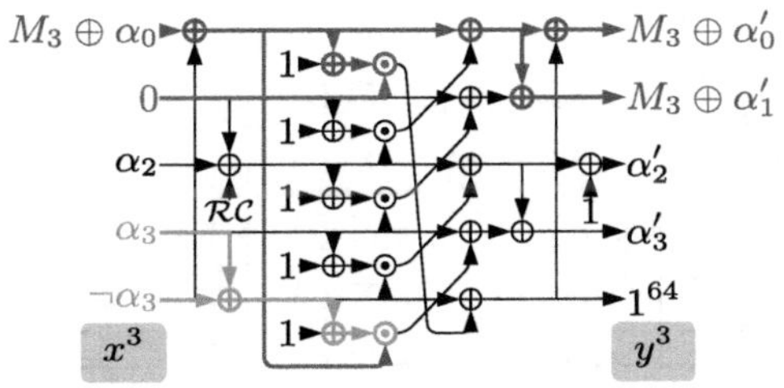

Fig. 6. Relevant initial conditions $x_1^3 = 0$ (■) and $x_3^3 = \neg x_4^3$ (■) limiting the diffusion of the message (■).

Ensuring $x_3^3 \oplus x_4^3 = 1^{64}$. To ensure all conditions are satisfied, we propose a brute-force approach. First, we pick two random messages M_0 and M_1 and process them. Next, we use M_2 to ensure $y_1^2 = 0$ as described above. If $x_3^3 \oplus x_4^3 = 1^{64}$ we are done; else, we try again. We expect to need about 2^{64} tries. In Sect. 4.2, we improve the time complexity for this step to ≈ 7.9 Gaussian eliminations.

3.3 Completing the Second-Preimage Attack

To complete the attack, we need to gather enough degrees of freedom to generate a system of equations that has a solution with a high probability. Hence, we linearize the Ascon permutation both in the forward direction as well as in the backward direction. Due to the initial conditions, we can linearize two permutation calls/rounds in the forward direction as depicted in Fig. 7. After the 2-round linearization in forward direction over the variables M_3 and M_4, the words x_1^M, x_2^M, and x_3^M can be described as linear functions of M_3 and M_4, while x_0^M and x_4^M can only be described as function of degree 2. For x_0^M, we do not really care, as this value is XORED with M_5 anyway. For x_4^M, we will exclude it from our equation system, and solve repeatedly until we find a solution that works for x_4^M. When linearizing the backward direction, we find that we can only reasonably linearize one permutation call as a function of M_6. In this case, all expressions for x^M are linear as there is only one equivalent message bit per S-box. If we try to linearize more permutation calls, we find that the we lose linear equations more quickly than we gain degrees of freedom by the additional message blocks.

We can formalize parts of the matching point x_1^M, x_2^M, and x_3^M as a linear function of M_3 and M_4 using the matrix A_f and in the backward direction as a function of M_6 using the matrix A_b:

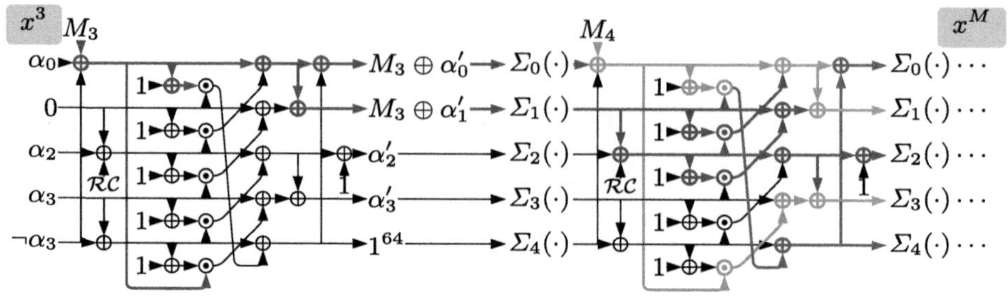

Fig. 7. Linearization over two 1-round permutation calls with initial conditions satisfied.

$$x_1^M \| x_2^M \| x_3^M = A_\mathrm{f} \cdot (M_3 \| M_4) \oplus b_\mathrm{f} \,,$$
$$x_1^M \| x_2^M \| x_3^M = A_\mathrm{b} \cdot M_6 \oplus b_\mathrm{b} \,.$$

Since the internal state needs to match, we write

$$(A_\mathrm{f} \| A_\mathrm{b}) \cdot (M_3 \| M_4 \| M_6) = b_\mathrm{f} \oplus b_\mathrm{b} \,,$$

and solve for the message blocks. Note that we can deduce M_5 in post-processing, to make sure the value in x_0^M matches. Since the final matrix has dimensions 192×192, we expect one solution on average. For each solution, we check whether x_4^M matches. Hence, we repeat this process about 2^{64} times. Further optimizations based on preprocessing the linear system are discussed in [Sch25].

Generating 2^{64} starting states x^3 would be too expensive for our attack. Instead, we add messages M_7 and M_8 (conforming to padding) before the target state $x^\star$ to generate random target states x^6 leading to new values for A_b and b_b.

Extension to Preimage Attack. To extend this attack to a first-preimage attack, we need to find the target state $x^\star$ based on a hash value/XOF output $h = (H_0 \| H_1 \| H_2 \| \ldots)$. We can accelerate this process by determining the state x^{H_0} when H_0 is squeezed. We set $x^{H_0} = (H_0, \epsilon_1, \epsilon_2, \Sigma_0^{-1}(H_1) \oplus \epsilon_3, \epsilon_4)$, where ϵ_1, ϵ_2, and ϵ_4 are arbitrary constants and $\epsilon_3 = H_0 \cdot \epsilon_1 \oplus H_0 \oplus \epsilon_1 \cdot \epsilon_2 \oplus \epsilon_1 \cdot \epsilon_4 \oplus \epsilon_1 \oplus \epsilon_2$ is calculated in such a way that we deterministically match H_1 in the next output block. Any additional output blocks are matched probabilistically, leading to an overall runtime of $2^{64} + 2^{n-128}$ to find a preimage for an n-bit output. This is below the 128-bit security claim for messages up to 255 bits. We believe this can be improved by more careful analysis of linearization properties.

4 Forgeries via Random-Prefix Preimages on Ascon-XOF

In this section, we outline our attack on the Ed25519+Ascon-XOF128 signature scheme construction by attacking Ascon-XOF128 when used as a commitment

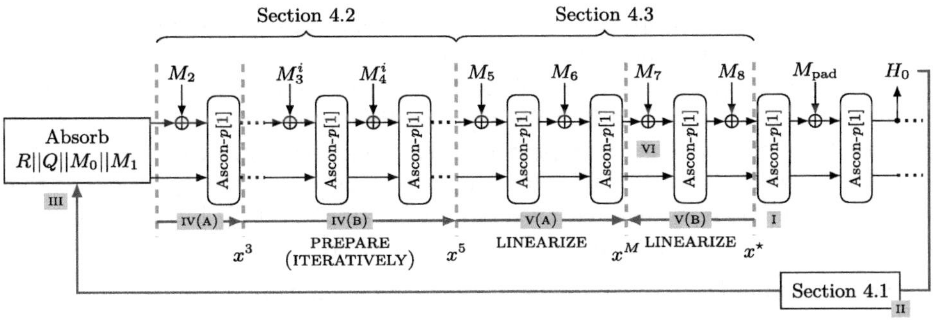

Fig. 8. Finding forgeries with random-prefix preimages on Ascon-XOF128.

scheme. That is, we choose an output for Ascon-XOF128 (commitment) and then find a preimage (opening) that fits the chosen output. Our attack proceeds in 3 steps as depicted in Fig. 8. First, we transform the problem of forging a signature into finding a *random-prefix preimage* for Ascon-XOF128 (Sect. 4.1). Next, we prepare the internal state of Ascon-XOF128 (Sect. 4.2). We repeat this step to prepare many candidates for the final step. Finally, we connect the prepared internal state with the target hash by solving an equation system over 4 message blocks (Sect. 4.3). In Sect. 4.4, we experimentally verify our attack.

4.1 Forgeries Based on Preimage Attacks

For this attack, we make use of the same forgery attack from Sect. 3.1 where no known signatures are needed. However, instead of utilizing a second-preimage attack on Ascon-XOF128, we will now exploit the fact that we can freely choose the target hash $h^\star$. Concretely, we will choose a suitable internal 320-bit Ascon state $x^\star$, absorb the padding block $M_{\text{pad}} = \texttt{0x0000000000000001}$ and generate the target hash $h^\star$. We will see that by choosing a suitable $x^\star$, we can amplify the probability that we find a solution by $2^{37.4}$ leading to a very practical attack.

4.2 Preparing the Internal State

As discussed in Sect. 3.2, we require the conditions $x_1 = 0$ and $x_3 \oplus x_4 = 1^{64}$ on the internal state (x^5, see Fig. 8) to limit the diffusion of the message blocks. This leads to better linearization enabling the rest of the attack.

In Sect. 3.2, we only needed one state that fulfills the conditions, as we could generate many target states by prepending message blocks to the actual target state $x^\star$. Compared to the second preimage attack, there is no incentive to randomize the target state $x^\star$, as we specifically choose $x^\star$ to make the equation system easier to solve. Instead, we need to generate a new state that fulfills the conditions each time we want to try to solve the system. That is, the complexity contributes a multiplicative factor to the total complexity instead of an additive one. Note that we can apply this improved method also to the previous attack as well, altough it does not affect the overall complexity.

Therefore, we propose a more efficient process: First, we use 1 message block to ensure $x_1 = 0$ like in Sect. 3.2. We expect a Hamming weight of 32 on average: $\mathrm{HW}(x_3 \oplus x_4) \approx 32$. Next, we repeatedly use a linearization procedure over two message blocks to maintain $x_1 = 0$ while increasing $\mathrm{HW}(x_3 \oplus x_4)$. We find that after 7.9 repetitions on average (see Sect. 4.4), all 128 single-bit conditions are satisfied. Next, we explain the main step of the iterative process.

Increasing the Hamming weight of $x_3 \oplus x_4$. At this point, we start with $x_1^3 = 0$, $x_2^3 = \alpha_2$, $x_3^3 = \alpha_3$, and $x_4^3 = \alpha_4$. For the first iteration, we expect $\mathrm{HW}(\alpha_3 \oplus \alpha_4) \approx 32$. We will now describe two permutation calls that process the messages M_3 and M_4 with a system of equations and solve the system to increase the Hamming weight. To prevent the diffusion of M_3 through the bottom AND gate (■ in Fig. 6 on page 13) we set the relevant message bits to zero. While this reduces our overall degrees of freedom by $64 - \mathrm{HW}(\alpha_3 \oplus \alpha_4)$, it ensures that M_3 only diffuses to the first two words of the Ascon state after the first permutation call. Then, after XORING the message M_4, XORING the round constant $\mathcal{RC}$, after the S-box but before linear layer, we arrive at the state $(y_0^4, y_1^4, y_2^4, y_3^4, y_4^4)$ as depicted in Fig. 9. The relevant part of the new state is calculated as follows:

$$
\begin{aligned}
y_1^4 &= M_3' \cdot \delta_{1a} \oplus M_4' \oplus \delta_{1b} \,, \\
y_3^4 &= M_3' \oplus M_4' \cdot \delta_{3a} \oplus \delta_{3b} \,, \\
y_4^4 &= M_3' \cdot (M_4' \oplus \delta_{4a}) \oplus \delta_{4b} \,,
\end{aligned}
$$

where $M_3' = \Sigma_1(M_3 \oplus \beta_1)$, $M_4' = M_4 \oplus \Sigma_0(M_3 \oplus \beta_0)$ and each lowercase Greek letter denotes some 64-bit constant and $\cdot$ denotes bitwise AND. Note that y_4^4 is a nonlinear combination of M_3' and M_4' leading to a nonlinear system. However, since we require $\Sigma_1(y_1^4) = 0$ or equivalently $y_1^4 = 0$, we can replace $M_4' = M_3' \cdot \delta_{1a} \oplus \delta_{1b}$:

$$
\begin{aligned}
y_3^4 &= M_3' \cdot \delta_{3a}' \oplus \delta_{3b}' \,, \\
y_4^4 &= M_3' \cdot \delta_{4a}' \oplus \delta_{4b} \,,
\end{aligned}
$$

with $\delta_{3a}' = \delta_{1a} \cdot \delta_{3a} \oplus 1^{64}$, $\delta_{3b}' = \delta_{1b} \cdot \delta_{3a} \oplus \delta_{3b}$, and $\delta_{4a}' = \delta_{1a} \oplus \delta_{1b} \oplus \delta_{4a}$. Now, we want to solve $\Sigma_3(M_3' \cdot \delta_{3a}' \oplus \delta_{3b}') \oplus \Sigma_4(M_3' \cdot \delta_{4a}' \oplus \delta_{4b}) = 1^{64}$. Note that the condition

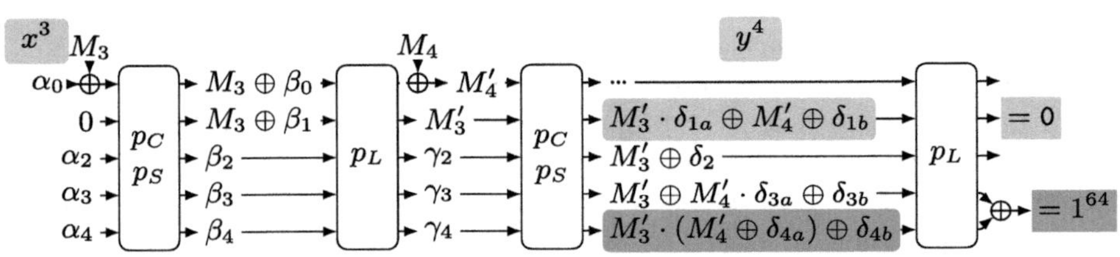

Fig. 9. Iteratively finding the initial conditions $x_1 = 0$ (■) and $x_3 = \neg x_4$ (■). Some bits of M_3 are used to compensate the missing initial conditions on $x_3 \oplus x_4$.

for $y_1^4 = 0$ is implicit in this system and will be satisfied when we calculate M_4' as a function of M_3'. However, we have already spent some degrees of freedom, so we have 64 equations and only $\mathrm{HW}(\alpha_3 \oplus \alpha_4)$ variables. Hence, the system of equation most will likely not have a (full) solution. Finding M_3' such that the Hamming weight is maximized is an instance of decoding a linear code. In our case, we use a greedy algorithm to find a good, but not necessarily optimal, solution. Concretely, we create a new system of equations that is initially empty and then add each of the 64 equations that does not contradict this new system. This process can be thought of as a variant of Gaussian elimination where a row of the matrix is discarded should it lead to a contradiction. With this process, we can effectively increase the Hamming weight of $\alpha_3 \oplus \alpha_4$ while keeping $\alpha_1 = 0$. We find that by repeating it on average 7.9 times, we can fulfill all 128 conditions and enable the next step of the attack.

4.3 Completing the Preimage Attack

Now, we have an efficient routine to generate a state $x^5 = (\alpha_0, 0, \alpha_2, \alpha_3, \neg\alpha_3)$ using 7.9 Gaussian eliminations on average. However, even with all initial conditions, a linearization attack like in Sect. 3.3 would still need approximately 2^{64} repetitions to be successful. Hence, we analyze how we can improve the attack by controlling the target value $x^\star$. We depict this part of the attack in Fig. 10.

Choosing a Suitable Target Value. To choose the target value $x^\star$, we first recall that $y_4^5 = 1^{64}$ due to the initial conditions (see Fig. 6 on page 13). This implies that $x_4^6 = 1^{64}$ since $\Sigma_4(1^{64}) = 1^{64}$. Based on this fact, we can derive that the difference $y_2^6 \oplus y_3^6$ is biased (see Fig. 10on page 18):

$$y_2^6 \oplus y_3^6 = M_6' \cdot \delta_{3a} \oplus 1^{64},$$

with δ_{3a} denoting a uniform 64-bit constant. So for those bits where the bit of δ_{3a} is zero, the difference is guaranteed to be 1, while for the other the difference is controlled by M_5'. We can also explain this fact by examining the linear approximation table of the Ascon S-box which confirms that $x_{4,i} = y_{2,i} \oplus y_{3,i}$ with $p = 75\%$ and we know that $x_4^6 = 1^{64}$.

To exploit this property, we analyze the algebraic normal form of the inverse S-box when the rate bits are set to a given constant in Table 2. We find that for $\mathcal{S}^{-1}(y\|\mathtt{1011})$, we get $x_2 = 1$ and $x_3 = 0$. Similarly, for $\mathcal{S}^{-1}(y\|\mathtt{1101})$, we get $x_2 = 0$ and $x_3 = 0$. By combining these two patterns ($\mathcal{S}^{-1}(y\|\mathtt{1011})$ for most bits and $\mathcal{S}^{-1}(y\|\mathtt{1101})$ for those bits where the round constant $\mathcal{RC}$ flips a bit of x_2), we can ensure that $x_3^7 = 1^{64}$ and $x_4^7 = 0$. Since these two constants are fixed points of the linear layer Σ_2/Σ_3, we get the same constants before the linear layer at the state y^6: $y_3^6 = 1^{64}$ and $y_2^6 = 0$. Consequently, we get $64 - \mathrm{HW}(\delta_{3a}) \approx 32$ equations for free, greatly improving the probability that we get a solution.

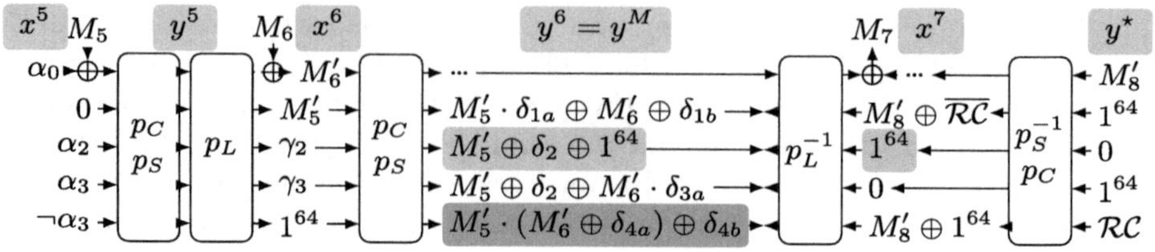

Fig. 10. Main part of the attack. The left side, satisfying the initial conditions x^5, is connected to the fixed target state $y^\star = p_L^{-1}(x^\star)$. We express y_6 from the left and from the right and match the equations. By inserting the green equation (■) into the red equation (■), we get a linear system.

With the target state selected, we can formulate the equation system:

$$\begin{aligned} \Sigma_1(M'_5 \cdot \delta_{1a} \oplus M'_6 \oplus \delta_{1b}) &= M'_8 \oplus \overline{\mathcal{RC}}\,, \\ \Sigma_2(M'_5 \oplus \delta_2 \oplus 1^{64}) &= 1^{64}\,, \\ \Sigma_3(M'_5 \oplus \delta_2 \oplus M'_6 \cdot \delta_{3a}) &= 0\,, \\ \Sigma_4(M'_5 \cdot (M'_6 \oplus \delta_{4a}) \oplus \delta_{4b}) &= M'_8 \oplus 1^{64}\,, \end{aligned}$$

where each δ is a 64-bit constant and $\overline{\mathcal{RC}} = \mathcal{RC} \oplus 1^{64}$.

Simplifying the Equation System by Changing Variables. At this point, the last word of the equation system is nonlinear, however, from the second equation we see that $M'_5 = \delta_2$. By simplifying, we get linear equations:

$$\begin{aligned} \Sigma_1(M'_6) \oplus M'_8 &= \overline{\mathcal{RC}} \oplus \Sigma_1(\delta_2 \cdot \delta_{1a} \oplus \delta_{1b})\,, \\ M'_6 \cdot \delta_{3a} &= 0\,, \\ \Sigma_4(M'_6 \cdot \delta_2) \oplus M'_8 &= 1^{64} \oplus \Sigma_4(\delta_{4a} \cdot \delta_2 \oplus \delta_{4b})\,. \end{aligned}$$

Here, we can already see the improvement by choosing a suitable target state $y^\star$, as the equation $M'_6 \cdot \delta_{3a} = 0$ is a tautology for $64 - \mathrm{HW}(\delta_{3a})$ bits. By substituting $M'_8 = \Sigma_1(M'_6) \oplus \overline{\mathcal{RC}} \oplus \Sigma_1(\delta_2 \cdot \delta_{1a} \oplus \delta_{1b})$, we can further simplify:

$$\begin{aligned} M'_6 \cdot \delta_{3a} &= 0\,, \\ \Sigma_4(M'_6 \cdot \delta_2) \oplus \Sigma_1(M'_6) &= \Sigma_4(\delta_{4a} \cdot \delta_2 \oplus \delta_{4b}) \oplus \Sigma_1(\delta_2 \cdot \delta_{1a} \oplus \delta_{1b}) \oplus \mathcal{RC}\,. \end{aligned}$$

Now, we have a linear equation system with 64 variables and $64 + \mathrm{HW}(\delta_{3a})$ equations. After we solve the equation system with Gaussian elimination, we can deduce M'_8 from M'_6. Then, we find $M_5 = \Sigma_1^{-1}(M'_5) \oplus \alpha_0$, M_6 by seeing what value we need to XOR to get $x_0^6 = M'_6$, M_7 by seeing what value we need to XOR to get $x_0^7 = M'_8 \cdot \overline{\mathcal{RC}} \oplus \mathcal{RC}$, and $M_8 = \Sigma_0(M'_8)$.

Table 2. Algebraic normal form of component functions of the inverse S-box. The highlighted values ensure $x_2 \oplus x_3 = 1$ after adding the round constant $\mathcal{RC}$.

	x_0	x_1	x_2	x_3	x_4
$\mathcal{S}^{-1}(y\|0000)$	1	y	$y+1$	0	0
$\mathcal{S}^{-1}(y\|0001)$	1	$y+1$	y	1	0
$\mathcal{S}^{-1}(y\|0010)$	0	y	$y+1$	1	1
$\mathcal{S}^{-1}(y\|0011)$	y	$y+1$	$y+1$	0	1
$\mathcal{S}^{-1}(y\|0100)$	0	0	0	y	y
$\mathcal{S}^{-1}(y\|0101)$	0	$y+1$	y	0	1
$\mathcal{S}^{-1}(y\|0110)$	y	1	1	$y+1$	0
$\mathcal{S}^{-1}(y\|0111)$	1	y	y	1	y
$\mathcal{S}^{-1}(y\|1000)$	y	$y+1$	y	1	y
$\mathcal{S}^{-1}(y\|1001)$	y	y	$y+1$	1	y
$\mathcal{S}^{-1}(y\|1010)$	$y+1$	$y+1$	1	0	$y+1$
$\mathcal{S}^{-1}(y\|1011)$	0	y	0	0	$y+1$
$\mathcal{S}^{-1}(y\|1100)$	$y+1$	1	y	y	1
$\mathcal{S}^{-1}(y\|1101)$	$y+1$	y	1	0	$y+1$
$\mathcal{S}^{-1}(y\|1110)$	1	0	0	$y+1$	$y+1$
$\mathcal{S}^{-1}(y\|1111)$	$y+1$	$y+1$	$y+1$	1	0

Probability of Finding a Solution. The overall complexity of the attack depends on the probability that the constructed system of equations has at least one solution. The final linear system of equations has 64 variables and $X_{\#\text{eq}} \sim 64 + B(n = 64, p = 0.5)$ equations, where B denotes a binomial distribution for n trials with probability p. So, for a single equation system, the logarithm of the probability to find at least one solution is distributed according to a binomial distribution: $p_{\text{sol}} \sim 2^{-B(n=64,p=0.5)}$. To predict the overall complexity, we calculate the expected value of p_{sol}:

$$\mathbb{E}(p_{\text{sol}}) = \sum_{k=0}^{64} 2^{-k} \cdot \binom{64}{k} \cdot 0.5^k \cdot 0.5^{64-k} \approx 2^{-26.56},$$

which we later also verify experimentally. This is an improvement by a factor of $2^{37.4}$ compared to the previous 2^{-64}.

Overall Complexity. We need 7.9 Gaussian eliminations on average to find a starting point and 1 Gaussian elimination to see whether we find a solution for this starting point. As we need to repeat this process on average $2^{26.56}$ times the expected complexity of the attack is $(7.9 + 1) \cdot 2^{26.56} \approx 2^{29.7}$.

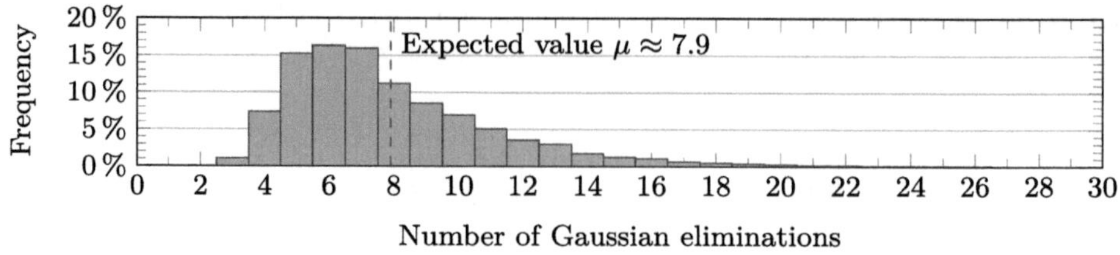

Fig. 11. Experimental complexity of finding initial state ($n = 5000$).

4.4 Experimental Evaluation

The code for this experimental evaluation is available online[1].

We implement the routine of Sect. 4.2 to find a state that matches the initial conditions. By trying 5000 different random states, we find that we need on average 7.9 Gaussian eliminations corresponding to 16.8 message blocks to find a state that fulfills all initial conditions. We show the distribution of the number of Gaussian eliminations needed in Fig. 11.

We implemented the random-prefix-preimage attack of Sect. 4 in C++ and performed it for the Ascon-Hash256 IV. Out of $2^{34.5}$ random prefixes $M_0 \| M_1$, we find that 294 of them lead to a successful preimage attack, corresponding to a rate of one solution every $2^{26.47}$ tries, which closely matches our statistical estimate. On our server with 2 AMD EPYC 9754 CPUs we find one random-prefix-preimage about every 27 s (3.2 core-hours). On the same hardware this corresponds to roughly $2^{35.3}$ brute-force attempts. Note that with a more optimized implementation of Guassian elimination this number would be lower.

5 Conclusion

In this paper, we have shown second-preimage and random-prefix-preimage attacks on 1-round Ascon-XOF128. These are the first preimage attacks on round-reduced Ascon-XOF128 with 256-bit output and Ascon-Hash256 with complexity below the claimed 128-bit security. For second-preimage attacks and random-prefix-preimage attacks, the security claim is also matched by a generic attack. Both our attacks apply in settings where Ascon-XOF128 or Ascon-Hash256 are used as a commitment scheme as they allow us to break the binding property. This property is required by the Fiat-Shamir transformation [FS86], which is commonly used to transform interactive zero-knowledge proofs into non-interactive zero-knowledge proves or signature schemes like in Ed25519.

We propose a second-preimage attack on 1-round Ascon Hash with complexity 2^{64}, which we also extend to a first-preimage attack on Ascon-XOF with outputs up to 255 bit for a complexity below 2^{128}. We find that by specifically

[1] http://github.com/isec-tugraz/ascon-rpp-preimages.

exploiting the fact that we can freely choose the hash output, our random-prefix-preimage attack is faster by a factor of $2^{34.3}$ compared to our second-preimage attack.

We believe our work can be built upon in future work. In particular, being able to choose the target state might allow improved cryptanalysis on other sponge-based hash functions as well using our techniques. Furthermore, increasing the number of attacked round is of high interest. However, since the core of our attack necessarily spans 3 permutation calls to get enough degrees of freedom, increasing the number of attacked rounds implies analyzing 6 rounds of Ascon over all capacity bits, which may be challenging given the 128-bit security level.

Acknowledgments. We would like to thank Fredrik Meisingseth for insightful discussions on probability theory. This research was funded in part by the European Research Council (ERC) Starting Grant KEYLESS (#101165216).

A Detailed Experimental Results

Table 3. Examplary random-prefix-preimage for 1-round Ascon-Hash256, breaking the binding property of the commitment scheme. Each row states a message block and the internal state after XORING the message and applying the Ascon permutation.

	M_i	x_0	x_1	x_2	x_3	x_4	Comment
		9b1e5494e934d681	4bc3a01e333751d2	ae65396c6b34b81a	3c7fd4a4d56a4db3	1a5c464906c5976d	Ascon-Hash256 IV
M_0	685903260457ea53	7970a54f7a956205	e9a17ea5020eaf64	d414b335e550a038	ce2b77bea3c33fae	6c4b2bc95f2b8612	randomize
M_1	af1cb14c5d612ec1	916deea6ca0c72b3	0a6160777409cca1	70870fd1dfdfed47	085e826fa9975606	f358a8241564bdab	randomize
M_2	18caa93c20b674b7	387d44f426400f5d	0000000000000000	20cd0294856ce9d9	e661109dca462fe5	a5ae5f097f76c9e7	$x_1 = 0$
M_3^0	02034e8424004000	7b5fd54cc3442713	79b3c813ba6959a9	8e981997454cb201	eb022c6a4ca098c2	8d1249789d7b6069	
M_4^0	01f669c9a1d2ac91	f8a9dabce0271af2	0000000000000000	5e954963f707cbff	93940c511e30a8b1	b0a4a03ea5cf574c	$\mathrm{HW}(x_3 \oplus x_4) = 44$
M_3^1	00002c0313ccfde0	08e2144b56261f9d	ce0ae2d036a6b480	5fea35b137080f08	ade02e27b0350c3a	eeab32c89a199854	
M_4^1	15a3f9744b803c32	00e92efb764370dc	0000000000000000	daae749cd5a45915	c38ee7010cc0932f	e458bcdef33f6cd0	$\mathrm{HW}(x_3 \oplus x_4) = 53$
M_3^2	00844284fede47b6	39714d7a7ada4901	ba0e93d81e0db0a2	45855c2dc2b33c60	867ea1897720a565	36660897bf93eb2d	
M_4^2	f0ecba1838f63fe3	ae7c216a92878d36	0000000000000000	d08ff4f28c946d24	67e6360c2c81f91f	ea19c9f3d37e06e0	$\mathrm{HW}(x_3 \oplus x_4) = 60$
M_3^3	84651c261793f7ac	f0b342b5edf85168	0b62ef4c276c5728	3640848a0a9f0819	1227e8b7b5b1f1c1	8d1bffffffc6ffff	
M_4^3	40cfd2b5adc1516c	3ad693c7c7a2c56b	0000000000000000	051854c4920ed35c	fbdc2a1e3a528196	4423d5e1c5ad7e69	$\mathrm{HW}(x_3 \oplus x_4) = 63$
M_3^4	12ea247b8325fbbc	76c4d6d49a7b27a3	0bad11bcb3f78c5c	065d504c96d30a8b	16bd4fa276b7e65b	bf7ffffffdfffff	
M_4^4	d44b76d580c036c3	e52f8615a999649f	0000000000000000	eb86bd4233149d27	b7aa2d4e2d66f7f0	4c55d2b1d299080f	$\mathrm{HW}(x_3 \oplus x_4) = 63$
M_3^5	701b354e4cb8b2d3	0bb9f7786ebb76c5	58a0a5c730f2b3ff	034a6a4a21329678	01f5d6d1c2c6be3e	fbf7ffffffdffff	
M_4^5	abb1f71862b2a4f7	e12feb45172b0c5b	0000000000000000	b864c997c9c9cc64	d5174e2ae7415ebf	aae8b1d518bea140	$\mathrm{HW}(x_3 \oplus x_4) = 63$
M_3^6	68cf246ff07f4737	e2614bcbe9faa9bb	ada27d29b6866f6f	1a7f8a7d4d76f992	aa62f368370fa547	7effffffffbfffff	
M_4^6	2b434b61edbc88fa	7c76c3ee03ffe1f7	0000000000000000	56927a3259d256c6	4f1fd664b03eb777	70e0299b4fc14888	$\mathrm{HW}(x_3 \oplus x_4) = 62$
M_3^7	1a442a5a23dc2146	07643ea2da87265e	b008f46aaa6d1b88	3f2d4cccc6bd2280	a15eca1a17a2f10e	3e7ffffff9fffff	
M_4^7	a66c7fabd8c72266	40f931a2dc9d06e2	0000000000000000	ec3d2628b747674a	455dd67eb2e95fa1	baa229814d16a05e	$\mathrm{HW}(x_3 \oplus x_4) = 64$
M_5	fbd9a0e8fd133565	512431250c059e61	e0b3d4c3f1117122	7f750bbc5f6f9c12	6039208051811284	ffffffffffffff	
M_6	47a0bf2fae0db670	45d9c05dee430635	d6ffe8ad49ad9387	ffffffffffffff	0000000000000000	d6ffe8ad49ad93cc	matching point x^M
M_7	932628f0a7ee95b1	01a0b14024b94fd2	ffffffffffffff	0000000000000000	ffffffffffffff	960000002580004b	$x_4 = \Sigma_4(\mathcal{RC})$
M_8	01a0b14024b94fd2	ce097679458004f9	d9b4fffef753fffb	ac0000000000006f	9625cb00258972c0	0000000000000000	cancel x_0
M_{pad}	0000000000000001	19970aba0d463889	333c724c2fe75a29	4d47ac0188d8b030	a6e0330b337df6e8	43d58d477b36f471	state after padding

References

BDPV07. Bertoni, G., Daemen, J., Peeters, M., Van Assche, G.: Sponge functions. Ecrypt Hash Workshop 2007 (2007). https://keccak.team/files/SpongeFunctions.pdf

BDPV11. Bertoni, G., Daemen, J., Peeters, M., Van Assche, G.: Cryptographic sponge functions (2011). https://keccak.team/files/CSF-0.1.pdf

Ber06. Bernstein, D.J.: Curve25519: new Diffie-Hellman speed records. In PKC 2006, volume 3958 of LNCS, pp. 207–228. Springer (2006). https://doi.org/10.1007/11745853_14

BKK24. Baek, S., Kim, G., Kim, J.: Preimage attacks on reduced-round Ascon-XOF. Des. Codes Cryptogr. **92**(8), 2197–2217 (2024). https://doi.org/10.1007/s10623-024-01383-0

BV96. Boneh, D., Venkatesan, R.: Hardness of computing the most significant bits of secret keys in Diffie-Hellman and related schemes. In: CRYPTO '96, volume 1109 of LNCS, pp. 129–142. Springer (1996). https://doi.org/10.1007/3-540-68697-5_11

DEMS14. Dobraunig, C., Eichlseder, M., Mendel, F., Schläffer, M.: Ascon v1. Submission to the CAESAR competition (2014). https://competitions.cr.yp.to/round1/asconv1.pdf

DEMS19a. Dobraunig, C., Eichlseder, M., Mendel, F., Schläffer, M.: Ascon v1.2. Submission to the NIST lightweight cryptography competition (2019). https://csrc.nist.gov/CSRC/media/Projects/Lightweight-Cryptography/documents/round-1/spec-doc/ascon-spec.pdf

DEMS19b. Dobraunig, C., Eichlseder, M., Mendel, F., Schläffer, M.: Preliminary analysis of Ascon-XOF and Ascon-Hash. IACR Cryptology ePrint Archive, Paper 2024/908 (2019). https://eprint.iacr.org/2024/908

DEMS21. Dobraunig, C., Eichlseder, M., Mendel, F., Schläffer, M.: Ascon v1.2: lightweight authenticated encryption and hashing. J. Cryptol. **34**(3), 1–42 (2021). https://doi.org/10.1007/s00145-021-09398-9

DEMS24. Dobraunig, C., Eichlseder, M., Mendel, F., Schläffer, M.: Ascon MAC, PRF, and short-input PRF – lightweight, fast, and efficient pseudorandom functions. In: CT-RSA 2024, volume 14643 of LNCS, pp. 381–403. Springer (2024). https://doi.org/10.1007/978-3-031-58868-6_15

DGL+24. Dong, X., Guo, J., Li, S., Pham, P., Zhang, T.: Improved meet-in-the-middle Nostradamus attacks on AES-like hashing. IACR Trans. Symmetric Cryptol. **2024**(1), 158–187 (2024). https://doi.org/10.46586/tosc.v2024.i1.158-187

DZQ+24. Dong, X., Zhao, B., Qin, L., Hou, Q., Zhang, S., Wang, X.: Generic MitM attack frameworks on sponge constructions. In: CRYPTO 2024, volume 14923 of LNCS, pp. 3–37. Springer (2024). https://doi.org/10.1007/978-3-031-68385-5_1

FLYS23. Fu, Q., Luo, Y., Yang, Q., Song, L.: Preimage and collision attacks on reduced Ascon using algebraic strategies. IACR Cryptology ePrint Archive, Paper 2023/1453 (2023). https://eprint.iacr.org/2023/1453

FS86. Fiat, A., Shamir, A.: How to prove yourself: practical solutions to identification and signature problems. In: CRYPTO '86, volume 263 of LNCS, pp. 186–194. Springer (1986). https://doi.org/10.1007/3-540-47721-7_12

GLS16. Guo, J., Liu, M., Song, L.: Linear structures: applications to cryptanalysis of round-reduced Keccak. In: ASIACRYPT 2016, volume 10031 of LNCS, pp. 249–274 (2016). https://doi.org/10.1007/978-3-662-53887-6_9

HM96. Halevi, S., Micali, S.: Practical and provably-secure commitment schemes from collision-free hashing. In: CRYPTO '96, volume 1109 of LNCS, pp. 201–215. Springer (1996). https://doi.org/10.1007/3-540-68697-5_16

JL17. Josefsson, S., Liusvaara, I.: Edwards-curve digital signature algorithm (EdDSA). RFC 8032 (2017). https://doi.org/10.17487/rfc8032

KK06. Kelsey, J., Kohno, T.: Herding hash functions and the Nostradamus attack. In: EUROCRYPT 2006, volume 4004 of LNCS, pp. 183–200. Springer (2006). https://doi.org/10.1007/11761679_12

LHC+23. Li, H., He, L., Chen, S., Guo, J., Qiu, W.: Automatic preimage attack framework on Ascon using a linearize-and-guess approach. IACR Trans. Symmetric Cryptol. **2023**(3), 74–100 (2023). https://doi.org/10.46586/tosc.v2023.i3.74-100

LM22. Lefevre, C., Mennink, B.: Tight preimage resistance of the sponge construction. In: CRYPTO 2022, volume 13510 of LNCS, pp. 185–204. Springer (2022). https://doi.org/10.1007/978-3-031-15985-5_7

MSP+23. Mattsson, J.P., Selander, G., Paavolainen, S., Karakoç, F., Tiloca, M., Moskowitz, R.: Proposals for standardization of the Ascon family. NIST Lightweight Cryptography Workshop 2023 (2023)

Nat23. National Institute of Standards and Technology. Digital signature standard (DSS). Technical Report Federal Information Processing Standards Publications (FIPS) 186-5 (2023). https://doi.org/10.6028/nist.fips.186-5

Nat25. National Institute of Standards and Technology. Ascon-based lightweight cryptography standards for constrained devices: Authenticated encryption, hash, and extendable output functions. Technical Report NIST Special Publication (SP) 800-232 (2025). https://doi.org/10.6028/nist.sp.800-232

NHS+24. Niu, Z., Hu, K., Sun, S., Zhang, Z., Wang, M.: Speeding up preimage and key-recovery attacks with highly biased differential-linear approximations. In: CRYPTO 2024, volume 14923 of LNCS, pp. 73–104. Springer (2024). https://doi.org/10.1007/978-3-031-68385-5_3

NSW09. Neven, G., Smart, N.P., Warinschi, B.: Hash function requirements for Schnorr signatures. J. Math. Cryptol. **3**(1), 69–87 (2009). https://doi.org/10.1515/jmc.2009.004

QHD+23. Qin, L., Hua, J., Dong, X., Yan, H., Wang, X.: Meet-in-the-middle preimage attacks on sponge-based hashing. In: EUROCRYPT 2023, volume 14007 of LNCS, pp. 158–188. Springer (2023). https://doi.org/10.1007/978-3-031-30634-1_6

Sch89. Schnorr, C.-P.: Efficient identification and signatures for smart cards. In: CRYPTO '89, volume 435 of LNCS, pp. 239–252. Springer (1989). https://doi.org/10.1007/0-387-34805-0_22

Sch25. Schmid, L.: Preimages for Ascon-Xof in EdDSA. Master's thesis, Graz University of Technology (2025). https://doi.org/10.3217/6jv2t-pgn22

ZSWH23. Zhang, Z., Sun, S., Wang, C., Hu, L.: Classical and quantum meet-in-the-middle Nostradamus attacks on AES-like hashing. IACR Trans. Symmetric Cryptol. **2023**(2), 224–252 (2023). https://doi.org/10.46586/tosc.v2023.i2.224-252

Collision Attacks on SPONGENT with Grouping Method

Keita Toyama[1(✉)], Kosei Sakamoto[2,3], and Takanori Isobe[3]

[1] University of Hyogo, Kobe, Japan
toyama.uoh.hyogo@gmail.com
[2] Mitsubishi Electric Corporation, Kamakura, Japan
sakamoto.kosei@dc.mitsubishielectric.co.jp
[3] Osaka University, Osaka, Japan
takanori.isobe@ist.osaka-u.ac.jp

Abstract. SPONGENT is a lightweight hash function based on the sponge construction, featuring a PRESENT-like round function. Although it is included in the ISO standard for lightweight cryptography, no third-party analysis of collision attacks has been conducted. This lack of analysis is primarily due to the inherent difficulty of identifying value pairs that satisfy differential characteristics in sponge-construction-based hash functions. In this paper, we propose a novel method to efficiently identify value pairs that satisfy differential characteristics for keyless permutations. To address the existing problems, we introduce a grouping method that classifies input variables into categories such as free bits, fixed bits, and interdependent groups. This categorization facilitates efficient computation of degrees of freedom by solving for valid states within each group independently. We apply this method to variants of SPONGENT and, for the first time, demonstrate collision and semi-free-start collision attacks on reduced variants.

Keywords: SPONGENT · SAT · differential attacks · collision

1 Introduction

1.1 Background

In recent years, lightweight cryptography for resource-constrained environments, such as IoT devices, has gained significant attention. While research on lightweight block ciphers is very active, the security evaluation of lightweight hash functions remains insufficient, particularly for sponge-based schemes such as Quark [2], PHOTON [12] and SPONGENT [7]. Although these schemes are included in the ISO standard for lightweight cryptography [13], it is surprising that no third-party evaluations of collision attacks, which is one of the most critical properties of a hash function, have been conducted. Existing research has only focused on distinguishing attacks targeting the underlying permutations [1,14,19,27,30,31].

C. Boura et al. (Eds.): SAC 2025, LNCS 16207, pp. 26–54, 2026.
https://doi.org/10.1007/978-3-032-10536-3_2

SPONGENT [7] is a sponge-based lightweight hash function proposed by Bogdanov et al. It is designed using a PRESENT-like primitive [8] and offers 13 variants with different security levels, allowing users to select an option based on resource constraints and specific security priorities.

Regarding security evaluation, Abdelraheem showed differential and linear distinguishers for the underlying permutations [1].

Zhang and Liu further performed distinguishing attacks and preimage attacks through truncated differential attacks with the meet-in-the-middle technique [31]. However, no effective evaluation of collision resistance has been conducted so far except designer's evaluation [7]. This lack of evaluation arises from the inherent difficulty of identifying value pairs that satisfy differential characteristics in sponge-construction-based hash functions. The difficulty is primarily due to the absence of key-insertion mechanisms in their underlying permutations. This imposes taking the dependency between values and differences in S-boxes over multiple rounds into account, making obtaining enough degrees of freedom (DoF) quite complex. Indeed, Liu et al. demonstrated that many differential characteristics in the previous studies on sponge-based hash functions are not valid [17].

1.2 Contribution

In this paper, to address the problem of collision attacks on sponge-based hash function, we present a new method to efficiently identify value pairs that satisfy a given differential characteristics for key-less permutations. Our method focuses on modeling dependencies between value and difference transitions, drawing from Liu et al.'s approach [17]. A truth table representing these transitions is constructed and then simplified using logic minimization tools like Espresso. Our contribution is summarized as follow.

- We propose an approach to categorize input variables based on their dependencies. These variables are classified into free bits, which are independent and maximize the DoF; fixed bits, which are constrained to specific values; and interdependent groups, which are analyzed incrementally using SAT solvers. This categorization ensures efficient computation of DoF by solving for valid states within each group independently. By integrating the solutions from these groups, we determine the total DoF, which is crucial for assessing the feasibility of collision attacks on sponge-construction-based hash functions.
- We apply our method to several variants of SPONGENT. Table 1 shows the summary of our results. We obtain collision and semi-free-start collision attacks on reduced variants of SPONGENT for the first time. To verify our approach, we present actual collision pairs for several variants. It should be noted that the results of our attacks do not immediately affect the security of Spongent as there are still enough security margin.

2 Preliminaries

In this section, we explain differential cryptanalysis and automatic exploration using SAT solvers. Finally, we outline the specifications of SPONGENT, the cryptographic hash function analyzed in this paper, and discuss limitations of existing evaluations.

Table 1. Summary of collision attack results. Rounds marked with * indicate actual collision pairs found. †: invalid attack as it is less efficient than generic attack

	Collision		Semi-free-start		Ref	Full round	Collision security
	Rounds	Time	Rounds	Time			
SPONGENT-88/80/8	-	-	8*	2^{17}	Ours	45	2^{40}
	6†	$2^{55.2}$	-	-	[6]		
SPONGENT-88/176/88	9	2^{42}	9*	2^{33}	Ours	135	2^{44}
	8*	2^{28}					
SPONGENT-128/128/8	-	-	8*	2^{22}	Ours	70	2^{64}
SPONGENT-128/256/128	12	2^{58}	14	2^{63}	Ours	195	2^{64}
	8*	2^{28}					
SPONGENT-160/160/16	-	-	7	2^{47}	Ours	90	2^{80}
SPONGENT-160/160/80	11	2^{61}	14	2^{78}	Ours	120	2^{80}
SPONGENT-160/320/160	11	2^{56}	13	2^{79}	Ours	240	2^{80}
	8*	2^{28}					
SPONGENT-224/224/16	-	-	8	2^{91}	Ours	120	2^{112}
SPONGENT-224/224/112	10	2^{60}	11	2^{62}	Ours	170	2^{112}
SPONGENT-224/448/224	10	2^{47}	11	2^{57}	Ours	340	2^{112}
	8*	2^{21}					
SPONGENT-256/256/16	-	-	11	2^{110}	Ours	140	2^{128}
SPONGENT-256/256/128	15	2^{79}	15	2^{75}	Ours	195	2^{128}
SPONGENT-256/512/256	15	2^{73}	15	2^{73}	Ours	385	2^{128}
	9*	2^{28}					

2.1 Specification of SPONGENT

SPONGENT is a lightweight hash function with a sponge-based structure, consisting of 13 variants [7]. Each variant is specified by its hash size n, capacity$c$, and rate r, and is denoted as SPONGENT-$n/c/r$. The size of the internal state, $b = r + c \geq n$, is called the width. The security requirement for collision attacks is $\min(2^{n/2}, 2^{c/2})$. The specifications of each variant are shown in Table 2.

The sponge construction follows an iterative design with three phases. In the initialization phase, the message is padded to a multiple of r bits. During the absorbing phase, each r-bit message block is XORed with the first r bits of the state. Finally, in the squeezing phase, an n-bit output is obtained. The overall view is shown in Fig. 1.

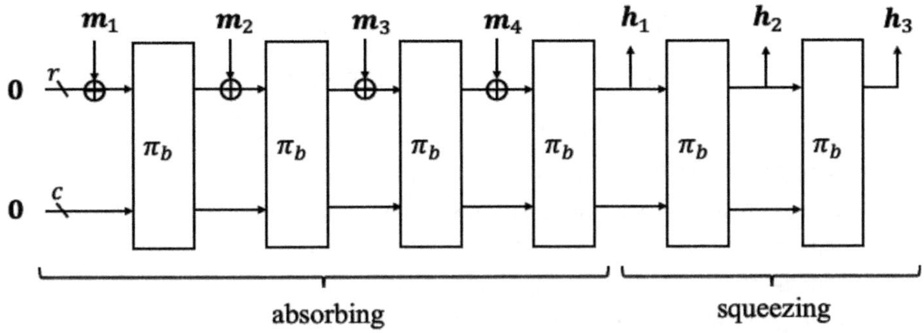

Fig. 1. Sponge construction based on a b-bit permutation π_b with capacity c bits and rate r bits. m_i are r-bit message blocks. h_i are parts of the hash value.

The round function uses an SPN (Substitution-Permutation Network) structure. The round function consists of the following three operations:

- **sBoxLayer**: The S-box operates on 4-bit inputs and produces 4-bit outputs, and it is applied in parallel $b/4$ times. The operation of the S-box in hexadecimal notation is shown as follows.

$$S[\cdot] = \{\texttt{0xE}, \texttt{0xD}, \texttt{0xB}, \texttt{0x0}, \texttt{0x2}, \texttt{0x1}, \texttt{0x4}, \texttt{0xF}, \texttt{0x7}, \texttt{0xA}, \texttt{0x8}, \texttt{0x5}, \texttt{0x9}, \texttt{0xC}, \texttt{0x3}, \texttt{0x6}\}$$

  The differential characteristics and internal states are interpreted with the leftmost bit as the least significant bit and represented in hexadecimal notation in this paper.
- **pLayer**: This is an extension of the (inverse) presentbit-permutation. The bit at position j of the state is moved to the bit position $P(j)$. Bit permutation is as shown in Fig. 2.

$$P_b(j) = \begin{cases} j \cdot b/4 \mod (b-1), & \text{if } j \in \{0, \ldots, b-2\} \\ -1, & \text{if } j = b-1. \end{cases}$$

- **lCounter**: A round-dependent constant is XORed with the state. The left end of the state is XORed with the round constant, and the right end is XORed with the round constant's bit-reversed value. These round constants are generated by an LFSR (Linear Feedback Shift Register). An LFSR is clocked once each time its state is used, ultimately reaching a final state where all bits are set to 1.

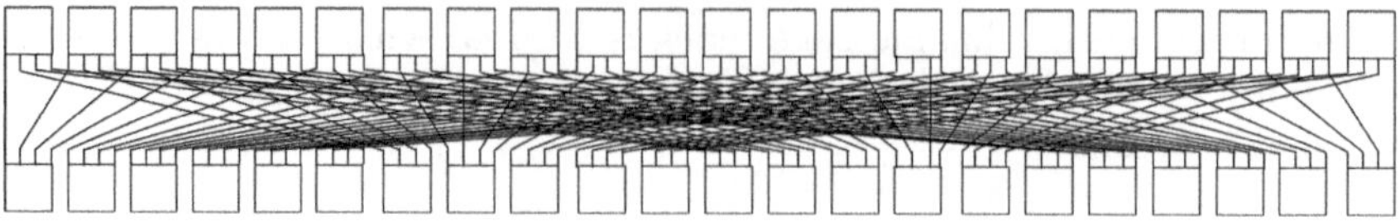

Fig. 2. The bit permutation layer of SPONGENT-88/80/8

Table 2. Parameters of SPONGENT

	n	b	c	r	Rounds	Collision security (bit)
SPONGENT-88/80/8	88	88	80	8	45	40
SPONGENT-88/176/88	88	264	176	88	135	44
SPONGENT-128/128/8	128	136	128	8	70	64
SPONGENT-128/256/128	128	384	256	128	195	64
SPONGENT-160/160/16	160	176	160	16	90	80
SPONGENT-160/160/80	160	240	160	80	120	80
SPONGENT-160/320/160	160	480	320	160	240	80
SPONGENT-224/224/16	224	240	224	16	120	112
SPONGENT-224/224/112	224	336	224	112	170	112
SPONGENT-224/448/224	224	672	448	224	340	112
SPONGENT-256/256/16	256	272	256	16	140	128
SPONGENT-256/256/128	256	384	256	128	195	128
SPONGENT-256/512/256	256	768	512	256	385	128

2.2 Variants of Collision Attacks

Let H, (m, m'), and IV be a hash function, a message pair, and an initial vector, respectively. A collision is a pair (m, m') satisfying $H(IV, m) = H(IV, m')$ where IV is set to 0 in SPONGENT. Let v be that is equal to the output of the previous block. A semi-free-start collision is a pair of (v, m) and (v, m') satisfying $H(v, m) = H(v, m')$ where $v \neq IV$.

2.3 Differential Characteristics

Differential cryptanalysis is one of the most powerful attacks on symmetric-key primitives proposed by Biham and Shamir [5]. In this attack, the attacker first tries to find a pair of input and output differences in which the input differences reach the output differences with a high probability and then mounts the key recovery on it. The time and data complexities depend on the ability to find an input-output pair difference with as high a probability as possible. Such search is the most important task in differential cryptanalysis. However, it is generally a hard task to find such pairs in practical time. Hence, we often use *differential characteristics* instead of calculating the probability of such pairs.

Let an r-round iterated block cipher be $E(\cdot) = f_r(\cdot) \circ \cdots \circ f_1(\cdot)$. Differential characteristic is defined as follows:

Definition 1 (Differential characteristic). *The differential characteristic is a sequence of differences over E defined as follows:*

$$\boldsymbol{D} = (\boldsymbol{d_0} \xrightarrow{f_1} \boldsymbol{d_1} \xrightarrow{f_2} \cdots \xrightarrow{f_r} \boldsymbol{d_r}) := (\boldsymbol{d_0}, \boldsymbol{d_1}, \cdots, \boldsymbol{d_r}),$$

where $\boldsymbol{d_i}$ is the difference at the output of i-th round for $0 < i \leq r$ and $\boldsymbol{d_0}$ is the difference at the input of the first round.

The Differential Characteristics Probability (DCP) is calculated by the product of the differential probability of each round on the well-known Markov cipher assumption [15] as follows:

$$DCP = \prod_{i=1}^{r} Prob.(\boldsymbol{d_{i-1}} \xrightarrow{f_i} \boldsymbol{d_i}).$$

For readability, we often use *weight* to express the probability of differential characteristics. A weight is defined as follows:

Definition 2 (Weight). *A weight w is a negated value of the binary logarithm of the probability P defined as follows:*

$$w = -\log_2 P$$

2.4 SAT-Based Automatic Search Method

SAT Problems. SAT problem is to solve whether a given Boolean formula can be made "True". A Boolean formula consists of only AND ($\wedge$), OR ($\vee$), and NOT ($\bar{\cdot}$) operations based on Boolean variables, and it can be converted into *Conjunctive Normal Form* (CNF). A CNF is constructed by the conjunction ($\wedge$) of the disjunction ($\vee$) on (possibly negated) Boolean variables, such as $\bigwedge_{a=0}^{i}(\bigvee_{b=0}^{j_a} x_{i,j})$, where $x_{i,j}$ is a Boolean variable. We call each disjunction $\bigvee_{b=0}^{j_a} c_{i,j}$ in a Boolean formula a *clause*. SAT solvers accept a CNF Boolean formula as their input.

Differential Characteristics Search by SAT. Recent studies demonstrated that the SAT-based automatic search method for identifying optimal differential characteristics can be much more efficient than the MILP- and CP-based ones [4, 29] for bit-oriented primitives. While the advantage is not clear in the case of byte-oriented ones, we opted for SAT and utilized Nicky and Bart's pure SAT-based method [23]. We leave for future research to test MILP- and CP-based techniques. Another possible research direction to improve our result is to integrate Sun et al.'s results into libraries like TAGADA, CASCADA, or CLAASP [3,16,26] to search for cipher vulnerabilities. In this case, rather than building a model directly, it is enough to represent the cipher in a specific format.

In the SAT-based search method for differential characteristics, we convert all differential propagation over primitives and its weight into a CNF. We call such a CNF a SAT model. Then, we give an objective function to identify the weight of the found differential characteristics, which is also expressed in a CNF, to a SAT model. Lastly, we give the created SAT model to a SAT solver. Hereafter, We briefly explain how to construct CNFs for each operation and the objective function.

Modeling for an XOR. Let $(a_0, a_1, \ldots, a_{i-1})$ and b be the input and output differences of an XOR operation with i inputs, respectively, i.e., $a_0 \oplus a_1 \oplus \cdots \oplus a_{i-1} = b$. Let X be the set $\{(x_0, x_1, \ldots, x_i) \in \mathbb{F}_2^{i+1} \mid (x_0 \oplus x_1 \oplus \cdots \oplus x_i) = 1\}$. The following variables and clauses are sufficient to express the differential propagation for an XOR with i inputs:

$$\mathcal{M}_{var} \leftarrow (a_0, a_1, \ldots, a_{i-1}, b, x_0, x_1, \ldots, x_i),$$
$$\mathcal{M}_{cla.xor} \leftarrow (a_0 \oplus x_0) \vee (a_1 \oplus x_1) \vee \cdots \vee (a_{i-1} \oplus x_{i-1}) \vee (b \oplus x_i),$$

where $\mathcal{M}_{var}$ and $\mathcal{M}_{cla.xor}$ denote the sets of Boolean variables and clauses, respectively.

Modeling for an XOR. Let (a_0, a_1) and b be the input and output differences of an XOR operation, respectively, i.e., $a_0 \oplus a_1 = b$. The following variables and clauses are sufficient to express the differential propagation for an XOR with i inputs:

$$\mathcal{M}_{var} \leftarrow (a_0, a_1, b),$$
$$\mathcal{M}_{cla.xor} \leftarrow \{(a_0 \vee a_1 \vee \bar{b}), (a_0 \vee \bar{a_1} \vee b), (\bar{a_0} \vee a_1 \vee b), (\bar{a_0} \vee \bar{a_1} \vee \bar{b}), \}$$

where $\mathcal{M}_{var}$ and $\mathcal{M}_{cla.xor}$ denote the sets of Boolean variables and clauses, respectively.

Modeling for an S-Box. Let $\boldsymbol{a} = (a_0, a_1, \ldots, a_{i-1})$ and $\boldsymbol{b} = (b_0, b_1, \ldots, b_{i-1})$ be the input and output differences of an i-bit S-box, respectively. Additionally, we introduce additional Boolean variables $\boldsymbol{p} = (p_0, p_1, \ldots, p_{j-1})$, where j is the maximum weight of the differential propagation through an i-bit S-box and $p_q \in \{0, 1\}$ for $1 \leq q \leq j-1$, to count the differential probability as an S-box is a probabilistic operation. With these Boolean variables, we construct the following Boolean formula:

$$f(\boldsymbol{a}, \boldsymbol{b}, \boldsymbol{p}) = \begin{cases} 1 & \textit{if } \Pr(\boldsymbol{a} \to \boldsymbol{b}) = 2^{-\sum_{q=0}^{j-1} p_q}, \\ 0 & \textit{otherwise.} \end{cases}$$

Then, we extract a set A, which contains all vectors satisfying $f(\boldsymbol{x}, \boldsymbol{y}, \boldsymbol{z}) = 0$ as follows:

$$A = \{(\boldsymbol{x}, \boldsymbol{y}, \boldsymbol{z}) \in \mathbb{F}_2^{2i+j} \mid f(\boldsymbol{x}, \boldsymbol{y}, \boldsymbol{z}) = 0\},$$

where $\boldsymbol{x} = (x_0, x_1, \ldots, x_{i-1})$, $\boldsymbol{y} = (y_0, y_1, \ldots, y_{i-1})$, and $\boldsymbol{z} = (z_0, z_1, \ldots, z_{j-1})$. Since A is a set of invalid patterns in a model of an S-box, we ban these patterns by the following clauses:

$$\bigvee_{c=0}^{i-1} (a_c \oplus x_c) \vee \bigvee_{d=0}^{i-1} (b_d \oplus y_d) \vee \bigvee_{e=0}^{j-1} (p_e \oplus z_e) = 1, \ (\boldsymbol{x}, \boldsymbol{y}, \boldsymbol{z}) \in A. \tag{1}$$

The remaining vectors, identical to $\overline{A}$, are a set of valid patterns. Therefore, these clauses extract the differential propagation with corresponding weight over an i-bit S-box. Note that the solution space of $|A|$ clauses about $(\boldsymbol{a}, \boldsymbol{b}, \boldsymbol{p})$ in Eq. (1) is identical to that of the following Boolean function:

$$g(\boldsymbol{a}, \boldsymbol{b}, \boldsymbol{p}) = \bigwedge_{(\boldsymbol{x}, \boldsymbol{y}, \boldsymbol{z}) \in \mathbb{F}_2^{2i+j}} \left(g(\boldsymbol{x}, \boldsymbol{y}, \boldsymbol{z}) \vee \bigvee_{c=0}^{i-1} (a_c \oplus x_c^{\eta}) \vee \bigvee_{d=0}^{i-1} (b_d \oplus y_d^{\eta}) \vee \bigvee_{e=0}^{j-1} (p_e \oplus z_e^{\eta}) \right).$$

This equation is called the *product-of-sum* of g. We know that we can reduce the number of clauses in g by Quine-McCluskey algorithm [21,24,25] and Espresso algorithm [9], shown in [18,28,29]. We use Espresso logic minimizer[1] to reduce clauses in g. Therefore, the following variables and clauses are sufficient to express the differential propagation with corresponding weight over an i-bit S-box:

$$\begin{aligned} &\mathcal{M}_{var} \leftarrow (a_0, a_1, \ldots, a_{i-1}, b_0, b_1, \ldots, b_{i-1}, p_0, p_1, \ldots, p_{j-1}), \\ &\mathcal{M}_{cla.sbox} \leftarrow min\left(g(\boldsymbol{a}, \boldsymbol{b}, \boldsymbol{p})\right), \end{aligned}$$

where $\mathcal{M}_{cla.xor}$ denotes the set of clauses.

For the evaluation to count the number of active S-boxes, we must consider whether an S-box is active instead of its weight. Therefore, we can implement it by replacing variables $\boldsymbol{p}$ to a, indicating whether an S-box is active. We represent it as $\mathcal{M}_{cla.sbox^*}$.

Objective Function. To identify the weight of the found differential characteristics, we set the objective function that suppresses the sum of all variables $(p_0, p_1, \ldots, p_{n-1})$ expressing weight by a specific value k as follows:

$$\sum_{i=0}^{n-1} p_i \leq k. \tag{2}$$

Equation 2 is called *Boolean cardinality constraints.* According to Erlacher et al.'s work [10], `kmtotalizer` [20] is a good choice to implement it. Therefore, the following variables and clauses are sufficient to express the objective function:

$$(\mathcal{M}_{cla.obj(k)}, \mathcal{M}_{var}) \leftarrow \texttt{kmtotalizer}(\Sigma_{i=0}^{n-1} p_i \leq k),$$

where $\mathcal{M}_{cla.obj(k)}$ denotes the set of clauses.

[1] https://ptolemy.berkeley.edu/projects/embedded/pubs/downloads/espresso/index.htm.

Modeling for an Entire SAT Model. We construct the whole SAT model $\mathcal{SAT}_{model}$ to identify the differential characteristics with the weight less than or equal to k with the above clauses and Boolean variables as follows:

$$\mathcal{SAT}_{model} \leftarrow (\mathcal{M}_{var}, \mathcal{M}_{cla.xor}, \mathcal{M}_{cla.sbox}, \mathcal{M}_{cla.obj(k)}).$$

Then, we give $\mathcal{SAT}_{model}$ to a SAT solver and solve it. If a SAT solver returns "SAT", we obtain the differential characteristic with the weight less than or equal to k. Otherwise, we increase k and repeat this procedure until a SAT solver returns "SAT". To count the number of active S-boxes, we can use the same model replaced $\mathcal{M}_{cla.sbox}$ to $\mathcal{M}_{cla.sbox^*}$ with the same procedure. It should be mentioned that this SAT model contains only CNFs for an XOR, S-box, and objective function because our target SPONGENT has only these operations.

Modeling of Difference and Value Transitions. Unlike block ciphers, the underlying permutation in permutation-based primitives does not involve round keys. Therefore, considering the dependence of differential transitions over multiple rounds, the risk of the actual state and differential characteristics becoming incompatible increases. In most MILP or SAT-based models for searching differential characteristics, only differential transitions are considered, and they are handled independently across different rounds, which may result in finding invalid differential characteristics for the actual state.

Liu et al. [17] designed a model that considers both differential transitions and value transitions in differential characteristics search. They independently construct models to describe differential transitions and value transitions, and connect them using a model that describes the differential value relationships in nonlinear operations.

2.5 Previous Results and Obstacles

The designers have performed a collision resistance evaluation using rebound attacks [22] on 6-round SPONGENT-88/80/8 [7]. However, the computational complexity is $2^{55.2}$, which is much larger than the claimed security of 2^{40}, making it an ineffective attack. Abdelraheem showed differential and linear distinguisher for the underlying permutations [1]. Zhang and Liu [32] demonstrated that an efficient distinguishing attack could be performed on all variations of SPONGENT permutations using a truncated differential attack with the meet-in-the-middle technique.

Despite these efforts, detailed analysis papers on collision attacks by third party are still lacking. To efficiently carry out collision attacks, bringing enough degrees of freedom is necessary, which is the number of value pairs satisfying the differential characteristics. For block-cipher-based hash functions, such as AES-like hashing, this can be conducted by counting the available DoF in each S-box independently, such as the super-S-box technique in the rebound attack [11].

In contrast, for sponge-construction-based hash functions, such as SPONGENT, finding value pairs satisfying the differential characteristics is challenging because their underlying permutations do not have a key-inserting operations. This imposes taking the dependency between values and differences in S-boxes over multiple rounds into account, making obtaining enough DoF quite complex. At CRYPTO 2020, Liu et al. showed that many differential characteristics in previous studies on sponge-based hash functions are invalid, i.e., there are no value pairs that satisfy the differential characteristics, and they presented an automatic search tool to find valid differential characteristics [17].

In our method, we first compute value pairs in selected parts of the hash function, similar to the rebound attack. However, bit dependencies in the internal state must be considered for both active and inactive bits.

3 Evaluation of the Number of Value Pairs Satisfying Differential Characteristics

To address this problem for collision attacks on sponge-construction-based hash functions, we propose a new method to efficiently evaluate the available degrees of freedom that satisfy a given set of differential characteristics for key-less permutations. The core idea of our method is to categorize the input bits by leveraging the dependency model of values and differences introduced by Liu et al. [17]. The proposed method consists of five steps, outlined as follows:

Step 1: Modeling by Liu et al.'s Method [17]. We describe the relationship between value transitions and difference transitions in the product of terms. To express these value-and-difference transitions, we adopt the method proposed by Liu et al. [17]. Specifically, to model these transitions, we construct a truth table that captures the value-and-difference transitions and utilize the Espresso tool to derive a corresponding Boolean function.

Step 2: Assigning a Given Differential Characteristic. We assign a given differential characteristic to the variables expressing the differences. Consequently, the product of terms exclusively consists of variables that represent value transitions satisfying a given differential characteristic.

Step 3: Expressing All Internal Variables by Input Variables. After creating the product of terms whose variables express a value transition with a given differential characteristic, we convert all internal-value variables into the input-value variables that can be easily conducted by analyzing the *Algebraic Normal Form* (ANF) of S-boxes in the case of SPONGENT. Then, we attempt to reduce the number of terms in the product of terms. This can be realized by simplify-logic tools. In this paper, we use simplify-logic() in SymPy library for Python.

Step 4: Grouping Input Variables. We analyze all terms in the product of terms and grouping the input variables depending on how they depend on each other, which is a core step of Grouping method.

Step 5: Calculating Total Available DoF. We count the number of value pairs for each group independently, which can be realized by solving the SAT model multiple times for each group. The obtained results are equivalent to the available DoF in each group. Therefore, the total available DoF is calculated by the product of the available DoF in each group.

Because Step 1 can be realized as a simple application of Liu et al.'s method [17] and Step 2 is just a process of the allocation for variables regarding a given differential characteristic, we will focus on elaborating on the detailed procedure of the Grouping method in Step 3, 4, and 5 in the next section. The conceptual diagram of the Grouping method is shown in Fig. 3.

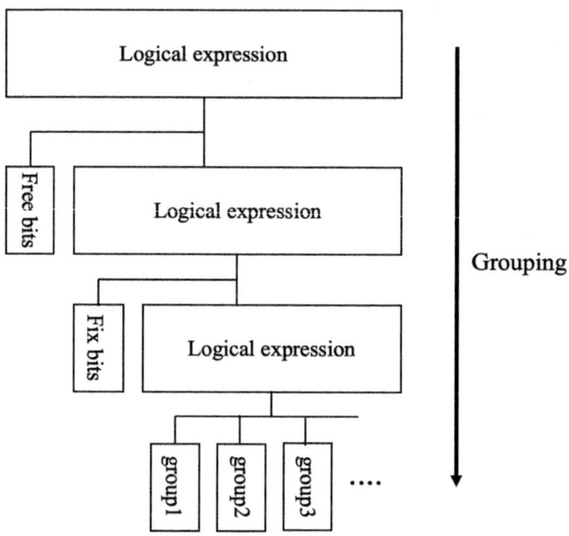

Fig. 3. Overview diagram of Grouping method

3.1 Grouping Method to Collect Value Pairs

Expressing All Internal Variables by Input Variables. After Step 1, and 2, the product of terms only consists of the variables expressing the internal values. Since the available DoF is brought from the message and the chaining value in semi-free-start collision setting, we need to express the product of terms only by these states, which are called the input values in this paper. This can be easily conducted by analyzing ANF of the S-box in the case of SPONGENT. This procedure allows us to investigate the dependency of the input values, which is necessary to efficiently estimate the available DoF in the later steps.

Grouping Input Variables and Enumerating Available DoF in Each Group. To verify a given value-and-difference transition model expressed in the product of terms, all terms must be "True". Therefore, we categorize variables,

Algorithm 1: Grouping of input-value variables.

Data: $\mathcal{C}$
Result: $\mathcal{G}$
$a = 1$
for $i = 1$ *to* α **do**
    for $j = 0$ *to* $l - 1$ **do**
        if v_i *in* $\mathcal{C}^j$ **and** v_i *is not in any group* **then**
            All literals in $\mathcal{C}^j$ are grouped to the a-th group
            $a \leftarrow a + 1$
        else if v_i *in* $\mathcal{C}^j$ **and** v_i *is already in* x*-th group* **then**
            All literals in $\mathcal{C}^j$ are grouped to the x-th group

which express the bits of the message and chaining value, into groups depending on which terms they are in. Then, we find all (or enough) assignments of literals in each group independently by solving the SAT model multiple times, equivalent to the number of valid value pairs with a given differential characteristic.

To find assignments of literals in a particular group, we first try to find one assignment for all literals. Then, we fix all literals to the found assignment except literals in a particular group in which we want to find all assignments of variables. This allows us to find all assignment by solving SAT models multiple times that can be efficiently carried out as this procedure can be viewed as an *incremental SAT problem.*

In the Grouping Method, dependencies between the internal values and differences can be categorized by "input values," which is essential to ensure valid differential characteristics and collect value pairs. Consequently, it is imperative to analyze it from the initial round and analyzing numerous rounds using the Grouping Method is challenging due to the computational cost.

Let $\mathcal{C} = \{C^0, C^1, \ldots, C^{l-1}\}$ and $C^i = \{c^i_0, c^i_1, \ldots, c^i_{m_i-1}\}$ be the Bool function describing value-and-difference transition and the term constructing $\mathcal{C}$ where c^i_j and m_i denote literals constructing C^i and the number of literals in C^i, respectively. Algorithm 1 shows how to categorize all input-value variables. In Algorithm 1, we assume to collect the value pairs satisfying a given differential characteristics regarding the function with the α-bit input, i.e., $c^i_j \in \{v_1, v_2, \ldots, v_\alpha\}$ where $0 \le i < l, 0 \le j < m_i$.

If a group has only one literal, we call this input-value variable as a *fixed bit* because it must be fixed to 0 or 1. If an input-value variable is not in any groups, we call it as a *free bit* because it can be either 0 or 1 not depending on other input-value variables.

We take the 2 rounds of `SPONGENT-160/160/80` as an example. Table 3 shows the differential characteristic in this example. We show the product of sums describing the value-and-difference transition regarding Table 3 as follows:

$$
\begin{aligned}
& v_{49} \bigwedge \neg v_{52} \bigwedge v_{57} \bigwedge \neg v_{60} \bigwedge v_{67} \bigwedge v_{75} \bigwedge (v_{65} | v_{68}) \bigwedge (v_{73} | v_{76}) \bigwedge (v_{50} | \neg v_{51}) \\
& \bigwedge (v_{51} | \neg v_{50}) \bigwedge (v_{58} | \neg v_{59}) \bigwedge (v_{59} | \neg v_{58}) \bigwedge (v_{66} | \neg v_{65}) \bigwedge (v_{74} | \neg v_{73}) \bigwedge (\neg v_{66} | \neg v_{68}) \\
& \bigwedge (\neg v_{74} | \neg v_{76}) \bigwedge (v_{78} \oplus v_{79} \oplus (v_{77} \wedge v_{80}) \oplus (v_{78} \wedge v_{79} \wedge v_{80})) \\
& \bigwedge (v_{61} \oplus (v_{61} \wedge v_{64}) \oplus (v_{62} \wedge v_{63}) \oplus (v_{62} \wedge v_{64}) \oplus (v_{63} \wedge v_{64}) \oplus (v_{62} \wedge v_{63} \wedge v_{64})) \\
& \bigwedge (v_{77} \oplus (v_{77} \wedge v_{80}) \oplus (v_{78} \wedge v_{79}) \oplus (v_{78} \wedge v_{80}) \oplus (v_{79} \wedge v_{80}) \oplus (v_{78} \wedge v_{79} \wedge v_{80})) \\
& \bigwedge \neg (v_{53} \oplus (v_{53} \wedge v_{56}) \oplus (v_{54} \wedge v_{55}) \oplus (v_{54} \wedge v_{56}) \oplus (v_{55} \wedge v_{56}) \oplus (v_{54} \wedge v_{55} \wedge v_{56})) \\
& \bigwedge \neg (v_{69} \oplus (v_{69} \wedge v_{72}) \oplus (v_{70} \wedge v_{71}) \oplus (v_{70} \wedge v_{72}) \oplus (v_{71} \wedge v_{72}) \oplus (v_{70} \wedge v_{71} \wedge v_{72})) \\
& \bigwedge ((v_{58} \wedge v_{59}) | \neg (v_{50} \wedge v_{51}) | (v_{61} \oplus (v_{61} \wedge v_{64}) \oplus (v_{62} \wedge v_{63}) \oplus (v_{62} \wedge v_{64}) \\
& \oplus (v_{63} \wedge v_{64}) \oplus (v_{62} \wedge v_{63} \wedge v_{64}))) \bigwedge ((v_{74} \oplus (v_{73} \wedge v_{76}) \oplus (v_{74} \wedge v_{76})) \\
& | \neg (v_{66} \oplus (v_{65} \wedge v_{68}) \oplus (v_{66} \wedge v_{68})) | (v_{78} \oplus v_{79} \oplus (v_{77} \wedge v_{80}) \oplus (v_{78} \wedge v_{79} \wedge v_{80}))) \\
& \bigwedge ((v_{65} \oplus v_{66} \oplus v_{68} \oplus (v_{65} \wedge v_{68})) | \neg (v_{73} \oplus v_{74} \oplus v_{76} \oplus (v_{73} \wedge v_{76})) \\
& | (v_{77} \oplus (v_{77} \wedge v_{80}) \oplus (v_{78} \wedge v_{79}) \oplus (v_{78} \wedge v_{80}) \oplus (v_{79} \wedge v_{80}) \oplus (v_{78} \wedge v_{79} \wedge v_{80}))) \\
& \bigwedge \neg (v_{70} \oplus v_{71} \oplus (v_{69} \wedge v_{72}) \oplus (v_{70} \wedge v_{71} \wedge v_{72}))
\end{aligned}
$$

,

where v_i denotes the input-value variable from the leftmost bit.

Table 3. The differential characteristic of the 2-round SPONGENT-160/160/80. Differences are displayed in hexadecimal.

Rounds	Differences at the input of each round
1(Input)	0000000000006060b0b00000000000000000000000000000000000000000
2	000000000000000000550000000000000050000000000000000000000000
3 (Output)	0000000000000000000000000000000000c000400000000000000000000

After applying Algorithm 1, the input-value variables are grouped as in Table 4. Since the input-value variables in the same group depends on each other and input-value variables in another group are independent, we can enumerate the assignment of the input-value variables group by group.

Calculating Total Available DoF. After Grouping the input-value variables, we attempt to find value pairs satisfying a given differential characteristic by solving the SAT model multiple times. We first try to find one solution. If there are no solutions, a given differential characteristic is invalid. Otherwise, we then count the number of value pairs satisfying differential characteristic by solving the SAT model multiple times. For the input-value variables categorized in free bits, they can take both 0 or 1. For the input-value variables categorized in

Table 4. Grouping results of the 2-round SPONGENT-160/160/80.

Category	Bits	Values
Free bits	48	v_{25}, v_{13}, v_{28}, v_{46}, v_{23}, v_{22}, v_{19}, v_{37}, v_{17}, v_{11}, v_{30}, v_{8}, v_{41}, v_{6}, v_{32}, v_{43}, v_{45}, v_{16}, v_{21}, v_{47}, v_{31}, v_{14}, v_{34}, v_{36}, v_{18}, v_{33}, v_{4}, v_{38}, v_{48}, v_{29}, v_{5}, v_{26}, v_{3}, v_{20}, v_{27}, v_{1}, v_{39}, v_{15}, v_{40}, v_{12}, v_{24}, v_{44}, v_{42}, v_{9}, v_{35}, v_{7}, v_{2}, v_{10}
Fixed bits	6	v_{49}, $\neg v_{52}$, v_{57}, $\neg v_{60}$, v_{67}, v_{75}
group1	4	v_{53}, v_{56}, v_{54}, v_{55}
group2	4	v_{69}, v_{72}, v_{70}, v_{71}
group3	8	v_{59}, v_{50}, v_{64}, v_{63}, v_{51}, v_{58}, v_{61}, v_{62}
group4	10	v_{80}, v_{78}, v_{77}, v_{73}, v_{68}, v_{66}, v_{65}, v_{76}, v_{79}, v_{74}

groups, we count the number of solutions by solving the SAT models multiple times. Let a, N_f, and N_x be the number of groups, the number of free bits, and the number of solutions in the x-th group, respectively. Since value pairs in each group can be calculated independently, the total number of value pairs satisfying a given differential characteristic can be calculated as follows:

$$2^{N_f} \times N_1 \times N_2 \times \cdots \times N_a.$$

which is equivalent to the available DoF.

3.2 Application to Collision Attacks

We apply the Grouping method to collision attacks by collecting enough number of the value pairs satisfying a part of differential characteristics and finding a collision pair satisfying the remaining part of differential characteristic as follows.

- Firstly, we divide a hash function H into an upper part H_u and a lower part H_b such that $H = H_b \circ H_u$. Then, we search the differential characteristics for H, which can occur collisions, taking only the weight in H_b into consideration.
- Next, we model the value-and-difference transitions with SAT by Liu et al.'s method [17] so as to confirm the validity of the differential characteristic in H_b. If there are no valid value pairs in H_b, we search the differential characteristic for H again.
- Then, we apply the Grouping method to H_u and obtain the enough number of DoFs to satisfy the differential characteristics in H_b. Let N_{DoF} and p be the available DoF in H_u and the probability of the differential characteristics found in the previous step, respectively. If $N_{DoF} \geq p^{-1}$, we can theoretically obtain $N_{DoF} \cdot p$ pairs satisfying the differential characteristic for H, meaning to find the colliding pairs.

Remarks. Above procedure only ensures the validity for the differential characteristics in H_u and H_b independently, i.e., the validity of the entire differential characteristic for H is not guaranteed. Therefore, we support the validity of the entire differential characteristic by showing the existence of numerous number of the value pairs satisfying the differential characteristics in H_u. Moreover, we show practical collision pairs for several variants of SPONGENT in Sect. 4 to enhance our assumption.

Besides, we always apply the Grouping method from the 1st round in all attacks because dependencies between the internal values and differences can be categorized by "input values," which is essential to ensure valid differential characteristics and collect value pairs in the Grouping method. Consequently, it is imperative to analyze it from the initial round, and analyzing numerous rounds using the Grouping method is challenging due to the computational cost. This is why we consistently apply the Grouping method from the first round. Introducing the Grouping method in a middle round is intriguing and remains as future work.

4 Applications to SPONGENT

In this section, we apply the grouping method to SPONGENT to construct a collision attack. First, we describe the method for searching differential characteristics suitable for the collision attack. Then, we apply the Grouping method to the identified differential characteristics to conduct the collision attacks to each variant of SPONGENT.

Overview. We first evaluate the optimal differential characteristics that can be used to find collisions. Then, we try to carry out the collision attacks with the procedure described in Sect. 3.2. For the number of rounds in H_u, we set it to at most 5 rounds because it can be too complex to carry out the Grouping method to more than 5 rounds regarding SPONGENT. Besides, we always apply the Grouping method from the first round since the distribution of differences at the middle rounds is complex, making the Grouping method quite expensive.

4.1 Searching Differential Characteristics for Collisions

For the variants with the parameters of $(r = n)$, we consider two cases:

1. Differences in the rate part after one block call is zero
2. Differences in the capacity part after one block call is zero and the difference in the second message will cancel out the differences in the internal state.

For the variants with the parameters $(r \neq n)$, we consider the case where differences in the capacity part after one block call is zero and the difference in the second message will cancel out the differences in the internal state. The results of the DCP evaluation for the collision attack are shown in Table 5.

Table 5. Summary of DCP for collision attacks on each variant, where - means that it was computationally infeasible.

Rounds	1	2	3	4	5	6	7	8	9	10	11	12	13	14	15	16	17
SPONGENT-88/80/8	2	7	-	-	54	58	60	61	68	72	85	89	97	107	107	118	119
SPONGENT-88/176/88	2	4	8	12	20	29	43	54	63	67	73	86	-	-	-	-	-
SPONGENT-128/128/8	2	-	-	-	-	93	86	88	90	92	96	107	-	-	-	-	-
SPONGENT-128/256/128	2	4	8	12	20	28	40	48	52	56	62	66	76	82	92	103	-
SPONGENT-160/160/16	2	6	-	-	-	69	51	75	85	84	80	88	-	-	-	-	-
SPONGENT-160/160/80	2	48	12	20	28	34	39	45	50	56	61	67	72	78	83	89	-
SPONGENT-160/320/160	2	4	8	12	20	28	41	52	61	71	-	-	-	-	-	-	-
SPONGENT-224/224/16	2	6	-	-	-	-	-	96	100	106	-	-	-	-	-	-	-
SPONGENT-224/224/112	2	4	8	12	20	30	45	56	66	76	-	-	-	-	-	-	-
SPONGENT-224/448/224	2	4	8	12	20	28	44	54	73	-	-	-	-	-	-	-	-
SPONGENT-256/256/16	2	6	-	-	-	-	-	81	85	87	102	120	-	-	-	-	-
SPONGENT-256/256/128	2	4	8	12	20	28	41	49	56	60	64	70	78	87	97	104	110
SPONGENT-256/512/256	2	4	8	12	20	28	40	48	52	56	62	68	76	86	94	-	-

4.2 Collision Attacks on the SPONGENT

We show the detailed procedure of collision attacks on several variants of SPONGENT. In addition, the procedure to find semi-free-start collisions on SPONGENT-128/256/128 and SPONGENT-160/160/80 are shown in the Appendix B. Due to the page limitation, the remaining results of (semi-free-start) collisions on other variants of SPONGENT are summarized in Appendix A. The implementation codes for the collision attacks on SPONGENT are available on https://anonymous.4open.science/r/SPONGENT-Collision-83F7/README.md

Attacks on 11-round SPONGENT-160/160/80

Step 1. Divide the round function into the first 2 rounds and the remaining 9 rounds such that $H = H_{(3\to 11)} \circ H_{(1\to 2)}$. Evaluate the differential characteristic for H taking the weight in $H_{(3\to 11)}$, which must be less than the weight of the claimed security, into consideration. As a result, we obtain the differential characteristics shown in Table 6 whose probability in $H_{(3\to 11)}$ is 2^{-61}.

Step 2. Construct the model for the value-and-difference transitions for $H_{(3\to 11)}$ by Liu et al.'s method [17], and verify that the differential characteristic is valid.

Step 3. Apply the Grouping method to $H_{(1\to 2)}$. Table 7 shows the results after applying the Grouping method. There are 48 free bits and 6 fixed bits. The other input bits are categorized into 4 groups.

Step 4. Since the differential probability of $H_{(3\to 11)}$ is 2^{-61}, at least 2^{61} DoF in $H_{(1\to 2)}$ is needed to obtain one collision pair on average. As we can obtain 2^{48} DoF by free bits, we need to get 2^{13} DoF by 4 groups. To this end, we construct the value-and-difference transition model by SAT and solve the constructed

SAT models multiple times. As a result, we found 2^3, 2^2, 2^5, and 2^4 in groups 1, 2, 3, and 4, respectively. Therefore, we obtain $2^{48} \times 2^3 \times 2^2 \times 2^5 \times 2^3 = 2^{61}$ DoF that is enough to find one collision pair.

Step 5. Finding the colliding pairs with 2^{61} in $H_{(1\to 2)}$, which satisfy the differential characteristic in $H_{(3\to 11)}$.

Complexity Analysis. The cost of Grouping input variables is negligible compared to those of enumerating the available DoF and finding a pair satisfying the differential characteristic in $H_{(3\to 11)}$ Time complexities of enumerating the available DoF and finding a pair satisfying the differential characteristic in $H_{(3\to 11)}$ are $\frac{2}{11} \times 2^{61}$ and $\frac{9}{11} \times 2^{61}$, respectively. Since these procedures can be independently conducted, the total time complexity is $\frac{2}{11} \times 2^{61} + \frac{9}{11} \times 2^{61} = 2^{61} < 2^{80}$.

Table 6. The differential characteristic of SPONGENT-160/160/80. Differences are displayed in hexadecimal.

Rounds	Differences at the input of each round	Prob.	Phase
1(Input)	0000000000006060b0b000000000000000000000000000000000000000000000		$H_{(1\to 2)}$
2	0000000000000000005500000000000000000050000000000000000000000000		
3	00000000000000000000000000000000000000c0004000000000000000000000	2^{-61}	$H_{(3\to 11)}$
4	0000000000000000000000000000000000000000004400000000000004400000		
5	0000000000000000000000000000000000000000000c00060000000000c00060		
6	0000000008800440000000000000000000000000000000000000000000000000		
7	0066000000000000066000000000000000000000000000000000000000000000		
8	c000600000000000000000000000000000000000000000000000000000000000		
9	1100000000000000000000000000000000000000000000000000000000000000		
10	3000000000000003000000000000000000000000000000000000000000000000		
11	0000000000000001008000000000000000000000000000000000000000000000		
Output	0008400000000000008400000000000000000000000000000000000000000000		

Attacks on 15-round SPONGENT-256/256/128

Step 1. Divide the round function into the first 2 rounds and the remaining 9 rounds such that $H = H_{(5\to 15)} \circ H_{(1\to 4)}$. Evaluate the differential characteristic for H taking the weight in $H_{(5\to 15)}$, which must be less than the weight of the claimed security, into consideration. As a result, we obtain the differential characteristics shown in Table 8 whose probability in $H_{(5\to 15)}$ is 2^{-79}.

Step 2. Construct the model for the value-and-difference transitions for $H_{(5\to 15)}$ by Liu et al.'s method [17], and verify that the differential characteristic is valid.

Step 3. Apply the Grouping method to $H_{(1\to 4)}$. Table 9 shows the results after applying the Grouping method. There are 64 free bits and 12 fixed bits. The other input bits are categorized into 2 groups.

Table 7. Grouping results of SPONGENT-160/160/80. The leftmost bit is denoted as v_1. Time of $H_{(1\to2)}$ represents the lower bound of the computational complexity required for collecting DoF in $H_{(1\to2)}$.

Category	Bits	Values
Free bits	48	v_{25}, v_{13}, v_{28}, v_{46}, v_{23}, v_{22}, v_{19}, v_{37}, v_{17}, v_{11}, v_{30}, v_8, v_{41}, v_6, v_{32}, v_{43}, v_{45}, v_{16}, v_{21}, v_{47}, v_{31}, v_{14}, v_{34}, v_{36}, v_{18}, v_{33}, v_4, v_{38}, v_{48}, v_{29}, v_5, v_{26}, v_3, v_{20}, v_{27}, v_1, v_{39}, v_{15}, v_{40}, v_{12}, v_{24}, v_{44}, v_{42}, v_9, v_{35}, v_7, v_2, v_{10}
Fixed bits	6	v_{49}, $\neg v_{52}$, v_{57}, $\neg v_{60}$, v_{67}, v_{75}
group1	4	v_{53}, v_{56}, v_{54}, v_{55}
group2	4	v_{69}, v_{72}, v_{70}, v_{71}
group3	8	v_{59}, v_{50}, v_{64}, v_{63}, v_{51}, v_{58}, v_{61}, v_{62}
group4	10	v_{80}, v_{78}, v_{77}, v_{73}, v_{68}, v_{66}, v_{65}, v_{76}, v_{79}, v_{74}
Time of $H_{(1\to2)}$	$2^{58.5}$	

Step 4. Since the differential probability of $H_{(5\to15)}$ is 2^{-79}, at least 2^{79} DoF in $H_{(1\to4)}$ is needed to obtain one collision pair on average. As we can obtain 2^{64} DoF by free bits, we need to get 2^{15} DoF by 4 groups. To this end, we construct the value-and-difference transition model by SAT and solve the constructed SAT models multiple times. As a result, we found 2^{12}, and 2^{13} in groups 1 and 2 respectively. Therefore, we obtain $2^{64} \times 2^{12} \times 2^{13} = 2^{79}$ DoF that is enough to find one collision pair.

Step 5. Finding the colliding pairs with 2^{79} in $H_{(1\to4)}$, which satisfy the differential characteristic in $H_{(5\to15)}$.

Complexity Analysis. The cost of Grouping input variables is negligible compared to those of enumerating the available DoF and finding a pair satisfying the differential characteristic in $H_{(5\to15)}$ Time complexities of enumerating the available DoF and finding a pair satisfying the differential characteristic in $H_{(5\to15)}$ are $\frac{4}{15} \times 2^{79}$ and $\frac{11}{15} \times 2^{79}$, respectively. Since these procedures can be independently conducted, the total time complexity is $\frac{4}{15} \times 2^{79} + \frac{11}{15} \times 2^{79} = 2^{79} < 2^{128}$.

4.3 Practical Collision Pairs on Several Variants of SPONGENT

To demonstrate the validity of the proposed method, we show the actual collision pairs for several variants. We show the detailed procedure of collision attacks on SPONGENT-88/176/88. The collision pairs and their input pairs are shown in Appendix C due to the page limitation.

Attacks on 8-round SPONGENT-88/176/88

Step 1. Divide the round function into the first 4 rounds and the remaining 4 rounds such that $H = H_{(1\to4)} \circ H_{(5\to8)}$. Evaluate the differential characteristic for H taking the weight in $H_{(5\to8)}$, which must be less than the weight of the claimed security, into consideration. As a result, we obtain the differential characteristics shown in Table 10 whose probability in $H_{(5\to8)}$ is 2^{-28}.

Table 8. The differential characteristic of SPONGENT-256/256/128. Differences are displayed in hexadecimal. The data is shown in a folded form, with each state listed sequentially from left to right.

Rounds	Differences at the input of each round	Prob.	Phase
1(Input)	0000000000000000ee800000295000000000000000000000000000000000000000000000000000000000000000000000		$H_{(1\to4)}$
2	0000e02000000000000000000000000000000000000000000000e0e00000000000000000000000000000000000000000		
3	050000000000050000000000000000000000000000000000005000000000050000000000000000000000000000000000		
4	000000000000000000000000000000000000000000000000020020000000200200000000000000000000000000000000		
5	000000000000000000000000000000000009009000000000000000000000000000000000000000000000900900000000	2^{-79}	$H_{(5\to15)}$
6	000000000000000000000000000000000000000000000000000000000000000000000900000000000900000000000000		
7	000000000000000000000000000000000000000002002000000000000000000000000000000000000000000000000000		
8	000000000021000000000000000000000000000000000000000000000021000000000000000000000000000000000000		
9	00c0000000000c000000000000000000000000000000000000c0000000000c0000000000000000000000000000000000		
10	400400000000400400000000000000000000000000000000000000000000000000000000000000000000000000000000		
11	000000000000000000000000000000000000000000000000900900000000000000000000900900000000000000000000		
12	000000000000000000000000000000000000000000000000000000000000000000000000000000000000900000900000		
13	000000000000000000000000000000000000000000000000000000000000000000000000000000000000000000000140		
14	000000000000000000000006000000000000000000000006000000000000000000000000000000000000000000000000		
15	000008000008000000000000000000000000000000000000000000000000000000000000000000000000000000000000		
Output	028000000000000000000000280000000000000000000000000000000000000000000000000000000000000000000000		

Table 9. Grouping results of SPONGENT-256/256/128. The leftmost bit is denoted as v_1. Time of $H_{(1\to4)}$ represents the lower bound of the computational complexity required for collecting DoF in $H_{(1\to4)}$.

Category	Bits	Values
Free bits	64	v_{13}, v_{23}, v_{12}, v_{43}, v_{53}, v_{60}, v_3, v_{34}, v_{37}, v_{14}, v_{11}, v_{30}, v_{19}, v_{49}, v_4, v_{25}, v_{59}, v_{64}, v_{18}, v_{22}, v_8, v_{24}, v_{51}, v_{58}, v_{21}, v_{16}, v_{56}, v_{17}, v_{39}, v_{33}, v_1, v_{15}, v_{32}, v_{28}, v_{55}, v_{62}, v_{52}, v_6, v_{50}, v_{42}, v_{54}, v_{10}, v_{38}, v_{48}, v_{45}, v_{46}, v_{26}, v_7, v_{47}, v_{40}, v_{44}, v_{31}, v_{35}, v_{27}, v_{29}, v_2, v_{63}, v_5, v_{57}, v_{36}, v_9, v_{20}, v_{41}, v_{61}
Fixed bits	12	v_{69}, v_{73}, v_{77}, v_{78}, $\neg v_{79}$, $\neg v_{101}$, $\neg v_{103}$, $\neg v_{104}$, $\neg v_{106}$, $\neg v_{107}$, v_{110}, $\neg v_{112}$
group1	16	v_{87}, v_{93}, v_{85}, v_{81}, v_{96}, v_{82}, v_{89}, v_{90}, v_{91}, v_{94}, v_{95}, v_{84}, v_{92}, v_{86}, v_{88}, v_{83}
group2	36	v_{100}, v_{65}, v_{67}, v_{68}, v_{105}, v_{75}, v_{115}, v_{123}, v_{66}, v_{119}, v_{114}, v_{74}, v_{99}, v_{109}, v_{124}, v_{71}, v_{120}, v_{122}, v_{127}, v_{108}, v_{102}, v_{111}, v_{116}, v_{128}, v_{72}, v_{80}, v_{117}, v_{97}, v_{113}, v_{118}, v_{125}, v_{70}, v_{76}, v_{121}, v_{98}, v_{126}
Time of $H_{(1\to4)}$	$2^{77.1}$	

Step 2. Construct the model for the value-and-difference transitions for $H_{(5\to8)}$ by Liu et al.'s method [17], and verify that the differential characteristic is valid.

Step 3. Apply the Grouping method to $H_{(1\to4)}$. Table 11 shows the results after applying the Grouping method. There are 32 free bits and 6 fixed bits. The other input bits are categorized into 1 group.

Step 4. Since the differential probability of $H_{(5\to8)}$ is 2^{-28}, at least 2^{28} DoF in $H_{(1\to4)}$ is needed to obtain one collision pair on average. As we can obtain 2^{32} DoF by free bits. To this end, we construct the value-and-difference transition model by SAT and solve constructed SAT models, and we found more than one state. Therefore, we obtain $2^{32}\times 1 = 2^{32}$ DoF that is enough to find one collision pair.

Step 5. Finding the colliding pairs with 2^{32} in $H_{(1\to4)}$, which satisfy the differential characteristic in $H_{(5\to8)}$.

Complexity Analysis. The cost of Grouping input variables is negligible compared to those of enumerating the available DoF and finding a pair satisfying the differential characteristic in $H_{(5\to8)}$ Time complexities of enumerating the available DoF and finding a pair satisfying the differential characteristic in $H_{(5\to8)}$ are $\frac{4}{8}\times2^{28}$ and $\frac{4}{8}\times2^{28}$, respectively. Since these procedures can be independently conducted, the total time complexity is $\frac{4}{8}\times2^{28}+\frac{4}{8}\times2^{28}=2^{28}<2^{43}$.

Table 10. The differential characteristic of SPONGENT-88/176/88. Differences are displayed in hexadecimal.

Rounds	Differences at the input of each round	Prob.	Phase
1(Input)	000000000d89b0000c6fa000000000000000000000000000000000000000000000		$H_{(1\to4)}$
2	006060000000000000000000000000000000000000000000000070700000000000		
3	000000000000050005000000000000000000000000000000000000000000000000		
4	000000000000000000000000000000000000220000000000000000000000000000		
5	0000000000000000000000000c00000000000000000000000000000000c0000000	2^{-28}	$H_{(5\to8)}$
6	000000200000000000000000000000000000000000000000000000000000000010		
7	000000000000000010100000000000000000000000000000010100000000000000		
8	000050000000a000000000000000000000000500000000a000000000000000000000		
Output	000000000000000000000000000000000010000000200000000040000000800000		

Table 11. Grouping results of SPONGENT-88/176/88. The leftmost bit is denoted as v_1. Time of $H_{(1\to4)}$ represents the lower bound of the computational complexity required for collecting DoF in $H_{(1\to4)}$.

Category	Bits	Values
Free bits	32	v_{19}, v_{26}, v_1, v_5, v_{15}, v_{12}, v_{23}, v_3, v_{20}, v_{17}, v_8, v_{18}, v_{30}, v_{31}, v_7, v_{16}, v_{13}, v_{25}, v_4, v_{29}, v_2, v_6, v_{22}, v_{11}, v_{24}, v_9, v_{14}, v_{10}, v_{21}, v_{27}, v_{28}, v_{32}
Fixed bits	6	v_{38}, v_{51}, v_{69}, $\neg v_{70}$, v_{81}, $\neg v_{83}$
group1	50	v_{82}, v_{57}, v_{55}, v_{85}, v_{78}, v_{74}, v_{50}, v_{88}, v_{52}, v_{39}, v_{53}, v_{67}, v_{79}, v_{63}, v_{60}, v_{87}, v_{84}, v_{75}, v_{73}, v_{76}, v_{37}, v_{47}, v_{40}, v_{48}, v_{56}, v_{34}, v_{42}, v_{54}, v_{62}, v_{49}, v_{58}, v_{65}, v_{64}, v_{41}, v_{86}, v_{35}, v_{45}, v_{61}, v_{59}, v_{71}, v_{44}, v_{66}, v_{46}, v_{80}, v_{36}, v_{33}, v_{77}, v_{43}, v_{72}, v_{68}
Time of $H_{(1\to4)}$	$2^{27.0}$	

5 Conclusion

In this paper, we proposed a novel method to efficiently identify value pairs that satisfy differential characteristics for keyless permutations. To address the existing problem, we introduced a grouping method that classifies input variables into categories such as free bits, fixed bits, and interdependent groups. We applied this method to variants of SPONGENT and, for the first time, demonstrated collision and semi-free-start collision attacks on reduced variants. It should be noted that the results of our attacks do not immediately affect the security of Spongent as there are still enough security margin.

Acknowledgments. This work was supported by JST AIP Acceleration Research JPMJCR24U1 Japan and JSPS KAKENHI Grant Number JP24H00696.

A Summary of Attacks on Other Variants of SPONGENT

In this section, we show the results of (semi-free start) collision attacks on the other variants of SPONGENT. Table 12 shows the summary of the results of our attacks. Due to the page limitations, we omit the detailed procedures of several our attacks. The procedures of all attacks are the same as described in Sect. 4.

B Applications of Semi-Free-Start Collisions

B.1 Attacks on 14-Round SPONGENT-128/256/128

Attack Procedure

Step 1. Divide the round function into the first 2 rounds and the remaining 9 rounds such that $H = H_{(5\to14)} \circ H_{(1\to4)}$. Evaluate the differential characteristic for H taking the weight in $H_{(5\to14)}$, which must be less than the weight of the claimed security, into consideration. As a result, we obtain the differential characteristics shown in Table 13 whose probability in $H_{(5\to14)}$ is 2^{-63}.

Step 2. Construct the model for the value-and-difference transitions for $H_{(5\to14)}$ by Liu et al.'s method [17], and verify that the differential characteristic is valid.

Step 3. Apply the Grouping method to $H_{(1\to4)}$. Table 14 shows the results after applying the Grouping method. There are 4 free bits and 33 fixed bits. The other input bits are categorized into 3 groups.

Step 4. Since the differential probability of $H_{(5\to14)}$ is 2^{-63}, at least 2^{63} DoF in $H_{(1\to4)}$ is needed to obtain one collision pair on average. As we can obtain 2^4 DoF by free bits, we need to get 2^{59} DoF by 4 groups. To this end, we construct the value-and-difference transition model by SAT and solve the constructed SAT models multiple times. As a result, we found 2^{20}, 2^{20}, 2^{29} in groups 1, 2, and 3 respectively. Therefore, we obtain $2^4 \times 2^{20} \times 2^{20} \times 2^{19} = 2^{63}$ DoF that is enough to find one collision pair.

Table 12. Summary of collision attack results. Rounds marked with * indicate actual collision pairs found. †: invalid attack as it is less efficient than generic attack

	Collision		Semi-free-start		Full round	Collision security
	Rounds	Time	Rounds	Time		
SPONGENT-88/80/8	-	-	8*	2^{17}	45	2^{40}
SPONGENT-88/176/88	9 8*	2^{42} 2^{28}	9*	2^{33}	135	2^{44}
SPONGENT-128/128/8	-	-	8*	2^{22}	70	2^{64}
SPONGENT-128/256/128	12 8*	2^{58} 2^{28}	14	2^{63}	195	2^{64}
SPONGENT-160/160/16	-	-	7	2^{47}	90	2^{80}
SPONGENT-160/160/80	11	2^{61}	14	2^{78}	120	2^{80}
SPONGENT-160/320/160	11 8*	2^{56} 2^{28}	13	2^{79}	240	2^{80}
SPONGENT-224/224/16	-	-	8	2^{91}	120	2^{112}
SPONGENT-224/224/112	10	2^{60}	11	2^{62}	170	2^{112}
SPONGENT-224/448/224	10 8*	2^{47} 2^{21}	11	2^{57}	340	2^{112}
SPONGENT-256/256/16	-	-	11	2^{110}	140	2^{128}
SPONGENT-256/256/128	15	2^{79}	15	2^{75}	195	2^{128}
SPONGENT-256/512/256	15 9*	2^{73} 2^{28}	15	2^{73}	385	2^{128}

Step 5. Finding the colliding pairs with 2^{63} in $H_{(1 \to 4)}$, which satisfy the differential characteristic in $H_{(5 \to 14)}$.

Table 13. The differential characteristic of SPONGENT-128/256/128 for semi-free-start collisions.

Rounds	Differences at the input of each round	Prob.	Phase
1(Input)	9dba9526599000003990e330037000000000000000000000000000000000000000000000000000000000000000000000		$H_{(1 \to 4)}$
2	cc00000000000000000000000000776000000000000000007770000000000000000000000000000000000000000000000		
3	300000070000070000000000000000000000000000000000000000000000000000000000000000000000000000000000		
4	000000000000000000000000180100000000000000000000000000000000000000000000000000000000000000000000		
5	000000b00000000000000000000000000000000000000000000000b00000000000000000000000000000000000000000	2^{-63}	$H_{(5 \to 14)}$
6	040000000000040000000000000000000000000000000000000000000000000000000000000000000000000000000000		
7	000000000000000000000000000000000000000000000000200200000000000000000000200200000000000000000000		
8	000000000000000000000000000000000000900000900000000000000000000000000000000000000000900000900000		
9	000000000000000000000000000000000000000000000000000000000000000000000000000000000140000000000140		
10	000000000000000000006006000000000000000000006006000000000000000000000000000000000000000000000000		
11	000009000009000000000000000000000000000000000000000000000000000000000000000000000000000000000000		
12	000000000000000000000000000000000000000000000000000000000000000000000000028000000000000000000000		
13	000000000000000060000000000000000000000000000000000000000000000000600000000000000000000000000000		
14	000040000000000000000000000000000000000000000000000000000000000040000000000000000000000000000000		
Output	000000000000000000000000000000000000000000000000010000000000000010000000010000000000000010000000		

Complexity Analysis. The cost of grouping input variables is negligible compared to those of enumerating the available DoF and finding a pair satisfying the differential characteristic in $H_{(5\to14)}$ Time complexities of enumerating the available DoF and finding a pair satisfying the differential characteristic in $H_{(5\to14)}$ are $\frac{4}{14} \times 2^{63}$ and $\frac{10}{14} \times 2^{63}$, respectively. Since these procedures can be independently conducted, the total time complexity is $\frac{4}{14} \times 2^{63} + \frac{10}{14} \times 2^{63} = 2^{63} < 2^{128}$.

B.2 Attacks on 14-Round SPONGENT-160/160/80

Attack Procedure

Step 1. Divide the round function into the first 2 rounds and the remaining 9 rounds such that $H = H_{(4\to14)} \circ H_{(1\to3)}$. Evaluate the differential characteristic for H taking the weight in $H_{(4\to14)}$, which must be less than the weight of the claimed security, into consideration. As a result, we obtain the differential characteristics shown in Table 15 whose probability in $H_{(4\to14)}$ is 2^{-78}.

Step 2. Construct the model for the value-and-difference transitions for $H_{(4\to14)}$ by Liu et al.'s method [17], and verify that the differential characteristic is valid.

Step 3. Apply the Grouping method to $H_{(1\to3)}$. Table 16 shows the results after applying the Grouping method. There are 160 free bits and 12 fixed bits. The other input bits are categorized into 3 groups.

Step 4. Since the differential probability of $H_{(4\to14)}$ is 2^{-78}, at least 2^{78} DoF in $H_{(1\to3)}$ is needed to obtain one collision pair on average. As we can obtain 2^{160} DoF by free bits if one or more states can be discovered from group 1. To this end, we construct the value-and-difference transition model by SAT and solve the constructed SAT model, and we found more than one state. Therefore, we obtain $2^{78} \times 1 = 2^{78}$ DoF that is enough to find one collision pair.

Step 5. Finding the colliding pairs with 2^{78} in $H_{(1\to3)}$, which satisfy the differential characteristic in $H_{(4\to14)}$.

Computational Cost Evaluation. Ignoring the cost of Grouping, the computational cost required to find one collision pair is $\frac{3}{14} \times 2^{78} + \frac{11}{14} \times 2^{78} = 2^{78} < 2^{80}$(claimed security). Therefore, the attack is successful.

The cost of grouping input variables is negligible compared to those of enumerating the available DoF and finding a pair satisfying the differential characteristic in $H_{(4\to14)}$ Time complexities of enumerating the available DoF and finding a pair satisfying the differential characteristic in $H_{(4\to14)}$ are $\frac{3}{14} \times 2^{78}$ and $\frac{11}{14} \times 2^{78}$, respectively. Since these procedures can be independently conducted, the total time complexity is $\frac{3}{14} \times 2^{78} + \frac{11}{14} \times 2^{78} = 2^{78} < 2^{128}$.

C Values of Practical Collision Pairs

Collision pairs for several variants of SPONGENT are shown in Table 17.

Table 14. Grouping results of SPONGENT-128/256/128 (semi-free-start). The leftmost bit is denoted as v_1. Time of $H_{(1\to4)}$ represents the lower bound of the computational complexity required for collecting DoF in $H_{(1\to4)}$.

Category	Bits	Values
Free bits	4	$v_{85}, v_{89}, v_{65}, v_{101}$
Fix bits	33	$v_{2}, \neg v_{3}, v_{6}, \neg v_{11}, v_{15}, \neg v_{13}, \neg v_{18}, \neg v_{19}, v_{22}, \neg v_{24}, \neg v_{25}, \neg v_{27}, \neg v_{28}, v_{34}, \neg v_{36}, \neg v_{38}, \neg v_{39}, \neg v_{42}, \neg v_{43}, v_{68}, \neg v_{67}, v_{70}, v_{71}, v_{74}, v_{75}, \neg v_{81}, v_{88}, \neg v_{87}, v_{92}, \neg v_{91}, v_{104}, \neg v_{103}, \neg v_{108}$
group1	64	$v_{172}, v_{132}, v_{163}, v_{140}, v_{187}, v_{162}, v_{159}, v_{155}, v_{179}, v_{185}, v_{157}, v_{176}, v_{165}, v_{149}, v_{186}, v_{150}, v_{183}, v_{169}, v_{166}, v_{152}, v_{175}, v_{133}, v_{168}, v_{171}, v_{147}, v_{144}, v_{154}, v_{181}, v_{164}, v_{170}, v_{135}, v_{138}, v_{174}, v_{178}, v_{190}, v_{151}, v_{161}, v_{158}, v_{130}, v_{184}, v_{156}, v_{131}, v_{191}, v_{173}, v_{137}, v_{142}, v_{180}, v_{134}, v_{192}, v_{182}, v_{160}, v_{177}, v_{167}, v_{136}, v_{188}, v_{139}, v_{146}, v_{148}, v_{143}, v_{145}, v_{153}, v_{141}, v_{189}, v_{129}$
group2	64	$v_{199}, v_{252}, v_{197}, v_{204}, v_{236}, v_{249}, v_{194}, v_{256}, v_{217}, v_{193}, v_{241}, v_{216}, v_{220}, v_{205}, v_{244}, v_{198}, v_{206}, v_{245}, v_{214}, v_{221}, v_{196}, v_{225}, v_{247}, v_{232}, v_{218}, v_{211}, v_{237}, v_{235}, v_{212}, v_{255}, v_{223}, v_{208}, v_{200}, v_{203}, v_{201}, v_{250}, v_{246}, v_{229}, v_{251}, v_{233}, v_{254}, v_{243}, v_{195}, v_{222}, v_{215}, v_{202}, v_{207}, v_{248}, v_{228}, v_{210}, v_{253}, v_{238}, v_{234}, v_{242}, v_{213}, v_{240}, v_{230}, v_{227}, v_{209}, v_{226}, v_{231}, v_{239}, v_{219}, v_{224}$
group3	219	$v_{279}, v_{260}, v_{60}, v_{31}, v_{10}, v_{370}, v_{78}, v_{100}, v_{119}, v_{295}, v_{267}, v_{53}, v_{300}, v_{96}, v_{61}, v_{304}, v_{272}, v_{265}, v_{5}, v_{90}, v_{259}, v_{283}, v_{297}, v_{326}, v_{51}, v_{312}, v_{26}, v_{356}, v_{35}, v_{372}, v_{1}, v_{41}, v_{76}, v_{348}, v_{357}, v_{340}, v_{328}, v_{266}, v_{371}, v_{57}, v_{378}, v_{375}, v_{55}, v_{365}, v_{368}, v_{287}, v_{257}, v_{123}, v_{301}, v_{84}, v_{284}, v_{341}, v_{360}, v_{20}, v_{319}, v_{44}, v_{63}, v_{107}, v_{369}, v_{285}, v_{327}, v_{110}, v_{308}, v_{269}, v_{21}, v_{268}, v_{350}, v_{324}, v_{331}, v_{353}, v_{99}, v_{258}, v_{344}, v_{111}, v_{9}, v_{296}, v_{80}, v_{128}, v_{77}, v_{307}, v_{336}, v_{298}, v_{325}, v_{321}, v_{50}, v_{73}, v_{349}, v_{310}, v_{333}, v_{12}, v_{105}, v_{17}, v_{359}, v_{280}, v_{282}, v_{37}, v_{367}, v_{126}, v_{30}, v_{289}, v_{347}, v_{292}, v_{95}, v_{7}, v_{122}, v_{98}, v_{261}, v_{47}, v_{276}, v_{278}, v_{45}, v_{115}, v_{106}, v_{262}, v_{293}, v_{313}, v_{62}, v_{97}, v_{270}, v_{315}, v_{291}, v_{116}, v_{381}, v_{361}, v_{317}, v_{314}, v_{127}, v_{329}, v_{380}, v_{383}, v_{355}, v_{377}, v_{29}, v_{338}, v_{311}, v_{303}, v_{306}, v_{16}, v_{286}, v_{121}, v_{273}, v_{332}, v_{274}, v_{364}, v_{352}, v_{343}, v_{376}, v_{305}, v_{345}, v_{83}, v_{8}, v_{363}, v_{366}, v_{263}, v_{125}, v_{281}, v_{290}, v_{112}, v_{46}, v_{49}, v_{66}, v_{120}, v_{316}, v_{48}, v_{358}, v_{384}, v_{79}, v_{373}, v_{117}, v_{102}, v_{342}, v_{58}, v_{323}, v_{64}, v_{351}, v_{322}, v_{362}, v_{109}, v_{288}, v_{379}, v_{339}, v_{86}, v_{124}, v_{118}, v_{69}, v_{275}, v_{23}, v_{354}, v_{72}, v_{277}, v_{56}, v_{33}, v_{309}, v_{318}, v_{4}, v_{271}, v_{302}, v_{334}, v_{113}, v_{54}, v_{114}, v_{93}, v_{59}, v_{264}, v_{330}, v_{94}, v_{14}, v_{320}, v_{346}, v_{337}, v_{382}, v_{335}, v_{32}, v_{82}, v_{374}, v_{294}, v_{52}, v_{299}, v_{40}$
Time of $H_{(1\to4)}$	$2^{61.2}$	

Table 15. The differential characteristic of SPONGENT-160/160/80 (semi-free-start). Differences are displayed in hexadecimal.

Rounds	Differences at the input of each round	Prob.	Phase
1(Input)	a0ac6660fff0000000000000000000000000000000000000000000000000		$H_{(1\to3)}$
2	000000000000000000000000000000d70000000000000d07000000000000		
3	0000000000000000000000c000a000000000000000000000000000000000		
4	000004400000000000000000000000000000000000000000000000000000	2^{-78}	$H_{(4\to14)}$
5	000000000000000000000000000000060000000000000060000000000000		
6	000000000000000000000080004000000000000000000000000000000000		
7	000004400000000000000440000000000000000000000000000000000000		
8	000000000000000000000000000000060003000000000060003000000000		
9	000000000000000000000088004400000000000000000000000000000000		
10	00000cc0000000000000cc00000000000000000000000000000000000000		
11	000000000000000000000000000000000000000000000060003000000000		
12	000000000000000000000000004400000000000000000000000000000000		
13	000000000000000000000000000000000000c00000000000000c00000000		
14	000000000100800000000000000000000000000000000000000000000000		
Output	002100000000000002100000000000000000000000000000000000000000		

Table 16. Grouping results of SPONGENT-160/160/80 (semi-free-start). The leftmost bit is denoted as v_1. Time of $H_{(1\to3)}$ represents the lower bound of the computational complexity required for collecting DoF in $H_{(1\to4)}$.

Category	Bits	Values
Free bits	160	v_{58}, v_{176}, v_{165}, v_{162}, v_{204}, v_{120}, v_{150}, v_{180}, v_{98}, v_{170}, v_{201}, v_{126}, v_{164}, v_{85}, v_{117}, v_{82}, v_{163}, v_{113}, v_{166}, v_{65}, v_{129}, v_{141}, v_{151}, v_{208}, v_{172}, v_{149}, v_{185}, v_{207}, v_{71}, v_{114}, v_{206}, v_{146}, v_{81}, v_{173}, v_{136}, v_{70}, v_{68}, v_{205}, v_{112}, v_{192}, v_{89}, v_{96}, v_{122}, v_{178}, v_{134}, v_{61}, v_{118}, v_{143}, v_{101}, v_{155}, v_{188}, v_{131}, v_{191}, v_{119}, v_{177}, v_{156}, v_{110}, v_{52}, v_{91}, v_{63}, v_{87}, v_{174}, v_{107}, v_{202}, v_{196}, v_{86}, v_{77}, v_{145}, v_{94}, v_{116}, v_{102}, v_{121}, v_{171}, v_{108}, v_{54}, v_{194}, v_{106}, v_{49}, v_{78}, v_{139}, v_{153}, v_{111}, v_{104}, v_{142}, v_{100}, v_{115}, v_{199}, v_{50}, v_{95}, v_{197}, v_{183}, v_{186}, v_{84}, v_{200}, v_{147}, v_{133}, v_{92}, v_{123}, v_{161}, v_{189}, v_{124}, v_{184}, v_{53}, v_{55}, v_{103}, v_{64}, v_{51}, v_{57}, v_{159}, v_{128}, v_{67}, v_{73}, v_{93}, v_{144}, v_{125}, v_{138}, v_{80}, v_{137}, v_{152}, v_{182}, v_{193}, v_{109}, v_{158}, v_{198}, v_{190}, v_{169}, v_{132}, v_{56}, v_{187}, v_{72}, v_{99}, v_{157}, v_{175}, v_{203}, v_{130}, v_{160}, v_{168}, v_{154}, v_{74}, v_{97}, v_{105}, v_{59}, v_{62}, v_{148}, v_{181}, v_{90}, v_{135}, v_{179}, v_{60}, v_{88}, v_{83}, v_{76}, v_{167}, v_{195}, v_{69}, v_{75}, v_{66}, v_{79}, v_{127}, v_{140}
Fix bits	12	v_1, $\neg v_3$, $\neg v_{11}$, $\neg v_9$, v_{14}, $\neg v_{13}$, v_{20}, $\neg v_{17}$, v_{24}, $\neg v_{21}$, v_{28}, $\neg v_{25}$
group1	68	v_8, v_{33}, v_{44}, v_{23}, v_{48}, v_{29}, v_{213}, v_{227}, v_{234}, v_4, v_{210}, v_{36}, v_{16}, v_{222}, v_7, v_{215}, v_{10}, v_{18}, v_{233}, v_{31}, v_{37}, v_{19}, v_{22}, v_{239}, v_6, v_{236}, v_{219}, v_{34}, v_{217}, v_{229}, v_{45}, v_{226}, v_5, v_{220}, v_{214}, v_{46}, v_{35}, v_{38}, v_{30}, v_{216}, v_{238}, v_{231}, v_{15}, v_{42}, v_{209}, v_{218}, v_{228}, v_{12}, v_{26}, v_{47}, v_{43}, v_{232}, v_2, v_{230}, v_{32}, v_{224}, v_{235}, v_{225}, v_{240}, v_{211}, v_{237}, v_{27}, v_{39}, v_{223}, v_{212}, v_{41}, v_{40}, v_{221}
Time of $H_{(1\to3)}$	$2^{75.8}$	

Table 17. Practical Value. The binary sequence is interpreted starting from the leftmost bit and then converted to a hexadecimal representation. The asterisk (*) indicates that the capacity part of the output difference after one block becomes zero. A collision occurs if, in the second message input, a message is chosen such that the message difference in the rate part becomes zero.

	Semi-free-start	Rounds	Collision Initial State Pair	Output state pair after one block
SPONGENT-88/80/8*	✓	8	99849783a23de4bef427d0	eac5019f85d14f1a00737a
			eb849783a23de4bef427d0	aac5019f85d14f1a00737a
SPONGENT-88/176/88		8	35fb4346c60adde3b1201b00000000000000000000000000000000000000000000	7b3b46e4d322a1d2df8a76699c9006f382975d94c6c2721c044aef94b4b2412f83
			35fb4346cb836de3bd4fbb00000000000000000000000000000000000000000000	7b3b46e4d322a1d2df8a76699c9006f382875d94c6e2721c044aaf94b4b2c12f83
SPONGENT-88/176/88	✓	9	d7d70b10f19bd790f78b2dc55a0b036d254d9134af34fdbebe860cbcf86a5847d5	47e569326d361e19bfcf46156a3855a24e6188f8846c540bbe30af0da266db4299
			6ed84110f14bd799422b2ac55a0b036d254d9134af34fdbebe860cbcf86a5847d5	47e569326d361e19bfcf46556a3855224e6188f8856c540bbc30af09a666db4a91
SPONGENT-128/128/8*	✓	7	c342f6693b4fb33ef56c4da6e1d9ce7d50	769f064e009136ef26462cb1beeeeafbd0
			4542f6693b4fb33ef56c4da6e1d9ce7d50	f59f064e009136ef26462cb1beeeeafbd0
SPONGENT-128/256/128		8	7170635ed5680d896650069ac6f1a8c70000000000000000 000000000000000000000000000000000000000000000000	b12cda2140dd3d1b4c2603576b93f5a86c725fef56dc1424d756cd33f93934a629d79a69475674db62852870867ca2b9
			7170635ed5680d896650260ca34dafa70000000000000000000000000000000000000000000000000000000000000000	b12cda2140dd3d1b4c2603576b93f5a86c725def76de1424d576ef33d93b36a629d59a6b477676db42872a70867ea2bb
SPONGENT-160/320/160*		8	27ddc249cbcc5cef966bfb0a748106559bb5932300000000000000000000	d79e0af164ad21793aada2f81d4c2f032bf75f312835c8743b1373f7c04d
			000000000000000000000000000000000000000000000000000000000000	e409f24a352042a16b6a932155fbdf694aedca90ab79f7497f51ab29628e
			27ddc249cbcc5ecd900bf1f3748100259775932300000000000000000000	879e0af574ad21793aada2f81d4c2f532bf75b212835c8743b1373f7c04d
			000000000000000000000000000000000000000000000000000000000000	e409f24a352042a16b6a932155fbdf694aedca90ab79f7497f51ab29628e
SPONGENT-224/448/224		8	c3a2eaac434f7793ddd32253323311a3777322567776ae483d4eba8d0000000000000000000000000000	a12e3217a8741ff53096e085ec41212f98127bfe26e05ff82c6e06cd7a37c635eb83e44451b7f83c3a1d
			000000000000000000000000000000000000000000000000000000000000000000000000000000000000	e1d0f25752d2546c4ff43852bed65003c66aa98b5258fa133842a704d1940deb93a75d006cbfc741f8b5
			c3a2eaac434f11a4000477b667667794111477b32223ae483d4eba8d0000000000000000000000000000	a12e3217a8741ff53096e085ec41212f98127bfe26e05ff82c6e06cd7a37c63deb83e54451b7f83c3a1d
			000000000000000000000000000000000000000000000000000000000000000000000000000000000000	e1d0f24752d0546c4ff43052bed75003c66aa98b5258fa132842a504d1940deb93a75c006cbfc741f8b5
SPONGENT-256/512/256		9	3bb916a152a19bb360105c2bfa68296932f7ea3933868ba9768292ca17c2d2d900000000000000000000000000000000	a3730378aaf6cc8dcbbb5a259d594688ab4926702cb7cf0481a7d99fdfa24f8189b7f6534c52a45a50c9788d9b0d0d2b
			000000000000000000000000000000000000000000000000000000000000000000000000000000000000000000000000	a20cad2fb189abb3fc2907670dbea12e3e78bb8b3e50b8199ca5e449ebc876f9715f7dbf59aa14778e9cd3f710f8b59d
			3bb916a152a19bb360105c2bfa68296967f2ea3966838ba9238792ca1717d2d900000000000000000000000000000000	a3730378aaf6cc8dcbbb5a259d594688ab4926702cb7cf0481a7d99fdfa24f8189b7f6534c52a45a50e97a8d9b0d0d0b
			000000000000000000000000000000000000000000000000000000000000000000000000000000000000000000000000	a20cad2fb189abb3fc2907670dbea12e3e78bb8b3e50b8399ca5e449ebc876f9715f7dbf5baa14778e9cd1f710f8b5bd

References

1. Abdelraheem, M.A.: Estimating the probabilities of low-weight differential and linear approximations on PRESENT-like ciphers. In: Kwon, T., Lee, M.-K., Kwon, D. (eds.) ICISC 2012. LNCS, vol. 7839, pp. 368–382. Springer, Heidelberg (2013). https://doi.org/10.1007/978-3-642-37682-5_26
2. Aumasson, J., Henzen, L., Meier, W., Naya-Plasencia, M.: Quark: a lightweight hash. J. Cryptol. **26**(2), 313–339 (2013). https://doi.org/10.1007/S00145-012-9125-6
3. Bellini, E., et al.: CLAASP: a cryptographic library for the automated analysis of symmetric primitives. In: Carlet, C., Mandal, K., Rijmen, V. (eds.) Selected Areas in Cryptography - SAC 2023 - 30th International Conference, Fredericton, Canada, 14–18 August 2023, Revised Selected Papers. LNCS, vol. 14201, pp. 387–408. Springer (2023). https://doi.org/10.1007/978-3-031-53368-6_19
4. Bellini, E., et al.: Differential cryptanalysis with SAT, SMT, MILP, and CP: a detailed comparison for bit-oriented primitives. Cryptology ePrint Archive, Paper 2024/105 (2024)
5. Biham, E., Shamir, A.: Differential cryptanalysis of DES-like cryptosystems. J. Cryptol. **4**(1), 3–72 (1991). https://doi.org/10.1007/BF00630563
6. Bogdanov, A., Knežević, M., Leander, G., Toz, D., Varıcı, K., Verbauwhede, I.: SPONGENT: a lightweight hash function. In: Preneel, B., Takagi, T. (eds.) CHES 2011. LNCS, vol. 6917, pp. 312–325. Springer, Heidelberg (2011). https://doi.org/10.1007/978-3-642-23951-9_21
7. Bogdanov, A., Knezevic, M., Leander, G., Toz, D., Varici, K., Verbauwhede, I.: SPONGENT: the design space of lightweight cryptographic hashing. IEEE Trans. Computers **62**(10), 2041–2053 (2013). https://doi.org/10.1109/TC.2012.196
8. Bogdanov, A.: PRESENT: an ultra-lightweight block cipher. In: Paillier, P., Verbauwhede, I. (eds.) CHES 2007. LNCS, vol. 4727, pp. 450–466. Springer, Heidelberg (2007). https://doi.org/10.1007/978-3-540-74735-2_31
9. Brayton, R.K., Hachtel, G.D., McMullen, C.T., Sangiovanni-Vincentelli, A.L.: Logic Minimization Algorithms for VLSI Synthesis, The Kluwer International Series in Engineering and Computer Science, vol. 2. Springer, New York (1984). https://doi.org/10.1007/978-1-4613-2821-6
10. Erlacher, J., Mendel, F., Eichlseder, M.: Bounds for the security of Ascon against differential and linear cryptanalysis. IACR Trans. Symmetric Cryptol. **2022**(1), 64–87 (2022)
11. Gilbert, H., Peyrin, T.: Super-Sbox Cryptanalysis: Improved Attacks for AES-Like Permutations. In: Hong, S., Iwata, T. (eds.) FSE 2010. LNCS, vol. 6147, pp. 365–383. Springer, Heidelberg (2010). https://doi.org/10.1007/978-3-642-13858-4_21
12. Guo, J., Peyrin, T., Poschmann, A.: The `PHOTON` family of lightweight hash functions. In: Rogaway, P. (ed.) CRYPTO 2011. LNCS, vol. 6841, pp. 222–239. Springer, Heidelberg (2011). https://doi.org/10.1007/978-3-642-22792-9_13
13. International Organization for Standardization: ISO/IEC 29192-2:2019 - information security – lightweight cryptography – part 2: Block ciphers (2019). https://www.iso.org/standard/67173.html
14. Jean, J., Naya-Plasencia, M., Peyrin, T.: Improved rebound attack on the finalist `Grøstl`. In: Canteaut, A. (ed.) FSE 2012. LNCS, vol. 7549, pp. 110–126. Springer, Heidelberg (2012). https://doi.org/10.1007/978-3-642-34047-5_7
15. Lai, X., Massey, J.L., Murphy, S.: Markov ciphers and differential cryptanalysis. In: Davies, D.W. (ed.) EUROCRYPT 1991. LNCS, vol. 547, pp. 17–38. Springer, Heidelberg (1991). https://doi.org/10.1007/3-540-46416-6_2

16. Libralesso, L., Delobel, F., Lafourcade, P., Solnon, C.: Automatic generation of declarative models for differential cryptanalysis. In: Michel, L.D. (ed.) 27th International Conference on Principles and Practice of Constraint Programming, CP 2021, Montpellier, France (Virtual Conference), 25–29 October 2021. LIPIcs, vol. 210, pp. 40:1–40:18. Schloss Dagstuhl - Leibniz-Zentrum für Informatik (2021). https://doi.org/10.4230/LIPICS.CP.2021.40
17. Liu, F., Isobe, T., Meier, W.: Automatic verification of differential characteristics: application to reduced Gimli. In: Micciancio, D., Ristenpart, T. (eds.) CRYPTO 2020, Part III. LNCS, vol. 12172, pp. 219–248. Springer, Cham (2020). https://doi.org/10.1007/978-3-030-56877-1_8
18. Liu, Y., Wang, Q., Rijmen, V.: Automatic search of linear trails in ARX with applications to SPECK and Chaskey. In: Manulis, M., Sadeghi, A.-R., Schneider, S. (eds.) ACNS 2016. LNCS, vol. 9696, pp. 485–499. Springer, Cham (2016). https://doi.org/10.1007/978-3-319-39555-5_26
19. Lu, X., Li, B., Liu, M., Lin, D.: Improved conditional differential attacks on lightweight hash family QUARK. Cybersecur. **5**(1), 12 (2022). https://doi.org/10.1186/S42400-021-00108-3
20. Martins, R., Joshi, S., Manquinho, V.M., Lynce, I.: Incremental cardinality constraints for MaxSAT. CoRR **abs/1408.4628** (2014)
21. McCluskey, E.J.: Minimization of Boolean functions. Bell Syst. Tech. J. **35**(6), 1417–1444 (1956)
22. Mendel, F., Rechberger, C., Schläffer, M., Thomsen, S.S.: The rebound attack: cryptanalysis of reduced whirlpool and Grostl. In: Dunkelman, O. (ed.) FSE 2009. LNCS, vol. 5665, pp. 260–276. Springer, Heidelberg (2009). https://doi.org/10.1007/978-3-642-03317-9_16
23. Mouha, N., Preneel, B.: A proof that the ARX cipher salsa20 is secure against differential cryptanalysis. IACR Cryptol. ePrint Arch. p. 328 (2013)
24. Quine, W.V.: The problem of simplifying truth functions. Am. Math. Mon. **59**(8), 521–531 (1952)
25. Quine, W.V.: A way to simplify truth functions. Am. Math. Mon. **62**(9), 627–631 (1955)
26. Ranea, A., Rijmen, V.: Characteristic automated search of cryptographic algorithms for distinguishing attacks (CASCADA). IET Inf. Secur. **16**(6), 470–481 (2022). https://doi.org/10.1049/ise2.12077. https://ietresearch.onlinelibrary.wiley.com/doi/abs/10.1049/ise2.12077
27. Shiba, R., Sakamoto, K., Liu, F., Minematsu, K., Isobe, T.: Integral and impossible-differential attacks on the reduced-round Lesamnta-LW-BC. IET Inf. Secur. **16**(2), 75–85 (2022). https://doi.org/10.1049/ISE2.12044
28. Sun, L., Wang, W., Wang, M.: More accurate differential properties of LED64 and midori64. IACR Trans. Symmetric Cryptol. **2018**(3), 93–123 (2018)
29. Sun, L., Wang, W., Wang, M.: Accelerating the search of differential and linear characteristics with the SAT method. IACR Trans. Symmetric Cryptol. **2021**(1), 269–315 (2021)
30. Wang, Q., Grassi, L., Rechberger, C.: Zero-sum partitions of PHOTON permutations. In: Smart, N.P. (ed.) CT-RSA 2018. LNCS, vol. 10808, pp. 279–299. Springer, Cham (2018). https://doi.org/10.1007/978-3-319-76953-0_15
31. Zhang, G., Liu, M.: A distinguisher on present-like permutations with application to SPONGENT. IACR Cryptol. ePrint Arch., 236 (2016). http://eprint.iacr.org/2016/236

32. Zhang, G., Liu, M.: A distinguisher on present-like permutations with application to SPONGENT. Sci. China Inf. Sci. **60**(7), 72101 (2017). https://doi.org/10.1007/S11432-016-0165-6

Practical Collision Attacks on Reduced-Round Xoodyak Hash Mode

Huina Li[1], Le He[2], and Weidong Qiu[1](✉)

[1] School of Cyber Science and Engineering, Shanghai Jiao Tong University, Shanghai, China
{lihuina,qiuwd}@sjtu.edu.cn

[2] School of Cyber Engineering, Xidian University, Xi'an, China
hele@xidian.edu.cn

Abstract. XOODYAK is a finalist of the NIST lightweight cryptography competition, offering both keyed and hash modes. After several years of cryptanalysis, the largest number of XOODYAK hash rounds for which actual collisions was still in vacancy. To the best of our knowledge, one of the most powerful collision attacks on hash functions based on sponge construction is the differential-based attacks using the S-box linearization technique proposed by Qiao *et al.* (EUROCRYPT 2017). However, the linearization technique requires a large number of degrees of freedom, making it challenging to apply to XOODYAK with a small outer part. On the other hand, the constraint-input and constraint-output imposed on the differential trail of XOODOO permutation make the exhaustive search for relatively high-probability differential trails in collision attacks extremely costly.

In this paper, we present critical observations regarding XOODOO round function, particularly focusing on its unique θ and χ operation. These properties can be leveraged to manually design specific differential trails, referred to as *loop* trails. To efficiently find practical collisions for up to 3 rounds, we develop a SAT model based on these *loop* trails. Finally, we present the first practical collision on 2 rounds and a practical semi-free-start collision on 3 rounds of XOODYAK hash mode. Besides, we improve Dong *et al.*'s (CRYPTO 2024) collision attack on 3-round XOODYAK-HASH from $2^{125.23}$ to $2^{100.93}$ using several linearization strategies. Since we focus on the analysis on collisions during the message absorbing phase of the hash modes, our results are applicable to both XOODYAK-HASH and XOODYAK-XOF.

Keywords: XOODYAK · XOODYAK hash mode · Collision attack · Semi-free-start collision attack

1 Introduction

With the rapid development of emerging networks such as the Internet of Things (IoT), sensor networks, and vehicular networks, symmetric cryptographic algorithms face new challenges. In 2018, the National Institute of Standards and

C. Boura et al. (Eds.): SAC 2025, LNCS 16207, pp. 55–78, 2026.
https://doi.org/10.1007/978-3-032-10536-3_3

Technology (NIST) launched a Lightweight Cryptography Competition [22] to solicit, evaluate, and standardize schemes providing authenticated encryption with associated data (AEAD) and optional hashing functionalities for constrained environments. In April 2019, NIST announced the first round of 56 candidate algorithms. Based on extensive security evaluations of the candidates by cryptanalysts, NIST announced the 10 finalists for the final round in March 2021. XOODYAK [8] is one of these finalists and has attracted considerable attention from cryptographers due to its unique design.

XOODYAK is an instance of the Cyclist mode of operation. Internally, it uses the XOODOO permutation [7], a 384-bit permutation whose design is inspired by KECCAK-p [3]. XOODYAK includes the keyed and the hash modes, while the keyed mode has been extensively studied [26,31], the hash mode has received comparatively less attention [11,18]. In this paper, we focus on the XOODYAK hash mode. The XOODYAK hash mode is based on the sponge construction [12], including the hash function XOODYAK-HASH and an eXtendable Output Function (XOF) XOODYAK-XOF.

A successful collision attack on a sponge-based hash function H is to find a pair of distinct messages M and M' such that $H_{IV}(M) = H_{IV}(M')$ with a time complexity of less than $2^{min(h/2,c/2)}$. One of the most powerful collision attacks on sponge-based hash function is based on the differential attack framework proposed by Dinur *et al.* in [10]. The full attack primarily consists of two parts: the first part is the high probability differential trail search that ensures collision on the digest bits, which we refer to as the colliding trail search phase, and the second part is constructing a 1-round connector with the target difference algorithm (TDA) in order to obtain a su?ciently large set of message pairs that simultaneously satisfy the colliding trail, as well as the constraints imposed by the padding rule and the initial value (IV) of the hash function. Qiao *et al.* [23] built upon the framework proposed by Dinur *et al.* [10] and introduced a novel algebraic technique to linearize all S-boxes in the first round, thereby extending 1-round connectors to 2-round connectors. Furthermore, 3-round connectors were designed in [13,27] using partial linearization techniques, resulting in the first practical 5-round collisions for SHA3-224 and SHA3-256.

To further address the inefficiency of differential trail search, Guo et al. in [14] introduced a SAT tool to accelerate multiple intermediate steps of the collision attacks. This approach demonstrated remarkably high efficiency in solving both differential trail search and connecting trail search problems encountered during the process, ultimately resulting in the first six-round collision attack on SHAKE128. Huang *et al.* [15] observed that the previously proposed linearization techniques [13,23,27] become impractical for variants with smaller input spaces, such as SHA3-384, which has only 832 initial degrees of freedom (ignoring padding bits). To address this limitation, they proposed an attack framework that utilizes 2-block messages instead of 1-block messages and transforms the connectivity problem into a Boolean Satisfiability (SAT) problem. Using SAT-based tools, they successfully presented the first practical attack on 4-round SHA3-384.

The Constrained-Input Constrained-Output (CICO) problem [12] inherent to sponge-based hash functions, significantly restricts the availability of high-probability differential trails for collision attacks. In the case of the XOODYAK hash mode, the rate part is considerably smaller, with only the first 128 bits having non-zero differences. Such trails are often extremely rare, requiring an exhaustive search of the entire space, which is computationally expensive. So far, differential trail search results on the XOODOO permutation have only been reported by its designers [7,21], who developed a dedicated tool for general trail search. This may explain why the first collision results for XOODYAK, relying on a meet-in-the-middle (MitM) attack, were recently presented in 2024, rather than through a differential-based attack.

At CRYPTO 2024, Dong *et al.* [11] proposed a generic MitM collision attack framework for sponge constructions for the first time and presented the first collision attack on 3-round XOODYAK-HASH with the time complexity of $2^{125.23}$. However, it required a huge memory complexity of 2^{124}. To the best of our knowledge, no further collision attacks against round-reduced instances of XOODYAK hash mode have been reported in the open literature.

1.1 Our Contributions

In this work, we improve the differential-based collision attacks against XOODYAK hash mode, as summarized below:

- We adopt a multi-block collision attack framework for the reduced-round XOODYAK hash mode. Unlike previous works that focused on the squeezing phase of KECCAK [10,13–15,23,27], our attack focuses on collisions during the message absorbing phase of hash modes. This distinction makes our framework applicable to both the hash mode (XOODYAK-HASH) and the extendable output function (XOODYAK-XOF).
- We utilize the property of the θ operation: when all columns in a sheet are odd, then the θ-effect cancels and there are no induced affected columns. Leveraging this property, along with the differential property of the non-linear operation χ, we manually design special differential trails (we refer to them as *loop* differential trails), each maintaining a probability of 2^{-64} per round[1]. To efficiently find practical collisions, we develop a collision search SAT model based on the *loop* trails. As a result, we obtain an actual 2-round collision in 64.7 s, and a practical 3-round semi-free-start (SFS) collision in 3.67 s. These are the first practical collision results on reduced rounds of the XOODYAK hash mode. For the source code, please refer to https://github.com/HuinaLi/Practical-Collision-Attacks-on-Xoodyak.
- Based on the 3-round *loop* trail with the probability of 2^{-192}, we propose a specific linearization technique that carefully selects the output bits of the first round to be linearized. We reduce the time complexity of Dong *et al.*'s

[1] It is noted that we have extensively explored SAT models to search for 2/3/4-round differential trails under the multi-block attack framework, yet no better alternatives than loop trails were identified.

3-round collision attacks on XOODYAK-HASH from $2^{125.23}$ to $2^{100.9311}$. It is worth noting that our approach has negligible memory complexity. The results are summarized in Table 1.

Table 1. Summary of collision attacks on Xoodyak-HASH

Methods	Rounds	Time	Memory	Reference
Differential	2	Practical	Negligible	Sect. 5
MitM	3	$2^{125.23}$	2^{124}	[11]
Differential	3	$2^{100.9311}$	Negligible	Sect. 5

1.2 Organization

In Sect. 2, we define some notations and properties that will be used in the paper and briefly describe XOODYAK hash mode and the underlying permutation XOODOO. In Sect. 3, we introduce our collision attack framework. In Sect. 4, we present an efficient SAT-based collision search model. In Sect. 5 we give some new collision results on XOODYAK hash mode. Finally, we summarize the full paper in Sect. 6.

2 Preliminary

2.1 XOODYAK Hash Mode

Xoodyak [8] is a versatile cryptographic primitive instantiated in the Cyclist mode of operation. It offers two modes including the keyed and the hash modes, one of which is selected upon initialization. In the case of hash mode illustrated in Fig. 1, it includes XOODYAK-HASH and the extanded output function XOODYAK-XOF.

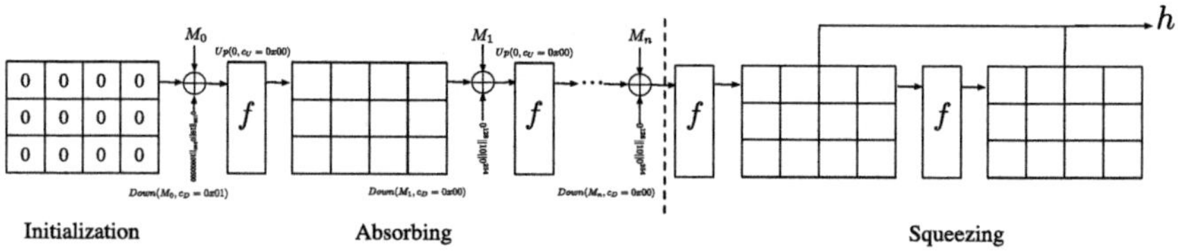

Fig. 1. The XOODYAK Hash Mode

The 384-bit state is initialized to the all-zero string like Cyclist, and a duplexing call corresponds to a sequence of Down() and Up()(Due to page limitations, specific details have been omitted. For more details, please refer to [8]). For Xoodyak hash mode with the parameters $b = 384, r = 130, c = 254$, the security claims are 2^{128} against any attacks.

The rate is set to $r = 130$ bits, which includes the maximum input message block size of 128 bits along with 2 bits from the padding. The sponge construction works on a b-bit internal state, which is divided into two phases (see Fig. 1): in the absorbing phase, it cuts the input message M in blocks of given length (after padding $r = 130$) and calls Down() and Up() appropriately. The Down(M_i, $c_D = 0x01$ if first block else 0×00) method absorbs one block of input message, by bitwise adding it to the state, together with a color c_D in the last byte of the state. The processed message is denoted by $\bar{M}_i$. The Up($0, c_U = 0x01$) method absorbs a color c_U in the last byte of the state, invokes the underlying permutation f and returns the output of the state. After absorbing all the message blocks, a 128-bit hash value is extracted during the squeezing process each time, until the desired hash length h is achieved.

2.2 Description of Xoodoo

Xoodoo is the underlying permutation of Xoodyak, first presented by Daemen et al. [7] at ToSC 2018. It operates on a 3-dimensional array of size 384 bits. The Xoodoo state, denoted as S, is a 3-dimensional array with bits indexed by the coordinates (x, y, z), where $0 \le x < 4$, $0 \le y < 3$, and $0 \le z < 32$. Each bit is indexed by $S[32 \times (x + 4 \times y) + z]$. The state can be decomposed into 1-dimensional arrays, such as rows, columns, and lanes, which refer to the x, y, and z directions, respectively. It can also be decomposed into two-dimensional arrays, such as plane and sheets, in the (x, z) and (y, z) directions, as shown in Fig. 2.

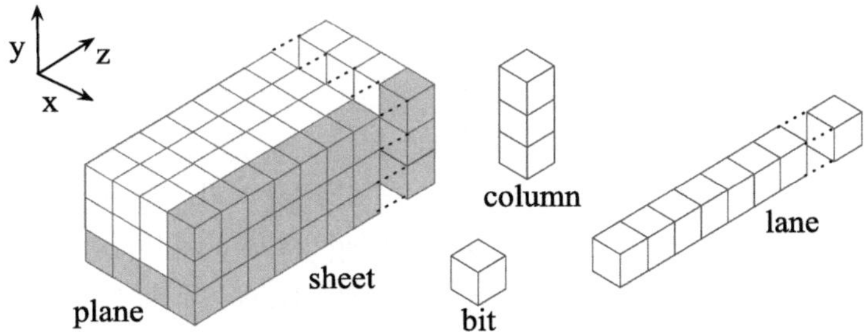

Fig. 2. The Xoodoo state

Xoodoo is an iterated permutation consisting of 12 rounds. The state is updated by repeatedly applying the round function. The round function of Xoodoo follows a design approach similar to Keccak-p with five steps per round: $R = \rho_{east} \circ \chi \circ \iota \circ \rho_{west} \circ \theta$. The five steps are given below, in order:
θ creates a parity plane P by adding the bit-wise sum of all columns, if the parity of a column is 1, which defines an odd (*resp.* even) column. Then, the θ-effect of

a state value S is E, which is calculated by adding two shifted parity planes with shift offsets $(1, 5)$ and $(1, 14)$. The θ-effect is then added to the original input state.

$$\begin{aligned} P[x][z] &\leftarrow \sum_{y=0}^{2} S[x][y][z] \\ E[x][z] &\leftarrow P[x-1][z-5] \oplus P[x-1][z-14] \\ S[x][y][z] &\leftarrow S[x][y][z] \oplus E[x][z] \end{aligned} \tag{1}$$

ρ_{west} shifts two planes of the state with offsets $(1, 0)$ and $(0, 11)$, respectively.

$$\begin{aligned} S[x][1][z] &\leftarrow S[x-1][1][z] \\ S[x][2][z] &\leftarrow S[x][2][z-11] \end{aligned} \tag{2}$$

ι adds a constant in each round. The round constants C_i in hexadecimal notation (see Table 2) are such that the least significant bit is at $z = 0$.

$$S[0][0][z] \leftarrow S[0][0][z] \oplus C_i$$

Table 2. Constants C_i used in the Xoodoo (round index i from -11 to 0)

Round i	Constant C_i	Round i	Constant C_i	Round i	Constant C_i
-11	0x00000058	-7	0x00000120	-3	0x00000380
-10	0x00000038	-6	0x00000014	-2	0x000000f0
-9	0x000003c0	-5	0x00000060	-1	0x000001a0
-8	0x000000d0	-4	0x0000002c	0	0x00000012

χ is the only non-linear layer. It operates in parallel on 3-bit columns and, as such, forms a layer of 128 3-bit S-boxes.

$$\begin{aligned} S[x][0][z] &\leftarrow S[x][0][z] \oplus \neg S[x][1][z] \wedge S[x][2][z] \\ S[x][1][z] &\leftarrow S[x][1][z] \oplus \neg S[x][2][z] \wedge S[x][0][z] \\ S[x][2][z] &\leftarrow S[x][2][z] \oplus \neg S[x][0][z] \wedge S[x][1][z] \end{aligned} \tag{3}$$

ρ_{east} shifts two planes of the state with offsets $(0, 1)$ and $(2, 8)$, respectively.

$$\begin{aligned} S[x][1][z] &\leftarrow S[x][1][z-1] \\ S[x][2][z] &\leftarrow S[x-2][2][z-8] \end{aligned} \tag{4}$$

2.3 Properties of θ

We first present the definition of *loop*, an important property of θ that allows us to manually design differential trails in Sect. 3.3 for improved collision attacks.

Definition 1 (Loop [7]). *A parity loop (or loop for short) is a state value with 32 active bits in a sheet, each in a distinct column.*

A *loop* is invariant through θ. According to Eq. 1, a *loop* generates 32 odd columns, that means all the columns in a sheet are odd, *i.e.*, $P[x-1][z-5] \oplus P[x-1][z-14] = 0$, then the θ-effect cancels and there are no induced affected columns.

It is worth noting that, as a linear function, the properties of θ remain the same whether it is applied to the absolute value of a state or to a difference. For a n-round differential trail, if all the internal differences consist solely of *loop* elements, we refer to such a differential trail as a *loop differential trail.* More details for constructing 2-round or 3-round *loop differential trails* will be introduced in Sect. 3.3.

2.4 Properties of χ

The non-linear component χ in the Xoodoo round function plays a key role in generating differential probabilities, which cause certain input and output differences to appear in a non-random manner. In Xoodoo it operates in parallel on 3-bit columns and as such forms a layer of 4×32 3-bit S-boxes. To better characterize its differential properties, we first present the difference distribution table (DDT) of the 3-bit S-box (see Table 3).

Definition 2 (Valid Differential Pattern). *In the DDT of* Xoodoo*'s 3-bit S-box, if the entry $\sigma(\alpha, \beta)$ for the input-output differential pair (α, β) is non-zero, we call the differential pattern valid; otherwise, it is referred to as invalid.*

Definition 3 (Active S-box). *A S-box is active if its input difference is non-zero; conversely, it is termed inactive if $(\alpha, \beta) = (0, 0)$.*

Each valid difference pattern (α, β) has a non-zero value, *i.e.*, the entry $\sigma(\alpha, \beta) \neq 0$. The differential weight of each valid pattern can be denoted by $w_{(\alpha,\beta)} = -log_2 \frac{\sigma(\alpha,\beta)}{8} = 2$.

Property 1. Given an input difference $\alpha \in \mathbb{F}_2^3$ and an output difference $\beta \in \mathbb{F}_2^3$ such that $\sigma(\alpha, \beta) \neq 0$, denote the value solution set $X = \{x \in \mathbb{F}_2^3 | \chi(x) \oplus \chi(x \oplus \alpha) = \beta\}$ and $\chi(X) = \{\chi(x) : x \in X\}$, then X is a linearizable a?ne subspace.

The algebraic degree of the 3-bit Xoodoo's S-box is 2 as shown in Eq. 5, which means that for any valid differential pattern (α, β), the set of input messages x that follow this pattern forming an affine subspace of size $2^{3-w_{(\alpha,\beta)}}$.

3-bit S-box Linearization. The linearization of a 3-bit S-box can be categorized into two classes.

- For active S-boxes, according to Property 1, when the input difference and the compatible output difference are given, two linear equations on the input bits x_i can be listed for each active S-box, such that the outputs y can be expressed as linear combinations of the input bits. From this algebraic perspective, these S-boxes are already fully linearized.

Table 3. DDT of XOODOO's S-box

Input difference (α)	Output difference (β)							
	0×0	0x1	0x2	0x3	0x4	0x5	0x6	0x7
0x0	8	0	0	0	0	0	0	0
0x1	0	2	0	2	0	2	0	2
0x2	0	0	2	2	0	0	2	2
0x3	0	2	2	0	0	2	2	0
0x4	0	0	0	0	2	2	2	2
0x5	0	2	0	2	2	0	2	0
0x6	0	0	2	2	2	2	0	0
0x7	0	2	2	0	2	0	0	2

- For non-active S-boxes, linearization can be achieved by introducing two additional equations involving the input bits (see Property 2).

Property 2. The algebraic normal form of χ mapping 3-bit $x = (x_0, x_1, x_2)$ into 3-bit $y = (y_0, y_1, y_2)$ can be written as $y_i = x_i \oplus (x_{i+1} \oplus 1)x_{i+2}$ as below,

$$\begin{aligned} y_0 &= x_0 \oplus (x_1 \oplus 1)x_2 \\ y_1 &= x_1 \oplus (x_2 \oplus 1)x_0 \\ y_2 &= x_2 \oplus (x_0 \oplus 1)x_1 \end{aligned} \tag{5}$$

Given the 3-bit input $x = (x_0, x_1, x_2)$, two bits of the output y_{i+1}, y_{i+2} can be linearized by introducing one linear equation on x_i. Furthermore, any bit of the output y can be represented as a linear function by adding two extra linear equations on the input x.

2.5 Difference-Value Relations

At CRYPTO 2021, Liu *et al.* [19] proposed an algebraic perspective on differential-linear cryptanalysis. This novel algebraic perspective pointed out that the output difference of a Boolean function is a special Boolean function of the input difference and input value. It is important to note that this forms the theoretical foundation for constructing the difference-value relations model, which will be presented in detail in Sect. 4.3.

Property 3. For a Boolean function $f_i : \mathbb{F}_2^n \to \mathbb{F}_2$ representing a certain output bit of a primitive, the output difference $\beta_i \in \mathbb{F}_2$ is the derivative of f with respect to input difference α at point $x \in \mathbb{F}_2^n$,

$$\beta_i = \mathcal{D}_\alpha f_i(x) = f_i(x) \oplus f_i(x \oplus \alpha) \tag{6}$$

This is equivalently expressed as the partial derivative of $f_i(x \oplus u \cdot \alpha)$ with respect to the boolean variable $u \in \mathbb{F}_2$. Formally, this relationship is defined as:

$$\mathcal{D}_\alpha f_i(x) = \mathcal{D}_u f_i(x \oplus u \cdot \alpha) \tag{7}$$

where the input message value x, the input difference α ($x, \alpha \in \mathbb{F}_2^n$), u is an auxiliary binary variable, $\mathcal{D}_u f_i(x \oplus u \cdot \alpha)$ is the partial derivative of $f_i(x \oplus u \cdot \alpha)$ with respect to u.

According to Eq. 3, the algebraic normal forms (ANFs) of the output bits are denoted by $\chi_i(x_i, x_{i+1}, x_{i+2}) = x_i \oplus \neg x_{i+1} \cdot x_{i+2}$. Based on Eq. (7), the relationship between the value and the differential can be illustrated as follows.

$$\begin{cases} \beta_0 = \mathcal{D}_u \chi_0(x_0 \oplus u \cdot \alpha_0, x_1 \oplus u \cdot \alpha_1, x_2 \oplus u \cdot \alpha_2) \\ \beta_1 = \mathcal{D}_u \chi_1(x_0 \oplus u \cdot \alpha_0, x_1 \oplus u \cdot \alpha_1, x_2 \oplus u \cdot \alpha_2) \\ \beta_2 = \mathcal{D}_u \chi_2(x_0 \oplus u \cdot \alpha_0, x_1 \oplus u \cdot \alpha_1, x_2 \oplus u \cdot \alpha_2) \end{cases} \tag{8}$$

Following the above Boolean equations, when the valid differential pattern (α, β) is determined, the linear equations on input bits x_i are directly listed.

Example 1. Let us consider an active S-box represented by $S(x_0, x_1, x_2)$, which follows a valid difference pattern ($\alpha = (1, 0, 0), \beta = (1, 0, 0)$). The input values $x = (x_0, x_1, x_2)$ of the S-box correspond to the solution space of the following linear equations, which are derived from Equation (8).

$$\begin{cases} 1 = 1 \\ 0 = x_2 \oplus 1 \\ 0 = x_1 \end{cases}$$

3 Overview of Our Collision Attack Framework

Following the collision attack framework by Dinur *et al.*'s [10], our differential-based collision attacks consist of two essential steps: one step is to find a n_1-round high probability collision-generating differential trail (we call it the colliding trail for simplicity). The second step is to construct a n_2-round connector that promises a subspace of message pairs which satisfy the colliding trail at the same time and the constraints imposed by the padding rule and IV of Xoodyak hash mode as depicted in Fig. 3.

In the n-round differential trail search of sponge-based hash functions, the Constrained-Input Constrained-Output (CICO) problem [12] arises. The CICO property imposes specific constraints on both the input and output differences. In our collision attack framework, there is no difference in the first $k-1$ message blocks, where the messages M_0, M_1, $\cdots$, M_{k-2} are chosen randomly. We focus our analysis on collisions occurring during the absorbing phase of the hash mode. Thus, the last 256 bits of the input difference A_0 and the output difference A_n are constrained to be zero.

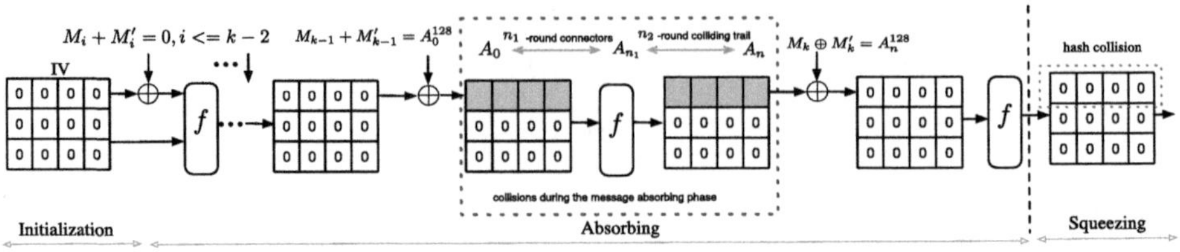

Fig. 3. Our Collision Attack Framework of XOODYAK Hash Mode

In our attack framework depicted in Fig. 3, assume there are $k+1$ message blocks, denoted by M_i for $i \in \{0, 1, ..., k\}$. During the middle absorbing phase, we introduce a message pair (M_{k-1}, M'_{k-1}) that satisfies the first 128 bits of the input difference A_0, denoted by A_0^{128}.

From this starting point, we generate an n-round differential trail, which includes a n_2-round colliding trail that ensure h-bit collision and a n_1-round differential trail (we refer to it as the connecting trail for simplicity) for constructing a connector that generates a subspace of messages linking the initial conditions of sponge construction and the input difference of the subsequent colliding trail.

Once we construct such a n-round differential trail and find a message pair $(M_0, \ldots, M_{k-1})$ and $(M'_0, \ldots, M'_{k-1})$ that follows this trail where $A_0^{128} = M_{k-1} \oplus M'_{k-1}$, we introduce one more pair of message blocks (M_k, M'_k) at the last absorbing phase that has the same difference in the first 128 bits, *i.e.*, $A_n^{128} = M_k \oplus M'_k$, the matching difference is then canceled out, resulting in zero difference during the squeezing phase, thus successfully converting it into a real collision.

3.1 Complexity Analysis

Suppose a n-round collision attack comprises a n_1-round connecting trail with weight w_1 and a n_2-round colliding trail with weight w_2, where $n_1 \leq 2$. The overall complexity includes both the complexity of the connector construction phase, denoted as T_1, and the complexity of the exhaustive search phase, denoted as T_2.

Connector Construction Complexity. The core idea of constructing n_1-round connector is to convert the problem to solving an algebraic system. For the attacker, the controllable initial degrees of freedom (DF) is 128.

Assume that an algebraic system of n_1-round connector is constructed, where the number of the linear equations denote by n_l, and the number of non-linear equations denote by n_q. The number of non-linear equations that can be linearized by guessing d_f extra equations (we call them guess equations which consume d_f DF) is denoted by n'_l. Thus, the final linear system includes $n_l + n'_l + d_f$ linear boolean equations in 128 Boolean variables.

Let us first recall the equivalent conversion of implementation efficiency between connector construction and n-round XOODOO. The total number of bit operations[2] for an n-round XOODOO is given by $n \times (1024 + 768 + 32) = 1824n$. If $n = 3$, The total number of bit operations $\approx 2^{12.4178}$.

Regarding this linear system, it is composed of $n_l + n_l' + d_f$ linear equations in 128 variables. Assume $n_l + n_l' + d_f \leq 128$, then the system has a non-trivial solution. The time complexity of Gaussian elimination T_g for a system of linear equations is approximately

$$T_g \approx \frac{1}{3}(n_l + n_l' + d_f)^2 \times 128.$$

Consequently, the complexity of solving a linear system can be calculated by taking the ratio of the number of bit operations required for one iteration of Gaussian elimination to the total number of bit operations in n-round XOODOO calls, *i.e.* $\frac{T_g}{1824n}$. During each iteration of Gaussian elimination, it is expected to obtain $2^{128-n_l-n_l'-d_f}$ solutions. The verification time complexity is estimated as $T_v = 2^{128-n_l-n_l'-d_f}$.

As each guess equation can be assigned a constant value of either 0 or 1. In this way, for one connector, we can construct 2^{d_f} linear systems.

To satisfy the remaining $n_q - n_l'$ non-linear equations and the w_2 conditions of the difference-value of the colliding trail, we need to prepare at least $2^{w_2+n_q-n_l'}$ solutions. Thus, the time complexity corresponds to the time required to construct $2^{(w_2+n_q-n_l')-(128-n_l-n_l'-d_f)-d_f} = 2^{w_2+n_q+n_l-128}$ connectors.

The total time complexity in connector construction is equivalent to,

$$T_1 = 2^{w_2+n_q+n_l-128} \times \left(2^{d_f} \times \left(\frac{T_g}{1824n} + T_v\right)\right) \tag{9}$$

Exhaustive Search Complexity. The remaining $n_q - n_l'$ equations and the w_2 conditions on the difference values of the colliding trail are satisfied via exhaustive search. In the exhaustive search phase of the attack, we try $2^{w_2+n_q-n_l'}$ different message pairs in order to find a pair whose difference evolves according to the specified n_2-round colliding trail. The time complexity is

$$T_2 = 2^{w_2+n_q-n_l'} \tag{10}$$

In total, the time complexity denoted by T_{total} of the n-round collision attack is

$$\begin{aligned} T_{total} &= T_1 + T_2 \\ &= \left(2^{w_2+n_q+n_l-128+d_f} \times \frac{\frac{1}{3}(n_l + n_l' + d_f)^2 \times 128}{1824n}\right) + 2^{w_2+n_q-n_l'} + 2^{w_2+n_q-n_l'} \end{aligned} \tag{11}$$

[2] where $2\times128+ 2\times384 = 1024$ bit operations are for the θ operation, $2\times3\times128 = 768$ bit operations are for the χ operation, and 32 bit operations are for the ι operation.

3.2 n-Round Differential Trail Search

Differential cryptanalysis is one of the most effective methods to attack cryptographic permutations or block ciphers. It was first proposed by Biham and Shamir in 1991 [5]. The idea of differential cryptanalysis is to choose an input difference such that output differences can be reliably predicted. If a certain input/output difference exists with an optimal probability, it can be used to construct a distinguisher. This distinguisher can then be used to recover the initial state in a collision attack or the key in a key recovery attack.

For the study of the differential trail propagation of XOODOO, we take a n-round differential trail as an example. A n-round differential trail starting from 0-th round has the following form:

$$A_0 \xrightarrow{\theta} B_0 \xrightarrow{\rho_{west}} C_0 \xrightarrow{\chi} D_0 \xrightarrow{\lambda} C_1 \xrightarrow{\chi} \dots \xrightarrow{\lambda} C_{n-1} \xrightarrow{\chi} D_{n-1} \xrightarrow{\rho_{east}} A_n \tag{12}$$

With i indexed from 0, let C_i denote the input difference and D_i denote the output difference of the i-th χ mapping. The last 256 bits of both the input and output differences (*i.e.*, A_0, A_n) are zero. We denote the linear layer as $\lambda = \rho_{\text{west}} \circ \theta \circ \rho_{\text{east}}$.

The weight of the j-th S-box in the i-th round is denoted by w_i^j, where i starts from 0. The weight of a n-round differential trail is defined as the sum of the weights of all 3-bit S-boxes:

$$w(A_0 \rightarrow A_n) = \sum_{i=0}^{r-1} \sum_{j=0}^{127} w_i^j$$

For all valid difference patterns, we have $w_{(c,d)} = 2$. This can be represented as twice the total number of active S-boxes (non-zero difference) in either C^k or D^k for simplicity.

$$w(A_0 \rightarrow A_n) = 2 \times \sum_{i=0}^{r-1} \sum_{j=0}^{4} \sum_{k=0}^{32} s_i[j][*][k] \tag{13}$$

In this context, $s_i[j][*][k]$ indicates the active status of the $32j + k$-th S-box in the i-th round, taking a value of 1 if it is active and 0 otherwise.

3.3 Loop Differential Trail

In this section, we introduce a specific differential trail with internal differences that consist solely of *loop* elements, based on the differential properties of the round function of XOODOO. We now provide a formal definition of such a differential trail as follows.

Definition 4 (Loop Differential Trail). *For a n-round differential trail, if all internal differences consist solely of loop elements, we refer to such a n-differential trail as a loop differential trail.*

It can be easily observed from Eq. 2 and Eq. 4 that, in order to eliminate the influence of ρ_{west} and ρ_{east}, only the first plane of $S[x][0][z]$ is allowed to have a non-zero difference. To ensure that only the first plane of the entire state retains a non-zero difference after the non-linear layer χ, we restrict the types of valid differential patterns. Specifically, we only allow $(C[x][0][z], C[x][1][z], C[x][2][z]) = (1, 0, 0)$ and $(D[x][0][z], D[x][1][z], D[x][2][z]) = (1, 0, 0)$.

To give a more formal definition of the weight of a n-round *loop* differential trail, we first define the notion of valid configuration of active S-boxes in Definition 5.

Definition 5 (Valid Configuration of Active S-boxes). *Let $r \geq 2$ be the number of rounds. We say a configuration $(s_0, \ldots, s_{r-1})$ is valid if there exists a r-round differential trail $(A_0, A_1, \ldots, A_r)$ with $s_0, \ldots, s_{r-1}$ active S-boxes at round 0, ..., $r-1$, respectively.*

With these constraints, we ensure that the output difference A_0 maintains the same differential state even after propagating through multiple rounds. For example, a one-round loop differential trail with a valid one-round configuration of active S-boxes ($s_0 = 32$) is illustrated in Fig. 4. In this way, we can extend it to a 2-round loop differential trail with the configuration ($s_0 = 32, s_1 = 32$), and to a 3-round loop differential trail with the configuration ($s_0 = 32, s_1 = 32, s_2 = 32$). In what follows, we describe how to use these *loop* trails to find practical collision results.

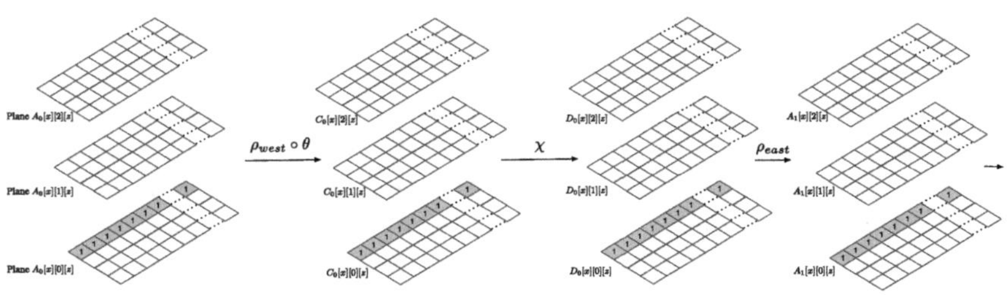

Fig. 4. 1-round Loop Differential Trail

4 SAT-Based Collision Search

In this section, we develop a SAT-based collision search method. This method effectively reduces the practical collision search problem into a SAT problem.

4.1 Overview of Our Collision Search Method

To search for a valid differential trail and conforming message pair simultaneously, Liu *et al.* [17] at the CRYPTO 2020 developed a novel MILP model.

Their MILP model independently constructed the difference transition and value transition of the target primitive as well as the difference-value relations model through the non-linear layer. Based on this MILP model, they present the ?rst practical Semi-Free-Start (SFS) collision for 6-round GIMLI-HASH.

Subsequently, Li *et al.* [16] presented a new method for finding a valid differential trail and message pair simultaneously. They formalized that the output difference of a Boolean function is a specific Boolean function of both the input difference and the input value, and utilized SageMath [30] as the symbolic computation tool to construct difference-value Boolean equations, employing the `Bosphorus` [6] as the solver. The `Bosphorus` supports the internal conversion of optimized Boolean equations into CNF clauses and invokes its underlying `CryptoMiniSat` solver to find the solutions. For GIMLI, they achieved a practical 6-round SFS collision in just 9.74 s, while Liu *et al.*'s MILP model took approximately 4 h for the same task.

Inspired by Li *et al.*'s verification approach [16], we propose a SAT model for collision search. For the value transitions model, unlike Li *et al.* [16] who constructed Boolean equations for the round function's non-linear layer and then converted them into CNF clauses, we provide a finer-grained approach. We directly encode the non-linear layers into CNF clauses by enumerating their truth tables. Although we find that this direct approach did not significantly improve the model's efficiency for Xoodoo, it did result in a more compact model than Li *et al.*'s verification model. For the difference-value relations model, following the same idea like Li *et al.*'s approach, we utilize Property 3 to derive the implicit difference-value relations for each round of XOODOO. It is noted that our model does not require a differential transition model; instead, the known differential trails are used as the constants.

We choose SAT tool for two main reasons. First, SAT is particularly well-suited for describing bit-level operations. At AISACRYPT 2022, Guo *et al.* [14] proved significant advantages of SAT models over MILP models when applied to differential trail search for KECCAK-f[1600]. In [9], Mathieu *et al.* reconstructed the MILP-based search model for the ASCON MitM attack proposed by Qin *et al.* [24] using a SAT model. This reconstruction not only significantly accelerated the solving process but also eliminated the need for heuristic algorithms, such as those relying on weak diffusion structures. To further study the impact of model and solver selection on cryptanalysis tasks, Bellini *et al.* [2] built SAT, SMT, MILP, and CP search models for various bit-oriented cryptographic primitives including block ciphers, permutations, and hash functions—targeting tasks such as optimal differential trail search, enumerating all optimal trails, and estimating differential probabilities. Their findings confirmed that SAT solvers generally outperform others for ARX primitives and SPN structures, demonstrating significant advantages.

On the other hand, the Sage [30] library includes a module named *sage.sat*, specifically designed for handling SAT problems. This module provides CNF encoding tools and functionalities for working with Boolean expressions and solving problems related to their satisfiability. Based on the *sage.sat* module, we can conveniently construct the corresponding SAT model for the linear layer as well as for the difference-value relations. Furthermore, it allows us to compatibly describe constraint models for nonlinear layers using truth table-based encoding methods [1,29]. Through this approach, we present an efficient SAT-based collision search model. In the next section, we will provide a detailed explanation of the construction process for the SAT-based collision search model.

4.2 Constructing SAT Model for Value Transitions

The Xoodoo permutation updates the initial state of 384 bits by applying the round function over a total of n rounds. A n-round value transition model can be expressed in the following form:

$$a_0 \xrightarrow{\theta} b_0 \xrightarrow{\iota \circ \rho_{west}} c_0 \xrightarrow{\chi} d_0 \xrightarrow{\rho_{east}} a_1 \xrightarrow{\theta} b_1 \xrightarrow{\iota \circ \rho_{west}} c_1 \xrightarrow{\chi} d_1 \dots \xrightarrow{\chi} d_{n-1} \qquad (14)$$

Modeling the Initialization. In terms of the SAT model, each round requires four sets a_i, b_i, c_i, d_i of 384 Boolean variables, with $b_i = \theta(a_i)$, $c_i = \iota \circ \rho_{west}(b_i)$, $d_i = \chi(c_i)$, $a_{i+1} = \rho_{east}(d_i)$. We omit the last ρ_{east}, as it does not influence our analysis. The initial state of Xoodyak hash mode in our model is denoted by a_0, the last 256 Boolean variables are assigned constant values according to the known padding rule and color bits.

Modeling the Linear Mappings. Linear mappings include θ, ρ_{west}, ρ_{east}, and ι, which involve a large number of XOR operations and cyclic shifts. We utilize the *sage.sat* module of SageMath [30] to simplify the cumbersome encoding of CNF clauses for the linear layer.

By simulating the linear mappings through symbolic computation, we generate the Boolean expressions of the internal state over n rounds. Using the *sage.sat* module, we can convert these Boolean expressions into the corresponding CNF clauses.

This approach enhances the flexibility of directly characterizing the SAT model for linear mappings but also broadens our capabilities for CNF clauses encoding of multivariate XOR operations. The specific process for modeling the linear layer is outlined in Algorithm 1.

Modeling the Non-Linear Mapping χ. According to Property 5, the lookup table of 3-bit χ is given in Table 4, where $x = (x_0, x_1, x_2)$; if $x = 4$, then $(x_0 = 1, x_1 = 0, x_2 = 0)$.

Table 4. Xoodoo's 3-bit S-box χ as a lookup table.

x	0	1	2	3	4	5	6	7
$\chi(x)$	0	5	3	2	6	1	4	7

The general encoding method of χ is to extract all items of Table 4 into a truth table and feed this table into existing mathematical software to automatically

Algorithm 1. Linear Layer SAT Model

Require: Input a_i, b_i, c_i, d_i, $0 \le i < n$, linear mappings $\theta, \rho_{west}, \iota, \rho_{east}$, number of rounds n.
Ensure: DIMACS format of the CNF clauses for the n-round iteration.

```
Initialize Q = ∅;
for i from 0 to n do
    Compute the Boolean expressions a_i ← θ(a_i);
    Add b_i ⊕ a_i to the set Q;
    Compute the Boolean expressions b_i ← ι ∘ ρ_west(b_i);
    Add c_i ⊕ b_i to the set Q;
    if i < n − 1 then
        Compute the Boolean expressions d_i ← ρ_east(d_i);
        Add a_{i+1} ⊕ d_i to the set Q;
    end if
end for
Convert the set Q into CNF clauses in DIMACS format using the sage.sat module.
```

generate minimized CNFs. For small-scale problems, such as those where the size of S-box is less than 5, we recommend using Logic Friday[3] which is a free tool specifically designed for Boolean logic analysis. Unfortunately, it only supports Windows systems. Fortunately, the POSform function[4] provided by the logic module in the SymPy library can achieve the same results and the logic module of SymPy, both of which employ the Quine-McCluskey algorithm [20,25] for minimizing logical functions. For larger-scale problems, particularly when the size of the S-box exceeds 5, the Espresso tool can be utilized.

4.3 Constructing Difference-Value Relations Through χ

The difference transitions and the value transitions are dependent only on the non-linear operation. For the $(j \times k)$-th S-box in the i-round, we denote the input difference and the output difference as $C_i[j][*][k]$ and$D_i[j][*][k]$, respectively, where $0 \le i < n$, $0 \le j < 4$, $0 \le k < 32$.

Our goal is to derive all relations between the differential pattern $(C_i[j][*][k], D_i[j][*][k])$ and the input value $c_i[j][*][k]$. Based on Property 3, the difference-value relations can be expressed as the following Boolean equations,

$$\begin{cases} D_i[j][0][k] \\ \quad = \mathcal{D}_u\chi_0(c_i[j][0][k] \oplus uC_i[j][0][k], c_i[j][1][k] \oplus uC_i[j][1][k], c_i[j][2][k] \oplus uC_i[j][2][k]) \\ D_i[j][1][k] \\ \quad = \mathcal{D}_u\chi_1(c_i[j][0][k] \oplus uC_i[j][0][k], c_i[j][1][k] \oplus uC_i[j][1][k], c_i[j][2][k] \oplus uC_i[j][2][k]) \\ D_i[j][2][k] \\ \quad = \mathcal{D}_u\chi_2(c_i[j][0][k] \oplus uC_i[j][0][k], c_i[j][1][k] \oplus uC_i[j][1][k], c_i[j][2][k] \oplus uC_i[j][2][k]) \end{cases} \tag{15}$$

[3] please refer to http://sontrak.com/.
[4] please refer to https://docs.sympy.org/latest/modules/logic.html.

Algorithm 2. Difference-Value Relations SAT Model

Require: $c_i, 0 \leq i < n$, the non-linear operations $\chi^{n-1} \circ \cdots \circ \chi^0$, the number of rounds n, a given differential trail $(A_0, B_0, C_0, D_0, A_1, \ldots, A_n)$(please refer to trail model 12), and an auxiliary binary variable u.

Ensure: The value of a_0 or "Invalid".

1: Initialize a set $Q = \emptyset$;
2: **for** i from 0 to n **do**
3: $\quad f^i = c_i \oplus uC_i$
4: $\quad$ Compute the output of the nonlinear operation: $f^{i+1} \leftarrow \chi^i(f^i)$;
5: $\quad$ Add $\mathcal{D}_u f^{i+1} \oplus D_i$ to the set Q;
6: **end for**
7: Convert the set Q into CNF clauses in DIMACS format using the *sage.sat* module.);

We utilize SageMath as the symbolic computation tool to construct difference-value Boolean equations and then use the sage.sat module to convert Boolean equations to CNF clauses in DIMACS format. The detailed process for modeling the difference-value relations is presented in Algorithm 2.

5 New Collision Attacks on Xoodyak Hash Mode

In this section, we present the first 2-round practical collision attack and a 3-round practical SFS collision attack based on our SAT-based collision search model.

5.1 2-Round Collision Attack

Our 2-round collision search can be divided into the following two phases:

1. Prepare a 2-round *loop* differential trail $(A_0, B_0, C_0, D_0, A_1, B_1, C_1, D_1)$ with the configuration $(s_0 = 32, s_1 = 32)$. In each 384-bit difference state, only the first 32 bits have non-zero difference.
2. Construct a 2-round collision search SAT model and invoke SAT solver to find a conforming message pairs satisfying the 2-round loop differential trail. This message pair can be viewed as actual colliding pairs.

Theoretical Complexity Analysis. The weight of the second round trail is $32 \times 2 = 64$. Based on the 1-round connector, we can construct a linear system with $n_l = 64$ linear equations induced by the difference-value relations. The remaining DF is 64, such that 1-round connector generates a subspace of 2^{64} message pairs. This enables us to exhaustively enumerate the message pairs generated with the connectors until we find a message pair that following our 1-round colliding trail. The time complexity of 2-round collision attack T_{total} is 2^{64}. Actually, T_{total} can be further reduced to $2^{37.2388}$ using the parameters $n_l = 64$, $n_q = 64$, $n_l' = 29$, and $d_f = 29$ based on our linearization strategy outlined in Sect. 5.3, by directly constructing the 2-round *loop* differential trails as 2-round connectors.

In the practical collision search on the 2-round XOODYAK hash mode, it typically requires at least $2^{37.2388}$ XOODYAK hash function calls to find an actual collision. In contrast, our SAT model demonstrates outstanding performance by enabling us to find a 2-round collision within minutes.

Practical 2-round Collision Search. We use different SAT solvers to solve our 2-round collision search model, the `Treengeling` solver performs well as shown in Appendix A (see Table 6).It takes only 64.7 s to find a practical collision. Thereal colliding pair is listed in Table 7.

5.2 Practical 3-Round SFS Collision Search

For the 3-round loop differential trail with weight 192, finding a practical collision is challenging due to the large search space and solver's limitation. In this section, we implement a practical SFS collision attack on the 3-round XOODOO hash mode. The theoretical collision attack will be analyzed in detail in Sect. 5.3.

In the Semi-Free-Start (SFS) collision attack, the attacker has the ability to select the initial chain value, specifically the initialization vector (IV), along with a pair of distinct messages, denoted as $M_0\|IV$ and $M_0'\|IV$. The goal is to find these messages such that their hash values, calculated with the chosen IV, are equal: $H(IV, M_0) = H(IV, M_0')$ [28].

The 3-round SFS collision search is conducted through the following steps:

1. Prepare a 3-round *loop* differential trail $(A_0, B_0, C_0, D_0, A_1, \ldots, D_2)$ with the configuration $(s_0 = 32, s_1 = 32, s_2 = 32)$. In each 384-bit difference state, only the first 32 bits have non-zero difference.
2. Construct a 3-round SFS collision search SAT model without imposing any constraints on the last 256 Boolean variables of the initial state a_0. We then invoke a SAT solver to find a conforming message pair that satisfy the 3-round loop differential trail. This message pair can be regarded as actual SFS colliding pair.

After constructing the 3-round SFS collision search model, We use `Treengeling` [4] solver to solve it, it takes just 3.67 s to find an actual 3-round SFS colliding pair. This actual colliding pair is presented in Table 5. However, for the 4-round model, we are unable to obtain an actual 4-round SFS colliding pair within a reasonable time (limited to 2 d).

5.3 Improved 3-Round Collision Attacks

Now, we have a 3-round *loop* differential trail with the configuration of $(s_0 = 32, s_1 = 32, s_2 = 32)$. For the last two rounds, the total weight equals the birthday bound (128 for both XOODOO-HASH and XOODOO-XOF). It is impractical to randomly select a 2-round colliding trail and construct a 1-round connector.

To make the collision attack on the XOODYAK hash mode theoretically feasible for up to 3 rounds, our 3-round collision attack is constructed using a 2-round

Table 5. 3-round Practical SFS Collision for Xoodyak Hash Mode $(\bar{M_0}, \bar{M_0'})$

$\bar{M_0}$			
0x89520d63	0x81dd4a10	0xfd153620	0x5f643139
0x87f72cf8	0x226e3ce7	0x6dd82fcb	0xc42eee67
0x683125fd	0xbd69af3d	0x859690da	0x84a2196b
$\bar{M_0'} \oplus A_0$			
0x76adf29c	0x81dd4a10	0xfd153620	0x5f643139
0x87f72cf8	0x226e3ce7	0x6dd82fcb	0xc42eee67
0x683125fd	0xbd69af3d	0x859690da	0x84a2196b

connector and a 1-round colliding trail with weight 64. We propose a linearization strategy in this section to partially linearize 64 quadratic conditions of the second-round connectors. Two rounds of Xoodoo permutation are expressed as

$$a_0 \xrightarrow{\iota \circ \rho_{west} \circ \theta} c_0 \xrightarrow{\chi} d_0 \xrightarrow{\iota \circ \rho_{west} \circ \theta \circ \rho_{east}} c_1 \xrightarrow{\chi} d_1 \xrightarrow{\rho_{east}} a_1. \tag{16}$$

In our 3-round *loop* trail, all S-boxes have the same valid difference pattern, $(1, 0, 0, 1, 0, 0)$, in the first round, we have $n_l = 64$ linear equations derived from the difference-value relations $D_0 = \mathcal{D}_u\chi(c_0 \oplus uC_0)$, *i.e.*, $c_0[0][1][z] = 0$ and $c_0[0][2][z] = 1$, where $0 \leq z < 32$. In the second round, the difference-value relations $D_1 = \mathcal{D}_u\chi(c_1 \oplus uC_1)$ give rise to $n_q = 64$ quadratic equations, *i.e.*, $c_1[0][1][z] = 0$ and $c_1[0][2][z] = 1$. Hence, the total complexity of 3-round collision attack can be computed based on Eq. 11,

$$T_{total} = 2^{51.5822+d_f} \times \frac{(64 + n_l' + d_f)^2 \times 128}{3} + 2^{128-n_l'} + 2^{128-n_l'} \tag{17}$$

Linearization Strategy. Our aim is to maximize the number of quadratic equations n_l' that can be linearized while minimizing the consumption of degrees of freedom is essential. This will reduce the overall complexity of collision attack.

As the inputs are already grouped to subset with the 64 linear constraints of differentials, the first 32 active S-boxes are already fully linearized. Thus, the output bits $d_0[0][*][z]$ of the 32 active S-boxes $c_0[0][*][z]$ after the first χ mapping must be linear bits *i.e.*, $(d_0[0][0][z], d_0[0][1][z], d_0[0][2][z], 0 \leq z < 32)$.

Let us consider a given state a_0, where only the first 128 bits are treated as Boolean variables, while the remaining 256 bits are fixed as constants. After propagation through the linear layer $\iota \circ \rho_{\text{west}} \circ \theta$, the resulting state c_0 satisfies the following property:

Property 4. If the bit $c_0[0][1][z]$ is imposed a linear equation, then the bit $c_0[3][2][z]$ is also imposed a linear equation equivalent to bit $c_0[0][1][z + 11]$, where $0 \leq z < 32$.

Property 5. If the bit $c_0[0][2][z]$ is imposed a linear equation, then the bit $c_0[1][1][z]$ is also imposed a linear equation equivalent to bit $c_0[0][2][z-11]$, where $0 \leq z < 32$.

This relationship is determined by the combined effects of the linear operations θ-effect and ρ_{west}. For brevity, the proof is omitted; Fig. 5 offers a graphical explanation of the linearization.

Based on Property 2, any two bit of the output can be linearized by adding one extra linear equations on the input. Thus, extra $2 \times 2 \times 32 = 128$ bits in d_0 can be linearized. We introduce 384 Boolean variables $x_{384}, \ldots, x_{767}$ to represent each bit of d_0. Among these, $96 + 128 = 224$ bits' ANF expressions are linear expressions with respect to the inputs x_i,$0 \leq i < 128$. We refer to such bits as linear bits. In contrast, the remaining 160 bits are referred to as non-linear bits, as their ANF expressions are non-linear with respect to the inputs x_i, $0 \leq i < 128$.

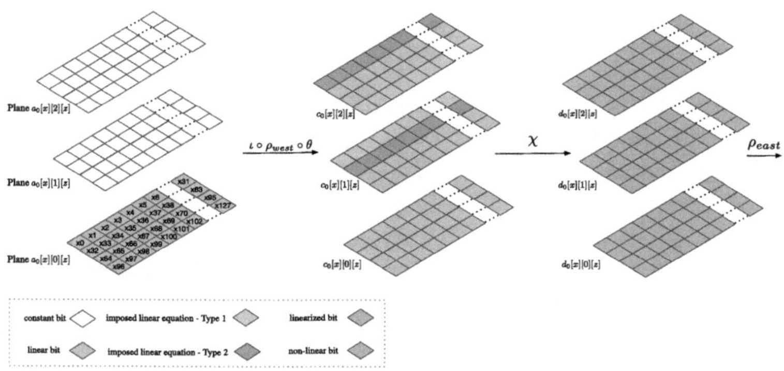

Fig. 5. Propagation of Boolean Variables in the First Round

Specially, for non-linear bits x_i, $704 \leq i \leq 735$, each non-linear bit require one extra linear equation to achieve linearization, resulting in the consumption of 1 DF. The quadratic terms involving these bits are listed below.

$$\begin{cases} x_{i+686} : (x_i + x_{i+9})(x_{i+32} + x_{i+41} + x_{i+46}), 18 \leq i \leq 22 \\ x_{i+709} : (x_i + x_{i+23})(x_{i+32} + x_{i+55} + x_{i+69}), 0 \leq i \leq 8 \\ x_{i+718} : (x_i + x_{i+9})(x_{i+32} + x_{i+41} + x_{i+78}), 0 \leq i \leq 17 \end{cases}$$

For example, if we set $x_7 + x_{30} = c$, where $c = 0$ or $c = 1$, x_{716} can be linearized. In this way, this process enables us to obtain one linearized quadratic equation at the cost of 1 DF, which can be mathematically expressed as $d_f = n'_l$.

Based on the above analysis, we can re-write Eq. 17 as below,

$$T_{total} = 2^{51.5822 + n'_l} \times \frac{(64 + 2n'_l)^2 \times 128}{3} + 2^{128 - n'_l + 1} \tag{18}$$

The above computation has the optimal choice when $n'_l = 29$, the time complexity of the 3-round collision attack reaches its minimum value, *i.e.*, $T_{total} = 2^{100.9311}$.

6 Conclusion

In this paper, we observed several key properties of the XOODOO round function, particularly its unique θ and non-linear operation χ. Leveraging these properties, we designed special differential trails referred to as *loop* differential trails to improve differential-based collision attacks. To quickly find practical collisions, we built a SAT-based collision search model for the round-reduced XOODYAK hash mode. We presented an actual 2-round collision and a 3-round SFS collision on the XOODYAK hash mode. Furthermore, by employing a linearization strategy, we reduced the best-known time complexity for 3-round collision attacks to $2^{100.9311}$. To the best of our knowledge, these are the best collision attacks on the round-reduced XOODYAK hash mode, covering both XOODYAK-`hash` and XOODYAK-XOF.

Acknowledgments. The authors would like to thank Kai Hu and the anonymous reviewers for their valuable suggestions to improve the quality of the paper. The research leading to these results has received funding from the National Key Research and Development Program of China under Grant 2023YFB3106501, the Fundamental Research Funds for the Central Universities (No. XJSJ25021).

Appendix

A Practical Collision Results

The real 2-round collision pair and the corresponding search time are listed as follows:

Table 6. 2-round Practical Collision Search Time

practical collision search time	solver	thread
64.7 s	`Treengeling`	10
966.4 s	`Plingeling`	10
1583.1 s	`CryptoMiniSat`	10
18983.3 s	`CaDiCaL`	1

B Quadratic Equations in the Second Round

To clearly illustrate the Boolean variables associated with the quadratic conditions, we present all quadratic equations in Table 8. We observe that each quadratic equation contains at least one non-linear bit or, in some instances, up to four non-linear bits.

Table 7. 2-round Practical Collision for XOODYAK Hash Mode $(\bar{M_0}, \bar{M_0'})$

$\bar{M_0}$			
0x2854a4be	0x3adea611	0xffffffff	0xaaaaaaab
0x01000000	0x00000000	0x00000000	0x00000000
0x00000000	0x00000000	0x00000000	0x00000001
$\bar{M_0'} \oplus A_0$			
0xd7ab5b41	0x3adea611	0xffffffff	0xaaaaaaab
0x01000000	0x00000000	0x00000000	0x00000000
0x00000000	0x00000000	0x00000000	0x00000001

Table 8. Statistics of 64 Quadratic Equations. $x(1,2,3) \triangleq x_1 \oplus x_2 \oplus x_3$; Orange bit is non-liner variable in d_0; Black bit is linear variable in d_0.

No.	Quadratic Equations	No.	Quadratic Equations
1	$x(466, 475, 593, 602, 639, 650, 659)$	33	$x(487, 496, 614, 623, 680, 703, 717)$
2	$x(467, 476, 594, 603, 608, 651, 660)$	34	$x(488, 497, 615, 624, 672, 681, 718)$
3	$x(468, 477, 595, 604, 609, 652, 661)$	35	$x(489, 498, 616, 625, 673, 682, 719)$
4	$x(469, 478, 596, 605, 610, 653, 662)$	36	$x(490, 499, 617, 626, 674, 683, 720)$
5	$x(470, 479, 597, 606, 611, 654, 663)$	37	$x(491, 500, 618, 627, 675, 684, 721)$
6	$x(448, 471, 598, 607, 612, 655, 664)$	38	$x(492, 501, 619, 628, 676, 685, 722)$
7	$x(449, 472, 576, 599, 613, 656, 665)$	39	$x(493, 502, 620, 629, 677, 686, 723)$
8	$x(450, 473, 577, 600, 614, 657, 666)$	40	$x(494, 503, 621, 630, 678, 687, 724)$
9	$x(451, 474, 578, 601, 615, 658, 667)$	41	$x(495, 504, 622, 631, 679, 688, 725)$
10	$x(452, 475, 579, 602, 616, 659, 668)$	42	$x(496, 505, 623, 632, 680, 689, 726)$
11	$x(453, 476, 580, 603, 617, 660, 669)$	43	$x(497, 506, 624, 633, 681, 690, 727)$
12	$x(454, 477, 581, 604, 618, 661, 670)$	44	$x(498, 507, 625, 634, 682, 691, 728)$
13	$x(455, 478, 582, 605, 619, 662, 671)$	45	$x(499, 508, 626, 635, 683, 692, 729)$
14	$x(456, 479, 583, 606, 620, 640, 663)$	46	$x(500, 509, 627, 636, 684, 693, 730)$
15	$x(448, 457, 584, 607, 621, 641, 664)$	47	$x(501, 510, 628, 637, 685, 694, 731)$
16	$x(449, 458, 576, 585, 622, 642, 665)$	48	$x(502, 511, 629, 638, 686, 695, 732)$
17	$x(450, 459, 577, 586, 623, 643, 666)$	49	$x(480, 503, 630, 639, 687, 696, 733)$
18	$x(451, 460, 578, 587, 624, 644, 667)$	50	$x(481, 504, 608, 631, 688, 697, 734)$
19	$x(452, 461, 579, 588, 625, 645, 668)$	51	$x(482, 505, 609, 632, 689, 698, 735)$
20	$x(453, 462, 580, 589, 626, 646, 669)$	52	$x(483, 506, 610, 633, 690, 699, 704)$
21	$x(454, 463, 581, 590, 627, 647, 670)$	53	$x(484, 507, 611, 634, 691, 700, 705)$
22	$x(455, 464, 582, 591, 628, 648, 671)$	54	$x(485, 508, 612, 635, 692, 701, 706)$
23	$x(456, 465, 583, 592, 629, 640, 649)$	55	$x(486, 509, 613, 636, 693, 702, 707)$
24	$x(457, 466, 584, 593, 630, 641, 650)$	56	$x(487, 510, 614, 637, 694, 703, 708)$
25	$x(458, 467, 585, 594, 631, 642, 651$	57	$x(488, 511, 615, 638, 672, 695, 709)$
26	$x(459, 468, 586, 595, 632, 643, 652)$	58	$x(480, 489, 616, 639, 673, 696, 710)$
27	$x(460, 469, 587, 596, 633, 644, 653)$	59	$x(481, 490, 608, 617, 674, 697, 711)$
28	$x(461, 470, 588, 597, 634, 645, 654)$	60	$x(482, 491, 609, 618, 675, 698, 712)$
29	$x(462, 471, 589, 598, 635, 646, 655)$	61	$x(483, 492, 610, 619, 676, 699, 713)$
30	$x(463, 472, 590, 599, 636, 647, 656)$	62	$x(484, 493, 611, 620, 677, 700, 714)$
31	$x(464, 473, 591, 600, 637, 648, 657)$	63	$x(485, 494, 612, 621, 678, 701, 715)$
32	$x(465, 474, 592, 601, 638, 649, 658)$	64	$x(486, 495, 613, 622, 679, 702, 716)$

References

1. Abdelkhalek, A., Sasaki, Y., Todo, Y., Tolba, M., Youssef, A.M.: MILP modeling for (large) S-boxes to optimize probability of differential characteristics. IACR Trans. Symmetric Cryptol. **2017**(4), 99–129 (2017)
2. Bellini, E., et al.: Differential cryptanalysis with SAT, SMT, MILP, and CP: a detailed comparison for bit-oriented primitives. In: CANS. Lecture Notes in Computer Science, vol. 14342, pp. 268–292 (2023)
3. Bertoni, Guido and Peeters, Michaël and Van Assche, Gilles and others: The Keccak reference (2011). http://keccak.noekeon.org
4. Biere, A.: CaDiCaL, Lingeling, Plingeling, Treengeling, YalSAT entering the SAT competition 2017. In: Balyo, T., Heule, M., Järvisalo, M. (eds.) Proc. of SAT Competition 2017 – Solver and Benchmark Descriptions. Department of Computer Science Series of Publications B, vol. B-2017-1, pp. 14–15 (2017)
5. Biham, E., Shamir, A.: Differential cryptanalysis of DES-like cryptosystems. J. Cryptol. **4**(1), 3–72 (1991). https://doi.org/10.1007/BF00630563
6. Choo, D., Soos, M., Chai, K.M.A., Meel, K.S.: Bosphorus: bridging ANF and CNF solvers. In: Design, Automation & Test in Europe Conference & Exhibition, DATE 2019. pp. 468–473 (2019)
7. Daemen, J., Hoffert, S., Assche, G.V., Keer, R.V.: The design of Xoodoo and Xoofff. IACR Trans. Symm. Cryptol. **2018**, 1–38 (2018)
8. Daemen, J., Hoffert, S., Peeters, M., Van Assche, G., Van Keer, R.: Xoodyak, a lightweight cryptographic scheme. IACR Trans. Symm. Cryptol. **2020**, 60–87 (2020)
9. Degré, M., Derbez, P., Lahaye, L., Schrottenloher, A.: New models for the cryptanalysis of Ascon. IACR Cryptol. ePrint Arch, p. 298 (2024)
10. Dinur, I., Dunkelman, O., Shamir, A.: New attacks on Keccak-224 and Keccak-256. In: Canteaut, A. (ed.) FSE 2012. LNCS, vol. 7549, pp. 442–461. Springer, Heidelberg (2012). https://doi.org/10.1007/978-3-642-34047-5_25
11. Dong, X., Zhao, B., Qin, L., Hou, Q., Zhang, S., Wang, X.: Generic MitM attack frameworks on sponge constructions. In: CRYPTO (4). Lecture Notes in Computer Science, vol. 14923, pp. 3–37. Springer (2024)
12. Guido, B., Joan, D., Michaël, P., Gilles, V.: Cryptographic sponge functions. https://keccak.team/files/CSF-0.1.pdf (2011)
13. Guo, J., Liao, G., Liu, G., Liu, M., Qiao, K., Song, L.: Practical collision attacks against round-reduced SHA-3. J. Cryptol. **33**(1), 228–270 (2020)
14. Guo, J., Liu, G., Song, L., Tu, Y.: Exploring SAT for cryptanalysis:(quantum) collision attacks against 6-round SHA-3. In: International Conference on the Theory and Application of Cryptology and Information Security, pp. 645–674. Springer (2022)
15. Huang, S., Ben-Yehuda, O.A., Dunkelman, O., Maximov, A.: Finding collisions against 4-round SHA3-384 in practical time. IACR Cryptol. ePrint Arch, p. 194 (2022)
16. Li, H., Zhang, H., Hu, K., Liu, G., Qiu, W.: AlgSAT - a SAT method for verification of differential trails from an algebraic perspective. In: ACISP (1). Lecture Notes in Computer Science, vol. 14895, pp. 450–471. Springer (2024)
17. Liu, F., Isobe, T., Meier, W.: Automatic verification of differential characteristics: application to reduced Gimli. In: Micciancio, D., Ristenpart, T. (eds.) CRYPTO 2020. LNCS, vol. 12172, pp. 219–248. Springer, Cham (2020). https://doi.org/10.1007/978-3-030-56877-1_8

18. Liu, G., Lu, J., Li, H., Tang, P., Qiu, W.: Preimage attacks against lightweight scheme Xoodyak based on deep learning. In: Arai, K. (ed.) FICC 2021. AISC, vol. 1364, pp. 637–648. Springer, Cham (2021). https://doi.org/10.1007/978-3-030-73103-8_45
19. Liu, M., Lu, X., Lin, D.: Differential-linear cryptanalysis from an algebraic perspective. In: Malkin, T., Peikert, C. (eds.) CRYPTO 2021. LNCS, vol. 12827, pp. 247–277. Springer, Cham (2021). https://doi.org/10.1007/978-3-030-84252-9_9
20. McCluskey, E.J.: Minimization of Boolean functions. Bell Syst. Techn. J. **35**(6), 1417–1444 (1956)
21. Mella, S., Daemen, J., Assche, G.V.: Tighter trail bounds for Xoodoo. IACR Trans. Symmetric Cryptol. **2023**(4), 187–214 (2023)
22. NIST: The NIST Lightweight Cryptography Project (2018). https://csrc.nist.gov/Projects/lightweight-cryptography
23. Qiao, K., Song, L., Liu, M., Guo, J.: New collision attacks on round-reduced Keccak. In: Coron, J.-S., Nielsen, J.B. (eds.) EUROCRYPT 2017. LNCS, vol. 10212, pp. 216–243. Springer, Cham (2017). https://doi.org/10.1007/978-3-319-56617-7_8
24. Qin, L., Hua, J., Dong, X., Yan, H., Wang, X.: Meet-in-the-middle preimage attacks on sponge-based hashing. In: EUROCRYPT (4). Lecture Notes in Computer Science, vol. 14007, pp. 158–188 (2023)
25. Quine, W.V.: A way to simplify truth functions. Am. Math. Mon. **62**(9), 627–631 (1955)
26. Song, L., Guo, J.: Cube-attack-like cryptanalysis of round-reduced Keccak using MILP. IACR Trans. Symmetric Cryptol. **2018**(3), 182–214 (2018)
27. Song, L., Liao, G., Guo, J.: Non-full Sbox linearization: applications to collision attacks on round-reduced KECCAK. In: Katz, J., Shacham, H. (eds.) CRYPTO 2017. LNCS, vol. 10402, pp. 428–451. Springer, Cham (2017). https://doi.org/10.1007/978-3-319-63715-0_15
28. Stevens, M., Karpman, P., Peyrin, T.: Freestart collision for full SHA-1. In: Fischlin, M., Coron, J.-S. (eds.) EUROCRYPT 2016. LNCS, vol. 9665, pp. 459–483. Springer, Heidelberg (2016). https://doi.org/10.1007/978-3-662-49890-3_18
29. Sun, L., Wang, W., Wang, M.: More accurate differential properties of LED64 and Midori64. IACR Trans. Symmetric Cryptol. **2018**(3), 93–123 (2018). https://doi.org/10.13154/tosc.v2018.i3.93-123
30. The Sage Developers: SageMath, the sage mathematics software system (version 9.5s) (2022). https://www.sagemath.org
31. Zhou, H., Li, Z., Dong, X., Jia, K., Meier, W.: Practical key-recovery attacks on round-reduced Ketje Jr. Xoodoo-AE and Xoodyak. Comput. J. **63**(8), 1231–1246 (2020)

Breaking the Twinkle Authenticated Encryption Scheme and Analyzing Its Underlying Permutation

Debasmita Chakraborty[1(✉)], Hosein Hadipour[2(✉)], Anup Kumar Kundu[3], Mostafizar Rahman[4], Prathamesh Ram[5], Yu Sasaki[6(✉)], Dilip Sau[7], and Aman Sinha[8]

[1] Graz University of Technology, Graz, Austria
debasmitachakraborty1@gmail.com
[2] Ruhr University Bochum, Bochum, Germany
hsn.hadipour@gmail.com
[3] Indian Statistical Institute, Kolkata 700108, India
anupkundumath@gmail.com
[4] Kyoto University, Kyoto, Japan
mrahman454@gmail.com
[5] Indian Institute of Technology Bhilai, Bhilai, India
rprathamesh@iitbhilai.ac.in
[6] NTT Social Informatics Laboratories and NIST Associate, Tokyo, Japan
yusk.sasaki@ntt.com
[7] Indian Institute of Technology Kharagpur, Kharagpur, India
dilip.sau@kgpian.iitkgp.ac.in
[8] Nanyang Technological University, Singapore, Singapore
aman0804@gmail.com

Abstract. This paper studies the `Twinkle` family of low-latency symmetric key schemes designed by Wang et al. (CiC 2024). In particular, it presents cryptanalysis of both the mode and the underlying primitive. `Twinkle` is a PRF-based design, and an authenticated encryption scheme `Twinkle-AE` is specified based on a dedicated PRF called `Twinkle-PRF`. To achieve low latency, `Twinkle-PRF` uses a large key and state to produce sufficient randomness in a single step. `Twinkle-AE` uses a 1024- or 512-bit key for authentication and generates a t-bit tag, where $t \in \{64, 128\}$. It claims to provide t bits of integrity. Several `Twinkle-AE` parameter sets claim higher confidentiality than integrity. In this setup, for any ciphertext, an adversary can obtain the message after $O(2^t)$ decryption attempts by guessing the tag, allowing attacks in the chosen-ciphertext setting. We show that a 1024- or 512-bit authentication key can be recovered using only $O(2^t)$ queries. The recovered authentication key enables the generation of valid ciphertexts for arbitrary plaintexts, thus achieving universal forgery. In the second part of the paper, we perform cryptanalysis on reduced-round variants of the 1280-bit public permutation `Twinkle-P`, which serves as a core component of `Twinkle-PRF`. We investigate impossible differential, zero-correlation linear, integral, and differential-linear distinguishers by developing automated analytic tools. We provide

C. Boura et al. (Eds.): SAC 2025, LNCS 16207, pp. 79–109, 2026.
https://doi.org/10.1007/978-3-032-10536-3_4

practical distinguishers for up to 5 rounds, and the longest distinguisher reaches 6 rounds with a complexity of $2^{74.32}$. This surpasses the round bounds evaluated by the designers. We stress that our attacks on mode exploits the gap between the claimed confidentiality and integrity levels, thus have no impact on the parameter sets having the same security level. Our attacks on the permutation do not have any significant impact on the whole specifications. Moreover, we note that `Twinkle-AE-512b`/`Twinkle-AE-1024b` and `Twinkle-PA` remain secure, and the versions we attacked would also be secure if the claimed confidentiality level matched the integrity level.

Keywords: Cryptanalysis · Lightweight cryptography · Low-latency primitive · `Twinkle` · authentication · confidentiality · permutation

1 Introduction

Evolving from general-purpose schemes, symmetric-key cryptography is increasingly adopting domain-specific designs tailored for particular use cases. This shift, driven by efforts such as NIST's lightweight cryptography standardization [3] and the CAESAR competition [1], reflects diverse requirements across domains, including lightweight applications, high throughput, and strong security guarantees. A prominent domain in this context is low-latency cryptography, which plays a vital role in securing memory and system components in modern computing environments. Some key ciphers in this area include PRINCE [13], MANTIS [9], QARMA [7], SPEEDY [25], Orthros [8], Gleeok [4], SCARF [14], and BipBip [10]. With rising threats from physical and software-based memory attacks, hardware vendors now integrate cryptographic protections through solutions like Intel Software Guard Extensions (SGX) [19], AMD Secure Encrypted Virtualization (SEV) [2], and ARM CCA [5]. These mechanisms reflect varying levels of protection offered by secure memory encryption engines (MEEs), including features like ciphertext uniqueness and replay protection [17].

While encryption for memory protection has received considerable attention, the design of authenticated encryption (AE) and message authentication codes (MACs) tailored for system-level security, such as Pointer Authentication (PA), remains less explored. Existing industrial implementations (e.g., ARM's PAC [6], Intel's C^3 [26]) often rely on domain-specific MACs or tweakable block ciphers optimized for minimal latency.

Building on these developments, Wang et al. introduced the `Twinkle` framework [33] to address the need for efficient cryptographic mechanisms at the system level. This framework provides two key components: (i) a nonce-based AE scheme designed for memory encryption, and (ii) a lightweight MAC optimized for pointer authentication. Both constructions are based on a compact and novel pseudorandom function (PRF), enabling efficient hardware implementation.

In this work, we present a comprehensive security analysis of the `Twinkle` family, a set of low-latency schemes designed to provide stronger protection against replay attacks in memory encryption scenarios. The design adopts a stream cipher structure combined with a Wegman-Carter message authentication code (WC-MAC) [34], deriving both the keystream and authentication mask from a single PRF, which helps reduce overall latency. This structure enables time-aligned encryption, plaintext-independent computation, and pre-processing when the nonce is known in advance. These features further minimize delay. The 1280-bit tailored PRF state allows efficient processing of entire cache lines, while the hardware-optimized round function, which includes diffusion-friendly S-boxes and double-lane rotations, improves both performance and security. `Twinkle-PA`, a matching MAC that uses the same PRF, supports compact and efficient integration on shared hardware.

A key challenge in analyzing `Twinkle-AE` stems from its large 1280-bit internal state. This design allows a greater number of active S-boxes per round, thereby improving security against differential and linear attacks. Additionally, at least 128 bits of the state remain concealed, complicating attempts at impossible differential and guess-and-determine attacks. Furthermore, the design introduces strong diffusion early in the computation: input data is spread across the state using multiple permutation matrices. Such a strong underlying structure leads the designers to claim the security of `Twinkle-AE` based on its underlying `Twinkle-PRF` and WC-MAC. Another aspect of `Twinkle-AE` is the use of the initialization vector (IV) as an only input to its underlying `Twinkle-PRF`, which makes it considerably more difficult to mount attacks targeting the PRF.

The designers claim that the security of the `Twinkle-AE` family fundamentally relies on the robustness of its underlying PRF, which is based on a large-state Even-Mansour construction. Assuming a random permutation and distinct key components, they argue that the construction achieves a security bound of $O(2^{640})$ for Twinkle's 1280-bit state, which is well beyond its intended security targets. The `Twinkle-PRF` has undergone extensive analysis against a wide range of classical cryptanalytic techniques, including differential, linear, integral, impossible differential, and meet-in-the-middle attacks. Based on these properties, the designers assert that the PRF is secure for use in both memory encryption and pointer authentication scenarios, under the assumption that the key is securely stored within the processor and not subject to related-key attacks.

The designers of `Twinkle` claim security based on the strength of the `Twinkle-PRF` and the WC-MAC components. Each part of `Twinkle-AE`, namely the encryption and MAC mechanisms, individually satisfies standard security guarantees. However, our analysis shows that the universal hash function introduces a weakness that an attacker can exploit when the number of queries can exceed the output size. Hence, as our first objective, we identify vulnerabilities that do not require directly targeting the underlying PRF.

In addition, although the designers have explored the security of the underlying permutation against cryptanalytic attacks, they have rarely presented concrete distinguishers. In particular, they have not examined the security of the permutation against differential-linear attacks, which often serve as some of the most powerful distinguishers for cryptographic permutations. To address this gap, we construct concrete differential-linear distinguishers and either significantly strengthen the existing analysis or provide the first known results in this direction.

1.1 Our Contributions

We provide a focused cryptanalytic evaluation of the Twinkle-AE scheme, addressing gaps in the analysis of the Twinkle-P permutation and key-recovery resistance. Our contributions are twofold:

1. **Authentication key-recovery attacks:** For AE, even if a nonce and a ciphertext are known, a corresponding M is not accessible without knowing a tag T. However as observed by Hosoyamada et al. [24] against Rocca [28], higher confidentiality than integrity allows an adversary to exhaustively guess T with 2^t queries, allowing M to be leaked to the adversary. By combining this idea with the structure of Twinkle-AE, we demonstrate authentication key-recovery attacks on Twinkle-AE for the versions claiming higher confidentiality than integrity, which allows an adversary to recover a 1024- or 512-bit authentication key K' with $O(2^t)$ queries in the nonce-respecting setting, where $t \in \{64, 128\}$. The recovered K' enables the generation of valid ciphertexts for arbitrary plaintexts, thus achieving universal forgery, which breaks the notion of indistinguishability under chosen-ciphertext attack (IND-CCA). Importantly, these attacks do not exploit weaknesses in the underlying Twinkle-PRF, but rather in the use of the universal hash function within the WC-MAC construction. Additionally, we present a variant of the attack that succeeds with only $O(1)$ queries in the nonce-misuse setting. Note that because the IV size is 128 bits, repeat of the same nonce is inevitable after 2^{128} queries for Twinkle-AE-512c and Twinkle-AE-1024c that claim 256-bit confidentiality even with the restriction that the attacker can only make queries in the chosen-plaintext setting. We also show that Twinkle-AE does not provide key-committing security, allowing an adversary to create distinct keys that produce the same ciphertext with $O(1)$ cost.
2. **Analysis of the underlying permutation:** We analyze the Twinkle-P permutation, the core component of Twinkle-AE, against several cryptanalytic distinguishers. Table 1 summarizes our findings. Notably, we present practical differential-linear (DL) distinguishers for up to 5 rounds of Twinkle-P, as well as a strong theoretical DL distinguisher for 6 rounds. For example, the data complexity of our 5-round differential-linear distinguisher is $2^{5.70}$ randomly chosen input pairs, or equivalently, $2 \cdot 2^{5.70}$ chosen inputs. While the designers claimed that no 7-round impossible differential trail could be constructed even with full adversarial control over all 1280 bits, we match this bound by explicitly constructing a 6-round impossible differential attack. Moreover, we provide zero-correlation (ZC) distinguishers for up to 6 rounds. We also leverage the connection between ZC and integral distinguishers, along with the constraint programming (CP) based search methods proposed in [21,23], to identify ZC-based integral attacks. Additionally, we use the bit-based division property to derive practical integral distinguishers for up to 5 rounds of Twinkle-P. We provide the source code of our tools as well as the experimental verifications at the following link: https://github.com/hadipourh/twinkle.

Table 1. Summary of distinguishers for `Twinkle-P`

Distinguisher	#Rounds	#Distinguishers	Attack complexity	Ref.
Differential	4	–	$> 2^{58}$	[33]
Linear	4	1	2^{60}	[33]
Truncated Differential	3.5	1	$2^{7.4}$	[33]
Differential-Linear	**4**	80	2	Subsect. 5.6
	5	80	$2 \cdot \mathbf{2^{5.70}}$	Subsect. 5.6
	6	80	$2 \cdot \mathbf{2^{73.32}}$	Subsect. 5.6
Impossible Differential	4	$80 \cdot 2^{1820}$	–	Subsect. 5.3
	5	$80 \cdot 2^{1148}$	–	Subsect. 5.3
	6	$80 \cdot 2^{356}$	–	Subsect. 5.3
Zero-Correlation Linear	4	$80 \cdot 2^{1278}$	–	Subsect. 5.4
	5	$80 \cdot 2^{1140}$	–	Subsect. 5.4
	6	$80 \cdot 2^{16}$	–	Subsect. 5.4
Integral	3	80	2	Subsect. 5.4
	4	80	2^4	Subsect. 5.4
	5	80	2^{12}	Subsect. 5.5

1.2 Paper Organization

The rest of the paper is organized as follows. Section 2 introduces the notation used throughout the paper. Section 3 describes the specification of `Twinkle`. Section 4 presents our attacks against `Twinkle-AE`. Section 5 provides the cryptanalysis of reduced rounds of `Twinkle-P`. Finally, Sect. 6 concludes the paper.

2 Notation

Let $\mathbb{Z}_m$ denote the set $\{0, 1, \ldots, m-1\}$ for a positive integer m. Assume that $S = S[m-1] \parallel \cdots \parallel S[1] \parallel S[0]$ is an m-bit string, where $S[0]$ (resp. $S[m-1]$) represents the least significant bit (LSB) (resp. most significant bit (MSB)). We assume that m is a multiple of 16, that is, $m = 16 \times \ell$ for some $\ell \in \mathbb{Z}_n$. According to the `Twinkle-AE` specification [33], the internal state of `Twinkle-P` is arranged into a $4 \times 4 \times \ell$ three-dimensional array, as illustrated in Fig. 1a. We use (x, y, z) or, alternatively, $S[x][y][z]$ to indicate the position of each bit within the 3D representation, where $x, y \in \{0, \ldots, 3\}$ and $0 \leq z \leq \ell - 1$. The entry $S[x][y][z]$ within the 3D representation corresponds to $S[x + 4 \cdot y + 16 \cdot z]$ within the one-dimensional (1D) representation. Similar to the specification [33], we use $\bullet$ to denote that one coordinate can take all possible values. For example, for a given pair (y, z), $S[\bullet][y][z]$ represents $S[x][y][z]$ for all $x \in \{0, \ldots, 3\}$. We refer to $S[\bullet][y][z]$, $S[x][\bullet][z]$, $S[x][y][\bullet]$, and $S[\bullet][\bullet][z]$ as *row*, *column*, *lane*, and *slice*, respectively.

Besides the 3D representation, we can also represent the internal state as a two-dimensional $16 \times \ell$ array, as shown in Fig. 1b. In this case, we assign $S[x][y][z]$ from the 3D representation to $S[i][j]$ in the 2D representation, where $j = z$ and $i = x + 4 \cdot y$. Therefore, the jth slice in the 3D representation corresponds to the jth column of the 2D representation, where each column is filled from top to bottom. That is, the topmost bit of each column in 2D representation is the first bit of each slice. Additionally, each row of the 2D representation corresponds to a lane of the 3D representation. For example, the cells marked by ■, ■, and ■ in Fig. 1b correspond to $S[0][0][0]$, $S[3][1][39]$, and $S[3][3][79]$ in the 3D representation, respectively. We recall that $S[0][0][0]$ is the LSB of the m-bit string S, and the leftmost bit in each row of the 2D representation represents the LSB of the corresponding lane. We denote left (i.e. from LSB to MSB) and

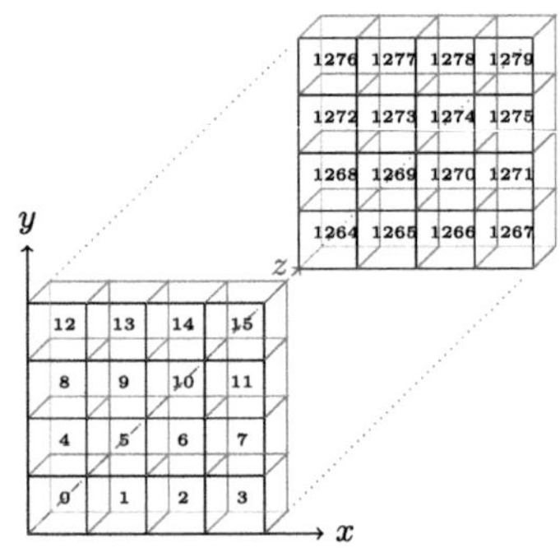

(a) 3D representation of a the `Twinkle` internal state

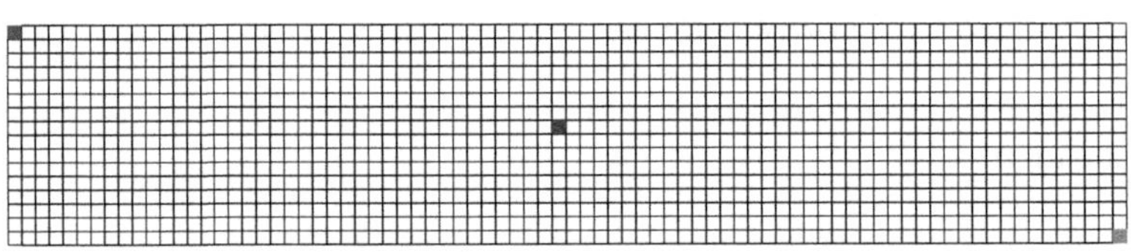

(b) 2D representation of the `Twinkle` internal state

Fig. 1. Different views of the `Twinkle` state.

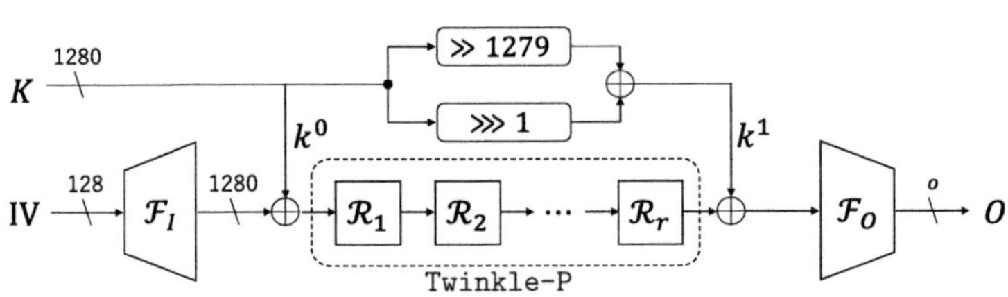

Fig. 2. Overview of `Twinkle-PRF`.

right (i.e. from MSB to LSB) bit rotations within an n-bit string by $\lll_n$ and $\ggg_n$, respectively.

3 Specification of Twinkle

Twinkle presents two modes of operations for a PRF; an AE mode Twinkle-AE and a MAC mode specialized for pointer authentication Twinkle-PA. Twinkle defines a specific instance by designing a dedicated PRF Twinkle-PRF, which is computed with a dedicated public permutation Twinkle-P.

3.1 Twinkle-PRF

Twinkle-PRF : $\{0,1\}^{1280} \times \{0,1\}^{128} \mapsto \{0,1\}^o$ is a function that takes a 1280-bit key K and 128-bit IV as input and returns an o-bit string where $o \in \{1, \ldots, 1152\}$. When a key is fixed, which is a more relevant scenario for attacking specific users, Twinkle-PRF is a 128-bit to o-bit function.

Overall, Twinkle-PRF performs the following three operations. First, an input expansion function $\mathcal{F}_I : \{0,1\}^{128} \mapsto \{0,1\}^{1280}$ is computed to create a 1280-bit state S from the 128-bit IV. Then, the Even-Mansour construction is computed with a 1280-bit key K and Twinkle-P. Finally, an output compression function $\mathcal{F}_O : \{0,1\}^{1280} \mapsto \{0,1\}^o$ is computed to produce an o-bit function. The overall structure of Twinkle-PRF is depicted in Fig. 2

$\mathcal{F}_I$ duplicates the 128-bit IV to make 10 copies of IV, each is applied a different bit-permutation σ_i. Namely, a 1280-bit state S is computed by $S \leftarrow \sigma_9(\mathrm{IV}) \| \sigma_8(\mathrm{IV}) \| \cdots \| \sigma_0(\mathrm{IV})$, where each σ_i moves the bit position j of IV to the bit position $a_i \cdot j + b_i \bmod 128$ for $j \in \{0, \ldots, 127\}$, and the values of a_i and b_i are defined in Table 2.

Table 2. Parameters of Bit Permutation σ_i.

i	0	1	2	3	4	5	6	7	8	9
a_i	1	3	5	7	11	13	17	19	23	29
b_i	0	1	2	3	4	5	6	7	8	9

$\mathcal{F}_O$ generates an o-bit string by computing $\mathrm{Trunc}_o(S \oplus (S \gg 128))$, where Trunc_n represents the least significant n bits of a bit string.

In the Even-Mansour construction in the middle, the 1280-bit state is updated by $S \leftarrow$ Twinkle-P$(S \oplus k^0) \oplus k^1$, where k^0 is the master key K, Twinkle-P is a 1280-bit public permutation specified later, and k^1 is another 1280-bit key computed by $k^1 \leftarrow (K \ggg 1) \oplus (K \gg 1279)$.

Note that the number of rounds inside Twinkle-P depends on the security level required by an upper-layer protocol, which is denoted by m, $m \in \{64, 128, 256\}$. This indicates that Twinkle-PRF also depends on m. Twinkle-

PRF is also parameterized by an output length o. To clarify those parameters, the designers introduced a notion of $\texttt{Twinkle}_o^m$ to denote the Twinkle-PRF with a security parameter of m and the output length of o.

3.2 Twinkle-AE

Twinkle-AE is an AE scheme specialized for encrypting the cache line, therefore, the plaintext size, denoted by c, is limited to two choices, either 512 bits or 1024 bits, i.e. $c \in \{512, 1024\}$, and the corresponding scheme is called Twinkle-AE-512 and Twinkle-AE-1024, respectively. IV serves as a unique nonce, which is never used more than once under the same key. Unlike standard AEAD schemes, Twinkle-AE does not take associated data as input. The ciphertext size is the same as the plaintext size, and it generates a t-bit tag for the message authentication, where $t \in \{64, 128\}$. Besides, Twinkle-AE supports two levels of confidentiality; 128 bits and 256 bits, in which the choice of the confidentiality level only affects the number of rounds inside Twinkle-P, and makes no difference as long as Twinkle-PRF is viewed as a block-box. Twinkle-AE specifies six valid combinations of c, t, and the confidentiality level as listed in Table 3.

Table 3. Twinkle-AE Versions and Security in Bits

Versions	Confidentiality	Integrity (t)
Twinkle-AE-512a	128	64
Twinkle-AE-512b	128	128
Twinkle-AE-512c	256	128
Twinkle-AE-1024a	128	64
Twinkle-AE-1024b	128	128
Twinkle-AE-1024c	256	128

Encryption. The diagram of the encryption procedure is depicted in Fig. 3. Encryption of Twinkle-AE takes as input a 1024-bit encryption key K, a c-bit authentication key K', a c-bit message M, and a 128-bit IV. It outputs a c-bit ciphertext C and t-bit tag T.

Encryption of Twinkle-AE first computes Twinkle-PRF to generate a $t + c$ bit string denoted by $O_t \| O_c$, from a 128-bit IV and a 1280-bit key K. Namely, $O_t \| O_c \leftarrow \texttt{Twinkle}_{t+c}^m(\text{IV}, K)$, where m is either 128 or 256 depending on the version of Twinkle-AE. O_c, c bits of the generated string, is used as a key stream. Namely, O_c is XORed to M, and the result is output as a c-bit ciphertext C.

O_t, t bits of the generated string, is used to generate a t-bit tag T in the WC-MAC paradigm. In details, M and K' are first divided into t-bits of strings $M_{c/t-1} \| \cdots \| M_1 \| M_0 \leftarrow M$ and $K'_{c/t-1} \| \cdots \| K'_1 \| K'_0 \leftarrow K'$, then a universal hash function $H = \sum_{i=0}^{c/t-1} M_i \otimes K'_i$ is computed, wherein $\otimes$ represents the multiplication in the finite field F_2^t, and finally $O_t \oplus H$ is output as a tag T.

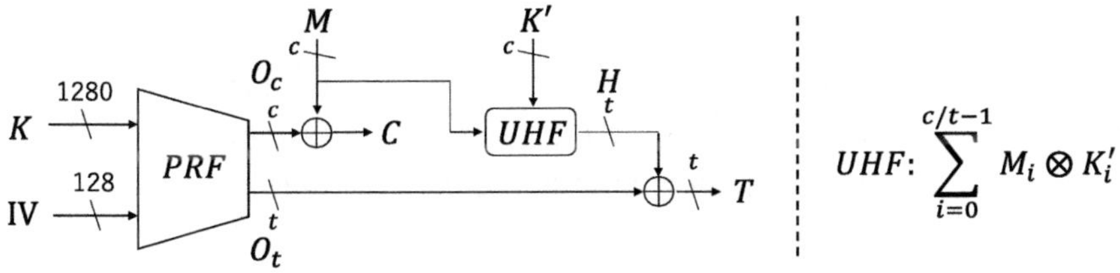

Fig. 3. Encryption Diagram of `Twinkle-AE`.

3.3 Twinkle-PA

`Twinkle-PA` is a MAC scheme designed for a pointer authentication, namely to authenticate a 64-bit pointer address PT and a 64-bit context CT. With a 1280-bit key K, it generates a t-bit tag T, where $1 \leq t \leq 32$.

`Twinkle-PA` consists of a single call of `Twinkle-PRF`. $CT \| PT$ forms a 128-bit IV, and the output of `Twinkle-PRF` is directly used as T. `Twinkle-PA` provides 64-bit security against offline attacks. Namely, $T \leftarrow \texttt{Twinkle}_t^{64}(CT \| PT, K)$.

3.4 Twinkle-P

Each round ($\mathcal{R}$) in `Twinkle-P` consists of five operations, namely `S-box` (SB), `LaneRotation`$_0$ (LR_0), `MixSlice` (MS), `LaneRotation`$_1$ (LR_1), and `AddConstant` (AC):

$$\mathcal{R} = AC \circ LR_1 \circ MS \circ LR_0 \circ SB.$$

S-box (SB): This step applies a 4-bit S-box S to each row of the internal state:

$$S[0][y][z] \| \cdots \| S[3][y][z] \leftarrow \texttt{S-box}(S[0][y][z] \| \cdots \| S[3][y][z]),$$

where $y \in \mathbb{Z}_4$ and $z \in \mathbb{Z}_{80}$. Table 4 shows the lookup table for `Twinkle`'s S-box.

Table 4. twinkle's S-box

x	0	1	2	3	4	5	6	7	8	9	a	b	c	d	e	f
$S(x)$	0	3	5	d	6	f	a	8	b	4	e	2	9	c	7	1

LaneRotation $_0$ (LR_0)*:* This step applies a right rotation using the offsets O_0 (defined in Table 5) to each lane of the state:

$$S[x][y][\cdot] \leftarrow S[x][y][\cdot] \ggg_{80} (O_0[x + 4y] \bmod 80), \quad \text{for all } x, y \in \mathbb{Z}_4.$$

MixSlice (MS): This step applies a linear transformation to each slice. For all $z \in \mathbb{Z}_{80}$, we compute:

$$S[\cdot][\cdot][z] \leftarrow S[\cdot][\cdot][z] \oplus (S[\cdot][\cdot][z] \lll_{16} 5) \oplus (S[\cdot][\cdot][z] \lll_{16} 12).$$

Table 5. Offsets for `LaneRotation`

i	0	1	2	3	4	5	6	7	8	9	10	11	12	13	14	15
O_0	20	24	38	77	49	66	30	40	76	15	46	50	17	18	61	62
O_1	63	45	34	39	32	43	60	66	54	26	55	36	61	12	15	35

LaneRotation $_1$ *(LR_1):* This operation is similar to LR_0 but uses the offset values O_1 from Table 5.
AddConstant (AC): At each round i, this step XORs a fixed 1280-bit round constant RC_i with the state.

As mentioned in Sect. 3.1, the number of rounds in `Twinkle-P` depends on the security level m. Specifically, for $m = 64$, 128, and 256, the total number of rounds is 5, 9.5, and 18.5, respectively. Here, "0.5 round" refers to an operation consisting of the application of `S-box` followed by a `LaneRotation`$_0$ on the 1280-bit state.

4 Generic Authentication Key Recovery for `Twinkle-AE`

By observing that some `Twinkle-AE` versions claim higher confidentiality than integrity, in Subsect. 4.1, we present authentication key-recovery attacks on `Twinkle-AE` mode, which recovers a c-bit key K' with $O(2^t)$ queries in the nonce-respecting setting. This eventually allows us, for an arbitrary choice of a message, to generate a ciphertext that passes the verification and is decrypted to the chosen message. This means that the generated plaintext by the decryption of `Twinkle-AE` is predictable, or more precisely, controllable in the chosen-ciphetext setting. Hence, our attacks break the IND-CCA security when confidentiality is higher than integrity, namely for `Twinkle-AE-512a`, `Twinkle-AE-512c`, `Twinkle-AE-1024a`, and `Twinkle-AE-1024c`. We then present variants of this attack that require only $O(1)$ queries in the nonce-misuse setting in Subsect. 4.2. Note that the attack does not exploit any property of `Twinkle-PRF`, but exploits the property of the universal hash function.

4.1 Nonce-Respecting Attacks with $O(2^t)$ Queries

Observations on Higher Confidentiality than Integrity. First, we observe that each of the encryption part and the MAC part of `Twinkle-AE` is rather solid. The ciphertext is generated by XORing the message with a PRF output, where a nonce IV is involved as a PRF input. This is a secure construction, identical to one-time pad, as long as the PRF output cannot be distinguished from a random string. The tag generation part is the simplest instantiation of the WC-MAC, where the message processed by a universal hash function is XORed with the PRF output. Hence, as long as the security of the encryption part and the MAC part are identical, the construction looks solid.

However, several `Twinkle-AE` versions are designed to provide higher confidentiality than integrity. This drastically changes the situation because attackers can make queries beyond the limit imposed by integrity, i.e. more than 2^t queries. As observed by Hosoyamada et al. [24], chosen-ciphertext attacks could be critical for confidentiality in this case. This contrasts with typical AE security, where such attacks usually have negligible impact because forgery attempts do not succeed below the integrity limit, and no plaintext is revealed from decryption.

Recovering K'**.** With the above observation, we show that the authentication key K' can be efficiently recovered. The attack is depicted in Fig. 4.

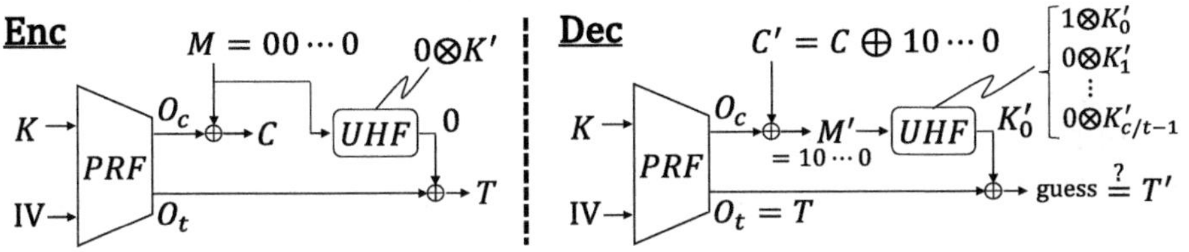

Fig. 4. Diagram of Nonce-Respecting Authentication Key Recovery.

The universal hash function (UHF) is a sum of field multiplications of M and K'. When M is set to 0, the output of UHF is $0 \otimes K' = 0$. Hence, when an encryption query $(\mathrm{IV}, 0)$ results in (C, T), T equals to the t-bit of the PRF output O_t. Similarly, since $M = 0$, C equals to the c-bit of the PRF output O_c.

We then play with the decryption oracle under the same IV. Let $C_0, \ldots, C_{c/t-1}$ denote the ciphertext C in every t bits. We then modify C to C' so that $C'_0 = C_0 \oplus 1$ and $C'_i = C_i$ for $i = 1, \ldots, c/t - 1$. This makes the value of $M' = 1\|0\| \cdots \|0$, and the output of UHF is $(1 \otimes K'_0) \oplus \sum_{i=1}^{c/t-1}(0 \otimes K'_i) = K'_0$. The challenge here is that an attacker does not know the new tag. However, as observed in above, the attacker can make 2^t decryption queries to exhaustively try all the tags, and obtain the corresponding tag T' after 2^t queries. Then, K'_0 is immediately recovered by $K'_0 = O_t \oplus T'$.

Other K'_i can be recovered in the same procedure by swapping t-bit block in C' to i-th block. Hence, the entire K' is recovered with $c/t \cdot 2^t$ queries. Recall that the possible parameter choices of c and t are $c \in \{512, 1024\}$ and $t \in \{64, 128\}$, so c/t is a small constant 4, 8, or 16.

A pseudo-code of the authentication key-recovery attack is given in Algorithm 1.

Universal Forgery with the Knowledge of K'**.** After the authentication key K' is recovered, along with a tuple of related values IV, O_t, and O_c, universal forgery can be performed with a negligible cost, i.e. for an arbitrary chosen value of the message M^*, the attacker can generate a ciphertext (IV, C^*, T^*) that passes the verification and is decrypted to M^*. The attack procedure is straightforward. With O_c, C^* can be computed by $C^* \leftarrow O_c \oplus M^*$. With O_t

Algorithm 1. Nonce-Respecting Authentication Key Recovery

Require: Accesses to decryption and encryption oracles with K, K'
Ensure: K'

Set IV to an arbitrary chosen value, and set M to 0.
Send (IV, M) to an encryption oracle to get corresponding (C, T).
Record $O_c = C$ and $O_t = T$.
for $i = 0, \ldots, c/t - 1$ **do**
  Set $C' = C$, then $C'_i \leftarrow C_i \oplus 1$.
  for $T' = 0, \ldots, 2^t - 1$ **do**
    Send (IV, C', T') to decryption oracle.
    if The decryption oracle returns a message M' **then**
      $K'_i \leftarrow O_t \oplus T'$.
    end if
  end for
end for
return K'.

and K', T^* can be computed by $T^* \leftarrow O_t \oplus \mathrm{UHF}_{K'}(M^*)$. Note that those can be computed offline, hence no additional query is required. A pseudo-code of universal forgery is given in Algorithm 2.

In addition, with the knowledge of K', universal forgery for any other IV is possible only with 1 additional known plaintext query. Given an encryption result $\tilde{C}, \tilde{T}$ for any $\tilde{\mathrm{IV}}, \tilde{M}$, the attacker can compute the corresponding $\tilde{O}_c$ and $\tilde{O}_t$ with K', and the rest of the attack is trivial.

Algorithm 2. Nonce-Respecting Universal Forgery

Require: K', IV, O_c, O_t, and a target message M^* that can be chosen arbitrary
Ensure: (IV, C^*, T^*) that is decrypted to M^*

Compute $C^* \leftarrow O_c \oplus M^*$ offline.
Compute $T^* \leftarrow O_t \oplus \mathrm{UHF}_{K'}(M^*)$ offline.
return (IV, C^*, T^*).

4.2 Nonce-Misuse Attack with $O(1)$ Queries

Due to the nature of the key-stream XOR in encryption and WC-MAC in authentication, it is natural that both confidentiality and integrity can be broken efficiently if the same IV is iterated more than once. However, it does not necessarily mean that authentication-key recovery or universal forgery is performed efficiently. Here we show that those strong attacks are possible with $O(1)$ queries in the nonce-misuse setting.

Note that because the size of IV is 128 bits, repeat of the same nonce is inevitable after 2^{128} queries for `Twinkle-AE-512c` and `Twinkle-AE-1024c` that claim 256-bit confidentiality with a 128-bit tag even with the restriction that the attacker can only make queries in the chosen-plaintext setting.

In the nonce-misuse setting, the procedure to recover K'_0 is as follows.

1. Make an encryption query of $(\mathrm{IV}, 0\|0\|\cdots\|0)$ to get (C_0, T_0).
2. Make an encryption query of $(\mathrm{IV}, 1\|0\|\cdots\|0)$ to get (C'_0, T'_0).
3. $K'_0 = T_0 \oplus T'_0$.

Other K'_i can be recovered similarly. We omit the details to avoid redundancy.

4.3 Remarks on Key-Committing Security

The key-committing security of symmetric-key cryptography was initiated by Farshim et al. [18], which was later generalized as CMT-1 security by Bellare and Hoang [11]. Its goal is to find a ciphetext (C, T) that can be decrypted with two distinct keys, i.e. to find (K, K', IV, M) and $(\tilde{K}, \tilde{K}', \tilde{\mathrm{IV}}, \tilde{M})$ with $K \neq \tilde{K}$ and $K' \neq \tilde{K}'$ such that the corresponding output of encryption queries will collide. It has been known that the lack of key-committing security may cause attacks in several real-world use-cases e.g. braking message franking [16] or accelerating password brute-force attacks [27].

The key-committing security of `Twinkle-AE` can be broken in the same way as the key-committing attack against `GCM` [16]. The attacker first randomly chooses $K, \tilde{K}, K', \tilde{K}'$, and $\mathrm{IV} = \tilde{\mathrm{IV}}$. Then, O_c, O_t, and $\tilde{O}_c, \tilde{O}_t$ can be computed by `Twinkle-PRF`.

Let ℓ be c/t, and O_c is separated into t-bit chunks denoted by $O_{c,0}, \ldots, O_{c,\ell-1}$, and the same is applied to $\tilde{O}_c$. Then the equations to compute T and $\tilde{T}$ can be written as follows.

$$T = (O_{c,0} \oplus C_0) \cdot K'_0 \oplus \cdots \oplus (O_{c,\ell-1} \oplus C_{\ell-1}) \cdot K'_{\ell-1} \oplus O_t,$$
$$\tilde{T} = (\tilde{O}_{c,0} \oplus C_0) \cdot \tilde{K}'_0 \oplus \cdots \oplus (\tilde{O}_{c,\ell-1} \oplus C_{\ell-1}) \cdot \tilde{K}'_{\ell-1} \oplus \tilde{O}_t.$$

The goal is to choose the value of C so that $T = \tilde{T}$ is satisfied. The attacker now fixes the values of $C_1, \ldots, C_{\ell-1}$ to arbitrary chosen values. Then, all the variables but C_0 become fixed constants. Denoting the sum of all the variables not including C_0 as X and $\tilde{X}$, the equation becomes

$$X \oplus C_0 \cdot K'_0 = \tilde{X} \oplus C_0 \cdot \tilde{K}'_0.$$

This is a linear equation with 1 free variable C_0 and the value of C_0 can be obtained immediately.

5 Analysis of the Underlying Primitive

The underlying permutation used in constructing AE schemes should resist most well-known cryptanalytic distinguishers, such as impossible differential, zero-correlation, integral, and differential-linear distinguishers. Here, we analyze the security of `Twinkle-P` as a standalone permutation, regardless of how it is used in the mode of operation.

5.1 Modeling the MixSlice Operation

To simplify the modeling of differential, linear, and integral property propagation through `MixSlice`, we derive its matrix representation. Let us represent each 16-bit slice $S[\bullet][\bullet][z]$ as a 16-bit vector $V \in \mathbb{F}_2^{16}$, such that $S[x][y][z] = V[x + 4 \cdot y]$ for all $x, y \in \mathbb{Z}_4$. Then, the `MixSlice` operation acts as a matrix multiplication $A \times V$, where A is a 16×16 circulant matrix. The ith rows of A and A^{-1} are as follows:

$$A[i] = \begin{bmatrix} 1\,0\,0\,0\,1\,0\,0\,0\,0\,0\,0\,0\,1\,0\,0\,0 \end{bmatrix} \ggg i,$$
$$A^{-1}[i] = \begin{bmatrix} 1\,0\,0\,0\,1\,1\,0\,1\,1\,0\,1\,0\,1\,0\,1\,1 \end{bmatrix} \ggg i,$$

for $i \in \mathbb{Z}_{16}$. We use A and A^{-1} to model the propagation of differences in the forward and backward directions, respectively.

To model the propagation of linear masks in the forward and backward directions, we use $\left(A^{-1}\right)^t$ and A^t, respectively. These are also circulant 16×16 matrices, and their ith rows are as follows:

$$\left(A^{-1}\right)^t[i] = \begin{bmatrix} 1\,1\,1\,0\,1\,0\,1\,0\,1\,1\,0\,1\,1\,0\,0\,0 \end{bmatrix} \ggg i,$$
$$A^t[i] = \begin{bmatrix} 1\,0\,0\,0\,0\,1\,0\,0\,0\,0\,0\,0\,1\,0\,0\,0 \end{bmatrix} \ggg i.$$

As can be seen, the diffusion of differences in the forward direction (resp. linear masks in the backward direction) is lower than that in the backward direction (resp. forward direction).

5.2 Modeling the S-Box

To model the propagation of differential, linear, and integral properties through `S-box`, we use the S-box Analyzer [21,22][1]. We model the S-box in three different ways: probabilistic with probabilities encoded, probabilistic without probabilities encoded, and deterministic. We use the probabilistic model with probabilities encoded to find regular differential and linear trails. We use the probabilistic model without probabilities encoded to model only the possibility of a differential or linear transition, regardless of the weight or probability of the transition. We use the deterministic model to represent differential and linear transitions with probability one. Such models are used to find impossible differential, zero-correlation, and differential-linear distinguishers. For more details on modeling the S-box using the S-box Analyzer, refer to Sect. A.

5.3 Impossible Differential Distinguishers

The designers of `Twinkle-AE` provided some bounds for impossible differential (ID) distinguishers by analyzing the full diffusion of `Twinkle-P` in both forward and backward directions [33]. However, they did not present any concrete ID

[1] https://github.com/hadipourh/sboxanalyzer.

distinguisher for `Twinkle-P`. Here, we fill this gap by providing concrete ID distinguishers.

We use two different techniques to find ID distinguishers: the negative CP (MILP/SAT)[2] model proposed in [15,29], and the positive CP (MILP/SAT) model proposed in [21,23]. In the negative model, we model the probabilistic propagation of differences (without encoding probabilities) and fix both the input and output differences. We then use a CP/MILP/SAT solver to check the satisfiability of the model. If the model is unsatisfiable, the chosen input and output differences yield an impossible differential.

In the positive model, we model the deterministic propagation of differences in both forward and backward directions. In this model, we encode the difference value of each bit using three symbols: 0, 1, and ?, where ? denotes an arbitrary difference or, equivalently, a free bit with respect to the difference value. We also add extra constraints to ensure that the forward and backward propagations contradict in at least one bit along the distinguisher. As a result, any feasible solution of the positive model corresponds to an ID distinguisher. For more details on how to construct the negative and positive models, we refer to [15,29] and [21,23], respectively.

Both negative and positive CP/MILP/SAT models can find ID distinguishers for up to 6 rounds of `Twinkle-P`. An advantage of the positive model is that we do not need to fix the input and output differences. Instead, we can define an objective function that maximizes the number of bits with arbitrary difference values at the input and output when solving a single instance of the model. In this way, we can find a truncated ID with more free bits at the input and output differences (i.e., a larger cluster of ID distinguishers), by solving only one instance of the positive model.

We present the distinguishers found using the positive model in Fig. 5a, Fig. 5b, and Fig. 5c. In these figures, the values "1" and "?" in the forward (resp. backward) difference propagation are represented using ◩ and ◩ (resp. ◪ and ◪). For example, ■ indicates that the corresponding bit takes an arbitrary difference in the forward propagation, while its difference is fixed and equal to "1" in the backward propagation. We represent zero differences using white (or no color). As a result, the presence of either ◩ or ◪ within a shape indicates a contradiction between the forward and backward propagations.

Note that the number of free bits at the input and output of the distinguisher in Fig. 9c (marked by ◩ and ◪, respectively) are 824 and 996, respectively. As a result, this figure represents $824 + 996 = 1820$ impossible differential (ID) distinguishers. Based on a similar argument, Fig. 5b and Fig. 5c illustrate 2^{1148} and 2^{356} ID distinguishers for 5 and 6 rounds of `Twinkle-P`, respectively. Moreover, since `Twinkle-P` remains invariant under rotation along the z-axis with respect to differential and linear trails, each ID distinguisher can be duplicated into 80 distinct ones. We recall that the distinguishers discovered using the positive CP

[2] CP stands for Constraint Programming, MILP stands for Mixed Integer Linear Programming, and SAT stands for the Satisfiability Problem. Here, we consider MILP and SAT as special cases of CP.

model were obtained from a single execution of the model. If we run the tool multiple times, it may yield additional solutions (i.e., distinguishers).

5.4 Zero-Correlation and ZC-Based Integral Distinguishers

We note that the designers of `Twinkle` neither provided any concrete zero-correlation (ZC) distinguisher nor leveraged the connection between ZC and integral distinguishers to construct integral distinguishers. Here, we fill this gap. Analogous to the approach used for impossible differential distinguishers, we search for ZC distinguishers using both positive and negative models. Both models are capable of identifying distinguishers up to 6 rounds. However, to obtain ZC distinguishers with a higher number of free input bits, we prefer the positive model. To this end, we configure the objective function of the positive model to maximize the number of free bits in the input linear mask. Finally, we apply Theorem 1 to transform our ZC distinguishers into ZC-based integral distinguishers.

Theorem 1. (Sun et al. [30]). *Let $F : \mathbb{F}_2^n \rightarrow \mathbb{F}_2^n$ be a vectorial Boolean function. Assume A is a subspace of $\mathbb{F}_2^n$ and $\beta \in \mathbb{F}_2^n \setminus \{0\}$ such that (α, β) is a ZC approximation for any $\alpha \in A$. Then, for any $\lambda \in \mathbb{F}_2^n$, $\langle \beta, F(x + \lambda) \rangle$ is balanced over the set*

$$A^{\perp} = \{x \in \mathbb{F}_2^n \mid \forall\, \alpha \in A : \langle \alpha, x \rangle = 0\}.$$

According to Theorem 1, having more free bits at the input linear mask of a ZC distinguisher (hull) results in fewer active bits in its corresponding integral distinguisher. Therefore, by maximizing the number of free bits at the input linear mask in the ZC distinguisher, we can obtain integral distinguishers with lower data complexity.

Similar to the representation used for ID distinguishers, we represent the values "1" and "?" in the forward (resp. backward) propagation of linear masks using ■ and ■ (resp. ■ and ■). Figure 7a, Fig. 7b, and Fig. 7c illustrate 2^{1278}, 2^{1140}, and 2^{16} ZC distinguishers that we obtained using the positive model for 4, 5, and 6 rounds of `Twinkle-P`, respectively.

We first applied our tool to 3 rounds of `Twinkle-P`. As shown in Fig. 6 we discovered a zero-correlation (ZC) linear hull whose input linear mask has only one inactive bit, while the remaining 1279 input bits take a free linear mask (marked by ■). As a result, its corresponding integral distinguisher has a data complexity of 2, where the input set assigns a fixed but random value to bits with free input linear mask (marked by ■) and takes all possible values over the single bit with inactive linear mask.

As another interesting result, the input linear mask of our 4-round ZC distinguisher contains 1276 free bits (marked by ■), while the remaining 4 bits are fixed to zero. Consequently, the corresponding 4-round integral distinguisher requires a data complexity of 2^4. In this distinguisher, the input set assigns fixed but random values to all free bits in terms of linear mask (marked by ■), while the remaining 4 bits take all possible combinations (see the input linear mask in Fig. 7). At the output, the XOR of the active cells (marked by ◪) satisfies a zero-sum property. We experimentally verified the validity of this 4-round integral distinguisher using at least 100 randomly chosen input sets that satisfy the required input structure, and in all cases, the distinguisher held as expected.

Our 5-round ZC distinguisher, shown in Fig. 7b, has an input linear mask with 1140 free bits (marked by ◩), while the remaining 140 bits in the mask are fixed to zero. As a result, the data complexity of the corresponding integral distinguisher is 2^{140}. Additionally, since `Twinkle-P` preserves zero-correlation linear hulls under rotation along the z-axis, we can derive 80 distinct ZC distinguishers from each initial one.

5.5 Division Property Based Integral Distinguishers

Here, we use the division property [31] and construct a MILP-based model [32,35] to identify integral distinguishers for `Twinkle-P`. We found a 4-round integral distinguisher for `Twinkle-P`, which originates from an input state featuring four active bits. As a result, the data complexity of the 4-round integral distinguisher is 2^4. Let S^i denote the i-th round state variable of `Twinkle-P`. Specifically, we set the four input bits $S^0[0][0][0]$, $S^0[1][0][0]$, $S^0[2][0][0]$, and $S^0[3][0][0]$ as active. Thus, by activating four input bits, we derive a 4-round integral distinguisher that exhibits 1152 balanced output bits (the detailed result can be found in Table 6). Additionally, we identify a 5-round integral distinguisher by setting 12 input bits as active bits. This distinguisher results in 38 balanced bits at the output, leading to a data complexity of 2^{12}. A summary of the 5-round integral distinguisher is provided in Table 7.

We also applied the division property to 6 rounds. The tool did not yield any integral distinguishers when fewer active bits (e.g., 4/12/36 bits) were set in the input; in this scenario, all output bits are unknown after 6 rounds. However, increasing the number of active bits in the input to search for 6-round integral distinguishers based on the division property significantly increased the running time. As a result, we could not find any 6-round integral distinguisher based on the division property.

We also employed the division property-based method proposed in [12] to compute an upper bound on the algebraic degree. Using this approach, we determine that the algebraic degree of `Twinkle-P` is upper bounded by 27, 81, and 243 for 3, 4, and 5 rounds, respectively, which aligns with the trivial bounds.

5.6 Differential-Linear Distinguishers

We observed that the designers of `Twinkle` did not analyze `Twinkle-P` against differential-linear (DL) distinguishers, even though DL distinguishers are often among the most effective techniques against cryptographic permutations. Here, we fill this gap by providing strong DL distinguishers for up to 6 rounds of `Twinkle-P`.

For $X = (x_0, x_1, \ldots, x_{n-1})$ and $Y = (y_0, y_1, \ldots, y_{n-1})$ in $\mathbb{F}_2^n$, we define the dot product as $X \cdot Y = \sum_{i=0}^{n-1} x_i \cdot y_i$. Let $F : \mathbb{F}_2^n \to \mathbb{F}_2^n$ be a vectorial Boolean function. For a given input difference Δ and output linear mask Γ, the correlation is defined as

$$\mathrm{corr}(\Delta \to \Gamma) = 2^{-n} \cdot \sum_{X \in \mathbb{F}_2^n} (-1)^{\Gamma \cdot (F(X)+F(X+\Delta))}, \tag{1}$$

where "+" denotes addition in $\mathbb{F}_2^n$ (i.e., bitwise XOR). Given a sample space $\mathcal{S} \subseteq \mathbb{F}_2^n$, the empirical correlation over $\mathcal{S}$ is defined by

$$\mathrm{corr}_{\mathcal{S}}(\Delta \to \Gamma) = 2^{-|\mathcal{S}|} \cdot \sum_{X \in \mathcal{S}} (-1)^{\Gamma \cdot (F(X)+F(X+\Delta))}. \tag{2}$$

The data complexity of a DL distinguisher with correlation c is in $\mathcal{O}(c^{-2})$.

To search for differential-linear (DL) distinguishers for `Twinkle-P`, we use a state-of-the-art technique proposed by Hadipour et al. in CRYPTO 2024 [20]. According to this method, we split the permutation E into three parts: $E = E_\ell \circ E_m \circ E_d$. We model the forward probabilistic differential propagation through E_d and the backward probabilistic linear propagation through E_ℓ. These sub-models allow us to find regular differential and linear trails for E_d and E_ℓ, respectively. We also model the deterministic difference propagation (forward) and deterministic linear mask propagation (backward) through E_m to encode the amount of overlap, measured by the number of shared active bits, between the differential and linear propagations in the middle part. Finally, we combine all these sub-models into a unified CP model, connect the junctions, and set the objective function to minimize the sum of the scaled weight of the differential trail through E_d, the scaled overlap weight through E_m, and the scaled weight of the linear trail through E_ℓ. For more details on this method, we refer to [20].

Figure 9a, Fig. 9b, and Fig. 9c illustrate the DL distinguishers for 4, 5, and 6 rounds of `Twinkle-P`, respectively. The colors and symbols in these figures follow the same convention as those used for the ID and ZC distinguishers. Let X_i denote the internal state before the `S-box` in round i, and let ΔX_i and ΓX_i represent the corresponding difference and linear mask, respectively. The input differences and output masks of the DL distinguishers are summarized in Table 8, Fig. 8, and Fig. 8.

For 4 rounds of `Twinkle-P`, we discovered a deterministic DL distinguisher, as shown in Fig. 9a. Table 8 represents the input difference and output mask of this distinguisher. As shown in Fig. 9a, the overlap between the deterministic forward differential and deterministic backward linear propagations for the output of `S-box` layer is zero. As a result, due to the (bit-wise) switching effect [20], the correlation of this 4-round DL distinguisher should be one and it is a deterministic distinguisher. We verified the correctness of this distinguisher in practice to ensure the soundness of both our model and the result.

For 5 rounds, we decomposed the permutation into a 1+3+1 round structure. Figure 9c illustrates this distinguisher, and Fig. 8 briefly describes its specification. The first round is covered by a pure differential distinguisher (E_d), the middle 3 rounds are handled by a combined DL distinguisher (E_m), and the last round is covered by a pure linear distinguisher (E_ℓ). The probability of the differential distinguisher over E_d is $p = \Pr(\Delta X_0 \to \Delta X_1) = 2^{-1.415}$. As shown in Fig. 9b, the overlap between the deterministic differential and linear propagations through E_m is zero, which implies that the correlation over the middle part is $r = \text{corr}(\Delta X_1 \rightarrow \Gamma X_4) = 1$. Moreover, the squared correlation of the linear distinguisher over E_ℓ is $q^2 = \text{corr}^2(\Gamma X_4 \rightarrow \Gamma X_5) = 2^{-2}$. As a result, we estimate the total correlation of the 5-round DL distinguisher as $c = prq^2 = 2^{-3.415}$. We conducted experiments and observed that the actual correlation is even higher in practice, with $c = 2^{-2.85}$ on average. Consequently, the data complexity of this distinguisher is approximately $2^{5.70}$.

For 6 rounds, we decomposed the permutation into a $1 + 4 + 1$ round structure, as shown in Fig. 9. We also specified the input difference and output mask of this distinguisher in Fig. 8. We have $p = \Pr(\Delta X_0 \rightarrow \Delta X_1) = 2^{-18.660}$ and $q^2 = \text{corr}^2(\Gamma X_5 \rightarrow \Gamma X_6) = 2^{-18}$. In addition, as seen in Fig. 9, the overlap between the deterministic differential and linear propagations through the middle 4 rounds (E_m) is zero, which implies that the correlation of the small DL distinguisher in the middle is $r = \text{corr}(\Delta X_1 \rightarrow \Gamma X_5) = 1$. As a result, we estimate the total correlation as $c = prq^2 = 2^{-36.66}$. Hence, the data complexity of our 6-round DL distinguisher is $2^{73.32}$. Moreover, since `Twinkle-P` preserves differential, and linear trails under rotation along the z-axis, we can generate 80 distinct DL distinguishers with almost the same correlation from each original one.

6 Conclusion

In this paper, we presented cryptanalysis against `Twinkle`. Our attacks on `Twinkle-AE` targeted variants that aim for a higher confidentiality than integrity. The attacker could make $O(2^t)$ queries to pass the verification, which made our attacks work in the nonce-respecting manner. We showed that c-bit authentication key is recovered only with $O(2^t)$ queries, which further allowed universal forgery attacks, i.e. for any plaintext, the attacker could generate the ciphertext that could be successfully decrypted to the target plaintext. We also pointed out that $O(1)$ attack is possible in the nonce-misuse setting, and key-commitment security can be attacked with a negligible cost. We also presented cryptanalyses on the underlying permutation `Twinkle-P` as a standalone permutation, and applied most well-known cryptanalytic approaches such as impossible differential, zero-correlation, integral, and differential-linear distinguishers by developing automated analytic tools. Our differential-linear distinguishers reach 6 rounds with $2^{73.32}$ complexity, which surpasses the round bounds evaluated by the designers. We stress that none of the results really change the current state of Twinkle because the attacks on the mode are only applicable in a degenerate case that the designers might want to disallow and the distinguishers on the permutation are unlikely to have any significant impact on the ciphers. Moreover, we note that `Twinkle-AE`-b and `Twinkle`-PA remain secure, and the versions we attacked would also be secure if the claimed confidentiality level matched the integrity level.

Acknowledgments. This work was initiated during ASK 2024. We want to appreciate the organizers of ASK 2024 for their efforts in creating a helpful and inspiring environment. The authors gratefully acknowledge support from their respective funding agencies. Hosein Hadipour was supported by the European Research Council (ERC) project SYMTRUST (#101097056). Debasmita Chakraborty was funded by the European Research Council (ERC) Starting Grant KEYLESS (#101165216).

A Modeling the S-Box Using the S-Box Analyzer

```
# Import the S-box Analyzer and define the S-box
from sboxanalyzer import *
sb = SboxAnalyzer([0x0,0x3,0x5,0xd,0x6,0xf,0xa,0x8,0xb,0x4,0xe,0x2,0x9,0xc,0x7,0x1])
# Model differential propagation with probabilities
cnf, milp, cp = sb.minimized_diff_constraints()
Number of constraints: 58
Input: a0||a1||a2||a3; msb: a0
Output: b0||b1||b2||b3; msb: b0
Weight: 3.0000 p0 + 2.0000 p1 + 1.4150 p2

# Model forward differential propagation without probabilities
cnf, milp,cp = sb.minimized_diff_constraints(subtable='star')
Number of constraints: 39
Input: a0||a1||a2||a3; msb: a0
Output: b0||b1||b2||b3; msb: b0

# Model backward differential propagation without probabilities
cnf, milp, cp = sbi.minimized_diff_constraints(subtable='star')
Number of constraints: 40
Input: a0||a1||a2||a3; msb: a0
Output: b0||b1||b2||b3; msb: b0

# Model deterministic differential propagation (forward)
temp = sb.encode_deterministic_differential_behavior()
cp = sb.generate_cp_constraints(temp); print(cp)
Input: a0||a1||a2||a3; msb: a0
Output: b0||b1||b2||b3; msb: b0
if(a0==0/\a1==0/\a2==0/\a3==0)then(b0=0/\b1=0/\b2=0/\b3=0)
elseif(a0==0/\a1==0/\a2==1/\a3==0)then(b0=-1/\b1=1/\b2=-1/\b3=-1)
elseif(a0==0/\a1==1/\a2==0/\a3==1)then(b0=-1/\b1=1/\b2=-1/\b3=1)
elseif(a0==0/\a1==1/\a2==1/\a3==1)then(b0=-1/\b1=0/\b2=-1/\b3=-1)
elseif(a0==1/\a1==0/\a2==0/\a3==0)then(b0=-1/\b1=-1/\b2=-1/\b3=1)
elseif(a0==1/\a1==1/\a2==0/\a3==1)then(b0=-1/\b1=-1/\b2=-1/\b3=0)
else(b0=-1/\b1=-1/\b2=-1/\b3=-1)
endif

# Model deterministic differential propagation (backward)
temp = sbi.encode_deterministic_differential_behavior()
cp = sbi.generate_cp_constraints(temp); print(cp)
Input:a0||a1||a2||a3;msb:a0
Output:b0||b1||b2||b3;msb:b0
if(a0==0/\a1==0/\a2==0/\a3==0)then(b0=0/\b1=0/\b2=0/\b3=0)
elseif(a0==0/\a1==0/\a2==0/\a3==1)then(b0=1/\b1=-1/\b2=1/\b3=-1)
elseif(a0==0/\a1==1/\a2==0/\a3==0)then(b0=1/\b1=-1/\b2=-1/\b3=-1)
elseif(a0==0/\a1==1/\a2==0/\a3==1)then(b0=0/\b1=-1/\b2=-1/\b3=-1)
elseif(a0==1/\a1==1/\a2==1/\a3==0)then(b0=-1/\b1=-1/\b2=1/\b3=-1)
elseif(a0==1/\a1==1/\a2==1/\a3==1)then(b0=-1/\b1=-1/\b2=0/\b3=-1)
else(b0=-1/\b1=-1/\b2=-1/\b3=-1)
endif
```

Listing 1.1. Encoding differential behavior of S-box

```
# Import the S-box Analyzer and define the S-box
from sboxanalyzer import *
sb = SboxAnalyzer([0x0,0x3,0x5,0xd,0x6,0xf,0xa,0x8,0xb,0x4,0xe,0x2,0x9,0xc,0x7,0x1])
sbi = SboxAnalyzer(sb.inverse())
# Model forward linear mask propagation with correlations
cnf, milp, cp = sb.minimized_linear_constraints()
Number of constraints: 39
Input: a0||a1||a2||a3; msb: a0
Output: b0||b1||b2||b3; msb: b0
Weight: 4.0000 p0 + 2.0000 p1

# Model forward linear mask propagation without correlations
cnf, milp, cp = sb.minimized_linear_constraints(subtable='star')
Number of constraints: 32
Input: a0||a1||a2||a3; msb: a0
Output: b0||b1||b2||b3; msb: b0

# Model backward linear mask propagation withoout correlations
cnf, milp,cp = sbi.minimized_linear_constraints(subtable='star')
Number of constraints: 33
Input: a0||a1||a2||a3; msb: a0
Output: b0||b1||b2||b3; msb: b0

# Model deterministic linear mask propagation (forward)
temp = sb.encode_deterministic_linear_behavior()
cp = sb.generate_cp_constraints(temp); print(cp)
Input:a0||a1||a2||a3;msb:a0
Output:b0||b1||b2||b3;msb:b0
if(a0==0/\a1==0/\a2==0/\a3==0)then(b0=0/\b1=0/\b2=0/\b3=0)
elseif(a0==0/\a1==0/\a2==1/\a3==0)then(b0=-1/\b1=-1/\b2=-1/\b3=1)
elseif(a0==1/\a1==0/\a2==0/\a3==0)then(b0=-1/\b1=1/\b2=-1/\b3=1)
elseif(a0==1/\a1==0/\a2==1/\a3==0)then(b0=-1/\b1=-1/\b2=-1/\b3=0)
else(b0=-1/\b1=-1/\b2=-1/\b3=-1)
endif

# Model deterministic linear mask propagation (backward)
temp = sbi.encode_deterministic_linear_behavior()
cp = sbi.generate_cp_constraints(temp); print(cp)
Input:a0||a1||a2||a3;msb:a0
Output:b0||b1||b2||b3;msb:b0
if(a0==0/\a1==0/\a2==0/\a3==0)then(b0=0/\b1=0/\b2=0/\b3=0)
elseif(a0==0/\a1==0/\a2==0/\a3==1)then(b0=1/\b1=-1/\b2=-1/\b3=-1)
elseif(a0==0/\a1==1/\a2==0/\a3==0)then(b0=-1/\b1=-1/\b2=1/\b3=-1)
else(b0=-1/\b1=-1/\b2=-1/\b3=-1)
endif

# Model monomial propagation in forward direction (MPT)
cnf, milp, cp = sb.minimized_integral_constraints()
Number of constraints: 38
Input: a0||a1||a2||a3; msb: a0
Output: b0||b1||b2||b3; msb: b0
```

Listing 1.2. Encoding linear and integral behaviors of S-box

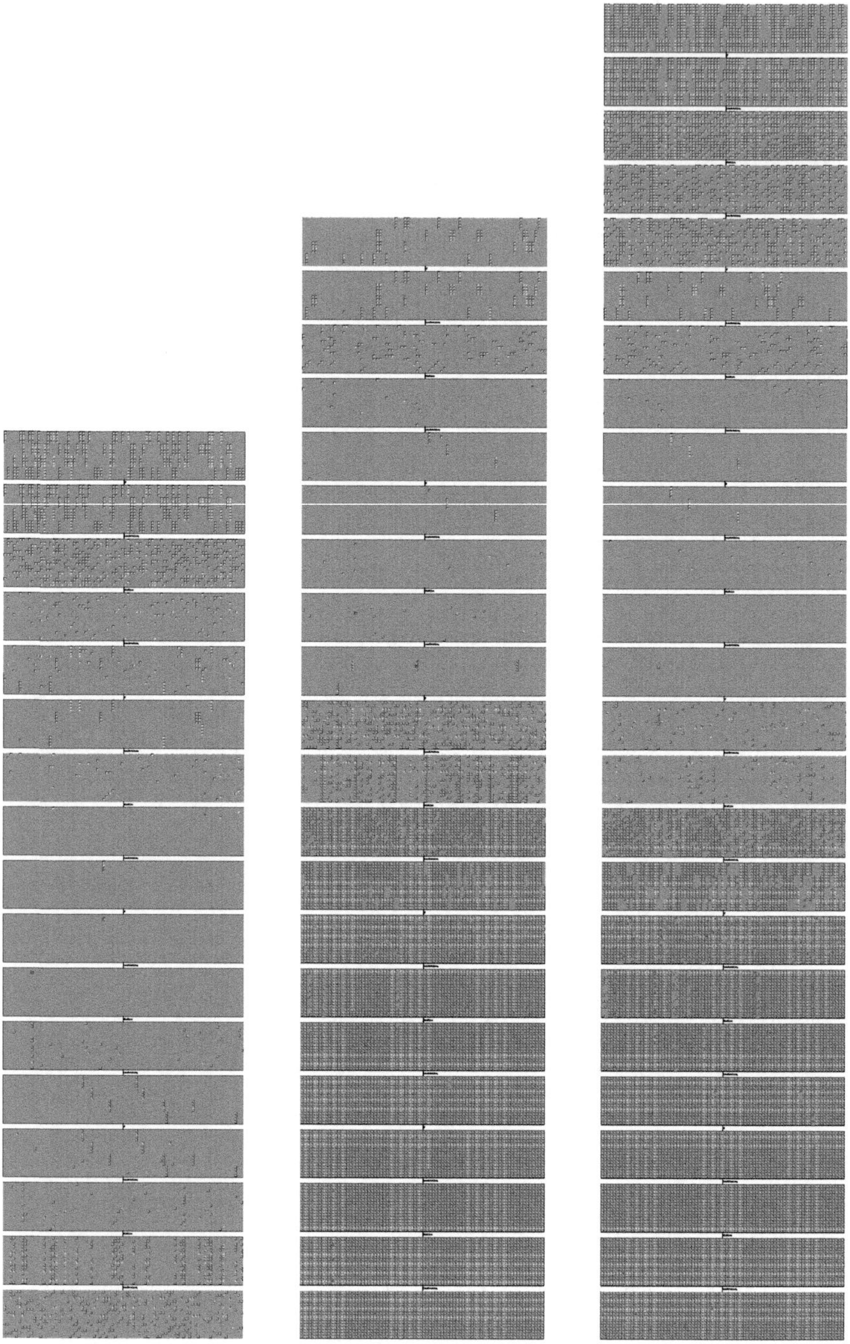

(a) ID distinguisher for 4 rounds of Twinkle-P

(b) ID distinguisher for 5 rounds of Twinkle-P

(c) ID distinguisher for 6 rounds of Twinkle-P

Fig. 5. ID distinguishers.

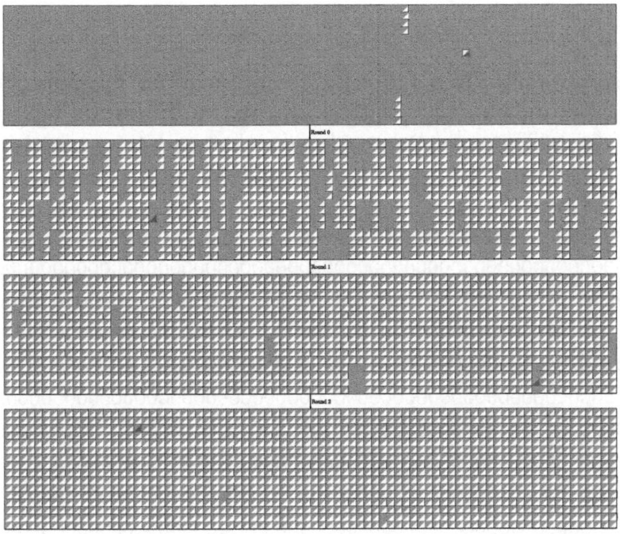

Fig. 6. ZC-based Integral distinguisher for 3 rounds of `Twinkle-P`. To see the complete figures refer to: https://github.com/hadipourh/twinkle

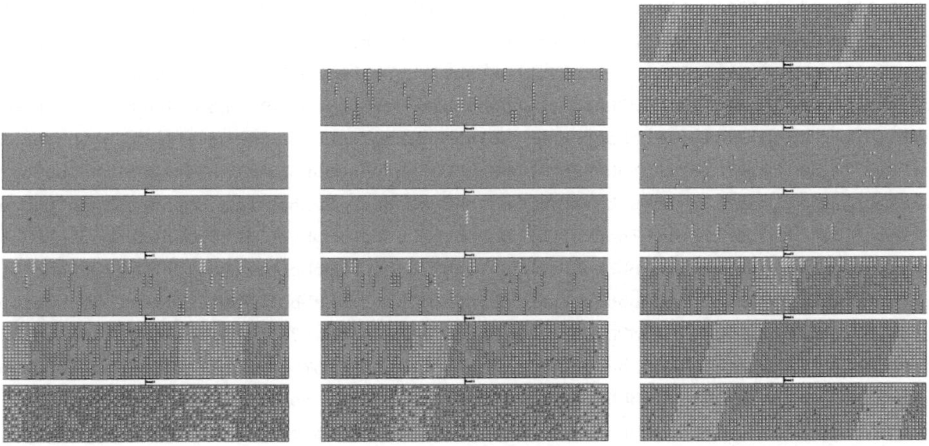

(a) ZC distinguisher for 4 rounds of `Twinkle-P`

(b) ZC distinguisher for 5 rounds of `Twinkle-P`

(c) ZC distinguisher for 6 rounds of `Twinkle-P`

Fig. 7. ZC distinguishers and ZC-based integral distinguishers. To see the complete figures refer to: https://github.com/hadipourh/twinkle

Table 6. Division-property-based integral distinguisher for 4 rounds. The symbols "1" and "0" at the input indicate the positions of active and constant bits, respectively. At the output, "b" and "?" denote balanced and unknown bits, respectively.

Input Division Property
10000000000000000000000000000000000000000000000000000000000000000000000000000000
10000000000000000000000000000000000000000000000000000000000000000000000000000000
10000000000000000000000000000000000000000000000000000000000000000000000000000000
10000000000000000000000000000000000000000000000000000000000000000000000000000000
00000000000000000000000000000000000000000000000000000000000000000000000000000000
00000000000000000000000000000000000000000000000000000000000000000000000000000000
00000000000000000000000000000000000000000000000000000000000000000000000000000000
00000000000000000000000000000000000000000000000000000000000000000000000000000000
00000000000000000000000000000000000000000000000000000000000000000000000000000000
00000000000000000000000000000000000000000000000000000000000000000000000000000000
00000000000000000000000000000000000000000000000000000000000000000000000000000000
00000000000000000000000000000000000000000000000000000000000000000000000000000000
00000000000000000000000000000000000000000000000000000000000000000000000000000000
00000000000000000000000000000000000000000000000000000000000000000000000000000000
00000000000000000000000000000000000000000000000000000000000000000000000000000000
Output Division Property
bbbbbbbbbbbbbbbbb?bb?bbbbbbbbbb?bb?bbbbbbb?bbbb?bbbbbbbbbbbbb?bb?bbb?bbbbbb?bb?
bbbbbb?bbbbbbbbbb?bbbb?bbbb?bbbbbb?b?bbbbb?bbbbbbbbbbbbbbbbbbbbbbbbb?bbbbbbbb
?bbbbbbbbbbbb?bbbbbbbbb?bbbbbb?bbbbbbbbb?bbbbbbbbbbbbbb?bb?bbbbbbbbbbbbbb?bb
bbbbbbbbbbbbbbbbbb?bbbbbb?bbbbbbbbbbbbbb?bbbbbbbbbb?bbbbbbbbbbbbbb??bbbbbbb?
bbbbb?bbbbbbbbbbbbbbbbbbbbbbbbbbbbb?bb?bbb?bbbbb?bbbb?bbbbbbbb?bbbbbb?b?bbbbbbb
bbbbbb?bbbbbbbbbb?bb?bbbbbbbbb?bbbbbbbbb?bbbbbbbbbbbbbbbbb?bb?bbb?bbbbbb?bb?
bbbbbbbbbbbbbbbbbb?b?bbbbbb?bbb?bbbbbbbbb?bbbbbbbbbbbbbbbbbbbbbbbbbbbbbb?bbbbb
?bbbbbbbbbbbb?bbbbbbbbb?bbbbbbbbbbbbbbbbbbbbbbbbbbbbb?bb?bbbbbbbbbbbbbb?bb
bbbbb?bbbbbbbbbbbb??bbb?bbbbbbbbbbb?b??bbb??bbbbbbbbbbbbbbbbbbbbbbbbb???bbbbbbb
bbbbbbbbbbbbbbbbbbbbbbbbbbbbbbbbbbbbbbb?bbbbbbbbbbb?bbbbbbbbbbbb?bbbbbbbbbbbbbbb
bbbbbb?bbbbbbbbbbbb?b?bbbb?bbbbbbbbbbbbbbb?bbbbbbbbbbb?bbbbbbbbbbbbbbb??bb?bbbb?
bbbbbbbbbbbbbbbbbbbbbbbbbbbbbbbbbbbbbbb?bbbbbbbbb?bbbbbbbbbb?bbbbbbbbbbbbbbbbbbbbbbbbb
bbbbbbbbbbbbbbbbb?bb?b?bbbbbbbb?bb?b?bbbbb?bbbbbbbbbbbbbbbbbb?bb?bbb??bbbbb?bb?
bbbbb?bbbbbbbbbbbbbbbbbbbbbbb?bbbbbbbbb?bbb?bbbbbbbbbbbbbbbbbbbbbbbbbb?b?bbbbbbb
?bbbbbbbbbbbb?bbbbbbbbbb??bbbbbbbbbbbbbb?bbbbbbbbbbb?bbb?bb?bbbbbbbb??bbbbb?b?
bbbbbbbbbbbbbbbbbb?b?bbbbbbbbbbbbbbbbbbbbbbbbbbbbbbbbb?bbbbbbbbbbbbbbbbbbb?bbbbb

Table 7. Division-property-based integral distinguisher for 5 rounds. The symbols "1" and "0" at the input indicate the positions of active and constant bits, respectively. At the output, "b" and "?" denote balanced and unknown bits, respectively.

Input Division Property
10000000000000000000000000000000000000000000000000000000000000000000000000000000
10000000000000000000000000000000000000000000000000000000000000000000000000000000
10000000000000000000000000000000000000000000000000000000000000000000000000000000
10000000000000000000000000000000000000000000000000000000000000000000000000000000
10000000000000000000000000000000000000000000000000000000000000000000000000000000
10000000000000000000000000000000000000000000000000000000000000000000000000000000
10000000000000000000000000000000000000000000000000000000000000000000000000000000
10000000000000000000000000000000000000000000000000000000000000000000000000000000
10000000000000000000000000000000000000000000000000000000000000000000000000000000
10000000000000000000000000000000000000000000000000000000000000000000000000000000
10000000000000000000000000000000000000000000000000000000000000000000000000000000
10000000000000000000000000000000000000000000000000000000000000000000000000000000
00000000000000000000000000000000000000000000000000000000000000000000000000000000
00000000000000000000000000000000000000000000000000000000000000000000000000000000
00000000000000000000000000000000000000000000000000000000000000000000000000000000
00000000000000000000000000000000000000000000000000000000000000000000000000000000
Output Division Property
??
??b???b?????????????????????
??
??????????b?????????????????????????b????????????????????b?????b????????????????
??
????????????????????????b??b??????????????????b????????????????????b????????????
??
??????b??????????????????????????????????????b???b????b?????????????????????????
??b?????????????????????????
?????????????????????????b???b???????b
??????????b?????????????????????????b???
??????????????????b?????????????????????b??????????????????????????b??????b????b
??
????b?b??b??b???????????????b?????????
??
????b?????b?????????b???????????????b??b??????????????????????b?b????b??????????

Table 8. Deterministic DL distinguisher for 4 rounds

ΔX_0
00000000000000000000000000000000000000000000000000000000000000000000000000000000
00000000000000000000000000000000000000000000000000000000000000000000000000000000
00000000000000000000000000000000000000000000000000000000000000000000000000000000
00000000000000000000000000000000000000000000000000000000000000000000000000000000
00000000000000000000000000000000000000000000000000000000000000000000000000000000
00000000000000000000000000000000000000000000000000000000000000000000000000000000
00000000000000000000000000000000000000000000000000000000000000000000000000000000
00000000000000000000000000000000000000000000000000000000000000000000000000000000
00000000000000000000000000000000000000000000000000000000000000000000000000000000
00000000000000000000000000000000000000000000000000000000000000000000000000000000
00000000000000000000000000000000000000000000000000000000000000000000000000000000
00000000000000000000000000000000000000000000000000000000000000000000000000000000
00000000000000000000000000000000000000000000000000000000000000000000000000000000
00000000000000000000000000000000000000000000000010000000000000000000000000000000
00000000000000000000000000000000000000000000000010000000000000000000000000000000
00000000000000000000000000000000000000000000000010000000000000000000000000000000
ΓX_4
00000100000000100100000000000000000000000000001000000110000000100000000000000000
00000000000000000100000100000000000010000000000000100000000000000000001000000000
00100000001000000000000000001000000000000000000000000000000000100000000000100000
00000100000000000000000100000000000000000100000000000000101000000000000000000100
00000000000000000000000000000000000000000000010000000000000000100000000000001000
01000000000000000000000001000000010010000000000000000000000000000000000000110000
00000000100000000000000000000000010000000000000010000001000000000000000000000000
00000000001001000000000000010100000000000010000001000000010000000000000000001000
00000000100000100000001001000000000000000100000001000000010000000000000000001000
00000000011000000010000000000000000000000010000000000100000000000001000000000000
00000001000000000000010000000000000000000100000000000000000001000000010000000000
10000000100000000000000000100000100000000000000000000000010100000000000000000001
00000000000000010000000000000000000000000000000100000000000000000000000000000000
01010000000000000010000001000000000000000000000000100000100000000001000000000000
00000000000000000000000000000000000000000000000000000000000001001000000000000010
11000000010000000000000000010000001000000100000000000000001010000000000001000000

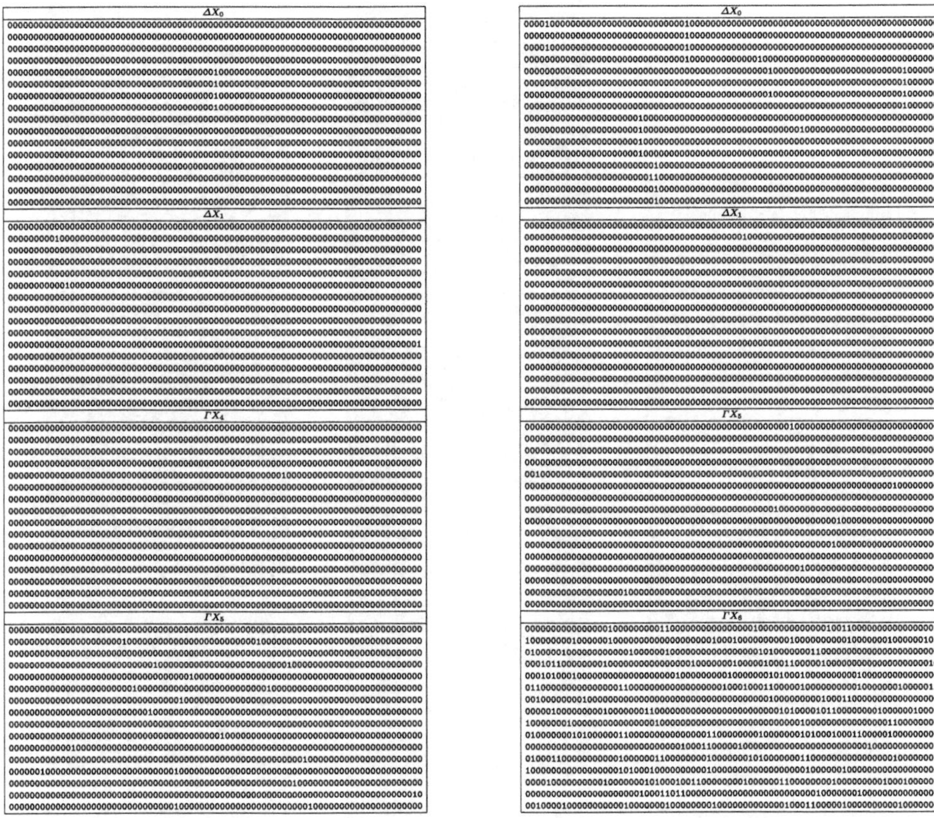

a) DL distinguisher for 5 rounds

b) DL distinguisher for 6 rounds

Fig. 8. Specification of DL distinguishers for `Twinkle-P`. a) DL distinguisher for 5 rounds b) DL distinguisher for 6 rounds

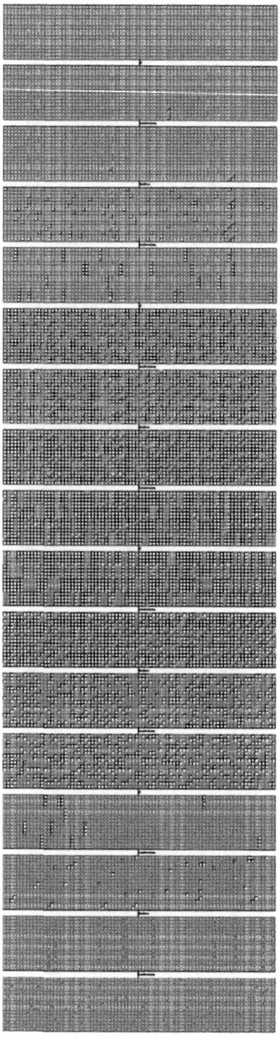

(a) DL distinguisher for 4 rounds of `Twinkle-P`

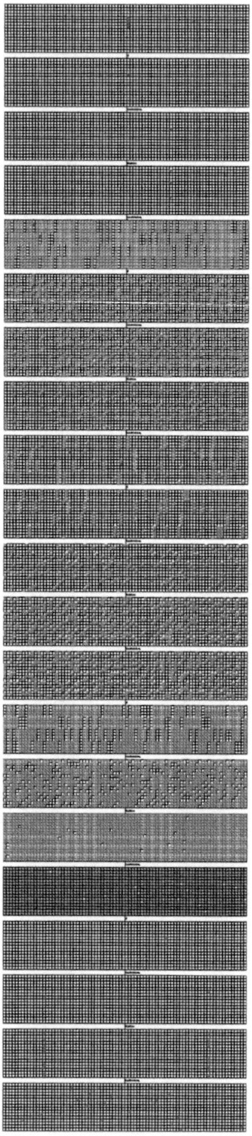

(b) DL distinguisher for 5 rounds of `Twinkle-P`

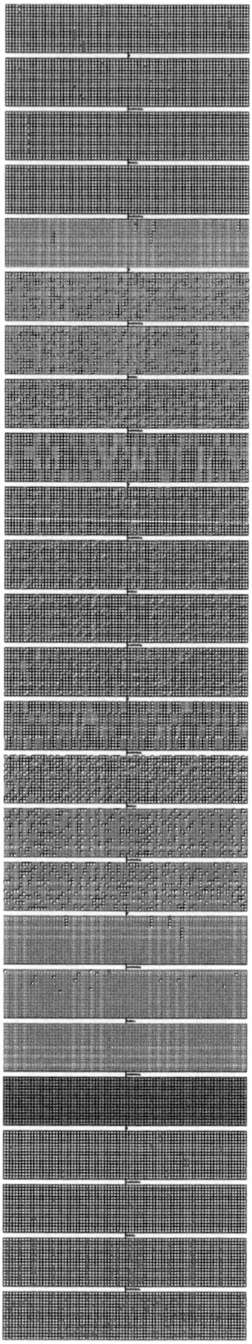

(c) DL distinguisher for 6 rounds of `Twinkle-P`

Fig. 9. DL distinguishers.

References

1. Caesar: Competition for authenticated encryption: security, applicability, and robustness (2014). https://competitions.cr.yp.to/caesar.html
2. AMD secure encrypted virtualization (SEV) — AMD (2019). https://www.amd.com/en/developer/sev.html
3. NIST lightweight cryptography competition (2021). https://csrc.nist.gov/projects/lightweight-cryptography/finalists
4. Anand, R., et al.: GLEEOK: a family of low-latency PRFS and its applications to authenticated encryption. IACR Trans. Cryptogr. Hardw. Embed. Syst. **2024**(2), 545–587 (2024). https://doi.org/10.46586/tches.v2024.i2.545-587
5. Architecture & Technology Group: Arm CCA Security Model 1.0. https://developer.arm.com/documentation/DEN0096/latest/ (2021). document number: DEN0096
6. ARM Holdings: introduction to PAC (2021). https://developer.arm.com/documentation/109576/0100/Pointer-Authentication-Code/Introduction-to-PAC
7. Avanzi, R.: The QARMA block cipher family. almost MDS matrices over rings with zero divisors, nearly symmetric even-mansour constructions with non-involutory central rounds, and search heuristics for low-latency s-boxes. IACR Trans. Symmetric Cryptol. **2017**(1), 4–44 (2017). https://doi.org/10.13154/tosc.v2017.i1.4-44
8. Banik, S., Isobe, T., Liu, F., Minematsu, K., Sakamoto, K.: Orthros: a low-latency PRF. IACR Trans. Symmetric Cryptol. **2021**(1), 37–77 (2021). https://doi.org/10.46586/tosc.v2021.i1.37-77
9. Beierle, C., et al.: The SKINNY family of block ciphers and its low-latency variant MANTIS. In: Robshaw, M., Katz, J. (eds.) CRYPTO 2016. LNCS, vol. 9815, pp. 123–153. Springer (2016). https://doi.org/10.1007/978-3-662-53008-5_5
10. Belkheyar, Y., Daemen, J., Dobraunig, C., Ghosh, S., Rasoolzadeh, S.: BipBip: a low-latency tweakable block cipher with small dimensions. IACR Trans. Cryptogr. Hardw. Embed. Syst. **2023**(1), 326–368 (2023). https://doi.org/10.46586/tches.v2023.i1.326-368
11. Bellare, M., Hoang, V.T.: Efficient schemes for committing authenticated encryption. In: EUROCRYPT 2022. LNCS, vol. 13276, pp. 845–875 (2022)
12. Bernstein, D.J., et al.: Gimli : a cross-platform permutation. In: Fischer, W., Homma, N. (eds.) CHES 2017. LNCS, vol. 10529, pp. 299–320. Springer (2017). https://doi.org/10.1007/978-3-319-66787-4_15
13. Borghoff, J., et al.: PRINCE - a low-latency block cipher for pervasive computing applications (full version). IACR Cryptol. ePrint Arch, p. 529 (2012). http://eprint.iacr.org/2012/529
14. Canale, F., Güneysu, T., Leander, G., Thoma, J.P., Todo, Y., Ueno, R.: SCARF - A low-latency block cipher for secure cache-randomization. In: Calandrino, J.A., Troncoso, C. (eds.) USENIX Security 2023, pp. 1937–1954. USENIX Association (2023). https://www.usenix.org/conference/usenixsecurity23/presentation/canale
15. Cui, T., Chen, S., Jia, K., Fu, K., Wang, M.: New automatic search tool for impossible differentials and zero-correlation linear approximations. IACR Cryptology ePrint Archive, Report 2016/689 (2016). https://eprint.iacr.org/2016/689
16. Dodis, Y., Grubbs, P., Ristenpart, T., Woodage, J.: Fast message franking: from invisible salamanders to encryptment. In: Shacham, H., Boldyreva, A. (eds.) CRYPTO 2018. LNCS, vol. 10991, pp. 155–186. Springer, Cham (2018). https://doi.org/10.1007/978-3-319-96884-1_6

17. Elbaz, R., Champagne, D., Gebotys, C.H., Lee, R.B., Potlapally, N.R., Torres, L.: Hardware mechanisms for memory authentication: a survey of existing techniques and engines. Trans. Comput. Sci. **4**, 1–22 (2009). https://doi.org/10.1007/978-3-642-01004-0_1
18. Farshim, P., Orlandi, C., Rosie, R.: Security of symmetric primitives under incorrect usage of keys. IACR Trans. Symmetric Cryptol. **2017**(1), 449–473 (2017)
19. Gueron, S.: Memory encryption for general-purpose processors. IEEE Secur. Priv. **14**(6), 54–62 (2016). https://doi.org/10.1109/MSP.2016.124
20. Hadipour, H., Derbez, P., and, M.E.: Revisiting differential-linear attacks via a boomerang perspective with application to AES, Ascon, CLEFIA, SKINNY, PRESENT, KNOT, TWINE, WARP, LBlock, Simeck, and SERPENT, pp. 38–72 (2024). https://doi.org/10.1007/978-3-031-68385-5_2
21. Hadipour, H., Gerhalter, S., Sadeghi, S., Eichlseder, M.: Improved search for integral, impossible differential and zero-correlation attacks application to ascon, forkskinny, skinny, mantis, PRESENT and qarmav2. IACR Trans. Symmetric Cryptol. **2024**(1), 234–325 (2024). https://doi.org/10.46586/TOSC.V2024.I1.234-325
22. Hadipour, H., Nageler, M., Eichlseder, M.: Throwing boomerangs into feistel structures application to clefia, warp, lblock, lblock-s and TWINE. IACR Trans. Symmetric Cryptol. **2022**(3), 271–302 (2022). https://doi.org/10.46586/tosc.v2022.i3.271-302
23. Hadipour, H., Sadeghi, S., Eichlseder, M.: Finding the impossible: automated search for full impossible differential, zero-correlation, and integral attacks. In: EUROCRYPT 2023. LNCS, vol. 14007, pp. 128–157. Springer (2023). https://doi.org/10.1007/978-3-031-30634-1_5
24. Hosoyamada, A., et al.: Cryptanalysis of ROCCA and feasibility of its security claim. IACR Trans. Symmetric Cryptol. **2022**(3), 123–151 (2022). https://doi.org/10.46586/TOSC.V2022.I3.123-151
25. Leander, G., Moos, T., Moradi, A., Rasoolzadeh, S.: The SPEEDY family of block ciphers engineering an ultra low-latency cipher from gate level for secure processor architectures. IACR Trans. Cryptogr. Hardw. Embed. Syst. **2021**(4), 510–545 (2021). https://doi.org/10.46586/TCHES.V2021.I4.510-545
26. LeMay, M., et al.: Cryptographic capability computing. In: MICRO 2021: 54th Annual IEEE/ACM International Symposium on Microarchitecture, Virtual Event, Greece, 18-22 October 2021, pp. 253–267. ACM (2021). https://doi.org/10.1145/3466752.3480076
27. Len, J., Grubbs, P., Ristenpart, T.: Partitioning oracle attacks. In: USENIX Security 2021, pp. 195–212 (2021)
28. Sakamoto, K., Liu, F., Nakano, Y., Kiyomoto, S., Isobe, T.: ROCCA: an efficient AES-based encryption scheme for beyond 5G. IACR Trans. Symmetric Cryptol. **2021**(2), 1–30 (2021). https://doi.org/10.46586/TOSC.V2021.I2.1-30, full version is available on IACR Cryptol. ePrint Arch. 2022/116
29. Sasaki, Y., Todo, Y.: New impossible differential search tool from design and cryptanalysis aspects. In: EUROCRYPT 2017. LNCS, vol. 10212, pp. 185–215. Springer (2017). https://doi.org/10.1007/978-3-319-56617-7_7
30. Sun, B., et al.: Links among impossible differential, integral and zero correlation linear cryptanalysis. In: CRYPTO 2015. LNCS, vol. 9215, pp. 95–115. Springer (2015). https://doi.org/10.1007/978-3-662-47989-6_5
31. Todo, Y.: Structural evaluation by generalized integral property. In: Oswald, E., Fischlin, M. (eds.) EUROCRYPT 2015. LNCS, vol. 9056, pp. 287–314. Springer (2015). https://doi.org/10.1007/978-3-662-46800-5_12

32. Todo, Y., Morii, M.: Bit-based division property and application to Simon family. In: Peyrin, T. (ed.) FSE 2016. LNCS, vol. 9783, pp. 357–377. Springer (2016). https://doi.org/10.1007/978-3-662-52993-5_18
33. Wang, J., Huang, T., Wu, S., Liu, Z.: Twinkle: a family of low-latency schemes for authenticated encryption and pointer authentication. IACR Commun. Cryptol. **1**(2) (2024). https://doi.org/10.62056/a3n59qgxq
34. Wegman, M.N., Carter, L.: New hash functions and their use in authentication and set equality. J. Comput. Syst. Sci. **22**(3), 265–279 (1981). https://doi.org/10.1016/0022-0000(81)90033-7
35. Xiang, Z., Zhang, W., Bao, Z., Lin, D.: Applying MILP method to searching integral distinguishers based on division property for 6 lightweight block ciphers. In: Cheon, J.H., Takagi, T. (eds.) ASIACRYPT 2016. LNCS, vol. 10031, pp. 648–678 (2016). https://doi.org/10.1007/978-3-662-53887-6_24

Impossible Differential Attacks

Minimalist Model for Impossible Differentials

Patrick Derbez[1] and Marie Euler[1,2](✉)

[1] Univ Rennes, Inria, Centre National de la Recherche Scientifique (CNRS), Institut de Recherche en Informatique et Systèmes Aléatoires (IRISA), Rennes, France
{patrick.derbez,marie.euler}@irisa.fr
[2] DGA MI, Bruz, France

Abstract. This paper introduces a new MILP modeling to find impossible differential (ID) distinguishers and attacks. Standard models for ID are negative models, in the sense that a differential is impossible if and only if the model has no solution. Our new modelling technique focuses on probable ID, differentials that are probably impossible. While this might lead to false positives, the main advantage is that searching for such probable ID can be achieved through a positive model. This facilitates the search for the best impossible differential attacks without first exhausting all possible ID distinguishers on a target. We also propose to simplify the modelling by only considering two possible states for internal cells: inactive and unknown. In this case there are no longer direct contradictions but only indirect ones, assuming that it is impossible that all cells are inactive.

With these two simple ideas, we are able to retrieve the longest impossible differentials distinguishers on `MIDORI`, `SKINNY`, `PRESENT`, `SIMON`, `Simeck` and `SPECK`. Furthermore, as the model looking for candidates is based on satisfiability, it can be incorporated in a larger model which looks directly for the best attacks in order to enumerate the distinguishers in the order of the complexity of the associated attacks, which we did for the `AES`, `ARADI`, `SIMON` and `SKINNY`.

Keywords: Impossible differential · MILP · AES · ARADI · MIDORI · PRESENT · SIMON · Simeck · SKINNY · SPECK

1 Introduction

Impossible differential (ID) cryptanalysis is a powerful method for eliminating incorrect keys by exploiting the observation of an impossible event. In this technique, the attacker partially encrypts and decrypts a pair of messages through a cipher while guessing round-key bits to uncover an impossible differential transition in the middle rounds. Specifically, this transition involves a pair of differences (Δ_X, Δ_Y) that occurs with zero probability in the remaining rounds of the cipher. Such a pair of differences is referred to as an *impossible differential distinguisher*. If this event is observed, the corresponding key guess is discarded as

C. Boura et al. (Eds.): SAC 2025, LNCS 16207, pp. 113–143, 2026.
https://doi.org/10.1007/978-3-032-10536-3_5

invalid. The attack concludes with an exhaustive search over the remaining key candidates.

This technique was introduced simultaneously in 1998 by Knudsen [22], who applied it to his `AES` candidate `DEAL`, and by Biham et al. [7], who successfully attacked 31 out of 32 rounds of `SkipJack`. Since its inception, ID cryptanalysis has proven to be a robust cryptanalytic tool. For instance, it remains one of the most effective techniques against 7 rounds of `AES-128` [9].

The complexity of an ID attack is largely determined by the *quality* of the impossible differential distinguisher. As such, much of the prior research has focused on techniques to identify long impossible distinguishers. The primary method relies on the *miss-in-the-middle* approach introduced by Biham et al. [7]. In this approach, the forward propagation of Δ_{in} with probability one contradicts the backward propagation of Δ_{out}, also with probability one, after a few rounds. Initially applied manually, this concept has been extended through a variety of automated techniques, including the $\mathcal{U}$-method [21], the UID-method [26], and the WW-method [39]. These methods rely on the propagation of four types of differences: zero difference, fixed nonzero difference, unspecified nonzero difference, and unknown difference.

In 2017, Sasaki and Todo [32] introduced a new approach leveraging Mixed-Integer Linear Programming (MILP). Their method involves modeling the difference propagation while fixing input and output activity patterns. If the MILP solver cannot find a solution (i.e., a valid differential characteristic), the differential is deemed impossible. However, for S-boxes operating on more than 4 bits, the MILP model often becomes too slow to yield results. To address this, they proposed an approximation using arbitrary S-boxes, where any active input bit implies a fully active output. Although this approximation simplifies the search, it sacrifices precision, as it does not account for detailed compatibility between successive S-boxes. This technique allows analysts to identify impossible differentials without requiring manual anticipation of contradiction patterns. However, it has drawbacks, such as a lack of explainability for why a differential is impossible and the need to test multiple input and output activity patterns separately, which becomes cumbersome for exhaustive security proofs.

To mitigate the issue of exhaustive testing, Sun et al. [34] demonstrated in 2016 that in the arbitrary S-box model, for SPNs or Feistel ciphers with SP-type round functions, any impossible differential of r rounds implies the existence of a weight-1 ID distinguisher for the same number of rounds. This result reduces the number of required activity pattern tests from 2^{2m} to m^2, where m is the number of bits or cells in the input.

In 2022, Hu, Peyrin, and Wang [19] introduced a new method for proving the security of specific ciphers without relying on the arbitrary S-box approximation. Their approach partitions the space of ID candidates and uses an MILP model incorporating the S-box difference distribution table (DDT). This advancement improves accuracy in identifying impossible differentials but retains the limitations of being a *negative model*, where a distinguisher's impossibility is proven only if no solutions exist.

Both MILP-based approaches share a key drawback: they are negative models that cannot be directly integrated into broader frameworks for finding the most efficient attacks. Furthermore, the low-weight ID distinguishers suggested by these models may not always lead to the most effective attacks.

Since 2023, Hadipour et al. [11,17,18] have introduced a Constraint Programming (CP)-based adaptation of the $\mathcal{U}$-method. Initially limited to strongly aligned ciphers with predefined contradiction locations [18], their models have evolved to handle bitwise representations, incorporate advanced key-recovery strategies [17], and even address indirect contradictions in ARX ciphers [11]. This line of research offers two major advantages: positive modeling, which facilitates integration into broader attack optimization frameworks, and flexibility in application across various cipher classes. Despite these advancements, Hadipour et al. have primarily focused on identifying *good* distinguishers before optimizing the corresponding key-recovery steps.

The first tool explicitly designed to find optimal ID attacks is that of Derbez and Fouque [14], which does not rely on generic solvers. However, their algorithm remains somewhat opaque, as the paper lacks detailed information on its inner workings, making it difficult to compare with other approaches. Recently, the automatic cryptanalysis tool CLAASP has been improved using the recent works of Hadipour *et al.* to generate CP models searching for attacks. It has been applied to both `LBlock` and `HIGHT` [5] but does not include the indirect contradiction search.

Our Contributions. In this work, we address the challenge of designing a simpler positive MILP model that can seamlessly handle cell-based ciphers, bit-oriented ciphers, AndRX and ARX ciphers. Our approach eliminates the need for analysts to exhaustively enumerate all contradictions manually. Furthermore, we demonstrate how this model can be integrated into a comprehensive framework for directly searching for the best impossible differential attacks in a unified process.

The core idea is to combine the validation strategy of Sasaki and Todo [32], which checks the validity of impossible differentials, with a novel positive model. This new model generates activity patterns that are likely to lead to valid impossible differential distinguishers. Furthermore, when included in full model searching directly for attacks, only few *probable* ID distinguishers are tried for. As a second contribution, we also propose to simplify the propagation of differences. Unlike the $\mathcal{U}$-method, which propagates four types of information (zero difference, fixed nonzero difference, unspecified nonzero difference, and unknown difference), our model simplifies this propagation to just two types: zero difference and unknown difference. This simplification reduces complexity while maintaining effectiveness.

The source code of our experiments is available at:

https://gitlab.inria.fr/capsule/idtool.git

Organisation. The rest of the paper is organized as follows. In Sect. 2, we review in more details impossible differential attacks, and in particular their complexity.

In Sect. 3, we explain in detail how our modeling works. Section 4 is dedicated to applications of the modeling to different contexts. Two full integrations in attack frameworks will be demonstrated with the cases of `AES` and `SKINNY-128` (and in appendix the low-latency design `ARADI`). More details on the distinguisher modeling will be given taking into example the word-oriented cipher `Midori`, the AndRX ciphers `SIMON` and the AddRX cipher `SPECK`. Distinguishers for the bit-oriented cipher `PRESENT` and the AndRX cipher `Simeck` are also presented in appendix.

2 Principle of ID Attacks

2.1 Impossible Differential Attacks

We begin by recalling the framework for impossible differential attacks on block ciphers, as outlined in [10]. Consider an n-bit block cipher with a k-bit master key K. The attack leverages a zero-probability differential distinguisher spanning r_d rounds, which begins with an n-bit input difference (or set of differences) Δ_X and concludes with an n-bit output difference (or set of differences) Δ_Y, as illustrated in Fig. 1. To extend the attack, r_{in} rounds are prepended to the distinguisher and r_{out} rounds are added afterward.

$$\Delta_{\text{in}} \xrightarrow{r_{\text{in}}} \Delta_X \xleftarrow{\quad r_{\text{D}} \quad} \!\!\!\!\!\times\!\!\!\!\! \xrightarrow{\quad} \Delta_Y \xleftarrow{r_{\text{out}}} \Delta_{\text{out}}$$

Fig. 1. The impossible differential attack principle : a central distinguisher surrounded by key recovery rounds

The set of potential differences at the plaintext side, denoted Δ_{in}, consists of differences that may propagate to Δ_X after r_{in} rounds. Similarly, Δ_{out} represents the set of differences at the ciphertext side that may result from Δ_Y after r_{out} rounds. The probability that a difference in Δ_{in} propagates to Δ_X is denoted as $2^{-c_{\text{in}}}$, while $2^{-c_{\text{out}}}$ represents the probability of a difference in Δ_{out} propagating to Δ_Y. Finally, the set of key bits involved in determining whether a difference in Δ_{in} leads to Δ_X is k_{in}, while k_{out} denotes the corresponding set of key bits at the ciphertext side.

Given a pair of messages with a plaintext difference in Δ_{in} and a ciphertext difference in Δ_{out}, the probability that a specific key guess results in Δ_X and Δ_Y (and is thus discarded) is $2^{-c_{\text{in}}-c_{\text{out}}}$. Consequently, the probability of not discarding a given key is $(1 - 2^{-c_{\text{in}}-c_{\text{out}}})$. When considering N such pairs, the probability of not discarding a given key becomes approximately $(1 - 2^{-c_{\text{in}}-c_{\text{out}}})^N \approx \exp(-N \cdot 2^{-c_{\text{in}}-c_{\text{out}}})$. Furthermore, to construct N pairs, the attacker organizes encryption queries into structures, either on the plaintext side or the ciphertext side. Depending on the required number of pairs, multiple structures may need to be encrypted, or in some cases, fewer than a full structure. Combining these scenarios, the data complexity D is given by the following formula also known as the *Limited Birthday formula* [10]:

$$D = \max\left\{ \min_{\Delta \in \{\Delta_{\text{in}}, \Delta_{\text{out}}\}} \left\{ \sqrt{N \cdot 2^{n+1-|\Delta|}} \right\}, N \cdot 2^{n+1-|\Delta_{\text{in}}|-|\Delta_{\text{out}}|} \right\},$$

where $2^{|\Delta_{\text{in}}|}$ and $2^{|\Delta_{\text{out}}|}$ represent the number of differences in Δ_{in} and Δ_{out}, respectively. In the classical scenario the data complexity must satisfy $D \leq 2^n$ (the full codebook size) but for tweakable block ciphers it might be extended by the size of the tweak.

The complexity of an impossible differential attack is then given by two main components: the generation of the pairs and the attack itself. As stated in [10] and confirmed in [13], a lower bound for the time complexity T is:

$$T = \left(D + \left(N + \frac{2^{|k_{\text{in}} \cup k_{\text{out}}|} \cdot N}{2^{c_{\text{in}}+c_{\text{out}}}} \right) C'_E \right) C_E,$$

where C_E represents the cost of a single encryption and C'_E the ratio of the cost of a partial encryption to that of a full encryption. This time complexity must satisfy $T < 2^k C_E$, otherwise the attack would not be faster than a brute force. Finally, the memory complexity corresponds to storing N pairs.

Note that the attacker's goal is to reduce the set of possible keys by at least a factor of 2 to ensure that the final exhaustive search step remains computationally feasible or to guess an extra bit and run another attack. We denote by N_{min} the minimum number of pairs required to achieve this reduction. We have:

$$(1 - 2^{-c_{\text{in}}-c_{\text{out}}})^{N_{\text{min}}} < \frac{1}{2}.$$

Using a well-known approximation, this can be simplified into $N_{\text{min}} > \ln(2) \cdot 2^{c_{\text{in}}+c_{\text{out}}}$, which can be rewritten as $N_{\text{min}} > 2^{c_{\text{in}}+c_{\text{out}}-0.53}$.

2.2 Searching for Impossible Differential Distinguishers

As explained in the introduction, searching for impossible differential distinguishers typically involves analyzing three trails: a **forward trail**, which propagates the input difference Δ_X with probability 1 in the forward direction; a **backward trail**, which propagates the output difference Δ_Y in the backward direction; and a **summary trail**, which consolidates the information deduced independently from the forward and backward trails.

In this context, a bit or cell (depending on the granularity) can take one of three possible states: 0 (no difference), 1 (non-zero difference), or $*$ (undetermined state). A *direct contradiction* arises when a cell is assigned conflicting values in the forward and backward trails (e.g., 0 in one trail and 1 in the other) or when a contradiction emerges during the evaluation of a cipher operation. For example, it may be impossible for an S-box to exhibit a transition such as $(1, 0, *, *) \to (0, *, *, 1)$.

An *indirect contradiction*, on the other hand, occurs when certain $*$ states must be resolved (to 0 or 1) before reaching a direct contradiction. For instance, in the MixColumns operation of AES, if there are four $*$ states and four 0 states, it is well known that the four $*$ states must resolve to 0. These newly determined values may then lead to a direct contradiction. The first paper pointing out the existence of indirect contradictions used the example of the SIMECK block cipher [30]. Initially found manually, these contradictions were later found with a MILP modeling in [31]. Yet, this was a negative model which therefore did not have to deal explicitly with the progressive deductions.

Indeed, the challenge with indirect contradictions lies in the iterative nature of the deductions required to reach a contradiction. For example, given two consecutive S-boxes, S_1 and S_2, it may be necessary to iteratively refine the $*$ states by alternating deductions between S_1 and S_2 multiple times before a contradiction is identified. Notably, the model proposed by Chakraborty *et al.* in [11] does not account for such indirect contradictions, as their approach limits deductions to a single pass from S_1 to S_2, even though it is unclear whether any of the best distinguishers requires multiple passes. More precisely, once the summary trail is computed, they start from one round (given by the user) and then propagate this state with probability one to both the input and output of the distinguisher and check whether a contradiction with either the forward or the backward trail occurs. They did so because in constraints programming new variables have to be used for each new pass, making the model very complex.

Moreover, some contradictions are not local: several deductions have to combined to obtain the source of the contradiction. It is the case of some impossible differentials on 9 rounds of the Feistel network Lilliput described in [32]: for $\alpha \in \{2, 3, 9, e, f\}$, the difference $(000000\alpha0; 00000000)$ cannot lead to the difference $(00000000; 00000\alpha00)$. The contradiction which uses the DDT of Lilliput's S-Box S comes from the fact that for such α there are no β, x, y, z such that

$$\begin{cases} S(x) \oplus S(x \oplus \alpha) = \beta; \\ S(y) \oplus S(y \oplus \alpha \oplus \beta) = \beta; \\ S(z) \oplus S(z \oplus \alpha) = \alpha \oplus \beta. \end{cases}$$

This set of contradictory equations arise from the observations of several Feistel XORs thus could not have been obtained with predefined local variables indicating potential sources of contradictions.

3 New Search Principle

Previous research has shown that handling all indirect contradictions using a *positive* model—where a solution represents an impossible distinguisher—is highly challenging. In this work, we focus on indirect contradictions, as they are the most difficult to address. Our approach is conceptually simple yet highly effective. Specifically, at the onset of an indirect contradiction, there exist $*$ states that must be resolved into either 0 or 1. This resolution is the core of our method for identifying impossible differential distinguishers and attacks.

Rather than directly searching for impossible differential distinguishers, our model targets distinguishers where, in the summary trail, at least one $*$ variable resolves to either 0 or 1. This approach allows us to identify *probable* impossible differential distinguishers, which can then be further analyzed externally to verify their validity.

To achieve this, we introduce two MILP models. The first, called the **generator model**, identifies probable impossible differential distinguishers. The second, referred to as the **validator model**, verifies the results of the generator model. While other constraint programming languages could be used to implement these models, it is crucial for the generator model to support callback functionality. This allows external programs to interact with the solver during the solving process, significantly enhancing efficiency. Additionally, it is preferable for the generator model to incorporate the full attack directly (not only the distinguisher part) and to optimize on the time complexity, ensuring it focuses only on probable distinguishers that lead to the best attacks. These two models are nested: the main interface is the one of the generator model which is parameterized by the number of rounds of either the distinguisher r_D or the respective parts of the attack $(r_{\text{in}}, r_D, r_{\text{out}})$ depending on whether the user wants to find a distinguisher or an attack. The validator model is called by the generator model to validate the distinguisher candidates as soon as they are generated. It never has to be called directly.

Finally, we emphasize that while the generator model is a positive model, the validator model does not need to be. This dual-model approach is deliberate and permits to simplify the modeling while handling all the contradictions that a *negative* model can find. However, its efficiency highly depends on how many candidates are generated by the generator model.

Simplifying the Model. In practice, the propagation of 1's in impossible differential distinguishers is highly ineffective within a cipher. At the cell level, the XOR of two 1's yields an indeterminate result, and at the bit level, it is uncommon for 1's to persist through more than few non-linear operations. Consequently, we propose simplifying the model by removing 1's and focusing solely on 0 and $*$ states. Under this approach, a differential is deemed impossible if and only if all the $*$ states in the summary trail must resolve to 0. In particular, a contradiction is necessary an indirect contradiction. The intuition behind this simplification is that, for the longest impossible differential, the contradiction arises not from the propagation of 1's from both the input and output of the distinguisher, but rather from the propagation of 0's from at least one of these two sides.

Hence, in the following we will describe a simplified model, with only two possible states for each variable – 0 and $*$ – and a distinguisher will be a probable impossible differential if and only if at least one of the $*$ variable of the summary trail has to resolve to 0 to be valid. However, the same approach can obviously be used in a model containing the 1's.

3.1 Generator Model: the Distinguisher Part

Classically, we use three trails in the distinguisher part of the generator model: the forward trail propagates Δ_X with probability 1 in the forward direction, the backward trail propagates Δ_Y in the backward direction and summary trail which merges the information of both these two trails. Each of the variables representing the state values considered in these trails are binary: it is zero if the cell is inactive (denoted 0) and 1 if the difference is unknown (denoted $*$).

We begin by describing the propagation of differences in the forward trail, constraints for the backward trail being similar.

Modeling the XOR and the AND. We know that the XOR (resp. the AND) of two inactive cells remains inactive while the result of the XOR (resp. the AND) of any unknown difference with another difference is unknown. Thus we model the XOR $c = a \oplus b$ and the AND $c = a \cdot b$ with the constraints $c \leq a + b \leq 2c$.

Modeling Arbitrary S-Boxes. We consider that except if all the inputs of a n-bit S-Box are inactive, the output difference bits of this S-Box are all unknown. Let us denote as $(a_i)_{0 \leq i < n}$ the input differences and $(b_i)_{0 \leq i < n}$ the output differences. The constraints we set on a and b are quite natural:

$$\begin{cases} b_0 = b_1 = \ldots = b_{n-1} \\ \sum a_i / n \leq b_0 \leq \sum a_i \end{cases}$$

Note that, for cell-oriented models, the constraint is even simpler since it simplifies to $a = b$.

Moreover, these kind of modeling naturally captures truncated distinguishers. Indeed, when the S-boxes are deemed arbitrary, the only important information in any bit activity pattern in Δ_X, is the knowledge of which cells are activated. Therefore, when only searching for distinguishers, we can fix an arbitrary bit pattern at the cell-level to indicate that the cell is active, for both the first and last layers of S-boxes. This will limit the number of equivalent solutions of the model. For instance, the constraint $a_0 = a_1 = \cdots = a_{n-1}$ can be applied on the input of the first S-box layer.

Modeling Specific S-Boxes. This only applies for bit-oriented models. Given a n-bit S-box, we need to determine for each $(a_0, \ldots, a_{n-1}) \in \{0, *\}^n$ at its input, what is the corresponding output. We first have to compute the list of all possible differential transitions through the S-box and then, for each input, we check which output bits (if any) are set to 0 for all the possible corresponding output differences. Next, we can construct the outputs $(b_0, \ldots, b_{n-1}) \in \{0, *\}^n$ associated to each $(a_0, \ldots, a_{n-1})$ step by step, ordering the inputs by their number of $*$. Finally, for each of the 2^n transitions $(a_0, \ldots, a_{n-1}) \to (b_0, \ldots, b_{n-1})$ we add the constraints:

$$\begin{cases} \sum\limits_{i, b_i = *} (1 - b_i) \leq |\{i, b_i = *\}| \times \sum\limits_{i, a_i = *} (1 - a_i) \\ \sum\limits_{i, b_i = 0} b_i \leq |\{i, b_i = 0\}| \times \sum\limits_{i, a_i = 0} a_i \end{cases}$$

Note that in practice, most of the constraints are redundant and do not need to be included. The final number of constraints only depends on the number of possible $(b_0, \ldots, b_{n-1})$. For instance, let assume we have the transitions $(0, *, 0, *) \rightarrow (0, 0, *, *)$ and $(*, *, 0, *) \rightarrow (0, 0, *, *)$. In this case we can keep only the constraints

$$(1 - b_2) + (1 - b_3) \leq 2((1 - a_1) + (1 - a_3)) \quad \text{and} \quad (1 - b_0) + (1 - b_1) \leq 2a_2,$$

since both $(1-b_2)+(1-b_3) \leq 2((1-a_0)+(1-a_1)+(1-a_3))$ and $(1-b_0)+(1-b_1) \leq 2(a_0 + a_2)$ are weaker. Note that most of the strong S-boxes do not have such patterns and thus the few constraints of the arbitrary S-box modeling are enough. Yet we can observe such weak diffusion pattern for some of the S-boxes used in lightweight ciphers. For example, there are two non-trivial transitions in the 4-bit S-box S of SKINNY-64: the third bit of $S(x) \oplus S(x \oplus 1)$ is always zero, which corresponds to the pattern $(*, 0, 0, 0) \rightarrow (*, *, 0, *)$, and the fourth bit of $S(x) \oplus S(x \oplus 2))$ is always zero, which is equivalent to the probability one transition $(0, *, 0, 0) \rightarrow (*, *, *, 0)$. For all other non null input patterns, the output pattern is merely $(*, *, *, *)$ that is none of the output bits is always inactive. Similarly, the only non-trivial pattern in the 5-bit S-Box of ASCON is $(0, 0, 0, 0, *) \rightarrow (*, *, 0, *, *)$.

Modeling Linear Layers. Since we are only looking for propagations of probability 1, the constraints are exactly the same as for XOR: an output bit/cell is 0 if and only if all the bits/cells it depends on the input are 0 as well.

Deduction of the Summary Trail. Let c be the deduction from the knowledge of the cell a in the forward trail and the cell b in the backward trail. The only case where the difference c is unknown is when the differences a and b are unknown. This can be modeled with the constraints $2c \leq a + b \leq 1 + c$.

Modeling the Deduction of New Zeros. This is the novelty of the model regarding the distinguisher. Given an operation f within the cipher, our goal is to identify all subsets of input and output bits or cells such that if all variables in a subset have a difference of 0, then at least one additional input or output bit/cell must also have a difference of 0. For linear layers, this process is straightforward and relies on basic linear algebra to determine which bits or cells can be expressed solely in terms of the subset's variables. For S-boxes, the process is similar to generating the constraints described earlier, but it differs in scale. The number of subsets that must be considered is larger, specifically 2^{n+m} for an n-to-m-bit function f.

We also have to introduce an auxiliary binary variable z into the model, which takes the value 1 for subsets that create a new zero and 0 otherwise. For sake of simplicity and efficiency, we only considered patterns which impose a new zero in a fixed place. While this results in 2^{n+m} inequalities, these can often be reduced using classical techniques such as the Quine-McCluskey algorithm [28] or similar methods.

Let us take as example the 4-bit S-Box of the `PRESENT` blockcipher whose table is [c, 5, 6, b, 9, 0, a, d, 3, e, f, 8, 4, 7, 1, 2]. There are 42 patterns leading to the creation of new zeros. They are presented in Table 1 and actually, all but the last one imply that the S-Box is fully inactive. Note that the $2^{4+4} = 256$ associated constraints are reduced by the Espresso logic minimizer to only 43 constraints.

Table 1. 42 input/output patterns leading to new zeros on the PRESENT S-box. Each pattern is given as the concatenation of the input and the output patterns.

$000*000*$	$000*00*0$	$000*00**$	$000*0*00$	$000*0*0*$	$000*0**0$
$000*0***$	$000**000$	$000**0*0$	$00*0000*$	$00*000*0$	$00*00*00$
$00*0*000$	$00*0**00$	$00**00*0$	$00***000$	$0*00000*$	$0*0000*0$
$0*000*00$	$0*00*000$	$0*00*00*$	$0*0*00*0$	$0*0**000$	$0**000*0$
$0**0*000$	$0***00*0$	$0****000$	$*000000*$	$*00000*0$	$*00000**$
$*0000*00$	$*0000*0*$	$*0000**0$	$*0000***$	$*000*000$	$*000*0*0$
$*00**000$	$*0*0000*$	$*0*00*00$	$**00000*$	$**000*00$	$*00**0*0$

Another interesting example is the specific case of Maximum Distance Separable (MDS) matrices for which the constraints can be significantly simplified. Consider, for instance, the `MixColumns` operation in `AES`, with inputs (a_0, a_1, a_2, a_3) and outputs (b_0, b_1, b_2, b_3). Subsets leading to a new zero must satisfy the following constraints:

$$\begin{cases} a_0 + a_1 + a_2 + a_3 \geq z, \\ b_0 + b_1 + b_2 + b_3 \geq z, \\ a_0 + a_1 + a_2 + a_3 + b_0 + b_1 + b_2 + b_3 \leq 8 - 4z. \end{cases}$$

In essence, this means that no more than three inputs and three outputs can simultaneously be zero; otherwise, new zeros would appear either in the forward or backward trail. However, at least four variables must be zero for new zeros to be created.

Removing Invalid Candidates. If the validator model confirms that a candidate (Δ_X, Δ_Y) is a valid differential, it becomes necessary to exclude this candidate from the solution space of the generator model. Furthermore, we can also eliminate all candidates that include this differential. This is achieved by enforcing a constraint in the model that ensures at least one of the $*$ variables in either Δ_X or Δ_Y is set to 0. This requires adding only a single inequality as a lazy constraint through the callback functionality.

3.2 Generator Model : Inclusion In An Attack Framework

The reason we propose a positive model is to include it in a larger model, directly searching for the best impossible differential attack. We describe here the main steps of the key-recovery part.

Active Cells. The r_{in} rounds of key recovery preceding the distinguisher and the r_{out} rounds following it are modeled in the standard way: Δ_X and Δ_Y are propagated with probability one toward the plaintext and the ciphertext. This process identifies the active cells at the inputs and outputs, as well as the *needed cells* whose values need to be determined to compute the active ones. These active and needed cells, in turn, dictate which key bits must be guessed during the key recovery step.

Entropy of the Key Bits. This is arguably the most challenging aspect and remains an open problem. When the key schedule is a permutation of bits or can be described with simple rules, as in the case of SKINNY, the modeling is relatively straightforward. However, even for linear key schedules, it can become complex to enumerate all possible relations, including key-bridging relations, and no systematic approach currently exists.

To address this limitation, users have two main options. They can either assume no relations exist between the key bits involved in the attack or artificially reduce the entropy estimated by the model and validate this assumption a posteriori.

Computing the Complexity. Given an n-bit cipher with m-bit cells and a key size of κ bits, we propose the following constraints to describe the complexity of the attack. Let us assume the model already set the variable p as the ($-\log_2$ of the) probability for a pair to satisfy the input and output of the impossible differential, the variable k as the ($-\log_2$ of the) entropy of $k_{in} \cup k_{out}$ and both the variables D_{in} and D_{out} representing the dimension of the active cells in the plaintext and the ciphertext respectively.

The first step is to model the data complexity D as well as the number of pairs N. This can be achieved with the following constraints:

$$\begin{cases} e \text{ binary variable}, \quad D_{max} \text{ continuous variable in } [0, n] \\ g \text{ continuous variable in } [1, m], \quad D \text{ continuous variable in } [0, n] \\ D_{max} \leq D_{in} + n \times e \\ D_{max} \leq D_{out} + n \times (1 - e) \\ N = p - 0.53 + g \\ D \geq (N + n + 1 - D_{max})/2 \\ D \geq N + n + 1 - D_{in} - D_{out} \end{cases}$$

If one tries to minimize D, he will reach the formula of the data complexity given in Sect. 2.1. The variable g represents the $-\log_2$ of the factor by which the key bits involved in the attack will be reduced and $2^{-0.53} \approx \ln(2)$. Then the time complexity of the attack can be constrained with the following inequalities:

$$\begin{cases} T \text{ continuous variable in } [0, \kappa], f \text{ binary variable} \\ T \geq D \\ T \geq N + c'_E \\ T \geq k - p + N + c'_E \\ T \geq \kappa - g - n \times f \\ g \geq m \times (1 - f) \end{cases}$$

The last two constraints are a bit different than the complexity formula given by Boura *et al.* in [10]. Here we propose to limit the reduction factor g to m-bit, since it is often more efficient to perform a second attack requiring one more guess than brute-forcing the remaining keys. But obviously, the constraints can be modified, depending on the target.

3.3 Validator Model

The validator model is a rather classical model searching for differential characteristics but for which both the input and output activity patterns are given. It only deals with the r_d rounds of the distinguishers. If the model is unsatisfiable, it implies that the activity patterns are incompatible, leading to the discovery of an impossible differential distinguisher. While, in theory, the validator model does not require the same granularity as the generator model, it would be unusual to adopt a different level of precision. In all applications described in Sect. 4, we used the same granularity for both models.

That said, the validator model differs from the generator model in its treatment of 1's. Although we decided to disregard them within the generator model, the validator model must account for them. Specifically, for each $*$ in Δ_X and Δ_Y we must decide whether it remains a $*$ or is set to 1 for the differential to be impossible. This consideration is particularly important in bit-oriented models, since the number of 1's directly affects the dimensions of Δ_X and Δ_Y which may, in turn, affect the time complexity of the associated attack.

A secondary goal of the validator model can therefore be to maximize $|\Delta_X|+|\Delta_Y|$. To achieve this, whenever the model finds a valid differential, we impose a new constraint that forces at least one of the $*$ bits previously set to 0 in either the input or output to be set to 1 and rerun the model. Asking the model to maximize the number of 1's will make the strategy highly effective. Finally, if the model eventually becomes unsatisfiable, we execute a simple model containing only the extra constraints previously added with the objective to minimize the number of 1's.

4 Applications

Our code was written using either the Python API or the C API for Gurobi. The computations run on a standard laptop, taking only seconds for the simplest cases and a few minutes for more complex ones.

We provide visualizations of some of the best impossible differential (ID) distinguishers across all applications, using a straightforward color-coding scheme. A red triangle in the upper-left corner of a cell (◩) indicates an unknown bit or cell in the forward trail, while a blue triangle in the lower-right corner (◪) represents an unknown bit or cell in the backward trail. Cells outlined in green correspond to the bits or cells used to deduce new zeros in the summary trail.

4.1 Application to the AES

The AES (Advanced Encryption Standard) is a block cipher with a block size of 128 bits. It comes in three variants, differing in key sizes—128, 192, or 256 bits—and the corresponding number of encryption rounds. The block state is represented as a 4×4 array of bytes. Encryption begins with an initial round-key addition, followed by multiple iterations of the same round function, which is identical across all AES versions. The round function consists of four byte-oriented transformations:

- **SubBytes (SB):** Applies the same S-box substitution to each byte of the state.
- **ShiftRows (SR):** Rotates the second, third, and fourth rows of the state to the left by one, two, and three bytes, respectively.
- **MixColumns (MC):** Multiplies each column of the state by a Maximum Distance Separable (MDS) matrix.
- **AddRoundKey (ARK):** XORs the state with the current round key.

In the final round, the **MixColumns** operation is omitted.

Modeling the Distinguisher. We use the arbitrary S-box model, and the propagation through the linear layers is encoded using the simplified constraints for modeling MDS matrices, as described in Sect. 3. Let X_f, X_b, and X_s denote arrays of $r_\mathrm{d} \times 16$ binary variables representing the states immediately before the **SB** operation for the forward, backward, and summary trails, respectively. For all r and i, the following inequalities hold:

$$2 \times X_s[r][i] \leq X_f[r][i] + X_b[r][i] \leq X_s[r][i] + 1,$$

relating these three trails and ensuring that a state byte in the summary trail is zero if and only if it is zero in either the forward or backward trails.

The propagation in the forward trail between rounds r and $r+1$ is encoded with only a few simple constraints. First, after MixColumns, a column is either fully active or fully inactive which can be translated into the constraints:

$$X_f[r+1][4i] = X_f[r+1][4i+j] \quad \text{for all } 0 \leq j < 4.$$

And then it is fully active if and only if at least one of the 4 cells involved in the MixColumns is active:

$$X_f[r+1][4i] \leq \sum_{j=0}^{3} X_f[r][4(i+j \mod 4)+j] \leq 4 \times X_f[r+1][4i].$$

Note that we combined here in one step the MixColumns and ShiftRows operations and that at the cell level, the SubBytes and AddRoundKey can be skipped as they do not alter the activity pattern.

Modeling the Key-Recovery. Let X_{in} be an array of $r_{\text{in}} \times 16$ binary variables representing the states immediately before the **SB** operation in the extension of the distinguisher to the plaintext. The end of X_{in} must match the input of the distinguisher, resulting in the constraint $X_{\text{in}}[r_{\text{in}}] = X_f[0]$. The transition between $X_{in}[r_{\text{in}}]$ and $X_{in}[r_{\text{in}} - 1]$ does not need to be deterministic since we can add any linear relation between the active bytes at the input of the distinguisher. Using the MDS property, the constraints between these two states are given as:

$$\begin{cases} e_{r_{\text{in}},i} \text{ is a binary variable,} \\ \sum_j X_{\text{in}}[r_{\text{in}} - 1][4(i+j \mod 4) + j] + X_{\text{in}}[r_{\text{in}}][4i+j] \geq 5e_{r_{\text{in}},i}, \\ \sum_j X_{\text{in}}[r_{\text{in}} - 1][4(i+j \mod 4) + j] + X_{\text{in}}[r_{\text{in}}][4i+j] \leq 8e_{r_{in},i}. \end{cases}$$

For the remaining rounds, propagation must occur with probability 1 up to the plaintext, so the constraints are identical to those for the backward trail. To compute the probability of a pair of plaintexts reaching the distinguisher's input, we define a variable $e_{r,i}$ for each column. The $-\log_2$ of the transition probability $p_{r,i}$ is then computed as:

$$p_{r,i} = 8(4e_{r,i} - \sum_j X_{\text{in}}[r][4i+j]), \quad \text{for } r \geq 1.$$

The dimension of the difference in the plaintext, D_{in}, is computed as $D_{\text{in}} = \sum_i X_{\text{in}}[0][i]$. Finally, the entropy k of the key material required for key recovery is obtained by counting the number of active variables in X_{in}, excluding $X_{\text{in}}[r_{\text{in}}]$. For each equation in the key schedule, if all variables in the equation are active, we subtract 1 from k. Note that our model includes only the original equations of the key schedule and does not account for advanced relations such as key bridging. A similar set of constraints can be derived for the extension of the distinguisher to the ciphertext.

Result. Our model efficiently identified the best impossible attack on AES-128, producing results instantly. The output matched the attack described by Mala *et al.* [27], which corresponds to the basic version of the best-known impossible differential attack against 7-round AES-128, as later refined by Leurent and Pernot [24]. Specifically, Leurent and Pernot enhanced the attack by leveraging multiple distinguishers and replacing the exhaustive search step with a clever procedure relying on their innovative representation of the AES key schedule.

4.2 Application to SKINNY

SKINNY is a family of tweakable block ciphers introduced in [3]. It is based on a Substitution-Permutation Network (SPN) structure. Each instance is denoted as SKINNY-n-zn, where n represents the block size (either 64 or 128 bits), and zn refers to the tweakey size, with $z \in \{1, 2, 3\}$. The state is composed of 16 cells, each of size $c \in \{4, 8\}$ bits. The round function consists of four main operations, similar to the ones of AES: the **SubCell (SC)** layer which applies the same

S-box on each cell of the state, the addition of round constants and $8c$-bit round tweakeys, a **ShiftRows (SR)** operation which is actually the inverse of the AES one, and a **MixColumns (MC)** operation which involves a non-MDS binary matrix.

Impossible differential cryptanalysis was included in the security analysis conducted by the designers. Using the *miss-in-the-middle* technique, they discovered distinguishers spanning 11 rounds and developed a 16-round attack on SKINNY-n-n based on this distinguisher. Subsequent research proposed attacks on SKINNY-n-n, SKINNY-n-$2n$, and SKINNY-n-$3n$ in both single-tweakey and related-tweakey settings [17,18,25,38,40]. In this work, we focused on the single-tweakey setting and aimed to recover the best known attacks, as described in [18].

Modeling the Distinguisher SKINNY is cell-oriented so we employed a cell-based model combined with the arbitrary S-box model. The generator model is tasked with identifying new zero cells in the only remaining complex layer, the MixColumns operation:

$$\begin{pmatrix} y_0 \\ y_1 \\ y_2 \\ y_3 \end{pmatrix} = \underbrace{\begin{pmatrix} 1\,0\,1\,1 \\ 1\,0\,0\,0 \\ 0\,1\,1\,0 \\ 1\,0\,1\,0 \end{pmatrix}}_{M} \begin{pmatrix} x_0 \\ x_1 \\ x_2 \\ x_3 \end{pmatrix}.$$

We exhaustively enumerated all possible patterns to identify those that result in new inactive cells. For instance, if $x_2 = y_2 = 0$, then $0 = y_2 = x_1 + x_2$, which implies $x_1 = 0$. Thus, the pattern $(*, *, 0, *, *, *, 0, *)$ leads to a new inactive cell (x_1). Using the Espresso logic minimizer, we derived compact constraints, yielding 31 inequalities.

Modeling the Key-Recovery. The key-recovery part of our model is similar to the one used for AES, but specific adaptations are required due to the particularities of SKINNY's tweakey schedule and the non-MDS matrix of the **MC** operation. Notably, inactive cells may occasionally need to be used to compute the value of an active cell, which is required to verify whether the partially encrypted pair of plaintexts belongs to ΔX. To account for this, we introduce a new binary variable, *needed*, for each cell. This variable encodes whether the value of the corresponding cell is necessary during the key-recovery step. The rules for identifying *needed* cells are as follows:

- **Active cells:** If a cell is *active*, it is also *needed.*
- **Propagation through MixColumns**: If any of the output cells y_j is *needed*, all the input cells x_i contributing to y_j are also *needed.* This propagation corresponds to the transpose of the MixColumns matrix M.
- **Round-tweakey cells:** If a round-tweakey cell is required to compute a *needed* state cell, the round-tweakey cell is included in k_{in}.

To identify k_{out}, we apply similar rules but swap the **AddTweakey** and **MixColumns** operations. The entropy of $k_{\text{in}} \cup k_{\text{out}}$ can then be accurately computed by, for instance, using the constraints provided by Qin *et al.* in [29]. More precisely, SKINNY-n-zn's tweakey schedule is merely a permutation, and guessing a cell in z round-tweakeys is sufficient to uniquely determine its value across all other round-tweakeys.

Results. For all variants of SKINNY, our model identifies optimal attacks in under 10 s, processing up to only five candidates suggested by the generator model. Using this approach, we successfully recover the three attacks described in [18] in the single-key setting. For SKINNY-n-n, our model identified three distinguishers leading to attacks with the same complexity, which is dominated by the data complexity (see Fig. 7 in Appendix D). Similarly, for SKINNY-n-$3n$, two distinct attacks with optimal complexity were found. One attack involves 42 round-tweakey bits, while the other involves 43 round-tweakey bits.

4.3 Recovering the Distinguishers of [32] on Midori-128

Midori [1] is a lightweight block cipher designed to minimize energy consumption during execution. It has two versions: Midori-64 (with a 64-bit block size) and Midori-128 (with a 128-bit block size). Since Midori-64 has been fully broken (see [6,16,37]), we focus on Midori-128.

The cipher uses four different 8-bit S-boxes, each defined as follows: a bit permutation p_i, followed by the parallel application of two 4-bit S-boxes, and finally the inverse bit permutation p_i^{-1}. A group of 8 bits entering an 8-bit S-box is referred to as a *cell*, while the cell's bits are divided into two *subcells*, processed by 4-bit S-boxes:

- The **upper subcell** consists of the 4 bits mapped by p_i to positions $\{0, \ldots, 3\}$.
- The **lower subcell** consists of the 4 bits mapped to positions $\{4, \ldots, 7\}$.

The first impossible differential attack on Midori was introduced in 2016 by Chen and Wang [42], using a 6-round distinguisher with two equal differences in the input pattern. Sasaki and Todo [32] later proposed 12 weight-1 distinguishers for 7 rounds of Midori-128. They also demonstrated that no weight-1 distinguishers exist for 8 rounds when the 4-bit S-boxes are treated as arbitrary.

Models. Due to the structured design of the 8-bit S-boxes, we implemented the generator model at the bit level, utilizing an arbitrary S-box model for the underlying 4-bit S-boxes. New zeros were only searched around the **MixColumns** operation, as described in Sect. 3.

The validator model used the same granularity as the generator model. Interestingly, we observed that adding redundant constraints for the inverse **MC** operation (*i.e.* since the matrix is involutive, it means swapping the input and output variables in the inequalities) significantly accelerated the solver—reducing runtime by approximately tenfold.

Results. We used Gurobi's `PoolSearchMode` option to exhaustively search for all ID distinguishers over 7 rounds of `Midori-128`. Without optimization, the model required 8 min to find all the 1,513 candidates, 36 of which were valid ID distinguishers. Recognizing that a complete 4-bit S-box must be inactive to produce an ID distinguisher, we added a constraint requiring at least four new zeros to be deduced from the summary trail. With this optimization, the same 36 distinguishers were identified in under 5 min, involving exactly 1,200 calls to the validator model.

The results are as follows: Among the 36 distinguishers, 12 correspond to the weight-1 distinguishers described in [32]. The remaining 24 are slight variations of these distinguishers.

Let us give more insight about the 12 original distinguishers. For any $i \in \{1, 4, 5, 8, 9, 12\}$, an input pattern where all cells are inactive except the **upper** (resp. **lower**) subcell of cell i is incompatible with an output pattern where all cells are inactive except the **lower** (resp. **upper**) subcell of cell i. Now the additional 24 distinguishers arise from the following observation: for each of the 12 distinguishers, replacing the active subcell in the input (resp. output) pattern with a fully active cell (*i.e.* both subcells active) still results in an impossible differential, provided the change is not applied to both input and output. In summary:

- At the cell level, there are 6 distinct ID patterns. Each pattern activates the same cell in both the input and output patterns.
- For each of these patterns, there are 6 valid subcell activation combinations, all leading to ID distinguishers.

An example of an ID distinguisher with both subcells active in an input cell is shown in Fig. 2.

Finally, the solver required only 2 min to confirm the absence of ID distinguishers over 8 rounds. Specifically, it demonstrated that no activity pattern exists that could lead to the deduction of new inactive cells.

Other kinds of SPNs such that the bit-oriented `PRESENT` and the LS-design low-latency `ARADI` can also be modeled in our framework. We give more details about this modeling in the appendix A and B and will focus here on bit-oriented Feistel networks: AndRX designs such as `SIMON` and ARX designs such as `SPECK`.

4.4 Application to AndRX and ARX Designs

`SIMON` The `SIMON` family of blockciphers is a NSA design introduced in [2]. It is a AndRX design based on Feistel structure. Let us call L^i_j (resp R^i_j) bit i of the left (resp. right) branch entering the round j. Let T^i be the result of the application of the non-linear function on L^i. All the registers have the same size n. Then, the round function works as follows

$$\begin{cases} R^{i+1}_j = L^i_j \\ T^i_j = L^i_{(j+8) \bmod n} L^i_{(j+1) \bmod n} \oplus L^i_{(j+2) \bmod n} \\ L^{i+1}_j = K^i_j \oplus R^i_j \oplus T^i_j. \end{cases}$$

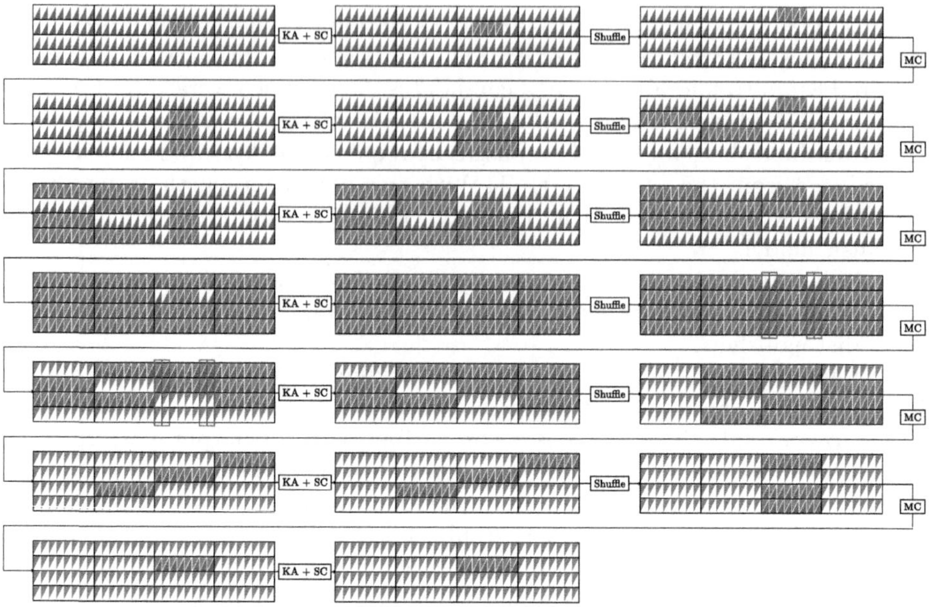

Fig. 2. Example of a new ID distinguisher on 7 rounds of MIDORI-128

SIMON has been the object of much scrutiny since its publication. Regarding impossible differential cryptanalysis, the first attacks were exposed by Boura *et al.* in [10]. Other distinguishers and attacks were manually obtained [12,23,35] and then automatically [14,32]. Note that Sasaki and Todo also proved the absence of impossible differential distinguisher of weight 1 on 12 rounds [32] of SIMON-32. More recently, Zhang *et al.* proved that the length of the known impossible differential distinguishers are optimal, even when considering indirect contradictions [43], but in 2024, Chakraborty *et al.* used their CP tool to improve the previously known attacks by at least one round on all versions [11].

Modeling. SIMON is bit-oriented cipher so is our model. New zeros can be obtained at two places through the round function. First if exactly two differences are null among the 3 bits L_j^{i+1}, R_j^i and T_j^i then the difference in the third one has to be null as well. The corresponding constraints are thus:

$$\begin{cases} L_j^{i+1} + R_j^i + T_j^i \geq z \\ L_j^{i+1} + R_j^i + T_j^i \leq 3 - 2z \end{cases}$$

Figure 3 zooms on the fourth round of a impossible differential distinguisher for SIMON-32 to give an example of the deduction of a new zero. The model detects a new zero around the XOR of bit number 8 of T^4 and R^4. Second, if the difference in $L^i_{(j+8) \bmod n}$ and $L^i_{(j+1) \bmod n}$ are null as well as the difference in either T_j^i or $L^i_{(j+2) \bmod n}$ then the difference in both T_j^i and $L^i_{(j+2) \bmod n}$ is null. This can be modeled by:

$$\begin{cases} L^i_{(j+8) \bmod n} + L^i_{(j+1) \bmod n} \leq 2(1-z) \\ T^i_j + L^i_{(j+2) \bmod n} \geq z \\ T^i_j + L^i_{(j+2) \bmod n} \leq 2 - z \end{cases}$$

Finally, we add a constraint to deal with the rotation invariance of the state by forcing the first bit of either the left or the right branch to be active: $L^0_0 + R^0_0 \geq 1$.

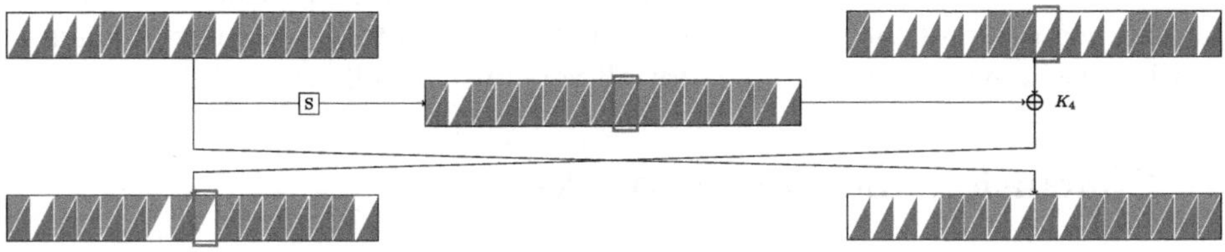

Fig. 3. New zeros in a Feistel Structure like SIMON.

Results. We recovered distinguishers of the same length as the previously known in less than 5 s for each version of `SIMON`. The number of candidates sent to the validator model until finding a valid ID was at most 20. We were also able to prove the absence of impossible differential for larger numbers of rounds in less than an hour on our laptop.

We can also include in our model the key recovery steps. Our modeling is looser than the one of [11] so the complexity bounds are less tight: contrary to [11], we cannot precisely define the filtering bits and therefore preferred to use the naive estimate of c_{in} as $D_{\text{in}} - D_X$ (respectively $c_{out} = D_{\text{out}} - D_Y$). Yet, we still obtain satisfactory results of attacks in a few minutes. For instance, we can reproduce the attack on 19 rounds of `SIMON-32-64` and also find one using fewer key bits (see Fig. 6 in Appendix C.1) for a total complexity of $2^{43.47}$. Similarly, we obtain attacks for all variants of `SIMON` in minutes but we needed to set up a time limit of 15 min in order to cut off long optimality proofs.

`Simeck`. We defer the analysis of `Simeck`, really close to the one of `SIMON` to the Appendix C.2.

`SPECK`. The `SPECK` family of blockciphers has been introduced with SIMON in [2]. It is an ARX design based on Feistel structure. Let us call L^i (resp R^i) the left (resp. right) branch entering the round i. All the registers have the same size n. Then, the round function works as follows

$$\begin{cases} L^{i+1} = ((L^i \lll \alpha) \boxplus R^i) \oplus K^i \\ R^{i+1} = (R^i \ggg \beta) \oplus L^{i+1} \end{cases}$$

Modeling. Obviously we used a bit-based modeling, mostly relying on the *full adder*, the function $f(x, y, c) = (x \oplus y \oplus c, xy \oplus cx \oplus cy)$, which can be used to iteratively compute the modular addition (see [11] for more details). We mainly considered it as an S-box and apply the same modeling techniques than for the other ciphers. The new zeros can be created around the XORs and the full adders. To simplify the problem, we removed the XOR of both branches in the last round since it is a linear operation.

Results. We were able to prove that there are no ID distinguisher on 7 rounds instantaneously and for all versions of `SPECK`. It also took only few seconds to find ID distinguishers on 6 rounds for all versions as well.

5 Conclusion and Future Works

This work mainly brings simplification in the field of automatic search for impossible differential distinguishers and attacks. This simplification comes with two main side advantages. The first is that it is really simple to get familiar with our model and thus we hope that many designers and cryptanalysts will apply it to various cryptographic algorithms. The second improvement is the solving time: a generic solver finds a solution nearly instantaneously for most of the applications we demonstrated.

Throughout our work, we noticed several areas for improvement in our model. The first limit is that we only considered the deduction of new zeros in a fixed position in the generator model. However, other behaviours could indicate a probable impossible differential transition. For example, if the dimension of the set of solutions to a $0/*$ pattern is smaller than the dimension of the pattern, it indicates that some zeros will appear in any instantiation of the pattern. Yet, taking into account this wider class of deduction may lead to too many false candidates flooding the validator model. Moreover, we are also convinced that the key recovery steps of our generator model could be adapted to the probabilistic propagation framework [33]. On a wider perspective, most of the previous works proposed both a model for zero-correlation cryptanalysis and for impossible differential cryptanalysis because of their duality. We did not demonstrate the ability of our model to detect the former but at least for the distinguisher part, it should be a straightforward application using the dual structures of the ciphers.

A Application to the Bit-Oriented Cipher `PRESENT`

`PRESENT` is a 64-bit lightweight blockcipher introduced by Bogdanov *et al.* in [8]. Its round function is composed of a S-box layer followed by a permutation of the state bits and a key addition.

Modeling the Distinguisher. Tezcan [36] provided ID distinguishers on 5 rounds in an arbitrary S-box model and on 6 rounds in the specific S-box model. The linear layer being a permutation, new zeros can only be obtained around an S-box. We applied the algorithm presented in Sect. 3 and found 42 possible patterns leading to new zeros. There is only one case where the deduction of a new zero occurs without completely inactivating the S-box: if we have the pattern $(*00*, *0*0)$ then we can deduce that the first bit of the output difference is actually zero. Regarding the validator model, we decided to do the more complete model possible by encoding the exact DDT in it.

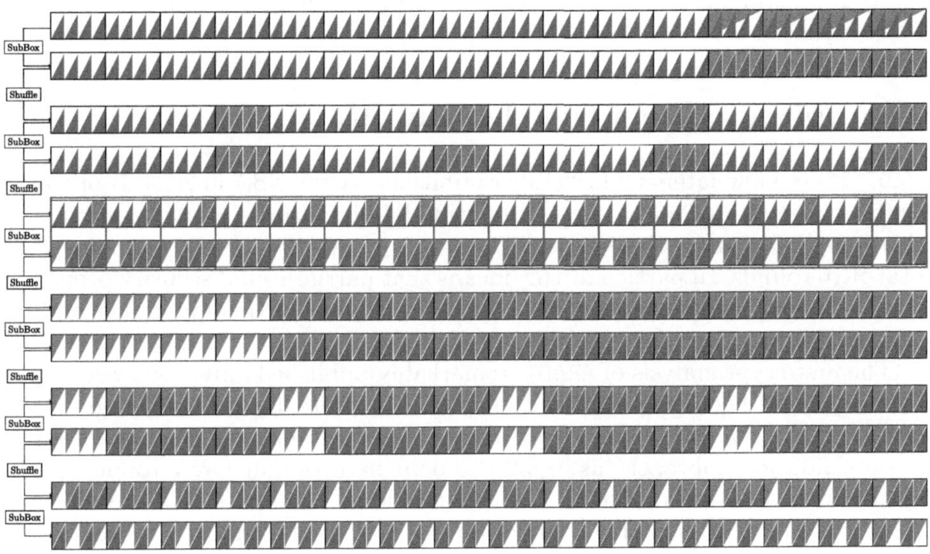

Fig. 4. A heavy ID distinguisher on 6 rounds of `PRESENT` (least significant bit on the left)

We faced our first challenge in reproducing these results without considering the propagation of 1's in the generator model. The main problem is that the 6-round distinguishers requires the transition $(1001) \to (***0)$ through the S-box to be valid within the model. Unfortunately, the transition $(*00*) \to (***0)$ cannot be added to the model since it does not happen with probability one. Hence, there are two choices. The first one is to consider 1's as well is the generator model, making it more complicated. The second option is to artificially allow the transition even though it is wrong and to let the validator model handle it. This is the option we selected. However, we only allowed it in the first S-box layer (note that a similar transition is also valid for S^{-1} and we allowed it in the last S-box layer) to avoid too many false positive for the generator model.

Results. Finding ID distinguishers on 6 rounds is instantaneous. The model decides also in less than one second that there is no ID in 7 rounds. Indeed, it does not find any candidate able to generate a new zero.

Interestingly, we were able to find a 6-round ID distinguisher such that all the S-boxes at the output are active. This heavy ID distinguisher is depicted in Fig. 4. It contradicts one of the heuristic commonly used in the search of Impossible Differential distinguisher that the longest IDs are caused by pairs with very few active bits because otherwise inactive values would not be able to propagate with probability one to the central rounds of the distinguisher. In particular, we emphasize that the result of Sun *et al.* [34] about the reduction of any ID distinguisher to a low weight distinguisher only applies to arbitrary S-box models.

B Application to a New Design ARADI

ARADI [15] is a low-latency blockcipher published by the NSA in 2024. It processes 128-bit blocks using 256-bit keys. An optimal 4-bit S-Box is used in combination with four different involutive linear layers Λ_i alternating every 4 rounds for a total of 16 rounds. In particular this means that partial-round security properties have to be evaluated regarding the number of rounds of this toy cipher and the index of the first linear layer used.

The first cryptanalysis of ARADI, remarkably published only a few weeks after the design, has been provided by the automatic tool CLAASP [4]. It gives first results against various types of attacks. Regarding impossible differentials, it uses a validation approach (as in [32]) to demonstrate that any 7-round pattern leading from 1 active nibble to 1 active nibble is an impossible differential. It seems that it only considers partial-round security beginning at round 0. A recent preprint presents a full round related-key Impossible Boomerang attack [20]. However it seems unverified as it needs 2^{130} data.

We applied our framework at the nibble based on of ARADI. We were able to obtain the first impossible differential attack against 13 rounds represented in Fig. 5. New zeros are obtained on the equations of the linear layer: sums of 4 nibbles having to be zeroed. Equations leading to new zeros are represented by nibbles being framed by the same color. We obtain $D_{\text{in}} = 4 \times 9 = 36$, $D_{\text{out}} = 4 \times 21 = 84$, $D_{\text{X}} = D_{\text{Y}} = 4$ and $|k_{\text{in}} \cup k_{\text{out}}| = 4 \times (16 + 39) = 220$. Finally, we get $c_{\text{in}} + c_{\text{out}} = 112$ and thus a data complexity of $c_{\text{in}} + c_{\text{out}} - 0.53 + n + 1 - |D_{\text{in}}| - |D_{\text{out}}| + g = 121.47$ (in log2) and a time complexity of $2^{220,47}$. Note that the last round does not completely appear in the figure as the missing step (S and Λ) will not change the dimension of the outer space.

The time complexity of the best 13-round attacks we obtain for other offsets are $2^{224.47}$ (for offset 1), $2^{252.47}$ (for offset 2) and $2^{240.47}$ (for offset 3). We did not found any attack on 14 rounds.

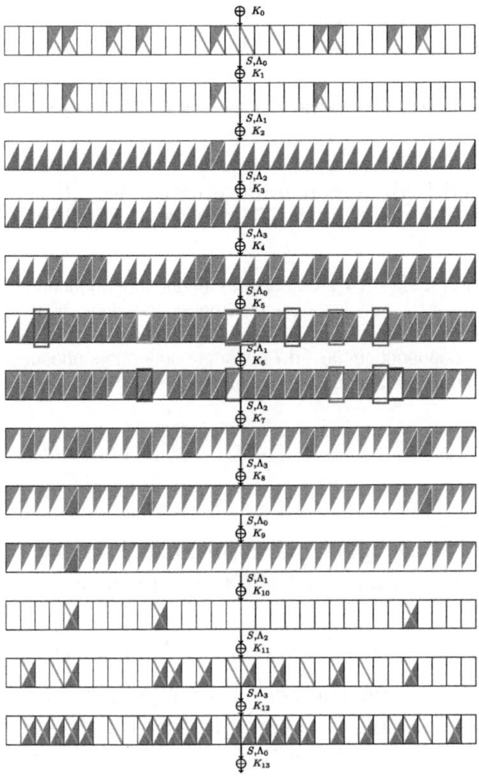

Fig. 5. The first ID attack on 13 rounds of `ARADI` beginning at round 0. Cells framed in the same colours are involved in the same deduction. The striped cells are the *needed* cells of the key recovery steps.

C More Results on the AndRX SIMON and Simeck

C.1 SIMON

We also ran the solver with the objective to find impossible differential of heavy weights. We used the technique from Sect. 3.3 to deduce clusters from these distinguishers. For exemple, the distinguisher on 11 rounds of `SIMON-32`

$$0000000000000000\ 1000000100000010 \not\rightarrow 1000000000000010\ 0000000000000000$$

is in fact the convex hull of the following impossible differential distinguisher cluster containing 16 characteristics

$$0000000000000000 * 0000001000000 * 0 \nrightarrow *0000000000000 * 00000000000000000.$$

Similarly, we obtained high dimensional clusters for all versions of `SIMON` in few seconds. The bigger one deals with 19 rounds of `SIMON-128` and has dimension 48:

$$\begin{array}{c}
0*0*000****00*****0********0000000000000000000000000000000000000 \\
00**0***************1*00000000000000000000000000000*0*000* \\
\not\downarrow \\
0000000000000000000000000*0*0000000000000000000000000000000000000 \\
0000000000000000000000000000000000000000000000000000000000000000
\end{array}$$

C.2 SIMECK

The `Simeck` family of blockciphers is an optimized version of `SIMON` introduced in [41]. It is structurally similar to `SIMON` except it uses a different non linear function :

$$T_j^i = L_j^i L_{(j+5) \bmod n}^i \oplus L_{(j+1) \bmod n}^i.$$

As for `SIMON`, we focused on the search of new zeros around the XOR of the Feistel structure and reduced the search space by forcing the first bit of either the left or the right branch to be active in the input pattern.

The designers of `Simeck` provided in their security analysis first estimations on the number of rounds that could be attacked by impossible differential distinguishers. However, it was only focused on direct contradiction between the forward and the backward trail. These attacks were later improved using indirect contradictions found manually ([30]) or automatically ([11,43]).

We did the same modeling as for `SIMON`, with only the slight modification of the rotation coefficients. We tried two approaches to generate distinguishers. The first one consists in searching for candidates with a maximum number of newly deduced inactived cells in the generator model. Indeed, intuitively, these candidates will lead to impossible transitions with high probability and thus the validator model will have to verify less candidates. Remarkably, we recovered distinguishers of the same length than the previously known in seconds without the burden of the modelisation of the propagation of deductions usually needed to find indirect contradiction. We are also able to prove the absence of impossible differential for larger number of rounds in less than a minute. The other approach is to consider heavy weight candidates. Indeed, as seen in the section about SIMON, they are associated to big clusters of candidates. This approach takes longer but most of the solving time is used to prove the optimality of the solutions. The best solution is indeed found in a few seconds so the search could have been stopped before the end of the process. The performances of the search are given in Table 2.

Table 2. Performances of the search for distinguishers on Simeck

Version	r_D	Generated candidates (Valid ones)	Time	Deduced inactive cells	Active bits
Simeck-32	11	7 (2)	0.8s	6	2
	12	805 (0)	37s	-	-
Simeck-48	15	8 (1)	1s	4	2
	16	22 (0)	2.7s	-	-
Simeck-64	17	25 (1)	5s	6	2
	18	184 (0)	30s	-	-

(a) Objective function : maximize the number of deduced inactive cells

Version	r_D	Generated candidates (Valid ones)	Time (Best solution)	Deduced inactive cells	Active bits
Simeck-32	11	39 (2)	2.6 s (2s)	3	11
Simeck-48	15	23 (2)	2.6 s (0s)	4	3
Simeck-64	17	5292 (1)	630s (0s)	4	6

(b) Objective function : Maximize the number of active bits

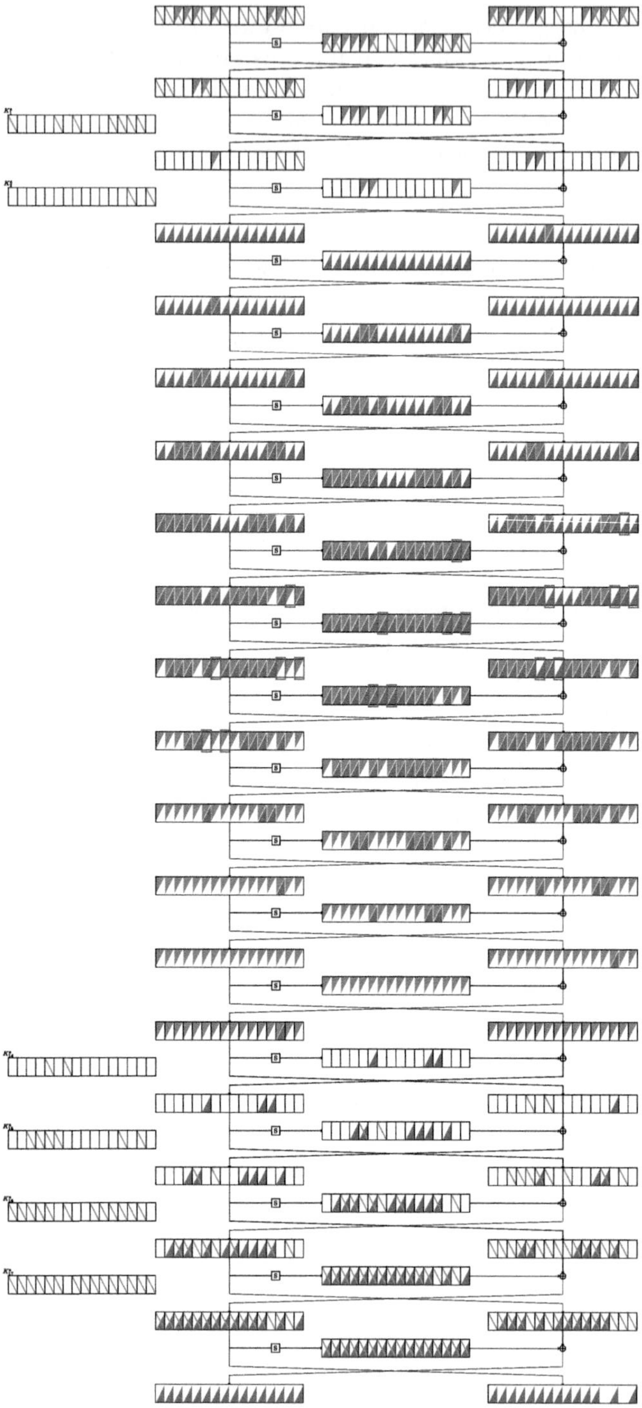

Fig. 6. A more efficient attack on 19 rounds of SIMON-32-64 than [11]. The striped cells are the *needed* cells of the key recovery steps.

D Attacks on 17 Rounds SKINNY-N-N

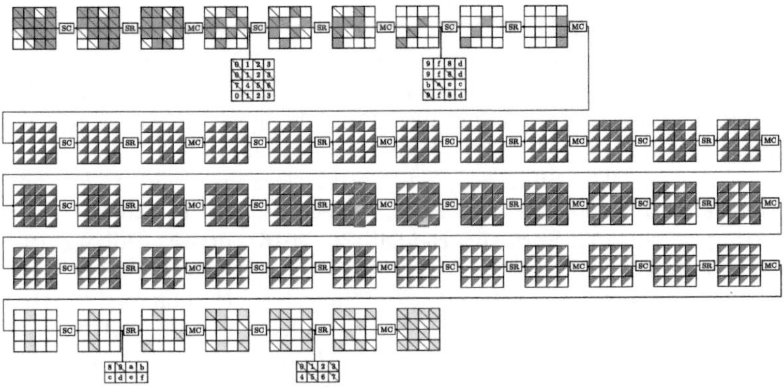

(a) $|k_{in} \bigcup k_{out}| = 10c$

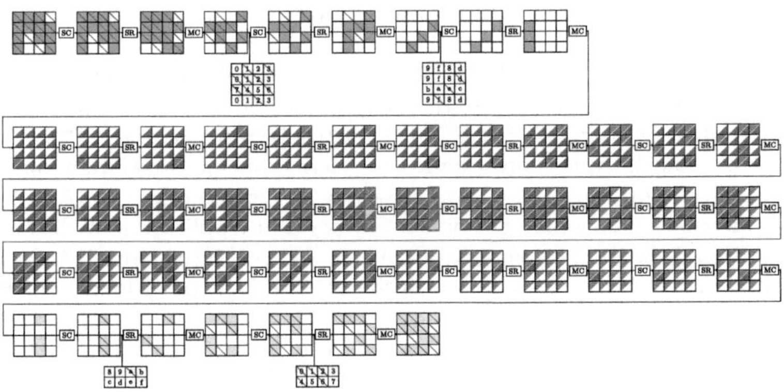

(b) $|k_{in} \bigcup k_{out}| = 11c$

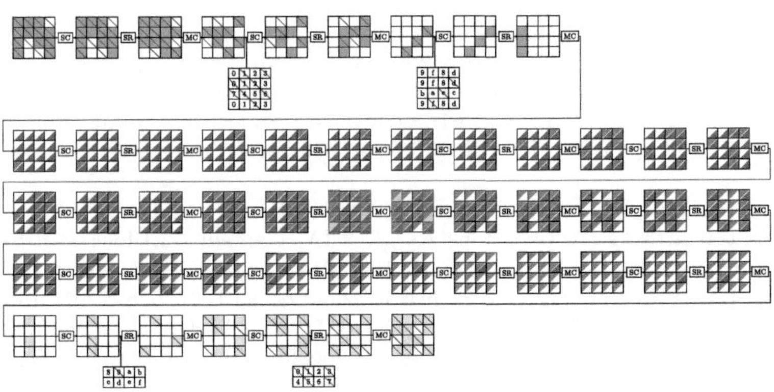

(c) $|k_{in} \bigcup k_{out}| = 12c$

Fig. 7. Three equivalent attacks on 17-round SKINNY-n-n. Green and yellow cells are the cells involved in the key recovery steps. In the three cases, they determine $c_{in} = c_{out} = 7c - c = 6c$.

References

1. Banik, S., et al.: MIDORI: a block cipher for low energy. In: Iwata, T., Cheon, J.H. (eds.) ASIACRYPT 2015, Part II. LNCS, vol. 9453, pp. 411–436. Springer, Heidelberg (2015). https://doi.org/10.1007/978-3-662-48800-3_17
2. Beaulieu, R., Shors, D., Smith, J., Treatman-Clark, S., Weeks, B., Wingers, L.: The SIMON and SPECK families of lightweight block ciphers. Cryptology ePrint Archive, Report 2013/404 (2013). https://eprint.iacr.org/2013/404
3. Beierle, C., et al.: The SKINNY family of block ciphers and its low-latency variant MANTIS. In: Robshaw, M., Katz, J. (eds.) CRYPTO 2016, Part II. LNCS, vol. 9815, pp. 123–153. Springer, Heidelberg (2016). https://doi.org/10.1007/978-3-662-53008-5_5
4. Bellini, E., Formenti, M., Gérault, D., Grados, J., Hambitzer, A., Huang, Y.J., Huynh, P., Rachidi, M., Rohit, R., Tiwari, S.K.: Claasping ARADI: automated analysis of the ARADI block cipher. In: Mukhopadhyay, S., Stanica, P. (eds.) Progress in Cryptology - INDOCRYPT 2024 - 25th International Conference on Cryptology in India, Chennai, India, 18-21 December 2024, Proceedings, Part II. LNCS, vol. 15496, pp. 90–113. Springer (2024). https://doi.org/10.1007/978-3-031-80311-6_5
5. Bellini, E., Huynh, P., Gerault, D., Visconti, A., Piccoli, A.D., Pelizzola, S.: Impossible differential automation: Model generation and new techniques. Cryptology ePrint Archive, Paper 2024/1998 (2024). https://eprint.iacr.org/2024/1998
6. Beyne, T.: Block cipher invariants as eigenvectors of correlation matrices. In: Peyrin, T., Galbraith, S.D. (eds.) Advances in Cryptology - ASIACRYPT 2018 - 24th International Conference on the Theory and Application of Cryptology and Information Security, Brisbane, QLD, Australia, 2-6 December 2018, Proceedings, Part I. LNCS, vol. 11272, pp. 3–31. Springer (2018). https://doi.org/10.1007/978-3-030-03326-2_1
7. Biham, E., Biryukov, A., Shamir, A.: Cryptanalysis of Skipjack reduced to 31 rounds using impossible differentials. In: Stern, J. (ed.) EUROCRYPT 1999. LNCS, vol. 1592, pp. 12–23. Springer, Heidelberg (1999). https://doi.org/10.1007/3-540-48910-X_2
8. Bogdanov, A., et al.: PRESENT: an ultra-lightweight block cipher. In: Paillier, P., Verbauwhede, I. (eds.) CHES 2007. LNCS, vol. 4727, pp. 450–466. Springer, Heidelberg (2007). https://doi.org/10.1007/978-3-540-74735-2_31
9. Boura, C., Lallemand, V., Naya-Plasencia, M., Suder, V.: Making the impossible possible. J. Cryptol. **31**(1), 101–133 (2017). https://doi.org/10.1007/s00145-016-9251-7
10. Boura, C., Naya-Plasencia, M., Suder, V.: Scrutinizing and improving impossible differential attacks: Applications to CLEFIA, Camellia, LBlock and Simon. In: Sarkar, P., Iwata, T. (eds.) ASIACRYPT 2014, Part I. LNCS, vol. 8873, pp. 179–199. Springer, Heidelberg (2014). https://doi.org/10.1007/978-3-662-45611-8_10
11. Chakraborty, D., Hadipour, H., Nguyen, P.H., Eichlseder, M.: Finding complete impossible differential attacks on andrx ciphers and efficient distinguishers for ARX designs. IACR Trans. Symmetric Cryptol. **2024**(3), 84–176 (2024). https://doi.org/10.46586/tosc.v2024.i3.84-176
12. Chen, Z., Wang, N., Wang, X.: Impossible differential cryptanalysis of reduced round SIMON. Cryptology ePrint Archive, Report 2015/286 (2015). https://eprint.iacr.org/2015/286

13. Derbez, P.: Note on impossible differential attacks. In: Peyrin, T. (ed.) FSE 2016. LNCS, vol. 9783, pp. 416–427. Springer, Heidelberg (2016). https://doi.org/10.1007/978-3-662-52993-5_21
14. Derbez, P., Fouque, P.A.: Automatic search of meet-in-the-middle and impossible differential attacks. In: Robshaw, M., Katz, J. (eds.) CRYPTO 2016, Part II. LNCS, vol. 9815, pp. 157–184. Springer, Berlin, Heidelberg (2016). https://doi.org/10.1007/978-3-662-53008-5_6
15. Greene, P., Motley, M., Weeks, B.: ARADI and LLAMA: low-latency cryptography for memory encryption. IACR Cryptol. ePrint Arch, p. 1240 (2024). https://eprint.iacr.org/2024/1240
16. Guo, J., Jean, J., Nikolic, I., Qiao, K., Sasaki, Y., Sim, S.M.: Invariant subspace attack against midori64 and the resistance criteria for s-box designs. IACR Trans. Symmetric Cryptol. **2016**(1), 33–56 (2016). https://doi.org/10.13154/tosc.v2016.i1.33-56
17. Hadipour, H., Gerhalter, S., Sadeghi, S., Eichlseder, M.: Improved search for integral, impossible differential and zero-correlation attacks application to Ascon, ForkSKINNY, SKINNY, MANTIS, PRESENT and QARMAv2. IACR Trans. Symm. Cryptol. **2024**(1), 234–325 (2024). https://doi.org/10.46586/tosc.v2024.i1.234-325
18. Hadipour, H., Sadeghi, S., Eichlseder, M.: Finding the impossible: Automated search for full impossible-differential, zero-correlation, and integral attacks. In: Hazay, C., Stam, M. (eds.) EUROCRYPT 2023, Part IV. LNCS, vol. 14007, pp. 128–157. Springer, Cham (2023). https://doi.org/10.1007/978-3-031-30634-1_5
19. Hu, K., Peyrin, T., Wang, M.: Finding all impossible differentials when considering the DDT. In: Smith, B., Wu, H. (eds.) SAC 2022. LNCS, vol. 13742, pp. 285–305. Springer, Cham (2024). https://doi.org/10.1007/978-3-031-58411-4_13
20. Hu, X., Jiao, L.: Pre-sieve, partial-guess, and accurate estimation: Full-round related-key impossible boomerang attack on ARADI. Cryptology ePrint Archive, Paper 2025/056 (2025). https://eprint.iacr.org/2025/056
21. Kim, J., Hong, S., Sung, J., Lee, C., Lee, S.: Impossible differential cryptanalysis for block cipher structures. In: Johansson, T., Maitra, S. (eds.) INDOCRYPT 2003. LNCS, vol. 2904, pp. 82–96. Springer, Heidelberg (2003). https://doi.org/10.1007/978-3-540-24582-7_6
22. Knudsen, L.: Deal-A 128-bit block cipher. Complexity **258**(2), 216 (1998)
23. Kondo, K., Sasaki, Y., Iwata, T.: On the design rationale of simon block cipher: Integral attacks and impossible differential attacks against simon variants. In: Manulis, M., Sadeghi, A.R., Schneider, S. (eds.) ACNS 16International Conference on Applied Cryptography and Network Security. LNCS, vol. 9696, pp. 518–536. Springer, Cham (2016). https://doi.org/10.1007/978-3-319-39555-5_28
24. Leurent, G., Pernot, C.: New representations of the AES key schedule. In: Canteaut, A., Standaert, F.X. (eds.) EUROCRYPT 2021, Part I. LNCS, vol. 12696, pp. 54–84. Springer, Cham (2021). https://doi.org/10.1007/978-3-030-77870-5_3
25. Liu, G., Ghosh, M., Song, L.: Security analysis of SKINNY under related-tweakey settings (long paper). IACR Trans. Symm. Cryptol. **2017**(3), 37–72 (2017). https://doi.org/10.13154/tosc.v2017.i3.37-72
26. Luo, Y., Lai, X., Wu, Z., Gong, G.: A unified method for finding impossible differentials of block cipher structures. Inf. Sci. **263**, 211–220 (2014). https://doi.org/10.1016/j.ins.2013.08.051
27. Mala, H., Dakhilalian, M., Rijmen, V., Modarres-Hashemi, M.: Improved impossible differential cryptanalysis of 7-round AES-128. In: Gong, G., Gupta, K.C. (eds.) INDOCRYPT 2010. LNCS, vol. 6498, pp. 282–291. Springer, Berlin, Heidelberg (2010). https://doi.org/10.1007/978-3-642-17401-8_20

28. McCluskey, E.J.: Minimization of Boolean functions. Bell Syst. Tech. J. **35**(6), 1417–1444 (1956)
29. Qin, L., Dong, X., Wang, X., Jia, K., Liu, Y.: Automated search oriented to key recovery on ciphers with linear key schedule. IACR Trans. Symm. Cryptol. **2021**(2), 249–291 (2021). https://doi.org/10.46586/tosc.v2021.i2.249-291
30. Sadeghi, S., Bagheri, N.: Improved zero-correlation and impossible differential cryptanalysis of reduced-round SIMECK block cipher. IET Inf. Secur. **12**(4), 314–325 (2018). https://doi.org/10.1049/iet-ifs.2016.0590
31. Sadeghi, S., Bagheri, N.: Security analysis of SIMECK block cipher against related-key impossible differential. Inf. Process. Lett. **147**, 14–21 (2019)
32. Sasaki, Y., Todo, Y.: New impossible differential search tool from design and cryptanalysis aspects - revealing structural properties of several ciphers. In: Coron, J.S., Nielsen, J.B. (eds.) EUROCRYPT 2017, Part III. LNCS, vol. 10212, pp. 185–215. Springer, Cham (2017). https://doi.org/10.1007/978-3-319-56617-7_7
33. Song, L., Yang, Q., Chen, Y., Hu, L., Weng, J.: Probabilistic extensions: a one-step framework for finding rectangle attacks and beyond. In: Joye, M., Leander, G. (eds.) EUROCRYPT 2024, Part I. LNCS, vol. 14651, pp. 339–367. Springer, Cham (2024). https://doi.org/10.1007/978-3-031-58716-0_12
34. Sun, B., Liu, M., Guo, J., Rijmen, V., Li, R.: Provable security evaluation of structures against impossible differential and zero correlation linear cryptanalysis. In: Fischlin, M., Coron, J.S. (eds.) EUROCRYPT 2016, Part I. LNCS, vol. 9665, pp. 196–213. Springer, Berlin, Heidelberg (2016). https://doi.org/10.1007/978-3-662-49890-3_8
35. Sun, S., et al.: Constructing mixed-integer programming models whose feasible region is exactly the set of all valid differential characteristics of SIMON. Cryptology ePrint Archive, Report 2015/122 (2015). https://eprint.iacr.org/2015/122
36. Tezcan, C.: Improbable differential attacks on present using undisturbed bits. J. Comput. Appl. Math. **259**, 503–511 (2014). https://doi.org/10.1016/j.cam.2013.06.023
37. Todo, Y., Leander, G., Sasaki, Y.: Nonlinear invariant attack - practical attack on full SCREAM, iSCREAM, and Midori64. In: Cheon, J.H., Takagi, T. (eds.) ASIACRYPT 2016, Part II. LNCS, vol. 10032, pp. 3–33. Springer, Berlin, Heidelberg (2016). https://doi.org/10.1007/978-3-662-53890-6_1
38. Tolba, M., Abdelkhalek, A., Youssef, A.M.: Impossible differential cryptanalysis of reduced-round SKINNY. In: Joye, M., Nitaj, A. (eds.) AFRICACRYPT 17. LNCS, vol. 10239, pp. 117–134. Springer, Cham (2017). https://doi.org/10.1007/978-3-319-57339-7_7
39. Wu, S., Wang, M.: Automatic search of truncated impossible differentials for word-oriented block ciphers. In: Galbraith, S.D., Nandi, M. (eds.) INDOCRYPT 2012. LNCS, vol. 7668, pp. 283–302. Springer, Berlin, Heidelberg (2012). https://doi.org/10.1007/978-3-642-34931-7_17
40. Yang, D., Qi, W., Chen, H.: Impossible differential attacks on the SKINNY family of block ciphers. IET Inf. Secur. **11**(6), 377–385 (2017). https://doi.org/10.1049/iet-ifs.2016.0488
41. Yang, G., Zhu, B., Suder, V., Aagaard, M.D., Gong, G.: The SIMECK family of lightweight block ciphers. In: Güneysu, T., Handschuh, H. (eds.) CHES 2015. LNCS, vol. 9293, pp. 307–329. Springer, Berlin, Heidelberg (2015). https://doi.org/10.1007/978-3-662-48324-4_16

42. Zhan, C., Xiaoyun, W.: Impossible differential cryptanalysis of MIDORI. Cryptology ePrint Archive, Report 2016/535 (2016). https://eprint.iacr.org/2016/535
43. Zhang, Please check and confirm if the inserted citations of Fig. 3 is correct. Please check and confirm if the inserted citations of Fig. 3 is correct. K., et al.: Impossible differential cryptanalysis and a security evaluation framework for AND-RX ciphers. IEEE Trans. Inf. Theory **70**(8), 6025–6040 (2024). https://doi.org/10.1109/TIT.2023.3292241

Impossible Differentials Automation: Model Generation and New Techniques

Emanuele Bellini[1], Alessandro De Piccoli[2], David Gerault[1], Paul Huynh[1], Simone Pelizzola[2](✉), and Andrea Visconti[2]

[1] Technology Innovation Institute, Abu Dhabi, UAE
{emanuele.bellini,david.gerault,paul.huynh}@tii.ae
[2] Università degli Studi di Milano, Milan, Italy
{alessandro.depiccoli,simone.pelizzola,andrea.visconti}@unimi.it

Abstract. In this paper, we propose new techniques for impossible differential cryptanalysis. The first one is a *hybrid* model for finding distinguishers on block ciphers that have both bit-oriented and word-oriented components; we apply this model to LBlock, and build an improbable differential for 18 rounds, improving over the previous 17-round results. Our second model builds impossible differential attacks for ARX ciphers automatically, including, for the first time, hash table based optimizations into the complexity evaluation of the attack. We apply this model to the HIGHT block cipher, and improve complexity of the state-of-the-art 27-round attack. Finally, we include these techniques in the cryptanalysis tool CLAASP, building the needed decryption functions automatically from the block cipher's graph representation; this inversion technique is of independent interest to other similar libraries, such as TAGADA.

Keywords: Impossible differential · LBlock · HIGHT · CLAASP · Automated cryptanalysis

1 Introduction

Block ciphers are a cornerstone of many secure applications, and serve as building blocks for various symmetric primitives; as such, their analysis is one of the most fundamental research areas in symmetric cryptography. A key step in the design of a new block cipher is evaluating its resistance to known cryptanalysis techniques, such as differential attacks, introduced in the late 1980s by Biham and Shamir [7], which evaluates the probability of a *differential* $\delta \rightarrow \gamma$ through the cipher, that is, the probability that a pair of plaintexts with XOR difference δ is encrypted to a pair of ciphertexts with XOR difference γ.

In this paper, we focus on impossible differential cryptanalysis [6,21], the study of *impossible differentials*, which no input satisfies. Such distinguishers allow invalid key guesses to be discarded, reducing the space for exhaustive search. This remains the best known attack on the cipher Camellia [9].

The search for differentials, possible or not, is a challenging problem, due to the inherent combinatorial explosion resulting from the probabilistic aspect of

C. Boura et al. (Eds.): SAC 2025, LNCS 16207, pp. 144–175, 2026.
https://doi.org/10.1007/978-3-032-10536-3_6

differential transitions through the building blocks of a cipher. In recent years, the community has put more focus towards generic tools, where the search process is automated through a dedicated solver, significantly simplifying the process. Libraries like TAGADA and CLAASP are now commonly used to analyze ciphers, given their representation in a specific language or format. For example, CLAASP was used to automatically evaluate the NSA's ARADI cipher shortly after its release, despite the lack of an official security analysis [3].

In this paper, we propose two new impossible differential models, as well as their automation in the CLAASP framework[1]. Our contributions are as follows.

- **Automation -** We extend CLAASP with a technique to automatically build the decryption function of a block cipher represented as graph; this technique can be adapted for libraries that use a similar representation, such as TAGADA. Using this automated inversion, we include the state of the art impossible differential search techniques from [16] to CLAASP, along with our new models in CLAASP.
- **Hybrid model -** We propose *hybrid* model that combines the cell-wise properties of [29] and the bit-wise granularity of [10] and [16]. Our hybrid model supports key-dependent probabilistic transitions and detects more incompatibilities than standard truncated models, by leveraging the impossible differential clustering effect.
- **Improved LBlock Cryptanalysis -** Using this model, we show that the 17-round improbable differential on LBlock presented in [10] is invalid and we exhibit the first 18-round *improbable* differential, valid for about $2^{-0.83}$ of the key space.
- **Hash Table Modeling -** We extend the automatic technique of [16] to integrate the use of hash-tables into the overall attack cost.
- **Improved HIGHT Cryptanalysis -** Using this model, we build a 27-round key recovery attack with time complexity $2^{118.9}$ and data complexity 2^{55}, improving the state-of-the-art complexity from $2^{120.58}$ time and $2^{59.3}$ data. Notably, our technique fully automates the highly sophisticated use of multiple hash tables to improve the attack complexity.

2 Automatic Impossible Differential Search Tools

Let $E : \mathbb{F}_2^n \times \mathbb{F}_2^k \rightarrow \mathbb{F}_2^n$ be a block cipher. An *impossible differential* for E is a pair of differences δ, γ, such that $E_K(X) \oplus E_K(X \oplus \delta) = \gamma$ never holds.

In differential cryptanalysis, the differential propagation rules associated with each operation of the cipher are used iteratively to build a sequence of transitions forming a *differential trail* from δ to γ. Impossible differentials are identified by proving that no such trail exists.

Since the introduction of Mixed Integer Linear Program (MILP) models for differential cryptanalysis [24], declarative techniques from the AI and operational

---

[1] https://github.com/Crypto-TII/claasp/blob/main/claasp/cipher_modules/models.

research communities have become the tool of choice for similar problems. In these frameworks, the differential propagation rules are encoded into a model, defined by *variables* and *constraints*: Boolean CNF formulas for SAT, linear inequalities for MILP, and generic constraints for CP. The model is then given to a specialized solver.

Two independent works by Sasaki and Todo [28] and Cui et al. [13] propose to find impossible differentials fixing the input and output difference of an MILP differential model, and checking the existence of a trail; a negative answer indicates an impossible differential. This method has the advantage of making no assumption on the type of contradiction, but is inherently limited by the size of the subspace of input and output differences that can be enumerated.

Alternatively, the contradiction can be modeled explicitly by encoding deterministic propagation rules in the forward and backwards direction and applying a miss-in-the-middle approach, requiring a contradiction between the reached intermediate states. This technique shifts the problem from proving unsatisfiability to proving satisfiability, removing the need for explicit enumeration. In the following section, we briefly review miss-in-the-middle approaches, focusing on the operations that are used in the ciphers we study.

Sun et al. [29]. In [29], Sun et al. propose a CP-based model for the deterministic propagation of truncated differences in cell-oriented ciphers. Their tool enumerates forward truncated trails $\Delta_{in_0} \rightarrow \Delta_{out_0}$ and backward truncated trails $\Delta_{out_1} \leftarrow \Delta_{in_1}$. Incompatibility between Δ_{out_0} and Δ_{out_1} is then verified outside the CP model.

Variables. Consider $\Delta X = (\Delta X_0, \Delta X_1, \ldots \Delta X_{m-1})$, the difference of the internal state X of size $m \cdot s$ bits, with $X_i \in \mathbb{F}_2^s$. For each cell difference ΔX_1, two variables are introduced: $\delta X_i \in \{0, 1, 2, 3\}$ represents the differential pattern of ΔX_i and $\zeta X_i \in \{-2, -1, 0, \ldots, 2^{s-1}\}$ represents the actual value of ΔX_i:

$$\delta X_i = \begin{cases} 0 & \text{if } \Delta X_i = 0\,(Z) \\ 1 & \text{if } \Delta X_i \text{ is nonzero and fixed } (N) \\ 2 & \text{if } \Delta X_i \text{ is nonzero } (N^*) \\ 3 & \text{if } \Delta X_i \text{ is unknown } (U) \end{cases} \qquad \zeta X_i \in \begin{cases} \{0\} & \text{if } \delta X_i = 0 \\ \{1, \ldots, 2^{s-1}\} & \text{if } \delta X_i = 1 \\ \{-1\} & \text{if } \delta X_i = 2 \\ \{-2\} & \text{if } \delta X_i = 3 \end{cases}$$

Constraints.

- For the **XOR** operation $Y = X_0 \oplus X_1$, the differential patterns satisfy:

$$\begin{aligned} &\text{if } \delta X_0 + \delta X_1 > 2 \text{ then } \delta Y 3 \text{ and } \zeta Y - 2 \\ &\text{elseif } \delta X_0 + \delta X_1 = 1 \text{ then } \delta Y 1 \text{ and } \zeta Y \zeta X_0 + \zeta X_1 \\ &\text{elseif } \delta X_0 = \delta X_1 = 0 \text{ then } \delta Y 0 \text{ and } \zeta Y 0 \\ &\text{elseif } \zeta X_0 + \zeta X_1 < 0 \text{ then } \delta Y 2 \text{ and } \zeta Y - 1 \\ &\text{elseif } \zeta X_0 = \zeta X_1 \text{ then } \delta Y 0 \text{ and } \zeta Y 0 \\ &\text{else } \delta Y 1 \text{ and } \zeta Y \zeta X_0 \oplus \zeta X_1 \text{ endif} \end{aligned}$$

- For the bijective **S-box** application $Y = S(X)$, the patterns satisfy:

$$\delta Y 1 \text{ and } \delta X + \delta Y \{0, 3, 4, 6\} \text{ and } \delta Y \delta X \text{ and } \delta Y \delta X \leq 1$$

Cao et al. [10]**.** Cao et al. extended Sun et al.'s technique to bit-oriented ciphers. Their MILP model relies on *undisturbed differential bits*, a concept previously defined by Teczan [30]. For an input difference Δ_{in}, an output bit Δ_{out_i} is said to be *undisturbed* if its value is deterministically fixed by Δ_{in}; such bits play a valuable role in identifying bit-level incompatibilities.

Variables. Consider $\Delta X = (\Delta X_0, \Delta X_1, \ldots \Delta X_{n-1})$, the difference of the internal state X of size n bits. Each bit of the state is associated with a variable $\delta X_i \in \{0, 1, 2\}$ that represents the value of ΔX_i:

$$\delta X_i = \begin{cases} 0 & \text{if } \Delta X_i = 0 \\ 1 & \text{if } \Delta X_i = 1 \\ 2 & \text{if } \Delta X_i \text{ is unknown} \end{cases}$$

Constraints.

- For the **XOR** operation $Y = X_0 \oplus X_1$, the differential patterns satisfy:

$$\begin{aligned} &\text{if } \delta X_0 = 2 \text{ or } \delta X_1 = 2 \text{ then } \delta Y 2 \\ &\text{else } \delta Y \delta X_0 \oplus \delta X_1 \text{ endif} \end{aligned}$$

- For the **Modular Addition** operation $Z = X \boxplus Y$, where $X = (x_{n-1}, \ldots, x_0)$, $Y = (y_{n-1}, \ldots, y_0)$ and $Z = (z_{n-1}, \ldots, z_0)$, the differential patterns satisfy:

$$\begin{aligned} &\delta z_0 = \delta x_0 \oplus \delta y_0,\ c_0 = f_1(\delta x_0, \delta y_0) \\ &\delta z_1 = \delta x_1 \oplus \delta y_1 \oplus c_0,\ c_1 = f_2(\delta x_1, \delta y_1, c_0) \\ &\vdots \\ &\delta z_{n-2} = \delta x_{n-2} \oplus \delta y_{n-2} \oplus c_{n-3},\ c_{n-2} = f_2(\delta x_{n-2}, \delta y_{n-2}, c_{n-3}) \\ &\delta z_{n-1} = \delta x_{n-1} \oplus \delta y_{n-1} \oplus c_{n-2} \end{aligned}$$

$$\text{where } f_1(x, y) = \begin{cases} 0 & \text{if } x + y = 0 \\ 2 & \text{otherwise} \end{cases}, \quad f_2(x, y, c) = \begin{cases} 0 & \text{if } x + y + c = 0 \\ 2 & \text{otherwise.} \end{cases}$$

- For the **S-box** application $Y = S(X)$, where $X = (x_{n-1}, \ldots, x_0)$, and $Y = (y_{m-1}, \ldots, y_0)$, the DDT restricted to undisturbed bits must be encoded. For each input difference ΔX, let us consider the set $\mathcal{P}_{\Delta X}$ of undisturbed bits positions of S under ΔX. For p in $\mathcal{P}_{\Delta X}$, we denote by b_p the undisturbed bit value at position p of the output, that is, $\Delta y_p = b_p$. If $\mathcal{P}_{\Delta X} \neq \emptyset$ then

$\delta X = (\delta X_{n-1}, \ldots, \delta X_0)$ propagates to the output difference pattern $\delta Y = (\delta Y_{m-1}, \ldots, \delta Y_0)$, where

$$\delta Y_i = \begin{cases} b_i & \text{if } i \in \mathcal{P}_{\Delta X} \\ 2 & \text{otherwise.} \end{cases}$$

In all the other cases, the output is all unknown: $(\delta Y_{m-1}, \ldots, \delta Y_0) = (2)_{i=0}^{m-1}$.

Limitations. In this model, if a nonzero input does not produce any undisturbed bits, an unknown value is assigned to the output. For bijective operations, this results in the loss of crucial information, as the output is guaranteed to be nonzero. Furthermore, the method requires fixing the input patterns, which represents a regression compared to the approach of [29]. Finally, some results in the paper appear to be incorrect, indicating potential issues in the model or its implementation; these are discussed in Subsect. 5.2.

Hadipour et al. [17]**.** `Zero` is a tool developed by Hadipour et al. for identifying impossible differential, zero-correlation and integral attacks on block ciphers. Like the approach in [29], it formulates the differential propagations as a constraint optimization problem. However, in this case, the forward and backward trail searches are integrated into a single unified model. The encoding is the one employed in [29] and thus we refer to Sect. 2 for the detailed definitions of variables and constraints. A key strength of this approach is that the tool additionally gives the time complexity of the corresponding key recovery, allowing to find full impossible differential attacks; however, it is limited to word-oriented constructions and the number of rounds forward and backward must be specified in advance.

Hadipour et al. [16]**.** Earlier this year, Hadipour et al. released `Zeroplus`, an improvement of `Zero` [17]. This updated version extends the tool to weakly aligned primitives by including bit-wise propagations for the branching, XOR and S-box operations, with the inclusion of undisturbed bits, following the approach of [10]. While `Zeroplus` still does not apply to ARX, it addresses the second limitation of the previous version of the tool, by automating the identification of the middle round, removing the need for manual specification. The case of ARX/AndRX constructions has partly been addressed in a recent work by Hadipour et al. [11].

Going Further. All the previously described approaches were implemented manually for specific ciphers. This process is often tedious and error-prone, and work towards more automation is important within the community. We propose a method to automatically generate the decryption function of a cipher within an automated tool, as a stepping stone towards the fully automatic generation of impossible differential models.

3 Automating Cipher Inversion

As noted in the previous section, automation can help limit the risk of human oversight. With this in mind, we aimed to push this principle further by eliminating the need to manually construct the corresponding impossible differential model for each cryptographic primitive. This approach aligns with the philosophy behind automated cryptanalysis tools such as CLAASP [4], which served as a starting point for our efforts. Indeed, CLAASP already supports the generation of SAT, SMT, CP, and MILP models for various attack scenarios. In particular, the tool can automate the search of differential and linear distinguishers. The first challenge was the systematic inversion of a cipher from its representation in CLAASP to model the backward propagations. We also notice that inversion is a fundamental step in many key recovery techniques. In CLAASP, a primitive is described as a list of connected components, forming a directed acyclic graph. Each component is a dictionary containing an identifier, a type, and a description specifying the operation. It also includes the identifiers of its input components, their bit positions, and the input and output sizes.

3.1 Method Description

To ensure generality, the inversion process operates sequentially on individual components, starting from the output and working backward through the cipher to the input, rather than processing groups of components.

First, each component type must have defined handling rules. For components representing a *bijective operation*, the inversion simply involves swapping the input and output and applying the inverse permutation. The condition for this component to be *inverted* successfully is that all output bits must be available by the time it is reached. *Non-bijective operations*, like bit shifts, require more careful consideration. If such a component is encountered during the inversion process, it needs to be *evaluated*; in other words, its input bits must be available for the inversion to succeed. For example, in a 2-branch Feistel structure where the Feistel function is a shift operation, inversion is possible because the input to the Feistel function is also available via the round output.

The XOR operation is another case to examine. Given $a \oplus b = c$, the operation can be evaluated if a and b are known. Alternatively, it can also be inverted as either $a = b \oplus c$ or $b = a \oplus c$, depending on which input is available first.

Given a target cipher C, the inversion process begins by establishing a list L of available components. Specifically, at any stage of the process, a component is considered available if it can either be evaluated or inverted, given the cipher output and the components previously made available up to that point. Initially, L only contains the output of the primitive to be inverted as it becomes an input to the inverse: $L =$ [`cipher_output`]. All the other components remain in a separate list T, representing components yet to be inverted. As the components are processed, they are moved from T to L. The inversion is complete once T is empty. The procedure is detailed in Algorithm 1. The `can_be_evaluated()` and `can_be_inverted()` functions are routines that verify whether enough input and/or output bits are available to process the component c, by establishing its connection to the elements of L. The functions `evaluate_component()` and `invert_component()` create a new component c' from c, based on the rule established for the operation it represents–as discussed above–and its connection to the elements of L. We illustrate this method on a toy example in Sect. A.

Algorithm 1: Cipher inversion algorithm

```
Input  : Target cipher C as a list of connected components
Output: Inverse cipher C_inv
L = [cipher_output]
T = [c — c ∈ C],
while |T| > 0 do
    for c in T do
        if can_be_evaluated(c, L) then
            c' = evaluate_component(c, L)
            L = L + [c']
            remove c from T
        else if can_be_inverted(c, L) then
            c' =invert_component(c, L)
            L = L + [c']
            remove c from T
Build C_inv from the components list L
```

3.2 Limitations of This Approach

This inversion method relies exclusively on local information and processes each component independently, rather than considering larger groups of operations. Consequently, certain components are challenging to invert. For instance, in the linear layer of Ascon [14], each row x is updated through a series of shifts and XORs. Specifically, x is shifted by two values, r_0 and r_1, and these shifted versions are then combined with the original x through an XOR: $y = x \oplus (x \ggg r_0) \oplus (x \ggg r_1)$. From this expression, the original value x can be recovered from y by solving the equation. However, consider an implementation where this transformation is broken into simpler components, as follows:

$$u = x \ggg r_0;\ v = x \ggg r_1;\ y = x \oplus u \oplus v.$$

In such a case, the component producing y is simply viewed as a 3-input XOR operation with no discernible connection to the earlier shifts. This lack of global context prevents the inversion process from reconstructing x. On the other hand, the entire linear layer of Ascon can be expressed as a binary matrix multiplication, which is inherently easy to invert. As such, the effectiveness of this inversion method heavily depends on how the cipher is described in terms of components.

4 Hybrid Model for the Distinguisher Search

The bit-wise model combined with undisturbed bits properties has been shown to be effective against weakly aligned ciphers like Present and Ascon [16]. In fact, even in the case of word-oriented cipher, it may provide extra information that can lead to the detection of more impossible trails such as the undisturbed bits of an S-box or the result an XOR operation between one fully known input and one partially known input: given $a =???1$ and $b = 0010$, the bit-wise representation is $a \oplus b =???1$ while the cell-wise model abstracts this operation as $N \oplus N^* = U$.

However, as already mentioned in Sect. 2, this model presents one limitation: it is unable to keep track of groups of bits that are undetermined yet nonzero. This typically happens when a bijective operation maps a nonzero input difference to a truncated output difference with no undisturbed bit. Let us consider the first S-box of LBLOCK as an example:

$$S_0 = (14, 9, 15, 0, 13, 4, 10, 11, 1, 2, 8, 3, 7, 6, 12, 5).$$

There are 6 differential transitions with undisturbed bits: $(0000 \xrightarrow{S_0} 0000), (0001 \xrightarrow{S_0} ???1), (0010 \xrightarrow{S_0} ???1), (0011 \xrightarrow{S_0} ??10), (1000 \xrightarrow{S_0} ??1?), (1011 \xrightarrow{S_0} ??0?)$.

In the bit-based model, all other cases are mapped to a fully undetermined output $\delta_{out} =????$, losing crucial information like the guarantee that a nonzero input implies a nonzero output. These observations motivated us to investigate a *hybrid model*, which integrates bit-based and cell-based representations into a unified framework. This approach eliminates the need to choose between the two models while retaining their respective advantages.

4.1 A Toy Example

Consider a simple Feistel cipher acting on an 8-bit state $(x_l||x_r)$, where the Feistel function F is defined by a round key addition followed by an S-box: $F(x_l, k_i) = S_0(x_l \oplus k_i)$, with S_0 being the first S-box used in LBLOCK, previously defined. For simplicity, the key schedule is linear, producing the 4-bit round key differences 1000, 0100, 1101, and 0101 for rounds 0 to 3. Fixing the input and output differences to (0000, 0000) and (0101, 0000), respectively, Fig. 1 shows that the regular cell- and bit-based models detect no incompatibility, while the hybrid model identifies the related-key differential as impossible. Indeed, one extra information that the hybrid model gains over the other models is that the right branch at the end of round 1 is undetermined but nonzero. More precisely, these models differ in their treatment of $S(S(0000 \oplus 1000) \oplus 0110)$:

- for the *cell-based* model, $S(0000 \oplus 1000)$ produces an undetermined nonzero value α, making $S(S(0000 \oplus 1000) \oplus 0110) = S(\alpha \oplus 0110)$ unknown[2].

[2] The XOR of an undetermined nonzero input with a fixed input is unknown.

- for the *bit-based* model, $S(0000 \oplus 1000) =??1?$ using the undisturbed bits of S, and thus $S(S(0000 \oplus 1000) \oplus 0101) = S(??1? \oplus 0101) = S(??1?)$ remains unknown since 1??? has no undisturbed bits;
- for the *hybrid-based* model, similar to the bit-based model, $S(S(0000 \oplus 1000) \oplus 0110) = S(??1? \oplus 0110) = S(??1?)$ but the result is evaluated as a bijective S-box on a nonzero input, so it is undetermined but nonzero.

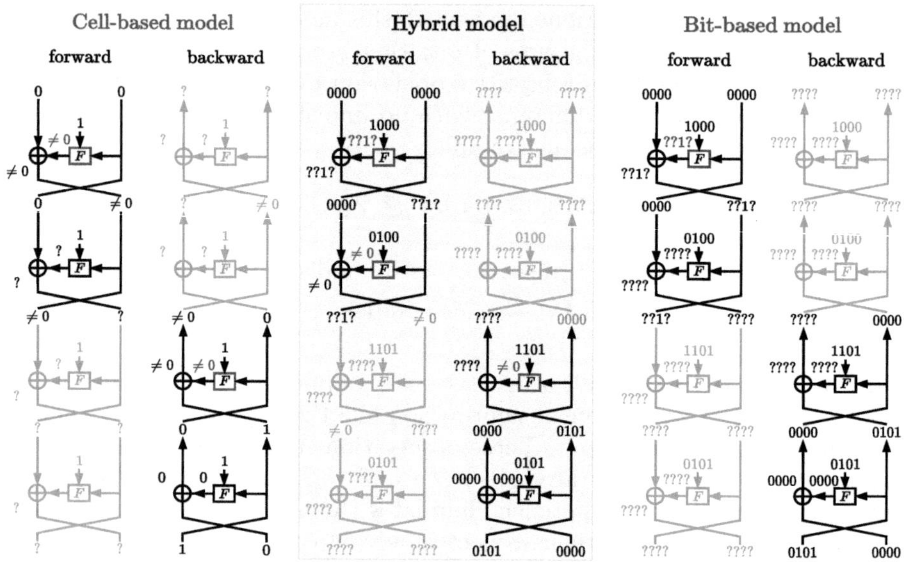

Fig. 1. Comparison of the cell-based, bit-based, and hybrid models.

4.2 Model Description

The hybrid model is an extension of the bit-wise model described in Sect. 2. The core idea is to capture both notions of undisturbed bits and of active groups of bits in S-box outputs and, more generally, in any nonlinear operation that is bijective. As such, it can be seen as an extension of the bit-wise model with undisturbed bits, to which cell-wise properties are added.

Data Representation. We recall that in bit-based approaches, for each round r, each bit difference is associated to an integer variable $\delta X_{i,r} \in \{0, 1, 2\}$, where 2 stands for the unknown bit. In the hybrid model, this domain is extended by introducing a unique integer $\texttt{id}_{s,r}$ for each n-bit S-box s of round r that serves as an identifier. The value should not intersect with the base domain of the bit-wise representation, meaning that for all s and r, $\texttt{id}_{s,r} > 2$.

$$\delta X_i = \begin{cases} 0 & \text{if } \Delta X_{i,r} = 0 \\ 1 & \text{if } \Delta X_{i,r} = 1 \\ 2 & \text{if } \Delta X_{i,r} \text{ is unknown} \\ \mathtt{id}_{s,r'} & \text{if } \Delta X_{i,r} \text{ is produced by S-box } s \text{ of round } r', \\ & \text{evaluated on a nonzero input difference} \end{cases}$$

Whenever a nonzero input difference has no undisturbed bits, the n bits of output are all set to $\mathtt{id}_{i,r}$ to indicate that even though the output is unknown, at least one of the bits is nonzero. Denoting n_{sb} the number of S-box per round and n_r the number of rounds, the new domain of each variable $\delta X_{r,i}$ thus becomes $\mathcal{D}(\delta X_{ri}) = \{0, 1, 2\} \bigcup_{s \in \mathcal{N}_{sb}, k \in \mathcal{N}_r} \{\mathtt{id}_{s,k}\}$, where $\mathcal{N}_{sb} = \{0, \dots, n_{sb} - 1\}$ and $\mathcal{N}_r = \{0, \dots, n_r - 1\}$. The modeling of the S-box and XOR operations needs to be changed to reflect this domain extension.

Extended Modeling of a Bijective S-Box. For the S-box application $Y = S(X)$, where S is the s-th S-box at round r, $X = (x_{n-1}, \dots, x_0)$, and $Y = (y_{n-1}, \dots, y_0)$, the encoding still uses information from the DDT restricted to undisturbed bits. For this, we introduce new variables $\beta X_i \in \{0, 1, 2\}$ for each bit difference ΔX_i. These variables satisfy the bit-wise constraints of the S-box. Consider the sets $\mathcal{P}_{\Delta X}$ and $\{b_p \mid p \in \mathcal{P}\}$ as defined in Sect. 2. If $\mathcal{P}_{\Delta X}$ is not empty then $\beta X = (\beta X_{n-1}, \dots, \beta X_0)$ propagates to the output difference $\beta Y = (\beta Y_{n-1}, \dots, \beta Y_0)$, where

$$\beta Y_i = \begin{cases} b_i & \text{if } i \in \mathcal{P}_{\Delta X} \\ 2 & \text{otherwise.} \end{cases}$$

In all the other cases, $(\beta Y_{n-1}, \dots, \beta Y_0) = (2)_{i=0}^{n-1}$. In turn, extended output patterns $\delta Y = (\delta Y_{n-1}, \dots, \delta Y_0)$ satisfy

$$\delta Y = \begin{cases} \beta Y \text{ or } \mathtt{id}_{s,r} & \text{if } \exists i \in \{0, \dots, n-1\},\ \delta X_i = 1 \\ \mathtt{id}_{s,r} & \text{if } \forall i \in \{0, \dots, n-1\},\ \delta X_i = \mathtt{id}_{s',r'} \\ 2 & \text{otherwise.} \end{cases}$$

Since the output bits can either be set to the truncated output with undisturbed bits or to the S-box identifier when the input has undisturbed bits and one of the output bits equals 1, this model can find multiple trails given fixed input/output differences, but one is enough.

Extended Modeling of the XOR. For the XOR operation $Y = X_0 \oplus X_1$, the propagation of the differential pattern follows:

$$\begin{aligned}&\text{if } \delta X_0 < 2 \wedge \delta X_1 < 2 \text{ then } \delta Y = \delta X_0 + \delta X_1\\&\text{elseif } \delta X_0 > 2 \wedge \delta X_1 = 0 \text{ then } \delta Y = \delta X_0\\&\text{elseif } \delta X_0 = 0 \wedge \delta X_1 > 2 \text{ then } \delta Y = \delta X_1\\&\text{else } \delta Y = 2\end{aligned}$$

Objective Function. With this extended approach, two types of incompatibilities can be detected. Denoting $\delta X u_{r,i}$ (respectively $\delta X l_{r,i}$) the difference in bit i of the internal state at round r in the forward (respectively backward) direction:

1. a **bit-based contradiction** occurs if there exist a round r and a bit position i for which $\delta X u_{r,i} + \delta X l_{r,i} = 1$;
2. a **word-based contradiction** occurs if there exist a round r, n bit positions $i_0, \ldots i_{n-1}$ and an S-box index s that verify:

$$\forall j \in \{i_0, \ldots, i_{n-1}\}, (\delta X u_{r,i_j} = \mathtt{id}_{s,r} \wedge \delta X l_{r,i_j} = 0).$$

5 Application to LBlock

LBlock is a lightweight block cipher proposed by Wu and Zhang at ACNS 2011 [32], described in Sect. B. Due to its 4-bit cell-aligned round function, and rotation of 29 bits to the left in the key schedule, the cipher seemed like a good target for our hybrid model. Since our approach builds upon the bit-wise model, it achieves the same results for weakly aligned ciphers as those reported by Hadipour et al. [16].

5.1 Previous ID Cryptanalysis Results on LBlock

The authors of LBlock demonstrated a 20-round single-key impossible differential attack using a 14-round distinguisher found with Kim et al.'s $\mathcal{U}$-method [20]. Karakoç et al. [19] extended this to 21 rounds using the same characteristic, while a 22-round attack was devised using a different 14-round impossible differential. Boura et al. broke 23 rounds with a similar characteristic [8]. Minier and Naya-Plasencia [23] performed the first related-key analysis, covering 22 rounds with a 15-round impossible differential path, exploiting the low diffusion of the key schedule. Wen et al. [31] improved this with a dedicated algorithm, reaching 16 rounds by splitting all key values into partitions of differential trails and checking their impossibility for the entire key space. Cui et al. [13] identified several 16-round differentials, the highest number of rounds with impossible differentials for the full key space, using MILP modeling with constraints on key, input, and output differences. In 2022, Cao et al. [10] introduced an automatic tool incorporating Teczan's undisturbed differential bits [30], discovering a 17-round impossible differential in the weak related-key model. A summary of LBlock's main results is presented in Table 1.

Table 1. Previous results of impossible differential distinguishers for LBlock

Setting	Rounds	Key Space Covered	Search Method	Ref.
Single-Key	14	Full	$\mathcal{U}$-method	[32]
Related-Key	15	Full	Dedicated	[23]
Related-Key	16	Full	Dedicated	[31]
Related-Key	16	Full	MILP (Infeasibility-based)	[13]
Related-Key	17	2^{-2}	MILP (Deterministic Truncated + Undisturbed Bits)	[10]

5.2 Disproving the Previous Result on LBlock

In the work by Cao et al. [10], the authors present a 17-round related-key *improbable* differential trail for LBlock. Rather than modeling the key schedule with deterministic propagation patterns, they employ probabilistic differential propagations, shown in Table 2. This approach leads to distinguishers that are longer but are not valid across the entire key space. However, we found out that the described key schedule trail follows invalid transitions.

Table 2. Subkeys used in the 17-round improbable trail by [10]. $\alpha \in \{0, 1, 2, 3\}, \beta \in \{0, 4, 8, 12\}, \gamma \in \{0, 1\}, \delta \in \{0, 2, 4, 6, 8, 10, 12, 14\}$.

Round	Subkey	Round	Subkey	Round	Subkey	Round	Subkey
0	00000000	5	00000000	10	00000000	15	00?00000
1	00030000	6	00000006	11	00000000	16	00000000
2	00000000	7	?0000000	12	000$\gamma\delta$000		
3	00000000	8	00000000	13	00000000		
4	01800000	9	00000$\alpha\beta$0	14	00000000		

More precisely, producing a subkey difference equal to `0x01800000` at round 5 is not possible if the subkey difference at round 2 equals `0x00030000`. Indeed, it is quite easy to observe that given any subkey $sk_i = (sk^i_{31}sk^i_{30}\dots sk^i_1, sk^i_0)$ of a round $i < 9$, the following equalities hold for the subkey of round $i + 3$[3]:

$$sk^{i+3}_{27\sim24} = S_8(sk^i_{20\sim17}). \tag{1}$$

For Δsk_2 = `0x00030000` and Δsk_5 = `0x01800000`, Eq. 1 would imply that `0x1` $\rightarrow$ `0x1` is a valid transition for S_8, which is false. The authors of [10] kindly shared their source code with us; their model mistakenly uses a state SBox in the key schedule (S_0 and S_1 are used in place of S_8 and S_9, respectively), which explains the discrepancy. We confirmed that using the same incorrect key schedule, our models retrieve the same results. It is clear how crafting models manually can be an error-prone process, not as with fully automatic modeling.

[3] This was also observed in [31].

5.3 New 18-Round Improbable Distinguisher for LBlock

The longest impossible differentials covering the full key space of LBlock were identified by Cui et al. [13], who presented several 16-round impossible differentials in the related-key setting. These results cannot be reproduced using the bit-based model due to the limitations discussed earlier in this section. In Sect. D, Table 7 and Table 8 detail the propagation in the subkeys and in the state under this model, for the differential $0 \xrightarrow{16r} 0$, with a single active bit located at k_{11} in the master key.

Table 3. New 16-round impossible differentials found with our model

Δin	Δout	ΔK
(0x00000000,0x00000000)	(0x00000000,0x00000000)	0x0b
(0x00000000,0x00000000)	(0x00000000,0x00000000)	0x580
(0x00000600,0x00000000)	(0x00000000,0x00000000)	0x580

Using the hybrid model, we recover this differential. The resulting state is shown in Table 9 of Sect. D. We also provide a script that can find other 16-round impossible differentials that were not listed in Cui et al.'s paper (Listing 1.1) and reported them in Table 3. This highlights the hybrid model's advantage in bridging gaps left by the bit-based approach. However, it is still unable to capture all the other differentials reported by Cui et al. due to differences in our approach compared to theirs.

The strategy described in [13] involves testing the feasibility of a differential model given specific constraints on the input and output; if no solution exists, the differential is deemed impossible. One limitation of this model is that the input and output differences must be fixed in advance but it offers one advantage over ours: if the set of all *differential characteristics* composing a differential can be partitioned into subsets $P = \cup_{p_i}$ such that, for each pair (p_i, p_j), the cell or bit positions of the incompatibility differ, Cui et al.'s model will successfully detect this differential as impossible. In contrast, our truncated deterministic approach will fail to do so. One example among the differentials by Cui et al. is

$$(\texttt{0x00000000}, \texttt{0x00000000}) \xrightarrow[\Delta K = \texttt{0x40}]{16r} (\texttt{0x00000000}, \texttt{0x00000000}).$$

An analysis of the key schedule propagations (shown in Table 10) reveals that the contradiction at round 9 depends on the value of the most significant bit of the first byte of the subkey from round 8: if 1, the differential is impossible due to an inconsistency at byte 15; otherwise, the inconsistency is always at byte 11.

5.4 A New Result Using Probabilistic Trails

As observed in Subsect. 5.3, for LBlock, given fixed plaintext, ciphertext, and key differences, it is possible for the incompatibility to occur at different locations, depending on the S-box outputs of the key schedule. Subkey partitioning has previously been used to manually find impossible differentials [23,31]. Thus, allowing probabilistic differential transitions for the key schedule in our model can lead to the identification of more impossible differentials.

The modeling of the two key schedule S-boxes S_8 and S_9 were changed to encode their standard DDT and the corresponding probability, as done for automated differential cryptanalysis [1,15]. Then, we used this probabilistic hybrid model to enumerate all trails of weight less than 20. Indeed, each transition of S_8 and S_9 has a probability of at least 2^{-3}, and with a small number of active bits in the key, we can expect to have very few active S-boxes even for a high number of rounds. The trails found are then merged to obtain differentials.

For *16 rounds*, we are able to retrieve more of the 16-round impossible differentials found by the authors of [13]. The results are summarized in Table 4. While some missing instances are due to a limitation of our approach, it should be noted we were unable to reproduce the paper's results when either bit k_0 or k_1 of the master key is active, even with the strategy described by the authors. In fact, the SAT differential model generated by CLAASP shows that the differentials are satisfiable.

Table 4. 16-round impossible trails found by [13] tested against our model.

Δin	Δout	ΔK	SAT differential model	our model
0	0 or $1 \ll j,\ j \in \{40, 41, 42, 43\}$	$1 \ll 11$	✓	only $\Delta_{out} = 0$ or $1 \ll j,\ j \in \{43, 42\}$
0	0 or $1 \ll j,\ j \in \{52, 53, 54, 55\}$	$1 \ll 10$	✓	✗
0	0	$1 \ll 6$	✓	✓
0	0 or $1 \ll j,\ j \in \{44, 45, 46, 47\}$	4	✓	✗
0	0	2	✗	✗ ($p = 2^{-0.093}$)
0	0	1	✗	✗ ($p = 2^{-0.093}$)

For *18 rounds*, among the 121 trails of weight less than 20, 6 are part of the following differential

$$(\texttt{0x00000000}, \texttt{0x00000008}) \xrightarrow[\Delta K = \texttt{0x40000000}]{18r} (\texttt{0x00000000}, \texttt{0x00000000}).$$

This impossible differential holds on average for 2^{45} keys and requires a subkey at round 10 of the form $\texttt{0x}\alpha\texttt{0000000}$, where $\alpha = \texttt{0x0}$ or $\texttt{0x8}$, which occurs with probability $2^{-0.83}$. This new trail is reported in Table 11 of Sect. E. Additionally, verification scripts based on CLAASP are provided in Listing 1.2 and Listing 1.3 of Sect. E.

6 Automated Key Recovery: Application to HIGHT

HIGHT is a lightweight block cipher proposed by Hong et al. at CHES 2006 [18]. Its description is provided in Section C. The security analysis performed by the authors showed impossible differential results up to 18 rounds. Later works brought that number up to 27 rounds for single-key impossible differential cryptanalysis and 31 rounds for the related-key setting. In [22], Lu presented new impossible differentials reaching 25 rounds (rounds 6-30) in the single-key scenario and 28 rounds (rounds 3–30) in related-key, while removing the initial transformation of the cipher. Ozen et al. extended the attack to 26 (rounds 1–26) and 31 rounds (rounds 1–31) respectively, again without the initial transformation. In [12] Chen et al. finally included the initial transformation, and attacked 27 rounds (rounds 4–30) in the single-key scenario, using hash tables to optimize the attack. This approach was refined by Azimi et al. in [2]. In [27], Rostami et al. show a full-round attack for a class of weak keys in the related-key setting. A summary of all the results can be found in Table 5.

Table 5. Previous results of impossible differential cryptanalysis of HIGHT

Scenario	Rounds	Transformations	Time	Data	Memory	Ref.
Single-key	18 (1–18)	Both	$2^{109.2}$ enc.	$2^{46.8}$ plaintexts	/	[18]
Single-key	25 (6–30)	Only final	$2^{126.75}$ enc.	2^{60} plaintexts	/	[22]
Single-key	26 (1–26)	Only final	$2^{119.53}$ enc.	2^{61} plaintexts	2^{109} B	[26]
Single-key	27 (4–30)	Both	$2^{126.6}$ enc.	2^{58} plaintexts	2^{120} B	[12]
Single-key	**27 (4–30)**	**Both**	$2^{124.5}$ **enc.**	2^{60} **plaintexts**	2^{116} **B**	**this work**
Single-key	27 (4–30)	Both	$2^{120.58}$ enc.[a]	$2^{59.3}$ plaintexts	$2^{107.4}$ B	[2]
Related-key	28 (3–30)	Only final	$2^{125.99}$ enc.	2^{59} plaintexts	/	[22]
Related-key	31 (1–31)	Only final	$2^{127.28}$ enc.	2^{64} plaintexts	2^{117} B	[26]
Related-key	32	Both	$2^{127.276}$ enc.	2^{64} plaintexts	2^{104} B	[27]

[a]Counts one hash table access as a quarter round encryption

6.1 The ID Attack

The general steps for a key recovery attack, given an impossible differential, are as follows.

1. **Distinguisher extension**: The attacker propagates the impossible differential trail to the plaintext and ciphertext. The propagation is performed in the backward direction from the start of the differential to the plaintext and in the forward direction from the output difference to the ciphertext.
2. **Pairs generation**: In this phase, pairs satisfying the extended differential are generated. This is usually done by generating structures of 2 sets of plaintexts (resp. ciphertexts), where fixed difference bits are constant, and free difference bits vary so that all plaintexts (resp. ciphertexts) pairs in the structure satisfy the expected difference. The structures are then encrypted (resp. decrypted), and the ones satisfying the output (resp. input) extended difference are kept.

3. **Pairs elimination**: The pairs satisfying each round's difference are propagated deterministically forward from the plaintext and backward from the ciphertext, exhaustively guessing the involved key bits. Since the starting states will contain more unknown difference bits than in the successive states, this process leads to the elimination of some of the initial pairs, namely the ones not satisfying at least one round difference.
4. **Subkeys elimination**: Once the last round of the distinguisher extension is reached, for each remaining pair, all guessed subkeys that satisfy the differential are eliminated.
5. **Exhaustive search**: The remaining keys are exhaustively checked until the correct one is found.

Chen et al. introduced a variation of the attack in [12] that uses hash tables to reduce the time complexity of the pairs elimination step, which is the heaviest one. In particular, portions of the distinguisher's extension are precomputed, in order to efficiently deduce the subkeys leading to the impossible differential when the guessed portion is reached during the pairs elimination phase. Therefore, instead of multiplying the complexities of each step, it is enough to add the sub-extension complexities of the evaluations. The hash table complexity gains are usually computed on top of an existing impossible differential, even though different impossible differentials may be better suited; in the following section, we account for this precomputation step in an impossible differential search model.

6.2 Modeling the Search for the Distinguisher and Its Extensions

Our model extends the approach of the bit-based version of [16]. In fact we obtain a finer-grained complexity analysis by including the hash tables precomputation [12] in the objective function.

HIGHT operates on words of 8 bits using the XOR, modular addition, and left rotation. To model these operations, we use the bit-based encoding of [10] (Sect. 2). We recall that each bit difference is represented by a variable with values in the set $\{0, 1, 2\}$, where 0 and 1 correspond to known bit differences of 0 and 1, and 2 represents an unknown bit difference.

We use the high-level language MiniZinc [25] to create this model. In Sect. F, we provide the MiniZinc implementations of the different functions (Listing 1.4). In our standard model (without the use of hash tables), we need the following variables, tables and functions:

- n_I, the end round of the initial extension and beginning round of the impossible differential.
- n_M, the meeting round of the impossible differential.
- n_F, the end round of the impossible differential and beginning round of the final extension.
- n_r the total number of rounds.
- S_r^b, $r \in \{0, \ldots, n_r\}$, $b \in \{0, \ldots, 7\}$, a table representing the state at round r and byte position b.

- IS_r^b, $r \in \{0,\ldots,n_I\} \bigcup \{n_F,\ldots,n_r\}$, $b \in \{0,\ldots,7\}$, a table representing the result of the deterministic propagation in the extension rounds from the plaintext and ciphertext.
- F_r^b, $r \in \{0,\ldots,n_I\} \bigcup \{n_F,\ldots,n_r\}$, $b \in \{0,\ldots,7\}$, A binary table listing filtering bytes, identified by the number of bit conditions they enforce.
- $FUse_r^b$, $r \in \{0,\ldots,n_I\} \bigcup \{n_F,\ldots,n_r\}$, $b \in \{0,\ldots,7\}$, a binary table containing the state bytes necessary to the evaluation of the filtering bytes, identified with a 1.
- KP_i, $i \in \{0,\ldots,15\}$, an array of variables containing a permutation of the key bytes determined by the model to optimize the guess and filtering phase.
- K_r^b, $r \in \{0,\ldots,n_I\} \bigcup \{n_F,\ldots,n_r\}$, $b \in \{0,\ldots,7\}$, a table with values in $\{-1,\ldots,15\}$ with, for each state byte active in $FUse$, the maximum of the indexes of the key bytes involved in its evaluation, with respect to the permutation KP (i.e. if the permutation is $(0,15,3,2,4,\ldots)$ and the byte (r,b) needs the key bytes $0,2,3$ it will be $K_r^b = 3$ since $KP_3 = 2$). The value will be a -1 if no key byte is needed or the state byte is not active in $FUse$.
- $H_R : \mathbb{F}_3^{64} \rightarrow \mathbb{F}_3^{64}$ a propagation function representing one round of deterministic progagation of HIGHT.
- $Dep : \{0,\ldots,n_r\} \times \{0,\ldots,7\} \times \{0,\ldots,n_r\} \times \{0,\ldots,7\} \rightarrow \{0,1\}$ a dependency function such that $Dep(r_1,b_1,r_2,b_2) = 1$ if and only if the byte in position (r_1,b_1) is necessary for the evaluation of (r_2,b_2).
- $KB : \{0,\ldots,n_r\} \times \{0,\ldots,7\} \rightarrow \{0,\ldots,15\}$ a function giving the key byte necessary for the evaluation of the input byte.

Given the start and end of the impossible differential, the deterministic propagation is modeled using the function H_R and its inverse, to obtain the table S. The same is done starting from the plaintext and ciphertext, using the states of S, to compute IS with the same propagation functions.

From S and IS is easy to compute the table F, just by setting $F_r^b = 1$ iff $S_r^b \neq IS_r^b$, and $FUse$ is then computed thanks to the function Dep.

Finally the table K is evaluated with the use of the functions KB and Dep, the idea is that $K_r^b = max(KB(r,b), max\{KB(i,j), s.t.\ Dep(i,j,r,b) = 1\})$.

The complexity of each step of the guess and filter phase is evaluated by looking at each key byte in the order in which they appear in KP and determining which bytes active in $FUse$ have a value in the table K equal to the index considered. In particular at step i the number of checks to make for each remaining pair is $C_i = C_{i-1} \cdot 2^{8-b_i}$, where $b_i = \sum_{K_r^b = i-1} F_r^b$.

6.3 Complexity Evaluation and Objective Function

The data complexity evaluation is similar to [17]. In practice, we implement the complexity of the pairs elimination phase with the set C_i. The heaviest complexity step is the maximum over i of $C_i + \log_2(|\{j\ s.t.\ C_j = C_i\}|)$, where for the logarithm we use the approximation $\log_2(x) = 2.2x - 2$ as in [5].

For the final exhaustive search, the complexity is as shown in [26],

$$\log_2\left(2^{128}\cdot\left(1-\frac{2^f}{2^{8\cdot(\max(MK)-1)}}\right)^{2^{IP-EP}}\right)$$

where f is the number of bits of the last filtering byte where a fixed known difference has to be forced and 2^{IP} is the number of initial pairs and $EP = \sum_{r,b} F_r^b$ is the logarithm of the number of eliminated pairs. We approximate the function as

$$\log_2\left(2^{128}\left(1-\frac{1}{2^k}\right)^{2^n}\right)\approx\log_2\left(2^{128}\cdot e^{-2^{n-k}}\right)=128-2^{n-k}\log_2(e)$$

Modeling the Hash Tables. The main improvement of our automatic model compared to others in the literature is the automation of the *hash tables approach* and its integration with the model of the distinguisher search.

Let $IT_1, IT_2, \ldots, IT_T$ denote T tables with binary elements, representing the modeling of T hash tables. A table entry equal to 1 means that the byte in that position will be guessed in the corresponding hash table. Another set of T tables, $OT_1, OT_2, \ldots, OT_T$, represents the bytes that are computed during the creation of the hash table. Among the bytes leading to pairs eliminations, we select T of them as representatives of the hash tables. The constraints used for these tables (apart from the relations among the bytes) represent two properties. First, every selected filtering byte must be active in at least one of the second set of tables. Moreover, as conditions for the first set of tables, given the filtering bytes related to a hash table, we set as 1 the nearest bytes to the filtering tables, which are involved in its computation and have already been evaluated as outputs in at least one previous table or in the pairs elimination part. An important addition to the model is the modification of the objective function. Next, the pairs filtering must be modeled only on the filtering bytes not involved in the hash tables, thus drastically reducing this part of the total complexity. On the other hand we have to take into account the generation of the tables and the memory accesses. Regarding the $\log_2$ of the first part of the evaluation, we have that

$$\max_{i=1}^{T}(8\cdot(\sum_{k=0}^{n_r}\sum_{j=0}^{7}(IT_i[k,j])+TK_i))$$

where TK_i is the number of key bytes to be guessed in the computation of table i. For the second part, in [2] each hash table access is counted as a quarter round encryption, while in [12] as a full round encryption. Given the size of the hash tables it is definitely better to count one access as a full round encryption and we would like to point out that in the second case, our structure would improve the attack of [2]. Each hash table is represented by some filtering bytes, which involve a total of CT_i bit conditions. Moreover, each table also determines as output some key bytes, denoted KT_i. Each table is then accessed a total number of times equal to the number of remaining pairs 2^{RP}, after filtering multiplied by 2 to the power of the sum of the numbers of the free bits after accessing the previous tables:

$$A_i = 2^{RP+\sum_{j=1}^{i-1}(8\cdot KT_i - CT_i)}$$

The $\log_2$ of the tables' access complexity is approximately

$$\max_{i=1}^{T}(RP + \sum_{j=1}^{i-1}(8\cdot KT_i - CT_i)) .$$

7 Single Key Attack Improvement

Using our model, we improve the attack complexity on 27-rounds HIGHT in the single-key setting with initial and final transformations. The extension of the trail can be found in Table 6. The hash tables filtering bytes are highlighted in red, and one of the pairs elimination processes is in blue. The bytes to be guessed in the pairs elimination process are highlighted in green. A detailed review of the attack procedure can be found in Sect. G, where the input bytes of each table have already been guessed or evaluated in previous steps, either the pairs elimination phase or in previous tables. We first detail the filtering process and give a description of the hash tables computation. The permutation of the key bytes guessed in the pairs elimination phase is $(13, 12, 0, 3, 2, 7, 1, 6, 5)$, while the hash tables involve the following filtering bytes (in order of computation): $(S_6^3), (S_8^3), (S_7^3), (S_{25}^0, S_{24}^2), (S_{26}^6)$.

Complexity Evaluation. We have to generate 2^{IP} initial pairs satisfying the plaintext and ciphertext truncated differences. From a fixed 64-bit string we can construct 2^{39} plaintexts having the same bit in the positions where the plaintext difference is fixed and another 2^{39} such that the difference with the first ones satisfies the plaintext difference. These sets can generate a total of 2^{78} pairs. Each one of these pairs satisfies the ciphertext condition with probability 2^{-9}, so for each structure, a total of 2^{69} good pairs will remain. Therefore we will need 2^{IP-69} structures of $2^{39} + 2^{39} = 2^{40}$ plaintexts each, resulting in a total amount of 2^{IP-29} initial plaintexts for our attack. A summary of the complexity evaluation of the attack follows (we count C_B as a quarter round encryption, $C_B = \frac{1}{108}C_E$):

- Initial pairs generation: the total complexity of the step is $C_0 = 2^{IP-29}C_E$
- Pairs elimination: the total complexity is the sum of the complexity of each guessing step, in our case $C_1 \leq 2^{IP+29}C_B$
- Hash tables computation: the total complexity is the sum of the complexity of each step, whose leading term in our case is $C_2 \leq (2^8)^{16}C_B$
- Hash tables access: the total complexity is the sum of each the complexity of table access, in our case $C_3 \leq 2^{IP-40} \cdot 2^{72} \cdot 9C_E$

Table 6. Our ID trail with extensions for a 27 rounds attack on HIGHT

PT	???????0	10000000	00000000	00000000	????????	????????	????????	????????	
R3	???????0	10000000	00000000	00000000	????????	????????	????????	????????	↑
R4	10000000	00000000	00000000	00000000	????????	????????	????????	???????1	↑
R5	00000000	00000000	00000000	00000000	????????	????????	???????1	10000000	↑
R6	00000000	00000000	00000000	00000000	????????	???????1	10000000	00000000	↑
R7	00000000	00000000	00000000	00000000	???????1	10000000	00000000	00000000	↑
R8	00000000	00000000	00000000	00000000	10000000	00000000	00000000	00000000	↑
	Trail start								
R9	00000000	00000000	00000000	10000000	00000000	00000000	00000000	00000000	↓
R10	00000000	?????100	10000000	00000000	00000000	00000000	00000000	00000000	↓
R11	?????100	10000000	00000000	00000000	00000000	00000000	00000000	????????	↓
R12	10000000	00000000	00000000	00000000	00000000	????????	????????	???????1	↓
R13	00000000	00000000	00000000	????????	????????	????????	???????1	10000000	↓
R14	00000000	????????	????????	????????	????????	???????1	10000000	00000000	↓
R15	????????	????????	????????	????????	???????1	10000000	00000000	????????	↓
R16	????????	????????	????????	???????0	10000000	????????	????????	????????	↓
	Middle point								
R16	????????	????????	????????	???????1	????????	????????	????????	????????	↑
R17	????????	????????	???????1	00000000	????????	????????	????????	????????	↑
R18	????????	???????1	00000000	00000000	????????	????????	????????	????????	↑
R19	???????1	00000000	00000000	00000000	????????	????????	????????	????????	↑
R20	00000000	00000000	00000000	00000000	????????	????????	????????	???????1	↑
R21	00000000	00000000	00000000	00000000	????????	????????	???????1	00000000	↑
R22	00000000	00000000	00000000	00000000	????????	???????1	00000000	00000000	↑
R23	00000000	00000000	00000000	00000000	???????1	00000000	00000000	00000000	↑
	Trail end								
R24	00000000	00000000	00000000	???????1	00000000	00000000	00000000	00000000	↓
R25	00000000	????????	???????1	00000000	00000000	00000000	00000000	00000000	↓
R26	????????	???????1	00000000	00000000	00000000	00000000	00000000	????????	↓
R27	???????1	00000000	00000000	00000000	00000000	????????	????????	????????	↓
R28	00000000	00000000	00000000	????????	????????	????????	????????	???????1	↓
R29	00000000	????????	????????	????????	????????	????????	???????1	00000000	↓
R30	????????	????????	????????	????????	????????	???????1	00000000	????????	↓
CT	????????	????????	????????	????????	????????	????????	???????1	00000000	

- Exhaustive search: $C_4 = 2^{128} \cdot (1 - \frac{2}{2^{48}})^{2^{IP-40}}$

By setting $IP = 89$, the data complexity is 2^{60} plaintexts and the total time complexity is $C_T = C_0 + C_1 + C_2 + C_3 + C_4 \leq 2^{60} C_E + (2^{118} + 2^{128}) C_B + 2^{124.2} C_E \leq$

$2^{124.5}C_E$. Moreover the memory required for storing the hash tables will be less than $2^{116}B$.

8 Conclusions and Future Work

We presented an extension of previous techniques to find impossible differential trails by introducing a hybrid model. The model is available in multiple formalisms and combines the advantages of the cell-wise propagation analysis with the precision of the bit-wise approach, while also supporting probabilistic transitions in the related-key setting. We also introduced an effective technique to automatically invert symmetric ciphers. We demonstrated the generality of the techniques above by implementing them in an automated tool, namely CLAASP. We effectively applied the tool to the LBlock cipher to not only recover state-of-the-art results for 16 rounds but also expand them with new 16-round impossible differentials and a new 18-round improbable differential.

Additionally, we developed a new CP model to evaluate the complexity of ID attacks and automatically identify the optimal impossible differential trail for key recovery in the HIGHT block cipher. Our model improves the key-recovery attacks on 27-round HIGHT by identifying a new trail and leveraging the hash tables approach presented in [12].

Future work will aim to generalize our ID attack model for HIGHT to enhance automated tools. This will involve expanding support for complexity evaluation of ID attacks for SAT, SMT, MILP, and CP, with the option to incorporate the hash tables approach. Another promising direction is integrating the differential clustering effect into the model for optimal distinguisher search, which is currently performed as a post-processing step in the hybrid probabilistic model.

A CLAASP Automatic Cipher Inversion: A Toy Example

The example depicted in Fig. 2 can be inverted as follows:

Step 1. L = [`cipher_output_0_2`]. The bits `plaintext[0:2]` can be obtained as they are equal to `cipher_output_0_2[3:5]`.
Step 2. L = [`cipher_output_0_2`, `plaintext[0:2]`]. The S-box `sbox_0_0` can be **evaluated** as its input bits `plaintext[0:2]` are available.
Step 3. L = [`cipher_output_0_2`, `plaintext[0:2]`, `sbox_0_0`]. The *XOR* operation `xor_0_1` can be **inverted** as its output `cipher_output_0_2[0:2]` and its second input `sbox_0_0` are available.
Step 4. L = [`cipher_output_0_2`, `plaintext[0:2]`, `sbox_0_0`, `inv_xor_0_1`]. Finally, the last bits `plaintext[3:5]` can be obtained as they are equal to the output of the inverted XOR.

```
cipher = {
...
'cipher_rounds' : [
[{# round = 0 - round component = 0
  'id': 'sbox_0_0',
  'type': 'sbox',
  'in_bit_size': 3,
  'in_id_link': ['plaintext'],
  'in_bit_positions': [[0, 1, 2]],
  'out_bit_size': 3,
  'description': [0, 5, 3, 2, 6, 1, 4, 7]},
 {# round = 0 - round component = 1
  'id': 'xor_0_1',
  'type': 'word_operation',
  'in_bit_size': 6,
  'in_id_link': ['sbox_0_0', 'plaintext'],
  'in_bit_positions': [[0, 1, 2], [3, 4, 5]],
   'out_bit_size': 3,
   'description': ['XOR', 2]},
 {# round = 0 - round component = 2
  'id': 'cipher_output_0_2',
  'type': 'cipher_output',
  'in_bit_size': 6,
  'in_id_link': ['xor_0_1', 'plaintext'],
  'in_bit_positions': [[0, 1, 2], [0, 1, 2]],
  'out_bit_size': 6,
  'description': ['cipher_output'],
 }]]
}
```

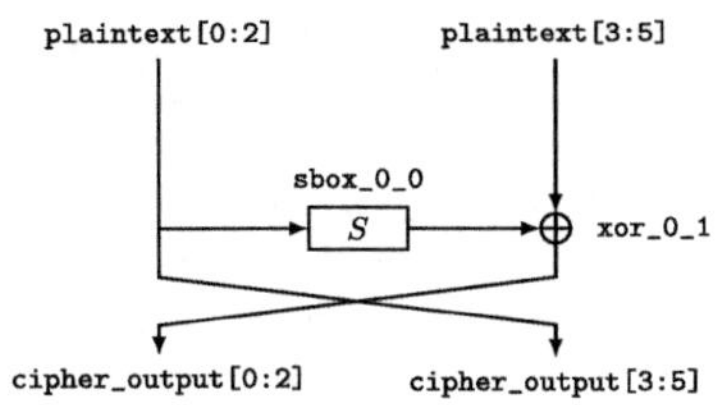

Fig. 2. A toy example and its CLAASP representation.

B Description of LBlock

LBlock is a lightweight block cipher proposed by Wu and Zhang at ACNS 2011 [32]. The round function acts on a 64-bit state. It follows a two-branched Feistel structure, where the receiving branch of the Feistel function is first rotated by 8 bits. The inner round function is made of one round key addition, a parallel application of 8 different 4-bit S-boxes and a nibble-wise permutation (Fig. 3).

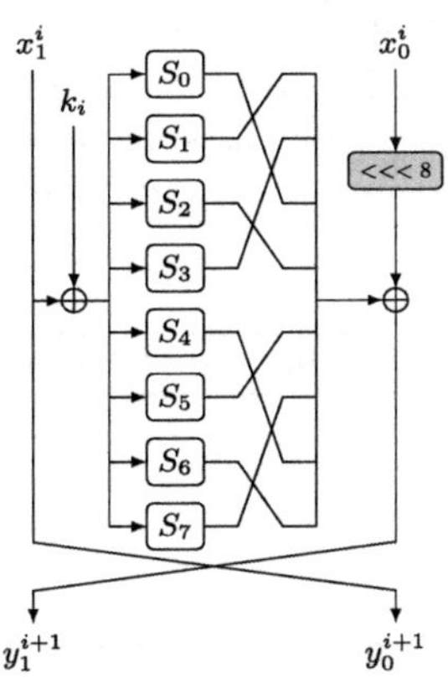

Fig. 3. One round of the LBlock cipher.

The 80-bit master key K is stored in a key register and denoted as $K = k_{79}k_{78}\cdots k_1k_0$. At each round i, the 32-bit round key sk_i consists of the 64 leftmost bits of the current key state: $k_i = k_{79\sim48}$. The key update is described in Algorithm 2.

Algorithm 2: Key schedule of LBlock

$sk_0 = K_{79\sim48}$;
for $1 \leq r \leq 31$ **do**
  $k_{79\sim0} \leftarrow k_{79\sim0} \lll 29$;
  $k_{79\sim76} \leftarrow S_9(k_{79\sim76})$;
  $k_{75\sim72} \leftarrow S_8(k_{75\sim72})$;
  $k_{50\sim47} \leftarrow k_{50\sim47} \oplus [i]_2$;
  $sk_{5r} \leftarrow k_{79\sim48}$;

C Description of HIGHT

HIGHT is a lightweight block cipher proposed by Hong et al. at CHES 2006 [18]. The round function acts on a 64-bit state. Its round function can be seen as a concatenation of 4 Feistel structures acting on pairs of bytes which are then rotated. The key is inducted alternately on the bytes by XOR and modular addition, while the state operations are rotations and either XOR, if the key is used with the modular addition, or modular addition. The 128-bit master key K is used for an initial transformation and then at each round the 32-bit subkey involved in the state is evaluated via modular addition with fixed constants of previous subkeys.

The 128-bit initial key MK is used for the computation of the 32-bit round keys SK_i and the initial and final whitening keys WK (Algorithm 3 and Algorithm 4). The initial and final whitening are performed at the beginning and end of the encryption by adding or XORing the whitening key to the plaintext and to the last round output respectively, as shown in Algorithm 5. From now on we will indicate the i-th byte of the r-th round output as S_r^i.

Algorithm 3: Whitening key schedule of HIGHT

for $0 \leq i \leq 3$ **do**
  $WK_i \leftarrow MK_{i+12}$;
for $4 \leq i \leq 7$ **do**
  $WK_i \leftarrow MK_{i-4}$;

Algorithm 4: Key schedule of HIGHT

$\delta_0 \leftarrow 1011010$;
for $1 \leq i \leq 127$ **do**
  $\delta_i \leftarrow ((\delta_{i-1} \oplus (\delta_{i-1} \gg 3)) \ll 6) \oplus (\delta_{i-1} \gg 1)$;
for $0 \leq i \leq 7$ **do**
  for $0 \leq j \leq 7$ **do**
    $SK_{16i+j} \leftarrow MK_{j-1 \bmod 8} \boxplus \delta_{16i+j}$;
  for $0 \leq j \leq 7$ **do**
    $SK_{16i+j+8} \leftarrow MK_{(j-1 \bmod 8)+8} \boxplus \delta_{16i+j+8}$;

Algorithm 5: Initial and final whitening of HIGHT

$S_0^0 \leftarrow P_0$; $S_0^1 \leftarrow P_1 \oplus WK_3$; $S_0^2 \leftarrow P_2$; $S_0^3 \leftarrow P_3 \boxplus WK_2$; $S_0^4 \leftarrow P_4$;
$S_0^5 \leftarrow P_5 \oplus WK_1$; $S_0^6 \leftarrow P_6$; $S_0^7 \leftarrow P_7 \boxplus WK_0$;
ENC(S);
$C_0 \leftarrow S_{32}^7$; $C_1 \leftarrow S_{32}^0 \oplus WK_7$; $C_2 \leftarrow S_{32}^1$; $C_3 \leftarrow S_{32}^2 \boxplus WK_6$; $C_4 \leftarrow S_{32}^3$;
$C_5 \leftarrow S_{32}^4 \oplus WK_5$; $C_6 \leftarrow S_{32}^5$; $C_7 \leftarrow S_{32}^6 \boxplus WK_4$;

The ENC(S) encryption function consists of 32 applications of the round function (described in Algorithm 6). This function needs the definition of two auxiliary functions, F_0 and F_1, which are defined as follows:

$$F_0(x) = (x \lll 1) \oplus (x \lll 2) \oplus (x \lll 7)$$

$$F_1(x) = (x \lll 3) \oplus (x \lll 4) \oplus (x \lll 6)$$

Algorithm 6: Round function of HIGHT

for $0 \leq r \leq 31$ **do**
  for $0 \leq i \leq 3$ **do**
    $S_{r+1}^{2i} \leftarrow S_r^{2i+1}$
  for $0 \leq i \leq 1$ **do**
    $S_{r+1}^{4i-1 \bmod 8} \leftarrow S_r^{4i} \oplus (F_1(S_{r-1}^{4i+1}) \boxplus SK_{4r+3-2i})$
  for $0 \leq i \leq 1$ **do**
    $S_{r+1}^{4i+1} \leftarrow S_r^{4i+2} \boxplus (F_1(S_{r-1}^{4i+3}) \oplus SK_{4r+2-2i})$

A graphic representation of the round function can be found in Fig. 4.

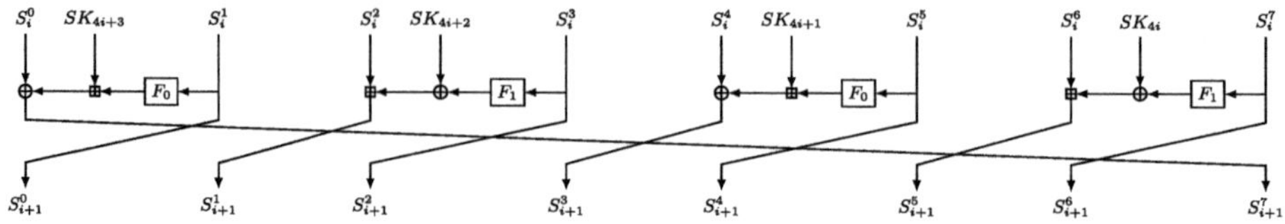

Fig. 4. One round of the HIGHT cipher.

D 16-Round Impossible Differential for LBlock by [13]

Table 7. Deterministic subkeys used in the 16-round impossible differential $0 \xrightarrow{\Delta k_{11}=1} 0$ of [13].

0000 0000 0000 0000 0000 0000 0000 0000
0000 0000 0000 0000 0000 0000 0000 0000
0000 0000 0010 0000 0000 0000 0000 0000
0000 0000 0000 0000 0000 0000 0000 0000
0000 0000 0000 0000 0000 0000 0000 0000
?1?? 0000 0000 0000 0000 0000 0000 0000
0000 0000 0000 0000 0000 0000 0000 0000
0000 0000 0000 0000 0000 00?1 ??00 0000
0000 0000 0000 0000 0000 0000 0000 0000
0000 0000 0000 000? 1??0 0000 0000 0000
0000 0000 0000 0000 0000 0000 0000 0000
0000 0000 ?1?? 0000 0000 0000 0000 0000
0000 0000 0000 0000 0000 0000 0000 0000
0000 0000 0000 0000 0000 0000 0000 00?1

Listing 1.1. CLAASP script to find 16-round impossible trails with the hybrid model, in the related-key setting

```
from claasp.cipher_modules.models.cp.mzn_models.
    mzn_hybrid_impossible_xor_differential_model import
    MznHybridImpossibleXorDifferentialModel
from claasp.ciphers.block_ciphers.lblock_block_cipher import
    LBlockBlockCipher
from claasp.cipher_modules.models.utils import set_fixed_variables
lblock = LBlockBlockCipher(number_of_rounds=16)
mzn = MznHybridImpossibleXorDifferentialModel(lblock)
rk_key = [set_fixed_variables('key', 'not_equal', range(80), [0]*80)]
mzn.find_all_impossible_xor_differential_trails(16, rk_key, 'Chuffed', 1, 8,
    16, intermediate_components=False)
```

Table 8. State of the the 16-round impossible differential $0 \xrightarrow{\Delta k_{11}=1} 0$ of [13] using a bit-wise model.

0000	0000	0000	0000	0000	0000	0000	0000	0000	0000	0000	0000	0000	0000	0000	0000
0000	0000	0000	0000	0000	0000	0000	0000	0000	0000	0000	0000	0000	0000	0000	0000
0000	0000	0000	0000	0000	0000	0000	0000	0000	0000	0000	0000	0000	0000	0000	0000
0000	0000	0000	???1	0000	0000	0000	0000	0000	0000	0000	0000	0000	0000	0000	0000
0000	????	0000	0000	0000	0000	0000	0000	0000	0000	0000	???1	0000	0000	0000	0000
????	???1	0000	0000	0000	0000	0000	0000	0000	????	0000	0000	0000	0000	0000	0000
????	0000	????	0000	0000	0000	0000	????	????	???1	0000	0000	0000	0000	0000	0000
0000	0000	????	????	0000	????	????	???1	????	0000	????	0000	0000	0000	0000	????
????	????	0000	????	????	????	????	????	0000	0000	????	????	0000	????	????	???1
????	????	????	????	????	????	????	????	????	????	????	????	????	????	????	????
????	????	????	????	????	????	????	????	????	????	????	????	????	????	????	????
0000	????	????	????	0000	????	0000	????	????	????	????	????	????	????	????	????
0000	????	????	0000	0000	0000	????	????	0000	????	????	????	0000	????	0000	????
0000	????	0000	0000	0000	????	0000	????	0000	????	????	0000	0000	0000	????	????
0000	0000	0000	0000	0000	0000	0000	????	0000	????	0000	0000	0000	????	0000	????
0000	0000	0000	0000	0000	0000	0000	0000	0000	0000	0000	0000	0000	0000	0000	0000
0000	0000	0000	0000	0000	0000	0000	0000	0000	0000	0000	0000	0000	0000	0000	0000

E 18-Round Improbable Differential for LBlock

Listing 1.2. CLAASP script to verify the improbable differential

```
from claasp.ciphers.block_ciphers.lblock_block_cipher import
    LBlockBlockCipher
lblock = LBlockBlockCipher(number_of_rounds=18)
from claasp.cipher_modules.models.utils import set_fixed_variables
from claasp.cipher_modules.models.sat.sat_models.sat_xor_differential_model
    import SatXorDifferentialModel
sat = SatXorDifferentialModel(lblock)
key = set_fixed_variables(component_id='key', constraint_type='equal',
    bit_positions=range(80), bit_values=[0]*49+[1]+[0]*30)
pt = set_fixed_variables(component_id='plaintext', constraint_type='equal',
    bit_positions= range(64), bit_values= [0]*60+[1,0,0,0])
ct = set_fixed_variables(component_id='intermediate_output_17_12',
    constraint_type='equal', bit_positions= range(64), bit_values= [0]*64)
key_proba = [set_fixed_variables(component_id='intermediate_output_10_0',
    constraint_type='equal', bit_positions = range(1,4), bit_values= [0]*3)]
sat.find_one_xor_differential_trail(fixed_values=key_proba + [key, pt, ct])
```

Listing 1.3. CLAASP script to verify the probability of the 18-round differential

```
from claasp.cipher_modules.models.cp.mzn_models.
    mzn_hybrid_impossible_xor_differential_model import
    MznHybridImpossibleXorDifferentialModel
from claasp.ciphers.block_ciphers.lblock_block_cipher import
    LBlockBlockCipher
from claasp.cipher_modules.models.utils import set_fixed_variables
lblock = LBlockBlockCipher(number_of_rounds=18)
```

Table 9. State of the 16-round impossible differential $0 \xrightarrow{\Delta k_{11}=1} 0$ of [13] using the hybrid model.

0000	0000	0000	0000	0000	0000	0000	0000	0000	0000	0000	0000	0000	0000	0000	0000
0000	0000	0000	0000	0000	0000	0000	0000	0000	0000	0000	0000	0000	0000	0000	0000
0000	0000	0000	0000	0000	0000	0000	0000	0000	0000	0000	0000	0000	0000	0000	0000
0000	0000	0000	2222	0000	0000	0000	0000	0000	0000	0000	0000	0000	0000	0000	0000
0000	5555	0000	0000	0000	0000	0000	0000	0000	0000	0000	2222	0000	0000	0000	0000
4444	2222	0000	0000	0000	0000	0000	0000	0000	5555	0000	0000	0000	0000	0000	0000
6666	0000	????	0000	0000	0000	0000	5555	4444	2222	0000	0000	0000	0000	0000	0000
0000	0000	8888	????	0000	2222	4444	2222	6666	0000	????	0000	0000	0000	0000	5555
????	????	0000	5555	????	????	6666	????	0000	0000	8888	????	0000	2222	4444	2222
4444	????	8888	????	????	????	5555	????	????	????	????	????	????	????	????	????
????	8888	????	????	6666	4444	8888	????	4444	????	8888	????	????	????	5555	????
0000	????	4444	6666	0000	6666	0000	????	????	8888	????	????	6666	4444	8888	????
0000	4444	6666	0000	0000	0000	????	8888	0000	????	4444	6666	0000	6666	0000	????
0000	6666	0000	0000	0000	????	0000	2222	0000	4444	6666	0000	0000	0000	????	8888
0000	0000	0000	0000	0000	0000	0000	4444	0000	6666	0000	0000	0000	????	0000	2222
0000	0000	0000	0000	0000	0000	0000	6666	0000	0000	0000	0000	0000	0000	0000	4444
0000	0000	0000	0000	0000	0000	0000	0000	0000	0000	0000	0000	0000	0000	0000	0000
0000	0000	0000	0000	0000	0000	0000	0000	0000	0000	0000	0000	0000	0000	0000	0000

```
mzn = MznHybridImpossibleXorDifferentialModel(lblock)
fixed_variables = [set_fixed_variables(component_id='key', constraint_type='
    equal', bit_positions=range(80), [0]*49+[1]+[0]*30)]
fixed_variables.append(set_fixed_variables(component_id='plaintext',
    constraint_type='equal', range(64), [0]*60 +[1,0,0,0]))
fixed_variables.append(set_fixed_variables('inverse_cipher_output_17_19', '
    equal', range(64), [0]*64))
mzn.find_all_impossible_xor_differential_trails(18, fixed_variables, 'Chuffed
    ', 1, 9, 18, intermediate_components=False, probabilistic=True)
```

F MiniZinc Predicates for the HIGHT Model

```
% Xor of two bits
function array[int] of var 0..2: Xor2(array[int] of var 0..2: a, array[int]
    of var 0..2: b)=
array1d(0..(length(a)-1), [if (a[j] == 2 \/ b[j] == 2) then 2 else ((a[j]+b[j
    ]) mod 2) endif | j in 0..(length(a)-1)]);

% Modular Addition of two words
predicate Modadd_2(array[int] of var 0..2: a, array[int] of var 0..2: b,array
    [int] of var 0..2: c) = (
  let {
    array [0..length(a)-1] of var 0..2: as = LShift(a,1),
    array [0..length(a)-1] of var 0..2: bs = LShift(b,1),
    array [0..length(a)-1] of var 0..2: cs = LShift(c,1),
    var 0..length(a)-1: pivot;
```

Table 10. The LBlock key schedule over 16 rounds, when $\Delta K = 0x40$, in the bit-wise deterministic truncated model. The differential $0 \xrightarrow{\Delta K=0x40} 0$ is impossible due to a contradiction at byte 11 of round 9 if $\alpha = 0$ and at byte 15 of round 9 otherwise.

Round	Subkey							
0	0000	0000	0000	0000	0000	0000	0000	0000
1	0000	0000	0000	0000	0000	0000	0000	0000
2	0000	0000	0000	0001	0000	0000	0000	0000
3	0000	0000	0000	0000	0000	0000	0000	0000
4	0000	0000	0000	0000	0000	0000	0000	0000
5	0000	0000	1000	0000	0000	0000	0000	0000
6	0000	0000	0000	0000	0000	0000	0000	0000
7	0000	0000	0000	0000	0000	0000	0000	0010
8	$\alpha\beta\gamma\delta$	0000	0000	0000	0000	0000	0000	0000
9	0000	0000	0000	0000	0000	0000	0000	0000
10	0000	0000	0000	0000	0000	$00\alpha\beta$	$\gamma\delta00$	0000
11	0000	0000	0000	0000	0000	0000	0000	0000
12	0000	0000	0000	0000	0000	0000	0000	0000
13	0000	0000	0000	000α	$\beta\gamma\delta0$	0000	0000	0000
14	0000	0000	0000	0000	0000	0000	0000	0000
15	0000	0000	0000	0000	0000	0000	0000	0000

```
  } in
  forall (i in 0..length(a)-1) (
    if i<pivot then c[i]=2 else (as[i]=0) /\ (bs[i]=0) /\ (cs[i]=0) endif
  ) /\
  xor_bit_p1_2(a[pivot],b[pivot],c[pivot])
  /\ if pivot>0 then a[pivot]+b[pivot]>0 else true endif
);

% Left Rotation
function array[int] of var 0..2: LRot(array[int] of var 0..2: X, var int: val
    )=
array1d(0..(length(X)-1), [X[(j+val) mod length(X)] | j in 0..(length(X)-1)])
    ;
```

Listing 1.4. The MiniZinc predicates representing the operations of HIGHT

G Full Procedure of the Attack on 27-Round HIGHT

See Table 12.

Table 11. Our 18-round improbable trail (cell-wise notation): 0 for null difference, * for unknown nonzero, and ? for fully undetermined. Conditional subkey transitions are highlighted in blue, with α = 0x0 or 0x8.

State (truncated)	Subkey
(00000000, 00000008)	00000000
(00000800, 00000000)	00000800
(00000000, 00000800)	00000000
(00080000, 00000000)	00000000
(0*000000, 00080000)	00040000
(*?000000, 0*000000)	00000000
(?*0*0000*, *?000000)	00000000
(00?*0**?, ?0*0000*)	0*000000
(?*0?*??*, 00?*0**?)	00000000
(???*??*?, ?*0?*??*)	000000?*
(?*?*?**?, ??*?????)	
(0?0*?***, ?*?*?**?)	α0000000
(? 00*0*?0, 0?0*?***)	00000000
(000*0*00, ?00*0*?0)	0000?*00
(000*0000, 000*0*00)	00000000
(000*0000, 000*0000)	00000000
(00000000, 000*0000)	000*0000
(00000000, 00000000)	00000000
(00000000, 00000000)	00000000
(00000000, 00000000)	

Table 12. Impossible differential attack procedure on 27 rounds of HIGHT

Step	Description	Time complexity
Pairs elimination		
1	Guess MK_{13} and compute S_3^5, S_4^3 by partial decryption for each initial pair, then eliminate those whose difference does not propagate to the expected one (on average 1 pair every 2^8 will remain)	$2 \cdot 2^{IP} \cdot (2 \cdot 2^8) C_B$
2	Guess MK_{12}, MK_0 and compute S_3^7, S_4^5, S_5^3 by partial encryption and S_{30}^6 by partial decryption for each remaining pair, and filter	$2 \cdot 2^{IP-8} \cdot (3 \cdot 2^{16} + 2^{24}) C_B$
3	Guess MK_3 and compute S_{30}^0, S_{29}^0 by partial decryption for each remaining pair, and filter	$2 \cdot 2^{IP-16} \cdot (2 \cdot 2^{32}) C_B$
4	Guess MK_2, MK_7 and compute $S_{30}^2, S_{29}^2, S_{28}^2$ by partial decryption for each remaining pair, and filter	$2 \cdot 2^{IP-24} \cdot (2^{40} + 2 \cdot 2^{48}) C_B$
5	Guess MK_1, MK_6 and then MK_{15} bit by bit and compute $S_{30}^4, S_{29}^4, S_{28}^4, S_{27}^4$ by partial decryption for each remaining pair, and filter	$2 \cdot 2^{IP-32} \cdot (2^{56} + 2 \cdot 2^{64} + 2^{65}) C_B$
Memory tables generation ($S_i^{j,\Delta} = \{S_i^j, \Delta S_i^j\}$)		
6	Build table T_0 by partial encryption, guessing bytes $P_0, \Delta P_0, P_1, P_7^{\Delta}, S_4^{5,\Delta}$, The condition $\Delta S_6^3 = 0$ is a 8-bit condition, therefore if we index the table by $P_0^{\Delta}, P_1, P_7^{\Delta}, S_4^{5,\Delta}, C_6, S_{29}^0, MK_0, MK_7, MK_{15}$ and take as outputs MK_4 and the implied $S_4^{7,\Delta}, S_5^{5,\Delta}, S_6^3, S_{28}^0$, for each set of inputs we get on average 1 output.	$2 \cdot (2^8)^{12} \cdot 2^7 C_B$
7	Build table T_1 by partial encryption, guessing bytes $P_1, S_3^2, P_3, S_4^3, S_4^{7,\Delta}$, The condition $\Delta S_8^3 = 0$ is a 7-bit condition, therefore if we index the table by $P_1, S_3^2, P_3, S_4^3, S_4^{7,\Delta}, S_{28}^0, S_{27}^2, MK_1, MK_2, MK_3, MK_6, MK_{12}, MK_{15}$ and take as outputs MK_{14} and the implied $S_4^1, S_5^1, S_5^7, S_6^7, S_6^{5,\Delta}, S_7^5, S_8^3$, for each set of inputs we get on average 2 outputs.	$2 \cdot (2^8)^{12} \cdot 2^7 C_B$
8	Build table T_2 by partial encryption, guessing bytes $S_5^{5,\Delta}, S_6^{5,\Delta}, S_{29}^0$, The condition $\Delta S_7^3 = 0$ is a 8-bit condition, therefore if we index the table by $S_5^{5,\Delta}, S_6^{5,\Delta}, S_{29}^0, S_{28}^0, S_{28}^2, MK_{12}$ and take as outputs MK_8 and the implied S_{27}^2, S_{26}^2, for each set of inputs we get on average 2 outputs.	$2 \cdot (2^8)^8 \cdot 2^7 C_B$
9	Build table T_3 by partial decryption, guessing bytes $S_{26}^2, S_{28}^0, S_{29}^{4,\Delta}, S_{30}^{4,\Delta}$, The conditions $\Delta S_{25}^0 = 0, \Delta S_{24}^2 = 0$ are a 16-bit condition, therefore if we index the table by $S_{26}^2, S_{28}^0, S_{29}^{4,\Delta}, S_{30}^{4,\Delta}, S_{30}^6, S_{30}^{5,\Delta}, MK_0, MK_1, MK_4, MK_{13}, MK_{14}$ and take as outputs MK_5, MK_9 and the implied $S_{27}^{6,\Delta}$, for each set of inputs we get on average 2 outputs.	$2 \cdot (2^8)^{15} \cdot 2^7 C_B$
10	Build table T_4 by partial decryption, guessing bytes $S_{27}^{6,\Delta}, S_{28}^{4,\Delta}, MK_{10}$. The condition $\Delta S_{26}^6 = 0$ is a 8-bit condition, therefore if we index the table by $S_{27}^{6,\Delta}, S_{28}^{4,\Delta}$ and take as outputs MK_{10}, for each set of inputs we get on average 2 valid outputs, and finally one can filter wrong keys.	$2 \cdot (2^8)^5 C_B$
11	Each evaluation of the first 5 steps corresponds to some evaluated bytes which will be the inputs of the hash tables, along with the outputs of the previous tables, therefore for each remaining pair and subkeys guesses for steps 1-5, the tables can be accessed and they produce some wrong subkeys (2 per guess in particular).	
12	The remaining keys are exhaustively tested.	

References

1. Abdelkhalek, A., Sasaki, Y., Todo, Y., Tolba, M., Youssef, A.M.: MILP modeling for (large) s-boxes to optimize probability of differential characteristics. IACR Trans, Symmetric Cryptol (2017)
2. Azimi, S.A., Ahmadi, S., Ahmadian, Z., Mohajeri, J., Aref, M.R.: Improved impossible differential and biclique cryptanalysis of HIGHT. Int. J. Commun. Syst. (2018)
3. Bellini, E., et al.: Claasping ARADI: automated analysis of the ARADI block cipher. IACR Cryptol. ePrint Arch. (2024)
4. Bellini, E., et al.: CLAASP: a cryptographic library for the automated analysis of symmetric primitives. In: Selected Areas in Cryptography - SAC (2023)
5. Bellini, E., Gérault, D., Grados, J., Makarim, R.H., Peyrin, T.: Fully automated differential-linear attacks against ARX ciphers. In: CT-RSA (2023)
6. Biham, E., Biryukov, A., Shamir, A.: Cryptanalysis of skipjack reduced to 31 rounds using impossible differentials. In: Stern, J. (ed.) EUROCRYPT 1999. LNCS, vol. 1592, pp. 12–23. Springer, Heidelberg (1999). https://doi.org/10.1007/3-540-48910-X_2
7. Biham, E., Shamir, A.: Differential cryptanalysis of DES-like cryptosystems. In: Menezes, A.J., Vanstone, S.A. (eds.) CRYPTO 1990. LNCS, vol. 537, pp. 2–21. Springer, Heidelberg (1991). https://doi.org/10.1007/3-540-38424-3_1
8. Boura, C., Minier, M., Naya-Plasencia, M., Suder, V.: Improved impossible differential attacks against round-reduced lblock. IACR Cryptol. ePrint Arch. (2014)
9. Boura, C., Naya-Plasencia, M., Suder, V.: Scrutinizing and improving impossible differential attacks: applications to CLEFIA, Camellia, LBlock and Simon. In: Sarkar, P., Iwata, T. (eds.) ASIACRYPT 2014. LNCS, vol. 8873, pp. 179–199. Springer, Heidelberg (2014). https://doi.org/10.1007/978-3-662-45611-8_10
10. Cao, W., Zhang, W., Zhou, C.: New automatic search tool for searching for impossible differentials using undisturbed bits. In: In: Deng, Y., Yung, M. (eds.) Inscrypt 2022. LNCS, vol. 13837, pp. 43–63. Springer, Cham (2022). https://doi.org/10.1007/978-3-031-26553-2_3
11. Chakraborty, D., Hadipour, H., Nguyen, P.H., Eichlseder, M.: Finding complete impossible differential attacks on andrx ciphers and efficient distinguishers for ARX designs. IACR Trans, Symmetric Cryptol (2024)
12. Chen, J., Wang, M., Preneel, B.: Impossible differential cryptanalysis of the lightweight block ciphers TEA, XTEA and HIGHT. In: Mitrokotsa, A., Vaudenay, S. (eds.) AFRICACRYPT 2012. LNCS, vol. 7374, pp. 117–137. Springer, Heidelberg (2012). https://doi.org/10.1007/978-3-642-31410-0_8
13. Cui, T., Chen, S., Fu, K., Wang, M., Jia, K.: New automatic tool for finding impossible differentials and zero-correlation linear approximations. Sci. China Inf. Sci. (2021)
14. Dobraunig, C., Eichlseder, M., Mendel, F., Schläffer, M.: Ascon v1.2: lightweight authenticated encryption and hashing. J. Cryptol. (2021)
15. Gérault, D., Minier, M., Solnon, C.: Constraint programming models for chosen key differential cryptanalysis. In: CP (2016)
16. Hadipour, H., Gerhalter, S., Sadeghi, S., Eichlseder, M.: Improved search for integral, impossible differential and zero-correlation attacks application to Ascon, ForkSKINNY, SKINNY, MANTIS, PRESENT and QARMAv2. IACR Trans. Symmetric Cryptol. (2024)

17. Hadipour, H., Sadeghi, S., Eichlseder, M.: Finding the impossible: Automated search for full impossible-differential, zero-correlation, and integral attacks. In: Hazay, C., Stam, M. (eds.) EUROCRYPT 2023. LNCS, vol. 14007, pp. 128–157. Springer, Cham (2023). https://doi.org/10.1007/978-3-031-30634-1_5
18. Hong, D., et al.: HIGHT: a new block cipher suitable for low-resource device. In: Goubin, L., Matsui, M. (eds.) CHES 2006. LNCS, vol. 4249, pp. 46–59. Springer, Heidelberg (2006). https://doi.org/10.1007/11894063_4
19. Moon, D., Hwang, K., Lee, W., Lee, S., Lim, J.: Impossible differential cryptanalysis of reduced round XTEA and TEA. In: Daemen, J., Rijmen, V. (eds.) FSE 2002. LNCS, vol. 2365, pp. 49–60. Springer, Heidelberg (2002). https://doi.org/10.1007/3-540-45661-9_4
20. Kim, J., Hong, S., Sung, J., Lee, S., Lim, J., Sung, S.: Impossible differential cryptanalysis for block cipher structures. In: Johansson, T., Maitra, S. (eds.) INDOCRYPT 2003. LNCS, vol. 2904, pp. 82–96. Springer, Heidelberg (2003). https://doi.org/10.1007/978-3-540-24582-7_6
21. Knudsen, L.: Deal-a 128-bit block cipher. Complexity (1998)
22. Lu, J.: Cryptanalysis of reduced versions of the HIGHT block cipher from CHES 2006. In: ICISC (2007)
23. Minier, M., Naya-Plasencia, M.: A related key impossible differential attack against 22 rounds of the lightweight block cipher lblock. Inf. Process. Lett. (2012)
24. Mouha, N., Wang, Q., Gu, D., Preneel, B.: Differential and linear cryptanalysis using mixed-integer linear programming. In: Wu, C.-K., Yung, M., Lin, D. (eds.) Inscrypt 2011. LNCS, vol. 7537, pp. 57–76. Springer, Heidelberg (2012). https://doi.org/10.1007/978-3-642-34704-7_5
25. Nethercote, N., Stuckey, P.J., Becket, R., Brand, S., Duck, G.J., Tack, G.: MiniZinc: towards a standard CP modelling language. In: Bessière, C. (ed.) CP 2007. LNCS, vol. 4741, pp. 529–543. Springer, Heidelberg (2007). https://doi.org/10.1007/978-3-540-74970-7_38
26. Özen, O., Varıcı, K., Tezcan, C., Kocair, Ç.: Lightweight block ciphers revisited: cryptanalysis of reduced round PRESENT and HIGHT. In: Boyd, C., González Nieto, J. (eds.) ACISP 2009. LNCS, vol. 5594, pp. 90–107. Springer, Heidelberg (2009). https://doi.org/10.1007/978-3-642-02620-1_7
27. Rostami, S., Chafjiri, S.B., Tabatabaei, S.A.H.: Related-key impossible differential cryptanalysis of full-round HIGHT. In: SECRYPT (2013)
28. Sasaki, Yu., Todo, Y.: New impossible differential search tool from design and cryptanalysis aspects. In: Coron, J.-S., Nielsen, J.B. (eds.) EUROCRYPT 2017. LNCS, vol. 10212, pp. 185–215. Springer, Cham (2017). https://doi.org/10.1007/978-3-319-56617-7_7
29. Sun, L., Gérault, D., Wang, W., Wang, M.: On the usage of deterministic (related-key) truncated differentials and multidimensional linear approximations for SPN ciphers. IACR Trans. Symmetric Cryptol. (2020)
30. Tezcan, C.: Improbable differential attacks on present using undisturbed bits. J. Comput. Appl. Math. (2014)
31. Wen, L., Wang, M., Zhao, J.: Related-key impossible differential attack on reduced-round lblock. J. Comput. Sci. Technol. (2014)
32. Wu, W., Zhang, L.: LBlock: a lightweight block cipher. In: Lopez, J., Tsudik, G. (eds.) ACNS 2011. LNCS, vol. 6715, pp. 327–344. Springer, Heidelberg (2011). https://doi.org/10.1007/978-3-642-21554-4_19

Symmetric Design Strategies and Security

Multiforked Iterated Even-Mansour and a Note on the Tightness of IEM Proofs

Elena Andreeva[1], Amit Singh Bhati[2,3], and Andreas Weninger[1(✉)]

[1] TU Wien, Vienna, Austria
{elena.andreeva,andreas.weninger}@tuwien.ac.at
[2] COSIC, KU Leuven, Leuven, Belgium
[3] 3milabs, Leuven, Belgium
amitsingh.bhati@3milabs.tech

Abstract. The Iterated Even-Mansour (IEM) construction was introduced by Bogdanov et al. at EUROCRYPT 2012 and can be seen as an abstraction or idealization of blockciphers like AES. IEM provides insights into the soundness of this blockcipher structure and the best possible security for any number of rounds. IEM with r permutations on n-bit blocks is secure up to $q \approx 2^{rn/(r+1)}$ queries to the cipher and each permutation.

Forkciphers, introduced at ASIACRYPT 2019 as expanding symmetric ciphers, have since found applications in encryption, authenticated encryption and key derivation. Kim et al. (ToSC 2020) proposed the first IEM-style forkcipher, FTEM, but their security proof is limited to a 2-round design with tweak processing based on XORing AXU hashes. This offers limited insight into practical forkciphers like ForkSkinny, which use 40 to 56 rounds and a different tweak schedule. No security results currently exist for forked IEM constructions with more than two rounds.

We propose a generalized forked IEM construction called GIEMwhich integrates any tweakey schedule (including tweak-dependent round keys or constant keys) and thus encompasses IEM, FTEM and similar IEM-related constructions. We define three forkcipher-related instantiations, FEM(2 branches and no tweaks), FTEM-ITS(2 branches and idealized tweakey schedule) and MFTEM(unlimited branches and AXU-based tweakey schedule). We prove that each construction achieves security similar to the respective non-forked construction. This shows the soundness of the forking design strategy and can serve as a basis for new constructions with more than two branches.

In their work, Bogdanov et al. also propose an attack against IEM using $q \approx 2^{rn/(r+1)}$ queries, which is used in a number of follow-up works to argue the tightness of IEM-related security bounds. In this work, we demonstrate that the attack is ineffective with the specified query complexity. To salvage the purported tightness results, we turn to an attack by Gaži (CRYPTO 2013) against cascading block ciphers and provide the necessary parameters to apply it to IEM. This validates the tightness of the known IEM security bound.

C. Boura et al. (Eds.): SAC 2025, LNCS 16207, pp. 179–208, 2026.
https://doi.org/10.1007/978-3-032-10536-3_7

Keywords: Iterated Even-Mansour · forkcipher · provable security

1 Introduction

Blockciphers are a fundamental building block in cryptography. Their design has been an important research focus in the last decades. In 1997 Even and Mansour [EM97] introduced the concept of building a blockcipher based on a public permutation P and a secret key $k = (k_1, k_2)$ as

$$c = P(m \oplus k_1) \oplus k_2 .$$

The Even-Mansour cipher (EM) [EM97] is provably secure up to roughly $2^{n/2}$ adversarial queries against adversaries that do not exploit the specific instantiation of the permutation. To formally model this, the permutation is randomly drawn from the set of all permutations and the adversary can query it arbitrarily. The security proof of the Even-Mansour cipher gives a generic security guarantee that shifts the difficulty of designing a secure blockcipher to the arguably simpler concept of designing a secure permutation. In 2012, Bogdanov et al. [BKL+12] extended the EM design to multiple rounds as

$$c = P_r(...P_2(P_1(m \oplus k_1) \oplus k_2)...) \oplus k_{r+1} ,$$

where $P_1, \ldots, P_r$ are independently and randomly sampled permutations. This construction is referred to as a Key Alternating Cipher (KAC) or Iterated Even-Mansour cipher (IEM) in the literature. While the original EM design is the basis for creating new blockciphers, IEM has an additional relevance, as it follows the internal (permute-round key XOR) alternating structure of popular ciphers, such as AES. Bogdanov et al. first provably analyzed the IEM structure. Since practical ciphers with a similar structure do not use independent random permutations, the security of existing ciphers does not surpass that of IEM. Hence the results on IEM give the minimum number of rounds of any secure key-alternating cipher.

In terms of provable security, the added rounds allow IEM to achieve beyond birthday bound security as a pseudo-random permutation. Bogdanov et al. [BKL+12] proved the security of IEM for information theoretic adversaries up to roughly $q \approx 2^{2n/3}$ queries when the number of rounds $r \geq 2$, and conjectured a security of $q \approx 2^{rn/(r+1)}$ in general.

The IEM work of Bogdanov et al. [BKL+12] sparked a broad body of follow-up works. In 2014, Chen and Steinberger [CS14] proved the IEM conjectured security up to about $2^{rn/(r+1)}$ queries for any number of rounds r. Later, Hoang and Tessaro [HT16] confirm this asymptotic bound with a proof in their new framework called the *expectation method.* This method both enables a simpler proof and an improved final bound. While asymptotically the same, the bound by Hoang and Tessaro gives better concrete security. For AES-like parameters ($n = 128$ and $r = 10$) and $q = 2^{110}$ queries to the cipher and each primitive, it gives still a reasonable bound on the maximum advantage of 2^{-50} whereas Chen and Steinberger's bound is already vacuous. Further, the expectation method gives a bound on the multi-user security of IEM. Multi-user security assumes each user to have independent keys but the same permutations, which better captures how blockciphers are deployed in the real world.

In a different line of work, Cogliati et al. [CLS15] proposed a tweakable variant of IEM called Tweakable Even-Mansour (TEM). Tweakable block ciphers (TBCs) are a generalization of traditional block ciphers that, aside from the message and key, take an additional tweak input, which may be adversarially controlled. For each distinct tweak, the tweakable cipher is supposed to behave like an independent random permutation. TBCs are used for length-preserving encryption modes [HR03, HR04], message authentication codes [LRW02, LST12] and authenticated encryption modes [RBBK01, LRW02, Rog04]. Cogliati et al. [CLS15] generate the round keys of TEM with almost XOR-universal (AXU) functions on input the current tweak. They proved security up to roughly $q \approx 2^{rn/(r+1)}$ queries in a dedicated proof for the 1- and 2-round construction, and security up to $q \approx 2^{rn/(r+2)}$ queries when $r \geq 3$, which is equivalent to the expected security of (regular) IEM with half as many rounds.

A number of works on IEM-like constructions [BKL+12, LPS12, Ste12, CS14, CLS15] argue about the tightness of their security bounds. Their arguments appear to be rooted in the attack by Bogdanov et al. [BKL+12] which uses $2^{rn/(r+1)}$ queries to each permutation and the cipher. However, to the best of our knowledge, a detailed analysis of this attack is missing in the existing literature.

In 2020, Kim et al. [KLL20] proposed FTEM, a novel key-alternating structure similar to a forkcipher. Forkciphers were introduced by Andreeva et al. [ALP+19]. They are expanding tweakable ciphers, that produce $2n$-bit ciphertext outputs from an n-bit input message. Intuitively, their output can be seen as the result of the application of two distinct tweakable blockciphers over the same input message. Forkciphers are used to build robust authenticated encryption schemes [ALP+19, ADP+20, ABV21, BAV24, BPA+23, BBDL23], generalized CTR mode encryption [ABPV21], tweakable enciphering scheme [BVA24], pseudorandom number generators [AW23, BDA+24], message authentication codes [BAMV24] and efficient PRFs [DGL22]. The work of Kim et al. [KLL20] follows the idea of Cogliati et al. [CLS15] and uses AXU functions to derive round keys from the tweak. They specify FTEMfor 2 branches and any number of rounds. Although FTEMprescribes a way to build new forkciphers, it does not capture existing forkciphers with a different key schedule such as ForkSkinny [ALP+19]. The mismatch stems from an optimization in FTEMto reduce the necessary number of AXU functions, which is not present in ForkSkinny. Widening the gap even further, the FTEMsecurity proof is limited to two rounds whereas ForkSkinny variants have 40 to 56 rounds. This brings up the question of how one can achieve a maximally secure "forked" TEM, that also encompasses ForkSkinny. Kim et al. [KLL20] prove the security of FTEMup to roughly $q \approx 2^{2n/3}$ queries, thus matching IEM with the same number of rounds and gaining tweakability and forking "for free". They conclude their work with two open questions:

"What is the security of this construction with more than 2 rounds and can it be extended to a multiforkcipher with more than 2 branches?"
A multiforkcipher [ABPV21] is an expanding cipher with more than two output branches. Multiforkciphers have immediate applications, for example, in CTR-style encryption where already $b = 2$ branch (multi)forkciphers have been shown to be approximately 20% more efficient than the regular blockcipher-based CTR encryption mode [ABPV21]. We give an overview of the different IEM variants in Fig. 1.

Name	r	b	Tweakable	Security (Queries)
IEM [CS14, HT16]	any	1	no	$2^{rn/(r+1)}$
TEM, $r \leq 2$ [CLS15]	2	1	yes (AXU)	$2^{2n/3}$
TEM [CLS15]	any	1	yes (AXU)	$2^{rn/(r+2)}$
FTEM [KLL20]	2	2	yes (AXU)	$2^{2n/3}$
FEM (this work)	any	2	no	$2^{rn/(r+1)}$
FTEM-ITS (this work)	any	2	yes (ideal)	$2^{rn/(r+1)}$
MFTEM (this work)	any	any	yes (AXU)	$\frac{1}{b^2}2^{rn/(r+2)}$

Fig. 1. Comparison of Iterated Even-Mansour variants. r denotes the number of rounds and b the number of (multiforkcipher) branches. For tweakable ciphers, we distinguish based on the tweakey schedule, using AXU (almost XOR universal) functions or an idealized tweakey schedule. Security is given in the number of adversarial queries that are roughly needed to attack successfully, so a higher number is better.

1.1 Contribution and Related Work

In support of additional analysis of forkciphers and similar iterative expanding structures, we introduce GIEM. GIEM is a generalization of IEM that allows an arbitrary choice for tweakey schedule functions, rounds and branches. As such GIEM can be instantiated to EM [EM97], IEM [BKL+12], TEM [CLS15] and FTEM [KLL20]. We provide 3 novel instantiations of GIEM, FEM (2 branches and no tweaks), FTEM-ITS (2 branches and idealized tweakey schedule) and MFTEM (unlimited branches and AXU-based tweakey schedule).

FEM is the forked version of IEM [BKL+12]. As mentioned, IEM starts from the message and then alternates between XORing the round key and applying a permutation, and after r rounds (i.e. permutations) gives a single ciphertext block as output. FEM also follows the IEM structure for $r/2$ rounds, after which the current state is used as the starting point for two branches, each of which performs the IEM structure for $r/2$ rounds again (with independent keys and permutations), resulting in two ciphertext blocks. We prove FEM to have security similar to IEM, i.e. up to $q \approx 2^{rn/(r+1)}$ queries. Due to the structural similarity to IEM, FEM gives direct insight into the security impact of the forking design strategy. Current forkciphers additionally take a tweak input, which is not the case for FEM.

This leads us to our second construction, MFTEM (Multi-Forked Tweakable iterated Even-Mansour), which is tweakable and answers the open questions of Kim et al. [KLL20]. MFTEM is a generalization of FTEM [KLL20], and is the first provably secure IEM-style construction with an arbitrary number of branches. In the two-branch case, MFTEM is similar to FEM, but MFTEM derives its round keys from the tweak input using AXU (almost XOR universal) functions. We prove the security of MFTEM for any number and rounds, unlike the two-round proof by Kim et al. For b branches, we prove security up to $q \approx \frac{1}{b^2} 2^{rn/(r+2)}$ queries. Here any small constant b has a negligible impact, and in particular for $b = 1$, MFTEM matches the best known bounds for TEM [CLS15]. Similar to FTEM, the tweakey schedule MFTEM is incompatible with ForkSkinny [ALP+19]. Yet, MFTEM can serve as the basis for new multiforkciphers with more than 2 branches.

Finally, we propose FTEM-ITS (2 branches and idealized tweakey schedule) as our third instantiation of GIEM and as an idealization of ForkSkinny. FTEM-ITS requires a stronger assumption than MFTEM (idealized tweakey schedule) but provides better security, up to roughly $q \approx 2^{rn/(r+1)}$ queries.

Overall, our results show that the security impact of the forking design strategy on the constructions we analyzed results in only a negligible security loss. At the same time, the forked constructions can provide two output blocks at the cost of only 1.5 times as many permutation calls. When we add tweaking based on AXU functions (MFTEM with $b = 2$ branches), the security up to $q \approx 2^{rn/(r+2)}$ is worse than that of IEM ($q \approx 2^{rn/(r+1)}$), but this loss is the same as for (single-branch) TEM [CLS15] versus IEM. When tweaking is done with an idealized key schedule, i.e. FTEM-ITS, we achieve security close to IEM (asymptotically up to $q \approx 2^{rn/(r+1)}$ queries). Compared to prior work, our results bring tweaking and forking to IEM (with idealized key schedule) and forking to TEM (with AXU-based key schedule) without weakening the asymptotic security.

In terms of security proofs, our single proof for FEM and FTEM-ITS provides the largest novelty. Our proof strategy follows the expectation method by Hoang and Tessaro [HT16], as well as their proof approach of creating a graph. We define a forked version of this graph. At the heart of our proof we provide a novel argument to bound the difference between sampling in this forked graph versus the regular graph. Combining this with results from the Chen and Steinberger proof for IEM [CS14] gives the final asymptotically tight bound. On the other hand, our MFTEM security proof is based on the proof by Cogliati et al. [CLS15] and has the benefit of being very concise compared to our proof for FEM and FTEM-ITS. The proof uses the probability distribution of IEM with half as many rounds to find the probability of producing a specific state in the middle layer. As a result the asymptotic security of our tweaked construction only matches the security of IEM with half as many rounds, similar to Cogliati's proof.

To answer whether our security bounds are tight, we take a detailed look at the attack by Bogdanov et al. [BKL+12]. Surprisingly, our analysis reveals a problem that renders the attack ineffective. Our analysis relies on the number of queries that Bogdanov et al. defined. While the concrete problem we describe does not apply if the number of queries is multiplied by some constant, the attack by Bogdanov et al. remains without a formal proof. In order to rely on proven results, we instead show that the generic attack by Gaži [Gaz13] against cascades of block ciphers applies to IEM. We describe how to use the attack by providing the necessary parameters.

2 Preliminaries

Notation. For any bitstring X, $|X|$ denotes its length and $X_{[a:b]}$ denotes the bitstring which is comprised of the bits of X at indices a to b. $X_{[1:|X|]} = X$. n is the security parameter, $N = 2^n$. For any set S, let 2^S denote the power set of S and $|S|$ the size of S. For a set S, $\min S$ denotes the minimum element of S, for a tuple (or finite sequence) $I = (i_b)_{b \in B}$, $\min I$ denotes $\min\{i_b | b \in B\}$, similarly $\max S$ the maximum element. For two bitstrings A, B, let $A||B$ denote their concatenation. We write $x \leftarrow_{\$} X$ to denote uniformly randomly sampling an element x from the set X.

Distributions. Given a finite event space Ω and probability distributions μ, ν defined on Ω, the total variation distance between μ and ν is $||\mu - \nu|| = \frac{1}{2}\sum_{x \in \Omega} |\mu(x) - \nu(x)|$.

Function Families. Let $\mathsf{Perm}(n)$ be the set of all permutations from $\{0,1\}^n$ to $\{0,1\}^n$, and $\mathsf{Func}(n)$ be the set of all functions from $\{0,1\}^n$ to $\{0,1\}^n$. Let $\mathcal{H}$ be a family of functions from some set $\mathtt{T}$ to $\{0,1\}^n$. $\mathcal{H}$ is *uniform* if for any $t \in \mathtt{T}$ and any $y \in \{0,1\}^n$, $\Pr[H \leftarrow_{\$} \mathcal{H} : H(t) = y] = 2^{-n}$. $\mathcal{H}$ is *ϵ-almost universal* (ϵ-AU) if for any distinct $t, t' \in \mathtt{T}$, $\Pr[H \leftarrow_{\$} \mathcal{H} : H(t) = H(t')] \leq \epsilon$. $\mathcal{H}$ is *ϵ-almost XOR-universal* (ϵ-AXU) if for any distinct $t, t' \in \mathtt{T}$ and any $y \in \{0,1\}^n$, $\Pr[H \leftarrow_{\$} \mathcal{H} : H(t) \oplus H(t') = y] \leq \epsilon$.

Multiforkcipher. We slightly adapt the multiforkcipher notion [ABPV21] to allow an arbitrary key K and tweak $\mathtt{T}$ spaces and fix each function to always produce the maximum number of outputs. We define a multiforkcipher (MFC) F_b (with b branches) as a pair of deterministic algorithms, the forward $F_b : K \times \mathtt{T} \times \{0,1\}^n \to \{0,1\}^{bn}$ (i.e. from the key, tweak and message it produces b blocks of n bits each), and the backward (or inverse) $F_b^{-1} : K \times \mathtt{T} \times \{0,1\}^n \times [b] \to \{0,1\}^{bn}$. The extra F_b^{-1} input is called the input indicator. The MFC is said to be *correct*, if for every call $F_b^{-1}(k, t, y)$, where y is one of the output blocks of a $F_b(k, t, x)$ call, the F_b^{-1} output is x followed by the other output blocks of the F_b call. We write $F_b[\mathbf{P}]$ to denote an MFC F that is based on a tuple of permutations $\mathbf{P}$.

The advantage of an adversary $\mathcal{A}$ in distinguishing F_b from a random multi-forked permutation $\tilde{P}$ (c.f. Sect. 3.2 [ABPV21]) is defined as

$$\mathsf{Adv}_{F_b}^{\mathbf{prtmfp}}(\mathcal{A}) = |\Pr[\mathcal{A}^{\mathbf{prtmfp\text{-}real}_{F_b}} \Rightarrow 1] - \Pr[\mathcal{A}^{\mathbf{prtmfp\text{-}ideal}_{F_b}} \Rightarrow 1]|.$$

where **prtmfp-real**$_{F_b}$ allows $\mathcal{A}$ to access $F_b(k,\cdot,\cdot), F_b^{-1}(k,\cdot,\cdot,\cdot)$, k is a random secret key. **prtmfp-ideal**$_{F_b}$ gives access to $\tilde{P} : K \times \mathtt{T} \times \{0,1\}^n \rightarrow \{0,1\}^{bn}$, which is equivalent to a randomly drawn permutation for each tweak $t \in \mathtt{T}$ and each branch $1,\ldots,b$. When F is based on some internal permutations $\mathbf{P}$, then they are drawn randomly at the start of both games and can be queried by $\mathcal{A}$ directly as well. A more detailed MFC definition is given in Sect. A.

H-coefficient Technique [Pat09]**.** We consider the interactions of a distinguisher $\mathcal{A}$ with an abstract system S that answers $\mathcal{A}$'s queries. The resulting interaction then generates a transcript $\tau = ((X_1,Y_1),...,(X_q,Y_q))$ of query-response pairs. S is entirely described by the probabilities $\mathsf{ps}(\tau)$ that correspond to the system S responding with answers as indicated by τ when queries in τ are made. We will generally describe systems informally, or more formally in terms of a set of oracles they provide, and only use the fact that they define corresponding probabilities $\mathsf{ps}(\tau)$ without explicitly giving these probabilities. We say that a transcript is valid for system S if $\mathsf{ps}(\tau) > 0$.

For any systems $\mathbf{S}_1$ and $\mathbf{S}_0$, let $\Delta_{\mathcal{A}}(\mathbf{S}_1, \mathbf{S}_0)$ denote the distinguishing advantage of the adversary $\mathcal{A}$ against the "real" system $\mathbf{S}_1$ and the "ideal" system $\mathbf{S}_0$.

We now describe the H-coefficient technique of Patarin [Pat09]. Generically, it considers a deterministic distinguisher $\mathcal{A}$ that tries to distinguish a "real" system $\mathbf{S}_1$ from an "ideal" system $\mathbf{S}_0$. The adversary's interactions with those systems define transcripts X_1 and X_0, respectively, and a bound on the distinguishing advantage of $\mathcal{A}$ is given by the statistical distance $\mathsf{SD}(X_1, X_0)$.

Lemma 1 (see [Pat09]). *Suppose we can partition the set of valid transcripts for the ideal system into good and bad ones. Further, suppose that there exists* $\epsilon \geq 0$ *such that* $1 - \frac{\mathsf{ps}_1(\tau)}{\mathsf{ps}_0(\tau)} \leq \epsilon$ *for every good transcript* τ*. Then,*

$$\mathsf{SD}(X_1, X_0) \leq \epsilon + \Pr[X_0 \textit{ is bad}].$$

Expectation Method. For the expectation method by Hoang and Tessaro [HT16], assume an adversary plays against a single-user security game $\mathsf{su\text{-}game}$ for a keyed construction Π that is built from some primitive P. The adversary is allowed q queries to the construction and p queries to each primitive, and shall output 0 if the construction queries were answered with the real Π or 1 if the queries where answered by the idealized system. Let $\mathbf{S}_0$ the system of the adversary interacting with the real system and $\mathbf{S}_1$ the random system. Further, let $\mathsf{mu\text{-}game}$ the multi-user security game corresponding to $\mathsf{su\text{-}game}$, where each user has its own key but the same primitive P. In $\mathsf{mu\text{-}game}$, the adversary has access to the same oracles as in $\mathsf{su\text{-}game}$ (e.g. for encryption and decryption), but each oracle has an additional input to select the index of the user whose key is used. A more detailed description of admissible security games is given by Hoang and Tessaro [HT16]. Let random variable S capture the key of Π (which we sample uniformly both in $\mathbf{S}_0$ and $\mathbf{S}_1$). $\mathsf{p}_{\mathbf{S}}(\tau, s)$ denotes the probability that $S = s$ and $\mathbf{S}$ behaves according to τ.

Lemma 2 (Lemma 2, Definition 1 and Lemma 3 in [HT16]). *If for any transcript τ for which $\mathsf{ps}_{\mathsf{S}_1}(\tau) > 0$ there exists a partition $\Gamma_{\mathsf{good}}, \Gamma_{\mathsf{bad}}$ of the range $\mathcal{U}$ of S, as well as a function $g : \mathcal{U} \to [0, \infty)$ such that $\Pr[S \in \Gamma_{\mathsf{bad}}] \leq \delta$ and for all $s \in \Gamma_{\mathsf{good}}$,*

$$1 - \frac{\mathsf{ps}_{\mathsf{S}_0}(\tau, s)}{\mathsf{ps}_{\mathsf{S}_1}(\tau, s)} \leq g(s).$$

Then, for $\epsilon(p, q) := \delta + \mathbb{E}[g(S)]$,

$$\begin{aligned}\mathsf{Adv}_{\Pi}^{\text{su-game}}(p, q) &\leq \epsilon(p, q),\\ \mathsf{Adv}_{\Pi}^{\text{mu-game}}(p, q) &\leq 2\epsilon(p + qm, q).\end{aligned}$$

3 The GIEMConstruction

We now describe our r-rounds b-branches GIEM(Generalized Iterated Even-Mansour) construction, where $r \geq 2$ is even, and $b \geq 1$.

Definition 1. *We define*

$$\begin{aligned}\mathbb{I} &= \{(0,1), \ldots, (0, r/2), (1, r/2+1), \ldots, (1, r), (2, r/2+1), \ldots, (b, r)\},\\ \mathbb{J} &= \{(0,1), \ldots, (0, r/2), (1, r/2+1), \ldots, (1, r+1), (2, r/2+1), \ldots, (b, r+1)\}.\end{aligned}$$

Let $\mathtt{T}$ denote the tweakspace. For all $i \in \mathbb{I}$, let $P_i : \{0,1\}^n \to \{0,1\}^n$ be a permutation. For all $j \in \mathbb{J}$, let $h_j : \mathtt{T} \to \{0,1\}^n$ be some function, and $\mathbf{H} = (h_j)_{j \in \mathbb{J}}$. $\mathsf{GIEM}_{\mathbf{H}}^{b,r}$ is defined in Fig. 2, and an example with $r = 4$ and $b = 2$ is given in Fig. 3. When we want to make the internally used permutations explicit we write $\mathsf{GIEM}_{\mathbf{H}}^{b,r}[\mathbf{P}]$, where $\mathbf{P} = (P_i)_{i \in \mathbb{I}}$.

$\mathsf{GIEM}_{\mathbf{H}}^{b,r}(t, m)$
$S \leftarrow m$
for $j = 1$ **to** $r/2$ **do**
$\quad S \leftarrow P_{0,j}(S \oplus h_{0,j}(t))$
for $i = 1$ **to** b :
$\quad S_i \leftarrow S$
$\quad$ **for** $j = r/2+1$ **to** r **do**
$\quad\quad S_i \leftarrow P_{i,j}(S \oplus h_{i,j}(t))$
$\quad S_i \leftarrow S_i \oplus h_{i,r+1}(t)$
return $S_1 \| \ldots \| S_b$

$(\mathsf{GIEM}^{-1})_{\mathbf{H}}^{b,r}(t, c, \beta)$
$S \leftarrow c \oplus h_{\beta,r+1}(t)$
for $j = r$ **to** $r/2+1$ **do**
$\quad S \leftarrow P_{\beta,j}^{-1}(S) \oplus h_{\beta,j}(t)$
for $j = r/2$ **to** 1 **do**
$\quad S \leftarrow P_{0,j}^{-1}(S) \oplus h_{0,j}(t)$
$Y_1 \| \ldots \| Y_b \leftarrow \mathsf{GIEM}_{\mathbf{H}}^{b,r}.\mathsf{Enc}(t, S)$
return $S \| Y_1 \| \ldots \| Y_{\beta-1} \| Y_{\beta+1} \| \ldots \| Y_b$

Fig. 2. $\mathsf{GIEM}_{\mathbf{H}}^{b,r}$ algorithms.

Related Constructions. If $b = 2$ and $\mathbf{H} = (h_{0,1}, h_{0,2} \oplus h_{0,1}, \ldots, h_{b,r-1} \oplus h_{b,r}, h_{b,r})$ where all h_j are sampled randomly and independently from a uniform AXU-family, then $\mathsf{GIEM}_{\mathbf{H}}^{2,r}$ is equivalent to FTEM by Kim et al. [KLL20]. Contrary to the idea of Kim et al., we fix the branching point to after the $r/2$-th permutation, instead of allowing the common initial part to have a different length than the branches. The reason is that the security appears to be limited by the shortest path from the message to one ciphertext block or from one ciphertext block to another. Our proof strategy requires having at least $r/2$ permutations after the branching point.

If $b = 1$ instead, then $\mathsf{GIEM}_{\mathbf{H}}^{1,r}$ is equivalent to TEM by Cogliati et al. [CLS15]. If $b = 1$, $|\mathtt{T}| = 1$ and $\mathbf{H} = (k_{0,1}, \ldots k_{1,r+1})$ where each k_i is a random value from $\{0,1\}^n$ (or more precisely, and to match our notation, a constant function pointing to this value) then $\mathsf{GIEM}_{\mathbf{H}}^{1,r}$ is equivalent to the original IEM by Bogdanov et al. [BKL+12].

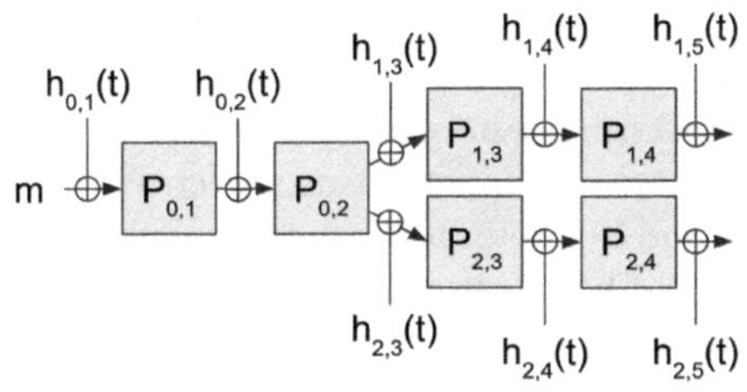

Fig. 3. $\mathsf{GIEM}_{\mathbf{H}}^{b,r}$ with $r = 4, b = 2$.

4 FEMand FTEM-ITS

We describe instantiations FEM and FTEM-ITS of GIEM. Let $\mathsf{FEM} = \mathsf{GIEM}_{\mathbf{H}}^{b,r}$, with $b = 2$ and each $h_{i,j} \in \mathbf{H}$ being a randomly sampled constant function, i.e. $\forall x : h_{i,j}(x) = k_{i,j}$ for some $k_{i,j} \in \{0,1\}^n$. Let the tweakspace $\mathtt{T} = \{0\}$. Since all queries must use the same tweak 0, FEMacts as a forkcipher with randomly sampled round keys and no tweaks, making it the 2-branch forked variant of IEM.

Let $\mathsf{FTEM\text{-}ITS} = \mathsf{GIEM}_{\mathbf{H}}^{b,r}$ with $b = 2$ and each $h \in \mathbf{H}$ being a randomly sampled function from an arbitrary tweakspace to $\{0,1\}^n$. Thus FTEMmodels a forkcipher with ideal tweakey schedule, giving independent round keys for each tweak.

Theorem 1. *For any adversary $\mathcal{A}$ making at most $q \leq N/2^{r+2}$ queries to each permutation and the cipher, we have*

$$\mathsf{Adv}_{\mathsf{FEM}}^{\mathrm{prtmfp}}(q) \leq 2 \cdot 10^r q^{r+1}/N^r,$$
$$\mathsf{Adv}_{\mathsf{FEM}}^{\mathrm{mu\text{-}prtmfp}}(q) \leq (3r/2+1)^{r+1} \cdot 4 \cdot 10^r q^{r+1}/N^r.$$

The proof is provided in the next section.

Relation to Tweaked Forkciphers. Since the multi-user security assumes independent keys for each user, our above bound for multi-user security of untweaked forkciphers also applies to the (single-user) security of forkciphers where the tweakey schedule is assumed to be ideal. Concretely,

$$\mathsf{Adv}^{\mathrm{prtmfp}}_{\mathsf{FTEM\text{-}ITS}}(q) \le (3r/2+1)^{r+1} \cdot 4 \cdot 10^r q^{r+1}/N^r \,.$$

Bound Interpretation. First, note that the restriction to $q \le N/2^{r+2}$ has little impact, for more queries q and AES-like parameters ($n = 128, r = 10$) the right-hand sides of the inequalities are larger than 1 anyways. The single-user advantage of FEMin Theorem 1 is similar to the bound for IEM of Hoang and Tessaro (Theorem 1 in [HT16]) with q primitive queries, except having $2 \cdot 10^r$ instead of 4^r as factor. Asymptotically, both bounds give security up to $q \approx N^{r/(r+1)}$ queries. The concrete security is also similar, an adversary attacking FEMwith q queries to the cipher and each permutation has less advantage than attacking IEM with $4q$ queries. Our multi-user security of FEMis obtained from the expectation method and holds for any number of users. Comparing multi-user to single-user security, our FEM bound has a similar loss as is the case for IEM (Theorem 2 in [HT16]) based on the number of permutations, which is larger in FEM, i.e. $3r/2$. Again, the asymptotic security of both is $q \approx N^{r/(r+1)}$ and attacking FEMin the multi-user setting with q queries has less advantage than the corresponding IEM bound [HT16] with $8q$ queries.[1] Thus the single-user and multi-user security of FEMis similar to that of regular IEM.

For FTEM-ITSthere is no construction that is the direct equivalent without forking. The only tweakable IEM construction, TEMby Cogliati et al. [CLS15], has security up to $q \approx N^{\frac{r}{r+2}}$ queries. For FTEM-ITSwe have security up to $q \approx N^{\frac{r}{r+1}}$ queries, which is better. However TEMis based on a specific key schedule with AXU functions, which is a weaker assumption than what we use for FTEM-ITS. Compared to regular IEM, the single-user security of FTEM-ITSfor q queries is better than the single-user security of IEM [CS14,HT16] with $8rq$ queries, while FTEM-ITSprovides additional tweaking and forking capabilities.

4.1 Proof of Theorem 1

We follow the IEM security proof by Hoang and Tessaro [HT16] in the expectation method (Lemma 2), adapted to our forked IEM structure. Let $\mathbf{S}_0, \mathbf{S}_1$ be the systems associated to the real and ideal game for prtmfp security. $\mathbb{I}, \mathbb{J}$ were defined in Definition 1. Transcripts τ contain two types of entries: For any $(i,j) \in \mathbb{I}$, $y = P_{i,j}(x)$ and $x = P^{-1}_{i,j}(y)$ queries result in entry $(\mathsf{Perm}, i, j, x, y)$,

[1] In our multi-user security bound, the factor $(3r/2+1)^{r+1}q^{r+1}$ matches the $(p+qt)^t$ term in Theorem 2 in [HT16] (for $t = r$ permutations and $p = q$ queries), except for having $3r/2$ rather than r permutations.

$\boldsymbol{c} = \mathsf{Enc}(m)$ and Dec queries result in entry $(\mathsf{Enc}, m, \boldsymbol{c})$, where $\boldsymbol{c} = (c^1, c^2)$ contains the ciphertext blocks of branch 1 and 2. (To maintain the same format, for forkcipher decryption queries of a ciphertext block at index $\beta \in \{1, 2\}$, put the query input in the position of c^β and the output blocks in the position of the message and the other ciphertext block.) We note that the direction of the queries does not impact the probabilities $\mathsf{p}_{\mathbf{S}_0}(\tau), \mathsf{p}_{\mathbf{S}_1}(\tau)$ of a transcript occurring in $\mathbf{S}_0$ or $\mathbf{S}_1$. Let $f = r/2$, i.e. the final round after which the construction forks into two branches. In the above definitions, i corresponds to the branch (0 for the initial part before forking) and j to the round. For notational convenience we will also use indexing as described in the following definition.

Notation 1. *Throughout this proof, whenever we use an index* (i, j) *with* $j \leq f$ *and* $i \in \{1, 2\}$ *it should be treated as* $(0, j)$.

Thus $P_{0,1} = P_{1,1} = P_{2,1}$, and we can always specify the permutation "to the left" of permutation $P_{i,j}$ as $P_{i,j-1}$.

Overview, Defining $G(s)$. Define $N = 2^n$. We have $q \leq N/4$ from the assumption in the theorem statement. Fix a transcript τ. We will use the expectation method (Lemma 2). Let S be the random variable for the key of FEMin $\mathbf{S}_0$. Let $\mathcal{K}$ be the keyspace, then S is uniformly distributed over $\mathcal{K}$. For each key $s = (L_j)_{j \in \mathbb{J}} \in \mathcal{K}$, define graph $G(s)$ as follows: Let $\mathbb{I}_0 = \mathbb{I} \cup \{(0, 0)\}$. Its set of vertices is partitioned into sets $V_\gamma, \gamma \in \mathbb{I}_0$ each of 2^n elements which are labelled $(\gamma, 0) \ldots (\gamma, 2^n - 1)$. For each entry $(\mathsf{Perm}, i, j, x, y)$ in τ, add an edge between $((i, j-1), x \oplus L_{j-1})$ and $((i, j), y)$. For a path F in $G(s)$, let $|F|$ be the number of edges in F. An example of such a graph is given in Fig. 4.

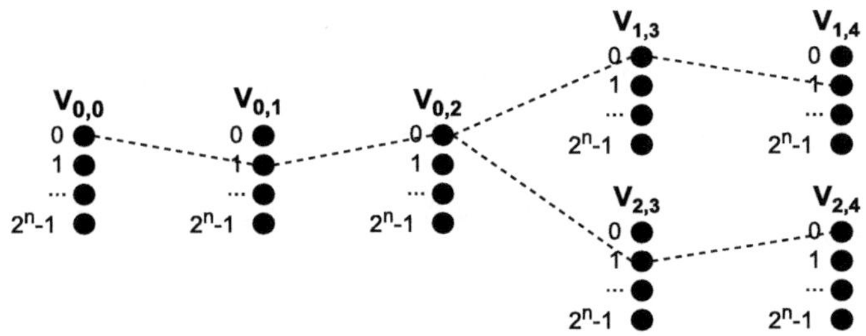

Fig. 4. Graph $G(s)$ for $\mathsf{FEM}$with $r = 4$. Here the transcript τ contains exactly the Perm queries that would be needed to evaluate the encryption of $m = 0$, the edges thus form a "forked" path. *In the example,* τ *contains queries* $(\mathsf{Perm}, 0, 1, 0, 1)$, $(\mathsf{Perm}, 0, 2, 5, 0)$, $(\mathsf{Perm}, 1, 3, 0, 0)$, $(\mathsf{Perm}, 1, 4, 0, 1)$, $(\mathsf{Perm}, 2, 3, 2, 1)$ *and* $(\mathsf{Perm}, 2, 4, 4, 0)$. $s_{0,1} = 0, s_{0,2} = 4, s_{1,3} = 0, s_{1,4} = 0, s_{2,3} = 2, s_{2,4} = 5$. ($s_{1,5}$ and $s_{2,5}$ *are irrelevant for the graph.*)

Following the expectation method, we now classify the keys as good or bad. Intuitively, for bad keys the adversary made the necessary Perm queries to verify if encrypting message m can result in $\boldsymbol{c}$ for at least one $(\mathsf{Enc}, m, \boldsymbol{c})$ in τ.

Definition 2 (Good and bad keys). *We say a key s is* bad *if τ contains an entry* $(\mathsf{Enc}, m, \boldsymbol{c})$ *such that in $G(s)$, there are paths F_0, F_1 starting from two distinct elements in $\{(0,0,m),(1,r,c^1 \oplus L_{1,r+1}),(2,r,c^2 \oplus L_{2,r+1})\}$ and some $\gamma \in \mathbb{I}_0$ such that F_0 contains some vertex in V_γ and F_1 contains some vertex in V_γ.*

If a key is not bad then we say it is good. *Let Γ_{bad} be the set of bad keys, and $\Gamma_{\mathsf{good}} = \mathcal{K} \setminus \Gamma_{\mathsf{bad}}$.*

We will show

$$\Pr[S \in \Gamma_{\mathsf{bad}}] \leq \frac{1}{2} \cdot 10^r \cdot \frac{q^{r+1}}{N^r}. \tag{1}$$

To see this, let $S = (S_j)_{j \in \mathbb{J}}$. First treat the case that F_0 starts from $(0,0,m)$ and F_1 in $(1,r,c_1 \oplus L_r)$. $S \in \Gamma_{\mathsf{bad}}$ means that τ contains entries

$$(\mathsf{Enc}, m, \boldsymbol{c}), (\mathsf{Perm}, 1, 1, u_1, v_1), \ldots, (\mathsf{Perm}, 1, r, u_r, v_r)$$

(indexing as in Definition 1) such that one of the following happens:

1. $u_1 = m \oplus S_{1,1}$ and $u_j = v_{j-1} \oplus S_{1,j}$ for every $j \in \{2,\ldots,r\}$, or
2. $v_r = c^i \oplus S_{1,r+1}$ and $u_j = v_{j-1} \oplus S_{1,j}$ for every $j \in \{2,\ldots,r\}$, or
3. $u_1 = m \oplus S_{1,1}$, $v_r = c^i \oplus S_{1,r+1}$ and there is an $\ell \in \{2,\ldots,r\}$ such that $u_j = v_{j-1} \oplus S_{1,j}$ for every $j \in \{2,\ldots,r\} \setminus \{\ell\}$.

There are q choices for the query $(\mathsf{Enc}, m, \boldsymbol{c})$ in τ and q choices for $(\mathsf{Perm}, 1, j, u_j, v_j)$ for each j, i.e. q^{r+1} choices in total for the list of queries. For each choice, there is only one $S_{1,j}$ for each $j \in \{1,\ldots,r\}$ to fulfill condition (1). Since all $S_{i,j}$ are uniform in $\{0,1\}^n$, the chance for condition (1) is at most q^{r+1}/N^r. For condition (2) and (3) for any ℓ the same is true, giving $(r+1)q^{r+1}/N^r$ in total. For the other 2 pairs of elements in $\{(0,0,m),(1,r,c_1 \oplus L_r),(2,r,c_2 \oplus L_r)\}$, the bound is analogous, resulting in $\Pr[S \in \Gamma_{\mathsf{bad}}] \leq 3(r+1)q^{r+1}/N^r \leq \frac{1}{2} \cdot 10^r \cdot \frac{q^{r+1}}{N^r}$.

Lemma 3. *There is a non-negative function $g : \mathcal{K} \to [0,\infty)$ such that for any $s \in \Gamma_{\mathsf{good}}$, it holds that*

$$1 - \frac{\mathsf{ps}_0(\tau, s)}{\mathsf{ps}_1(\tau, s)} \leq g(s) \quad \text{and} \quad \mathbb{E}[g(s)] \leq \frac{3}{2} \cdot 10^r \cdot \frac{q^{r+1}}{N^r}.$$

The proof is given in Sect. 4.2. Using Lemma 2 with Lemma 3 and Eq. (1) proves Theorem 1.

4.2 Proof of Lemma 3

Defining $\alpha, \beta, Z_s^i(a,b)$. Fix some $s = (L_j)_{j \in \mathbb{J}}$. Let $Z_s^i(a,b)$ be the number of paths from vertices $V_{i,a}$ to vertices in $V_{i,b}$ of $G(s)$. Let the Enc entries of τ be $(\mathsf{Enc}, m_1, \boldsymbol{c}_1) \ldots (\mathsf{Enc}, m_q, \boldsymbol{c}_q)$. For $k \in \{1,\ldots,q\}$ let $\alpha_k[s]$ be the length of the longest path starting from $(0,0,m_k)$ and for $i \in \{1,2\}$, let $r - \beta_k^i[s]$ be the length of the longest path ending at $(i, r, c_k^i \oplus L_{i,r+1})$. Note that if s is good then $\alpha_k[s] \le \beta_k^i[s]$ for every $k \in \{1, \dots, q\}, i \in \{1, 2\}$.

Defining G_k, PathSample. Let G_0 be $G(s)$. For each $k \in \{1, \dots, q\}$, let G_k be defined from G_{k-1} by running the following procedure, which we refer to as $\mathsf{PathSample}_k$. Intuitively, $\mathsf{PathSample}_k$ simulates the evaluation of the cipher on input m_k, represented as a forkpath through the graph G_k.

Definition 3. $\mathsf{PathSample}_k$: *Let* $z_{0,0} \leftarrow m_k \oplus L_{0,1}, z_{0,1} \leftarrow P_{0,1}(z_{0,0})$ *and for each* $(i, j) \in \mathbb{I} \setminus \{(0, 1)\}$, *let* $z_{i,j} \leftarrow P_{i,j}(z_{i,j-1} \oplus L_{i,j})$. *For all* $(i, j) \in \mathbb{I}$ *connect vertices* $((i, j-1), z_{i,j-1})$ *and* $((i, j), z_{i,j})$ *if this edge is not yet in graph* G_{k-1}.

Defining $m_k \rightarrow^* \boldsymbol{c}_k, m_k \rightarrow^i \boldsymbol{c}_k$. Fix some $k \in \{1, \dots, q\}$. Let G be a graph in the support of random variable G_{k-1}. We define a forkpath F as a triple of paths F_0, F_1, F_2 that have a common endpoint in $V_{0,r/2}$ and otherwise each path contains only vertices from branch 0, 1 or 2, respectively. F is said to connect vertices x and y if $x, y \in F_0 \cup F_1 \cup F_2$. We say that G is *well-formed* if there is a forkpath in G connecting $((0, 0), m_j)$ to $((r, 1), c_j^1 \oplus L_{1,r+1})$ and $((r, 2), c_j^2 \oplus L_{2,r+1})$ for every $j \in \{1, \dots, k-1\}$. If G is well-formed then let $\Pr[m_k \rightarrow^i c_k^i]$ (for $i \in \{1, 2\}$) be the probability that in $\mathbf{S}_0$, if S agrees with s, and the permutation oracles behave according to G for every $j \in \{1, \dots, k-1\}$, then querying m_k to Enc results in the block c_k^i in branch i. Let $\Pr[m_k \rightarrow^* \boldsymbol{c}_k] = \Pr[m_k \rightarrow^1 c_k^1 \wedge m_k \rightarrow^2 c_k^2]$, i.e. the probability that m_k results in both blocks of $\boldsymbol{c}_k$. Then from the definition of PathSample, $\Pr[m_k \rightarrow^i c_k^i]$ is equal to the probability that the corresponding vertices are connected in G_k, i.e. $((0, 0), m_k \oplus L_{0,1})$ connected to $((i, r), c_k^i \oplus L_{i,r+1})$.

Defining $\bar{\mathsf{U}}_G^i(a, b)$. Let G^* be the graph obtained from G by deleting the paths connecting $((0, 0), x_j)$ to $((r, 1), c_j^1)$ and $((0, 0), x_j)$ to $((r, 2), c_j^2)$ for every $j \in \{1, \dots, k-1\}$. Let $U_G^i(a, b)$ be the number of paths F from vertices in $V_{i,a}$ to $V_{i,b}$ in G^*, such that there is no vertex in $V_{i,a-1}$ connected to the first vertex in F. Let $\bar{\mathsf{U}}_G^i(a, b)$ be the vertices of such paths F in $V_{i,a}$ (i.e. the endpoints of these paths). We have

$$U_G^i(a, b) \le Z_s^i(a, b), \tag{2}$$

since all paths contributing to $U_G^i(a, b)$ also contribute to $Z_s^i(a, b)$.

Preparing the Expectation Method. We turn to establishing a bound on $1 - \frac{\mathsf{ps}_0(\tau, s)}{\mathsf{ps}_1(\tau, s)}$.

Lemma 4. *We have*

$$1 - \frac{\mathsf{ps}_0(\tau, s)}{\mathsf{ps}_1(\tau, s)} \le \sum_{k=1}^{q} \left(1 - (N - k + 1)^2 \Pr[m_k \rightarrow^* \boldsymbol{c}_k]\right) .$$

The proof is given in Appendix A.2, and follows similar steps to Hoang and Tessaro [HT16]. To continue, we define

$$\Theta_k = \Pr[m_k \rightarrow^* \boldsymbol{c}_k] - \Pr[m_k \rightarrow^1 c_k^1] \Pr[m_k \rightarrow^2 c_k^2] .$$

Intuitively, this is the difference between receiving the correct ciphertext from FEM (which has a single set of permutations before forking) versus two IEM instances that use independent permutations (from the set of permutations that are consistent with the permutation queries in the transcript). Then,

$$\Pr[m_k \to^* \boldsymbol{c}_k] = \Pr[m_k \to^1 c_k^1] \Pr[m_k \to^2 c_k^2] + \Theta_k \,. \tag{3}$$

We will bound $\Pr[m_k \to^i c_k^i]$ using existing results on (non-forked) IEM. The main challenge lies in establishing a lower bound for Θ_k. Note that event $m_k \to^* \boldsymbol{c}_k$ happens when the forkpath F that is created from following the permutations P connects m_k to $c_k^1 \oplus L_{1,r+1}$ and $c_k^2 \oplus L_{2,r+1}$. Since $m_k \to^* \boldsymbol{c}_k$ is conditioned on the permutations agreeing with the Perm queries, F must contain the paths associated to $\alpha_k[s], \beta_k^1[s], \beta_k^2[s]$. Consider some graph G with $a = \alpha_k[s], b_1 = \beta_k^1[s], b_2 = \beta_k^2[s]$. Since we fixed the transcript τ and the key s, the remaining randomness lies in the unqueried permutation inputs. In the case that $a > f$, the path F must contain the path associated to $\alpha_k[s]$. $m_k \to^1 c_k^1$ therefore only depends on sampling the permutations of branch 1, and $m_k \to^2 c_k^2$ only on permutations in branch 2, making them independent. Thus $\Theta_k = 0$. In the case that $f \geq b_1$, F again contains the path for $b_1 = \beta_k^1[s]$, $m_k \to^1 c_k^1$ now depends only on permutations in branch 0 and $m_k \to^2 c_k^2$ only on permutations in branch 2, again $\Theta_k = 0$. The case of $f \geq b_2$ is analogous. The rest of this proof is on proving a bound for Θ_k in general, which is worse than $\Theta_k = 0$. Thus from this point on we restrict our focus to

$$a \leq f < \min\{b_1, b_2\} \,.$$

Defining $u_{i,j}, w_{i,j}$. Fix any $k \in \{1, \dots, q\}$ and $a = \alpha_k[s], b_1 = \beta_k^1[s], b_2 = \beta_k^2[s]$. We now define an alternative algorithm $\mathsf{PathSample}'_k$ to obtain G_k from G_{k-1}, and will show that it is equivalent to $\mathsf{PathSample}_k$. Let $\mathbb{M} = \{(0, a+1), \dots, (0, f), (1, f+1), \dots, (1, b_1), (2, f+1), \dots, (2, b_2)\}$. For $(i, j) \in \mathbb{M}$ we define $u_{i,j}$ to be a randomly sampled vertex among the vertices in $V_{i,j}$, that do not have an edge to $V_{i,j-1}$. Then define $w_{0,a}$ as the endpoint of the path associated to $\alpha_k[s]$ in $V_{0,a}$ (recall our assumption $a \leq f$). For $(i, j) \in \mathbb{M}$, if there is an edge between $w_{i,j-1}$ and some vertex $v \in V_{i,j}$, then $w_{i,j} := v$. Otherwise, $w_{i,j} := u_{i,j}$. Note the vertices w_i define a forkpath F that has the same distribution as the original sampling algorithm, the first condition captures when $P_{i,j}$ was queried on the relevant input already, and the second condition captures lazy sampling of the unqueried permutation inputs. Similar to $\mathsf{PathSample}_k$, the edges of F are added to the graph G_{k-1} to obtain G_k.

Defining $\odot, \otimes, \Delta$. For $(i, x) \in \mathbb{M}, y \in \{x+1, \dots, r\}$, let $\odot_{xy}^i = \Pr[u_{i,x} \in \bar{\mathsf{U}}_{x,y}^i]$ and $\otimes_{xy}^i = \Pr[w_{i,x} \in \bar{\mathsf{U}}_{x,y}^i]$. Intuitively, $\odot_{xy}^i$ is the probability that $\mathsf{PathSample}'$ "tries" to select a path from $V_{i,x}$ to $V_{i,y}$, whereas $\otimes_{xy}^i$ is the probability that such a path is in fact selected.[2] We sometimes write $\odot_{x,y}^i$ instead of $\odot_{xy}^i$ for clarity. For pairs $X = (x_1, x_2), Y = (y_1, y_2)$, we define the following symbols.

[2] This notation resembles the one by Chen and Steinberger [CS14] in their Lemma 1 proof. However they defined $\odot, \otimes$ as the corresponding events, i.e. our $\odot_{xy}^1$ is equal to $\Pr[\odot_{xy}]$ in their notation. They use unconventional arithmetic notation $(+, -, \dots)$ for operations on these events, we chose our different definition to avoid this.

$$\bar{\odot}_{XY} = \Pr[u_{1,x_1} \in \bar{\mathsf{U}}^1_{x_1,y_1} \wedge u_{2,x_2} \in \bar{\mathsf{U}}^2_{x_2,y_2}]$$
$$\bar{\otimes}_{XY} = \Pr[w_{1,x_1} \in \bar{\mathsf{U}}^1_{x_1,y_1} \wedge w_{2,x_2} \in \bar{\mathsf{U}}^2_{x_2,y_2}]$$
$$\dot{\odot}_{XY} = \odot^1_{x_1,y_1} \odot^2_{x_2,y_2}$$
$$\dot{\otimes}_{XY} = \otimes^1_{x_1,y_1} \otimes^2_{x_2,y_2}$$
$$\Delta_{XY} = \bar{\otimes}_{XY} - \dot{\otimes}_{XY}$$

To give an intuition, one may interpret $\bar{\odot}_{XY}, \bar{\otimes}_{XY}$ as related to our forked graph, unlike the single-branch $\odot^i_{xy}, \otimes^i_{xy}$. Then $\dot{\odot}_{XY}, \dot{\otimes}_{XY}$ could be thought of as relating to two IEM instances with independent permutations. Indeed, if for $i \in \{1,2\}$, $x \leq f < y_i$, then $u_{1,x} = u_{2,x} = u_{0,x}$ and thus for $X = (x,x), Y = (y_1, y_2)$, $\bar{\odot}_{XY} > 0$ requires the existence of a joint path through $V_{0,x}, \ldots, V_{0,f}$ which then splits into paths for each branch, whereas $\dot{\odot}_{XY} > 0$ is possible if there are two separate paths from a vertex in $V_{0,x}$ to V_{1,y_1} and V_{2,y_2}, respectively.

Characterizations and Defining M, B, R. Recall we fixed $a = \alpha_k[s], b_1 = \beta^1_k[s], b_2 = \beta^2_k[s]$. For natural number x, define $[x] = \{a+1, \ldots, x-1\}$. For $X = (x_1, x_2), Y = (y_1, y_2)$ define $X \prec Y \Leftrightarrow x_1 < y_1 \wedge x_2 < y_2, X \preceq Y \Leftrightarrow x_1 \leq y_1, x_2 \leq y_2$. For notational convenience, we consider G with additional vertices $V_{i,r+1}$ for $i \in \{1,2\}$, with a single edge from c^i_k in $V_{i,r}$ to vertex $((i, r+1), 0)$. Let $M := N - k + 1$. Then for all $\gamma \in \mathbb{I}_0$, we have $M = |V_\gamma|$ in G^*. Let $B = (b_1, b_2)$. Let $R = (r+1, r+1)$. Let $X = (x_1, x_2) \in [b_1+1] \times [b_2+1], Y = (y_1, y_2)$ with $X \prec Y \preceq R$. We now give a list of equations to characterize our $\odot, \otimes$ expressions, and prove all of them below. The following first equations allow us to translate our prior probabilities.

$$\Pr[m_k \to^i c^i_k] = \otimes^i_{b_i, r+1} \tag{4}$$
$$\Pr[m_k \to^* \mathbf{c}_k] = \bar{\otimes}_{BR} \tag{5}$$

The next equations will help us to compute the concrete values for $\otimes^i_{b_i,r+1}, \bar{\otimes}_{BR}$ by deconstructing the $\otimes$ expressions step-by-step.

$$\otimes^i_{xy} = \odot^i_{xy}(1 - \sum_{j \in [x]} \otimes^i_{jx}) \tag{6}$$

$$\dot{\otimes}_{XY} = \dot{\odot}_{XY}\left(1 - \sum_{i \in \{1,2\}} \sum_{j \in [x_i]} \otimes^i_{j,x_i} + \sum_{J \in [x_1] \times [x_2]} \dot{\otimes}_{JX}\right) \tag{7}$$

$$\bar{\otimes}_{XY} = \bar{\odot}_{XY}\left(1 - \sum_{i \in \{1,2\}} \sum_{j \in [x_i]} \otimes^i_{j,x_i} + \sum_{J \in [x_1] \times [x_2]} \bar{\otimes}_{JX}\right) \tag{8}$$

$$\bar{\otimes}_{XY} \leq \bar{\odot}_{XY} \tag{9}$$
$$\dot{\odot}_{XY} = \bar{\odot}_{XY} \quad \text{if } \max X > f \tag{10}$$
$$\dot{\odot}_{XY} \leq 4\frac{Z^1_s(x_1,y_1)Z^2_s(x_2,y_2)}{N^2} \tag{11}$$
$$\dot{\odot}_{BR} \leq \frac{2}{M^2} \tag{12}$$

We justify the equations in Appendix A.2.

Continuing the Proof. For the above characterizations, we fixed some arbitrary k. To continue the proof, we make this fixed k explicit by writing $\dot{\odot}_{BR}[k]$. Comparing the definitions, we find $\Theta_k = \Delta_{BR}[k]$ due to Eqs. (4) and (5). Using Lemma 4 and (3) with Eq. (4) results in

$$1 - \frac{\mathsf{ps}_0(\tau, s)}{\mathsf{ps}_1(\tau, s)} \leq g(s) \quad \text{with} \quad g(s) = \sum_{k=1}^{q} \left[1 - (N-k+1)^2(\dot{\otimes}_{BR}[k] + \Delta_{BR}[k])\right]. \tag{13}$$

To apply the expectation method, what is left is to compute an upper bound for $\mathbb{E}[g(S)]$. From the linearity of expectation,

$$\mathbb{E}[g(S)] = \sum_{k=1}^{q} \left[1 - (N-k+1)^2(\mathbb{E}[\dot{\otimes}_{BR}[k]] + \mathbb{E}[\Delta_{BR}[k]])\right]. \tag{14}$$

Bounding $\dot{\otimes}_{BR}[k]$. We turn to $\dot{\otimes}_{BR}[k] = \Pr[m_k \to^1 c_k^1] \cdot \Pr[m_k \to^2 c_k^2]$.

Lemma 5. *We have*

$$\mathbb{E}[\dot{\otimes}_{BR}[k]] \geq \frac{1}{(N-k+1)^2}\left(1 - 2\frac{4^r q^r}{N^r}\right).$$

The proof is given in Appendix A.2 and utilizes results by Chen and Steinberger [CS14] and Hoang and Tessaro [HT16].

Bounding $\Delta_{BR}[k]$. We now turn to $\Delta_{BR}[k]$. For notational convenience, we fix an arbitrary $k \in \{1, \ldots, q\}$ for now and omit the $[k]$.

Let $X = (x_1, x_2) \in [b_1 + 1] \times [b_2 + 1], Y = (y_1, y_2)$ with $X \prec Y \preceq R$. By Eqs. (7) and (8),

$$\begin{aligned}\Delta_{XY} &= \bar{\otimes}_{XY} - \dot{\otimes}_{XY} \\ &= \bar{\odot}_{XY}\left(1 - \sum_{i\in\{1,2\}}\sum_{w\in[x_i]} \otimes^i_{w,x_i} + \sum_{W\in[x_1]\times[x_2]} \bar{\otimes}_{WX}\right) \\ &\quad - \dot{\odot}_{XY}\left(1 - \sum_{i\in\{1,2\}}\sum_{w\in[x_i]} \otimes^i_{w,x_i} + \sum_{W\in[x_1]\times[x_2]} \dot{\otimes}_{WX}\right).\end{aligned}$$

We make two observations. (1) In general, $\Delta_{XY} \geq -\dot{\otimes}_{XY} \geq -\dot{\odot}_{XY}$ (by Eq. (9)). (2) Additionally, if $\max X > f$ then $\bar{\odot}_{XY} = \dot{\odot}_{XY}$ (Eq. (10)) and

$$\Delta_{XY} = \dot{\odot}_{XY} \sum_{W\in[x_1]\times[x_2]} (\bar{\otimes}_{WX} - \dot{\otimes}_{WX}) = \dot{\odot}_{XY} \sum_{W\in[x_1]\times[x_2]} \Delta_{WX}.$$

We utilize these two rules to lower bound Δ. Define

$$\tilde{\Delta}_{XY} := \begin{cases} -\dot{\odot}_{XY} & \text{if } \max X \le f, \\ \dot{\odot}_{XY} \sum_{W \in [x_1] \times [x_2]} \tilde{\Delta}_{WX} & \text{else.} \end{cases}$$

$\tilde{\Delta}$ is well defined, since applying the "else" case lowers the first index, i.e. $W \prec X$, meaning that eventually the first case is applied. We have $\Delta_{XY} \ge \tilde{\Delta}_{XY}$. The explicit form for $\tilde{\Delta}_{XY}$ is quite unwieldy, so instead we show several properties to characterize $\tilde{\Delta}_{XY}$. Firstly, there is a set $\mathfrak{S}$ which contains sets $\sigma \in \mathfrak{S}$, which in turn contain pairs $(C, D) \in \sigma$, such that $C = (c_1, c_2), D = (d_1, d_2)$ are pairs, and

$$\tilde{\Delta}_{XY} = -\sum_{\sigma \in \mathfrak{S}} \prod_{(C,D) \in \sigma} \dot{\odot}_{CD}\,.$$

To see that this set exists, note that applying the $\tilde{\Delta}$ definition to unwrap $\tilde{\Delta}_{XY}$ repeatedly multiplies $\dot{\odot}$ expressions, with one final negative $-\dot{\odot}$ expression, making any $\tilde{\Delta}_{XY}$ negative. Furthermore, after writing out all sum expressions explicitly and applying the distributive law, results in a sum of $\dot{\odot} \cdot \dot{\odot} \cdots \dot{\odot}$ products.

Lemma 6. *For any X, Y, there is a set $\mathfrak{S}$ such that*

$$\tilde{\Delta}_{XY} = -\sum_{\sigma \in \mathfrak{S}} \prod_{(C,D) \in \sigma} \dot{\odot}_{CD}$$

where all $\sigma \in \mathfrak{S}$ are of the form $\sigma = \{(C_1, C_2), (C_2, C_3), \dots (C_{\ell-1}, C_\ell)\}$ (for some $\ell, C_1, \dots, C_\ell$) and

$$\forall i : C_i \prec C_{i+1}, \tag{15}$$
$$\max C_1 \le f, \;\; \max C_2 > f \tag{16}$$
$$C_{\ell-1} = X, \;\; C_\ell = Y \tag{17}$$
$$|\sigma| \le \max X - f + 1 \tag{18}$$
$$|\mathfrak{S}| \le f 2^{x_1 + x_2 - f - 1} \tag{19}$$

Proof. To see that σ follows the form $(C_1, C_2), (C_2, C_3), \dots$, note that the second case in the $\tilde{\Delta}_{XY}$ definition always uses X as the second index for the inner $\tilde{\Delta}_{WX}$ expressions. Equation (15) is due to taking $W \in [x_1] \times [x_2]$, Eq. (16) since unfolding $\tilde{\Delta}$ only stops with the first case of the $\tilde{\Delta}$ definition and Eq. (17) is justified because $\tilde{\Delta}_{XY}$ always resolves to a $\dot{\odot}_{XY}$ expression when applying the definition of $\tilde{\Delta}$ the first time. For Eq. (18), note that for any $\sigma \in \mathfrak{S}$, Eq. (15) implies that each C_i must have both elements smaller than C_{i+1}. Now $\max C_{\ell-1} = \max X$, $\max C_{\ell-2} \le \max X - 1, \dots$, in general $\max C_{\ell-1-z} \le \max X - z$. Thus $\max C_{\ell-1-(\max X - f)} \le f$ if it exists and from Eq. (16) $C_{\ell-1-(\max X - f)} = C_1$. Comparing the C indices gives $1 \ge \ell - 1 - (\max X - f)$, hence $\ell - 1 \le 1 + \max X - f$. Since $|\sigma| = \ell - 1$ this proves the Eq. (18). We will use a similar argument for Eq. (19). Let $\Pi_1((a, b)) = a, \Pi_2((a, b)) = b$. Fix any $\sigma \in \mathfrak{S}$, let C_i the sets as in Lemma 6. From Eq. (16), consider $\Pi_1(C_1) \le f < \Pi_1(C_2)$

as case (1). Let $E_1 = \{f+1, \ldots, x_1 - 1\}, E_2 = \{1, \ldots, x_2 - 1\}$. Note that $\{\Pi_1(C_2), \ldots, \Pi_1(C_{\ell-2})\} \subseteq E_1$, due to $C_{\ell-1} = X$. Further $\Pi_1(C_1) \in \{1, \ldots, f\}$. Similarly $\{\Pi_2(C_1), \ldots, \Pi_2(C_{\ell-2})\} \subseteq E_2$. Therefore each $\sigma \in \mathfrak{S}$ where case (1) applies can be represented as an element from $E = \{1, \ldots, f\} \times 2^{E_1} \times 2^{E_2}$. With $|E_1| = x_1 - f - 1, |E_2| = x_2 - 1$, we have $|E| \leq f 2^{x_1+x_2-f-2}$. Case (2), i.e. $\Pi_2(C_1) \leq f < \Pi_2(C_2)$, is analogous. Each such $\sigma \in \mathfrak{S}$ can be mapped into set E' with $|E'| \leq f 2^{x_1+x_2-f-2}$. The sum over both cases gives Eq. (19). □

We use this bound to derive a lower bound of Δ_{BR}. Since $\mathfrak{S}$ depends on $\beta^* = (\beta_k^1[s], \beta_k^2[s])$, we write it as $\mathfrak{S}(\beta^*)$. When fixing β^* to a specific value $B = (b_1, b_2)$, we write $\mathfrak{S}(B)$. Let $R_{B,k}^i[s] = 1$ if $\beta_k^1[s] \leq b_1$ and $\beta_k^2[s] \leq b_2$, and let $R_{a,b,k}^i[s] = 0$ otherwise. Let $\bar{\mathsf{B}} = \{f+1, \ldots, r\} \times \{f+1, \ldots, r\}$. From $\Delta_{BR} \geq \tilde{\Delta}_{BR} \geq -\sum_{\sigma \in \mathfrak{S}(\beta^*)} \prod_{(C,D) \in \sigma} \dot{\odot}_{CD}$,

$$\Delta_{BR} \geq -\frac{2}{M^2} \sum_{\sigma \in \mathfrak{S}(\beta^*)} \prod_{(C,D) \in \sigma \setminus \{(B,R)\}} 4 \frac{Z_s^1(c_1, d_1) Z_s^2(c_2, d_2)}{N^2} \tag{20}$$

$$\geq -\frac{2}{M^2} \sum_{B \in \bar{\mathsf{B}}} R_{B,k}[s] \cdot \sum_{\sigma \in \mathfrak{S}(B)} \prod_{(C,D) \in \sigma \setminus \{(B,R)\}} 4 \frac{Z_s^1(c_1, d_1) Z_s^2(c_2, d_2)}{N^2} \tag{21}$$

where the first line follows from Eq. (11), the fact that $(B, R) \in \sigma$ (Eq. (17)) allowing us to factor out $\dot{\odot}_{BR}$ and apply Eq. (12). For the second line it suffices that $R_{B,k}^i[s] = 1$ if $\beta_k^1[s] = b_1$ and $\beta_k^2[s] = b_2$.

For any $c < c' < d$,

$$Z_s^i(c, d) \leq Z_s^i(c', d) \tag{22}$$

because any path that is counted by $Z_s(c, d)$ also contributes to $Z_s^i(c, k), Z_s^i(k, d)$. Take any $\sigma \in \mathfrak{S}(B)$ from Eq. (21). Let $(C_1, \ldots, C_\ell)$ according to Lemma 6, i.e. $\sigma = \{(C_1, C_2), \ldots\}$. Let $(c_1^1, c_1^2) := C_1, (c_2^1, c_2^2) := C_2$. From Eq. (16), there is an $i \in \{1, 2\}$ s.t. $c_1^i \leq f < c_2^i$. Without loss of generality, assume $i = 2$. We will now *prune* branch 2, specifically we create $\phi(\sigma)$ as copy of $\sigma \setminus \{(B, R)\}$, except that $c_1^2 := f$. We then use ϕ inside Eq. (21). Due to Eq. (22),

$$\Delta_{BR} \geq -\frac{2}{M^2} \sum_{B \in \bar{\mathsf{B}}} R_{B,k}[s] \cdot \sum_{\sigma \in \mathfrak{S}(B)} \prod_{(C,D) \in \phi(\sigma)} 4 \frac{Z_s^1(c_1, d_1) Z_s^2(c_2, d_2)}{N^2} \tag{23}$$

As a result, for any fixed $\sigma \in \mathfrak{S}(B)$, the $\prod_{(C,D) \in \phi(\sigma)} 4 \frac{Z_s^1(c_1, d_1) Z_s^2(c_2, d_2)}{N^2}$ expression only contains independent random variables $Z_s^i(c_i, d_i)$. This is because the Perm queries are fixed in the transcript and thus $Z_s^i(c_i, d_i)$ depends only on the subkeys $s_{i,c_i+1}, \ldots, s_{i,d_1-1}$ ($d_i - c_i - 1$ subkeys). We have

$$\mathbb{E}[Z_s^i(c_i, d_i)] = q^{d_i - c_i} / N^{d_i - c_i - 1} \tag{24}$$

since there are q edges in $G(s)$ that can start the path from V_{i,c_i} and each will be connected to one of the q subsequent edges if the subkey is one of the q

corresponding keys out of N keys. Due to pruning one of the branches for ϕ, the relevant subkeys for different $Z_s^i(c_i, d_i)$ expressions do not overlap. Further, for any fixed B, $R_{B,k}[s]$ is independent from the $Z_s^i(c_i, d_i)$, as $R_{B,k}$ depends on subkeys $(i, b_i + 1), \ldots, (i, r + 1)$ for $i \in \{1, 2\}$, which are not part of any $\phi(\sigma)$ due to removing (B, R). Since $R_{B,k}[s]$ depends on $2r - b_1 - b_2$ subkeys,

$$\mathbb{E}[R_{B,k}[s]] = (q/N)^{2r-b_1-b_2}\,. \tag{25}$$

Starting from Eq. (23),

$$\begin{aligned}\mathbb{E}[\Delta_{BR}] &\geq -\frac{2}{M^2}\sum_{B\in\bar{\mathsf{B}}}\mathbb{E}\left[R_{B,k}[s]\right]\cdot\mathbb{E}\left[\sum_{\sigma\in\mathfrak{S}(B)}\prod_{(C,D)\in\phi(\sigma)}4\frac{Z_s^1(c_1,d_1)Z_s^2(c_2,d_2)}{N^2}\right]\\ &\geq -\frac{2}{M^2}\sum_{B\in\bar{\mathsf{B}}}\mathbb{E}\left[R_{B,k}[s]\right]\cdot\sum_{\sigma\in\mathfrak{S}(B)}\prod_{(C,D)\in\phi(\sigma)}4\frac{\mathbb{E}\left[Z_s^1(c_1,d_1)\right]\mathbb{E}\left[Z_s^2(c_2,d_2)\right]}{N^2}\end{aligned}$$

due to linearity of expectation, and $R_{B,k}[s]$ and the Z_s depending on different subkeys. Now fix some $\sigma \in \mathfrak{S}(B)$, and let $(C_1, \ldots, C_\ell) := \phi(\sigma)$.

$$\prod_{(C,D)\in\phi(\sigma)}4\frac{\mathbb{E}\left[Z_s^1(c_1,d_1)\right]\mathbb{E}\left[Z_s^2(c_2,d_2)\right]}{N^2} = 4^{|\phi(\sigma)|}\prod_{(C,D)\in\phi(\sigma)}\frac{\mathbb{E}\left[Z_s^1(c_1,d_1)\right]\mathbb{E}\left[Z_s^2(c_2,d_2)\right]}{N^2}$$

Without loss of generality, assume we pruned branch 2 for ϕ. Either (a) $C_1 = (f, f)$ or (b) $C_1 = (h, f)$ with $h < f$ (Eq. (16)). In case (a), we have $|\phi(\sigma)| \leq \min B - f$. Using Eq. (24), since the $C_1 = (f, f)$ and $C_\ell = (b_1, b_2)$,

$$4^{|\phi(\sigma)|}\prod_{(C,D)\in\phi(\sigma)}\frac{\mathbb{E}\left[Z_s^1(c_1,d_1)\right]\mathbb{E}\left[Z_s^2(c_2,d_2)\right]}{N^2} \leq 4^{\min B-f}(q/N)^{b_1+b_2-2f}$$

In case (b), Eqs. (18) and (24),

$$4^{|\phi(\sigma)|}\prod_{(C,D)\in\phi(\sigma)}\frac{\mathbb{E}\left[Z_s^1(c_1,d_1)\right]\mathbb{E}\left[Z_s^2(c_2,d_2)\right]}{N^2} \leq 4^{\max B-f+1}(q/N)^{b_1+b_2-f-h}\,.$$

Using $h \leq f - 1$ and $\max B - f + 1 \leq (\min B - f) + f + 1$,

$$4^{\max B-f+1}(q/N)^{b_1+b_2-f-h} \leq 4^{\min B-f}(q/N)^{b_1+b_2-2f}(4^{f+1}q/N)\,.$$

From assuming $4^{f+1}q/N \leq 1$, both case (a) and (b) have the same bound. Thus,

$$\mathbb{E}[\Delta_{BR}] \geq -\frac{2}{M^2}\sum_{B\in\bar{\mathsf{B}}}\mathbb{E}\left[R_{B,k}[s]\right]\cdot\sum_{\sigma\in\mathfrak{S}(B)}4^{\min B-f}(q/N)^{b_1+b_2-2f}$$

Then,

$$
\begin{aligned}
\mathbb{E}[\Delta_{BR}] &\geq -\frac{2}{M^2}\sum_{B\in\bar{\mathsf{B}}}(q/N)^{2r-b_1-b_2}\cdot\sum_{\sigma\in\mathfrak{S}(B)}4^{\min B-f}(q/N)^{b_1+b_2-2f}\\
&\geq -\frac{2}{M^2}\sum_{B\in\bar{\mathsf{B}}}(q/N)^{2r-b_1-b_2}\cdot f2^{b_1+b_2-f-1}4^{\min B-f}(q/N)^{b_1+b_2-r}\\
&\geq -\frac{2}{M^2}\sum_{B\in\bar{\mathsf{B}}}(q/N)^{r}\cdot f2^{5r/2-1}\geq -\frac{1}{M^2}(r/2)^3 2^{5r/2}(q/N)^r\\
\mathbb{E}[\Delta_{BR}] &\geq -\frac{1}{(N-k+1)^2}10^r(q/N)^r
\end{aligned}
$$

where the first line is obtained using Eq. (25), the second using Eq. (19), the third from $\min B, b_1, b_2 \leq r, f = r/2, |B| = (r/2)^2$ and the final line from the definition of M. Thus with Eq. 14 and Lemma 5, and $M_k = N - k + 1$,

$$
\begin{aligned}
\mathbb{E}[g(S)] &\leq \sum_{k=1}^{q}\left[1-(N-k+1)^2(\mathbb{E}[\dot{\otimes}_{BR}[k]]+\mathbb{E}[\Delta_{BR}[k]])\right]\\
&\leq \sum_{k=1}^{q}\left[1-M_k^2\left(\frac{1}{M_k^2}(1-2\frac{4^r q^r}{N^r})-\frac{1}{M_k^2}10^r(q/N)^r\right)\right]\\
\mathbb{E}[g(S)] &\leq \frac{3}{2}\cdot 10^r\cdot\frac{q^{r+1}}{N^r}
\end{aligned}
$$

This proves Lemma 3.

5 The MFTEMConstruction

We define MFTEM(multi-forked tweakable iterated Even-Mansour) as a specific instantiation of GIEM. It is the b-branch generalization of FTEM by Kim et al. [KLL20] (which has 2 branches) and TEM by Cogliati et al. [CLS15] (which has 1 branch).

Let $\mathbf{H} = (h_{0,1}, \ldots, h_{b,r})$ where all h_j are functions from $\mathtt{T}$ to $\{0,1\}^n$. Let $\mathbf{H}' = (h_{0,1}, h_{0,1} \oplus h_{0,2}, \ldots, h_{b,r-1} \oplus h_{b,r}, h_{b,r})$. Then define $\mathsf{MFTEM}^{b,r}_{\mathbf{H}}[\mathbf{P}] := \mathsf{GIEM}^{b,r}_{\mathbf{H}'}[\mathbf{P}]$.

5.1 Security of MFTEM

Let q_e denote the number of queries by the adversary to the cipher and q the number of queries to each oracle.

Theorem 2. *Let* $\mathsf{MFTEM}^{b,r}_{\mathbf{H}}$ *as defined above and* $r \geq 2$ *be an even number. Let all* $h_i \in \mathbf{H}$ *be sampled from a uniform and* ϵ*-AXU function family.*

$$
\mathsf{Adv}^{\mathrm{prtmfp}}_{\mathsf{MFTEM}^b_r}(q_e, q) \leq 2(b+1)\sqrt{q(2q\epsilon + \frac{2q_e}{N})^{r/2}}
$$

Hence if we set $q = q_e$ and $\mathbf{H}$ to an ϵ-AXU function family with $\epsilon \approx \frac{1}{N}$ then MFTEM achieves security up to roughly $q \approx \frac{N^{\frac{r}{r+2}}}{b^2}$ queries.

Proof Sketch. We use a strategy similar to Cogliati et al. [CLS15] (specifically their Theorem 4), and are able to reuse some of their lemmas. Thus we only sketch the proof idea here. Our full proof is given in Sect. A.3.

The r round MFTEM can be seen as $r/2$ rounds of TEM, and each branch then as inverse call of the corresponding $r/2$ round TEM. We reuse Lemma 10 by Cogliati et al. [CLS15], which gives us the distribution of the internal state of MFTEMat the branching point when the inputs from the transcript are used. Similarly for the ciphertext blocks in the transcript, we obtain the distribution of previous internal MFTEMstates. From this we derive a set of internal states, that have a high probability of (a) occurring from the input and (b) resulting in the ciphertext blocks from the transcript, and thereby probability of the transcript occurring in the real world.

6 Attacks Against IEM

In Sect. A.4, we show that the attack by Bogdanov et al. (Section 3.1 in [BKL+12]) is ineffective, i.e. succeeds with probability less than $\frac{1}{N/2}$ when using the specified number of queries, and instead point to a different attack by Gaži [Gaz13] (Sect. 5) with slightly more queries (depending on the number of rounds). Thus the asymptotic tightness of IEM proofs is retained.

Acknowledgements. Elena Andreeva and Andreas Weninger are supported in part by the Austrian Science Fund (FWF) SFB project SPyCoDe 10.55776/F85. Amit Singh Bhati was supported by CyberSecurity Research Flanders with reference number VR20192203, in part by the Research Council KU Leuven C1 on Security and Privacy for Cyber-Physical Systems and the Internet of Things with contract number C16/15/058 and by the Flemish Government through FWO Project G.0835.16 A security Architecture for IoT.

A Appendix (Supplementary)

A.1 Supporting Definitions

Multiforkcipher and Security. A multiforkcipher (MFC) F_b (with b branches) is a pair of deterministic algorithms, the forward $F_b : K \times \mathtt{T} \times \{0,1\}^n \rightarrow \{0,1\}^{bn}$, and the backward (or inverse) $F_b^{-1} : K \times \mathtt{T} \times \{0,1\}^n \times [b] \rightarrow \{0,1\}^{bn}$.

The forward evaluation algorithm takes a key k, a tweak T and an input block X. It outputs the blocks $Y_1, \ldots, Y_b$. The backward evaluation algorithm F_b^{-1} takes in a key k, a tweak T, a block Y and an input indicator β. It then outputs blocks $X, Y_1, \ldots, Y_{\beta-1}, Y_{\beta+1}, \ldots, Y_b$. We omit b from the notation if it is fixed and clear from the context, and we will also write $F_k(T, X)$ for $F_b(k, T, X)$ (F_k^{-1} analogously).

MFC is *correct* if for every $k \in K, T \in \mathtt{T}, X \in \{0,1\}^n$ and $\beta \in [b]$ it satisfies:

$$F_k^{-1}(T, F_k(T,X)_{[(\beta-1)n+1:\beta n]}, \beta) = X||Z$$

where Z is $F_k(T,X)_{[1:(\beta-1)n]}||F_k(T,X)_{[\beta n+1:bn]}$. We write $F[\mathbf{P}]$ to denote a multiforkcipher F based on a tuple of permutations $\mathbf{P} = (P_i)_{i \in I}$ for some index set I.

The advantage of an adversary $\mathcal{A}$ at distinguishing F_b from a random multi-forked permutation $\tilde{P}$ (c.f. Section [ABPV21]) is defined w.r.t. Fig. 5 as

$$\mathsf{Adv}_{F_b}^{\mathbf{prtmfp}}(\mathcal{A}) = |\Pr[\mathcal{A}^{\mathbf{prtmfp\text{-}real}_{F_b}} \Rightarrow 1] - \Pr[\mathcal{A}^{\mathbf{prtmfp\text{-}ideal}_{F_b}} \Rightarrow 1]|.$$

Note that for $b = 1$ branch (thus β fixed to 1) and $|\mathtt{T}| = 1$ this game is equivalent to the pseudorandom permutation (PRP) game as it is used for IEM proofs [BKL+12, CS14].

Game $\mathbf{prtmfp\text{-}real}_{F_b}$	Game $\mathbf{prtmfp\text{-}ideal}_{F_b}$
$k \leftarrow K$	**for** $T \in \mathtt{T}$ **do** $\pi_{T,1}, \ldots, \pi_{T,b} \leftarrow\$ \mathsf{Perm}(n)$
$\mathbf{P} \leftarrow\$ \mathsf{Perm}(n)^{\lvert I \rvert}$	$\mathbf{P} \leftarrow\$ \mathsf{Perm}(n)^{\lvert I \rvert}$
$b \leftarrow \mathcal{A}^{\mathcal{E},\mathcal{D},\mathbf{P}}$	$b \leftarrow \mathcal{A}^{\mathcal{E},\mathcal{D},\mathbf{P}}$
return b	**return** b
Oracle $\mathcal{E}(T,X)$	**Oracle** $\mathcal{E}(T,X)$
return $F_k[\mathbf{P}](T,X)$	**return** $\pi_{T,1}(X)\|\|\ldots\|\|\pi_{T,b}(X)$
Oracle $\mathcal{D}(T,Y,\beta)$	**Oracle** $\mathcal{D}(T,Y,\beta)$
return $F_k^{-1}[\mathbf{P}](T,Y,\beta)$	$X \leftarrow \pi_{T,\beta}^{-1}(Y)$
	return $X\|\|\pi_{T,1}(X)\|\|\ldots\|\|\pi_{T,\beta-1}(X)\|\|$ $\pi_{T,\beta+1}(X)\|\|\ldots\|\|\pi_{T,b}(X)$

Fig. 5. Games $\mathbf{prtmfp\text{-}real}_{F_b}$ and $\mathbf{prtmfp\text{-}ideal}_{F_b}$ defining security of the multiforkcipher F_b. When $\mathbf{P}$ is made available to the adversary, the inverse permutations are implicitly made available as well.

A.2 Details for the Proof of Theorem 1

Proof of Lemma 4. Let Prim_b be the event that S_b behaves according to Primentries in (τ, s). Then $\Pr[\mathsf{Prim}_0] = \Pr[\mathsf{Prim}_1]$. On the one hand

$$\mathsf{ps}_{S_1}(\tau, s) = \frac{\Pr[\mathsf{Prim}_1]}{N^{|\mathbb{J}|} \cdot (N(N-1)\ldots(N-q+1))^2}$$

where $\frac{1}{N^{|\mathbb{J}|}}$ is from hitting the key s and $\frac{1}{(N(N-1)\ldots(N-q+1))^2}$ from both construction branches outputting the correct ciphertexts. On the other hand, for $\mathbf{S}_0$ to behave according to according to (τ, s), it means that (i) S must agree with s, and the system must behave according to $\mathsf{Primentries}$ in (τ, s), and (ii) for every $k = 1, \ldots, q-1$, if condition (i) holds and querying $m_1, \ldots, m_{k-1}$ to $\mathsf{Encoracles}$ in $\mathbf{S}_0$ results in $\boldsymbol{c}_1, \ldots, \boldsymbol{c}_{k-1}$, respectively, then querying m_k results in $\boldsymbol{c}_k$. Then

$$\mathsf{ps}_{\mathbf{S}_0}(\tau, s) = \frac{\Pr[\mathsf{Prim}_0]}{N^{|\mathbb{J}|}} \prod_{k=1}^{q} \Pr[m_k \to^* \boldsymbol{c}_k].$$

Thus,

$$1 - \frac{\mathsf{ps}_{\mathbf{S}_0}(\tau, s)}{\mathsf{ps}_{\mathbf{S}_1}(\tau, s)} = 1 - \prod_{k=1}^{q} (N-k+1)^2 \Pr[m_k \to^* \boldsymbol{c}_k].$$

We use the fact that for all reals $c_k \in [0; 1]$, $\prod_{k=1}^{q}(1-c_k) \geq 1 - \sum_{k=1}^{q} c_k$, and hence $1 - \prod_{k=1}^{q} c_k = 1 - \prod_{k=1}^{q}(1-(1-c_k)) \leq 1 - (1 - \sum_{k=1}^{q}(1-c_k)) = \sum_{k=1}^{q}(1-c_k)$ to obtain the claimed bound.

Proof of Lemma 5

Lemma 7 (Eq. 21 in [HT16]**).** *We have*

$$\Pr[m_k \to^i c_k^i] \geq \frac{1}{N-k+1} \left(1 - \sum_{\sigma \in \mathfrak{B}(\alpha_k[s], \beta_k^i[s])} \prod_{(a,b)\in\sigma} \frac{Z_s^i(a,b)}{N-2q}\right).$$

For $0 \leq a < b \leq r$, let $R_{a,b,k}^i[s] = 1$ if $\alpha_k[s] \geq a$ and $\beta_k^i[s] \leq b$, and let $R_{a,b,k}^i[s] = 0$ otherwise. Similar to Hoang and Tessaro in their proof of Lemma 4 we use $q \leq N/4$, to find

$$\Pr[m_k \to^i c_k^i] \geq \frac{1}{N-k+1} \left(1 - \sum_{0 \leq a < b \leq r} R_{a,b,k}^i[s] \cdot \sum_{\sigma \in \mathfrak{B}(a,b)} \prod_{(a,b)\in\sigma} \frac{2Z_s^i(a,b)}{N}\right).$$

To see that the inequality holds, it suffices that $R_{a,b,k}^i[s] = 1$ if $a = \alpha_k[s], b = \beta_k^i[s]$. Then from $(1-c)(1-d) \geq 1 - c - d$ for all $c, d \in [0; 1]$ and $\dot{\otimes}_{BR}[k] = \Pr[m_k \to^1 c_k^1] \cdot \Pr[m_k \to^2 c_k^2]$,

$$\dot{\otimes}_{BR}[k] \geq \frac{1}{(N-k+1)^2} \left(1 - \sum_{i \in \{1,2\}} \sum_{0 \leq a < b \leq r} R_{a,b,k}^i[s] \cdot \sum_{\sigma \in \mathfrak{B}(a,b)} \prod_{(a,b)\in\sigma} \frac{2Z_s^i(a,b)}{N}\right).$$

By linearity of expectation,

$$\mathbb{E}[\dot{\otimes}_{BR}[k]] \geq \frac{1}{(N-k+1)^2} \left(1 - \sum_{i \in \{1,2\}} \mathbb{E}\left[\sum_{0 \leq a < b \leq r} R_{a,b,k}^i[s] \cdot \sum_{\sigma \in \mathfrak{B}(a,b)} \prod_{(a,b)\in\sigma} \frac{2Z_s^i(a,b)}{N}\right]\right). \tag{26}$$

Lemma 8 (Lemma 5 in [HT16]). *We have*

$$\mathbb{E}\left[\sum_{0\leq a<b\leq r} R^i_{a,b,k}[s] \cdot \sum_{\sigma\in\mathfrak{B}(a,b)} \prod_{(a,b)\in\sigma} \frac{2Z^i_s(a,b)}{N}\right] \leq \frac{4^r q^r}{N^r}.$$

Using the above lemma and Eq. (26) we obtain the claimed bound.

Proof of Characterizations. We now justify Eqs. 4 to 12. As discussed before, PathSample′ is equivalent to PathSample. To justify Eq. (4), note that from $b^i = \beta^i_k[s]$ we know there is a path from some vertex in V_{i,b^i} to $(i, r+1, c^i_k \oplus L_{i,r+1})$, and from there the additional edge to $V_{i,r+2}$ that we added. If the sampled path connects m to $c^i_k \oplus L_{i,r+1}$, then it must follow that path, i.e. w_{i,b^i} must select this path (which is the only path to $V_{i,r+2}$). The analogous is true for Eq. (5).

For Lemma 6, the event corresponding to $\otimes^i_{xy}$ can only happen if the event corresponding to $\odot^i_{xy}$ happened (i.e. $u_{i,x}$ must be the start of a path to a vertex in $V_{i,y}$) and $w_{i,x}$ was not "hijacked" by a previous path (thus probability $1 - \sum_{j\in[x]} \otimes^i_{jx}$). These two events are indeed independent, since the sampling of $u_{i,x}$ is independent of what happened on previous layers. This result was also used by Chen and Steinberger (Eq. 30 in [CS14]). Equation (7) is the result of $\dot{\otimes}_{XY} = \otimes^1_{x_1y_1}\otimes^2_{x_2y_2}$ and multiplying out Lemma 6. For Lemma 8 a similar argument applies as for Lemma 6, now the event corresponding to $\bar{\odot}_{XY}$ is a requirement. In this case, the expression in brackets is the result of the inclusion exclusion principle on the hijacking paths. Specifically, any of the events corresponding to $\otimes^i_{j,x_i}$ makes $\bar{\otimes}_{XY}$ impossible, but the sum over all $\otimes^i_{j,x_i}$ counts the events twice, where any $\otimes^1_{j_1,x_1}$ and $\otimes^2_{j_2,x_2}$ happen at the same time.

Equation (9) is due to any $w_{i,j}$ only being able to choose a vertex from $\bar{U}_{i,j}$ if $w_{i,j} = u_{i,j}$ (otherwise $w_{i,j}$ is the endpoint of an existing edge, which cannot be in $\bar{U}_{i,j}$ per definition of $\bar{U}_{i,j}$). For Eq. (10), since $i_1, i_2 > f$, u_{1,i_1} and u_{2,i_2} are independent random variables, so the multiplication rule for independent events applies. For Eq. (11), we have

$$\dot{\odot}_{XY} = \odot^1_{x_1y_1}\odot^2_{x_2y_2} = \prod_{i\in\{1,2\}} \frac{U^i_{G_{k-1}}(x_i,y_i)}{M-q} \leq 4\frac{U^1_{G_{k-1}}(x_1,y_1)}{N} \cdot \frac{U^2_{G_{k-1}}(x_2,y_2)}{N}$$

The first equation is the definition of $\dot{\odot}_{XY}$, the second is from the fact that u_{1,x_1} is sampled from the vertices without an edge to the left in G_{k-1}. From the N total vertices, $k-1$ are used from prior paths and up to q additional edges exist due to Perm queries, so in total $M-q$ possible choices. There are $U^i_{G_{k-1}}(x_i,y_i)$ such paths. The inequality follows from $M - q = N - k + 1 - q \geq N - 2q$ and $q \leq N/4$. Together with Eq. (2) this proves Eq. (11). Equation (12) uses a similar argument, and the fact that only the one edge we considered for notational convenience exists to a vertex from $V_{i,r+2}$ for each $i \in \{1,2\}$.

A.3 Proof of Theorem 2

Preliminaries. We also identify h_i with k_i. Before starting our proof, we recall some lemmas from Cogliati et al. [CLS15].

Lemma 9 (Lemma 8 in [CLS15]**).** *Let Ω be some finite event space and μ^* be the uniform probability distribution on Ω. Let μ be a probability distribution on Ω such that $||\mu - \mu^*|| \leq \epsilon$. Then there is a set $S \subset \Omega$ such that:*

- $|S| \geq (1 - \sqrt{\epsilon})|\Omega|$,
- $\forall x \in S, \mu(x) \geq (1 - \sqrt{\epsilon})\mu^*(x)$.

Let $\mathsf{TEM}^r_{\mathbf{H}}[\mathbf{P}] := \mathsf{MFTEM}^{1,r}_{\mathbf{H}}[\mathbf{P}]$. For a given sequence of tweaks $t = (t_1, \ldots, t_{q_e})$, let

$$\Omega_t = \{(x_1, \ldots, x_{q_e}) \in (\{0,1\}^n)^{q_e} | \forall i \neq j : (t_i, x_i) \neq (t_j, x_j)\}.$$

Definition 4. *For a given set of tweaks t and cipher inputs x and any attainable queries transcript $Q_{\mathbf{P}}$, define the tuple of random variables*

$$\mathsf{TEM}^r_{\mathbf{H}}[\mathbf{P}](t, x) := (\mathsf{TEM}^r_{\mathbf{H}}[\mathbf{P}](t_1, x_1), \ldots, \mathsf{TEM}^r_{\mathbf{H}}[\mathbf{P}](t_{q_e}, x_{q_e}))$$

and let μ_{t,x,Q_P} denote the distribution of the tuple conditioned on the event $\mathbf{P} \vdash Q_{\mathbf{P}}$ (i.e. when the key $\mathbf{H}$ is uniformly random and the permutations $\mathbf{P}$are uniformly random among permutations that are consistent with $Q_{\mathbf{P}}$).

Lemma 10 (Lemma 10 in [CLS15]**).**
Let μ^*_t denote the uniform distribution on Ω_t. Fix any attainable queries transcript $Q_{\mathbf{P}}$ and any $t \in \mathrm{T}^{q_e}, x \in \Omega_t$

$$||\mu_{t,x,Q_{\mathbf{P}}} - \mu^*_t|| \leq q_e(2q_e\epsilon + \frac{2q}{N})^r$$

Proof (of Theorem 2). We will follow a similar strategy to [CLS15] in order to separate the full r-round forked construction into smaller, single branch parts with $r/2$ rounds each.

We use the H-coefficient technique, and there will be no bad transcripts. Let the query transcript $\tau = (Q_C, Q_{P_{0,1}}, \ldots, Q_{P_{b,r}})$ be arbitrary from all attainable transcripts but fixed. Let $\mathbf{P}_0 = (P_{0,1}, \ldots, P_{0,r/2})$ and for all $0 < i \leq b$ let $\mathbf{P}_i = (P_{i,r/2+1}, \ldots, P_{i,r})$. Define $\mathbf{P}_i^{-1} = (P_{i,r}^{-1}, \ldots, P_{i,r/2+1}^{-1})$. Similarly $\mathbf{H}_0 = (h_{0,1}, \ldots, h_{0,r/2})$ and for all $0 < i \leq b$ let $\mathbf{H}_i = (h_{i,r/2+1}, \ldots, h_{i,r})$ and $\mathbf{H}_i^{-1} = (h_{i,r}, \ldots, h_{i,r/2+1})$.

Let $\gamma_i = (\mathsf{TEM}^{-1})^{r/2}_{\mathbf{H}_i^{-1}}[P_i^{-1}]$. Note that $\mathsf{MFTEM}^{b,r}_{\mathbf{H}}[\mathbf{P}](x) = \gamma_1(z)|| \ldots ||\gamma_b(z)$ where $z = \mathsf{TEM}^{r/2}_{\mathbf{H}_0}(x)$.

From the transcript τ, let $t = (t_1, \ldots, t_{q_e})$ be the tweaks in Q_C, $m = (m_1, \ldots, m_{q_e})$ the messages and for all $1 \leq i \leq b$, $c^i = (c^i_1, \ldots, c^i_{q_e})$ the i-th ciphertext blocks. Let $\mu^0(z) = \mu^0_{t,m,Q_{\mathbf{P}_0}}(z)$ be the distribution of tuple

$\mathsf{TEM}_{\mathbf{H}_0}^{r/2}[\mathbf{P}_0](t,m)$ like in Definition 4. Let $\mu^i(z) = \mu^i_{t,c^i,Q^{-1}_{\mathbf{P}_i}}(z)$ be the distribution of tuple $\mathsf{TEM}_{\mathbf{H}_i^{-1}}^{r/2}[\mathbf{P}_i^{-1}](t,c^i)$, where $Q^{-1}_{\mathbf{P}_i}$ is $Q_{\mathbf{P}_i}$ with the elements in the tuples in reverse order (to invert the permutations) and the permutations in reverse order. Intuitively, each of the $\mu^i(z)$, with $z = (z_1, \ldots, z_{q_e})$, gives the "local" probability that, for $1 \le \ell \le q_e$, the intermediate state z_ℓ occurred during the ℓ-th execution of MFTEM.

Let $r' = r/2$. We denote $\alpha = 2^{r'}\frac{q_e(N\epsilon q_e+q_p)^{r'}}{N^{r'}}$. We can apply the bound of Lemma 10 to each μ^i. Hence by Lemma 9 for each $0 \le i \le b$ there exists a set $S_i \subset \Omega_t$ of size at least $(1-\sqrt{\alpha})|\Omega_t|$ such that for all $z \in S_i$: $\mu^i(z) \ge \frac{1-\sqrt{\alpha}}{|\Omega_t|}$.

Let $S = S_0 \cap \cdots \cap S_b$. Note that $|S| \ge (1-(b+1)\sqrt{\alpha})|\Omega_t|$. Recall that $\gamma_i = (\mathsf{TEM}^{-1})^{r/2}_{\mathbf{H}_i^{-1}}[P_i^{-1}]$ and we will again use the tuples m, c^i of all messages and ciphertext blocks. We will also use c^0 to refer to m. Let $\gamma_0 = \mathsf{TEM}_{\mathbf{H}_0}^{r/2}[P_0]$. Since the permutations and keys are uniformly random and independent, we have

$$\begin{aligned}
\Pr[T_{re} = \tau'] &= \sum_{z \in (\{0,1\}^n)^{q_e}} \Pr[\mathbf{P} \vdash Q_{\mathbf{P}} \wedge \gamma_0(m) = z \wedge \bigwedge_{1 \le i \le b} \gamma_i(z) = c^i] \\
&\ge \sum_{z \in S} \prod_{i=0}^{b} \Pr[\mathbf{P} \vdash Q_{\mathbf{P}} \wedge \mathsf{TEM}_{\mathbf{H}_i}^{r/2}[\mathbf{P}_i](t,c^i) = z] \\
&\ge \sum_{z \in S} \prod_{i=0}^{b} \Pr[\mathbf{P} \vdash Q_{\mathbf{P}}]\mu^i(z) \ge \Pr[\mathbf{P} \vdash Q_{\mathbf{P}}] \sum_{z \in S} \prod_{i=0}^{b} \mu^i(z) \\
&\ge \Pr[\mathbf{P} \vdash Q_{\mathbf{P}}] \sum_{z \in S} \frac{(1-\sqrt{\alpha})^{b+1}}{|\Omega_t|^{b+1}} \ge \Pr[\mathbf{P} \vdash Q_{\mathbf{P}}] \frac{|S|(1-(b+1)\sqrt{\alpha})}{|\Omega_t|^{b+1}} \\
&\ge \Pr[\mathbf{P} \vdash Q_{\mathbf{P}}] \frac{(1-(b+1)\sqrt{\alpha})^2}{|\Omega_t|^{b}} \ge \Pr[\mathbf{P} \vdash Q_{\mathbf{P}}] \frac{(1-2(b+1)\sqrt{\alpha})}{|\Omega_t|^{b}}
\end{aligned}$$

Let us turn to $\Pr[T_{id} = \tau']$. Let $\tilde{P}$ be a random multiforked permutation. All (multiforked) permutations are independent, thus we have $\Pr[T_{id} = \tau'] = \Pr[\mathbf{P} \vdash Q_{\mathbf{P}}] \Pr[\tilde{P} \vdash Q_C]$, $\Pr[\tilde{P} \vdash Q_C] = \frac{1}{|(\Omega_t)^b|}$. Finally, this results in $\frac{\Pr[T_{re}=\tau']}{\Pr[T_{id}=\tau']} \ge 1 - 2(b+1)\sqrt{\alpha}$. □

A.4 Attack by Bogdanov Et Al.

For completeness, Bogdanov et al. noted: *"To get a better reduction on key-candidates, a bit more [...] queries are sufficient"*. We argue that the way they presented their attack could at least make readers assume that the attack already works decently for q as specified. Indeed, the follow-up literature [LPS12, Ste12, CS14, CLS15] treated it as such, and we suspect it was also what the authors assumed. Furthermore, only slightly increasing the number of queries, say by adding a constant, does not fix the problem. It remains unclear if multiplying the number of queries by a constant solves the problem (and which constant would be needed), due to the lack of a proof.

We instead point to a similar attack by Gaži [Gaz13] (Sect. 5). Both attacks make random queries at the start and then iterate over all possible keys to output the first candidate. The main difference is that the Bogdanov et al. attack accepts the first key candidate where no inconsistencies were found, which includes keys for which we cannot evaluate even a single message-ciphertext pair. On the other hand the Gaži attack only accepts a key if it has a minimum number of verifiable message-ciphertext pairs. This minimum number is given as a parameter. To achieve our desired asymptotic query complexity and success probability (Sect. A.5), we need to use slightly more queries than the Bogdanov et al. attack (a multiplicative factor depending on the number of rounds). Gaži provides a security proof, which aids to preserve the asymptotic tightness of IEM proofs.

Below we first describe the attack by Bogdanov et al. [BKL+12]. We denote $N = 2^n$. For consistency with the notation by Bogdanov et al., we use t as the number of rounds in the construction, rather than r as in our constructions.

Definitions. IEM is defined as $E_k = P_t(\dots P_1(m \oplus k_0) \oplus k_1 \dots) \oplus k_t$ for random public permutations $P_1, \dots, P_t$. We define the following predicates.

- $\mathsf{Connect}$: For key k, queried message m and integer $r, 1 \leq r \leq t$, $\mathsf{Connect}(m, r)$ is true if and only if we have made queries (see attack below) of the form

$$c := E(m), y_1 := P_1(m \oplus k_0), y_2 := P_2(y_1 \oplus k_1), ..., y_r := P_r(y_{r-1} \oplus k_{r-1}).$$

  In other words, there are some $c, y_1, y_2, \dots$ s.t. $(m, c) \in \mathcal{M}, (m \oplus k_0, y_1) \in \mathcal{P}_1, \dots$ (see set definitions in the attack below).
- Path: For key k and queried message m, $\mathsf{Path}(k, m) :\Leftrightarrow \mathsf{Connect}(k, m, t)$ (i.e. all relevant queries including to the final permutation have been made).
- $\mathsf{ConsistentPath}$: For key k and queried message m, $\mathsf{ConsistentPath}(k, m) :\Leftrightarrow \mathsf{Path}(k, m) \wedge y_t \oplus k_t = c$ (i.e. the cipher query result matches the permutation query results).
- $\mathsf{InconsistentPath}$: For key k and queried message m, $\mathsf{InconsistentPath}(k, m) :\Leftrightarrow \mathsf{Path}(k, m) \wedge y_t \oplus k_t \neq c$.

IEM Attack.

1. For each oracle $P_1, \dots P_t$ and E, make q random queries. (Bogdanov et al. [BKL+12] use $q = N^{t/(t+1)}$.) The results are stored in $\mathcal{P}_i, \mathcal{M}$ as input output pairs, e.g. if $(x, y) \in \mathcal{P}_1$, then this means we queried $P_1(x)$ and received y.
2. For each key candidate $k = (k_0, k_1, \dots, k_t) \in \{0, 1\}^{n(t+1)}$ do:
   (a) For each message m: If $\mathsf{InconsistentPath}(k, m)$: Continue to the next key candidate (since this key is definitely wrong).
   (b) If for no message $\mathsf{InconsistentPath}(k, m)$ holds, output k as the key guess.

Analysis on the IEM Attack. Note that in the IEM attack the first key candidate without an inconsistent path is output. Given the number of such candidates, the probability that the attack succeeds is thus 1 divided by the number of candidates.

Lemma 11. *The above attack, when executed with $q = N^{t/(t+1)}$, has probability of less than $\frac{1}{N/2}$ of success.*

Proof. For all k_0, let M_{k_0} denote the set of messages $m, \exists c : (m, c) \in \mathcal{M}$, for which we have $\exists (x, y) \in \mathcal{P}_1 : m \oplus k_0 = x$. Note that if any $M_{k_0} = \emptyset$, then any key k containing partial key k_0 will not have $\mathsf{Connect}(k, m, 1)$ for any message m, let alone have $\mathsf{Path}(k, m)$ or $\mathsf{InconsistentPath}(k, m)$ for any message m. Thus, the attack would give at least N^t candidates.

Observe that any m from $\mathcal{M}$ will be in M_{k_0} for exactly q different k_0 ($k_0 = m \oplus x$ for each $(x, y) \in \mathcal{P}_1$). Thus, the q elements of $\mathcal{M}$ cause a total of q^2 elements spread over some or all M_{k_0}. How they are distributed depends on the randomly selected queries of step 1 of the attack. If they are distributed evenly, then every M_{k_0} contains q^2/N elements, since $k_0 \in \{0, 1\}^n$. In any case, there are at least $N/2$ sets M_{k_0} which have strictly less than $2q^2/N$ elements. We will show that each of these keys k_0 can be extended into (at least) one key candidate, which proves the lemma.

Let k_0 s.t. $|M_{k_0}| < 2q^2/N$ elements. By a similar argument as above, there is a subkey k_1, such that strictly fewer than $2\frac{q^2}{N}\frac{q}{N}$ messages m have $\mathsf{Connect}(k, m, 2)$ by a key k containing k_0, k_1. Repeating this for each of t permutations, we have a partial key $k = (k_0, \ldots, k_{t-1})$, where there are less than $2\frac{q^{t+1}}{N^t}$ messages m for which $\mathsf{Connect}(k, m, t)$ is true. Thus, for fewer than $2\frac{q^{t+1}}{N^t} = 2$ messages i.e. at most for one message m we have $\mathsf{Path}(k, m)$. If no such m exists, any final subkey $k_t \in \{0, 1\}^n$ can be used to complete the key $k^* = (k_0, \ldots, k_t)$ without having $\mathsf{InconsistentPath}(k^*, m)$. On the other hand, if a single such m exists, where $(m, c) \in \mathcal{M}$, then we can set $k_t = y_t \oplus c$ which results in $\mathsf{ConsistentPath}(k^*, m)$. $\square$

A.5 Instantiating Gaži's Attack

To apply Gaži's attack [Gaz13] (Sect. 5) to IEM, fix $k_1 := 1, \ldots, k_\ell := \ell$ (independent of k'), which effectively extracts several public random permutations from the ideal cipher. We define k' as being comprised of all IEM round keys $k' = (k'_0, \ldots k'_\ell)$ and define $Q_{i,k'}(x) := x \oplus k'_i$. To asymptotically match the desired query number, we use the trade-off that Gaži described at the end of Sect. 5.

References

[ABPV21] Andreeva, E., Bhati, A.S., Preneel, B., Vizár, D.: 1, 2, 3, fork: Counter mode variants based on a generalized forkcipher. IACR Trans. Symm. Cryptol. **2021**(3), 1–35 (2021)

[ABV21] Andreeva, E., Bhati, A.S., Vizár, D.: Nonce-misuse security of the SAEF authenticated encryption mode. In: Dunkelman, O., Jacobson, Jr., M.J., O'Flynn, C. (eds.) SAC 2020. LNCS, vol. 12804, pp. 512–534. Springer, Cham (2021). https://doi.org/10.1007/978-3-030-81652-0_20

[ADP+20] Andreeva, E., Deprez, A., Pittevils, J., Roy, A., Bhati, A.S., Vizár, D.: New results and insighs on forkae, In: NIST LWC workshop (2020)

[ALP+19] Andreeva, E., Lallemand, V., Purnal, A., Reyhanitabar, R., Roy, A., Vizár, D.: Forkcipher: a new primitive for authenticated encryption of very short messages. In: Galbraith, S.D., Moriai, S. (eds.) ASIACRYPT 2019. LNCS, vol. 11922, pp. 153–182. Springer, Cham (2019). https://doi.org/10.1007/978-3-030-34621-8_6

[AW23] Andreeva, E., Weninger, A.: A forkcipher-based pseudo-random number generator. In: Tibouchi, M., Wang, X. (eds.) Applied Cryptography and Network Security, pp. 3–31. Springer, Cham (2023)

[BAMV24] Bhati, A.S., Andreeva, E., Müller, S., Vizar, D.: Sonikku: Gotta Speed, Keed! A Family of Fast and Secure MACs. Cryptology ePrint Archive, Paper 2024/1980 (2024)

[BAV24] Bhati, A.S., Andreeva, E., Vizár, D.: OAE-RUP: a strong online AEAD security notion and its application to SAEF. In: International Conference on Security and Cryptography for Networks, pp. 117–139. Springer, Heidelberg (2024). https://doi.org/10.1007/978-3-031-71073-5_6

[BBDL23] Bhattacharjee, A., Bhaumik, R., Dutta, A., List, E.: PAE: Towards more efficient and bbb-secure ae from a single public permutation. Cryptology ePrint Archive, Paper 2023/978 (2023). https://eprint.iacr.org/2023/978

[BDA+24] Bhati, A.S., Dufka, A., Andreeva, E., Roy, A., Preneel, B.: Skye: an expanding PRF based fast KDF and its applications. In: Proceedings of the 19th ACM Asia Conference on Computer and Communications Security, pp. 1082–1098 (2024)

[BKL+12] Bogdanov, A., Knudsen, L.R., Leander, G., Standaert, F.-X., Steinberger, J., Tischhauser, E.: Key-alternating ciphers in a provable setting: encryption using a small number of public permutations. In: Pointcheval, D., Johansson, T. (eds.) EUROCRYPT 2012. LNCS, vol. 7237, pp. 45–62. Springer, Heidelberg (2012). https://doi.org/10.1007/978-3-642-29011-4_5

[BPA+23] Bhati, A.S., Pohle, E., Abidin, A., Andreeva, E., Preneel, B.: Let's go eevee! a friendly and suitable family of AEAD modes for IoT-to-cloud secure computation. In: Proceedings of the 2023 ACM SIGSAC Conference on Computer and Communications Security, pp. 2546–2560 (2023)

[BVA24] Bhati, A.S., Verbauwhede, M., Andreeva, E.: Breaking, Repairing and Enhancing XCBv2 into the Tweakable Enciphering Mode GEM. Cryptology ePrint Archive (2024). https://eprint.iacr.org/2024/1554

[CLS15] Cogliati, B., Lampe, R., Seurin, Y.: Tweaking even-mansour ciphers. In: Gennaro, R., Robshaw, M. (eds.) CRYPTO 2015. LNCS, vol. 9215, pp. 189–208. Springer, Heidelberg (2015). https://doi.org/10.1007/978-3-662-47989-6_9

[CS14] Chen, S., Steinberger, J.: Tight security bounds for key-alternating ciphers. In: Nguyen, P.Q., Oswald, E. (eds.) EUROCRYPT 2014. LNCS, vol. 8441, pp. 327–350. Springer, Heidelberg (2014). https://doi.org/10.1007/978-3-642-55220-5_19

[DGL22] Dutta, A., Guo, J., List, E.: Forking sums of permutations for optimally secure and highly efficient prfs. Cryptology ePrint Archive, Paper 2022/1609 (2022). https://eprint.iacr.org/2022/1609

[EM97] Even, S., Mansour, Y.: A construction of a cipher from a single pseudorandom permutation. J. Cryptol. **10**(3), 151–162 (1997)

[Gaz13] Gaži, P.: Plain versus randomized cascading-based key-length extension for block ciphers. In: Canetti, R., Garay, J.A. (eds.) CRYPTO 2013. LNCS, vol. 8042, pp. 551–570. Springer, Heidelberg (2013). https://doi.org/10.1007/978-3-642-40041-4_30

[HR03] Halevi, S., Rogaway, P.: A tweakable enciphering mode. In: Boneh, D. (ed.) CRYPTO 2003. LNCS, vol. 2729, pp. 482–499. Springer, Heidelberg (2003). https://doi.org/10.1007/978-3-540-45146-4_28

[HR04] Halevi, S., Rogaway, P.: A parallelizable enciphering mode. In: Okamoto, T. (ed.) CT-RSA 2004. LNCS, vol. 2964, pp. 292–304. Springer, Heidelberg (2004). https://doi.org/10.1007/978-3-540-24660-2_23

[HT16] Hoang, V.T., Tessaro, S.: Key-alternating ciphers and key-length extension: exact bounds and multi-user security. In: Robshaw, M., Katz, J. (eds.) CRYPTO 2016. LNCS, vol. 9814, pp. 3–32. Springer, Heidelberg (2016). https://doi.org/10.1007/978-3-662-53018-4_1

[KLL20] Kim, H., Lee, Y., Lee, J.: Forking tweakable even-mansour ciphers. IACR Trans. Symm. Cryptol. **2020**(4), 71–87 (2020)

[LPS12] Lampe, R., Patarin, J., Seurin, Y.: An asymptotically tight security analysis of the iterated even-mansour cipher. In: Wang, X., Sako, K. (eds.) ASIACRYPT 2012. LNCS, vol. 7658, pp. 278–295. Springer, Heidelberg (2012). https://doi.org/10.1007/978-3-642-34961-4_18

[LRW02] Liskov, M., Rivest, R.L., Wagner, D.: Tweakable block ciphers. In: Yung, M. (ed.) CRYPTO 2002. LNCS, vol. 2442, pp. 31–46. Springer, Heidelberg (2002). https://doi.org/10.1007/3-540-45708-9_3

[LST12] Landecker, W., Shrimpton, T., Terashima, R.S.: Tweakable blockciphers with beyond birthday-bound security. In: Safavi-Naini, R., Canetti, R. (eds.) CRYPTO 2012. LNCS, vol. 7417, pp. 14–30. Springer, Heidelberg (2012). https://doi.org/10.1007/978-3-642-32009-5_2

[Pat09] Patarin, J.: The "Coefficients H" technique. In: Avanzi, R.M., Keliher, L., Sica, F. (eds.) SAC 2008. LNCS, vol. 5381, pp. 328–345. Springer, Heidelberg (2009). https://doi.org/10.1007/978-3-642-04159-4_21

[RBBK01] Rogaway, P., Bellare, M., Black, J., Krovetz, T.: OCB: a block-cipher mode of operation for efficient authenticated encryption. In: Reiter, M.K., Samarati, P. (eds.) ACM CCS 2001, Philadelphia, PA, USA, 5–8 November 2001, pp. 196–205. ACM Press (2001)

[Rog04] Rogaway, P.: Efficient instantiations of tweakable blockciphers and refinements to modes OCB and PMAC. In: Lee, P.J. (ed.) ASIACRYPT 2004. LNCS, vol. 3329, pp. 16–31. Springer, Heidelberg (2004). https://doi.org/10.1007/978-3-540-30539-2_2

[Ste12] Steinberger, J.: Improved security bounds for key-alternating ciphers via hellinger distance. Cryptology ePrint Archive, Report 2012/481 (2012). https://eprint.iacr.org/2012/481

Blockcipher-Based Key Commitment for Nonce-Derived Schemes

Panos Kampanakis(✉), Shai Halevi, Nevine Ebeid, and Matt Campagna

Amazon Web Services, Seattle, USA
{kpanos,shaihal,nebeid,campagna}@amazon.com

Abstract. AES-GCM has seen great adoption for the last 20 years to protect data in various use-cases because of its optimal performance. It has also posed some challenges to modern applications due to its nonce, block size, and lack of key commitment. Nonce-derived schemes address these challenges by deriving a different key from random values and using GCM with the derived key. In this work, we explore efficient key commitment methods for nonce-derived schemes. For concreteness, we focus on expanding XAES-256-GCM, a derived key scheme originally introduced by Filippo Valsorda. We propose an efficient CMAC-based key commitment solution, and prove its security in the ideal-cipher model. This proposal yields a FIPS-compliant mode and offers much better data bounds than GCM. Finally, we benchmark the new mode's performance to demonstrate that the additional cost affects mostly small plaintexts.

Keywords: XAES · KC-XAES · Key Committing AEAD · CMAC based key commitment

1 Introduction

AES-GCM has been the status quo for efficient symmetric encryption for decades. As technology and cryptographic applications evolved over time, AES-GCM has posed some challenges to certain use-cases due to its default 96-bit nonce size, 128-bit block size, and lack of key commitment. Some of these challenges, in the context of demanding applications in cloud environments, were discussed in [21].

Nonce-derived schemes are one way of addressing these challenges: Such schemes derive multiple keys from nonce values, then apply standard AES-GCM with the derived keys (and possibly another 96-bit nonce). The approach overcomes the nonce length and data limit issues since each derived key is only used to encrypt a few messages. One example of a derived mode is used in the AWS Encryption SDK (ESDK) and AWS Key Management Service (KMS) [30] which employ HMAC-based PRFs for key derivation. Other examples include DNDK [16,17] and XAES-256-GCM [14]. Below we refer to the latter as XAES, for brevity. By itself, the use of nonce-derived keys does not address key commitment, however. Some schemes such as DNDK and the AWS ESDK chose to

C. Boura et al. (Eds.): SAC 2025, LNCS 16207, pp. 209–234, 2026.
https://doi.org/10.1007/978-3-032-10536-3_8

include a built-in key commitment mechanism, while others such as XAES left it out of scope.

In this work, we explore efficient key commitment methods that can be added to any nonce-derived scheme in a black-box manner. Our focus is on options that use the underlying block cipher, are efficient, and only use standard primitives which are FIPS-approved. We propose an efficient CMAC-based key commitment solution, and prove its security in the ideal-cipher model. We argue that adding this solution to XAES yields a FIPS-compliant mode, quantify the data and message length limits of this mode and compare this combination to other nonce-derived schemes. We also benchmark our key committing XAES performance.

Recently, after its Accordion mode workshop [26], US National Institute of Standards and Technology (NIST) has been exploring a new wide-block cipher [28] which could be used in a new AEAD mode [27] to alleviate some of AES-GCM challenges [21]. The blockcipher-based key commitment proposed in this work is generic and could be used in any new wide-block derived key mode variant by leveraging similar constructions with a wide block cipher instead of AES256.

1.1 Related Work

As we said above, there has been significant work in the literature trying the address the practical shortcomings of GCM. Prior works that use GCM in a nonce-derived mode include AWS' implementation that addressed key rotation at scale using a solution based on HMAC-SHA256 [7], Gueron's DNDK-GCM mode [16], Bhaumik and Degabriele's strong blockcipher-based PRF for GCM derived key modes [6], and Valsorda's XAES mode [13,14]. XAES is the focus of our work. Gueron and Risternpart subsequently improved DNDK by introducing DNDK version 2 [17,18] which uses less blockcipher calls to derive the key and commitment string. One more related proposal is the new accordion mode AES-GEM [2], which has large nonces, a derived key and a tweaked 64-bit internal AES-GCM counter.

Another relevant area deals with key (and context) commitment [1,3,22, 24], with some works showing that GCM does not provide these properties and proposing various solutions. For example, [15] introduced key commitment to AES-GCM by using a pseudorandom function to generate a derived key and a key commitment string from the main key and a random value. The AWS ESDK and AWS KMS added key commitment in 2020 based on this work [30]. DNDK [16] and DNDK version 2 [17,18] introduced key commitment by using a beyond birthday bound PRF and a large nonce.

1.2 Organization

The rest of this document is organized as follows: In Sect. 2 we recall the notions of key commitment security, in Sect. 3 we review Valsorda's XAES mode [14] and describe our construction for adding key commitment, and in Sect. 4 we discuss the usage of this mode, its data limits, and FIPS-compliance. We prove the security of our key commitment function in Sect. 5, and provide performance numbers in Sect. 6. The Appendices provide more details about the implementation of the schemes and other key commitment options we considered.

2 Key Commitment

Standard notions of security for authenticated encryption (AEAD, e.g., [4]) assume that all keys are chosen at random by legitimate users, but there are settings in which the entity choosing the keys may itself be adversarial. Perhaps surprisingly, [12] showed that AES-GCM and other common authenticated encryption schemes are susceptible to such attacks: It is rather easy to come up with two different keys and a ciphertext which would pass the authentication test relative to both keys and decrypt to two different plaintexts. It turns out that some meaningful notions of security can be achieved even in these cases. Specifically, Farshim et al. [12] and follow up works [1,3,15,22,29] described a *key commitment* property, where even a key-choosing adversary cannot come up with a ciphertext that decrypts to different plaintext messages under different keys.

As described in [1,12], key commitment turns out to be important in several real-world settings where an adversary may be able to trick different parties into using different keys to decrypt the same ciphertext. For example, in storage environments that support key rotation, an adversary could theoretically encrypt a file with one key, then rotate the key and trick the system into decrypting with the new key, causing readers to get the wrong file upon decryption. Similarly, in systems that use key-wrapping for hierarchical key management, the adversary can wrap different data keys under different high-level keys, causing different users to decrypt the same ciphertext to different plaintexts.

The literature contains a few different formal definitions for the key-commitment requirement. All of these definitions consider AEAD schemes with the following encryption/decryption interfaces:

$$\mathsf{Encrypt}(K, N, A, P) \mapsto C, \ \mathsf{Decrypt}(K, A, C) \mapsto P/\perp,$$

where K is the key, N is a nonce, A is some context information or additional data that needs authentication (A is called "additional authenticated data" (AAD) in AES-GCM), P is the message to be encrypted, and C is the ciphertext. These formal key commitment definitions are summarized below in order from weakest to strongest:

- The weakest notion was put forward by Farshim et al. [12]. It asserts that it is hard for the adversary to come up with two different keys, $K \neq K'$, one nonce value N, and two pairs $(A, P), (A', P')$ such that $\mathsf{Encrypt}(K, N, A, P) = \mathsf{Encrypt}(K', N, A', P')$. Below we refer to this notion as FOR-KC.
- A stronger notion called CMT-1, put forward by Bellare and Hoang [3], asserts that it is hard for the adversary to come up with two different keys, $K \neq K'$ and two tuples $(N, A, P), (N', A', P')$ such that $\mathsf{Encrypt}(K, N, A, P) = \mathsf{Encrypt}(K', N', A', P')$.

- Yet a stronger notion is CMT-2, implicit in [3] and mentioned explicitly by Takeuchi et al. [29], asserting that it is hard for the adversary to come up with two different pairs $(K, N) \neq (K', N')$ and two other pairs $(A, P), (A', P')$, such that $\mathsf{Encrypt}(K, N, A, P) = \mathsf{Encrypt}(K', N', A', P')$.
- Bellare and Hoang [3] also defined the strongest notion of this type, called CMT-4 (and also referred to as *context commitment* [24]), asserting that it is hard for the adversary to come up with two different tuples $(K, N, A, P) \neq (K', N', A', P')$ such that $\mathsf{Encrypt}(K, N, A, P) = \mathsf{Encrypt}(K', N', A', P')$. This last notion asks for all, key, nonce, additional data, and plaintext values to be committed to which differs from FOR-KC, CMT-1, and CMT-2. Achieving efficient context commitment (while keeping the ciphertext length independent of the length of A) requires two passes on the additional data and plaintext and newer constructions like truncated Davies-Meyer or iterative truncated-permutation [3], and we do not consider it in this manuscript.

FOR-KC vs. CMT-1 vs. CMT-2: While the three notions, FOR-KC, CMT-1, CMT-2, are different, the distinction turns out to be meaningless for most common AEAD use-cases. Specifically, these notions are the same if the nonce value N is part of the output ciphertext C, which is usually the case. Note, however, that the distinction could be important in applications where the nonce value is implied and is not included explicitly in the ciphertext. For example, a storage system that does not include the nonce in the ciphertext but instead uses the object index as the nonce (bad idea) could be vulnerable to key commitment attacks even if it satisfied the FOR-KC property. In this manuscript, we focus on AEAD schemes that include the nonce explicitly with the ciphertext, hence we only consider FOR-KC.

3 Adding Key Commitment to XAES

3.1 XAES

XAES-256-GCM by Filippo Valsorda [14] specified XAES as a variant of AES-GCM which takes a 192-bit (24-byte) nonce and a 256-bit main key. It derives a new AES-GCM key from the main key and half the nonce for every invocation. The other half of the nonce is used as the Initialization Vector (IV) to encrypt the message with AES-GCM and the derived key.

In more detail, the input to XAES is a 256-bit main key K, a 24-byte nonce N, Plaintext P, and Additional Authenticated Data A. The output is the ciphertext C. Denote the first 12 bytes of the nonce by U and the last 12-bytes by V. XAES uses CMAC-AES-256 to derive another 256-bit key K_U from K and U, and then encrypts the message using AES-256-GCM with key K_U and nonce V. We provide a pseudo-code below for self-containment. The two 32-bit constants in that code are $\text{const}_1 = \texttt{0x00015800}$ and $\text{const}_2 = \texttt{0x00025800}$. (Note that the GCM ciphertext includes in particular the nonce value V, so the output of XAES includes the entire nonce N.)

XAES-Encrypt(Key K, Nonce N, AAD A, Plaintext P):

0. $U = N[0:12]$, $V = N[12:24]$ // U, V are the two halves of N
1. $K1 = X \times \text{AES}_K(0^{128})$ // Multiplication by $X \in GF(2^{128})$

2a. $M_1 = (\text{const}_1 \parallel U) \oplus K1$

2b. $M_2 = (\text{const}_2 \parallel U) \oplus K1$

3. $K_U = \text{AES}_K(M_1) \parallel \text{AES}_K(M_2)$ // CMAC-based key derivation
4. Output $U \mid \text{AES-GCM}_{K_U}(V, A, P)$ // AES-GCM encryption

Note that the blockcipher-based key derivation in XAES is used beyond the birthday bound. In a separate analysis manuscript [5], we prove that this use of CMAC maintains the security of XAES, showing that it is safe to derive close to 2^n keys using an n-bit blockcipher in counter mode as in XAES.

3.2 KC-XAES

XAES is a derived key mode of AES-GCM. Like with plain AES-GCM, an adversary could find two different derived keys, K_U and K'_U which could have been produced from the same main key K and lead to the same ciphertext and authentication tag. Decrypting the ciphertext with the two derived keys would lead to two different plaintexts. Thus, XAES does not provide key commitment for any of the notions defined in Sect. 2.

One solution for derived key modes is PRF-based key commitment, as proposed by Gueron in [15], which provides key-commitment by using a hash-based PRF (e.g., HMAC-SHA256), at the cost of the PRF performance. An alternative is to implement the generic solution of Albertini et al. [1, Sec 5.4], adding to the ciphertext a key commitment value $F_{com}(K, N)$ that is verified upon decryption. While Albertini et al. say that $F_{com}(K, \cdot)$ should be a PRF (which is independent of the one used to derive data key), it is clear that this PRF must also be collision-resistant. Specifically, for this construction to yield FOR-KC, it must be hard for an attacker to find two keys $K \neq K'$ and a nonce N such that $F_{com}(K, N) = F_{com}(K', N)$.

Our aim in this work is to describe an efficient construction using only the underlying blockcipher, so in particular we need to describe a blockcipher-based construction that offers collision-resistance and does not leak information about the main key K. To achieve this, we propose:

$$F_{com}(K, N) = CMAC_K(c\|U\|V\|c') \parallel CMAC_K(c\|U\|V\|c''),$$

where c, c', and c'' are different 32-bit constants (that are also different from the constants used for key derivation), which are defined later. With the 192-bit nonce of XAES, the length of each of the CMAC inputs $c\|N\|c'$ and $c\|N\|c''$ is 256 bits, or two AES blocks. We note that computing $F_{com}(K, N)$ only takes three more block encryption operations on top XAES, since the first block is the same in both CMAC calls. A depiction of the function $F_{com}(K, N)$ is given in Fig. 1, and a pseudocode for the combined XAES with key commitment is given in Fig. 2. Note that all the derived values (both derived keys and key-commitment values) are obtained by CMAC with the same main key on different inputs, so they are pseudorandom and (pseudo)independent of each other. In other words, revealing the key-commitment values does not weaken the derived keys of XAES.

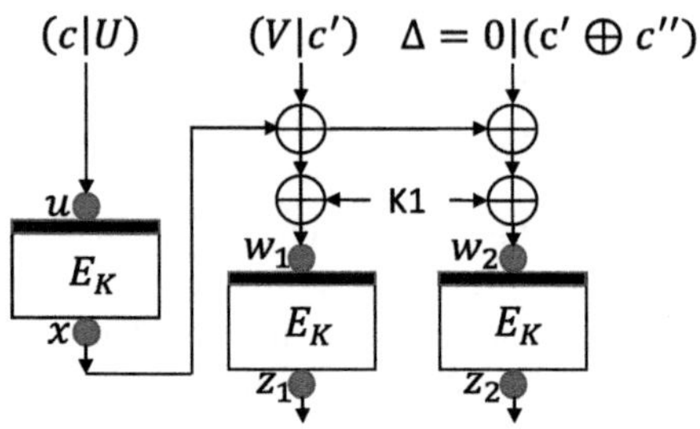

Fig. 1. The function F_{com}, applied to the 192-bit nonce $N = (U \parallel V)$. c, c', c'' are 32-bit constants. The 256-bit output is $K_C = (z_1 \parallel z_2)$.

KC-XAES-Encrypt(Key K, Nonce N, AAD A, Plaintext P):

0. $U = N[0:12]$, $V = N[12:24]$	// U, V are the two halves of N
1. $K1 = X \times \text{AES256}_K(0^{128})$	// Multiplication by $X \in GF(2^{128})$
2a. $M_1 = (\text{const}_1 \parallel U) \oplus K1$	// CMAC-based key derivation
2b. $M_2 = (\text{const}_2 \parallel U) \oplus K1$	
3. $K_U = \text{AES256}_K(M_1) \parallel \text{AES}_K(M_2)$	//$K_U = CMAC_K(\text{const}_1 \Vert U) \parallel CMAC_K(\text{const}_2 \Vert U)$
4. $CT = \text{AES256-GCM}_{K_U}(V, A, P)$	// AES-GCM encryption
5. $X_1 = \text{AES256}_K(\text{const}_3 \parallel U)$	// CMAC-based key commitment
6a. $W_1 = X_1 \oplus (V \parallel \text{const}_4) \oplus K1$	
6b. $W_2 = X_1 \oplus (V \parallel \text{const}_5) \oplus K1$	
7. $K_C = \text{AES256}_K(W_1) \parallel \text{AES256}_K(W_2)$	// $K_C = CMAC_K(\text{const}_3 \Vert U \Vert V \Vert \text{const}_4)$
8. Output $U \Vert\ CT \Vert\ K_C$	// $\parallel CMAC_K(\text{const}_3 \Vert U \Vert V \Vert \text{const}_5)$

Fig. 2. The KC-XAES256 Specification. The constants are defined as $\text{const}_1 =$ 0x00015800, $\text{const}_2 =$ 0x00025800, $\text{const}_3 = c =$ "XCMT" $=$ 0x58434D54, $\text{const}_4 = c' =$ 0x00010001, $\text{const}_5 = c'' =$ 0x00010002. Prepending constant const_3 to the input of $CMAC_K$ and appending const_4 and const_5 allows us to re-use X_1 and omit an extra AES256 call while remaining FIPS compliant as per [9].

Appendix A breaks down Fig. 2 into a prescriptive implementation specification. Appendix B abstracts the specification to allow for smaller nonces useful to constrained use-cases and Appendix C lays out other $F_{com}(K, N)$ options we considered and did not pick.

4 KC-AES Usage and Data Limits

We analyze below the usage, data limits, and FIPS certification considerations for the KC-XAES construction as specified in Fig. 2.

4.1 Uses

XAES-256-GCM [14] introduces three additional AES-256 calls on top of AES-256-GCM (one of which can be computed only once and cached for all the XAES calls with the same main key). Our CMAC-based key commitment adds three more AES-256 calls. The impact of these extra calls is very small when we use this mode to encrypt large messages, since we anyways need many AES-256 calls to produce the ciphertext.

Some of the use-cases that could benefit from XAES are described in [21]. These include high encryption rate uses that can run through 2^{32} 96-bit AES-GCM IVs in seconds and where deterministic IVs pose challenges due to their statefulness. Other uses include encryption clients and servers like the AWS ESDK with AWS Key Management Service that encrypt many messages from one main key and require key commitment without maintaining state.

4.2 Data Limits

XAES is a nonce-derived mode that derives a random data-key K_U and IV for GCM per invocation. Hence XAES remains as secure as AES-GCM as long as the pair (K_U, IV) does not repeat, and as long as the data bounds per key K_U do not violate AES-GCM's limits. There are various works that analyze the security of AES-GCM which set the maximum data bounds based on the desired confidentiality and integrity level [19,20,23]. These bounds still apply to XAES and we consider them below when we calculate the maximum data size per derived key K_U. Additionally, a separate manuscript [5] proves that using blockcipher-based key derivation beyond the birthday bound maintains the security of the scheme to 2^n keys for n-bit blockcipher in counter mode.

First, we focus on the (K_U, V) collision probability. Clearly, the pair (K_U, V) would repeat if the 24-byte nonce N was re-used with the same main key K. As long as the nonces N do not collide, we will not have (K_U, V) collisions under the same main key K. To see that, observe that since AES is a permutation, then the two blocks of K_U can only collide if the corresponding AES inputs (M_1, M_2 from Fig. 2) repeat. $K1$ is fixed for the same K which means we can have a K_U collision (under the same main key K) only when we have a U collision. Thus, a (K_U, V) collision requires a full nonce (U, V) collision.[1]

It follows that when the nonce N is chosen at random, a full (K_U, V) collision will only happen after roughly $2^{|N|/2} = 2^{96}$ calls. If we want to limit the probability of such collisions to less than 2^{-32}, then it is sufficient to limit the number of calls below 2^{80}. To see that, note that by the union bound the probability of having a collision among a set of 2^{80} random 192-bit (24-byte) strings is at most

$$\binom{2^{80}}{2} \cdot 2^{-192} \leq 2^{2 \cdot 80 - 1} \cdot 2^{-192} = 2^{-33}.$$

[1] While it is theoretically possible to have a (K_U, V) collision under *different* main keys $K \neq K'$, if these main keys are chosen at random then the K_U's will be pseudorandom and so will not collide except with insignificant probability.

An AES-GCM (key, IV) collision probability $\leq 2^{-32}$ is typically considered satisfactory. It was initially introduced by NIST in [11] and it usually dictates AES-GCM's rekey frequency when IVs are generated at random. We note that while the analysis above rules out full-nonce collisions, we still could have collisions for $U = N[0:12]$, the portion of the nonce that is used for key-derivation. Collisions like that would have us use the same data key K_U to encrypt multiple messages, which is not a problem as long as these different encryptions use different GCM nonces V (which is ensured by the analysis above). By the analysis above, we can use each main key K to encrypt at most 2^{80} messages.

Let m be a parameter (to be determined later), then the probability of the same value $U \in \{0,1\}^{96}$ occurring m times among 2^{80} messages (assuming random nonces) is bounded using the union bound by

$$\binom{2^{80}}{m} \cdot 2^{-96(m-1)} \approx \frac{2^{80\,m-96(m-1)}}{m!} = \frac{2^{96-16\,m}}{m!}. \tag{1}$$

Setting $m = 8$, Eq. (1) tells us that the probability of seeing an eight-way collision is bounded by $2^{96-(96-80)\cdot 8}/8! \approx 2^{-47.3}$. Hence we can safely assume that we will not see more than seven collisions (with probability $> 2^{-32}$), which means that no derived data-key K_U will be used to encrypt more than seven messages. In settings where we can enforce fewer messages per main key, the K_U occurrence bound m is lower.

Some applications need to enforce usage limit for keys (say, no more than X-bytes-per-GCM-key). In such applications, we need to ensure that no single data key K_U is used to encrypt more than X bytes. The bound from Eq. (1) above implies that except with probability $\epsilon < 2^{-47}$, we will only see at most $m-1 = 7$ messages encrypted under the same data key K_U. Hence, an application that wants to enforce X-bytes-per-GCM-key limit can achieve this by limiting the length of the encrypted messages to no more than $X/7$ bytes each. (Note there is still an inherent limit on each AES-GCM invocation where the plaintext cannot exceed $2^{36} - 32 \approx 2^{36}$ bytes [11, § 5.2.1.1]. Thus, the KC-XAES message limit ought to be bound by $\min(X/7, 2^{36})$ bytes). As an example, NIST [11] defines a data limit of 2^{64} blocks per GCM key which means $X = 2^{68}$. In that case, each message could be up to 2^{36} bytes ($\ll 2^{68}/7$). Other X values for AES-GCM depending on the attack success probability can be found in [23] which calculates the bounds based on the analysis in [20]. [19] includes a tighter AES-GCM data bound analysis.

Are 2^{80} Messages Enough? Some prior work such as [21] expressed a desire to support as many as 2^{112} messages encrypted under a single key (which is what we would get from a straightforward adaptation of GCM mode to a 256-bit block cipher). XAES with 24-byte random nonces does not satisfy this desire because, as we point out above, it only supports up to 2^{80} messages under a single main key. Nonetheless, 2^{80} messages is still much better than what we have today with AES-GCM, and it seems sufficient for most of today's use-cases. Indeed, for most of today's workloads it is enough to encrypt only 2^{64} messages under one key.

Multi-key XAES: The analysis above is only concerned with the case where a single XAES main key is used for encrypting many messages. When dealing with multiple keys, ensuring a small enough collision probability requires that we bound not only the number of messages per key but also the total number of messages under all keys. For example, if we use XAES 24-byte random nonces and limit ourselves to 2^{64} messages per main key, then for each key we get a nonce N collision probability of at most 2^{-65}, and we can use as many as 2^{33} keys for a total of $2^{64+33} = 2^{97}$ messages before the multi-key-IV collision probability increases to 2^{-32}. Note that GCM's multi-key-IV collision probability is far worse. It becomes 2^{-32} after using just two keys to encrypt 2^{32} messages with each key (assuming random 96-bit IVs).

4.3 FIPS Compliance

Here we argue that KC-XAES falls under the NIST FIPS 140-3 program [25] approved algorithms, and systems that use it could be FIPS validated. FIPS 140-3 defines a set of approved cryptographic algorithms and certifies their implementations. Only certified cryptographic modules and approved algorithms can be used in Federal Government systems in the USA and Canada. Other government and International requirements like Common Criteria [10] sometimes require FIPS too.

Valsorda explains briefly in [14] how XAES maps to FIPS-compliant key derivation and use of AES-GCM. We argue that KC-XAES can be used in environments that require FIPS compliance by showing that the derived K_U key, the IV used in the AES-GCM calls of XAES, and the derived K_C follow FIPS requirements.

In KC-XAES, a new 256-bit data key K_U is derived from the main key K as

$$\begin{aligned} K_U = \ & \text{CMAC-AES256}_K(\text{0x00015800} \| N[:12]) \ \| \\ & \text{CMAC-AES256}_K(\text{0x00025800} \| N[:12]). \end{aligned}$$

This translates to a Counter Mode Key Derivation Function (KDF) as defined in NIST SP 800-108 [9], where CMAC-AES256 is the PRF, the fixed input data is $\text{0x5800} \| N[:12]$, and the counter $i = 1, 2$ is two bytes. Thus, the derived key is FIPS approved as a Key Based Key Derivation Function (KBKDF) specified in [9, §4.1]. Note that one issue with key derivation using CMAC-AES256 discussed in [9, §6.7] is Key Control Security for inputs that span more than one 128-bit blocks. XAES' derived key K_U does not have this concern because the CMAC input is always one block.

Subsequently, KC-XAES uses the derived key K_U and the last 12-bytes of the nonce $V = N[12:24]$ in AES-GCM-256. If $N[12:24]$ was generated by using a FIPS-approved entropy source (or any other approved way of generating nonces), then the KC-XAES encryption is FIPS approved because it encrypts with AES-GCM which is FIPS-approved and a key K_U and IV generated with FIPS-approved methods. Of course, the message and data limits laid out in Sect. 4.2 apply to ensure the NIST security bounds for AES-GCM hold.

Regarding key commitment, the key commitment string generation K_C is

$$K_C = \text{CMAC-AES256}_K(\text{“XCMT”} \| N[: 24] \| \text{0x00010001}) \; \| \\ \text{CMAC-AES256}_K(\text{“XCMT”} \| N[: 24] \| \text{0x00010002}).$$

This translates to a Counter Mode KDF as defined in [9], where CMAC-AES256 is the PRF, the fixed input data is “XCMT”$\|N[: 24] \|$ 0x000100, and the counter $i = 1, 2$ is one byte. Thus, the derived commitment string is generated with a FIPS approved KBKDF [9, §4.1], although it admittedly is not used as an encryption key.

5 Key Commitment Security

This section uses the notations from Fig. 1.

5.1 CMT-2 Insecurity

In Sect. 5.2 below we show that in the ideal-cipher model with n-bit blockcipher, our construction offers roughly n bits of security against “FOR-KC collision attacks”, where the adversary must use the same nonce for the two keys. Before that, and in order to build some intuition, we describe an attack against the stronger CMT-2 notion, where the attacker can use different nonces with the different keys. We recall again that in most use-cases, where the nonce is included as part of the ciphertext, FOR-KC implies also CMT-1 and CMT-2. The attack below does not apply in those cases.

We now show a CMT-2 attack with complexity roughly $2^{n/2}$, even though the key-commitment length is $2n$ bits. That is, it only takes about $2^{n/2}$ queries to the blockcipher to find two different keys $K \neq K'$ and two sets of nonces U, V, U', V', such that $F_{com}(K, U, V) = F_{com}(K', U', V')$ for the function F_{com} from Fig. 1. The collision attack proceeds as follows (with the the blockcipher being AES and with the constants $c, c', c'' \in \{0,1\}^{32}$): Denote $\Delta = 0|(c' \oplus c'') \in \{0,1\}^{128}$.

1. Choose an arbitrary 128-bit block $z_1 \in \{0,1\}^{128}$.
2. For $i = 1, 2, 3, \ldots$, choose a random key K^i and compute:

   $$w_1^i \leftarrow AES_{K^i}^{-1}(z_1), \quad w_2^i \leftarrow w_1^i \oplus \Delta, \quad z_2^i \leftarrow AES_{K^i}(w_2^i).$$

   Repeat until you find a collision, $z_2^i = z_2^j$ for different keys $K^i \neq K^j$.
   Below we denote the colliding value by $z_2 := z_2^i = z_2^j$. We also denote $K := K^i, w_1 := w_1^i, w_2 := w_2^i$ and $K' := K^j, w_1' := w_1^j, w_2' := w_2^j$.
3. Let $K1 = X \times E_K(0)$ and $K_1' = X \times E_{K'}(0)$ (multiplication by X in $GF(2^n)$).
4. Try many values for $U \in \{0,1\}^{96}$, for each value compute $x \leftarrow AES_K(c\|U)$, until $x \oplus K1 \oplus w_1 = (V\|c')$ for some $V \in \{0,1\}^{96}$.
5. Similarly try many values for $U' \in \{0,1\}^{96}$, for each one compute $x' \leftarrow AES_{K'}(c\|U')$, until $x' \oplus K_1' \oplus w_1' = (V'\|c')$ for some $V' \in \{0,1\}^{96}$.
6. Output (K, U, V) and (K', U', V').

The complexity of step 2 is roughly 2^{64}, and the complexity of steps 4, 5 is roughly $2^{|c'|}$ (which is 2^{32} in our construction). Overall the complexity of this attack is about 2^{64}. This collision attack on the key-commitment function can then be extended to a full CMT-2 attack on XAES with this function, using the known key-commitment attacks on AES-GCM [24].

5.2 FOR-KC Security

We now show that for the weaker FOR-KC notion, when the attacker must use the same nonce for both keys, we get roughly n bits of security. We note that proving the hardness of collision-finding for a blockcipher-based construction often requires resorting to idealized models such as the ideal-cipher model, and our proof is no different. Drawing conclusions from such a proof takes some caution, especially when using AES256 for which related-key attacks are known. The specific related-key attacks on AES256 do not seem to apply directly to our construction, but more cryptanalysis may be needed before accepting the numbers of our ideal-cipher analysis. This is an interesting topic for future work.

Fix an n-bit blockcipher and some n-bit block $\Delta \neq 0$, and consider the function

$$F_{com} : \mathsf{Keys} \times (\{0,1\}^n)^2 \to \{0,1\}^{2n}, \quad F_{com}(K,U,V) = CMAC_K(U\|V) \,\| \, CMAC_K(U\|V \oplus \Delta). \tag{2}$$

(This is exactly our construction, except that in this section we give the adversary a little more freedom by not insisting on the specific constants c, c', c'' from Fig. 1.) Below we prove that in the ideal-cipher model, an adversary asking $q \ll 2^n$ blockcipher queries has probability $O(q)/2^n$ of finding a collision, i.e. two keys $K \neq K'$ and inputs U, V such that $F_{com}(K,U,V) = F_{com}(K',U,V)$.

One high-level intuition is that a blockcipher query made by the adversary can only induce a collision if it satisfies four equalities over n-bit blocks (i.e., the two nonce blocks and two output blocks). The adversary can force at most two of these equalities to hold (e.g. by going backward from one of the output blocks and choosing U as in the attack from above), but this leaves two n-bit equalities to chance. After making i blockcipher applications, a new application would therefore only induce collision with probability about $i/2^{2n}$. Hence, the overall probability of finding a collision after q blockcipher queries cannot be much more than $\binom{q}{2}/2^{2n}$.

Technically, what we need to prove is that even though an attacker can induce "partial collisions" as per the attack from above with complexity $2^{n/2}$, they cannot get too many of them. In particular, in Lemma 1 we show that with high probability, no key will induce partial collisions with too many other keys. Once this is established, the rest of the proof proceeds via a straightforward (if somewhat tedious) case analysis, resulting in the following lemma:

Theorem 1. *With an n-bit blockcipher in the ideal-cipher model, an adversary making at most q blockcipher queries (in either direction) has probability at most*

$$\mathsf{adv}(q,n) = \min_{\beta\in\mathbb{N}} \left\{ \frac{q\cdot\binom{q-1}{\beta}}{(2^n-2q)^\beta} + \frac{4(\beta-1)q}{2^n-2q} \right\} + \frac{3\binom{q}{2}}{(2^n-2q)^2}$$

of finding two keys $K' \neq K$ and inputs U, V such that $F(K,U,V) = F(K',U,V)$.

For example, with $n = 128$ and $q = 2^{80}$, using $\beta = 3$ yields a bound of $\mathsf{adv}(q,n) < 2^{-44} = \frac{16q}{2^n}$.

Proof (of Theorem 1). We will use the notations from Fig. 1, where for each key K we have $K1 = X \times E_K(0^{128})$, and the inputs and outputs of the block cipher are denoted u, w_1, w_2 and correspondingly x, z_1, z_2. (Presumably the inputs are computed by the adversary as $u = (c\|U)$, $w_1 = x \oplus (V\|c') \oplus K1$ and $w_2 = x \oplus (V\|c'') \oplus K1$ for the nonce value $N = (U\|V)$ and constants c, c', c''.) We also denote the 128-bit block $\Delta = 0\|(c' \oplus c'')$.

To slightly simplify the case analysis below, we consider a *principled adversary* such that: (a) they never make a redundant blockcipher query that they already know the answer to; (b) with each forward-query to a block cipher $s = E_K(a)$ the adversary also makes another forward query $s' = E_K(a \oplus \Delta)$ with the same key K; and (c) with each backward-query $a = E_K^{-1}(s)$ the adversary also makes the forward query $s' = E_K(a \oplus \Delta)$ with the same key K. Below we call the two queries $((a,s)(a',s'))$ a query pair. It is a forward pair if the first query in that pair is forward, and otherwise (if the first query is backward) it is a backward pair.

Clearly, any q-query adversary can be converted into a principled adversary making at most q pairs of queries. Also, note that query pairing is a partition of the queries relative to each key into disjoint pairs. This means that if $((a,s),(a',s'))$ is a query pair for key K, then neither (a,s) nor (a',s') belongs to any other pair for that key.

Fix a principled adversary $\mathcal{A}$, making at most q query pairs to the underlying block cipher and also fix the randomness of $\mathcal{A}$. The *transcript* of the interaction between $\mathcal{A}$ and the scheme consists of entries of the form $(K, \mathsf{dir}, (a,s), (a' = a \oplus \Delta, s'))$, where $\mathsf{dir} \in \{+,-\}$ denotes whether this is a forward or backward pair.[2] The transcript is a random variable over the choice of the random permutations in the ideal cipher model. We use the following notations:

- We write $(K, \mathsf{dir}, (a,s), (a',s')) \in \Pi$ when this query pair appears in the transcript Π. We replace some of these quantities with '·' (or omit them completely) when we mean them to remain unspecified. For a few examples:
  - We write $K \in \Pi$ to denote that some query pair in Π was made with respect to K;
  - $(K,(a,s)) \in \Pi$ means that Π includes either query $s = E_K(a)$ or $a = E_K^{-1}(s)$;

[2] Note that specifying a' is redundant, it is there just to aid readability.

- $(K, \cdot, (a_1, s_1), (a_2, s_2)) \in \Pi$ means that this query pair is in Π without specifying the direction;
- $(K, \{z, z'\}) \in \Pi$ means that $(\cdot, z), (\cdot, z')$ showed up in some query pair under K, in either order. Namely, either $(K, \cdot, (\cdot, z), (\cdot, z')) \in \Pi$ or $(K, \cdot, (\cdot, z'), (\cdot, z)) \in \Pi$.

– Two query pairs, $(K, \cdot, (\cdot, z_1), (\cdot, z_2))$, $(K', \cdot, (\cdot, z'_1), (\cdot, z'_2)) \in \Pi$, are called a *partial collision* if $K \neq K'$ but $\{z_1, z_2\} = \{z'_1, z'_2\}$ as sets, irrespective of order. These are important since a collision between K and K' requires a partial collision, in addition to using the same nonces U, V under both keys. A partial collision between two query pairs is either a *forward partial collision* or a *backward partial collision*, depending on whether the latter query pair is forward or backward.[3]

– For any key $K \in \Pi$, let $\mathsf{col}_\Pi(K)$ denote the set of partial collisions involving K,

$$\mathsf{col}_\Pi(K) = \{(K', \{z, z'\}) \in \Pi : K' \neq K, (K, \{z, z'\}) \in \Pi\}. \tag{3}$$

Let maxCol be the largest number of partial collisions for any key, $\mathsf{maxCol}(\Pi) = \max_{K\in\Pi} (|\mathsf{col}(K)|)$.

– A *full collision* between two keys $K \neq K'$ involves a partial collision $(K, \cdot, (w_1, z_1), (w_2, z_2))$, $(K', \cdot, (w'_1, z'_1), (w'_2, z'_2)) \in \Pi$ with $\{z_1, z_2\} = \{z'_1, z'_2\}$, and in addition queries $(K, (u, x))$, $(K', (u, x')) \in \Pi$ (with the same u) such that either $x \oplus K1 \oplus w_1 = x' \oplus K'_1 \oplus w'_1$ or $x \oplus K1 \oplus w_1 = x' \oplus K'_1 \oplus w'_1 \oplus \Delta$. (Recall that $w'_2 = w'_1 \oplus \Delta$.)

With these notations, we prove below the following three technical claims:

Lemma 1. *For a transcript of $q < 2^{n-1}$ query pairs,*

$$\Pr[\exists \text{ any forward partial collisions}] \leq \frac{2\binom{q}{2}}{(2^n - 2q)^2}.$$

Lemma 2. *For a transcript of $q < 2^{n-1}$ query pairs and any bound $\beta \in \mathbb{N}$,*

$$\Pr[\mathsf{maxCol}_\Pi \geq \beta \text{ with no forward partial collisions}] \leq \frac{q \cdot \binom{q-1}{\beta}}{(2^n - 2q)^\beta}.$$

Lemma 3. *For a transcript of $q < 2^{n-1}$ query pairs and any bound $\beta \in \mathbb{N}$,*

$$\Pr[\text{any full collision with } \mathsf{maxCol}_\Pi < \beta \text{ and no forward partial collisions}]$$

$$\leq \frac{4(\beta - 1)q}{2^n - 2q} + \frac{\binom{q}{2}}{(2^n - 2q)^2}.$$

Theorem 1 is deduced just by adding the bounds in the three lemmas above.

[3] It is insignificant if the earlier query pair is forward or backward, only the direction of the latter pair matters.

Proof (of Lemma 1). A forward query pair $(K^i, +, (\cdot, z_1^i), (\cdot, z_2^i)) \in \Pi$ can only induce a partial collision with some prior query $(K^j, \cdot, (\cdot, z_1^j), (\cdot, z_2^j)) \in \Pi$ if both z_1^i, z_2^i appeared in that prior query. This being a forward query, both z_1^i and z_2^i are drawn at random from a set of size at least $2^n - 2i \geq 2^n - 2q$, so the probability that it collides with the prior pair j is bounded by $2/(2^n - 2q)^2$. (The factor 2 in the numerator is because it could collide in either order: $z_1^i = z_1^j$ and $z_2^i = z_2^j$, or $z_1^i = z_2^j$ and $z_2^i = z_1^j$.) Hence, the probability of any partial collision being induced by a forward pair is bounded by $2\binom{q}{2}/(2^n - 2q)^2$ as in Lemma 1.

Proof (of Lemma 2). For any specific key K, a *neighboring query pair* to K (or just a neighbor, for short) is a query pair using some other key $K' \neq K$, which is involved in a partial collision with K. Our goal is to bound the probability of any key K having β neighbors, where all the partial collisions are induced by backward queries.

We start by numbering all the keys that are used in the transcript (e.g., by the order in which they appeared there), then fix one of these keys (call it K^*) by choosing its number $i \leq q$. We also fix a set of β query pairs *under keys other than* K^* by choosing $j_1 < j_2 < \cdots < j_\beta < q$ out of the indexes of pairs that are not using K^*. There are at most $q \cdot \binom{q-1}{\beta}$ ways to select this key and those pairs. Below we prove that for each such choice, the probability of all these β query pairs being neighbors of K^* is bounded by $1/(2^n - 2q)^\beta$. The claim then follows by the union bound.

To prove our bound, we build a labeled directed graph whose nodes are (the indexes of) all these β query pairs, as well as all the query pairs under the key K^*. We start by having a fixed set of (indexes of) query pairs $J = \{j_1, j_2, \ldots, j_\beta\}$, and a fixed (index of) another query pair i that determines the key K^*. Initially the nodes of this graph include only the set J. Every time the adversary makes a query pair under K^*, then the index of that query pair is added as another node to the graph. We label each node by the key that was used in the corresponding query pair. A directed edge $m \to \ell$ is *tentatively* added to the graph if all the following conditions hold:

- $m > \ell$;
- the m-th pair is a backward query pair, $(K^m, -, (\cdot, z_1^m), (\cdot, \cdot))$;
- the ℓ-th query pair is $(K^\ell, \cdot, (\cdot, z_1^\ell), (\cdot, z_2^\ell))$ with $K^\ell \neq K^m$ and $z_1^m \in \{z_1^\ell, z_2^\ell\}$;
- the ℓ-th query pair has no other incoming edges.

Intuitively, the adversary is making the query pair m in an attempt to create a partial collision with the query pair ℓ, starting with a backward query with one of the blocks in the ℓ-th pair. The edge becomes *permanent* if the attempt is successful, namely $\{z_1^m, z_2^m\} = \{z_1^\ell, z_2^\ell\}$, which happens with probability at most $1/(2^n - 2q)$, independently of anything that had happened before. Otherwise the edge is removed from the graph and the adversary is moving to the next query pair.

This process continues until the transcript is done, at which point the neighbors of K^* from among the nodes J are those that are connected to some K^*-labeled node in the underlying undirected graph. A crucial observation is that any tentative edge in this process that does not turn into a permanent edge, implies that the nodes in J cannot all be neighbors of K^*. Recall that a tentative edge means that the two nodes share one of the z blocks, and it fails to turn into a permanent edge if they do not share also the other z block.

Consider the case where one of these nodes (call it k^*) is labeled by K^* and the other is $j \in J$ which is labeled by another key $K \neq K^*$. Then no node labeled by K^* will be connected to node j in the underlying undirected graph, because the node k^* is the only K^*-labeled node that has the z block on which they agree, and the other z block in that node differs.

For the same reason, if two nodes that are labelled by two keys other than K^* had a tentative edge that did not turn into a permanent edge, then a K^*-labeled node can be a neighbor of one of them or the other, but then the node that was left out cannot be a neighbor of any K^*-labelled node.

Therefore, assuming no forward partial collisions, the only way in which this process ends up with all the nodes in J being neighbors of K^* is if the graph only ever had β tentative edges that all turned into permanent edges. This happens with probability at most $1/(2^n - 2q)^\beta$, which is what we needed to show for Lemma 2.

Proof (of Lemma 3*).* Consider a particular query pair i in Π, labeled by key K, and we bound the probability that it is the first query that induces a full collision. The full collision induced by this pair includes in particular a partial collision, either between two prior query pairs or between the i-th query pair itself and a prior pair. Either way, one of the keys in that partial collision is K and the other is some $K' \neq K$ (or else the i'th pair could not have induced a full collision). We analyze these two cases separately.

Case 1. A prior partial collision: In this case the partial collision happened before the i-th query pair. Note that before the i-th query pair, the key K could have been involved in several partial collisions, but no more than $\beta - 1$ of them. Below we fix one of them (say between the query pairs j and j') and bound the probability that the i-th query pair completes that partial collision into a full collision.

For this case we denote the i-th query by $(K = K^i, \mathsf{dir}^i, (u_1^i, x_1^i), (u_2^i, x_2^i))$ (with $u_2^i = u_1^i \oplus \Delta$), and denote the prior partial collision involving K by $(K = K^j, \cdot, (w_1^j, z_1), (w_2^j, z_2))$ and $(K' = K^{j'}, \cdot, (w_1^{j'}, z_1), (w_2^{j'}, z_2))$, with the same z_1, z_2 but $K' \neq K$. For the i-th query pair to complete this partial collision into a full collision, it must be the case that:

- The same u block is queried under K and K', so at least one of u_1^i and u_2^i must have been queried as a pre-image of $E_{K'}(\cdot)$. Since this is a principled adversary, it means that they both appears in the same query pair (since pre-images always come in pairs that are Δ apart).
  Let $(K' = K^{i'}, \cdot, (u_1^{i'}, x_1^{i'}), (u_2^{i'}, x_2^{i'}))$ be query pair i' where theses values were queried with key K', to have full collision we must have $\{u_1, u_2\} = \{u_1^{i'}, u_2^{i'}\}$ (as sets, in either order).

– A full collision means in particular the same block v was used, so at least one of the following equalities must hold:

$$\begin{array}{lll} 1.\ x_1^i \oplus w_1^j \oplus K1 = x_1^{i'} \oplus w_1^{j'} \oplus K_1' & \#\ u = u_1^i,\ v \in \{x_1^i \oplus w_1^j \oplus K1, \\ & \quad x_1^i \oplus w_1^j \oplus K1 \oplus \Delta\} \\ 2.\ x_1^i \oplus w_1^j \oplus K1 = x_1^{i'} \oplus w_1^{j'} \oplus K_1' \oplus \Delta & \#\ \text{(as above)} \\ 3.\ x_2^i \oplus w_1^j \oplus K1 = x_2^{i'} \oplus w_1^{j'} \oplus K_1' & \#\ u = u_2^i,\ v \in \{x_2^i \oplus w_1^j \oplus K1, \\ & \quad x_2^i \oplus w_1^j \oplus K1 \oplus \Delta\} \\ 4.\ x_2^i \oplus w_1^j \oplus K1 = x_2^{i'} \oplus w_1^{j'} \oplus K_1' \oplus \Delta & \#\ \text{(as above)} \end{array} \tag{4}$$

We now analyze separately the cases where query pair i is a forward pair or a backward pair.

– If this is a forward pair then u_1^i, u_2^i are set by the adversary (with difference Δ) and x_1^i, x_2^i are drawn at random from a set of size $> 2^n - 2q$. In this case each of the equalities 1–4 from Eq. (4) holds with probability at most $1/(2^n - 2q)$.
– If this is a backward pair then x_1^i is set by the adversary, u_1^i is drawn at random from a set of size $> 2^n - 2q$, u_2^i is set to $u_1^i \oplus \Delta$ and x_2^i is drawn at random from a set of size $> 2^n - 2q$. Clearly, equalities 3–4 still only hold with probability at most $1/(2^n - 2q)$ each, but we claim that the same is true also for equalities 1–2.
To see this, recall that at this point the keys K, K' are fixed, and so are all the queries up to (but not including) the i-th pair. Denote the set of pre-images under $E_{K'}(\cdot)$ that are known so far by $U(K') = \{u_1, u_2, \ldots, u_\ell\}$ (for some ℓ), and the corresponding images by $X(K') = \{x_i = E_{K'}(u_i) : u_i \in U(K')\}$.
To satisfy equality 1, the value u_1^i must be equal to some $u_k \in U(K')$. Moreover, once x_1^i is set by the adversary, there is at least one such value that would make equality 1 hold, namely the value u_k corresponding to $x_k = x_1^i \oplus w_1^j \oplus w_1^{j'} \oplus K1 \oplus K_1'$. Hence once the adversary sets x_1^i, the probability of equality 1 holding is at most $1/(2^n - 2q)$, i.e. the chance of hitting just the right value $u_1^i = u_k$. The exact same argument is true also for equality 2.

We conclude that the case where the i-th query pair completes any specific prior partial collision into a full collision only happens with probability at most $4/(2^n - 2q)$. Since key K has at most $\beta - 1$ prior partial collisions, it means that this case happens with probability at most $4(\beta - 1)/(2^n - 2q)$ which satisfies the bound in Lemma 3.

Case 2. In this case, it is a partial collision between the i-th pair itself and a prior query pair that gives us the full collision. Here we denote the i-th query by $(K = K^i, \cdot, (w_1^i, z_1^i), (w_2^i, z_2^i))$ (where $w_2^i = s_1^i \oplus \Delta$ and $\{z_1^i, z_2^i\}$ were obtained before for some other key).

We already bound the probability of any forward partial collision, here we only need to analyze the case where the i-th query pair is a backward pair. Namely the adversary sets z_1^i, then w_1^i is drawn from a set of size $> 2^n - 2q$, w_2^i is set as $w_2^i = w_1^i \oplus \Delta$ and z_2^i is drawn from a set of size $\geq 2^n - 2q$. We want to bound the probability of the event where:

- The $z_\star^i$'s collide with some prior query pair i', denoted $(K' = K^{i'}, \cdot, (w_1^{i'}, z_1^{i'}), (w_2^{i'}, z_2^{i'}))$. Namely $\{z_1^i, z_2^i\} = \{z_1^{i'}, z_2^{i'}\}$ as sets irrespective of order, which happens with probability at most $i/(2^n - 2q)$.
- In addition, there were two other query pairs involving K and K', denoted $(K = K^j, \cdot, (u_1^j, x_1^j), (u_2^j, x_2^j))$ and $(K' = K^{j'}, \cdot, (u_1^{j'}, x_1^{j'}), (u_2^{j'}, x_2^{j'}))$ (where j, j' can be the same as or different from i, i'), such that at least one of the following equalities hold:

$$
\begin{aligned}
&1.\ x_1^j \oplus w_1^i \oplus K1 = x_1^{j'} \oplus w_1^{i'} \oplus K_1' && \#\ u = u_1^j,\ v \in \{x_1^j \oplus w_1^j \oplus K1,\\
& && \qquad x_1^j \oplus w_1^i \oplus K1 \oplus \Delta\}\\
&2.\ x_1^j \oplus w_1^i \oplus K1 = x_1^{j'} \oplus w_1^{i'} \oplus K_1' \oplus \Delta\ \# && \text{(as above)}\\
&3.\ x_2^j \oplus w_1^i \oplus K1 = x_2^{j'} \oplus w_1^{i'} \oplus K_1' && \#\ u = u_2^j,\ v \in \{x_2^j \oplus w_1^i \oplus K1,\\
& && \qquad x_2^j \oplus w_1^i \oplus K1 \oplus \Delta\}\\
&4.\ x_2^j \oplus w_1^i \oplus K1 = x_2^{j'} \oplus w_1^{i'} \oplus K_1' \oplus \Delta\ \# && \text{(as above)}
\end{aligned}
$$

(These are exactly the same equalities as in Eq. (4), except with $i \leftrightarrow j$ and $i' \leftrightarrow j'$.)

The partial collision happens with probability at most $i/(2^n - 2q)$, and since w_1^i is drawn at random then each of the equalities above holds with probability at most $1/(2^n - 2q)$, so this case only happens with probability at most $4i/(2^n - 2q)^2$.

By the above, the probability of the i-th query inducing the first full collision (when $\mathsf{maxCol} < \beta$ and no forward partial collisions) is bounded by $4(\beta - 1)/(2^n - 2q) + 4i/(2^n - 2q)^2$. Therefore, Pr[any full collision with $\mathsf{maxCol}_\Pi < \beta$ and no forward partial collisions] $\leq 4(\beta - 1)q/(2^n - 2q) + \binom{q}{2}/(2^n - 2q)^2$, as needed by Lemma 3.

6 Performance

XAES introduces three additional AES256 calls to AES-GCM and KC-XAES introduces six. For comparison, DNDK [16], another efficient derived key mode, adds six AES256 calls without key commitment and ten with key commitment. DNDK version 2 [17,18], on the other hand, adds three and five, respectively. Note that DNDK v2 requires more frequent rekeys to keep the K_C collision probability conservatively low than every 2^{80} messages mandated by (KC-)XAES. Regardless, the impact of a few extra AES256 calls per invocation is minimal especially when XAES encrypts large plaintexts. To investigate this impact, we implemented XAES and KC-XAES and benchmarked them against AES-GCM in `x86_64` and `AArch64`-based platforms. Note that our implementation could be further sped up by taking advantage of vectorization and optimizing the AES256 calls (by parallelizing $\text{AES256}_K(0^{128})$ with $\text{AES256}_K(\text{const}_3 \parallel U)$ and $\text{AES256}_K(M_1)$ with $\text{AES256}_K(M_2)$, $\text{AES256}_K(W_1)$, and $\text{AES256}_K(W_2)$ from Fig. 2).

Table 1. AES-GCM, XAES, and KC-XAES cost in μs/operation with small and large plaintexts in x86_64 and AArch64-based platforms.

		Intel® Xeon® Platinum 8375C			AWS Graviton4 - Neoverse V2		
		AES-GCM	XAES	KC-XAES	AES-GCM	XAES	KC-XAES
Init		0.134	0.053	0.054	0.082	0.041	0.042
Encrypt	32B	0.087	0.244	0.296	0.089	0.209	0.251
	1KB	0.219	0.376	0.432	0.250	0.411	0.454
	16KB	1.448	1.620	1.686	2.644	2.767	2.810
	1MB	91.24	90.74	90.13	164.2	164.4	164.5
Decrypt	32B	0.094	0.242	0.298	0.096	0.217	0.258
	1KB	0.225	0.373	0.431	0.254	0.415	0.457
	16KB	1.457	1.618	1.671	2.587	2.711	2.752
	1MB	85.40	86.33	85.93	160.4	160.3	160.6

Table 1 shows the performance of each mode in microseconds spent per operation in x86_64-based Intel® Xeon® Platinum 8375C and AArch64-based AWS Graviton4 (Neoverse V2) processors, respectively. The Init operation for AES-GCM includes a) the key scheduling, b) one AES256 encryption of a counter (for the AES-GCM tag T) and c) a pre-computation of the GHASH constants which depend on the implementation; the more blocks processed in parallel (i.e. the more optimized the implementation), the more constants are pre-computed. In the case of (KC-)XAES, Init includes only the AES256 encryption to produce $K1$ used in key derivation (and commitment). Note that (KC-)XAES Encrypt and Decrypt include the AES256 calls to derive the key (two calls) and the commitment string (three calls). They also include a), b) and c) for the newly-derived K_U as (KC-)XAES initializes GCM with every invocation. We can see that for small plaintexts, XAES and KC-XAES encryption and decryption cost $\times 2 - \times 3$ than AES-GCM respectively because of the cost of deriving K_U and K_C and initializing GCM for K_U. As the plaintext size increases this cost is amortized over the cost of plaintext encryption and it ends up being unnoticeable for large 1MB plaintexts. The difference between AES-GCM and (KC-)XAES is almost constant because the overhead for the key derivation and commitment does not depend on the size of the plaintext.

Table 2 shows the percentage overhead for each mode in both the Intel® and AWS Graviton4 platforms. Init is ~60% slower for GCM since (KC-)XAES only includes the $K1$ derivation. Encrypt and Decrypt starts much slower for (KC-)XAES for small plaintexts and drops as the cost of the GCM initialization and K_U, K_C derivation for every invocation of (KC-)XAES becomes insignificant compared to the cost of encryption/decryption of the plaintext.

Table 2. (KC-)XAES impact comparison against AES-GCM with small and large plaintexts in `x86_64`-based and `AArch64`-based platforms.

		Intel® Xeon® Platinum 8375C		AWS Graviton4 - Neoverse V2	
		XAES vs GCM	KC-XAES vs GCM	XAES vs GCM	KC-XAES vs GCM
Init		−60.45%	−59.70%	−50.00%	−48.78%
Encrypt	32B	180.46%	240.23%	134.83%	182.02%
	1KB	71.69%	97.26%	64.40%	81.60%
	16KB	11.88%	16.44%	4.65%	6.28%
	1MB	−0.55%	−1.22%	0.12%	0.18%
Decrypt	32B	157.45%	217.02%	126.04%	168.75%
	1KB	65.78%	91.56%	63.39%	79.92%
	16KB	11.05%	14.69%	4.79%	6.38%
	1MB	1.09%	0.62%	−0.06%	0.12%

Table 3 compares the schemes for small plaintexts in an Intel® Xeon® Platinum 8375C. `Init` remains cheaper for (KC-)XAES. Encryption and decryption is still expensive for (KC-)XAES especially since the plaintexts are small. Note that the amortization of the (KC-)XAES overhead compared to AES-GCM is not linear because GCM's performance also increases as the plaintext grows in size.

Table 3. AES-GCM, XAES, and KC-XAES cost with small plaintexts in Intel® Xeon® Platinum 8375C.

		AES-GCM	XAES		KC-XAES	
		μs/op	μs/op	vs GCM	μs/op	vs GCM
Init		0.134	0.054	−60.29%	0.055	−59.56%
Encrypt	32B	0.087	0.247	183.91%	0.303	248.28%
	128B	0.096	0.258	168.75%	0.313	226.04%
	256B	0.123	0.285	131.71%	0.341	177.24%
	512B	0.176	0.333	89.20%	0.388	120.45%
	1KB	0.220	0.377	71.36%	0.429	95.00%
Decrypt	32B	0.092	0.250	171.74%	0.303	229.35%
	128B	0.096	0.252	162.50%	0.306	218.75%
	256B	0.116	0.269	131.90%	0.326	181.03%
	512B	0.180	0.334	85.56%	0.388	115.56%
	1KB	0.224	0.379	69.20%	0.433	93.30%

To confirm that blockcipher-based key derivation is more performant that HMAC-based key derivation, we also compared (KC-)XAES against HMAC-based derived key modes. AES256 is generally one order of magnitude faster than HMAC in common

Table 4. AES-GCM, HMAC-based Derived Key AES-GCM (H-AES-GCM), and HMAC-based Derived Key and Key Committing AES-GCM (H-KC-AES-GCM) cost with small and large plaintexts on **x86_64** and **AArch64** processors. H-(KC-)XAES is shown much more expensive than CMAC-based (KC-)XAES in Table 2.

		AES-GCM	H-AES-GCM		H-KC-AES-GCM	
		μs/op	μs/op	vs GCM	μs/op	vs GCM
		Intel® Xeon® Platinum 8375C				
Init		0.136	0.142	4%	0.142	4%
Encrypt	32B	0.086	0.357	314%	0.501	481%
	1KB	0.219	0.487	122%	0.637	191%
	16KB	1.462	1.718	17%	1.882	29%
	1MB	87.23	86.64	−1%	88.11	1%
Decrypt	32B	0.093	0.361	289%	0.506	445%
	1KB	0.225	0.493	119%	0.640	184%
	16KB	1.458	1.726	18%	1.879	29%
	1MB	85.33	85.22	0%	85.10	1%
		AWS Graviton4 - Neoverse V2				
Init		0.083	0.091	10%	0.091	10%
Encrypt	32B	0.089	0.285	220%	0.395	344%
	1KB	0.250	0.485	94%	0.594	138%
	16KB	2.643	2.841	7%	2.951	12%
	1MB	164.6	164.3	0%	164.8	0%
Decrypt	32B	0.096	0.290	202%	0.399	316%
	1KB	0.254	0.487	92%	0.595	134%
	16KB	2.587	2.784	8%	2.892	12%
	1MB	160.8	160.4	0%	160.6	0%

implementations. An HMAC derived key mode is described in [7] with a goal to prevent frequent re-keying in high-scale cloud environments. HMAC-based key derivation and key commitment implementations in our experiments included the exact same operations in all `Init`, `Encrypt` and `Decrypt` operations of (KC-)XAES with the only difference being the PRF function. Table 4 shows the experimental results. We can see that when HMAC-SHA256 is used as the PRF instead of CMAC-AES256 for (KC-)XAES key derivation and key commitment, both the `Init` and `Encrypt`/`Decrypt` operations for messages up to 16KB introduce more overhead to GCM than the overhead of (KC-)XAES (Table 2). When the plaintext increases to 1MB, the cost of AES-GCM encryption and decryption diminishes the performance benefit of cheaper key derivation and commitment. Using other HMAC-based PRF functions like HKDF instead of HMAC would be of similar or worse performance.

7 Conclusion

In conclusion, we revisited Valsorda's XAES [14] and described how to add key commitment to it, resulting in a scheme that we call KC-XAES. We showed that in the ideal-cipher model, KC-XAES provides n-bit security against the FOR-KC key commitment attacks of Farshim et al. [12]. We established usage- and data-bounds for (KC-)XAES, and argued that these modes are FIPS-compliant. We confirmed XAES is very performant, especially for larger plaintexts where the additional key derivation and/or key commitment are amortized over the encryption of the whole message. Finally, we briefly discussed applications where KC-XAES would be suitable.

Acknowledgements. The authors would like to thank Fabrice Benhamouda and Hugo Krawczyk from AWS for their valuable input and help.

A KC-XAES Specification Breakdown

Specification 1 below breaks down the code in Fig. 2 to its AES256 calls to eliminate three unnecessary subkey $K1$ and one subciphertext X_1 calculations in the CMAC-AES256 calls.

Specification 1 KC-XAES with a 24-byte random nonce and a 256-bit key

Input: $K[0:32]$, $N[0:24]$, P, AAD
Output: C, T, $K_C[0:32]$
$T1 = \text{AES256}_K(0\text{x}(00)^{16})$.
if $MSB_1(T1) = 0$ **then**
  $K1[0:16] = T1 \ll 1$
else
  $K1[0:16] = (T1 \ll 1) \oplus 0\text{x}(00)^{15}87$ ▷ $X \times AES_K(0^{128})$
end if
$M_1[0:16] \leftarrow (0\text{x}00015800 \parallel N[0:12]) \oplus K1[0:16]$
$K_U[0:16] \leftarrow \text{AES256}_K(M_1[0:16])$ ▷ $\text{CMAC-AES256}_K(0\text{x}00015800 \parallel U[:12])$
$M_2[0:16] \leftarrow (0\text{x}00025800 \parallel N[0:12]) \oplus K1[0:16]$
$K_U[16:32] \leftarrow \text{AES256}_K(M_2[0:16])$ ▷ $\text{CMAC-AES256}_K(0\text{x}00025800 \parallel U[:12])$
$V[0:12] \leftarrow N[12:24]$
$(C, T) \leftarrow \text{AES-256-GCM}(K_U[0:32], AAD, IV = V, P)$
$X_1[0:16] \leftarrow \text{AES256}_K(0\text{x}58434\text{D}54 \parallel N[0:12])$
$W_1[0:16] \leftarrow X_1[0:16] \oplus (N[12:24] \parallel 0\text{x}00010001) \oplus K1[0:16]$
$K_C[0:16] \leftarrow \text{AES256}_K(W_1)$ ▷ $\text{CMAC-AES256}_K(\text{"XCMT"} \parallel U \parallel V \parallel 0\text{x}00010001)$
$W_2[0:16] \leftarrow X_1[0:16] \oplus (N[12:24] \parallel 0\text{x}00010002) \oplus K1[0:16]$
$K_C[16:32] \leftarrow \text{AES256}_K(W_2)$ ▷
$\text{CMAC-AES256}_K(\text{"XCMT"} \parallel U \parallel V \parallel 0\text{x}00010002)$
$K_C \leftarrow K_C[0:16] \parallel K_C[16:32]$

As shown in Sect. 4.3, an implementation of Specification 1 could be FIPS certified. To do that, someone would need to certify the underlying AES-GCM implementation, the nonce N generation method, and the K_U derivation (which can be certified as a KBKDF [9]). For a KBKDF FIPS validation of the K_U derivation, the ACVP "KDF"//"1.0" module test [8] will include

```
"kdfMode":"counter",
"macMode":"CMAC-AES256",
"counterLocation":"before fixed data",
"counterLength":16,
```

For the K_C derivation, the ACVP "KDF"//"1.0" module test will include

```
"kdfMode":"counter",
"macMode":"CMAC-AES256",
"counterLocation":"after fixed data",
"counterLength":8,
```

The module registration for both the K_U and K_C derivation will include

```
"supportedLengths":[ {"min":256, "max":256, "increment":1 } ]
```

The fixed data field in the ACVP test vector response will be

"fixedData":"0x5800$\langle U \rangle$"

and

"fixedData":"0x58434D54$\langle U \rangle \langle V \rangle$000100"

for the K_U and K_C derivation respectively.

B An Extension that Supports Shorter Nonces

Some constrained use-cases may not be able to use 24-byte nonce N or generate 24-byte entropy fast enough. Such scenarios could benefit from slightly smaller b-byte nonces. Figure 3 breaks down KC-XAES by using a b-byte nonce $N[: b]$ instead of constant 24-bytes, where $20 \leq b \leq 24$. To avoid trivial K_C collisions between nonces of different lengths under the same main key K, we redefine the two constants from Fig. 2, depending on the length b of the nonce, as $\text{const}_4 = \langle 24 - b \rangle \parallel \text{0x010001}$ and $\text{const}_5 = \langle 24 - b \rangle \parallel \text{0x010002}$. XAES as specified in Fig. 2 follows exactly Fig. 3 for $b = 24$.

Note that when $b < 24$, $N[b - 12 : 12]$ is used as-is in the AES-GCM IV, but it passes through a pseudorandom permutation for deriving K_U. The collision-resistance analysis from Sect. 5 applies to this setting too; using $b < 24$ does not affect the key-collision security of KC-XAES. It is worth mentioning that even in the theoretical scenario where $b = 12$, XAES is not less secure than plain AES-GCM. Additionally, K_C's derivation function remains a FIPS approved KBKDF [9, §4.1] as explained in Sect. 4.3 with the fixed input data becoming "XCMT"$\parallel U \parallel V \parallel \langle 24 - b \rangle \parallel$ 0x0100.

Also, it is easy to adjust the data limit analysis from Sect. 4.2 to this case. For example, for $b = 20$ we need to bound the number of messages encrypted under one main key to at most 2^{64} to ensure a nonce collision probability of 2^{-33}. Setting the K_U re-occurrence bound $m = 4$, we get $\Pr[\text{4-collisions}] \leq \binom{2^{64}}{4} \cdot 2^{-96 \cdot 3} \approx 2^{64 \cdot 4 - 96 \cdot 3}/4! \approx 2^{-36.6} < 2^{-32}$. We can therefore assume that there will be no four-way K_U collisions for the life of the main key K, which means that every data key K_U will be used to encrypt at most three messages. The data bound per message will then be $\min(X/3, 2^{36})$, where X is the use-case specific X-bytes-per-GCM-key limit as defined in Sect. 4.2.

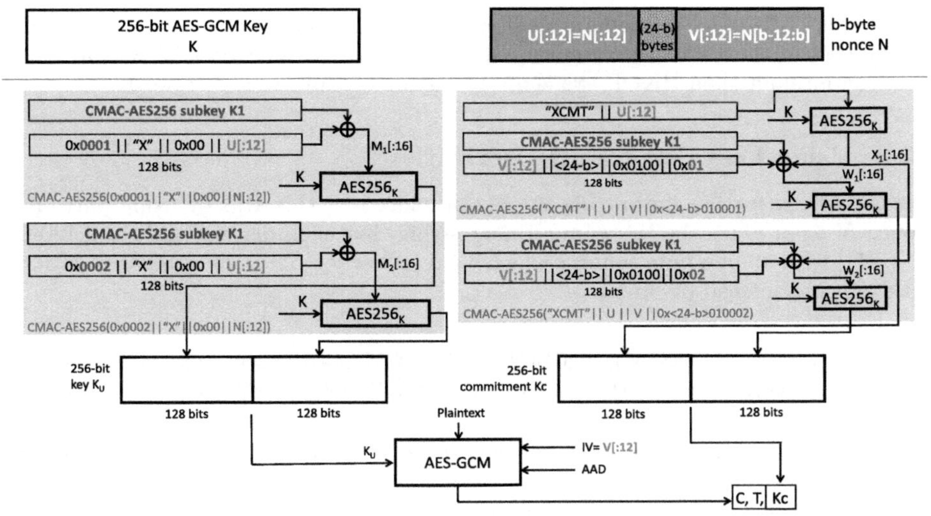

Fig. 3. KC-XAES with a b-byte random nonce N and a 256-bit key, where $20 \leq b \leq 24$

C Other Key Commitment Options

Additionally to the commitment scheme proposed in this work, we considered other constructions, some of which had already been proposed in the literature.

C.1 Padding Fix

Since XAES uses AES-GCM for encryption, then perhaps the simplest way to add key-commitment to it is using the GCM-specific padding-fix mechanism from [1]. Namely, instead of computing just $\text{AES-GCM}_{K_U}(V; P)$, prepend ℓ zero bits to the plaintext and compute $\text{AES-GCM}_{K_U}(V; 0^\ell | P)$. Albertini et al. proved in [1, Thm 1] that this yields $\ell/2$ bits of security, in the sense of FOR-KC. In particular, to get 128-bit security we need to prepend two 128-bit blocks to the plaintext before encrypting it. Decryption needs to verify that the plaintext begins with ℓ zeros, then remove those zeros and return the rest of the plaintext.

In terms of performance, this proposal adds two blocks to the ciphertext, and uses only two additional AES block encryption and two GF 128-bit block multiplication operations. The practical disadvantages of padding key commitment is its lack of modularity and the requirement for the application layer to be aware of the encryption layer which violates common programming abstractions. It also needs for decryption to take place before the commitment string can be verified to confirm that the ciphertext was produced with the expected key.

C.2 HKDF

The AWS ESDK and KMS have introduced key commitment by using HKDF with a random 256-bit `salt` and an `info` string to generate a 32-byte commitment string.

$$K_C = HKDF_K(\textsf{salt}, \textsf{"COMMITKEY"}, 32)$$

This is PRF-based key commitment as described in [15]. It achieves CMT-2 security at the cost of the PRF performance. Given that CMAC-AES-based PRFs are much more performant than HKDF, we chose to pursue the former in this work.

C.3 Using Less Bits for K_C Derivation

We considered further optimizing the performance of KC-XAES by using part of the nonce N to produce the key commitment string. For example, we could use 120-bits ($N[:15]$) with an one-byte counter which would allow for K_C to be generated with two AES256 calls instead of three.

$$\begin{aligned} K_C &= \text{CMAC-AES256}_K(0\text{x}01\|N[:15]) \ \| \ \text{CMAC-AES256}_K(0\text{x}02\|N[:15]) \\ &= \text{AES256}_K((0\text{x}01\|N[:15]) \oplus K1) \ \| \ \text{AES256}_K((0\text{x}02\|N[:15]) \oplus K1). \end{aligned}$$

Of course, that would mean we can encrypt up to 2^{48} messages before a K_C collision with 2^{-32} probability.

[17,18] follow this approach. Gueron et al. consider the collision probability and conclude that by limiting DNDK v2 to 2^{50} queries, the collision probability remains below 2^{-21} which is satisfactory as a K_C collision reveals information about the re-use of the main key and part of the nonce, but it does not reveal information about the plaintext. Although KC-XAES could have used part of the nonce for deriving the key commitment string to save an AES256 call, we decided against it because because we considered the performance advantage marginal versus the K_C collision disadvantage.

References

1. Albertini, A., Duong, T., Gueron, S., Kölbl, S., Luykx, A., Schmieg, S.: How to abuse and fix authenticated encryption without key commitment. In: Butler, K.R.B., Thomas, K. (eds.) 31st USENIX Security Symposium, USENIX Security 2022, Boston, MA, USA, 10-12August 2022, pp. 3291–3308. USENIX Association (2022)
2. Arciszewski, S.: AES with Galois Extended Mode (AES-GEM). NIST Workshop on the Requirements for an Accordion Cipher Mode (2024). https://csrc.nist.gov/csrc/media/Events/2024/accordion-cipher-mode-workshop-2024/documents/papers/galois-extended-mode.pdf
3. Bellare, M., Hoang, V.T.: Efficient schemes for committing authenticated encryption. In: Dunkelman, O., Dziembowski, S. (eds.) Advances in Cryptology - EUROCRYPT 2022. pp, pp. 845–875. Springer International Publishing, Cham (2022). https://doi.org/10.1007/978-3-031-07085-3_29
4. Bellare, M., Namprempre, C.: Authenticated encryption: relations among notions and analysis of the generic composition paradigm. In: Okamoto, T. (ed.) ASIACRYPT 2000. LNCS, vol. 1976, pp. 531–545. Springer, Heidelberg (2000). https://doi.org/10.1007/3-540-44448-3_41
5. Benhamouda, F., Halevi, S., Kampanakis, P., Krawczyk, H.: BlockCipher-based key derivation without PRP/PRF switching. Cryptology ePrint Archive, Paper 2025/878 (2025)
6. Bhaumik, R., Degabriele, J.P.: Pencil: a domain-extended PRF with full n-bit security for strengthening GCM and more. Cryptology ePrint Archive, Paper 2025/383 (2025)

7. Campagna, M., Gueron, S.: Key management systems at the cloud scale. Cryptography **3**(3) (2019)
8. Celi, C.: ACVP SP800-108 Key derivation function JSON specification. nist.gov (2024). https://pages.nist.gov/ACVP/draft-celi-acvp-kbkdf.html
9. Chen, L.: Recommendation for key derivation using pseudorandom functions. NIST Special Publication 800-108 Rev1 Upd1 (2024). https://doi.org/10.6028/NIST.SP.800-108r1-upd1
10. Common Criteria Recognition Arrangement (CCRA) Members. Common Criteria for Information Technology Security Evaluation. commoncriteriaportal.org (2024). https://www.commoncriteriaportal.org/index.cfm
11. Dworkin, M.: Recommendation for block cipher modes of operation: Galois/counter mode (GCM) and GMAC. Technical Report NIST Special Publication (SP) 800-38D (Final), November 28, 2007, U.S. Department of Commerce, Washington, D.C. (2007)
12. Farshim, P., Orlandi, C., Rosie, R.: Security of symmetric primitives under incorrect usage of keys. IACR Trans. Symmetric Cryptol. **2017**(1), 449–473 (2017)
13. Valsorda, F.: XAES-256-GCM. Personal Blog (2024). https://words.filippo.io/dispatches/xaes-256-gcm/
14. Valsorda, F.: XAES-256-GCM specification. GitHub (2024). https://github.com/C2SP/C2SP/blob/main/XAES-256-GCM.md
15. Gueron, S.: Key committing AEADs. Cryptology ePrint Archive, Paper 2020/1153 (2020). https://eprint.iacr.org/2020/1153
16. Gueron, S.: Double Nonce Derive Key AES-GCM (DNDK-GCM). Internet-Draft draft-gueron-cfrg-dndkgcm-01, Internet Engineering Task Force (2024). Work in Progress
17. Gueron, S.: Double Nonce Derive Key AES-GCM (DNDK-GCM). Internet-Draft draft-gueron-cfrg-dndkgcm-02, Internet Engineering Task Force (2025). Work in Progress
18. Gueron, S., Ristenpart, T.: DNDK: combining nonce and key derivation for fast and scalable AEAD. Cryptology ePrint Archive, Paper 2025/785 (2025)
19. Hoang, V.T., Tessaro, S., Thiruvengadam, A.: The multi-user security of GCM, revisited: tight bounds for nonce randomization. In: Proceedings of the 2018 ACM SIGSAC Conference on Computer and Communications Security, CCS 2018, pp. 1429–1440, New York, NY, USA (2018). Association for Computing Machinery
20. Iwata, T., Ohashi, K., Minematsu, K.: Breaking and repairing GCM security proofs. Cryptology ePrint Archive, Paper 2012/438 (2012)
21. Kampanakis, P., Crocket, E., Campagna, M., Petcher, A., Gueron, S.: Practical Challenges with AES-GCM and the need for a new cipher. NIST 3rd Workshop on Block Cipher Modes of Operation (2023). https://csrc.nist.gov/csrc/media/Events/2023/third-workshop-on-block-cipher-modes-of-operation/documents/accepted-papers/Practical%20Challenges%20with%20AES-GCM.pdf
22. Len, J., Grubbs, P., Ristenpart, T.: Partitioning oracle attacks. In: Bailey, M.D., Greenstadt, R. (eds.) 30th USENIX Security Symposium, USENIX Security 2021, 11-13 August 2021, pp. 195–212. USENIX Association (2021)
23. Luykx, A., Paterson, K.G.: Limits on authenticated encryption use in TLS. Cryptology ePrint Archive, Paper 2024/051 (2024)
24. Menda, S., Len, J., Grubbs, P., Ristenpart, T.: Context discovery and commitment attacks. In: Hazay, C., Stam, M. (eds.) Advances in Cryptology - EUROCRYPT 2023. pp, pp. 379–407. Springer Nature Switzerland, Cham (2023). https://doi.org/10.1007/978-3-031-30634-1_13

25. National Institute of Standards and Technology. Security Requirements for Cryptographic Modules. csrc.nist.gov (2019). https://csrc.nist.gov/pubs/fips/140-3/final
26. NIST: NIST Workshop on the requirements for an accordion cipher mode 2024. Workshop Report. NIST NIST Interagency Report (2024). https://nvlpubs.nist.gov/nistpubs/ir/2024/NIST.IR.8537.pdf
27. NIST: Pre-draft call for comments: GCM and GMAC block cipher modes of operation. NIST SP 800-38D Rev. 1 (Initial Preliminary Draft) (2024). https://csrc.nist.gov/pubs/sp/800/38/d/r1/iprd
28. NIST: PRE-DRAFT Call for Comments: NIST proposes to standardize a wider variant of AES. NIST SP 800-197 (Initial Preliminary Draft) (2024). https://csrc.nist.gov/pubs/sp/800/197/iprd
29. Takeuchi, R., Todo, Y., Iwata, T.: Key recovery, universal forgery, and committing attacks against revised Rocca: how finalization affects security. IACR Trans. Symmetric Cryptol. **2024**(2), 85–117 (2024)
30. Tribble, A.: Improved client-side encryption: explicit KeyIds and key commitment. AWS Security Blog (2020). https://aws.amazon.com/blogs/security/improved-client-side-encryption-explicit-keyids-and-key-commitment

The Revisited Hidden Weight Bit Function

Pierrick Méaux[1], Tim Seuré[1(✉)], and Deng Tang[2]

[1] University of Luxembourg, Esch-sur-Alzette, Luxembourg
{pierrick.meaux,tim.seure}@uni.lu
[2] Shanghai Jiao Tong University, Shanghai, China
dengtang@sjtu.edu.cn

Abstract. The Hidden Weight Bit Function (HWBF) has drawn considerable attention for its simplicity and cryptographic potential. Despite its ease of implementation and favorable algebraic properties, its low nonlinearity limits its direct application in modern cryptographic designs. In this work, we revisit the HWBF and propose a new weightwise quadratic variant obtained by combining the HWBF with a bent function. This construction offers improved cryptographic properties while remaining computationally efficient. We analyze the balancedness, nonlinearity, and other criteria of this function, presenting theoretical bounds and experimental results to highlight its advantages over existing functions in similar use cases. The different techniques we introduce to study the nonlinearity of this function also enable us to bound the nonlinearity of a broad family of weightwise quadratic functions, both theoretically and practically. We believe these methods are of independent interest.

Keywords: Boolean functions · HWBF · Nonlinearity

1 Introduction

The Hidden Weight Bit Function (HWBF) has attracted significant attention since its introduction by Bryant in 1991 [7]. It has been regarded as the simplest example of a function whose binary decision diagram has exponential size [5,7]. The ease of implementing this function across various computational models—owing to its reliance on computing the Hamming weight of the input and applying a simple linear function—combined with its relatively strong cryptographic properties as demonstrated in [46] (*e.g.*, balancedness, nonlinearity, degree, and algebraic immunity), has made it a noteworthy candidate for use as a filter function in stream cipher constructions.

Recent developments in stream ciphers have reignited interest in this function. The emergence of new applications for stream ciphers with filter functions on a larger number of variables—such as Hybrid Homomorphic Encryption (HHE) [40]—has further emphasized the relevance of such functions. HHE requires Boolean functions that can be efficiently evaluated in an input-oblivious algorithm. For instance, several new binary stream ciphers have been proposed since 2016, including Kreyvium [9], FLIP [37], Rasta [25], FiLIP [36],

C. Boura et al. (Eds.): SAC 2025, LNCS 16207, pp. 235–263, 2026.
https://doi.org/10.1007/978-3-032-10536-3_9

Dasta [4] and Fasta [19]. Currently, designs employing Boolean functions with more than one hundred variables as filters lead to HHE schemes with the best latency [1,20,28,39].

The HWBF, while efficient to compute, suffers from low nonlinearity, which limits its direct application as a filter function. Consequently, various generalizations have been explored to enhance this parameter while preserving or improving other cryptographically relevant properties, such as balancedness, algebraic degree, and algebraic immunity. Notable examples include functions introduced in [13,16] and [38]. The latter work considers functions obtained by computing the Hamming weight of the input and applying a quadratic Boolean function, so-called weightwise quadratic functions.

In this article, we propose a new generalization of the HWBF, a weightwise quadratic function constructed by XOR-ing the HWBF with a bent quadratic function. This leads to a family of Boolean functions that are computationally efficient and feature superior cryptographic properties compared to previous constructions. Additionally, the techniques we introduce to analyze nonlinearity have broader applicability and provide bounds on the maximum absolute Walsh spectrum for a wider class of weightwise quadratic functions. Our contributions are as follows:

- *Balancedness analysis* (Sect. 3): We define the revisited HWBF in n variables, hereafter denoted by f, and analyze its balancedness. This involves studying the (restricted) Walsh transform of specific quadratic functions over sets of fixed Hamming weights (called slices). By establishing recursive relations for these values, we determine for which values of n the function is balanced.
- *Nonlinearity bounds* (Sect. 4): We relate the maximum Walsh coefficients of the revisited HWBF to the coefficients of generating functions and employ complex analysis techniques to prove lower bounds on the nonlinearity of f. Unlike most studies on Boolean functions used in cryptography, this approach yields strong nonlinearity bounds for a broader class of functions in an even number of variables.
- *Experimental results and comparisons* (Sect. 5): For bounded values of n, we employ specific techniques to refine the nonlinearity bounds of f, providing tighter estimates up to $n = 80$. Through experiments, we compare these bounds with actual nonlinearity values for f and other weightwise quadratic functions, such as the majority function, the HWBF, and the two main examples in [38]. Our results highlight the revisited HWBF's superior nonlinearity relative to functions with similar computational costs.
- *Analysis of other cryptographic parameters* (Sect. 6): We evaluate other cryptographically relevant parameters of f, including degree, algebraic immunity, and fast algebraic immunity. Similar to the nonlinearity analysis, the revisited HWBF outperforms or matches other functions with comparable computational costs.

2 Preliminaries

Throughout this paper, $n \geqslant 0$ will always denote a non-negative integer. Further, our intervals will only contain integers, so that for instance $[0, n] = \{0, 1, \dots, n\}$. The set of binary vectors of length n will be denoted by $\mathbb{F}_2^n$, with the zero vector written as 0_n. The canonical basis of $\mathbb{F}_2^n$ will be written as $\{e_1, \dots, e_n\}$; therefore, $e_i \in \mathbb{F}_2^n$ is the vector which is zero everywhere except at position i. The entries of a binary vector $x \in \mathbb{F}_2^n$ will always be denoted by $x_1, \dots, x_n$. Given a permutation $\pi : [1, n] \to [1, n]$ and a vector $x \in \mathbb{F}_2^n$, we define $\pi(x) = (x_{\pi(i)})_{i \in [1,n]} \in \mathbb{F}_2^n$. We write the scalar product of two binary vectors $x, y \in \mathbb{F}_2^n$ as $x \cdot y = \sum_{i=1}^n x_i y_i \in \mathbb{F}_2$. The Hamming weight of a binary vector $x \in \mathbb{F}_2^n$ is denoted by $\mathsf{w_H}(x) = |\{i \in [1, n] : x_i = 1\}|$.

2.1 Boolean Functions and Cryptographic Parameters

In this part, we recall general concepts on Boolean functions and their cryptographic properties we use in this article. For a deeper introduction on Boolean functions and their cryptographic parameters, we refer to the book [12], and to [15] for properties on slices, so-called weightwise properties.

Definition 1 (Slice). *For any integer k, we introduce the set $\mathsf{E}_{k,n} = \{x \in \mathbb{F}_2^n : \mathsf{w_H}(x) = k\}$, and call it the k-th slice of the Boolean hypercube (of dimension n); note that if $k \notin [0, n]$, then $\mathsf{E}_{k,n} = \varnothing$.*

Definition 2 (Boolean function). *A Boolean function in n variables is a function from $\mathbb{F}_2^n$ to $\mathbb{F}_2$. The set of all Boolean functions in n variables is denoted by $\mathcal{B}_n$, and we denote this set without the null function by $\mathcal{B}_n^*$.*

Below, for a Boolean function $f \in \mathcal{B}_n$, we write $f+1$ for the Boolean function $g \in \mathcal{B}_n$ which satisfies $g(x) = f(x) + 1$ for every $x \in \mathbb{F}_2^n$.

Definition 3 (Algebraic normal form, degree). *We call algebraic normal form of a Boolean function $f \in \mathcal{B}_n$ its unique representation as an element of the ring $\mathbb{F}_2[x_1, \dots, x_n]/(x_1^2 + x_1, \dots, x_n^2 + x_n)$, and we express it as $f(x_1, \dots, x_n) = \sum_{I \subseteq [1,n]} a_I \left(\prod_{i \in I} x_i\right)$, where $a_I \in \mathbb{F}_2$. The (algebraic) degree of f is defined by $\mathsf{deg}(f) = 0$ in case f is the null function, and $\mathsf{deg}(f) = \max\{|I| : I \subseteq [1, n], a_I = 1\}$ otherwise.*

Definition 4 (Walsh transform). *The Walsh transform at $a \in \mathbb{F}_2^n$ of $f \in \mathcal{B}_n$ restricted to a subset $S \subseteq \mathbb{F}_2^n$ is defined as $\mathcal{W}_{f,S}(a) = \sum_{x \in S} (-1)^{f(x)+a \cdot x}$. The (unrestricted) Walsh transform of f is then defined as $\mathcal{W}_f = \mathcal{W}_{f,\mathbb{F}_2^n}$. For any integer k, we also set $\mathcal{W}_{f,k} = \mathcal{W}_{f,\mathsf{E}_{k,n}}$.*

Definition 5 (Balancedness). *A Boolean function $f \in \mathcal{B}_n$ is called balanced if $|\{x \in \mathbb{F}_2^n : f(x) = 0\}| = 2^{n-1} = |\{x \in \mathbb{F}_2^n : f(x) = 1\}|$. Equivalently, f is balanced if and only if $\mathcal{W}_f(0_n) = 0$.*

Definition 6 (Nonlinearity, *e.g.*, page 79 in [12]). *The nonlinearity* $\mathsf{NL}(f)$ *of a Boolean function* $f \in \mathcal{B}_n$ *is the minimum Hamming distance between* f *and all the affine functions in* $\mathcal{B}_n$*, that is,* $\mathsf{NL}(f) = \min\{\mathsf{d_H}(f, g) : g \in \mathcal{B}_n, \mathsf{deg}(g) \leqslant 1\}$*, where the Hamming distance between* f *and* g *is defined as* $\mathsf{d_H}(f, g) = |\{x \in \mathbb{F}_2^n : f(x) \neq g(x)\}|$*. Alternatively, the nonlinearity of* $f \in \mathcal{B}_n$ *can also be defined in terms of its Walsh transform:* $\mathsf{NL}(f) = 2^{n-1} - \frac{1}{2}\max_{a\in\mathbb{F}_2^n} |\mathcal{W}_f(a)|$.

When n is even, the nonlinearity of a Boolean function in n variables can reach at most $2^{n-1} - 2^{n/2-1}$. Functions reaching this maximum are called bent functions. Due to their broad applications and importance, they have been the focus of multiple works, *e.g.*, [8,24,33,42,45]. The quadratic function $d_n \in \mathcal{B}_n$ given by $d_n(x) = \sum_{i=1}^{n/2} x_{2i-1}x_{2i}$ is an example for such a bent function.

The algebraic degree of multiples of a Boolean function is a crucial quantity for various attacks on stream ciphers that utilize a Boolean function as a filter. The well-known algebraic attack [22] and fast algebraic attack [21] on filtered LFSRs have motivated the study of cryptographic properties such as algebraic immunity and fast algebraic immunity, *e.g.*, [2,27,29]. Nowadays, these parameters are systematically determined for any function considered as a filter.

Definition 7 (Annihilator, algebraic immunity [32]). *Let* $f \in \mathcal{B}_n$ *be a Boolean function. Then a function* $g \in \mathcal{B}_n^*$ *is called an annihilator of* f *if it satisfies* $fg = 0$*. The algebraic immunity of* f *is then defined as* $\mathsf{AI}(f) = \min\{\mathsf{deg}(g) : g \in \mathcal{B}_n^* \text{ is an annihilator of } f \text{ or } f+1\}$.

Definition 8 (Fast algebraic immunity, *e.g.*, [3,17,30]). *The fast algebraic immunity of* $f \in \mathcal{B}_n$ *is defined as* $\mathsf{FAI}(f) = \min\{2\mathsf{AI}(f), \min\{\mathsf{deg}(g) + \mathsf{deg}(fg) : g \in \mathcal{B}_n, 1 \leqslant \mathsf{deg}(g) < \mathsf{AI}(f)\}\}$.

2.2 Symmetric Functions, HWBF and Weightwise Degree-*d* Functions

Recall that the Boolean symmetric functions in n variables are those that are constant on the slice $\mathsf{E}_{k,n}$ for every $k \in [0, n]$. This class of functions has been thoroughly studied in the context of cryptography, see *e.g.*, [6,10,11,14,18,34, 35,41,44]. In this article, the symmetric functions that we consider will mainly be the slice indicator function and the majority function.

Definition 9 (Slice Indicator Functions). *The indicator function of the slice of weight* $k \in [0, n]$ *is the function* $\varphi_{k,n} \in \mathcal{B}_n$ *defined by* $\varphi_{k,n}(x) = 1$ *if and only if* $\mathsf{w_H}(x) = k$.

Definition 10 (Majority function). *The majority function in* n *variables is the Boolean function* $\mathsf{Maj}_n \in \mathcal{B}_n$ *defined by* $\mathsf{Maj}_n(x) = 1$ *if and only if* $\mathsf{w_H}(x) \geqslant n/2$.

Bigger families of functions can be obtained by considering functions of bounded degree on each slice. This corresponds to the concept of weightwise degree-d functions introduced in [26] for $d = 1$ and [38] for the general case.

Definition 11 (Weightwise degree-d functions, Definition 12 in [38]). *A Boolean function $f \in \mathcal{B}_n^*$ is called weightwise degree-d if it can be written under the form $f = \sum_{k=0}^{n} f_k \varphi_{k,n}$ with $f_k \in \mathcal{B}_n$ of degree at most d. The set of weightwise degree-d functions is denoted by $\mathcal{WD}_n^d$. Additionally, a weightwise degree-d function $f = \sum_{k=0}^{n} f_k \varphi_{k,n}$ is called a cyclic weightwise degree-d function if for all $k \in [0, n]$ and all $x \in \mathbb{F}_2^n$, it holds that $f_k(x) = f_0(O^k(x))$, where $O^k : \mathbb{F}_2^n \rightarrow \mathbb{F}_2^n$ is the cyclic shift by k positions, defined by $O^k(x_1, \ldots, x_n) = (x_{(1+k) \bmod n}, \ldots, x_{(n+k) \bmod n})$, the representatives modulo n being taken as integers in $[1, n]$.*

Various weightwise affine functions (*i.e.*, belonging to $\mathcal{WD}_n^1$) have been exhibited, such as in [15] where the bent functions in Propositions 1 and 2 are weightwise affine, or in [26] to show that no weightwise perfectly balanced function is weightwise affine for $n \geqslant 8$. The arguably best known example of weightwise affine function is the Hidden Weight Bit Function introduced in [7], the one obtained by fixing $f_0 = 0$ and $f_k = x_k$ for $k \in [1, n]$. The cryptographic properties of this function have been studied in [46], showing good algebraic properties for this function.

Definition 12 (Hidden Weight Bit Function). *We call Hidden Weight Bit Function (HWBF) the Boolean function $h \in \mathcal{B}_n$ defined as:*

$$h(x) = \sum_{k=1}^{n} x_k \varphi_{k,n}(x).$$

In [38], the parameters of different functions from $\mathcal{WD}_n^1$ and $\mathcal{WD}_n^2$ are studied experimentally for $n \leqslant 20$, and lower bounds are given for the nonlinearity for all n. These bounds focus on cyclic weightwise quadratic functions and involve sums of binomial coefficients. For simplicity, in the following, we provide only the nonlinearity values of the majority function and HWBF, as these bounds will be used for comparison.

Property 1.

- (*E.g.*, Theorem 3 and Theorem 2 in [23]) The majority function $\mathsf{Maj}_n \in \mathcal{B}_n$ satisfies $\mathsf{NL}(\mathsf{Maj}_n) = 2^{n-1} - \binom{n-1}{\frac{n}{2}}$ and $\mathsf{deg}(\mathsf{Maj}_n) = 2^{\lfloor \log_2(n) \rfloor}$ for even $n \geqslant 2$.
- (Theorem 3 and Theorem 1 in [46]) The HWBF $h \in \mathcal{B}_n$ satisfies $\mathsf{NL}(h) = 2^{n-1} - 2\binom{n-2}{\frac{n-2}{2}}$ for even $n \geqslant 2$ and $\mathsf{deg}(h) = n - 1$ for even $n \geqslant 4$.

2.3 Krawtchouk Polynomials

We use Krawtchouk polynomials and some of their properties to prove one of our main results. We give the necessary definition here and refer to [31] for more details, for instance.

Definition 13 (Krawtchouk polynomials). *The n-th Krawtchouk polynomial of degree $k \in \mathbb{Z}$ is given by $\mathsf{K}_k(x, n) = \sum_{j=0}^{k}(-1)^j \binom{x}{j}\binom{n-x}{k-j}$. Alternatively, the Krawtchouk polynomials can be characterized as the coefficients in the generating function for $(1+z)^{n-x}(1-z)^x$ in the variable z, that is, $(1+z)^{n-x}(1-z)^x = \sum_{k\in\mathbb{Z}} \mathsf{K}_k(x, n)z^k$.*

3 Revisited HWBF and Balancedness

In this part, we will formally define the revisited HWBF function and introduce a quantity that allows us to study its balancedness and nonlinearity.

3.1 Definition and Basic Properties

Definition 14 (Revisited Hidden Weight Bit Function). *For an even integer $n \geqslant 0$, we call revisited HWBF the Boolean function $f \in \mathcal{B}_n$ defined as:*

$$f(x) = \sum_{k=1}^{n} x_k \varphi_{k,n}(x) + \sum_{i=1}^{n/2}(x_i + 1)x_{i+n/2}.$$

Since f is the sum of a quadratic function and a weightwise affine function, it is a weightwise quadratic function. Note that, while the HWBF can be computed by first computing the Hamming weight of the input and then applying a linear function, the revisited HWBF can be computed by first computing the Hamming weight of the input and then applying a quadratic function, leading to a similar computational cost for both.

Using the formalism of Definition 11, f is the weightwise quadratic function defined by $f_0(x) = 0$ and $f_k(x) = x_k + \sum_{i=1}^{n/2}(x_i + 1)x_{i+n/2}$ for $k \in [1, n]$. This form allows to derive the restricted Walsh transform of f, which can be a useful tool to study the balancedness and bound the nonlinearity of a function.

Proposition 1. *Let $n \geqslant 0$ be an even integer, and let $f \in \mathcal{B}_n$ be the revisited HWBF. Consider any binary vector $a \in \mathbb{F}_2^n$ and any integer $k \in [1, n]$. Define $c = a + e_k + \sum_{i=n/2+1}^{n} e_i$. Then the restricted Walsh transform of f satisfies:*

$$\mathcal{W}_{f,k}(a) = \sum_{x\in\mathsf{E}_{k,n}} (-1)^{\sum_{i=1}^{n/2} x_i x_{i+n/2} + c\cdot x}.$$

Proof. By definition, we have $\mathcal{W}_{f,k}(a) = \sum_{x\in\mathsf{E}_{k,n}} (-1)^{x_k + \sum_{i=1}^{n/2}(x_i+1)x_{i+n/2} + a\cdot x}$. Therefore:

$$\begin{aligned}
\mathcal{W}_{f,k}(a) &= \sum_{x\in\mathsf{E}_{k,n}} (-1)^{\sum_{i=1}^{n/2} x_i x_{i+n/2} + \left(x_k + \sum_{i=n/2+1}^{n} x_i + a\cdot x\right)} \\
&= \sum_{x\in\mathsf{E}_{k,n}} (-1)^{\sum_{i=1}^{n/2} x_i x_{i+n/2} + c\cdot x}.
\end{aligned}$$

□

Accordingly, we can study the restricted Walsh transform of the revisited HWBF by analyzing the following Boolean function $d_n \in \mathcal{B}_n$.

Definition 15. *Let $n \geqslant 0$ be an even integer. Then we define the Boolean function $d_n \in \mathcal{B}_n$ by:*

$$d_n(x) = \sum_{i=1}^{n/2} x_{2i-1}x_{2i}.$$

Further, for an integer k and a binary vector $a \in \mathbb{F}_2^n$, we define:

$$\mathsf{D}_{k,n}(a) = \mathcal{W}_{d_n,k}(a) = \sum_{x \in \mathsf{E}_{k,n}} (-1)^{d_n(x)+a\cdot x}.$$

The $\mathsf{D}_{k,n}(a)$ satisfy a recursive relation.

Proposition 2. *Let $n \geqslant 0$ be an even integer. Then for all integers k and all binary vectors $a \in \mathbb{F}_2^n$, the following hold:*

- *We have $\mathsf{D}_{0,0}(a) = 1$ and $\mathsf{D}_{k,0}(a) = 0$ if $k \neq 0$.*
- *If $n \geqslant 2$, then for $b = (a_1, \ldots, a_{n-2}) \in \mathbb{F}_2^{n-2}$, we have:*

$$\begin{aligned}\mathsf{D}_{k,n}(a) = \mathsf{D}_{k,n-2}(a) &+ ((-1)^{a_{n-1}} + (-1)^{a_n})\,\mathsf{D}_{k-1,n-2}(a) \\ &+ (-1)^{1+a_{n-1}+a_n}\,\mathsf{D}_{k-2,n-2}(a).\end{aligned}$$

Proof. We have that $\mathsf{D}_{0,0}(a) = (-1)^0 = 1$ since $\mathsf{E}_{0,0} = \{\varepsilon\}$ for the empty vector $\varepsilon = a \in \mathbb{F}_2^0$. That $\mathsf{D}_{k,0}(a) = 0$ if $k \neq 0$ follows from $\mathsf{E}_{k,0}$ being empty if $k \neq 0$. Assume now that $n \geqslant 2$. By considering binary vectors $x \in \mathbb{F}_2^n$ as $x = (y, x_{n-1}, x_n)$ for $y \in \mathbb{F}_2^{n-2}$, we get:

$$\begin{aligned}\mathsf{D}_{k,n}(a) &= \sum_{x \in \mathsf{E}_{k,n}} (-1)^{d_n(x)+a\cdot x} \\ &= \sum_{y \in \mathsf{E}_{k,n-2}} (-1)^{d_{n-2}(y)+b\cdot y} + \sum_{y \in \mathsf{E}_{k-1,n-2}} (-1)^{d_{n-2}(y)+b\cdot y+a_{n-1}} \\ &\quad + \sum_{y \in \mathsf{E}_{k-1,n-2}} (-1)^{d_{n-2}(y)+b\cdot y+a_n} \\ &\quad + \sum_{y \in \mathsf{E}_{k-2,n-2}} (-1)^{d_{n-2}(y)+b\cdot y+1+a_{n-1}+a_n} \\ &= \mathsf{D}_{k,n-2}(a) + ((-1)^{a_{n-1}} + (-1)^{a_n})\,\mathsf{D}_{k-1,n-2}(a) \\ &\quad + (-1)^{1+a_{n-1}+a_n}\,\mathsf{D}_{k-2,n-2}(a).\end{aligned}$$

□

Remark 1. We note that Proposition 2 gives three different cases depending on the values of the two last elements of a:

- if $a_{n-1} = 0 = a_n$, then $\mathsf{D}_{k,n}(a) = \mathsf{D}_{k,n-2}(a) + 2\mathsf{D}_{k-1,n-2}(a) - \mathsf{D}_{k-2,n-2}(a)$,
- if $a_{n-1} \neq a_n$, then $\mathsf{D}_{k,n}(a) = \mathsf{D}_{k,n-2}(a) + \mathsf{D}_{k-2,n-2}(a)$,
- if $a_{n-1} = 1 = a_n$, then $\mathsf{D}_{k,n}(a) = \mathsf{D}_{k,n-2}(a) - 2\mathsf{D}_{k-1,n-2}(a) - \mathsf{D}_{k-2,n-2}(a)$.

Remark 2. The recursive formula of Proposition 2 gives different cases depending on the values of the pair (a_{n-1}, a_n). However, the same reasoning applies to any pair of the form (a_{2i-1}, a_{2i}) for $i \in [1, n/2]$. Therefore, the value of $\mathsf{D}_{k,n}(a)$ depends only on the number of pairs (a_{2i-1}, a_{2i}) in a being $(0,0)$, $(1,1)$, $(0,1)$ or $(1,0)$. We give the values of $\mathsf{D}_{k,2}(a)$ for $n = 2$ in Table 1. These values together with Proposition 2 are sufficient to determine any $\mathsf{D}_{k,n}(a)$.

Table 1. Values of $\mathsf{D}_{k,2}(a)$.

a	$(0,0)$	$(0,1)$	$(1,1)$
$\mathsf{D}_{0,2}(a)$	1	1	1
$\mathsf{D}_{1,2}(a)$	2	0	-2
$\mathsf{D}_{2,2}(a)$	-1	1	-1

In the following, we show how the Walsh transform of the revisited HWBF $f \in \mathcal{B}_n$ can be written in terms of the $\mathsf{D}_{k,n}(a)$. Then, in Sect. 3.2, we use Proposition 2 to determine the balancedness of f, and in Sect. 4.1 we study the value of $\mathsf{D}_{k,n}(a)$ using generating functions.

Proposition 3. *Let $n \geqslant 0$ be an even integer, and let $f \in \mathcal{B}_n$ be the revisited HWBF. Denote by $\pi : [1, n] \to [1, n]$ the permutation sending the first $n/2$ elements to the odd positions and the $n/2$ last ones to the even positions. Let $a \in \mathbb{F}_2^n$ be a binary vector, and let $b = \pi^{-1}(a) + \sum_{i=1}^{n/2} e_{2i}$. Then the following holds true:*

$$\mathcal{W}_f(a) = 1 + \sum_{k=1}^{n} \mathsf{D}_{k,n}(a).$$

Proof. For every $k \in [1, n]$, we have by Proposition 1 that:

$$\begin{aligned}
\mathcal{W}_{f,k}(a) &= \sum_{x \in \mathsf{E}_{k,n}} (-1)^{f(x) + a \cdot x} \\
&= \sum_{\pi(x) \in \mathsf{E}_{k,n}} (-1)^{f(\pi(x)) + a \cdot \pi(x)} \\
&= \sum_{\pi(x) \in \mathsf{E}_{k,n}} (-1)^{\sum_{i=1}^{n/2} x_{\pi(i)} x_{\pi(i+n/2)} + x_{\pi(k)} + a \cdot \pi(x) + \sum_{i=1}^{n/2} x_{\pi(i+n/2)}} \\
&= \sum_{\pi(x) \in \mathsf{E}_{k,n}} (-1)^{d_n(x) + x_{\pi(k)} + \pi^{-1}(a) \cdot x + \sum_{i=1}^{n/2} x_{2i}} \\
&= \sum_{x \in \mathsf{E}_{k,n}} (-1)^{d_n(x) + (b + \pi(e_k)) \cdot x} \\
&= \mathsf{D}_{k,n}(a).
\end{aligned}$$

We conclude by applying $\mathcal{W}_f(a) = 1 + \sum_{k=1}^{n} \mathcal{W}_{f,k}(a)$. □

3.2 Balancedness of f

In this part, we determine for which values of n the revisited HWBF $f \in \mathcal{B}_n$ is balanced, using the expression of its Walsh transform in terms of the $\mathsf{D}_{k,n}(a)$ and the recursive relation of these quantities.

Theorem 1. *Let $n \geqslant 2$ be an even integer. Then the Walsh transform of the revisited HWBF $f \in \mathcal{B}_n$ at 0_n satisfies:*

$$\mathcal{W}_f(0_n) = \begin{cases} 0 & \text{if } n \equiv 0 \bmod 4, \\ -2\binom{(n-2)/2}{(n-2)/4} & \text{if } n \equiv 2 \bmod 4. \end{cases}$$

Accordingly, f is balanced if and only if $n \equiv 0 \bmod 4$.

Proof. We use Proposition 3, applying Remark 2 and that $\pi^{-1}(0_n) = 0_n$:

$$\begin{aligned} \mathcal{W}_f(0_n) &= 1 + \sum_{k=1}^{n} \mathsf{D}_{k,n}(a) \\ &= 1 + \sum_{k=1}^{n/2} \mathsf{D}_{k,n}(a) + \sum_{k=n/2+1}^{n} \mathsf{D}_{k,n}(a). \end{aligned}$$

Using the recursive relation from Proposition 2, we obtain:

$$\begin{aligned} \mathsf{D}_{k,n}(a) = \mathsf{D}_{k,n-2}(a) \\ + \mathsf{D}_{k-2,n-2}(a). \end{aligned}$$

By reapplying this $n/2 - 1$ times, we obtain:

$$\begin{aligned} \mathsf{D}_{k,n}(a) &= \sum_{i=0}^{n/2-1} \binom{n/2-1}{i} \mathsf{D}_{k-2i,2}(a) \\ &= \binom{n/2-1}{k/2} \mathsf{D}_{0,2}(a) + \binom{n/2-1}{(k-1)/2} \mathsf{D}_{1,2}(a) \\ &\quad + \binom{n/2-1}{k/2-1} \mathsf{D}_{2,2}(a) \\ &= \binom{n/2-1}{k/2} - 2\binom{n/2-1}{(k-1)/2} - \binom{n/2-1}{k/2-1}. \end{aligned}$$

We similarly get:

$$\mathsf{D}_{k,n}(a) = \binom{n/2-1}{k/2} + 2\binom{n/2-1}{(k-1)/2} - \binom{n/2-1}{k/2-1}.$$

Then, combining both, we obtain:

$$\begin{aligned}
\mathcal{W}_f(0_n) &= 1 + \sum_{k=1}^{n/2} \mathsf{D}_{k,n}(a) + \sum_{k=n/2+1}^{n} \mathsf{D}_{k,n}(a) \\
&= \sum_{k=0}^{n/2} \left(\binom{n/2-1}{k/2} - 2\binom{n/2-1}{(k-1)/2} - \binom{n/2-1}{k/2-1} \right) \\
&\quad + \sum_{k=n/2+1}^{n} \left(\binom{n/2-1}{k/2} + 2\binom{n/2-1}{(k-1)/2} - \binom{n/2-1}{k/2-1} \right) \\
&= \sum_{k=0}^{n} \left(\binom{n/2-1}{k/2} - \binom{n/2-1}{k/2-1} \right) \\
&\quad + 2 \left(\sum_{k=n/2+1}^{n} \binom{n/2-1}{(k-1)/2} - \sum_{k=0}^{n/2} \binom{n/2-1}{(k-1)/2} \right) \\
&= 0 + 2 \left(\sum_{k=n/2+1}^{n} \binom{n/2-1}{(k-1)/2} - \sum_{k=0}^{n/2} \binom{n/2-1}{(k-1)/2} \right) \\
&= 2 \left(\sum_{i=\lceil n/4 \rceil}^{n/2-1} \binom{n/2-1}{i} - \sum_{i=0}^{\lfloor (n-2)/4 \rfloor} \binom{n/2-1}{i} \right).
\end{aligned}$$

The result follows by applying that $\binom{n}{k} = \binom{n}{n-k}$ for all integers $n \geqslant 0$ and k. □

4 Extensive Study of the $\mathsf{D}_{k,n}(a)$ and Bounds on the Walsh Spectrum of f

This section examines the values of $\mathsf{D}_{k,n}(a)$ through the use of generating functions. To begin, in Sect. 4.1, we determine essential characteristics of these values. Subsequently, in Sect. 4.2, we employ Cauchy's estimate to bound the absolute value of the $\mathsf{D}_{k,n}(a)$. This approach allows us to also bound the absolute value of the Walsh transform of the revisited HWBF, thereby constraining the nonlinearity. Lastly, in Sect. 4.3, we illustrate how this result can be extended to bound the nonlinearity of a family of weightwise quadratic functions.

4.1 Study of the $\mathsf{D}_{k,n}(a)$ Through Generating Functions

Definition 16. *Let $n \geqslant 0$ be an even integer. For $a \in \mathbb{F}_2^n$, we denote by $p = p(a)$ the number of $i \geqslant 1$ for which $(a_{2i-1}, a_{2i}) = (0,0)$, by $q = q(a)$ the number of $i \geqslant 1$ for which $(a_{2i-1}, a_{2i}) = (1,1)$, and by $r = r(a)$ the number of $i \geqslant 1$ for which $(a_{2i-1}, a_{2i}) \in \{(0,1),(1,0)\}$. We then have $p + q + r = n/2$. We further introduce the integer polynomial $P_a(z)$ given by the following expression:*

$$P_a(z) = (-z^2 + 2z + 1)^p \cdot (-z^2 - 2z + 1)^q \cdot (z^2 + 1)^r.$$

Proposition 4. *For every even integer $n \geqslant 0$ and every binary vector $a \in \mathbb{F}_2^n$, the following holds:*

$$\sum_{k\in\mathbb{Z}} \mathsf{D}_{k,n}(a)z^k = P_a(z).$$

Proof. We proceed by induction on even $n \geqslant 0$. For the base case $n = 0$, we consider the empty vector $a = \varepsilon \in \mathbb{F}_2^0$; it satisfies $P_a(z) = 1$, while $\mathsf{D}_{0,0}(a) = 1$ and $\mathsf{D}_{k,0}(a) = 0$ if $k \neq 0$ by Proposition 2. For the inductive step, let $n \geqslant 2$ be even, and assume that the corresponding formula holds for $n - 2$. Using the recursive formula for $\mathsf{D}_{k,n}(a)$ from Proposition 2 with $b = (a_1, \ldots, a_{n-2}) \in \mathbb{F}_2^{n-2}$, we have:

$$\begin{aligned}\sum_{k\in\mathbb{Z}} \mathsf{D}_{k,n}(a)z^k &= \sum_{k\in\mathbb{Z}} \mathsf{D}_{k,n-2}(a)z^k + \left((-1)^{a_{n-1}} + (-1)^{a_n}\right)\sum_{k\in\mathbb{Z}} \mathsf{D}_{k-1,n-2}(a)z^k \\ &\quad + (-1)^{1+a_{n-1}+a_n}\sum_{k\in\mathbb{Z}} \mathsf{D}_{k-2,n-2}(a)z^k \\ &= P_b(z) + \left((-1)^{a_{n-1}} + (-1)^{a_n}\right)zP_b(z) + (-1)^{1+a_{n-1}+a_n}z^2P_b(z) \\ &= P_b(z)\cdot\left(z^2(-1)^{1+a_{n-1}+a_n} + z\left((-1)^{a_{n-1}} + (-1)^{a_n}\right) + 1\right) \\ &= P_a(z).\end{aligned}$$

□

Remark 3. We have already argued in Remark 2 that $\mathsf{D}_{k,n}(a)$ only depends on $p(a)$, $q(a)$ and $r(a)$. This observation can also be obtained from Proposition 4: since $P_a(z)$ only depends on $p(a)$, $q(a)$ and $r(a)$ (by definition), we deduce that also $\mathsf{D}_{k,n}(a)$ only depends on $p(a)$, $q(a)$ and $r(a)$. Therefore, for any $p, q, r \geqslant 0$ satisfying $p + q + r = n/2$, it makes sense to introduce the notation $\mathsf{D}_{k,n}^{p,q,r} = \mathsf{D}_{k,n}(a)$, where $a \in \mathbb{F}_2^n$ is any vector with $(p(a), q(a), r(a)) = (p, q, r)$. We will make use of this notation in Sect. 5.1.

Proposition 5. *For every even integer $n \geqslant 0$, for every binary vector $a \in \mathbb{F}_2^n$, and for every integer k, the following holds:*

$$\mathsf{D}_{n-k,n}(a) = (-1)^{p+q+k}\mathsf{D}_{k,n}(a).$$

Proof. We define the reverse polynomial $Q_a(z)$ as the degree n polynomial where each coefficient of z^k in $Q_a(z)$, for any k, is equal to the coefficient of z^{n-k} in $P_a(z)$. Then we have:

$$\begin{aligned}Q_a(z) &= z^n P_a(1/z) \\ &= (z^2 + 2z - 1)^p \cdot (z^2 - 2z - 1)^q \cdot (z^2 + 1)^r \\ &= (-1)^{p+q}(-z^2 - 2z + 1)^p \cdot (-z^2 + 2z + 1)^q \cdot (z^2 + 1)^r \\ &= (-1)^{p+q}P_a(-z).\end{aligned}$$

Therefore, the coefficient of z^k in $Q_a(z)$, which is $\mathsf{D}_{n-k,n}(a)$, is equal to the coefficient of z^k in $(-1)^{p+q}P_a(-z)$, which is $(-1)^{p+q+k}\mathsf{D}_{k,n}(a)$. □

Corollary 1. *Let $n \geqslant 0$ be an even integer, and let $a \in \mathbb{F}_2^n$ be a binary vector. If $r = r(a)$ is odd, then it holds that $\mathsf{D}_{n/2,n}(a) = 0$.*

Proof. By Proposition 5, it holds that $\mathsf{D}_{n/2,n}(a) = (-1)^{p+q+n/2}\mathsf{D}_{n/2,n}(a) = -\mathsf{D}_{n/2,n}(a)$ because $p+q+n/2$ is odd: $p+q+n/2 \equiv n/2-p-q \equiv r \equiv 1 \bmod 2$. □

Another immediate case for zero coefficients is the following.

Proposition 6. *Let $n \geqslant 0$ be an even integer, and let $a \in \mathbb{F}_2^n$ be a binary vector. If k is an odd integer and $p = q$, then it holds that $\mathsf{D}_{k,n}(a) = 0 = \mathsf{D}_{n-k,n}(a)$.*

Proof. If $p = q$, we have $P_a(z) = (z^4 - 6z^2 + 1)^p \cdot (z^2 + 1)^r$, which can be seen as a polynomial in z^2. Thus, the coefficient $\mathsf{D}_{k,n}(a)$ in $P_a(z)$ of z^k for odd k must be zero. It also follows that $\mathsf{D}_{n-k,n}(a) = 0$ by Proposition 5. □

Remark 4. We can also use Proposition 4 to obtain $\mathsf{D}_{k,n}(a)$ through differentiation and evaluation at $z = 0$, to get $k! \cdot \mathsf{D}_{k,n}(a) = \frac{\mathrm{d}^k}{\mathrm{d}^k z} P_a(z)|_{z=0}$. Using this formula, we can for instance use a computer algebra system to deduce $\mathsf{D}_{k,n}(a)$ for small values of k, see Table 2. Note that even though the expression for $\mathsf{D}_{3,n}(a)$ involves a division by 3, its evaluation at specific values for (p, q, r) will always yield integers. Indeed, either $p - q \equiv 0 \bmod 3$, or $(p-q)^2 \equiv 1 \bmod 3$, in which case $2(p-q)^2 + 7 \equiv 0 \bmod 3$.

Table 2. Values of $\mathsf{D}_{k,n}(a)$ for small values of k.

k	$\mathsf{D}_{k,n}(a)$
0	1
1	$2(p-q)$
2	$2(p-q)^2 - 3(p+q) + r$
3	$\frac{2}{3}(p-q)\left(2(p-q)^2 - 9(p+q) + 3r + 7\right)$

From differentiation, we can get more cases in which $\mathsf{D}_{k,n}(a) = 0$.

Proposition 7. *Let $n \geqslant 0$ be an even integer, and let $a \in \mathbb{F}_2^n$ be a binary vector.*

1. *For every integer $s \geqslant 0$, define $\ell_s = s(s-1)$. If $n = 16m$ and $\{p, q\} = \{m + \ell_s, m + \ell_{s+1}\}$ for integers $m, s \geqslant 0$, then $\mathsf{D}_{2,n}(a) = 0 = \mathsf{D}_{n-2,n}(a)$.*
2. *For every integer $s \geqslant 0$, define $\ell_s = \left(6s^2 + 6s + (-1)^s(2s+1) - 1\right)/8$. If $n = 16m + 2$ and $\{p, q\} = \{m + \ell_s, m + \ell_{s+2}\}$ for integers $m, s \geqslant 0$, then $\mathsf{D}_{3,n}(a) = 0 = \mathsf{D}_{k-3,n}(a)$.*
3. *For every integer $s \geqslant 0$, define $\ell_s = s^2$. If $n = 16m + 4$ and $\{p, q\} = \{m + \ell_s, m + \ell_{s+1}\}$ for integers $m, s \geqslant 0$, then $\mathsf{D}_{2,n}(a) = 0 = \mathsf{D}_{n-2,n}(a)$.*
4. *For every integer $s \geqslant 0$, define $\ell_s = \left(6s^2 + 6s - (-1)^s(2s+1) + 1\right)/8$. If $n = 16m + 6$ and $\{p, q\} = \{m + \ell_s, m + \ell_{s+2}\}$ for integers $m, s \geqslant 0$, then $\mathsf{D}_{3,n}(a) = 0 = \mathsf{D}_{n-3,n}(a)$.*

Proof. We use the expressions from Table 2, and replace p, q and r by their respective values. For instance, for the case $n = 16m$, we replace p, q and r by $m + s(s-1)$, $m + s(s+1)$ and $6m - 2s^2$, respectively, in the expression $\mathsf{D}_{2,n}(a) = 2(p-q)^2 - 3(p+q) + r$, which yields $\mathsf{D}_{2,n}(a) = 0$. This checking can be automatized by a computer algebra system, for which we provide a SageMath implementation.[1] □

Remark 5. There are other instances where $\mathsf{D}_{k,n}(a) = 0$ which have not been described by any of the previous results. For instance, we have $\mathsf{D}_{4,34}(a) = 0$ if $\{p, q\} = \{1, 2\}$.

Using Proposition 4, we can also deduce some sums involving the $\mathsf{D}_{k,n}(a)$.

Proposition 8. *Let $n \geqslant 0$ be an even integer, and let $a \in \mathbb{F}_2^n$ be a binary vector.*

1. *The sum and alternating sum over k of the $\mathsf{D}_{k,n}(a)$ are, respectively:*

$$\sum_{k \in \mathbb{Z}} \mathsf{D}_{k,n}(a) = (-1)^q 2^{n/2}, \qquad \sum_{k \in \mathbb{Z}} (-1)^k \mathsf{D}_{k,n}(a) = (-1)^p 2^{n/2}.$$

2. *The sum over the even and the odd k of the $\mathsf{D}_{k,n}(a)$ are, respectively:*

$$\sum_{k \in \mathbb{Z}} \mathsf{D}_{2k,n}(a) = 2^{n/2-1}\big((-1)^q + (-1)^p\big),$$
$$\sum_{k \in \mathbb{Z}} \mathsf{D}_{2k+1,n}(a) = 2^{n/2-1}\big((-1)^q - (-1)^p\big).$$

Proof. For the sum and the alternating sum, we compute $P_a(1)$ and $P_a(-1)$, respectively. The sum of the $\mathsf{D}_{k,n}(a)$ over the even (respectively, odd) k is obtained by adding (respectively, subtracting) these two sums and dividing by 2. □

4.2 Bounding the Walsh Transform of f Using the Cauchy Estimate

We recall Cauchy's estimate on holomorphic functions.

*Property 2 (Cauchy's estimate, **e.g.**, Theorem 10.26 in* [43]*).* Let w be a complex number, and let $R > 0$ be some radius. Let $D \subseteq \mathbb{C}$ be a set containing every complex number z satisfying $|z - w| \leqslant R$. Let $f : D \to \mathbb{C}$ be a holomorphic function, and let M_R be the maximum of the absolute value of f on the circle defined by $|z - w| = R$. Then for every integer $k \geqslant 0$, the k-th derivative of f evaluated at w can be bounded, in absolute value, by $\left| \frac{\mathrm{d}^k}{\mathrm{d}^k z} f(z)|_{z=w} \right| \leqslant \frac{k! \cdot M_R}{R^k}$.

[1] https://github.com/se-tim/Revisited-HWBF.git.

Theorem 2. *Let $n \geqslant 0$ be an even integer, and let $a \in \mathbb{F}_2^n$ be a binary vector. Then, for every integer $k \in [0, n]$, it holds that:*

$$|\mathsf{D}_{k,n}(a)| \leqslant 2^{3n/4}.$$

Proof. From Remark 4 we have $k! \cdot \mathsf{D}_{k,n}(a) = \frac{\mathrm{d}^k}{\mathrm{d}^k z} P_a(z)|_{z=0}$. Choosing $f = P_a$, $w = 0$ and $R = 1$ in Property 2 then gives $|\mathsf{D}_{k,n}(a)| = \frac{1}{k!}\left|\frac{\mathrm{d}^k}{\mathrm{d}^k z} P_a(z)|_{z=0}\right| \leqslant M$, where M is the maximum of $|P_a(z)|$ on the complex circle $\mathsf{c}_1 = \{z \in \mathbb{C} : |z| = 1\}$. We claim, and prove below, that the maximum of $\left|-z^2 + 2z + 1\right|$ on c_1 is $2\sqrt{2}$. This implies that the maximum of $\left|-z^2 - 2z + 1\right|$ on c_1 is $2\sqrt{2}$ as well because $-z^2 - 2z + 1 = -(-z)^2 + 2(-z) + 1$. Since the maximum of $\left|z^2 + 1\right|$ on c_1 is $2 < 2\sqrt{2}$, it follows that $|\mathsf{D}_{k,n}(a)| \leqslant M \leqslant (2\sqrt{2})^{p+q}2^r \leqslant (2\sqrt{2})^{n/2}$.

We prove that the maximum of $|-z^2 + 2z + 1|$ on c_1 is $2\sqrt{2}$ by showing that the one of $|-z^2 + 2z + 1|^2$ on c_1 equals 8. Using that $|w|^2 = w\overline{w}$ for every complex number w, we obtain for all $z \in \mathsf{c}_1$:

$$\left|-z^2 + 2z + 1\right|^2 = \left(z^2 - 2z - 1\right)\left(\overline{z}^2 - 2\overline{z} - 1\right) = 6 - \left(z^2 + \overline{z}^2\right) = 6 - 2\mathrm{Re}\left(z^2\right).$$

Since the minimum of $\mathrm{Re}\left(z^2\right)$ on c_1 is -1, we conclude that the maximum of $|-z^2 + 2z + 1|^2$ on c_1 is $6 - 2(-1) = 8$. □

Corollary 2. *Let $n \geqslant 0$ be an even integer, and let $f \in \mathcal{B}_n$ be the revisited* HWBF. *Then for every binary vector $a \in \mathbb{F}_2^n$, it holds that:*

$$|\mathcal{W}_f(a)| \leqslant 1 + n \cdot 2^{3n/4}.$$

Equivalently, it holds that $\mathsf{NL}(f) \geqslant 2^{n-1} - \frac{1}{2} - 2^{3n/4 + \log_2(n) - 1}$.

Proof. It is enough to prove the bound on $|\mathcal{W}_f(a)|$; the bound on the nonlinearity of f comes from the second expression of Definition 6. We have previously established in Proposition 3 that $\mathcal{W}_f(a) = 1 + \sum_{k=1}^{n} \mathsf{D}_{k,n}(a)$ for some vectors $b_k \in \mathbb{F}_2^n$. Then, applying the triangle inequality together with Theorem 2 yields $|\mathcal{W}_f(a)| \leqslant 1 + \sum_{k=1}^{n} |\mathsf{D}_{k,n}(a)| \leqslant 1 + n \cdot 2^{3n/4}$. □

4.3 Generalization to a Family of Weightwise Quadratic Functions

In this part, we generalize the results of Sect. 4.2 to all weightwise quadratic functions f such that, for every $k \in [1, n]$, the function f_kÂă(as defined in Definition 11) contains exactly t quadratic terms with no shared variables. We skip the proofs of the following results; they are provided in the appendix, see Sect. A.

Definition 17. *For an even integer $n \geqslant 0$ and an integer $t \in [0, n/2]$, we define the Boolean function $d_{t,n} \in \mathcal{B}_n$ by:*

$$d_{t,n}(x) = \sum_{i=1}^{t} x_{2i-1}x_{2i}.$$

Further, for an integer k and a binary vector $a \in \mathbb{F}_2^n$, we define:

$$\mathsf{D}_{t,k,n}(a) = \mathcal{W}_{d_{t,n},k}(a) = \sum_{x \in \mathsf{E}_{k,n}} (-1)^{d_{t,n}(x)+a\cdot x}.$$

In particular, it holds that $d_{n/2,n}(x) = d_n(x)$ and $\mathsf{D}_{n/2,k,n}(a) = \mathsf{D}_{k,n}(a)$. We now focus on the $\mathsf{D}_{t,k,n}(a)$.

Proposition 9. *Let $n \geqslant 0$ be an even integer, and let $t \in [0, n/2]$. Let $a \in \mathbb{F}_2^n$ be a binary vector, and write $a = (b, c)$ with $b \in \mathbb{F}_2^{2t}$ and $c \in \mathbb{F}_2^{n-2t}$. Then the following holds for all integers k:*

$$\mathsf{D}_{t,k,n}(a) = \sum_{\ell=0}^{2t} \mathsf{D}_{\ell,2t}(a) \cdot \mathsf{K}_{k-\ell}(\mathsf{w_H}(c), n-2t).$$

Definition 18. *Let $n \geqslant 0$ be an even integer, and let $t \in [0, n/2]$. Let $a = (b, c) \in \mathbb{F}_2^n$ be a binary vector with $b \in \mathbb{F}_2^{2t}$ and $c \in \mathbb{F}_2^{n-2t}$. By letting $u = u_t(a) = n - 2t - \mathsf{w_H}(c)$ and $v = v_t(a) = \mathsf{w_H}(c)$, we introduce the polynomial $P_{t,a}(z)$ given by the following expression:*

$$P_{t,a}(z) = P_b(z) \cdot (1+z)^u \cdot (1-z)^v.$$

Proposition 10. *For every even integer $n \geqslant 0$, every integer $t \in [0, n/2]$ and every binary vector $a \in \mathbb{F}_2^n$, the following holds:*

$$\sum_{k \in \mathbb{Z}} \mathsf{D}_{t,k,n}(a) z^k = P_{t,a}(z).$$

This result can in turn be used to bound the $\mathsf{D}_{t,k,n}(a)$. The following result is a direct generalization of Theorem 2.

Theorem 3. *Let $n \geqslant 0$ be an even integer, and let $t \in [0, n/2]$. We define $\lambda = t/n$, as well as:*

$$\mu = \mu(\lambda) = \begin{cases} \frac{\lambda+1}{2} + \frac{1}{2}\log_2\left(\frac{\left(-\lambda^2+2\lambda+\lambda\sqrt{\lambda^2-4\lambda+2}\right)^{\lambda}}{\left(1-\lambda+\sqrt{\lambda^2-4\lambda+2}\right)^{2\lambda-1}}\right) & \text{if } \lambda > \frac{1}{6}, \\ 1-\lambda & \text{if } \lambda \leqslant \frac{1}{6}. \end{cases}$$

Then, for all $a \in \mathbb{F}_2^n$ and all $k \in [0, n]$, the following hold:

$$|\mathsf{D}_{t,k,n}(a)| \leqslant 2^{\mu n}, \qquad |\mathcal{W}_{d_{t,n}}(a)| \leqslant 1 + n \cdot 2^{\mu n}.$$

The curve of $\lambda \mapsto \mu(\lambda)$ defined in the above Theorem 3 is represented in Fig. 1. Observe that $\mu(1/2) = 3/4$, which corresponds to Theorem 2.

5 Experiments and Comparisons

In this section, we establish a tighter bound on the absolute value of the Walsh transform of the revisited HWBF for even $n \in [1, 80]$. We then compare the nonlinearity of this function to that of other functions suited to similar use cases, such as the HWBF or the weightwise cyclic functions from [38].

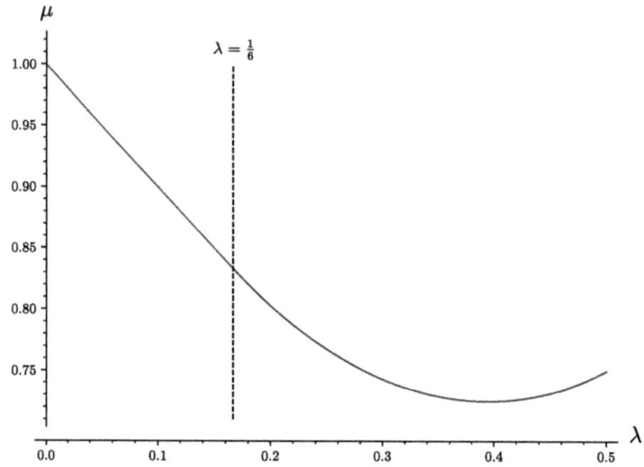

Fig. 1. The curve of $\lambda \mapsto \mu(\lambda)$ with $0 \leqslant \lambda \leqslant \frac{1}{2}$ from Theorem 3.

5.1 Experimentally Bounding the Walsh Transform of *f*

Following Corollary 2, we deduce that $|\mathcal{W}_f(a)| \leqslant 1 + n \cdot 2^{3n/4}$ for every even integer $n \geqslant 0$ and every binary vector $a \in \mathbb{F}_2^n$, where $f \in \mathcal{B}_n$ denotes the revisited HWBF. This is a somewhat pessimistic bound. In this part, we discuss how a tighter bound on $|\mathcal{W}_f(a)|$ can be obtained in polynomial time in n.

This method is based on the identity given in Proposition 3. For this, consider a vector $b \in \mathbb{F}_2^n$; we write $(p, q, r) = (p(b), q(b), r(b))$. Also, for $k \in [1, n]$, let $b_k = b + \pi(e_k)$ and $(p_k, q_k, r_k) = (p(b_k), q(b_k), r(b_k))$, where $\pi : [1, n] \to [1, n]$ is again the permutation sending the first $n/2$ elements to the odd positions and the $n/2$ last ones to the even positions. Notice first that for every integer $k \in [1, n]$, it holds that $(p_k, q_k, r_k) \in \{(p \pm 1, q, r \mp 1), (p, q \pm 1, r \mp 1)\}$. Furthermore, observe that if $k \in [0, n/2]$ and $(p_k, q_k, r_k) = (p + \alpha, q + \beta, r + \gamma)$ for $\{\alpha, \beta, \gamma\} = \{0, \pm 1\}$ with $\gamma \neq 0$, then we have $(p_{k+n/2}, q_{k+n/2}, r_{k+n/2}) = (p + \alpha', q + \beta', r + \gamma')$ for some $\{\alpha', \beta', \gamma'\} = \{0, \pm 1\}$ with $\gamma' \neq 0$, where α',β' and γ' only depend on α, β and γ. Explicitly, we have $(\alpha', \beta', \gamma') = (\alpha, \beta, \gamma)$ if $\gamma = 1$ and $(\alpha', \beta', \gamma') = (\beta, \alpha, \gamma)$ if $\gamma = -1$.

In the following discussion, we outline a method to determine an upper bound on $\max_{a \in \mathbb{F}_2^n} \mathcal{W}_f(a)$. A similar approach can be applied to find a lower bound on $\min_{a \in \mathbb{F}_2^n} \mathcal{W}_f(a)$, and by utilizing both, we can also obtain an upper bound on $\max_{a \in \mathbb{F}_2^n} |\mathcal{W}_f(a)|$ by making use of the following identity:

$$\max_{a \in \mathbb{F}_2^n} |\mathcal{W}_f(a)| = \max\left(\max_{a \in \mathbb{F}_2^n} \mathcal{W}_f(a), -\min_{a \in \mathbb{F}_2^n} \mathcal{W}_f(a) \right).$$

For each $k \in [1, n/2]$, we select $\{\alpha_k, \beta_k, \gamma_k\} = \{0, \pm 1\}$ with $\gamma_k \neq 0$ such that the following expression, based on the notation introduced in Remark 3, is defined and maximized:

$$B_k^{p,q,r} = \mathsf{D}_{k,n}^{p+\alpha_k, q+\beta_k, r+\gamma_k} + \mathsf{D}_{k+n/2,n}^{p+\alpha'_k, q+\beta'_k, r+\gamma'_k}.$$

This implies that $\mathsf{D}_{k,n}(a) + \mathsf{D}_{k+n/2,n}(a) \leqslant B_k^{p,q,r}$ for every $k \in [1, n/2]$, leading to the conclusion that $\sum_{k=1}^{n} \mathsf{D}_{k,n}(a) \leqslant \sum_{k=1}^{n/2} B_k^{p,q,r}$. As a result, we derive the following upper bound:

$$\max_{a \in \mathbb{F}_2^n} \mathcal{W}_f(a) \leqslant 1 + \max_{p+q+r=n/2} \sum_{k=1}^{n/2} B_k^{p,q,r}. \tag{1}$$

Under the assumption that the values of $\mathsf{D}_{k,n}^{p,q,r}$ have already been computed for all $k \in [1, n]$ and for all triplets (p, q, r) satisfying $p+q+r = n/2$, the bound in equation (1) can be determined with a computational complexity of $\mathcal{O}(n^3)$. This is because there are $\mathcal{O}(n^2)$ possible triplets (p, q, r) that meet the condition $p+q+r = n/2$, and the summation itself can be computed in $\mathcal{O}(n)$ steps.

We consider now the complexity involved in computing the values of $\mathsf{D}_{k,n}^{p,q,r}$ for all $k \in [1, n]$ and all triplets (p, q, r) satisfying $p+q+r = n/2$. We claim that this computation has a complexity of $\mathcal{O}(n^3 \log n)$. Towards this, it is sufficient to expand $(-z^2+2z+1)^p \cdot (-z^2-2z+1)^q \cdot (z^2+1)^r$ for all triplets (p, q, r) such that $p+q+r = n/2$; this is due to Proposition 4.

To achieve this, we first precompute the expanded polynomial $(-z^2+2z+1)^p$ for each $p \in [0, n/2]$. This can be done recursively using the formula $(-z^2+2z+1)^{p+1} = (-z^2+2z+1) \cdot (-z^2+2z+1)^p$. For each p, this requires $\mathcal{O}(n)$ arithmetic computations. Performing this for every p results in a total complexity of $\mathcal{O}(n^2)$. The same approach can be used to expand the polynomials $(-z^2-2z+1)^q$ and $(z^2+1)^r$, resulting in an overall complexity of $\mathcal{O}(n^2)$ for all $p, q, r \in [0, n/2]$.

Finally, for each triplet (p, q, r) satisfying $p+q+r = n/2$, we multiply the three expanded polynomials $(-z^2+2z+1)^p$, $(-z^2-2z+1)^q$ and $(z^2+1)^r$. These two multiplications are performed in $\mathcal{O}(n \log n)$ operations by using the fast Fourier transform. Given that there are $\mathcal{O}(n^2)$ triplets (p, q, r) to consider, we conclude that precomputing the values $\mathsf{D}_{k,n}^{p,q,r}$ for all $k \in [1, n]$ and all triplets (p, q, r) has a complexity of $\mathcal{O}(n^3 \log n)$, making the overall complexity of the procedure also $\mathcal{O}(n^3 \log n)$.

In Table 3, we compare the exact values of $\max_{a \in \mathbb{F}_2^n} |\mathcal{W}_f(a)|$ for small values of n (calculated using SageMath) to the bound B_n obtained through the above method and to the bound from Corollary 2. Additionally, Table 4 provides the values of the bound B_n for all even values of $n \in [1, 80]$. The method described above offers a tighter bound compared to Corollary 2. Its polynomial complexity makes it possible to extend the analysis well beyond the limitations imposed by a full computation of the Walsh spectrum, which requires a complexity of $\mathcal{O}(n2^n)$. We provide a SageMath implementation to obtain the bound B_n.[2]

5.2 Comparison of the Nonlinearity

In this part, we compare the nonlinearity of the revisited HWBF with other weightwise quadratic functions considered for similar use-cases, such as the majority function, the HWBF and the cyclic weightwise functions studied in [38].

[2] https://github.com/se-tim/Revisited-HWBF.git.

Table 3. The actual $\max_{a \in \mathbb{F}_2^n} |\mathcal{W}_f(a)|$ compared to the bound B_n and the theoretical bound from Corollary 2.

n	$\max_a \|\mathcal{W}_f(a)\|$	B_n	$\lfloor 1 + n \cdot 2^{3n/4} \rfloor$
2	2	2	6
4	8	8	33
6	20	28	136
8	52	76	513
10	108	212	1 811
12	292	596	6 145
14	700	1 828	20 275
16	2 176	5 196	65 537
18	4 964	14 668	208 535
20	14 968	41 468	655 361
22	34 232	118 544	2 039 002
24	109 648	325 188	6 291 457

Table 4. Approximate values of B_n for various values of n.

n	$\approx B_n$	n	$\approx B_n$	n	$\approx B_n$	n	$\approx B_n$
2	$2.00 \cdot 10^0$	22	$1.19 \cdot 10^5$	42	$4.01 \cdot 10^9$	62	$1.32 \cdot 10^{14}$
4	$8.00 \cdot 10^0$	24	$3.25 \cdot 10^5$	44	$1.12 \cdot 10^{10}$	64	$3.66 \cdot 10^{14}$
6	$2.80 \cdot 10^1$	26	$9.59 \cdot 10^5$	46	$3.21 \cdot 10^{10}$	66	$1.05 \cdot 10^{15}$
8	$7.60 \cdot 10^1$	28	$2.68 \cdot 10^6$	48	$8.91 \cdot 10^{10}$	68	$2.93 \cdot 10^{15}$
10	$2.12 \cdot 10^2$	30	$7.65 \cdot 10^6$	50	$2.56 \cdot 10^{11}$	70	$8.40 \cdot 10^{15}$
12	$5.96 \cdot 10^2$	32	$2.14 \cdot 10^7$	52	$7.12 \cdot 10^{11}$	72	$2.33 \cdot 10^{16}$
14	$1.83 \cdot 10^3$	34	$6.25 \cdot 10^7$	54	$2.05 \cdot 10^{12}$	74	$6.71 \cdot 10^{16}$
16	$5.20 \cdot 10^3$	36	$1.76 \cdot 10^8$	56	$5.73 \cdot 10^{12}$	76	$1.87 \cdot 10^{17}$
18	$1.47 \cdot 10^4$	38	$5.03 \cdot 10^8$	58	$1.65 \cdot 10^{13}$	78	$5.39 \cdot 10^{17}$
20	$4.15 \cdot 10^4$	40	$1.40 \cdot 10^9$	60	$4.59 \cdot 10^{13}$	80	$1.51 \cdot 10^{18}$

In Fig. 2, we compare bounds for the values of $\max_{a \in \mathbb{F}_2^n} |\mathcal{W}_f(a)|$ for various functions $f \in \mathcal{B}_n$, where a smaller maximum indicates better nonlinearity, see Definition 6. We present values for n up to 80, which is sufficient for examining the asymptotic behavior of the different bounds. The bound on the cyclic weightwise linear functions stems from [38]. With the notation from Definition 11, these functions f satisfy $f_0(x) = b \cdot x$ for $\mathsf{w_H}(b)$ odd; therefore, this represents, for instance, an upper bound for the HWBF. The bound also applies to the cyclic weightwise quadratic function f defined by $f_0(x) = x_1 + x_2x_3$. Next, the bound for the majority function and the HWBF comes from Property 1; we use a single curve here because the nonlinearity difference between these two functions is too small to be distinguished on a logarithmic scale. The theoretical and experimental bounds for the revisited HWBF come from Corollary 2 and Sect. 5.1, respectively.

The revisited HWBF demonstrates significantly better performance compared to the majority function, the original HWBF and the functions studied in [38]. Its theoretical bound on $\max_{a \in \mathbb{F}_2^n} |\mathcal{W}_f(a)|$ reveals an asymptotic slope of 3/4 on a logarithmic scale, contrasting with the slope of 1 for the majority function, the HWBF, and the bounds proven in [38]. Notably, the two curves for the revisited

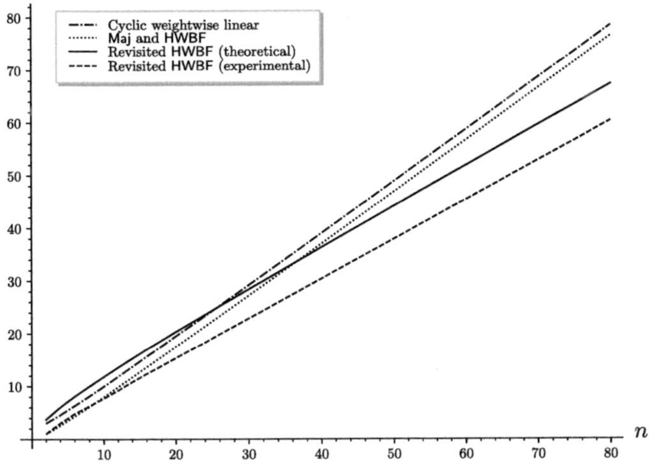

Fig. 2. Bounds on $\max_{a\in\mathbb{F}_2^n} |\mathcal{W}_f(a)|$ for various functions $f \in \mathcal{B}_n$ for even n, shown on a logarithmic scale. The bound for the cyclic weightwise linear functions stems from [38]. The bound for the majority function and the HWBF comes from Property 1. The theoretical bound for the revisited HWBF is from Corollary 2, and the experimental bound is from Sect. 5.1.

HWBF appear to share this asymptotic slope of 3/4, supporting the effectiveness of Corollary 2 and the stronger Theorem 3 in capturing asymptotic behavior.

We also compare in Table 5 the precise nonlinearity values of the functions under consideration. Among the various weightwise quadratic functions studied so far, we observe that the revisited HWBF has the highest nonlinearity from $n = 10$ onward.

Table 5. Comparison of the nonlinearity.

n	4	6	8	10	12	14	16
HWBF	4	20	88	372	1 544	6 344	25 904
Majority	5	22	93	386	1 586	6 476	26 333
t [38]	4	22	96	404	1 672	6 854	27 884
u [38]	4	24	104	456	1 888	7 816	31 616
Revisited HWBF	4	22	102	458	1 902	7 842	31 680

6 Other Parameters

In this section, we present additional cryptographic parameters for the revisited HWBF. While Theorem 1 describes its balancedness and Sects. 4.2 and 5 thoroughly explore its nonlinearity, our focus here will be on its algebraic characteristics. Specifically, we will examine the degree, the algebraic immunity, and the fast algebraic immunity, and offer comparisons with other weightwise quadratic functions.

Proposition 11. *Let $n \geqslant 4$ be even, and let $f \in \mathcal{B}_n$ be the revisited HWBF. Then $\mathsf{deg}(f) = n - 1$.*

Proof. We write $f = q + h$, where $q \in \mathcal{B}_n$ is given by $q(x) = \sum_{i=1}^{n/2}(x_i + 1)x_{i+n/2}$ and $h \in \mathcal{B}_n$ is the HWBF. The function h has degree $n-1 \geqslant 3$ by Property 1, and the function q has no monomial of degree higher than 2, so $\mathsf{deg}(f) = \mathsf{deg}(h) = n - 1$. □

In Table 6, we display the algebraic degree of different weightwise quadratic functions. We observe that the revisited HWBF has the highest degree along with the original HWBF when n is not a power of 2. However, when n is a power of 2, the majority function has a degree that is one higher than that of the other two functions, as explained by Property 1 and Proposition 11.

Table 6. Comparison of the degree and algebraic immunity.

n	4	6	8	10	12	14	16
HWBF	3, 2	5, 3	7, 4	9, 4	11, 5	13, 5	15, 6
Majority	4, 2	4, 3	8, 4	8, 5	8, 6	8, 7	16, 8
t [38]	2, 2	5, 3	6, 4	9, 5	11, 5	13, 6	14, 7
u [38]	2, 2	4, 3	6, 4	8, 5	10, 6	12, 6	14, 7
Revisited HWBF	3, 2	5, 3	7, 4	9, 5	11, 6	13, 6	15, 7

Proposition 12. *Let $n \geqslant 4$ be even, let $f \in \mathcal{B}_n$ be the revisited HWBF, and let $h \in \mathcal{B}_n$ be the HWBF. Then $\mathsf{AI}(f) \geqslant \mathsf{AI}(h) - 2$.*

Proof. Let $q \in \mathcal{B}_n$ be given by $q(x) = \sum_{i=1}^{n/2}(x_i + 1)x_{i+n/2}$, so that $h = f + q$. Let $g \in \mathcal{B}_n^*$ with $\mathsf{deg}(g) = \mathsf{AI}(f)$ be an annihilator of $f + \varepsilon$ for some $\varepsilon \in \{0, 1\}$. Then the following holds:

$$\begin{aligned} g \cdot (q+1) \cdot (h+\varepsilon) &= g \cdot (q+1) \cdot (f+q+\varepsilon) \\ &= g \cdot (q+1) \cdot (f+\epsilon) + g \cdot (q+1) \cdot q \\ &= 0 + 0 \\ &= 0. \end{aligned}$$

Hence, $g \cdot (q + 1)$ is an annihilator of $h + \varepsilon$. If $g \cdot (q + 1) \neq 0$, it follows that $\mathsf{AI}(h) \leqslant \mathsf{deg}(g \cdot (q+1)) \leqslant \mathsf{deg}(g) + \mathsf{deg}(q+1)$, and therefore that $\mathsf{AI}(f) = \mathsf{deg}(g) \geqslant \mathsf{AI}(h) - \mathsf{deg}(q + 1) = \mathsf{AI}(h) - 2$. If $g \cdot (q + 1) = 0$, then $0 = g \cdot (f + \epsilon + q + 1) = g \cdot (h + \epsilon + 1)$, showing that $\mathsf{AI}(f) = \mathsf{deg}(g) \geqslant \mathsf{AI}(h)$. □

From Theorem 4 in [46], the algebraic immunity of the HWBF is at least $\lfloor n/3 \rfloor + 1$, which leads to $\lfloor n/3 \rfloor - 1$ for the revisited HWBF. In Table 6, we present the algebraic immunity of various weightwise quadratic functions. We observe that the revisited HWBF demonstrates the best performance after the majority function; the latter is known to achieve optimal algebraic immunity.

Lastly, we also considered the fast algebraic immunity of the revisited HWBF f. In Table 7, we give the best couples (d, e) encountered for the function f, where $\mathsf{deg}(g) = d$ and $\mathsf{deg}(h) = e$ for functions g and h satisfying $fg = h$.

These various results on the algebraic properties of the revisited HWBF suggest that it possesses strong resistance against standard attacks. Furthermore, its high nonlinearity makes it a well-suited candidate for use as a filter function in contexts such as filtered LFSRs or in homomorphically-friendly schemes like FLIP and FiLIP. For example, the best current FiLIP filters in HHE [1,20,39] are XOR-threshold functions—the sum of a k-variable linear function and an m-variable threshold function (generalizing majority). By Proposition 7 in [14], their nonlinearity is at most $2^{k+m-1} - 2^k \cdot M$, where $M = \binom{m-1}{\frac{m-1}{2}}$ if M is odd, and $M = (1/2) \cdot \binom{m}{\frac{m}{2}}$ if M is even. This is similar to the majority function, whereas the revisited HWBF achieves higher nonlinearity for the same size, offering better resistance to correlation-like attacks with fewer variables.

Table 7. Lowest possible values of (d, e) for different values of n.

n	4	6	8	10	12	14	16	18
(d, e)	$(1, 2)$	$(1, 3)$	$(1, 5)$	$(1, 7)$	$(1, 9)$	$(1, 11)$	$(1, 13)$	$(1, 15)$
			$(2, 4)$	$(2, 6)$	$(2, 8)$	$(2, 10)$	$(2, 12)$	$(2, 14)$
				$(3, 5)$	$(3, 6)$	$(3, 9)$	$(3, 11)$	$(3, 13)$
							$(4, 9)$	$(4, 11)$
								$(5, 10)$

7 Conclusion and Open Questions

In this work, we introduced the revisited Hidden Weight Bit Function, a weightwise quadratic Boolean function with improved cryptographic properties over existing constructions. We analyzed its balancedness, and using generating functions in combination with complex analysis, we derived interesting lower bounds on its nonlinearity, demonstrating that the revisited HWBF achieves superior nonlinearity compared to other functions with similar computational costs. We further examined other cryptographic parameters such as degree, algebraic immunity, and fast algebraic immunity, confirming that the revisited HWBF matches or outperforms comparable functions in these aspects.

Our approach utilizes generating functions and Cauchy's estimate to establish lower bounds on the nonlinearity of weightwise quadratic functions. This naturally raises the question: can the employed techniques, particularly the use of Cauchy's estimate, be extended to other families of Boolean functions? Specifically, this approach appears feasible for other weightwise-degree-d functions f where the f_k are direct sums. Investigating this could potentially lead to the discovery of new functions with comparable computational costs and even better cryptographic properties.

Acknowledgments. Pierrick Méaux was funded by the European Research Council (ERC) under the Advanced Grant program (reference number: 787390). Tim Seuré acknowledges the support of the Luxembourgish "Fonds National de la Recherche" (FNR) through an Individual Grant (reference number: 17936291). The work of Deng Tang was supported in part by the National Natural Science Foundation of China (NSFC, reference number: 62272303). We would also like to thank Claude Carlet for discussing the function introduced in this work with Deng Tang some years ago.

Disclosure of Interests. The authors have no competing interests to declare that are relevant to the content of this article.

A Proofs for Section 4.3

In this section, we provide the missing proofs for Sect. 4.3.

Proof of Proposition 9. By considering binary vectors $x \in \mathbb{F}_2^n$ as $x = (y, z)$ with $y \in \mathbb{F}_2^{2t}$ and $z \in \mathbb{F}_2^{n-2t}$, we get:

$$\begin{aligned}
\mathsf{D}_{t,k,n}(a) &= \sum_{x \in \mathsf{E}_{k,n}} (-1)^{d_{t,n}(x)+a\cdot x} \\
&= \sum_{(y,z)\in \mathsf{E}_{k,n}} (-1)^{d_{t,2t}(y)+b\cdot y + c\cdot z} \\
&= \sum_{\ell=0}^{2t} \sum_{\substack{y \in \mathsf{E}_{\ell,2t} \\ z \in \mathsf{E}_{k-\ell,n-2t}}} (-1)^{d_{t,2t}(y)+b\cdot y+c\cdot z} \\
&= \sum_{\ell=0}^{2t} \left(\sum_{y\in \mathsf{E}_{\ell,2t}} (-1)^{d_{2t}(y)+b\cdot y} \right) \left(\sum_{z \in \mathsf{E}_{k-\ell,n-2t}} (-1)^{c\cdot z} \right) \\
&= \sum_{\ell=0}^{2t} \mathsf{D}_{\ell,2t}(a) \cdot \mathsf{K}_{k-\ell}(\mathsf{w_H}(c), n-2t).
\end{aligned}$$

□

Proof of Proposition 10. Applying Proposition 9, we get:

$$\begin{aligned}\sum_{k\in\mathbb{Z}} \mathsf{D}_{t,k,n}(a)z^k &= \sum_{\ell=0}^{2t} \mathsf{D}_{\ell,2t}(a)z^\ell \sum_{k\in\mathbb{Z}} \mathsf{K}_{k-\ell}(\mathsf{w_H}(c), n-2t)z^{k-\ell} \\ &= \left(\sum_{\ell=0}^{2t} \mathsf{D}_{\ell,2t}(a)z^\ell\right) \cdot (1+z)^u \cdot (1-z)^v \\ &= P_b(z) \cdot (1+z)^u \cdot (1-z)^v \\ &= P_{t,a}(z).\end{aligned}$$

□

Lastly, we provide a proof for Theorem 3. We start with a preliminary result that will be required for the proof.

Lemma 1. *Let $N \geqslant 1$ be an integer and $D \subseteq \mathbb{C}$ a set of complex numbers. For every $i \in [1, N]$, consider integers $m_i \geqslant 0$ and $k_i \geqslant 1$, as well as complex functions $f_{i,1}, \ldots, f_{i,k_i} : D \to \mathbb{C}$. Assume that the following maximum exists (which holds for instance if the functions $f_{i,j}$ are continuous and D is topologically compact):*

$$M = \max_{\substack{\forall i\in[1,N]:\, p_{i,1}+\cdots+p_{i,k_i}=m_i \\ z\in D}} \left| \prod_{i=1}^{N} \prod_{j=1}^{k_i} f_{i,j}(z)^{p_{i,j}} \right|.$$

Then there exist integers $j_1, \ldots, j_N$ with $j_i \in [1, k_i]$ such that the following holds:

$$M = \max_{z\in D} \left| \prod_{i=1}^{N} f_{i,j_i}(z)^{m_i} \right|.$$

Proof. Let us choose the integers $p_{i,j} \geqslant 0$ satisfying $\sum_{j=1}^{k_i} p_{i,j} = m_i$ for every $i \in [1, N]$ together with the complex number $z \in D$ to maximize the quantity $\left|\prod_{i=1}^{N} \prod_{j=1}^{k_i} f_{i,j}(z)^{p_{i,j}}\right|$. Next, for every $i \in [1, N]$, choose $j_i \in [1, k_i]$ such that $|f_{i,j_i}(z)| \geqslant |f_{i,j}(z)|$ for every $j \in [1, k_i]$. Then we have:

$$\begin{aligned}M &= \left| \prod_{i=1}^{N} \prod_{j=1}^{k_i} f_{i,j}(z)^{p_{i,j}} \right| \\ &\leqslant \left| \prod_{i=1}^{N} \prod_{j=1}^{k_i} f_{i,j_i}(z)^{p_{i,j}} \right| \\ &= \left| \prod_{i=1}^{N} f_{i,j_i}(z)^{\sum_{j=1}^{k_i} p_{i,j}} \right| \\ &= \left| \prod_{i=1}^{N} f_{i,j_i}(z)^{m_i} \right| \\ &\leqslant M.\end{aligned}$$

□

Proof of Theorem 3. To begin, we observe that the inequality $|\mathcal{W}_{d_{t,n}}(a)| \leqslant 1 + n \cdot 2^{\mu n}$ will follow from the inequality $|\mathsf{D}_{t,k,n}(a)| \leqslant 2^{\mu n}$ using precisely the arguments of the proof of Corollary 2, so that we are only required to prove the first inequality. Also, since the case $\lambda = 1/2$ corresponds to Theorem 2, we will henceforth assume $\lambda < 1/2$.

Similarly to the proof of Theorem 2, we want to bound the maximum of $|P_{t,a}(z)|$ on $\mathsf{c}_1 = \{z \in \mathbb{C} : |z| = 1\}$ for $a \in \mathbb{F}_2^n$, and this will then be an upper bound on $|\mathsf{D}_{t,k,n}(a)|$ for every $k \in [0, n]$. We write $a = (b, c)$ with $b \in \mathbb{F}_2^{2t}$ and $c \in \mathbb{F}_2^{n-2t}$, and define $(p, q, r) = (p(b), q(b), r(b))$, and further consider $u = n - 2t - \mathsf{w_H}(c)$ and $v = \mathsf{w_H}(c)$ as in Definition 18. To find a bound for $|P_{t,a}(z)|$ on c_1 that applies to all $a \in \mathbb{F}_2^n$, we would like to bound the quantity $\max_{a \in \mathbb{F}_2^n, z \in \mathsf{c}_1} |P_{t,a}(z)|$. Moving through all $a \in \mathbb{F}_2^n$ is equivalent to moving through all tuples $(p, q, r; u, v)$ of non-negative integers which satisfy $p + q + r = t$ and $u + v = n - 2t$. It follows from Lemma 1 that it is enough to consider only the cases for which only one of p, q, r is non-zero, and for which only one of u, v is non-zero. This leaves us with the following cases to consider for $(p, q, r; u, v)$:

$$(t, 0, 0; n - 2t, 0), \quad (0, t, 0; n - 2t, 0), \quad (0, 0, t; n - 2t, 0),$$
$$(t, 0, 0; 0, n - 2t), \quad (0, t, 0; 0, n - 2t), \quad (0, 0, t; 0, n - 2t).$$

Since simultaneously replacing (p, q) by (q, p) and (u, v) by (v, u) has the same effect as replacing z by $-z$ in $P_{t,a}(z)$ and therefore does not change the maximum of $|P_{t,a}(z)|$ on c_1, we can restrict ourselves to the following tuples for $(p, q, r; u, v)$:

$$(t, 0, 0; n - 2t, 0), \quad (0, t, 0; n - 2t, 0), \quad (0, 0, t; n - 2t, 0).$$

Let us start by bounding $|P_{t,a}(z)|$ on c_1 in the case $(p, q, r; u, v) = (t, 0, 0; n - 2t, 0)$. Since $t = \lambda n$, we can write:

$$P_{t,a}(z) = \left((-z^2 + 2z + 1)^{\lambda}(1 + z)^{1-2\lambda}\right)^n.$$

Writing $z = \mathrm{e}^{\mathrm{i}\alpha}$ and $z^2 = \mathrm{e}^{2\mathrm{i}\alpha}$ for $\alpha \in [-\pi, \pi]$, and using that $|w|^2 = w\overline{w}$ for every complex number w, we get:

$$|-z^2 + 2z + 1|^2 = \left(-\mathrm{e}^{2\mathrm{i}\alpha} + 2\mathrm{e}^{\mathrm{i}\alpha} + 1\right)\left(-\mathrm{e}^{-2\mathrm{i}\alpha} + 2\mathrm{e}^{-\mathrm{i}\alpha} + 1\right).$$

Expanding yields $|-z^2 + 2z + 1|^2 = 6 - \mathrm{e}^{2\mathrm{i}\alpha} - \mathrm{e}^{-2\mathrm{i}\alpha} = 6 - 2\cos(2\alpha)$ because $\mathrm{e}^{2\mathrm{i}\alpha} = \cos(2\alpha) + \mathrm{i}\sin(2\alpha)$. We similarly obtain that $|1 + z|^2 = 2 + 2\cos\alpha$. Combining both, we get:

$$\begin{aligned} P_{t,a}(z)|^2 &= \left(\left|-z^2 + 2z + 1\right|^{2\lambda} |1 + z|^{2(1-2\lambda)}\right)^n \\ &= \left((6 - 2\cos(2\alpha))^{\lambda}(2 + 2\cos\alpha)^{1-2\lambda}\right)^n. \end{aligned}$$

The goal will be to prove that the maximum of the function $g(\alpha) = g^{(\lambda)}(\alpha) = (6 - 2\cos(2\alpha))^{\lambda}(2 + 2\cos\alpha)^{1-2\lambda}$ for $\alpha \in [-\pi, \pi]$ is equal to $2^{2\mu}$; the maximum of $|P_{t,a}(z)|$ on c_1 will then be $\left(2^{2\mu}\right)^{n/2} = 2^{\mu n}$. Note that g is an even function,

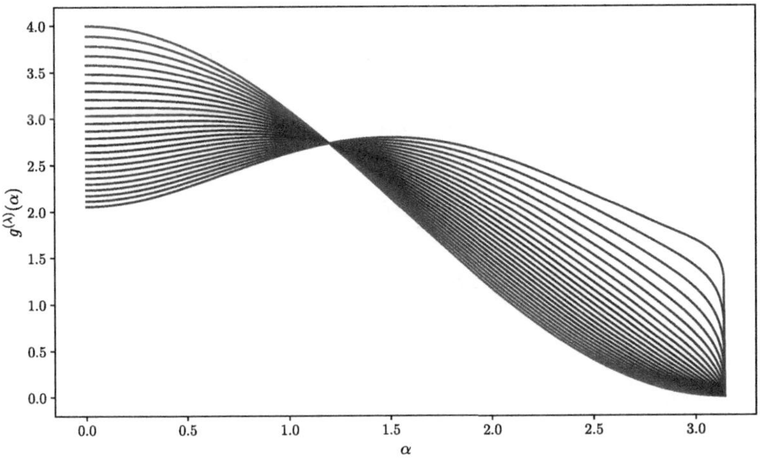

Fig. 3. The curves of $\alpha \mapsto g^{(\lambda)}(\alpha)$ for the values $\lambda = \frac{i}{50}$ from $i = 0$ (the curve with the highest value at $\alpha = 0$) to $i = 24$ (the curve with the lowest value at $\alpha = 0$).

so it is enough to focus on the interval $\alpha \in [0, \pi]$; the function g is represented for several values of $0 \leqslant \lambda < 1/2$ in Fig. 3.

Writing $g(\alpha) = g_1(\alpha)^\lambda g_2(\alpha)^{1-2\lambda}$ for $g_1(\alpha) = 6 - 2\cos(2\alpha)$ and $g_2(\alpha) = 2 + 2\cos\alpha$, we compute the first derivative of g, and apply the double angle formulas $\cos(2\alpha) = 2\cos^2\alpha - 1$ and $\sin(2\alpha) = 2\cos\alpha\sin\alpha$:

$$\begin{aligned}
\frac{\mathrm{d}}{\mathrm{d}\alpha} g(\alpha) &= g_1(\alpha)^{\lambda-1} g_2(\alpha)^{-2\lambda} \left(\lambda g_2(\alpha) \frac{\mathrm{d}}{\mathrm{d}\alpha} g_1(\alpha) + (1-2\lambda) g_1(\alpha) \frac{\mathrm{d}}{\mathrm{d}\alpha} g_2(\alpha)\right) \\
&= g_1(\alpha)^{\lambda-1} g_2(\alpha)^{-2\lambda} (\lambda(2 + 2\cos\alpha) \cdot 4\sin(2\alpha) \\
&\qquad + (1-2\lambda)(6 - 2\cos(2\alpha))(-2\sin\alpha)) \\
&= g_1(\alpha)^{\lambda-1} g_2(\alpha)^{-2\lambda} (\lambda(2 + 2\cos\alpha) \cdot 4 \cdot 2\cos\alpha\sin\alpha \\
&\qquad + (1-2\lambda)\left(8 - 4\cos^2\alpha\right)(-2\sin\alpha)) \\
&= 8 g_1(\alpha)^{\lambda-1} g_2(\alpha)^{-2\lambda} \sin\alpha \big(2\lambda\cos\alpha(1 + \cos\alpha) \\
&\qquad - (1-2\lambda)\left(2 - \cos^2\alpha\right)\big) \\
&= 8 g_1(\alpha)^{\lambda-1} g_2(\alpha)^{-2\lambda} \sin\alpha \left(\cos^2\alpha + 2\lambda\cos\alpha + 4\lambda - 2\right).
\end{aligned}$$

The only interesting zeros of $\frac{\mathrm{d}}{\mathrm{d}\alpha} g(\alpha)$ are those of the last factor $\cos^2\alpha + 2\lambda\cos\alpha + 4\lambda - 2$: the factor $8g_1(\alpha)^{\lambda-1} g_2(\alpha)^{-2\lambda}$ has none, and those for $\sin\alpha$ are $\alpha = 0$ and $\alpha = \pi$, with corresponding values $g(0) = 2^{2-2\lambda}$ and $g(\pi) = 0$.

Our first claim is that the equation $\mathcal{E} : \cos^2\alpha + 2\lambda\cos\alpha + 4\lambda - 2 = 0$ has a unique solution $\cos\alpha = -\lambda + \sqrt{\lambda^2 - 4\lambda + 2}$ if $\lambda \geqslant 1/6$ and has no solution $\cos\alpha$ otherwise. To see this, we consider $\mathcal{E}$ as an equation of second degree in $\cos\alpha$, which leads to the two solution candidates $\cos\alpha = -\lambda \pm \sqrt{\lambda^2 - 4\lambda + 2}$.

We can exclude the solution $\cos\alpha = -\lambda - \sqrt{\lambda^2 - 4\lambda + 2}$ since $\cos\alpha \in [-1, 1]$ and $\lambda \in [0, 1/2)$. The other solution needs to be excluded for the same reason if $\lambda < 1/6$.

Our second claim is that $\frac{\mathrm{d}^2}{\mathrm{d}^2\alpha} g(\alpha)|_{\alpha=0}$ has the same sign as $6\lambda - 1$. To see why, we apply the definition of the second derivative:

$$\begin{aligned}\frac{\mathrm{d}^2}{\mathrm{d}^2\alpha} g(\alpha)|_{\alpha=0} &= \lim_{\alpha\to 0} \frac{\frac{\mathrm{d}}{\mathrm{d}\alpha} g(\alpha)}{\alpha} \\ &= \lim_{\alpha\to 0} 8(6 - 2\cos(2\alpha))^{\lambda-1}(2 + 2\cos\alpha)^{-2\lambda} \\ &\quad \cdot \frac{\sin\alpha}{\alpha} \cdot \left(\cos^2\alpha + 2\lambda\cos\alpha + 4\lambda - 2\right) \\ &= 8 \cdot 4^{\lambda-1} \cdot 4^{-2\lambda} \cdot 1 \cdot (6\lambda - 1) \\ &= 2^{1-2\lambda}(6\lambda - 1).\end{aligned}$$

Therefore, in case $\lambda < 1/6$, we can conclude from the two claims that $g(\alpha)$ reaches its maximum at $\alpha_0 = 0$, and this maximum is then equal to $2^{2-2\lambda} = 2^{2\mu}$, as required. For $\lambda = 1/6$, the solution to the equation $\mathcal{E}$ is $\cos\alpha = 1$, again implying that $g(\alpha)$ reaches its maximum at $\alpha_0 = 0$, and we obtain the same maximum of $2^{2\mu}$. In case $\lambda > 1/6$, the two claims imply that $g(\alpha)$ reaches its maximum at the unique $\alpha_0 \in [0, \pi]$ for which $\cos\alpha_0 = -\lambda + \sqrt{\lambda^2 - 4\lambda + 2}$. For this α_0, the double angle formula for the cosine implies that $\cos(2\alpha_0) = 4\lambda^2 - 8\lambda + 3 - 4\lambda\sqrt{\lambda^2 - 4\lambda + 2}$. If we replace $\cos\alpha_0$ and $\cos(2\alpha_0)$ by their respective values, we obtain that the maximum of $g(\alpha)$ for $\alpha \in [0, \pi]$ is given by the following value:

$$g(\alpha_0) = \frac{\left(-8\lambda^2 + 16\lambda + 8\lambda\sqrt{\lambda^2 - 4\lambda + 2}\right)^{\lambda}}{\left(2 - 2\lambda + 2\sqrt{\lambda^2 - 4\lambda + 2}\right)^{2\lambda-1}} = 2^{2\mu}.$$

With this, we have covered the case $(p, q, r; u, v) = (t, 0, 0; n - 2t, 0)$ entirely. Similarly, it can be proven that $|P_{t,a}(z)|$ is also bounded by $2^{\mu n}$ on c_1 for the remaining two cases of $(p, q, r; u, v)$. For $(p, q, r; u, v) = (0, t, 0; n - 2t, 0)$, one can proceed in exactly the same way, and for $(p, q, r; u, v) = (0, 0, t; n - 2t, 0)$, it is enough to replace $g(\alpha)$ by $h(\alpha) = (2 + 2\cos(2\alpha))^{\lambda}(2 + 2\cos\alpha)^{1-2\lambda}$, whose maximum is bounded by the maximum of $g(\alpha)$ since $0 \leqslant h(\alpha) \leqslant g(\alpha)$. □

References

1. Aranha, D.F., Guimarães, A., Hoffmann, C., Méaux, P.: Secure and Efficient Transciphering for FHE-Based MPC. IACR Cryptology ePrint Archive (2024)
2. Armknecht, F.: Improving fast algebraic attacks. In: Fast Software Encryption, Springer, Heidelberg (2004)
3. Armknecht, F., Carlet, C., Gaborit, P., Künzli, S., Meier, W., Ruatta, O.: Efficient computation of algebraic immunity for algebraic and fast algebraic attacks. In: Advances in Cryptology, EUROCRYPT 2006. Springer, Heidelberg (2006)
4. Beierle, C., Leander, G.: 4-uniform permutations with null nonlinearity. Crypt. Commun. **12** (2020)

5. Bollig, B., Löbbing, M., Sauerhoff, M., Wegener, I.: On the complexity of the hidden weighted bit function for various BDD models. RAIRO Theoret. Inf. Appl. **33**(2) (1999)
6. Braeken, A., Preneel, B.: On the Algebraic Immunity of Symmetric Boolean Functions. In: Progress in Cryptology, INDOCRYPT 2005. Springer, Heidelberg (2005)
7. Bryant, R.E.: On the complexity of VLSI implementations and graph representations of Boolean functions with application to integer multiplication. IEEE Trans. Comput. **40**(2) (1991)
8. Budaghyan, L., Carlet, C., Helleseth, T.: On Bent functions associated to AB functions. In: IEEE Information Theory Workshop 2011. IEEE (2011)
9. Canteaut, A., et al.: Stream ciphers: a practical solution for efficient homomorphic-ciphertext compression. J. Cryptol. **31**(3), 885–916 (2018). https://doi.org/10.1007/s00145-017-9273-9
10. Canteaut, A., Videau, M.: Symmetric Boolean functions. IEEE Trans. Inf. Theor. (2005)
11. Carlet, C.: On the degree, nonlinearity, algebraic thickness, and nonnormality of Boolean functions, with developments on symmetric functions. IEEE Trans. Inf. Theor. (2004)
12. Carlet, C.: Boolean Functions for Cryptography and Coding Theory. Cambridge University Press (2021)
13. Carlet, C.: A wide class of Boolean functions generalizing the hidden weight bit function. IEEE Trans. Inf. Theor. **68**(2) (2022)
14. Carlet, C., Méaux, P.: A complete study of two classes of boolean functions: direct sums of monomials and threshold functions. IEEE Trans. Inf. Theor. (2021)
15. Carlet, C., Méaux, P., Rotella, Y.: Boolean functions with restricted input and their robustness; application to the FLIP cipher. IACR Trans. Symmetric Cryptol. **2017** (2017)
16. Carlet, C., Sarkar, P.: Constructions of efficiently implementable Boolean functions possessing high nonlinearity and good resistance to algebraic attacks. IACR Cryptology ePrint Archive (2024)
17. Carlet, C., Tang, D.: Enhanced Boolean functions suitable for the filter model of pseudo-random generator. Des. Codes Crypt. **76**(3) (2015)
18. Chen, Y., Lu, P.: Two classes of symmetric Boolean functions with optimum algebraic immunity: construction and analysis. IEEE Trans. Inf. Theor. **57** (2011)
19. Cid, C., Indrøy, J.P., Raddum, H.: FASTA – a stream cipher for fast FHE evaluation. In: Topics in Cryptology, CT-RSA 2022. Springer, Heidelberg (2022)
20. Cong, K., Das, D., Park, J., Pereira, H.V.L.: SortingHat: efficient private decision tree evaluation via homomorphic encryption and transciphering. In: Proceedings of the 2022 ACM SIGSAC Conference on Computer and Communications Security. ACM (2022)
21. Courtois, N.T.: Fast algebraic attacks on stream ciphers with linear feedback. In: Advances in Cryptology, CRYPTO 2003. Springer, Heidelberg (2003)
22. Courtois, N.T., Meier, W.: Algebraic attacks on stream ciphers with linear feedback. In: Biham, E. (ed.) EUROCRYPT 2003. LNCS, vol. 2656, pp. 345–359. Springer, Heidelberg (2003). https://doi.org/10.1007/3-540-39200-9_21
23. Dalai, D.K., Maitra, S., Sarkar, S.: Basic theory in construction of Boolean functions with maximum possible annihilator immunity. Des. Codes Crypt. (2006)
24. Dobbertin, H.: Construction of Bent functions and balanced Boolean functions with high nonlinearity. In: Fast Software Encryption. Springer, Heidelberg (1995)

25. Dobraunig, C., et al.: Rasta: a cipher with low ANDdepth and few ANDs per bit. In: Shacham, H., Boldyreva, A. (eds.) CRYPTO 2018. LNCS, vol. 10991, pp. 662–692. Springer, Cham (2018). https://doi.org/10.1007/978-3-319-96884-1_22
26. Gini, A., Méaux, P.: On the weightwise nonlinearity of weightwise perfectly balanced functions. Discrete Appl. Math. **322** (2022)
27. Hawkes, P., Rose, G.G.: Rewriting variables: the complexity of fast algebraic attacks on stream ciphers. In: Franklin, M. (ed.) CRYPTO 2004. LNCS, vol. 3152, pp. 390–406. Springer, Heidelberg (2004). https://doi.org/10.1007/978-3-540-28628-8_24
28. Hoffmann, C., Méaux, P., Ricosset, T.: Transciphering, using FiLIP and TFHE for an efficient delegation of computation. In: Bhargavan, K., Oswald, E., Prabhakaran, M. (eds.) INDOCRYPT 2020. LNCS, vol. 12578, pp. 39–61. Springer, Cham (2020). https://doi.org/10.1007/978-3-030-65277-7_3
29. Jiao, L., Zhang, B., Wang, M.: Establishing equations: the complexity of algebraic and fast algebraic attacks revisited. In: Information Security. Springer, Heidelberg (2013)
30. Liu, M., Lin, D., Pei, D.: Fast algebraic attacks and decomposition of symmetric Boolean functions. IEEE Trans. Inf. Ther. **57**(7) (2011)
31. MacWilliams, F.J., Sloane, N.J.A.: The Theory of Error-Correcting Codes. North-Holland Publishing Company (1978)
32. Meier, W., Pasalic, E., Carlet, C.: Algebraic attacks and decomposition of Boolean functions. In: Advances in Cryptology, EUROCRYPT 2004. Springer, Heidelberg (2004)
33. Mesnager, S.: Bent Functions. Springer, Heidelberg (2016)
34. Méaux, P.: On the fast algebraic immunity of majority functions. In: Schwabe, P., Thériault, N. (eds.) LATINCRYPT 2019. LNCS, vol. 11774, pp. 86–105. Springer, Cham (2019). https://doi.org/10.1007/978-3-030-30530-7_5
35. Méaux, P.: On the fast algebraic immunity of threshold functions. Crypt. Commun. **13** (2021)
36. Méaux, P., Carlet, C., Journault, A., Standaert, F.-X.: Improved filter permutators for efficient FHE: better instances and implementations. In: Hao, F., Ruj, S., Sen Gupta, S. (eds.) INDOCRYPT 2019. LNCS, vol. 11898, pp. 68–91. Springer, Cham (2019). https://doi.org/10.1007/978-3-030-35423-7_4
37. Méaux, P., Journault, A., Standaert, F.-X., Carlet, C.: Towards stream ciphers for efficient FHE with low-noise ciphertexts. In: Fischlin, M., Coron, J.-S. (eds.) EUROCRYPT 2016. LNCS, vol. 9665, pp. 311–343. Springer, Heidelberg (2016). https://doi.org/10.1007/978-3-662-49890-3_13
38. Méaux, P., Ozaim, Y.: On the cryptographic properties of weightwise affine and weightwise quadratic functions. Discrete Appl. Math. **355** (2024)
39. Méaux, P., Park, J., Pereira, H.V.L.: Towards practical transciphering for FHE with setup independent of the plaintext space. IACR Commun. Cryptol. **1**(1) (2024)
40. Naehrig, M., Lauter, K.E., Vaikuntanathan, V.: Can homomorphic encryption be practical? In: Proceedings of the 3rd ACM Cloud Computing Security Workshop, CCSW 2011. ACM (2011)
41. Qu, L., Feng, K., Liu, F., Wang, L.: Constructing symmetric boolean functions with maximum algebraic immunity. IEEE Trans. Inf. Theor. (2009)
42. Rothaus, O.S.: On "Bent" functions. J. Comb. Theor. Ser. A **20** (1976)
43. Rudin, W.: Real and Complex Analysis. McGraw-Hill Book Company (1987)
44. Sarkar, P., Maitra, S.: Balancedness and correlation immunity of symmetric Boolean functions. Discrete Math. (2007)

45. Tokareva, N.: Bent Functions: Results and Applications to Cryptography. Academic Press (2015)
46. Wang, Q., Carlet, C., Stanica, P., Tan, C.H.: Cryptographic properties of the hidden weighted bit function. Discrete Appl. Math. **174** (2014)

Bit Security of Quantum Key Search

Marc Fischlin and Evangelos Gkoumas(✉)

Cryptoplexity, Technische Universität Darmstadt, Darmstadt, Germany
{marc.fischlin,evangelos.gkoumas}@tu-darmstadt.de

Abstract. A common presumption in cryptography is that quantum key search effectively halves the level of bit security compared to the classical setting, leading, for example, to the recommendation to use AES with 256-bit keys instead of 128-bit keys. From a very coarse point of view, this is perspicuous by the speed-up obtained via Grover's search algorithm. On closer inspection, however, it lacks a formal justification, especially if the AES key is not perfectly random but only statistically close to uniform if generated by a quantum key distribution scheme. In other words, the question is how the statistical distance influences the quantum key search, or, viewed from an implementation point of view, how one should choose the statistical distance to achieve the best security bounds.

Our starting points are the recent works about bit security of Micciancio and Walter (Eurocrypt 2018), Watanabe and Yasunaga (Asiacrypt 2021), and Lee (Communication in Cryptology 2024) in the classical setting. We transfer them to the quantum setting and discuss the security against quantum key search if the keys are close to uniform. We then argue that to achieve an optimal bit security level of $\lambda/2$ bits for λ-bit keys against quantum search, it is advisable to set the statistical distance of the keys from uniform to a value in the range from $2^{-\lambda}$ to $2^{-\lambda/2}$. Going below these bounds does not yield any advantage for the bit security, and going above this range gives worse bit security guarantees.

Keywords: Bit Security · Quantum Key Search · Hellinger distance

1 Introduction

An easy way to compare the strength of cryptographic primitives like block ciphers, hash functions, or even public-key schemes is via the *bit security* of the primitives. For example, a hash function like SHA-256 is attributed a security level of $\lambda' = 128$, and thus in the same realm as 256-bit elliptic curves. This is based on the observation that the currently best attack on SHA-256 via the general birthday collision search requires approximately $O(2^{\lambda/2})$ steps for $\lambda = 256$. Similarly, for λ-bit elliptic curves, Pollard's rho method also needs $O(2^{\lambda/2})$ steps. Hence, for a hash-and-sign signature scheme of security level $\lambda' = 128$, one could deploy SHA-256 with a 256-bit curve (albeit one would need to take the security loss due to the combination in the signature protocol into account). The

C. Boura et al. (Eds.): SAC 2025, LNCS 16207, pp. 264–290, 2026.
https://doi.org/10.1007/978-3-032-10536-3_10

bit security levels of cryptographic primitives and their comparison have thus also entered recommendations for cryptographic primitives for security agencies [2,6].

1.1 Defining Bit Security

Lenstra [17] informally defined a cryptographic system to offer λ'-bit security if any attacker is expected to require the effort of at least $2^{\lambda'}$ to break the system. A more rigorous and common approach is to measure bit security by the logarithm of time divided by the success probability, $\log T/\epsilon$, and taking the minimum over all adversaries. More specifically, in the setting of search problems, a scheme has bit security λ' if no adversary can exceed a success probability of ϵ in less than $\epsilon \cdot 2^{\lambda'}$ steps for any ϵ.

Recently, there were several proposals how to capture bit security more formally and more broadly. Micciancio and Walter [20] proposed definitions for search and decision games based on entropy notions. Bit security in this case is defined as

$$\min_{\mathcal{A}} \log\left(T_{\mathcal{A}}/\mathsf{adv}(\mathcal{A})\right),$$

where $\mathsf{adv}(\mathcal{A})$ is the adversary's advantage in term of entropy. Building on this, Watanabe and Yasunaga [34] presented a new framework for defining bit security, focusing on demonstrating the advantage of the adversary. This demonstrates the advantage measures how often an outer adversary $\mathcal{B}$ needs to invoke an inner adversary $\mathcal{A}$ (with some success probability $\epsilon_{\mathcal{A}}$) to find a correct answer with overwhelming probability. The bit security for search problems is then defined as

$$\min_{\mathcal{A},\mathcal{B}} \log\left(N_{\mathcal{B}} \cdot T_{\mathcal{A}}\right),$$

where $N_{\mathcal{B}}$ is the number of invocations of $\mathcal{A}$. Note that the success probability $\epsilon_{\mathcal{A}}$ is implicit in $N_{\mathcal{B}}$: For any $\epsilon_{\mathcal{A}}$ one usually requires $N_{\mathcal{B}} = 1/\epsilon_{\mathcal{A}}$ many runs of adversary $\mathcal{A}$ to find a solution. The approaches were shown to be equivalent [19].

More recently, Lee [16] conducted a comparative analysis of the frameworks proposed by Micciancio and Walter [20] and by Watanabe and Yasunaga [34]. Lee gave a more comprehensive framework for capturing search and decision games simultaneously, with the help of a so-called dummy adversary $\mathcal{A}^{\text{dummy}}$, which defines a baseline probability. The dummy adversary can be considered the best non-adaptive strategy to win the game in the same time as the adversary $\mathcal{A}$. As in [34], Lee then defines bit security via an observational advantage of an adversary $\mathcal{B}$, amplifying the distinguishing probability between the adversary $\mathcal{A}$ and the dummy adversary $\mathcal{A}^{\text{dummy}}$ of the same complexity $T_{\mathcal{A}}$ as $\mathcal{A}$. This also results in the definition of the bit security level of $\min_{\mathcal{A},\mathcal{B}} \log(N_{\mathcal{B}} \cdot T_{\mathcal{A}})$, but the definition is now independent of the structure of the security game.

Both the work of Watanabe and Yasunaga [34] and of Lee [16], referring to an earlier work by Yasunaga [11,35], also pointed out the importance of the Hellinger distance in determining the observational advantage. Namely, the number $N_{\mathcal{B}}$ of invocations of the adversary $\mathcal{A}$ is roughly in the order of the square of the Hellinger distance (between the probability of $\mathcal{A}$ winning and the probability of the dummy adversary $\mathcal{A}^{\text{dummy}}$ winning), such that bit security can be well approximated by

$$\min_{\mathcal{A}} \log\left(\frac{T_{\mathcal{A}}}{d_{\text{Hell}}(\Pr^{\mathsf{G}}_{\mathcal{A}}, \Pr^{\mathsf{G}}_{\mathcal{A}^{\text{dummy}}})^2}\right).$$

1.2 From Statistical Distance to Bit Security

We are interested in the following question:

> *Suppose that one aims to derive an AES key of* 256 *bits to protect against a key search of a quantum adversary. The key generation is not perfectly uniform but has a slight statistical distance from the uniform distribution. What is the reasonable range for this statistical distance?*

The question appears naturally when the key is derived via quantum key distribution. In this case, privacy amplification as the final step of the protocol is usually implemented via randomness extractors [12,38], generating secret keys that are statistically close to uniform keys. Making the statistical distance arbitrarily small is inefficient because the smaller the distance, the more bits have to be truncated. Specifically, for a statistical distance Δ, one must roughly sacrifice $2 \log 1/\Delta$ bits [12].

The problem also appears in any modern hybrid key exchange setting combining classical and quantum-safe keys. Any protocol like TLS 1.3 [27] is based on Krawczyk's extract-and-expand paradigm [14], implemented either via HKDF [15] or some AES-based function [7]. The quality of the extraction steps in terms of statistical distance from uniform depends on properties of the underlying cryptographic primitive [9,10]. This is also true for multi-input key derivation functions, such as the hybrid version of TLS 1.3 [28].

We note that in the classical setting, with the interpretation of bit security λ' that no adversary can exceed a success probability of ϵ in less than $\epsilon \cdot 2^{\lambda'}$ steps for any ϵ, one can easily compute an upper bound on the bit security in terms of the statistical distance. For this, consider an adversary $\mathcal{A}$ testing at most $T_{\mathcal{A}}$ potential key values of λ bits. The best strategy of $\mathcal{A}$ is to sort the keys in decreasing likelihood, i.e., testing the most likely keys first, where we assume that determining the order is for free. The situation is depicted in Fig. 1.

Then we can upper bound the success probability of the adversary $\mathcal{A}$ when testing the most likely $T_{\mathcal{A}}$ keys first by

$$\epsilon \leq T_{\mathcal{A}} \cdot 2^{-\lambda} + \Delta,$$

where Δ is the statistical distance of the key distribution from uniform (the shaded area in Fig. 1). The reason is that the probability of finding the right value for a uniform key would be $T_{\mathcal{A}} \cdot 2^{-\lambda}$, also taking into account the increased probability via the statistical distance in the first steps. Using

$$T_{\mathcal{A}} \cdot 2^{-\lambda} + \Delta \leq T_{\mathcal{A}} \cdot (2^{-\lambda} + 2^{-\log 1/\Delta}) \leq T_{\mathcal{A}} \cdot 2^{\max\{-\lambda, -\log 1/\Delta\}+1},$$

we hence get a bit security of $\lambda' = \min\{\lambda, \log 1/\Delta\} - 1$. This bound is quasi-tight since, in general, the statistical distance may concentrate on a single key only, such that an adversary outputting this key would succeed with probability $2^{-\lambda} + \Delta \geq 2 \cdot \min\{2^{-\lambda}, 2^{-\log 1/\Delta}\}$ with a single guess.

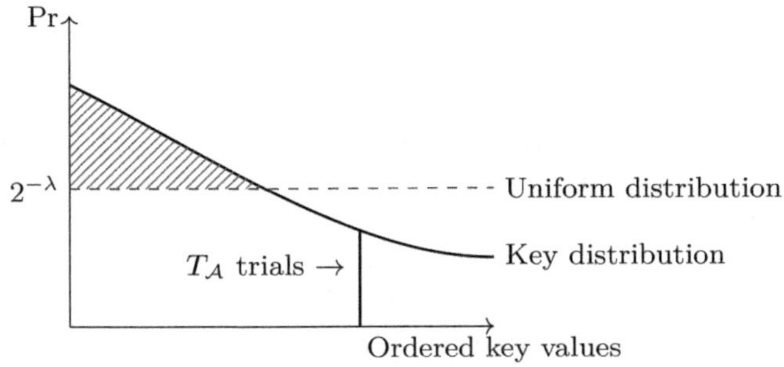

Fig. 1. Optimal search strategy in the classical setting (neglecting ordering effort): Check the most probable keys first.

Setting the statistical distance to $\Delta \leq 2^{-\lambda}$ maximizes the above bound $\min\{\lambda, \log 1/\Delta\} - 1$ for bit security, meaning that the classical setting with the straightforward interpretation of bit security suggests using a statistical distance close to $2^{-\lambda}$. However, it is unclear if this is also true in the quantum setting. For one, the approach here uses a simple approach to define bit security. Then, when a quantum adversary searches for a key, we cannot easily argue about the optimal strategy to order keys in sequential order.

We note that Micciancio and Walter [20] as well as Yasunaga [35] already discuss the relationship of closeness of distributions and bit security for classical games. As mentioned by Yasunaga [35], if the statistical distance of two distributions is $2^{-\lambda}$, e.g., the distance of a uniform key vs. an almost uniform key as in our setting, then the game preserves λ-bit security (up to additive terms). Micciancio and Walter [20] showed that this also holds if the max-log distance of the distributions is at most $2^{-\lambda/2}$, and Yasunaga [35] extended this to a difference in the Hellinger distance of $2^{-\lambda/2}$. He also proves, by presenting a specific game, that this generally does not hold if the distributions have a statistical distance of $2^{-\lambda/2}$. In contrast, we investigate here quantum key search games and the precise effect of the more common notion of statistical distance on the actual bit security for this game.

1.3 Our Results

We start with the bit security notion of Lee [16] according to observational advantages. This model is independent of the game's structure (but not the run time of the adversary and the dummy adversary). Yet, the structural simplicity allows us to transfer the setting to the case of quantum adversaries. We model, for example, the interaction of the adversary with the challenger in the game as a joint quantum computation, such that the dummy adversary, implementing the best non-adaptive strategy, will only act in the first stage of the interaction. We note that the observational distinguisher $\mathcal{B}$, receiving information about the effectiveness of the quantum or dummy adversary, will remain classical. Its task is to distinguish two worlds and amplify the advantage; quantum power is only used to search for the key.

We then define a quantum key search game in which we randomly select a secret key and allow the adversary to test candidates. This corresponds to a black-box search on, say, an AES key space $\{0,1\}^\lambda$ for $\lambda = 256$ where the adversary can trial decrypt a given ciphertext and verify its guess. The distribution of keys will not be perfectly random but instead have a statistical distance Δ from the uniform distribution. Using an upper bound for quantum searches for skewed input distributions by Montanaro [22], in a version by He et al. [13], we present an upper bound on the adversary's success probability in terms of its run time $T_{\mathcal{A}}$ in our setting. This bound is roughly $T_{\mathcal{A}}^2 \cdot 2^{-\lambda} + \Delta$ for any quantum adversary with run time $T_{\mathcal{A}}$.

It turns out that the optimal strategy of the dummy adversary in our setting is to guess the most likely key and win with probability at most $2^{-\lambda} + \Delta$, independently of its run time. We can then use the two probabilities, the one for $\mathcal{A}$ and the one for $\mathcal{A}^{\text{dummy}}$, to compute the Hellinger distance and use it to estimate the post-quantum bit security of the key search game. In doing so, we derive the following results:

1. Statistical distance smaller than $2^{-\lambda}$ will not yield an improved security level. This is shown by upper and lower bounds for the bit security of key search, which match up to additive terms.
2. Statistical distances in the range $2^{-\lambda}$ and $2^{-\lambda/2}$ yield the optimal bound of bit security $\lambda' = \lambda/2$, again shown via corresponding upper and lower bounds. Here, $2^{-\lambda}$ is the conservative choice, giving tight bounds also in cases where, for instance, quantum adversaries cannot rely on arbitrary run times but are bounded in computing power.
3. Statistical distance larger than $2^{-\lambda/2}$ give worse security guarantees than $\lambda' = \lambda/2$.

These conclusions match common intuition but now rely on a proper formal foundation. We present the technical statements in Sect. 4 and discuss their meaning in Sect. 5.

We also discuss in Sect. 6 our findings in light of quantum key distributions and suggestions for parameter choices in this area. Specifically, there appears to be a general tendency in the literature [5,18,21,23–26,30,31] to choose the security parameter ε close to $10^{-10} \approx 2^{-33}$, where ε can be roughly viewed as our value for statistical distance.[1] However, this choice of $\varepsilon = 10^{-10}$ is not well

[1] The situation is more complex than outlined here, partly because it is common to capture both correctness and security with this single parameter ε, where the correctness error could be the dominating part. See Sect. 6 for details.

motivated from our viewpoint. In fact, our results indicate that if the quantum key distribution should be used to generate 256-bit AES keys, then setting $\varepsilon = 10^{-10}$ may be too optimistic.

2 Preliminaries

2.1 Notation

We consider a classical adversary $\mathcal{A}$ that interacts in a game with a challenger X. All parties in a game receive the security parameter $\lambda \in \mathbb{N}$ in unary as input. The symbols win or lose, eventually output by the challenger, indicate if the adversary has won or lost the game. When considering quantum parties, we usually use a subscript Q and write $\mathcal{A}_Q$ and X_Q. We denote by $T_{\mathcal{A}_Q}$ the run time of adversary $\mathcal{A}_Q$. The run time usually depends on the security parameter λ. When calling a quantum oracle O, it is understood that we use the common approach to make it a unitary operation by considering the map $|x\rangle|y\rangle \mapsto |x\rangle|y \oplus \mathsf{O}(x)\rangle$, where $x \in \{0,1\}^n$ and $y \in \{0,1\}^m$.

Calligraphic letters like $\mathcal{P}$ or $\mathcal{Q}$ usually represent probability distributions or sets. For a distribution $\mathcal{P}$ we write $\mathcal{P}(x)$ for the probability that the distribution outputs x. The notation $x \leftarrow\!\$\ \mathbf{S}$ means that x is chosen uniformly from a finite set $\mathbf{S}$. The key space is denoted as $\mathcal{K}$ such that sampling a random key is denoted as $\mathsf{k} \leftarrow\!\$\ \mathcal{K}$. Unless mentioned differently, all logarithms log are to base 2.

2.2 Probability Metrics

This section goes over the primary definitions and properties of the two metrics used to formulate our concepts: *total variation distance* and *Hellinger distance.*

Definition 1 (Statistical/Total Variation distance). *The total variation (aka. statistical) distance between two discrete distributions $\mathcal{P}$ and $\mathcal{Q}$ on the same domain Ω is defined as*

$$\Delta(\mathcal{P}, \mathcal{Q}) = \frac{1}{2} \sum_{x \in \Omega} \mid \mathcal{P}(x) - \mathcal{Q}(x) \mid .$$

The Hellinger distance is frequently used in information theory to measure the closeness between distributions. It is the probabilistic equivalent of the Euclidean distance. It has turned out to be an important notion in cryptography [8,11,16,29,34,35].

Definition 2 (Hellinger distance). *The Hellinger distance d_{Hell} between two discrete distributions $\mathcal{P}$ and $\mathcal{Q}$ on the same domain $\boldsymbol{\Omega}$ is defined as*

$$d_{Hell}(\mathcal{P}, \mathcal{Q}) = \frac{1}{\sqrt{2}} \sqrt{\sum_{x \in \Omega} (\sqrt{\mathcal{P}(x)} - \sqrt{\mathcal{Q}(x)})^2}.$$

A different formulation associates the Hellinger distance with the Bhattacharyya coefficient (BC):

$$d_{\text{Hell}}(\mathcal{P}, \mathcal{Q}) = \sqrt{1 - \text{BC}(\mathcal{P}, \mathcal{Q})},$$

where

$$\text{BC}(\mathcal{P}, \mathcal{Q}) = \sum_{x \in \Omega} \sqrt{\mathcal{P}(x) \cdot \mathcal{Q}(x)}.$$

The Bhattacharyya coefficient quantifies the similarity of two random statistical samples. Furthermore, the Bhattacharyya coefficient is closely related to fidelity, which is known from quantum information theory to measure the closeness of density matrices.

For binary distributions $\mathcal{P}, \mathcal{Q}$ with $\epsilon_{\mathcal{P}} = \mathcal{P}(1)$ and $\epsilon_{\mathcal{Q}} = \mathcal{Q}(1)$ the Hellinger distance is thus given by

$$d_{\text{Hell}}(\mathcal{P}, \mathcal{Q}) = \sqrt{1 - \sqrt{\epsilon_{\mathcal{P}} \cdot \epsilon_{\mathcal{Q}}} - \sqrt{(1 - \epsilon_{\mathcal{P}}) \cdot (1 - \epsilon_{\mathcal{Q}})}}.$$

Both distances serve as metrics for assessing the similarity between distributions. They adhere to the classical analogue of the Fuchs van de Graaf inequalities:

$$d_{\text{Hell}}(\mathcal{P}, \mathcal{Q})^2 \leq \Delta(\mathcal{P}, \mathcal{Q}) \leq \sqrt{2} \cdot d_{\text{Hell}}(\mathcal{P}, \mathcal{Q}).$$

For additional properties and proofs pertaining to statistical distances, we refer the reader to [1,29,35].

3 Definitions

3.1 Quantum Security Game

We consider a cryptographic game $\mathsf{G} = (\mathsf{X}, \mathsf{W})$ interacting with an adversary $\mathcal{A}$ as in [16] abstractly as an interaction between the challenger X and the adversary $\mathcal{A}$, where both parties receive the security parameter λ as unary input. At the end of the interaction, the challenger outputs a bit win or lose to indicate if the adversary has won or not. Formally, in [16], the decision is captured through the condition predicate W, which evaluates the challenger's view, consisting of the input, the internal randomness, and the incoming messages from $\mathcal{A}$, to win or lose. This predicate is only used for a better comparison with previous approaches, and we keep it here as well for compatibility reasons.

First, we introduce the quantum variants of the classical definitions provided by Lee [16] to capture security games. We envision the interaction of the quantum adversary $\mathcal{A}_Q$ with the quantum challenger X_Q in the security game as a joint computation in a Hilbert space $\mathcal{H}_{\mathcal{A}_Q} \otimes \mathcal{H}_{\mathcal{A}_Q\mathsf{X}_Q} \otimes \mathcal{H}_{\mathsf{X}_Q}$, where $\mathcal{H}_{\mathcal{A}_Q}$ is attributed to algorithm $\mathcal{A}_Q$, $\mathcal{H}_{\mathsf{X}_Q}$ to X_Q, and $\mathcal{H}_{\mathcal{A}_Q\mathsf{X}_Q}$ is a joint space for communication. Formally, we thus decompose algorithm $\mathcal{A}_Q$ (and likewise X_Q) into sequences $\mathcal{A}_Q^{(1)}, \mathcal{A}_Q^{(2)}, \mathcal{A}_Q^{(3)}, \ldots$ operating on $\mathcal{H}_{\mathcal{A}_Q} \otimes \mathcal{H}_{\mathcal{A}_Q\mathsf{X}_Q}$. See Fig. 2. Note that we let the challenger access the following query of $\mathcal{A}_Q$ in each round for clarity, whereas we can assume that $\mathcal{A}_Q$ may already access all joint registers from the beginning.

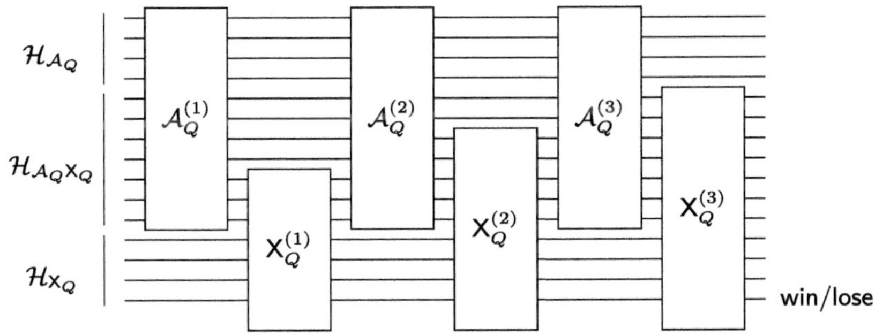

Fig. 2. Interactive computation of $\mathcal{A}_Q$ and X_Q. Both algorithms receive 1^λ as input in their corresponding registers.

Definition 3 (Quantum Security Game). *A quantum security game $G_Q = (\mathsf{X}_Q, \mathsf{W}_Q)$ against quantum adversary $\mathcal{A}_Q$ consists of a quantum challenger X_Q and a winning condition W_Q. The game is parameterized by the security parameter λ. In this game, the quantum adversary $\mathcal{A}_Q(1^\lambda)$ interacts with the quantum challenger $\mathsf{X}_Q(1^\lambda)$ as depicted in Fig. 2. The challenger eventually outputs a bit* win *or* lose. *We say that the adversary wins (loses) the game for security parameter λ if the challenger's output is* win *(*lose*) when executing the game for parameter λ. We write*

$$\Pr_{\mathcal{A}_Q}^{G_Q}(\lambda) := \Pr[\mathcal{A}_Q \textit{ wins game } G_Q \textit{ for security parameter } \lambda].$$

In Fig. 3, we give a protocol-based view of the interactive game between the parties. This notation will be supportive of understanding observational games.

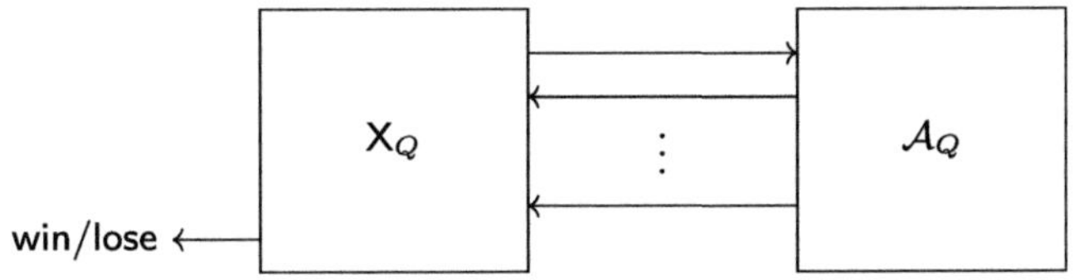

Fig. 3. Protocol-based view on game between $\mathcal{A}_Q$ and X_Q. Both algorithms receive 1^λ as input (omitted here in the presentation).

3.2 Baseline Probabilities

We define the quantum version of dummy adversary following [16]. There, classical dummy adversaries are defined as being independent of the challenger's responses. We note that such adversaries can be considered even more simplistic than trivial adversaries whose output may depend on the challenger's behavior.

The example in [16] is a security game where the challenger sends a random string s to the adversary, and the adversary wins the game if it responds with that string s. A trivial adversary duplicating the incoming message s can easily win this game, while a dummy adversary whose output does not depend on the challenger's messagey only has a success probability of $2^{-|s|}$.

For the quantum case, we can translate the independence of the dummy adversary of the challenger by demanding that $\mathcal{A}_Q$ creates all game queries at the outset. The situation is depicted in Fig. 4. Note that the challenger's processing steps remain unchanged. This is necessary as we consider fixed games with identical challengers; only the adversary may change.

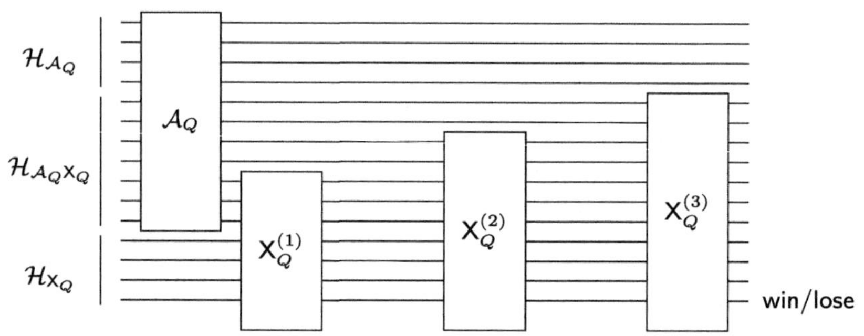

Fig. 4. Interactive computation of dummy adversary $\mathcal{A}_Q$ with X_Q

Definition 4 (Quantum Dummy Adversary). *In a quantum security game* G_Q *against a quantum adversary* $\mathcal{A}_Q$*, the adversary is called a* quantum dummy adversary *if* $\mathcal{A}_Q^{(i)}$ *is the identity operation for all* $i \geq 2$*. That is,* $\mathcal{A}_Q$ *prepares all queries in advance, and the challenger processes all queries sequentially, eventually outputting* win *or* lose *(see Fig. 4).*

By construction, every quantum dummy adversary is a quantum adversary, but in general, the converse does not hold.

We next define the baseline probability as the success probability of dummy adversaries of a particular time complexity bound T_Q.

Definition 5 (Bounded Quantum Baseline Probability). *A quantum baseline probability for time complexity* T_Q *for a quantum security game* G_Q *is defined as*

$$\Pr^{\mathsf{G}_Q}_{\mathbf{D}[T_Q]}(\lambda) = \max_{dummy\ \mathcal{A}_Q : T_{\mathcal{A}_Q} \leq T_Q} \Pr^{\mathsf{G}_Q}_{\mathcal{A}_Q}(\lambda),$$

where the maximum is over all quantum dummy adversaries of time complexity T_Q*. A quantum dummy adversary* $\mathcal{A}_Q$ *against a quantum security game* G_Q *is a quantum baseline adversary if it achieves the maximum,* $\Pr^{\mathsf{G}_Q}_{\mathcal{A}_Q}(\lambda) = \Pr^{\mathsf{G}_Q}_{\mathbf{D}[T_Q]}(\lambda)$.

We note that the maximum in the definition is a point-wise maximum over the security parameter λ. If we assume a fixed representation of quantum circuits, e.g., described via some universal gate set, then for given λ, run time bound T_Q and game G, the number of dummy adversaries $\mathcal{A}_Q$ with run time $T_{\mathcal{A}_Q} \leq T_Q$ is finite and the maximum thus reached. In the following, we use a similar line of reasoning for the point-wise minimum over quantum search algorithms, which we implicitly bound in run time by $T_Q \leq 2^{\lambda/2}$.

To normalize the advantage of an adversary $\mathcal{A}_Q$, running in time $T_{\mathcal{A}_Q}$, over the dummy adversary of the same complexity, we follow [16] and use the notion of the conventional advantage:

Definition 6 (Quantum Conventional Advantage). *We denote the quantum conventional advantage of $\mathcal{A}_Q$ for the game G_Q as follows:*

$$QAdv_{\mathcal{A}_Q}^{G_Q}(\lambda) = \max\left\{\Pr_{\mathcal{A}_Q}^{G_Q}(\lambda) - \Pr_{\mathbf{D}[T_Q]}^{G_Q}(\lambda), 0\right\}.$$

3.3 Hybrid Observation Game

The *(advantage) observation game* in [16] captures the advantage of distinguishing the success of an adversary over a baseline adversary. The idea of the observation game is to have a meta-game between an adversary $\mathcal{B}$ and a "meta-challenger" $\hat{\mathsf{X}}$. Adversary $\mathcal{B}$ can ping the meta-challenger multiple times. Each time $\hat{\mathsf{X}}$ runs the game G with either the adversary $\mathcal{A}$ or with the baseline adversary $\mathcal{A}^{\text{dummy}}$, the choice depends on a secret random bit b held by $\hat{\mathsf{X}}$. As in [16], we stipulate that the adversary $\mathcal{A}_Q$ has a success probability that is at least as large as that of the baseline adversary (of the same complexity). The meta-challenger returns the game's outcome win or lose to adversary $\mathcal{B}$. Adversary $\mathcal{B}$ eventually needs to predict b almost with certainty.

Based on the conceptual framework in [16], we propose a modification of the observation game to the quantum setting. In this setting, the game and the adversary may be quantum, and since we assume the execution of the game to be part of the meta-challenger, we also make the meta-challenger quantum. The observation algorithm $\mathcal{B}$, however, is still classical. The reason is that we are interested in the quantum adversary $\mathcal{A}_Q$ finding the classical key, i.e., the search game is supposed to use quantum power to solve a classical problem. We, therefore, call this type of observation game a hybrid game.

Definition 7 (Hybrid Observation Game). *Let $\mathcal{A}_Q$ be a quantum adversary of run-time $T_{\mathcal{A}_Q}$ for a quantum game $G_Q = (X_Q, W_Q)$.*

Consider a classical adversary $\mathcal{B}$ and a quantum meta-challenger $\hat{\mathsf{X}}_Q$ in the following hybrid observation game (see Fig. 5):

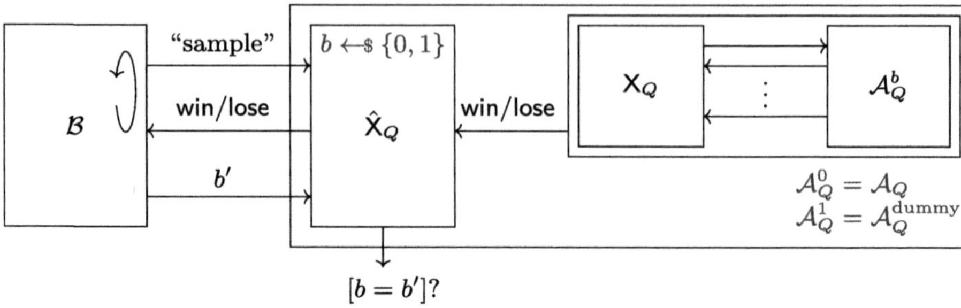

Fig. 5. Protocol-based view on hybrid observation game between $\mathcal{B}$ and $\hat{X}_Q$. Both algorithms receive 1^λ as input (omitted here in the presentation).

Hybrid Observation Game

Challenge: *At the beginning of the game the quantum meta-challenger $\hat{X}_Q(1^\lambda)$ chooses a secret bit $b \leftarrow_{\$} \{0,1\}$. This secret bit b determines in the following if we execute the game G_Q with the adversary $\mathcal{A}_Q^0 = \mathcal{A}_Q$ or with a quantum baseline adversary $\mathcal{A}_Q^1 = \mathcal{A}_Q^{dummy}$ of complexity $T_{\mathcal{A}_Q}$ for the game.*

Sample Queries: *Adversary $\mathcal{B}(1^\lambda)$ may repeatedly send the special symbol "sample" to $\hat{X}_Q$. The meta-challenger then invokes the quantum game G_Q with $\mathcal{A}_Q^b$ for security parameter λ. When the game invocation eventually returns* win *or* lose, *then algorithm $\hat{X}_Q$ returns the value to $\mathcal{B}$.*

Decision: *The adversary $\mathcal{B}$ eventually returns a prediction b' for the secret bit. The meta-challenger $\hat{X}_Q$ outputs* win *if $b = b'$ and $\Pr^{G_Q}_{\mathcal{A}_Q}(\lambda) \geq \Pr^{G_Q}_{\mathbf{D}[T_{\mathcal{A}_Q}]}(\lambda)$, and* lose *otherwise.*

Remark 1. The hybrid observation game can be viewed as a game $\hat{G}_Q$ between the meta-challenger $\hat{X}_Q$ and adversary $\mathcal{B}$, such that we can, for example, immediately transfer the notation $\Pr^{\hat{G}_Q}_{\mathcal{B}}(\lambda)$ to describe the success probability of $\mathcal{B}$ in the observation game.

For the definition of bit security in our setting, we use the approach proposed by [34], which is also used in [16]. The starting point is Definition 7 of the hybrid observation game. We define the bit security as the cost to demonstrate the advantage of the $\mathcal{A}_Q$ against the quantum game G_Q. This cost reflects the overall effort needed to repeatedly invoke $\mathcal{A}_Q$, enabling the classical algorithm $\mathcal{B}$ to win the hybrid observation game with sufficiently large probability. Precisely, we measure the total cost $T_{\mathcal{A}_Q}$ of $\mathcal{A}_Q$ multiplied by the query complexity $N_{\mathcal{B}}$ of $\mathcal{B}$ against the hybrid observation game. To distinguish this setting from the classical scenario and because it corresponds to quantum attacks on otherwise classical key derivation schemes, we call this the post-quantum bit security (PQBS).

Definition 8 (Post-Quantum Bit Security as Cost to Demonstrate Advantage). *For any quantum security game G_Q we define the* Post-Quantum Bit Security *(PQBS) with error probability* $0 < \delta(\lambda) < \frac{1}{2}$ *as follows:*

$$PQBS^{G_Q,\delta}_{Dem}(\lambda) = \min_{\mathcal{A}_Q,\mathcal{B}}\{\log(T_{\mathcal{A}_Q} \cdot N_{\mathcal{B}}) \ : \ \Pr^{\hat{G}_Q}_{\mathcal{B}}(\lambda) \geq 1 - \delta(\lambda)\}.$$

3.4 Estimating the Post-quantum Bit Security

Lee [16] relates the bit security, as defined above, via the Hellinger distance. Namely, the number of (classical) samples N_δ to distinguish two probability distributions $\mathcal{P}$ and $\mathcal{Q}$ with success probability $1 - \delta$ for $0 < \delta < \frac{1}{2}$ is tightly bounded by the inverse square of the Hellinger distance of the two distributions:

$$\frac{1}{4\ln 2} \cdot \frac{\ln(\frac{1}{4\delta(1-\delta)})}{d_{\text{Hell}}(\mathcal{P},\mathcal{Q})^2} \leq N_\delta(\mathcal{P},\mathcal{Q}) \leq \frac{\ln(\frac{1}{2\delta})}{d_{\text{Hell}}(\mathcal{P},\mathcal{Q})^2}.$$

Here, the upper bound holds unconditionally and the lower bound holds if $d_{\text{Hell}}(\mathcal{P},\mathcal{Q})^2 \leq \frac{1}{2}$. Since we consider a classical adversary $\mathcal{B}$ in our hybrid observation game, we can also apply this bound and derive the same conclusion as in [16].

Theorem 1 (Estimation of Post-Quantum Bit Security [16]). *For* $0 < \delta < \frac{(2-\sqrt{3})}{4}$*, we have the following estimation of the quantum demonstration bit security, up to a small additive error* α*, satisfying* $0 \leq \alpha \leq 1 + \log(\ln(\frac{1}{2\delta}))$ *:*

$$PQBS^{G_Q,\delta}_{Dem}(\lambda) = \min_{\mathcal{A}_Q} \log\left(\ln\left(\frac{1}{2\delta}\right) \cdot \frac{T_{\mathcal{A}_Q}}{d_{Hell}(\Pr^{G_Q}_{\mathcal{A}_Q}(\lambda), \Pr^{G_Q}_{\mathbf{D}[T_{\mathcal{A}_Q}]}(\lambda))^2}\right) - \alpha,$$

where the minimum is over all quantum adversaries $\mathcal{A}_Q$ *satisfying* $\Pr^{G_Q}_{\mathcal{A}_Q}(\lambda) \geq \Pr^{G_Q}_{\mathbf{D}[T_{\mathcal{A}_Q}]}(\lambda)$.

For small δ this bound can be simplified in terms of the quantum Hellinger advantage:

Definition 9 (Quantum Hellinger Advantage). *In a quantum security game G_Q with a quantum adversary $\mathcal{A}_Q$ we denote the quantum Hellinger advantage as:*

$$QAdv^{G_Q,\mathcal{A}_Q}_{Hell^2}(\lambda) = \begin{cases} d_{Hell}(\Pr^{G_Q}_{\mathcal{A}_Q}(\lambda), \Pr^{G_Q}_{\mathbf{D}[T_{\mathcal{A}_Q}]}(\lambda))^2 & \text{if } \Pr^{G_Q}_{\mathcal{A}_Q}(\lambda) \geq \Pr^{G_Q}_{\mathbf{D}[T_{\mathcal{A}_Q}]}(\lambda), \\ 0 & \text{if } \Pr^{G_Q}_{\mathcal{A}_Q}(\lambda) < \Pr^{G_Q}_{\mathbf{D}[T_{\mathcal{A}_Q}]}(\lambda). \end{cases}$$

Then, we get a simplified approximation of post-quantum bit security:

Definition 10 (Hellinger Post-Quantum Bit Security). *Let G_Q be a quantum security game. Then, the Hellinger Post-Quantum Bit Security is defined as:*

$$PQBS^{G_Q}_{Hell^2}(\lambda) = \min_{\mathcal{A}_Q} \log \left(\frac{T_{\mathcal{A}_Q}}{QAdv^{G_Q,\mathcal{A}_Q}_{Hell^2}(\lambda)} \right).$$

4 Bit Security of Quantum Key Search

In this section, we examine the bit security within the context of the quantum key search game, where the adversary endeavors to find an unknown key for a distribution with a small statistical distance from the uniform distribution. One can view this game as reflecting the best adversarial strategy in settings where the deployment of the keys does not introduce collateral weaknesses. For example, one may think of a key used in a secure AES-based authenticated encryption scheme, such that the adversary can check a key guess via trial decryption. Still, neither the usage of AES nor of the authenticated encryption scheme is known to facilitate the key search.

We determine the upper and lower bounds for the success probabilities associated with any adversary participating in the quantum key search game. We adopt here the definition of bit security, defined via Hellinger distance:

$$\mathrm{PQBS}^{\mathsf{G}_Q}_{\mathrm{Hell}^2}(\lambda) = \min_{\mathcal{A}^{\mathrm{ks}}_Q} \log \left(\frac{T_{\mathcal{A}_Q}}{\mathrm{QAdv}^{\mathsf{G}_Q}_{\mathrm{Hell}^2}\mathcal{A}_Q(1^\lambda)} \right),$$

where the quantum Hellinger advantage is articulated through the Hellinger distance $d_{\mathrm{Hell}}\big(\Pr^{\mathsf{G}_Q}_{\mathcal{A}^{\mathrm{ks}}_Q}(\lambda), \Pr^{\mathsf{G}_Q}_{\mathbf{D}[T_{\mathcal{A}^{\mathrm{ks}}_Q}]}(\lambda)\big)^2$ for successful adversaries $\mathcal{A}_Q$. Within this framework, the derivation of an *upper* bound on post-quantum bit security requires a *lower* bound on the Hellinger distance, whereas deriving a *lower* bound on post-quantum bit security requires an *upper* bound on the Hellinger distance.

4.1 Quantum Key Search Game and Baseline Probability

The quantum key search game is parameterised by some distribution μ, which assigns a probability to each of the possible λ-bit keys $\mathsf{k} \leftarrow\!\!\$\, \mathcal{K} = \{0,1\}^\lambda$. The distribution μ has a statistical distance Δ from the uniform distribution. The goal of the adversary is to find a randomly sampled key. For this, it can query the challenger in superposition about the candidate keys. Finally, it outputs a classical prediction for the secret key.

Definition 11 (Quantum Key Search Game). *The quantum key search game $G^{ks,\mu,\Delta}_Q = (X^{ks}_Q, W^{ks}_Q)$ with quantum key search adversary $\mathcal{A}^{ks}_Q$ is defined as follows:*

> *Quantum Key Search Game*
>
> **Challenge:** *At the beginning of the game the quantum challenger* $X_Q^{ks}(1^\lambda)$ *chooses a secret key* $\mathsf{k} \in \{0,1\}^\lambda$ *according to distribution* $\mu(\lambda)$.
>
> **Queries:** *Adversary* $\mathcal{A}_Q^{ks}$ *can repeatedly query the challenger about any quantum state* $\sum \alpha_{xy}|x\rangle|y\rangle$ *to receive the answer* $\sum \alpha_{xy}|x\rangle|y \oplus I_{\mathsf{k}}(x)\rangle$, *where* $I_{\mathsf{k}}(x)$ *is the indicator function returning* 1 *if and only if* $x = \mathsf{k}$.
>
> **Decision:** *The adversary* $\mathcal{A}_Q^{ks}$ *eventually sends a prediction* k' *to the challenger* X_Q^{ks}. *The challenger outputs* win *if* $\mathsf{k} = \mathsf{k}'$, *and* lose *otherwise.*

We consider the baseline probability for the key search game. Recall that dummy adversaries against the key search game must prepare all queries and their output at the beginning of the game. In particular, this means for our search game that the dummy adversary must compute its guess k' for the challenger's secret key k before it learns any information about the actual secret. This implies that the best strategy is to pick the most likely key, whose probability is bounded from above by $2^{-\lambda} + \Delta$. At the same time, at least one key must be hit with probability at least $2^{-\lambda}$, giving us a lower bound for the optimal dummy adversary. We conclude that

$$2^{-\lambda} \leq \mathrm{Pr}_{\mathbf{D}[T_Q]}^{\mathsf{G}_Q^{\mathrm{ks},\mu,\Delta}}(\lambda) \leq 2^{-\lambda} + \Delta.$$

This holds independently of the run time of the dummy adversary.

4.2 Bounds for Quantum Key Search Adversaries

We now turn to lower and upper bounds on the success probabilities of adversaries $\mathcal{A}_Q^{\mathrm{ks}}$ against the quantum key search game $\mathsf{G}_Q^{\mathrm{ks},\mu,\Delta}$. He et al. [13], optimizing Montanaro's algorithm [22], give a quantum search algorithm for *known* input distribution $p_i = \mathcal{P}(i)$ for $i = 1, 2, \ldots, N$. The idea of their search algorithm is to run Grover's algorithm but use an initial state $|s\rangle = \sum_{i=1}^{N} \sqrt{q_i}|i\rangle + \sqrt{q_0}|0\rangle$ for non-negative values q_i and $q_0 = 1 - \sum_{i=1}^{N} q_i \geq 0$. The values q_i can be chosen arbitrarily, yielding different bounds on the success probability after T_Q steps of the search algorithm. Specifically, He et al. [13] show that the expected success probability $\mathsf{ESP}_{T_Q}(p,q)$ of finding the key in T_Q steps when using q as a starting vector as

$$\mathsf{ESP}_{T_Q}(p,q) = \sum_{i=1}^{N} p_i \cdot \sin^2((2T_Q + 1)\arcsin\sqrt{q_i}).$$

Each term $\sin^2((2T_Q + 1) \cdot \arcsin\sqrt{q_i})$ reaches its maximum 1 for $q_i = \sin^2 \frac{\pi}{2(2T_Q+1)}$.

For our quantum key search problem, we assume that the probabilities p_i are given in non-increasing order, i.e., that the adversary has already ordered the keys according to their likelihood (see Fig. 1 on page 4).[2] Given a bound T_Q on the run time, we now set the q_i as

$$q_i = \begin{cases} \sin^2 \frac{\pi}{2(2T_Q+1)} & \text{if } i \leq {T_Q}^2 \\ 0 & \text{otherwise} \end{cases},$$

such that the sum over all q_i's is bounded by 1 as required. Then, we get a lower bound for the expected success probability of

$$\mathsf{ESP}_{T_Q}(p,q) \geq \sum_{i=1}^{{T_Q}^2} p_i \cdot \sin^2((2T_Q+1)\arcsin\sqrt{q_i}) = \sum_{i=1}^{{T_Q}^2} p_i.$$

Since the p_i-values are in non-increasing order, the sum over the first ${T_Q}^2$ values can never be smaller than ${T_Q}^2 \cdot 2^{-\lambda}$. To see this, let I be the index where the probability p_i drops below $2^{-\lambda}$, i.e., where keys are less likely than uniformly distributed keys, and the curve of the actual key distribution lies below the curve of the uniform distribution in Fig. 1. Then we can split the sum of the probabilities in the values up to index I and after I (if I exceeds ${T_Q}^2$):

$$\sum_{i=1}^{{T_Q}^2} p_i = \sum_{i=1}^{\min\{I,{T_Q}^2\}} p_i + \sum_{i=I+1}^{{T_Q}^2} p_i.$$

Noting that the first sum equals the "uniform contribution" plus the statistical distance, and the second sum at least the "uniform contribution" minus the statistical distance, we conclude:

$$\begin{aligned} &\geq \min\{I, {T_Q}^2\} \cdot 2^{-\lambda} + \Delta + \max\{0, {T_Q}^2 - I\} \cdot 2^{-\lambda} - \Delta \\ &\geq {T_Q}^2 \cdot 2^{-\lambda}. \end{aligned}$$

He et al. [13] also show that their algorithm is optimal. That is, they show that any quantum search algorithm has a success probability of at most

$$\max_q \mathsf{ESP}_{T_Q}(p,q) \quad \text{where } q_i \geq 0 \text{ and } \sum q_i \leq 1.$$

Letting $q^*(p)$ denote the optimal choice for q given a specific distribution p,

$$q^*(p) = \arg\max_q \mathsf{ESP}_{T_Q}(p,q),$$

they argue that for any other distribution $\hat{p}$ we have

$$\mathsf{ESP}_{T_Q}(\hat{p}, q^*(\hat{p})) \geq \mathsf{ESP}_{T_Q}(\hat{p}, q^*(p))$$

[2] Computing this ordering may nonetheless be quite expensive in practice and significantly increase the run time of the adversary [33]. This depends on the concrete key generation algorithm and its specific manifestation of the statistical distance. We assume here, in favor of the adversary, that this step is inexpensive.

because $q^*(p)$ cannot yield a better probability than the maximizing value $q^*(\hat{p})$. Exploiting linearity in the probabilities, we conclude further

$$= \mathsf{ESP}_{T_Q}(p, q^*(p)) + \mathsf{ESP}_{T_Q}(\hat{p} - p, q^*(p))$$

Noting that the squared sin-values lie between 0 and 1 and that $\hat{p}_i - p_i \geq -|\hat{p}_i - p_i|$, we obtain the lower bound

$$\begin{aligned} &\geq \mathsf{ESP}_{T_Q}(p, q^*(p)) - \sum_{i=1}^{N} |\hat{p}_i - p_i| \\ &= \mathsf{ESP}_{T_Q}(p, q^*(p)) - 2 \cdot \Delta \end{aligned}$$

for the statistical distance Δ between $\hat{p}$ and p. It follows that we can bound the value $\mathsf{ESP}_{T_Q}(p, q^*(p))$ via the expected success probability for the *uniform* distribution $\hat{p}$ on the values and (twice) the statistical distance from uniform.

For the uniform distribution over all inputs and a single positive entry, we can apply the common upper bounds for any search algorithm [4] in the slightly optimized version of [36]: The probability ρ that any quantum search algorithm for the uniform distribution on a set of N elements (with a single matching element) is found after T_Q steps, satisfies

$$4{T_Q}^2 \geq 2N - 2\sqrt{N}\sqrt{\rho} - 2\sqrt{N}\sqrt{N-1}\sqrt{1-\rho}.$$

Using $\sqrt{1-\rho} \leq 1 - \frac{\rho}{2}$, we obtain:

$$\begin{aligned} 4{T_Q}^2 &\geq 2N - 2\sqrt{N}\sqrt{\rho} - 2\sqrt{N}\sqrt{N-1}\sqrt{1-\rho} \\ &\geq 2N - 2\sqrt{N\rho} - 2N(1 - \frac{\rho}{2}) \\ &\geq N\rho - 2\sqrt{N\rho} \\ &= (\sqrt{N\rho} - 1)^2 - 1. \end{aligned}$$

Since $T_Q \geq 1$ we can write this as

$$5{T_Q}^2 \geq 4{T_Q}^2 + 1 \geq (\sqrt{N\rho} - 1)^2$$

Since we can assume that $\rho \geq \frac{1}{N}$ to surpass the dummy adversary, we have $N\rho \geq 1$ and the value $\sqrt{N\rho} - 1$ is thus non-negative. On the left-hand side, we also have $T_Q \geq 1$ such that we can take roots to obtain:

$$\sqrt{5}T_Q \geq \sqrt{N\rho} - 1$$

and thus $4T_Q \geq \sqrt{5}T_Q + 1 \geq \sqrt{N\rho}$ which implies

$$\frac{16{T_Q}^2}{N} \geq \rho.$$

We can now put the bounds together to obtain a sharp bound (up to constants and additive terms) on the adversary's success probability in relation to the number of steps $T_{\mathcal{A}_Q^{\mathrm{ks}}}$, the search space $N = 2^\lambda$, and the statistical distance Δ of the key distribution from uniform:

$$T^2_{\mathcal{A}_Q^{\mathrm{ks}}} \cdot 2^{-\lambda} \leq \Pr^{\mathsf{G}_Q^{\mathrm{ks},\mu,\Delta}}_{\mathcal{A}_Q^{\mathrm{ks}}}(\lambda) \leq 16 T^2_{\mathcal{A}_Q^{\mathrm{ks}}} \cdot 2^{-\lambda} + 2 \cdot \Delta$$

The upper bound holds for adversaries $\mathcal{A}_Q^{\mathrm{ks}}$ with success probability at least $2^{-\lambda}$, which equals the dummy adversary's success probability.

4.3 Upper Bound for the Post-quantum Bit Security

We give the upper bound of

$$\mathrm{PQBS}^{\mathsf{G}_Q}_{\mathrm{Hell}^2}(\lambda) = \min_{\mathcal{A}_Q^{\mathrm{ks}}} \log \left(\frac{T_{\mathcal{A}_Q}}{\mathrm{QAdv}^{\mathsf{G}_Q, \mathcal{A}_Q}_{\mathrm{Hell}^2}(\lambda)} \right)$$

in terms of the given statistical distance Δ. Since the bit security is defined over the minimum over all adversaries, we may pick a specific adversary and its run time in dependence on Δ to get an upper bound. Specifically, we assume that $T_{\mathcal{A}_Q^{\mathrm{ks}}} \geq 48$. For the bounds, we also need that $T_{\mathcal{A}_Q^{\mathrm{ks}}} \leq 2^{\lambda/2}$, which matches the known upper bound on the run time of Grover's search algorithm.

For the statistical distance, we stipulate for technical reasons that $\Delta \leq \frac{1}{48^2}$. In other words, we do not consider constant statistical distances $\Delta > \frac{1}{48^2}$. This is not a major restriction since constant distances are considered insecure in the first place, because then a small set of keys, even a single key, can have a constant probability of being chosen by the key generation algorithm. Technically, this may also imply that the success probabilities $2^{-\lambda} + \Delta$ of the dummy adversary can be quite very large. With the assumption about Δ, we can conclude that $\Delta \leq \frac{1}{48^2} \cdot T^2_{\mathcal{A}_Q^{\mathrm{ks}}} \cdot 2^{-\lambda}$. This can always be accomplished by picking $T_{\mathcal{A}_Q^{\mathrm{ks}}}$ as its maximum $2^{\lambda/2}$. We can therefore write the distance Δ for factor $\gamma \leq \frac{1}{48^2}$ as

$$\Delta = \gamma \cdot {T_{\mathcal{A}_Q^{\mathrm{ks}}}}^2 \cdot 2^{-\lambda}.$$

To derive an upper bound on the bit security, we need a lower bound on the Hellinger distance. Recall that for binary probability distributions $\mathcal{P}$, $\mathcal{Q}$, as in the case of our key search game, the square of the Hellinger distance can be written as

$$d_{\mathrm{Hell}}(\mathcal{P}, \mathcal{Q})^2 = 1 - \sqrt{\epsilon_{\mathcal{P}} \cdot \epsilon_{\mathcal{Q}}} - \sqrt{(1 - \epsilon_{\mathcal{P}}) \cdot (1 - \epsilon_{\mathcal{Q}})},$$

where $\epsilon_{\mathcal{P}} = \mathcal{P}(1)$ and $\epsilon_{\mathcal{Q}} = \mathcal{Q}(1)$ denote the success probabilities. In our setting, the distributions are given by an arbitrary quantum key search adversary $\mathcal{A}_Q^{\mathrm{ks}}$ playing the game $\mathsf{G}_Q^{\mathrm{ks},\mu,\Delta}$, and a baseline dummy adversary $\mathcal{A}_Q^{\mathrm{dummy,ks}}$ in the game. Hence, to give an upper bound on the bit security—and therefore a lower bound on the squared Hellinger distance—we plug in upper bounds for $\epsilon_{\mathcal{P}}, \epsilon_{\mathcal{Q}}$ in the first term (taking into account the negative sign) and lower bounds for $\epsilon_{\mathcal{P}}, \epsilon_{\mathcal{Q}}$ in the second term (taking into account the inner and outer negative sign).

Recall that we have $\epsilon_{\mathcal{P}} \leq 16{T_{\mathcal{A}_Q^{\text{ks}}}}^2 \cdot 2^{-\lambda} + 2\Delta$ for the key search adversaries and $\epsilon_{\mathcal{Q}} \leq 2^{-\lambda} + \Delta$ for any dummy adversary. Similarly, we have $\epsilon_{\mathcal{P}} \geq {T_{\mathcal{A}_Q^{\text{ks}}}}^2 \cdot 2^{-\lambda}$ for the key search adversaries and $\epsilon_{\mathcal{Q}} \geq 2^{-\lambda}$ for dummy adversaries. This yields the following.

$$
\begin{aligned}
&d_{\text{Hell}}\left(\Pr^{\mathsf{G}_Q}_{\mathcal{A}_Q}(\lambda), \Pr^{\mathsf{G}_Q}_{\mathbf{D}[T_{\mathcal{A}_Q^{\text{ks}}}]}(\lambda)\right)^2 \\
&\geq 1 - \sqrt{(16{T_{\mathcal{A}_Q^{\text{ks}}}}^2 \cdot 2^{-\lambda} + 2 \cdot \Delta) \cdot (2^{-\lambda} + \Delta)} - \sqrt{(1 - {T_{\mathcal{A}_Q^{\text{ks}}}}^2 \cdot 2^{-\lambda}) \cdot (1 - 2^{-\lambda})} \\
&\geq 1 - \sqrt{16{T_{\mathcal{A}_Q^{\text{ks}}}}^2 \cdot 2^{-2\lambda} + 2 \cdot \Delta^2 + 16{T_{\mathcal{A}_Q^{\text{ks}}}}^2 \cdot 2^{-\lambda} \cdot \Delta + 2^{-\lambda+1} \cdot \Delta} \\
&\qquad - \sqrt{1 - 2^{-\lambda} - {T_{\mathcal{A}_Q^{\text{ks}}}}^2 \cdot 2^{-\lambda} + {T_{\mathcal{A}_Q^{\text{ks}}}}^2 \cdot 2^{-2\lambda}}.
\end{aligned}
$$

We start to simplify the second square root by dropping the negative term $-2^{-\lambda}$ and bounding the term ${T_{\mathcal{A}_Q^{\text{ks}}}}^2 \cdot 2^{-2\lambda} \leq \frac{1}{2} \cdot {T_{\mathcal{A}_Q^{\text{ks}}}}^2 \cdot 2^{-\lambda}$ for $\lambda \geq 1$. The gives:

$$
\sqrt{1 - 2^{-\lambda} - {T_{\mathcal{A}_Q^{\text{ks}}}}^2 \cdot 2^{-\lambda} + {T_{\mathcal{A}_Q^{\text{ks}}}}^2 \cdot 2^{-2\lambda}} \leq \sqrt{1 - \tfrac{1}{2}{T_{\mathcal{A}_Q^{\text{ks}}}}^2 \cdot 2^{-\lambda}}.
$$

Using the bound $(1 + x)^r \leq 1 + rx$ (Bernoulli's inequality) for $r \in [0, 1]$ and for $x \geq -1$ (which holds in our case because we presume $T_{\mathcal{A}_Q^{\text{ks}}} \leq 2^{\lambda/2}$) we thus obtain

$$
\sqrt{1 - \tfrac{1}{2}{T_{\mathcal{A}_Q^{\text{ks}}}}^2 \cdot 2^{-\lambda}} \leq 1 - \tfrac{1}{4}{T_{\mathcal{A}_Q^{\text{ks}}}}^2 \cdot 2^{-\lambda}.
$$

Hence, the Hellinger distance is lower bounded by

$$
\begin{aligned}
&d_{\text{Hell}}\left(\Pr^{\mathsf{G}_Q}_{\mathcal{A}_Q}(\lambda), \Pr^{\mathsf{G}_Q}_{\mathbf{D}[T_{\mathcal{A}_Q^{\text{ks}}}]}(\lambda)\right)^2 \\
&\geq \tfrac{1}{4}{T_{\mathcal{A}_Q^{\text{ks}}}}^2 \cdot 2^{-\lambda} - \sqrt{16{T_{\mathcal{A}_Q^{\text{ks}}}}^2 \cdot 2^{-2\lambda} + 2 \cdot \Delta^2 + 16{T_{\mathcal{A}_Q^{\text{ks}}}}^2 \cdot 2^{-\lambda} \cdot \Delta + 2^{-\lambda+1} \cdot \Delta}.
\end{aligned}
$$

Next, we bound the remaining square root. We make a case distinction:

- Case $\Delta \leq 2^{-\lambda}$. In this case, we can upper-bound the square root expression as

$$
\begin{aligned}
&\sqrt{16{T_{\mathcal{A}_Q^{\text{ks}}}}^2 \cdot 2^{-2\lambda} + 2 \cdot \Delta^2 + 16{T_{\mathcal{A}_Q^{\text{ks}}}}^2 \cdot 2^{-\lambda} \cdot \Delta + 2^{-\lambda+1} \cdot \Delta} \\
&\qquad \leq \sqrt{16{T_{\mathcal{A}_Q^{\text{ks}}}}^2 \cdot 2^{-2\lambda} + 2 \cdot 2^{-2\lambda} + 16{T_{\mathcal{A}_Q^{\text{ks}}}}^2 \cdot 2^{-2\lambda} + 2^{-2\lambda+1}} \\
&\qquad \leq \sqrt{32{T_{\mathcal{A}_Q^{\text{ks}}}}^2 \cdot 2^{-2\lambda} + 4 \cdot 2^{-2\lambda}} \\
&\qquad \leq \sqrt{36{T_{\mathcal{A}_Q^{\text{ks}}}}^2 \cdot 2^{-2\lambda}} \\
&\qquad = 6T_{\mathcal{A}_Q^{\text{ks}}} \cdot 2^{-\lambda}
\end{aligned}
$$

For $T_{\mathcal{A}_Q^{\text{ks}}} \geq 48$ we thus obtain

$$d_{\text{Hell}}\left(\Pr_{\mathcal{A}_Q}^{\mathsf{G}_Q}(\lambda), \Pr_{\mathbf{D}[T_{\mathcal{A}_Q^{\text{ks}}}]}^{\mathsf{G}_Q}(\lambda)\right)^2 \geq \tfrac{1}{4}T_{\mathcal{A}_Q^{\text{ks}}}{}^2 \cdot 2^{-\lambda} - 6T_{\mathcal{A}_Q^{\text{ks}}} \cdot 2^{-\lambda} \geq \tfrac{1}{8}T_{\mathcal{A}_Q^{\text{ks}}}{}^2 \cdot 2^{-\lambda}.$$

Therefore, the upper bound for the post-quantum Hellinger bit security $\text{PQBS}_{\text{Hell}^2}^{\mathsf{G}_Q}(\lambda)$ becomes:

$$\text{PQBS}_{\text{Hell}^2}^{\mathsf{G}_Q}(\lambda) \leq \min_{\mathcal{A}_Q^{\text{ks}}} \log \frac{T_{\mathcal{A}_Q^{\text{ks}}}}{\frac{1}{8}T_{\mathcal{A}_Q^{\text{ks}}}{}^2 \cdot 2^{-\lambda}} \leq \min_{\mathcal{A}_Q^{\text{ks}}}(\lambda - \log T_{\mathcal{A}_Q^{\text{ks}}} + 3).$$

– Case $\Delta > 2^{-\lambda}$. In this case, we can bound the square root expression due to $\Delta > 2^{-\lambda}$ and $\Delta \leq \frac{1}{48^2}T_{\mathcal{A}_Q^{\text{ks}}}{}^2 \cdot 2^{-\lambda}$ as follows:

$$\begin{aligned}
&\sqrt{16T_{\mathcal{A}_Q^{\text{ks}}}{}^2 \cdot 2^{-2\lambda} + 2 \cdot \Delta^2 + 16T_{\mathcal{A}_Q^{\text{ks}}}{}^2 \cdot 2^{-\lambda} \cdot \Delta + 2^{-\lambda+1} \cdot \Delta} \\
&\leq \sqrt{16T_{\mathcal{A}_Q^{\text{ks}}}{}^2 \cdot 2^{-\lambda} \cdot \Delta + 2 \cdot \frac{1}{48^2}T_{\mathcal{A}_Q^{\text{ks}}}{}^2 \cdot 2^{-\lambda} \cdot \Delta + 16T_{\mathcal{A}_Q^{\text{ks}}}{}^2 \cdot 2^{-\lambda} \cdot \Delta + 2 \cdot 2^{-\lambda} \cdot \Delta} \\
&\leq \sqrt{36T_{\mathcal{A}_Q^{\text{ks}}}{}^2 \cdot 2^{-\lambda} \cdot \Delta} \\
&= 6T_{\mathcal{A}_Q^{\text{ks}}} \cdot 2^{-\lambda/2} \cdot \sqrt{\Delta}
\end{aligned}$$

We thus get from the condition $\Delta = \gamma \cdot T_{\mathcal{A}_Q^{\text{ks}}}{}^2 \cdot 2^{-\lambda}$ that this is equal to

$$= 6T_{\mathcal{A}_Q^{\text{ks}}} \cdot 2^{-\lambda/2} \cdot \sqrt{\gamma} \cdot T_{\mathcal{A}_Q^{\text{ks}}} \cdot 2^{-\lambda/2} = 6\sqrt{\gamma} \cdot T_{\mathcal{A}_Q^{\text{ks}}}{}^2 \cdot 2^{-\lambda}.$$

Plugging this in, and using that $\sqrt{\gamma} \leq \frac{1}{48}$, we thus get

$$d_{\text{Hell}}\left(\Pr_{\mathcal{A}_Q}^{\mathsf{G}_Q}(\lambda), \Pr_{\mathbf{D}[T_{\mathcal{A}_Q^{\text{ks}}}]}^{\mathsf{G}_Q}(\lambda)\right)^2 \geq \tfrac{1}{4}T_{\mathcal{A}_Q^{\text{ks}}}{}^2 \cdot 2^{-\lambda} - 6\sqrt{\gamma} \cdot T_{\mathcal{A}_Q^{\text{ks}}}{}^2 \cdot 2^{-\lambda} \geq \tfrac{1}{8}T_{\mathcal{A}_Q^{\text{ks}}}{}^2 \cdot 2^{-\lambda}.$$

This gives us, once more, the upper bound on the post-quantum Hellinger bit security:

$$\text{PQBS}_{\text{Hell}^2}^{\mathsf{G}_Q}(\lambda) \leq \min_{\mathcal{A}_Q^{\text{ks}}} \log \frac{T_{\mathcal{A}_Q^{\text{ks}}}}{\frac{1}{8}T_{\mathcal{A}_Q^{\text{ks}}}{}^2 \cdot 2^{-\lambda}} \leq \min_{\mathcal{A}_Q^{\text{ks}}}(\lambda - \log T_{\mathcal{A}_Q^{\text{ks}}} + 3).$$

4.4 Lower Bound for the Post-quantum Bit Security

To determine a lower bound on post-quantum bit security, yielding an upper bound on the squared Hellinger distance, we use the upper bound of the squared Hellinger distance in terms of the statistical distance:

$$d_{\text{Hell}}(\mathcal{P}, \mathcal{Q})^2 \leq d_{\text{TV}}(\mathcal{P}, \mathcal{Q}).$$

The statistical distance for the binary random variables $\mathcal{P}$ and $\mathcal{Q}$ is given by $|\epsilon_{\mathcal{P}} - \epsilon_{\mathcal{Q}}|$, which, in our case, can be upper bounded by

$$d_{\mathrm{TV}}\left(\Pr^{\mathsf{G}_Q}_{\mathcal{A}_Q}(\lambda), \Pr^{\mathsf{G}_Q}_{\mathbf{D}[T_{\mathcal{A}_Q^{\mathrm{ks}}}]}(\lambda)\right) \le 16{T_{\mathcal{A}_Q^{\mathrm{ks}}}}^2 \cdot 2^{-\lambda} + 2 \cdot \Delta - 2^{-\lambda} \le 16{T_{\mathcal{A}_Q^{\mathrm{ks}}}}^2 \cdot 2^{-\lambda} + 2 \cdot \Delta.$$

We make a case distinction:

– Case $\Delta \le {T_{\mathcal{A}_Q^{\mathrm{ks}}}}^2 \cdot 2^{-\lambda}$. Then we conclude that

$$d_{\mathrm{Hell}}\left(\Pr^{\mathsf{G}_Q}_{\mathcal{A}_Q}(\lambda), \Pr^{\mathsf{G}_Q}_{\mathbf{D}[T_{\mathcal{A}_Q^{\mathrm{ks}}}]}(\lambda)\right)^2 \le d_{\mathrm{TV}}\left(\Pr^{\mathsf{G}_Q}_{\mathcal{A}_Q}(\lambda), \Pr^{\mathsf{G}_Q}_{\mathbf{D}[T_{\mathcal{A}_Q^{\mathrm{ks}}}]}(\lambda)\right) \le 18{T_{\mathcal{A}_Q^{\mathrm{ks}}}}^2 \cdot 2^{-\lambda},$$

such that we derive a lower bound for the post-quantum bit security as

$$\mathrm{PQBS}^{\mathsf{G}_Q}_{\mathrm{Hell}^2}(\lambda) \ge \min_{\mathcal{A}_Q^{\mathrm{ks}}} \log \frac{T_{\mathcal{A}_Q^{\mathrm{ks}}}}{18{T_{\mathcal{A}_Q^{\mathrm{ks}}}}^2 \cdot 2^{-\lambda}} \ge \min_{\mathcal{A}_Q^{\mathrm{ks}}}(\lambda - \log T_{\mathcal{A}_Q^{\mathrm{ks}}} - 5).$$

– Case $\Delta > {T_{\mathcal{A}_Q^{\mathrm{ks}}}}^2 \cdot 2^{-\lambda}$. In this case the dominating term in the upper bound $16{T_{\mathcal{A}_Q^{\mathrm{ks}}}}^2 \cdot 2^{-\lambda} + 2 \cdot \Delta$ is the statistical distance Δ and we can conclude that

$$\mathrm{PQBS}^{\mathsf{G}_Q}_{\mathrm{Hell}^2}(\lambda) \ge \min_{\mathcal{A}_Q^{\mathrm{ks}}} \log \frac{T_{\mathcal{A}_Q^{\mathrm{ks}}}}{18\Delta} \ge \min_{\mathcal{A}_Q^{\mathrm{ks}}}(\log T_{\mathcal{A}_Q^{\mathrm{ks}}} - \log \Delta - 5).$$

If we rewrite Δ as $\Delta = \gamma \cdot {T_{\mathcal{A}_Q^{\mathrm{ks}}}}^2 \cdot 2^{-\lambda}$ for factor $\gamma > 1$ then we derive

$$\mathrm{PQBS}^{\mathsf{G}_Q}_{\mathrm{Hell}^2}(\lambda) \ge \min_{\mathcal{A}_Q^{\mathrm{ks}}}(\lambda - \log T_{\mathcal{A}_Q^{\mathrm{ks}}} - \log \gamma - 5).$$

Hence, we only get a slightly worse bound, losing $\log \gamma$ additional bits. Note that $\gamma > 1$ in this case here, such that we indeed reduce the lower bound for post-quantum bit security compared to the other case.

5 Interpretation of Results

We discuss here the significance of our results in light of the potential choices of the statistical distance Δ. We note that we technically require that $\Delta \le \frac{1}{48^2}$ as well as $48 \le T_{\mathcal{A}_Q^{\mathrm{ks}}} \le 2^{\lambda/2}$ for the upper bounds. For the lower bounds, we usually also make the assumption that any adversary, over which we minimize, is bounded by run time $2^{\lambda/2}$, as quantum key search already succeeds with probability close to 1 in this case.

5.1 The Case $\Delta \leq 2^{-\lambda}$

If we choose the statistical to be very small, $\Delta \leq 2^{-\lambda}$, we have a matching upper and lower bound. The upper bound tells us

$$\mathrm{PQBS}^{\mathsf{G}_Q}_{\mathrm{Hell}^2}(\lambda) \leq \min_{\mathcal{A}_Q^{\mathrm{ks}}}(\lambda - \log T_{\mathcal{A}_Q^{\mathrm{ks}}} + 3),$$

and the lower bound for $\Delta \leq 2^{-\lambda} \leq {T_{\mathcal{A}_Q^{\mathrm{ks}}}}^2 \cdot 2^{-\lambda}$ says

$$\mathrm{PQBS}^{\mathsf{G}_Q}_{\mathrm{Hell}^2}(\lambda) \geq \min_{\mathcal{A}_Q^{\mathrm{ks}}}(\lambda - \log T_{\mathcal{A}_Q^{\mathrm{ks}}} - 5).$$

Hence, both bounds match up to a constant number of bits. Furthermore, if we consider adversaries with run time $T_{\mathcal{A}_Q^{\mathrm{ks}}} = \Theta(2^{\lambda/2})$, then we can conclude that we get a bit security of approximately $\lambda - \lambda/2 = \lambda/2$. This matches the known expectations for the quadratic speed-up for search with quantum computers, e.g., a uniform 256-bit AES key gives bit security of 128. Our result here confirms that this is indeed the case according to formal models and still holds if the statistical distance of the key distribution from uniform is $\Delta \leq 2^{-\lambda}$.

Remarkably, our result also shows that decreasing the statistical distance further, e.g., to $\Delta \leq 2^{-2\lambda}$, does not yield any advantage in terms of bit security. Our lower bound indicates that this is not known to increase bit security since the bound is independent of the statistical distance Δ in case $\Delta \leq 2^{-\lambda}$. Our upper bound proves that this is not only due to a loose lower bound, but that the bit security, indeed, cannot increase.

5.2 The Case $2^{-\lambda} \leq \Delta \leq 2^{-\lambda/2}$

The quadratic speed-up in quantum search halves the bit security. A natural idea is then to also allow for a larger statistical distance, say, $\Delta = 2^{-\lambda/2}$, which reduces, for example, the number of truncated bits for privacy amplification. In this case, the upper bounds remain unchanged. For the lower bound, we then have $2^{-\lambda/2} \geq \Delta = \gamma \cdot {T_{\mathcal{A}_Q^{\mathrm{ks}}}}^2 \cdot 2^{-\lambda}$ and therefore $\gamma \leq {T_{\mathcal{A}_Q^{\mathrm{ks}}}}^{-2} \cdot 2^{\lambda/2}$. This gives us

$$\begin{aligned}\mathrm{PQBS}^{\mathsf{G}_Q}_{\mathrm{Hell}^2}(\lambda) &\geq \min_{\mathcal{A}_Q^{\mathrm{ks}}}(\lambda - \log T_{\mathcal{A}_Q^{\mathrm{ks}}} + 2\log T_{\mathcal{A}_Q^{\mathrm{ks}}} - \lambda/2 - 5) \\ &= \min_{\mathcal{A}_Q^{\mathrm{ks}}}(\lambda/2 + \log T_{\mathcal{A}_Q^{\mathrm{ks}}} - 5).\end{aligned}$$

Hence, we get a lower bound of at least $\lambda/2$ bits, matching the upper bound, if we consider $T_{\mathcal{A}_Q^{\mathrm{ks}}} = 1$.

Note that the run time $T_{\mathcal{A}_Q^{\mathrm{ks}}}$ for the upper and lower bound may differ. For the upper bound, any choice of $T_{\mathcal{A}_Q^{\mathrm{ks}}}$ gives an upper limit for $\mathrm{PQBS}^{\mathsf{G}_Q}_{\mathrm{Hell}^2}(\lambda)$ which is defined over the minimum over all adversaries. For the lower bound, we therefore have to consider all adversaries with all possible choices of $T_{\mathcal{A}_Q^{\mathrm{ks}}}$ and then take the minimum of all these values. In the example above, we would thus take $T_{\mathcal{A}_Q^{\mathrm{ks}}} = 1$ for the minimum, whereas we choose $T_{\mathcal{A}_Q^{\mathrm{ks}}} = 2^{\lambda/2}$ for the upper bound.

It may now seem as if the statistical distance $\Delta = 2^{-\lambda/2}$ should be preferable over $\Delta = 2^{-\lambda}$ since it yields the same bound at a relaxed requirement. This interpretation, however, crucially relies on the estimated global upper bound of $T_{\mathcal{A}_Q^{\mathrm{ks}}}$. Above, we assume that this is at most $2^{\lambda/2}$. If one instead assumes that the best quantum algorithm can make at most $2^{\lambda/8}$ steps, e.g., because of engineering constraints, then we obtain a different picture. In this case, the upper bound would be in the order of $\lambda - \lambda/8 = 7\lambda/8$, whereas the lower bound would still be $\lambda/2$. This is because we get the negative term $\log\gamma$ in the lower bound in this case here, unless in the first case of $\Delta \leq 2^{-\lambda}$, and this value $\log\gamma$ can be quite significant if the run time $T_{\mathcal{A}_Q^{\mathrm{ks}}}$ is smaller.

In summary, a conservative choice, which works independently of some upper bound on $T_{\mathcal{A}_Q^{\mathrm{ks}}}$ beyond $2^{\lambda/2}$, is to set $\Delta = 2^{-\lambda}$.

5.3 The Case $\Delta > 2^{-\lambda/2}$

Increasing the statistical distance even beyond $2^{-\lambda/2}$ may be tempting. Recall that we have $\Delta = \gamma \cdot {T_{\mathcal{A}_Q^{\mathrm{ks}}}}^2 \cdot 2^{-\lambda}$ and that the lower bound tells us

$$\mathrm{PQBS}^{\mathsf{G}_Q}_{\mathrm{Hell}^2}(\lambda) \geq \min_{\mathcal{A}_Q^{\mathrm{ks}}}(\lambda - \log T_{\mathcal{A}_Q^{\mathrm{ks}}} - \log\gamma - 5).$$

We may pick $T_{\mathcal{A}_Q^{\mathrm{ks}}} = 1$ such that $\gamma = \Delta \cdot 2^{\lambda}$ and $\log\gamma = \lambda + \log\Delta$; we discuss below that this indeed minimizes the bound. Plugging this into the inequality, we derive

$$\mathrm{PQBS}^{\mathsf{G}_Q}_{\mathrm{Hell}^2}(\lambda) \geq -\log\Delta - 5.$$

If the statistical distance Δ now goes significantly above the bound $2^{-\lambda/2}$, then this yields a notably decreased lower bound. For example, if we choose $\Delta = 2^{-\lambda/4}$, we only get a guarantee of $\lambda/4$ bits of security. In this case, however, our upper bound is not tight. This leaves the possibility that the actual bit security may be higher.

We note that picking $T_{\mathcal{A}_Q^{\mathrm{ks}}} = 1$ and thus adversaries which only test a single key is not surprising in this context. In the worst case, only one key may encompass the entire (large) statistical distance Δ such that testing only this key may be a valid strategy. In terms of our bound, both negative terms $\log T_{\mathcal{A}_Q^{\mathrm{ks}}}$ and $\log\gamma$ enter linearly into the bound for bit security. Yet, in $\Delta = \gamma \cdot {T_{\mathcal{A}_Q^{\mathrm{ks}}}}^2 \cdot 2^{-\lambda}$ for given Δ the run time enters quadratically. We thus maximize the loss in bits by setting $T_{\mathcal{A}_Q^{\mathrm{ks}}} = 1$ and picking γ as large as possible.

6 Implications to Quantum Key Distribution

Several works in the area of quantum key distribution investigate the security bounds from a cryptographic point of view [5,18,21,23–26,30,31]. These works usually divide the error $\varepsilon = \varepsilon_{\text{correct}} + \varepsilon_{\text{secure}}$ of the overall protocol into an error $\varepsilon_{\text{correct}}$ for the two parties not arriving at the same key, and an error $\varepsilon_{\text{secure}}$ for an adversary learning information about the secret. Our work does not consider the former type of error because we only investigate key generation as a monolithic inner process. The latter error somewhat corresponds to our notion of statistical distance: In particular, the final step in the protocols consists of the privacy amplification step, resulting in a close-to-uniform key. In this step, the works [5,23–26,31] consider the trace distance as the quantum analogue to the statistical distance; still, the trace and statistical distances are tightly related [24].[3]

One can argue whether one should combine the errors for correctness and secrecy within a single parameter $\varepsilon = \varepsilon_{\text{correct}} + \varepsilon_{\text{secure}}$. If the two parties do not derive the same key, then it may be easy for the parties to check, e.g., by running a key confirmation protocol before any sensitive data is transmitted. A small but non-negligible error $\varepsilon_{\text{correct}}$ of, say, 10^{-6} may be acceptable, forcing the parties to restart the execution occasionally. This issue has also been pointed out in [30], but that work still uses the sum to discuss example figures.

Conversely, secrecy is generally not verifiable, i.e., the parties cannot easily determine that the adversary can learn more information than desired. A smaller value $\varepsilon_{\text{secure}} \ll \varepsilon_{\text{correct}}$ may thus be preferable. In the combined sum, however, the value $\varepsilon_{\text{correct}}$ then overshadows the other term, suggesting that $\varepsilon_{\text{secure}}$ could be chosen close to 10^{-6}, too. Some practical demonstrations like [3] confirm the use such a choice with $\varepsilon_{\text{secure}} = \varepsilon_{\text{correct}} = 10^{-9}$.

Indeed, the mix-up of the correctness and secrecy parameters also makes it hard to interpret the suggested figures for ε in [5,18,21,26,30,31] with respect to the choice for $\varepsilon_{\text{secret}}$. The works [18,30,31] give a bound of $\varepsilon = 10^{-10}$. Mizutani et al. [21] set ε to be 10^{-8} or 10^{-10}. Renner and Wolf [26] list typical values for parameter ε in the range of 10^{-6} to 10^{-12}. The work by Bunandar et al. [5] states explicitly in their example that $\varepsilon_{\text{correct}} = 10^{-15}$ and $\varepsilon_{\text{secure}} = 10^{-10}$. Müller-Quade and Renner [23] explicitly mention $\varepsilon_{\text{secure}} = 10^{-10}$ as an example instantiation. We are unaware of the origin of these figures, e.g., whether they are based on values used in practice, recommendations, or merely provide numerical examples. It is also unclear whether these figures have been evaluated against a concrete security goal, like the key search game in our work here. Remarkably, the work by Zhang et al. [37] nonetheless states for instance that a choice of $\varepsilon = 10^{-5}$ "is considered to be realistic for cryptography applications."

One may now interpret the suggested parameter $\varepsilon = 10^{-10}$ in [18,21,26,30, 31] to use $\varepsilon_{\text{secure}} \approx \varepsilon_{\text{correct}}$, approximately also matching the concrete suggestions in [5,23] for $\varepsilon_{\text{secure}}$. However, this parameter selection appears optimistic in light of our results regarding bit security. Even for a short 256-bit AES key of quantum security level 128, choosing, for example, $\varepsilon_{\text{secure}} \approx 10^{-12} \approx 2^{-40}$

[3] We note that some works in this domain also define a third criterion, robustness (see, for example, [23,24]). This property can be roughly described as correctness in the absence of an adversary, i.e., noise resilience. In cryptography, one usually uses the two terms correctness and robustness oppositely.

may be insufficient. According to our results, a more conservative choice with a significantly smaller value is advisable unless one has further information about the actual distributions.

If, on the other hand, one assumes that the aforementioned works suggest using significantly smaller $\varepsilon_{\text{secure}} \ll \varepsilon_{\text{correct}}$ for $\varepsilon = 10^{-10}$, then they leave open how to choose $\varepsilon_{\text{secure}}$, as the term $\varepsilon_{\text{correct}}$ dominates the sum. This is even more remarkable because the actual choice of $\varepsilon_{\text{secure}}$ can influence the key rate notably, challenging the practical results in this area: Computing, for example, a 256-bit AES key for $\varepsilon_{\text{secure}} = 2^{-40}$ requires to cut approximately $2 \log 1/\varepsilon_{\text{secure}} = 80$ bits for privacy amplification (also in the quantum case [32]), whereas for $\varepsilon_{\text{secure}} = 2^{-256}$ one loses $2 \log 1/\varepsilon_{\text{secure}} = 512$ bits. Hence, in one case, one requires at least 336 reconciled bits to produce an AES key; in the other case, at least 768 reconciled bits. This even neglects the overhead of maintaining the seed for privacy amplification and the extra time needed to evaluate the amplification step for the smaller statistical bound.

7 Conclusion

When one implements a key generation procedure for λ-bit keys close to uniform, our results suggest using a statistical distance Δ equal to $2^{-\lambda}$. This gives the best bit security level against quantum key search one can hope for. It guarantees a level of approximately $\lambda - \log T_Q$ where $T_Q \leq 2^{\lambda/2}$ is an upper bound on the run time of quantum algorithms. In particular, one achieves the expected bit security bound of at least $\lambda/2$.

Choosing a smaller statistical distance than $2^{-\lambda}$ gives no additional advantage according to our results. If necessary, one may increase Δ up to $2^{-\lambda/2}$, in which case one still gets the expected security lower bound of $\lambda/2$ bits. However, this lower bound is not known to match potentially improved bounds if the global time bound T_Q of quantum adversaries is actually smaller than $2^{\lambda/2}$. Choosing statistical distances (significantly) larger than $2^{-\lambda/2}$ is generally not recommended. Depending on the concrete distribution, one may, however, achieve better results than via the abstract view on the statistical distance.

We emphasise that our results give conservative bounds for general key distributions for which only the statistical distance from uniform is known. If one has specific information about the distribution of keys, one could, in principle, derive more exact bounds. This may be relevant for the case of quantum key distribution (cf. Sect. 6) where smaller statistical distances are often preferred for efficiency reasons. Additionally, our results assume that ordering the keys according to the likelihood comes for free. Quantifying the effort for this part may also allow to argue bounds for smaller statistical distances.

Acknowledgments. We thank the anonymous reviewers for their valuable and constructive feedback, and Gonne Kretschmer for comments. This research has been funded by the German Federal Ministry of Education and Research (BMBF) as part of the program "High-performance components and optimized materials for quantum communication" under project grant CBQD (16KIS1942).

References

1. Bar-Yossef, Z., Jayram, T.S., Kumar, R., Sivakumar, D.: An information statistics approach to data stream and communication complexity. J. Comput. Syst. Sci. **68**(4), 702–732 (2004). (Preliminary Version in 43rd FOCS, 2002). https://doi.org/10.1016/j.jcss.2003.11.006
2. Barker, E.: NIST SP 800-57 Part 1 Rev. 5: recommendation for key management: part 1 – general. Technical report, National Institute of Standards and Technology (2020)
3. Boaron, A., et al.: Secure quantum key distribution over 421 km of optical fiber. Phys. Rev. Lett. **121**, 190502 (2018). https://doi.org/10.1103/PhysRevLett.121.190502. https://link.aps.org/doi/10.1103/PhysRevLett.121.190502
4. Boyer, M., Brassard, G., Høyer, P., Tapp, A.: Tight bounds on quantum searching. Fortschr. Phys. **46**(4–5), 493–505 (1998)
5. Bunandar, D., Govia, L., Krovi, H., Englund, D.: Numerical finite-key analysis of quantum key distribution. npj Quant. Inf. **6** (2020). https://doi.org/10.1038/s41534-020-00322-w
6. Bundesamt für Sicherheit in der Informationstechnik: BSI TR-02102-1: cryptographic mechanisms: recommendations and key lengths. Technical report, Bundesamt für Sicherheit in der Informationstechnik (2024)
7. Chen, L.: Recommendation for key derivation using pseudorandom functions. Technical report. NIST Special Publication (SP) 800-108-r1-upd1. National Institute of Standards and Technology (NIST), Gaithersburg, MD (2024). https://doi.org/10.6028/NIST.SP.800-108r1-upd1
8. Cogliati, B., Fouque, P.A., Goubin, L., Minaud, B.: New security proofs and techniques for hash-and-sign with retry signature schemes. Cryptology ePrint Archive, Paper 2024/609 (2024). https://eprint.iacr.org/2024/609
9. Dodis, Y., Gennaro, R., Håstad, J., Krawczyk, H., Rabin, T.: Randomness extraction and key derivation using the CBC, Cascade and HMAC modes. In: Franklin, M. (ed.) CRYPTO 2004. LNCS, vol. 3152, pp. 494–510. Springer, Heidelberg (2004). https://doi.org/10.1007/978-3-540-28628-8_30
10. Fouque, P.A., Pointcheval, D., Zimmer, S.: HMAC is a randomness extractor and applications to TLS. In: Abe, M., Gligor, V. (eds.) 3rd ACM Symposium on Information, Computer and Communications Security, ASIACCS 08, Tokyo, Japan, 18–20 March 2008, pp. 21–32. ACM Press (2008). https://doi.org/10.1145/1368310.1368317
11. Gentry, C., Wichs, D.: Separating succinct non-interactive arguments from all falsifiable assumptions. Cryptology ePrint Archive, Paper 2010/610 (2010). https://eprint.iacr.org/2010/610
12. Håstad, J., Impagliazzo, R., Levin, L.A., Luby, M.: A pseudorandom generator from any one-way function. SIAM J. Comput. **28**(4), 1364–1396 (1999)
13. He, X., Sun, X., Zhang, J.: Quantum search with prior knowledge. Sci. China Inf. Sci. **67**(9), 192503 (2024). https://doi.org/10.1007/s11432-023-3972-y
14. Krawczyk, H.: Cryptographic extraction and key derivation: the HKDF scheme. In: Rabin, T. (ed.) CRYPTO 2010. LNCS, vol. 6223, pp. 631–648. Springer, Heidelberg (2010). https://doi.org/10.1007/978-3-642-14623-7_34
15. Krawczyk, H., Eronen, P.: HMAC-based Extract-and-Expand Key Derivation Function (HKDF). RFC 5869, May 2010. https://doi.org/10.17487/RFC5869. https://www.rfc-editor.org/info/rfc5869

16. Lee, K.: Bit security as cost to demonstrate advantage **1**(1), 1 (2024). https://doi.org/10.62056/an5txol7
17. Lenstra, A.K.: Key lengths. In: Bidgoli, H. (ed.) The Handbook of Information Security, pp. 617–635. Wiley, Hoboken (2005). Contribution to The Handbook of Information Security
18. Liu, H., et al.: Tight finite-key analysis for quantum key distribution without monitoring signal disturbance. npj Quant. Inf. **7** (2021). https://doi.org/10.1038/s41534-021-00428-9
19. Micciancio, D., Schultz-Wu, M.: Bit security: optimal adversaries, equivalence results, and a toolbox for computational-statistical security analysis. In: Boyle, E., Mahmoody, M. (eds.) Theory of Cryptography - 22nd International Conference, TCC 2024, Proceedings, Part II. LNCS, Milan, Italy, 2–6 December 2024, vol. 15365, pp. 224–254. Springer, Cham (2024). https://doi.org/10.1007/978-3-031-78017-2_8
20. Micciancio, D., Walter, M.: On the bit security of cryptographic primitives. In: Nielsen, J.B., Rijmen, V. (eds.) EUROCRYPT 2018. LNCS, vol. 10820, pp. 3–28. Springer, Cham (2018). https://doi.org/10.1007/978-3-319-78381-9_1
21. Mizutani, A., Curty, M., Imoto, N., Tamaki, K.: Finite-key security analysis of quantum key distribution with imperfect light sources. New J. Phys. **17** (2015). https://doi.org/10.1088/1367-2630/17/9/093011
22. Montanaro, A.: Quantum search with advice. In: van Dam, W., Kendon, V.M., Severini, S. (eds.) TQC 2010. LNCS, vol. 6519, pp. 77–93. Springer, Heidelberg (2011). https://doi.org/10.1007/978-3-642-18073-6_7
23. Müller-Quade, J., Renner, R.: Composability in quantum cryptography. New J. Phys. **11**, 085006 (2009). https://api.semanticscholar.org/CorpusID:7735175
24. Portmann, C., Renner, R.: Security in quantum cryptography. Rev. Mod. Phys. **94**, 025008 (2022). https://doi.org/10.1103/RevModPhys.94.025008. https://link.aps.org/doi/10.1103/RevModPhys.94.025008
25. Renner, R., König, R.: Universally composable privacy amplification against quantum adversaries. In: Kilian, J. (ed.) TCC 2005. LNCS, vol. 3378, pp. 407–425. Springer, Heidelberg (2005). https://doi.org/10.1007/978-3-540-30576-7_22
26. Renner, R., Wolf, R.: Quantum advantage in cryptography. AIAA J. **61**(5), 1895–1910 (2023). https://doi.org/10.2514/1.J062267
27. Rescorla, E.: The Transport Layer Security (TLS) Protocol Version 1.3. RFC 8446 (2018). https://doi.org/10.17487/RFC8446, https://www.rfc-editor.org/info/rfc8446
28. Stebila, D., Fluhrer, S., Gueron, S.: Hybrid key exchange in TLS 1.3. Internet-Draft: draft-ietf-tls-hybrid-design-11. Internet Engineering Task Force (2024, work in progress). https://datatracker.ietf.org/doc/draft-ietf-tls-hybrid-design/11/
29. Steinberger, J.: Improved security bounds for key-alternating ciphers via Hellinger distance. Cryptology ePrint Archive, paper 2012/481 (2012). https://eprint.iacr.org/2012/481
30. Tomamichel, M., Gisin, N., Renner, R.: Tight finite-key analysis for quantum cryptography. Nat. Commun. **3**, 634 (2012). https://doi.org/10.1038/ncomms1631
31. Tomamichel, M., Leverrier, A.: A largely self-contained and complete security proof for quantum key distribution. Quantum **1**, 14 (2017). https://doi.org/10.22331/q-2017-07-14-14
32. Tomamichel, M., Schaffner, C., Smith, A., Renner, R.: Leftover hashing against quantum side information. IEEE Trans. Inf. Theor. **57**, 5524–5535 (2011). https://doi.org/10.1109/TIT.2011.2158473

33. Viamontes, G.F., Markov, I.L., Hayes, J.P.: Is Quantum search practical? Comput. Sci. Eng. **7**(3), 62–70 (2005). https://doi.org/10.1109/MCSE.2005.53
34. Watanabe, S., Yasunaga, K.: Bit security as computational cost for winning games with high probability. In: Tibouchi, M., Wang, H. (eds.) ASIACRYPT 2021. LNCS, vol. 13092, pp. 161–188. Springer, Cham (2021). https://doi.org/10.1007/978-3-030-92078-4_6
35. Yasunaga, K.: Replacing probability distributions in security games via Hellinger distance. In: Tessaro, S. (ed.) 2nd Conference on Information-Theoretic Cryptography, ITC 2021. Leibniz International Proceedings in Informatics (LIPIcs), vol. 199, pp. 17:1–17:15. Schloss Dagstuhl – Leibniz-Zentrum für Informatik, Dagstuhl, Germany (2021). https://doi.org/10.4230/LIPIcs.ITC.2021.17. https://drops.dagstuhl.de/entities/document/10.4230/LIPIcs.ITC.2021.17
36. Zalka, C.: Grover's quantum searching algorithm is optimal. Phys. Rev. A **60**(4), 2746–2751 (1999). https://doi.org/10.1103/physreva.60.2746. http://dx.doi.org/10.1103/PhysRevA.60.2746
37. Zhang, W., et al.: A device-independent quantum key distribution system for distant users. Nature **607**, 687–691 (2022). https://doi.org/10.1038/s41586-022-04891-y
38. Zuckerman, D.: General weak random sources. In: 31st Annual Symposium on Foundations of Computer Science, St. Louis, MO, USA, 22–24 October 1990, pp. 534–543. IEEE Computer Society Press (1990). https://doi.org/10.1109/FSCS.1990.89574

Efficient Implementations

High-Throughput EdDSA Verification on Intel Processors with Advanced Vector Extensions

Bowen Zhang[1], Hao Cheng[2,3,4](✉), Johann Großschädl[1], and Peter Y. A. Ryan[1]

[1] DCS and SnT, University of Luxembourg, Esch-sur-Alzette, Luxembourg
bowen.zhang.002@student.uni.lu, {johann.groszschaedl,peter.ryan}@uni.lu
[2] School of Cyber Science and Technology, Shandong University, Qingdao, China
hao.cheng@sdu.edu.cn
[3] State Key Laboratory of Cryptography and Digital Economy Security, Shandong University, Qingdao, China
[4] Key Laboratory of Cryptologic Technology and Information Security, Ministry of Education, Shandong University, Qingdao, China

Abstract. The Edwards-curve Digital Signature Algorithm (EdDSA) is a deterministic digital signature scheme that has recently been adopted in a range of popular security protocols. Verifying an EdDSA signature involves the computation of a double-scalar multiplication of the form $SB - hA$, which is a costly operation. The vector extensions of modern Intel processors, such as AVX2 and AVX-512, offer a variety of options to speed up double-scalar multiplication thanks to their massive SIMD-parallel processing capabilities. However, in certain application domains like fintech or e-voting, several or many EdDSA verifications have to be performed, and what counts in the end is not the execution time of one single signature verification, but how long it takes to verify a certain number of signatures. For such applications, it makes more sense to use SIMD instructions to maximize the throughput of a batch of verification operations instead of minimizing the latency of one verification. In this paper, we introduce high-throughput AVX2/AVX-512 implementations of EdDSA verification executing four (resp., eight) instances of double-scalar multiplication in a SIMD-parallel fashion, whereby each instance uses a 64-bit element of the 256-bit (resp., 512-bit) vectors. We analyze three techniques for double-scalar multiplication, one that separates the computation of SB and hA, while the other two integrate or interleave them based on a joint-sparse form or non-adjacent form representation of the scalars S and h. Our experiments with 256-bit AVX2 vectorization on an Intel Cascade Lake CPU show that the separate method achieves the best results and reaches a single-core throughput of 48,182 double-scalar multiplications per second, which exceeds the throughput of the currently fastest latency-optimized implementation by 33%.

C. Boura et al. (Eds.): SAC 2025, LNCS 16207, pp. 293–314, 2026.
https://doi.org/10.1007/978-3-032-10536-3_11

1 Introduction

The Edwards-curve Digital Signature Algorithm (EdDSA) [5] can be described as a variant of the classic Schnorr signature scheme [25] with some adaptations to improve both efficiency and security. Most importantly, EdDSA replaces the multiplicative group $\mathbb{Z}_p^*$ by the additive group of points on a twisted Edwards curve [4] that is birationally-equivalent to Curve25519 [3], thereby reducing the execution time and the size of keys and signatures, respectively. The designers of EdDSA also slightly modified the procedure for signature generation so as to support *batch verification*, which allows for verifying a set of $n > 1$ signatures faster than when the conventional verification function is executed n times. As reported in [5], verifying a batch of 64 EdDSA signatures on an Intel Nehalem processor is about 52% faster than computing 64 single-signature verifications separately. On the security side, the improvements include the insertion of the signer's public key in the hash computation (to address concerns about multi-target attacks) and a deterministic generation of the per-message secret scalars (as a hedge against "bad randomness"). Thanks to all these tweaks, EdDSA is a robust, yet efficient, signature scheme that has enjoyed wide adoption in the past 15 years. Besides major security protocols like TLS and IKEv2, EdDSA is also an integral part of numerous other applications, ranging from block chains (e.g., Monero[1]) over anonymity tools (e.g., Tor) to electronic voting systems.

When the message to be signed is short, the most costly computation of the signature generation is a scalar multiplication rB, where B is a generator of an additive subgroup of large prime order ℓ and r is in the range of $[0, \ell - 1]$. The optimized EdDSA software described in [5] performs this scalar multiplication using a fixed-base comb method [7] with a radix-16 signed-digit representation of r and employs a look-up table of 256 pre-computed points. In this way, the scalar multiplication needs only 64 point additions (and exactly as many table queries) and four point doublings. On the other hand, the verification involves a more costly *Double-Scalar Multiplication (DSM)* of the form $SB - hA$, where B is fixed while A becomes only known at run-time. Most optimized software libraries perform this computation in an interleaved or a simultaneous fashion with "joint doublings," which roughly halves the number of point doublings to be performed in total compared to a separate computation of SB and hA. The simplest variant of the *simultaneous technique* (in [16] referred to as "Shamir's trick") pre-computes the point $B - A$ and performs the DSM via the double-and-add method, whereby the addend is either B, $-A$ or $B - A$, depending on value of the bits of S and h at a certain position. More advanced variants aim to reduce the number of additions by lowering the joint Hamming weight of the two scalars (e.g., through a representation in Joint Sparse Form (JSF) or some similar low-weight form [27]) and using a table containing linear combinations of B and A, i.e., the points $\pm uB \pm vA$ for small u and v [16].

The *interleaving technique* to perform a DSM differs from the simultaneous technique since it does not pre-compute $B - A$ (and also no other combination

---

[1] See https://www.susanka.eu/coins-crypto (accessed 2025-01-20).

of B and A) [16]. A basic interleaved computation of $SB - hA$ uses the normal binary representation of the scalars and adds B and A individually, though the point doublings are still performed "jointly." More sophisticated variants of the interleaving method take advantage of a low-weight expansion of S and h, like the width-w Non-Adjacent Form (NAF), in combination with two tables, one containing multiples of B and the other multiples of A [16]. For example, the EdDSA implementation introduced in [5] leverages a width-5 NAF expansion of the scalars, i.e., each of the tables contains $2^{w-2} = 8$ points. However, since one point, namely B, is fixed, it can be beneficial to use tables of different size along with different representations of the two scalars. Most of these algorithms for comb or window-based (double-)scalar multiplication are additive variants of older methods for (multi-)exponentiation, which were widely studied in the context of classic discrete-logarithm cryptosystems [2,20]. Some exponentiation techniques can even be traced back to papers from the 1960s, e.g., [1,24].

Vector Extensions. Basically any modern high-performance processor architecture comes with vector instructions to increase the performance of a multitude of tasks that can take advantage of SIMD-level parallelism, most notably video processing and computer gaming. Examples of common vector instruction sets include Intel's Advanced Vector eXtensions (AVX) and successors (e.g., AVX2 and AVX-512, which support 256-bit and 512-bit vectors, respectively) and the NEON extensions for the ARM architecture. AVX2 adds 16 vector registers to the x64 architecture (`ymm0`–`ymm15`) and provides instructions for SIMD-parallel loads/stores and arithmetic operations with a granularity of bytes, half-words (16 bits), words (32 bits), as well as double-words (64 bits). For example, the AVX2 instruction `vpmuludq` performs a 4-way-parallel multiplication on packed 64-bit unsigned integers and yields four 64-bit results. On the other hand, the ordinary x64 `mul` instruction executes only a single (64×64)-bit multiplication that produces a 128-bit result. AVX-512 further enriches the x64 architecture with 32 vector registers of a length of 512 bits (`zmm0`–`zmm31`). Accordingly, the `vpmuludq` instruction is able to execute eight $(64 \times 64 \rightarrow 64)$-bit multiplications in parallel, i.e., AVX-512 has twice the multiplication-power of AVX2.

Implementation results presented in the literature indicate that the massive parallel processing capabilities of AVX2 and AVX-512 are relatively difficult to exploit for elliptic curve cryptosystems like X25519 and Ed25519. An example of such results are the performance figures of LIB25519 [6] for the computation of a shared secret key for X25519 (i.e., variable-base scalar multiplication). The fastest vectorized AVX2 implementation contained in LIB25519 uses 10 limbs per field-element and reaches an execution time of 87,870 cycles on a Skylake CPU. On the other hand, an ordinary (unvectorized) x64 implementation has an execution time of about 133,947 Skylake cycles, i.e., the AVX2 vector engine reduces the latency by a factor of 1.52. At a first glance, this performance gain is relatively disappointing when taking into account that `vpmuludq` can execute four times more (64×64)-bit multiplications than `mul` or `mulx`. However, there are a number of reasons for this modest speed-up, which range from differences in the representation of the field-elements (i.e., 10 versus four or five limbs) to micro-architectural properties (i.e., instruction latencies and throughputs). An additional aspect that deserves attention is the fact that the number of limbs used by the AVX2 implementation (i.e., 10) can not be evenly divided by the number of 64-bit elements of a vector (i.e., four), which means that numerous AVX2 instructions are executed on vectors that are half empty. The situation becomes even worse for AVX-512 because many vectors are 75% empty and, as a consequence, only two out of the eight 64-bit elements of a vector contribute to the computation of the result. This under-utilization of vector instructions causes sub-optimal performance and also wastes a lot of energy.

Vectorization Bottlenecks. Elliptic curve schemes offer different options to take advantage of parallel processing. Besides the field arithmetic itself, such options do also exist for the point arithmetic (e.g., certain formulae for point addition or doubling support the parallel execution of two or more field-operations) and the scalar multiplication (e.g., some scalar multiplication algorithms allow two point operations to be carried out in parallel). The actual speed-up a software developer can achieve by taking advantage of SIMD-parallel processing at the layer of the field arithmetic, point arithmetic, and scalar multiplication is often restricted by dependencies between operations that enforce a sequential execution. This explains why the speed-up factor due to vectorization (compared to conventional execution) is always below the degree of parallelism offered by the vector instructions. However, in the case of X25519, it seems the performance one can gain by increasing the parallel-processing capabilities of an execution environment is significantly below the theoretical maximum. To give a concrete example, the benchmarking results released in [17] demonstrate that vectorized implementations of X25519 do not scale particularly well when migrating from one generation of AVX to the next. While AVX-512 (theoretically) doubles the degree of parallelism versus AVX2 (since it is possible to execute operations on eight 64-bit elements instead of four), the actual reduction in execution time is much smaller, namely only 25% (74,368 versus 99,400 Skylake cycles [17]).

The parallelization bottlenecks sketched above (i.e., partially empty vectors and sequential dependencies) are highly challenging to overcome, which implies that latency-optimized implementations are not capable to utilize the massive computing power of vector engines like AVX2 in an ideal way. This observation initiated research on how to use vector engines to optimize throughput instead of latency and paved the way to vectorized implementations of cryptosystems that have the goal of minimizing the execution time of several instances of an operation instead of a single instance. For example, such throughput-optimized implementations have been described for X25519 key exchange [10] and isogeny-based elliptic curve cryptosystems [8,9]. The variable-base scalar multiplication on Curve25519 introduced in [10] reached significantly higher throughput than any of the latency-optimized implementations from [11–13,18,22]. There are some important differences between optimization for latency and optimization for throughput. Of course, minimizing the latency of one scalar multiplication also reduces the total execution time of several scalar multiplications, but due to the mentioned parallelization bottlenecks, optimizing for low latency entails a sub-optimal utilization of vector engines. High-throughput implementations effectively overcome these bottlenecks by executing, for example, four instances of scalar multiplication in parallel with AVX2 instructions, where each instance uses a single 64-bit element of a 256-bit vector. This approach naturally solves the problem of partially empty (or even largely empty) vectors and also reduces the issues with sequential dependencies because the vast majority of operations can now be executed in a SIMD-parallel fashion (in essence, the only operation that is not parallelizable for high throughput is table look-up).

Our Contributions. Previous research on throughput-optimized implementation of elliptic curve cryptography solely considered key exchange schemes such as X25519. In this paper, we introduce the first high-throughput implementation of the Ed25519 signature system, especially the verification. More precisely, we present a vectorized implementation of Ed25519 verification that can execute four instances of a DSM of the form $SB - hA$ (with a fixed point B) in parallel using AVX2 instructions, whereby each instance occupies a 64-bit element of the 256-bit vectors. Both scalars, as well as point A, can be different in each of the four instances. Such a throughput-optimized implementation of the verification has many real-world use cases. For example, it allows one to quickly check the validity of a chain of (typically three) certificates used by TLS to authenticate web servers. This validation can take advantage of a parallel execution of the DSMs needed to verify the three signatures in the certificates. Blockchains, like those used by crypto currencies, require verifications of large numbers of signatures to confirm the validity of the transactions in a block before the block can be added to the chain. What counts in the end is the time needed for all these verification operations and not for a single one. Similarly, (very) large numbers of signatures have to be verified by e-voting systems, which is much faster when the DSM implementation targets high throughput instead of low latency.

Our main contribution is a detailed analysis and comparison of algorithms for DSM to identify the best one for maximizing throughput. These algorithms include simultaneous and interleaved techniques, which are widely used by low-latency implementations, but also an uncommon approach that fully separates the computation of SB and hA. This separated method exploits the individual arithmetic strengths of the twisted Edwards model and the Montgomery model by performing the fixed-base scalar multiplication SB with a comb method on the twisted Edwards curve, but the variable-base scalar multiplication hA on the birationally-equivalent Montgomery curve using a Montgomery ladder, as proposed in [15]. Our results for AVX2 show that, somewhat surprisingly, the separated method achieves the best results and outperforms the simultaneous and interleaving techniques. Consequently, DSM algorithms that are efficient in terms of latency are not (necessarily) the best option in a throughput-oriented setting, and this seems to hold also for AVX-512. We mainly focus on AVX2 in this paper as AVX2 instructions are supported by basically any modern Intel CPU, while relatively few come with AVX-512. However, we also present some (preliminary) results for an AVX-512 implementation executing eight instances in parallel. These results show that AVX-512 instructions almost double the throughput of the AVX2 implementation, which confirms the scalability of the separated technique for DSM. In addition, the comparison between AVX2 and AVX-512 results indicates that the implementation makes near-ideal use of the enormous parallel processing power of modern Intel CPUs.

2 Background

2.1 Notation

This section presents the symbols used throughout the paper. For prime-field operations, we use q to denote the prime defining the underlying field, and the prime field with q elements is written as $\mathbb{F}_q$. The SIMD-parallel field arithmetic operates on *limb vectors* and *limb vector sets*, with the same representation as defined in [10]. In the case of AVX2, a limb vector consists of four limbs (each of a length of 29 bits), but these four limbs belong to four different field elements and not to one and the same field-element. Since we use 29-bit limbs, four field elements can be stored in nine limb vectors, called a limb vector set. A limb vector is represented by a bold lowercase letter (e.g., $\boldsymbol{v}$), and a limb vector set by a bold uppercase letter (e.g., $\boldsymbol{V}$). Furthermore, we denote a twisted Edwards curve as E_T, and a curve over $\mathbb{F}_q$ as $E_T(\mathbb{F}_q)$. The base point (generator) of E_T is represented by B, its order by ℓ, and d denotes the curve parameter. An uppercase letter in script style (e.g., $\mathcal{P}$) represents a point vector set. Specifically, $\mathcal{O}$ is used for a point vector set containing only neutral elements. We use $||$ to indicate the concatenation of strings.

2.2 Intel AVX2 Extensions

In this work, we take advantage of the 256 bit vector extensions, namely using AVX2 instructions, to enhance the throughput of our software. Intel's Advanced Vector eXtension 2 (AVX2) is an instruction set extension designed for the SIMD parallel computing paradigm. It was first introduced with the Haswell microarchitecture in 2013, and is now supported by most of the main stream processors. AVX2 is built upon its original AVX, by expanding the width of the vector to 256-bit, and increasing the operand number from two to three in instruction format. AVX2 has sixteen 256-bit vector registers (`ymm0-ymm15`) and hundreds of vector instructions. We test our software on an Intel Cascade Lake processor. As a super-scalar processor, Cascade Lake follows an out-of-order fashion when assigning the micro-operations decoded from the AVX instructions to different execution ports. The Cascade Lake has a very identical architecture to its predecessor Skylake [28], which means it has eight execution ports (port 0 to 7). Ports 0, 1, and 5 can handle vector instructions, while ports 2, 3, 4, and 7 are used for memory access instructions. Branching and other instructions are assigned to port 6. Taking some arithmetic and logical operation instructions as an example, we summarize their latency, CPI, and execution ports[2] in Table 1.

[2] See https://uops.info/table.html.

To be specific, the registers of three operands in use for AVX2 instructions are `ymm, ymm, ymm`.

As mentioned in the last section, we will describe the implementation details of our throughput-optimized EdDSA software using AVX2 as a case study because AVX2 is more widely available than AVX-512. However, we also developed a prototype for AVX-512, which was relatively simple since AVX2 and AVX-512 are very similar when optimizing for high throughput. As will be shown in Sect. 4, the throughput almost doubled when we migrated our software from AVX2 to AVX-512.

Table 1. Execution details of example instructions.

Operation	Instruction	Latency	CPI	Ports
ADD	`vpaddq`	1	0.33	0, 1, and 5
MUL	`vpmuludq`	5	0.50	0 and 1
AND	`vpand`	1	0.33	0, 1, and 5
OR	`vpor`	1	0.33	0, 1, and 5
XOR	`vpxor`	1	0.33	0, 1, and 5

2.3 Ed25519

Ed25519 is an instance of EdDSA based on an elliptic curve known as Edwards25519. It is defined by the formulae:

$$x^2 + y^2 = 1 + dx^2y^2,$$

where d is a specific constant with $d = -121665/121666$, and all operations are performed over the prime field $\mathbb{F}_q$ with $q = 2^{255} - 19$. Ed25519 plays a key role in transport layer protocols such as TLS and was included in the FIPS185-6 Digital Signature Standard by NIST in 2023. In the following, we provide a brief overview of the main algorithms of Ed25519. For more details, we refer the reader to [5].

Point Encoding and Decoding. All integers are coded in the little-endian format. A point $P = (x, y)$ on $E_T(\mathbb{F}_q)$ is encoded as follows. First, clear the most significant bit of the y-coordinate and encode it as a 256-bit string in little-endian format. Then, copy the least significant bit of the x-coordinate to the place of the most significant bit of the final bit-string. The point encoding can be defined formally as:

$$Encode(P) = (x \, mod \, 2) \, || \, y.$$

The point decoding takes a 256-bit string s as input. First, it extracts the y-coordinate from s with $y = (s_{255}, ..., s_0)_2$. Then, it recovers the x-coordinate by calculating $x = \sqrt{(y^2 - 1)/(dy^2 + 1)}$. If $s_{255} \neq x$ mod 2 then set $x = q - x$. The point decoding fails if either $y \notin \mathbb{F}_q$ or the square root does not exist. The point decoding can be defined formally as:

$$Decode(s) = (x, y).$$

Key Generation. The private key and public key are generated using Algorithm 1. The execution time of key generation is dominated by the fixed-base scalar multiplication sB.

Algorithm 1. Ed25519 key generation

Output:(sk, pk).

1: $sk \leftarrow \{0,1\}^{256}$ ▷ Generate a random 256-bit integer
2: $\text{HASH}(sk) = (h_{511}, ..., h_0)_2$
3: $s = 2^{254} + \sum_{3 \leq i \leq 253} 2^i h_i$
4: $pk = Encode(sB)$
5: **return** (sk, pk)

Signature Generation. The input to the signing procedure is the signer's key pair (sk, pk), and a message M of arbitrary size. The signature is calculated as shown in Algorithm 2. The execution time of signature generation is dominated by the fixed-base scalar multiplication rB.

Algorithm 2. Ed25519 signature generation

Input:(sk, pk), message M.
Output:$(R\,||\,S)$.

1: $\text{HASH}(sk) = (h_{511}, ..., h_0)_2$
2: $r = \text{HASH}((h_{511}, ..., h_{256})_2\,||\,pk\,||\,M) \bmod \ell$
3: $R = Encode(rB)$
4: $S = r + \text{HASH}(R\,||\,pk\,||\,M)s \bmod \ell$ ▷ s is obtained at key generation
5: **return** $(R\,||\,S)$

Signature Verification. To verify a signature $(R\,||\,S)$ on message M, given signer's public key pk, the signature verification proceeds as specified in Algorithm 3. The verification time primarily depends on the DSM, i.e., the computation of $SB - hA$, for which we discuss some efficient implementations in Sect. 3.

Algorithm 3. Ed25519 signature verification

Input: pk, message M, $(R\,||\,S)$.
Output: *Accept* or *Reject*.

```
R' = Decode(R)
A = Decode(pk)
if any Decode fails then
    return Reject
end if
h = HASH(R || pk || M) mod ℓ
if R' = SB − hA then
    return Accept
end if
return Reject
```

3 Implementation

When assuming that the message M to be signed is not excessively long, the most time-consuming operation in EdDSA verification is the DSM of the form $R = SB - hA$, which contains a fixed-base scalar multiplication SB and a variable-base scalar multiplication hA. From a high-level perspective, there exist two main techniques for computing a DSM, namely (i) the *combined* approach that computes SB and hA with joint doublings (two variants of this approach, namely the simultaneous and interleaving technique, were sketched in Sect. 1), and (ii) the *separate* approach that computes SB and hA sequentially and independently of each other. The former approach usually takes advantage of a special representations of the scalars to reduce the number of point operations, e.g., Non-Adjacent Form (NAF) or Joint-Sparse Form (JSF), whereas the latter utilizes the birational equivalence between the twisted Edwards model and the Montgomery model.

In this section, we show how the Intel AVX2 instructions can be used to execute four DSM instances in parallel, each with different points and scalars, to improve the throughput of EdDSA verification, whereby the NAF-based, JSF-based, and separate approaches are considered. Our throughput-optimized software enables a "batch execution" of EdDSA verification since four EdDSA signatures are verified simultaneously (the number of parallel instances increases to eight in the case of AVX-512). Therefore, our throughput-optimized implementation is somewhat similar to the (algorithmic) batch verification described in [5]. However, this batch verification has two disadvantages compared to our approach. First, batch verification is only effective when the size of the batch is relatively large (in Sect. 1 we mentioned a speed-up of 52% for a batch size of 64), whereas our implementation is able to boost throughput with a batch of only four (AVX2) or eight (AVX-512) signatures. Second, when the verification of a batch fails, each signatures still needs to be verified separately. In addition to describing throughput-optimization with AVX2 (resp., AVX-512), we also study how one can further improve the throughput by applying multiprocessing.

3.1 Limb Vector Sets

Similar to [10], the data structure we operate on for the field arithmetic is a (4×1)-way *limb vector set*. For each field element, we employ a 29-bit-per-limb (i.e., radix-2^{29}) representation, meaning nine limbs are needed in total. Given four field elements a, b, c, and d, the (4×1)-way limb vector $\boldsymbol{V}$ is defined formally as

$$\begin{aligned}\boldsymbol{V} = [a, b, c, d] &= [\sum_{i=0}^{8} 2^{29i} a_i, \sum_{i=0}^{8} 2^{29i} b_i, \sum_{i=0}^{8} 2^{29i} c_i, \sum_{i=0}^{8} 2^{29i} d_i] \\ &= \sum_{i=0}^{8} 2^{29i} [a_i, b_i, c_i, d_i] = \sum_{i=0}^{8} 2^{29i} \boldsymbol{v}_i,\end{aligned}$$

where $\boldsymbol{v}_i = [a_i, b_i, c_i, d_i]$ is called a limb vector. As explained in the previous section, in the case of AVX2 a limb vector set consists of nine limb vectors, each containing four limbs from four different field elements. Analogous to [10], a *point vector set* is then used for the elliptic curve arithmetic. Given four points A, B, C, and D in affine coordinates, the point vector set $\mathcal{P}$ is defined formally as

$$\begin{aligned}\mathcal{P} &= [A, B, C, D] \\ &= [(x_A, y_A), (x_B, y_B), (x_C, y_C), (x_D, y_D)] \\ &= ([x_A, x_B, x_C, x_D], [y_A, y_B, y_C, y_D]) \\ &= (x_{\mathcal{P}}, y_{\mathcal{P}}),\end{aligned}$$

where the limb vector set $x_{\mathcal{P}}$ (resp. $y_{\mathcal{P}}$) represents the x-coordinate (resp. y-coordinate) of four points. For points in projective coordinates, the corresponding point vector set is $\mathcal{P} = (X_{\mathcal{P}}, Y_{\mathcal{P}}, Z_{\mathcal{P}})$. We adopt the formulas for point addition/doubling from [19].

3.2 Implementation Using NAF-Based Approach

The first implementation option uses the ω-NAF representation [26] for the scalars, applied with a so-called interleaving technique [14]. This NAF-based approach relies on two look-up tables, one for the fixed point B and the other for the variable point A, using a coefficient of the ω-NAF expansion (of the scalar) as the input for a table. Taking scalar h and point A as an example, the ω_A-NAF expansion of h is $h = \sum_{i=0}^{l-1} h_i 2^i$, where each coefficient $|h_i| < 2^{\omega_A - 1}$, i.e., the range of the coefficients and the size of the look-up table is determined by ω_A. In addition, in this expansion, the most significant coefficient h_{l-1} is non-zero, and all non-zero coefficients are odd. The associated look-up table is composed of the points

$$\left\{A_i = (2i + 1)A \mid 0 \le i < 2^{\omega_A - 2}\right\}.$$

Note the specific parameters $\omega_B = 7$ and $\omega_A = 5$ are used in state-of-the-art NAF-based implementations, e.g., [12] and [6], and therefore we adopt the same setting for our implementation.

```c
#include <immintrin.h>
/* 4-way arithmetic operations on packed 64-bit integers */
#define VSUB(X, Y)          _mm256_sub_epi64(X, Y)
#define VABS32(X)           _mm256_abs_epi32(X)
/* 4-way bitwise logical operations on packed 64-bit integers */
#define VXOR(X, Y)          _mm256_xor_si256(X, Y)
#define VAND(X, Y)          _mm256_and_si256(X, Y)
#define VOR(X, Y)           _mm256_or_si256(X, Y)
#define VSHR(X, Y)          _mm256_srli_epi64(X, Y)
/* Other 4-way operations on packed 64-bit integers */
#define VSET164(X)          _mm256_set1_epi64(X)
#define VSET64(W, X, Y, Z) _mm256_set_epi64x(W, X, Y, Z)
#define VZERO               _mm256_setzero_si256()
/* Structure for projective point representation */
typedef struct projective_point {
    __m256i x[NWORDS];
    __m256i y[NWORDS];
    __m256i z[NWORDS];
} ProPoint;
```

Listing 1. Defined macros for AVX intrinsics and structure for point representation.

```c
void table_query(ProPoint *r, ProPoint *table, __m256i b)
{
  const __m256i babs = VABS32(b), one = VSET164(1);
  __m256i xP[9], yP[9], zP[9], t[9], temp, bsign, bmask;
  uint32_t xcoor[4][9], ycoor[4][9], zcoor[4][9], index[4];
  int i, j;

  /* Extract the coefficients from a vector */
  for (i = 0; i < 4; i++) index[i] = (((uint32_t*) &babs)[i*2] + 1) / 2;
  /* Start table query*/
  for (i = 0; i < 4; i++) {
    for (j = 0; j < 9; j++) {
      xcoor[i][j] = ((uint32_t*) &table[index[i]].x[j])[i*2];
      ycoor[i][j] = ((uint32_t*) &table[index[i]].y[j])[i*2];
      zcoor[i][j] = ((uint32_t*) &table[index[i]].z[j])[i*2];
    }
  }
  /* Form the point vector set with query results */
  for (i = 0; i < 9; i++) {
    xP[i] = VSET64(xcoor[3][i], xcoor[2][i], xcoor[1][i], xcoor[0][i]);
    yP[i] = VSET64(ycoor[3][i], ycoor[2][i], ycoor[1][i], ycoor[0][i]);
    zP[i] = VSET64(zcoor[3][i], zcoor[2][i], zcoor[1][i], zcoor[0][i]);
  }
  /* Conditional negation */
  bsign = VSHR(b, 31);
  bmask = VSUB(zero, bsign);
  for (i = 0; i < 9; i++) {
    temp  = VAND(VXOR(xP[i], yP[i]), bmask);
    xP[i] = VXOR(xP[i], temp);
    yP[i] = VXOR(yP[i], temp);
  }
  mpi29_copy_avx2(t, zP);
  mpi29_gfp_neg_avx2(t);
  mpi29_cswap_avx2(zP, t, bsign);
  /* Copy final result to the point vector set */
  mpi29_copy_avx2(r->x, xP);
  mpi29_copy_avx2(r->y, yP);
  mpi29_copy_avx2(r->z, zP);
}
```

Listing 2. Simplified C source code of batch table query.

Algorithm 4. Batch DSM implementation using NAF-based approach.

Input: Fixed base point vector set $\mathcal{B}$, variable base point vector set $\mathcal{A}$, scalar sets $\boldsymbol{S}$ and $\boldsymbol{H}$, a precomputed table $\mathcal{T}_{\mathcal{B}}$ for $\mathcal{B}$, and window sizes $\omega_{\mathcal{A}}$ and $\omega_{\mathcal{B}}$
Output: $\mathcal{R} = \boldsymbol{S}\mathcal{B} - \boldsymbol{H}\mathcal{A}$

1: $\mathcal{T}_{\mathcal{A}} \leftarrow$ TableComputation($\mathcal{A}$) ▷ Compute the look-up table for $\mathcal{A}$
2: $\boldsymbol{S}' \leftarrow \omega_{\mathcal{B}}$-NAF($\boldsymbol{S}$), $\boldsymbol{H}' \leftarrow \omega_{\mathcal{A}}$-NAF($\boldsymbol{H}$)
3: $t \leftarrow$ MaxLength($\boldsymbol{S}', \boldsymbol{H}'$)
4: $\mathcal{R} \leftarrow \mathcal{O}$, $\mathcal{P} \leftarrow \mathcal{O}$
5: **for** i from $t-1$ to 0 by 1 **do**
6: $\quad \mathcal{R} \leftarrow$ PointDoubling($\mathcal{R}$)
7: $\quad$ **if** $\boldsymbol{S}'_i \neq \boldsymbol{0}$ **then**
8: $\quad\quad \mathcal{P} \leftarrow$ TableQuery($\mathcal{T}_{\mathcal{B}}, \lfloor \frac{|\boldsymbol{S}'_i|+1}{2} \rfloor$) ▷ Refer to Listing 2
9: $\quad\quad \mathcal{R} \leftarrow$ PointAddition($\mathcal{R}, \mathcal{P}$)
10: $\quad$ **end if**
11: $\quad$ **if** $\boldsymbol{H}'_i \neq \boldsymbol{0}$ **then**
12: $\quad\quad \mathcal{P} \leftarrow$ TableQuery($\mathcal{T}_{\mathcal{A}}, \lfloor \frac{|\boldsymbol{H}'_i|+1}{2} \rfloor$) ▷ Refer to Listing 2
13: $\quad\quad \mathcal{R} \leftarrow$ PointAddition($\mathcal{R}, \mathcal{P}$)
14: $\quad$ **end if**
15: **end for**
16: **return** $\mathcal{R}$

Algorithm 4 describes our batch DSM implementation using the NAF-based approach. After getting the NAF representations of the scalars, we first identify the longest NAF expansion among all instances and pad others with zeros on the MSB side. Then, the main loop (line 5 to 15) starts, in which each iteration processes a single coefficient of each expansion. Note that, if a coefficient is zero in an instance, the related table query and point addition could be skipped for this instance. However, due to the SIMD pattern, we will skip the computation only if *all* coefficients in the four (resp., eight) instances are zero. A slightly simplified version of the batch table-query is shown in Listing 2, which is implemented using the AVX2 intrinsics and projective point representation detailed in Listing 1. The table query loads points in extended affine coordinates[3], and to handle the case that some coefficients in a vector are zero, the point at infinity (again in extended affine coordinates) is included in the look-up table.

3.3 Implementation Using JSF-Based Approach

The second implementation option uses the JSF [27] representation for scalars, and needs only one joint look-up table containing besides the two points B and $-A$ also their sum and difference. The JSF expansion uses a signed coefficient set $\{-1, 0, 1\}$ to represent two scalars s and h in a matrix of the form:

$$\begin{pmatrix} s_{l-1} & s_{l-2} & \cdots & s_0 \\ h_{l-1} & h_{l-1} & \cdots & h_0 \end{pmatrix},$$

[3] An extended affine point has the form (u, v, w), where $u = (x+y)/2$, $v = (y-x)/2$, $w = dxy$, and d is the parameter of the twisted Edwards curve [5].

Algorithm 5. Batch DSM implementation using JSF-based approach.

Input: Fixed base point vector set $\mathcal{B}$, variable base point vector set $\mathcal{A}$, and two scalar sets $\boldsymbol{S}$ and $\boldsymbol{H}$

Output: $\mathcal{R} = \boldsymbol{S}\mathcal{B} - \boldsymbol{H}\mathcal{A}$

$(\boldsymbol{S}', \boldsymbol{H}') \leftarrow$ JOINTSPARSEFORM$(\boldsymbol{S}, \boldsymbol{H})$
$t \leftarrow \max(\boldsymbol{S}', \boldsymbol{H}')$
$\mathcal{T} \leftarrow [-\mathcal{A}, \mathcal{B} + \mathcal{A}, \mathcal{B}, \mathcal{B} - \mathcal{A}]$ ▷ Compute the look-up table
$\mathcal{R} \leftarrow \mathcal{O}$, $\mathcal{P} \leftarrow \mathcal{O}$
for i from $t-1$ to 0 by 1 **do**
    $\mathcal{R} \leftarrow$ POINTDOUBLING$(\mathcal{R})$
    $\boldsymbol{D}_i \leftarrow 3\boldsymbol{S}'_i + \boldsymbol{H}'_i$
    if $\boldsymbol{D}_i \neq \boldsymbol{0}$ **then**
        $\mathcal{P} \leftarrow$ TABLEQUERY$(\mathcal{T}, \boldsymbol{D}_i)$ ▷ Refer to Listing 2
        $\mathcal{R} \leftarrow$ POINTADDITION$(\mathcal{R}, \mathcal{P})$
    end if
end for
return $\mathcal{R}$

where $s = \sum_{i=0}^{l-1} s_i 2^i$ and $h = \sum_{i=0}^{l-1} h_i 2^i$. Thus, the corresponding look-up table contains four entries, namely $[-A, B+A, B, B-A]$. The JSF of two scalars has, in the average case, a joint Hamming weight of 0.5 and, therefore, reduces the number of point additions by 25% compared t o a conventional implementation. The idea of reducing the joint Hamming weight of two scalars can be extended in two directions. First, one can extend the digit set from $\{0, \pm 1\}$ to $\{0, \pm 1, \pm 3\}$ or $\{0, \pm 1, \pm 3, \pm 5\}$ to further reduce the Joint Hamming weight (e.g., from 0.5 to roughly 0.38 when ± 3 is included in the digit set) at the expense of a larger table. A second direction is to generalize the JSF to support more than two scalars, e.g., to minimize the joint Hamming weight of eight scalars, which is relevant in the case when four DSMs are computed in parallel.

Algorithm 5 presents our batch DSM implementation using JSF-based approach. Compared to the NAF-based implementation (Algorithm 4), the main difference is that the processed coefficient is now a linear combination d_i of a column (s_i, h_i) from the matrix, instead of the JSF expansion itself. On the other hand, a similarity is that we will skip the table query and point addition in an iteration only if all coefficients being processed are zero.

3.4 Implementation Using the Separate Approach

The third implementation option is computing two scalar multiplications SB and hA separately. Cheng et al. [10] present a batch implementation of fixed-base scalar multiplication used in X25519 key generation[4], whereby the table query operation loads all possible points (related to a scalar nibble) from a

[4] From a high-level perspective, this implementation is a SIMD-parallel variant of the fixed-base scalar multiplication in [5], which, as mentioned in Sect. 1, uses a look-up table with 256 points and executes 64 point additions and four doublings.

pre-computed table and employs a mask to extract the right one to ensure constant-time execution. Their implementation prevents cache-timing attacks at the cost of additional operations, which is not necessary for our implementation since the two scalars used in EdDSA verification are not secret. Our implementation therefore selects the corresponding points straightforwardly, and thus reduces the execution time[5].

Algorithm 6. Scalar multiplication on TE curve using Montgomery ladder [15]

Input: Twisted Edwards curve E_T over $\mathbb{F}_q$ of cardinality $h\ell$ where ℓ is prime, rational point $P = (x, y) \in E_T(\mathbb{F}_q)$ with $\text{ord}(P) \geq \ell$, scalar $k \in [0, \ell - 1]$.
Output: Point $Q = kP$ in projective coordinates.
1: if $k = 0$ then return $(0 : 1 : 1)$
2: if $k = \ell - 1$ then return $(-x : y : 1)$
3: $P_m \leftarrow \text{TedToMon}(P)$
4: $(Q_1, Q_2) \leftarrow \text{MonLadder}(P_m)$
5: $Q_r \leftarrow \text{RecoveryY}(Q_1, Q_2, P_m)$
6: $Q \leftarrow \text{MonToTed}(Q_r)$
7: return Q

The basic idea is to use the twisted-Edwards model of the curve for the fixed-base scalar multiplication SB and the birationally-equivalent Montgomery model for the variable-base scalar multiplication hA. Algorithm 6 describes the computation of hA more formally. We compute hA using the Montgomery ladder on a Montgomery curve that is birationally-equivalent to the twisted Edwards curve, which requires a mapping of points from one curve model to the other. These mappings utilize the point conversion formula in [4]. The mapping from twisted Edwards to Montgomery involves a conversion from projective to affine coordinates (so that we can use the conventional Montgomery ladder), for which our implementation adopts a simultaneous inversion technique [21]. Given a point $P' = (X_{P'}, Y_{P'}, Z_{P'})$ in projective coordinates on the twisted Edwards curve, the corresponding point $P = (X_P, Y_P, Z_P)$ in projective coordinates on the birationally-equivalent Montgomery curve (i.e., constant $a = 486662$) can be computed as shown on the left side of the formulae below

$$
\begin{aligned}
X_P &= (Z_{P'} + Y_{P'})X_{P'} & X_{P'} &= \text{ModSqrt}(-a)X_P Y_P (X_P + Z_P)\\
Y_P &= \text{ModSqrt}(-a)(Z_{P'} + Y_{P'})Z_{P'} & Y_{P'} &= (X_P - Z_P)Y_P Z_P\\
Z_P &= (Z_{P'} - Y_{P'})X_{P'} & Z_{P'} &= Y_P Z_P (X_P + Z_P).
\end{aligned}
$$

The mapping in the other direction can use the formulae on the right side. After the mapping of point A, we take advantage of the Montgomery ladder [21] to compute the scalar multiplication kP, which operates on only the affine x-coordinate of the point P, i.e., X_P and Z_P. Then, to recover the affine y-coordinate of the point P needed by EdDSA, we use the *y recovery* formula

[5] One should switch back to constant-time table query when processing sensitive values.

```
void ted_mul_varbase(ProPoint *r, ProPoint *p, const __m512i *k)
{
  ProPoint h, q1, q2, q3;
  AffPoint s;
  __m256i t[9];
  /* Convert point on Ed25519 to Curve25519 */
  conv_ted_to_mon(&h, p);
  /* Obtain the affine coordinate of the input point on Curve25519 */
  mpi29_gfp_inv_4x1w(t, h.z);
  mpi29_gfp_mul_4x1w(s.x, t, h.x);
  mpi29_gfp_mul_4x1w(s.y, t, h.y);
  /* Perform variable base multiplication on Curve25519 */
  mon_mul_varbase(&q1, &q2, k, s.x);
  /* Perform point recovery on Curve25519 */
  point_recovery(&q3, &s, &q1, &q2);
  /* Convert point on Curve25519 to Ed25519 */
  conv_mon_to_ted(r, &q3);
}
```

Listing 3. Simplified code of (4×1)-way variable-base multiplication

from [23]. Given the two points $Q_1 = kP = (X_1, Z_1)$ and $Q_2 = (k+1)P = (X_2, Z_2)$ output from Montgomery ladder and $P = (x_P, y_P)$, we can recover the full projective coordinate $(X_{rec}, Y_{rec}, Z_{rec})$ on Curve25519 by:

$$
\begin{aligned}
X_{\text{rec}} &= 2By_P Z_1 Z_2 X_1 \\
Y_{\text{rec}} &= Z_2[(X_1 + x_P Z_1 + 2aZ_1)(X_1 + x_P Z_1)] - 2aZ_1^2 - (X_1 - x_P Z_1)^2 X_2 \\
Z_{\text{rec}} &= 2By_P Z_1 Z_2 Z_1.
\end{aligned}
$$

Finally, the recovered point is converted back to its corresponding point on the twisted Edwards curve. The associated code is shown in Listing 3.

While the basic principle is relatively simple, one has to pay attention to certain corner cases in the point mappings and the recovery of the y-coordinate, which can fail the implementation. All these corner cases were analyzed in [15]. In short, encountering these corner cases can be avoided when we insist that the scalar is fully reduced (i.e., in the range $[0, \ell - 1]$) and the point A does not have low order. These are exactly t he requirements imposed by widely-used software libraries like LibSodium (see [15] for details).

3.5 Applying Multiprocessing

To further improve software throughput, we take advantage of thread-level parallelism in addition to the parallelism offered by the vector instructions, for which we use OpenMP[6]. The provided directive `#pragma omp parallel` allows the user to distribute a computation across multiple threads. Since in the batch implementation each instance of DSA is independent, which implies that no synchronization between threads is actually needed, applying multiprocessing to our software is straightforward. To be specific, we simply use the OpenMP API directives `sections` and `section` to allocate a single (4×1)-way DSM to

[6] https://www.openmp.org.

```
void multiprocessing_example()
{
  /* Set thread number to 3 */
  omp_set_num_threads(3);
  /* Start the multiprocessing implementation */
  #pragma omp parallel
  {
    #pragma omp sections
    {
      #pragma omp section
        double_scalar_mul_4x1w();
      #pragma omp section
        double_scalar_mul_4x1w();
      #pragma omp section
        double_scalar_mul_4x1w();
    }
  }
}
```

Listing 4. Example code of a multiprocessing implementation of batch DSM using three threads.

each thread. Taking a multiprocessing implementation using three threads as an example, the associated code snippet is shown in Listing 4.

4 Evaluation

To measure the performance of our software, we use an Intel Xeon W-2245 Cascade Lake CPU, which is clocked at 3.9 GHz. Both Turbo Boost and Hyper-Threading are disabled during the measurements. Our source code is compiled using Clang version 14.0.0 with the optimization flag[7] `-O2`, to ensure alignment with other benchmark implementations [6,12]. The source code of the field-arithmetic operations was taken from the implementation described in [10], for which the source code is linked in the paper.

Table 2. Latency and throughput of our AVX2 software on Intel Xeon W-2245 Cascade Lake CPU (latency is the execution time of four parallel instances).

DSM implementation	Latency	Throughput
NAF-based approach	494,376 cycles	31,654 ops/sec
JSF-based approach	502,868 cycles	31,117 ops/sec
separate approach	324,772 cycles	48,182 ops/sec

We benchmarked our three different DSM implementations described in Sect. 3 on said CPU, and present the measured results in Table 2. The separate approach clearly turns out to be the most efficient implementation option

[7] The optimization level does not have a significant impact on the results in our experiment.

Table 3. Probability of skipping the table query and point addition in a single iteration.

Representation	#Instances	Probability
5-NAF	1	83.6%
	4	48.7%
7-NAF	1	87.7%
	4	59.0%
JSF	1	49.5%
	4	6.2%

for batch DSM, showing an improvement of the throughput by more than 52% compared to the other two options. A major reason is that the execution time for the separate approach does not depend on the representation of the scalars. In the NAF- and JSF-based implementations, the execution time is affected by the "density" of zero coefficients in their scalar representations since they allow one to skip operations (i.e., table query and point addition). Most latency-optimized implementations (e.g., [6,12,15]) adopt either a NAF- or JSF-based approach because it can yield fewer table lookups and point additions. However, the probability of skipping operations in NAF- and JSF-based implementations is much lower in a batch implementation, as shown more concretely in Table 3. The probability data are obtained from the experiments, where for each case, we examined one million random 255-bit integers (i.e., scalars). Per Table 3, the table query and point addition are skipped with a high probability in the single-instance case, but becomes much lower when four-instance are computed in parallel, as these operations will be skipped only if *all* the processed coefficients of the batch are zero. Furthermore, this issue will be even amplified if a more powerful vector extension is used, such as AVX-512, which allows one to compute eight DSMs in parallel instead of four. As a result, the separate method is a better implementation option for batch DSM software since it is completely unaffected by this issue.

We also carried out some experiments with variants of the JSF that try to minimize the joint Hamming weight of eight scalars, but the probability for skipping a table-query and point addition was always below 10%. Since this is only a marginal improvement over the conventional JSF representation, we did not consider it in the implementation described below. However, we remark that the throughput for the JSF-based implementation could be further improved by a few percent when an advanced JSF variant is used.

Table 4 shows the comparison between our most efficient implementation, i.e., the implementation based on the separate approach, and the currently best latency-optimized AVX2 implementations of DSM on Ed25519. We compiled the implementation of [12] with the same Clang version and `-O2` flag, whereas the implementation of [6] was compiled with GCC 11.4.0 and `-O2` flag since the GCC executable achieved better performance for this implementation than Clang. Notably, both [12] and [6] implementations use the NAF-based approach

Table 4. Comparison between our implementation (based on separate approach) and other AVX2 implementations of DSM on an Intel Xeon W-2245 Cascade Lake CPU, and the most efficient latency-optimized implementation is used as the baseline for throughput comparison.

Reference	Latency	#Instances	Throughput	Ratio
[12]	142,119 cycles	1	27,526 ops/sec	0.76
[6]	108,253 cycles	1	36,138 ops/sec	1.00
This work	324,772 cycles	4	48,182 ops/sec	1.33

where $\omega_B = 7$ and $\omega_A = 5$ (as mentioned in Sect. 3.2). In Table 4, the ratio is calculated by comparing the throughput between the baseline and the targeted implementation, which indicates that our software achieves a 33% higher throughput than the best latency-optimized implementation.

Table 5. Latency and throughput of our separate-approach-based DSM implementation using AVX2 on an Intel Xeon W-2245 Cascade Lake CPU, where the multiprocessing is applied.

#Thread	Latency	#Instances	Throughput	Ratio
1	324,772 cycles	4	48,182 ops/sec	1.00×
2	328,932 cycles	8	95,173 ops/sec	1.98×
4	328,790 cycles	16	190,400 ops/sec	3.95×
8	330,135 cycles	32	379,251 ops/sec	7.87×
16	678,912 cycles	64	368,843 ops/sec	7.66×

Table 5 and Fig. 1 present the performance data of our AVX2 implementation when multiple threads are used to further improve the software throughput, where the throughput improvement ratio increases linearly until eight threads. Beyond eight threads, the improvement diminishes and plateaus at a certain level. We also use the Intel Vtune Profiler[8] to investigate the logical core usage at different thread numbers, which shows the usage of logical cores matches the thread number when the number is below eight. Once the thread number exceeds eight, the logical core usage stabilizes at approximately 7.8 out of 16 cores. The reason is that there are eight physical cores and 16 logical cores on an Intel Xeon W-2245 CPU, with one set of AVX units per physical core. As a result, the overhead caused by the thread context switching will be introduced when the enabled thread number exceeds the actual physical core number. Therefore, the optimal thread number for our parallel implementation equals the number

[8] https://www.intel.com/content/www/us/en/developer/tools/oneapi/vtune-profiler.html.

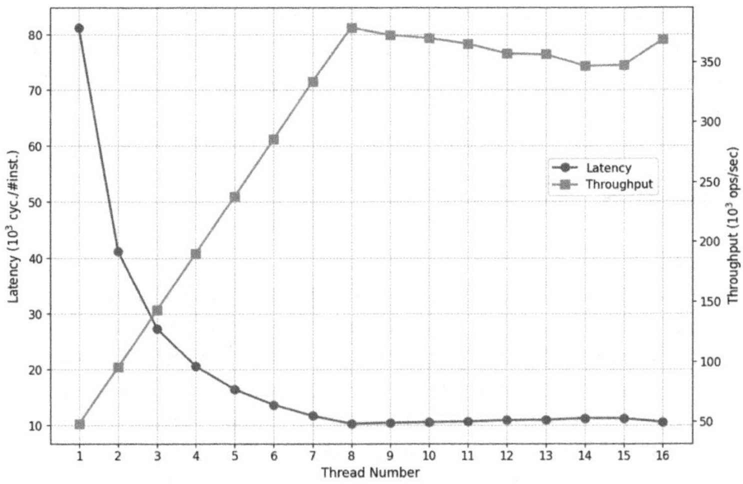

Fig. 1. Latency (This is obtained by dividing the overall latency by the number of instances, entry for latency is 10^3 cycles/# inst., entry for throughput is 10^3 ops/sec) and throughput of our separate-approach-based DSM implementation using AVX2 on an Intel Xeon W-2245 Cascade Lake CPU, where the different numbers of threads are enabled.

of physical cores of the CPU, which is eight on Intel Xeon W-2245 CPU. In this setting, the throughput is 379, 251 DSMs per second, as shown in Table 5.

Finally, we carried out some experiments with an AVX-512 implementation that computes eight DSMs in a SIMD-parallel fashion; the results can be found in Table 6. These results show that the throughput almost doubles when migrating from AVX2 to AVX-512. This is an important result since it confirms that optimizing for throughput allows one to overcome the parallelization bottlenecks of latency-oriented implementations (i.e., half-empty vectors and sequential dependencies) discussed in Sect. 1. However, we note that the throughput gain is a bit below the (theoretical) factor of two in practice when shifting to AVX-512. We

Table 6. Latency and throughput of our separate-approach-based DSM implementation using AVX-512 on an Intel Xeon W-2245 Cascade Lake CPU, where the multiprocessing is applied.

#Thread	Latency	#Instances	Throughput	Ratio
1	415,177 cycles	8	75,385 ops/sec	1.00×
2	420,727 cycles	16	148,867 ops/sec	1.97×
4	424,115 cycles	32	295,184 ops/sec	3.92×
8	423,650 cycles	64	591,326 ops/sec	7.84×
16	807,653 cycles	128	623,011 ops/sec	8.26×

believe that one of the reasons is a higher Cycles-Per-Instruction (CPI) count for some instructions in AVX-512 than in AVX2. For example, for the addition (`vpaddq`) and `XOR` (`vpxor`), the CPI count is 0.33 in the AVX2 instruction set, while it is 0.5 in AVX-512.

5 Conclusions

Driven by its efficiency and robustness, the EdDSA signature scheme has found adoption across a broad spectrum of applications, ranging from security protocols over block chains to electronic voting systems. These applications include settings where several or many signatures need to be verified, which means the key performance metric is the number of verifications executable within a given time period (i.e., the verification throughput), rather than the latency of one single verification. However, all software optimizations for EdDSA verification described in the literature focused on minimizing the latency of one execution of the verification operation. In this paper, we proposed using the vector engine of modern Intel CPUs to maximize verification throughput by a SIMD-parallel execution of either four (AVX2) or eight (AVX-512) instances of DSM.

We analyzed three state-of-the-art options to implement DSM, namely the interleaving technique using a NAF representation of scalars, the simultaneous technique (using a JSF representation), and a separated method that exploits the birational equivalence between the twisted Edwards curve model and the Montgomery model. Our experiments showed that the separated method is the best option for 4-way (resp., 8-way) parallel DSM execution and reaches a 52% higher throughput than its two competitors. The interleaving and simultaneous approaches, which are widely adopted in low-latency EdDSA libraries because they significantly reduce the number of point additions, are much less effective in a throughput-oriented setting. Our separated AVX2 implementation reaches a throughput of 48,182 DSMs/second on one core of a Xeon W-2245 CPU; this exceeds the throughput of the currently best latency-optimized implementation (i.e., LIB25519) by 33%. We further improved throughput by utilizing multiprocessing and found that, ideally, the number of execution threads equals the number of physical cores. The CPU we used for benchmarking has eight cores and is capable to perform 379,251 DSMs/second. However, there exist Cascade Lake models with up to 28 cores, which means a single CPU could potentially execute more than one million DSMs/second thanks to the AVX2 engine.

We envision that this paper will serve as inspiration for future research in high-throughput cryptographic software, motivated by our observation that the best implementation option for low latency is not necessarily ideal if one aims for maximum throughput. As part of our future work, we intend to develop an EdDSA implementation using powerful AVX-512IFMA instructions, which we expect to boost throughput roughly four times compared to AVX2.

Acknowledgments. This research has been supported by the Luxembourg National Research Fund (FNR) via the CORE projects "Advanced Cryptography for Finance and Privacy" (C22/IS/17415825/CryptoFin) and "Real-World Implementation and Human-Centered Design of PAKE Technologies" (C21/IS/16221219/ImPAKT), as well as by the Lux4QCI project. The source code is available under an open-source license at https://github.com/zh-bw/AVXEd25519.

References

1. Bellman, R., Straus, E.: Addition chains of vectors. Am. Math. Mon. **71**(7), 806–808 (1964)
2. Bernstein, D.J.: Pippenger's exponentiation algorithm. Preprint (2002). https://cr.yp.to/papers.html#pippenger
3. Bernstein, D.J.: Curve25519: new Diffie-Hellman speed records. In: Yung, M., Dodis, Y., Kiayias, A., Malkin, T. (eds.) PKC 2006. LNCS, vol. 3958, pp. 207–228. Springer, Heidelberg (2006). https://doi.org/10.1007/11745853_14
4. Bernstein, D.J., Birkner, P., Joye, M., Lange, T., Peters, C.: Twisted edwards curves. In: Vaudenay, S. (ed.) AFRICACRYPT 2008. LNCS, vol. 5023, pp. 389–405. Springer, Heidelberg (2008). https://doi.org/10.1007/978-3-540-68164-9_26
5. Bernstein, D.J., Duif, N., Lange, T., Schwabe, P., Yang, B.-Y.: High-speed high-security signatures. J. Cryptogr. Eng. **2**(2), 77–89 (2012). https://doi.org/10.1007/s13389-012-0027-1
6. Bernstein, D.J., Nath, K.: Artifact: Lib25519, a microlibrary for the x25519 encryption system and the ed25519 signature system (2024). https://lib25519.cr.yp.to
7. Brickell, E.F., Gordon, D.M., McCurley, K.S., Wilson, D.B.: Fast exponentiation with precomputation. In: Workshop on the Theory and Application of of Cryptographic Techniques, pp. 200–207. Springer (1992)
8. Cheng, H., Fotiadis, G., Großschädl, J., Ryan, P.Y.A.: Highly vectorized SIKE for AVX-512. IACR Trans. Cryptogr. Hardw. Embed. Syst. (TCHES) **2022**(2), 41–68 (2022). https://doi.org/10.46586/tches.v2022.i2.41-68
9. Cheng, H., Fotiadis, G., Großschädl, J., Ryan, P.Y.A., Rønne, P.B.: Batching CSIDH group actions using AVX-512. IACR Trans. Cryptogr. Hardw. Embed. Syst. (TCHES) **2021**(4), 618–649 (2021). https://doi.org/10.46586/tches.v2021.i4.618-649
10. Cheng, H., Großschädl, J., Tian, J., Rønne, P.B., Ryan, P.Y.A.: High-throughput elliptic curve cryptography using AVX2 vector instructions. In: Dunkelman, O., Jacobson, Jr., M.J., O'Flynn, C. (eds.) SAC 2020. LNCS, vol. 12804, pp. 698–719. Springer, Cham (2021). https://doi.org/10.1007/978-3-030-81652-0_27
11. Chou, T.: Sandy2x: new Curve25519 speed records. In: Dunkelman, O., Keliher, L. (eds.) SAC 2015. LNCS, vol. 9566, pp. 145–160. Springer, Cham (2016). https://doi.org/10.1007/978-3-319-31301-6_8
12. Faz-Hernández, A., López, J., Dahab, R.: High-performance implementation of elliptic curve cryptography using vector instructions. ACM Trans. Math. Softw. (TOMS) **45**(3), 1–35 (2019). https://doi.org/10.1145/3309759
13. Faz-Hernández, A., López, J.: Fast implementation of Curve25519 using AVX2. In: Lauter, K., Rodríguez-Henríquez, F. (eds.) LATINCRYPT 2015. LNCS, vol. 9230, pp. 329–345. Springer, Cham (2015). https://doi.org/10.1007/978-3-319-22174-8_18
14. Gallant, R.P., Lambert, R.J., Vanstone, S.A.: Faster point multiplication on elliptic curves with efficient endomorphisms. In: Kilian, J. (ed.) CRYPTO 2001. LNCS, vol. 2139, pp. 190–200. Springer, Heidelberg (2001). https://doi.org/10.1007/3-540-44647-8_11

15. Großschädl, J., Franck, C., Liu, Z.: Lightweight EdDSA signature verification for the ultra-low-power internet of things. In: Deng, R., et al. (eds.) ISPEC 2021. LNCS, vol. 13107, pp. 263–282. Springer, Cham (2021). https://doi.org/10.1007/978-3-030-93206-0_16
16. Hankerson, D., Menezes, A.J., Vanstone, S.: Guide to Elliptic Curve Cryptography. Springer (2004). https://doi.org/10.1007/b97644
17. Hişil, H., Eğrice, B., Yassi, M.: Fast 4 way vectorized ladder for the complete set of Montgomery curves. Cryptology ePrint Archive, Report 2020/388 (2020). https://eprint.iacr.org
18. Hisil, H., Egrice, B., Yassi, M.: Fast 4 way vectorized ladder for the complete set of Montgomery curves. Cryptology ePrint Archive, Paper 2020/388 (2020). https://eprint.iacr.org/2020/388
19. Hisil, H., Wong, K.K.-H., Carter, G., Dawson, E.: Twisted edwards curves revisited. Cryptology ePrint Archive, Paper 2008/522 (2008). https://eprint.iacr.org/2008/522
20. Möller, B.: Public-Key CryptographyTheory and Practice. Ph.D. thesis, Technische Universität Darmstadt (2003)
21. Montgomery, P.: Speeding the Pollard and elliptic curve methods of factorization. Math. Comput. (MCOM) **48**(177), 243–264 (1987). https://doi.org/10.1090/S0025-5718-1987-0866113-7
22. Nath, K., Sarkar, P.: Efficient 4-way vectorizations of the Montgomery ladder. IEEE Trans. Comput. (TOC) **71**(3), 712–723 (2021). https://doi.org/10.1109/TC.2021.3060505
23. Okeya, K., Sakurai, K.: Efficient elliptic curve cryptosystems from a scalar multiplication algorithm with recovery of the y-coordinate on a Montgomery-form elliptic curve. In: Koç, Ç.K., Naccache, D., Paar, C. (eds.) CHES 2001. LNCS, vol. 2162, pp. 126–141. Springer, Heidelberg (2001). https://doi.org/10.1007/3-540-44709-1_12
24. Pippenger, N.: On the evaluation of powers and related problems. In: 17th Annual Symposium on Foundations of Computer Science (SFCS 1976), pp. 258–263. IEEE Computer Society (1976)
25. Schnorr, C.P.: Efficient identification and signatures for smart cards. In: Brassard, G. (ed.) CRYPTO 1989. LNCS, vol. 435, pp. 239–252. Springer, New York (1990). https://doi.org/10.1007/0-387-34805-0_22
26. Solinas, J.A.: Efficient arithmetic on koblitz curves. Des. Codes Cryptogr. (DCC) **19**(2/3), 195–249 (2000). https://doi.org/10.1023/A:1008306223194
27. Solinas, J.A.: Low-weight binary representation for pairs of integers. Combinatorics and Optimization Research Report CORR 2001-41 (2001)
28. WikiChip. Intel microarchitectures: Cascade lake. https://en.wikichip.org/wiki/intel/microarchitectures/cascade_lake. Accessed 06 Oct 2024

Air-FRI: Acceleration of the FRI Protocol on the GPU for ZkSNARK Applications

Tanmayi Jandhyala(✉) and Guang Gong

Department of Electrical and Computer Engineering, University of Waterloo, Waterloo, ON, Canada
{tjandhyala,ggong}@uwaterloo.ca

Abstract. Blockchain holds the potential to support the privacy of its participants by integrating zero-knowledge proofs into its design. zkSNARK schemes can effectively prove the validity of blockchain transactions to their owners without disclosing user data. However, the efficiency and scalability of the underlying cryptographic protocols that enable these schemes remain a challenge to realize in practice. This paper presents Air-FRI, a novel GPU-enabled software implementation of the Fast Reed-Solomon Interactive Oracle Proof of Proximity (FRI) protocol, which is a core component in post-quantum zkSNARKs that reduces computational complexity in systems with substantial mathematical instances. Existing schemes that implement the FRI protocol entail significant computational times due to large proof sizes. Our optimized solution includes a parallelized computation of Reed-Solomon codewords, the pre-computation of time-intensive finite field operations, non-interactiveness, and the application of a unified Merkle tree commitment to authenticate the entire proof. Together, the implemented optimizations yield a solution that significantly reduces prover and verifier times while minimizing proof size, addressing both scalability and performance challenges in zkSNARK-based algorithms. Performance evaluations conducted by us across two security levels confirm the implementation's high throughput, establishing it as a promising solution for practicable privacy-preservation. Our results show a 93.3% improvement on an average in the speed of the protocol on the GPU as compared to a non-GPU solution for the same parameters, which includes the execution time of all of its sub-phases: the commit phase, the query phase, and the round consistency checks to ensure correctness of the proof. This work establishes a foundation for advancing privacy-preserving post-quantum cryptography, supporting the development of secure, transparent, and decentralized digital infrastructures for the future.

Keywords: FRI · zkSNARKs · GPUs · Software

1 Introduction

In a digitally-driven society, the balance between data privacy and trust is often compromised. While individuals expect sensitive data, such as medical or financial records, to remain secure and accessible only with explicit consent, these

C. Boura et al. (Eds.): SAC 2025, LNCS 16207, pp. 315–338, 2026.
https://doi.org/10.1007/978-3-032-10536-3_12

expectations are frequently violated or undermined by institutional misconduct or technological vulnerabilities [8] respectively. Such breaches erode the foundational trust of centralized systems. Blockchain technology [39] offers a decentralized and persistent framework for recording transactions and has been adopted across financial services [43], smart contracts [34], and public services [1]. However, its reliance on distributed public ledgers introduces significant privacy concerns, as all participants must maintain identical copies of data. Addressing these challenges is crucial for organizations to ensure trust while leveraging blockchain's potential [48].

A significant concern within these privacy challenges is the de-anonymization of data recorded on blockchains. Transactions on public ledgers, once verified, are permanently stored in open databases. Past network-based de-anonymization attacks [14,15,35] have linked blockchain transactions to real-world identifiers, such as IP addresses. Additionally, user interactions with the blockchain such as querying transactions, checking account balances, or requesting information about specific blocks can inadvertently reveal their areas of interest. For instance, repeatedly checking the balance of a particular wallet may suggest ownership or a financial association with that wallet [3].

Researchers have developed several cryptographic techniques to address privacy challenges on the blockchain. Among these, Zero-Knowledge Proofs (ZKPs) [27], introduced to prove possession of information without revealing it, play a pivotal role. While initially interactive [4,25], non-interactive proofs were later proposed [6,17], enabling their integration into modern cryptographic systems. Notably, ZCash [32] (based on ZeroCash [10]) was among the first blockchain frameworks to employ ZKPs for user anonymity. Zero-Knowledge Succinct Non-Interactive Arguments of Knowledge (zkSNARKs) [30,31] extend ZKPs, offering short, efficient proofs that verify knowledge of computations while preserving privacy. Such systems also find utility in zk-oriented digital signature schemes [24].

The challenge is that such systems involve handling extensive computations which must be efficiently verified. To address scalability, Ben-Sasson et al. introduced the ***Fast Reed-Solomon Interactive Oracle Proofs of Proximity*** (FRI) protocol [7], which leverages algebraic structures for verifying mathematical computations, particularly in polynomial commitment schemes [18], where large polynomials are checked for their degree efficiently. FRI employs a transparent setup, meeting the requirements of blockchain infrastructures, and operates as an Interactive Oracle Proof [12] to verify the low-degree property of functions over finite fields with minimal communication complexity and verification costs. The protocol has been adopted in notable works such as Polaris [24], Aurora [11], STARK [9], Fractal [21], Spartan [46], and PREON [20] which builds on Aurora's FRI.

This paper presents a GPU-based implementation of the FRI protocol which employs Reed-Solomon (RS) codewords, as demonstrated in prior works [7,20]. RS codewords encode messages as polynomials over finite fields, evaluated at distinct field points to form codewords. Our implementation, initially programmed in C, incorporates optimizations identified within the protocol and further parallelizes computationally intensive parts on the GPU. Our optimized GPU implementation achieves a remarkable **93%** performance improvement compared to its unoptimized, CPU-only counterpart. Additionally, this work introduces a *specialized* Merkle Tree, designed to accelerate verification while ensuring the protocol's authenticity and integrity.

Our Contributions

The contributions in this paper are **fourfold**, focusing on the optimizing the performance of the FRI protocol in implementation for effective low-degree testing of polynomials for zkSNARK schemes.

1. *Precomputation of inverse elements and implementing repeated hashing of a random element by the prover for every round.*
   The FRI protocol operates through multiple rounds, performing low-degree testing of polynomials represented as Reed-Solomon codewords. At each round, it needs to compute a finite field inverse element. Our first optimization method is to move this computation to a pre-computation done prior to the start of the protocol and the data is stored to be retrieved during the execution of the protocol versus on-the-fly. Secondly, we adopt a method implemented in Factal's [21] FRI and we realize this in our standalone implementation to make the protocol non-interactive by having the prover sample the random element only once before the FRI protocol begins. This also reduces the communication cost, since the prover is given this random element only once at the beginning, facilitating non-interativeness of the protocol in practice.
2. *Implementation and parallelization of a specialized Merkle tree for efficient commitment and verification in the FRI Protocol.*
   We implement an *integrated, verifiable* Merkle tree, designed to efficiently commit all codewords in one go. Specifically, the prover commits to its codewords using a single, specially-constructed Merkle tree, enabling the verifier to verify the authenticity of all committed codewords without requiring the prover to construct an independent Merkle tree for the commitment of each codeword. This implementation not only substantially reduced the proof size but also enhanced the overall performance of the algorithm.
3. *Parallelization of FRI's Commit Phase.*
   As a key contribution, this work presents for the first time to the best of our knowledge, an implementation of the commit phase of the FRI protocol (that follows an additive-FFT for polynomial evaluation) on a GPU, leveraging the parallel computability of all elements in a codeword round. In this approach, each thread is assigned to compute the next codeword element for a specific index during each round, with thread synchronization ensuring that the hierarchical structure of all indices is preserved across all rounds of the protocol.
4. *Implementation and Performance Report*
   As a final contribution, we provide a detailed performance evaluation of our

optimized FRI implementation. Our benchmarks measure prover and verifier runtimes across different field sizes and optimization levels, illustrating the tangible performance gains from GPU acceleration and from the integrated Merkle tree. These results demonstrate the practical viability of our approach, offering a pathway for deploying FRI-based zkSNARKs in computation-intensive settings. Table 1 introduces performance comparisons between having no optimizations (CPU-only implementation) versus Air-FRI. The L3 and L5 parameter sets defined in Preon [20] correspond to security levels based on the size of the finite field and degree of the tested polynomial. Specifically, L3 uses a 256-bit field $\mathbb{F}_{2^{256}}$, while L5 operates over a larger 320-bit field $\mathbb{F}_{2^{320}}$, with correspondingly larger codewords and deeper recursive rounds. These configurations represent realistic zkSNARK security levels, allowing us to evaluate our optimizations under practical, high-assurance cryptographic workloads.

This work together is termed *Air-FRI*, where 'Air' indicates the fast performance factor of the FRI Protocol, and doubles to mean 'Acceleration'.

Table 1. Prover time comparison between CPU and GPU implementations of FRI protocol

Security Parameters	CPU Time	GPU Time (Air-FRI)	Speedup (%)
L3	22.00 s	1.49 s	93.3%
L5	400.00 s	13.89 s	96.5%

Outline. The rest of the paper has the following structure. Section 2 provides background on how the FRI Protocol came to be introduced in zkSNARK schemes. Section 3 mathematically describes the FRI Protocol and its phases. Section 4 discusses our optimizations in depth. Section 5 and Sect. 6 detail our implementation and its results. While Sect. 7 presents limitations of our work, Sect. 8 provides concluding remarks and future work.

2 Background and Related Work

Zero-Knowledge Proofs are a cryptographic tool that allow two parties, a prover P and a verifier V to engage in a 'proof' that attests to the validity of a statement without revealing any information beyond the truth of the statement itself. First introduced [27] in 1985, ZKP systems must satisfy three essential properties, as interpreted from the definitions in the article by [26]: *completeness, soundness,* and *zero-knowledge.*

The evolution of zero-knowledge proofs (ZKPs) introduced non-interactive variants, with Goldwasser and Bellare [6] presenting NIZK, enabling generic theorem validity to be proven without repeated interactions. A NIZK proof system involves a setup phase to establish shared information, followed by a non-interactive phase for proof generation. Building on Blum et al.'s work [17], Rackoff and Simon [44] developed non-interactive proofs of knowledge, securing public-key cryptosystems against chosen ciphertext attacks and demonstrating proofs for **NP** using trapdoor functions. Micali [38] introduced Succinct Non-Interactive Arguments (SNARGs) to enhance efficiency by reducing proof sizes and verification times, which paved way for Bitansky et al. [16] to formalize SNARKs using assumptions like extractable collision-resistant hash functions. zkSNARKs, an advanced class of non-interactive proofs, offer succinct, computationally secure verification and have become pivotal for blockchain privacy by enabling efficient, verifiable transaction ownership without revealing sensitive data. Zero-knowledge digital signatures play a critical role in blockchain by ensuring integrity, authentication, and non-repudiation of transactions. While traditional digital signatures possess zero-knowledge-like properties, non-interactive zero-knowledge proofs offer additional benefits, including *public verifiability*, as highlighted by [6]. This enables proofs to be validated by any party in the setup, whether trusted or transparent.

Practical zkSNARKs rely on Arithmetic Circuits (ACs) and Quadratic Arithmetic Programs (QAPs) [12] to transform computational problems into succinct proofs. QAPs represent circuits as polynomial equations, allowing zkSNARKs to prove correctness without revealing inputs, while maintaining small proof sizes and efficient verification [13]. These characteristics make zkSNARKs highly scalable for blockchain applications. Ben-Sasson [8] introduced zkSTARKs, which ensure transparency and post-quantum resilience without requiring a trusted setup. However, zkSTARKs produce proofs roughly 1000 times larger than zkSNARKs [8,42], and zkSNARKs generally exhibit better performance for smaller proof sizes and verification times. The primary advantage of zkSTARKs lies in their transparent setup and quantum-resistant primitives, such as collision-resistant hash functions.

Efficient zkSNARK systems often rely on the FRI-IOP protocol to handle large polynomials without revealing them, employing Reed-Solomon codes to encode these polynomials into finite field elements [7]. This approach supports transparent polynomial commitment schemes (PCS) for constructing short proofs and ensuring efficient verification with minimal or no interaction. The FRI protocol, utilized in systems like Polaris [24], Aurora [11], and STARK [8], enables zkSNARK scalability by producing logarithmically growing proof sizes while maintaining transparency.

3 The FRI Protocol

In our work, we were able to translate the following information-theoretic math into code that can efficiently run on the GPU. The mathematical workings of the protocol and the notations used in this paper is referenced from the authors of [24] and [5].

3.1 Notations

Let $\mathbb{F} = \mathbb{F}_{2^N}$ be a finite field of characteristic 2, and let $L \subset \mathbb{F}$ be a linear subspace of dimension n, spanned by the basis $\{\beta_0, \beta_1, \cdots, \beta_{n-1}\}$. Each element $\alpha_i \in L$ is formed via binary linear combinations of these basis vectors using coefficients $i_j \in \mathbb{F}_2$, such that $i = i_0 + i_1 2^1 + \cdots + i_{n-1}2^{n-1}$ and $\alpha_i = i_0\beta_0 + i_1\beta_1 + \cdots + i_{n-1}\beta_{n-1}$. The space L thus contains 2^n elements indexed as $L = \{\alpha_0, \alpha_1, \ldots, \alpha_{2^n-1}\}$. A Reed-Solomon code of rate $\sigma \in (0,1)$ over L is denoted $\mathsf{RS}[L,\sigma]$ and defined as the set $\mathsf{RS}[L,\sigma] = \{\boldsymbol{f}_L \mid f \in \mathbb{F}[x], \deg(f) < k' = 2^n\sigma\}$, where $\boldsymbol{f}_L = (f(\alpha_0), f(\alpha_1), \ldots, f(\alpha_{2^n-1}))$. This code is linear with (the Hamming distance of) at least $2^n - k'$, since any polynomial f of degree less than k' has at most k' roots, and hence at most k' zero entries in the codeword. This follows from the classical Reed-Solomon distance bound [37].

3.2 Phases of the FRI Protocol [5,29]

The FRI Protocol is designed to have three functions/phases: (i) the commit phase, (ii) the query phase, (iii) the round-consistency check. We denote this as $FRI(com, query, RC-test)$. Our optimizations in the protocol are not presented here yet.

Let $L_0 = L$ and $\mathsf{RS}[L,\sigma]$. Let $f(x) \in \mathbb{F}[x]$ with degree $< \sigma 2^n = 2^k$ ($\sigma = 2^{n-k}$), so $\boldsymbol{f}_L \in RS[L_0,\sigma]$. Given $f(x)$ and $\boldsymbol{f}_L \in RS[L_0,\sigma]$, the protocol intends to prove to a verifier the following NP statement:

$$\deg(f(x)) < 2^k.$$

The process is to iteratively reduce the degree of f *by half* at each step of the proof computation. The protocol begins with the input consisting of a polynomial function $f(x)$, the initial subspace L_0, σ, and the RS codeword $\boldsymbol{f}_L \in RS[L_0,\sigma]$. The output is a binary value $b \in \{0,1\}$, indicating whether the verification passed.

Commit Phase. The commit phase of the FRI protocol involves both the prover and verifier interacting to commit to codewords derived from a polynomial over several rounds. The prover starts with the input $f^{(0)} : L_0 \to \mathbb{F}$, which represents an initial Reed-Solomon (RS) codeword corresponding to the polynomial $f_0(X)$ with a rate ρ. The commitment process is described. For each round $k = 0, \ldots, \mathsf{r}-1$, the following steps occur:

1. Prover Commitment:
   The prover recursively defines codewords $\boldsymbol{f}^{(k)} : L_k \to \mathbb{F}$ for each round.
   It then computes a Merkle tree commitment for each codeword and sends the Merkle root to the verifier.
2. Verifier Challenge:
   The verifier sends a uniformly random element $\alpha^{(k)} \in \mathbb{F}$ to the prover.

3. Codeword Definition:
   The prover constructs the next codeword $\boldsymbol{f}^{(k+1)}$ with domain L_{k+1} such that, for every i where $0 \leq i < |L_{k+1}|$, the following holds:

$$q_k(L_k[2i]) = q_k(L_k[2i+1]) = L_{k+1}[i].$$

   Each element of the new codeword $\boldsymbol{f}^{(k+1)}$ is derived from the previous codeword:

$$f_{k+1}(L_{k+1}[i]) = \frac{f_k(L_k[2i]) - f_k(L_k[2i+1])}{L_k[2i] - L_k[2i+1]}(\alpha^{(k)} - L_k[2i]) + f_k(L_k[2i]). \quad (1)$$

   The term $L_k[2i] - L_k[2i+1]$ is $\beta_0^{(k)}$ [5,28,29].
   At the final round $k = \mathsf{r}$, the prover constructs the codeword $\boldsymbol{f}^{(\mathsf{r})} : L_{\mathsf{r}} \rightarrow \mathbb{F}$. This last codeword is directly sent to the verifier as the final commitment.

Query Phase. In the query phase, the verifier extracts the Merkle roots, the challenges $\alpha^{(0)}, \alpha^{(1)}, \ldots, \alpha^{(\mathsf{r}-1)}$, and the final codeword $\boldsymbol{f}^{(\mathsf{r})}$. The verifier also gains oracle access to all intermediate codewords $\boldsymbol{f}^{(0)}, \boldsymbol{f}^{(1)}, \ldots, \boldsymbol{f}^{(\mathsf{r}-1)}$. In symbol, this is represented as $\boldsymbol{f}^{(k)} = (\boldsymbol{f}_{k,0}, \boldsymbol{f}_{k,1}, \cdots, \boldsymbol{f}_{k,|L|_k-1})$.

First, the verifier performs *Interpolant Verification* by computing the interpolant polynomial $f_{\mathsf{r}}(X)$ using points from $\boldsymbol{f}^{(\mathsf{r})}$. If the degree of $f_{\mathsf{r}}(X)$ exceeds $\rho \cdot |L_{\mathsf{r}}| - 1$, the verifier **rejects** the proof. Second, the *Round Consistency Check* ensures consistency between consecutive codewords through ℓ iterations. In each iteration, a random index $s^{(0)} = i$ is selected, where $0 \leq i < |L_0|$, and for every $0 \leq k < \mathsf{r} - 1$, the index is updated as $s^{(k+1)} = \lfloor s^{(k)}/2 \rfloor$. If $s^{(\mathsf{r})}$ is sampled more than once, the verifier resamples $s^{(0)}$. Lastly, during the *Verification of Codeword Values*, the verifier queries the values $f_{k+1}(L_{k+1}[s^{(k+1)}])$, $f_k(x_1^{(k)})$, and $f_k(x_2^{(k)})$, where $x_1^{(k)} = L_k[2\,s^{(k+1)}]$ and $x_2^{(k)} = L_k[2\,s^{(k+1)} + 1]$. The correctness of these queried points is ensured by verifying their Merkle paths.

Round Consistency Check. The verifier checks the following equation for every $k \in \{0, 1, \ldots, \mathsf{r} - 1\}$:

$$f_{k+1}(L_{k+1}[s^{(k+1)}]) = \frac{f_k(x_1^{(k)}) - f_k(x_2^{(k)})}{x_1^{(k)} - x_2^{(k)}}(\alpha^{(k)} - x_1^{(k)}) + f_k(x_1^{(k)}).$$

If any of these checks fail, the verifier rejects the proof.
Acceptance: If all checks pass, the verifier accepts the proof, confirming that the original polynomial $f_0(X)$ has a degree no more than $\rho \cdot |L_0| - 1$.

4 Air-FRI

As zkSNARKs progress to support more intricate circuits and transparent setups, achieving computational and memory challenges encountered during their deployment for large-scale cryptographic applications remains a challenge. In traditional zkSNARK implementations, the prover faces substantial overhead when managing large arithmetic circuits or evaluating polynomials, especially when encoding computations into Rank-1 Constraint Satisfiable (R1CS) systems. This bottleneck becomes even more pronounced in protocols like Aurora [11] and Fractal [21], where polynomial commitments using FRI demand significant memory management and intensive field operations [36,45].

A key challenge addressed in this work is the prover's time complexity. Existing FRI-based zkSNARK systems, while providing post-quantum security and transparent setups, often present a trade-off between proof size and prover efficiency. For instance, Aurora achieves proof sizes in the range of 100–150 KB with logarithmic verification times but incurs increased prover workload scaling with $O(n \log n)$ for large circuits. Similarly, Fractal reduces verification time but imposes considerable computational demands on the prover due to multi-round polynomial evaluations. These limitations underscore the need for novel optimizations to reduce the prover's computational burden while preserving the succinctness and transparency of FRI-based proofs.

This paper introduces optimizations aimed at parallelizing polynomial computations and integrating Merkle tree commitments into GPU-accelerated workflows. By utilizing CUDA-enabled GPU kernels to offload polynomial evaluations and streamline Merkle commitments, our proposed solution reduces memory overhead and prover time without compromising on the transparency and security guarantees inherent to FRI-based systems. These enhancements are expected to accelerate proof generation and improve the scalability of zkSNARK applications, particularly in blockchain environments, where throughput and latency are critical for adoption.

The optimizations proposed in this paper are categorized into four main contributions, as detailed below.

4.1 Precomputation of Inverse Elements and Repeated Hashing of a Random Element

The **line computation** in the FRI protocol plays a critical role in recursively transforming polynomial evaluations across rounds to ensure proximity to low-degree polynomials. This transformation is mathematically expressed by Eq. (1), where the verifier provides a uniformly random challenge $\alpha^{(k)}$, and the transformation depends on the denominator term

$$\beta_0^{(k)} = L_k[2i] - L_k[2i+1].$$

Computing the inverse of $\beta_0^{(k)}$ in each round introduces considerable overhead due to the cost of division operations in finite fields $\mathbb{F}_p$. To mitigate this bottleneck, we precompute these inverses before the recursion begins. The stored values are then retrieved during protocol execution, replacing expensive on-the-fly inverse computations with efficient multiplications, which are more favorable in field arithmetic [11,21]. This optimization substantially reduces the prover's computational load, especially for large circuits with many recursive steps.

Additionally, rather than following an interactive protocol, we implement a non-interactive variant by having the prover sample a random element α_0 once from the extension field at the start of the protocol. This element is reused across all rounds by computing the challenges deterministically through repeated hashing. Specifically, the next round's challenge is computed as

$$\alpha_1 = \text{Hash}(\alpha_0 \parallel \text{root}),$$

and for all subsequent rounds,

$$\alpha_{k+1} = \text{Hash}(\alpha_k), \quad 1 \leq k \leq r,$$

where r denotes the total number of FRI rounds. The verifier reconstructs the challenges using the initial α_0 and the hash function, eliminating the need for back-and-forth communication. This non-interactive design adheres to the **Fiat-Shamir heuristic** [23] and aligns with techniques used in prior work such as Fractal [21] and the framework of Interactive Oracle Proofs [12]. By minimizing interaction, this strategy improves scalability and seamlessly supports GPU-based acceleration for both hashing and proof generation [11,21].

4.2 Integrated FRI Merkle Tree Construction

The primary motivation to the following contribution of our work is to reduce the prover's computational overhead while ensuring the verifier's ability to validate the integrity of the proof through a recursive structure of polynomial evaluations. This construction, as described in the previous section, is based on Reed-Solomon (RS) codewords evaluated over a sequence of domains and committed using a single Merkle tree, ensuring both scalability and security in the zkSNARK setting [11,21].

As our second essential contribution, we construct and employ a verifiable and integrated Merkle tree for simultaneous commitment of all codewords. Specifically, the construction combines codewords and Merkle hash computations into one tree structure. The details are as described below.

RS Tree Structure. The recursive nature of the FRI protocol can be represented as a binary tree. The elements of the initial codeword $\boldsymbol{f}_0$ are placed as the leaf nodes at layer 0. Each subsequent layer $k+1$ is constructed from the elements of layer k using the linear combination described earlier in (1). At the final layer r, there are $|L_r|$ nodes. This recursive binary structure is referred to as the RS tree with height r and initial codeword $\boldsymbol{f}_0$. The tree is denoted by $RST(f_0, r)$, where $f_0(x)$ is the original polynomial evaluated over L_0.

Merkle Tree Commitment of RS Codewords. To guarantee the integrity of Reed-Solomon (RS) codewords, we construct a Merkle tree that integrates seamlessly with the RS tree structure. This Merkle tree provides an efficient commitment scheme by hashing pairs of codeword elements along with their corresponding RS codeword values at each index at each layer. The construction proceeds as follows.

For layers $0 \leq k \leq r$, we compute hash values iteratively:

$$\begin{aligned} h_{1,i} &= h(f_{0,2i}, f_{0,2i+1}), & 0 \leq i < |L_1|, \\ h_{2,i} &= h(h_{1,2i} \parallel f_{1,2i}, h_{1,2i+1} \parallel f_{1,2i+1}), & 0 \leq i < |L_2|, \\ &\vdots \\ h_{k+1,i} &= h(h_{k,2i} \parallel f_{k,2i}, h_{k,2i+1} \parallel f_{k,2i+1}), & 0 \leq i < |L_{k+1}|. \end{aligned}$$

For subsequent layers, where $r \leq k < n$, we compute hashes without appending RS values:

$$h_{k+1,i} = h(h_{k,2i}, h_{k,2i+1}), \quad 0 \leq i < 2^{n-k}.$$

The final hash at the top layer provides the Merkle root:

$$h_{n,0} = h(h_{n-1,0}, h_{n-1,1}).$$

This root serves as the commitment for the FRI protocol's Merkle tree, thereby ensuring that all RS codewords are securely and efficiently committed. We use SHA3-256, which outputs 256-bit hashes, and allows an input size of up to 1320 bits, enabling efficient processing of codeword elements: 1024-bit inputs are used for layers $0 < k < r$, while 512-bit inputs are employed for layers beyond r.

Figure 1 shows the structure of our specialized Merkle tree constructed for the purpose of efficiently parallelizing the FRI protocol.

Time Efficiency of This Optimization. As compared to that of the CPU implementation (sequentially committing the codeword elements), the number of computations that are reduced is highlighted here. For simplicity, we denote $N = 2^n$, where n is the dimension of the first codeword $\boldsymbol{f}_0$. The number of computations for codewords looks like $\boldsymbol{f}_0 = 2^n$, $\boldsymbol{f}_1 = 2^{n-1}$, and so on. So, for the entire Integrated FRI Merkle Tree leading up to the root, the total number of sequential computations (including computing all codewords and Merkle hashes) is:

$$2^{n+1} - 1 - n$$

where the final subtraction accounts for structural hash reuse across FRI rounds.

If a separate Merkle tree is constructed for each codeword $\boldsymbol{f}_k$, then each such tree would require:

$$2^{n-k} \text{ codeword elements} + (2^{n-k-1} + \cdots + 1) \text{ hashes} = 2^{n-k+1} - 1 \text{ computations.}$$

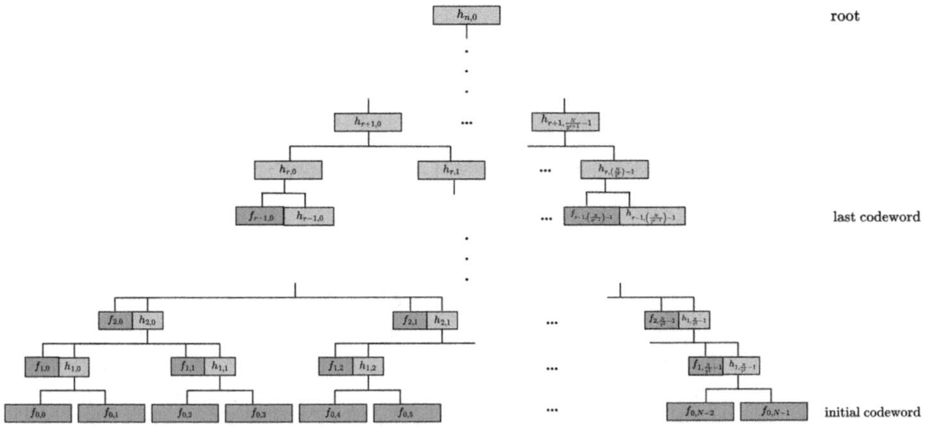

Fig. 1. Integrated FRI Merkle Tree.

Summing this across all n layers, the total number of sequential computations for the Merkle commitment model yields:

$$\sum_{k=0}^{n-1}(2^{n-k+1}-1) = 2^{n+2}-1-n.$$

In contrast, the integrated Merkle tree design requires only $2^{n+1}-1-n$ computations, as it avoids redundant hashing at each round by committing to the FRI structure in a unified tree. Thus, the total number of operations saved is:

$$(2^{n+2}-1-n)-(2^{n+1}-1-n) = 2^{n+1}.$$

This shows that the integrated Merkle tree design improves efficiency by eliminating 2^{n+1} unnecessary operations, making it particularly well-suited for high-performance GPU-based implementations.

Verification and Authentication Paths. To verify the authenticity of two neighboring points, starting with $s_0 \in L_0$ at layer 0 and extending to $s_k \in L_k$ for $0 < k < r$, the verifier uses authentication paths in the Merkle tree. These paths contain the concatenated hash values of the queried elements and their corresponding RS codewords. Notably, while the leaf layer hashes $\boldsymbol{f}_0$ separately, the intermediate layers $\boldsymbol{f}_k$ (for $1 \leq k < r$) do not require separate hashing, as their values are integrated into the hash tree structure.

The integration of RS codewords with Merkle tree commitments within the FRI protocol ensures both scalability and security. The recursive construction of the RS tree enables efficient polynomial evaluations, while the Merkle tree offers a compact and secure method for committing to the underlying codewords. We believe that these combined structures could be crucial for deploying zkSNARKs in practical applications, such as blockchain networks, where performance and security are of utmost importance.

4.3 Parallel Computation of Codeword Elements on the GPU

zkSNARK systems that have the FRI protocol as one of their core components have large parameter sets to conduct proofs, despite ironically being termed 'succinct'. Depending on the security requirement of the system, arithmetic is performed over finite fields of varying bit-widths. For instance, elements from different domains are represented as 192-bit, 256-bit, or 320-bit field elements, as noted in Preon's documentation [20]. Direct computation of these elements in a sequential fashion is both time- and memory-intensive. To address this, GPU parallelization is employed to distribute the computation of codeword elements across multiple threads, substantially accelerating proof generation.

A novel contribution of this paper is elucidated below. The FRI protocol reduces the codeword size recursively at each round. For a given round k, the next codeword element $f_{k+1}(L_{k+1}[i])$ is computed from two elements of the previous codeword, as described in (1). Each GPU thread computes one element of the next codeword in parallel, avoiding sequential bottlenecks. CUDA kernels assign threads to independently compute each codeword element.

4.4 Implementation and Performance Report

To support our proposed optimizations, we developed a modular and extensible implementation of the FRI protocol tailored for GPU acceleration. The codebase is designed to run both serially on the CPU and in parallel on the GPU, enabling comparative analysis and performance benchmarking. Key computational subroutines including codeword generation, line computations, and Merkle tree hashing are implemented in CUDA-C, while orchestration and memory management are handled in C.

The implementation carefully manages data transfer between host and device memory, pre-allocating buffers for each FRI round to ensure scalability across increasing security parameters. GPU kernels were written with thread-block synchronization to preserve the hierarchical structure of codeword indices across rounds. Where necessary, bit-width precision was customized to handle 256-bit and 320-bit field elements as required by zkSNARK parameter sets.

The modularity of the implementation allows seamless integration into zkSNARK frameworks such as Polaris [24] or Aurora [11]. In the following section, we outline the software components, toolchains, and dependencies involved in building the system, while Sect. 6 evaluates the empirical performance under various cryptographic parameter settings.

5 Implementation

The architectural details of the protocol, on a system level, can be broken down into several key modules, each handling different aspects of the protocol. Our implementation is available on GitHub[1].

[1] https://github.com/tanmayij/airfri.

5.1 Components

Figure 2 shows the overview of the software components that make the implementation. The tiles in green represent code that is borrowed from Preon's [20] implementation. The purple tiles show our code. The blue tile represents open-source library functions.

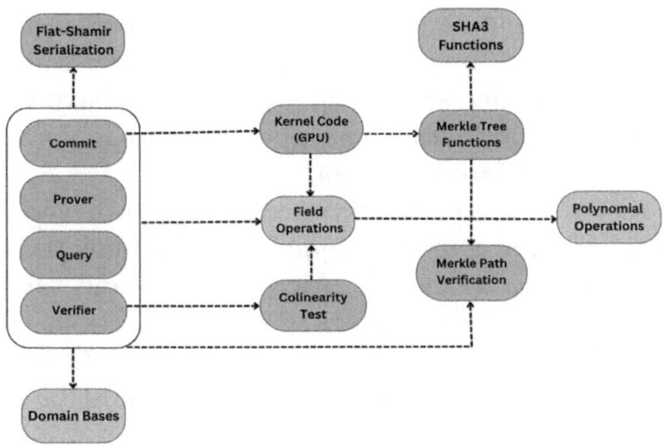

Fig. 2. Software Components of Our Implementation.

Implementation Assumptions. The implementation of this FRI protocol is based on several key assumptions that ensure both functionality and performance in cryptographic settings. First and foremost, it is assumed that any entities or participants involved in using this protocol have access to GPU systems capable of executing CUDA-based applications. The use of CUDA-C allows the protocol to take full advantage of modern GPU architectures, enabling the parallel execution of tasks like polynomial evaluation, hashing, and consistency checks in the commit and verify phases. The CUDA toolkit and NVCC compiler are dependencies to compile and execute the code.

We use Keccak [33] (or more specifically, the SHA3-256 variant) to compute cryptographic commitments such as Merkle tree roots and authentication paths. The open-source implementation of Keccack's SHA3-256 is made GPU-compatible for use in our implementation. On the performance side, libcudart facilitates interaction between the code and the GPU, managing tasks such as memory allocation, kernel execution, and synchronization of GPU threads. In particular, it is responsible for handling CUDA-specific operations such as transferring data between the host (CPU) and device (GPU) and launching the parallel kernels that compute the polynomial evaluations and Merkle tree commitments.

Borrowing Preon's [20] Parameters. To make the protocol work, our code uses the FRI Domain parameters, finite field functions, and Polynomial evaluation functions as used in Preon's Optimised Implementation, which is available in the public domain. These functions were made compatible with the GPU nodes using CUDA-related function qualifiers.

5.2 Proof Stream and Verification

The proof stream serves as the main interaction channel between the prover and verifier in the protocol. The prover adds commitments, authentication paths, and related data into the stream, while the verifier retrieves this data during verification. Proper memory management is noted to be essential to ensure that all proof elements remain accessible and valid, particularly when dealing with dynamically generated proof paths. This guarantees that the verifier has all the information needed to validate the proof.

For non-interactiveness of the protocol, a custom serialization method inspired by the Fiat-Shamir heuristic is employed, enabling the prover to sequentially add objects such as codewords, Merkle roots, and sampled values to a global proof stream. The verifier processes these objects in the same order to verify correctness. However, since the serializer used in C does not track data types, the sequence of adding and retrieving objects must be precisely aligned.

5.3 Testing

We highlight and discuss the performance of our implementation. Mainly, the section aims to bring to light the various metrics for our performance testing, how much time the prover and verifier take for their respective execution, and a bit about the memory management that went into the code. We outline the test plan employed for evaluating the performance and correctness of the Fast Reed-Solomon Interactive Oracle Proof of Proximity (FRI) protocol here. The tests are divided into two main categories: unit tests to verify functional correctness and performance tests to assess execution times under various optimization levels. Description of unit tests are assumed to be self-evident and are omitted from this paper.

Performance Test Design. The performance tests are divided into two categories: CPU-based tests and GPU-accelerated tests. Each test is run multiple times (up to 100 iterations) to ensure the consistency and reliability of the timing results.

1. **CPU-based tests:** The performance of the C-based FRI protocol is measured for baseline comparison. Initial tests use no optimizations, followed by tests with precomputed inverses, repeated hashes (Fiat-Shamir), and FRI Merkle tree implementation.
2. **GPU-accelerated tests:** Performance is evaluated on the GPU version of the code. The tests include precomputed inverses and parallel line computation, with the final implementation featuring FRI Merkle tree optimizations. These tests assess how GPU parallelism improves the runtime of each phase of the protocol.

Test Environment & Test Metrics
The tests were conducted on a system with the following configuration. The system's CPU was a standard ARM processor with 8 CPU cores and 8GB of unified memory. For GPU acceleration, an NVIDIA A40 GPU was used, equipped with 10,752 CUDA cores and 48GB of VRAM [40]. The time was measured in seconds, and the system clock was used for recording execution times. The performance evaluation of the FRI protocol focuses on execution times across different implementations. Key metrics include **prover time**, measuring the time taken for proof commitment, and **verifier time**, capturing proof validation tasks. To ensure reliability, the *average time* is calculated over multiple iterations, while the *minimum* and *maximum times* represent the best- and worst-case scenarios. Additionally, the *speedup factor* quantifies performance gains from GPU acceleration compared to CPU implementations. These metrics provide a comprehensive assessment of the protocol's performance.

6 Results

This section presents the results for various parameters and briefly compares them with existing implementations.

6.1 Performance of the Code Run with L3 Parameters

The code for our implementation is majorly written for Preon's [20] L3 parameters.

Parameter Mapping. Throughout this section, we instantiate the symbolic parameters used in earlier sections as follows: (1) $N = 2^{17}$ is the length of the initial codeword, corresponding to the size of the evaluation domain $L \subset \mathbb{F}_{2^{256}}$. (2) $n = \log_2 N = 17$ is the height of the Merkle tree used to commit to the initial codeword. (3) $k = 2^{12}$ is the degree bound of the polynomial being tested in the FRI protocol. (4) The field $\mathbb{F} = \mathbb{F}_{2^{256}}$ is used throughout the protocol's L3 security implementation to represent codeword elements and evaluate polynomial values. (5) The codeword is reduced over $r = 12$ rounds of FRI folding, from size $N = 2^{17}$ down to 2^5, with each round halving the domain size. (6) An expansion factor of 32 is used, implying a rate $\rho = \frac{k}{N} = \frac{2^{12}}{2^{17}} = \frac{1}{32}$.

To verify the correctness of the protocol, 14 co-linearity tests are conducted during the process. The hash function used in the Merkle tree commitment processes inputs of 1024 bits and generates outputs of 256 bits.

Table 2 shows the progressive decrease in Average Time taken to run the protocol for the same parameters with each optimization implementation. Rows 1, 2, 3 show the times taken by the implementation in C, while 4 and 5 clearly show the advantages of our major and novel optimizations using the GPU.

For the implementation of the protocol for the low-degree test of 4096, we measure the individual prover and verifier times over 10 iterations to account for additional overhead incurred outside the isolated prover and verifier functions, including memory transfers and proof stream serialization costs, the results

Table 2. Performance Comparison of the FRI protocol on CPU vs GPU for L3 Parameters

S.No.	Category	Iterations	Average (s)	Max (s)	Min (s)
1	C Code - No Optimizations	100	22.516272	24.487644	21.283454
2	C Code - Precomputed Inverses & Fiat-Shamir	100	17.949764	18.285129	17.674678
3	C Code - Precomputed Inverses, Non-interactiveness, & Verifiable FRI Merkle Tree	100	13.466491	14.387460	12.974454
4	GPU Code - Precomputed Inverses, Non-interactiveness, Parallel Line Computation	100	9.355615	10.225553	9.138932
5	**GPU Code - Parallel Line Computation & Verifiable FRI Merkle Tree**	**100**	**1.490716**	**1.626001**	**1.459887**

of which are shown in Table 3. As such, the timings in Table 3 represent a lower bound on computational performance, whereas Table 2 captures end-to-end system-level costs.

Table 3. Minimum, Maximum, and Average Times for Prover and Verifier for degree 2^{12} over 10 iterations

Metric	Prover Time (s)	Verifier Time (s)
Minimum	0.66909	0.16506
Maximum	0.67360	0.16651
Average	0.67026	0.16586

The Fig. 4 below shows the times for various degrees as tested on the GPU. One of the implications of an uneven curve could be the fact that time efficiency is also dependent on the number of threads and blocks that a GPU kernel is allocated before invocation. This is in-turn dependent on the length of the input. Effective scheduling and memory coalescing techniques can reduce bottlenecks in such GPU workloads by ensuring that memory access is streamlined across multiple threads, thus improving throughput for numerically-driven computations.

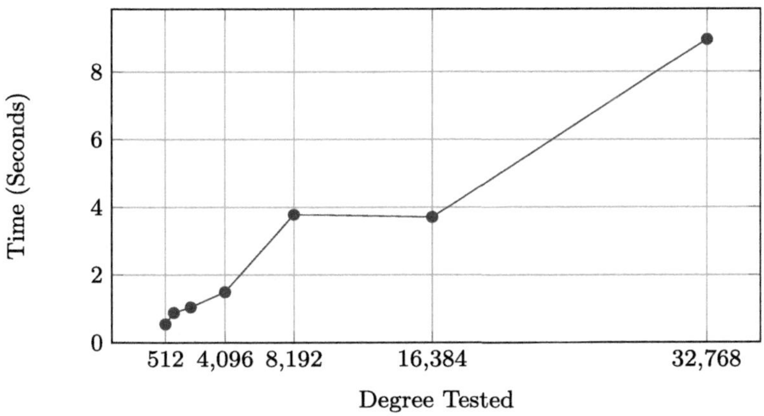

Fig. 3. FRI Degree Testing Time on the GPU with L3 Parameters.

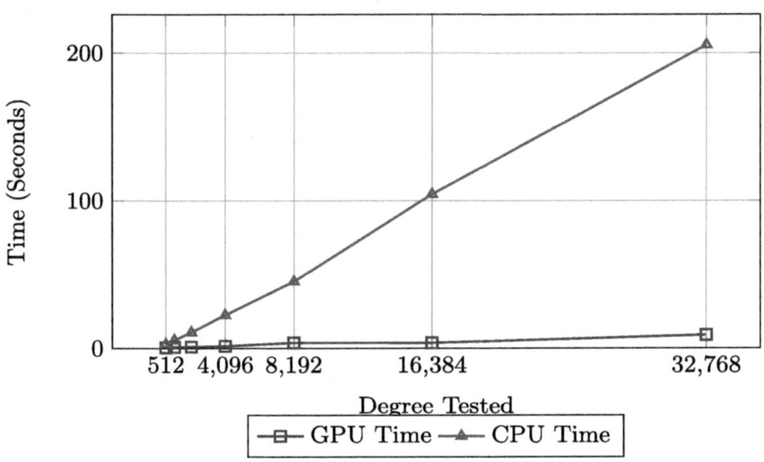

Fig. 4. CPU vs GPU Execution Times for FRI Degree Testing for L3 Parameters

Based on the CPU and GPU times for the same degrees, we measure the percentage in performance efficiency termed as the 'Speedup Factor' (Table 4). Since the degree test for 2^{12} is the main focus of our implementation, we consider the speedup factor of this degree as the benchmark for our work.

6.2 Performance on L5 Parameters

For L5 security, Air-FRI's results show notably seminal performance despite large codeword lengths to begin the protocol with.

The parameters for the L5 implementation of the FRI protocol are carefully chosen to ensure robust performance and security. The finite field used is $\mathbb{F}_{2^{320}}$, and the protocol tests polynomials with a degree of 2^{16}. An expansion factor of

Table 4. Speedup Factor (%) of GPU over CPU for Various Degrees for L3 Parameters

Degree	CPU Time (s)	GPU Time (s)	Speedup Factor (%)
512	2.798574	0.543291	80.59%
1024	5.476513	0.881827	83.90%
2048	10.856021	1.043323	90.39%
4096	**22.425451**	**1.490716**	**93.35%**
8192	45.155425	3.776132	91.64%
16384	104.365670	3.696402	96.46%
32768	205.366330	8.953130	95.64%

32 is applied, with the initial codeword length set to 2^{21} $(2,097,152)$ and the least codeword length reduced to 2^5 (32) after successive rounds. The protocol undergoes 16 rounds of codeword reductions, with 10 co-linearity tests conducted to verify correctness. To secure commitments, a Merkle tree with a height of 21 is constructed, where each node involves a hash computation that takes 1152 bits as input and produces a 256-bit output.

Tested on the metrics mentioned above, Table 5 shows the prover and verifier times measured over 10 iterations on the GPU. As compared to L3's results, it is shown that the proof generation takes only a few seconds more even when the codeword constraints are large. This shows significant promise in realizing our implementation in *post-quantum secure* algorithms which require such large constraints and strong security levels.

Table 5. Minimum, Maximum, and Average Times for Prover and Verifier over 10 iterations using L5 parameters ($\mathbb{F}_{2^{320}}$, degree 2^{16}). The estimated sequential CPU prover time was approximately 400 s, which is not practical at all.

Metric	GPU Prov. (s)	GPU Verif. (s)	CPU Prov. (s)	CPU Verif. (s)
Minimum	13.85859	1.12372	~400	~1.9
Maximum	13.88316	1.12699		
Average	13.87129	1.12488		

6.3 Performance of Current FRI Implementations

To compare our test results with the existing FRI implementations, which are currently compatible to be run only on the CPU, we ran the pre-written tests of the libiop library [45], which Aurora [11], Ligero [2], and Fractal [21] use to run their entire protocol. The tests are generated with the library's build and metrics like the vector size and subgroup size **are much lesser** as compared to those tested for in our implementation. Table 6 shows the times for the three algorithms that use the libiop library for their low-degree test implementation. Further, to compare the entire performance, we also consider the Merkle tree test times for these algorithms.

Table 6. Performance Comparison of Existing FRI Implementations on the CPU

Implementation	Prover Time (s)	Verifier Time (s)	Vector Size	Subgroup Size
Aurora (libiop)	0.077	0.006	2^9	2^{12}
Fractal (libiop)	0.071	0.009	2^9	2^{12}
Ligero (libiop)	0.049	0.022	2^9	2^{12}

The Merkle tree test for libiop implementations recorded an execution time of 1.008 s, with verification requiring approximately 1 s per index in a single tree.

Note: Preon's [20] FRI implementation is tested for a large polynomial of degree 2^{12} with a subgroup size of 2^{17}, while the Aurora, Fractal, and Ligero implementations from the libiop library are tested for a smaller polynomial degree of 2^9 within a subgroup of 2^{12}. In scale, when the size of the extension field exponentially increases, the prover time approximately doubles (see Fig. 3). This is why, although Preon calls Aurora for its inner working, including for running the FRI Low-Degree Test, the time taken by Preon's code is much greater to account to the exponential growth in codeword sizes and to cater to parameters of larger extension basis. This is shown in Table 7 below.

These timings on the CPU shown in Table 7, when compared with our implementation the GPU, has significant performance improvements through our optimizations. This shows promise that our software-oriented solution for accelerating the FRI protocol can serve algorithmic efficiency when carefully deployed in those zkSNARK schemes which contain the FRI as one of their core components.

Table 7. Preon's Prover and Verifier Times for Testing of Degree 2^{12} over 50 Iterations on the CPU

Metric	Prover Time (seconds)	Verifier Time (seconds)
Minimum	126.926	0.803
Maximum	139.683	1.167
Average	129.248	0.875

7 Limitations

Our implementation does not account for software-induced vulnerabilities, such as susceptibility to side-channel attacks, which remains a limitation. Further, the proof system dynamically allocates memory in C to manage objects of varying sizes, but there is a risk of memory mismanagement if more memory is allocated than utilized. To enhance memory safety while leveraging GPU performance, Rust and Rustacuda [47] could be explored as alternatives. Additionally, the integrated Merkle tree implementation does not facilitate on-the-fly computation of authentication paths, requiring the prover to either store the Merkle tree data or access all codewords across FRI rounds during the query phase, increasing memory management complexity and security vulnerabilities.

8 Conclusions and Future Work

This paper presents novel and efficient optimizations of the FRI protocol for low-degree polynomial testing, implemented on the GPU. Implementation parameters, particularly the domain elements, are adapted from Preon's values [20]. Key optimizations include the pre-computation of domain base inverses to accelerate codeword generation and the sampling of a random element by the prover, which is repeatedly hashed by the verifier during co-linearity checks, enabling a non-interactive protocol. Further performance gains are achieved by parallelizing codeword computations and constructing a verifiable Merkle tree on GPU kernels using NVIDIA's CUDA-C, significantly reducing proof size and improving scalability. Compared to a CPU-based implementation, our GPU-based approach achieves a 93.3% efficiency gain for codeword computations in $\mathbb{F}_{2^{256}}$, reducing prover time from an average of 22 s to 1.49 s. For $\mathbb{F}_{2^{320}}$, corresponding to `L5` security parameters, the prover time is 13.89 s, only 11 s higher than for `L3` parameters, despite larger codewords and more reduction rounds. As expected, verifier times remain significantly lower than prover times, reflecting the protocol's efficiency-focused design. These results underscore the importance of optimization in cryptographic implementations, particularly for scalable systems. While this implementation was developed for integration with Polaris [24], it remains broadly applicable to any system utilizing the FRI protocol as a core component. Future work may explore additional performance refinements and broader deployment contexts.

Further Reduction of the Proof Size. For a finite field byte size of 256, the current implementation shares approximately 9,000 objects with the verifier via the proof stream, primarily for co-linearity tests across all rounds. Reducing this number could involve adjusting localization parameters and decreasing the number of co-linearity tests while maintaining protocol correctness.

Implementing Zero-Knowledge with This FRI Protocol. To integrate this code with any zkSNARK-based system, the zero-knowledge property can be achieved by masking the polynomial whose degree is being tested. At each reduction step of the FRI protocol, an additive masking polynomial can be applied to conceal the original polynomial. This ensures that the verifier learns nothing beyond the degree bound. The masking terms are designed to cancel during verification, maintaining proof integrity while preserving privacy.

Comparison of Energy Consumption Between CPU and GPU Implementations of the Protocol. While GPUs improve protocol performance, it is important to assess their energy consumption to understand the ecological trade-offs. Uncoalesced global memory accesses are known to significantly impact energy use in NVIDIA GPUs [19], and nearly half of a 100A GPU's energy is consumed by a static kernel [22]. Future work should aim to quantify the energy differences between CPU and GPU implementations, balancing performance with sustainability.

Memory Profiling of the GPU Code. Since the protocol's performance relies heavily on shared memory between the host (CPU) and device (GPU kernel), a robust implementation should incorporate memory profiling results to make optimization decisions about thread and block usage, ensuring efficient GPU kernel launches across varying codeword lengths and Merkle tree computations. Specifically, a GPU-oriented memory profiling using nvprof or nsys profile [41] tools provided within the cuda-toolkit can be employed.

Integrating Air-FRI with Full-Fledged ZkSNARKs and Blockchain Applications. An important direction for future work is the integration of Air-FRI into complete zkSNARK systems, particularly for scalable blockchain applications. This requires extending Air-FRI's GPU-accelerated commitment and verification phases to support the various models in zkSNARKs. Additionally, replacing the current FFT implementation (borrowed from Preon [20]) with a more efficient FFT algorithm such as one using specialized bases and subfield structures [29] could further accelerate polynomial evaluation and improve overall system performance.

Acknowledgement. This work is supported by MITACS-BTQ research grant.

References

1. Akins, B., Ng, J., Verdi, R.S.: The use of blockchain for public services. J. Public Econ. (2013)
2. Ames, S., Hazay, C., Ishai, Y., Venkitasubramaniam, M.: Ligero: lightweight sublinear arguments without a trusted setup. In: Proceedings of the 2017 ACM SIGSAC Conference on Computer and Communications Security, pp. 2087–2104 (2017)
3. Aslam, S., Tošić, A., Mrissa, M.: Secure and privacy-aware blockchain design: requirements, challenges and solutions. J. Cybersecur. Priv. **1**(1), 164–194 (2021). https://doi.org/10.3390/jcp1010009

4. Babai, L.: Trading group theory for randomness. In: Proceedings of the Seventeenth Annual ACM Symposium on Theory of Computing (STOC), pp. 421–429 (1985)
5. Badakhshan, M., Luo, G., Jandhyala, T., Gong, G.: URSA minor: the implementation framework for polaris. In: International Workshop on the Arithmetic of Finite Fields (WAIFI), Ottawa, Canada (2024, accepted for publication)
6. Bellare, M., Goldwasser, S.: New paradigms for digital signatures and message authentication based on non-interactive zero knowledge proofs. In: Brassard, G. (ed.) CRYPTO 1989. LNCS, vol. 435, pp. 194–211. Springer, New York (1990). https://doi.org/10.1007/0-387-34805-0_19
7. Ben-Sasson, E., Bentov, I., Horesh, Y., Riabzev, M.: Fast reed-solomon interactive oracle proofs of proximity. In: Chatzigiannakis, I., Kaklamanis, C., Marx, D., Sannella, D. (eds.) 45th International Colloquium on Automata, Languages, and Programming, ICALP 2018, 9–13 July 2018, Prague, Czech Republic. LIPIcs, vol. 107, pp. 14:1–14:17. Schloss Dagstuhl - Leibniz-Zentrum für Informatik (2018). https://doi.org/10.4230/LIPIcs.ICALP.2018.14
8. Ben-Sasson, E., Bentov, I., Horesh, Y., Riabzev, M.: Scalable, transparent, and post-quantum secure computational integrity. In: Advances in Cryptology – CRYPTO 2018, pp. 201–234 (2018)
9. Ben-Sasson, E., Bentov, I., Horesh, Y., Riabzev, M.: Scalable, transparent, and post-quantum secure computational integrity. Cryptology ePrint Archive, Paper 2018/046 (2018). https://eprint.iacr.org/2018/046
10. Ben-Sasson, E., et al.: Zerocash: decentralized anonymous payments from bitcoin. In: Proceedings of the 2014 IEEE Symposium on Security and Privacy, pp. 459–474 (2014)
11. Ben-Sasson, E., Chiesa, A., Riabzev, M., Spooner, N., Virza, M., Ward, N.P.: Aurora: transparent succinct arguments for R1CS. In: Ishai, Y., Rijmen, V. (eds.) EUROCRYPT 2019. LNCS, vol. 11476, pp. 103–128. Springer, Cham (2019). https://doi.org/10.1007/978-3-030-17653-2_4
12. Ben-Sasson, E., Chiesa, A., Spooner, N.: Interactive oracle proofs. In: Hirt, M., Smith, A. (eds.) TCC 2016. LNCS, vol. 9986, pp. 31–60. Springer, Heidelberg (2016). https://doi.org/10.1007/978-3-662-53644-5_2
13. Ben-Sasson, E., Chiesa, A., Tromer, E., Virza, M.: Succinct non-interactive zero knowledge for a von neumann architecture. In: Proceedings of the 23rd USENIX Conference on Security Symposium, SEC 2014, pp. 781–796. USENIX Association (2014)
14. Biryukov, A., Khovratovich, D., Pustogarov, I.: Deanonymisation of clients in bitcoin P2P network. In: Proceedings of the 2014 ACM SIGSAC Conference on Computer and Communications Security, CCS 2014, p. 15 29. Association for Computing Machinery (2014). https://doi.org/10.1145/2660267.2660379
15. Biryukov, A., Tikhomirov, S.: Deanonymization and linkability of cryptocurrency transactions based on network analysis. In: 2019 IEEE European Symposium on Security and Privacy (EuroS&P), pp. 172–184. IEEE (2019)
16. Bitansky, N., Canetti, R., Chiesa, A., Tromer, E.: From extractable collision resistance to succinct non-interactive arguments of knowledge, and back again. In: Proceedings of the 3rd Innovations in Theoretical Computer Science Conference, pp. 326–349. Association for Computing Machinery (2012). https://doi.org/10.1145/2090236.2090263
17. Blum, M., Feldman, P., Micali, S.: Non-interactive zero-knowledge and its applications. In: Proceedings of the Twentieth Annual ACM Symposium on Theory of Computing, pp. 103–112. Association for Computing Machinery, New York (1988). https://doi.org/10.1145/62212.62222

18. Boneh, D., Drake, J., Fisch, B., Gabizon, A.: Halo infinite: recursive zk-snarks from any additive polynomial commitment scheme. Cryptology ePrint Archive (2020)
19. Chen, J., Li, B., Zhang, Y., Peng, L., Peir, J.K.: Statistical GPU power analysis using tree-based methods. In: 2011 International Green Computing Conference and Workshops, pp. 1–6 (2011). https://doi.org/10.1109/IGCC.2011.6008582
20. Chen, M.S., et al.: Preon: zk-snark based signature scheme (2023)
21. Chiesa, A., Ojha, D., Spooner, N.: Fractal: post-quantum and transparent recursive proofs from holography. In: Canteaut, A., Ishai, Y. (eds.) EUROCRYPT 2020. LNCS, vol. 12105, pp. 769–793. Springer, Cham (2020). https://doi.org/10.1007/978-3-030-45721-1_27
22. Delestrac, P., et al.: Analyzing GPU energy consumption in data movement and storage. In: 2024 IEEE 35th International Conference on Application-specific Systems, Architectures and Processors (ASAP), pp. 143–151. IEEE Computer Society (2024). https://doi.org/10.1109/ASAP61560.2024.00038
23. Fiat, A., Shamir, A.: How to prove yourself: practical solutions to identification and signature problems. In: Odlyzko, A.M. (ed.) Advances in Cryptology – CRYPTO' 86, pp. 186–194. Springer, Heidelberg (1987)
24. Fu, S., Gong, G.: Polaris: transparent succinct zero-knowledge arguments for R1CS with efficient verifier. Proc. Priv. Enhancing Technol. (2022)
25. Goldreich, O., Micali, S., Wigderson, A.: Proofs that yield nothing but their validity. In: Proceedings of the 27th Annual Symposium on Foundations of Computer Science (FOCS), pp. 174–187 (1986)
26. Goldreich, O., Oren, Y.: Definitions and properties of zero-knowledge proof systems. J. Cryptol. **7**(1), 1–32 (1994). https://doi.org/10.1007/BF00195207
27. Goldwasser, S., Micali, S., Rackoff, C.: The knowledge complexity of interactive proof systems. SIAM J. Comput. **18**(1), 186–208 (1989). https://doi.org/10.1137/0218012
28. Gong, G.: Fri. Unpublished note. Department of Electrical and Computer Engineering. University of Waterloo, Waterloo, ON, Canada (2023)
29. Gong, G.: Uni/multi variate polynomial embeddings for zkSNARKs. Cryptogr. Commun. 1–32 (2024)
30. Groth, J.: Short pairing-based non-interactive zero-knowledge arguments. In: Abe, M. (ed.) ASIACRYPT 2010. LNCS, vol. 6477, pp. 321–340. Springer, Heidelberg (2010). https://doi.org/10.1007/978-3-642-17373-8_19
31. Groth, J.: On the size of pairing-based non-interactive arguments. In: Fischlin, M., Coron, J.-S. (eds.) EUROCRYPT 2016. LNCS, vol. 9666, pp. 305–326. Springer, Heidelberg (2016). https://doi.org/10.1007/978-3-662-49896-5_11
32. Hopwood, D., Bowe, S., Hornby, T., Wilcox, N., et al.: Zcash protocol specification. GitHub: San Francisco, CA, USA **4**(220), 32 (2016)
33. Keccak Team: Keccak specifications summary (2024). https://keccak.team/keccak_specs_summary.html. Accessed 11 Nov 2024
34. Kosba, A., Miller, A., Shi, E., Wen, Z., Papamanthou, C.: Hawk: the blockchain model of cryptography and privacy-preserving smart contracts. In: Proceedings of the IEEE Symposium on Security and Privacy, pp. 839–858 (2016)
35. Koshy, P., Koshy, D., McDaniel, P.: An analysis of anonymity in bitcoin using P2P network traffic. In: Christin, N., Safavi-Naini, R. (eds.) Financial Cryptography and Data Security, pp. 469–485. Springer, Heidelberg (2014)
36. Levinin, A.: libiop-fp2: A C++ library for IOP-based zkSNARKs over elliptic curves (2023). https://github.com/levanin/libiop-fp2. Accessed 13 Oct 2024
37. MacWilliams, F.J., Sloane, N.J.A.: The theory of error-correcting codes. Elsevier (1977)

38. Micali, S.: CS proofs (extended abstract). In: Proceedings of the 35th Annual Symposium on Foundations of Computer Science (FOCS), pp. 436–453 (1994)
39. Nakamoto, S., Bitcoin, A.: A peer-to-peer electronic cash system. Bitcoin **4**(2), 15 (2008). https://bitcoin.org/bitcoin.pdf
40. NVIDIA Corporation: NVIDIA A40 datasheet (2020). https://images.nvidia.com/content/Solutions/data-center/a40/nvidia-a40-datasheet.pdf. Accessed 23 Oct 2024
41. NVIDIA Corporation: Cuda profiler user's guide (2024). https://docs.nvidia.com/cuda/profiler-users-guide/. Accessed 12 Nov 2024
42. Panait, A.-E., Olimid, R.F.: On using zk-SNARKs and zk-STARKs in blockchain-based identity management. In: Maimut, D., Oprina, A.-G., Sauveron, D. (eds.) SecITC 2020. LNCS, vol. 12596, pp. 130–145. Springer, Cham (2021). https://doi.org/10.1007/978-3-030-69255-1_9
43. Peters, G.W., Panayi, E.: Understanding modern banking ledgers through blockchain technologies: future of transaction processing and smart contracts on the internet of money. J. Bank. Regul. **16**(3–4), 217–233 (2015). https://doi.org/10.1057/jbr.2015.19
44. Rackoff, C., Simon, D.R.: Non-interactive zero-knowledge proof of knowledge and chosen ciphertext attack. In: Annual International Cryptology Conference, pp. 433–444. Springer (1991)
45. SCIPR Lab, contributors: libiop: A C++ library for IOP-based zksnarks (2017–2024). https://github.com/scipr-lab/libiop. Accessed 13 Oct 2024
46. Setty, S.: Spartan: efficient and general-purpose zkSNARKs without trusted setup. Cryptology ePrint Archive, Paper 2019/550 (2019). https://eprint.iacr.org/2019/550
47. The RustaCUDA Developers: Rustacuda: A safe wrapper for the CUDA driver API (2024). https://docs.rs/rustacuda/latest/rustacuda/. Accessed 10 Nov 2024
48. Zhang, R., Xue, R., Liu, L.: Security and privacy on blockchain. ACM Comput. Surv. (CSUR) **52**(3), 1–34 (2019)

Accelerating Post-quantum Secure zkSNARKs by Optimizing Additive FFT

Mohammadtaghi Badakhshan(✉), Susanta Samanta, and Guang Gong

Department of Electrical and Computer Engineering, University of Waterloo, Waterloo, ON, Canada
{mbadakhshan,ssamanta,ggong}@uwaterloo.ca

Abstract. Zero-Knowledge Succinct Non-Interactive Arguments of Knowledge (zkSNARKs) are increasingly utilized across diverse applications. While significant advances have been made in the development of post-quantum secure zkSNARKs, these schemes face challenges, including substantial computational complexity. In this paper, we propose leveraging the Cantor special basis in post-quantum secure zkSNARKs operating over binary extension fields. This approach enables the optimization of the additive Fast Fourier Transform (FFT) algorithm in Aurora, a post-quantum secure zkSNARK, by replacing the previously used Gao–Mateer FFT with the Cantor and LCH FFTs. Our implementation demonstrates a significant reduction in computation time for Aurora, with the potential to accelerate other zkSNARKs utilizing additive FFTs. Additionally, we present a detailed theoretical analysis of the computational costs of the Cantor FFT algorithm, providing exact counts of additions, multiplications, and precomputation overhead. Furthermore, we analyze the FFT call complexity within the encoding of the Rank-1 Constraint System in the Aurora zkSNARK.

Keywords: Post-quantum secure zkSNARK · R1CS · Aurora · Additive FFT · Cantor Algorithm · Gao–Mateer Algorithm

1 Introduction

Zero-Knowledge Succinct Non-Interactive Argument of Knowledge (zkSNARK) protocols are cryptographic schemes involving a prover and a verifier. The prover generates a publicly verifiable and succinct proof that demonstrates knowledge of a witness vector (secret inputs) satisfying a given constraint system. The proof does not reveal any information about the witness itself. These protocols have a wide range of applications, from post-quantum secure digital signature algorithms [2,17,18,32] to privacy preserving applications over blockchains [8,14,43,47], and blockchain scalability solutions using rollups [16,44]. The efficiency of the prover and verifier algorithms, along with the proof size of the zkSNARK protocol, are crucial factors influencing the cost-effectiveness and overall practicality of the aforementioned applications. Additionally, two other

C. Boura et al. (Eds.): SAC 2025, LNCS 16207, pp. 339–368, 2026.
https://doi.org/10.1007/978-3-032-10536-3_13

important factors are: whether the zkSNARK protocol relies on a trusted setup or employs a transparent setup, and, whether it offers plausible post-quantum security against a malicious prover with quantum capabilities.

Optimizing or accelerating the implementation of algorithms in zkSNARKs is an active and popular area of research [5,6,23,31,40]. In parallel, optimizing the *Fast Fourier Transform (FFT)* over additive groups has been a significant focus of study [15,26,27,36,37]. The FFT over additive groups can be utilized in various zkSNARK protocols operating over binary extension fields. Examples of such protocols include Ligero [1], STARK [4], Aurora [10], Fractal [21], and Polaris [25].

The FFT over additive groups, known as the *additive FFT*, over finite fields was developed in the late 1980s. Wang and Zhu [46] first introduced this concept, followed independently by Cantor [15]. These algorithms evaluate polynomials of degree less than $n = 2^m$ over m-dimensional *affine subspaces* of $\mathbb{F}_{2^k}$, where $k = 2^\ell$. This was later generalized to arbitrary k by von zur Gathen and Gerhard [27], but this incurred a higher computational cost. Subsequently, Gao and Mateer [26] proposed two algorithms based on Taylor expansions: one applicable to arbitrary k, with lower complexity than the method of von zur Gathen and Gerhard, and another optimized for additive *FFTs of length* 2^m, where m is a power of two, reducing the number of additions while matching Cantor's multiplication count.

Lin et al. [38] later introduced the LCH basis, constructed from the *vanishing polynomials*, enabling FFTs with $O(n \log n)$ additions and multiplications. They also developed conversion algorithms [37] between the LCH and monomial bases, requiring $O(n \log n \log \log n)$ additions and no multiplications under the *Cantor special basis*, with further refinements in [22]. These methods have been applied to fast binary polynomial multiplication [19,20,35]. Since additive FFTs require input lengths that are powers of two, a polynomial with $(t + 1)$ coefficients (i.e., of degree t) must be zero-padded to length 2^m if $t + 1 < 2^m$. Bernstein et al. [13] addressed this by modifying the Gao–Mateer algorithm to skip operations on known-zero coefficients. Further improvements were made by Bernstein and Chou [12], incorporating the Cantor special basis and tower field constructions, particularly for FFTs of length up to 64.

For this study, we select Aurora [10] to demonstrate the performance improvements achieved by optimizing the FFT algorithm using the Cantor special basis. While our optimization is applicable to all the aforementioned zkSNARKs, Aurora was chosen due to its small proof size, which makes it a strong candidate for post-quantum secure digital signature schemes. Accordingly, Aurora serves as the foundation of Preon [18], a post-quantum digital signature scheme that was a first-round candidate in NIST's PQC standardization process [42].

Contributions. Our main contributions are summarized as follows:

- In the Cantor FFT algorithm, we present a theoretical analysis of the vanishing polynomials, providing a precise count of their terms based on Hamming weight. To the best of our knowledge, prior works have only reported upper

Table 1. Comparison of the number of finite field additions (#A) and multiplications (#M) in the Gao–Mateer (GM), LCH, and Cantor additive FFT algorithms of length n over general and Cantor special basis.

FFT	Basis	Basis Conversion	Evaluation
GM	General (Sect. 4.3)	#A: $\frac{1}{4}n(\log_2 n)^2 - \frac{1}{4}n\log_2 n$ #M: $n\log_2 n - n + 1$	#A: $n\log_2 n$ #M: $\frac{1}{2}n\log_2 n$
	Cantor (Sect. 4.4)	#A: $\frac{1}{4}n(\log_2 n)^2 - \frac{1}{4}n\log_2 n$ #M: 0	#A: $n\log_2 n$ #M: $\frac{1}{2}n\log_2 n$
LCH	General [37]	#A: $O(n(\log_2 n)^2)$ #M: $O(n\log_2 n)$	#A: $n\log_2 n$ #M: $\frac{1}{2}n\log_2 n$
	Cantor [37]	#A: $O(n\log_2 n\log_2\log_2 n)$ #M: 0	#A: $n\log_2 n$ #M: $\frac{1}{2}n\log_2 n$
Cantor	Cantor (Sect. 3.4)	N/A	#A: $\frac{1}{2}n\log_2 n + \frac{1}{2}n\sum_{r=0}^{\log_2(n)-1} 2^{\mathrm{wt}(r)}$ #M: $\frac{1}{2}n\log_2 n$

bounds. We also efficiently compute the vanishing polynomials and multiplication factors, improving efficiency even without precomputation.

- We propose Cantor FFT building blocks and demonstrate notable performance gains in the current Aurora implementation [9] over the Gao–Mateer algorithm across all input sizes and the LCH algorithm for smaller circuits, which are prevalent in many zkSNARK applications [18,29]. Table 2 shows how our FFT optimizations using the Cantor special basis can accelerate both prover and verifier algorithms in Aurora.
- We provide a detailed breakdown of the Gao–Mateer algorithm's core components, Expand and Aggregate, and enhance their computational and space efficiency using the Cantor special basis. We also introduce precomputation techniques that substantially reduce overhead in the Cantor algorithm, along with two levels of precomputation for Gao–Mateer.
- We analyze the FFT call complexity in the Aurora zkSNARK, evaluating the number and size of each FFT/IFFT call based on R1CS constraints, variables, and the target security parameter. We also show how selecting the shift element in Aurora's affine subspaces reduces precomputation space complexity significantly in the Cantor FFT by leveraging the Cantor special basis.
- We provide a C++ implementation of the Cantor algorithm, along with the Gao–Mateer and LCH algorithms using the Cantor special basis, as well as our

precomputation techniques. A comprehensive comparison of these algorithms is presented in Fig. 1.

Table 2. Runtime (in seconds) of the Aurora [10] algorithms over $\mathbb{F}_{2^{256}}$ on the platform described in Sect. 6, based on the number of constraints N and the size of the codeword domain $|L|$.

$\log_2(N)$	$\log_2(\|L\|)$	Aurora Prover			Aurora Verifier		
		GM* libiop [9]	Cantor (this work)	LCH (this work)†	GM* libiop [9]	Cantor (this work)	LCH (this work)†
9	16	0.44	0.33	0.35	0.04	0.04	0.04
10	17	0.90	0.67	0.71	0.05	0.05	0.05
11	18	1.87	1.36	1.44	0.07	0.06	0.07
12	19	3.99	2.91	2.93	0.10	0.09	0.10
13	20	8.53	6.02	5.95	0.17	0.15	0.16
14	21	19.47	12.01	12.44	0.29	0.26	0.28
15	22	41.05	25.27	25.41	0.54	0.48	0.52
16	23	84.26	50.83	50.63	1.02	0.93	1.00
17	24	176.67	104.26	102.95	1.98	1.79	1.93
18	25	373.83	216.00	213.61	3.88	3.51	3.78
19	26	771.42	443.88	441.51	7.78	6.91	7.44

* Gao–Mateer FFT using standard basis.

† The LCH FFT using Cantor special basis from [19] is reimplemented in C++ to become compatible with `libiop` [9] and polymorphism over finite fields.

The paper is structured as follows. Section 2 covers mathematical preliminaries, including the Cantor and Gao–Mateer algorithms and R1CS encoding in Aurora. Section 3 presents Cantor algorithm optimizations, while Sect. 4 details the Gao–Mateer algorithm and its precomputations. Section 5 analyzes FFT call complexity in Aurora, and Sect. 6 benchmarks the FFT algorithms and Aurora. Finally, Sect. 7 summarizes the findings and future directions.

2 Preliminaries

This section presents key definitions and preliminaries essential to our study.

2.1 Algebraic Foundations

Finite Field. Let $\mathbb{F}_{2^k}$ be the finite field of order 2^k. We know that there exists a vector space isomorphism from $\mathbb{F}_{2^k}$ to $\mathbb{F}_2^k$ defined by $\mathbf{x} = (x_0\beta_0 + x_1\beta_1 + \cdots + x_{k-1}\beta_{k-1}) \mapsto (x_0, x_1, \ldots, x_{k-1})$, where $\{\beta_0, \beta_1, \ldots, \beta_{k-1}\}$ is a basis of $\mathbb{F}_{2^k}$. The polynomial ring over $\mathbb{F}_{2^k}$ in the variable x is denoted by $\mathbb{F}_{2^k}[x]$.

Affine Subspace. Let us define the subspace W_m of $\mathbb{F}_{2^k}$ as the linear combinations of $\{\beta_0, \beta_1, \ldots, \beta_{m-1}\}$. We order the elements of the subspace W_m by $\{\eta_0 = 0, \eta_1, \eta_2, \ldots, \eta_{2^m-1}\}$ where $\eta_j = \sum_{i=0}^{m-1} x_i\beta_i$ and $j = \sum_{i=0}^{m-1} x_i 2^i, x_i \in \{0,1\}$.

Note that for any $0 \leq m < k$, we can decompose the elements of W_{m+1} into two disjoint sets: the subspace W_m and the *affine subspace* $\beta_m + W_m$, where $\beta_m + W_m$ is the set obtained by translating (or shifting) the subspace W_m by the vector β_m.

Vanishing Polynomial. The polynomial $\mathbb{Z}_{W_m}(x) = \prod_{a\in W_m}(x-a)$ which is a linearized polynomial, is given by $\mathbb{Z}_{W_m}(x) = \sum_{i=0}^{m} c_i x^{2^i}, c_i \in \mathbb{F}_{2^k}$. This polynomial is called the *vanishing polynomial* for the subspace W_m. Since $W_{m+1} = W_m \cup (\beta_m + W_m)$, we have $\mathbb{Z}_{W_{m+1}}(x) = (\mathbb{Z}_{W_m}(x))^2 - \mathbb{Z}_{W_m}(\beta_m) \cdot \mathbb{Z}_{W_m}(x)$.

Univariate Polynomials Vectorial Representation. For any univariate polynomial $f(x) = \sum_{i=0}^{n-1} c_i x^i, c_i \in \mathbb{F}_{2^k}$, where $\deg(f) < n = 2^m$, the coefficients are represented as a vector of n elements, ordered from the constant term to the highest degree term. Namely, $\mathbf{f} = (c_0, \ldots, c_{n-1}), c_i \in \mathbb{F}_{2^k}$ represents the polynomial $f(x)$, where $\deg(f) < n$.

Additive Discrete Fourier Transform. Now we will discuss the evaluation of a univariate polynomial $f(x)$ over the subspace W_m. The evaluation of $f(x)$ at the points $\eta_0, \eta_1, \ldots, \eta_{2^m-1}$ is given by $\hat{\mathbf{f}} = (f(\eta_0), f(\eta_1), \ldots, f(\eta_{2^m-1}))$.

This set of evaluations is referred to as the additive discrete Fourier transform (DFT) of $f(x)$ over the subspace W_m. We sometimes refer to the vector $\hat{\mathbf{f}}$ as the *discrete Fourier transform of length* $n = 2^m$ for the function $f(x)$, denoted by $\text{DFT}(f, W_m)$. *The additive FFT* is an efficient method for computing $\text{DFT}(f, W_m)$, which we will denote as $\text{FFT}(f, W_m)$.

2.2 Cantor Algorithm

The evaluation of a polynomial $f(x)$ of degree less than $n = 2^m$ over the subspace W_m using Cantor's algorithm is valid only when W_m is a subspace of the field (or subfield) $\mathbb{F}_{2^k}$, where $k = 2^\ell$. Cantor introduced a special basis to facilitate the efficient evaluation of $f(x)$.

The Cantor Special Basis. Consider the function $S : \mathbb{F}_{2^k} \to \mathbb{F}_{2^k}$ defined by $S(x) = x^2 + x$, and let the following sequence of functions be defined recursively: $S^0(x) = x$ and $S^m(x) = S(S^{m-1}(x))$. A nonrecursive formula for $S^m(x)$ is $S^m(x) = \sum_{i=0}^{m} \binom{m}{i} x^{2^i}$, where $\binom{m}{i}$ denotes the binomial coefficient reduced modulo 2. For $m = 2^t$, we have $S^{2^t} = x^{2^{2^t}} + x$. The *Cantor special basis* $\{\beta_0, \beta_1, \ldots, \beta_{m-1}\}$ for the subspace W_m is defined as $S(\beta_i) = \beta_{i-1}$ for $i = 1, \ldots, m-1$ with $\beta_0 = 1$. With this basis, we have $S^i(\beta_i) = 1$ for $i = 0, 1, \ldots, m-1$. Consequently, in the context of the Cantor special basis, the vanishing polynomial of the subspaces simplifies to $\mathbb{Z}_{W_i}(x) = S^i(x)$ for $i = 0, 1, \ldots, m$.

Polynomial Evaluation. Let $f(x) \in \mathbb{F}_{2^k}[x]$ be a polynomial of degree less than $n = 2^m$ and we want to evaluate $f(x)$ over the affine subspace $\theta + W_m = \theta + \langle \beta_0, \beta_1, \ldots, \beta_{m-1} \rangle$, where $\{\beta_0 = 1, \beta_1, \ldots, \beta_{m-1}\}$ is a Cantor special basis. The evaluation of $f(x)$ using the Cantor algorithm proceeds as follows: first, compute two polynomials $f_0(x)$ and $f_1(x)$ such that $f_0(x) = f(x)$ for all $x \in \theta + W_{m-1}$ and $f_1(x) = f(x)$ for all $x \in \theta + \beta_{m-1} + W_{m-1}$. The polynomials $f_0(x)$ and $f_1(x)$ can be obtained by taking the remainders of $f(x)$ when divided by the vanishing polynomials of the affine subspaces. Specifically, we have

$$f_0(x) = f(x) \mod S^{m-1}(x+\theta) \quad \text{and} \quad f_1(x) = f(x) \mod S^{m-1}(x+\theta+\beta_{m-1}).$$

We then proceed by recursively evaluating $f_0(x)$ and $f_1(x)$ over the affine subspaces $\theta + W_{m-1}$ and $\theta + \beta_{m-1} + W_{m-1}$, respectively. The recursion continues until all the resulting polynomials $f_0(x)$ and $f_1(x)$ are constants. This is summarized in Algorithm 6 in Appendix A.

2.3 Gao–Mateer Algorithm

Note that the evaluation of $f(x)$ over $\theta + W_m$ is equivalent to the evaluation of the function $g(x) = f(\beta_{m-1}x)$ over

$$\beta_{m-1}^{-1}(\theta + W_m) = \beta_{m-1}^{-1}\theta + \beta_{m-1}^{-1} \cdot W_m = (\theta_0 + G) \cup (1 + \theta_0 + G),$$

where $\theta_0 = \beta_{m-1}^{-1}\theta$ and G is a $m-1$ dimensional subspace given by $G = \langle \gamma_0, \ldots, \gamma_{m-2} \rangle$, where $\gamma_i = \beta_i \cdot \beta_{m-1}^{-1}$ for $i = 0, 1, \ldots, m-2$.

Now, consider the Taylor expansion of $g(x)$ at $x^2 + x$ to obtain $f_0(x)$ and $f_1(x)$. Specifically, express $g(x)$ as

$$g(x) = \sum_{i=0}^{\ell-1} (g_{i0} + g_{i1}x)(x^2 + x)^i, \text{ where } \ell = 2^{m-1} \text{ and } g_{ij} \in \mathbb{F}_{2^k}$$

and define $f_0(x) = \sum_{i=0}^{\ell-1} g_{i0}x^i$ and $f_1(x) = \sum_{i=0}^{\ell-1} g_{i1}x^i$. Then, the FFT of $g(x)$ over $\beta_{m-1}^{-1}(\theta + W_m)$ can be derived from the evaluation of $f_0(x)$ and $f_1(x)$ over $\theta_0^2 + \theta_0 + D$, where $D = \langle \delta_0, \delta_1, \ldots, \delta_{m-2} \rangle$ is a $m-1$ dimensional subspace with $\delta_i = \gamma_i^2 + \gamma_i$ for $i = 0, 1, \ldots, m-2$. By applying this reduction step again to $\text{FFT}(f_0, \theta_0^2 + \theta_0 + D)$ and $\text{FFT}(f_1, \theta_0^2 + \theta_0 + D)$, we continue until D has a dimension of 1. This is summarized in Algorithm 7 in Appendix A.

2.4 Aurora zkSNARK

Aurora [10] is a zkSNARK for R1CS relations. It encodes an R1CS instance into entries of Reed–Solomon (RS) codewords and to generate an argument regarding the R1CS instance, it employs the fast RS interactive oracle proof (IOP) of proximity (FRI) [3] to prove that the given codewords are close to a low-degree polynomial.

Definition 1 (Rank-1 Constraint System (R1CS)). *Let d_1, d_2, and d_3 denote the number of constraints, variables, and public inputs. The R1CS relation consists of* $\mathbf{A}, \mathbf{B}, \mathbf{C} \in \mathbb{F}_{2^k}^{d_1 \times (d_2+1)}$ *and public inputs* $\mathbf{v} \in \mathbb{F}_{2^k}^{d_3}$. $\mathbf{w} \in \mathbb{F}_{2^k}^{d_2-d_3}$, *denoting private (auxiliary) inputs, satisfies the system if* $\mathbf{Az} \circ \mathbf{Bz} = \mathbf{Cz}$, *where* $\mathbf{z} := (1, \mathbf{v}, \mathbf{w}) \in \mathbb{F}_{2^k}^{d_2+1}$ *and "$\circ$" denotes the Hadamard product.*

Definition 2 (Reed–Solomon (RS) Code). *Let $L \subseteq \mathbb{F}_{2^k}$ denote the codeword domain and $\rho \in [0,1]$ denote the rate parameter. $RS[L, \rho]$ is the set of all codewords $\hat{\mathbf{f}} : L \to \mathbb{F}_{2^k}$ that are the evaluation of polynomials over L with degree $< \rho|L|$.*

At the beginning of the Aurora protocol, the prover and verifier establish a finite field $\mathbb{F}_{2^k}$, a security parameter $\boldsymbol{\lambda}$, an RS rate ρ, an FRI localization parameter η, an R1CS instance, and two subspaces $H_1, H_2 \subset \mathbb{F}_{2^k}$, where $|H_1| = d_1$ and $|H_2| = d_2 + 1$ such that $H_1 \subseteq H_2$ or $H_2 \subseteq H_1$. We can write $H_1 \cup H_2 = \{h_0, \ldots, h_{t-1}\}$, where $t = |H_1 \cup H_2| = \max(d_1, d_2 + 1)$. Finally, the codeword domain L is determined such that $t \leq \rho|L|$ and $L \cap (H_1 \cup H_2) = \emptyset$. Section 5 describes how $|L|$ is determined. Given these parameters, the repetition counts λ_i for the *lincheck* protocol and λ_i' for the *FRI low-degree testing* (FRI-LDT) protocol, Aurora's two main sub-protocols, are determined.

The prover algorithm starts by interpolating a polynomial $f_{(1,\mathbf{v})}(x)$ of degree $d_3 + 1$ such that $f_{(1,\mathbf{v})}(h_0) = 1$ and $f_{(1,\mathbf{v})}(h_{i+1}) = v_i$ for $i = 0, \ldots, d_3 - 1$, where v_i denotes the i-th element in $\mathbf{v}$. Then, during each round $\ell = 1, \ldots, \lambda_i$ of the lincheck protocol, four public-coin random numbers $\alpha_\ell, s_\ell^A, s_\ell^B, s_\ell^C \in_R \mathbb{F}_{2^k}$ are sampled. Then, both prover and verifier interpolate

1. A polynomial $p_{\alpha_\ell}(x)$ of degree $t - 1$, such that $p_{\alpha_\ell}(h_i) = {\alpha_\ell}^{i+1}$ for $i = 0, \ldots, d_1 - 1$ and if $t > d_1$, then $p_{\alpha_\ell}(h_i) = 0$ for $i = d_1, \ldots, t - 1$.
2. Three polynomials $p_{\alpha_\ell}^{\mathbf{A}}(x)$, $p_{\alpha_\ell}^{\mathbf{B}}(x)$, and $p_{\alpha_\ell}^{\mathbf{C}}(x)$ of degree $t - 1$, such that $p_{\alpha_\ell}^{\mathbf{M}}(h_j) = \sum_{i=0}^{d_1-1} \mathbf{M}_{i,j} {\alpha_\ell}^{i+1}$ for $j = 0, \ldots, d_2$ and $M \in \{A, B, C\}$. If $t > d_2 + 1$, then $p_{\alpha_\ell}^{\mathbf{M}}(h_j) = 0$ for $j = d_2 + 1, \ldots, t - 1$.
3. A polynomial $p_{\alpha_\ell}^{ABC}(h_j) = \sum_{M \in \{A,B,C\}} s_\ell^{\mathbf{M}} p_{\alpha_\ell}^{\mathbf{M}}(h_j)$, which is a random combination of defined $p_{\alpha_\ell}^{\mathbf{A}}(x)$, $p_{\alpha_\ell}^{\mathbf{B}}(x)$, and $p_{\alpha_\ell}^{\mathbf{C}}(x)$.

Table 6 in Appendix C lists the primary codewords obtained by encoding the R1CS instance, together with the polynomials subsequently derived during the prover's computation. To ensure zero-knowledge against a b-query bounded malicious verifier, every degree is raised by b; hence any b evaluations from of the polynomials in L are independent and uniform in $\mathbb{F}_{2^k}$ [7]. Finally, the codewords' low degree is proven with the FRI protocol.

3 Cantor Algorithm Building Blocks

The Cantor FFT of length $n = 2^m$ consists of m iterative rounds to evaluate a polynomial $f(x) \in \mathbb{F}_{2^k}[x]$ of degree $< 2^m$ over the affine subspace $\theta + W_m$, where $\theta \in \mathbb{F}_{2^k}$ and W_m must be generated by the Cantor special basis as described in

Sect. 2.2. Also, for the Cantor special basis, we know that $\mathbb{Z}_{W_i}(x) = S^i(x)$ for $i = 0, 1, \ldots, m$. Thus, the coefficients of the vanishing polynomials $\mathbb{Z}_{W_i}(x)$ are in $\mathbb{F}_2$. Additionally, we have $S^i(\beta_i) = 1$.

Let $0 \leq r \leq m-1$ be the round number. In each round r, the algorithm processes 2^r polynomials of degree $< 2^{m-r}$, resulting in 2^{r+1} polynomials of degree $< 2^{m-r-1}$ at the end of the round. $f(x)$ is represented by $\mathbf{f}$, a vector of size 2^m that stores the coefficients as described in Sect. 2. We use the same vector to store all intermediate polynomials during each round. For example, in round r, $\mathbf{f}$ stores the concatenation of the 2^{r+1} polynomials. Finally, in round $r = m-1$, the algorithm outputs 2^m constant values stored in the vector $\mathbf{f}$, representing the evaluations of $f(x)$ over $\theta + W_m$.

Before presenting the details of our Cantor algorithm implementation, we first explain the selection process of the Cantor special basis of length m, denoted by $\{\beta_0, \beta_1, \ldots, \beta_{m-1}\}$. From [26, Appendix], we know that $W_m = \langle \beta_0, \beta_1, \ldots, \beta_{m-1} \rangle$ must be a subspace of the field (or subfield) $\mathbb{F}_{2^{2^\ell}}$. To determine the Cantor special basis for $\mathbb{F}_{2^{2^\ell}}$, we begin by defining a basis $\{\beta_0, \beta_1, \ldots, \beta_{2^\ell-1}\}$ such that $\mathrm{Tr}_{\mathbb{F}_{2^{2^\ell}}/\mathbb{F}_2}(\beta_{2^\ell-1}) = 1$. Then, we recursively determine the remaining basis elements by $\beta_{j-1} = \beta_j^2 + \beta_j$ for $1 \leq j \leq 2^\ell - 1$. We then select the first m elements from this basis to construct our Cantor special basis of dimension m. In our implementation, we randomly try different values of $\beta_{2^\ell-1}$ and compute their trace. With a probability of 0.5, the trace 1.

3.1 Vanishing Polynomials

In the Cantor additive FFT of length 2^m, the vanishing polynomials $\mathbb{Z}_{W_0}, \mathbb{Z}_{W_1}, \ldots, \mathbb{Z}_{W_{m-1}}$ must be computed to perform the division algorithm. The coefficients in each $\mathbb{Z}_{W_i}(x)$ are derived from

$$\mathbb{Z}_{W_i}(x) = \sum_{j=0}^{i} \left[\binom{i}{j} \mod 2 \right] x^{2^j}.$$

Employing Lucas's theorem [39], we efficiently compute $\binom{i}{j} \equiv \prod_{k=0}^{t-1} \binom{i_k}{j_k} \bmod 2$, where

$$i = i_0 + i_1 2 + i_2 2^2 + \ldots + i_{t-1} 2^{t-1} \quad (i_k \in \{0, 1\}),$$
$$j = j_0 + j_1 2 + j_2 2^2 + \ldots + j_{t-1} 2^{t-1} \quad (j_k \in \{0, 1\}).$$

Theorem 1. *[24, Theorem 2] The number of integers j not exceeding i for which $\binom{i}{j} \not\equiv 0 \pmod 2$ is $\prod_{k=0}^{t}(i_k + 1)$.*

Thus, by the above theorem we conclude that the number of non-zero coefficients in $\mathbb{Z}_{W_i}(x)$ equals $2^{\mathrm{wt}(i)}$, where $\mathrm{wt}(i)$ denotes the Hamming weight of i, i.e., the number of bits equal to 1. Since the number of non-zero coefficients in most vanishing polynomials is considerably less than its degree (i.e., 2^i), we avoid using vectorial representation of univariate polynomials described in Sect. 2 for these polynomials. Otherwise, the polynomial division algorithm would require excessive addition operation on zero coefficients.

To efficiently represent the vanishing polynomials, we store the index number of the coefficients in the reverse order. Specifically, let $\mathbf{z}_i$ represent $\mathbb{Z}_{W_i}(x) = \sum_{j=0}^{i} c_j x^{2^j}$ in our implementation. We define

$$\mathbf{z}_i = (\zeta_0, \zeta_1, \ldots, \zeta_{2^{\mathrm{wt}(i)}-1}) = (2^i - 2^j | c_j = 1 \text{ in } \mathbb{Z}_{W_i}(x)),$$

where Algorithm 1 describes how $\mathbf{z}_i$ is computed.

Algorithm 1: Vanishing Polynomial (i, θ)

Input: $i \in \mathbb{N}$ and $\theta \in \mathbb{F}_{2^k}$
Output: $\mathbf{z}_i$, eval.
$\ell \leftarrow 0$
eval $\leftarrow \theta$
for $j = 0$ **to** $i - 1$ **do**
  $t \leftarrow \lceil \log_2(j+1) \rceil$
  $k \leftarrow 0$
  while $(i_k \vee \neg j_k) \wedge (k < t)$ **do**
    $k \leftarrow k + 1$
  end
  if $k = t$ **then**
    $\zeta_\ell \leftarrow 2^i - 2^j$
    eval $\leftarrow$ eval $+ \theta^{2^j}$
    $\ell \leftarrow \ell + 1$
  end
end
eval $\leftarrow$ eval $+ \theta^{2^i}$ `// As the highest degree term is not in` $\mathbf{z}_i$
assert $\ell = 2^{\mathrm{wt}(i)} - 2$
return $\mathbf{z}_i \leftarrow (\zeta_0, \zeta_1, \ldots, \zeta_{2^{\mathrm{wt}(i)}-2})$, eval.

Algorithm 1 also computes the evaluation of $\mathbb{Z}_{W_i}(\theta)$ which is used later in Sect. 3.3. Reversing the order (i.e., measuring the distance from 2^i rather than from 0) eliminates the need for degree shifting in $\mathbb{Z}_{W_i}(x)$ during the division rounds. Additionally, since $\binom{i}{i} = 1$, c_i is always one, and $\zeta_{2^{\mathrm{wt}(i)}-1}$ is zero which can be omitted from $\mathbf{z}_i$. This omission excludes this coefficient from the polynomial division algorithm, saving one addition per division round while keeping the quotient in the same vector as the dividend.

3.2 Polynomial Division

In round r of the Cantor algorithm, the 2^r polynomials $f_{i,r}(x)$, each of degree $< 2^p$, are divided by $\mathbb{Z}_{W_{p-1}}(x+\theta_{i,r})$ and $\mathbb{Z}_{W_{p-1}}(x+\theta_{i,r}+\beta_{p-1})$, where $p = m-r$ and $0 \leq i \leq 2^r - 1$. The corresponding remainders of these divisions for each $f_{i,r}(x)$ are outputted to be processed in the next round. Since the vanishing polynomials are linearized polynomials, we have

$$\mathbb{Z}_{W_{p-1}}(x + \theta_{i,r}) = \mathbb{Z}_{W_{p-1}}(x) + \mathbb{Z}_{W_{p-1}}(\theta_{i,r}), \text{ and}$$
$$\mathbb{Z}_{W_{p-1}}(x + \theta_{i,r} + \beta_{p-1}) = \mathbb{Z}_{W_{p-1}}(x) + \mathbb{Z}_{W_{p-1}}(\theta_{i,r}) + \mathbb{Z}_{W_{p-1}}(\beta_{p-1}),$$

where $\mathbb{Z}_{Wp-1}(\beta_{p-1}) = 1$. Since $\deg(f_i(x)) < 2\deg(\mathbb{Z}_{Wp-1}(x))$, we reduce the two divisions required for each $f_i(x)$ to a single division by $\mathbb{Z}_{Wp-1}(x)$, and then compute the remainders of the original divisions accordingly.

Since the coefficients in $\mathbb{Z}_{W_{p-1}}(x)$ are in $\mathbb{F}_2$, division by $\mathbb{Z}_{W_{p-1}}(x)$ requires only additions. In the division algorithm, the dividend polynomial, denoted by $f_{i,r}(x)$, is added to scaled degree-shifts of $\mathbb{Z}_{W_{p-1}}(x)$. However, we eliminate the need for degree shifts by using the reversed index order in $\mathbf{z}_i$, which represents the distance of each non-zero coefficient from the highest degree (i.e., 2^p).

Dividing $f_{i,r}(x)$, a polynomial of degree $< 2^p$, by $\mathbb{Z}_{W_{p-1}}(x)$ yields the quotient $q_{i,r}(x)$ and the remainder $r_{i,r}(x)$, each with degree $< 2^{p-1}$. Let $\mathbf{f}_{i,r}$ represent the $(i+1)$-th sub-vector of 2^p elements in the vector $\mathbf{f}$ at the beginning of round r. This sub-vector stores the coefficients of $f_{i,r}(x)$, ordered from the constant term to the highest degree term. Our polynomial division algorithm begins with the coefficient of the highest degree term in $\mathbf{f}_{i,r}$ and subtracts that coefficient from the lower-degree coefficients, spaced by distances determined by $\mathbf{z}_i$. Since $\mathbf{z}_i$ does not include zero, the coefficient of the highest degree term remains unaffected. In the next round of the polynomial division, the algorithm repeats this process with the second highest degree term. After 2^{p-1} rounds, the higher-degree (right) half of $\mathbf{f}_{i,r}$ stores the coefficients of $q_{i,r}(x)$, while the lower-degree (left) half stores the coefficients of $r_{i,r}(x)$. Then, the algorithm processes inputs to the next round

$$\begin{aligned} f_{2i,r+1}(x) &= r_{i,r}(x) - \mathbb{Z}_{W_{p-1}}(\theta_{i,r})\, q_{i,r}(x), \text{ and} \\ f_{2i+1,r+1}(x) &= f_{2i,r+1}(x) - q_{i,r}(x), \end{aligned}$$

where $\mathbb{Z}_{W_{p-1}}(\theta_{i,r})$ denotes the evaluation of the vanishing polynomial at $\theta_{i,r}$. Figure 2 in Appendix D illustrates the computation of the polynomials for the next round from the quotient and remainder in each round. Our polynomial division algorithm implementation integrates the computation of the quotient, remainder, and the polynomials for the next round.

Algorithm 2: Polynomial Division ($\mathbf{f}_{\text{in}}$, $\mathbf{z}_{p-1}$, $\mathbb{Z}_{W_{p-1}}(\theta_{i,r})$, p, i)

Input: $\mathbf{f}_{\text{in}} = (c_0, c_1, \dots, c_{n-1})$, $\mathbf{z}_{p-1} = (\zeta_0, \zeta_1, \dots, \zeta_{2^{\text{wt}(p-1)}-2})$, $\mathbb{Z}_{W_{p-1}}(\theta_{i,r}) \in \mathbb{F}_{2^k}$, $p = m - r$, and i determines the polynomial $f_{i,r}(x)$, of degree $< 2^p$, in $\mathbf{f}_{\text{in}}$.
Output: $\mathbf{f}_{\text{out}}$.

offset $\leftarrow i \times 2^p$ `// The offset at which the coefficients of` $f_{i,r}(x)$ `are in` $\mathbf{f}_{\text{in}}$
for $k = 2^p +$ offset $- 1$ **to** $2^{p-1} +$ offset **do**
  `// Iterates over the higher-degree half in decreasing order`
  for $\ell = 0$ **to** $2^{wt(p-1)} - 2$ **do**
    $c_{(k-\zeta_\ell)} \leftarrow c_{(k-\zeta_\ell)} + c_k$
  end
  $c_{(k-2^{p-1})} \leftarrow c_{(k-2^{p-1})} + c_k \times \mathbb{Z}_{W_{p-1}}(\theta_{i,r})$ `// Computes` $f_{2i,r+1}(x)$
end
for $k = 2^{p-1} +$ offset **to** $2^p +$ offset $- 1$ **do**
  $c_k \leftarrow c_k + c_{(k-2^{p-1})}$ `// Computes` $f_{2i+1,r+1}(x)$
end
return $\mathbf{f}_{\text{out}} \leftarrow (c_0, c_1, \dots, c_{n-1})$.

The Canopy module, described in the next section, is responsible for providing all of the inputs of the polynomial division algorithm.

3.3 Canopy Module

The Cantor algorithm is implemented by Canopy modules of varying input sizes 2^p and indices i, denoted by $\mathsf{Canopy}_{p,i}$. The index i indicates the module number in each round and determines the offset from the start of the $\mathbf{f}$ vector, where the coefficients of the input polynomial begin with $\mathsf{offset} = i2^p$.

The $\mathsf{Canopy}_{p,i}$ determines $\theta_{i,r}$ and then evaluate $\mathbb{Z}_{W_{p-1}}(\theta_{i,r})$, which is necessary for running Algorithm 2. Let the Cantor algorithm evaluate $f(x)$ of degree $< 2^m$ over $\theta + \langle \beta_0 = 1, \beta_1, \ldots, \beta_{m-1} \rangle$. Let $\theta_{0,0} = \theta$, and for $1 \leq r \leq m-1$ and $0 \leq i \leq 2^r - 1$, $\theta_{i,r}$ is determined recursively according to the following rules:

$$\theta_{i,r} = \begin{cases} \theta_{i/2,r-1} & \text{if } i \bmod 2 = 0, \\ \theta_{(i-1)/2,r-1} + \beta_p & \text{if } i \bmod 2 = 1, \end{cases}$$

where $p = m - r$. This equation can be simplified to $\theta_{i,r} = \theta_{\lfloor i/2 \rfloor, r-1} + (i \bmod 2)\beta_p$, and can be written as

$$\theta_{i,r} = \theta + \sum_{j=0}^{r-1} \left(\lfloor \frac{i}{2^j} \rfloor \bmod 2 \right) \beta_{p+j} = \theta + \sum_{j=0}^{r-1} i_j \, \beta_{p+j},$$

where $i = i_0 + i_1 2 + i_2 2^2 + \ldots + i_{r-1} 2^{r-1}$ ($i_j \in \mathbb{F}_2$), denotes the binary representation of i. Then, to evaluate $\mathbb{Z}_{W_{p-1}}(\theta_{i,r})$, we employ the rule $S^i(\beta_{i+\ell}) = \beta_\ell$ provided earlier in this section to simplify the computation. Specifically, we write $\mathbb{Z}_{W_{p-1}}(\beta_{p-1+j}) = \beta_j$. Therefore, $\mathbb{Z}_{W_{p-1}}(\theta_{i,r})$ can be evaluated as

$$\mathbb{Z}_{W_{p-1}}(\theta_{i,r}) = \mathbb{Z}_{W_{p-1}}(\theta) + \sum_{j=0}^{r-1} i_j \, \beta_{j+1},$$

where $\mathbb{Z}_{W_{p-1}}(\theta)$ is evaluated at each round while constructing $\mathbf{z}_{p-1}$ from $\mathbb{Z}_{W_{p-1}}(x)$ during Algorithm 1. The computation of $\mathbb{Z}_{W_{p-1}}(\theta)$ is shared across all the Canopy modules in each row since the vanishing polynomial remains consistent.

Algorithm 8 in Appendix D details the steps within the $\mathsf{Canopy}_{p,i}$ module, and Algorithm 3 describes the implementation of the Cantor algorithm based on those modules.

3.4 Detailed Cost Analysis

At the r-th iteration of the algorithm, we perform 2^r divisions by the polynomial $\mathbb{Z}_{W_{m-r-1}}(x)$. Moreover, as discussed in Sect. 3.1, each of these divisions results in the saving of one addition per division iteration. Consequently, the total number of additions resulting from polynomial division in the Cantor additive FFT is given by

Algorithm 3: Cantor Algorithm ($\mathbf{f}_{\text{in}}$, θ, $\{\beta_0, \beta_1, \ldots, \beta_{m-1}\}$)

Input: $\mathbf{f}_{\text{in}}$ is a vector of size 2^m which represents the coefficients in $f(x)$ (where $\deg f < 2^m$), $\theta \in \mathbb{F}_{2^k}$ is the affine shift, and $\{\beta_0, \beta_1, \ldots, \beta_{m-1}\}$ is the Cantor special basis.

Output: $\mathbf{f}_{\text{out}}$ is the vector of the evaluations of $f(x)$ over $\theta + \langle \beta_0, \beta_1, \ldots, \beta_{m-1} \rangle$.

for $r = 0$ **to** $m - 1$ **do**
  $p \leftarrow m - r$
  $\mathbf{z}_{p-1}$, eval $\leftarrow$ Vanishing Polynomial ($p - 1$, θ) // `Algorithm 1`
  for $i = 0$ **to** $2^r - 1$ **do**
    Canopy$_{p,i}$ ($\mathbf{f}_{\text{in}}$, $\{\beta_0, \beta_1, \ldots, \beta_{m-1}\}$, $\mathbf{z}_{p-1}$, eval, p, i) // `Algorithm 8`
  end
end
return $\mathbf{f}_{\text{out}}$.

$$\sum_{r=0}^{m-1} 2^r \cdot 2^{m-r-1}\left(2^{\text{wt}(m-r-1)} - 1\right) = 2^{m-1}\sum_{r=0}^{m-1} 2^{\text{wt}(r)} - m2^{m-1}$$

From Steps 6 and 9 of Algorithm 2, we know that for the input polynomial in the r-th iteration, we require 2×2^r polynomial additions, each of degree less than 2^{m-r-1}. This leads to a total of $\sum_{r=0}^{m-1} 2 \cdot 2^r \cdot 2^{m-r-1} = 2^m m$ additions. Therefore, the total number of additions in the Cantor additive FFT is given by

$$2^m m + 2^{m-1}\sum_{r=0}^{m-1} 2^{\text{wt}(r)} - m2^{m-1} = \frac{1}{2}n\log_2 n + \frac{1}{2}n \sum_{r=0}^{\log_2(n)-1} 2^{\text{wt}(r)}. \quad (1)$$

On the other hand, from Step 6 of Algorithm 2, we know that for the input polynomial in the r-th iteration, we require $2^r \times 2^{m-r-1} = 2^{m-1}$ multiplications. Thus, the number of multiplications in the Cantor additive FFT is given by $\sum_{r=0}^{m-1} 2^{m-1} = \frac{1}{2}n\log_2 n$.

If the Cantor additive FFT is performed over a subspace W_m, due to Step 6 of the Algorithm 2, we must account for a reduction of $\sum_{r=0}^{m-1} 2^{m-r-1} = 2^m - 1 = n - 1$ in both additions and multiplications. Thus, the costs for additions and multiplications are changed to $\frac{1}{2}n\log_2 n + \frac{1}{2}n\sum_{r=0}^{\log_2(n)-1} 2^{\text{wt}(r)} - n + 1$ and $\frac{1}{2}n\log_2 n - n + 1$, respectively.

Remark 1. Equation 1 provides an exact count of the additions required in the Cantor additive FFT, while, to our knowledge, previous studies have only established upper bounds, such as $O(n(\log_2 n)^{1.58})$ [22] or, more precisely, as shown in [41], $\frac{1}{2}n(\log_2 n)^{1.58} + n\log_2 n$. Our exact count offers a significant improvement over these bounds on the number of additions. For example, when $n = 2^4$, the Cantor additive FFT requires only 104 additions, while [41] estimates 136 additions.

3.5 Precomputation

The multiplication factors $\mathbb{Z}_{W_{p-1}}(\theta_{i,r})$ depend only on the input size and the affine shift that defines the evaluation domain. Likewise, the vanishing polynomials are fixed and independent of input. The storage required to store the precomputed values for the Cantor algorithm of length $n = 2^m$ is $2^m - 1$ field elements to store multiplication factors and $\sum_{i=0}^{m-1} \left(2^{\mathrm{wt}(i)} - 1\right)$ integers to store vanishing polynomials which is negligible compared to the field elements. Over $\mathbb{F}_{2^{256}}$ this translates to 32 KB, 1 MB, and 32 MB for $m = 10, 15, 20$, respectively.

In the *special case* where the affine shift θ lies in the Cantor special basis, the multiplication factors are simply linear combinations of the basis vectors in the subspace $W_m = \langle \beta_0, \ldots, \beta_{m-1} \rangle$. So, a single lookup table that lists these combinations therefore suffices. With a practical upper bound of $m = 32$ for the FFT input size, precomputing the entire span of W_m is infeasible. Instead, the basis is partitioned into four blocks, and the spans

$$\langle \beta_0, \ldots, \beta_7 \rangle, \langle \beta_8, \ldots, \beta_{15} \rangle, \langle \beta_{16}, \ldots, \beta_{23} \rangle, \langle \beta_{24}, \ldots, \beta_{31} \rangle$$

are precomputed. Each block contributes 2^8 field elements, so the complete table contains $4 \times 2^8 = 1024$ elements (compact enough to hard-code). For $\mathbb{F}_{2^{256}}$ this table occupies only 32 KB. Note that this special case applies in Aurora, where the domain L is an affine subspace whose affine shift is itself a basis element.

Table 3. Runtime speedup of the Cantor FFT general (gen.) precomputation method over $\mathbb{F}_{2^{256}}$ for an arbitrary θ versus the special (spec.) choice $\theta = \beta_{31}$ (see Sect. 6 for platform details).

m	5	6	7	8	9	10	11	12	13	14	15	16	17	18	19	20
Gen.	1.38	1.29	1.21	1.13	1.09	1.07	1.07	1.37	1.47	1.49	1.46	1.45	1.51	1.49	1.47	1.43
Spec.	1.24	1.17	1.09	1.06	1.09	1.08	1.08	1.38	1.49	1.51	1.48	1.45	1.43	1.42	1.41	1.37

4 Gao–Mateer Algorithm Building Blocks

The Gao–Mateer FFT implementation of length $n = 2^m$ consists of $2m$ iterative rounds to evaluate a polynomial $f(x) \in \mathbb{F}_{2^k}[x]$ of degree $< 2^m$ over the affine subspace $\theta + W_m$, where $\theta \in \mathbb{F}_{2^k}$ and $W_m = \langle \beta_0, \beta_1, \ldots, \beta_{m-1} \rangle$.

We describe the Gao–Mateer algorithm through two primary modules: the Expand module and the Aggregate module. Expand is an r-round algorithm where in each round $0 \leq r \leq m - 1$, it expands 2^r polynomials of degree $< 2^{m-r}$ into 2^{r+1} smaller polynomials of degree $< 2^{m-r-1}$. Similar to our Cantor algorithm implementation, only one vector of length 2^m denoted by $\mathbf{f}$ is required to store all the polynomials in each round. Aggregate is an r-round algorithm that takes the output of Expand, and iteratively folds them over r rounds, ultimately producing the evaluations of $f(x)$ on $\theta + W_m$.

4.1 Expand Module

The Expand module involves multiple invocations of Taylor expansion, polynomial scaling (e.g., $f(\beta_m x)$), and computing basis vectors and shift elements for the Aggregate module. The Taylor expansion algorithm implemented in [9] is described in Algorithm 9 in Appendix D. To have the vector representation of coefficients in the Gao–Mateer algorithm, it is required to have even-odd rearrangement of indices after each Taylor expansion, however, Algorithm 9 lets us omit those arrangements, instead add one bit-reversal rearrangement at the end of the Expand module. This also keeps the coefficients of terms with the same degree placed next to each other, thus allowing multiplying consecutive elements by the same scaling factor.

Algorithm 4: Expand $(\mathbf{f}_{\text{in}}, \theta, \{\beta_{0,0}, \ldots, \beta_{0,m-1}\})$

Input: $\mathbf{f}_{\text{in}} = (c_0, c_1, \ldots, c_{n-1})$, which represents $f(x) \in \mathbb{F}[x]$ of degree $< n = 2^m$, $\theta \in \mathbb{F}_{2^k}$ is the affine shift, and $\beta_{0,i} \in \mathbb{F}_{2^k}$ are the basis of W_m.
Output: $\mathbf{f}_{\text{out}}$, $\boldsymbol{\theta} = (\theta_0, \ldots, \theta_{m-1})$, $\boldsymbol{\Gamma} = (\mathbf{G}_0 = \emptyset, \mathbf{G}_1, \ldots, \mathbf{G}_{m-1})$, where θ_r and $\mathbf{G}_r = \{\gamma_{r,0}, \ldots, \gamma_{r,r-1}\}$ denote the affine shift and basis corresponding to round r of the Aggregate module respectively.

for $r = 0$ **to** $m-1$ **do**
  // Scaling polynomials:
  $\psi \leftarrow 1$ // ψ denotes the scaling factor of each term
  offset $\leftarrow 2^r$
  while offset $\leq 2^m - 1$ **do**
    for $i = 0$ **to** $2^r - 1$ **do**
      $c_{\text{offset}+i} \leftarrow c_{\text{offset}+i} \times \psi$
    end
    $\psi \leftarrow \psi \times \beta_{r,m-r-1}$
    offset $\leftarrow$ offset $+ 2^r$
  end
  $(c_0, \ldots, c_{n-1}) \leftarrow$ Taylor Expansion $((c_0, \ldots, c_{n-1}), r)$ // Algorithm 9
  for $i = 0$ **to** $m - r - 2$ **do**
    $\gamma_{m-r-1,i} \leftarrow \beta_{r,i} \times \beta^{-1}_{r,m-r-1}$
    $\beta_{r+1,i} \leftarrow \gamma^2_{m-r-1,i} + \gamma_{m-r-1,i}$
  end
  $\mathbf{G}_{m-r-1} \leftarrow (\gamma_{m-r-1,0}, \ldots, \gamma_{m-r-1,m-r-2})$
  $\theta_{m-r-1} \leftarrow \theta \times \beta^{-1}_{r,m-r-1}$
  $\theta \leftarrow \theta^2_{m-r-1} + \theta_{m-r-1}$
end
$(c_0, \ldots, c_{n-1}) \leftarrow$ Bit-reversal Rearrangement $(c_0, \ldots, c_{n-1})$
return $\mathbf{f}_{\text{out}} \leftarrow (c_0, c_1, \ldots, c_{n-1})$

4.2 Aggregate Module

For $0 \leq r \leq m-1$, let $\theta_r + \mathbf{G}_r = \langle \gamma_{r,0}, \ldots, \gamma_{r,r-1} \rangle$ be provided in round $m-r-1$ of the Expand module, the round r of the Aggregate module spans $\theta_r + \mathbf{G}_r$ and combines 2^r adjacent elements in $\mathbf{f}$. Algorithm 5 describes the Aggregate module.

4.3 Detailed Cost Analysis

We now compute the number of multiplications and additions required by the algorithm. From Algorithm 4, we know that at the r-th iteration, we need to scale 2^r polynomials, each of degree 2^{m-r}. Thus, the multiplication for the scaling is given by $\sum_{r=0}^{m-1} 2^r \cdot (2^{m-r} - 1) = 2^m m - \sum_{r=0}^{m-1} 2^r = n \log_2 n - n + 1$.

From Algorithm 5, we know that at the r-th iteration, the number of required multiplications is $2^r \cdot 2^{m-r-1} = 2^{m-1}$. Thus, the total multiplication cost in Algorithm 5 is $\sum_{r=0}^{m-1} 2^{m-1} = \frac{1}{2} n \log_2 n$. Therefore, the total number of multiplications in the Gao–Mateer algorithm is given by $n \log_2 n - n + 1 + \frac{1}{2} n \log_2 n = \frac{3}{2} n \log_2 n - n + 1$.

Algorithm 5: Aggregate $(\mathbf{f}_{\text{in}}, \boldsymbol{\Gamma}, \boldsymbol{\theta})$

Input: $\mathbf{f}_{\text{in}} = (c_0, c_1, \ldots, c_{n-1})$ is a vector of length $n = 2^m$, $\boldsymbol{\theta} = (\theta_0, \ldots, \theta_{m-1})$, $\boldsymbol{\Gamma} = (\mathbf{G}_0 = \emptyset, \mathbf{G}_1, \ldots, \mathbf{G}_{m-1})$, where θ_r and $\mathbf{G}_r = \{\gamma_{r,0}, \ldots, \gamma_{r,r-1}\}$ denote the affine shift and basis corresponding to round r.

Output: $\mathbf{f}_{\text{out}}$ is the vector of the evaluations of $f(x)$ over $\theta + W_m$

```
1  for r = 0 to m − 1 do
2      {η_0, η_1, ..., η_{2^r − 1}} ← Span(G_r, θ_r)
3      for j = 0 to 2^{m−r−1} − 1 do
4          d ← j2^{r+1}
5          for i = 0 to 2^r − 1 do
6              c_{d+i} ← c_{d+i} + c_{d+2^r+i} × η_i
7              c_{d+2^r+i} ← c_{d+2^r+i} + c_{d+i}
8          end
9      end
10 end
11 return f_out ← (c_0, c_1, ..., c_{n−1})
```

From Algorithm 9, we know that in the r-th iteration, the number of additions due to the Taylor expansion is $2^{m-1}(m - r - 1)$. Thus, the total number of additions required for the Taylor expansions is $\sum_{r=0}^{m-2} 2^{m-1}(m - r - 1) = 2^{m-2} m(m-1)$. Also, in Algorithm 5, we know that at the r-th iteration, the number of required additions is $2 \cdot 2^r \cdot 2^{m-r-1} = 2^m$. Therefore, the total addition cost for the algorithm is given by $2^{m-2} m(m-1) + m \cdot 2^m = \frac{1}{4} n (\log_2 n)^2 + \frac{3}{4} n \log_2 n$.

When performing the FFT over a subspace, at the r-th iteration of Algorithm 5, we have $\eta_0 = 0$. Thus, for Steps 6 and 7, we need no multiplications, and only one addition is needed. Consequently, we must account for a reduction of $\sum_{r=0}^{m-1} 2^{m-r-1} = 2^m - 1 = n - 1$ in both additions and multiplications. Therefore, the costs for multiplications and additions are changed to $\frac{3}{2} n \log_2 n - 2n + 2$ and $\frac{1}{4} n (\log_2 n)^2 + \frac{3}{4} n \log_2 n - n + 1$, respectively.

4.4 Optimization for Cantor Special Basis

If we have a Cantor special basis of dimension m, we can avoid the scaling in every iteration. We know that a Cantor special basis satisfies the following

$$\beta_0 = 1 \quad \text{and } S(\beta_i) = \beta_i^2 + \beta_i = \beta_{i-1} \quad \text{for } 1 \leq i \leq m-1,$$

where $S(x) = x^2 + x$. In addition, we know that $S^i(\beta_i) = \beta_0 = 1$ for $0 \le i \le m-1$ and $S^{i+\ell}(\beta_{i+\ell}) = \beta_\ell$ for any $i, \ell \ge 0$ with $i+\ell \le m-1$. Now, consider the Cantor special basis in the reversed order, i.e.,

$$W_m = \langle \beta_{m-1}, \beta_{m-2}, \ldots, \beta_1, 1 \rangle = \langle \beta_{m-1}, S(\beta_{m-1}), \ldots, S^{m-2}(\beta_{m-1}), 1 \rangle.$$

Thus, we have $G = \langle \beta_{m-1}, S(\beta_{m-1}), \ldots, S^{m-2}(\beta_{m-1}) \rangle$ and

$$D = \langle S(\beta_{m-1}), S^2(\beta_{m-1}), \ldots, S^{m-1}(\beta_{m-1}) \rangle = \langle S(\beta_{m-1}), S^2(\beta_{m-1}), \ldots, 1 \rangle.$$

Thus, we do not need the scaling for the functions $f_0(x)$ and $f_1(x)$. Also, at the j-th iteration, G and D will be of the form

$$G^{(j)} = \langle S^j(\beta_{m-1}), S^{j+1}(\beta_{m-1}), \ldots, S^{m-2}(\beta_{m-1}) \rangle \quad \text{and}$$
$$D^{(j)} = \langle S^{j+1}(\beta_{m-1}), S^{j+2}(\beta_{m-1}), \ldots, S^{m-1}(\beta_{m-1}) = 1 \rangle.$$

Therefore, at each iteration, there is no need for scaling. Also, due to the chosen basis, computing the basis elements in $G^{(j)}$ and $D^{(j)}$ does not require any multiplications or additions. This can be done simply by selecting one fewer element from $G^{(j-1)}$ and $D^{(j-1)}$.

Detailed Cost Analysis of the Optimized Algorithm. When using the Cantor special basis in Algorithm 4, no scaling is required for the polynomials. All other steps in Algorithms 4 and 5 remain unchanged. Thus, the number of additions remains the same, as evaluated in Sect. 4.3. Consequently, the multiplication and addition costs are $\frac{1}{2}n \log_2 n$ and $\frac{1}{4}n(\log_2 n)^2 + \frac{3}{4}n \log_2 n$, respectively.

Furthermore, as discussed in Sect. 4.3, when performing the FFT over a subspace, the total multiplication and addition costs for the algorithm are $\frac{1}{2}n \log_2 n - n + 1$ and $\frac{1}{4}n(\log_2 n)^2 + \frac{3}{4}n \log_2 n - n + 1$, respectively. Thus, by using Cantor special basis in the Gao–Mateer algorithm, we can efficiently compute the additive FFT of $f(x) \in \mathbb{F}_{2^k}[x]$ over $\theta + W_m$ where $\mathbb{F}_{2^k}$ contains a subfield $\mathbb{F}_{2^{2^\ell}}$ with $m \le 2^\ell$.

Note that the basis conversion (Expand Module) in the Gao–Mateer FFT involves scaling followed by a Taylor expansion with respect to $x^2 + x$. In the Cantor special basis, scaling is eliminated, reducing the multiplication cost; but the Taylor expansion remains. More efficient methods, such as that of Lin et al. [37], could improve this step, but would diverge from the original Gao–Mateer framework and yield a different FFT. We retain the original structure to allow fair comparison with the Cantor and LCH FFTs. Optimized conversions in this broader context are left for future work.

4.5 Precomputation

In this section, we introduce two levels of precomputation. The first level precomputes the scaling factors $\boldsymbol{\beta} = \{\beta_{0,m-1}, \beta_{1,m-2} \ldots, \beta_{m-1,0}\}$, basis vectors $\boldsymbol{\Gamma} = (\mathbf{G}_0 = \emptyset, \mathbf{G}_1, \ldots, \mathbf{G}_{m-1})$ and shift elements $\boldsymbol{\theta} = (\theta_0, \ldots, \theta_{m-1})$. Each of $\boldsymbol{\beta}$

and $\boldsymbol{\theta}$ requires m finite field elements and $\boldsymbol{\Gamma}$ needs $\sum_{i=0}^{m-1} i = m(m-1)/2$. Consequently, this algorithm stores a total of $(m^2+3m)/2$ finite field elements. Over $\mathbb{F}_{2^{256}}$ this translates to 2 KB, 4.2 KB, and 7.2 KB for $m = 10, 15, 20$, respectively. This precomputation is inapplicable for the optimized Gao–Mateer algorithm for the Cantor special basis (see Sect. 4.4), because the scaling step is omitted and each basis vector reduces to $\mathbf{G}_r$ is simply $\{\beta_0, \beta_1, \ldots, \beta_{r-1}\}$, where the β_i are the Cantor special basis elements.

The second level precomputes all required powers of the scaling factors and all elements in each affine subspace $\theta_r + \mathbf{G}_r$. This requires storing $\sum_{r=0}^{m-1}(2^{m-r} - 1) = 2^{m+1} - m - 2$ finite field elements for the powers of the scaling factors, and $\sum_{r=0}^{m-1} 2^r = 2^m - 1$ finite field elements for $\theta_r + \mathbf{G}_r$. Consequently, this algorithm stores a total of $3 \cdot 2^m - m - 3$ finite field elements. Over $\mathbb{F}_{2^{256}}$ this translates to 95.6 KB, 3 MB, and 96 MB for $m = 10, 15, 20$, respectively. For the optimized Gao–Mateer algorithm for the Cantor special basis, the powers of the scaling factor are not required and the elements in $\theta + \langle \beta_0, \beta_1, \ldots, \beta_{m-1} \rangle$ are computed, which equals 2^m finite field elements.

Table 4. Runtime speedup of the Gao–Mateer additive FFT level 1 (L1) versus level 2 (L2) precomputation methods over $\mathbb{F}_{2^{256}}$ (see Sect. 6 for platform details).

m	4	5	6	7	8	9	10	11	12	13	14	15	16	17	18	19
L1	11.5	6.41	3.81	2.48	1.80	1.46	1.29	1.20	1.12	1.07	1.06	1.05	1.05	1.06	1.06	1.05
L2	15.8	8.33	4.70	2.94	2.09	1.58	1.38	1.27	1.17	1.11	1.09	1.08	1.08	1.07	1.06	1.09

5 Aurora FFT Complexity Analysis

The FFT complexity of Aurora depends on the R1CS dimensions (d_1, d_2, d_3), the codeword domain size $|L|$, and the repetition parameters λ_i and λ'_i introduced in Sect. 2.4. While (d_1, d_2, d_3), λ_i, and λ'_i are fixed at setup, determining $|L|$ requires an iterative procedure since several constraints are mutually dependent.

Initialization. Set $|L| = 4t/\rho$.

Iterative Check. Repeat the following steps until no parameter changes:

1. For the target security level $\boldsymbol{\lambda}$, the RS rate ρ, and the FRI localization parameter η, the required number of codeword queries is $\mathtt{b}$ (see Appendix B).
2. Given $\mathtt{b}$, the maximum lincheck degree is $d' = 2t + \mathtt{b} - 1$ (see Table 6).
3. The number of FRI reductions (rounds) is $\mathtt{r} := \lfloor \log(\rho|L|)/\eta \rfloor$. Consequently, $d' \equiv 0 \pmod{2^{\mathtt{r}\eta}}$. If not, replace d' with the next multiple of $2^{\mathtt{r}\eta}$.
4. If $d' > \rho|L|$, enlarge the domain by one dimension (i.e. set $|L| \leftarrow 2|L|$)

The loop terminates when $\mathtt{b}$ and $|L|$ stabilize; at that point, $|L|$ satisfies all constraints.

Now, we construct the evaluation domains H_1, H_2, and L. Let $\{\beta_0, \beta_1, \ldots, \beta_{k-1}\}$ be the basis of $\mathbb{F}_{2^k}$,

$$H_1 = \langle \beta_0, \beta_1, \cdots \beta_{\lceil \log d_1 \rceil} \rangle, \quad H_2 = \langle \beta_0, \beta_1, \cdots \beta_{\lceil \log(d_2+1) \rceil} \rangle,$$
$$L = \beta_{\lceil \log(|L|) \rceil + 1} + \langle \beta_0, \beta_1, \cdots \beta_{\lceil \log(|L|) \rceil} \rangle,$$

where L is an affine subspace that is disjoint from the linear subspaces H_1 and H_2; specifically, $L \cap (H_1 \cup H_2) = \varnothing$. If the basis elements are the Cantor special basis, all three domains admit the Cantor additive FFT. Moreover, because the affine shift in L is a basis element, the special precomputation in Sect. 3.5 applies. Table 5 shows the FFT and IFFT calls in the Aurora prover algorithm.

Table 5. The FFT and IFFT calls in the Aurora zkSNARK protocol.

FFT Calls	Description
$\lambda_i \times$FFT of len. $\lvert L\rvert$	$\hat{\mathbf{r}}_\ell$: Evaluate $r_\ell(X)$ of degree $< 2t + b - 1$ over L $(\ell = 1, \ldots, \lambda_i)$.
1) IFFT of len. $d_3 + 1$ 2) FFT of len. $d_2 + 1$ 3) IFFT of len. $d_2 + 1$ 4) FFT of len $\lvert L\rvert$	1) Interpolate $f_{(1,\mathbf{v})}(X)$ of degree $< d_3 + 1$. 2) Evaluate $f_{(1,\mathbf{v})}(X)$ over H_2 to compute $\mathbf{f}_{(1,\mathbf{v})}$. Then, compute $\mathbf{f}'_{\mathbf{w}} = \mathbf{w}[0 : d_2 - d_3 - 1] - \mathbf{f}_{(1,\mathbf{v})}[d_3 + 1 : d_2]$ 3) Interpolate $\mathbf{f}'_{\mathbf{w}}$ over H_2 to get $f'_{\mathbf{w}}(X)$ of degree $< d_2 + 1$. Then, divide $f'_{\mathbf{w}}(X)$ by $\mathbb{Z}_{\{h_0,\ldots,h_{d_3}\}}(X)$ to compute $f^*_{\mathbf{w}}(X)$. 4) Evaluate $f^*_{\mathbf{w}}(X)$ over L to compute $\hat{\mathbf{f}}_{\mathbf{w}}$.
1) 3×IFFT of len. d_1 2) 3×FFT of len. $\lvert L\rvert$	For $\mathbf{M} \in \{\mathbf{A}, \mathbf{B}, \mathbf{C}\}$: 1) Interpolate $\mathbf{Mz}$ to get $f^*_{\mathbf{Mz}}(X)$ of degree $< d_1$. 2) Evaluate $f^*_{\mathbf{Mz}}(X)$, over L to compute $\hat{\mathbf{f}}_{\mathbf{Mz}}$.
$\lambda'_i \times$FFT of len. $\lvert L\rvert$	$\hat{\mathbf{r}}'_\ell$: Evaluate $r'_\ell(X)$ of degree $< 2t + 2b$ over L $(\ell = 1, \ldots, \lambda'_i)$.
$2\lambda_i \times$IFFT of len. t	Interpolate $p_{\alpha_\ell}(X)$ and $p^{ABC}_{\alpha_\ell}(X)$ $(\ell = 1, \ldots, \lambda_i)$.
FFT of len. $\lvert L\rvert$	Evaluate $f_{(1,\mathbf{v})}(X)$ over L to compute $\hat{\mathbf{f}}_{\mathbf{z}} = \hat{\mathbf{f}}_{\mathbf{w}} \cdot (\mathbb{Z}_{\{h_0,\ldots,h_\kappa\}}(X)\lvert_L) + \hat{\mathbf{f}}_{(1,\mathbf{v})}$.
$2\lambda_i \times$FFT of len. $\lvert L\rvert$	Evaluate $p_{\alpha_\ell}(X)$ and $p^{ABC}_{\alpha_\ell}(X)$ over L to compute $\hat{\mathbf{q}}^{\mathbf{M}}_\ell := \hat{\mathbf{f}}_{\mathbf{Mz}} \cdot \hat{\mathbf{p}}_{\alpha_\ell} - \hat{\mathbf{f}}_{\mathbf{z}} \cdot \hat{\mathbf{p}}^{ABC}_{\alpha_\ell}$ $(\ell = 1, \ldots \lambda_i$ and $\mathbf{M} \in \{\mathbf{A}, \mathbf{B}, \mathbf{C}\})$.
1) $\lambda_i \times$IFFT of len. d where $d = 2^{\lceil \log(t+b) \rceil}$ 2) $\lambda_i \times$FFT of len. $\lvert L\rvert$	1) Interpolate $\sum_{\mathbf{M} \in \{\mathbf{A},\mathbf{B},\mathbf{C}\}} s^{\mathbf{M}}_\ell \hat{\mathbf{q}}^{\mathbf{M}}_\ell$ to get a polynomial of degree $< 2^{\lceil \log(t+b) \rceil}$. Then, compute $h(X)$ (see Table 6). 2) Evaluate $h(X)$ over L to compute $\hat{\mathbf{h}}_\ell$.

6 Implementation and Benchmarking

With the goal of accelerating Aurora, we implemented the Cantor FFT in C++, making it compatible with the `libiop` library [9], which implements Aurora.

We also converted the C implementation of the LCH FFT for subspaces over the Cantor special basis provided by [19] to C++, and extended it to support affine subspaces, when the affine shift is one of the basis elements and made it compatible with `libiop`. Additionally, we optimized the Gao–Mateer implementation by using the Cantor special basis. The `libff` library [11] is used for finite field operations in `libiop` as well as in our FFT implementations, enabling polymorphism over finite fields. Notably, the Cantor special basis must exist in a finite field in order to enable the use of FFT algorithms over that basis. We computed and hardcoded the Cantor special basis for $\mathbb{F}_{2^{128}}$, $\mathbb{F}_{2^{192}}$, and $\mathbb{F}_{2^{256}}$. Our implementation of additive FFT algorithms is available on GitHub[1].

Using our FFT implementations, we extended the `libiop` library to support switching between the standard basis, which was originally used, and the Cantor special basis, which we hardcoded for $\mathbb{F}_{2^{128}}$, $\mathbb{F}_{2^{192}}$, and $\mathbb{F}_{2^{256}}$ and the dimensions less than 32. Consequently, the Gao–Mateer algorithm is used for the standard basis, while either our Cantor or LCH implementation is employed for the Cantor special basis. Our implementation of the accelerated `libiop` is available on GitHub[2].

Benchmark Setup. All measurements were taken with Google Benchmark [28], with a minimum 10-s warm-up period, on an AMD Ryzen 9 9950X @ 5.7 GHz, with 64 GB of DDR5 RAM and running Debian 12 with kernel 6.12.12.

Standalone FFT Benchmark. For each input size $n = 2^m$, the reported runtime of every additive FFT implementation is the mean of 1,000 independent evaluations when $m \leq 20$ and over 300 evaluations when $m > 20$. In each trial a polynomial $f(x) \in \mathbb{F}_{2^{256}}[x]$ of degree $< 2^m$ is sampled uniformly at random and evaluated on the affine subspace $W_m = \langle \beta_0, \ldots, \beta_{m-1} \rangle + \theta \subset \mathbb{F}_{2^{256}}$ where the shift $\theta \in \mathbb{F}_{2^{256}}$ is chosen uniformly at random for that trial. For the special case discussed in Sect. 3.5, the shift is fixed to $\theta = \beta_{31}$. The 99.9% confidence interval of the measurements is no greater than 1%.

Aurora Benchmark. We benchmark the Aurora protocol using three FFT implementations: Gao–Mateer, our Cantor implementation, and our C++ version of the LCH algorithm implemented in [37]. In this benchmarking, the multiplication factors in both Cantor and LCH are precomputed based on the method described in Sect. 3.5, and the coefficients of the vanishing polynomials in the Cantor algorithm are also precomputed. For each input size N, the reported runtime is the average proving and verifying time measured over 100 randomly generated satisfiable R1CS instances. Each R1CS instance uses $d_1 = N$, $d_2 = N - 1$, and $d_3 = 31$ (Definition 1). The codeword length is $|L| = 2^7 N$ by adopting Preon's choice of $\rho = 2^{-5}$ (Definition 2), to tighten the FRI soundness error [18], and two extra dimensions are added as described in Sect. 5. The 99.9% confidence interval of the measurements is no greater than 1%.

[1] https://github.com/mtbadakhshan/additive-fft.

[2] https://github.com/mtbadakhshan/cantor-libiop.

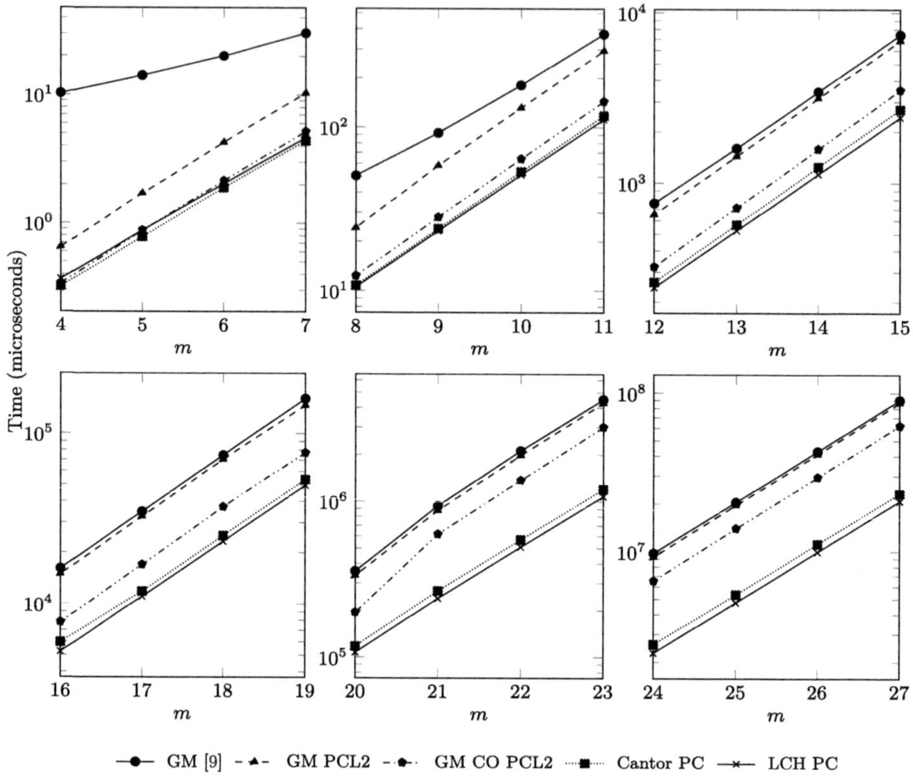

Fig. 1. Log-scale runtime of additive FFTs of length 2^m over $\mathbb{F}_{2^{256}}$ for Gao–Mateer (GM), GM with level-2 precomputation (GM PCL2), Cantor optimized GM with level-2 precomputation (GM CO PCL2), and Cantor with precomputation (Cantor PC), and LCH with special-case precomputation (LCH PC)

Comparisons. Figure 1 compares the runtime of the FFT algorithms. It shows that the savings in Cantor PC are consistent across different input lengths. Table 3 presents the runtime improvements achieved through precomputations in the Cantor FFT. Table 4 shows the runtime gains from L1 and L2 precomputations in Gao–Mateer. However, these improvements become insignificant for larger m since Gao–Mateer requires extensive memory access for Taylor expansion, which suppresses the savings gained from the precomputations. Figure 3 in Appendix D depicts the fraction of each sub-algorithm in Gao–Mateer.

Note that the Gao–Mateer FFT with Cantor special basis, the LCH FFT with Cantor special basis, and the Cantor FFT require the same number of multiplications (see Table 1), but differ in their addition counts. The Gao–Mateer FFT uses $\frac{1}{4}n(\log_2 n)^2 + \frac{3}{4}n\log_2 n$ additions, while the Cantor FFT uses $\frac{1}{2}n\log_2 n + \frac{1}{2}n\sum_{r=0}^{\log_2(n)-1} 2^{\mathrm{wt}(r)}$, with $\mathrm{wt}(r)$ denoting the Hamming weight. No closed-form expression is known for the LCH FFT. Numerical evaluation shows that the Cantor FFT consistently requires fewer additions than the Gao–Mateer FFT for the m values in Fig. 1; this, along with the basis conversion overhead in the Gao–Mateer algorithm, accounts for its slower performance. Furthermore, Fig. 1 shows that, when used as standalone FFT algorithms, Cantor outperforms LCH for smaller dimensions (specifically, $m \leq 7$), while LCH exhibits better performance for $8 \leq m \leq 27$, though the performance difference remains marginal even at higher dimensions. It should also be noted that, similar to the Gao–Mateer FFT, the LCH FFT incurs a basis conversion overhead [37], while the Cantor FFT completely avoids this by employing a pure divide-and-conquer structure.

Table 2 shows that integrating our optimized Cantor algorithm into the Aurora prover results in nearly twice the speed compared to using the Gao–Mateer FFT for large input sizes. It also outperforms our C++ integration of the LCH algorithm [19] into Aurora for smaller inputs. This performance differential highlights how the interaction between FFT algorithms and the underlying protocol structure significantly influences overall system efficiency, beyond what is captured in the standalone benchmarks. The observed slowdown in the LCH-based Aurora implementation for smaller input sizes is likely attributable to the memory overhead incurred by basis conversion. As a result, the Cantor FFT is more suitable for the circuit sizes commonly found in practical zkSNARK applications. For example, the Preon [18] proposes multiple security levels, where the number of constraints ranges from 2^{12} to 2^{14}. Additionally, constructing a circuit that proves knowledge of a Merkle tree leaf in a tree of 2^{30} elements using the POSEIDON-128 [29] hash function typically requires $2^{12} \leq N \leq 2^{13}$ constraints, depending on the arity of the Merkle tree.

7 Conclusions and Future Works

This work demonstrates how leveraging the Cantor special basis enables the integration of the Cantor and LCH additive FFTs into post-quantum secure zkSNARKs, focusing on Aurora [10]. We show that replacing the Gao–Mateer FFT with the Cantor and LCH additive FFTs significantly reduces computation time and Cantor is generally the best choice in typical zkSNARK applications. Our implementation is supported by a detailed cost analysis, including exact counts of additions and multiplications for both FFTs, and a complexity evaluation of FFT calls in Aurora's R1CS encoding, parameterized by constraints, variables, and the security level. We also propose optimized building blocks for the Cantor FFT and precomputation techniques that reduce overhead for both Cantor and Gao–Mateer FFTs when the affine subspace basis is fixed.

Building on the presented optimizations, several promising directions can be explored for future research. One possibility is optimizing other components of Aurora, such as the FRI protocol, or applying tower field constructions to accelerate field multiplications. Additionally, the proposed optimizations may extend to other post-quantum secure zkSNARKs over binary extension fields, such as STARK [4], which is used by zk-rollups and requires heavy CPU/GPU computation for proof generation [16].

Another direction is improving additive FFT throughput through parallelization. The Cantor FFT supports pure divide-and-conquer parallelism [45] as it does not require basis conversion. Thus, in hierarchical memory architectures, radix-4 or radix-8 variations could reduce rounds. Additive FFTs could also benefit from processing-in-memory (PIM) architectures, improving data locality like in multiplicative FFT [34].

Additionally, exploring more efficient basis conversion methods, such as replacing the Taylor expansion in Gao–Mateer FFT with the approach by Lin et al. [37], could reduce addition complexity, offering new FFT variants with better trade-offs. Comparing these with Cantor and LCH FFTs remains a valuable avenue. Finally, thorough side-channel analysis of additive FFT implementations is essential for security-critical applications such as post-quantum zkSNARKs and code-based cryptosystems, as demonstrated leakages in Gao–Mateer implementations reveal critical vulnerabilities [30,33].

Acknowledgments. This work was supported by a MITACS–BTQ research grant. We sincerely appreciate the constructive feedback from the anonymous reviewers, which significantly enhanced the clarity and precision of this manuscript.

A The Cantor and Gao–Mateer FFT Algorithm

In this section, we present two additive FFT algorithms central to our contributions: the Cantor algorithm [15] and the algorithm by Gao and Mateer [26]. While Gao and Mateer propose two algorithms based on Taylor expansion for additive FFT, we focus on the first one, which applies to lengths $n = 2^m$ for any m. This algorithm is originally designed for the subspace $W_m = \langle \beta_0, \beta_1, \ldots, \beta_{m-1} \rangle$, but we adapt it for use over the affine subspace $\theta + W_m$. Algorithms 6 and 7 provide the algorithmic formulations of the Cantor and Gao–Mateer algorithms, respectively.

Algorithm 6: Cantor additive FFT of length $n = 2^m$

Input: $f(x) \in \mathbb{F}_{2^k}[x]$ of degree $< n = 2^m$, where $k = 2^\ell$ and the affine subspace $\theta + W_m = \theta + \langle \beta_0, \beta_1, \ldots, \beta_{m-1} \rangle$, where $\{\beta_0 = 1, \beta_1, \ldots, \beta_{m-1}\}$ is a Cantor special basis.

Output: $\mathrm{FFT}(f, \theta + W_m)$.

if $m = 0$ **then**
  return $f(\theta)$.
end
Compute

$$f_0(x) = f(x) \mod S^{m-1}(x + \theta), \quad \text{and}$$

$$f_1(x) = f(x) \mod S^{m-1}(x + \theta + \beta_{m-1}).$$

return $\mathrm{FFT}(f_0, \theta + W_{m-1}) \| \mathrm{FFT}(f_1, \theta + \beta_{m-1} + W_{m-1})$.

Algorithm 7: Gao–Mateer additive FFT of length $n = 2^m$

Input: $f(x) \in \mathbb{F}_{2^k}[x]$ of degree $< n = 2^m$ and the affine subspace $\theta + W_m = \theta + \langle \beta_0, \beta_1, \ldots, \beta_{m-1} \rangle$
Output: $\mathrm{FFT}(f, \theta + W_m)$.
if $m = 1$ **then**
  return $(f(\theta), f(\theta + \beta_0))$.
end
else
  Compute $g(x) = f(\beta_{m-1} x)$
  Compute the Taylor expansion of $g(x)$ at $x^2 + x$ to obtain $f_0(x)$ and $f_1(x)$. Specifically, express $g(x)$ as $g(x) = f_0(x^2 + x) + x f_1(x^2 + x)$.
  Compute $\gamma_i = \beta_i \cdot \beta_{m-1}^{-1}$ and $\delta_i = \gamma_i^2 + \gamma_i$ for $0 \le i \le m - 2$.
  Let $\theta_0 = \beta_{m-1}^{-1} \theta$. Consider the affine subspaces

$$\theta_0 + G = \theta_0 + \langle \gamma_0, \ldots, \gamma_{m-2} \rangle \quad \text{and} \quad \theta_0^2 + \theta_0 + D = \theta_0^2 + \theta_0 + \langle \delta_0, \ldots, \delta_{m-2} \rangle.$$

  Let $\ell = 2^{m-1}$ and

$$\mathrm{FFT}(f_0, \theta_0^2 + \theta_0 + D) = (u_0, \ldots, u_{\ell-1}) \text{ and } \mathrm{FFT}(f_1, \theta_0^2 + \theta_0 + D) = (v_0, \ldots, v_{\ell-1}).$$

  For $0 \le i \le \ell - 1$, set $\omega_i = u_i + \eta_i \cdot v_i$ and $\omega_{\ell+i} = \omega_i + v_i$.
  return $(\omega_0, \ldots, \omega_{n-1})$.
end

B FRI Soundness Errors: Number of Queries Analysis

The FRI of proximity parameter is defined as

$$\delta := \min\left(\frac{1 - 2\rho}{2}, \frac{1 - \rho}{3}, 1 - \rho\right). \tag{2}$$

Given $\boldsymbol{\lambda}$, $\boldsymbol{\epsilon_q}$ and $\boldsymbol{\epsilon_i}$ represents query and interactive soundness errors such that $\boldsymbol{\epsilon_q} + \boldsymbol{\epsilon_i} < 2^{-\boldsymbol{\lambda}}$, where $2^{-\boldsymbol{\lambda}-1}$ is allocated to each. According to [10, Theorem 4],

$$\boldsymbol{\epsilon_i} = \left(\frac{d_1 + 1}{|\mathbb{F}|}\right)^{\lambda_i} + \left(\frac{|L|}{|\mathbb{F}|}\right)^{\lambda_i'} + \epsilon_i^{\mathrm{FRI}}, \text{ and } \boldsymbol{\epsilon_q} = \epsilon_q^{\mathrm{FRI}},$$

where $\left(\frac{\eta+1}{|\mathbb{F}|}\right)^{\lambda_i}$ and $\left(\frac{|L|}{|\mathbb{F}|}\right)^{\lambda_i'}$ denote the lincheck and LDT soundness errors respectively. $\epsilon_i^{\mathrm{FRI}}$ and $\epsilon_q^{\mathrm{FRI}}$ denote the interactive and query soundness errors in FRI, respectively. Each term in $\boldsymbol{\epsilon_i}$ gets $2^{-\boldsymbol{\lambda}-3}$ and $\boldsymbol{\epsilon_q}$ gets $2^{-\boldsymbol{\lambda}-1}$ soundness error bound. The codeword is queried during FRI. Given the target proximity parameter in (2), the number of query repetitions in FRI is:

$$\lambda_q^{\mathrm{FRI}} = \frac{\log(\epsilon_q^{\mathrm{FRI}})}{\log\left(1 - \min\left(\delta, \frac{1 - 3\rho - 2^{\eta}/\sqrt{|L|}}{4}\right)\right)}. \tag{3}$$

The number of queries to the codeword is set to $\mathsf{b} = \lambda_q^{\mathrm{FRI}} \cdot 2^{\eta}$ to ensure zero-knowledge.

C Aurora Codewords

Table 6. The primary codewords encoded by prover. The mechanism for randomizing polynomials is omitted for the sake of simplicity.

Codeword	Description
$\hat{\mathbf{f}}_{\mathbf{w}} \in \mathrm{RS}[L, \frac{d_2-d_3+\mathtt{b}}{\lvert L\rvert}]$	$\hat{\mathbf{f}}_{\mathbf{w}} := f^*_{\mathbf{w}}\lvert_L$, where $f^*_{\mathbf{w}}$ is a random polynomial of degree $< d_2 - d_3 + \mathtt{b}$ such that for $d_3 < i \leq d_2$, $f_{\mathbf{w}}(h_i) = (w_{i-d_3-1} - f_{(1,\mathbf{v})}(h_i))/\mathbb{Z}_{\{h_0,\ldots,h_{d_3}\}}(h_i)$ (w_i denotes the i-th element in $\mathbf{w}$).
$\hat{\mathbf{f}}_{\mathbf{Az}} \in \mathrm{RS}[L, \frac{d_1+\mathtt{b}}{\lvert L\rvert}]$, $\hat{\mathbf{f}}_{\mathbf{Bz}} \in \mathrm{RS}[L, \frac{d_1+\mathtt{b}}{\lvert L\rvert}]$, $\hat{\mathbf{f}}_{\mathbf{Cz}} \in \mathrm{RS}[L, \frac{d_1+\mathtt{b}}{\lvert L\rvert}]$	$\hat{\mathbf{f}}_{\mathbf{Mz}} := f^*_{\mathbf{Mz}}\lvert_L$ for $\mathbf{M} \in \{\mathbf{A}, \mathbf{B}, \mathbf{C}\}$, where $f^*_{\mathbf{Mz}}$ is a random polynomial of degree $< d_1 + \mathtt{b}$ such that for $i = 0, \ldots, d_1 - 1$, $f_{\mathbf{Mz}}(h_i) = (\mathbf{Mz})_i$, where $(\mathbf{Mz})_i$ denotes the i-th element of the matrixâĂŞvector product $\mathbf{Mz}$.
$\hat{\mathbf{r}}_\ell \in_R \mathrm{RS}[L, \frac{2t+\mathtt{b}-1}{\lvert L\rvert}]$	For $\ell = 1, \ldots, \lambda_i$, $\hat{\mathbf{r}}_\ell$ is a random lincheck masking codeword.
$\hat{\mathbf{h}}_\ell \in \mathrm{RS}[L, \frac{t+\mathtt{b}}{\lvert L\rvert}]$, $\hat{\mathbf{g}}_\ell \in \mathrm{RS}[L, \frac{t-1}{\lvert L\rvert}]$	For $\ell = 1, \ldots, \lambda_i$, $\hat{\mathbf{h}}_\ell := h_\ell\lvert_L$, where h_ℓ is a polynomial of degree $< t + b$ derived from the following polynomial division: $r_\ell(X) + \sum_{\mathbf{M}\in\{\mathbf{A},\mathbf{B},\mathbf{C}\}} s^{\mathbf{M}}_\ell \left(f_{\mathbf{Mz}}(X)p_{\alpha_\ell}(X) - f_{\mathbf{z}}(X)p^{\mathbf{M}}_{\alpha_\ell}(X)\right) = g_\ell(X) + \frac{\sum_{a\in H_1 \cup H_2} r_\ell(a)}{\sum_{a\in H_1 \cup H_2} a^{t-1}} \cdot X^{t-1} + \mathbb{Z}_{H_1 \cup H_2}(X) \cdot h_\ell(X)$
$\hat{\mathbf{r}}'_{\ell'} \in_R \mathrm{RS}[L, \frac{2t+2\mathtt{b}}{\lvert L\rvert}]$	For $\ell' = 1, \ldots, \lambda'_i$, $\hat{\mathbf{r}}'_{\ell'}$ is a random LDT masking codeword.

D Additional Algorithms

Algorithm 8 outlines the procedures within the $\mathsf{Canopy}_{p,i}$ module, while Fig. 2 illustrates how the polynomials for the subsequent round are derived from the quotient and remainder at each step.

Algorithm 8: $\mathsf{Canopy}_{p,i}$ ($\mathbf{f}_{\text{in}}$, $\{\beta_0, \beta_1, \ldots, \beta_{m-1}\}$, $\mathbf{z}_{p-1}$, $\mathbb{Z}_{W_{p-1}}(\theta)$, p, i)

Input: $\mathbf{f}_{\text{in}}$, $\{\beta_0, \beta_1, \ldots, \beta_{m-1}\}$ is the Cantor special basis, $\mathbf{z}_{p-1} = (\zeta_0, \zeta_1, \ldots, \zeta_{2^{\mathrm{wt}(i)}-2})$, $\mathbb{Z}_{W_{p-1}}(\theta) \in \mathbb{F}_{2^k}$, $p = m - r$, and $i = (i_0, i_1, i_2, \ldots, i_r)$.
Output: $\mathbf{f}_{\text{out}}$.

```
ψ_{i,r} ← Z_{W_{p-1}}(θ)
for j = 0 to r − 1 do
  | ψ_{i,r} ← ψ_{i,r} + i_j × β_{j+1}
end
f_out ← Polynomial Division (f_in, z_{p−1}, ψ_{i,r}, p, i) // Algorithm 2, where
    Z_{W_{p−1}}(θ_{i,r}) = ψ_{i,r}
return f_out.
```

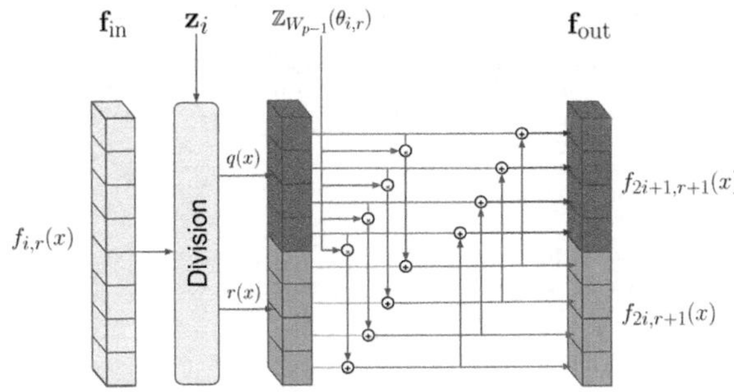

Fig. 2. Computing the polynomials for the next round from the outputs of dividing $f_{i,r}(x)$ (of degree < 8) by $\mathbb{Z}_{W_{p-1}}$, represented by $\mathbf{z}_{p-1}$.

We now present the Taylor expansion algorithm, which constitutes the core of the Expand module. Let $f(x) = \sum_{i=0}^{m-1} c_i x^i, c_i \in \mathbb{F}_q$, $\delta(x) = x^2 + x$. We denote $y = \delta(x)$. Then we may write f as

$$f(x) = f_0(y) + xf_1(y). \tag{4}$$

Here, f_i, $i \in \{0, 1\}$, are polynomials in $\mathbb{F}_{2^k}$ with degree $< 2^{m-1}$. The representation of f by (4) is referred to as the Taylor expansion in [26]. The polynomials f_i can be obtained iteratively as follows. Let $\mathbf{f} = (c_0, \dots, c_{n-1})$, referred to as the coefficient vector of $f(x)$, where $n = 2^m$, denoted by $f(x) \leftrightarrow \mathbf{f}$. Let $t = m - 2$, we define a *quadrant concatenation* of $\mathbf{f}$ as $\mathbf{f} = (\mathbf{c}_0, \mathbf{c}_1, \mathbf{c}_2, \mathbf{c}_3)$ where $c_i = (c_{i \cdot 2^t}, c_{i \cdot 2^t + 1}, \dots, c_{(i+1) \cdot 2^t - 1})$. In the following, we model the Taylor expansion of f in terms of the concept of T_n module. The T_n module operation on f is defined as $\mathbf{b} = (\mathbf{c}_0, \mathbf{c}_1 + \mathbf{h}, \mathbf{h}, \mathbf{c}_3)$, where $\mathbf{h} = \mathbf{c}_2 + \mathbf{c}_3$. From $\mathbf{b} = (\mathbf{b}_0, \mathbf{b}_1, \mathbf{b}_2, \mathbf{b}_3)$, we have the following result.

Lemma 1. *With the above notation, we have*

$$f(x) = g_0(x) + g_1(x)y^{2^t}, \text{ where } y = \delta(x) \tag{5}$$

where $g_0(x) \leftrightarrow (\mathbf{b}_0, \mathbf{b}_1)$ *and* $g_1(x) \leftrightarrow (\mathbf{b}_2, \mathbf{b}_3)$.

Now, to compute the Taylor expansion of $f(x) \in \mathbb{F}[x]$ of degree $< n = 2^m$, the Taylor expansion of $f(x)$ at $\delta(x) = x^2 + x$, denoted by $\mathsf{TE}(f, n, 2)$ can be computed through the Taylor expansions of two polynomials:

$$\mathsf{TE}(f, n, 2) = (\mathsf{TE}(g_0, \frac{n}{2}, 2), \mathsf{TE}(g_1, \frac{n}{2}, 2)) \tag{6}$$

where g_0 and g_1 are computed in Lemma 1 by T_n module.

Theorem 2. *Let* $\mathbf{u} = (u_0, u_1, \dots, u_{n-1})$ *be the output at the recursion* t *in (6), then the Taylor expansion of* f*, defined by (4), is given by*

$$f_0 \leftrightarrow (u_0, u_2, \dots, u_{2i}, \dots, u_{2\lfloor n/2 \rfloor})$$
$$f_1 \leftrightarrow (u_1, u_3, \dots, u_{2i+1}, \dots, u_{2\lfloor n/2 \rfloor + 1}),$$

where f_0 *and* f_1*, are polynomials each of degree* $< \lfloor n/2 \rfloor = 2^{m-1}$.

Algorithm 9: Taylor Expansion ($\mathbf{f}_{\text{in}}, r$)

```
Input: f_in = (c_0, c_1, ..., c_{n-1}) and r denotes the number of rounds reduction.
Output: f_out.
k ← m − 2
while k ≥ r do
    j ← 0
    while j ≤ n − 4 · 2^k do
        for i = 0 to 2^k − 1 do
            c_{2·2^k+i+j} ← c_{2·2^k+i+j} + c_{3·2^k+i+j}
            c_{2^k+i+j} ← c_{2^k+i+j} + c_{2·2^k+i+j}
        end
        j ← j + 4 · 2^k
    end
    k ← k − 1
end
return f_out ← (c_0, c_1, ..., c_{n-1})
```

As described in the above theorem, the polynomials f_0 and f_1 are constructed by performing an even-odd rearrangement on $\mathbf{u}$. Subsequently, as described in Algorithm 7, the evaluations $\mathsf{TE}(f_0, n/2, 2)$ and $\mathsf{TE}(f_1, n/2, 2)$ also need to be computed and so on their outputs as well. Alternatively, as implemented in [9], instead of performing the even-odd rearrangements, the positions of the coefficients of these two polynomials can be retained within $\mathbf{u}$. This allows us to compute a single $\mathsf{TE}(u, n/2, 2)$ on the entire polynomial $u(x)$, represented by $\mathbf{u}$, in $t-1$ recursive steps (one fewer recursion than required for f). Finally, to account for the skipped even-odd rearrangements, in the last round the resulting vector is rearranged in bit-reversal order as discussed below:

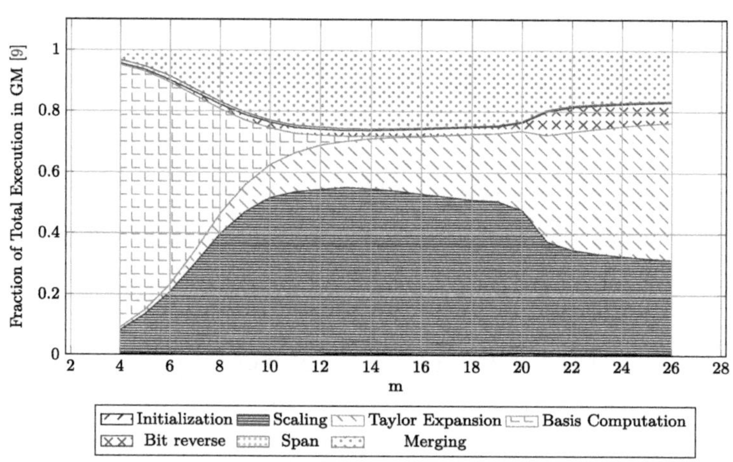

Fig. 3. The fraction of execution time for sub-algorithms in Gao–Mateer over $\mathbb{F}_{2^{256}}$ in [9]. The execution times of the Taylor expansion and bit-reversal sub-algorithms increase more rapidly with m. *Initialization* is a one-time computing for copying the input polynomial to a new vector. *Span* and *Merging* are the Span function and the nested for loop in the $\mathsf{Aggregate}$ Module.

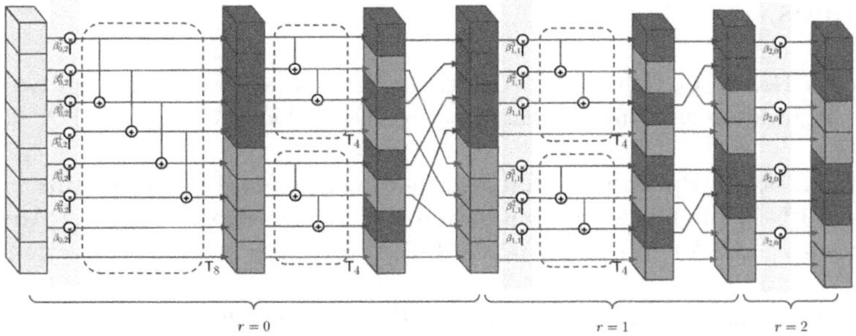

(a) Original Approach: Groups even and odd indices after each Taylor expansion

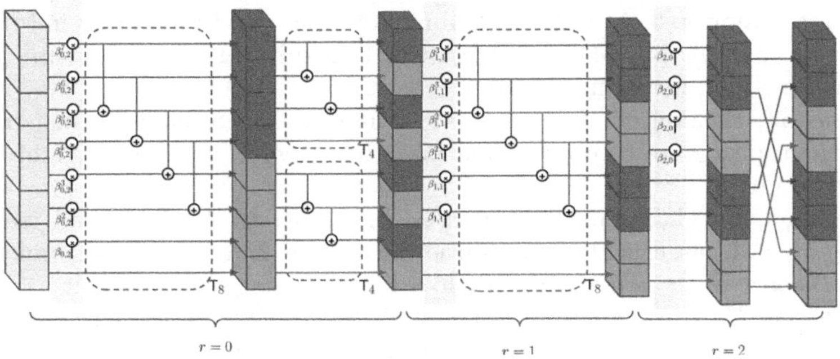

(b) Alternative Approach: Bit-reversal rearrangement in the final round

Fig. 4. The Expand module in Gao–Mateer of length $n = 2^3$, which evaluates a polynomial $f(x) \in \mathbb{F}[x]$ of degree < 8 over $\theta + W_3$, where $W_3 = \langle \beta_0, \beta_1, \beta_2 \rangle$. In Figure (a), the Expand module groups even and odd indices after each Taylor expansion. In contrast, Figure (b) skips these rearrangements by using one T_8 module instead of two T_4 modules in round $r = 1$ then performs the bit-reversal in the final round.

Define a recursive process that partitions the index set $\{0, 1, \ldots, 2^n - 1\}$ by the least significant bit (LSB): indices with LSB 0 form the even group, and those with LSB 1 form the odd group. This splitting is applied recursively to each group using the next least significant bit, continuing until each group contains exactly two indices. The resulting arrangement corresponds to the bit-reversal permutation of the original sequence.

Figure 3 illustrates the contribution of each sub-algorithm in the Gao–Mateer FFT implementation from [9]. The basis computations, which are precomputed in GM PCL1, require fewer resources as m increases. In contrast, the computational cost of bit-reversal rearrangement and Taylor expansion grows more rapidly for larger m, significantly impacting the overall FFT runtime.

References

1. Ames, S., Hazay, C., Ishai, Y., Venkitasubramaniam, M.: Ligero: lightweight sublinear arguments without a trusted setup. Des. Codes Crypt. **91**(11), 3379–3424 (2023)
2. Baum, C., et al.: Publicly verifiable zero-knowledge and post-quantum signatures from VOLE-in-the-head. In: Handschuh, H., Lysyanskaya, A. (eds.) Advances in Cryptology – CRYPTO 2023, pp. 581–615. Springer Nature Switzerland, Cham (2023)
3. Ben-Sasson, E., Bentov, I., Horesh, Y., Riabzev, M.: Fast reed-Solomon interactive oracle proofs of proximity. In: Chatzigiannakis, I., Kaklamanis, C., Marx, D., Sannella, D. (eds.) 45th International Colloquium on Automata, Languages, and Programming (ICALP 2018). Leibniz International Proceedings in Informatics (LIPIcs), vol. 107, pp. 14:1–14:17. Schloss Dagstuhl – Leibniz-Zentrum für Informatik, Dagstuhl, Germany (2018)
4. Ben-Sasson, E., Bentov, I., Horesh, Y., Riabzev, M.: Scalable, transparent, and post-quantum secure computational integrity. Cryptology ePrint Archive, Paper 2018/046 (2018)
5. Ben-Sasson, E., Carmon, D., Kopparty, S., Levit, D.: Scalable and transparent proofs over all large fields, via elliptic curves. In: Kiltz, E., Vaikuntanathan, V. (eds.) Theory of Cryptography, pp. 467–496. Springer, Cham (2022)
6. Ben-Sasson, E., Carmon, D., Kopparty, S., Levit, D.: Elliptic curve fast Fourier transform (ECFFT) part I: low-degree extension in time $o(n \log n)$ over all finite fields. In: Proceedings of the 2023 Annual ACM-SIAM Symposium on Discrete Algorithms (SODA), pp. 700–737 (2023)
7. Ben-Sasson, E., Chiesa, A., Forbes, M.A., Gabizon, A., Riabzev, M., Spooner, N.: Zero knowledge protocols from succinct constraint detection. In: Kalai, Y., Reyzin, L. (eds.) TCC 2017. LNCS, vol. 10678, pp. 172–206. Springer, Cham (2017). https://doi.org/10.1007/978-3-319-70503-3_6
8. Ben-Sasson, E., et al.: Zerocash: decentralized anonymous payments from bitcoin. In: 2014 IEEE Symposium on Security and Privacy, pp. 459–474 (2014)
9. Ben-Sasson, E., et al.: Libiop: a C++ library for zero knowledge proofs. https://github.com/scipr-lab/libiop. Accessed 10 Jan 2025
10. Ben-Sasson, E., Chiesa, A., Riabzev, M., Spooner, N., Virza, M., Ward, N.P.: Aurora: transparent succinct arguments for R1CS. In: Ishai, Y., Rijmen, V. (eds.) EUROCRYPT 2019. LNCS, vol. 11476, pp. 103–128. Springer, Cham (2019). https://doi.org/10.1007/978-3-030-17653-2_4
11. Ben-Sasson, E., et al.: libff: C++ library for finite fields and elliptic curves. https://github.com/scipr-lab/libff. Accessed 10 Jan 2025
12. Bernstein, D.J., Chou, T.: Faster binary-field multiplication and faster binary-field MACs. In: Joux, A., Youssef, A. (eds.) SAC 2014. LNCS, vol. 8781, pp. 92–111. Springer, Cham (2014). https://doi.org/10.1007/978-3-319-13051-4_6
13. Bernstein, D.J., Chou, T., Schwabe, P.: McBits: fast constant-time code-based cryptography. In: Bertoni, G., Coron, J.-S. (eds.) CHES 2013. LNCS, vol. 8086, pp. 250–272. Springer, Heidelberg (2013). https://doi.org/10.1007/978-3-642-40349-1_15
14. Bünz, B., Agrawal, S., Zamani, M., Boneh, D.: Zether: towards privacy in a smart contract world. In: Bonneau, J., Heninger, N. (eds.) FC 2020. LNCS, vol. 12059, pp. 423–443. Springer, Cham (2020). https://doi.org/10.1007/978-3-030-51280-4_23

15. Cantor, D.G.: On arithmetical algorithms over finite fields. J. Comb. Theory Ser. A **50**(2), 285–300 (1989)
16. Chaliasos, S., Reif, I., Torralba-Agell, A., Ernstberger, J., Kattis, A., Livshits, B.: Analyzing and benchmarking ZK-rollups. In: Böhme, R., Kiffer, L. (eds.) 6th Conference on Advances in Financial Technologies (AFT 2024). Leibniz International Proceedings in Informatics (LIPIcs), vol. 316, pp. 6:1–6:24. Schloss Dagstuhl – Leibniz-Zentrum für Informatik, Dagstuhl, Germany (2024)
17. Chase, M., et al.: Post-quantum zero-knowledge and signatures from symmetric-key primitives. In: Proceedings of the 2017 ACM SIGSAC Conference on Computer and Communications Security, CCS 2017, pp. 1825–1842. Association for Computing Machinery, New York, NY, USA (2017)
18. Chen, M.-S., et al.: Preon: zk-SNARK based Signature Scheme. Technical report, NIST (2023)
19. Chen, M.-S., Cheng, C.-M., Kuo, P.-C., Li, W.-D., Yang, B.-Y.: Faster multiplication for long binary polynomials. arXiv: 1708.09746 (2018). https://arxiv.org/abs/1708.09746
20. Chen, M.-S., Cheng, C.-M., Kuo, P.-C., Li, W.-D., Yang, B.-Y.: Multiplying Boolean polynomials with Frobenius partitions in additive fast Fourier transform. arXiv: 1803.11301 (2018). https://arxiv.org/abs/1803.11301
21. Chiesa, A., Ojha, D., Spooner, N.: Fractal: post-quantum and transparent recursive proofs from holography. In: Canteaut, A., Ishai, Y. (eds.) EUROCRYPT 2020. LNCS, vol. 12105, pp. 769–793. Springer, Cham (2020). https://doi.org/10.1007/978-3-030-45721-1_27
22. Coxon, N.: Fast transforms over finite fields of characteristic two. J. Symb. Comput. **104**, 824–854 (2021)
23. Diamond, B.E., Posen, J.: Succinct arguments over towers of binary fields. In: Fehr, S., Fouque, P.-A. (eds.) Advances in Cryptology – EUROCRYPT 2025, pp. 93–122. Springer, Cham (2025)
24. Fine, N.J.: Binomial coefficients modulo a prime. Am. Math. Mon. **54**(10), 589–592 (1947)
25. Fu, S., Gong, G.: Polaris: transparent succinct zero-knowledge arguments for R1CS with efficient verifier. In: Proceedings on Privacy Enhancing Technologies (2022)
26. Gao, S., Mateer, T.: Additive fast Fourier transforms over finite fields. IEEE Trans. Inf. Theory **56**(12), 6265–6272 (2010)
27. von zur Gathen, J., Gerhard, J.: Arithmetic and factorization of polynomial over $\mathbb{F}_2$ (extended abstract). In: Proceedings of the 1996 International Symposium on Symbolic and Algebraic Computation, ISSAC 1996, pp. 1–9. Association for Computing Machinery, New York, NY, USA (1996)
28. Google Inc. and contributors. Benchmark - a microbenchmark support library. https://github.com/google/benchmark. Accessed 10 Jan 2025
29. Grassi, L., Khovratovich, D., Rechberger, C., Roy, A., Schofnegger, M.: POSEIDON: a new hash function for Zero-Knowledge proof systems. In: 30th USENIX Security Symposium (USENIX Security 21), pp. 519–535. USENIX Association, August 2021
30. Guo, Q., Johansson, A., Johansson, T.: A key-recovery side-channel attack on classic McEliece implementations. IACR Trans. Cryptograph. Hardware Embedded Syst. **2022**(4), 800–827 (2022)
31. Jandhyala, T.: Air-FRI: acceleration of the FRI protocol on the GPU for low-degree polynomial testing in zk-SNARK applications. Master's thesis, University of Waterloo, Canada (2024)

32. Katz, J., Kolesnikov, V., Wang, X.: Improved non-interactive zero knowledge with applications to post-quantum signatures. In: Proceedings of the 2018 ACM SIGSAC Conference on Computer and Communications Security, CCS 2018, pp. 525–537. Association for Computing Machinery, New York, NY, USA (2018)
33. Lahr, N., Niederhagen, R., Petri, R., Samardjiska, S.: Side channel information set decoding using iterative chunking. In: Moriai, S., Wang, H. (eds.) ASIACRYPT 2020. LNCS, vol. 12491, pp. 881–910. Springer, Cham (2020). https://doi.org/10.1007/978-3-030-64837-4_29
34. Li, D., Pakala, A., Yang, K.: MeNTT: a compact and efficient processing-in-memory number theoretic transform (NTT) accelerator. IEEE Trans. Very Large Scale Integr. (VLSI) Syst. **30**(5), 579–588 (2022)
35. Li, W.-D., Chen, M.-S., Kuo, P.-C., Cheng, C.-M., Yang, B.-Y.: Frobenius additive fast Fourier transform. In: Proceedings of the 2018 ACM International Symposium on Symbolic and Algebraic Computation, ISSAC 2018, pp. 263–270 (2018)
36. Lin, S.-J., Al-Naffouri, T.Y., Han, Y.S.: FFT algorithm for binary extension finite fields and its application to Reed–Solomon codes. IEEE Trans. Inf. Theory **62**(10), 5343–5358 (2016)
37. Lin, S.-J., Al-Naffouri, T.Y., Han, Y.S., Chung, W.-H.: Novel polynomial basis with fast fourier transform and its application to Reed–Solomon erasure codes. IEEE Trans. Inf. Theory **62**(11), 6284–6299 (2016)
38. Lin, S.-J., Chung, W.-H., Han, Y.S.: Novel polynomial basis and its application to Reed-Solomon erasure codes. In: 2014 IEEE 55th Annual Symposium on Foundations of Computer Science, pp. 316–325 (2014)
39. Lucas, E.: Théorie des fonctions numériques simplement périodiques. Am. J. Math. **1**(4), 289–321 (1878)
40. Luo, G., Shihui, F., Gong, G.: Speeding up multi-scalar multiplication over fixed points towards efficient zkSNARKs. IACR Trans. Cryptograph. Hardware Embedded Syst. **2023**(2), 358–380 (2023)
41. Mateer, T.: Fast Fourier transform algorithms with applications. Ph.D. thesis. Clemson University (2008). https://open.clemson.edu/all_dissertations/231/
42. National Institute of Standards and Technology: Post-Quantum Cryptography: Standardization Process (2023). https://csrc.nist.gov/projects/pqc-dig-sig/round-1-additional-signatures. Accessed 10 Jan 2025
43. Steffen, S., Bichsel, B., Baumgartner, R., Vechev, M.: ZeeStar: private smart contracts by homomorphic encryption and zero-knowledge proofs. In: 2022 IEEE Symposium on Security and Privacy (SP), pp. 179–197 (2022)
44. Thibault, L.T., Sarry, T., Hafid, A.S.: Blockchain scaling using rollups: a comprehensive survey. IEEE Access **10**, 93039–93054 (2022)
45. Van Nieuwpoort, R.V., Wrzesińska, G., Jacobs, C.J.H., Bal, H.E.: Satin: a high-level and efficient grid programming model. ACM Trans. Program. Lang. Syst. **32**(3) (2010)
46. Wang, Y., Zhu, X.: A fast algorithm for the Fourier transform over finite fields and its VLSI implementation. IEEE J. Sel. Areas Commun. **6**(3), 572–577 (1988)
47. Xiong, A.L., et al.: VeriZexe: decentralized private computation with universal setup. In: 32nd USENIX Security Symposium (USENIX Security 23), pp. 4445–4462. USENIX Association, Anaheim, CA, August 2023

Multi-precision PMNS with CIOS Reduction

Nicolas Méloni, François Palma(✉), and Pascal Véron

Université de Toulon, Institut de Mathématiques, Toulon, France
{nicolas.meloni,francois.palma,pascal.veron}@univ-tln.fr

Abstract. The Polynomial Modular Number System (PMNS) is a representation system that has shown its effectiveness for finite-field arithmetic with ECC-size integers [4,7,9]. Efforts have also been made to adapt it to larger integers [8,19,24] with mixed results. In particular in [19], a gap in the 2048-bit to 8192-bit integer sizes was highlighted, for which PMNS seemed incapable of overcoming the competition. In this work, we propose a new way of using PMNS for larger sizes, which involves multi-precision polynomial coefficients and utilizes the Montgomery CIOS reduction, thus closing said gap.

Keywords: Modular Arithmetic, PMNS, Montgomery CIOS, Toeplitz Matrices

1 Introduction

Finite-field arithmetic is key to many cryptographic protocols, with Elliptic Curve Cryptography, for example, being used in the "vast majority" of TLS handshakes [18, footnote 2 page 8] with TLS 1.3 reported by Cloudflare to be "93% of the connections" [27] in 2024. Meanwhile, Post Quantum Cryptography (PQC) also uses finite-field arithmetic, with the preeminent example being Kyber [3], the new NIST standard for PQC [21] (although Modular Lattices do not need multi-precision due to their characteristic fields generally being much smaller). Another example in PQC is CSIDH whose prime sizes range from 1024 bits [6] up to 8192 bits [5].

PMNS are usable in any finite-field arithmetic context but mostly as a replacement for traditional multi-precision arithmetic. Instead of the usual 2^w-ary multi-precision where an integer a can be written as $a = \sum_{i=0}^{m-1} a_i 2^{wi}$, a corresponding polynomial $A(X) = \sum_{i=0}^{n-1} A_i X^i$ is chosen to represent a with the main advantages being the lack of carry propagation and the independence of each coefficient during multiplication. In practice, the efficiency of PMNS has been shown in [7], which described a specific library for ECC, named MPHELL, and compared it with other dedicated cryptographic libraries. The results show that on a 64-bit architecture, the PMNS representation gives the best results

C. Boura et al. (Eds.): SAC 2025, LNCS 16207, pp. 369–390, 2026.
https://doi.org/10.1007/978-3-032-10536-3_14

inside MPHELL for ECDSA/EdDSA signatures (generation and verification). Moreover, it also offers competitive timings on an ARM v8 architecture or an STM32F4 board. More recently, PMNS have been implemented as a faster alternative to the standard finite-field arithmetic provided in the Zcash library, which is a cryptocurrency based on bitcoin [11]. Furthermore, PMNS are well-suited to both SIMD [13] and multithreading approaches [19]. However, the number of coefficients required to represent integers in memory seems to balloon out in size as we consider larger prime fields, as noted in [19]. In that paper, the authors increased the size of the coefficients by using a 128-bit type made available by GCC on x86_64 CPUs, with mixed results.

In this work, we explain the observed degradation in size efficiency with concrete formulas. We also propose an adaptation of the well-established Montgomery CIOS method [16], originally designed for integer modular arithmetic, to a polynomial context using the PMNS representation. Furthermore, we incorporate the use of Toeplitz matrices into our methodology, which are particularly well-suited for polynomial modular reduction. Finally, we establish an alternative way to handle multi-precision sized coefficients in PMNS through the use of "reduced coefficients" [2]. By multi-precision, we mean that each coefficient of a polynomial is stored across multiple machine words. Together, these methods achieve very convincing results and finally bridge the gap for PMNS on large integers highlighted in [19]. Furthermore, we also improve the results with regard to the SIMD implementation presented in [8].

In Sect. 2 we provide background information related to PMNS. In Sect. 3 we provide a new bound for the minimal number of symbols required to represent an integer in PMNS. In Sect. 4 we adapt the Montgomery CIOS algorithm to PMNS in order to manage polynomial coefficients stored on multiple machine words. Finally, in Sects. 5 and 6 we present a complexity analysis of our new algorithm followed by the implementation results.

2 Background

In this section, we give a brief overview of PMNS and the way operations are performed.

2.1 PMNS

Definition 1. *Let* $p \geqslant 3$, $n \geqslant 2$, $\gamma \in [1, p-1]$ *and* $\rho \in [1, p-1]$. *Let* $E \in \mathbb{Z}[X]$ *be a monic polynomial of degree* n, *such that* $E(\gamma) \equiv 0 \pmod{p}$. *A PMNS is a set* $\mathcal{B} \subset \mathbb{Z}[X]$ *such that :*

1. $\forall A \in \mathcal{B}$, $\deg(A) < n$,
2. $\forall A(X) = \sum_{i=0}^{n-1} a_i X^i \in \mathcal{B}$, $-\rho < a_i < \rho$ *for all* i,
3. $\forall a \in \mathbb{Z}/p\mathbb{Z}$, $\exists A \in \mathcal{B}$ *such that* $A(\gamma) \equiv a \pmod{p}$.

Since we want $\|A\|_\infty < \rho$, bounds must be put on ρ to guarantee that each element of $\mathbb{Z}/p\mathbb{Z}$ will have at least one polynomial in $\mathcal{B}$ to represent it. This bound is given in [1, Theorem 4.2].
The condition is as follows. Let $\mathfrak{L} = \left\{(x_0, \ldots, x_{n-1}) \in \mathbb{Z}^n : \sum_{i=0}^{n-1} x_i\gamma^i \equiv 0 \pmod{p}\right\}$, which corresponds to the lattice of all vectors of size n for which the associated polynomials vanish in γ modulo p. Let $\mathbf{B}$ be any basis of $\mathfrak{L}$. Then, as long as $\rho > \frac{1}{2}\|\mathbf{B}\|_1$, every element of $\mathbb{Z}/p\mathbb{Z}$ can be represented in $\mathcal{B}$. The way to construct a basis of $\mathfrak{L}$ is also explained by [1], which gives the following canonical basis:

$$\mathbf{B} = \begin{pmatrix} p & 0\,0\ldots0\,0 \\ -\gamma & 1\,0\ldots0\,0 \\ -\gamma^2 & 0\,1\ldots0\,0 \\ \vdots & \ddots\quad\vdots \\ -\gamma^{n-2} & 0\,0\ldots1\,0 \\ -\gamma^{n-1} & 0\,0\ldots0\,1 \end{pmatrix} \qquad (1)$$

The first row of $\mathbf{B}$ corresponds to $(p, 0, \ldots, 0)$ and we have $p \equiv 0 \pmod{p}$. The next $n-1$ rows are $(-\gamma^i, 0, \ldots, 0, 1, 0, \ldots, 0)$ which correspond to the polynomials $X^i - \gamma^i$ and we indeed have that $\gamma^i - \gamma^i \equiv 0 \pmod{p}$.

In practice, we can choose a short basis, since we generally want ρ to be as small as possible, originally to fit inside a machine word. Such a short basis can be obtained, for example, through the application of LLL [17]. For parameter consistency, it has been shown in [12, Section 3.2] that taking $\rho = \|\mathbf{B}_{LLL}\| - 1$ (with $\mathbf{B}_{LLL}$ being the LLL-reduced form of $\mathbf{B}$) is optimal as long as negative polynomial coefficients are allowed.

Remark 1. Note that the determinant of $\mathfrak{L}$ is $det(\mathbf{B}) = p$.

Remark 2. Note that any lattice reduction algorithm can be used, such as BKZ [26]. For small sizes, LLL often finds the shortest basis. Meanwhile, for larger sizes, the gain that can be obtained with regard to ρ using another algorithm is often negligible at the cost of a much longer execution time.

2.2 Operations

Let $\mathcal{B} = (p, n, \gamma, \rho, E)$, a PMNS. Let $a \in \mathbb{Z}/p\mathbb{Z}$ and $b \in \mathbb{Z}/p\mathbb{Z}$ with $A \in \mathcal{B}$ such that $A(\gamma) \equiv a \pmod{p}$ and $B \in \mathcal{B}$ such that $B(\gamma) \equiv b \pmod{p}$.
Performing $c = a \odot b \pmod{p}$ through our PMNS $\mathcal{B}$ is done by computing $C(X) = A(X) \odot B(X) \pmod{E(X)}$ with $\odot$ being either addition, subtraction or multiplication. $E(X)$ is called the *external reduction* polynomial and, since it is a monic polynomial of degree n, it allows the polynomial degree to remain bounded by n after each step. Indeed, since $E(\gamma) \equiv 0 \pmod{p}$, modular reduction by E does not change the value of the result and hence we will properly have $C(\gamma) \equiv c \pmod{p}$.

However, there is no guarantee that we will have $\|C\|_\infty < \rho$, so another step is performed called the *internal reduction* which computes from C another polynomial $\tilde{C} \in \mathcal{B}$ such that $\tilde{C}(\gamma) \equiv c \pmod{p}$ and $\|\tilde{C}\|_\infty < \rho$.

External Reduction. External reduction in PMNS is generally performed by choosing $E(X) = X^n - \lambda$ with small λ. The existence of such a polynomial in $\mathbb{Z}/p\mathbb{Z}$ only presupposes the existence of a sufficiently small nth residue. Since a polynomial modular reduction is performed, the shape of E has an impact on performance. Other shapes of E have been highlighted in [13] but, for our purposes, we will always consider E to be of shape $X^n - \lambda$. This is because it allows the use of sub-quadratic algorithms for the computation of $A(X) \times B(X) \pmod{E(X)}$, as noted in [19].

Indeed, let $A(X) = a_0 + a_1X + \cdots + a_{n-1}X^{n-1}$ and $B(X) = b_0 + b_1X + \cdots + b_{n-1}X^{n-1}$, let $C(X) = A(X) \times B(X) \pmod{E(X)}$ with $E(X) = X^n - \lambda$. We can write each c_i as $c_i = \sum_{j=0}^{i} a_j b_{i-j} + \lambda \sum_{j=1}^{n-i-1} a_{i+j} b_{n-j}$.
Hence, computing $C(X)$ can be viewed as the following vector-matrix computation:

$$(c_0, c_1, \ldots, c_{n-1}) = (a_0, a_1, \ldots, a_{n-1}) \times \begin{pmatrix} b_0 & b_1 & \ldots & b_{n-2} & b_{n-1} \\ \lambda b_{n-1} & b_0 & \ldots & b_{n-3} & b_{n-2} \\ \vdots & \ddots & \ddots & \ddots & \vdots \\ \lambda b_2 & \lambda b_3 & \ldots & b_0 & b_1 \\ \lambda b_1 & \lambda b_2 & \ldots & \lambda b_{n-1} & b_0 \end{pmatrix} \tag{2}$$

The matrix being a Toeplitz matrix, we can use the recursive Toeplitz vector-matrix algorithm [15], which is a sub-quadratic algorithm, much like the Karatsuba or Toom-Cook algorithms. However, this algorithm has been shown to be slightly faster than a Karatsuba multiplication followed by a reduction in [19, Proposition 5.2].

Internal Reduction. The Internal Reduction in a PMNS is closely related to the Closest Vector Problem (CVP). Indeed, considering the lattice $\mathfrak{L}$ defined in Sect. 2.1, if we find the element closest to a vector C we want to reduce, we can subtract that element without changing the value of the evaluation in γ, since the elements of $\mathfrak{L}$ vanish in γ modulo p. In doing so, we can reduce the norm of C. CVP is known to be NP-hard [14], but in our context, solving a ρ-approximation suffices. As such, we can use polynomial-time approximation algorithms instead. Several reduction methods have been proposed, the state-of-the-art being the Montgomery Internal Reduction from [22] (see Algorithm 1), which is an adaptation of the classical Montgomery modular reduction to polynomial coefficients. Note that it does not solve the CVP or an approximation, but it does allow us to obtain vectors with reduced norms. Let $M \in \mathbb{Z}[X]$ be such that $M(\gamma) \equiv 0 \pmod{p}$. To reduce $\|C\|_\infty$, the main idea is to compute a polynomial Q such that every coefficient of $C(X) + Q(X) \times M(X) \pmod{E(X)}$ is divisible by a parameter ϕ. Since Q must satisfy $C(X) + Q(X) \times M(X) \equiv 0 \pmod{E(X), \phi}$, we conclude that $Q(X) \equiv C(X)(-M^{-1}(X)) \pmod{E(X), \phi}$. We note $M'(X) \equiv -M^{-1}(X) \pmod{E(X), \phi}$ in the sequel. Hence, $M(X)$ necessarily needs to be invertible modulo $E(X)$ modulo ϕ. Note that the parameter ϕ is often chosen as a power of 2 so that divisions can be performed with a simple binary shift.

Algorithm 1. Coefficients reduction [22]

Require: $\mathcal{B} = (p, n, \gamma, \rho, E)$ a PMNS, $V \in \mathbb{Z}_{n-1}[X]$, $M \in \mathbb{Z}[X]$ such that $M(\gamma) \equiv 0 \pmod{p}$, $\phi \in \mathbb{N} \setminus \{0\}$ and $M' = -M^{-1} \bmod (E, \phi)$.
Ensure: $S(\gamma) = V(\gamma)\phi^{-1} \pmod{p}$, with $S \in \mathbb{Z}_{n-1}[X]$
1: $Q \leftarrow V \times M' \bmod (E, \phi)$
2: $T \leftarrow Q \times M \bmod E$
3: $S \leftarrow (V + T)/\phi$
4: **return** S

Note that similarly to the External Reduction step, computing a polynomial multiplication by $M(X)$ and $M'(X) \bmod E(X)$ can be done through the Toeplitz vector-matrix algorithm. We call $\mathcal{M}$ and $\mathcal{M}'$ the Internal Reduction Matrices associated with M and M' which correspond to the Toeplitz matrices needed for the computation of the previous algorithm. They are as follows:

$$\mathcal{M} = \begin{pmatrix} m_0 & m_1 & \dots & m_{n-1} \\ \lambda m_{n-1} & m_0 & \dots & m_{n-2} \\ \vdots & \vdots & \ddots & \vdots \\ \lambda m_1 & \lambda m_2 & \dots & m_0 \end{pmatrix} \begin{matrix} \leftarrow M \\ \leftarrow X.M \bmod E \\ \vdots \\ \leftarrow X^{n-1}.M \bmod E \end{matrix} \tag{3}$$

and

$$\mathcal{M}' = \begin{pmatrix} m'_0 & m'_1 & \dots & m'_{n-1} \\ \lambda m'_{n-1} & m'_0 & \dots & m'_{n-2} \\ \vdots & \vdots & \ddots & \vdots \\ \lambda m'_1 & \lambda m'_2 & \dots & m'_0 \end{pmatrix} \begin{matrix} \leftarrow M' \\ \leftarrow X.M' \bmod E \\ \vdots \\ \leftarrow X^{n-1}.M' \bmod E \end{matrix} \tag{4}$$

Consequently, internal reduction has a non-negligible cost, since it is at best sub-quadratic in n. As such a parameter δ has been introduced in [9] that refers to the number of "free" additions one can perform without needing to execute an internal reduction step before a multiplication.

Remark 3. $\mathcal{M}$ is a basis of a sub-lattice $\mathfrak{L}' \subset \mathfrak{L}$ as shown in [1, Proposition 4.1].

Remark 4. The use of the Montgomery Internal Reduction algorithm implies the need to use the Montgomery domain for operational consistency. This means that we will have $A(X) \equiv a\phi \pmod{p}$ to represent a and $B(X) \equiv b\phi \pmod{p}$ to represent b so that $C(X) = A(X) \times B(X) \times \phi^{-1} \pmod{E(X)}$ will be such that $C(\gamma) \equiv (a \times b)\phi \pmod{p}$.

Notice that since the multiplication in PMNS is a polynomial multiplication, we can improve this operation when the two operands are the same. We do not consider this case because we prioritize constant-time implementations for modular arithmetic.

Due to the redundancy inherent to PMNS, equality tests cannot be performed in a straightforward fashion like in a classical binary representation. Equality tests, if needed, should be performed either through Horner polynomial evaluation in γ or by testing the membership in a modular lattice. Indeed, let $\mathcal{B}$ be a PMNS. Let $A \in \mathcal{B}$ and $B \in \mathcal{B}$. Then $A(\gamma) \equiv B(\gamma) \pmod{p} \iff (A - B) \in \mathfrak{L} = \left\{(x_0, \ldots, x_{n-1}) \in \mathbb{Z}^n : \sum_{i=0}^{n-1} x_i\gamma^i \equiv 0 \pmod{p}\right\}$. The authors in [10] present PMNS with increased size parameters for faster equality tests, but the performance for standard operations is reduced as a result. In this paper, we only consider PMNS with optimal parameters with regard to the performance of modular multiplication. Hence, we only consider PMNS without equality tests.

3 A New Definition of Optimal N for PMNS

The parameter n_{opt} has been introduced in previous papers as the optimal value of n for a given prime size for generation purposes. More explicitly, no PMNS can exist with $n < n_{opt}$ without coefficients potentially overflowing from machine words in the middle of operations.

The complexity of the external and internal reductions depends mainly on the parameter n, which is the number of coefficients used to represent an element of $\mathbb{Z}/p\mathbb{Z}$ by a polynomial. Therefore, it is critical to minimize the parameter as much as possible.

Let σ be the number of values in a machine word (for example, 2^{64} for a 64-bit processor). In previous works, authors often set the optimal value of n as $n_{opt} = \left\lfloor \frac{\log_2(p)}{\log_2(\sigma)} \right\rfloor + 1$.

Table 1. size in number of 64-bit machine words.

Prime size	256	512	1024	2048	4096	6144	8192
n_{opt}	5	9	17	33	65	97	129
n_{actual}	5	9	18	36	72	108	144

Table 1 shows empirical results for the actual values of n for various integer sizes compared to the naive evaluation of n_{opt}, assuming 64-bit machine words.

As can be seen, while for smaller integer sizes, this bound can be reached, the gap widens as we increase in integer size. This has been highlighted in [19, Proposition 4.1]. In this section, we give an explanation for this gap and give a more accurate expression for the theoretical minimum value of n.

3.1 Minkowski's Bound on the 1-Norm of Lattices

Let us first recall Minkowski's theorem from [20].
Minkowski's Theorem. *Let $\mathfrak{L} \subseteq \mathbb{R}^n$, a full-rank lattice. Let $S \subseteq \mathbb{R}^n$ be a convex centrally symmetric set. If $vol(S) > 2^n \det(\mathfrak{L})$, then S contains at least one non-zero lattice vector.*

Proposition 1. *Let $\mathfrak{L} \subseteq \mathbb{R}^n$, a full-rank lattice.*
Let $v \in \mathfrak{L}$ such that $\forall x \in \mathfrak{L} \setminus \{0\}, \|x\|_1 \geqslant \|v\|_1$. Then $\|v\|_1 \leqslant (n! \det(\mathfrak{L}))^{\frac{1}{n}}$.

Proof. Let $v \in \mathfrak{L}$ such that $\forall x \in \mathfrak{L} \setminus \{0\}, \|x\|_1 \geqslant \|v\|_1$. In other words, v is the shortest non-zero vector of $\mathfrak{L}$ in terms of 1-norm. Let $S = \{x \in \mathbb{R}^n : \|x\|_1 < \|v\|_1\}$. S is both convex and centrally symmetric, verifying the requirements for Minkowski's Theorem. S is a n-ball in L^1 norm of radius $\|v\|_1$ by construction, thus its volume is $vol(S) = \frac{2^n}{n!}(\|v\|_1)^n$. If we assume $\|v\|_1 > (n! \det(\mathfrak{L}))^{\frac{1}{n}}$, then we have $vol(S) > 2^n \det(\mathfrak{L})$. In that case, S contains at least one non-zero lattice vector according to Minkowski's theorem. This contradicts the assumption that v is the shortest non-zero vector of $\mathfrak{L}$ in terms of 1-norm since all elements of S have a smaller 1-norm than v by construction. Therefore, it follows that $\|v\|_1 \leqslant (n! \det(\mathfrak{L}))^{\frac{1}{n}}$. □

This is a classical result on lattices that helps us in establishing a realistic bound on the 1-norm of $\mathcal{M}$. This is important because ρ, which provides a bound for our polynomial coefficients, directly depends on it. Since $\mathcal{M}$ is a sub-lattice of $\mathfrak{L}$ (see Remark 3), then, from [13, Proposition 3], a PMNS exists as soon as $\rho > \frac{1}{2}\|\mathcal{M}\|_1$. The matrix $\mathcal{M}$ is constructed from a short vector of $\mathfrak{L}$ which means the result from Proposition 1 helps us bound its 1-norm. Indeed, assuming that we choose the shortest vector, v_1, it follows that $\|\mathcal{M}\|_1 \leqslant |\lambda| \|v_1\|_1$. This gives us

$$\|\mathcal{M}\|_1 \leqslant |\lambda|(n!p)^{\frac{1}{n}} \tag{5}$$

by remarking that $\det(\mathfrak{L}) = p$ (see Remark 1).
Being able to construct $\mathcal{M}$ with v_1 is not guaranteed and, in the first place, finding the shortest vector in a lattice is an NP-hard problem, but this gives us a bound in the optimal case, which is the premise behind the choice of n_{opt}. Similarly, the optimal value of $|\lambda|$ is 1 in the case of $E(X) = X^n + 1$ with n a power of 2. This gives us $\|\mathcal{M}\|_1 \leqslant (n!p)^{\frac{1}{n}}$ in the optimal case.

3.2 New Expression for n_{opt}

We want $\sigma \geqslant 2\rho$ so as to be able to fit our polynomial coefficients in a single machine word. Indeed, having $\sigma \geqslant \rho$ does not suffice, seeing as coefficients can be both positive and negative, so an extra bit is needed. As explained in the previous section, we cannot construct a PMNS such that $\rho < \frac{1}{2}\|\mathcal{M}\|_1$. Which means, since we want $\sigma \geqslant 2\rho$, we will at least need to have $\sigma \geqslant \|\mathcal{M}\|_1$. Hence, we can set a requirement on n to be $\sigma \geqslant (n!p)^{\frac{1}{n}}$. Which means:

$$p \leqslant 2^{n\log_2(\sigma)-\log_2(n!)},$$

thus $\log_2(p) \leqslant n\log_2(\sigma) - \log_2(n!)$. We can then set n_{opt} as the smallest n which verifies the above inequality. This gives us the following table (Table 2):

Table 2. size in number of 64-bit machine words.

Prime size	256	512	1024	2048	4096	6144	8192
old n_{opt}	5	9	17	33	65	97	129
new n_{opt}	5	9	17	34	70	105	141
n_{actual}	5	9	18	36	72	108	144

The new approximation fits better with reality. The remaining difference can be attributed to the approximation error from LLL [23] (since we generally obtain our short bases with LLL in practice).

Note that we can write $n_{opt} = \left\lceil \frac{\log_2(p)+\log_2(n_{opt}!)}{\log_2(\sigma)} \right\rceil$ or, alternatively,

$$n_{opt} = \left\lfloor \frac{\log_2(p) + \log_2(n_{opt}!)}{\log_2(\sigma)} \right\rfloor + 1$$

Proposition 2. *Let p be such that $\log_2\left(\left(\left\lfloor \frac{\log_2(p)}{\log_2(\sigma)} \right\rfloor + 1\right)!\right) \geqslant \log_2(\sigma)$, then*

$$n_{opt} > \left\lfloor \frac{\log_2(p)}{\log_2(\sigma)} \right\rfloor + 1$$

Proof. First, notice that $\left\lfloor \frac{\log_2(p)+\log_2(n_{opt}!)}{\log_2(\sigma)} \right\rfloor + 1 \geqslant \left\lfloor \frac{\log_2(p)}{\log_2(\sigma)} \right\rfloor + 1$. Hence, since $n_{opt} = \left\lfloor \frac{\log_2(p)+\log_2(n_{opt}!)}{\log_2(\sigma)} \right\rfloor + 1$, then

$$n_{opt} \geqslant \left\lfloor \frac{\log_2(p)}{\log_2(\sigma)} \right\rfloor + 1$$

Then, as soon as $\log_2\left(\left(\left\lfloor \frac{\log_2(p)}{\log_2(\sigma)} \right\rfloor + 1\right)!\right) \geqslant \log_2(\sigma)$, then $\frac{\log_2(n_{opt}!)}{\log_2(\sigma)} \geqslant 1$.

Therefore

$$n_{opt} = \left\lfloor \frac{\log_2(p) + \log_2(n_{opt}!)}{\log_2(\sigma)} \right\rfloor + 1 \geqslant \left\lfloor \frac{\log_2(p)}{\log_2(\sigma)} + 1 \right\rfloor + 1 > \left\lfloor \frac{\log_2(p)}{\log_2(\sigma)} \right\rfloor + 1$$

□

For example, for $\sigma = 2^{64}$, this bound is achieved for $p \geqslant 2^{1280}$. This is simply because 1280 is 64 times 20 and $21! > 2^{64}$ while $20! < 2^{64}$. Hence, past this bound, our new expression of n_{opt} will be strictly superior to the old expression, making the old bound impossible to reach.

4 Adaptations to Make Multi-precision PMNS More Efficient

This section details the adaptations necessary to switch to multi-precision polynomial coefficients for our PMNS.

4.1 Reduced Coefficients

To address the expansion of n as the size of p increases, it is suggested in [19] to switch to $\phi = \sigma^2$ (using the 128-bit type made available by GCC on x86_64 CPUs). In so doing, an integer from $\mathbb{Z}/p\mathbb{Z}$ is now represented by a polynomial with coefficients stored over two machine words (128 bits) rather than a single one. However, the multi-precision used was a naive implementation with carry propagation.
A better method is to instead split the coefficients in equal parts among several machine words. This is reminiscent of non-saturated integer arithmetic with a radix chosen to minimize carry chains used in some cryptographic schemes. For example, for $\rho = 2^{108}$ with $\sigma = 2^{64}$, instead of storing the first 64 bits of a coefficient on the first machine word and the next 44 bits on another, we split the coefficients into two 54-bit values on the two machine words. All coefficients are thus bounded, which means we can anticipate any overflows and remove the need for carry propagation until the end step of operations to ensure that the result is back to the initial bounds on our coefficients. This technique is similar to the one used in [2] where it is called "reduced coefficients" polynomials, which is how we shall refer to it in the sequel of this paper.

For the sequel of this section, we assume that PMNS coefficients are larger than one machine word, and thus multi-precision is required. Let s be the number of machine words needed to fit a single coefficient. Since we want to perform the division by ϕ in s steps, we split each coefficient such that only values from $-\lceil \sqrt[s]{\phi} \rceil$ to $\lceil \sqrt[s]{\phi} \rceil - 1$ are contained in each machine word at the start. That is to say, let $a \in \mathbb{Z}/p\mathbb{Z}$, a polynomial A representing a in a PMNS will thus be written as $A(X) = \sum_{k=0}^{n-1} a_k X^k$ with $a_k = \sum_{i=0}^{s-1} a_{k_i} \lceil \sqrt[s]{\phi} \rceil^i$. Thus, $A(X) = \sum_{i=0}^{s-1} (\sum_{k=0}^{n-1} a_{k_i} X^k) \lceil \sqrt[s]{\phi} \rceil^i = \sum_{i=0}^{s-1} A_i \lceil \sqrt[s]{\phi} \rceil^i$ where

$$A_i = \sum_{k=0}^{n-1} a_{k_i} X^k \tag{6}$$

.

Traditionally, authors set ϕ as the size of a machine word and a given PMNS is valid if $2w\rho(\delta + 1)^2 < \phi$ with δ a parameter introduced in [9] that refers to the number of "free" additions one can perform without needing to execute an internal reduction step before a multiplication and $w = |\lambda|(n-1)+1$ for $E(X) = X^n - \lambda$ [13]. As such, we can, for now, set the value of ϕ to $2^{\lceil \log_2(2w\rho(\delta+1)^2) \rceil}$.

Carry-Less Operations. The main purpose of reduced coefficients is to delay all carry propagation to the last step. As such, for efficiency reasons, we must ensure that $|\lambda|\lceil \sqrt[s]{\phi} \rceil < \sigma$ otherwise we will not be able to construct the Toeplitz matrix from Eq. (2) in such a way that all coefficients fit in a machine word. Furthermore, since we are using the Toeplitz vector-matrix algorithm, some additions are performed before the multiplication step. The maximum number of addition performed for one coefficient is n, with coefficients of size bounded by $|\lambda|\lceil \sqrt[s]{\phi} \rceil$, hence we need to enlarge the bound to be:

$$n|\lambda|\lceil \sqrt[s]{\phi} \rceil < \sigma \tag{7}$$

Note that some fine-tuning can be done depending on the number of recursion steps and the way the splitting is performed, but this bound is sufficient for a general approach.

Division by ϕ. As noted in Sect. 4.1, we can set $\phi = 2^{\lceil \log_2(2w\rho(\delta+1)^2) \rceil}$. However, by necessity from Eq. (7), we cannot set $\sqrt[s]{\phi} = \sigma$. Traditionally in PMNS, ϕ is set to σ. This is done for efficiency reasons, since a division by the size of a machine word in practice translates to a simple MOV instruction. Similarly, a modular reduction can be performed "for free" since anything above σ will overflow. In our case, since this isn't possible, we will need to perform actual divisions and modular reductions.

One of the most efficient ways to perform a modular reduction consists of simply applying a binary mask in memory. However, this is only possible for powers of 2. Similarly, powers of 2 allow the use of bit-shifting to perform divisions. Hence, it seems logical to choose ϕ to be a power of 2.

In our case, the divisions and reductions performed will be done with $\lceil \sqrt[s]{\phi} \rceil$. Thus, we also want $\lceil \sqrt[s]{\phi} \rceil$ to be a power of 2. This gives us, for efficiency reasons:

$$\phi = 2^{s \left\lceil \frac{\log_2(2w\rho(\delta+1)^2)}{s} \right\rceil} \tag{8}$$

4.2 Generation

In this section, we detail the generation process for multi-precision PMNS. A sample generation code is available at https://github.com/francoispalma/PMNS/tree/master/multiprecision_pmns.

Adaptation to Multi-precision. In previous works, authors generate a PMNS for a given p in the following manner:

1. ϕ is chosen (often the size of a machine word)
2. n_{opt} is computed with regards to ϕ and we set $n \leftarrow n_{opt}$ at the start
3. we find λ, a small nth root in $\mathbb{Z}/p\mathbb{Z}$ such that $E(X) = X^n - \lambda$ is irreducible in $\mathbb{Z}$
4. we choose γ among the roots of $E(X)$ in $\mathbb{Z}/p\mathbb{Z}$

5. we construct $\mathbf{B}$ as detailed in Eq. (1) and apply LLL. We note $\mathbf{B}_{LLL}$ the LLL reduced form of $\mathbf{B}$
6. we set $\rho = \|\mathbf{B}_{LLL}\|_1 - 1$ (as explained in Sect. 2.1). If ρ is small enough with respect to ϕ (we need $\phi > 2w\rho(\delta+1)^2$ as explained in Sect. 4.1), the generation process ends. Else, we set $n \leftarrow n+1$ and go to step 3.

Note that this is a generalization of the process and does not necessarily fit all previous works. This process works and is good enough for us to expand on.

Remark 5. Note that in step 3 we choose the smallest possible λ. Notice that since the value of w is proportional to λ, and ϕ must satisfy $\phi > 2w(\delta+1)^2$, it is natural to choose λ as small as possible.

When switching to multi-precision, the value of ϕ is necessarily set differently. One can choose s, the number of machine words necessary for a single polynomial coefficient, at the start of the generation process and compute n_{opt} as detailed in Sect. 3.2. The process thus ends up being very similar to the one we have just described. However, another approach is possible:

1. we choose n
2. we find λ, a small nth root in $\mathbb{Z}/p\mathbb{Z}$ such that $E(X) = X^n - \lambda$ is irreducible in $\mathbb{Z}$
3. we choose γ among the roots of $E(X)$ in $\mathbb{Z}/p\mathbb{Z}$
4. we construct $\mathbf{B}$ as detailed in Eq. (1) and apply LLL. We note $\mathbf{B}_{LLL}$ the LLL reduced form of $\mathbf{B}$. From it, we set $\rho = \|\mathbf{B}_{LLL}\|_1 - 1$ as explained in Sect. 2.1
5. We set s so that $\sigma^s \geqslant \rho$ (with σ the number of values in a machine word, for example, 2^{64} for a 64-bit processor) from which we compute ϕ as detailed in Eq. (8).

Choosing n however we want is beneficial because it allows us to choose it to be optimal in terms of complexity (see Sect. 5 for more details) but also with many small factors for the Toeplitz recursive splitting. Note also that this process always yields a PMNS.

Choice of M. Since Algorithm 1 requires $-M^{-1} \pmod{E(X), \phi}$, then necessarily M needs to have an inverse mod $E(X), \phi$. Previous works [9,13] provide more details as to the exact conditions for M to be invertible. In this section, we explain a process for choosing M among the valid possibilities such that the 1-norm is minimal.

After constructing $\mathbf{B}$ as detailed in Eq. (1) and applying LLL, M is often chosen as the row such that the associated Internal Reduction Matrix $\mathcal{M}$ has the smallest 1-norm and is invertible mod ϕ. However, some small optimizations can be performed.

Proposition 3. *Let $v = (v_0, v_1, \ldots, v_{n-1}) \in \mathfrak{L}$ and $\mathcal{V}$ be the internal reduction matrix associated with v (see Eq. (3)). Let $w = (v_1, \ldots, v_{n-1}, \frac{v_0}{\lambda})$ and $\mathcal{W}$ be the internal reduction matrix associated with w. If $v_0 \equiv 0 \pmod{\lambda}$, then $w \in \mathfrak{L}$ and $\|\mathcal{W}\|_1 \leqslant \|\mathcal{V}\|_1$.*

Proof. Let $v = (v_0, v_1, \ldots, v_{n-1}) \in \mathfrak{L}$. We note $V(X)$ the polynomial associated with v. Let $w = (v_1, \ldots, v_{n-1}, \frac{v_0}{\lambda})$. We note $W(X)$ the polynomial associated with w. Then, if $v_0 \equiv 0 \pmod{\lambda}$, $W(X) \in \mathbb{Z}[X]$. Furthermore, notice that $W(X) \times X \equiv V(X) \pmod{E(X)}$ since $\frac{v_0}{\lambda} X^n \equiv v_0 \pmod{E(X)}$. Since $v \in \mathfrak{L}$, we have $V(\gamma) \equiv 0 \pmod{p}$ and therefore $W(\gamma) \equiv \frac{V(\gamma)}{\gamma} \equiv 0 \pmod{p}$ and thus $w \in \mathfrak{L}$.

For $M(X) = m_0 + m_1 X + \cdots + m_{n-1} X^{n-1}$ then $\|\mathcal{M}\|_1 = |m_0| + |\lambda| \sum_{i=1}^{n-1} |m_i|$ since the first column of $\mathcal{M}$ is always the one with the largest coefficients. Hence $\|\mathcal{W}\|_1 \leqslant \|\mathcal{V}\|_1$. □

Remark 6. It is easy to see that the process can be repeated as long as the coefficient in the first position is divisible by λ. Note in particular that for $\lambda = 2$, this process will give a vector whose first coefficient is odd. This is notable because it has been shown in [9, Proposition 8] that it is a sufficient condition to guarantee that M is invertible by ϕ when ϕ is a power of 2, as is our case here.

Thus, selecting M can be done with the following heuristic:

1. We compute $\mathbf{B}_{LLL}$, the LLL-reduced form of $\mathbf{B}$.
2. For the first row of $\mathbf{B}_{LLL}$ which we can note as r_1, compute R_1 the corresponding polynomial.
3. Compute the successive $R_1/X^i \bmod E(X)$ as long as $R_1/X^i \bmod E(X)$ has integer coefficients.
4. Choose $M_1 = R_1/X^j \pmod{E(X)}$ with j the largest value such that M_1 is invertible mod $E(X)$ mod ϕ.
5. Repeat for each row of $\mathbf{B}_{LLL}$.
6. Choose M as the smallest 1-norm vector among the M_k.

Note that a given row is not guaranteed to yield a polynomial that is invertible mod $E(X)$ mod ϕ through this heuristic unless $\lambda = 2$. It has been shown in [9, Propositions 8 and 11] that for $E(X) = X^n - \lambda$ with even λ, at least one row of $\mathbf{B}_{LLL}$ is invertible, but for odd λ the question remains open for nonspecific n. In [9, Proposition 12] and [13, Proposition 7], the authors show that a valid M can be found by performing binary linear combinations of the rows of $\mathbf{B}_{LLL}$ for odd λ although this may need a 2^n step exhaustive search.

Another consideration is sign. PMNS are well-suited for the use of vectorized instructions, and in particular they make great use of the AVX512IFMA set of instructions, as shown in [8]. However, those instructions only exist in unsigned form. It is possible to perform all operations in the PMNS using only unsigned coefficients; however, this requires finding a M with only positive coefficients. This also means that the value of ρ must be doubled to account for the necessity of every element of $\mathbb{Z}/p\mathbb{Z}$ having a polynomial representation with only positive coefficients, which halves the number of potential candidates.

The authors of [8] use a generation process that involves iterating over various random vectors whose norms are close to the upper bound on the shortest vector until one is found that is all positive and invertible. The considerations for our new multi-precision PMNS variant are opposite in that we do not necessarily require a very short vector since we can increase the size of our coefficients as needed. Instead, having a process that is guaranteed to find a positive invertible vector in $\mathfrak{L}$ is more useful.

We propose the following heuristic that systematically finds a positive linear combination of the rows of the reduced basis that is also guaranteed to be invertible for even λ.

1. We initialize $C(X)$ as the polynomial corresponding to the vector $(\|\mathbf{B_{LLL}}\|_1+1, \|\mathbf{B_{LLL}}\|_1+1, \ldots, \|\mathbf{B_{LLL}}\|_1+1)$ and set $\rho' = \|\mathbf{B_{LLL}}\|_1$, a temporary ρ for generation purposes.
2. We compute $\phi' = 2^{s\left\lceil \frac{\log_2(2w\rho'(\delta+1)^2)}{s} \right\rceil}$, a temporary ϕ for generation purposes. We have a temporary valid PMNS for use in conversion operations.
3. We compute $c \in \mathbb{Z}/p\mathbb{Z}$ with $C(\gamma) \equiv c \pmod p$.
4. Using algorithm 5 from [12], we compute $\overline{C}(X)$, a polynomial representing c in our temporary PMNS. This guarantees $\|\overline{C}\|_\infty \leqslant \frac{1}{2}\|\mathbf{B}_{LLL}\|_1 + 1$ (as shown in [12, Proposition 1]).
5. Since $C(\gamma) \equiv \overline{C}(\gamma) \equiv c \pmod p$, we set $M(X) = C(X) - \overline{C}(X)$ and we properly have $M(\gamma) \equiv 0 \pmod p$. Furthermore, we know by construction that $\forall i, \frac{1}{2}\rho' \leqslant m_i \leqslant \frac{3}{2}\rho' + 2$. Hence, all coefficients of M are positive.

This M is not necessarily invertible. Assuming even λ, a sufficient condition can be found to construct an invertible M, using [9, Proposition 11] which shows that at least one row of $\mathbf{B}_{LLL}$ is such that its first coefficient is odd. As mentioned above, [9, Proposition 8] states that it is sufficient for even λ that the first coefficient of M is odd for M to be invertible mod E, ϕ with ϕ a power of 2, which is our case here.

Thus, the construction is as follows. Let us note $R_k(X)$ the polynomial equivalent of one of the rows of $\mathbf{B}_{LLL}$ whose first coefficient is odd. Since no coefficient of $\mathbf{B}_{LLL}$ is bigger than $\|\mathbf{B}_{LLL}\|_1$ (which is ρ') by definition of the 1-norm of a matrix, then $2 \times M(X) - R_k(X)$ will have all coefficients positive and the first coefficient odd. Indeed, as noted earlier, $\forall i, \frac{1}{2}\rho' \leqslant m_i \leqslant \frac{3}{2}\rho' + 2$. Hence $\forall i, \rho' \leqslant 2 \times m_i \leqslant 3\rho' + 4$. Hence subtracting $R_k(X)$ from $2 \times M(X)$ will not have any coefficient go negative. Also since the first coefficient of $R_k(X)$ is odd, then the first coefficient of the result of $2 \times M(X) - R_k(X)$ will always be odd. Hence this new polynomial will be invertible and all positive. Since we are subtracting an element of $\mathfrak{L}$ from another element of $\mathfrak{L}$, the result will be in $\mathfrak{L}$.

We can then continue as normal in the generation and set the real value of ρ as $\rho > 2 \times (\frac{1}{2}\|\mathcal{M}\|_1 + 1)$ with $\mathcal{M}$ the internal reduction matrix from Eq. (3) and $\phi = 2^{s\left\lceil \frac{\log_2(2w\rho(\delta+1)^2)}{s} \right\rceil}$. As noted above, the value of ρ needs to be doubled, compared to a system where negative coefficients are allowed in order to represent all elements of $\mathbb{Z}/p\mathbb{Z}$.

One demerit of this heuristic is that we have $\|2\times M(X) - R_k(X)\|_\infty \leqslant 4\rho' + 4$, which is much larger in terms of ∞-norm than a row of $\mathbf{B}_{LLL}$. Thus, this process is useful from a theoretical standpoint, but in practice we can improve on it. Indeed, one can continuously add and subtract rows of the short basis matrix, as long as the result is positive. The end result is not guaranteed to be invertible, however for $\lambda = 2$, we can always obtain an invertible polynomial from Remark 6.

4.3 Montgomery CIOS

As explained in Sect. 2.2, internal reduction in PMNS is done through the use of an adaptation of the Montgomery algorithm to polynomials. However, the classic Montgomery algorithm has several variants. In [16], Koç et al. proposed various ways to schedule the operations of the Montgomery algorithm, notably the Montgomery CIOS (Coarsely Integrated Operand Scanning) and FIOS (Finely Integrated Operand Scanning) methods. In [24], Noyez et al. show how to adapt the FIOS variant to PMNS in a hardware context, since this variant is well adapted. Meanwhile, in a software context, the CIOS variant is the state-of-the-art for many cryptographic protocols that rely on modular multiplication. The widely used OpenSSL and GMP libraries both propose software implementations, for example. Another example would be the reference implementation of [6] (https://csidh.isogeny.org/software.html). From our testing (see Sect. 6), Montgomery CIOS seems to have the edge over regular Montgomery until the 2048-bit range. For our purposes, this means that as long as $\sigma^s < 2^{2048}$, using the CIOS version seems logical. Algorithm 2 paraphrases the Montgomery CIOS algorithm from [16].

The parameter w from Algorithm 2 refers to the wordsize and the parameter W is set to $W = 2^w$. The principle is to first compute a times ($b \pmod W$) before zeroing out the last w bits using the Montgomery reduction mod W and divide by W (which is seamless here due to the division being the size of a machine word). We then compute a times ($\lceil \frac{b}{W} \rceil \pmod W$) and add it to the running total before repeating the process. The end result is the same as the classical Montgomery algorithm, although we only need to compute the least significant word of the modular inverse of n (the modulus) by r (a power of 2 such that $\frac{r}{2} < n < r$) and the operations are scheduled differently.

We adapt it to PMNS in Algorithm 3. In it, $\mathbb{Z}_{n-1}[X]$ refers to the polynomials of degree of at most $n-1$ with coefficients in $\mathbb{Z}$. Each polynomial $P(X)$ is such that $P(X) = \sum_{i=0}^{s-1} P_i(\sqrt[s]{\phi})^i$ with $\forall i$, $\|P_i\|_\infty < \sqrt[s]{\phi}$ (see Eq. (6)). In a similar fashion to the integer version, instead of computing $A(X) \times B(X) \pmod{E(X)}$ in one step, this CIOS variant first computes $A(X) \times B_0 \pmod{E(X)}$. Then, we compute a polynomial Q to zero out the lower bits of the result as normal

Algorithm 2. Montgomery CIOS modular multiplication [16]

Require: $n \in \mathbb{N}$ the modulus, $a \in \mathbb{N}$ and $b \in \mathbb{N}$ the operands, w the wordsize of the computer with $W = 2^w$, r the smallest power of 2 such that $r > n$, $z = \lceil \frac{r}{W} \rceil$ and $n' \equiv -n^{-1} \pmod{r}$
Ensure: $t \equiv a \times b \times r^{-1} \pmod{n}$

for $i = 0 \ldots z-1$ **do**
  $C \leftarrow 0$
  for $j = 0 \ldots z-1$ **do**
    $C, S \leftarrow a_j \times b_i + C$
    $t_j \leftarrow S$
  end for
  $(C, S) \leftarrow t_z + C$
  $t_z \leftarrow S$
  $t_{z+1} \leftarrow C$
  $C \leftarrow 0$
  $m \leftarrow t_0 \times n'_0 \pmod{W}$
  for $j = 0 \ldots z-1$ **do**
    $(C, S) \leftarrow t_j + m \times n_j + C$
    $t_j \leftarrow S$
  end for
  $(C, S) \leftarrow t_z + C$
  $t_z \leftarrow S$
  $t_{z+1} \leftarrow t_{z+1} + C$
  for $j = 0 \ldots z-1$ **do**
    $t_j \leftarrow t_{j+1}$
  end for
end for
return t

and divide by $\sqrt[s]{\phi}$. We then compute $A(X) \times B_1 \pmod{E(X)}$ and add it to the running total before repeating the process of finding Q and so on. This is equivalent to the normal Montgomery Internal Reduction algorithm, just scheduled differently.

Each multiplication step in the algorithm makes use of the Toeplitz vector-matrix multiplication algorithm to ensure sub-quadratic complexity.

Algorithm 3. Multi-precision PMNS Montgomery CIOS modular multiplication

Require: (p, n, γ, ρ, E) a PMNS with $E(X) = X^n - \lambda$, $A, B \in \mathbb{Z}_{n-1}[X]$ with $\|A\|_\infty < \rho$ and $\|B\|_\infty < \rho$, s the number of chunks coefficients are split into, $\phi = 2^h$ with $h \in \mathbb{N}^*$ a multiple of s, $M(X) \in \mathbb{Z}_{n-1}[X]$ such that $M(\gamma) \equiv 0 \pmod p$ and $M' \equiv -M^{-1} \pmod{E(X), \phi}$.

Ensure: $C(\gamma) \equiv A(\gamma)B(\gamma)\phi^{-1} \pmod p$, with $C \in \mathbb{Z}_{n-1}[X]$ such that $\forall i$, $\|C_i\|_\infty < \sqrt[s]{\phi}$ and $\|C\|_\infty < \rho$

$R \leftarrow (0, \ldots, 0)$
for $i = 0 \ldots s-1$ **do**
  for $j = 0 \ldots s-1$ **do**
    $R_{i+j} \leftarrow R_{i+j} + A_j \times B_i \pmod{E(X)}$
  end for
  $T \leftarrow R_i \times M'_0 \pmod{E(X), \sqrt[s]{\phi}}$
  for $j = 0 \ldots s-1$ **do**
    $Q_j \leftarrow T \times M_j \pmod{E(X)}$
  end for
  for $j = 0 \ldots s-1$ **do**
    $R_{i+j} \leftarrow R_{i+j} + Q_j$
  end for
  $R_{i+1} \leftarrow R_i / \sqrt[s]{\phi}$ # Exact Division
end for
for $i = 0 \ldots s-1$ **do**
  $C_i \leftarrow R_{s+i} \pmod{\sqrt[s]{\phi}}$
  $R_{s+i+1} \leftarrow R_{s+i} / \sqrt[s]{\phi}$ # Euclidean Division
end for
return C

5 Complexity Analysis

In this section we analyze the Multi-precision CIOS algorithm for PMNS and compare it to the single-precision classical Montgomery version from [22].

Table 3 summarizes the differences in terms of the number of multiplications, with n_{sp} being the single-precision version of the parameter n, s being the number of machine words needed to represent a single coefficient in our new multi-precision version of the PMNS and n_m being the multi-precision version of the parameter n. To clarify, in all cases we will have $s \times n_m \leqslant n_{sp}$. Obviously, for $s = 1$, the complexity of our new algorithm is identical to the single-precision version.

Not shown in the table is the fact that the division steps are performed through binary shifts in the multi-precision version, whereas they are performed by using MOV instructions in the single-precision version. In the same vein, modular reductions are considered to be "free" in the single-precision version because they are the result of natural overflow behavior of machine word sized multiplications, whereas they are performed with binary masks in the multi-

Table 3. Complexity of the various step of each algorithm in the number of multiplications.

Step\Method	Single-precision Montgomery	Multi-precision Montgomery CIOS
A times B	$n_{sp}^{2-\log_{n_{sp}}(2)}$	$s^2 \times n_m^{2-\log_{n_m}(2)}$
Multiplication by $\mathcal{M}'$	$n_{sp}^{2-\log_{n_{sp}}(2)}$	$s \times n_m^{2-\log_{n_m}(2)}$
Multiplication by $\mathcal{M}$	$n_{sp}^{2-\log_{n_{sp}}(2)}$	$s^2 \times n_m^{2-\log_{n_m}(2)}$
Total	$3n_{sp}^{2-\log_{n_{sp}}(2)}$	$s \times (2s+1) \times n_m^{2-\log_{n_m}(2)}$

precision version.

The exponent on the respective n of each variant comes from the usage of the Toeplitz vector-matrix algorithm, whose complexity was detailed in [15, Equation 22]. In this case, we assume the worst case which is prime n. The more n can be decomposed into small factors, the lower the exponent, which means that in the general case it is more favorable to choose $s \leqslant n_m$ since the overall complexity is quadratic in s but sub-quadratic in n_m.

The choice of s and n_m in the multi-precision case should be made according to the value of n_{opt} detailed in Sect. 3.2. That is to say:

$$n_m \times s \geqslant n_{opt} \text{ with } n_m \geqslant s$$

However, while choosing $s = 1$ may look the best on paper, reducing s too much means increasing n_m to the point where the value of w, with $w = |\lambda|(n_m - 1) + 1$, becomes much too large and we no longer have $2w\rho(\delta+1)^2 \leqslant \sigma$ with σ the number of values in a single machine word (for example, 2^{64} for a 64-bit processor). Table 4 shows some empirical results of the value of $s \times n_m$ for various PMNS found with corresponding parameters.

Table 4. Evaluation of $s \times n_m$ for various values of s with $\sigma = 2^{64}$ compared with n_{opt} for various prime sizes.

Prime size	1024	2048	4096	6144	8192
n_{opt} from 3.2	17	34	69	105	141
$s = 1$	19	39	83	130	183
$s = 2$	18	36	80	120	160
$s = 3$	18	36	72	108	144
$s = 4$	20	36	72	108	144

Hence, the method should be to select the smallest value of $s \times n_m$, among which the smallest value of s should give a better time complexity.

6 Implementation Results

Clock cycle measurements are performed according to the following recommendation from the relevant Intel white paper [25] with slight adaptation (taking the median instead of the minimum measurement) :

- We deactivate the *Turbo-Boost*®
- We try to minimize potential cache misses by "heating" the cache memory with 501 runs that are not measured
- Then we generate 1001 appropriate data sets for which 501 runs are executed and the clock cycles are measured by interrogating the Time Stamp Counter with calls to the RDTSC instruction.
- The performance is the median value

The source code is available at https://github.com/francoispalma/PMNS/tree/master/multiprecision_pmns.

6.1 Sequential

Table 5. Cycle count for modular multiplication on large integers using GCC 12.3.0 on intel processor i9-11900KF.

Method\Prime size	1024	2048	4096	6144	8192
GMP Montgomery	1539	4653	14524	28028	44587
GMP Montgomery CIOS	1187	4607	16793	35283	61478
PMNS from [19]	1709	7491	33471	87671	169070
PMNS128 from [19]	2363	10304	39446	80726	146895
This work $s = 2$	1173	3874	16254	30795	54146
This work $s = 3$	1195	3901	**13444**	**26497**	**43835**
This work $s = 4$	1511	4218	14766	30973	45392
OpenSSL Montgomery CIOS	**968**	**3684**	14889	33506	58723

Note that our code is compiled with the flag **-fno-tree-vectorize** to ensure that no vectorized instructions are used. This is so that we can compare ourselves fairly to GMP which does not use vectorized instructions.

We can see in Table 5 that this new multi-precision method is better than the naive one from [19]. This new method makes PMNS competitive with GMP in the 2048 to 8192-bit range, which was highlighted as not being very favorable in [19]. The comparison with OpenSSL shows that the 1024 to 2048-bit range is, while still competitive, not better than the alternative. However, our choices allow for much better performances on larger integer sizes.

6.2 AVX512IFMA

The instruction set AVX512IFMA available on many modern CPUs has been noted in [8] to be particularly well-suited to PMNS. Although AVX2 allows for full vectorized 32-bit multiplication, in our tests this does not lead to better performance than regular sequential instructions due to the large increase in n from taking $\sigma = 2^{32}$. The trade-off of using AVX512IFMA compared to normal sequential instructions is that we will have $\sigma = 2^{52}$ because this instruction set only allows for full vectorized 52-bit multiplication and only positive coefficients can be used. This naturally leads to an increase in the value of the parameter n for a given prime size, but the speedup still seems to be worth the cost.

Table 6. Cycle count for modular multiplication on large integers with AVX512IFMA instructions using GCC 12.3.0 on intel processor i9-11900KF.

Method\Prime size	1024	2048	4096	6144	8192
This work $s = 2$	747	1574	5227	12725	25220
This work $s = 3$	457	1577	5132	10891	15896
This work $s = 4$	-	-	5563	12844	19012

Table 7. Ratio of above table values with the best sequential version of the same integer size.

Method\Prime size	1024	2048	4096	6144	8192
This work $s = 2$	1.570	2.461	2.572	2.082	1.738
This work $s = 3$	2.566	2.457	2.619	2.433	2.758
This work $s = 4$	-	-	2.417	2.063	2.306

In Table 6 we show the results we get for the same integer sizes as the one used in Table 5. In Table 7 we perform a ratio of the results in Table 6 by the best result of any PMNS variant in each column of Table 5. It is clear from those results that the vectorized instructions are faster at all sizes, which shows that they are indeed worth both the increase in parameter size and the slower generation process. In theory, we would expect to see a factor 4 improvement. However, memory management of 512-bit registers and the reduced σ mean that the ratio is lower. Furthermore, the sub-quadratic algorithms we use require subtraction, which may lead to negative coefficients. This needs to be handled manually through the use of sign masks, which adds an additional cost.

Table 8. Comparison of cycle count for modular multiplication on large integers with available sizes in OpenSSL using AVX512IFMA instructions with GCC 12.3.0 on intel processor i9-11900KF.

Method\Prime size	1024	1536	2048
OpenSSL Montgomery CIOS	505	846	1177
This work	453	1065	1492

In Table 8 we compare ourselves with the AVX512IFMA OpenSSL implementation of Montgomery CIOS. Note that comparatively to Tables 4, 4, 5 and 7 OpenSSL only provides AVX512IFMA versions for integers of size 1024, 1536 and 2048 bits. As can be seen, our version seems to be worse for prime sizes above 1024-bit. This can be attributed in part to our code being written in C and comparing ourselves with the optimized assembly code used by OpenSSL. The performance of this work remains relatively competitive and further optimizations may lead to better results in the future.

Table 9. Comparison of cycle count for modular multiplication on PMNS, $\delta = 5$, with [8] using AVX512IFMA instructions with GCC 12.3.0 on intel processor i9-11900KF.

Method\Prime size	807	1214	1621	2029	2436	2844	3251
Results in [8]	779	1004	1965	3764	6233	9093	19157
This work	457	747	1573	2443	3244	5124	5125

In Table 9 we compare ourselves with the results in [8] at the same exact integer sizes. In that paper, they set the parameter δ to 5 so the parameters we generated for this table similarly set δ to 5 for a fair comparison. As can be seen, this new multi-precision method seems to lead to better performance overall. The comparison is made with the code made available by the authors "as is" in [8], only switching the compiler to the same version of GCC for a fair comparison.

7 Conclusion

In this work, we give a more accurate bound on the number of symbols needed to represent an integer in a PMNS. We also present an adaptation of the Montgomery CIOS algorithm to PMNS, utilizing multi-precision oriented optimizations. We show that these changes allow for better performance on large integer sizes and help alleviate a deficiency in the 2048-bit to 8192-bit range for PMNS.

Furthermore, we provide an efficient heuristic that solves the problem of finding a suitable polynomial M in an AVX512IFMA context. Combined with the new multi-precision CIOS algorithm, we obtain better performances than the previous results.

References

1. Bajard, J.C., Marrez, J., Plantard, T., Véron, P.: On polynomial modular number systems over $\mathbb{Z}/p\mathbb{Z}$. Adv. Math. Commun. **18**(3), 674–695 (2024). https://doi.org/10.3934/amc.2022018
2. Bernstein, D.J.: Curve25519: New Diffie-Hellman speed records. In: Public Key Cryptography - PKC 2006, 9th International Conference on Theory and Practice of Public-Key Cryptography. LNCS, vol. 3958, pp. 207–228. Springer (2006). https://doi.org/10.1007/11745853_14
3. Bos, J., et al.: Crystals - KYBER: A CCA-secure module-lattice-based KEM. In: 2018 IEEE European Symposium on Security and Privacy (EuroS&P), pp. 353–367 (2018). https://doi.org/10.1109/EuroSP.2018.00032
4. Bouvier, C., Imbert, L.: An alternative approach for SIDH arithmetic. In: Garay, J.A. (ed.) Public-Key Cryptography – PKC 2021, pp. 27–44. Springer International Publishing, Cham (2021). https://doi.org/10.1007/978-3-030-75245-3_2
5. Campos, F., et al.: Optimizations and practicality of high-security CSIDH. IACR Communications in Cryptology (2024). https://doi.org/10.62056/anjbksdja
6. Castryck, W., Lange, T., Martindale, C., Panny, L., Renes, J.: CSIDH: an efficient post-quantum commutative group action. In: Peyrin, T., Galbraith, S. (eds.) ASIACRYPT 2018. LNCS, vol. 11274, pp. 395–427. Springer, Cham (2018). https://doi.org/10.1007/978-3-030-03332-3_15
7. Coladon, T., Elbaz-Vincent, P., Hugounenq, C.: MPHELL: a fast and robust library with unified and versatile arithmetics for elliptic curves cryptography. In: ARITH 2021. Transactions on Emerging Topics in Computing, Torino, Italy (2021). https://doi.org/10.1109/ARITH51176.2021.00026
8. Didier, L.S., Robert, J.M., Dosso, F.Y., El Mrabet, N.: A software comparison of RNS and PMNS . In: 2022 IEEE 29th Symposium on Computer Arithmetic (ARITH), pp. 86–93. IEEE Computer Society, Los Alamitos, CA, USA (2022). https://doi.org/10.1109/ARITH54963.2022.00025
9. Didier, L.-S., Dosso, F.-Y., Véron, P.: Efficient modular operations using the adapted modular number system. J. Cryptogr. Eng. **10**(2), 111–133 (2020). https://doi.org/10.1007/s13389-019-00221-7
10. Dosso, F.Y., Berzati, A., Mrabet, N.E., Proy, J.: PMNS revisited for consistent redundancy and equality test. Cryptology ePrint Archive, Paper 2023/1231 (2023). https://eprint.iacr.org/2023/1231
11. Dosso, F.Y., Duquesne, S., Mrabet, N.E., Gautier, E.: PMNS arithmetic for elliptic curve cryptography. Cryptology ePrint Archive, Paper 2025/467 (2025). https://eprint.iacr.org/2025/467
12. Dosso, F.Y., Mrabet, N.E., Méloni, N., Palma, F., Véron, P.: Friendly primes for efficient modular arithmetic using the polynomial modular number system. Cryptology ePrint Archive, Paper 2025/090 (2025). https://eprint.iacr.org/2025/090
13. Dosso, F.Y., Robert, J.M., Véron, P.: PMNS for efficient arithmetic and small memory cost. IEEE Trans. Emerg. Top. Comput. **10**(3), 1263–1277 (2022). https://doi.org/10.1109/tetc.2022.3187786

14. van Emde Boas, P.: Another np-complete problem and the complexity of computing short vectors in a lattice. Tech. Rep. 81-04, University of Amsterdam, Department of Mathematics, Netherlands (1981)
15. Hasan, M.A., Nègre, C.: Multiway splitting method for toeplitz matrix vector product. IEEE Trans. Comput. **62**, 1467–1471 (2013). https://doi.org/10.1109/TC.2012.95
16. Kaya Koc, C., Acar, T., Kaliski, B.: Analyzing and comparing montgomery multiplication algorithms. IEEE Micro **16**(3), 26–33 (1996). https://doi.org/10.1109/40.502403
17. Lenstra, A.K., Lenstra, H.W., Lovász, L.: Factoring polynomials with rational coefficients. Math. Ann. **261**, 515–534 (1982). https://doi.org/10.1007/BF01457454
18. Mankowski, D., Wiggers, T., Moonsamy, V.: TLS post-quantum TLS: inspecting the TLS landscape for PQC adoption on android . In: 2023 IEEE European Symposium on Security and Privacy Workshops (EuroS&PW), pp. 526–538. IEEE Computer Society, Los Alamitos, CA, USA (2023). https://doi.org/10.1109/EuroSPW59978.2023.00065, https://doi.ieeecomputersociety.org/10.1109/EuroSPW59978.2023.00065
19. Méloni, N., Palma, F., Véron, P.: PMNS for cryptography : a guided tour. Advances in mathematics of communications, pp. 342–359 (2023). https://doi.org/10.3934/amc.2023033
20. Minkowski, H.: Zur Geometrie der Zahlen. Teubner, Leipzig (1905)
21. National Institute of Standards and Technology: Module-lattice-based key-encapsulation mechanism standard. Tech. Rep. Federal Information Processing Standards Publications (FIPS) 203, U.S. Department of Commerce, Washington, D.C. (2024). https://doi.org/10.6028/NIST.FIPS.203
22. Negre, C., Plantard, T.: Efficient modular arithmetic in adapted modular number system using lagrange representation. In: Information Security and Privacy, 13th Australasian Conference, ACISP 2008, Wollongong, Australia, pp. 463–477 (2008). https://doi.org/10.1007/978-3-540-70500-0_34
23. Nguyen, P.Q., Stehlé, D.: Lll on the average. In: Hess, F., Pauli, S., Pohst, M. (eds.) Algorithmic Number Theory, pp. 238–256. Springer Berlin Heidelberg, Berlin, Heidelberg (2006). https://doi.org/10.1007/11792086_18
24. Noyez, L., El Mrabet, N., Potin, O., Véron, P.: Modular multiplication in the AMNS representation: hardware implementation. In: Selected Areas in Cryptography. Montréal (Québec), France (2024). https://hal.science/hal-04691484, to appear in LNCS vol 15516
25. Paoloni, G.: White paper: how to benchmark code execution times on intel® IA-32 and IA-64 instruction set architectures. intel corporation, Tech. rep. (2010)
26. Schnorr, C.P., Euchner, M.: Lattice basis reduction: improved practical algorithms and solving subset sum problems. In: Budach, L. (ed.) FCT 1991. LNCS, vol. 529, pp. 68–85. Springer, Heidelberg (1991). https://doi.org/10.1007/3-540-54458-5_51
27. Westerbaan, B.: The state of the post-quantum internet (2024). https://blog.cloudflare.com/pq-2024/. Accessed 23 Oct 2024

Unified MEDS Accelerator

Sanjay Deshpande[1(✉)], Yongseok Lee[2], Mamuri Nawan[3], Kashif Nawaz[3], Ruben Niederhagen[4,5], Yunheung Paek[2], and Jakub Szefer[6]

[1] CASLAB, DEE, Yale University, New Haven, USA
sanjay.deshpande@yale.edu
[2] ECE and ISRC, Seoul National University, Seoul, South Korea
yslee@sor.snu.ac.kr, ypaek@snu.ac.kr
[3] CRC, Technology Innovation Institute, Abu Dhabi, UAE
{mamuri,kashif.nawaz}@tii.ae
[4] IIS, Academia Sinica, Taipei, Taiwan
ruben@polycephaly.org
[5] IMADA, University of Southern Denmark, Odense, Denmark
[6] Northwestern University, Evanston, USA
jakub.szefer@northwestern.edu

Abstract. The Matrix Equivalence Digital Signature (MEDS) scheme, a code-based candidate in the first round of NIST's Post-Quantum Cryptography (PQC) standardization process, offers competitively small signature sizes but incurs high computational costs for signing and verification. This work explores how a high-performance FPGA-based hardware implementation can enhance MEDS performance by leveraging the inherent parallelism of its computations, while examining the trade-offs between performance gains and resource costs. This work in particular proposes a unified hardware architecture capable of efficiently performing both signing and verification operations within a single combined design. The architecture jointly supports all security parameters, including the dynamic, run-time handling of different prime fields without the need to re-configure the FPGA. This work also evaluates the resource overhead of supporting different prime fields in a single design, which is relevant not only for MEDS but also for other cryptographic schemes requiring similar flexibility. This work demonstrates that custom hardware for PQC signature schemes can flexibly support different prime fields with limited resource overhead. For example, for NIST security Level I, our implementation achieves signing times of 4.5 ms to 65.2 ms and verification times of 4.2 ms to 64.5 ms utilizing 22k to 72k LUTs and 66 to 273 DSPs depending on design variant and optimization goal.

Keywords: Post-Quantum Cryptography · Digital Signature Algorithm · Matrix Equivalence Digital Signature (MEDS)

1 Introduction

Matrix Equivalence Digital Signature (MEDS) is a code-based digital signature scheme based on the hardness assumption of the Matrix Code Equivalence

C. Boura et al. (Eds.): SAC 2025, LNCS 16207, pp. 391–421, 2026.
https://doi.org/10.1007/978-3-032-10536-3_15

(MCE) problem. It was submitted to the National Institute of Standards and Technology (NIST) Post-Quantum Cryptography (PQC) Signature standardization process launched in 2023, but it did not advance to the second round due to its comparatively low performance (e.g., according to data from the PQM4 project[1], when evaluated in software on an embedded evaluation board, MEDS is 25×, 244×, 856× slower in key generation, signing, and verification times respectively when compared to NIST standard ML-DSA Dilithium [KKPY24] on security level I) and the novelty of its security assumptions. Given the importance of ensuring the practicality of the cryptographic schemes, this paper focuses on developing a unified high-performance hardware implementation of the MEDS signing and verification operation. We present a joint design that supports all security parameter sets, selectable at runtime, and evaluate the overhead of accommodating arithmetic for different finite fields in a single design. Our results on the overhead generalize well and can be transferred to other schemes with similar parameter set specifications such as the NIST PQC Signature Round 2 submission CROSS [BBB+24a], which has parameter sets for $\mathbb{F}_{127}$ and $\mathbb{F}_{509}$. Other related schemes such as LESS [BBB+24b] and PERK [ABB+24] that currently are using a single small binary field might benefit from investigating trade-offs of offering parameter sets with different fields.

By addressing the computational challenges associated with MEDS, we aim to contribute to the broader goal of making post-quantum cryptography viable for widespread adoption in the face of advancing quantum computing technologies. To the best of our knowledge, this work presents the first hardware implementation of MEDS. Our implementation operates in constant time (i.e., there are no timing variations depending on secret data), though it does not include additional side-channel protections.

Related Work. Gaussian elimination is an important step in MEDS as well as many other PQC schemes. Early work [HQR89] used processor arrays as large as the matrix being processed. The work in [SWM+10] presented one of the first hardware accelerators for the code-based Niederreiter cryptosystem. The work used a systolic processor array for performing Gaussian systemization. Later work on Classic McEliece also used a systemizer similar to [SWM+10] with smaller processor array. For example, in [WSN16, WSN17] the authors present a hardware design of a key-generation module for the Niederreiter cryptosystem. In [CCD+22], the authors implemented a complete design of Classic McEliece compliant with the specification submitted to NIST standardization process including binary field systemizers. We are using a similar systemizer in our work.

Although there are similar computations in regard to matrix systemization between MEDS and Classic McEliece, compared to Classic McEliece, instead of working with binary fields, MEDS requires $\mathbb{F}_q$ with prime q. As a result, the latencies (in overall wall-clock time) of finite field operations are larger compared to when using $\mathbb{F}_2$ or a small binary extension filed $\mathbb{F}_q^m$. This difference necessitates

[1] https://github.com/mupq/pqm4.

significant design effort for the systemizer design, e.g., a different control logic and a more complex pipelining process.

Within current NIST standardization process for digital signatures schemes, in [SMA+24,HSK+23] the authors develop hardware implementations of the MAYO digital signature scheme. In [DHSY24], authors present the first hardware implementation of the SDitH digital signature scheme. [dPRS23] describes hardware FPGA implementations of the Raccoon digital signature scheme.

In [WJW+19], the authors present several hardware accelerators that work with a RISC-V core to accelerate the XMSS signature scheme. In [BCH+23], the authors present hardware implementation of the Oil and Vinegar (OV) signature scheme. In [TYD+11] authors presented an FPGA-based implementation of the multivariate-based signature scheme Rainbow. Later, in [FG18] authors presented high-speed, FPGA-based implementation of Rainbow with updated parameters for NIST's first round of PQC standardization process. Both designs are operating on small binary fields using a processor array similar to the code-based designs discussed above. Among ASIC designs, in [ZZL+23] authors present a processor designed specifically for PQC algorithms, which can support schemes such as Saber, Kyber, Dilithium, NTRU, McEliece, and Rainbow. This design also includes a module for the systemization of matrices over small binary fields, but instead of a processor array composed of several vector units, the authors here are using only a single a vector unit.

Hardware architectures for algorithms already being standardized by NIST include [SAW+23], where the authors implement a hardware design of the FALCON scheme and [LSG21,BNG21] where the authors explore hardware implementations of CRYSTALS-Dilithium (being standardized under the name "ML-DSA"). [ALCZ20,Saa24,DLK+25] explores implementations of SPHINCS+ (being standardized under the name "SLH-DSA").

We are not aware of any other hardware implementation of MEDS and our work presents a hardware design of MEDS that provides a competitive performance and resource utilization compared hardware implementations of other signature schemes.

Contributions. This paper introduces the first hardware implementation of the sign and verify operations for the PQC signature scheme MEDS. Our implementation combines both operations into a single design sharing most resources between sign and verify. We further provide joint support of all security parameter sets in one single design selectable at runtime.

We aim to address the following research questions:

Q1: Does MEDS provide sufficient inherent parallelism to accelerate the sign and verify operations to a competitive level? What are the associated resource costs for achieving such a speed-up?

Q2: To what extent can resources be shared in a combined design for the sign and verify operations?

Q3: What is the overhead of supporting all security parameters at runtime, particularly concerning arithmetic in two distinct finite fields?

The source code of our hardware designs is available under an open source license at https://github.com/caslab-code/pqc-hw-meds.

2 Preliminaries

We first introduce our notation in Sect. 2.1 and then explain the relevant details of the MEDS specification in Sect. 2.2.

2.1 Notation

We are following the notation of the MEDS specification document [CNP+23a] and denote matrices with bold capital letters, e.g., $\mathbf{M}$, $\mathbf{A}$, and $\mathbf{B}$. We follow the MEDS specification in denoting submatrices with square brackets, e.g., $\mathbf{M}[a, b; c, d]$ denotes the submatrix of the intersection of rows a to b and columns c to d of matrix $\mathbf{M}$ [CNP+23a, Section 2.1]. If no row or column range is provided, all rows or columns are included. $\mathbb{F}_q$ is a finite field with q elements. We define an $[m \times n, k]$ matrix rank metric code over $\mathbb{F}_q$ as k-dimensional subspace of $\mathbb{F}_q^{m\times n}$. Here, m and n are the codeword sizes and k the code dimension.

The operation $\mathsf{SF}(\mathbf{M})$ returns the systematic form of a matrix $\mathbf{M}$ if it exists or $\perp$ if not. The operation $\pi_{\mathbf{A},\mathbf{B}}(\mathbf{M})$ with $\mathbf{A} \in \mathbb{F}_q^{m\times m}$, $\mathbf{B} \in \mathbb{F}_q^{n\times n}$, and $\mathbf{M} \in \mathbb{F}_q^{k\times mn}$ first maps each row $i \in \{0, \ldots, k-1\}$ of $\mathbf{M}$ to a matrix $\mathbf{P}_i \in \mathbb{F}_q^{m\times n}$ such that $\mathbf{P}_i[\lfloor j/n \rfloor; j \bmod n] = \mathbf{M}[i, j]$ for $j \in \{0, \ldots, mn-1\}$. It then computes $\mathbf{P}'_i \in \mathbb{F}_q^{m\times n}$ as $\mathbf{P}'_i = \mathbf{A}\mathbf{P}_i\mathbf{B}$, maps the $\mathbf{P}'_i$ back to the rows i of a matrix $\mathbf{M}' \in \mathbb{F}_q^{k\times mn}$, and finally returns $\mathbf{M}'$ as result.

2.2 MEDS

The MEDS scheme [CNP+23a, CNP+23b] was a submissions to the on-ramp to the NIST PQC signature standardization process[2] but it did not advance to the second round. It is based on the notion of Matrix Code Equivalence (MCE):

Definition 1 (Matrix Code Equivalence). *Let $\mathcal{C}$ and $\mathcal{D}$ be two $[m \times n, k]$ matrix codes over $\mathbb{F}_q$. We say that $\mathcal{C}$ and $\mathcal{D}$ are* equivalent *if there exist two invertible matrices $\mathbf{A} \in \mathbb{F}_q^{m\times m}$ and $\mathbf{B} \in \mathbb{F}_q^{n\times n}$ such that $\mathcal{D} = \mathbf{A} \cdot \mathcal{C} \cdot \mathbf{B}$, i.e., for all $\mathbf{C} \in \mathcal{C}$, $\mathbf{A} \cdot \mathbf{C} \cdot \mathbf{B} \in \mathcal{D}$.*

This gives rise to the MCE problem:

Problem 1 (Matrix Code Equivalence Problem). Given two k-dimensional matrix codes $\mathcal{C}, \mathcal{D} \subset \mathbb{F}_q^{m\times n}$, find two invertible matrices $\mathbf{A} \in \mathbb{F}_q^{m\times m}$, $\mathbf{B} \in \mathbb{F}_q^{n\times n}$ such that $\mathcal{D} = \mathbf{A} \cdot \mathcal{C} \cdot \mathbf{B}$.

The MCE problem is at least as hard as the linear code equivalence problem and as hard as the isomorphism of polynomials problem [BFV13], and as hard

[2] https://csrc.nist.gov/Projects/pqc-dig-sig/round-1-additional-signatures.

as the alternating trilinear form equivalence problem [GQT21, TDJ+22]. Please refer to [CNP+23a, CNP+23b] for a concrete security analysis.

MEDS uses the MCE problem to construct a signature scheme from an interactive Σ-protocol using the Fiat-Shamir (FS) transform [FS87] with t rounds and by applying some tricks to improve signature size and performance, i.e., by using s matrix codes in the public key, by using challenges with a fixed weight w, by seeding 0-responses, and by generating these seeds from a seed tree.

MEDS Parameters. Table 1 shows the parameter sets of MEDS from the first round of the NIST PQC signature scheme standardization. In May 2024, the MEDS submission team announced new parameter sets in the NIST PQC mailing list[3] as reaction to refined attacks [NQT24]. However, they suggest to combine these new parameter sets with signature-size optimization techniques introduced in [CNRS24]. These optimizations require algorithmic changes compared to the MEDS Round 1 specification document [CNP+23a]. We decided to provide a hardware implementation that follows the MEDS Round 1 specification and therefore do not implement the optimization from [CNRS24] since there is no concrete specification for that MEDS variant and since we are interested in analyzing the effect of supporting different prime fields in a joint design.

Table 1. MEDS parameter sets.

Level	Parameter Set	q	n	m	k	s	t	w	pk (byte)	sig(byte)
MEDS Parameter Sets [CNP+23a, Table 2]:										
Level I	MEDS-9923	4093	14	14	14	4	1152	14	9923	9896
Level I	MEDS-13 220	4093	14	14	14	5	192	20	13 220	12 976
Level III	MEDS-41711	4093	22	22	22	4	608	26	41 711	41 080
Level III	MEDS-69497	4093	22	22	22	5	160	36	55 604	54 736
Level V	MEDS-134180	2039	30	30	30	5	192	52	134 180	132 528
Level V	MEDS-167717	2039	30	30	30	6	112	66	167 717	165 464
New Parameter Sets May 2024 (signature bytes with seed tree)[3]:										
Level I		4093	26	25	25	2	144	48	21 595	5456
Level III		4093	35	34	34	2	208	75	55 520	10 786
Level V		4093	45	44	44	2	272	103	122 000	21 052

MEDS Key Generation. To generate a key pair, first chose a random $\mathbf{G}_0 \in \mathbb{F}_q^{k \times mn}$. Then choose random invertible matrices $\mathbf{A}_1, \ldots, \mathbf{A}_{s-1} \in \mathbb{F}_q^{m \times m}$ and $\mathbf{B}_1, \ldots, \mathbf{B}_{s-1} \in \mathbb{F}_q^{n \times n}$. Finally, compute the matrices $\mathbf{G}_1, \ldots, \mathbf{G}_{s-1} \in \mathbb{F}_q^{k \times mn}$

[3] https://groups.google.com/a/list.nist.gov/g/pqc-forum/c/pbT_DnPrc2A/m/ZPrIVSmFCQAJ.

as $\mathbf{G}_i = \mathsf{SF}(\pi_{\mathbf{A}_i,\mathbf{B}_i}(\mathbf{G}_0))$, $i \in \{1,\ldots,s-1\}$. The public key of MEDS consists of the seed for randomly generating $\mathbf{G}_0 \in \mathbb{F}_q^{k\times mn}$ and $s-1$ matrices $\mathbf{G}_1,\ldots,\mathbf{G}_{s-1} \in \mathbb{F}_q^{k\times mn}$. The secret key of $s-1$ pairs of invertible matrices $(\mathbf{A}_1^{-1},\mathbf{B}_1^{-1}),\ldots,(\mathbf{A}_{s-1}^{-1},\mathbf{B}_{s-1}^{-1}) \in \mathbb{F}_q^{m\times m} \times \mathbb{F}_q^{n\times n}$.

MEDS Signing. During signing, the signer commits to t matrices $\tilde{\mathbf{G}}_i \in \mathbb{F}_q^{k\times mn}$, $i \in \{0,\ldots,t-1\}$ using t maps of pairs of random invertible matrices $(\tilde{\mathbf{A}}_0,\tilde{\mathbf{B}}_0),\ldots,(\tilde{\mathbf{A}}_{t-1},\tilde{\mathbf{B}}_{t-1}) \in \mathbb{F}_q^{m\times m}\times\mathbb{F}_q^{n\times n}$ such that $\tilde{\mathbf{G}}_i = \mathsf{SF}(\pi_{\tilde{\mathbf{A}}_i,\tilde{\mathbf{B}}_i}(\tilde{\mathbf{G}}_0))$, $i \in \{0,\ldots,t-1\}$. The signer then hashes the $\tilde{\mathbf{G}}_i$ to the commitment hash d and parses d to the challenge vector $h_0,\ldots,h_{t-1}$ of weight w with $h_i \in \{0, s-1\}$. The signature finally is composed by providing d as well as the seeds $\tilde{\mathbf{A}}_i$ and $\tilde{\mathbf{B}}_i$ for all i where $h_i = 0$ and $\mu_i = \tilde{\mathbf{A}}_i \cdot \mathbf{A}_{h_i}^{-1}$ and $\nu_i = \mathbf{A}_{h_i}^{-1} \cdot \tilde{\mathbf{B}}_i$ for all i where $h_i > 0$.

MEDS Verification. For verification, the verifier parses the challenge vector $h_0,\ldots,h_{t-1}$ from d. The verifier then computes $\hat{\mathbf{G}}_i \in \mathbb{F}_q^{k\times mn}$, $i \in \{0,\ldots,t-1\}$ as $\hat{\mathbf{G}}_i = \mathsf{SF}(\pi_{\mu_i,\nu_i}(\mathbf{G}_{h_i}))$, where the matrices $\mu_i = \tilde{\mathbf{A}}_i$ and $\nu_i = \tilde{\mathbf{B}}_i$ are regenerated from the seed-tree seeds for all i with $h_i = 0$, and $\mu_i = \tilde{\mathbf{A}}_i \cdot \mathbf{A}_{h_i}^{-1}$ and $\nu_i = \mathbf{A}_{h_i}^{-1} \cdot \tilde{\mathbf{B}}_i$ are parsed from the signature for all i with $h_i > 0$. If the hash of the $\hat{\mathbf{G}}_i$ equals the commitment hash d, the verification is successful.

Cost. The most expensive sub-operations in MEDS are SF with a cost of $\mathrm{O}(mnk^2)$ finite field operations for performing Gaussian elimination on a matrix of size $k \times mn$ and π with a cost of $\mathrm{O}(kmn^2 + km^2n)$ for performing k matrix products of sizes $\mathbb{F}_q^{m\times m}$ times $\mathbb{F}_q^{m\times n}$ times $\mathbb{F}_q^{n\times n}$. Hence, the computational cost of SF and π is quartic in the security parameters with $k \approx m \approx n$.

For key generation, we need to compute SF and π each only s times, where $s \in \{4, 5, 6\}$—but for signing and verification, we need to perform these costly operations t times with $t \in \{112, 160, 192, 608, 1152\}$. Therefore, signing and verification are 18.6 to 288 times more expensive than key generation and hence benefit the most from hardware acceleration. Since verification performs almost the same computations as signing with only little difference in the control flow, we combine both operations in a single design, sharing as many resources between these operations as possible.

3 Unified MEDS Design

We call our hardware design of MEDS a *unified* design, since it *combines* both the MEDS signing and verification operations into a single design, and it provides *joint* support for all parameter sets selectable at runtime, while sharing hardware resources between both operations and all parameter sets as much as possible.

Algorithms 1 and 2 in the Appendix show the signing and verification operations in detail [CNP+23a, Algorithms 11 and 12]. The inputs to the signing operation are the secret key sk and the message msg that needs to be signed. The inputs to the verify operation are the public key pk and the signed message to be verified. Comparing the main loop in Algorithms 1 to 2 in Algorithm 1 with the main loop in Algorithms 1 to 2 in Algorithm 2 shows that the main operations of obtaining invertible matrices, applying the π and SF operations, and computing a commitment hash are structurally identical. Hence, in our combined design, resources for performing these computations can be shared efficiently between the sign and the verify operation with little control overhead.

3.1 Top-Down Overview of Our MEDS Hardware Design

Figure 1 shows the operation flow of our combined hardware implementation. Data flow unique to the sign operation is shown in red and unique to the verify operation in blue. First, both operations expand $\mathbf{G}_0$ from seed $\sigma_{\mathbf{G}_0}$, which is parsed from sk or pk respectively, using the module `ExpandSystMat`.

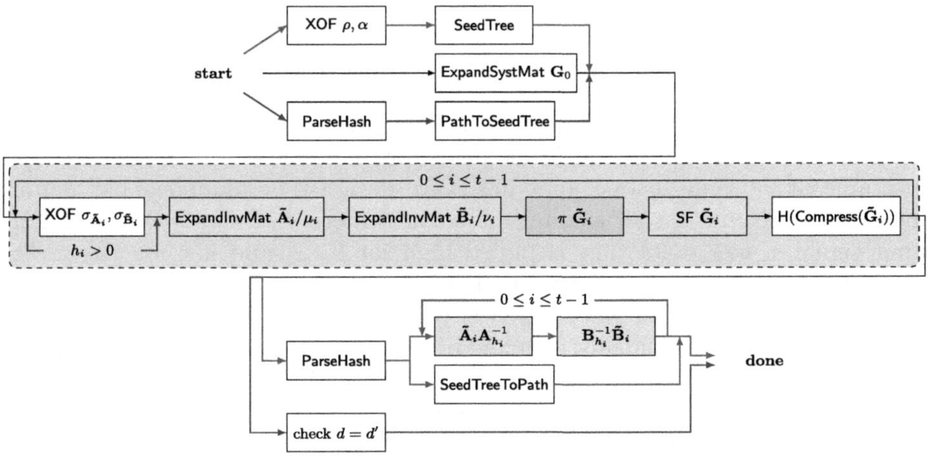

Fig. 1. Overview of the operational flow of our combined sign and verify module, red lines for sign only, blue lines for verify only. (Color figure online)

Signature generation starts with the generation of the seed δ of length $\ell_{\mathsf{sec\_seed}}$ from a randomness source. We assume that the seed δ will be initialized by a top-level hardware module, e.g., by interfacing to a True Random Number Generator (TRNG) or by implementing the NIST Known Answer Test (KAT) Pseudo Random Number Generator (PRNG). The seed δ is then expanded using the module `XOF` to the root seed ρ of length $\ell_{\mathsf{tree\_seed}}$ of the seed tree and a salt α of length ℓ_{salt}. In our hardware design, we accomplish this again using a `SHAKE256` module via a `XOF` wrapper. Then the next step is the seed tree generation using the root seed ρ and the salt α with the `SeedTree` module. Verification instead parses the hash and then generates the partial seed tree from the signature. We implement this in the modules `ParseHash` and `PathToSeedTree`.

For the main loop in sign and verify we need to expand the seeds σ_i from the seed tree leaves into seeds $\sigma_{\tilde{\mathbf{A}}_i}$ and $\sigma_{\tilde{\mathbf{B}}_i}$ and expand these seeds to $\tilde{\mathbf{A}}_i$ and

$\tilde{\mathbf{B}}_i$ (i.e., μ_i and ν_i respectively for verify) using a `ExpandInvMat` module. For signing, we store each σ_i in a memory which is later used to recompute $\sigma_{\tilde{\mathbf{A}}_i}$ and $\sigma_{\tilde{\mathbf{B}}_i}$ and then expand these seeds to $\tilde{\mathbf{A}}_i$ and $\tilde{\mathbf{B}}_i$ for computation of μ_i and ν_i. We then feed the matrices into a `Pi` module together with the matrix $\mathbf{G}_0$, compute the systematic form $\tilde{\mathbf{G}}_i$ of the result using the module `SF`. We pull the absorb-function of the hash function H into the loop to avoid the need to store all $\tilde{\mathbf{G}}_i$. We will describe the implementation of this loop in detail in Sect. 4.5.

The steps after the main loop are different for sign and verify. For sign, we also absorb the message msg into the hash state and finalize H to obtain the challenge vector. Then, to compute the final loop, we recompute $\sigma_{\tilde{\mathbf{A}}_i}$ and $\sigma_{\tilde{\mathbf{B}}_i}$ using σ_i, and then expand them to generate $\tilde{\mathbf{A}}_i$ and $\tilde{\mathbf{B}}_i$ for the computation of μ_i and ν_i using a matrix-matrix multiplication module. Eventually, we compute the seed tree path for the signature using `SeedTreeToPath`. For verify, we only need to check that $d = d'$ and set the return value of the module correspondingly.

3.2 Joint Security Parameter Design

One of the main questions we want to investigate in this work is the hardware overhead of supporting several prime fields for different security parameter sets selectable at runtime in one joint hardware design. For modules that require both 11-bit arithmetic in $\mathbb{F}_{2039}$ and 12-bit arithmetic in $\mathbb{F}_{4093}$, we are using an input signal `i_sel_4093` that is pulled high for $\mathbb{F}_{4093}$ and low for $\mathbb{F}_{2039}$. The bus width for field elements is set to 12 bit for the joint design, with the most significant bit set to zero when $\mathbb{F}_{2039}$ is being selected. Therefore, the cost for memory storing field elements is defined by the larger field in the joint design. A similar design approach of constructing field arithmetic modules capable of operating over two distinct prime fields was adopted in [AMI+23, MR24], where the authors integrated CRYSTALS-Kyber (which operates over a 12-bit prime field polynomial coefficients) and CRYSTALS-Dilithium (which utilizes a 23-bit prime field polynomial coefficients). In contrast, MEDS features prime fields that differ by only a single bit, enabling support for multiple fields with minimal overhead.

If the Verilog code is synthesised for one specific field only, we are fixing `i_sel_4093` to constant 0 or 1 respectively so that the optimization step during synthesis can remove unnecessary logic automatically. This enables us to get precised resource estimates for hardware designs supporting only one respective field and for the joint design with otherwise identical logic.

The remaining security parameters besides the prime field are matrix dimensions n, m, and k, the number s of pk matrices, as well as t and s for the challenge vector. All these other parameters mostly affect the upper limit of loops and can easily be selected using multiplexers at runtime at little resource overhead. We pre-compute related pre-defined constant values (e.g., counter widths) and provide them as macros and module parameters during synthesis (and simulation).

4 Implementation

For the description of our implementation of the MEDS signature scheme, we take a bottom-up approach. The different building blocks and sub-modules are described in the following including finite field arithmetic, matrix operations, and the complete sign and verify module.

4.1 Finite Field Arithmetic

As described in specified in Sect. 2.2, all underlying arithmetic operations multiplication, addition, and inversion in the MEDS signature scheme are performed in the prime field $\mathbb{F}_q$ where q is either the 11-bit prime $2039 = 2^{11} - 9$ or the 12-bit prime $4093 = 2^{12} - 3$. We implement these operations as integer arithmetic modulo the prime q. An overview of the resource consumption and performance for each module is provided in Table 2.

Table 2. Resource consumption and performance of the $\mathbb{F}_q$ arithmetic functions targeting an Xilinx Artix 7 (`xc7a200t`) FPGA.

Operation	q	Resources				Cycles	Freq.	Time	Time×Area
		Area		Memory					
		(LUT)	(DSP)	(FF)	(BRAM)	(cyc.)	(MHz)	(us)	
Addition	2 039	27	0	23	—	1	244	0.004	0.110×10^3
	4 093	28	0	25	—	1	221	0.005	0.127×10^3
	both	33	0	25	—	1	201	0.005	0.164×10^3
Multiplication	2 039	30	1	40	—	4	361	0.011	0.333×10^3
	4 093	44	1	41	—	4	357	0.011	0.494×10^3
	both	46	1	45	—	4	343	0.012	0.536×10^3
Inverse 2× parallel	2 039	0	0	1	1	1	392	0.003	—
	4 093	0	0	1	1.5	1	392	0.003	—
	both	12	0	1	2.5	1	269	0.004	0.045×10^3

Modular Multiplication. Since the size of each element in $\mathbb{F}_q$ is 11 or 12 bits, we can use the DSPs available on the target FPGA (AMD Artix 7 `xc7a200t-3`) to perform integer multiplication followed by full reduction. Using the DSPs helps to avoid long critical paths in the FPGA design. For modular reduction after integer multiplication, we design a specific modular reduction unit targeting the q value. As q is in a pseudo-Mersenne form ($q = 2^{11} - 9 = 2039$ or $q = 2^{12} - 3 = 4093$), we use the folding technique to perform the modular reduction [HGG07]. As the size of the multiplied output is up to $2\lceil \log_2(q) \rceil$ bits (i.e., 22 resp. 24 bits), we take the most-significant $\lceil \log_2(q) \rceil$ bits (i.e., 11 resp. 12 bits), of the output, multiply them by $2^{\lceil \log_2(q) \rceil} - q$ (i.e., $9 = 1001_b$ or $3 = 11_b$—since the binary representation of the factor is sparse, we simple shift-and-add instead of multiplying), and add this to the least significant $\lceil \log_2(q) \rceil$ bits (i.e., 11 resp. 12 bits). As the result of the addition may have more than $\lceil \log_2(q) \rceil$ bits, we repeat this folding process until all most-significant bits are folded and until there is no more carry generated from addition after folding. Eventually, we use a multiplexer at the intermediate folded result r to identify corner cases $r \geq q$ and in case we detect one of these cases, we subtract the modulus q from r.

Many computations in the joint design are the same for both fields. The only difference in the folding reduction step is that for $q = 2039$ we need to multiply the top bits by 9 and for $q = 4093$ by 3, which only requires an additional multiplexer. Also the final conditional subtraction just requires a multiplexer to select the prime.

The input-independent latency for our modular multiplication unit for all variants is four clock cycles. One register is placed after the multiplication unit followed by two registers to pipeline the reduction unit efficiently to reduce the overall critical path. The output is not registered by default.

Modular Inversion. This operation is mostly required for matrix systemization (described in detail in Sect. 4.3). To perform that computation efficiently, we require low-latency field inversion. To achieve this and since the size of the finite field $\mathbb{F}_q$ with 11 and 12 bits is relatively small, we decided not to use expensive, high-latency inversion algorithms like the extended Euclidean algorithm, Fermat's little theorem or Montgomery inversion for our modular inversion module. Instead, we trade computation for memory and precompute the inverse of all elements in $\mathbb{F}_q$ at synthesis time and store them as look-up table in Block RAM (BRAM). Hence, we have a input-independent latency of only one clock-cycle for performing modular inversion. To use the memory resources as efficiently as possible, we are exploiting the dual-ported interface of the BRAM to perform two independent inversions in parallel, hence halving the effective resource cost.

The joint design for this operation provides look-up tables for both primes and some additional logic for selecting the output of the requested field. The resource requirements are shown on Table 2.

Summary. The resource evaluation in Table 2 demonstrates that hardware support for multiple fields imposes only a small additional cost, provided the fields are "related," meaning they share the same reduction algorithm. Similar works that support two distinct prime fields [AMI+23, MR24] do not present a fine-grained analysis of the overhead introduced at the modular arithmetic level due to dual-field support; instead, they primarily emphasize the associated overhead at the level of polynomial multiplication units. In our reduction module, when employing the folding technique, efficient resource sharing can be achieved under the condition that the primes have a low Hamming distance. Consequently, supporting different prime fields in hardware is not prohibitively resource-intensive if the fields are selected carefully. This can make using different prime fields a viable design choice for cryptographic primitives when using different fields offers meaningful benefits, such as reduced signature or ciphertext sizes.

4.2 Matrix Multiplication

Matrix multiplication is one of the most used operations in the MEDS It is used in the π operation and for computing the μ_i and ν_i during signing. Consequently, we take care to design an efficient matrix multiplication unit that is parameterizable at synthesis time to enable performance trade-offs. As mentioned in Sect. 3.1, matrices in MEDS are specified to be sampled in row-wise order.

The general task of this module is to compute $\mathbf{C} = \mathbf{A} \cdot \mathbf{B}$. Instead of traditional schoolbook matrix multiplication with limited parallelism, we are using a vector-based approach similar to standard SIMD techniques in our matrix multiplication design.

Asymptotically more efficient matrix multiplication algorithms, e.g., Strassen or CoppersmithWinograd, do not apply to MEDS due to the relatively small matrix dimensions. Additionally, techniques such as the trick by Arlazarov, Dinic, Kronrod, and Faradžev [ADKF70], which are not asymptotically faster and are most effective for small fields when the matrix dimension exceeds the field size (e.g., GF(16) with matrix dimension up to 133 in [BCC+24]), are also not applicable in the context of MEDS due to the relatively large fields $\mathbb{F}_{2039}$ and $\mathbb{F}_{4093}$ and small matrix dimension of up to 30.

This approach allows us to take advantage of the pipelining of the $\mathbb{F}_q$ multiplier and also allows us to perform single-element additions in each iteration. This design also allows us to stream the inputs to the multiplication unit and to make best use of all pipelining registers. The latency l_{mm} of our matrix multiplication unit can be computed from the matrix dimensions d_1, d_2, and d_3, the number of pipeline stages l_{mmpipe}, and the performance parameter p_{mm} (i.e., the column-block width) as $l_{\mathrm{mm}} = l_{\mathrm{mmpipe}} + \frac{d_1 \cdot d_2 \cdot d_3}{p_{\mathrm{mm}}}$.

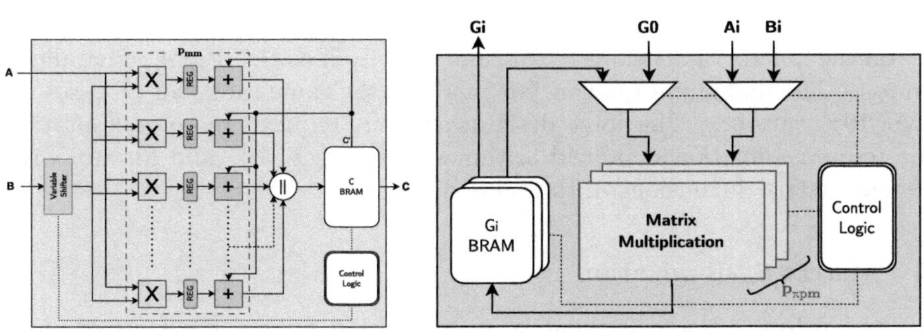

(a) matrix multiplication module. (b) π module.

Fig. 2. Hardware design of the matrix multiplication and π modules.

Performance and resource demands for the different parameter sets and design variants are shown in Table 3. Since the arithmetic latencies of the field-specific variants and the joint design are identical, the number of cycles depends

Table 3. Comparison of the time and area for our Matrix Multiplication module targeting Xilinx Artix 7 (xc7a200t) FPGA.

d_1, d_2, d_3	p_{mm}	q	Resources				Cycles	Freq.	Time	Time×**Area**
			Area		Memory					
			(LUT)	(DSP)	(FF)	(BRAM)	(cyc.)	(MHz)	(us)	
Parameter-set specific designs:										
14, 14, 14	2	4 093	279	2	197	0.5	1 380	218	6.34	2×10^3
22, 22, 22	2	4 093	294	2	206	0.5	5 332	218	24.50	7×10^3
30, 30, 30	2	2 039	298	2	206	0.5	13 508	195	69.20	21×10^3
14, 14, 14	4	4 093	383	4	317	1	792	218	3.64	1×10^3
22, 22, 22	4	4 093	396	4	332	1	2 912	218	13.38	5×10^3
30, 30, 30	4	2 039	387	4	320	1	7 208	218	33.11	13×10^3
14, 14, 14	8	4 093	598	8	565	1.5	400	218	1.84	1×10^3
22, 22, 22	8	4 093	625	8	580	1.5	1 460	199	7.32	5×10^3
30, 30, 30	8	2 039	606	8	556	1.5	3 608	199	18.09	11×10^3
Joint designs:										
14, 14, 14							1 380		6.93	2×10^3
22, 22, 22	2	both	335	2	220	0.5	5 332	199	26.79	9×10^3
30, 30, 30							13 508		67.88	23×10^3
14, 14, 14							792		3.65	2×10^3
22, 22, 22	4	both	460	4	348	1	2 912	217	13.42	6×10^3
30, 30, 30							7 208		33.23	15×10^3
14, 14, 14							400		2.04	2×10^3
22, 22, 22	8	both	753	8	612	1.5	1 460	196	7.43	6×10^3
30, 30, 30							3 608		18.36	14×10^3

only on the matrix dimensions d_1, d_2, and d_3 as well as the degree of parallelization p_{mm}. The maximum frequency is in about the same range for all cases with about 10% variance. The joint design, however, requires more computational logic resources for the joint field arithmetic (see Sect. 4.1) and for supporting different matrix dimensions in the same design.

4.3 Matrix Systemization

Our hardware design for matrix systemization follows the state-of-the art such as [SWM+10, WSN16, WSN17, CCD+22, ZZC+23, BCH+23]: We are using a processor array of a quadratic shape that processes column-blocks of the input matrix in several rounds consisting of several steps. For a detailed description of the operation of the systemizer, we refer to [CCD+22, Section 3].

The design in [BCH+23] combines matrix systemization and matrix multiplication in one design with the goal to share resources between these two operations. However, we are using a pipelined overall design to increase signing and verification performance and hence we need individual modules for matrix

Table 4. Comparison of the time and area for our Systemizer module targeting Xilinx Artix 7 (`xc7a200t`) FPGA.

Matrix Size rows×cols	p_{mm}	q	Resources				Cycles	Freq.	Time	Time×Area
			Area		Memory					
			(LUT)	(DSP)	(FF)	(BRAM)	(cyc.)	(MHz)	(us)	
Parameter-set specific designs:										
14 × 196	2	4 093	943	6	1 076	1.5	9 345	185	50.52	48×10^3
22 × 484	2	4 093	1 067	6	1 334	1.5	57 393	177	324.21	346×10^3
30 × 900	2	2 039	1 178	6	1 511	1.0	199 393	199	1002.15	$1\,181 \times 10^3$
14 × 196	4	4 093	2 172	20	2 670	3.0	2 718	177	15.39	33×10^3
22 × 484	4	4 093	2 288	20	3 155	3.0	15 702	183	85.94	197×10^3
30 × 900	4	2 039	2 388	20	3 408	2.0	53 222	173	308.32	736×10^3
14 × 196	8	4 093	6 442	72	7 030	7.5	794	193	4.12	27×10^3
22 × 484	8	4 093	6 645	72	8 192	7.5	4 069	166	24.54	163×10^3
30 × 900	8	2 039	6 783	72	8 939	5.0	13 490	170	79.24	537×10^3
Joint designs:										
14 × 196							9 345		52.67	67×10^3
22 × 484	2	both	1 263	6	1595	2.5	57 393	177	323.47	409×10^3
30 × 900							199 393		1123.78	$1\,419 \times 10^3$
14 × 196							2 718		15.72	44×10^3
22 × 484	4	both	2 778	20	3685	5.0	15 702	173	90.82	252×10^3
30 × 900							53 222		307.84	855×10^3
14 × 196							794		4.69	39×10^3
22 × 484	8	both	8 333	72	9138	10.0	4 069	169	24.04	200×10^3
30 × 900							13 490		79.71	664×10^3

systemization and multiplication. Due to the pipelined overall design, all modules are under load most of the time (as shown in Table 7) and resources are in use in parallel—and hence do not need to be shared to achieve efficiency.

The design in [ZZC+23] reduces memory cost by streaming out parts of the systemized matrix as complete columns become available during computation without storing the entire matrix on-chip. This optimization does not apply to MEDS (except if external memory is used), since the large $k \times nm$ matrices $\tilde{\mathbf{G}}_\mathbf{i}$ and $\hat{\mathbf{G}}_\mathbf{i}$ need to be fed row-wise into the hash function.

In contrast to earlier designs aiming at the systemization of matrices over $\mathbb{F}_2$ as they appear, e.g., in binary codes used for the code-based McEliece cryptosystem [SWM+10, WSN16, CCD+22] or matrices over binary fields as used, e.g., in code-based [WSN17] as well as multivariate cryptosystems [FG18, BCH+23], we are dealing with matrices over medium-sized prime fields, which means that we are dealing with a longer arithmetic latency: while binary field arithmetic in earlier work has a latency of one cycle, we decided to deal with the larger arithmetic latency by using several clock cycles for multiplication and addition. This does not affect the overall process of the systemization, but we need to take the latencies into consideration to avoid race conditions during the parallel processing of that data. For example, our design needs to wait for different amounts of overhead cycles between consecutive rounds to wait for data of the previous round being written back to memory depending on the number of column blocks that are being processed in between. Depending on the size of the processor array, the arithmetic latencies add up and we quickly get an overall latency of the processor array of dozens of cycles. However, in contrast to earlier designs [WSN16, WSN17, CCD+22] we do pipeline computation between consecutive rounds as much as possible.

Similar to [BCH+23], we are not too concerned about systemization failures, which happen only very rarely for our field sizes:

The probability that a random $n \times m$ matrix ($m \geq n$) over a finite field $\mathbb{F}_q$ has a systematic form is the same as that of an $n \times n$ matrix over $\mathbb{F}_q$ being full rank. For large n and q, this probability is approximately $1 - \frac{1}{q}$. Hence, for $q = 4093$, we have a probability of success for the SF operation in Algorithm 1 of about 99.98% and for $q = 2039$ of about 99.96%. In other words, we expect a failure to systemize a matrix over $\mathbb{F}_q$ roughly every q attempts—for $q = 4093$ we expect one failure roughly every 4093 and for $q = 2039$ roughly every 2039 systemization attempts. Therefore, we omit some of the tweaks described in [CCD+22]: As we do not require a mechanism to detect failure as early as possible but only at the end of systemization, we do not need store all operations that are generated in pivoting steps in-place in the data memory for later use. Instead, we can use a relatively small additional memory as in [WSN16, WSN17, BCH+23] to store the operations only of the current pivoting step, overwriting those of previous steps. Similar to these designs, we detect systemization failure at the end of the computation in the final pivoting step.

Figure 3 shows an overview of the systemizer module. We use the performance parameter p_{sys} to specify the number of both rows and columns of the processor array. The number of columns corresponds to the column-block width of the corresponding BRAM that stores the matrix data. We are grouping the processor elements of each row into a vector Arithmetic Logic Units (ALUs) of width p_{sys}.

The design operates by feeding matrix data in column blocks row-by-row into the processor array, one row in each cycle. Once a pivot matrix row reaches the corresponding processor row, it is stored in registers `SAR[i,j]`. The pivoting rows need to be normalized, which requires a scalar inversion and a scalar-vector multiplication. Later in the process, incoming rows are reduced by the pivoting row, which requires a scalar multiplication and a subtraction.

Now, as mentioned before, the prime-filed arithmetic operations have a considerable latency. Since processor array operates in a pipelined fashion, the result of the normalization is already required for the next input. Overcoming the latencies of the normalization would require several buffer stages. Also, we would like to use only one vector unit computing scalar-vector multiplication and vector addition, not two for normalization and reduction.

Our solution to this problem is to delay the normalization of pivoting rows until they are read out of the processor array. This means that a new pivot row can be stored in `SAR[i,j]` unmodified and is available without further latency

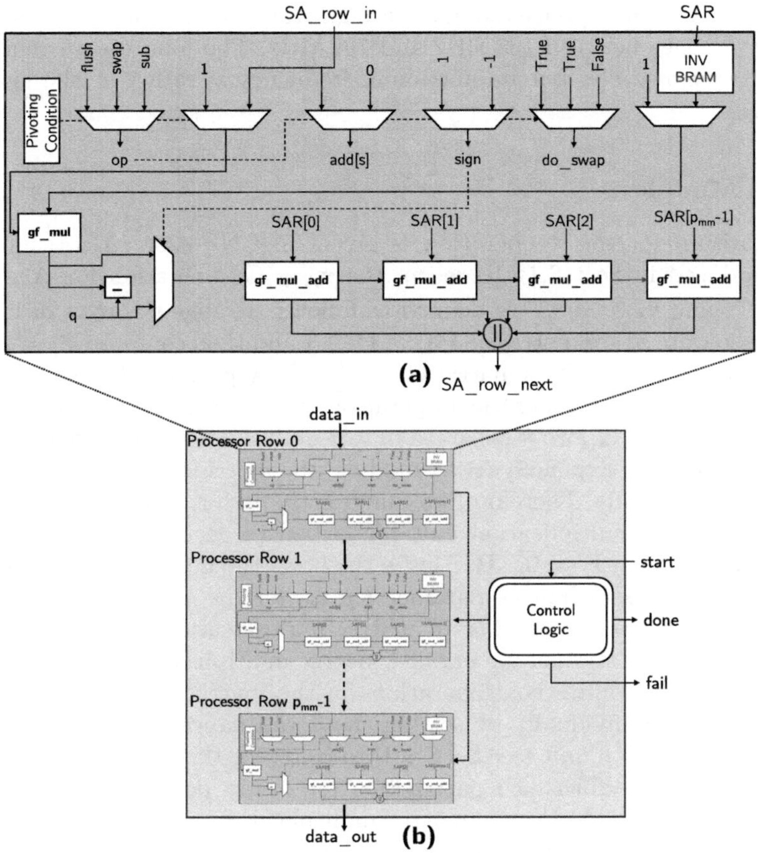

Fig. 3. Systemizer module with p_{sys} vector ALUs of width p_{sys}.

in the next cycle. For the normalization and reduction we now can use just one single vector ALU, but we need to prepare the respective inputs at the cost of several cycles of latency. The vector ALU now always multiplies `SAR[i,j]` by a scalar factor either for normalization or for reduction and adds an input vector to the result which is either all zero for normalization or input matrix data for reduction. We need one additional scalar-scalar multiplication per processor row for normalizing the pivot row towards reducing follow-up rows.

The top part of Fig. 3 shows the pipelined modules that prepare the inputs for and control the behavior of the vector unit and the bottom part shows the vector unit itself with p_{sys} multiply-and-add units. The overall latency of each processor row is defined by the sequential operation of the top part and the parallel latency of bottom part as the latencies of one multiplication, one addition, and one multiply-and-add operation plus some additional latencies to optimize data paths of control logic.

The performance of our systemizer design is shown in Table 4. The maximum frequency ranges between 166 MHz and 199 MHz. The joint design requires the same number of cycles but its maximum frequency is rather at the low end of the range.

4.4 Pi Module

The algorithm for the π operation is given in [CNP+23a, Algorithm 7] and was introduced in Sect. 2.1. To recap, the $\pi_{\mathbf{A},\mathbf{B}}(\mathbf{G})$ operation for $\mathbf{A} \in \mathbb{F}_q^{m\times m}$, $\mathbf{B} \in \mathbb{F}_q^{n\times n}$, and $\mathbf{G} \in \mathbb{F}_q^{k\times mn}$ is defined as follows: arrange the rows of matrix $\mathbf{G}$ into a k separate $m \times n$ matrices $\{\mathbf{P}_0, ..., \mathbf{P}_{k-1}\}$ and then compute $\mathbf{P}'_i = \mathbf{A}\cdot\mathbf{P}_i\cdot\mathbf{B}$. Finally, we get the result as matrix $\mathbf{G}' \in \mathbb{F}_q^{k\times mn}$ by packing $\mathbf{P}'_i$ into row i of $\mathbf{G}'$.

In our implementation of the π operation, we avoid the first step of arranging the rows of matrix $\mathbf{G}$ into k separate $m \times n$ matrices. Instead, while generating matrix $\mathbf{G}$ using the `ExpandSystMat` module, the matrix is already arranged in k separate BRAM units. Therefore, we can directly perform the $\mathbf{A}\cdot\mathbf{P}_i\cdot\mathbf{B}$ operation using our matrix multiplication unit (described in Sect. 4.2). We first perform $\mathbf{T} = \mathbf{A} \cdot \mathbf{P}$ and then $\mathbf{P}' = \mathbf{T} \cdot \mathbf{B}$. Figure 2b shows the design of our π module.

We provide a performance parameter $p_{\pi\text{pm}}$ for the k matrix multiplications such that we can select number of matrix multiplications to be performed in parallel (the "pm" strands for parallel matrix multiplications). We control the number of parallel finite field operations in the matrix multiplication units of the π operation individually by setting the performance parameter p_{mm} of the matrix multiplication unit (see Sect. 4.2) to $p_{\pi\text{mm}}$ for the π operation. This gives us two different performance parameters for our π design: first, the number $p_{\pi\text{mm}}$ of prime field ALUs per matrix multiplication and second, the number $p_{\pi\text{pm}}$ of parallel matrix multiplications. The latency l_π of our π operation is $l_\pi = \frac{k}{p_{\pi\text{pm}}}\left(2l_{\text{mmpipe}} + \frac{mmn+mnn}{p_{\pi\text{mm}}}\right)$ with l_{mm} and l_{mmpipe} as defined in Sect. 4.2.

The synthesis results for our `Pi` module for different configurations are shown in Table 5. The maximum frequency is similar for all variants. The larger matrix dimensions for $k, m, m = 30$ seem to outweigh the smaller resource requirement of $\mathbb{F}_{2039}$ arithmetic. The resource overhead of the joint design compared to the field-specific variants is moderate.

4.5 Signing and Verification

Figure 4 shows the block diagram of the overall hardware design combining both MEDS sign and verify algorithms detailed in Algorithms 1 and 2 respectively by sharing hardware modules between both operations.

In sign, we assume that byte deserialization of the input data for the secret key `sk` into the seed $\sigma_{\mathbf{G}_0}$ and the matrices $\mathbf{A}_i^{-1}$ and $\mathbf{B}_i^{-1}$ using the `Decompress` module are performed on a higher layer. We also leave the composition of the signed message $\mathsf{msg}_{\mathsf{sig}}$ including the serialization of output data μ_i and ν_i using the `Compress` module to a higher layer and just provide read ports to its components as output ports to the design. We also omit the implementation of the

Table 5. Comparison of the time and area for our Pi module targeting Xilinx Artix 7 (`xc7a200t`) FPGA for $p_{\pi mm} = 4$.

k, m, n	$p_{\pi pm}$	q	Resources				Cycles	Freq.	Time	Time×Area
			Area		Memory					
			(LUT)	(DSP)	(FF)	(BRAM)	(cyc.)	(MHz)	(us)	
Parameter-set specific designs:										
14, 14, 14	2	4 093	1 329	8	660	2	25 474	218	117.03	155.0×10^3
22, 22, 22	2	4 093	1 610	8	706	2	91 354	218	419.68	675.0×10^3
30, 30, 30	2	2 039	1 655	8	688	2	223 474	218	1 026.64	$1\,697.0 \times 10^3$
14, 14, 14	4	4 093	2 172	16	1 248	4	13 588	218	62.42	135.0×10^3
22, 22, 22	4	4 093	2 204	16	1 313	4	48 724	196	249.17	548.0×10^3
30, 30, 30	4	2 039	2 457	16	1 269	4	119 188	196	609.53	$1\,494.0 \times 10^3$
14, 14, 14	8	4 093	3 350	32	2 438	8	6 796	218	31.22	104.0×10^3
22, 22, 22	8	4 093	3 526	32	2 536	8	24 364	218	111.93	394.0×10^3
30, 30, 30	8	2 039	4 028	32	2 437	8	59 596	218	273.78	$1\,101.0 \times 10^3$
Joint designs:										
14, 14, 14							25 474		117.44	197.0×10^3
22, 22, 22	2	both	1 891	8	751	2	91 354	217	421.14	705.0×10^3
30, 30, 30							223 474		1 030.22	$1\,725.0 \times 10^3$
14, 14, 14							13 588		62.64	190.0×10^3
22, 22, 22	4	both	2 856	16	1 392	4	48 724	217	224.62	682.0×10^3
30, 30, 30							119 188		549.46	$1\,668.0 \times 10^3$
14, 14, 14							6 796		31.33	174.0×10^3
22, 22, 22	8	both	4 732	32	2 661	8	24 364	217	112.32	623.0×10^3
30, 30, 30							59 596		274.74	$1\,523.0 \times 10^3$

random number generator Randombytes and instead assume that the random seed δ is provided from a higher level.

Similarly, in verification, we assume that byte deserialization of the input data for the public key pk into the seed $\sigma_{\mathbf{G}_0}$ and deserialization of signed message $\mathsf{msg}_{\mathsf{sig}}$ into p, d, α, and msg are performed at a higher layer.

We note that, in our hardware design, the operations `XOF`, `ExpandInvMat`, `SeedTree`, and `PathToSeedTree` share the same SHAKE256 module as shown in Fig. 4 but that we use a separate SHAKE256 module that is shared between `ExpandSystMat`, `ParseHash` for the combined `Compress` and `Hash` operation (Algorithm 1 in Algorithm 1 and Algorithm 2 in Algorithm 2). The reason for this will be described in the discussion of the loop pipeline later on in this section.

The most expensive operations π and `SF` are in the main for-loops of the sign and verify operations i.e., Algorithm 1 to Algorithm 1 in Algorithm 1 and Algorithm 2 to Algorithm 2 in Algorithm 2 respectively. Initially, we had considered to construct a large finite field vector ALU for the use in both π and `SF`. However, the required multiplexing and control logic likely would have been inef-

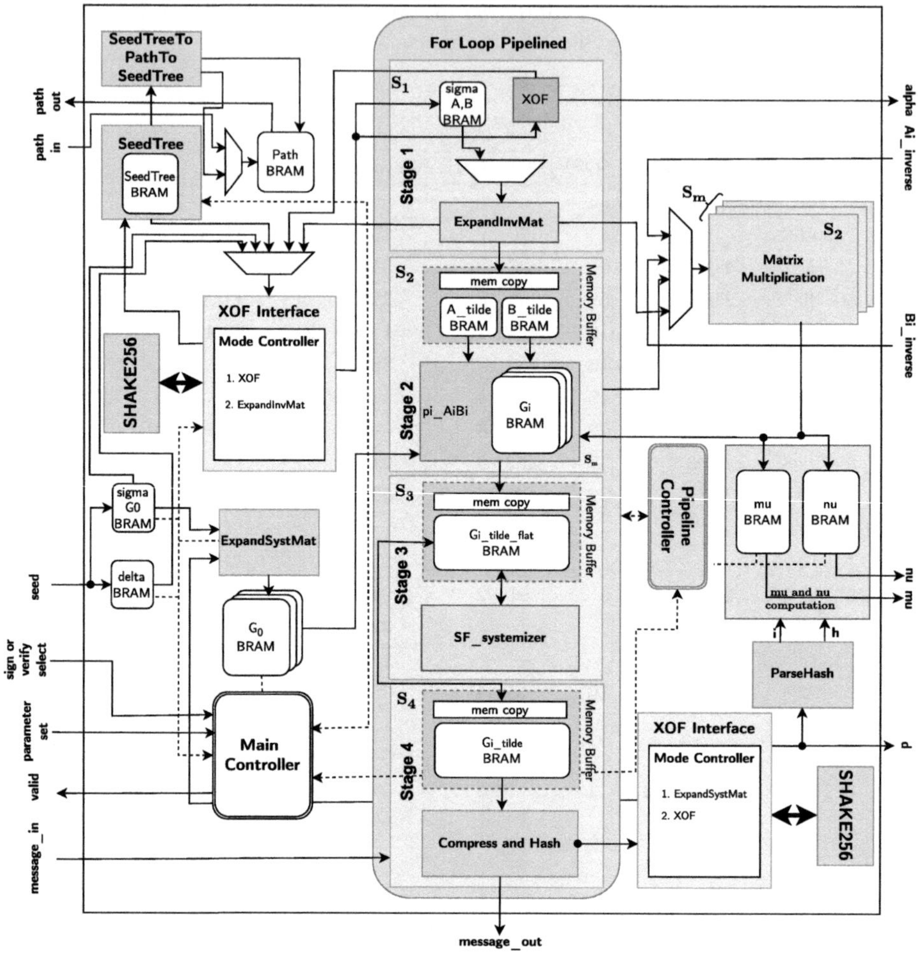

Fig. 4. High-level design overview of the MEDS signing operation.

ficient, complex, error prone, and hard to maintain. Also, π requires about two times more finite field multiplications compared to SF but no finite field inversions and the different matrices that are systemized in SF and ExpandInvMat have different dimensions. A joint large finite field vector ALU would hence lead to a less fine-grained control over performance vs. area trade-offs between those operations. Therefore, to obtain high performance and high efficiency, we decided to implement this loop in a pipelined fashion with four pipeline stages.

Stage 1: This stage consists of operations involved in Algorithms 1 to 1 of Algorithm 1 and Algorithms 2 to 2 and Algorithms 2 and 2 of Algorithm 2. In signing, first a leaf seed (σ_i) concatenated with the salt (α) and the iteration number (i) is extended into two seeds $\sigma_{\tilde{A}_i}$, $\sigma_{\tilde{B}_i}$ using the XOF module. Then

$\sigma_{\tilde{A}_i}$ and $\sigma_{\tilde{B}_i}$ are used to generate invertible matrices $\tilde{A}_i$ and $\tilde{B}_i$. In our hardware design, we accomplish the generation of $\sigma_{\tilde{A}_i}$ and $\sigma_{\tilde{B}_i}$ using the `SHAKE256` module and the `XOF` interface module by selecting the "XOF mode". The expanded seeds are stored in `sigmaAB` BRAM. Then, the `ExpandInvMat` module uses the seed $\sigma_{\tilde{A}_i}$ and the `XOF` interface and `SHAKE256` module by selecting the "ExpandInvMat" mode. This generates data for matrix $\tilde{A}_i$ and the `Systemizer` module inside the `ExpandInvMat` module is used to check if the matrix is invertible or not. If it is not invertible then, the module draws another matrix from the current `SHAKE256` state and performs another check for invertability of the matrix. This process is repeated until an invertible matrix is found. Once it is ensured that the matrix is invertible then $\tilde{B}_i$ is generated in similar fashion. We note that, for each iteration i, we store the related σ_i value in a BRAM inside Stage 1 for later use in computing μ_i and ν_i matrices.

In verification, if the value of $h_i = 0$ then all operations in stage 1 are similar to signing except here we use $\sigma_{\hat{A}_i}$ and $\sigma_{\hat{B}_i}$ and generate invertible matrices μ_i and ν_i. And in the case of $h_i > 0$, we skip the sampling part inside the `ExpandInvMat` and instead copy the μ_i and ν_i from the input into the BRAM where sampled μ_i and ν_i are stored and check for their invertability. In case the μ_i or ν_i are non-invertible, then a global "systemization fail" signal is generated, which will trigger "invalid signature" output.

Stage 2: This stage consists of the π operation (i.e., Algorithm 1 of Algorithm 1 and Algorithm 2 of Algorithm 2). In signing, this operation involves matrix multiplication of rows of $\mathbf{G}_0 \in \mathbb{F}_q^{k\times mn}$ with matrix $\tilde{\mathbf{A}}_i \in \mathbb{F}_q^{m\times m}$ and with $\tilde{\mathbf{B}}_i \in \mathbb{F}_q^{n\times n}$. As shown in Fig. 4, in our hardware design, this operation is accomplished by the `Pi` module using $\mathbf{G}_0$ from `G0 BRAM` and $\tilde{\mathbf{A}}_i$, $\tilde{\mathbf{B}}_i$ (generated in Stage 1). For verification, similar operations are performed as for signing except that $\mathbf{G}_{hi}$, μ_i, and ν_i are being processed in place of $\mathbf{G}_0$, $\tilde{\mathbf{A}}_i$, and $\tilde{\mathbf{B}}_i$.

Stage 3: This stage consists of operation SF and the checking if the $\tilde{\mathbf{G}}_i$ has systematic form (i.e., Algorithm 1 of Algorithm 1 or Algorithm 2 of Algorithm 2). We use a `Systemizer` module (described in Sect. 4.3) to compute the systematic form. As described in Sect. 4.3, there is a possibility that the input matrix does not have a systematic form. We describe how we handle this situation in detail below. This step is the same for sign and verify with corresponding inputs.

Stage 4: This stage consists of operations for compressing and hashing matrices $\tilde{\mathbf{G}}_i$ together with the message msg (i.e., Algorithm 1 of Algorithm 1). Although the compress and hash operation are not part of the for loop in the algorithm, in our hardware design we move the compression and the hash-absorb operation inside the for loop. This avoids the need to store all $\tilde{\mathbf{G}}_i$ values in the memory, which would require a significant amount of BRAM storage on the FPGA. For this, we use a dedicated `SHAKE256` module for Stage 4. This `SHAKE256` module digests each $\tilde{\mathbf{G}}_i$ and maintains the hash state. Hence, we only need to store one $\tilde{\mathbf{G}}_i$ in the memory at a given time. This step is the same for sign and verify.

After finishing all t iterations of the loop, the message input is absorbed into the state as well and finally we squeeze the hash state to compute the hash value d.

Pipeline Control and Memory Buffering. The pipelined part of our hardware design is highlighted in blue in Fig. 4. The pipelining in our hardware design varies from the traditional register-based pipelining: Since the data we move from one stage to another are relatively large matrices, we use BRAMs as buffers between the pipeline stages. These memory buffers are shown as blush pink blocks in Fig. 4. The `MemCopy` modules copy the data from the internal memories of each stage and move the data to the memory buffers, which can then be consumed in the next stage.

As the workload of each stage is different, the number of clock cycles taken by each stage is also different. Therefore, to balance the clock cycles taken by each stage, we introduce the following five performance parameters:

- S_1: Stage 1 performance parameter that corresponds to the performance parameter p_{sys} (see Sect. 4.3) of the matrix systemizer for checking the invertability of $\tilde{A}_i$ and $\tilde{B}_i$ in the sign operation respective μ_i and ν_i in verify. S_1 controls the number of rows and columns in the processor array used inside the matrix systemizer.
- S_2: Stage 2 performance parameter that corresponds to the performance parameter $p_{\pi\text{mm}}$ (see Sect. 4.4) of the matrix multiplication unit inside the `Pi` module. S_2 controls the vector width inside the matrix multiplication unit.
- S_{mat}: Stage 2 performance parameter that corresponds to the performance parameter $p_{\pi\text{pm}}$ of the `Pi` module used inside stage 2. S_{mat} controls number of matrix multiplications performed in parallel.
- S_3: Stage 3 performance parameter that corresponds to the performance parameter p_{sys} (see Sect. 4.3) of the large $k \times m \cdot n$ matrix systemizer used inside stage 3 for computing the systematic form of $\tilde{G}_i$ in sign respective $\hat{G}_i$ in verify. S_3 controls the number of rows and columns in the processor array used inside the matrix systemizer.
- S_4: Stage 4 performance parameter that corresponds to the shifter width used inside the compress and hash module. Larger S_4 leads to fewer memory accesses while compressing and hashing the matrices $\tilde{G}_i$ respective $\hat{G}_i$.

Choosing Suitable Performance Parameters. Recall that the goal behind choosing the performance parameters is to balance the pipeline stages so that all the modules in the pipeline are busy with their respective workloads. Let us look at the methodology we followed using the example (shown in Table 6) for the Security Level I parameter sets: Firstly, we fix the value of $S_{mat} = 1$ and then we assign all possible values to S_1, S_2, S_3, and S_4 based on the MEDS parameters up to $m = n = k = 14$ as shown in Table 6. To further lower the latency of stage 2, the S_{mat} parameter can be tweaked. The latencies reported in Table 6 also include the clock cycles required for buffering data from one stage to another. Based on these latencies, we chose a value for each S_1, S_2, S_3, and S_4 to meet our optimization goal (performance or resource consumption),

As an example for parameters with moderate resource requirement, we can select $S_1 = 1, S_2 = 7, S_3 = 6$, and $S_4 = 6$ (marked in Table 6) such that the cycles counts are roughly equal. Setting $S_{mat} = 4$ in this example brings down the cycle count of stage 2 to about $12\,132/4 = 3033$ (plus the unaffected overhead for data movement between the stages).

Based on this method, we propose different configurations for specific parameter sets as well as for a unified design that aim at balancing the pipeline stages in all parameter sets as shown in Table 7. We propose two variants of configurations: 1) a balanced design choice and 2) a high performance design choice as shown in Table 7. The choice to parameters is not just limited to the combinations provided in Table 7. Several such parameter combinations can be constructed based on resources available on the target device. We note that when selecting the parameters for a unified design, to avoid resource wastage, we limit the values of parameters based on m, n, and k values of smallest parameter set.

Table 6. Latencies of all pipeline stages for the Security Level 1 parameter sets with performance parameter $S_{mat} = 1$.

$S_1 = S_2 = S_3 = S_4$	Stage 1	Stage 2	Stage 3	Stage 4
1	3534	83364	48191	16599
2	1432	41812	14877	8521
3	1142	29926	8350	5883
4	1104	23990	5702	4503
5	1042	18054	4020	3751
6	1120	18054	3557	3178
7	980	12132	2477	2782
8	1032	12118	2294	2522
9	1084	12118	2153	2484
10	1136	12118	2054	2371
11	1188	12118	1955	2652
12	1240	12118	1912	2197
13	1292	12118	1869	2137
14	975	6195	1643	1796

Data Flow. To cope with the different ready-times of each stage that results from the different cycle counts, we resort to a handshake-based control mechanism to control the flow of data between the stages. After each stage is done with its computation, it sends a handshake signal to the next stage to indicate that the output data is ready for consumption and waits for the response from the next stage. This handshake mechanism is handled by the `PipelineController` module shown in Fig. 4.

As mentioned above in Stage 3, an additional challenge in the pipeline design is the handling of possible systemization failures in some iteration i in Stage 3. In this case, we need to repeat the operations of the previous stages starting again at iteration i. We flush all the data from Stages 1 and 2, which are working on data that belongs to iterations $i + 1$ and $i + 2$, restart Stage 1 from iteration i, and step by step refill the pipeline. Stage 4 is not affected by this as it is working on data that belongs to iteration $i - 1$. The reason we restart from iteration i is

Table 7. Configuration table showing selected configurations for $S_1, S_2, S_3, S_4, S_{mat}$ and idle percentages for the different stages for each configuration. In case of the unified design the idle percentages are average of different security levels.

Design Choice	Parameter Set	q	Perf. Metrics					Stage-wise Idle %			
			S_1	S_2	S_3	S_4	S_{mat}	1	2	3	4
Balanced	Level I	4093	1	7	6	6	3	3.6%	0.0%	3.4%	6.1%
	Level III	4093	1	11	8	9	5	0.5%	1.7%	0.0%	0.5%
	Level V	2039	1	10	10	12	5	0.0%	4.4%	2.8%	5.8%
	Unified Level I–V	both	1	10	10	12	5	3.4%	5.5%	15.4%	15.7%
High Perf.	Level I	4093	2	14	14	14	4	5.7%	3.8%	2.4%	0.0%
	Level III	4093	2	11	22	22	8	1.5%	0.3%	0.0%	3.9%
	Level V	2039	2	15	14	15	8	0.2%	2.7%	0.6%	0.0%
	Unified Level I–V	both	2	14	14	14	4	18.4%	1.3%	17.5%	13.9%

because of the on-the-fly `CompressHash` operation in Stage 4. The data fed into the `SHAKE256` module has to be in sequential order to produce the correct hash value. This means that we would need memory buffers after Stage 3 to store data related to iterations $i + 1$ and $i + 2$ and wait until data from iteration i becomes ready to be loaded into module `CompressHash`. We avoid this expensive memory buffering by simply restarting the pipeline. As the failure probability of the systemizer is low (as specified in Sect. 4.3), the overhead of restarting the pipeline is marginal. To restart Stage 1 with iteration i, Stage 1 requires to backup the seed for i, i.e., σ_i generated in Algorithm 1 of Algorithm 1. After Stage 3 has completed successfully, the stored σ_i is discarded. The logic related to flushing and restarting is also handled by the `PipelineController` module.

Other Operations. After the loop is finished, the `CompressHash` module requests the message `msg` as data stream from input port `message_in` and the message is loaded into the `SHAKE256` module to compute the hash value d. Following that, for verification, this d value is compared against the input d value to ensure the verification of the signature. Where as for signing, the value d is then loaded into the `ParseHash` module shown in Fig. 4, which parses the hash value and generates the vector h. The `ParseHash` module also captures i values where $h_i > 0$ while generating t. This is useful for the following computation of μ_i and ν_i. Rather than iterating over all t values, we only iterate over the w indices where $h_i > 0$. To compute matrices μ_i and ν_i, We first generate the matrices $\tilde{\mathbf{A}}_i$ and $\tilde{\mathbf{B}}_i$ using the σ_i seeds stored in Stage 1 and by reusing the logic from Stage 1. The reason for regenerating the matrices $\tilde{\mathbf{A}}_i$ and $\tilde{\mathbf{B}}_i$ is to avoid storing the t - $n \times n$ matrices and t - $m \times m$ matrices, which would otherwise consume a significant amount of BRAM. Therefore, we opted for regenerating the matrices instead. Then, we reuse the `MatMul` units of the `Pi` module. The result is then stored in BRAMs `mu` and `nu` respectively. If the `Pi` module is configured to use multiple matrix multiplication units, the `MuNuComputation` module computes μ_i and ν_i matrices in parallel. In parallel to the computation of μ_i and ν_i, the h vector along with

ρ and α are loaded into the `SeedTreeToPath` module, which generates the seed path. The μ_i, ν_i, p, d, α values finally can be accessed by a top-level module through the output ports `mu`, `nu`, `path`, `d`, and `alpha` respectively as shown in Fig. 4.

5 Evaluation

Table 8 shows the time and area results for our MEDS signing and verification hardware design for all parameter sets targeting an AMD `xc7a200t-3` FPGA. We note that the maximum clock frequency is limited by two different factors: 1) In case of MEDS-9923, the critical path lies inside the duplicate detection logic inside the `ParseHash` module. We use a bit-vector mapping technique to perform the duplicate detection and since the value t is large in case of MEDS-9923, the fully combinatorial variable shifter and comparator is quite large. 2) In all other cases, the critical path lies inside the sampling unit of `XOF` interface.

As discussed in Sect. 4.5, we propose two different design variants for our implementation: "Balanced" and "High Performance". The results for these choices are presented in Table 8. While the high performance design requires only 4.5 ms to 29.5 ms for signing and a similar amount of time for verification, it also takes up significant resources, mainly in terms of BRAM utilization. We note that while the storage required for the data remains the same in both the design choices, due to the wider memory word width in the High Performance variant, the synthesis tool needs to use multiple BRAM units.

Additionally, for each of the design variants, the design allows further flexibility to be synthesized for a specific parameter set or for a unified design that allows us to choose any of the six different parameter choices at run-time. While the unified design does not impact the cycles taken for signing and verification compared to specific designs, it does have an impact on resource utilization. However, it can be seen from Table 8 that the resource utilization of the unified design is close to the utilization of the parameter set specific designs for the biggest parameter sets (i.e., MEDS-134180 and MEDS-167717).

We note that to the best of our knowledge this is the first and only MEDS hardware implementation. Therefore, our primary comparison is with the optimized software implementation provided along with the MEDS specification [CNP+23a]. We note that while our design is running at a frequency range of 115 MHz to 133 MHz, the software implementations results are reported for a CPU running at a frequency of 1.9 GHz. We note that both of our design choices outperform the optimized software implementation by a significant margin as shown in Table 8. Our hardware implementation achieves a speed-up of 69× to 322× in sign + verify cycles compared to the software implementation. Similarly, it achieves a speed-up of 4.1× to 21.5× in sign + verify time, despite operating at a significantly lower frequency than the processor used in the software implementation. This answers Research Question 1 positively, showing that MEDS algorithms provide inherent parallelism which can be exploited through hardware implementation to provide substantial speed-up as demonstrated by our results (in Table 8).

Table 8. Performance data for our `Sign` and `Verify` modules targeting a Xilinx Artix 7 (`xc7a200t`) FPGA. Improvements are calculated as $T \times A = (t_{sign} + t_{verify}) \times LUT$ $cyc = \frac{(Sign+Verify\ Cycles\ for\ Software)}{(Sign+Verify\ Cycles\ for\ Hardware)}$, $t = \frac{(Sign+Verify\ time\ for\ Software)}{(Sign+Verify\ time\ for\ Hardware)}$.

MEDS Parameter Set	Resources				Time					Improvement		
	Area		Memory		Freq.	Sign		Verify		cyc	t	T×A
	LUT $\times 10^3$	DSP	FF $\times 10^3$	BRAM	MHz	Mcyc	ms	Mcyc	ms			$\times 10^6$
Balanced – $\{S_1, S_2, S_3, S_4, S_{mat}\} = \{1, 7, 6, 6, 3\}$												
MEDS-9923	24.3	66	20.5	111.5	116	7.5	65	7.4	64	69	4.1	3.1
MEDS-13220	21.6	66	19.5	69.5	130	1.3	10	1.2	10	68	4.6	0.4
High Performance – $\{S_1, S_2, S_3, S_4, S_{mat}\} = \{2, 14, 14, 14, 3\}$												
MEDS-9923	46.8	259	44.8	192.5	115	3.3	29	3.3	29	154	9.3	2.7
MEDS-13220	44.1	259	43.8	150.5	132	0.6	4	0.6	4	154	10.6	0.4
Balanced – $\{S_1, S_2, S_3, S_4, S_{mat}\} = \{1, 11, 8, 9, 5\}$												
MEDS-41711	34.0	130	31.2	205.5	123	9.8	80	9.5	78	151	9.8	5.3
MEDS-69497	33.1	130	30.7	187	125	2.9	23	2.5	20	141	9.2	1.4
High Performance – $\{S_1, S_2, S_3, S_4, S_{mat}\} = \{2, 11, 22, 22, 8\}$												
MEDS-41711	80.5	601	91.0	204.5	129	6.1	47	5.9	46	242	16.4	7.6
MEDS-69497	79.6	601	90.5	186	129	1.8	14	1.5	12	227	15.4	2.1
Balanced – $\{S_1, S_2, S_3, S_4, S_{mat}\} = \{1, 10, 10, 12, 5\}$												
MEDS-134180	38.3	163	39.5	284.5	130	11.2	87	9.0	70	160	10.9	5.9
MEDS-167717	38.0	163	39.4	327.5	133	8.1	61	5.3	40	141	9.8	3.9
High Performance – $\{S_1, S_2, S_3, S_4, S_{mat}\} = \{2, 15, 14, 15, 8\}$												
MEDS-134180	61.5	337	60.9	290	127	5.4	43	4.5	36	322	21.5	4.9
MEDS-167717	60.6	337	60.9	288	131	3.9	29	2.7	21	290	19.9	3.0
Unified Design												
Balanced – $\{S_1, S_2, S_3, S_4, S_{mat}\} = \{1, 10, 10, 12, 5\}$												
MEDS-9923	44.8	163	43.1	344.5	113	5.2	46	5.1	46	100	5.9	4.1
MEDS-13220						0.9	8	0.8	8	98	5.8	0.7
MEDS-41711						13.4	119	13.1	116	110	6.5	10.6
MEDS-69497						3.8	34	3.4	31	105	6.2	2.9
MEDS-134180						11.2	100	9.0	80	160	9.4	8.0
MEDS-167717						8.1	72	5.3	47	141	8.3	5.3
High Performance – $\{S_1, S_2, S_3, S_4, S_{mat}\} = \{2, 14, 14, 14, 4\}$												
MEDS-9923	72.8	273	63.4	386.5	113	3.3	33	3.3	33	154	8.2	4.2
MEDS-13220						0.5	6	0.5	5	154	8.2	0.7
MEDS-41711						10.2	100	10.1	99	144	7.7	12.9
MEDS-69497						2.7	27	2.6	25	145	7.7	3.3
MEDS-134180						11.1	109	10.7	104	149	7.9	13.7
MEDS-167717						6.7	67	6.2	61	146	7.8	8.2
Reference Software Implementation on an AMD Ryzen 7 PRO 5850U CPU [CNP+23a]												
MEDS-9923	—	—	—	—	1 900	518.0	273	515.5	271	—	—	—
MEDS-13220	—	—	—	—	1 900	88.9	47	87.4	46	—	—	—
MEDS-41711	—	—	—	—	1 900	1 467.0	772	1 461.9	769	—	—	—
MEDS-55604	—	—	—	—	1 900	387.2	204	380.7	200	—	—	—
MEDS-134180	—	—	—	—	1 900	1 629.8	858	1 612.5	849	—	—	—
MEDS-167717	—	—	—	—	1 900	961.8	506	938.8	494	—	—	—

Comparison to Related Work. Table 9 presents a comparison to a number of other PQC signature schemes that have been presented in literature. We are unaware of other MEDS hardware implementations, so no other MEDS works are included in the table. Many works present data for the same XC7A100T FPGA that we use and they generally report similar frequencies as we. Specific comparisons with these schemes to our implementation is difficult as different schemes are based on different mathematical problems. Further, some related works use high-end FPGAs, which generally give much better performance.

Table 9. Existing FPGA-based hardware implementations of various PQC signature schemes. For the listed related work, if the prior work implemented different variants of an algorithm, the fastest design is listed. The "—" indicates that the corresponding parameter was not specified or not implemented. $\mathbf{T}\times\mathbf{A} = \frac{(t_{sign}+t_{verify})\times LUT}{10^6}$

Design	Algorithm	FPGA	Freq. (MHz)	Sign (ms)	Verify (ms)	Resources (LUT/FF/DSP/BR)	T×A
[BCH+23]	ov-Ip-pkc	XC7A200T	100	0.08	0.69	37k/25k/2/81	0.03
[BCH+23]	ov-V-pkc+skc	XC7A200T	100	28.57	3.93	83k/41k/4/359	2.70
[SMA+24]	MAYO 1	Arm/Zynq-7020	100	28.6	—	21k/13k/11/129	0.60
[HSK+23]	MAYO 1	Artix-7	75	0.43	0.05	106k/38k/2/45.5	0.05
[DHSY24]	SDitH L1 GF256	XC7A200T	164	41.0	52.9	17k/9k/0/164.5	1.60
[DHSY24]	SDitH L3 GF251	XC7A200T	164	276.1	183.6	34k/31k/472/521.5	15.63
[dPRS23]	Raccoon-128 2 shares	RISC-V/XC7A100T	78	30.7	18.4	10k/4k/3/—	0.49
[dPRS23]	Raccoon-128 32 shares	RISC-V/XC7A100T	78	284.10	17.86		3.02
[WJW+19]	XMSS SHA256 $h = 10$	RISC-V/Cyclone V	145	9.95	5.80	7k/10k/—/145	0.11
[LSG21]	Dilithium-III F	XC7A100T	145	0.85	0.23	30k/11k/45/21	0.03
[BNG21]	Dilithium-V	Artix-7	116	0.21	0.12	53k/28k/16/29	0.02
[Saa24]	SLH-DSA-SHAKE-128f	RISC-V/XC7A100T	100	49.0	4.4	14k/—/—/—	0.75
[Saa24]	SLH-DSA-SHA2-256 s	RISC-V/XC7A100T	100	69620.1	8.9		974.81
[ALCZ20]	SPHINCS+-128f-simple	XC7A100T	250	1.01	0.16	48k/73k/1/11.5	0.06
[ALCZ20]	SPHINCS+-256 s-robust	XC7A100T	250	36.1	0.20	50k/76k/1/30	1.82
[SAW+23]	Falcon-512	ZCU104	187.5	4.2	—	23k/26k/101/23	0.17
[SAW+23]	Falcon-512	ZCU104	214.3	—	0.62	12k/8k/15/13	
[SAW+23]	Falcon-1024	ZCU104	187.5	8.7	—	45k/41k/182/37	0.58
[SAW+23]	Falcon-1024	ZCU104	214.3	—	1.3	13k/9k/2/4	

Compared to the hardware (co-)designs of some other PQC schemes shown in Table 9, our hardware implementation of MEDS (results shown in Table 8) makes MEDS a competitive choice when the time area product ($\mathbf{T}\times\mathbf{A}$) is considered. Some of the other designs are much more efficient than our implementation, however this is due to the high computational cost inherent to the MEDS specification in particular compared to lattice-based schemes. Nevertheless, the performance of our implementation is comparable to several other PQC schemes such as SPHINCS+/SLH-DSA, SDitH, and Raccoon. We believe that this shows that the quality of our implementation is on par with other work in this field.

Our results emphasize that MEDS is computationally expensive but that FS-schemes with a large round number can be parallelized efficiently and can achieve high performance (at high resource cost). Possible future works include the implementation of key generation and of recent proposals for the optimization of MEDS as well as the exploration of supporting different fields in one joint design for other applicable schemes such as CROSS [BBB+24a], LESS [BBB+24b], and PERK [ABB+24].

6 Conclusion

In the introduction in Sect. 1, we raised three research questions:

Research Question 1 asks if there is sufficient inherent parallelism in MEDS to speed up the sign and verify operations. Given that there is plenty parallelism on the low level multiplying and systemizing matrices as well as on the high level iterating over t independent computations, there is indeed ample opportunity to accelerate MEDS. We provide performance parameters to control the low level parallelization and we pipeline the main loop, achieving a significant speed up for MEDS signing and verification. For e.g., for security level I, our balanced design achieves a speed-up of 4-5× for both signing and verification times, whereas our high-performance design achieves a speed-up of 9-10× for both signing and verification times when compared to the optimized software reference implementation. Notably, these gains are achieved while our design operates in the frequency range of 115 MHz to 132 MHz, whereas the optimized software implementation runs at 1.9 GHz. However, 1 also asks about the resource cost of accelerating MEDS. Since the computational cost of MEDS sign and verification is significant, selecting large performance parameters for a high-performance design results in high resource cost.

Research Question 1 asks to what extent resources can be shared between the sign and verify operations in a shared design implementing both operations. Since the main loop operates very similar in both sign and verify, the resources of sign can be reused by verify with only little control logic overhead. Sign requires some additional computations at the end to compute the responses for the signature, which can simply be skipped by verify.

Research Question 1 asks about the overhead of supporting all parameter sets selectable at runtime in a single joint design. The overhead for additional control logic for supporting different matrix dimensions and challenge lengths is marginal. To our surprise, supposing arithmetic in multiple prime fields also comes at only a small overhead as for the fields specified in MEDS, most resources can be shared between both fields. Only slightly more logic than needed for the larger field is required to support both fields. We conclude that—if the fields are chosen carefully—supporting multiple fields in a joint hardware implementation is very much feasible. Specifically our results show that arithmetic for pseudo-Mersenne primes with small Hamming distance can be implemented jointly with small overhead.

Acknowledgements. This research has been partially supported by the US government through NSF grant 2332406, by the Korean government through the BK21 FOUR Education and Research Program for Future ICT Pioneers, the IITP grant IITP-2023-RS-2023-00256081, and the NRF grant RS-2023-00277326, and by the Taiwanese government through the NSTC grant 113-2221-E-001-024-MY3.

Appendix

Algorithm 1: MEDS sign (from [CNP+23a])

Input: secret key $\mathsf{sk} \in \mathcal{B}^{\ell_{\mathsf{sk}}}$, message $\mathsf{msg} \in \mathcal{B}^{\ell_{\mathsf{msg}}}$
Output: signed message $\mathsf{msg}_{\mathsf{sig}} \in \mathcal{B}^{\ell_{\mathsf{sig}}+\ell_{\mathsf{msg}}}$

1 $f_{\mathsf{sk}} \leftarrow \ell_{\mathsf{sec\_seed}}$;
2 $\sigma_{\mathbf{G}_0} \leftarrow \mathsf{sk}[f_{\mathsf{sk}}, f_{\mathsf{sk}} + \ell_{\mathsf{pub\_seed}} - 1]$;
3 $f_{\mathsf{sk}} \leftarrow f_{\mathsf{sk}} + \ell_{\mathsf{pub\_seed}}$;
4 $\mathbf{G}_0 \in \mathbb{F}_q^{k \times mn} \leftarrow \mathsf{ExpandSystMat}(\sigma_{\mathbf{G}_0})$;
5 **forall the** $i \in \{1, \dots, s-1\}$ **do**
6 $\quad \mathbf{A}_i^{-1} \in \mathbb{F}_q^{m \times m} \leftarrow \mathsf{Decompress}(\mathsf{sk}[f_{\mathsf{sk}}, f_{\mathsf{sk}} + \ell_{\mathbb{F}_q^{m \times m}}], m, m)$;
7 $\quad f_{\mathsf{sk}} \leftarrow f_{\mathsf{sk}} + \ell_{\mathbb{F}_q^{m \times m}}$;
8 **forall the** $i \in \{1, \dots, s-1\}$ **do**
9 $\quad \mathbf{B}_i^{-1} \in \mathbb{F}_q^{n \times n} \leftarrow \mathsf{Decompress}(\mathsf{sk}[f_{\mathsf{sk}}, f_{\mathsf{sk}} + \ell_{\mathbb{F}_q^{n \times n}}], n, n)$;
10 $\quad f_{\mathsf{sk}} \leftarrow f_{\mathsf{sk}} + \ell_{\mathbb{F}_q^{n \times n}}$;
11 $\delta \in \mathcal{B}^{\ell_{\mathsf{sec\_seed}}} \leftarrow \mathsf{Randombytes}(\ell_{\mathsf{sec\_seed}})$;
12 $\rho \in \mathcal{B}^{\ell_{\mathsf{tree\_seed}}}, \alpha \in \mathcal{B}^{\ell_{\mathsf{salt}}} \leftarrow \mathsf{XOF}(\delta, \ell_{\mathsf{tree\_seed}}, \ell_{\mathsf{salt}})$;
13 $\sigma_0, \dots, \sigma_{t-1} \in \mathcal{B}^{\ell_{\mathsf{tree\_seed}}} \leftarrow \mathsf{SeedTree}_t(\rho, \alpha)$;
14 **forall the** $i \in \{0, \dots, t-1\}$ **do**
15 $\quad \sigma_i' \in \mathcal{B}^{\ell_{\mathsf{salt}}+\ell_{\mathsf{tree\_seed}}+4} \leftarrow (\alpha | \sigma_i | \mathsf{ToBytes}(2^{1+\lceil \log_2(t) \rceil} + i, 4))$;
16 $\quad \sigma_{\tilde{\mathbf{A}}_i}, \sigma_{\tilde{\mathbf{B}}_i} \in \mathcal{B}^{\ell_{\mathsf{pub\_seed}}}, \sigma_i \in \mathcal{B}^{\ell_{\mathsf{tree\_seed}}} \leftarrow \mathsf{XOF}(\sigma_i', \ell_{\mathsf{pub\_seed}}, \ell_{\mathsf{pub\_seed}}, \ell_{\mathsf{tree\_seed}})$;
17 $\quad \tilde{\mathbf{A}}_i \in \mathrm{GL}_m(q) \leftarrow \mathsf{ExpandInvMat}(\sigma_{\tilde{\mathbf{A}}_i}, m)$;
18 $\quad \tilde{\mathbf{B}}_i \in \mathrm{GL}_n(q) \leftarrow \mathsf{ExpandInvMat}(\sigma_{\tilde{\mathbf{B}}_i}, n)$;
19 $\quad \tilde{\mathbf{G}}_i \in \mathbb{F}_q^{k \times mn} \leftarrow \pi_{\tilde{\mathbf{A}}_i, \tilde{\mathbf{B}}_i}(\mathbf{G}_0)$;
20 $\quad \tilde{\mathbf{G}}_i \in \mathbb{F}_q^{k \times mn} \cup \{\perp\} \leftarrow \mathsf{SF}(\tilde{\mathbf{G}}_i)$;
21 $\quad$ **if** $\tilde{\mathbf{G}}_i = \perp$ **then**
22 $\quad\quad$ **goto** line 15;
23 $d \in \mathcal{B}^{\ell_{\mathsf{digest}}} \leftarrow \mathsf{H}(\mathsf{Compress}(\tilde{\mathbf{G}}_0[;k, mn-1]) \mid \dots \mid \mathsf{Compress}(\tilde{\mathbf{G}}_{t-1}[;k, mn-1]) \mid \mathsf{msg})$;
24 $h_0, \dots, h_{t-1} \in \{0, \dots, s-1\} \leftarrow \mathsf{ParseHash}_{s,t,w}(d)$;
25 $f_v \leftarrow 0$;
26 **forall the** $i \in \{0, \dots, t-1\}$ **do**
27 $\quad$ **if** $h_i > 0$ **then**
28 $\quad\quad \mu_i \in \mathbb{F}_q^{m \times m} \leftarrow \tilde{\mathbf{A}}_i \cdot \mathbf{A}_{h_i}^{-1}$;
29 $\quad\quad \nu_i \in \mathbb{F}_q^{n \times n} \leftarrow \mathbf{B}_{h_i}^{-1} \cdot \tilde{\mathbf{B}}_i$;
30 $\quad\quad v_{f_v} \in \mathcal{B}^{\ell_{\mathbb{F}_q^{m \times m}}+\ell_{\mathbb{F}_q^{n \times n}}} \leftarrow (\mathsf{Compress}(\mu_i) \mid \mathsf{Compress}(\nu_i))$;
31 $\quad\quad f_v \leftarrow f_v + 1$;
32 $p \in \mathcal{B}^{\ell_{\mathsf{path}}} \leftarrow \mathsf{SeedTreeToPath}_t(h_0, \dots, h_{t-1}, \rho, \alpha)$;
33 **return** $\mathsf{msg}_{\mathsf{sig}} \in \mathcal{B}^{w(\ell_{\mathbb{F}_q^{m \times m}}+\ell_{\mathbb{F}_q^{n \times n}})+\ell_{\mathsf{path}}+\ell_{\mathsf{digest}}+\ell_{\mathsf{salt}}+\ell_{\mathsf{msg}}=\ell_{\mathsf{sig}}+\ell_{\mathsf{msg}}} =$
$(v_0 \mid \dots \mid v_{w-1} \mid p \mid d \mid \alpha \mid \mathsf{msg})$;

Algorithm 2: MEDS verify (adapted from [CNP+23a])

Input: public key $\mathsf{pk} \in \mathcal{B}^{\ell_{\mathsf{pk}}}$, signed message $\mathsf{msg}_{\mathsf{sig}} \in \mathcal{B}^{\ell_{\mathsf{sig}}+\ell_m}$

Output: message $\mathsf{msg} \in \mathcal{B}_m^{\ell}$ or $\perp$

$\sigma_{\mathbf{G}_0} \leftarrow \mathsf{pk}[0, \ell_{\mathsf{pub\_seed}} - 1]$;

$\mathbf{G}_0 \in \mathbb{F}_q^{k \times mn} \leftarrow \mathsf{ExpandSystMat}(\sigma_{\mathbf{G}_0})$;

$f_{\mathsf{pk}} \leftarrow \ell_{\mathsf{pub\_seed}}$;

forall the $i \in \{1, \dots, s-1\}$ **do**

  $\mathbf{G}_i \in \mathbb{F}_q^{k \times mn} \leftarrow \mathsf{DecompressG}(\mathsf{pk}[f_{\mathsf{pk}}, f_{\mathsf{pk}} + \ell_{G_i}])$;

  $f_{\mathsf{pk}} \leftarrow f_{\mathsf{pk}} + \ell_{G_i}$;

$p \in \mathcal{B}^{\ell_{\mathsf{path}}} \leftarrow \mathsf{msg}_{\mathsf{sig}}[\ell_{\mathsf{sig}} - \ell_{\mathsf{digest}} - \ell_{\mathsf{salt}} - \ell_{\mathsf{path}}, \ell_{\mathsf{sig}} - \ell_{\mathsf{digest}} - \ell_{\mathsf{salt}} - 1]$;

$d \in \mathcal{B}^{\ell_{\mathsf{digest}}}, \alpha \in \mathcal{B}^{\ell_{\mathsf{salt}}}, \mathsf{msg} \in \mathcal{B}^* \leftarrow$
$\mathsf{msg}_{\mathsf{sig}}[\ell_{\mathsf{sig}} - \ell_{\mathsf{digest}} - \ell_{\mathsf{salt}}, \ell_{\mathsf{sig}} - \ell_{\mathsf{salt}} - 1], \mathsf{msg}_{\mathsf{sig}}[\ell_{\mathsf{sig}} - \ell_{\mathsf{salt}}, \ell_{\mathsf{sig}} - 1], \mathsf{msg}_{\mathsf{sig}}[\ell_{\mathsf{sig}},]$;

$h_0, \dots, h_{t-1} \in \{0, \dots, s-1\} \leftarrow \mathsf{ParseHash}_{s,t,w}(d)$;

$\sigma_0, \dots, \sigma_{t-1} \in \mathcal{B}^{\ell_{\mathsf{tree\_seed}}} \leftarrow \mathsf{PathToSeedTree}_t(h_0, \dots, h_{t-1}, p, \alpha)$;

$f_{m_s} \leftarrow 0$;

forall the $i \in \{0, \dots, t-1\}$ **do**

  if $h_i > 0$ **then**

    $\mu_i \in \mathbb{F}_q^{m \times m} \leftarrow \mathsf{Decompress}(\mathsf{msg}_{\mathsf{sig}}[f_{m_s}, f_{m_s} + \ell_{\mathbb{F}_q^{m \times m}} - 1], m, m)$;

    $\nu_i \in \mathbb{F}_q^{n \times n} \leftarrow$
    $\mathsf{Decompress}(\mathsf{msg}_{\mathsf{sig}}[f_{m_s} + \ell_{\mathbb{F}_q^{m \times m}}, f_{m_s} + \ell_{\mathbb{F}_q^{m \times m}} + \ell_{\mathbb{F}_q^{n \times n}} - 1], n, n)$;

    $f_{m_s} \leftarrow f_{m_s} + \ell_{\mathbb{F}_q^{m \times m}} + \ell_{\mathbb{F}_q^{n \times n}}$;

    if $\mu_i \notin \mathrm{GL}_m(q)$ **or** $\nu_i \notin \mathrm{GL}_n(q)$ **then**

      return $\perp$;

  else

    $\sigma_i' \in \mathcal{B}^{\ell_{\mathsf{salt}} + \ell_{\mathsf{tree\_seed}} + 4} \leftarrow \left(\alpha | \sigma_i | \mathsf{ToBytes}(2^{1 + \lceil \log_2(t) \rceil} + i, 4)\right)$;

    $\sigma_{\hat{\mathbf{A}}_i}, \sigma_{\hat{\mathbf{B}}_i} \in \mathcal{B}^{\ell_{\mathsf{pub\_seed}}}, \sigma_i \in \mathcal{B}^{\ell_{\mathsf{tree\_seed}}} \leftarrow \mathsf{XOF}(\sigma_i', \ell_{\mathsf{pub\_seed}}, \ell_{\mathsf{pub\_seed}}, \ell_{\mathsf{tree\_seed}})$;

    $\mu_i \in \mathrm{GL}_m(q) \leftarrow \mathsf{ExpandInvMat}(\sigma_{\hat{\mathbf{A}}_i}, m)$;

    $\nu_i \in \mathrm{GL}_n(q) \leftarrow \mathsf{ExpandInvMat}(\sigma_{\hat{\mathbf{B}}_i}, n)$;

  $\hat{\mathbf{G}}_i \in \mathbb{F}_q^{k \times mn} \leftarrow \pi_{\mu_i, \nu_i}(\mathbf{G}_{h_i})$;

  $\hat{\mathbf{G}}_i \in \mathbb{F}_q^{k \times mn} \cup \{\perp\} \leftarrow \mathsf{SF}(\hat{\mathbf{G}}_i)$;

  if $\hat{\mathbf{G}}_i = \perp$ **then**

    return $\perp$;

$d' \in \mathcal{B}^{\ell_{\mathsf{digest}}} \leftarrow$
$\mathsf{H}(\mathsf{Compress}(\hat{\mathbf{G}}_0[; k, mn-1]) \mid \dots \mid \mathsf{Compress}(\hat{\mathbf{G}}_{t-1}[; k, mn-1]) \mid \mathsf{msg})$;

if $d = d'$ **then**

  return msg;

else

  return $\perp$;

References

ABB+24. Aaraj, N., et al.: PERK. Technical report, National Institute of Standards and Technology (2024). https://csrc.nist.gov/Projects/pqc-dig-sig/round-2-additional-signatures

ADKF70. Arlazarov, V., Dinic, E., Kronrod, M., Faradzev, I.: On economical construction of the transitive closure of a directed graph. Soviet Math. Doklady **11**(5), 1209–1210 (1970)

ALCZ20. Amiet, D., Leuenberger, L., Curiger, A., Zbinden, P.: FPGA-based SPHINCS$^+$ implementations: mind the glitch. In: 23rd Euromicro Conference on Digital System Design, DSD 2020, Kranj, Slovenia, August 26–28, 2020, pp. 229–237. IEEE (2020)

AMI+23. Aikata, A., Can Mert, A., Imran, M., Pagliarini, S., Sinha Roy, S.: KaLi: a crystal for post-quantum security using Kyber and Dilithium. IEEE Trans. Circ. Syst. I Reg. Pap. **70**(2), 747–758 (2023)

BBB+24a. Baldi, M., et al.: CROSS—codes and restricted objects signature scheme. Technical report, National Institute of Standards and Technology (2024). https://csrc.nist.gov/Projects/pqc-dig-sig/round-2-additional-signatures

BBB+24b. Baldi, M., et al.: LESS—linear equivalence signature scheme. Technical report, National Institute of Standards and Technology (2024). https://csrc.nist.gov/Projects/pqc-dig-sig/round-2-additional-signatures

BCC+24. Beullens, W., Campos, F., Celi, S., Hess, B., Kannwischer, M.J.: Nibbling MAYO: optimized Implementations for AVX2 and Cortex-M4. IACR Trans. Cryptographic Hardware Embed. Syst. **2024**(2), 252–275 (2024)

BCH+23. Beullens, W., et al.: Oil and vinegar: modern parameters and implementations. IACR TCHES **2023**(3), 321–365 (2023)

BFV13. Bouillaguet, C., Fouque, P.-A., Véber, A.: Graph-theoretic algorithms for the "Isomorphism of Polynomials" problem. In: Johansson, T., Nguyen, P.Q. (eds.) EUROCRYPT 2013. LNCS, vol. 7881, pp. 211–227. Springer, Heidelberg (2013). https://doi.org/10.1007/978-3-642-38348-9_13

BNG21. Beckwith, L., Tri Nguyen, D., Gaj, K.: High-performance hardware implementation of CRYSTALS-dilithium. In: International Conference on Field-Programmable Technology, (IC)FPT 2021, Auckland, New Zealand, December 6–10, 2021, pp. 1–10. IEEE (2021)

CCD+22. Chen, P.-J., et al.: Complete and improved FPGA implementation of classic McEliece. IACR TCHES **2022**(3), 71–113 (2022)

CNP+23a. Chou, T., et al.: MEDS—matrix equivalence digital signature. Technical report, National Institute of Standards and Technology (2023). https://csrc.nist.gov/Projects/pqc-dig-sig/round-1-additional-signatures

CNP+23b. Chou, T., et al.: Take your MEDS: digital signatures from matrix code equivalence. In: El Mrabet, N., De Feo, L., Duquesne, S. (eds.) AFRICACRYPT 23, volume 14064 of LNCS, pp. 28–52. Springer, Cham (2023). https://doi.org/10.1007/978-3-031-37679-5_2

CNRS24. Chou, T., Niederhagen, R., Ran, L., Samardjiska, S.: Reducing signature size of matrix-code-based signature schemes. In: Saarinen, M.-J.O., Smith-Tone, D. (eds.) Post-Quantum Cryptography - 15th International Workshop, PQCrypto 2024, Oxford, UK, June 12-14, 2024, Proceedings, Part I, volume 14771 of Lecture Notes in Computer Science, pp. 107–134. Springer (2024)

DHSY24. Deshpande, S., Howe, J., Szefer, J., Yue, D.: SDitH in hardware. IACR Trans. Cryptogr. Hardw. Embed. Syst. **2024**(2), 215–251 (2024)

DLK+25. Deshpande, S., Lee, Y., Karakuzu, C., Szefer, J., Paek, Y.: SPHINCSLET: an area-efficient accelerator for the full SPHINCS+ digital signature algorithm. ACM Trans. Embed. Comput. Syst. (2025). Just Accepted

dPRS23. del Pino, R., Prest, T., Rossi, M., Saarinen, M.-J.O.: High-order masking of lattice signatures in quasilinear time. In: 2023 IEEE Symposium on Security and Privacy, pp. 1168–1185. IEEE Computer Society Press (2023)

FG18. Ferozpuri, A., Gaj, K.: High-speed FPGA implementation of the NIST round 1 rainbow signature scheme. In: 2018 International Conference on ReConFigurable Computing and FPGAs (ReConFig), pp. 1–8 (2018)

FS87. Fiat, A., Shamir, A.: How to prove yourself: practical solutions to identification and signature problems. In: Odlyzko, A.M. (ed.) CRYPTO'86. LNCS, vol. 263, pp. 186–194. Springer, Heidelberg (1987)

GQT21. Grochow, J.A., Qiao, Y., Tang, G.: Average-case algorithms for testing isomorphism of polynomials, algebras, and multilinear forms. In: Bläser, M., Monmege, B. (eds.) 38th International Symposium on Theoretical Aspects of Computer Science, STACS 2021, March 16–19, 2021, Saarbrücken, Germany (Virtual Conference), volume 187 of LIPIcs, pp. 38:1–38:17. Schloss Dagstuhl - Leibniz-Zentrum für Informatik (2021)

HGG07. Hasenplaugh, W., Gaubatz, G., Gopal, V.: Fast modular reduction. In: 18th IEEE Symposium on Computer Arithmetic (ARITH-18 2007), 25–27 June 2007, Montpellier, France, pp. 225–229. IEEE Computer Society (2007)

HQR89. Hochet, B., Quinton, P., Robert, Y.: Systolic Gaussian elimination over GF(p) with partial pivoting. IEEE Trans. Computers **38**(9), 1321–1324 (1989)

HSK+23. Hirner, F., Streibl, M., Krieger, F., Can Mert, A., Sinha Roy, S.: Whipping the MAYO signature scheme using hardware platforms. Cryptology ePrint Archive, Paper 2023/1267 (2023). https://eprint.iacr.org/2023/1267

KKPY24. Kannwischer, M.J., Krausz, M., Petri, R., Yang, S.-Y.: pqm4: benchmarking NIST additional post-quantum signature schemes on microcontrollers. Cryptology ePrint Archive, Paper 2024/112 (2024)

LSG21. Land, G., Sasdrich, P., Güneysu, T.: A hard crystal - implementing dilithium on reconfigurable hardware. In: Grosso, V., Pöppelmann, T. (eds.) Smart Card Research and Advanced Applications - 20th International Conference, CARDIS 2021, Lübeck, Germany, November 11–12, 2021, Revised Selected Papers, volume 13173 of Lecture Notes in Computer Science, pp. 210–230. Springer (2021)

MR24. Mandal, S., Basu Roy, D.: KiD: a hardware design framework targeting unified NTT multiplication for CRYSTALS-Kyber and CRYSTALS-Dilithium on FPGA. In: 2024 37th International Conference on VLSI Design and 2024 23rd International Conference on Embedded Systems (VLSID), pp. 455–460 (2024)

NQT24. Kumar Narayanan, A., Qiao, Y., Tang, G.: Algorithms for matrix code and alternating trilinear form equivalences via new isomorphism invariants. In: Joye, M., Leander, G. (eds.) Advances in Cryptology - EUROCRYPT 2024 - 43rd Annual International Conference on the Theory and Applications of Cryptographic Techniques, Zurich, Switzerland, May 26–30, 2024, Proceedings, Part III, volume 14653 of Lecture Notes in Computer Science, pp. 160–187. Springer (2024)

Saa24. Saarinen, v: Accelerating SLH-DSA by two orders of magnitude with a single hash unit. IACR Cryptol. ePrint Arch., pp. 367 (2024). To appear in CRYPTO 2024, August 2024

SAW+23. Schmid, M., Amiet, D., Wendler, J., Zbinden, P., Wei, T.: Falcon takes off - a hardware implementation of the falcon signature scheme. IACR Cryptol. ePrint Arch., p. 1885 (2023)

SMA+24. Sayari, O., Marzougui, S., Aulbach, T., Krämer, J., Seifert, J.-P.: HaMAYO: a fault-tolerant reconfigurable hardware implementation of the MAYO signature scheme. In: Wacquez, R., Homma, N. (eds.) Constructive Side-Channel Analysis and Secure Design - 15th International Workshop, COSADE 2024, Gardanne, France, April 9-10, 2024, Proceedings, volume 14595 of Lecture Notes in Computer Science, pp. 240–259. Springer (2024)

SWM+10. Shoufan, A., Gregor Molter, T.W.H., Huss, S.A., Kohnert, E.: A novel cryptoprocessor architecture for the McEliece public-key cryptosystem. IEEE Trans. Comput. **59**(11), 1533–1546 (2010)

TDJ+22. Tang, G., Hoang Duong, D., Joux, A., Plantard, T., Qiao, Y., Susilo, W.: Practical post-quantum signature schemes from isomorphism problems of trilinear forms. In: Dunkelman, O., Dziembowski, S. (eds.) EUROCRYPT 2022, Part III, volume 13277 of LNCS, pp. 582–612. Springer, Heidelberg (2022)

TYD+11. Tang, S., Yi, H., Ding, J., Chen, H., Chen, G.: High-speed hardware implementation of rainbow signature on FPGAs. In: Yang, B.-Y. (ed.) Post-Quantum Cryptography, pp. 228–243. Springer, Heidelberg (2011)

WJW+19. Wang, W., et al.: XMSS and embedded systems. In: Paterson, K.G., Stebila, D. (eds.) SAC 2019. LNCS, vol. 11959, pp. 523–550. Springer, Heidelberg (2019)

WSN16. Wang, W., Szefer, J., Niederhagen, R.: Solving large systems of linear equations over GF(2) on FPGAs. In: Athanas, P.M., Cumplido, R., Feregrino, C., Sass, R. (eds.) International Conference on ReConFigurable Computing and FPGAs, ReConFig 2016, Cancun, Mexico, November 30–Dec. 2, 2016, pp. 1–7. IEEE (2016)

WSN17. Wang, W., Szefer, J., Niederhagen, R.: FPGA-based key generator for the Niederreiter cryptosystem using binary Goppa Codes. In: Fischer, W., Homma, N. (eds.) CHES 2017. LNCS, vol. 10529, pp. 253–274. Springer, Heidelberg (2017)

ZZC+23. Zhu, Y., et al.: Mckeycutter: a high-throughput key generator of classic McEliece on hardware. In: 60th ACM/IEEE Design Automation Conference, DAC 2023, San Francisco, CA, USA, July 9–13, 2023, pp. 1–6. IEEE (2023)

ZZL+23. Yihong Zhu, et al.: RePQC: a 3.4-uJ/Op 48-kOPS post-quantum cryptoprocessor for multiple-mathematical problems. IEEE J. Solid-State Circ. **58**(1), 124–140 (2023)

Public Key Encryption

Bounded CCA2-Secure Proxy Re-encryption from Lattices

Shingo Sato[1,2(✉)] and Junji Shikata[1,3]

[1] Institute of Advanced Sciences, Yokohama National University, Yokoaham, Japan
{sato-shingo-zk,shikata-junji-rb}@ynu.ac.jp
[2] Organization for the Promotion of Education, Yokohama National University, Yokoaham, Japan
[3] Graduate School of Environment and Information Sciences, Yokohama National University, Yokoaham, Japan

Abstract. Proxy re-encryption (PRE) allows a semi-honest party (called a proxy) to convert ciphertexts under a public key into ciphertexts under another public key. Due to this functionality, there are various applications such as encrypted email forwarding, key escrow, and secure distributed file systems. On the other hand, post-quantum cryptography (PQC) is one of the most important research areas. However, there is no post-quantum PRE scheme with security against adaptive chosen ciphertext attacks (denoted by CCA2 security) while many PRE schemes have been proposed so far. In this paper, we propose a bounded CCA2-secure PRE scheme based on CRYSTALS-Kyber (Kyber, for short) which is a selected algorithm in the NIST PQC competition. To this end, we present a generic construction of bounded CCA2-secure PRE. Our generic construction starts from PRE with (a variant of) security against chosen plaintext attacks (denoted by CPA security) and a new PRE's property introduced in this paper. In order to instantiate our generic construction, we present a lattice-based PRE scheme with the required property. As a result, we can construct a bounded CCA2-secure PRE scheme from lattices.

Keywords: Proxy re-encryption · Bounded CCA2 security · Post-quantum cryptography

1 Introduction

1.1 Background and Related Work

The notion of proxy re-encryption (PRE) was introduced in [5], and PRE is public key encryption (PKE) which allows a semi-honest party (called a proxy) to convert an encryption of a message under a public key into another encryption of the same message under another public key. More concretely, the procedures of PRE are as follows: A user Alice with a public key pk_A can generate a re-encryption key $\mathsf{rk}_{A \to B}$ converting ciphertexts under pk_A into ciphertexts under

C. Boura et al. (Eds.): SAC 2025, LNCS 16207, pp. 425–455, 2026.
https://doi.org/10.1007/978-3-032-10536-3_16

a public key pk_B of another user Bob and give $\mathsf{rk}_{A \to B}$ to a proxy. Then, this proxy can transform ciphertexts under pk_A into ciphertexts under pk_B, without knowledge of underlying messages. Security of PRE ensures confidentiality of messages even though the adversary has several re-encryption keys. Additionally, PRE is classified into several types, as follows:

Unidirectional vs. Bidirectional. A PRE scheme is said to be *bidirectional* if $\mathsf{rk}_{A \to B}$ also allows to convert from ciphertexts under pk_B to pk_A. Meanwhile, *unidirectional* PRE just allows re-encryption from pk_A to pk_B, and not vice versa. Unidirectional PRE is more desirable because the proxies of bidirectional PRE are authorized in order to realize re-encryption functionalities.
Single-hop vs. Multi-hop. Suppose that ct_A is transformed to ct_B by using $\mathsf{rk}_{A \to B}$, and pk_C is another user's public key. A PRE scheme is said to be *single-hop* if a re-encryption key $\mathsf{rk}_{B \to C}$ cannot convert ct_B to another ciphertext ct_C under pk_C. In contrast, *multi-hop* PRE allows convert a ciphertext ct_B into a ciphertext ct_C under pk_C by using $\mathsf{rk}_{B \to C}$.

Due to PRE's functionality, there are various applications such as encrypted email forwarding [5], key escrow [21], secure distributed file systems [3], and secure publish-subscribe system [28]. Accordingly, there are many PRE schemes such as Diffie-Hellman-based schemes (e.g., [5,7,11,27]), pairing-based schemes (e.g., [2,3,8,23]), and obfuscation-based schemes [9,10].

In particular, we focus on post-quantum PRE because post-quantum cryptography (PQC) is one of the most important research areas, and there are many researches on selected algorithms and candidates in the NIST (National Institute of Standards and Technology) PQC standardization process (e.g., [1,15,19,26]), due to advancement of quantum computers. As post-quantum PRE, several lattice-based PRE schemes have been proposed so far (e.g., [9,16,28,31,32]). However, there is no post-quantum PRE scheme with security against adaptive chosen ciphertext attacks (denoted by CCA2 security) which was formalized in [8]. To the best of our knowledge, all the existing lattice-based schemes satisfy *security against chosen plaintext attacks, non-adaptive chosen ciphertext attacks, or honest re-encryption attacks* (denoted by CPA, CCA1, or HRA security, respectively). CPA and CCA1 security are strictly weaker than CCA2 security and may be insufficient in PRE's applications, as discussed in [12]. Additionally, the relation between CCA2 and HRA security is not known. Achieving CCA2 security is important because this security is one of the most desirable security notions and provides a wide range of applications for PRE.

Related Work. Blaze, Bleumer, and Strauss [5] introduced the notion of PRE and proposed a PRE scheme based on the DDH assumption. This scheme is bidirectional, multi-hop, and CPA secure. Ateniese, Fu, Green, and Hohenberger [4] presented the first (single-hop) unidirectional PRE scheme with CPA security by using bilinear maps. Since Canetti and Hohenberger [8] formalized CCA2 security for PRE, CCA2-secure PRE schemes have been proposed in [7,8,11,23].

As post-quantum PRE, there are only lattice-based constructions. Lattice-based PRE schemes with CPA security have been proposed in [9,17,22,28,32].

Fan and Liu [16] gave tag-based PRE schemes based on the learning with errors (LWE) assumption and these achieve CCA1 security. On the other hand, Cohen [12] introduced the notion of HRA security and showed that one of practical lattice-based (CPA-secure) PRE schemes of [28] was insecure in the HRA security model. Furthermore, Fuchsbauer et al. [17] formalized adaptive CPA and HRA security notions and proposed adaptive HRA-secure schemes based on the PRE schemes of [9,18]. Zhou, Liu, and Han [31] presented a LWE-based construction of HRA-secure fine-grained PRE whose notion was introduced in [32].

From the above, all the existing post-quantum PRE schemes do not satisfy CCA2 security.

1.2 Our Contribution

Our goal is to propose a bounded CCA2-secure post-quantum PRE scheme with compact ciphertexts. In the bounded CCA2 security game of PRE, the numbers of queries which the adversary can issue to the decryption and re-encryption oracles are at most a-priori parameters t_d and t_r, respectively. Although bounded CCA2 security is a weak variant of CCA2 security, there are practical applications where PKE's bounded CCA2 security is sufficient (e.g., see [13,20,30]). Here, compact ciphertexts for bounded CCA2-secure PRE mean that ciphertext size does not depend on the parameters t_d, t_r linearly.

To achieve our goal, we propose a generic construction of bounded CCA2-secure PRE. This construction is based on the generic construction of bounded CCA2-secure PKE [13], and its building blocks are PRE with a variant of CPA security and one-time signatures (OTSs). To achieve compact ciphertexts, we require the underlying PRE to satisfy an additional property, and we present a lattice-based PRE scheme with this additional property, so that we can instantiate our generic construction. Details on our contribution are as follows:

- We formalize a notion of bounded CCA2 security for single-hop unidirectional PRE. This formalization is based on the definition of bounded CCA2 security for PKE [13]. The formalized security notion is a bounded variant of the standard CCA2 security (concretely, [11, Definition 2]) for single-hop unidirectional PRE.
- As a new property of PRE, we introduce re-encrytption key homomorphism in order to construct the objective bounded CCA2-secure PRE scheme. Accordingly, we also formalize a new security notion: RKH-CPA security, which is a variant of CPA security.
- We propose a generic construction of bounded CCA2-secure (single-hop unidirectional) PRE with compact ciphertexts. This is based on the bounded CCA2-secure PKE scheme [13]. The building blocks of our scheme are re-encryption key homomorphic PRE with RKH-CPA security and strongly unforgeable OTS. An overview of this construction appears in Sect. 1.3.
- In order to instantiate our generic construction, we present a RKH-CPA secure PRE scheme with re-encryption key homomorphism, from lattices. This scheme

is based on the underlying PKE scheme of CRYSTALS-Kyber (Kyber, for short) [6] which is a selected algorithm in the NIST PQC competition. We have chosen Kyber since this is intended to be used widely as one of standard PQC algorithms.

As a result, we can obtain a bounded CCA2-secure post-quantum PRE scheme with compact ciphertexts by applying our generic construction to our lattice-based PRE scheme. Furthermore, our lattice-based PRE is simple and practical because this scheme is constructed just by adding the re-encryption key generation and re-encryption algorithms to slightly modified Kyber's key generation, encryption, and decryption algorithms. Hence, the resulting bounded CCA2-secure PRE scheme is also constructed simply.

1.3 Technical Overview

We explain an overview of technical aspects of our bounded CCA2-secure PRE with compact ciphertexts.

Bounded CCA2-secure PRE from CPA secure PRE. To construct bounded CCA2-secure PRE with compact ciphertexts, we first consider a basic generic construction of bounded CCA2-secure PRE $\Pi_{\mathsf{B\text{-}PRE}}$. This construction is based on the generic construction [13] of bounded CCA2-secure PKE, so that $\Pi_{\mathsf{B\text{-}PRE}}$ achieves the bounded CCA2 security of PRE. Furthermore, $\Pi_{\mathsf{B\text{-}PRE}}$ is constructed from CPA-secure PRE and OTS in order to achieve the re-encryption functionality, while the generic construction [13] starts from CPA secure PKE and OTS.

More concretely, a public key pk and a secret key sk of $\Pi_{\mathsf{B\text{-}PRE}}$ consist of u public keys $\mathsf{pk}'_1, \ldots, \mathsf{pk}'_u$ and u secret keys $\mathsf{sk}'_1, \ldots, \mathsf{sk}'_u$ of the underlying PRE, respectively, where a positive integer u is a parameter of a cover-free family[1]. Then, for a user $i \in \{A, B\}$, let $\mathsf{pk}_i = (\mathsf{pk}'_{i,1}, \ldots, \mathsf{pk}'_{i,u})$ and $\mathsf{sk}_i = (\mathsf{sk}'_{i,1}, \ldots, \mathsf{sk}'_{i,u})$ denote the user i's public key and secret key, respectively. A ciphertext ct_A under pk_A consists of $(\mathsf{vk}_A, \mathsf{ct}'_{\mathsf{vk}_A}, \sigma_A)$, where vk_A is a verification key of the underlying OTS, $\mathsf{ct}'_{\mathsf{vk}_A} = (\mathsf{ct}'_1, \ldots, \mathsf{ct}'_v)$ is a tuple of v ciphertexts of the underlying PRE, and σ_A is an OTS signature on $\mathsf{ct}'_{\mathsf{vk}_A}$. Here, $\mathsf{ct}'_{\mathsf{vk}_A} = (\mathsf{ct}'_1, \ldots, \mathsf{ct}'_v)$ is a ciphertext associated with vk_A, as follows: Let $\alpha_1, \ldots, \alpha_v \in \{1, \ldots, u\}$ be indices determined by vk_A and a cover-free family, and ct'_i is a PRE ciphertext under pk'_{α_i} for each $i \in \{1, \ldots, v\}$. Then the correctness of the ciphertext ct_A is ensured in the same way as the PKE scheme of [13].

We consider converting ct_A into a ciphertext $\mathsf{ct}_B = (\mathsf{vk}_B, \mathsf{ct}'_{\mathsf{vk}_B}, \sigma_B)$ under pk_B. A re-encryption key of $\Pi_{\mathsf{B\text{-}PRE}}$ consists of u^2 re-encryption keys $\mathsf{rk}'_{(A,1)\to(B,1)}, \ldots, \mathsf{rk}'_{(A,u)\to(B,u)}$ of the underlying PRE. Notice that each re-encryption $\mathsf{rk}_{(A,i)\to(B,j)}$ transforms a ciphertext under $\mathsf{pk}_{(A,i)}$ into a ciphertext under $\mathsf{pk}_{(B,j)}$ (where $i \in [u]$ and $j \in [u]$). When re-encrypting a ciphertext ct_A, it is possible to generate a tuple of PRE ciphertexts $\mathsf{ct}'_{\mathsf{vk}_B} = (\mathsf{ct}'_{B,1}, \ldots, \mathsf{ct}'_{B,v})$ on another OTS verification key vk_B since it is possible to convert $\mathsf{ct}'_{A,i}$ into a

[1] For simplicity, we employ disjunct matrices in our PRE, instead of cover-free families. Notice that the notion of such matrices is identical to that of cover-free families.

ciphertext $\mathsf{ct}'_{B,i}$ under pk'_{B,β_i} by using a re-encryption key $\mathsf{rk}_{(A,\alpha_i)\to(B,\beta_i)}$, where the indices $\beta_1,\ldots,\beta_v \in \{1,\ldots,u\}$ are determined by vk_B in the same way as the indices $\alpha_1,\ldots,\alpha_v$. Because a new verification/signing key-pair $(\mathsf{vk}_B, \mathsf{sigk}_B)$ of OTS is generated in the re-encryption procedure, we can generate a signature σ_B on $\mathsf{ct}'_{\mathsf{vk}_B} = (\mathsf{ct}'_{B,1},\ldots,\mathsf{ct}'_{B,v})$ by using sigk_B. Since each $\mathsf{ct}_{B,i}$ is a valid ciphertext of the underlying PRE, the correctness of the transformed ciphertext $\mathsf{ct}_B = (\mathsf{vk}_B, \mathsf{ct}'_{\mathsf{vk}_B}, \sigma_B)$ is also ensured.

Hence, this basic scheme $\Pi_{\mathsf{B\text{-}PRE}}$ achieves the re-encryption functionality. This concrete construction and its security proof are given in Appendix A.

Bounded CCA2-secure PRE with Compact Ciphertexts. We explain an overview of our bounded CCA2-secure PRE $\Pi_{\mathsf{C\text{-}PRE}}$ with compact ciphertexts. This construction is based on the basic scheme $\Pi_{\mathsf{B\text{-}PRE}}$. The main difference between these schemes is how to create $\mathsf{ct}'_{\mathsf{vk}_A}$ when generating a ciphertext $\mathsf{ct}_A = (\mathsf{vk}_A, \mathsf{ct}'_{\mathsf{vk}_A}, \sigma_A)$ under pk_A. More concretely, $\mathsf{ct}'_{\mathsf{vk}_A}$ is an encryption of a message under a compressed public key $\mathsf{pk}'_{\mathsf{vk}_A} = \sum_{i\in\{1,\ldots,v\}} \mathsf{pk}'_{\alpha_i}$. In order to ensure the correctness of this encryption, we require the underlying PRE to satisfy a property: secret-key to public-key homomorphism, which was formalized in [29].

Problem of Re-encryption of Our Scheme. One may think that the secret-key to public-key homomorphism is sufficient to construct the objective PRE scheme; however, we cannot ensure the correctness of re-encrypted ciphertexts just by requiring secret-key to public-key homomorphism. A re-encryption key of $\Pi_{\mathsf{B\text{-}PRE}}$ consists of $\mathsf{rk}'_{(A,1)\to(B,1)},\ldots,\mathsf{rk}'_{(A,u)\to(B,u)}$. When re-encrypting $\mathsf{ct}_A = (\mathsf{vk}_A, \mathsf{ct}'_{\mathsf{vk}_A}, \sigma_A)$ by using re-encryption keys $\mathsf{rk}'_{(A,\alpha_1)\to(B,\beta_1)},\ldots,\mathsf{rk}'_{(A,\alpha_v)\to(B,\beta_v)}$ in the same way as $\Pi_{\mathsf{B\text{-}PRE}}$, there are no ciphertexts $\mathsf{ct}_{A,\alpha_1},\ldots,\mathsf{ct}_{A,\alpha_v}$ since $\mathsf{ct}'_{\mathsf{vk}_A}$ is a single ciphertext under the public key $\mathsf{pk}'_{\mathsf{vk}_A}$.

In order to resolve this, we introduce a new property of PRE called re-encryption key homomorphism. This property guarantees the homomorphic evaluation of $\mathsf{rk}'_{(A,\alpha_1)\to(B,\beta_1)},\ldots,\mathsf{rk}'_{(A,\alpha_v)\to(B,\beta_v)}$. Intuitively, we can convert $\mathsf{ct}'_{\mathsf{vk}_A}$ under $\mathsf{pk}'_{\mathsf{vk}_A}$ into a single ciphertext $\mathsf{ct}'_{\mathsf{vk}_B}$ under $\mathsf{pk}'_{\mathsf{vk}_B} = \sum_{i\in\{1,\ldots,v\}} \mathsf{pk}'_{\beta_i}$ by using a re-encryption key $\mathsf{rk}'_{\mathsf{vk}_A\to\mathsf{vk}_B} = \sum_{i\in\{1,\ldots,v\}} \mathsf{rk}'_{(A,\alpha_i)\to(B,\beta_i)}$. Due to the introduced property, it is possible to ensure the correctness of the transformed ciphertext $\mathsf{ct}_B = (\mathsf{vk}_B, \mathsf{ct}'_{\mathsf{vk}_B}, \sigma_B)$. Furthermore, we need to consider a new security notion related to re-encryption key homomorphism, as the remaining problem. We formalize RKH-CPA security for PRE with this homomorphic property. This security is defined in the same way as CPA security except that the adversary can access homomorphic re-encryption key generation oracle which returns re-encryption keys $\{\mathsf{rk}'_{(A,i)\to(B,j)}\}_{i\in\{1,\ldots,u\},j\in\{1,\ldots,u\}}$ such that the homomorphic computation $\sum_{i\in\{1,\ldots,v\}} \mathsf{rk}'_{(A,\alpha_i)\to(B,\beta_i)}$ is possible. Finally, we give a security proof for $\Pi_{\mathsf{C\text{-}PRE}}$ by assuming the RKH-CPA security of the underlying PRE.

Instantiation of Our Generic Construction. We construct a lattice-based PRE scheme to instantiate our generic construction. As mentioned beforehand, the key generation, encryption, and decryption algorithms of our scheme are constructed by slightly modifying those of Kyber PKE scheme. Although we need the introduced property re-encryption key homomorphism, all the existing post-quantum scheme cannot generate re-encryption keys satisfying such homomorphism. Hence, we present a new re-encryption key generation algorithm so that our lattice-based PRE scheme satisfies the objective homomorphism. Additionally, we can use existing strongly unforgeable OTS schemes [24,25] based on lattice assumptions, to instantiate our generic construction. As a result, we can obtain the objective bounded CCA2-secure post-quantum PRE scheme.

2 Preliminaries

Throughout this paper, we use the following notation: For a positive integer n, let $[n] := \{1, \ldots, n\}$. For n values $x_1, \ldots, x_n$ and a subset $\mathcal{I} \subseteq [n]$, let $(x_i)_{i \in \mathcal{I}}$ (resp. $\{x_i\}_{i \in \mathcal{I}}$) be the sequence (resp. the set) of values whose indices are included in $\mathcal{I}$. For a value v, let $|v|$ be its bit-length. If a function $f : \mathbb{N} \to \mathbb{R}$ satisfies $f(\lambda) = o(\lambda^{-c})$ for any constant $c > 0$ and sufficiently large $\lambda \in \mathbb{N}$, then f is said to be negligible in λ and denoted by $f(\lambda) \leq \mathsf{negl}(\lambda)$. A probability is an overwhelming probability if it is at least $1 - \mathsf{negl}(\lambda)$. "Probabilistic polynomial-time" is abbreviated as PPT. For a positive integer λ, let $\mathsf{poly}(\lambda)$ be a universal polynomial of λ.

Matrices and vectors. For consistency, we use capital bold letters for matrices, non-capital letters for scalars, and bold letters for (column) vectors. For a (binary) matrix $\boldsymbol{M} \in \{0,1\}^{u \times n}$, we use the standard notation $\boldsymbol{M} = (m_{i,j})$. For a n-dimensional vector $\boldsymbol{v}$, v_i is the i-th entry, namely $\boldsymbol{v} = (v_1, \ldots, v_n)^\top$. For a binary matrix $\boldsymbol{x} \in \{0,1\}^n$, let $\mathsf{supp}(\boldsymbol{x}) := \{i \in [n] \mid x_i = 1\}$. For a binary matrix $\boldsymbol{M} = (m_{i,j}) \in \{0,1\}^{u \times n}$ and a binary vector $\boldsymbol{x} \in \{0,1\}^n$, the binary vector $\boldsymbol{y} = \boldsymbol{M} \odot \boldsymbol{x} \in \{0,1\}^u$ is defined as $\forall i \in [u], y_i = \bigvee_{j \in [n] \text{ s.t. } m_{i,j}=1} x_j$, where $\bigvee$ is the bitwise-OR. For a binary matrix $\boldsymbol{M} = (m_{i,j}) \in \{0,1\}^{u \times n}$ and $c \in [n]$, let $\phi_{\boldsymbol{M}}(c) := \{i \in [u] \mid m_{i,c} = 1\}$.

Moreover, following [14], we describe the definition of disjunct matrices. Notice that the notion of disjunct matrices is identical to that of cover-free families.

Definition 1 (t-disjunct matrices). *Let $\bar{n}, u$ be positive integers. A binary matrix $\boldsymbol{M} = (m_{i,j}) \in \{0,1\}^{u \times \bar{n}}$ is t-disjunct if for every distinct $s_1, \ldots, s_t \in [\bar{n}]$ and every $j \in [\bar{n}] \backslash \{s_1, \ldots, s_t\}$, there exists a row $q \in [u]$ such that $m_{q,j} = 1$ and $\forall j' \in \{s_1, \ldots, s_t\}$, $m_{q,j'} = 0$.*

Without loss of generality, we suppose that the Hamming weight of each column vector of a t-disjunct matrix $\boldsymbol{M}$ is some positive integer v. For t-disjunct matrices, u is bounded by $u = \Omega(t^2 \log \bar{n})$ and there are concrete constructions with order-optimal values of u and $v = O(t \log \bar{n})$ (e.g., see [14]).

Rings and distributions. Let $R := \mathbb{Z}[X]/(X^N + 1)$ and $R_q := \mathbb{Z}_q[X]/(X^N + 1)$, where $N = 2^{N'}$ such that $X^N + 1$ is the $2^{N'-1}$-th cyclotomic polynomial. For a set S, $s \xleftarrow{\$} S$ means that an element $s \in S$ is chosen uniformly at random. For a probability distribution D, $d \leftarrow D$ denotes that d is drawn from the distribution D. Following [6], we describe the definition of the central binomial distribution B_η for a positive integer η, as follows: B_η chooses $\{(a_i, b_i)\}_{i\in[\eta]} \xleftarrow{\$} (\{0,1\} \times \{0,1\})^\eta$ and outputs $\sum_{i=1}^{\eta}(a_i - b_i)$. Here $v \leftarrow \beta_\eta$ denotes that $v \in R$ is drawn from a distribution β_η where each of its coefficients is chosen according to B_η. In the same way as this, $\boldsymbol{v} \leftarrow \beta_\eta^k$ means that a k-dimensional vector $\boldsymbol{v} \in R^k$ is chosen from β_η^k.

Furthermore, we describe definitions of cryptographic primitives and computational assumptions used in our schemes.

Proxy Re-encryption. Following [2], we describe the syntax of (single-hop) unidirectional proxy re-encryption (PRE), as follows:

Definition 2 (Unidirectional PRE). *For a security parameter λ, let $\mathcal{M} = \mathcal{M}(\lambda)$ be a message space. A (single-hop) unidirectional PRE scheme consists of six polynomial-time algorithms* $(\mathsf{Setup}, \mathsf{KeyGen}, \mathsf{Enc}, \mathsf{Dec}, \mathsf{ReKeyGen}, \mathsf{ReEnc})$*:*

- $\mathsf{Setup}(1^\lambda) \rightarrow \mathsf{pp}$*: The randomized algorithm* Setup *takes as input a security parameter* 1^λ *and outputs a public parameter* pp.
- $\mathsf{KeyGen}(\mathsf{pp}) \rightarrow (\mathsf{pk}, \mathsf{sk})$*: The randomized algorithm* KeyGen *takes as input a public parameter* pp *and outputs a public key* pk *and a secret key* sk.
- $\mathsf{Enc}(\mathsf{pk}, \mathsf{m}) \rightarrow \mathsf{ct}$*: The randomized algorithm* Enc *takes as input a pubic key* pk *and a message* $\mathsf{m} \in \mathcal{M}$*, and outputs a ciphertext* ct.
- $\mathsf{Dec}(\mathsf{sk}, \mathsf{ct}) \rightarrow \mathsf{m}/\bot$*: The deterministic algorithm* Dec *takes as input a secret key* sk *and a ciphertext* ct*, and outputs a message* m *or the rejection symbol* $\bot$.
- $\mathsf{ReKeyGen}(\mathsf{sk}_i, \mathsf{pk}_j) \rightarrow \mathsf{rk}_{i\rightarrow j}$*: The randomized or deterministic algorithm takes as input a secrete key* sk_i *and a public key* pk_j*, and outputs a re-encryption key* $\mathsf{rk}_{i\rightarrow j}$.
- $\mathsf{ReEnc}(\mathsf{rk}_{i\rightarrow j}, \mathsf{ct}_i) \rightarrow \mathsf{ct}_j$*: The randomized or deterministic algorithm* ReEnc *takes as input a re-encryption key* $\mathsf{rk}_{i\rightarrow j}$ *and a ciphertext* ct_i*, and outputs a new ciphertext* ct_j.

For simplicity, we suppose that a public parameter pp *is implicitly contained in the inputs of the algorithms* $\mathsf{Enc}, \mathsf{Dec}, \mathsf{ReKeyGen}, \mathsf{ReEnc}$.

Definition 3 (Correctness). *A single-hop unidirectional PRE scheme* $(\mathsf{Setup}, \mathsf{KeyGen}, \mathsf{Enc}, \mathsf{Dec}, \mathsf{ReKeyGen}, \mathsf{ReEnc})$ *is said to be* correct *if, for every* $\mathsf{pp} \leftarrow \mathsf{Setup}(1^\lambda)$ *and every* $\mathsf{m} \in \mathcal{M}$*, the following conditions hold:*

Encryption Correctness. *For every* $(\mathsf{pk}, \mathsf{sk}) \leftarrow \mathsf{KeyGen}(\mathsf{pp})$*, it holds that* $\mathsf{Dec}(\mathsf{sk}, \mathsf{ct}) = \mathsf{m}$ *with overwhelming probability, where* $\mathsf{ct} \leftarrow \mathsf{Enc}(\mathsf{pk}, \mathsf{m})$.

Re-encryption Correctness. *For every* $(\mathsf{pk}_i, \mathsf{sk}_i) \leftarrow \mathsf{KeyGen}(\mathsf{pp}), (\mathsf{pk}_j, \mathsf{sk}_j) \leftarrow \mathsf{KeyGen}(\mathsf{pp})$*, and every* $\mathsf{rk}_{i\rightarrow j} \leftarrow \mathsf{ReKeyGen}(\mathsf{sk}_i, \mathsf{pk}_j)$*, it holds that* $\mathsf{Dec}(\mathsf{sk}_j, \mathsf{ct}_j) = \mathsf{m}$ *with overwhelming probability, where* $\mathsf{ct}_j \leftarrow \mathsf{ReEnc}(\mathsf{rk}_{i\rightarrow j}, \mathsf{ct}_i)$ *and* $\mathsf{ct}_i \leftarrow \mathsf{Enc}(\mathsf{pk}_i, \mathsf{m})$.

Following [8,11], we describe definitions of oracles in security games of PRE.

Definition 4. *For a security parameter, let* $n = \mathsf{poly}(\lambda)$. *An adversary against a PRE scheme* (Setup, KeyGen, Enc, Dec, ReKeyGen, ReEnc) *is given access to the following oracles in a security game of PRE: Suppose that a public parameter* pp *and* n *key-pairs* $(\mathsf{pk}_1, \mathsf{sk}_1), \ldots, (\mathsf{pk}_n, \mathsf{sk}_n)$ *are generated by* Setup *and* KeyGen, *respectively.*

- *Challenge Oracle* $\mathtt{O.Challenge}_b(i^*, \mathsf{m}_0^*, \mathsf{m}_1^*)$: *Given a challenge query* $(i^*, \mathsf{m}_0^*, \mathsf{m}_1^*)$ *(where* $i^* \in [n]$ *and* $(\mathsf{m}_0^*, \mathsf{m}_1^*) \in \mathcal{M} \times \mathcal{M}$*), the oracle* $\mathtt{O.Challenge}_b$ *with* $b \in \{0, 1\}$ *returns* $\bot$ *if* $i^* \in \mathcal{L}_{\mathtt{Corrupt}}$ *or* $|\mathsf{m}_0^*| \neq |\mathsf{m}_1^*|$ *holds, and returns* $\mathsf{ct}^* \leftarrow \mathsf{Enc}(\mathsf{pk}_{i^*}, \mathsf{m}_b^*)$ *otherwise.*
- *Re-Encryption Key Generation Oracle* $\mathtt{O.ReKeyGen}(i, j)$: *Given a re-encryption key query* $(i, j) \in [n] \times [n]$, *the oracle* $\mathtt{O.ReKeyGen}$ *returns* $\bot$ *if* $i = i^* \wedge j \in \mathcal{L}_{\mathtt{Corrupt}}$ *or* $i = j$ *holds (where* i^* *is the user-index issued to the challenge oracle); otherwise, this oracle does the following:*
  - *If* $\mathsf{T}_{\mathsf{rk}}[i, j] = \mathsf{rk}_{i \to j}$, $\mathtt{O.ReKeyGen}$ *returns* $\mathsf{rk}_{i \to j}$, *where* T_{rk} *is the list of re-encryption key query-response pairs.*
  - *If* $\mathsf{T}_{\mathsf{rk}}[i, j] = \emptyset$, *it returns* $\mathsf{rk}_{i \to j} \leftarrow \mathsf{ReKeyGen}(\mathsf{sk}_i, \mathsf{pk}_j)$ *and sets* $\mathsf{T}_{\mathsf{rk}}[i, j] \leftarrow \mathsf{rk}_{i \to j}$.
- *Decryption Oracle* $\mathtt{O.Dec}(i, \mathsf{ct}_i)$: *Given a decryption query* (i, ct_i), *the oracle* $\mathtt{O.Dec}$ *returns* $\bot$ *if* (i, ct_i) *is a* derivative *of* (i^*, ct^*) *(Definition 5), and returns* $\mathsf{Dec}(\mathsf{sk}_i, \mathsf{ct}_i)$ *otherwise.*
- *Re-Encryption Oracle* $\mathtt{O.ReEnc}(i, j, \mathsf{ct}_i)$: *Given a re-encryption query* (i, j, ct_i), *the oracle* $\mathtt{O.ReEnc}$ *returns* $\bot$ *if* (i, ct_i) *is a* derivative *of* (i^*, ct^*) *and* $j \in \mathcal{L}_{\mathtt{Corrupt}}$ *holds; otherwise, this oracle does the following:*
  - *If* $\mathsf{T}_{\mathsf{rk}}[i, j] = \mathsf{rk}_{i \to j}$, $\mathtt{O.ReEnc}$ *returns* $\mathsf{ct}_j \leftarrow \mathsf{ReEnc}(\mathsf{rk}_{i \to j}, \mathsf{ct}_i)$.
  - *If* $\mathsf{T}_{\mathsf{rk}}[i, j] = \emptyset$, *it computes* $\mathsf{rk}_{i \to j} \leftarrow \mathsf{ReKeyGen}(\mathsf{sk}_i, \mathsf{pk}_j)$, *returns* $\mathsf{ct}_j \leftarrow \mathsf{ReEnc}(\mathsf{rk}_{i \to j}, \mathsf{ct}_i)$, *and sets* $\mathsf{T}_{\mathsf{rk}}[i, j] \leftarrow \mathsf{rk}_{i \to j}$.

Additionally, we describe the definition of *derivatives* of single-hop unidirectional PRE ciphertexts in a CCA2 game, by following [11]:

Definition 5 (Derivatives for CCA2 security [11]). *Let* Π_{PRE} = (Setup, KeyGen, Enc, Dec, ReKeyGen, ReEnc) *be a single-hop unidirectional PRE scheme. Suppose that the challenge ciphertext* ct^* *under a public key* pk_{i^*} *is defined in a security game of PRE.* Derivatives *of* (i^*, ct^*) *are defined as follows:*

- (i^*, ct^*) *is a* derivative *of itself.*
- *If the adversary against* Π_{PRE} *has queried the re-encryption oracle* $\mathtt{O.ReEnc}$ *on input* (i, i', ct_i) *and obtained the response* $\mathsf{ct}_{i'}$, *then* $(i', \mathsf{ct}_{i'})$ *is a* derivative *of* (i, ct_i).
- *If the adversary against* Π_{PRE} *has queried the re-encryption key generation oracle* $\mathtt{O.ReKeyGen}$ *on input* (i, i'), *and* $\mathsf{Dec}(\mathsf{pk}_{i'}, \mathsf{ct}_{i'}) \in \{\mathsf{m}_0^*, \mathsf{m}_1^*\}$, *then* $(i', \mathsf{ct}_{i'})$ *is a* derivative *of* (i, ct_i).

As a new security notion of PRE, we formalize a bounded variant of *security against chosen ciphertext attacks* (denoted as bounded CCA2 security) by following [11,13]. For simplicity, we consider security notions under selective corruptions, rather than adaptive corruptions, throughout this paper.

Definition 6 (Bounded CCA2 security). *Let t_d, t_r be positive integers. For a security parameter, let $n = \mathsf{poly}(\lambda)$ be a positive integer. A single-hop unidirectional PRE scheme $\Pi_{\mathsf{PRE}} = (\mathsf{Setup}, \mathsf{KeyGen}, \mathsf{Enc}, \mathsf{Dec}, \mathsf{ReKeyGen}, \mathsf{ReEnc})$ is said to be (t_d, t_r)-CCA2-secure if for any PPT adversary $\mathcal{A} = (\mathcal{A}_0, \mathcal{A}_1, \mathcal{A}_2)$ against Π_{PRE}, its advantage*

$$\mathsf{Adv}^{(t_d,t_r)\text{-cca2}}_{\Pi_{\mathsf{PRE}},\mathcal{A},n}(\lambda) := \left|\Pr[\mathsf{Expt}^{(t_d,t_r)\text{-cca2}}_{\Pi_{\mathsf{PRE}},\mathcal{A},n}(\lambda) = 1] - 1/2\right|$$

is negligible in λ, where the experiment $\mathsf{Expt}^{(t_d,t_r)\text{-cca2}}_{\Pi_{\mathsf{PRE}},\mathcal{A},n}(\lambda)$ is defined as follows:

$\underline{\mathsf{Expt}^{(t_d,t_r)\text{-cca2}}_{\Pi_{\mathsf{PRE}},\mathcal{A},n}(\lambda)}$:

Generate $\mathsf{pp} \leftarrow \mathsf{Setup}(1^\lambda)$ *and set* $\mathsf{T_{rk}} \leftarrow \emptyset$;
$(\mathcal{L}_{\mathtt{Corrupt}}, \mathsf{st}_0) \leftarrow \mathcal{A}_0(\mathsf{pp})$;
$\forall i \in [n]$, *generate* $(\mathsf{pk}_i, \mathsf{sk}_i) \leftarrow \mathsf{KeyGen}(\mathsf{pp})$;
$(i^*, \mathsf{m}_0^*, \mathsf{m}_1^*, \mathsf{st}_1) \leftarrow \mathcal{A}_1^{\mathtt{O.ReKeyGen},\mathtt{O.Dec},\mathtt{O.ReEnc}}(\mathsf{st}_0, \{\mathsf{pk}_i\}_{i\in[n]}, \{\mathsf{sk}_i\}_{i\in\mathcal{L}_{\mathtt{Corrupt}}})$;
Sample $b \xleftarrow{\$} \{0.1\}$ *and run* $\mathsf{ct}^* \leftarrow \mathtt{O.Challenge}_b(i^*, \mathsf{m}_0^*, \mathsf{m}_1^*)$;
$b' \leftarrow \mathcal{A}_2^{\mathtt{O.ReKeyGen},\mathtt{O.Dec},\mathtt{O.ReEnc}}(\mathsf{st}_1, \mathsf{ct}^*)$;
Return 1 *if* $b = b'$; *otherwise, return* 0,

where $\mathcal{A}$ is allowed to issue at most t_d queries to $\mathtt{O.Dec}$ *and at most t_r queries to* $\mathtt{O.ReEnc}$, *$\mathcal{L}_{\mathtt{Corrupt}}$ is a subset of $[n]$, and $(\mathsf{st}_0, \mathsf{st}_1)$ is internal state information.*

One-Time Signatures. We describe the syntax of one-time signatures (OTSs), as follows.

Definition 7 (OTS). *For a security parameter λ, let $\mathcal{M} = \mathcal{M}(\lambda)$ be a message space. An OTS scheme consists of three polynomial-time algorithms* $(\mathsf{KeyGen}, \mathsf{Sign}, \mathsf{Vrfy})$*:*

- $\mathsf{KeyGen}(1^\lambda) \rightarrow (\mathsf{vk}, \mathsf{sigk})$*: The randomized algorithm* KeyGen *takes as input a security parameter 1^λ and outputs a verification key* vk *and a signing key* sigk.
- $\mathsf{Sign}(\mathsf{sigk}, \mathsf{m}) \rightarrow \sigma$*: The randomized or deterministic algorithm* Sign *takes as input a signing key* sigk *and a message $\mathsf{m} \in \mathcal{M}$, and outputs a signature σ.*
- $\mathsf{Vrfy}(\mathsf{vk}, \mathsf{m}, \sigma) \rightarrow \top/\bot$*: The deterministic algorithm* Vrfy *takes as input a verification key* vk*, a message $\mathsf{m} \in \mathcal{M}$, and a signature σ, and it outputs $\top$ (accept) or $\bot$ (reject).*

Definition 8 (Correctness). *An OTS scheme* $(\mathsf{KeyGen}, \mathsf{Sign}, \mathsf{Vrfy})$ *is said to be* correct *if, for every* $(\mathsf{vk}, \mathsf{sigk}) \leftarrow \mathsf{KeyGen}(1^\lambda)$ *and every $\mathsf{m} \in \mathcal{M}$, it holds that* $\mathsf{Vrfy}(\mathsf{vk}, \mathsf{m}, \sigma) = \top$ *with overwhelming probability, where* $\sigma \leftarrow \mathsf{Sign}(\mathsf{sigk}, \mathsf{m})$.

As a security notion of OTSs, we describe the definition of *strong unforgeability*, as follows:

Definition 9 (Strong unforgeability). *An OTS scheme* $\Pi_{\mathsf{OTS}} = (\mathsf{KeyGen}, \mathsf{Sign}, \mathsf{Vrfy})$ *is said to be* strongly unforgeable *if, for any PPT adversary against* Π_{OTS}*, its advantage* $\mathsf{Adv}^{\text{suf-ot}}_{\Pi_{\mathsf{OTS}},\mathcal{A}}(\lambda) = \Pr[\mathcal{A} \text{ wins}]$ *is negligible in* λ*, where* $[\mathcal{A} \text{ wins}]$ *is the event that* $\mathcal{A}$ *wins in the following game between a challenger and* $\mathcal{A}$*:*

Setup. *The challenger generates* $(\mathsf{vk}, \mathsf{sigk}) \leftarrow \mathsf{KeyGen}(1^\lambda)$*, sets* $\mathcal{L}_{\mathsf{Sign}} \leftarrow \emptyset$*, and gives* vk *to* $\mathcal{A}$*.*

Queries. $\mathcal{A}$ *is allowed to access the signing oracle* $\mathtt{O.Sign}$*, where* $\mathtt{O.Sign}$ *on input a signing query* $\mathsf{m} \in \mathcal{M}$ *returns* $\perp$ *if* $\mathcal{L}_{\mathsf{Sign}} \neq \emptyset$*; otherwise it returns* $\sigma \leftarrow \mathsf{Sign}(\mathsf{sigk}, \mathsf{m})$ *and sets* $\mathcal{L}_{\mathsf{Sign}} \leftarrow \mathcal{L}_{\mathsf{Sign}} \cup \{(\mathsf{m}, \sigma)\}$*.*

Forgery. $\mathcal{A}$ *outputs a forgery* (m^*, σ^*)*.* $\mathcal{A}$ *wins if it holds that* $(\mathsf{m}^*, \sigma^*) \notin \mathcal{L}_{\mathsf{Sign}}$ *and* $\mathsf{Vrfy}(\mathsf{vk}, \mathsf{m}^*, \sigma^*) = \top$*.*

Module-Learning with Errors. Following [6], we describe the definition of the module-learning with errors (MLWE) assumption, as follows:

Definition 10 (MLWE assumption). *For a security parameter* λ*, let* $n = n(\lambda), k = k(\lambda), \eta = \eta(\lambda)$ *denote positive integers. The module-LWE problem is to distinguish between uniform samples* $(\boldsymbol{a}_i, b_i) \in R_q^k \times R_q$ *from* m *samples* $(\boldsymbol{a}_i, b_i) \in R_q^k \times R_q$ *for* $i \in [m]$*, where* $\boldsymbol{a}_i \xleftarrow{\$} R_q^k$*,* $\boldsymbol{s} \xleftarrow{\$} \beta_\eta^k$*, and* $e_i \xleftarrow{\$} \beta_\eta$ *are samples (uniformly) at random, and* $b_i = \boldsymbol{a}_i^T \boldsymbol{s} + e_i$*.*

The MLWE assumption $\mathsf{MLWE}_{m,k,\eta}$ *holds if for any PPT algorithm* $\mathcal{A}$ *solving the module-LWE problem, its advantage*

$$\mathsf{Adv}^{\mathrm{mlwe}}_{m,k,\eta}(\mathcal{A}) := \left| \Pr\left[b' = 1 \;\middle|\; \begin{array}{l} \boldsymbol{A} \xleftarrow{\$} R_q^{m \times k}; (\boldsymbol{s}, \boldsymbol{e}) \leftarrow \beta_\eta^k \times \beta_\eta^m; \\ \boldsymbol{b} = \boldsymbol{A}\boldsymbol{s} + \boldsymbol{e}; b' \leftarrow \mathcal{A}(\boldsymbol{A}, \boldsymbol{b}) \end{array} \right] \right.$$
$$\left. - \Pr\left[b' = 1 \;\middle|\; \boldsymbol{A} \xleftarrow{\$} R_q^{m \times k}; \boldsymbol{b} \xleftarrow{\$} R_q^m; b' \leftarrow \mathcal{A}(\boldsymbol{A}, \boldsymbol{b}) \right] \right|$$

is negligible in λ*.*

3 Bounded CCA2-Secure PRE with Compact Ciphertexts

In this section, we propose a generic construction of bounded CCA2-secure PRE with compact ciphertexts. To achieve this, we introduce re-encryption key homomorphism and a security notion associated with this property. Then, we propose a generic construction starting from re-encryption key homomorphic PRE with our formalized security and strongly unforgeable OTS, and give a security proof for this construction.

3.1 Re-encryption Key Homomorphism of PRE

In order to construct a bounded CCA2-secure PRE with compact ciphertexts, we introduce *re-encryption key homomorphism* as a new property of PRE. This property is inspired by the *secret-to-public key homomorphism* defined in [29].

Definition 11 (Re-encryption key homomorphism). *Throughout this section, we consider a PRE scheme* $\Pi_{\mathsf{PRE}} = (\mathsf{Setup}, \mathsf{KeyGen}, \mathsf{Enc}, \mathsf{Dec}, \mathsf{ReKeyGen}, \mathsf{ReEnc})$ *with the property that the secret keys, public keys and re-encryption keys are elements of groups* $\mathcal{K}_{\mathsf{sk}}$, $\mathcal{K}_{\mathsf{pk}}$, *and* $\mathcal{K}_{\mathsf{rk}}$, *respectively. For simplicity, we suppose that all of the group operations of* $\mathcal{K}_{\mathsf{sk}}$, $\mathcal{K}_{\mathsf{pk}}$, *and* $\mathcal{K}_{\mathsf{rk}}$ *are* $+$. *The PRE scheme* Π_{PRE} *is said to be* re-encryption key homomorphic *if there exist the following map* $\mu : \mathcal{K}_{\mathsf{sk}} \to \mathcal{K}_{\mathsf{pk}}$ *and polynomial-time algorithms* $(\mathsf{HReKeyGen}, \mathsf{ReKeyEval})$*:*

- *Every* $(\mathsf{pk}, \mathsf{sk})$ *generated by* KeyGen *satisfies* $\mathsf{pk} = \mu(\mathsf{sk})$*;*
- μ *is a homomorphism: i.e., for all* $\mathsf{sk}, \mathsf{sk}' \in \mathcal{K}_{sk}$, *it holds that* $\mu(\mathsf{sk} + \mathsf{sk}') = \mu(\mathsf{sk}) \cdot \mu(\mathsf{sk}')$*;*
- $\mathsf{HReKeyGen}((\mathsf{sk}_{A,i})_{i\in[u]}, (\mathsf{pk}_{B,j})_{j\in[u]}) \to (\mathsf{rk}_{(A,i)\to(B,j)})_{i\in[u],j\in[u]}$*: The randomized or deterministic algorithm* $\mathsf{HReKeyGen}$ *takes as input* u *secret keys* $(\mathsf{sk}_{A,i})_{i\in[u]}$ *and* u *public keys* $(\mathsf{pk}_{B,j})_{j\in[u]}$ *(where* $\forall i \in [u], \forall j \in [u] : \mathsf{pk}_{A,i} \neq \mathsf{pk}_{B,j}$*), and outputs* u^2 *re-encryption keys* $(\mathsf{rk}_{(A,i)\to(B,j)})_{i\in[u],j\in[u]}$.
- $\mathsf{ReKeyEval}((\mathsf{rk}_{(A,\alpha_i)\to(B,\beta_i)})_{i\in[u]}) \to \mathsf{rk}_{A\to B}$*: The randomized or deterministic algorithm* $\mathsf{ReKeyEval}$ *takes as input* v *re-encryption keys* $(\mathsf{rk}_{(A,\alpha_i)\to(B,\beta_i)})_{i\in[v]}$ *(where* $v \leq u$ *and* $\forall i \in [v] : \alpha_i \in [u] \wedge \beta_i \in [u]$*) and outputs a new re-encryption key* $\mathsf{rk}_{A\to B}$.
- *For every* $n = \mathsf{poly}(\lambda)$, $u = \mathsf{poly}(\lambda)$, *every* $\mathsf{pp} \leftarrow \mathsf{Setup}(\lambda)$, *every* $\{(\mathsf{pk}_{i,j}, \mathsf{sk}_{i,j}) \leftarrow \mathsf{KeyGen}(\mathsf{pp})\}_{i\in\{A,B\},j\in[u]}$, *every* $(\mathsf{rk}_{(A,i)\to(B,j)})_{i\in[u],j\in[u]} \leftarrow \mathsf{HReKeyGen}((\mathsf{sk}_{A,i})_{i\in[u]}, (\mathsf{pk}_{B,i})_{i\in[u]})$, *every* $\mathsf{rk}_{A\to B} \leftarrow \mathsf{ReKeyEval}((\mathsf{rk}_{(A,\alpha_i)\to(B,\beta_i)})_{i\in[v]})$ *(for any* $\{(\alpha_i, \beta_i) \in [u]\times[u]\}_{i\in[v]}$*), and every* $\mathsf{m} \in \mathcal{M}$, *it holds that* $\mathsf{Dec}(\mathsf{sk}_B, \mathsf{ct}_B) = \mathsf{m}$ *with overwhelming probability, where* $\mathsf{ct}_B \leftarrow \mathsf{ReEnc}(\mathsf{rk}_{A\to B}, \mathsf{ct}_A)$, $\mathsf{ct}_A \leftarrow \mathsf{Enc}(\mathsf{pk}_A, \mathsf{m})$, $\mathsf{pk}_A = \mu(\mathsf{pk}_{A,\alpha_1}, \ldots, \mathsf{pk}_{A,\alpha_u})$, *and* $\mathsf{sk}_B = \mu(\mathsf{sk}_{B,\beta_1}, \ldots, \mathsf{sk}_{B,\beta_u})$.

Due to the additional property above, we need to introduce *security against chosen plaintext attacks with re-encryption key homomorphism* (denoted by RKH-CPA security) as a new security notion, since the two algorithms ReKeyGen and HReKeyGen are not compatible. This security is defined in the same way as the definition of CPA security (Definition 13) except that the adversary is given access to the homomorphic re-encryption key generation oracle `O.HReKeyGen`, instead of `O.ReKeyGen`. This formalization is Definition 12. Notice that, for simplicity, user-indices in Definition 12 are regarded as index-pairs $(i, j) \in [n] \times [u]$ rather than $i \in [n]$.

Definition 12 (RKH-CPA security). *For a security parameter* λ, *let* $n = \mathsf{poly}(\lambda), u = \mathsf{poly}(\lambda)$ *be positive integers. A* re-encryption key homomorphic *PRE scheme* $\Pi_{\mathsf{PRE}} = (\mathsf{Setup}, \mathsf{KeyGen}, \mathsf{Enc}, \mathsf{Dec}, \mathsf{ReKeyGen}, \mathsf{ReEnc})$ *with* $(\mathsf{HReKeyGen}, \mathsf{ReKeyEval})$ *is said to be* u*-*RKH-CPA*-secure if, for any PPT adversary* $\mathcal{A} = (\mathcal{A}_0, \mathcal{A}_1, \mathcal{A}_2)$ *against* Π_{PRE}, *its advantage* $\mathsf{Adv}^{u\text{-rkh-cpa}}_{\Pi_{\mathsf{PRE}},\mathcal{A},n}(\lambda) := \left|\Pr[\mathsf{Expt}^{u\text{-rkh-cpa}}_{\Pi_{\mathsf{PRE}},\mathcal{A},n}(\lambda) = 1] - 1/2\right|$ *is negligible in* λ, *where the experiment*

$\mathsf{Expt}^{u\text{-rkh-cpa}}_{\Pi_{\mathsf{PRE}},\mathcal{A},n}(\lambda)$ *is defined as follows:*

$\underline{\mathsf{Expt}^{u\text{-rkh-cpa}}_{\Pi_{\mathsf{PRE}},\mathcal{A},n}(\lambda)}$:

Generate $\mathsf{pp} \leftarrow \mathsf{Setup}(1^\lambda)$;
$(\mathcal{L}_{\mathtt{Corrupt}}, \mathsf{st}_0) \leftarrow \mathcal{A}_0(\mathsf{pp})$;
$\forall i \in [n], \forall j \in [u]$, *generate* $(\mathsf{pk}_{i,j}, \mathsf{sk}_{i,j}) \leftarrow \mathsf{KeyGen}(\mathsf{pp})$;
$((i^*, j^*), \mathsf{m}_0^*, \mathsf{m}_1^*, \mathsf{st}_1) \leftarrow \mathcal{A}_1^{\mathtt{O.HReKeyGen}}(\mathsf{st}_0, \{\mathsf{pk}_{i,j}\}_{i\in[n],j\in[u]}, \{\mathsf{sk}_{i,j}\}_{(i,j)\in\mathcal{L}_{\mathtt{Corrupt}}})$;
Sample $b \xleftarrow{\$} \{0.1\}$ *and run* $\mathsf{ct}^* \leftarrow \mathtt{O.Challenge}_b((i^*, j^*), \mathsf{m}_0^*, \mathsf{m}_1^*)$;
$b' \leftarrow \mathcal{A}_2^{\mathtt{O.HReKeyGen}}(\mathsf{st}_1, \mathsf{ct}^*)$;
Return 1 *if* $b = b'$; *otherwise, return* 0,

where $\mathcal{L}_{\mathtt{Corrupt}}$ *is a subset of* $[n] \times [u]$ *in the experiment above,* $(\mathsf{st}_0, \mathsf{st}_1)$ *is internal state information, and the oracle* O.HReKeyGen *is defined as follows:*

- *Homomorphic re-encryption key generation oracle* O.HReKeyGen *given a homomorphic re-encryption key query* $((A,i)_{i\in[u]}, (B,j)_{j\in[u]})$ *(where* $A, B \in [n]$*) returns* $\perp$ *if there exists some index* $(\hat{i}, \hat{j}) \in [u] \times [u]$ *such that* $((A, \hat{i}) = (i^*, j^*) \wedge (B, \hat{j}) \in \mathcal{L}_{\mathtt{Corrupt}})$ *or* $(A, \hat{i}) = (B, \hat{j})$ *(where* $\mathcal{L}_{\mathtt{Honest}} = [n]\backslash\mathcal{L}_{\mathtt{Corrupt}}$*); otherwise, it returns* $(\mathsf{rk}_{(A,i)\to(B,j)})_{i\in[u],j\in[u]} \leftarrow \mathsf{HReKeyGen}((\mathsf{sk}_{A,i})_{i\in[u]}, (\mathsf{pk}_{B,j})_{j\in[u]})$.

Regarding the relation between CPA security and RKH-CPA security, it is clear that RKH-CPA security implies CPA security. However, it seems that CPA security does not necessarily imply RKH-CPA security. This is because O.HReKeyGen in the RKH-CPA game needs to return re-encryption keys such that homomorphic evaluation is possible, while O.ReKeyGen in the CPA game does not necessarily return such re-encryption keys.

3.2 Construction from Re-encryption Key Homomorphic PRE

We give a generic construction of bounded CCA2-secure PRE scheme $\Pi_{\mathsf{C\text{-}PRE}}$ with compact ciphertexts. As described before, this is constructed from RKH-CPA-secure PRE and strongly unforgeable OTS. To achieve compact ciphertexts, we require the underlying PRE scheme to be re-encryption key homomorphic (Definition 11).

The proposed scheme $\Pi_{\mathsf{C\text{-}PRE}}$ employs the following cryptographic primitives:

- a re-encryption key homomorphic PRE scheme $\Pi'_{\mathsf{PRE}} = (\Pi'_{\mathsf{PRE}}.\mathsf{Setup}, \Pi'_{\mathsf{PRE}}.\mathsf{KeyGen}, \Pi'_{\mathsf{PRE}}.\mathsf{Enc}, \Pi'_{\mathsf{PRE}}.\mathsf{Dec}, \Pi'_{\mathsf{PRE}}.\mathsf{ReKeyGen}, \Pi'_{\mathsf{PRE}}.\mathsf{ReEnc})$ with two PPT algorithms $\Pi'_{\mathsf{PRE}}.\mathsf{HReKeyGen}, \Pi'_{\mathsf{PRE}}.\mathsf{ReKeyEval}$; and
- an OTS scheme $\Pi_{\mathsf{OTS}} = (\Pi_{\mathsf{OTS}}.\mathsf{KeyGen}, \Pi_{\mathsf{OTS}}.\mathsf{Sign}, \Pi_{\mathsf{OTS}}.\mathsf{Vrfy})$.

The proposed PRE scheme $\Pi_{\mathsf{C\text{-}PRE}} = (\mathsf{Setup}, \mathsf{KeyGen}, \mathsf{Enc}, \mathsf{Dec}, \mathsf{ReKeyGen}, \mathsf{ReEnc})$ is constructed as follows:

- $\mathsf{Setup}(1^\lambda) \to \mathsf{pp}$: Generate $\mathsf{pp}' \leftarrow \Pi'_{\mathsf{PRE}}.\mathsf{Setup}(\mathsf{pp})$. Let $\mathcal{M} = \mathcal{M}(\lambda)$ be the message space, which is the same as that space of Π'_{PRE}, let $\bar{n} = \bar{n}(\lambda), u = u(\lambda)$ be positive integers, and let $[\bar{n}]$ be the verification key space of Π_{OTS}[2]. Let $\boldsymbol{M} = (m_{i,j}) \in \{0,1\}^{u \times \bar{n}}$ be a t-disjunct matrix. Output $\mathsf{pp} = (\mathsf{pp}', \bar{n}, u, \boldsymbol{M})$.
- $\mathsf{KeyGen}(\mathsf{pp}) \to (\mathsf{pk}, \mathsf{sk})$: Parse $\mathsf{pp} = (\mathsf{pp}', \bar{n}, u, \boldsymbol{M})$ and generate $(\mathsf{pk}'_i, \mathsf{sk}'_i) \leftarrow \Pi'_{\mathsf{PRE}}.\mathsf{KeyGen}(\mathsf{pp}')$ for $i \in [u]$. Output $\mathsf{pk} = (\mathsf{pk}'_i)_{i\in[u]}$ and $\mathsf{sk} = (\mathsf{sk}'_i)_{i\in[u]}$.
- $\mathsf{Enc}(\mathsf{pk}, \mathsf{m}) \to \mathsf{ct}$:
  1. Parse $\mathsf{pk} = (\mathsf{pk}'_i)_{i\in[n]}$.
  2. Generate $(\mathsf{vk}, \mathsf{sigk}) \leftarrow \Pi_{\mathsf{OTS}}.\mathsf{KeyGen}(1^\lambda)$.
  3. Compute $\{\tau_1, \ldots, \tau_v\} \leftarrow \phi_{\boldsymbol{M}}(\mathsf{vk})$, where all $\tau_1, \ldots, \tau_v \in [u]$ are distinct.
  4. Compute $\mathsf{pk}'_{\mathsf{vk}} \leftarrow \sum_{i\in[v]} \mathsf{pk}'_{\tau_i}$ and $\mathsf{ct}'_{\mathsf{vk}} \leftarrow \Pi'_{\mathsf{PRE}}.\mathsf{Enc}(\mathsf{pk}'_{\mathsf{vk}}, \mathsf{m})$.
  5. Compute $\sigma \leftarrow \Pi_{\mathsf{OTS}}.\mathsf{Sign}(\mathsf{sigk}, \mathsf{ct}'_{\mathsf{vk}})$.
  6. Output $\mathsf{ct} = (\mathsf{vk}, \mathsf{ct}'_{\mathsf{vk}}, \sigma)$.
- $\mathsf{Dec}(\mathsf{sk}, \mathsf{ct}) \to \mathsf{m}/\bot$: Parse $\mathsf{sk} = (\mathsf{sk}'_i)_{i\in[u]}$ and $\mathsf{ct} = (\mathsf{vk}, \mathsf{ct}'_{\mathsf{vk}}, \sigma)$. Output $\bot$ if $\Pi_{\mathsf{OTS}}.\mathsf{Vrfy}(\mathsf{vk}, \mathsf{ct}'_{\mathsf{vk}}, \sigma) = \bot$ holds; otherwise, compute $\{\tau_1, \ldots, \tau_v\} \leftarrow \phi_{\boldsymbol{M}}(\mathsf{vk})$, $\mathsf{sk}'_{\mathsf{vk}} \leftarrow \sum_{i\in[v]} \mathsf{sk}'_{\tau_i}$, and output $\mathsf{m}' \leftarrow \Pi'_{\mathsf{PRE}}.\mathsf{Dec}(\mathsf{sk}'_{\mathsf{vk}}, \mathsf{ct}'_{\mathsf{vk}})$.
- $\mathsf{ReKeyGen}(\mathsf{sk}_A, \mathsf{pk}_B) \to \mathsf{rk}_{A\to B}$:
  1. Parse $\mathsf{sk}_A = (\mathsf{sk}'_{A,i})_{i\in[u]}$ and $\mathsf{pk}_B = (\mathsf{pk}'_{B,i})_{i\in[u]}$.
  2. Compute $(\mathsf{rk}_{(A,i)\to(B,j)})_{i\in[u],j\in[u]} \leftarrow \Pi'_{\mathsf{PRE}}.\mathsf{HReKeyGen}((\mathsf{sk}'_{A,i})_{i\in[u]}, (\mathsf{pk}'_{B,j})_{j\in[u]})$.
  3. Output $\mathsf{rk}_{A\to B} = (\mathsf{rk}_{(A,i)\to(B,j)})_{i\in[u],j\in[u]}$.
- $\mathsf{ReEnc}(\mathsf{rk}_{A\to B}, \mathsf{ct}_A) \to \mathsf{ct}_B$:
  1. Parse $\mathsf{rk} = (\mathsf{rk}_{(A,i)\to(B,j)})_{i\in[u],j\in[u]}$ and $\mathsf{ct}_A = (\mathsf{vk}_A, \mathsf{ct}'_{\mathsf{vk}_A}, \sigma_A)$.
  2. Output $\bot$ if $\Pi_{\mathsf{OTS}}.\mathsf{Vrfy}(\mathsf{vk}_A, \mathsf{ct}'_{\mathsf{vk}_A}, \sigma_A) = \bot$ holds.
  3. Generate $(\mathsf{vk}_B, \mathsf{sigk}_B) \leftarrow \Pi_{\mathsf{OTS}}.\mathsf{KeyGen}(1^\lambda)$.
  4. Compute $\{\alpha_1, \ldots, \alpha_v\} \leftarrow \phi_{\boldsymbol{M}}(\mathsf{vk}_A)$ and $\{\beta_1, \ldots, \beta_v\} \leftarrow \phi_{\boldsymbol{M}}(\mathsf{vk}_B)$.
  5. Compute $\mathsf{rk}_{\mathsf{vk}_A\to\mathsf{vk}_B} \leftarrow \Pi'_{\mathsf{PRE}}.\mathsf{ReKeyEval}((\mathsf{rk}_{(A,\alpha_i)\to(B,\beta_i)})_{i\in[v]})$.
  6. Compute $\mathsf{ct}'_{\mathsf{vk}_B} \leftarrow \Pi'_{\mathsf{PRE}}.\mathsf{ReEnc}(\mathsf{rk}_{\mathsf{vk}_A\to\mathsf{vk}_B}, \mathsf{ct}'_{\mathsf{vk}_A})$.
  7. Compute $\sigma_B \leftarrow \Pi_{\mathsf{OTS}}.\mathsf{Sign}(\mathsf{sigk}_B, \mathsf{ct}'_{\mathsf{vk}_B})$.
  8. Output $\mathsf{ct}_B = (\mathsf{vk}_B, \mathsf{ct}'_{\mathsf{vk}_B}, \sigma_B)$.

Due to the correctness of $\Pi'_{\mathsf{PRE}}, \Pi_{\mathsf{OTS}}$ and the re-encryption key homomorphism of Π'_{PRE}, the correctness of $\Pi_{\mathsf{C\text{-}PRE}}$ holds. Proposition 1 shows this correctness, and we omit the proof of this proposition because this is proved clearly.

Proposition 1 (Correctness of $\Pi_{\mathsf{C\text{-}PRE}}$). *If the PRE scheme* Π'_{PRE} *is* correct *and* re-encryption key-homomorphic*, and the OTS scheme* Π_{OTS} *is* correct*, then the resulting PRE scheme* $\Pi_{\mathsf{C\text{-}PRE}}$ *is* correct.

3.3 Security Proof

The following theorem shows the bounded CCA2 security of $\Pi_{\mathsf{C\text{-}PRE}}$:

[2] By using a collision resistant hash function, we can compress the verification key size of Π_{OTS} into the space $[\bar{n}]$ in order to reduce the public key size of $\Pi_{\mathsf{C\text{-}PRE}}$.

Theorem 1 (Security of $\Pi_{\mathsf{C\text{-}PRE}}$). *Suppose that the matrix $\boldsymbol{M} \in \{0,1\}^{u \times \bar{n}}$ is a t-disjunct matrix and n (resp. n_h) is the total number of users (resp. honest users) in the (t,t)-CCA2 game. If the PRE scheme Π'_{PRE} is u-RKH-CPA-secure, and the OTS scheme Π_{OTS} is strongly unforgeable, then the resulting PRE scheme $\Pi_{\mathsf{C\text{-}PRE}}$ is (t,t)-CCA2-secure.*

In particular, if there exists a PPT algorithm $\mathcal{A}$ against a (t,t)-CCA2-secure PRE scheme $\Pi_{\mathsf{C\text{-}PRE}}$, then there exists a PPT algorithm $\mathcal{B}$ against a u-RKH-CPA-secure PRE scheme Π'_{PRE} and a PPT algorithm $\mathcal{F}$ against strongly unforgeable OTS scheme Π_{OTS}, such that

$$\mathsf{Adv}^{(t,\,t)\text{-cca2}}_{\Pi_{\mathsf{C\text{-}PRE}},\mathcal{A},n}(\lambda) \le n_h^3 u^2 \cdot \mathsf{Adv}^{u\text{-rkh-cpa}}_{\Pi'_{\mathsf{PRE}},\mathcal{B},n}(\lambda) + \mathsf{Adv}^{\text{suf-ot}}_{\Pi_{\mathsf{OTS}},\mathcal{F}}(\lambda).$$

Proof. Let $\mathcal{A}$ be a PPT adversary against the PRE scheme $\Pi_{\mathsf{C\text{-}PRE}}$. Let $\mathsf{ct}^* = (\mathsf{vk}^*, \mathsf{ct}'^*_{\mathsf{vk}^*}, \sigma^*)$ be the challenge ciphertext and let $\mathcal{L}_{\mathtt{Honest}} = [n] \backslash \mathcal{L}_{\mathtt{Corrupt}}$ be the set of honest users. In order to prove Theorem 1, we consider security games $\mathsf{Game}_0, \mathsf{Game}_1$. For $i \in \{0,1\}$, let W_i be the event that the experiment outputs 1 in Game_i.

$\underline{\mathsf{Game}_0}$: This game is the same as the ordinary (t,t)-CCA2 game. Then, we have $\mathsf{Adv}^{(t,\,t)\text{-cca2}}_{\Pi_{\mathsf{C\text{-}PRE}},\mathcal{A},n}(\lambda) = |\Pr[W_0] - 1/2|$.

$\underline{\mathsf{Game}_1}$: This game is the same as Game_0 except for the following procedures of the decryption oracle $\mathtt{O.Dec}$ and the re-encryption oracle $\mathtt{O.ReEnc}$: At the beginning of the game, the experiment generates $(\mathsf{vk}^*, \mathsf{sigk}^*) \leftarrow \Pi_{\mathsf{OTS}}.\mathsf{KeyGen}(1^\lambda)$. For a decryption query (i, ct_i) (resp. a re-encryption query (i, j, ct_i)) (where $\mathsf{ct}_i = (\mathsf{vk}_i, \mathsf{ct}'_{\mathsf{vk}_i}, \sigma_i)$), the experiment aborts if it holds that $\mathsf{vk}_i = \mathsf{vk}^*$, $\mathsf{ct}_i \ne \mathsf{ct}^*$, and $\Pi_{\mathsf{OTS}}.\mathsf{Vrfy}(\mathsf{vk}_i, \mathsf{ct}'_{\mathsf{vk}_i}, \sigma_i) = \top$ (this event is denoted as Bad); otherwise, it returns the result of $\mathtt{O.Dec}(i, \mathsf{ct}_i)$ (resp., $\mathtt{O.ReEnc}(i, j, \mathsf{ct}_i)$).

It is clear that Game_0 and Game_1 are identical unless Bad occurs. Thus, we construct a PPT algorithm $\mathcal{F}$ breaking the strongly unforgeable OTS scheme Π_{OTS} so that we bound the probability that Bad occurs.

On input a verification key vk^* of Π_{OTS}, $\mathcal{F}$ generates $\mathsf{pp} \leftarrow \mathsf{Setup}(1^\lambda)$ and $(\mathsf{pk}_i, \mathsf{sk}_i) \leftarrow \mathsf{KeyGen}(\mathsf{pp})$ for every $i \in [n]$ and gives $(\mathsf{pp}, \{\mathsf{pk}_i\}_{i \in [n]})$ to $\mathcal{A}$. Given $\mathcal{L}_{\mathtt{Corrupt}}$, $\mathcal{F}$ returns $\{\mathsf{sk}_i\}_{i \in \mathcal{L}_{\mathtt{Corrupt}}}$. By using the generated key-pairs, this algorithm simulates the oracles $\mathtt{O.ReKeyGen}$, $\mathtt{O.Dec}$, and $\mathtt{O.ReEnc}$ except for the following: For a decryption query (resp. a re-encryption query) on $\mathsf{ct}_i = (\mathsf{vk}_i, \mathsf{ct}'_{\mathsf{vk}_i}, \sigma_i)$, $\mathcal{F}$ aborts and outputs $(\mathsf{ct}'_{\mathsf{vk}_i}, \sigma_i)$ as a forgery in the strong unforgeability game, if Bad occurs; otherwise, this algorithm checks whether (i, ct_i) is a derivative of the challenge ciphertext (i^*, ct^*) if (i^*, ct^*) is defined. If so, it returns $\perp$. Otherwise it returns $\mathsf{m}' \leftarrow \mathsf{Dec}(\mathsf{sk}_i, \mathsf{ct}_i)$ (resp. $\mathsf{ct}_j \leftarrow \mathsf{ReEnc}(\mathsf{rk}_{i \to j}, \mathsf{ct}_i)$). Additionally, when $\mathcal{A}$ submits $(i^*, \mathsf{m}_0^*, \mathsf{m}_1^*)$, $\mathcal{F}$ chooses $b \xleftarrow{\$} \{0,1\}$ and computes $\mathsf{ct}'^*_{\mathsf{vk}^*}$ by following the procedure of $\mathsf{Enc}(\mathsf{pk}_{i^*}, \mathsf{m}_b^*)$. Then, this algorithm issues $\mathsf{ct}'^*_{\mathsf{vk}^*}$ to the signing oracle $\mathtt{O.Sign}$ in the strong unforgeability game and obtains σ^*. $\mathcal{F}$ returns the challenge ciphertext $\mathsf{ct}^* = (\mathsf{vk}^*, \mathsf{ct}'^*_{\mathsf{vk}^*}, \sigma^*)$. Finally, when $\mathcal{A}$ outputs $b' \in \{0,1\}$ and Bad has not occurred, $\mathcal{F}$ halts and aborts.

It is clear that the output of $\mathcal{F}$ is a valid forgery in the strong unforgeability game if Bad occurs. Additionally, $\mathcal{F}$ completely simulates the oracles in the

(t,t)-CCA2 game since it has all key-pairs $(\mathsf{pk}_i, \mathsf{sk}_i)$. Hence, we have $\Pr[\mathsf{Bad}] \le \mathsf{Adv}^{\text{suf-ot}}_{\Pi_{\mathsf{OTS}},\mathcal{F}}(\lambda)$, and it holds that $|\Pr[W_0] - \Pr[W_1]| \le \mathsf{Adv}^{\text{suf-ot}}_{\Pi_{\mathsf{OTS}},\mathcal{F}}(\lambda)$.

In order to bound the winning probability of $\mathcal{A}$ in Game_1, we construct a PPT algorithm $\mathcal{B}$ against the u-RKH-CPA security of Π'_{PRE}, as follows: On input $(\mathsf{pp}', \{\mathsf{pk}'_{i,j}\}_{i\in[n],j\in[u]})$ in the u-RKH-CPA game, $\mathcal{B}$ sets $\mathsf{pp} = (\mathsf{pp}', \bar{n}, u, \boldsymbol{M})$, generates $(\mathsf{vk}^*, \mathsf{sigk}^*) \leftarrow \mathsf{KeyGen}(1^\lambda)$, and gives pp to $\mathcal{A}$. When $\mathcal{A}$ submits $\mathcal{L}_{\mathtt{Corrupt}} \subset [n]$, $\mathcal{B}$ chooses $i^* \xleftarrow{\$} [n]\backslash\mathcal{L}_{\mathtt{Corrupt}}, j^* \xleftarrow{\$} \phi_{\boldsymbol{M}}(\mathsf{vk}^*)$, and obtains $\{\mathsf{sk}'_{i,j}\}_{(i,j)\in[n]\times[u]\backslash\{(i^*,j^*)\}}$ by issuing (i^*, j^*) to the u-RKH-CPA game. Here, let $\mathcal{L}_{\mathtt{Honest}} := [n]\backslash\mathcal{L}_{\mathtt{Corrupt}}$. Then, $\mathcal{B}$ sets $\mathsf{pk}'_{i^*,j^*} := \mathsf{pk}'_{i^*,j^*} \cdot \left(\sum_{j\in\phi_{\boldsymbol{M}}(\mathsf{vk}^*)\backslash\{j^*\}}(\mathsf{pk}'_{i^*,j})^{-1}\right)$ and $\mathsf{pk}_i = (\mathsf{pk}'_{i,j})_{j\in[u]}$ for $i \in [n]$ and then returns $(\{\mathsf{pk}_i\}_{i\in[n]}\{\mathsf{sk}_i\}_{i\in\mathcal{L}_{\mathtt{Corrupt}}})$, where let $\mathsf{sk}_i := (\mathsf{sk}'_{i,j})_{j\in[u]}$ for every $i \in [n]\backslash\{i^*\}$, and let $\mathsf{sk}_{i^*} := (\mathsf{sk}'_{i^*,j})_{j\in[u]\backslash\{j^*\}}$. Additionally, $\mathcal{B}$ simulates the oracles $\mathtt{O.ReKeyGen}$, $\mathtt{O.Dec}$, $\mathtt{O.ReEnc}$, $\mathtt{O.Challenge}_b$, as follows:

- $\mathtt{O.ReKeyGen}(A, B)$: $\mathcal{B}$ returns $\perp$ if $A = i^* \wedge B \in \mathcal{L}_{\mathtt{Corrupt}}$ holds. If $\mathsf{T}_{\mathsf{rk}}[A, B] = \mathsf{rk}_{A\to B}$, $\mathcal{B}$ returns $\mathsf{rk}_{A\to B}$; otherwise, it obtains $(\mathsf{rk}_{(A,i)\to(B,j)})_{i\in[u],j\in[u]}$ by issuing $((A,i)_{i\in[u]}, (B,j)_{j\in[u]})$ to the oracle $\mathtt{O.HReKeyGen}$ in the u-RKH-CPA game, returns $\mathsf{rk}_{A\to B} = (\mathsf{rk}_{(A,i)\to(B,j)})_{i\in[u],j\in[u]}$, and sets $\mathsf{T}_{\mathsf{rk}}[A, B] \leftarrow \mathsf{rk}_{A\to B}$.
- $\mathtt{O.Dec}(A, \mathsf{ct}_A)$: For $\mathsf{ct}_A = (\mathsf{vk}_A, \mathsf{ct}'_A, \sigma_A)$, $\mathcal{B}$ returns $\perp$ if the challenge ciphertext is defined and ct_A is its $\mathsf{derivative}$. Otherwise, it does the following:
  1. Abort and output a random bit if $A = i^* \wedge j^* \in \phi_{\boldsymbol{M}}(\mathsf{vk}_A)$ holds.
  2. Return $\perp$ if it holds that $\mathsf{vk}_A = \mathsf{vk}^*$, $\mathsf{ct}_A \ne \mathsf{ct}^*$, and $\Pi_{\mathsf{OTS}}.\mathsf{Vrfy}(\mathsf{vk}_A, \mathsf{ct}'_{\mathsf{vk}_A}, \sigma_A) = \top$.
  3. Return $\perp$ if $\Pi_{\mathsf{OTS}}.\mathsf{Vrfy}(\mathsf{vk}_A, \mathsf{ct}'_{\mathsf{vk}_A}, \sigma_A) = \perp$ holds.
  4. Compute $\mathsf{sk}_{\mathsf{vk}_A} \leftarrow \sum_{i\in[v]} \mathsf{sk}'_{\alpha_i}$, where $\{\alpha_1, \dots, \alpha_v\} = \phi_{\boldsymbol{M}_A}(\mathsf{vk}_A)$.
  5. Return $\mathsf{m}' \leftarrow \Pi'_{\mathsf{PRE}}.\mathsf{Dec}(\mathsf{sk}_{\mathsf{vk}_A}, \mathsf{ct}'_{\mathsf{vk}_A})$.
- $\mathtt{O.ReEnc}(A, B, \mathsf{ct}_A)$: For $\mathsf{ct}_A = (\mathsf{vk}_A, \mathsf{ct}'_{\mathsf{vk}_A}, \sigma_A)$, $\mathcal{B}$ returns $\perp$ if (A, ct_A) is a $\mathsf{derivative}$ of (i^*, ct^*) and $B \in \mathcal{L}_{\mathtt{Corrupt}}$ holds. Otherwise, this algorithm does the following:
  1. Abort and output a random bit if $A = i^* \wedge j^* \in \phi_{\boldsymbol{M}}(\mathsf{vk}_A)$ holds.
  2. Return $\perp$ if $\mathsf{vk}_A = \mathsf{vk}^*$, $\mathsf{ct}_A \ne \mathsf{ct}^*$, and $\Pi_{\mathsf{OTS}}.\mathsf{Vrfy}(\mathsf{vk}_A, \mathsf{ct}'_A, \sigma_A) = \top$ hold.
  3. Return $\perp$ if $\Pi_{\mathsf{OTS}}.\mathsf{Vrfy}(\mathsf{vk}_A, \mathsf{ct}'_{\mathsf{vk}_A}, \sigma_A) = \perp$ holds.
  4. Generate $(\mathsf{vk}_B, \mathsf{sigk}_B) \leftarrow \Pi_{\mathsf{OTS}}.\mathsf{KeyGen}(1^\lambda)$.
  5. Compute $\{\alpha_1, \dots, \alpha_v\} \leftarrow \phi_{\boldsymbol{M}}(\mathsf{vk}_A)$, $\{\beta_1, \dots, \beta_v\} \leftarrow \phi_{\boldsymbol{M}}(\mathsf{vk}_B)$.
  6. If $\mathsf{T}_{\mathsf{rk}}[A, B] = \mathsf{rk}_{A\to B}$, parse $\mathsf{rk}_{A\to B} = (\mathsf{rk}_{(A,i)\to(B,j)})_{i\in[u],j\in[u]}$.
  7. If $\mathsf{T}_{\mathsf{rk}}[A, B] = \emptyset$ and $A \ne i^*$ hold, compute $(\mathsf{rk}_{(A,i)\to(B,j)})_{i\in[u],j\in[u]} \leftarrow \mathsf{HReKeyGen}((\mathsf{sk}_{A,i})_{i\in[u]}, (\mathsf{pk}_{B,j})_{j\in[u]})$ and set $\mathsf{T}_{\mathsf{rk}}[A, B] \leftarrow (\mathsf{rk}_{(A,i)\to(B,j)})_{i\in[u],j\in[u]}$.
  8. If $\mathsf{T}_{\mathsf{rk}}[A, B] = \emptyset$ and $A = i^*$ hold, set $\mathsf{sk}_{A,i} \leftarrow \emptyset$ for all $i \notin \{\alpha_1, \dots, \alpha_v\}$ and then compute $(\mathsf{rk}_{(A,i)\to(B,j)})_{i\in[u],j\in[u]} \leftarrow \mathsf{HReKeyGen}((\mathsf{sk}_{A,i})_{i\in[u]}, (\mathsf{pk}_{B,j})_{j\in[u]})$.
  9. Compute $\mathsf{rk}_{\mathsf{vk}_A\to\mathsf{vk}_B} \leftarrow \sum_{i\in[v]} \mathsf{rk}_{(A,\alpha_i)\to(B,\beta_i)}$.
  10. Compute $\mathsf{ct}'_{\mathsf{vk}_B} \leftarrow \mathsf{ReEnc}(\mathsf{rk}_{\mathsf{vk}_A\to\mathsf{vk}_B}, \mathsf{ct}'_{\mathsf{vk}_A})$.
  11. Compute $\sigma_B \leftarrow \Pi_{\mathsf{OTS}}.\mathsf{Sign}(\mathsf{sigk}_B, \mathsf{ct}'_{\mathsf{vk}_B})$.
  12. Return $\mathsf{ct}_B = (\mathsf{vk}_B, \mathsf{ct}'_{\mathsf{vk}_B}, \sigma_B)$.

- $\mathtt{O.Challenge}_b(i', \mathsf{m}_0^*, \mathsf{m}_1^*)$:
  1. Abort and output a random bit if $i^* \neq i'$ holds.
  2. Obtain the ciphertext $\mathsf{ct}'^*_{\mathsf{vk}^*}$ by issuing $((i^*, j^*), \mathsf{m}_0^*, \mathsf{m}_1^*)$ to the challenge oracle in the u-RKH-CPA game.
  3. Compute $\sigma^* \leftarrow \Pi_{\mathsf{OTS}}.\mathsf{Sign}(\mathsf{sigk}^*, \mathsf{ct}'^*_{\mathsf{vk}^*})$.
  4. Return $\mathsf{ct}^* = (\mathsf{vk}^*, \mathsf{ct}'^*_{\mathsf{vk}^*}, \sigma^*)$.

Finally, when $\mathcal{A}$ outputs $b' \in \{0,1\}$, $\mathcal{B}$ also outputs b'.

We analyze the algorithm $\mathcal{B}$. $\mathcal{B}$ simulates the environment of $\mathcal{A}$ unless $\mathcal{B}$ aborts in the simulation of all the oracles. To estimate the winning probability of $\mathcal{B}$, we define Abort as the event that this algorithm aborts in the simulation above (namely, $A = i^* \wedge j^* \in \phi_M(\mathsf{vk}_A)$ holds in the oracle $\mathtt{O.Dec}$ or $\mathtt{O.ReEnc}$, or $i^* \neq i'$ holds in the oracle $\mathtt{O.Challenge}$). Additionally, let $W_{\mathcal{B}}$ denote the event that $\mathcal{B}$ outputs a bit $b' \in \{0,1\}$ such that $b = b'$. Then, $\Pr[W_{\mathcal{B}} \mid \mathsf{Abort}] = 1/2$ and $\Pr[\neg\mathsf{Abort}] \geq 1/(n_h^3 u^2)$ hold since Abort can occur in the simulation of the oracles $\mathtt{O.Dec}, \mathtt{O.ReEnc}, \mathtt{O.Challenge}_b$. Hence, we have

$$\begin{aligned}\Pr[W_{\mathcal{B}}] &= \Pr[\mathsf{Abort}] \cdot \Pr[W_{\mathcal{B}} \mid \mathsf{Abort}] + \Pr[\neg\mathsf{Abort}] \cdot \Pr[W_{\mathcal{B}} \mid \neg\mathsf{Abort}] \\ &\geq \frac{1}{2}\left(1 - \frac{1}{n_h^3 u^2}\right) + \frac{1}{n_h^3 u^2} \cdot \Pr[W_{\mathcal{B}} \mid \neg\mathsf{Abort}] \\ &= \frac{1}{2} + \frac{1}{n_h^3 u^2}\left(\Pr[W_{\mathcal{B}} \mid \neg\mathsf{Abort}] - \frac{1}{2}\right).\end{aligned}$$

Since the $\mathcal{A}$'s advantage $\varepsilon_{\mathcal{A}}$ in Game_1 is equivalent to $|\Pr[W_{\mathcal{B}} \mid \neg\mathsf{Abort}] - 1/2|$, the $\mathcal{B}$'s advantage $\varepsilon_{\mathcal{B}} = |\Pr[W_{\mathcal{B}}] - 1/2|$ is at least $\varepsilon_{\mathcal{A}}/(n_h^3 u^2)$.

From the above discussion, we obtain

$$\mathsf{Adv}^{(t,t)\text{-cca2}}_{\Pi_{\mathsf{C\text{-}PRE}},\mathcal{A},n}(\lambda) \leq n_h^3 u^2 \cdot \mathsf{Adv}^{u\text{-kh-cpa}}_{\Pi'_{\mathsf{PRE}},\mathcal{B},n}(\lambda) + \mathsf{Adv}^{\text{suf-ot}}_{\Pi_{\mathsf{OTS}},\mathcal{F}}(\lambda),$$

and complete the proof. □

4 Re-encryption Key Homomorphic PRE from Lattices

In order to instantiate our generic construction with compact ciphertexts, we give a lattice-based PRE scheme $\Pi_{\mathsf{L\text{-}PRE}}$ with re-encryption key homomorphism and prove that $\Pi_{\mathsf{L\text{-}PRE}}$ is RKH-CPA secure. The algorithms Setup, KeyGen, Enc, Dec of $\Pi_{\mathsf{L\text{-}PRE}}$ are similar to those of Kyber's underlying PKE scheme [6]. For simplicity, we consider a modified Kyber's algorithms in which procedures with compression functions used in Kyber's PKE scheme are omitted. Then, we add the algorithms ReKeyGen, ReEnc, HReKeyGen, ReKeyEval in order to guarantee the re-encryption functionality and re-encryption key homomorphic property of PRE.

To construct the PRE scheme $\Pi_{\mathsf{L\text{-}PRE}}$, we employ the following functions:

- The bit-decomposition function BitDecomp given a vector $x \in \mathbb{Z}_q^N$ decomposes x into its bit representation.

- The powers-of-two function $\mathsf{Powersof2}$ with $\ell = \lceil \log q \rceil$, on input a (column) vector $s \in \mathbb{Z}_q^N$, outputs $(1, 2, \ldots, 2^\ell)^\top \otimes s = (s, 2s, \ldots, 2^{\ell-1}s) \in \mathbb{Z}_q^{N\ell}$, where $\otimes$ is the standard tensor product.

The PRE scheme $\Pi_{\mathsf{L\text{-}PRE}} = (\mathsf{Setup}, \mathsf{KeyGen}, \mathsf{Enc}, \mathsf{Dec}, \mathsf{ReKeyGen}, \mathsf{ReEnc})$ with $(\mathsf{HReKeyGen}, \mathsf{ReKeyEval})$ is constructed as follows:

- $\mathsf{Setup}(1^\lambda) \to \mathsf{pp}$:
  - Let $\mathcal{M} = \{0,1\}^\mu$ be the message space, where $\mu = \mu(\lambda)$ is a positive integer.
  - Let η, k be positive integers, and let $\ell := \lceil \log q \rceil$.
  - Sample $\boldsymbol{A} \xleftarrow{\$} R_q^{k \times k}$.

  Output $\mathsf{pp} = (\lambda, \mu, N, N', q, \eta, k, \ell, \boldsymbol{A})$.
- $\mathsf{KeyGen}(\mathsf{pp}) \to (\mathsf{pk}, \mathsf{sk})$: Parse $\mathsf{pp} = (\lambda, \mu, N, N', q, \ell, \eta, k, \boldsymbol{A})$. Sample $(\boldsymbol{s}, \hat{\boldsymbol{s}}) \leftarrow \beta_\eta^k \times \beta_\eta^k$ and $(\boldsymbol{e}, \hat{\boldsymbol{e}}) \leftarrow \beta_\eta^k \times \beta_\eta^k$. Compute $\boldsymbol{t} \leftarrow \boldsymbol{A}\boldsymbol{s} + \boldsymbol{e}$ and $\hat{\boldsymbol{t}} \leftarrow \boldsymbol{A}\hat{\boldsymbol{s}} + \hat{\boldsymbol{e}}$. Output $\mathsf{pk} = (\boldsymbol{t}, \hat{\boldsymbol{t}}) \in R_q^k \times R_q^k$ and $\mathsf{sk} = (\boldsymbol{s}, \hat{\boldsymbol{s}}) \in R^k \times R^k$.
- $\mathsf{Enc}(\mathsf{pk}, \mathsf{m}) \to \mathsf{ct}$: Parse $\mathsf{pk} = (\boldsymbol{t}, \hat{\boldsymbol{t}})$. Sample $(\boldsymbol{r}, \boldsymbol{e}_1, e_2) \leftarrow \beta_\eta^k \times \beta_\eta^k \times \beta_\eta.$, and compute $\boldsymbol{u} \leftarrow \boldsymbol{A}^\top \boldsymbol{r} + \boldsymbol{e}_1^\top$ and $v \leftarrow \boldsymbol{t}^\top \boldsymbol{r} + e_2 + \lceil \frac{q}{2} \rfloor \cdot \mathsf{m}$. Output $\mathsf{ct} = (\boldsymbol{u}, v) \in R_q^k \times R_q$.
- $\mathsf{Dec}(\mathsf{sk}, \mathsf{ct}) \to \mathsf{m}$:
  1. Parse $\mathsf{sk} = (\boldsymbol{s}, \hat{\boldsymbol{s}})$ and $\mathsf{ct} = (\boldsymbol{u}, v)$.
  2. Set $\tilde{\boldsymbol{s}} \leftarrow \boldsymbol{s}$ if ct is generated by the algorithm Enc. Set $\tilde{\boldsymbol{s}} \leftarrow \hat{\boldsymbol{s}}$ if ct is generated by the algorithm ReEnc.
  3. Output $\mathsf{m} \leftarrow \lceil 2(v - \tilde{\boldsymbol{s}}^\top \boldsymbol{u})/q \rfloor \bmod 2$.
- $\mathsf{ReKeyGen}(\mathsf{sk}_A, \mathsf{pk}_B) \to \mathsf{rk}_{A \to B}$:
  1. Parse $\mathsf{sk}_A = (\boldsymbol{s}_A, \hat{\boldsymbol{s}}_A)$ and $\mathsf{pk}_B = (\boldsymbol{t}_B, \hat{\boldsymbol{t}}_B)$.
  2. Choose $\boldsymbol{R}_{A \to B,1}, \boldsymbol{R}_{A \to B,2} \leftarrow \beta_\eta^{k \times k\ell}$ and $\boldsymbol{r}_{A \to B,3} \leftarrow \beta_\eta^{k\ell}$.
  3. Compute $\boldsymbol{U}_{A \to B} \leftarrow \boldsymbol{A}^\top \boldsymbol{R}_{A \to B,1} + \boldsymbol{R}_{A \to B,2} \in R_q^{k \times k\ell}$.
  4. Compute $\boldsymbol{v}_{A \to B} \leftarrow \hat{\boldsymbol{t}}_B^\top \boldsymbol{R}_{A \to B,1} + \boldsymbol{r}_{A \to B,3}^\top - \mathsf{Powersof2}(\boldsymbol{s}_A^\top) \in R_q^{k\ell}$.
  5. Output $\mathsf{rk}_{A \to B} = (\boldsymbol{U}_{A \to B}, \boldsymbol{v}_{A \to B})$.
- $\mathsf{ReEnc}(\mathsf{rk}_{A \to B}, \mathsf{ct}_A) \to \mathsf{ct}_B$:
  1. Parse $\mathsf{rk}_{A \to B} = (\boldsymbol{U}_{A \to B}, \boldsymbol{v}_{A \to B})$ and $\mathsf{ct}_A = (\boldsymbol{u}_A, v_A)$.
  2. Compute $\boldsymbol{u}_B \leftarrow \boldsymbol{U}_{A \to B} \cdot \mathsf{BitDecomp}(\boldsymbol{u}_A)$.
  3. Compute $v_B \leftarrow v_A + \boldsymbol{v}_{A \to B}^\top \cdot \mathsf{BitDecomp}(\boldsymbol{u}_A)$.
  4. Output $\mathsf{ct}_B = (\boldsymbol{u}_B, v_B)$.
- $\mathsf{HReKeyGen}((\mathsf{sk}_{(A,i)})_{i \in [u]}, (\mathsf{pk}_{(B,j)})_{j \in [u]}) \to (\mathsf{rk}_{(A,i) \to (B,j)})_{i \in [u], j \in [u]}$:
  1. Parse $\mathsf{sk}_{A_i} = (\boldsymbol{s}_{A_i}, \hat{\boldsymbol{s}}_{A_i})$ and $\mathsf{pk}_{B,j} = (\boldsymbol{t}_{B,j}, \hat{\boldsymbol{t}}_{B,j})$ for every $i \in [u]$ and $j \in [u]$.
  2. Choose $\boldsymbol{R}_{A \to B,1}, \boldsymbol{R}_{A \to B,2} \leftarrow \beta_\eta^{k \times k\ell}$, and $\boldsymbol{r}_{(A,i) \to (B,j)} \leftarrow \beta_\eta^{k\ell}$ for every $i \in [u]$ and $j \in [u]$.
  3. Compute $\boldsymbol{U}_{A \to B} \leftarrow \boldsymbol{A}^\top \boldsymbol{R}_{A \to B,1} + \boldsymbol{R}_{A \to B,2}$.
  4. Compute $\boldsymbol{v}_{(A,i) \to (B,j)} \leftarrow \hat{\boldsymbol{t}}_{B,j}^\top \boldsymbol{R}_{A \to B,1} + \boldsymbol{r}_{(A,i) \to (B,j),3} - \mathsf{Powersof2}(\boldsymbol{s}_{A,i}^\top)$ for every $i \in [u]$ and every $j \in [u]$.
  5. Output $(\mathsf{rk}_{(A,i) \to (B,j)})_{i \in [u], j \in [u]}$, where $\mathsf{rk}_{(A,i) \to (B,j)} = (\boldsymbol{U}_{A \to B}, \boldsymbol{v}_{(A,i) \to (B,j)})$.

– $\mathsf{ReKeyEval}((\mathsf{rk}_{(A,\alpha_i)\to(B,\beta_i)})_{i\in[v]}) \to \mathsf{rk}_{A\to B}$: Parse $\mathsf{rk}_{(A,\alpha_i)\to(B,\beta_i)} = (\boldsymbol{U}_{A\to B}, \boldsymbol{v}_{(A,\alpha_i)\to(B,\beta_i)})$ for every $i \in [v]$. Compute $\boldsymbol{v}_{A\to B} \leftarrow \sum_{i\in[v]} \boldsymbol{v}_{(A,\alpha_i)\to(B,\beta_i)} \in R_q^{k\ell}$. Output $\mathsf{rk}_{A\to B} = (\boldsymbol{U}_{A\to B}, \boldsymbol{v}_{A\to B})$.

The scheme $\Pi_{\mathsf{L\text{-}PRE}}$ is correct and re-encryption key homomorphic with overwhelming probability. The formal propositions and these proofs appear in Appendix B. We give informal propositions, as follows:

Proposition 2 (Correctness of $\Pi_{\mathsf{L\text{-}PRE}}$ (informal)). *The proposed PRE scheme $\Pi_{\mathsf{L\text{-}PRE}}$ is* correct *with overwhelming probability, under a suitable parameter setting by the algorithm* Setup.

Proposition 3 (Re-encryption key homomorphism of $\Pi_{\mathsf{L\text{-}PRE}}$ (informal)). *The proposed PRE scheme $\Pi_{\mathsf{L\text{-}PRE}}$ is* re-encrytpion key homomorphic *with overwhelming probability, under a suitable parameter setting by the algorithm* Setup.

Furthermore, the following theorem shows the security of $\Pi_{\mathsf{L\text{-}PRE}}$:

Theorem 2 (RKH-CPA **security of $\Pi_{\mathsf{L\text{-}PRE}}$).** *For a security parameter λ, suppose that $n = \mathsf{poly}(\lambda)$ is a positive integer and u is a positive integer which may be independent of λ. If the $\mathsf{MLWE}_{k+1,k,\eta}$ assumption holds, the proposed PRE scheme $\Pi_{\mathsf{L\text{-}PRE}}$ is u-RKH-CPA-secure.*

In particular, if there exists a PPT adversary $\mathcal{A}$ against the u-RKH-CPA security of $\Pi_{\mathsf{L\text{-}PRE}}$, then there exists a PPT algorithm $\mathcal{B}$ against the $\mathsf{MLWE}_{k+1,k,\eta}$ problem, such that

$$\mathsf{Adv}^{u\text{-rkh-cpa}}_{\Pi_{\mathsf{L\text{-}PRE}},\mathcal{A},n}(\lambda) \le n_h(q_{rk}k\ell + 3) \cdot \mathsf{Adv}^{\mathrm{mlwe}}_{k+1,k,\eta}(\mathcal{B}),$$

where n_h is the number of honest users, and q_{rk} is the maximum number of queries issued to the re-encryption key generation oracle.

Proof. Let $\mathcal{A}$ denote a PPT adversary against the u-RKH-CPA security of the PRE scheme $\Pi_{\mathsf{L\text{-}PRE}}$. Let $n \cdot u\ (= n_h + n_c)$ be the total number of users whose key-pairs are generated in the u-RKH-CPA game, where n_h and n_c are the numbers of honest users and corrupted users, respectively. Let q_{rk} be the maximum number of queries issued to the oracle $\mathtt{O.HReKeyGen}$. The challenge ciphertext under the public key of the user $(i^*, j^*) \in [n] \times [u]$ is defined as $\mathsf{ct}^* = (\boldsymbol{u}^*, v^*)$. For simplicity, without loss of generality, the index $(i_\kappa, j_\kappa) \in \mathcal{L}_{\mathtt{Honest}}$ of the κ-th honest user (where $i_\kappa \in [n], j_\kappa \in [u]$, and $\mathcal{L}_{\mathtt{Honest}} = [n] \times [u] \backslash \mathcal{L}_{\mathtt{Corrupt}}$) is denoted by $\kappa = (i_\kappa, j_\kappa)$.

In order to prove Theorem 2, we consider a sequence of security games $\mathsf{Game}_0, (\mathsf{Game}_1^{(\kappa)})_{\kappa\in[n_h]}, (\mathsf{Game}_2^{(\kappa)})_{\kappa\in[n_h]}, (\mathsf{Game}_3^{(\kappa)})_{\kappa\in[n_h]}, \mathsf{Game}_4$. For $i \in [3]$ and $\kappa \in [n_h]$, let $W_i^{(\kappa)}$ be the events that the experiment in $\mathsf{Game}_i^{(\kappa)}$ outputs 1 (i.e., $b = b'$ holds for the output $b' \in \{0,1\}$ of $\mathcal{A}$). Let W_0 and W_4 denote the events that the experiments in Game_0 and Game_4 output 1, respectively. The games $\mathsf{Game}_0, (\mathsf{Game}_1^{(\kappa)})_{\kappa\in[n_h]}, (\mathsf{Game}_2^{(\kappa)})_{\kappa\in[n_h]}, (\mathsf{Game}_3^{(\kappa)})_{\kappa\in[n_h]}, \mathsf{Game}_4$ are defined as follows:

<u>Game_0</u>: This game is the original $\mathsf{RKH\text{-}CPA}$ game. Then, we have $\mathsf{Adv}^{u\text{-rkh-cpa}}_{\Pi_{\mathsf{PRE}},\mathcal{A},n}(\lambda) = |\Pr[W_0] - 1/2|$.

Let $\mathsf{Game}_1^{(0)}$ be the same game as Game_0. For each $\kappa \in [n_h]$, we consider a security game $\mathsf{Game}_1^{(\kappa)}$.

<u>$\mathsf{Game}_1^{(\kappa)}$</u>: This game is the same as $\mathsf{Game}_1^{(\kappa-1)}$ except that $\hat{\boldsymbol{t}}_\kappa = \boldsymbol{A}\hat{\boldsymbol{s}}_\kappa + \hat{\boldsymbol{e}}_\kappa \in R_q^k$ is replaced by a uniformly random $\hat{\boldsymbol{t}}_\kappa \in R_q^k$, when generating the public key $\mathsf{pk}_\kappa = (\boldsymbol{t}_\kappa, \hat{\boldsymbol{t}}_\kappa)$ of the honest user κ.

Assuming the existence of the adversary $\mathcal{A}$ against $\Pi_{\mathsf{L\text{-}PRE}}$, there exists a PPT algorithm $\mathcal{B}_1^{(\kappa)}$ against the $\mathsf{MLWE}_{k,k,\eta}$ problem, because the secret value $\hat{\boldsymbol{s}}_\kappa$ is not necessary to simulate the environments of $\mathcal{A}$ in both $\mathsf{Game}_1^{(\kappa-1)}$ and $\mathsf{Game}_1^{(\kappa)}$. By using $\mathcal{A}$'s output, $\mathcal{B}_1^{(\kappa)}$ can distinguish between a $\mathsf{MLWE}_{k,k,\eta}$ sample and a uniformly random one, in the straightforward way. Hence, we have $\left|\Pr[W_1^{(\kappa-1)}] - \Pr[W_1^{(\kappa)}]\right| \leq \mathsf{Adv}^{\mathrm{mlwe}}_{k,k,\eta}(\mathcal{B}_1^{(\kappa)})$ for $\kappa \in [n_h]$.

Here, we define $\mathsf{Game}_2^{(0)}$ as the same game as $\mathsf{Game}_1^{(n_h)}$, and consider the security game $\mathsf{Game}_2^{(\kappa)}$ for $\kappa \in \mathcal{L}_{\mathtt{Honest}}$.

<u>$\mathsf{Game}_2^{(\kappa)}$</u>: This game is the same as $\mathsf{Game}_2^{(\kappa-1)}$ except that, on input a homomorphic re-encryption key query $((A,i)_{i\in[u]}, (B,j)_{j\in[u]})$ such that $\kappa = (A,\hat{i})$ and $(B,\hat{j}) \in \mathcal{L}_{\mathtt{Honest}}$ for some $\hat{i} \in [u]$ and every $\hat{j} \in [u]$, $\mathtt{O.HReKeyGen}$ generates a uniformly random $\boldsymbol{U}_{A\to B} \in R_q^{k\times k\ell}$ and a uniformly random $\boldsymbol{v}_{(A,\hat{i})\to(B,j)} \in R_q^{k\ell}$ for every $j \in [u]$, instead of $\boldsymbol{U}_{A\to B} \leftarrow \boldsymbol{A}^\top \boldsymbol{R}_{A\to B,1} + \boldsymbol{R}_{A\to B,2}$ and $\boldsymbol{v}_{(A,\hat{i})\to(B,j)} \leftarrow \hat{\boldsymbol{t}}_{B,j}^\top \boldsymbol{R}_{A\to B,1} + \boldsymbol{r}_{(A,\hat{i})\to(B,j)} - \mathsf{Powersof2}(\boldsymbol{s}_{A,\hat{i}}^\top)$.

For each $m \in [k\ell]$, there exists a PPT algorithm $\mathcal{B}_2^{(m,\kappa)}$ distinguishing whether the m-th row of $[\boldsymbol{U}_{A\to B} \| \boldsymbol{v}_{(A,\hat{i})\to(B,1)} \| \cdots \| \boldsymbol{v}_{(A,\hat{i})\to(B,u)}]$ is an $\mathsf{MLWE}_{k+1,k,\eta}$ sample or uniformly random sample. Hence, we have $\left|\Pr[W_2^{(\kappa-1)}] - \Pr[W_2^{(\kappa)}]\right| \leq q_{rk} k\ell \cdot \mathsf{Adv}^{\mathrm{mlwe}}_{k+1,k,\eta}(\mathcal{B}_2^{(\kappa)})$ by letting $\mathcal{B}_2^{(\kappa)}$ be the PPT algorithm against the $\mathsf{MLWE}_{k+1,k,\eta}$ assumption, such that $\mathsf{Adv}^{\mathrm{mlwe}}_{k+1,k,\eta}(\mathcal{B}_2^{(m,\kappa)}) \leq \mathsf{Adv}^{\mathrm{mlwe}}_{k+1,k,\eta}(\mathcal{B}_2^{(\kappa)})$ for all $m \in [k\ell]$.

Here, let $\mathsf{Game}_3^{(0)}$ be the same game as $\mathsf{Game}_2^{(n_h)}$, and we define the security game $\mathsf{Game}_3^{(\kappa)}$ for every $\kappa \in \mathcal{L}_{\mathtt{Honest}}$.

<u>$\mathsf{Game}_3^{(\kappa)}$</u> : This game is the same as $\mathsf{Game}_3^{(\kappa-1)}$ except that $\boldsymbol{t}_\kappa = \boldsymbol{A}^\top \boldsymbol{s}_\kappa + \boldsymbol{e}_\kappa \in R_q^k$ is replaced by a uniformly random $\boldsymbol{t}_\kappa \in R_q^k$, when generating the public key $\mathsf{pk}_\kappa = (\boldsymbol{t}_\kappa, \hat{\boldsymbol{t}}_\kappa)$ of the honest user $\kappa \in \mathcal{L}_{\mathtt{Honest}}$.

There exists a PPT algorithm $\mathcal{B}_3^{(\kappa)}$ against the $\mathsf{MLWE}_{k,k,\eta}$ problem. Since $\boldsymbol{s}_\kappa$ is not used in both $\mathsf{Game}_3^{(\kappa-1)}$ and $\mathsf{Game}_3^{(\kappa)}$, it is possible to simulate the views of $\mathcal{A}$ in the two games and construct $\mathcal{B}_3^{(\kappa)}$. Hence, we have $\left|\Pr[W_3^{(\kappa-1)}] - \Pr[W_3^{(\kappa)}]\right| \leq \mathsf{Adv}^{\mathrm{mlwe}}_{k,k,\eta}(\mathcal{B}_3^{(\kappa)})$.

$\underline{\mathsf{Game}_4}$: This game is the same as $\mathsf{Game}_3^{(n_h)}$ except that the challenge ciphertext $(\boldsymbol{u}^*, v^*) \leftarrow \mathsf{Enc}(\mathsf{pk}_{i^*,j^*}, \mathsf{m}_b^*)$ is replaced by a uniformly random vector $(\boldsymbol{u}^*, v^*) \in R_q^k \times R_q$.

The secret key $(\boldsymbol{s}_\kappa, \hat{\boldsymbol{s}}_\kappa)$ for every $\kappa \in [n_h]$ is not used in both $\mathsf{Game}_3^{(n_h)}$ and Game_4. Thus, in these games, it is possible to simulate the environments of $\mathcal{A}$ without using that secret key, and construct a PPT algorithm $\mathcal{B}_4^{(i^*)}$ against the $\mathsf{MLWE}_{k+1,k,\eta}$ problem. Hence, we have $\left|\Pr[W_3^{(n_h)}] - \Pr[W_4]\right| \le n_h \cdot \mathsf{Adv}_{k+1,k,\eta}^{\mathrm{mlwe}}(\mathcal{B}_4^{(i^*)})$. Furthermore, $\Pr[W_4] = 1/2$ holds since the challenge ciphertext ct^* is independent of $b \in \{0,1\}$ in Game_4.

From the discussion above, we obtain

$$
\begin{aligned}
\mathsf{Adv}_{\Pi_{\mathsf{L\text{-}PRE}},\mathcal{A},n}^{u\text{-rkh-cpa}}(\lambda) \le& \sum_{i=1}^{3}\sum_{\kappa=1}^{n_h}\left|\Pr[W_i^{(\kappa-1)}] - \Pr[W_i^{(\kappa)}]\right| \\
&+ \left|\Pr[W_3^{(n_h)}] - \Pr[W_4]\right| + \left|\Pr[W_4] - \frac{1}{2}\right| \\
\le& \, n_h(q_{rk}k\ell + 3) \cdot \mathsf{Adv}_{k+1,k,\eta}^{\mathrm{mlwe}}(\mathcal{B}),
\end{aligned}
$$

where $\mathcal{B}$ is a PPT algorithm against the $\mathsf{MLWE}_{k+1,k,\eta}$ assumption, such that $\mathsf{Adv}_{k+1,k,\eta}^{\mathrm{mlwe}}(\mathcal{B}_i^{(\kappa)}) < \mathsf{Adv}_{k+1,k,\eta}^{\mathrm{mlwe}}(\mathcal{B})$ for all $i \in [4]$ and $\kappa \in \mathcal{L}_{\mathtt{Honest}}$. Therefore, this completes the proof. □

5 Conclusion

We aimed at constructing a bounded CCA2-secure post-quantum PRE scheme with compact ciphertexts. To this end, we formalized the notions of re-encryption key homomorphism and RKH-CPA security for PRE, and proposed a generic construction of bounded CCA2-secure PRE with compact ciphertexts, which starts from re-encryption key homomorphic PRE with RKH-CPA security and strongly unforgeable OTS. To instantiate this generic construction, we presented a lattice-based re-encryption key homomorphic PRE scheme with RKH-CPA security.

As a result, we can construct a bounded CCA2-secure post-quantum PRE scheme with compact ciphertexts by applying the generic construction to our lattice-based PRE and an existing lattice-based OTS scheme.

Although we just discussed single-hop PRE schemes, we can consider a multi-hop variant of our PRE schemes, $\Pi_{\mathsf{C\text{-}PRE}}, \Pi_{\mathsf{L\text{-}PRE}}$ as an extension of these schemes.

Acknowledgements. This work was supported by JST K Program Grant Number JPMJKP24U2, Japan. The authors would like to thank the anonymous referees for their helpful comments.

A Bounded CCA2 Secure PRE from CPA Secure PRE

In this section, we propose a generic construction of bounded CCA2-secure PRE, which starts from any CPA secure PRE and strongly unforgeable OTS, and then give a security proof for this construction.

A.1 Building Blocks

We describe the definitions of CPA security and *all-or-nothing transforms*, which are used for presenting a generic construction of bounded CCA2-secure PRE.

Definition 13 (CPA **security**). *For a security parameter* λ, *let* $n = \mathsf{poly}(\lambda)$ *be a positive integer. A unidirectional PRE scheme* $\Pi_{\mathsf{PRE}} = (\mathsf{Setup}, \mathsf{KeyGen}, \mathsf{Enc}, \mathsf{Dec}, \mathsf{ReKeyGen}, \mathsf{ReEnc})$ *is* CPA*-secure if, for any PPT adversary* $\mathcal{A} = (\mathcal{A}_0, \mathcal{A}_1, \mathcal{A}_2)$ *against* Π_{PRE}, *its advantage* $\mathsf{Adv}^{\mathrm{cpa}}_{\Pi_{\mathsf{PRE}},\mathcal{A},n}(\lambda) := \left|\Pr[\mathsf{Expt}^{\mathrm{cpa}}_{\Pi_{\mathsf{PRE}},\mathcal{A},n}(\lambda) = 1] - 1/2\right|$ *is negligible in* λ, *where the experiment* $\mathsf{Expt}^{\mathrm{cpa}}_{\Pi_{\mathsf{PRE}},\mathcal{A},n}(\lambda)$ *is defined as follows:*

$\underline{\mathsf{Expt}^{\mathrm{cpa}}_{\Pi_{\mathsf{PRE}},\mathcal{A},n}(\lambda)}$:
Generate $\mathsf{pp} \leftarrow \mathsf{Setup}(1^\lambda)$ *and set* $\mathsf{T}_{\mathsf{rk}} \leftarrow \emptyset;$;
$(\mathcal{L}_{\mathtt{Corrupt}}, \mathsf{st}_0) \leftarrow \mathcal{A}_0(\mathsf{pp})$;
$\forall i \in [n]$, *generate* $(\mathsf{pk}_i, \mathsf{sk}_i) \leftarrow \mathsf{KeyGen}(\mathsf{pp})$;
$(i^*, \mathsf{m}_0^*, \mathsf{m}_1^*, \mathsf{st}_1) \leftarrow \mathcal{A}_1^{\mathtt{O.ReKeyGen}}(\mathsf{st}_0, \{\mathsf{pk}_i\}_{i\in[n]}, \{\mathsf{sk}_i\}_{i\in\mathcal{L}_{\mathtt{Corrupt}}})$;
Sample $b \xleftarrow{\$} \{0.1\}$ *and run* $\mathsf{ct}^* \leftarrow \mathtt{O.Challenge}_b(i^*, \mathsf{m}_0^*, \mathsf{m}_1^*)$;
$b' \leftarrow \mathcal{A}_2^{\mathtt{O.ReKeyGen}}(\mathsf{st}_1, \mathsf{ct}^*)$;
Return 1 *if* $b = b'$; *otherwise, return* 0,

where $\mathcal{L}_{\mathtt{Corrupt}}$ *is a subset of* $[n]$, *and* $(\mathsf{st}_0, \mathsf{st}_1)$ *is internal state information.*

All-or-Nothing Transform. An all-or-nothing transform (AONT) splits a message X into v secret shares $x_1, \ldots, x_v$ and a public share z and recovers X from the shares $(x_1, \ldots, x_v, z)$.

Definition 14 (AONT). *A PPT algorithm* Trans *is* $(\mu, \bar{\mu}, v)$-AONT *if the following conditions hold:*

1. *Given* $X \in \{0,1\}^\mu$, Trans *outputs* $v+1$ *blocks* $(x_1, \ldots, x_v, z) \in (\{0,1\}^{\bar{\mu}})^{v+1}$, *where for* $i \in [v]$, x_i *is a secret share, and* z *is a public share.*
2. *There exists a polynomial-time inverse function* $\mathsf{Inverse}$ *which, on input* $(x_1, \ldots, x_v, z) \in (\{0,1\}^{\bar{\mu}})^{v+1}$, *outputs* $X \in \{0,1\}^\mu$.
3. Trans *satisfies* indistinguishability, *as follows: For any PPT algorithm* $\mathcal{A}$ *against* Trans, *its advantage*

$$\mathsf{Adv}^{\mathrm{ind}}_{\mathsf{Trans},\mathcal{A}}(\lambda) := \left|\Pr\left[b = b' \mid b \xleftarrow{\$} \{0,1\}; b' \leftarrow \mathcal{A}^{\mathtt{O.LR}}(1^\lambda)\right] - \frac{1}{2}\right|$$

is negligible in λ, *where* $\mathsf{O.LR}$ *is the* left-or-right *oracle which, on input* $(j, X_0, X_1) \in [v] \times (\{0,1\}^\mu)^2$, *returns* $(x_1, \ldots, x_{j-1}, x_{j+1}, \ldots, x_v, z)$.

A.2 Construction from CPA Secure PRE

We present a bounded CCA2-secure PRE scheme $\Pi_{\mathsf{B\text{-}PRE}}$ which is based on a generic construction [13] of bounded CCA2-secure PKE. To ensure the re-encryption functionality, we use CPA-secure PRE while the PKE scheme of [13] uses CPA-secure PKE. For simplicity, we employ disjunct matrices while the bound CCA2-secure PKE [13] uses cover-free families. Notice that the notion of disjunct matrices is identical to that of cover-free families. In order to construct the proposed PRE scheme, we use the following building blocks:

- a CPA-secure PRE scheme $\Pi'_{\mathsf{PRE}} = (\Pi'_{\mathsf{PRE}}.\mathsf{Setup}, \Pi'_{\mathsf{PRE}}.\mathsf{KeyGen}, \Pi'_{\mathsf{PRE}}.\mathsf{Enc}, \Pi'_{\mathsf{PRE}}.\mathsf{Dec}, \Pi'_{\mathsf{PRE}}.\mathsf{ReKeyGen}, \Pi'_{\mathsf{PRE}}.\mathsf{ReEnc})$ with the message space $\mathcal{M}' = \{0,1\}^{\bar{\mu}}$, where $\bar{\mu} = \bar{\mu}(\lambda)$ is a positive integer for a security parameter λ;
- a strongly unforgeable OTS scheme $\Pi_{\mathsf{OTS}} = (\Pi_{\mathsf{OTS}}.\mathsf{KeyGen}, \Pi_{\mathsf{OTS}}.\mathsf{Sign}, \Pi_{\mathsf{OTS}}.\mathsf{Vrfy})$;
- a $(\mu, \bar{\mu}, v)$-AONT Trans with an efficient inverse function Inverse, where $\mu = \mu(\lambda)$ and $v = v(\lambda)$ are positive integers for a security parameter λ.

The proposed PRE scheme $\Pi_{\mathsf{B\text{-}PRE}} = (\mathsf{Setup}, \mathsf{KeyGen}, \mathsf{Enc}, \mathsf{Dec}, \mathsf{ReKeyGen}, \mathsf{ReEnc})$ is constructed as follows:

- $\mathsf{Setup}(1^\lambda) \to \mathsf{pp}$:
  - Generate $\mathsf{pp}' \leftarrow \Pi'_{\mathsf{PRE}}.\mathsf{Setup}(\mathsf{pp})$.
  - Let $\mu = \mu(\lambda)$, $\bar{\mu} = \bar{\mu}(\lambda)$, and $v = v(\lambda)$ be positive integers.
  - Let $\mathcal{M} = \{0,1\}^{\mu}$ be the message space.
  - Let $\bar{n} = \bar{n}(\lambda)$ and $u = u(\lambda)$ be positive integers, and let $[\bar{n}]$ be the verification key-space of Π_{OTS}.
  - Let $\boldsymbol{M} = (m_{i,j}) \in \{0,1\}^{u \times \bar{n}}$ be a t-disjunct matrix, where the Hamming weight of each column vector is v.

  Output $\mathsf{pp} = (\mathsf{pp}', \mu, \bar{\mu}, v, \bar{n}, u, \boldsymbol{M})$.
- $\mathsf{KeyGen}(\mathsf{pp}) \to (\mathsf{pk}, \mathsf{sk})$: Parse $\mathsf{pp} = (\mathsf{pp}', \mu, \bar{\mu}, v, \bar{n}, u, \boldsymbol{M})$ and generate $(\mathsf{pk}'_i, \mathsf{sk}'_i) \leftarrow \Pi'_{\mathsf{PRE}}.\mathsf{KeyGen}(\mathsf{pp}')$ for $i \in [u]$. Output $\mathsf{pk} = (\mathsf{pk}'_i)_{i \in [u]}$ and $\mathsf{sk} = (\mathsf{sk}'_i)_{i \in [u]}$.
- $\mathsf{Enc}(\mathsf{pk}, \mathsf{m}) \to \mathsf{ct}$:
  1. Parse $\mathsf{pk} = (\mathsf{pk}'_i)_{i \in [u]}$.
  2. Generate $(\mathsf{vk}, \mathsf{sigk}) \leftarrow \Pi_{\mathsf{OTS}}.\mathsf{KeyGen}(1^\lambda)$.
  3. Compute $\{\tau_1, \ldots, \tau_v\} \leftarrow \phi_{\boldsymbol{M}}(\mathsf{vk})$, where all $\tau_1, \ldots, \tau_v \in [u]$ are distinct.
  4. Compute $(x_1, \ldots, x_v, z) \leftarrow \mathsf{Trans}(\mathsf{m})$.
  5. Compute $\mathsf{ct}'_i \leftarrow \Pi'_{\mathsf{PRE}}.\mathsf{Enc}(\mathsf{pk}_{\tau_i}, x_i)$ for every $i \in [v]$.
  6. Compute $\sigma \leftarrow \Pi_{\mathsf{OTS}}.\mathsf{Sign}(\mathsf{sigk}, (\mathsf{ct}'_1 \parallel \cdots \parallel \mathsf{ct}'_v \parallel z))$.
  7. Output $\mathsf{ct} = (\mathsf{vk}, (\mathsf{ct}'_i)_{i \in [v]}, z, \sigma)$.
- $\mathsf{Dec}(\mathsf{sk}, \mathsf{ct}) \to \mathsf{m}/\perp$:
  1. Parse $\mathsf{sk} = (\mathsf{sk}'_i)_{i \in [u]}$ and $\mathsf{ct} = (\mathsf{vk}, (\mathsf{ct}'_i)_{i \in [v]}, z, \sigma)$.
  2. Output $\perp$ if $\Pi_{\mathsf{OTS}}.\mathsf{Vrfy}(\mathsf{vk}, (\mathsf{ct}'_1 \parallel \cdots \parallel \mathsf{ct}'_v \parallel z), \sigma) = \perp$ holds.
  3. Compute $\{\tau_1, \ldots, \tau_v\} \leftarrow \phi_{\boldsymbol{M}}(\mathsf{vk})$.
  4. Compute $x'_i \leftarrow \Pi'_{\mathsf{PRE}}.\mathsf{Dec}(\mathsf{sk}'_{\tau_i}, \mathsf{ct}'_i)$ for every $i \in [v]$.
  5. Output $\mathsf{m}' \leftarrow \mathsf{Inverse}(x'_1, \ldots, x'_v, z)$ if $x'_i \neq \perp$ holds for every $i \in [v]$; otherwise, output $\perp$.
- $\mathsf{ReKeyGen}(\mathsf{sk}_A, \mathsf{pk}_B) \to \mathsf{rk}_{A \to B}$: Parse $\mathsf{sk}_A = (\mathsf{sk}'_{A,i})_{i \in [u]}$ and $\mathsf{pk}_B = (\mathsf{pk}'_{B,i})_{i \in [u]}$, and compute $\mathsf{rk}_{(A,i) \to (B,j)} \leftarrow \Pi'_{\mathsf{PRE}}.\mathsf{ReKeyGen}(\mathsf{sk}'_{A,i}, \mathsf{pk}'_{B,j})$ for $i \in [u]$ and $j \in [u]$. Output $\mathsf{rk}_{A \to B} = (\mathsf{rk}_{(A,i) \to (B,j)})_{i \in [u], j \in [u]}$.
- $\mathsf{ReEnc}(\mathsf{rk}_{A \to B}, \mathsf{ct}_A) \to \mathsf{ct}_B$:

1. Parse $\mathsf{rk}_{A\to B} = (\mathsf{rk}_{(A,i)\to(B,j)})_{i\in[u],j\in[u]}$ and $\mathsf{ct}_A = (\mathsf{vk}_A, (\mathsf{ct}'_{A,i})_{i\in[v]}, z, \sigma_A)$.
2. Output $\bot$ if $\Pi_{\mathsf{OTS}}.\mathsf{Vrfy}(\mathsf{vk}_A, (\mathsf{ct}'_{A,1} \parallel \cdots \parallel \mathsf{ct}'_{A,v} \parallel z), \sigma_A) = \bot$ holds.
3. Generate $(\mathsf{vk}_B, \mathsf{sigk}_B) \leftarrow \Pi_{\mathsf{OTS}}.\mathsf{KeyGen}(1^\lambda)$.
4. Compute $\{\alpha_1, \ldots, \alpha_v\} \leftarrow \phi_M(\mathsf{vk}_A)$ and $\{\beta_1, \ldots, \beta_v\} \leftarrow \phi_M(\mathsf{vk}_B)$.
5. For every $i \in [v]$, compute $\mathsf{ct}'_{B,i} \leftarrow \Pi'_{\mathsf{PRE}}.\mathsf{ReEnc}(\mathsf{rk}_{(A,\alpha_i)\to(B,\beta_i)}, \mathsf{ct}'_{A,i})$.
6. Compute $\sigma_B \leftarrow \Pi_{\mathsf{OTS}}.\mathsf{Sign}(\mathsf{sigk}_B, (\mathsf{ct}'_{B,1} \parallel \cdots \parallel \mathsf{ct}'_{B,v} \parallel z))$.
7. Output $\mathsf{ct}_B = (\mathsf{vk}_B, (\mathsf{ct}'_{B,i})_{i\in[v]}, z, \sigma_B)$.

The correctness of $\Pi_{\mathsf{B\text{-}PRE}}$ follows that of the underlying primitives Π'_{PRE}, Π_{OTS}, and $(\mu, \bar{\mu}, v)$-AONT Trans. Because this is proven in the straightforward way, we omit the proof.

A.3 Security Proof

Theorem 3 shows the bounded CCA2 security of the proposed scheme $\Pi_{\mathsf{B\text{-}PRE}}$.

Theorem 3 (**(t,t)-CCA2 security of $\Pi_{\mathsf{B\text{-}PRE}}$**). *Suppose that the matrix $\boldsymbol{M} \in \{0,1\}^{u\times\bar{n}}$ is a t-disjunct matrix, and n_h is the number of honest users in the (t,t)-CCA2 game. If the PRE scheme Π'_{PRE} is CPA-secure, the OTS scheme Π_{OTS} is strongly unforgeable, and the algorithm Trans is $(\mu, \bar{\mu}, v)$-AONT, then the resulting PRE scheme $\Pi_{\mathsf{B\text{-}PRE}}$ is (t,t)-CCA2-secure.*

In particular, if there exists a PPT algorithm $\mathcal{A}$ against the (t,t)-CCA2-secure PRE $\Pi_{\mathsf{B\text{-}PRE}}$, then there exist PPT adversaries $\mathcal{B}_1$ against the CPA-secure PRE Π'_{PRE}, $\mathcal{F}$ against the strongly unforgeable OTS Π_{OTS}, and $\mathcal{B}_2$ against $(\mu, \bar{\mu}, v)$-AONT Trans such that

$$\mathsf{Adv}^{(t,\,t)\text{-cca2}}_{\Pi_{\mathsf{B\text{-}PRE}},\mathcal{A},n}(\lambda) \leq n_h^3 u^2 \cdot \mathsf{Adv}^{\mathsf{cpa}}_{\mathcal{B}_1,\Pi'_{\mathsf{PRE}},nu}(\lambda) + \mathsf{Adv}^{\text{suf-ot}}_{\Pi_{\mathsf{OTS}},\mathcal{F}}(\lambda) + n_h^3 u^2 \cdot \mathsf{Adv}^{\mathsf{ind}}_{\mathcal{B}_2,\mathsf{AONT}}(\lambda).$$

Proof. Let $\mathcal{A}$ be a PPT adversary against the PRE scheme $\Pi_{\mathsf{B\text{-}PRE}}$. Let $\mathsf{ct}^* = (\mathsf{vk}^*, (\mathsf{ct}'^*_i)_{i\in[v]}, z^*, \sigma^*)$ denote the challenge ciphertext under pk_{i^*}. To prove Theorem 3, we consider security games $\mathsf{Game}_0, \mathsf{Game}_1$.

<u>Game_0</u>: This game is the same as the (t,t)-CCA2 security game.

<u>Game_1</u>: This game is the same as Game_0 except for the following procedures of the decryption oracle O.Dec and the re-encryption oracle O.ReEnc: For a decryption or re-encryption query on $\mathsf{ct}_i = (\mathsf{vk}_i, (\mathsf{ct}'_{i,j})_{j\in[v]}, z_i, \sigma_i)$, the oracle O.Dec or O.ReEnc checks whether it holds that $\mathsf{vk}_i = \mathsf{vk}^*$, $\mathsf{ct}_i \neq \mathsf{ct}^*$, and $\Pi_{\mathsf{OTS}}.\mathsf{Vrfy}(\mathsf{vk}_i, (\mathsf{ct}'_{i,1} \| \cdots \| \mathsf{ct}'_{i,v} \| z_i), \sigma_i) = \top$ (this event is defined as Bad). If so, the experiment aborts; otherwise, O.Dec computes $\mathsf{m}' \leftarrow \mathsf{Dec}(\mathsf{sk}_i, \mathsf{ct}_i)$ and returns $\mathsf{m}' \in \mathcal{M} \cup \{\bot\}$.

Game_0 and Game_1 are identical unless Bad occurs. In order to estimate the upper bound of the probability that Bad occurs, we construct a PPT algorithm $\mathcal{F}$ breaking the strongly unforgeable OTS scheme Π_{OTS}.

On input a verification key vk^* of Π_{OTS}, $\mathcal{F}$ gives $(\mathsf{pp}, \{\mathsf{pk}_i\}_{i\in[n]}, \{\mathsf{sk}_i\}_{i\in\mathcal{L}_{\mathsf{Corrupt}}})$ to $\mathcal{A}$ by generating $(\mathsf{pp}, \{(\mathsf{pk}_i, \mathsf{sk}_i)\}_{i\in[n]})$ by itself. By using the generated key-pairs, $\mathcal{F}$ simulates O.ReKeyGen. Additionally, the oracle O.Dec (resp., O.ReEnc) is simulated as follows: For a decryption query (i, ct_i) (resp., (i, j, ct_i)) (where $\mathsf{ct}_i =$

$(\mathsf{vk}_i, (\mathsf{ct}'_{i,j})_{j\in[v]}, z_i, \sigma_i))$, $\mathcal{F}$ aborts and outputs a forgery $((\mathsf{ct}'_{i,1}\|\cdots\|\mathsf{ct}'_{i,v}\|z_i), \sigma_i)$ in the strong unforgeability game of Π_{OTS}, if it holds that $\mathsf{vk}_i = \mathsf{vk}^*$, $\mathsf{ct}_i \neq \mathsf{ct}^*$, and $\Pi_{\mathsf{OTS}}.\mathsf{Vrfy}(\mathsf{vk}_i, (\mathsf{ct}'_{i,1}\|\cdots\|\mathsf{ct}'_{i,v}\|z_i), \sigma_i)) = \top$ (i.e., Bad occurs); otherwise, the algorithm computes $\mathsf{m}' \leftarrow \mathsf{Dec}(\mathsf{sk}_i, \mathsf{ct}_i)$ and returns $\mathsf{m}' \in \mathcal{M} \cup \{\bot\}$ (resp., computes $\mathsf{ct}_j \leftarrow \mathsf{ReEnc}(\mathsf{rk}_{i\to j}, \mathsf{ct}_i)$ and returns ct_j). Furthermore, when $\mathcal{A}$ submits a challenge query $(i^*, \mathsf{m}_0^*, \mathsf{m}_1^*)$, $\mathcal{F}$ chooses $b \xleftarrow{\$} \{0,1\}$, computes $((\mathsf{ct}_i'^*)_{i\in[v]}, z^*)$ by following the procedure of $\mathsf{Enc}(\mathsf{pk}_{i^*}, \mathsf{m}_b^*)$. Then, this algorithm issues $(\mathsf{ct}_1'^*\|\cdots\|\mathsf{ct}_v'^*\|z^*)$ to the signing oracle in the strong unforgeability game and obtains σ^*. And then, $\mathcal{F}$ returns the challenge ciphertext $\mathsf{ct}^* = (\mathsf{vk}^*, (\mathsf{ct}_i'^*)_{i\in[v]}, z^*, \sigma^*)$. Finally, when $\mathcal{A}$ outputs $b' \in \{0,1\}$ and Bad has not occurred, $\mathcal{F}$ halts and outputs 0.

We analyze the algorithm $\mathcal{F}$. It is clear that the output of $\mathcal{F}$ is a valid forgery in the strong unforgeability game if Bad occurs. Hence, the probability Pr[Bad] is at most the advantage $\mathsf{Adv}^{\text{suf-ot}}_{\Pi_{\mathsf{OTS}},\mathcal{F}}(\lambda)$ of $\mathcal{F}$, and the two games are distinguishable with probability at most $\mathsf{Adv}^{\text{suf-ot}}_{\Pi_{\mathsf{OTS}},\mathcal{F}}(\lambda)$.

Simulation of Game_1. To bound the winning probability of $\mathcal{A}$ in Game_1, we consider the following experiment $\mathcal{B}$: At the beginning of the game, $\mathcal{B}$ generates $(\mathsf{vk}^*, \mathsf{sigk}^*) \leftarrow \Pi_{\mathsf{OTS}}.\mathsf{KeyGen}(1^\lambda)$, chooses indices $i^* \xleftarrow{\$} [n_h]$, $j^* \xleftarrow{\$} \phi_{\boldsymbol{M}}(\mathsf{vk}^*)$, and simulates Game_1 except for the following procedure: $\mathcal{B}$ aborts and outputs a random bit if $\mathcal{A}$ issues a decryption or re-encryption query on $(i^*, (\mathsf{vk}_{i^*}, (\mathsf{ct}'_{i^*,j})_{j\in[v]}, z_{i^*}, \sigma_{i^*}))$ such that $j^* \in \phi_{\boldsymbol{M}}(\mathsf{vk}_{i^*})$; or a challenge query $(i', \mathsf{m}_0^*, \mathsf{m}_1^*)$ such that $i^* \neq i'$. When $\mathcal{A}$ finally outputs $b' \in \{0,1\}$, $\mathcal{B}$ also outputs b'.

We estimate the probability that $\mathcal{B}$ outputs b' such that $b = b'$ (this event is defined as $W_{\mathcal{B}}$). Let Abort be the event that $\mathcal{B}$ aborts in the above simulation of oracles. Notice that $\Pr[W_{\mathcal{B}} \mid \mathsf{Abort}] = 1/2$. Due to the t-disjunct property of $\boldsymbol{M}$, it holds that $\Pr[\neg\mathsf{Abort}] \geq 1/(n_h^3 u^2)$. Then, we have

$$\begin{aligned}
\Pr[W_{\mathcal{B}}] &= \Pr[\mathsf{Abort}] \cdot \Pr[W_{\mathcal{B}} \mid \mathsf{Abort}] + \Pr[\neg\mathsf{Abort}] \cdot \Pr[W_{\mathcal{B}} \mid \neg\mathsf{Abort}] \\
&\geq \frac{1}{2}\left(1 - \frac{1}{n_h^3 u^2}\right) + \frac{1}{n_h^3 u^2} \cdot \Pr[W_{\mathcal{B}} \mid \neg\mathsf{Abort}] \\
&= \frac{1}{2} + \frac{1}{n_h^3 u^2}\left(\Pr[W_{\mathcal{B}} \mid \neg\mathsf{Abort}] - \frac{1}{2}\right).
\end{aligned}$$

The $\mathcal{A}$'s advantage $\varepsilon_{\mathcal{A}}$ in Game_1 is equivalent to $|\Pr[W_{\mathcal{B}} \mid \neg\mathsf{Abort}] - 1/2|$. Hence, the $\mathcal{B}$'s advantage $\varepsilon_{\mathcal{B}} = |\Pr[W_{\mathcal{B}}] - 1/2|$ is at least $\varepsilon_{\mathcal{A}}/(n_h^3 u^2)$. Here, let $\phi_{\boldsymbol{M}}(\mathsf{vk}^*) := \{\tau_1^*, \ldots, \tau_v^*\}$ (where $\tau_1^*, \ldots, \tau_v^* \in [u]$). In order to bound $\varepsilon_{\mathcal{B}}$, we change the environment of $\mathcal{A}$. In this modified environment, the j^*-th share $x_{j^*}^*$ generated by Trans is replaced with the all-zero string $0^{\bar{\mu}}$ whose bit-length is $\bar{\mu}$, when producing the challenge ciphertext. The probability $\Pr[W_{\mathcal{B}}]$ is defined as $p^{(0)}$, and the probability that $W_{\mathcal{B}}$ occurs in the modified environment is defined as $p^{(1)}$. Then we have $\varepsilon_{\mathcal{B}} \leq |p^{(0)} - p^{(1)}| + |p^{(1)} - 1/2|$.

Reduction to CPA security. To bound $|p^{(0)} - p^{(1)}|$, we construct a PPT algorithm $\mathcal{B}_1$ against the CPA security of Π'_{PRE}, as follows: On input the public parameter pp' in the CPA game, $\mathcal{B}_1$ generates pp by following the algorithm Setup and gives pp to $\mathcal{A}$. When $\mathcal{A}$ submits $\mathcal{L}_{\mathtt{Corrupt}}$, $\mathcal{B}_1$ generates $(\mathsf{vk}^*, \mathsf{sigk}^*) \leftarrow \Pi_{\mathsf{OTS}}.\mathsf{KeyGen}(1^\lambda)$, chooses $i^* \xleftarrow{\$} [n], j^* \xleftarrow{\$} \phi_M(\mathsf{vk}^*)$, and obtains $\{\mathsf{pk}_{i,j}\}_{(i,j)\in[n]\times[u]}$ and $\{\mathsf{sk}'_{i,j}\}_{(i,j)\in[n]\times[u]\setminus\{(i^*,j^*)\}}$ by issuing $\mathcal{L}'_{\mathtt{Corrupt}} = \{(i,j)\}\setminus\{(i^*,j^*)\}$ in the CPA game. Here, for simplicity, $(i,j) \in [n] \times [u]$ represents a user-index in the CPA game. Then $\mathcal{B}_1$ returns $\{\mathsf{pk}_i\}_{i\in[n]}$ and $\{\mathsf{sk}_i\}_{i\in\mathcal{L}_{\mathtt{Corrupt}}}$, where let $\mathsf{sk}_i := (\mathsf{sk}'_{i,j})_{j\in[u]}$ for every $i \in [n]\setminus\{i^*\}$, and let $\mathsf{sk}_{i^*} := (\mathsf{sk}'_{i^*,j})_{j\in[u]\setminus\{j^*\}}$, and let $\mathsf{pk}_i := (\mathsf{pk}'_{i,j})_{j\in[u]}$ for every $i \in [n]$. Furthermore, $\mathcal{B}_1$ simulates the oracles $\mathtt{O.ReKeyGen}, \mathtt{O.Dec}, \mathtt{O.ReEnc}, \mathtt{O.Challenge}_b$, as follows:

- $\mathtt{O.ReKeyGen}(A, B)$: If $(A = i^* \wedge B \in \mathcal{L}_{\mathtt{Corrupt}})$ or $A = B$ holds, $\mathcal{B}_1$ returns $\perp$; otherwise it does the following:
  - (Case $A = i^*$): Obtain $\mathsf{rk}_{(i^*,j^*)\to(B,j)}$ by issuing a re-encryption query $((i^*,j^*),(B,j))$ in the CPA game, for every $j \in [u]$. For every $i \in [u]\setminus\{j^*\}$ and every $j \in [u]$, compute $\mathsf{rk}_{(i^*,i)\to(B,j)} \leftarrow \Pi'_{\mathsf{PRE}}.\mathsf{ReKeyGen}(\mathsf{sk}'_{i^*,i}, \mathsf{pk}'_{B,j})$.
  - (Case $A \neq i^*$): Compute $\mathsf{rk}_{(A,i)\to(B,j)} \leftarrow \Pi'_{\mathsf{PRE}}.\mathsf{ReKeyGen}(\mathsf{sk}'_{A,i}, \mathsf{pk}'_{B,j})$ for every $i \in [u]$ and every $j \in [u]$.

  $\mathcal{B}_1$ returns $\mathsf{rk}_{A\to B} = (\mathsf{rk}_{(A,i)\to(B,j)})_{i\in[u],j\in[u]}$ and sets $\mathsf{T}_{\mathsf{rk}}[A,B] \leftarrow \mathsf{rk}_{A\to B}$.
- $\mathtt{O.Dec}(A, \mathsf{ct}_A)$: For $\mathsf{ct}_A = (\mathsf{vk}_A, (\mathsf{ct}'_{A,i})_{i\in[v]}, z, \sigma_A)$, $\mathcal{B}_1$ does the following:
  1. Return $\perp$ if (A, ct_A) is a derivative of (i^*, ct^*).
  2. Abort and output a random bit if $A = i^* \wedge j^* \in \phi_M(\mathsf{vk}_A)$ holds.
  3. Return $\perp$ if it holds that $\mathsf{vk}_A = \mathsf{vk}^*$, $\mathsf{ct}_A \neq \mathsf{ct}^*$ and $\Pi_{\mathsf{OTS}}.\mathsf{Vrfy}(\mathsf{vk}_A, (\mathsf{ct}'_{A,1}\|\cdots\|\mathsf{ct}'_{A,v}\|z), \sigma_A) = \top$.
  4. Compute $\mathsf{m}' \leftarrow \mathsf{Dec}(\mathsf{sk}_A, \mathsf{ct}_A)$ and return $\mathsf{m}' \in \mathcal{M} \cup \{\perp\}$.
- $\mathtt{O.ReEnc}(A, B, \mathsf{ct}_A)$: $\mathcal{B}_1$ parses $\mathsf{ct}_A = (\mathsf{vk}_A, (\mathsf{ct}'_{A,i})_{i\in[v]}, z, \sigma_A)$ and does the following:
  1. Return $\perp$ if $B \in \mathcal{L}_{\mathtt{Corrupt}}$ holds and (A, ct_A) is a derivative of (i^*, ct^*).
  2. Abort and output a random bit if $A = i^* \wedge j^* \in \phi_M(\mathsf{vk}_A)$ holds.
  3. Return $\perp$ if it holds that $\mathsf{vk}_A = \mathsf{vk}^*$, $\mathsf{ct}_A \neq \mathsf{ct}^*$ and $\Pi_{\mathsf{OTS}}.\mathsf{Vrfy}(\mathsf{vk}_A, (\mathsf{ct}'_{A,1}\|\cdots\|\mathsf{ct}'_{A,v}\|z), \sigma_A) = \top$.
  4. If $\mathsf{T}_{\mathsf{rk}}[A,B] = \emptyset$, compute $\mathsf{rk}_{A\to B} \leftarrow \mathsf{ReKeyGen}(\mathsf{sk}_A, \mathsf{pk}_B)$. If $\mathsf{T}_{\mathsf{rk}}[A,B] = \widehat{\mathsf{rk}}_{A\to B}$ $(\neq \emptyset)$, set $\mathsf{rk}_{A\to B} \leftarrow \widehat{\mathsf{rk}}_{A\to B}$.
  5. Return $\mathsf{ct}_B \leftarrow \mathsf{ReEnc}(\mathsf{rk}_{A\to B}, \mathsf{ct}_A)$.
- $\mathtt{O.Challenge}_b(i', \mathsf{m}_0^*, \mathsf{m}_1^*)$:
  1. Abort and output a random bit if $i^* \neq i'$.
  2. Compute $\{\tau_1^*, \ldots, \tau_v^*\} \leftarrow \phi_M(\mathsf{vk}^*)$, $(x_1^*, \ldots, x_v^*, z^*) \leftarrow \mathsf{Trans}(\mathsf{m}_b^*)$.
  3. Obtain $\mathsf{ct}'^*_{j^*}$ by submitting a challenge query $(x^*_{j^*}, 0^{\bar{\mu}})$ to the CPA game.
  4. For every $j \in [v]\setminus\{j^*\}$, compute $\mathsf{ct}'^*_j \leftarrow \Pi'_{\mathsf{PRE}}.\mathsf{Enc}(\mathsf{pk}'_{\tau_j^*}, x_j^*)$.
  5. Compute $\sigma^* \leftarrow \Pi_{\mathsf{OTS}}.\mathsf{Sign}(\mathsf{sigk}^*, (\mathsf{ct}'^*_1\|\cdots\|\mathsf{ct}'^*_v\|z^*))$.
  6. Return $\mathsf{ct}^* = (\mathsf{vk}^*, (\mathsf{ct}'^*_i)_{i\in[v]}, z^*, \sigma^*)$.

When $\mathcal{A}$ finally outputs the guessing bit $b' \in \{0,1\}$, $\mathcal{B}_1$ outputs 1 if $b = b'$; otherwise, it outputs 0.

We analyze the algorithm $\mathcal{B}_1$. Unless $\mathcal{A}$ issues a decryption query or re-encryption query on $(A, (\mathsf{vk}_A, (\mathsf{ct}'_{A,i})_{i\in[v]}, z_A, \sigma_A))$ such that $A = i^* \wedge j^* \in \phi_M(\mathsf{vk}_A)$, $\mathcal{B}_1$ can simulate $\mathtt{O.Dec}$ and $\mathtt{O.ReEnc}$. The t-disjunct property of $\boldsymbol{M}$

ensures that $\mathcal{A}$ cannot issue such a query. Additionally, $\mathcal{B}_1$ wins the CPA game by employing $\mathcal{A}$'s output, in the straightforward way. Hence, we have $\left|p^{(0)} - p^{(1)}\right| \leq \mathsf{Adv}^{\mathrm{cpa}}_{\Pi'_{\mathsf{PRE}},\mathcal{B}_1,nu}(\lambda)$.

Reduction to AONT's Indistinguishability. To bound $|p^{(1)} - 1/2|$, we construct a PPT algorithm $\mathcal{B}_2$ against $(\mu, \bar{\mu}, v)$-AONT Trans. Suppose that $\mathcal{B}_2$ is given the oracle $\mathtt{O.LR}$ in the indistinguishability game of AONT: $\mathcal{B}_2$ generates all n key-pairs $\{(\mathsf{pk}_i, \mathsf{sk}_i)\}_{i\in[n]}$ by itself and simulates the environment of $\mathcal{A}$ except for the following procedure of the oracle $\mathtt{O.Challenge}_b(i', \mathsf{m}_0^*, \mathsf{m}_1^*)$:

1. Abort and output a random bit if $i^* = i'$.
2. Obtain $((x_i^*)_{i\in[v]\setminus\{j^*\}}, z^*)$ by issuing $(j^*, \mathsf{m}_0^*, \mathsf{m}_1^*)$ to $\mathtt{O.LR}$.
3. Compute $\mathsf{ct}'^*_{j^*} \leftarrow \Pi'_{\mathsf{PRE}}.\mathsf{Enc}(\mathsf{pk}_{\tau^*_{j^*}}, 0^{\bar{\mu}})$ and $\mathsf{ct}'^*_i \leftarrow \Pi'_{\mathsf{PRE}}.\mathsf{Enc}(\mathsf{pk}_{\tau^*_i}, x_i^*)$ for every $i \in [v]\setminus\{j^*\}$, where $\{\tau_1^*, \ldots, \tau_v^*\} = \phi_M(\mathsf{vk}^*)$.
4. Compute $\sigma^* \leftarrow \Pi_{\mathsf{OTS}}.\mathsf{Sign}(\mathsf{sigk}^*, (\mathsf{ct}'^*_1 \parallel \cdots \parallel \mathsf{ct}'^*_v \parallel z^*))$.
5. Return $\mathsf{ct}^* = (\mathsf{vk}^*, (\mathsf{ct}'^*_i)_{i\in[v]}, z^*, \sigma^*)$.

When $\mathcal{A}$ outputs the guessing bit $b' \in \{0, 1\}$, $\mathcal{B}_2$ also outputs b'.

$\mathcal{B}_2$ simulates $\mathtt{O.KeyGen}$, $\mathtt{O.ReKeyGen}$, $\mathtt{O.Dec}$, $\mathtt{O.ReEnc}$ completely since it has the key-pairs of all users. $\mathtt{O.Challenge}$ is also simulated correctly since $\mathcal{B}_2$ can generate the challenge ciphertext without knowledge of $x^*_{j^*}$. Hence, the $\mathcal{B}_2$' advantage $\mathsf{Adv}^{\mathrm{ind}}_{\mathsf{Trans},\mathcal{B}_2}(\lambda)$ is at least $\left|p^{(1)} - 1/2\right|$. Therefore, we have $\mathsf{Adv}^{\mathrm{cpa}}_{\Pi'_{\mathsf{PRE}},\mathcal{B}_1,nu}(\lambda) + \mathsf{Adv}^{\mathrm{ind}}_{\mathsf{Trans},\mathcal{B}_2}(\lambda) \geq \varepsilon_{\mathcal{A}}/(n_h^3 u^2)$.

From the discussion above, we obtain

$$\mathsf{Adv}^{(t,t)\text{-cca2}}_{\Pi_{\mathsf{PRE}},\mathcal{A},n}(\lambda) \leq n_h u^2 \cdot \mathsf{Adv}^{\mathrm{cpa}}_{\mathcal{B}_1,\Pi'_{\mathsf{PRE}},nu}(\lambda) + n_h^3 u^2 \cdot \mathsf{Adv}^{\mathrm{ind}}_{\mathsf{AONT},\mathcal{B}_2}(\lambda) + \mathsf{Adv}^{\mathrm{suf}}_{\Pi_{\mathsf{OTS}},\mathcal{F}}(\lambda).$$

and complete the proof. □

B Omitted Proofs for Our Lattice-Based PRE Scheme

In this section, we give proofs for the correctness and re-encryption key homomorphism of our scheme $\Pi_{\mathsf{L\text{-}PRE}}$.

Proposition 4 (Correctness of $\Pi_{\mathsf{L\text{-}PRE}}$). *Let* $\mathsf{pp} = (\lambda, \mu, N, N', q, \eta, k, \ell, \boldsymbol{A})$ *be a public parameter determined by running* $\mathsf{Setup}(1^\lambda)$ *and let A, B be distinct users. Then, the key-pairs of these users and a ciphertext under the user A 's public key are defined as follows:*

- *Let* $(\mathsf{pk}_A, \mathsf{sk}_A) = ((\boldsymbol{t}_A, \hat{\boldsymbol{t}}_A), (\boldsymbol{s}_A, \hat{\boldsymbol{s}}_A))$ *and* $(\mathsf{pk}_B, \mathsf{sk}_B) = ((\boldsymbol{t}_B, \hat{\boldsymbol{t}}_B), (\boldsymbol{s}_B, \hat{\boldsymbol{s}}_B))$ *be the key-pairs of the users A and B, respectively, where for $i \in \{A, B\}$,* $\boldsymbol{t}_i = \boldsymbol{A}\boldsymbol{s}_i + \boldsymbol{e}_i$ *and* $\hat{\boldsymbol{t}}_i = \boldsymbol{A}\hat{\boldsymbol{s}}_i + \hat{\boldsymbol{e}}_i$.
- *Let* $\mathsf{ct}_A := (\boldsymbol{u}_A, v_A) \leftarrow \mathsf{Enc}(\mathsf{pk}_A, \mathsf{m})$ *for an arbitrary message* $\mathsf{m} \in \mathcal{M}$.

Denote $w := \boldsymbol{e}_A^\top \boldsymbol{r} + e_2 - \boldsymbol{s}_A^\top \boldsymbol{e}_1$ *and* $\hat{w} := w + \hat{\boldsymbol{e}}_B^\top \cdot \mathsf{BitDecomp}(\boldsymbol{u}_A) + \boldsymbol{r}_{A\to B,3}^\top \cdot \mathsf{BitDecomp}(\boldsymbol{u}_A) - \hat{\boldsymbol{s}}_B^\top \cdot \boldsymbol{R}_{A\to B,2} \cdot \mathsf{BitDecomp}(\boldsymbol{u}_A)$*, where* $\boldsymbol{r}, \boldsymbol{e}_1, e_2, \boldsymbol{R}_{A\to B,2}, \boldsymbol{r}_{A\to B,3}$ *are random values generated by running* $\mathsf{Enc}(\mathsf{pk}_A, \mathsf{m})$ *and* $\mathsf{ReKeyGen}(\mathsf{sk}_A, \mathsf{pk}_B)$*. Then, the proposed PRE scheme* $\Pi_{\mathsf{L\text{-}PRE}}$ *is* correct *with probability* $1 - \Pr\left[\|\hat{w}\|_\infty \geq q/4\right]$.

Proof. We consider an arbitrary message $\mathsf{m} \in \mathcal{M}$ throughout the proof of Proposition 4. First, we show the encryption-correctness of $\Pi_{\text{L-PRE}}$. Then, the public value $\boldsymbol{t}_A$ is represented as $\boldsymbol{t}_A = \boldsymbol{A}\boldsymbol{s}_A + \boldsymbol{e}_A$. Additionally, the value $\boldsymbol{u}_A$ of the ciphertext $\mathsf{ct}_A = (\boldsymbol{u}_A, v_A)$ under pk_A is $\boldsymbol{u}_A = \boldsymbol{A}^\top \boldsymbol{r} + \boldsymbol{e}_1$, and the value v_A is $v_A = \boldsymbol{t}_A^\top \boldsymbol{r} + e_2 + \lceil \frac{q}{2} \rfloor \cdot \mathsf{m} = (\boldsymbol{A}\boldsymbol{s}_A + \boldsymbol{e}_A)^\top \boldsymbol{r} + e_2 + \lceil \frac{q}{2} \rfloor \cdot \mathsf{m}$. Then, we have

$$
\begin{aligned}
v_A - \boldsymbol{s}_A^\top \boldsymbol{u}_A &= (\boldsymbol{A}\boldsymbol{s}_A + \boldsymbol{e}_A)^\top \boldsymbol{r} + e_2 + \left\lceil \frac{q}{2} \right\rfloor \cdot \mathsf{m} - \boldsymbol{s}_A^\top (\boldsymbol{A}^\top \boldsymbol{r} + \boldsymbol{e}_1) \\
&= \left\lceil \frac{q}{2} \right\rfloor \cdot \mathsf{m} + \boldsymbol{e}_A^\top \boldsymbol{r} + e_2 - \boldsymbol{s}_A^\top \boldsymbol{e}_1.
\end{aligned}
$$

By setting $w = \boldsymbol{e}_A^\top \boldsymbol{r} + e_2 - \boldsymbol{s}_A^\top \boldsymbol{e}_1$, m is correctly recovered by the algorithm Dec, due to the assumption $||w||_\infty < q/4$. Hence, the proof of the encryption correctness is completed.

Next, we show the re-encryption correctness of $\Pi_{\text{L-PRE}}$. For simplicity, we also employ the above value of $(\boldsymbol{t}_A, \boldsymbol{u}_A, v_A)$. Then, a re-encryption key $\mathsf{rk}_{A\to B} = (\boldsymbol{U}_{A\to B}, \boldsymbol{v}_{A\to B})$ generated by running $\mathsf{ReKeyGen}(\mathsf{sk}_A, \mathsf{pk}_B)$ is

$$
\begin{aligned}
\boldsymbol{U}_{A\to B} &= \boldsymbol{A}^\top \boldsymbol{R}_{A\to B,1} + \boldsymbol{R}_{A\to B,2} \in R_q^{k\times k\ell}; \text{ and} \\
\boldsymbol{v}_{A\to B}^\top &= \hat{\boldsymbol{t}}_B^\top \boldsymbol{R}_{A\to B,1} + \boldsymbol{r}_{A\to B,3}^\top - \mathsf{Powersof2}(\boldsymbol{s}_A^\top) \in R_q^{k\ell}.
\end{aligned}
$$

Additionally, a re-encrypted ciphertext $\mathsf{ct}_B = (\boldsymbol{u}_B, v_B)$ is generated by using the value of $(\boldsymbol{U}_{A\to B}, \boldsymbol{v}_{A\to B})$, as follows:

$$
\begin{aligned}
\boldsymbol{u}_B &= \left(\boldsymbol{A}_B^\top \boldsymbol{R}_{A\to B,1} + \boldsymbol{R}_{A\to B,2}\right) \cdot \mathsf{BitDecomp}(\boldsymbol{u}_A); \text{ and} \\
v_B &= v_A + (\hat{\boldsymbol{t}}_B^\top \boldsymbol{R}_{A\to B,1} + \boldsymbol{r}_{A\to B,3}^\top - \mathsf{Powersof2}(\boldsymbol{s}_A^\top)) \cdot \mathsf{BitDecomp}(\boldsymbol{u}_A).
\end{aligned}
$$

Then, we have

$$
\begin{aligned}
&v_B - \hat{\boldsymbol{s}}_B^\top \boldsymbol{u}_B \\
&= (v_A - \boldsymbol{s}_A^\top \boldsymbol{u}_A) + \hat{\boldsymbol{t}}_B^\top \boldsymbol{R}_{A\to B,1} \cdot \mathsf{BitDecomp}(\boldsymbol{u}_A) + \boldsymbol{r}_{A\to B,3}^\top \cdot \mathsf{BitDecomp}(\boldsymbol{u}_A) \\
&\quad - \hat{\boldsymbol{s}}_B^\top (\boldsymbol{A}^\top \boldsymbol{R}_{A\to B,1} \cdot \mathsf{BitDecomp}(\boldsymbol{u}_A) + \boldsymbol{R}_{A\to B,2} \cdot \mathsf{BitDecomp}(\boldsymbol{u}_A)) \\
&= \left(w + \left\lceil \frac{q}{2} \right\rfloor \mathsf{m}\right) + \hat{\boldsymbol{e}}_B^\top \cdot \mathsf{BitDecomp}(\boldsymbol{u}_A) \\
&\quad + \boldsymbol{r}_{A\to B,3}^\top \cdot \mathsf{BitDecomp}(\boldsymbol{u}_A) - \hat{\boldsymbol{s}}_B^\top \boldsymbol{R}_{A\to B,2} \cdot \mathsf{BitDecomp}(\boldsymbol{u}_A).
\end{aligned}
$$

The error-term $\hat{w}$ of $(v_B - \hat{\boldsymbol{s}}_B^\top \boldsymbol{u}_B)$ is defined as

$$
\begin{aligned}
\hat{w} := w &+ \hat{\boldsymbol{e}}_B^\top \cdot \mathsf{BitDecomp}(\boldsymbol{u}_A) \\
&+ \boldsymbol{r}_{A\to B,3}^\top \cdot \mathsf{BitDecomp}(\boldsymbol{u}_A) - \hat{\boldsymbol{s}}_B^\top \boldsymbol{R}_{A\to B,2} \cdot \mathsf{BitDecomp}(\boldsymbol{u}_A).
\end{aligned}
$$

Due to the assumption $||\hat{w}||_\infty < q/4$, m is recovered correctly. Hence, the proof of the re-encryption correctness is completed.

Therefore, we complete the proof of the correctness of $\Pi_{\text{L-PRE}}$. □

Proposition 5 (Re-encryption key homomorphism of $\Pi_{\mathsf{L\text{-}PRE}}$). *Suppose that u, v be positive integers such that $v \leq u$. Let* $\mathsf{pp} = (\lambda, \mu, N, N', q, \eta, k, \ell, \boldsymbol{A}) \leftarrow \mathsf{Setup}(1^\lambda)$, *and let* $\{\alpha_1, \ldots, \alpha_v\} \in [u]^v$ *and* $\{\beta_1, \ldots, \beta_v\} \in [u]^v$ *be two sets of distinct user-indices. Then, users' key-pairs and a ciphertext are defined as follows:*

- *For every $i \in [u]$, let* $(\mathsf{pk}_{A,i}, \mathsf{sk}_{A,i}) = ((\boldsymbol{t}_{A,i}, \hat{\boldsymbol{t}}_{A,i}), (\boldsymbol{s}_{A,i}, \hat{\boldsymbol{s}}_{A,i}))$ *(resp.* $(\mathsf{pk}_{B,i}, \mathsf{sk}_{B,i}) = ((\boldsymbol{t}_{B,i}, \hat{\boldsymbol{t}}_{B,i}), (\boldsymbol{s}_{B,i}, \hat{\boldsymbol{s}}_{B,i}))$*) be the key-pair of the user (A, i) (resp. the user (B, i)), where* $\boldsymbol{t}_{A,i} = \boldsymbol{A}\boldsymbol{s}_{A,i} + \boldsymbol{e}_{A,i}$ *and* $\hat{\boldsymbol{t}}_{B,i} = \boldsymbol{A}\hat{\boldsymbol{s}}_{B,i} + \hat{\boldsymbol{e}}_{B,i}$*;*
- *Let* $\mathsf{ct}_A := (\boldsymbol{u}_A, v_A) \leftarrow \mathsf{Enc}(\boldsymbol{t}_A, \mathsf{m})$ *for an arbitrary message* $\mathsf{m} \in \mathcal{M}$*, where* $\boldsymbol{t}_A = \sum_{i\in[v]} \boldsymbol{t}_{A,\alpha_i}$, $\boldsymbol{u}_A = \boldsymbol{A}^\top \boldsymbol{r} + \boldsymbol{e}_1^\top$ *and* $v_A = \boldsymbol{t}_A^\top \boldsymbol{r} + e_2 + \lceil \frac{q}{2} \rfloor \cdot \mathsf{m}$.

Denote $w_A := \boldsymbol{e}_A^\top \boldsymbol{r} + e_2 - \boldsymbol{s}_A^\top \boldsymbol{e}_1$ *and*

$$w_B := w_A + \left(\sum_{i\in[v]} \boldsymbol{r}^\top_{(A,\alpha_i)\to(B,\beta_i),3} \right) \mathsf{BitDecomp}(\boldsymbol{u}_A) + \left(\hat{\boldsymbol{e}}_B^\top \boldsymbol{R}_{A\to B,1} - \hat{\boldsymbol{s}}_B^\top \boldsymbol{R}_{A\to B,2}\right) \mathsf{BitDecomp}(\boldsymbol{u}_A),$$

where $\hat{\boldsymbol{s}}_B = \sum_{i\in[v]} \hat{\boldsymbol{s}}_{B,\beta_i}$, $\hat{\boldsymbol{e}}_B = \sum_{i\in[v]} \hat{\boldsymbol{e}}_{B,\beta_i}$, *and random values* $\boldsymbol{R}_{A\to B,1}, \boldsymbol{R}_{A\to B,2}$, *and* $\boldsymbol{r}_{(A,\alpha_i)\to(B,\beta_i),3}$ *for* $i \in [v]$ *are generated by running* $\mathsf{HReKeyGen}((\mathsf{sk}_{A,i})_{i\in[u]}, (\mathsf{pk}_{B,i})_{j\in[u]})$.

Then, the proposed PRE scheme $\Pi_{\mathsf{L\text{-}PRE}}$ *is* re-encryption key homomorphic *with probability* $1 - \Pr\left[\|w_B\|_\infty \geq q/4\right]$.

Proof. We consider an arbitrary message $\mathsf{m} \in \mathcal{M}$ throughout the proof of Proposition 5. For every $i \in [u]$, the values of $\boldsymbol{t}_{A,i}$ and $\hat{\boldsymbol{t}}_{B,i}$ are $\boldsymbol{t}_{A,i} = \boldsymbol{A}\boldsymbol{s}_{A,i} + \boldsymbol{e}_{A,i}$ and $\hat{\boldsymbol{t}}_{B,i} = \boldsymbol{A}\hat{\boldsymbol{s}}_{B,i} + \hat{\boldsymbol{e}}_{B,i}$, respectively. Then, let $\boldsymbol{t}_A := \sum_{i\in[v]} \boldsymbol{t}_{A,\alpha_i} = \boldsymbol{A}\sum_{i\in[v]} \boldsymbol{s}_{A,\alpha_i} + \sum_{i\in[v]} \boldsymbol{e}_{A,\alpha_i} = \boldsymbol{A}\boldsymbol{s}_A + \boldsymbol{e}_A$; and $\hat{\boldsymbol{t}}_B := \sum_{i\in[v]} \hat{\boldsymbol{t}}_{B,\beta_i} = \boldsymbol{A}\sum_{i\in[v]} \hat{\boldsymbol{s}}_{B,\beta_i} + \sum_{i\in[v]} \hat{\boldsymbol{e}}_{B,\beta_i} = \boldsymbol{A}\hat{\boldsymbol{s}}_B + \hat{\boldsymbol{e}}_B$, where $\boldsymbol{s}_A = \sum_{i\in[v]} \boldsymbol{s}_{A,\alpha_i}$, $\boldsymbol{e}_A = \sum_{i\in[v]} \boldsymbol{e}_{A,\alpha_i}$, $\hat{\boldsymbol{s}}_B = \sum_{i\in[v]} \hat{\boldsymbol{s}}_{B,\beta_i}$, and $\hat{\boldsymbol{e}}_B = \sum_{i\in[v]} \hat{\boldsymbol{e}}_{B,\beta_i}$.

Since $\mathsf{ct}_A = (\boldsymbol{u}_A, v_A)$ is an encryption of m under $\boldsymbol{t}_A$, we have $\boldsymbol{u}_A = \boldsymbol{A}^\top \boldsymbol{r} + \boldsymbol{e}_1$ and $v_A = \boldsymbol{t}_A^\top \boldsymbol{r} + e_2 + \lceil q/2 \rfloor \cdot \mathsf{m}$. Let $(\mathsf{rk}_{(A,i)\to(B,j)})_{i\in[u],j\in[u]} \leftarrow \mathsf{HReKeyGen}((\mathsf{sk}_{A,i})_{i\in[u]}, (\mathsf{pk}_{B,j})_{j\in[u]})$. For $i \in [u]$ and $j \in [u]$, the values of $(\boldsymbol{U}_{A\to B}, \boldsymbol{v}_{(A,i)\to(B,j)})$ are

$$\boldsymbol{U}_{A\to B} = \boldsymbol{A}^\top \boldsymbol{R}_{A\to B,1} + \boldsymbol{R}_{A\to B,2}; \text{ and}$$
$$\boldsymbol{v}_{(A,i)\to(B,j)} = \hat{\boldsymbol{t}}_{B,j}^\top \boldsymbol{R}_{A\to B,1} + \boldsymbol{r}^\top_{(A,i)\to(B,j),3} - \mathsf{Powersof2}(\boldsymbol{s}_{A,i}^\top).$$

Then, the value $\boldsymbol{v}_{A\to B}$ for $(\boldsymbol{U}_{A\to B}, \boldsymbol{u}_{A\to B}) \leftarrow \mathsf{ReKeyEval}((\mathsf{rk}_{(A,\alpha_i)\to(B,\beta_i)})_{i\in[v]})$ is $\boldsymbol{v}_{A\to B} := \sum_{i\in[v]} \boldsymbol{v}_{(A,\alpha_i)\to(B,\beta_i)} = \sum_{i\in[v]} \hat{\boldsymbol{t}}_{B,\beta_i}^\top \boldsymbol{R}_{A\to B,1} + \sum_{i\in[v]} \boldsymbol{r}^\top_{(A,\alpha_i)\to(B,\beta_i),3} - \sum_{i\in[v]} \mathsf{Powersof2}(\boldsymbol{s}_{A,\alpha_i}^\top)$. Since $\mathsf{ct}_B = (\boldsymbol{u}_B, v_B)$ is a re-encrypted ciphertext generated by using $(\boldsymbol{U}_{A\to B}, \boldsymbol{v}_{A\to B})$, we have

$$\boldsymbol{u}_B = (\boldsymbol{A}^\top \boldsymbol{R}_{A\to B,1} + \boldsymbol{R}_{A\to B,2}) \cdot \mathsf{BitDecomp}(\boldsymbol{u}_A); \text{ and}$$

$$\begin{aligned} v_B &= v_A + \left(\sum_{i\in[v]} \hat{\boldsymbol{t}}_{B,\beta_i}^\top \boldsymbol{R}_{A\to B,1} + \sum_{i\in[v]} \boldsymbol{r}_{(A,\alpha_i)\to(B,\beta_i),3}^\top - \sum_{i\in[v]} \mathsf{Powersof2}(\boldsymbol{s}_{A,\alpha_i}^\top) \right) \mathsf{BitDecomp}(\boldsymbol{u}_A) \\ &= v_A - \boldsymbol{s}_A^\top \boldsymbol{u}_A + \left((\boldsymbol{A}\hat{\boldsymbol{s}}_B + \hat{\boldsymbol{e}}_B)^\top \boldsymbol{R}_{A\to B,1} + \sum_{i\in[v]} \boldsymbol{r}_{(A,\alpha_i)\to(B,\beta_i),3}^\top \right) \mathsf{BitDecomp}(\boldsymbol{u}_A). \end{aligned}$$

Hence, it holds that

$$\begin{aligned} v_B - \hat{\boldsymbol{s}}_B^\top \boldsymbol{u}_B = v_A &- \boldsymbol{s}_A^\top \boldsymbol{u}_A \\ &+ \left((\boldsymbol{A}\hat{\boldsymbol{s}}_B + \hat{\boldsymbol{e}}_B)^\top \boldsymbol{R}_{A\to B,1} + \sum_{i\in[v]} \boldsymbol{r}_{(A,\alpha_i)\to(B,\beta_i),3}^\top \right) \mathsf{BitDecomp}(\boldsymbol{u}_A) \\ &- \hat{\boldsymbol{s}}_B^\top \left(\boldsymbol{A}^\top \boldsymbol{R}_{A\to B,1} \cdot \mathsf{BitDecomp}(\boldsymbol{u}_A) + \boldsymbol{R}_{A\to B,2} \cdot \mathsf{BitDecomp}(\boldsymbol{u}_A) \right) \\ = v_A &- \boldsymbol{s}_A^\top \boldsymbol{u}_A + \left(\sum_{i\in[v]} \boldsymbol{r}_{(A,\alpha_i)\to(B,\beta_i),3}^\top \right) \mathsf{BitDecomp}(\boldsymbol{u}_A) \\ &+ \left(\hat{\boldsymbol{e}}_B^\top \boldsymbol{R}_{A\to B,1} - \hat{\boldsymbol{s}}_B^\top \boldsymbol{R}_{A\to B,2} \right) \mathsf{BitDecomp}(\boldsymbol{u}_A). \end{aligned}$$

The error-term w_B of $v_B - \hat{\boldsymbol{s}}_B^\top \boldsymbol{u}_B$ is defined as

$$\begin{aligned} w_B := w_A &+ \left(\sum_{i\in[v]} \boldsymbol{r}_{(A,\alpha_i)\to(B,\beta_i),3}^\top \right) \mathsf{BitDecomp}(\boldsymbol{u}_A) \\ &+ \left(\hat{\boldsymbol{e}}_B^\top \boldsymbol{R}_{A\to B,1} - \hat{\boldsymbol{s}}_B^\top \boldsymbol{R}_{A\to B,2} \right) \mathsf{BitDecomp}(\boldsymbol{u}_A), \end{aligned}$$

where w_A is the error-term of $v_A - \boldsymbol{s}_A^\top \boldsymbol{u}_A$, i.e., $w_A = \boldsymbol{e}_A^\top \boldsymbol{r} + e_2 - \boldsymbol{s}_A^\top \boldsymbol{e}_1$.

Therefore, Dec correctly recovers m due to the assumption $\|w_B\|_\infty < q/4$, and this completes the proof. □

References

1. Almeida, J.B., et al.: Formally verifying KYBER - episode V: machine-checked IND-CCA security and correctness of ML-KEM in easycrypt. In: CRYPTO (2). LNCS, vol. 14921, pp. 384–421. Springer (2024). https://doi.org/10.1007/978-3-031-68379-4_12
2. Ateniese, G., Benson, K., Hohenberger, S.: Key-private proxy re-encryption. In: Fischlin, M. (ed.) CT-RSA 2009. LNCS, vol. 5473, pp. 279–294. Springer, Heidelberg (2009). https://doi.org/10.1007/978-3-642-00862-7_19
3. Ateniese, G., Fu, K., Green, M., Hohenberger, S.: Improved proxy re-encryption schemes with applications to secure distributed storage. In: NDSS. The Internet Society (2005)
4. Ateniese, G., Fu, K., Green, M., Hohenberger, S.: Improved proxy re-encryption schemes with applications to secure distributed storage. ACM Trans. Inf. Syst. Secur. **9**(1), 1–30 (2006)

5. Blaze, M., Bleumer, G., Strauss, M.: Divertible protocols and atomic proxy cryptography. In: EUROCRYPT. LNCS, vol. 1403, pp. 127–144. Springer (1998). https://doi.org/10.1007/bfb0054122
6. Bos, J.W., Ducas, L., Kiltz, E., Lepoint, T., Lyubashevsky, V., Schanck, J.M., Schwabe, P., Seiler, G., Stehlé, D.: CRYSTALS - kyber: A cca-secure module-lattice-based KEM. In: EuroS&P, pp. 353–367. IEEE (2018)
7. Canard, S., Devigne, J., Laguillaumie, F.: Improving the security of an efficient unidirectional proxy re-encryption scheme. J. Internet Serv. Inf. Secur. **1**(2/3), 140–160 (2011)
8. Canetti, R., Hohenberger, S.: Chosen-ciphertext secure proxy re-encryption. In: CCS, pp. 185–194. ACM (2007)
9. Chandran, N., Chase, M., Liu, F.-H., Nishimaki, R., Xagawa, K.: Re-encryption, functional re-encryption, and multi-hop re-encryption: a framework for achieving obfuscation-based security and instantiations from lattices. In: Krawczyk, H. (ed.) PKC 2014. LNCS, vol. 8383, pp. 95–112. Springer, Heidelberg (2014). https://doi.org/10.1007/978-3-642-54631-0_6
10. Chandran, N., Chase, M., Vaikuntanathan, V.: Functional re-encryption and collusion-resistant obfuscation. In: Cramer, R. (ed.) TCC 2012. LNCS, vol. 7194, pp. 404–421. Springer, Heidelberg (2012). https://doi.org/10.1007/978-3-642-28914-9_23
11. Chow, S.S.M., Weng, J., Yang, Y., Deng, R.H.: Efficient unidirectional proxy re-encryption. In: AFRICACRYPT. LNCS, vol. 6055, pp. 316–332. Springer (2010). https://doi.org/10.1007/978-3-642-12678-9_19
12. Cohen, A.: What about bob? The inadequacy of CPA security for proxy Reencryption. In: Lin, D., Sako, K. (eds.) PKC 2019. LNCS, vol. 11443, pp. 287–316. Springer, Cham (2019). https://doi.org/10.1007/978-3-030-17259-6_10
13. Cramer, R., et al.: Bounded CCA2-Secure Encryption. In: Kurosawa, K. (ed.) ASIACRYPT 2007. LNCS, vol. 4833, pp. 502–518. Springer, Heidelberg (2007). https://doi.org/10.1007/978-3-540-76900-2_31
14. Du, D.Z., Hwang, F.K.: Combinatorial Group Testing and Its Applications (2nd Edition), Series on Applied Mathematics, vol. 12. World Scientific (2000)
15. Duman, J., Hövelmanns, K., Kiltz, E., Lyubashevsky, V., Seiler, G.: Faster lattice-based KEMS via a generic Fujisaki-Okamoto transform using prefix hashing. In: CCS, pp. 2722–2737. ACM (2021)
16. Fan, X., Liu, F.-H.: Proxy re-encryption and re-signatures from lattices. In: Deng, R.H., Gauthier-Umaña, V., Ochoa, M., Yung, M. (eds.) ACNS 2019. LNCS, vol. 11464, pp. 363–382. Springer, Cham (2019). https://doi.org/10.1007/978-3-030-21568-2_18
17. Fuchsbauer, G., Kamath, C., Klein, K., Pietrzak, K.: Adaptively secure proxy re-encryption. In: Lin, D., Sako, K. (eds.) PKC 2019. LNCS, vol. 11443, pp. 317–346. Springer, Cham (2019). https://doi.org/10.1007/978-3-030-17259-6_11
18. Gentry, C.: Fully homomorphic encryption using ideal lattices. In: STOC, pp. 169–178. ACM (2009)
19. Grubbs, P., Maram, V., Paterson, K.G.: Anonymous, robust post-quantum public key encryption. In: EUROCRYPT (3). LNCS, vol. 13277, pp. 402–432. Springer (2022). https://doi.org/10.1007/978-3-031-07082-2_15
20. Huguenin-Dumittan, L., Vaudenay, S.: On ind-qcca security in the ROM and its applications - CPA security is sufficient for TLS 1.3. In: EUROCRYPT (3). LNCS, vol. 13277, pp. 613–642. Springer (2022). https://doi.org/10.1007/978-3-031-07082-2_22

21. Ivan, A., Dodis, Y.: Proxy cryptography revisited. In: NDSS. The Internet Society (2003)
22. Liang, X., Weng, J., Yang, A., Yao, L., Jiang, Z., Wu, Z.: Attribute-based conditional proxy re-encryption in the standard model under LWE. In: Bertino, E., Shulman, H., Waidner, M. (eds.) ESORICS 2021. LNCS, vol. 12973, pp. 147–168. Springer, Cham (2021). https://doi.org/10.1007/978-3-030-88428-4_8
23. Libert, B., Vergnaud, D.: Unidirectional chosen-ciphertext secure proxy re-encryption. In: Cramer, R. (ed.) PKC 2008. LNCS, vol. 4939, pp. 360–379. Springer, Heidelberg (2008). https://doi.org/10.1007/978-3-540-78440-1_21
24. Lyubashevsky, V., Micciancio, D.: Asymptotically efficient lattice-based digital signatures. In: Canetti, R. (ed.) TCC 2008. LNCS, vol. 4948, pp. 37–54. Springer, Heidelberg (2008). https://doi.org/10.1007/978-3-540-78524-8_3
25. Lyubashevsky, V., Micciancio, D.: Asymptotically efficient lattice-based digital signatures. J. Cryptol. **31**(3), 774–797 (2018)
26. Maram, V., Xagawa, K.: Post-quantum anonymity of KYBER. In: Public Key Cryptography (1). LNCS, vol. 13940, pp. 3–35. Springer (2023). https://doi.org/10.1007/978-3-031-31368-4_1
27. Miao, P., Patranabis, S., Watson, G.J.: Unidirectional updatable encryption and proxy re-encryption from DDH. In: Public Key Cryptography (2). LNCS, vol. 13941, pp. 368–398. Springer (2023). https://doi.org/10.1007/978-3-031-31371-4_13
28. Polyakov, Y., Rohloff, K., Sahu, G., Vaikuntanathan, V.: Fast proxy re-encryption for publish/subscribe systems. ACM Trans. Priv. Secur. **20**(4), 14:1–14:31 (2017)
29. Tessaro, S., Wilson, D.A.: Bounded-collusion identity-based encryption from semantically-secure public-key encryption: generic constructions with short ciphertexts. In: Krawczyk, H. (ed.) PKC 2014. LNCS, vol. 8383, pp. 257–274. Springer, Heidelberg (2014). https://doi.org/10.1007/978-3-642-54631-0_15
30. Zhou, B., Jiang, H., Zhao, Y.: Cpa-secure kems are also sufficient for post-quantum TLS 1.3. In: ASIACRYPT (3). LNCS, vol. 15486, pp. 433–464. Springer (2024). https://doi.org/10.1007/978-981-96-0891-1_14
31. Zhou, Y., Liu, S., Han, S.: Multi-hop fine-grained proxy re-encryption. In: Public Key Cryptography (4). LNCS, vol. 14604, pp. 161–192. Springer (2024). https://doi.org/10.1007/978-3-031-57728-4_6
32. Zhou, Y., Liu, S., Han, S., Zhang, H.: Fine-grained proxy re-encryption: Definitions and constructions from LWE. In: ASIACRYPT (6). LNCS, vol. 14443, pp. 199–231. Springer (2023). https://doi.org/10.1007/978-981-99-8736-8_7

Public-Key Encryption and Injective Trapdoor Functions from LWE with Large Noise Rate

Liheng Ji[1,2](✉) and Yilei Chen[1,2,3]

[1] Tsinghua University, Beijing 100084, China
jlh23@mails.tsinghua.edu.cn, chenyilei@mail.tsinghua.edu.cn
[2] Shanghai Qi Zhi Institute, Shanghai 200232, China
[3] Shanghai Artificial Intelligence Laboratory, Shanghai 200232, China

Abstract. The hardness of the learning with errors (LWE) problem increases as its noise rate grows. However, all existing LWE-based public-key encryption schemes require the noise rate to be no greater than $o(1/(\sqrt{n}\log n))$. Breaking through this limitation presents an intriguing challenge.

In this paper, we construct public-key encryption (PKE) schemes based on the sub-exponential hardness of decisional LWE with polynomial modulus and noise rate ranging from $O(1/\sqrt{n})$ to $o(1/\log n)$. More concretely, we demonstrate the existence of CPA-secure PKE schemes as long as one of the following three assumptions holds.

(i) $(n^{\omega(1)}, n^{-\omega(1)})$−hardness of decisional LWE with noise rate $O(1/\sqrt{n})$.

(ii) $(2^{\omega(n^{1/c_1})}, 2^{-\omega(n^{1/c_1})})$-hardness of decisional LWE with noise rate $O(1/\sqrt{n^{1-1/c_1}\log n})$ for some constant $c_1 > 1$.

(iii) $(2^{\omega(n/\log^{c_2} n)}, 2^{-\omega(n/\log^{c_2} n)})$-hardness of decisional LWE with noise rate $O(1/\sqrt{\log^{c_2+1} n})$ for some constant $c_2 > 0$.

Here, (t, ϵ)-hardness means no adversary running in time t can gain advantage exceeding ϵ.

We also construct injective trapdoor function (iTDF) families based on similar hardness assumption as our PKE. To achieve this, we give a generalization of Babai's nearest plane algorithm, which finds a "common closest lattice point" for a set of vectors.

In addition, we propose a PKE based on the $(2^{\omega(n^{1/2})}, 2^{-\omega(n^{1/2})})$-hardness of constant noise learning parity with noise (LPN) problem. Our construction is simpler than the construction of Yu and Zhang [CRYPTO 2016] while achieving the same security.

Keywords: Lattice · Learning with Errors · Public-Key Encryption · Injective Trapdoor Function · Learning Parity with Noise

C. Boura et al. (Eds.): SAC 2025, LNCS 16207, pp. 456–485, 2026.
https://doi.org/10.1007/978-3-032-10536-3_17

1 Introduction

1.1 Background

Recently, cryptographers have shown fervent interest in the study of the learning with errors problem (LWE). This enthusiasm is not only due to its capability of constructing traditional cryptographic primitives, such as public-key encryption (PKE) schemes [Reg05], signatures [GPV08], but also for more advanced usages like fully homomorphic encryption [BV11,GSW13], identity-based encryption [GPV08], and attribute-based encryption [GVW13]. Furthermore, the LWE problem is also conjectured to be hard against quantum computers.

Let us give a brief introduction to the LWE problem. Given a public matrix $\mathbf{A} \in \mathbb{Z}_q^{n\times m}$, a secret $\mathbf{s} \leftarrow \chi_s^n$, an error $\mathbf{e} \leftarrow \chi_e^m$, the search LWE problem asks the adversary to recover $\mathbf{s}$ from $(\mathbf{A}, \mathbf{A}^T\mathbf{s}+\mathbf{e})$. The decision LWE problem asks the distinguisher to tell whether the LWE samples are sampled according to the real LWE distribution or the uniform random distribution. For certain parameters, decision LWE is proven to be as hard as the search version [Reg05,MP12]. In this paper, we focus on a canonical variant of LWE in [Reg05], where χ_s is the uniform distribution on $\mathbb{Z}_q$, and $\chi_e \sim \Psi_{\alpha,q}$ is the rounded Gaussian distribution with width αq. We call this problem by $\mathsf{LWE}(n, q, \alpha)$, and call α its noise rate. Reductions from hard lattice problems (e.g. SIVP,GapSVP) to LWE have been well studied [Reg05,PRS17]. We present the recent reduction by Aggarwal et al. [ABB+23] which allows the reduction to run in subexponential time.

Lemma 1 ([ABB+23], Theorem 5.5). *Let $n, q \in \mathbb{N}^+$, $\alpha \in (0,1)$, $\gamma \geq \frac{10\sqrt{n}}{\alpha}$ satisfy $\alpha q \geq 2\sqrt{n}$. There is a quantum reduction from GapSVP_γ for all lattices to decision $\mathsf{LWE}(n, q, \alpha)$ that runs in time $(1 - \frac{4n}{(\alpha\gamma)^2})^{-n/2} \cdot \mathrm{poly}(n)$.*

In the lecture notes of Vaikuntanathan [Vai20], he mentioned the problem of constructing a public-key encryption scheme from LWE with $\alpha \in O(1)$ as an open problem. Currently, most constructions of LWE-PKE require the noise rate to be upper-bounded by $o(1/(\sqrt{n}\log n))$, while some other primitives even need the LWE noise to be sub-exponentially small. This naturally sparks the following questions.

- *What is the largest possible noise rate of LWE that enables public-key encryption?*
- *Can we use large noise LWE to achieve other cryptographic primitives?*

In this paper, we explore answers to the questions above, and the main results are presented in the following subsection.

1.2 Main Results

Public-Key Encryption Schemes from Large Noise LWE. We manage to construct PKE schemes with chosen-plaintext attack (CPA) security on LWE with polynomial modulus and noise rate ranging from $O(1/\sqrt{n})$ to $o(1/\log n)$.

Theorem 1. *Let n be the security parameter, and $q := q(n) \in \mathsf{poly}(n)$ be the modulus such that $q > \omega(n)$. There exists a PKE scheme with CPA-security if one of the following three conditions holds.*

(i) The $(n^{\omega(1)}, n^{-\omega(1)})$-hardness of decision $\mathsf{LWE}(n, q(n), O(1/\sqrt{n}))$.
(ii) The $(2^{\omega(n^{\frac{1}{c_1}})}, 2^{-\omega(n^{\frac{1}{c_1}})})$-hardness of decision $\mathsf{LWE}(n, q(n), O(1/\sqrt{n^{1-\frac{1}{c_1}} \log n}))$, for some constant $c_1 > 1$.
(iii) The $(2^{\omega(\frac{n}{\log^{c_2} n})}, 2^{-\omega(\frac{n}{\log^{c_2} n})})$-hardness of decision $\mathsf{LWE}(n, q(n), O(1/\sqrt{\log^{c_2+1} n}))$, for some constant $c_2 > 0$.

Here, (t, ϵ)-hardness means any adversary with running time t has an advantage bounded by ϵ.

Combining with Lemma 1, we show that PKE exists assuming the subexponential hardness of worst-case lattice problems like GapSVP_γ for the approximation factor γ as small as $\tilde{O}(\sqrt{n})$, improving upon the previous best result of $\gamma \in \tilde{O}(n)$. In particular, by letting $\alpha = O(1/\sqrt{\log^{c_2+1} n})$ for some constant $c_2 > 0$, we can choose any $\gamma \in \omega(\sqrt{n \log^{c_2+1} n})$ in Lemma 1 and show PKE exists assuming no quantum algorithm solves GapSVP_γ in time $2^{o(n)}$.

Injective Trapdoor Functions from Large Noise LWE. Building on the results of [MP12], we construct a family of injective trapdoor functions (injective TDFs, iTDFs) on the same hardness of search LWE with the same noise rate as our PKE.

Theorem 2. *Let n be the security parameter and $q = q(n) \in \mathsf{poly}(n)$ be a prime such that $q > \omega(n)$. There exists a TDF family if one of the following three conditions holds.*

(i) The $(n^{\omega(1)}, n^{-\omega(1)})$-hardness of search $\mathsf{LWE}(n, q(n), O(1/\sqrt{n}))$.
(ii) The $(2^{\omega(n^{\frac{1}{c_1}})}, 2^{-\omega(n^{\frac{1}{c_1}})})$-hardness of search $\mathsf{LWE}(n, q(n), O(1/\sqrt{n^{1-\frac{1}{c_1}} \log n}))$, for some constant $c_1 > 1$.
(iii) The $(2^{\omega(\frac{n}{\log^{c_2} n})}, 2^{-\omega(\frac{n}{\log^{c_2} n})})$-hardness of search $\mathsf{LWE}(n, q(n), O(1/\sqrt{\log^{c_2+1} n}))$, for some constant $c_2 > 0$.

Specifically, assuming condition (i) or condition (ii) with $c_1 \geq 2$, the TDF family is injective.

In the construction, we need to extend Babai's nearest plane algorithm [Bab86] to identify a "common closest lattice point" for a set of vectors. This is presented in Sect. 4.

Public-Key Encryption Schemes from Constant Noise LPN. In [YZ16], Yu and Zhang proposed a PKE scheme based on the $(2^{\omega(n^{1/2})}, 2^{-\omega(n^{1/2})})$-hardness of LPN with constant noise. Using a construction similar to our LWE scheme, we get a PKE scheme which is simpler than that in [YZ16] while achieving the same security.

Theorem 3. *Let n be the security parameter. There exists a PKE scheme with CPA-security assuming the $(2^{\omega(n^{1/2})}, 2^{-\omega(n^{1/2})})$-hardness of $\mathsf{LPN}(n, \mu)$, for some constant $0 < \mu < 1/2$.*

1.3 Technique Overview

Public-Key Encryption Schemes from Large Noise LWE. Our starting point is Regev's PKE scheme [Reg05]. Let λ be the security parameter of this PKE scheme. Let $q = q(\lambda) = \mathsf{poly}(\lambda)$ be a prime such that $q > \omega(\lambda)$, $n = \Omega(\lambda \log q) = \Omega(\lambda \log \lambda)$. Let $\Psi_{\alpha,q} := \lfloor D_{\alpha,q} \rceil$ denote the discretized Gaussian distribution with width αq (see Appendix A.2 for a detailed explanation). The key generation algorithm samples $\mathbf{A} \leftarrow \mathbb{Z}_q^{\lambda \times n}, \mathbf{s} \leftarrow \mathbb{Z}_q^{\lambda}$, $\mathbf{e} \leftarrow \Psi_{\alpha,q}^n$, computes $\mathbf{b} = \mathbf{A}^T\mathbf{s} + \mathbf{e} \bmod q$, and sets $(pk, sk) = ((\mathbf{A}, \mathbf{b}), \mathbf{s})$. For any message $\mathfrak{m} \in \{0,1\}$, the encryption algorithm samples $\mathbf{r} \leftarrow \{0,1\}^n$, and outputs the ciphertext $\mathfrak{c} = (\mathbf{c}_1, c_2) = (\mathbf{A}\mathbf{r}, \langle \mathbf{r}, \mathbf{b}\rangle + \lfloor q/2 \rceil \cdot \mathfrak{m})$. Finally, the decryption algorithm computes $\Delta := c_2 - \mathbf{c}_1^T\mathbf{s} = \langle \mathbf{r}, \mathbf{e}\rangle + \lfloor q/2 \rceil \cdot \mathfrak{m}$, checks whether Δ is closer to 0 or $\lfloor q/2 \rceil$, and outputs 0 or 1 accordingly. Since $\langle \mathbf{r}, \mathbf{e}\rangle \sim \Psi_{\alpha,q}^{\star O(n)}$ ($\Psi_{\alpha,q}^{\star t}$ denotes the distribution of summing up t elements sampled independently from $\Psi_{\alpha,q}$), we have when $\alpha = o(1/(\sqrt{n \log \lambda}))$, this scheme is correct with probability $1 - \mathsf{negl}(\lambda)$ (see Corollary 2 for the calculation). By the hardness of LWE and the leftover hash lemma (Lemma 7), we have $(\mathbf{A}, \mathbf{b}, \mathbf{A}\mathbf{r}, \langle \mathbf{r}, \mathbf{b}\rangle) \approx_c (\mathbf{A}, \mathbf{b}', \mathbf{A}\mathbf{r}, \langle \mathbf{r}, \mathbf{b}'\rangle) \approx_s (\mathbf{A}, \mathbf{b}', \mathcal{U}_q^{\lambda+1})$, where $\mathbf{b}' \sim \mathcal{U}_q^n$, $\approx_c$, $\approx_s$ stands for computational and statistical indistinguishability. This suffices to prove the security of the encryption scheme.

Now we modify this scheme by the following steps.

- **Step 1: Raise the noise rate to $\alpha = O(1/\sqrt{n})$, while keeping the setting of the other parameters unchanged.** Now the new scheme is correct with probability 2/3, which is still sufficient since we can improve the correctness by applying parallel repetition.
- **Step 2: Replace the distribution of $\mathbf{r}$ by $\Xi^{[n;k]}$, where $k = \Theta(\lambda \log \lambda / \log n)$, and $\Xi^{[n;k]}$ represents the uniform distribution over the set**

  $$\{\mathbf{v} \in \{0,1\}^n | \text{ the Hamming weight of } \mathbf{v} \text{ is } k\}.$$

  We also let $n = \Omega(\lambda^{>1})$, and $\alpha = O(1/\sqrt{k}) = O(1/\sqrt{\lambda \log \lambda / \log n})$.
  - Security: Since $k = O(n^{<1})$, we have $H_\infty(\Xi^{[n;k]}) = \Theta(k \log n) = \Theta(\lambda \log \lambda)$ (by Lemma 10). Using the leftover hash lemma, we have $(\mathbf{A}, \mathbf{b}', \mathbf{A}\mathbf{r}, \langle \mathbf{r}, \mathbf{b}'\rangle) \approx_s (\mathbf{A}, \mathbf{b}', \mathcal{U}_q^{\lambda+1})$. So the security still holds.
  - Correctness: We have $\langle \mathbf{r}, \mathbf{e}\rangle \sim \Psi_{\alpha,q}^{\star k}$. Since we set $\alpha = O(1/\sqrt{k})$, the scheme is correct with probability 2/3.

  We remark that if the scheme is not required to be efficient, we can let n be subexponential in λ, and then the noise rate ($\alpha = O(1/\sqrt{\lambda \log \lambda / \log n})$) will become even larger. The next step applies this idea more cleverly.
- **Step 3: Change the security parameter of the PKE scheme from λ to n, and let $\lambda \in (\omega(\log n), O(n^{<1})]$.** This modification makes n subexponential in λ, while maintaining the efficiency of the scheme. However, the security

assumption becomes tricky: we need to assume the $(n^{\omega(1)}, n^{-\omega(1)})$-hardness of $\mathsf{LWE}(\lambda, q(\lambda), O(1/\sqrt{\lambda \log \lambda / \log n}))$ to make the scheme secure. Actually, this hardness assumption aligns with the subexponential hardness assumption in Theorem 1, and we provide a detailed explanation for this in Lemma 2. We also note that this step works only if α is larger than $O(1/\sqrt{\lambda})$, which means the previous two steps are indeed necessary.

Using a similar method, we can also construct a PKE scheme based on the $(n^{\omega(1)}, n^{-\omega(1)})$-hardness of $\mathsf{LPN}(\lambda, \mu)$, where $\lambda = \Theta(\log^2 n)$, and $0 < \mu < \frac{1}{2}$ is a constant. This aligns with the result in Theorem 3.

Injective Trapdoor Function from Large Noise LWE. Next, we construct an iTDF family from LWE with a large noise rate.

We first recall the trapdoor function in [MP12]. Let λ be the security parameter, $q = q(\lambda) = \mathsf{poly}(\lambda)$ be a prime such that $q > \omega(\lambda)$, $\kappa = \lceil \log_2 q \rceil$, $w = \lambda\kappa$. Let $\mathbf{G}_\lambda$ be the gadget matrix. For a random matrix $\bar{\mathbf{A}} \leftarrow \lambda \times (n - w)$, an invertible matrix $\mathbf{H} \in \mathbb{Z}_q^{\lambda \times \lambda}$, the trapdoor generation algorithm samples $\mathbf{R} \leftarrow \{0,1\}^{(n-w) \times w}$, and outputs the public evaluation key $\mathbf{A} = (\bar{\mathbf{A}} \| \mathbf{H}\mathbf{G}_\lambda - \bar{\mathbf{A}}\mathbf{R})$, along with the private inversion key (trapdoor) $\mathbf{R}$. On input $(\mathbf{s}, \mathbf{e})$ such that $\mathbf{s} \leftarrow \mathbb{Z}_q^\lambda$ and $\mathbf{e} \leftarrow \Psi^n_{o(1/(\sqrt{\lambda}\log\lambda)),q}$, the evaluation algorithm (accessible to $\mathbf{A}$) outputs $\mathbf{b} := \mathbf{A}^T\mathbf{s} + \mathbf{e}$. The inversion algorithm (accessible to $\mathbf{A}, \mathbf{R}$), on input $\mathbf{b}$, computes $[\mathbf{R}^T \| \mathbf{I}]\mathbf{b} = \mathbf{G}_\lambda^T \mathbf{H}^T \mathbf{s} + [\mathbf{R}^T \| \mathbf{I}]\mathbf{e}$, uses Babai's nearest plane algorithm on $\Lambda(\mathbf{G}_\lambda^T)$ (the q-ary lattices is defined in Eqn. (2)) to get $\mathbf{H}^T\mathbf{s}$, and then recovers $\mathbf{s}, \mathbf{e}$ in the end.

Our idea is applying a transformation resembling what we do for PKE, except that we use the truncated Bernoulli distribution $\tilde{\mathcal{B}}^{\bar{n}}_{k/\bar{n}}$ (see Definition 10) instead of $\Xi^{[\bar{n};k]}$, which has a similar min-entropy to $\Xi^{[\bar{n};k]}$ but enables us to calculate independent bounds for different errors. More concretely, we replace the security parameter by n, and let $\ell = \omega(\log n)$, $\bar{n} = n - \ell w$, $k = \Theta(\lambda \log \lambda / \log n)$. For a random $\bar{\mathbf{A}} \leftarrow \mathbb{Z}_q^{\lambda \times \bar{n}}$ and $\mathbf{H} \in \mathbb{Z}_q^{\lambda \times \lambda}$, the trapdoor generation algorithm samples $\mathbf{R}_1, \ldots, \mathbf{R}_\ell \leftarrow (\tilde{\mathcal{B}}^{\bar{n}}_{k/\bar{n}})^{\otimes w}$, and outputs $\mathbf{A} = (\bar{\mathbf{A}} \| \mathbf{H}\mathbf{G}_\lambda - \bar{\mathbf{A}}\mathbf{R}_1 \| \ldots \| \mathbf{H}\mathbf{G}_\lambda - \bar{\mathbf{A}}\mathbf{R}_\ell)$ with trapdoor $(\mathbf{R}_1, \ldots, \mathbf{R}_\ell)$. On input $(\mathbf{s}, \mathbf{e})$ such that $\mathbf{s} \leftarrow \mathbb{Z}_q^\lambda$ and $\mathbf{e} \leftarrow \Psi^n_{O(1/\sqrt{k}),q}$, the evaluation algorithm outputs $\mathbf{b} := \mathbf{A}^T\mathbf{s} + \mathbf{e}$. As for the inversion algorithm, on input $\mathbf{b}$, it first parses $\mathbf{b} = (\bar{\mathbf{b}}^T \| \underline{\mathbf{b}}_1^T \| \ldots \| \underline{\mathbf{b}}_\ell^T)^T \in \mathbb{Z}_q^{\bar{n}} \times (\mathbb{Z}_q^w)^{\otimes \ell}$, $\mathbf{e} = (\bar{\mathbf{e}}^T \| \underline{\mathbf{e}}_1^T \| \ldots \| \underline{\mathbf{e}}_\ell^T)^T \in \mathbb{Z}_q^{\bar{n}} \times (\mathbb{Z}_q^w)^{\otimes \ell}$, and computes $\hat{\mathbf{b}}_i = \mathbf{R}_i^T \bar{\mathbf{b}} + \underline{\mathbf{b}}_i = \mathbf{G}_\lambda^T \mathbf{H}^T \mathbf{s} + \mathbf{R}_i^T \bar{\mathbf{e}} + \underline{\mathbf{e}}_i$. Then, it only needs to recover $\mathbf{H}^T\mathbf{s}$ from $\{\hat{\mathbf{b}}_i\}_{1 \le i \le \ell}$, which enables the calculation of $\mathbf{s}, \mathbf{e}$.

However, the error vector $\mathbf{R}_i^T \bar{\mathbf{e}} + \underline{\mathbf{e}}_i$ is so large that merely applying the traditional nearest plane algorithm results in a very low probability of successfully recovering $\mathbf{H}^T\mathbf{s}$. In other words, we need many times of parallel repetitions to achieve strong correctness (ℓ should be $\omega(2^\lambda)$), which will destroy the structure of our trapdoor function. To deal with this, we make a non-trivial modification to Babai's algorithm, which improves its error correction ability.

Nearest-Plane Algorithm for Large Noise Vectors. Let L be any n-dimensional lattice, $\mathbf{v} \in L$ be a lattice vector, $\mathbf{e}^{(1)}, \ldots, \mathbf{e}^{(\ell)} \in \mathbb{R}^n$ be independent random error vectors. Our goal is to recover $\mathbf{v}$ from $\{\mathbf{v} + \mathbf{e}^{(i)}\}_{1 \le i \le \ell}$ when the errors are small.

Let $\mathbf{B} = (\mathbf{b}_1, \ldots, \mathbf{b}_n)$ be an ordered basis of L, then we can write $\mathbf{v} = \sum_{j=1}^{n} c_j \mathbf{b}_j$ for some $c_1, \ldots, c_n \in \mathbb{Z}$. The idea is to follow the process of Babai's nearest-plane algorithm [Bab86], except that we do a parallel repetition (error correction) when computing each c_j. More concretely, if for most of $\mathbf{e}^{(i)}$, its projection to every orthogonal basis vector $\tilde{\mathbf{b}}_j$ is of length less than $\|\tilde{\mathbf{b}}_j\|/2$, then, by computing the projection of every $\mathbf{v} + \mathbf{e}^{(i)}$ to $\tilde{\mathbf{b}}_j$ and taking a majority, we will recover the projection of $\mathbf{v}$ to $\tilde{\mathbf{b}}_j$. Using the property of Gram-Schmidt orthogonalization, we can recover $c_n, c_{n-1}, \ldots, c_1$ one by one.

1.4 Applications

Oblivious Transfers from Large Noise LWE and Constant Noise LPN. Gertner et al. [GKM+00] demonstrated that for a PKE scheme with CPA-security, if its public key can be sampled without the knowledge of the corresponding secret key and remains indistinguishable from a legitimately generated public key, then the scheme can be transformed into an oblivious transfer (OT) in a black-box manner. It is straightforward to verify that our PKE schemes, derived from both large noise LWE and constant noise LPN, satisfy these criteria, thereby guaranteeing the existence of OTs based on the same hardness assumptions.

Applications of iTDF from Large Noise LWE. Bartusek et al. [BKP23] proved the existence of PKE and commitment schemes with publicly-verifiable deletion (PVD) under the assumption that post-quantum iTDF exists, therefore our result directly implies that PKE and commitment with PVD exist assuming large noise LWE is hard against quantum attackers. Furthermore, for any post-quantum primitive $X \in$ {attribute-based encryption, quantum fully-homomorphic encryption, witness encryption, time-revocable encryption}, they also established the existence of X with PVD, assuming the availability of both X and iTDFs. We can therefore plug in our iTDF construction in those constructions.

2 Preliminary

Let n be the security parameter. For a distribution or a set $\mathcal{X}$, $x \leftarrow \mathcal{X}$ denotes sampling x according to the distribution or uniformly at random from $\mathcal{X}$. For any $k \in \mathbb{N}$, define $\chi^{\star k}$ as the distribution obtained by the sum of k elements sampled independently from the distribution χ. For $x \in \mathbb{R}$, let $\lfloor x \rceil$ be the integer closest to x (and the smaller one if there are two closest candidates). For any integer $q \ge 2$, let $\mathcal{U}_q$ denote the uniform distribution on $\mathbb{Z}_q$, and we use $\mathcal{U}$ to denote $\mathcal{U}_2$. For any $a \in \mathbb{Z}_q$, define $|a| := \min\{a, q-a\}$ to represent the absolute difference in modular arithmetic. For any $a \in \mathbb{Z}_q$ and $b \in \mathbb{Z}$, define the value of

$(a+b)$ (resp. $(a-b)$, $a \cdot b$) by treating a as an element of $\{0, \ldots, q-1\} \subseteq \mathbb{Z}$ and then adding (resp. subtracting, multiplying) it by b. For any $x > 0$, we use $\log x$ to denote $\log_2 x$.

We use bold uppercase letters to denote matrices, bold lowercase letters to denote column vectors, and standard lowercase letters to represent scalar values. For any matrix $\mathbf{A}$, use $\mathbf{A}^T$ to denote its transpose. If $\mathbf{A}$ is invertible, use $\mathbf{A}^{-1}$ to denote its inverse, and define $\mathbf{A}^{-T} = (\mathbf{A}^{-1})^T$. For any n-dimensional vector $\mathbf{v}$ and any integer $i \in [1, n]$, let $v(i)$ denote the ith component of $\mathbf{v}$. For any $t \in [1, \infty]$, the ℓ_t-norm of vector $\mathbf{v}$ is denoted by $\|\mathbf{v}\|_t$, with the ℓ_2-norm simply represented as $\|\mathbf{v}\|$. For any two positive integers $k \leq m$, $\Xi^{[m;k]}$ denotes the uniform distribution on the set $\{\mathbf{v} \in \{0,1\}^m \mid \mathsf{Ham}(\mathbf{v}) = k\}$, where $\mathsf{Ham}(\mathbf{v})$ denotes the Hamming weight of the vector $\mathbf{v}$.

For any $\mu \in (0, 1)$, let $\mathcal{B}_\mu$ denote the Bernoulli distribution with parameter μ. For any finite set $\mathcal{S}$, denote by $|\mathcal{S}|$ the number of elements in $\mathcal{S}$. Denote by $\mathsf{poly}(n)$ some polynomial function of n, by $\mathsf{negl}(n)$ some negligible function of n, and by $n^{<1}$ (resp. $n^{>1}$) some function n^c where c is a constant in $(0, 1)$ (resp. $(1, \infty)$). When we say some event $\mathcal{E}$ happens with overwhelming probability, it means $\Pr[\mathcal{E}] = 1 - \mathsf{negl}(n)$. "PPT" stands for probabilistic polynomial time. The statistical distance between two random variables X and Y is defined as $\mathsf{SD}(X, Y) := \frac{1}{2}\sum_x |\Pr[X = x] - \Pr[Y = x]|$, where the sum is over all possible outcomes x. If $\mathsf{SD}(X, Y) = \mathsf{negl}(n)$, we say X, Y are statistically indistinguishable, denoted by $X \approx_s Y$. If for every PPT adversary $\mathcal{A}$, $|\Pr[\mathcal{A}(X) = 1] - \Pr[\mathcal{A}(Y) = 1]| = \mathsf{negl}(n)$, we say X, Y are computationally indistinguishable, denoted by $X \approx_c Y$. We have $X \approx_s Y$ implies $X \approx_c Y$. Denote the min-entropy of X by $H_\infty(X) := -\log(\max_x \Pr[X = x])$. The statistical distance, indistinguishability, and min-entropy of probability distributions are defined similarly. Due to space limitations, we postpone the rest of this section to Appendix A.

3 Public-Key Encryption Scheme from LWE with Large Noise

In this section, we construct CPA-secure PKE schemes on subexponential hardness of LWE with large noise rates. Concretely, Subsect. 3.1 and 3.2 are dedicated to proving the following theorem.

Theorem 4. *Let n be the security parameter for the PKE scheme. For any $\lambda \in (\omega(\log n), O(n^{<1})]$, and any prime $q = q(\lambda) \in \mathsf{poly}(\lambda)$ such that $q > \omega(\lambda)$, there exists a PKE scheme with CPA-security assuming the $(n^{\omega(1)}, n^{-\omega(1)})$-hardness of decision $\mathsf{LWE}(\lambda, q(\lambda), O(1/\sqrt{\lambda \log \lambda / \log n}))$.*

The following lemma gives a better illustration of the hardness assumption in Theorem 4.

Lemma 2. *For any $\lambda \in (\omega(\log n), O(n^{<1})]$, and any $q(\lambda) \in \mathsf{poly}(\lambda)$,*

(i) if $\lambda = \Theta(n^{c_0})$ *for some constant* $0 < c_0 < 1$, *we have the* $(n^{\omega(1)}, n^{-\omega(1)})$*-hardness of decision (resp., search)* $\mathsf{LWE}(\lambda, q(\lambda), O(1/\sqrt{\lambda \log \lambda / \log n}))$ *is implied by the hardness of the decision (resp., search)* $\mathsf{LWE}(n, q(n), O(1/\sqrt{n}))$.

(ii) if $\lambda = \Theta(\log^{c_1} n)$ *for some constant* $c_1 > 1$, *we have the* $(n^{\omega(1)}, n^{-\omega(1)})$*-hardness of decision (resp., search)* $\mathsf{LWE}(\lambda, q(\lambda), O(1/\sqrt{\lambda \log \lambda / \log n}))$ *is implied by the* $(2^{\omega(n^{\frac{1}{c_1}})}, 2^{-\omega(n^{\frac{1}{c_1}})})$*-hardness of the decision (resp., search)* $\mathsf{LWE}(n, q(n), O(1/\sqrt{n^{1-\frac{1}{c_1}} \log n}))$.

(iii) if $\lambda = \Theta(\log n (\log \log n)^{c_2})$ *for some constant* $c_2 > 0$, *we have the* $(n^{\omega(1)}, n^{-\omega(1)})$*-hardness of decision (resp., search)* $\mathsf{LWE}(\lambda, q(\lambda), O(1/\sqrt{\lambda \log \lambda / \log n}))$ *is implied by the* $(2^{\omega(\frac{n}{\log^{c_2} n})}, 2^{-\omega(\frac{n}{\log^{c_2} n})})$*-hardness of the decision (resp., search)* $\mathsf{LWE}(n, q(n), O(1/\sqrt{\log^{c_2+1} n}))$.

Remark 1. The PKE proposed by Regev [Reg05] is based on the $(n^{\omega(1)}, n^{-\omega(1)})$-hardness of decision $\mathsf{LWE}(n, q(n), o(1/(\sqrt{n} \log n)))$. The LWE problem in (i) improves the noise by an $\omega(\log n)$ factor, and thus has a stronger hardness. As for the LWE problems in (ii) and (iii), we do not know how to compare their hardness to that in (i). However, they can be viewed as a trade-off between the secret length λ and the noise rate, which has not appeared in Regev's PKE [Reg05].

Proof. In the following, we do not distinguish between the search problem and the decision problem, as their proofs are the same.

(i) When $\lambda = \Theta(n^{c_0})$, we have $n^{\omega(1)} = \lambda^{\omega(1)}$, and $O(1/\sqrt{\lambda \log \lambda / \log n}) = O(1/\sqrt{\lambda \log \lambda / \log(\lambda^{1/c_0})}) = O(1/\sqrt{\lambda})$.
The $(n^{\omega(1)}, n^{-\omega(1)})$-hardness of $\mathsf{LWE}(n, q(n), O(1/\sqrt{n}))$ implies the $(\lambda^{\omega(1)}, \lambda^{-\omega(1)})$-hardness of $\mathsf{LWE}(\lambda, q(\lambda), O(1/\sqrt{\lambda}))$, which is exactly the $(n^{\omega(1)}, n^{-\omega(1)})$-hardness of $\mathsf{LWE}(\lambda, q(\lambda), O(1/\sqrt{\lambda \log \lambda / \log n}))$.

(ii) When $\lambda = \Theta(\log^{c_1} n)$, we have $n^{\omega(1)} = 2^{\Theta(\lambda^{1/c_1})}$, and $O(1/\sqrt{\lambda \log \lambda / \log n}) = O(1/\sqrt{(\lambda \log \lambda)/\lambda^{1/c_1}}) = O(1/\sqrt{\lambda^{1-1/c_1} \log \lambda})$.
The $(2^{\omega(n^{\frac{1}{c_1}})}, 2^{-\omega(n^{\frac{1}{c_1}})})$-hardness of $\mathsf{LWE}(n, q(n), O(1/\sqrt{n^{1-\frac{1}{c_1}} \log n}))$ implies the $(2^{\omega(\lambda^{\frac{1}{c_1}})}, 2^{-\omega(\lambda^{\frac{1}{c_1}})})$-hardness of $\mathsf{LWE}(\lambda, q(\lambda), O(1/\sqrt{\lambda^{1-\frac{1}{c_1}} \log \lambda}))$, which is exactly the $(n^{\omega(1)}, n^{-\omega(1)})$-hardness of $\mathsf{LWE}(\lambda, q(\lambda), O(1/\sqrt{\lambda \log \lambda / \log n}))$.

(iii) When $\lambda = \Theta(\log n (\log \log n)^{c_2})$, we have $\log \lambda = \Theta(\log \log n + c_2 \log \log \log n) = \Theta(\log \log n)$. Substituting back, we find $\lambda = \Theta(\log n \log^{c_2} \lambda)$, leading to $\log n = \Theta(\frac{\lambda}{\log^{c_2} \lambda})$. Then $n^{\omega(1)} = 2^{\omega(\frac{\lambda}{\log^{c_2} \lambda})}$, and $O(1/\sqrt{\lambda \log \lambda / \log n}) = O(1/\sqrt{\lambda \log \lambda / (\frac{\lambda}{\log^{c_2} \lambda})}) = O(1/\sqrt{\log^{c_2+1} \lambda})$.
The $(2^{\omega(\frac{n}{\log^{c_2} n})}, 2^{-\omega(\frac{n}{\log^{c_2} n})})$-hardness of $\mathsf{LWE}(n, q(n), O(1/\sqrt{\log^{c_2+1} n}))$ implies the $(2^{\omega(\frac{\lambda}{\log^{c_2} \lambda})}, 2^{-\omega(\frac{\lambda}{\log^{c_2} \lambda})})$-hardness of $\mathsf{LWE}(\lambda, q(\lambda), O(1/\sqrt{\log^{c_2+1} \lambda}))$, which is exactly the $(n^{\omega(1)}, n^{-\omega(1)})$-hardness of $\mathsf{LWE}(\lambda, q(\lambda), O(1/\sqrt{\lambda \log \lambda / \log n}))$.

□

By combining Theorem 4 and Lemma 2, we have the following corollary.

Corollary 1 (Theorem 1). *Let n be the security parameter, and $q = q(n) \in \mathsf{poly}(n)$ be a prime such that $q > \omega(n)$. There exists a construction of PKE scheme with CPA-security assuming one of the following three conditions.*

(i) The $(n^{\omega(1)}, n^{-\omega(1)})$-hardness of decision $\mathsf{LWE}(n, q(n), O(1/\sqrt{n}))$.

(ii) The $(2^{\omega(n^{\frac{1}{c_1}})}, 2^{-\omega(n^{\frac{1}{c_1}})})$-hardness of decision $\mathsf{LWE}(n, q(n), O(1/\sqrt{n^{1-\frac{1}{c_1}} \log n}))$, for some constant $c_1 > 1$.

(iii) The $(2^{\omega(\frac{n}{\log^{c_2} n})}, 2^{-\omega(\frac{n}{\log^{c_2} n})})$-hardness of decision $\mathsf{LWE}(n, q(n), O(1/\sqrt{\log^{c_2+1} n}))$, for some constant $c_2 > 0$.

3.1 Single-Bit LWE-PKE Scheme with Weak Correctness

In this subsection, we transform Regev's LWE-PKE [Reg05] into a single-bit public-key encryption scheme $\Pi_\lambda^{LWE} = (\mathsf{KeyGen}, \mathsf{Enc}, \mathsf{Dec})$ with 2/3-correctness.

Construction. Let n be the security parameter of the PKE scheme, $\lambda \in (\omega(\log n), O(n^{<1})]$ be the dimension of the LWE secret, $q = q(\lambda) \in \mathsf{poly}(\lambda)$ be a prime such that $q > \omega(\lambda)$. Let $k = \Theta(\lambda \log \lambda / \log n)$ s.t. $H_\infty(\Xi^{[n:k]}) > 2(\lambda+1)\log q$. (For the existence of such a k, please refer to Lemma 10.) Let $\chi_r \sim \Xi^{[n;k]}$, $\alpha \le \frac{1}{10\sqrt{k}}$.

- The message space is $\mathcal{M} = \{0, 1\}$.
- $\mathsf{KeyGen}(1^n)$: Given the security parameter 1^n, it samples $\mathbf{A} \leftarrow \mathbb{Z}_q^{\lambda \times n}$, as well as $\mathbf{s} \leftarrow \mathbb{Z}_q^{\lambda}$, $\mathbf{e} \leftarrow (\Psi_{\alpha,q})^n$. Then it computes $\mathbf{b} := (\mathbf{A}^T\mathbf{s} + \mathbf{e}) \bmod q$, and sets $(pk, sk) := ((\mathbf{A}, \mathbf{b}), \mathbf{s})$.
- $\mathsf{Enc}(pk, \mathtt{m})$: Given the public key $pk = (\mathbf{A}, \mathbf{b})$ and the message $\mathtt{m} \in \mathcal{M}$, it samples $\mathbf{r} \leftarrow \chi_r$, and output $\mathfrak{c} := (\mathbf{c}_1, c_2)$ as ciphertext, where $\mathbf{c}_1 := \mathbf{Ar}$ and $c_2 := (\mathbf{r}^T\mathbf{b} + \lfloor q/2 \rceil \cdot \mathtt{m}) \mod q$.
- $\mathsf{Dec}(sk, \mathfrak{c})$: Given the secret key $sk = \mathbf{s}$ and the ciphertext $\mathfrak{c}$, parse $\mathfrak{c}$ into $(\mathbf{c}_1, c_2)$, calculate $\Delta := (c_2 - \mathbf{c}_1^T\mathbf{s}) \bmod q$. If $|\Delta| < \lfloor q/2 \rceil / 2$, output 0. Otherwise, output 1.

Theorem 5 (Weak correctness). *Let $\lambda \in (\omega(\log n), O(n^{<1})]$, $q = q(\lambda) \in \mathsf{poly}(\lambda)$ be a prime such that $q > \omega(\lambda)$, $k = \Theta(\lambda \log \lambda / \log n)$ s.t. $H_\infty(\Xi^{[n:k]}) > 2(\lambda+1)\log q$, $\alpha \le \frac{1}{10\sqrt{k}}$. Then Π_λ^{LWE} has $\frac{2}{3}$-correctness.*

Proof. $\Delta = (c_2 - \mathbf{c}_1^T\mathbf{s}) \bmod q = (\mathbf{r}^T\mathbf{e} + \lfloor q/2 \rceil \cdot \mathtt{m}) \bmod q$. Let $e' := \mathbf{r}^T\mathbf{e}$, then $e' \sim (\Psi_{\alpha,q})^{\star k}$. By Corollary 2, $\Pr[|e'| < \lfloor q/2 \rceil / 2] > 1 - \exp(-\frac{(100k)\pi}{72k}) > 2/3$. □ The CPA security of Π_λ^{LWE} follows straightforwardly from the hardness of decision $\mathsf{LWE}(\lambda, q, \alpha)$ and an application of LHL (the leftover hash lemma, Lemma 7), and we postpone the formal proof to Appendix B.

Theorem 6 (CPA security). *Let $\lambda \in (\omega(\log n), O(n^{<1})]$, $q = q(\lambda) \in \mathsf{poly}(\lambda)$ such that $q > \omega(\lambda)$, $k = \Theta(\lambda \log \lambda / \log n)$ s.t. $H_\infty(\Xi^{[n:k]}) > 2(\lambda+1)\log q$, $\alpha \le \frac{1}{10\sqrt{k}}$. Assume decision $\mathsf{LWE}(\lambda, q, \alpha)$ is hard, then Π_λ^{LWE} is IND-CPA secure.*

3.2 Multi-bit LWE-PKE Scheme with Strong Correctness

In this subsection, we transform the scheme Π_λ^{LWE} in Subsect. 3.1 into a strongly correct one, denoted by $\widetilde{\Pi}_\lambda^{LWE} = (\widetilde{\mathsf{KeyGen}}, \widetilde{\mathsf{Enc}}, \widetilde{\mathsf{Dec}})$. The idea is to use a similar transformation as in [PVW08, Subsection 7.2], along with an error-correcting code.

Construction. Let $\lambda \in (\omega(\log n), O(n^{<1})]$, $q = q(\lambda) \in (\omega(\lambda), \mathsf{poly}(\lambda))$ be a prime, $\ell = O(\lambda)$, $k = \Theta((\lambda + \ell)\log\lambda/\log n)$ s.t. $H_\infty(\Xi^{[n:k]}) > 2(\lambda+\ell)\log q$. Let $\chi_r \sim \Xi^{[n;k]}$, $\alpha \leq \frac{1}{10\sqrt{k}}$. Let $\mathbf{C} \in \{0,1\}^{\ell\times m}$ be a binary error correcting code that corrects $\ell/3$ independent errors, where $m = O(\ell)$. (The construction of such error-correcting code can be found in [Jus72].)

- The message space is $\mathcal{M} = \{0,1\}^m$.
- $\widetilde{\mathsf{KeyGen}}(1^n)$: Let $\mathbf{A} \leftarrow \mathbb{Z}_q^{\lambda\times n}$. Let $\mathbf{s}_1,\dots,\mathbf{s}_\ell \leftarrow \mathbb{Z}_q^\lambda$, $\mathbf{e}_1,\dots,\mathbf{e}_\ell \leftarrow (\Psi_{\alpha,q})^n$, and set $\mathbf{S} := [\mathbf{s}_1\|\dots\|\mathbf{s}_\ell] \in \mathbb{Z}_q^{\lambda\times\ell}$, $\mathbf{E} := [\mathbf{e}_1\|\dots\|\mathbf{e}_\ell] \in \mathbb{Z}^{n\times\ell}$. Compute $\mathbf{B} := (\mathbf{A}^T\mathbf{S} + \mathbf{E}) \bmod q$, and set $(pk, sk) := ((\mathbf{A},\mathbf{B}),\mathbf{S})$.
- $\widetilde{\mathsf{Enc}}(pk, \mathfrak{m})$: Given the public key $pk = (\mathbf{A},\mathbf{B})$ and the message $\mathfrak{m} \in \mathcal{M}$, it samples $\mathbf{r} \leftarrow \chi_r$, and output $\mathfrak{c} := (\mathbf{c}_1^T, \mathbf{c}_2)$ as ciphertext, where $\mathbf{c}_1 := \mathbf{A}\mathbf{r}$ and $\mathbf{c}_2 := (\mathbf{r}^T\mathbf{B} + \lfloor q/2\rceil \cdot \mathbf{C}\cdot\mathfrak{m}) \bmod q$.
- $\widetilde{\mathsf{Dec}}(sk, \mathfrak{c})$: Parse $\mathfrak{c}$ into $(\mathbf{c}_1, \mathbf{c}_2)$, calculate $(\Delta_1,\dots,\Delta_\ell)^T := (\mathbf{c}_2 - \mathbf{c}_1^T\cdot\mathbf{S}) \bmod q$. Define $\mathbf{d} := (d_1,\dots,d_\ell)^T$, where

$$\forall 1 \leq i \leq \ell,\ d_i := \begin{cases} 0 \text{ if } |\Delta_i| < \lfloor q/2\rceil/2 \\ 1 \quad \text{otherwise.}\end{cases}$$

  Output $\mathbf{C}^{-1}\cdot\mathbf{d}$, where $\mathbf{C}^{-1}$ is the decoding function.

Theorem 7 (Strong correctness). *Let $\lambda \in (\omega(\log n), O(n^{<1})]$, $q = q(\lambda) \in \mathsf{poly}(\lambda)$ be a prime such that $q > \omega(\lambda)$, $\ell = O(\lambda)$, $k = \Theta((\lambda+\ell)\log\lambda/\log n)$ s.t. $H_\infty(\Xi^{[n:k]}) > 2(\lambda+\ell)\log q$. Let $\chi_r \sim \Xi^{[n;k]}$, $\alpha \leq \frac{1}{10\sqrt{k}}$. Then $\widetilde{\Pi}_\lambda^{LWE}$ is correct.*

Proof (sketch). Assume $(u_1,\dots,u_\ell)^T = \mathbf{C}\cdot\mathfrak{m}$ Through a calculation similar to the proof in Theorem 5, we have $\Pr[d_i = u_i] > 2/3$ for every $i \in [1,\ell]$. Therefore, we can successfully decode $\mathfrak{m}$ from $\mathbf{d}$ with overwhelming probability. □

Theorem 8 (CPA security). *Let $\lambda \in (\omega(\log n), O(n^{<1})]$, $q = q(\lambda) \in \mathsf{poly}(\lambda)$ be a prime such that $q > \omega(\lambda)$, $\ell = O(\lambda)$, $k = \Theta((\lambda+\ell)\log\lambda/\log n)$ s.t. $H_\infty(\Xi^{[n:k]}) > 2(\lambda+\ell)\log q$. Let $\chi_r \sim \Xi^{[n;k]}$, $\alpha \leq \frac{1}{10\sqrt{k}}$. Assume decision $\mathsf{LWE}(\lambda,q,\alpha)$ is hard, then $\widetilde{\Pi}_\lambda^{LWE}$ is IND-CPA secure.*

Proof (sketch). The hybrid argument is similar to the proof of Theorem 6. First, by the hardness of $\mathsf{LWE}(\lambda,q,\alpha)$, we can replace every column of $\mathbf{B}$ by a uniform vector sequentially. Then, an application of LHL (Lemma 7) concludes the proof. □

4 Nearest-Plane Algorithm for Large Noise Vectors

In this section, we give a generalization of Babai's nearest-plane algorithm [Bab86], which finds a "common closest lattice point" for a set of real vectors. More concretely, let $\tilde{\mathbf{B}} = (\tilde{\mathbf{b}}_1, \ldots, \tilde{\mathbf{b}}_\kappa)$ be an orthogonal basis of some lattice L. For any vector $\mathbf{v} \in L$, consider a set of independent error vectors $\{\mathbf{e}^{(i)} \in \mathbb{R}^\kappa\}_{1 \le i \le \ell}$. For each i, define $\mathbf{z}^{(i)} := \mathbf{v} + \mathbf{e}^{(i)}$. We show in the following theorem that, if for every i and j, the length of the projection of $\mathbf{e}^{(i)}$ onto $\tilde{\mathbf{b}}_j$ is less than $\|\tilde{\mathbf{b}}_j\|_2/2$ with a probability greater than $2/3$, then $\mathbf{v}$ and $\{\mathbf{e}^{(i)}\}_{1 \le i \le \ell}$ can be recovered with overwhelming probability.

Theorem 9. *Let $\kappa = \kappa(n) \in \mathsf{poly}(n)$, $\mathbf{B} = (\mathbf{b}_1, \ldots, \mathbf{b}_\kappa)$ be an ordered basis of any κ-dimensional lattice L, and let its orthogonal basis be $\tilde{\mathbf{B}} = (\tilde{\mathbf{b}}_1, \ldots, \tilde{\mathbf{b}}_\kappa)$. Let $\ell = \omega(\log n)$. For random vectors $\mathbf{e}^{(1)}, \ldots, \mathbf{e}^{(\ell)}$ sampled independently from some distribution over $\mathbb{R}^\kappa$, if*

$$\forall 1 \le i \le \ell, 1 \le j \le \kappa, \ \Pr_{\mathbf{e}^{(i)}}\left[|\langle \mathbf{e}^{(i)}, \tilde{\mathbf{b}}_j \rangle| < \frac{\|\tilde{\mathbf{b}}_j\|^2}{2}\right] > \frac{2}{3},$$

then there is a PPT algorithm, which takes $\mathbf{B}$ and $\{\mathbf{v}+\mathbf{e}^{(i)}\}_{1 \le i \le \ell}$ for some $\mathbf{v} \in L$ as input, outputs $\mathbf{v}$ and $\{\mathbf{e}^{(i)}\}_{1 \le i \le \ell}$ correctly with $1 - \mathsf{negl}(n)$ probability.

Algorithm 1. Nearest-Plane Algorithm for Larger Noise Vectors

function FINDCLOSESTVECTOR$^{\kappa,\ell}(L, \mathbf{B}, \{\mathbf{z}^{(i)}\}_{1 \le i \le \ell})$
  Orthogonalize $\mathbf{B} = (\mathbf{b}_1, \ldots, \mathbf{b}_\kappa)$ in the forward order and get $\tilde{\mathbf{B}} = (\tilde{\mathbf{b}}_1, \ldots, \tilde{\mathbf{b}}_\kappa)$.
  for $i = 1$ **to** ℓ **do**
    Initialize $\mathbf{x}^{(i)} := \mathbf{z}^{(i)}$
  end for
  for $j = \kappa$ **to** 1 **do**
    Find majority in $\{\lfloor \frac{\langle \mathbf{x}^{(i)}, \tilde{\mathbf{b}}_j \rangle}{\langle \tilde{\mathbf{b}}_j, \tilde{\mathbf{b}}_j \rangle} \rceil\}_{1 \le i \le \ell}$, and denote it by c_j.
    for $i = 1$ **to** ℓ **do**
      $\mathbf{x}^{(i)} \leftarrow \mathbf{x}^{(i)} - c_j \mathbf{b}_j$.
    end for
  end for
  Let $\mathbf{v} := \mathbf{z}^{(1)} - \mathbf{x}^{(1)}$, and $\mathbf{e}^{(i)} := \mathbf{x}^{(i)}$ for each $1 \le i \le \ell$.
  return $\mathbf{v}, \{\mathbf{e}^{(i)}\}_{1 \le i \le \ell}$.
end function

Proof. The detailed steps of the algorithm are given in Algorithm 1, and we show its correctness in the following. Assume the hidden lattice vector is $\mathbf{v} = \sum_{j=1}^{\kappa} c'_j \mathbf{b}_j$, where $c'_j \in \mathbb{Z}$. We abuse the notation that as j goes from κ to 1, we denote by $\mathbf{x}_j^{(i)}$ the value of $\mathbf{x}^{(i)}$ at the *beginning* of each corresponding iteration. Denote by $\mathbf{x}_0^{(i)}$ the value of $\mathbf{x}^{(i)}$ *after* all κ iterations. If we have with overwhelming probability that

$$\mathbf{x}_0^{(i)} = \mathbf{e}^{(i)} \wedge (\forall 1 \leq j \leq \kappa,\ \mathbf{x}_j^{(i)} = \sum_{h=1}^{j} c'_h \mathbf{b}_h + \mathbf{e}^{(i)}),$$

then we can get the correct $\mathbf{v}$ by subtracting $\mathbf{e}^{(1)}$ from $\mathbf{z}^{(1)}$. To show this, we only need to prove $c'_j = c_j$ with overwhelming probability for all $1 \leq j \leq \kappa$.

We prove this by induction on j downward from κ to 1. For every $j = \kappa - 1, \ldots, 1$, assume for all $h = j+1, \ldots, \kappa$, we have $c_h = c'_h$ holds with overwhelming probability. (In the base case where $j = \kappa$, we do not make any assumption.) Then we have for $i = 1, \ldots, \ell$, $\mathbf{x}_j^{(i)} = \sum_{h=1}^{j} c'_h \mathbf{b}_h + \mathbf{e}^{(i)}$. By the property of Gram-Schmidt orthogonalization, it holds that

$$\langle \mathbf{x}_j^{(i)}, \tilde{\mathbf{b}}_j \rangle = \langle \sum_{h=1}^{j} c'_h \mathbf{b}_h + \mathbf{e}^{(i)}, \tilde{\mathbf{b}}_j \rangle = \langle c'_j \tilde{\mathbf{b}}_j + \mathbf{e}^{(i)}, \tilde{\mathbf{b}}_j \rangle.$$

Let $\tilde{\mathbf{e}}_j^{(i)} := \frac{\langle \mathbf{e}^{(i)}, \tilde{\mathbf{b}}_j \rangle}{\langle \tilde{\mathbf{b}}_j, \tilde{\mathbf{b}}_j \rangle} \cdot \tilde{\mathbf{b}}_j$ be the projection of $\mathbf{e}^{(i)}$ to $\tilde{\mathbf{b}}_j$ for each $j = 1, \ldots, \kappa$. It follows that $\langle \mathbf{x}_j^{(i)}, \tilde{\mathbf{b}}_j \rangle = \langle c'_j \tilde{\mathbf{b}}_j + \tilde{\mathbf{e}}_j^{(i)}, \tilde{\mathbf{b}}_j \rangle$, which gives $\lfloor \frac{\langle \mathbf{x}_j^{(i)}, \tilde{\mathbf{b}}_j \rangle}{\langle \tilde{\mathbf{b}}_j, \tilde{\mathbf{b}}_j \rangle} \rceil = c'_j + \lfloor \frac{\|\tilde{\mathbf{e}}_j^{(i)}\|_2}{\|\tilde{\mathbf{b}}_j\|_2} \rceil$. Additionally, we have by our assumption that

$$\Pr[|\langle \tilde{\mathbf{e}}_j^{(i)}, \tilde{\mathbf{b}}_j \rangle| < \frac{\|\tilde{\mathbf{b}}_j\|_2^2}{2}] = \Pr[|\langle \mathbf{e}^{(i)}, \tilde{\mathbf{b}}_j \rangle| < \frac{\|\tilde{\mathbf{b}}_j\|_2^2}{2}] > \frac{2}{3},$$

therefore, $\Pr[\frac{\|\tilde{\mathbf{e}}_j^{(i)}\|_2}{\|\tilde{\mathbf{b}}_j\|_2} < 1/2] > 2/3$. Define $\xi_j^{(i)}$ as the indicator function for the event that $\lfloor \frac{\|\tilde{\mathbf{e}}_j^{(i)}\|_2}{\|\tilde{\mathbf{b}}_j\|_2} \rceil = 0$. Then we have $\Pr[\xi_j^{(i)} = 1] > 2/3$. Let $\xi_j = \sum_{i=1}^{\ell} \xi_j^{(i)}$, we have $\mathbb{E}[\xi_j] > 2\ell/3$. By Chernoff bound, we have

$$\Pr[\xi_j > \ell/2] > 1 - e^{-\frac{1}{2} \cdot \frac{2\ell}{3} \cdot (\frac{1}{4})^2} = 1 - n^{-\omega(1)}.$$

Therefore, with overwhelming probability, for more than a half of $i \in [1, \ell]$, the event $\lfloor \frac{\|\tilde{\mathbf{e}}_j^{(i)}\|_2}{\|\tilde{\mathbf{b}}_j\|_2} \rceil = 0$ happens. And then we can get $c_j = c'_j$ by taking a majority in $\{\lfloor \frac{\langle \mathbf{x}^{(i)}, \tilde{\mathbf{b}}_j \rangle}{\langle \tilde{\mathbf{b}}_j, \tilde{\mathbf{b}}_j \rangle} \rceil\}_{1 \leq i \leq \ell}$. □

5 Injective Trapdoor Functions from Large Noise LWE

This section focuses on proving the following theorem.

Theorem 10 (Theorem 2). *Let n be the security parameter, and $q = q(n) \in \mathsf{poly}(n)$ be a prime such that $q > \omega(n)$. There exists a construction of TDF family assuming one of the following three conditions.*

(i) The $(n^{\omega(1)}, n^{-\omega(1)})$*-hardness of search* $\mathsf{LWE}(n, q(n), O(1/\sqrt{n}))$.

(ii) The $(2^{\omega(n^{\frac{1}{c_1}})}, 2^{-\omega(n^{\frac{1}{c_1}})})$*-hardness of search* $\mathsf{LWE}(n, q(n), O(1/\sqrt{n^{1-\frac{1}{c_1}}\log n}))$*, for some constant* $c_1 > 1$.

(iii) The $(2^{\omega(\frac{n}{\log^{c_2} n})}, 2^{-\omega(\frac{n}{\log^{c_2} n})})$*-hardness of search* $\mathsf{LWE}(n, q(n), O(1/\sqrt{\log^{c_2+1} n}))$*, for some constant* $c_2 > 0$.

Specifically, assuming condition (i) or condition (ii) with $c_1 \geq 2$*, we have the TDF family is injective.*

In order to prove Theorem 10, we generalize the trapdoor in [MP12], and construct a TDF family $\mathcal{T}_\lambda$ from search $\mathsf{LWE}(\lambda, q, \alpha)$, where $\lambda \in (\omega(\log n), O(n^{<1})]$, $q = q(\lambda) \in \mathsf{poly}(\lambda)$ is a prime such that $q > \omega(\lambda)$, $k = \Theta(\lambda \log \lambda / \log n)$, $\alpha \leq \frac{1}{10\sqrt{k}}$. When $\lambda = \Omega(\log^2 n)$, we prove the injectivity of $\mathcal{T}_\lambda$. The result in Theorem 10 then follows straightforwardly by applying Lemma 2.

The organization of this section is as follows. In Subsect. 5.1, we revisit the concepts of primitive lattices from [MP12] and establish several bounds pertinent to our analysis. In Subsect. 5.2, we show how to invert LWE on primitive lattices. In Subsect. 5.3, we show how to generate an LWE instance with auxiliary information (trapdoor) that enables us to recover the secret and the noise. In Subsect. 5.4, we give the formal construction of injective trapdoor function family $\mathcal{T}_\lambda$, as well as the proof of its injectivity and invertibility. We also remark that the conclusions in Subsect. 5.1 and Subsect. 5.2 do not require q to be prime.

5.1 Primitive Lattices

We first recall some notions in [MP12]. Let $\kappa = \lceil \log_2 q \rceil$, and define $\mathbf{g} := (1, 2, \ldots, 2^{\kappa-1})^T$. A short basis for $\Lambda^\perp(\mathbf{g}^T)$ (the q-ary lattices is defined in Eqn. (2)), denoted by $\mathbf{T_g}$, is constructed as follows.

- When $q = 2^\kappa$, let

$$\mathbf{T_g} := (\mathbf{t}_1, \ldots, \mathbf{t}_\kappa) := \begin{bmatrix} 2 & & & & \\ -1 & 2 & & & \\ & -1 & \ddots & & \\ & & & 2 & \\ & & & -1 & 2 \end{bmatrix}.$$

- Alternatively, if q is not a power of 2, let

$$\mathbf{T_g} := (\mathbf{t}_1, \ldots, \mathbf{t}_\kappa) := \begin{bmatrix} 2 & & & & q_0 \\ -1 & 2 & & & q_1 \\ & -1 & \ddots & & q_2 \\ & & & 2 & q_{\kappa-2} \\ & & & -1 & q_{\kappa-1} \end{bmatrix},$$

where $(q_0, \ldots, q_{k-1}) \in \{0,1\}^\kappa$ is the bit decomposition of $q = \sum_{i=0}^{\kappa-1} 2^i \cdot q_i$.

Since $\mathbf{T}_{\mathbf{g}}^* := (\mathbf{t}_1^*, \ldots, \mathbf{t}_\kappa^*)$ is a basis of $\Lambda^\perp(\mathbf{g}^T)^*$, we have $q \cdot \mathbf{T}_{\mathbf{g}}^*$ is a basis for $\Lambda(\mathbf{g}) = q\Lambda^\perp(\mathbf{g}^T)^*$.

Define the gadget matrix as $\mathbf{G}_n := \mathsf{diag}(\mathbf{g}^T, \mathbf{g}^T, \ldots, \mathbf{g}^T) \in \mathbb{Z}_q^{n \times n\kappa}$, and let $\mathbf{T}_{\mathbf{G}_n} := \mathsf{diag}(\mathbf{T}_{\mathbf{g}}, \mathbf{T}_{\mathbf{g}}, \ldots, \mathbf{T}_{\mathbf{g}}) \in \mathbb{Z}_q^{n\kappa \times n\kappa}$, then we have $\mathbf{T}_{\mathbf{G}_n}$ is a basis for $\Lambda^\perp(\mathbf{G}_n)$. When $q = 2^\kappa$, orthogonalize $\mathbf{T}_{\mathbf{g}}$ in the reverse order, and we have $\tilde{\mathbf{T}}_{\mathbf{g}} = 2 \cdot \mathbf{I}_\kappa$. When q is not a power of 2, orthogonalize $\mathbf{T}_{\mathbf{g}}$ in the forward order, and we have $\tilde{\mathbf{T}}_{\mathbf{g}}$ is still a short basis by the following lemma.

Lemma 3. *When q is not a power of 2, let $\tilde{\mathbf{T}}_{\mathbf{g}} := (\tilde{\mathbf{t}}_1, \ldots, \tilde{\mathbf{t}}_\kappa)$ be the orthogonalization of $\mathbf{T}_{\mathbf{g}}$ in the forward order. It holds that*

- $\forall 1 \leq i < \kappa,\ \|\tilde{\mathbf{t}}_i\|_1 = \frac{2^{i+2}+1}{2^i+1} \in [3, 4)$;
- $\|\tilde{\mathbf{t}}_\kappa\|_1 = \frac{3q}{2^\kappa+1} \in (\frac{3}{2}, 3)$;
- $\forall 1 \leq i < \kappa,\ \|\tilde{\mathbf{t}}_i\|_2 = \sqrt{\frac{4^{i+1}-1}{4^i-1}} \in (2, \sqrt{5}]$;
- $\|\tilde{\mathbf{t}}_\kappa\|_2 = \sqrt{\frac{3q^2}{4^\kappa-1}} \in (\frac{\sqrt{3}}{2}, \sqrt{3})$.

In Lemma 3, we extend [MP12, Lemma 4.3] by figuring out more details on the bounds of both ℓ_1-norm and ℓ_2-norm for each $\tilde{\mathbf{t}}_i$. The proof is postponed to Appendix C.

5.2 Inverting Large Noise LWE on Primitive Lattices

For $\mathbf{s} \in \mathbb{Z}_q^n$ and specific errors $\mathbf{e}_1, \mathbf{e}_2, \ldots, \mathbf{e}_\ell \in \mathbb{Z}_q^{n\kappa}$, let $\mathbf{b}_i := \mathbf{G}_n^T\mathbf{s} + \mathbf{e}_i$ for all $1 \leq i \leq \ell$. We then describe an algorithm that, given $(\mathbf{b}_1, \ldots, \mathbf{b}_\ell)$, recovers $\mathbf{s}$ and $\mathbf{e}_1, \mathbf{e}_2, \ldots, \mathbf{e}_\ell$ with overwhelming probability.

For simplicity, we set $n = 1$ without loss of generality. (In cases where $n > 1$, we can decompose each $\mathbf{b}_i$ into n vectors in $\mathbb{Z}_q^\kappa$, apply the inversion algorithm to each of them, and then concatenate the results.) Now our task is to recover $s \in \mathbb{Z}_q$ and $\mathbf{e}_1, \mathbf{e}_2, \ldots, \mathbf{e}_\ell \in \mathbb{Z}_q^\kappa$ from $(\mathbf{b}_1 = s\mathbf{g} + \mathbf{e}_1, \ldots, \mathbf{b}_\ell = s\mathbf{g} + \mathbf{e}_\ell)$.

If we view $s\mathbf{g}$ as a lattice point on $\Lambda(\mathbf{g})$, then we can use the generalized nearest plane algorithm in Sect. 4 to recover it. We further explain this in the following lemma.

Lemma 4. *Adopt the notations of $\mathbf{g}, \mathbf{T}_{\mathbf{g}}, \mathbf{T}_{\mathbf{g}}^*, \tilde{\mathbf{T}}_{\mathbf{g}}$, and $\{\mathbf{t}_j, \mathbf{t}_j^*, \tilde{\mathbf{t}}_j\}_{1 \leq j \leq \kappa}$ in Subsect. 5.1. If $\mathbf{e}_1, \ldots, \mathbf{e}_\ell \in \mathbb{Z}^\kappa$ are independent random vectors and satisfy*

$$\forall 1 \leq i \leq \ell, 1 \leq j \leq \kappa,\ \Pr_{\mathbf{e}_i}[|\langle \mathbf{e}_i, \tilde{\mathbf{t}}_j \rangle| < q/2] > \frac{2}{3},$$

then there is an algorithm that for any $s \in \mathbb{Z}_q$, it takes $(\mathbf{b}_1 = s\mathbf{g} + \mathbf{e}_1, \ldots, \mathbf{b}_\ell = s\mathbf{g} + \mathbf{e}_\ell)$ as input, and recovers $(s, \mathbf{e}_1, \mathbf{e}_2, \ldots, \mathbf{e}_\ell)$ with overwhelming probability.

Particularly, when $q = 2^\kappa$, the condition is simplified as

$$\forall 1 \leq i \leq \ell, 1 \leq j \leq \kappa,\ \Pr_{\mathbf{e}_i}[|e_i(j)| < q/4] > \frac{2}{3}.$$

Proof. Since $s\mathbf{g} \in \Lambda(\mathbf{g})$, we can view it as a "common closest lattice vector" of $\{\mathbf{b}_i\}_{1\le i\le \ell}$. Denote by $\tilde{\mathbf{T}}_{\mathbf{g}}^*$ the orthogonalization of $\mathbf{T}_{\mathbf{g}}^*$. Since $q \cdot \mathbf{T}_{\mathbf{g}}^*$ is a basis for $\Lambda(\mathbf{g})$, we have $q \cdot \tilde{\mathbf{T}}_{\mathbf{g}}^*$ is an orthogonal basis of $\Lambda(\mathbf{g})$. By Theorem 9, we only need to prove

$$\forall 1 \le i \le \ell, 1 \le j \le \kappa, \Pr_{\mathbf{e}_i}[|\langle \mathbf{e}_i, q\tilde{\mathbf{t}}_j^* \rangle| < \|q\tilde{\mathbf{t}}_j^*\|^2/2] > 2/3,$$

which is easy to prove since

$$\Pr_{\mathbf{e}_i}[|\langle \mathbf{e}_i, q\tilde{\mathbf{t}}_j^* \rangle| < \|q\tilde{\mathbf{t}}_j^*\|^2/2] = \Pr_{\mathbf{e}_i}[|\langle \mathbf{e}_i, \tilde{\mathbf{t}}_j \rangle| < q/2] > 2/3,$$

where the equation holds by $\tilde{\mathbf{t}}_j = \frac{\tilde{\mathbf{t}}_j^*}{\|\tilde{\mathbf{t}}_j^*\|^2}$, and the "$>$" holds by assumption.

Particularly, when $q = 2^\kappa$, we do Gram-Schmidt orthogonalization in the reverse order and get $\tilde{\mathbf{T}}_{\mathbf{g}} = 2\mathbf{I}$. Then $\tilde{\mathbf{T}}_{\mathbf{g}}^* = \mathbf{I}/2$, and thus

$$\forall 1 \le i \le \ell, 1 \le j \le \kappa, \Pr_{\mathbf{e}_i}[|\langle \mathbf{e}_i, \tilde{\mathbf{t}}_j \rangle| < q/2] = \Pr_{\mathbf{e}_i}[|e_i(j)| < q/4].$$

Substitute this back into the condition and then we finish the proof. □

For completeness, we present the inversion process for $\mathbf{b} = \mathbf{G}_n^T \mathbf{s} + \mathbf{e}$ in Algorithm 2.

Algorithm 2. Inverting Large Noise LWE on Primitive Lattices

function INVERTPRIMITIVELWE$^{n,\kappa,\ell}(\{\mathbf{b}_i\}_{1\le i\le\ell})$
  if $q = 2^\kappa$ **then**
    Let $\hat{\mathbf{T}}_{\mathbf{g}}^* := (\mathbf{t}_\kappa^*, \mathbf{t}_{\kappa-1}^*, \ldots, \mathbf{t}_1^*)$.
    Let $\hat{\mathbf{T}}_{\mathbf{G}_n}^* := \mathsf{diag}(\hat{\mathbf{T}}_{\mathbf{g}}^*, \hat{\mathbf{T}}_{\mathbf{g}}^*, \ldots, \hat{\mathbf{T}}_{\mathbf{g}}^*) \in \mathbb{Z}_q^{n\kappa\times n\kappa}$
    return FINDCLOSESTVECTOR$(\Lambda(\mathbf{G}_n^T), \hat{\mathbf{T}}_{\mathbf{G}_n}^*, \{\mathbf{b}_i\}_{1\le i\le\ell})$
  else
    return FINDCLOSESTVECTOR$(\Lambda(\mathbf{G}_n^T), \mathbf{T}_{\mathbf{G}_n}^*, \{\mathbf{b}_i\}_{1\le i\le\ell})$
  end if
end function

5.3 Generating Large Noise LWE with Trapdoor

Trapdoor Generation. Let $\lambda \in (\omega(\log n), O(n^{<1})]$, $q = q(\lambda) \in \mathsf{poly}(\lambda)$ be a prime such that $q > \omega(\lambda)$, $k = \Theta(\lambda \log\lambda/\log n)$, $\alpha \le \frac{1}{10\sqrt{k}}$, $\ell = \omega(\log n)$, $\kappa = \lceil \log q \rceil$, $w = \lambda\kappa$, $\bar{n} = n - \ell w$. Let χ_r be some distribution on $\mathbb{Z}_q^{\bar{n}}$ such that $H_\infty(\chi_r) > 2\lambda \log q$. We present the trapdoor generation algorithm in Algorithm 3, which takes as input a matrix $\bar{\mathbf{A}} \in \mathbb{Z}_q^{\lambda\times\bar{n}}$ and an invertible matrix $\mathbf{H} \in \mathbb{Z}_q^{\lambda\times\lambda}$, (If there is no input, it randomly picks $\bar{\mathbf{A}} \leftarrow \mathbb{Z}_q^{\lambda\times\bar{n}}$, and set $\mathbf{H} = \mathbf{I}$.) and outputs a pseudo random matrix $\mathbf{A} \in \mathbb{Z}_q^{\lambda\times n}$ with trapdoor $(\mathbf{R}_1, \ldots, \mathbf{R}_\ell)$.

Algorithm 3. Trapdoor Generation

function $\text{TrapGen}^{n,\lambda,\ell,\chi_r}(\bar{\mathbf{A}}, \mathbf{H})$
  Sample $r_1, \ldots, r_{w\ell} \leftarrow \chi_r$.
  for $i = 1$ **to** ℓ **do**
    Let $\mathbf{R}_i = (r_{(i-1)w+1} \| \cdots \| r_{iw})$.
    Compute $\underline{\mathbf{A}}_i = \mathbf{H}\mathbf{G}_\lambda - \bar{\mathbf{A}}\mathbf{R}_i$
  end for
  Compute $\mathbf{A} := [\bar{\mathbf{A}} \| \underline{\mathbf{A}}_1 \| \underline{\mathbf{A}}_2 \| \cdots \| \underline{\mathbf{A}}_\ell]$
  return $\mathbf{A}, (\mathbf{R}_1, \ldots, \mathbf{R}_\ell)$
end function

Theorem 11. *Let $\lambda \in (\omega(\log n), O(n^{<1})]$, $q = q(\lambda) \in \mathsf{poly}(\lambda)$ be a prime such that $q > \omega(\lambda)$, $k = \Theta(\lambda \log \lambda / \log n)$, $\alpha \leq \frac{1}{10\sqrt{k}}$, $\ell = \omega(\log n)$, $\kappa = \lceil \log q \rceil$, $w = \lambda\kappa$, $\bar{n} = n - \ell w$. Let χ_r be some distribution on $\mathbb{Z}_q^{\bar{n}}$ such that $H_\infty(\chi_r) > 2\lambda \log q$. For a random matrix $\bar{\mathbf{A}} \leftarrow \mathbb{Z}_q^{\lambda \times \bar{n}}$, and an invertible matrix $\mathbf{H} \in \mathbb{Z}_q^{\lambda \times \lambda}$, let $(\mathbf{A}, (\mathbf{R}_1, \ldots, \mathbf{R}_\ell)) \leftarrow \text{TrapGen}^{n,\lambda,\ell,\chi_r}(\bar{\mathbf{A}}, \mathbf{H})$. Then $\mathbf{A}$ is statistically indistinguishable from uniform.*

Proof. By Lemma 7, we have

$$\mathsf{SD}((\bar{\mathbf{A}}, (\bar{\mathbf{A}}\mathbf{R}_1, \bar{\mathbf{A}}\mathbf{R}_2, \ldots, \bar{\mathbf{A}}\mathbf{R}_\ell)), (\bar{\mathbf{A}}, (\mathcal{U}_q^{\lambda \times w})^{\otimes \ell})) \leq 2^{(\lambda w \ell \log q - w\ell H_\infty(\chi_r))/2} = \mathsf{negl}(n).$$

So

$$\mathsf{SD}((\bar{\mathbf{A}}, (\mathbf{H}\mathbf{G}_\lambda - \bar{\mathbf{A}}\mathbf{R}_1, \mathbf{H}\mathbf{G}_\lambda - \bar{\mathbf{A}}\mathbf{R}_2, \ldots, \mathbf{H}\mathbf{G}_\lambda - \bar{\mathbf{A}}\mathbf{R}_\ell)), (\bar{\mathbf{A}}, (\mathcal{U}_q^{\lambda \times w})^{\otimes \ell})) = \mathsf{negl}(n).$$

Then we have $\mathbf{A}$ is statistically indistinguishable from uniform. □

Inversion. Assume $(\mathbf{A}, (\mathbf{R}_1, \ldots, \mathbf{R}_\ell)) \leftarrow \mathsf{TrapGen}(\bar{\mathbf{A}}, \mathbf{H})$ is generated by the algorithm above. Let $\mathbf{s} \leftarrow \mathbb{Z}_q^\lambda, \mathbf{e} \leftarrow \Psi_{\alpha,q}^n$. For LWE instance $\mathbf{b} = \mathbf{A}^T\mathbf{s} + \mathbf{e}$, we show that Algorithm 4 takes as input $\mathbf{A}, (\mathbf{R}_1, \ldots, \mathbf{R}_\ell), \mathbf{H}, \mathbf{b}$, and outputs the correct $\mathbf{s}$ and $\mathbf{e}$ with $1 - \mathsf{negl}(n)$ probability.

Algorithm 4. Inverting LWE with Trapdoor

function $\text{InvertLWE}^{n,\lambda,\ell}(\mathbf{A}, (\mathbf{R}_1, \ldots, \mathbf{R}_\ell), \mathbf{H}, \mathbf{b})$
  Parse $\mathbf{b} = (\bar{\mathbf{b}}^T, \underline{\mathbf{b}}_1^T, \ldots, \underline{\mathbf{b}}_\ell^T)^T \in \mathbb{Z}_q^{\bar{n}} \times (\mathbb{Z}_q^w)^{\otimes \ell}$
  for $i = 1$ **to** ℓ **do**
    Compute $\hat{\mathbf{b}}_i := \mathbf{R}_i^T \bar{\mathbf{b}} + \underline{\mathbf{b}}_i$
  end for
  Let $(\hat{\mathbf{s}}, \{\hat{\mathbf{e}}_i\}_{1 \leq i \leq \ell}) \leftarrow \text{InvertPrimitiveLWE}^{\lambda,\kappa,\ell}(\{\hat{\mathbf{b}}_i\}_{1 \leq i \leq \ell})$
  Compute $\mathbf{s} := \mathbf{H}^{-T}\hat{\mathbf{s}}$.
  Compute $\mathbf{e} := \mathbf{b} - \mathbf{A}^T\mathbf{s}$
  return $\mathbf{s}, \mathbf{e}$
end function

We begin our analysis of Algorithm 4 by parsing $\mathbf{e} = (\bar{\mathbf{e}}^T, \underline{\mathbf{e}}_1^T, \ldots, \underline{\mathbf{e}}_\ell^T)^T \in \mathbb{Z}^{\bar{n}} \times (\mathbb{Z}^w)^{\otimes \ell}$ for clarity. This yields $\bar{\mathbf{b}} = \bar{\mathbf{A}}^T\mathbf{s} + \bar{\mathbf{e}}$ and $\underline{\mathbf{b}}_i = \underline{\mathbf{A}}^T\mathbf{s} + \underline{\mathbf{e}}_i$ for each $1 \leq i \leq \ell$. Then $\hat{\mathbf{b}}_i := \mathbf{R}_i^T\bar{\mathbf{b}} + \underline{\mathbf{b}}_i = \mathbf{R}_i^T\bar{\mathbf{A}}^T\mathbf{s} + \mathbf{R}_i^T\bar{\mathbf{e}} + \underline{\mathbf{A}}^T\mathbf{s} + \underline{\mathbf{e}}_i = \mathbf{G}_\lambda^T\mathbf{H}^T\mathbf{s} + \mathbf{R}_i^T\bar{\mathbf{e}} + \underline{\mathbf{e}}_i$. Let $\hat{\mathbf{s}} = \mathbf{H}^T\mathbf{s}$, $\hat{\mathbf{e}}_i = \mathbf{R}_i^T\bar{\mathbf{e}} + \underline{\mathbf{e}}_i$, the remaining thing to do is giving a bound for every $\hat{\mathbf{e}}_i$. Concretely, parse $\hat{\mathbf{e}}_i = (\hat{\mathbf{e}}_{i,1}^T \| \ldots \| \hat{\mathbf{e}}_{i,\lambda}^T)^T \in (\mathbb{Z}^\kappa)^{\otimes\lambda}$. For every $h = 1, \ldots, \lambda$, we need to prove $\Pr[\langle \hat{\mathbf{e}}_{i,h}, \tilde{\mathbf{t}}_j \rangle < q/2] > 2/3$, which enables us to recover $\hat{s}(h)$ by Lemma 4 (note that $\hat{\mathbf{s}} = (\hat{s}(1), \ldots, \hat{s}(h))$). Then the secret $\mathbf{s}$ can be calculated by $\mathbf{s} = \mathbf{H}^{-T}\hat{\mathbf{s}}$.

We first give a bound for $\mathbf{R}_i\bar{\mathbf{e}}$. Attentive readers may have realized that the distribution of $\mathbf{R}_i$ (or χ_r) has not yet been specified. Here, we need every $\mathbf{R}_i\bar{\mathbf{e}}$ to have an independent bound conditioned on the choice of $\bar{\mathbf{e}}$. Therefore, instead of letting $\chi_r \sim \varXi^{[\bar{n}:k]}$ as in our PKE construction, we let $\chi_r \sim \tilde{\mathcal{B}}_{k/\bar{n}}^{\bar{n}}$, namely the truncated Bernoulli distribution (see Definition 10). This enables us to bound the projection length of $\mathbf{R}_i\bar{\mathbf{e}}$ on $\tilde{\mathbf{t}}_j$, which is presented in the following lemma.

Lemma 5 (Bound for $\mathbf{R}_i\bar{\mathbf{e}}$). *Let $\lambda \in (\omega(\log n), O(n^{<1})]$, $q = q(\lambda) \in \mathsf{poly}(\lambda)$ be a prime such that $q > \omega(\lambda)$, $\ell = \omega(\log n)$, $\kappa = \lceil \log q \rceil$, $w = \lambda\kappa$, $\bar{n} = n - \ell w$, $k = \Theta(\lambda \log \lambda / \log n)$ s.t. $H_\infty(\tilde{\mathcal{B}}_{k/\bar{n}}^{\bar{n}}) > 2\lambda \log q$. Let $\mathbf{r}_1, \ldots, \mathbf{r}_\kappa \leftarrow \tilde{\mathcal{B}}_{k/\bar{n}}^{\bar{n}}$, and $\mathbf{R} := (\mathbf{r}_1 \| \ldots \| \mathbf{r}_\kappa)$. For any fixed $\mathbf{e}' \in \mathbb{R}^{\bar{n}}$ with the following two properties,*

(i) $|\sum_{i=1}^{\bar{n}} e'(i)| < 0.01\sqrt{\frac{\bar{n}\log\bar{n}}{k}}$,
(ii) $\sum_{i=1}^{\bar{n}} e'(i)^2 < \frac{0.16\bar{n}}{100k}$,

let $\bar{\mathbf{e}} = \lfloor q\mathbf{e}' \rceil$, and we have $\forall 1 \leq j \leq \kappa$, $\Pr[\langle \mathbf{R}^T\bar{\mathbf{e}}, \tilde{\mathbf{t}}_j \rangle < q/4] > 0.79$.

We postpone the proof of Lemma 5 to Appendix D.

In the following we show when we generate a matrix $\mathbf{A}$ with trapdoor $\mathbf{R}_1, \ldots, \mathbf{R}_\ell$ using $\chi_r \sim \tilde{\mathcal{B}}_{k/\bar{n}}^{\bar{n}}$ in Algorithm 3, we can invert large noise LWE with overwhelming probability by Algorithm 4.

Theorem 12 (Correctness of inversion). *Let $\lambda \in (\omega(\log n), O(n^{<1})]$, $q = q(\lambda) \in \mathsf{poly}(\lambda)$ be a prime such that $q > \omega(\lambda)$, $\ell = \omega(\log n)$, $\kappa = \lceil \log q \rceil$, $w = \lambda\kappa$, $\bar{n} = n - \ell w$, $k = \Theta(\lambda \log \lambda / \log n)$ s.t. $H_\infty(\tilde{\mathcal{B}}_{k/\bar{n}}^{\bar{n}}) > 2\lambda \log q$, $\alpha \leq 1/(10\sqrt{k})$. Let $\mathbf{s} \in \mathbb{Z}_q^\lambda, \mathbf{e} \sim \Psi_{\alpha,q}^n$. Assume $(\mathbf{A}, (\mathbf{R}_1, \ldots, \mathbf{R}_\ell)) \leftarrow \textsc{TrapGen}^{n,\lambda,\ell,\tilde{\mathcal{B}}_{k/\bar{n}}^{\bar{n}}}(\bar{\mathbf{A}}, \mathbf{H})$, and let $\mathbf{b} = \mathbf{A}^T\mathbf{s} + \mathbf{e}$. Then*

$$\Pr[\textsc{InvertLWE}^{n,\lambda,\ell}(\mathbf{A}, (\mathbf{R}_1, \ldots, \mathbf{R}_\ell), \mathbf{H}, \mathbf{b}) = (\mathbf{s}, \mathbf{e})] = 1 - \mathsf{negl}(n).$$

The proof of this theorem is just a combination of previous lemmas (Lemma 12, Lemma 5, Lemma 13 and Lemma 4), and we postpone its proof to Appendix E.

5.4 Construction of iTDF Family

Now, we are ready to construct iTDF family $\mathcal{T}_\lambda$. Let $\lambda \in [\Omega(\log^2 n), O(n^{<1})]$, $q = q(\lambda) \in \mathsf{poly}(\lambda)$ be a prime such that $q > \omega(\lambda)$, $\ell = \omega(\log n)$, $\kappa = \lceil \log q \rceil$,

$w = \lambda\kappa$, $\bar{n} = n - \ell w$, $k = \Theta(\lambda \log \lambda / \log n)$ such that $H_\infty(\tilde{\mathcal{B}}^{\bar{n}}_{k/\bar{n}}) > 2\lambda \log q$, $\alpha \leq \frac{1}{10\sqrt{k}}$. Let $\mathcal{D} := \mathbb{Z}_q^\lambda \times [-q\alpha\sqrt{\log n}, q\alpha\sqrt{\log n}]^n$, $\mathcal{R} := \mathbb{Z}^n$ be the domain and range of $\mathcal{T}_\lambda$ respectively, and we construct its syntax as follows.

- $\mathsf{Sample}(1^n)$: Randomly sample a matrix $\bar{\mathbf{A}} \leftarrow \mathbb{Z}_q^{\lambda\times\bar{n}}$ and an invertible matrix $\mathbf{H} \in \mathbb{Z}_q^{\lambda\times\lambda}$. Compute $(\mathbf{A}, (\mathbf{R}_1, \ldots, \mathbf{R}_\ell)) \leftarrow \textsc{TrapGen}^{n,\lambda,\ell,\tilde{\mathcal{B}}^{\bar{n}}_{k/\bar{n}}}(\bar{\mathbf{A}}, \mathbf{H})$. Output $(ek, ik) = (\mathbf{A}, (\mathbf{A}, (\mathbf{R}_1, \ldots, \mathbf{R}_\ell), \mathbf{H}))$.
- $\mathsf{Eval}(ek, (\mathbf{s}, \mathbf{e}))$ takes as input the evaluation key $ek = \mathbf{A}$ and $(\mathbf{s}, \mathbf{e}) \in \mathbb{Z}_q^\lambda \times [-q\alpha\sqrt{\log n}, q\alpha\sqrt{\log n}]$, and outputs $\mathbf{y} = \mathbf{A}^T\mathbf{s} + \mathbf{e}$.
- $\mathsf{Invert}(ik, \mathbf{y})$ takes as input an image $\mathbf{y} \in \mathbb{Z}^n$ and the inversion key $ik = (\mathbf{A}, (\mathbf{R}_1, \ldots, \mathbf{R}_\ell), \mathbf{H})$. It computes $(\mathbf{s}, \mathbf{e}) \leftarrow \textsc{InvertLWE}^{n,\lambda,\ell}(\mathbf{A}, (\mathbf{R}_1, \ldots, \mathbf{R}_\ell), \mathbf{H}, \mathbf{A}^T\mathbf{s} + \mathbf{e})$, and outputs $(\mathbf{s}, \mathbf{e})$ (or output $\perp$ if $\textsc{InvertLWE}$ returns $\perp$).

Theorem 13 (Injectivity). *Let $\lambda \in [\Omega(\log^2 n), O(n^{<1})]$, $q = q(\lambda) \in \mathsf{poly}(\lambda)$ be a prime such that $q > \omega(\lambda)$, $\ell = \omega(\log n)$, $\kappa = \lceil \log q \rceil$, $w = \lambda\kappa$, $\bar{n} = n - \ell w$, $k = \Theta(\lambda \log \lambda / \log n)$ such that $H_\infty(\tilde{\mathcal{B}}^{\bar{n}}_{k/\bar{n}}) > 2\lambda \log q$, $\alpha \leq \frac{1}{10\sqrt{k}}$. Then*

$$\Pr_{(ek,ik)\leftarrow\mathsf{Sample}(1^n)}\Big[\exists \mathbf{s}_1, \mathbf{s}_2 \in \mathbb{Z}_q^\lambda, \mathbf{e}_1, \mathbf{e}_2 \in [-q\alpha\sqrt{\log n}, q\alpha\sqrt{\log n}]^n \text{ s.t. } (\mathbf{s}_1, \mathbf{e}_1) \neq (\mathbf{s}_2, \mathbf{e}_2) \wedge \mathsf{Eval}(ek, (\mathbf{s}_1, \mathbf{e}_1)) = \mathsf{Eval}(ek, (\mathbf{s}_2, \mathbf{e}_2))\Big] = \mathsf{negl}(n). \quad (1)$$

Proof. We have

$$\begin{aligned}
&\text{the left hand side of Eqn. (1)}\\
=&\mathsf{negl}(n) + \Pr_{\mathbf{A}\leftarrow\mathbb{Z}_q^{\lambda\times n}}\Big[\exists \mathbf{s}_1, \mathbf{s}_2 \in \mathbb{Z}_q^\lambda, \mathbf{e}_1, \mathbf{e}_2 \in [-q\alpha\sqrt{\log n}, q\alpha\sqrt{\log n}]^n \text{ s.t. }\\
&(\mathbf{s}_1, \mathbf{e}_1) \neq (\mathbf{s}_2, \mathbf{e}_2) \wedge \mathbf{A}^T\mathbf{s}_1 + \mathbf{e}_1 = \mathbf{A}^T\mathbf{s}_2 + \mathbf{e}_2\Big]\\
<&\mathsf{negl}(n) + \Pr_{\mathbf{A}\leftarrow\mathbb{Z}_q^{\lambda\times n}}\Big[\exists \mathbf{s}_1, \mathbf{s}_2 \in \mathbb{Z}_q^\lambda, \mathbf{e}_1, \mathbf{e}_2 \in [-q/8, q/8]^n \text{ s.t. } (\mathbf{s}_1, \mathbf{e}_1) \neq (\mathbf{s}_2, \mathbf{e}_2) \wedge \mathbf{A}^T\mathbf{s}_1 + \mathbf{e}_1 = \mathbf{A}^T\mathbf{s}_2 + \mathbf{e}_2\Big]\\
=&\mathsf{negl}(n) + \Pr_{\mathbf{A}\leftarrow\mathbb{Z}_q^{\lambda\times n}}\Big[\exists \mathbf{s}_1, \mathbf{s}_2 \in \mathbb{Z}_q^\lambda, \mathbf{e}_1, \mathbf{e}_2 \in [-q/8, q/8]^n \text{ s.t. } \mathbf{s}_1 \neq \mathbf{s}_2 \wedge \mathbf{A}^T\mathbf{s}_1 + \mathbf{e}_1 = \mathbf{A}^T\mathbf{s}_2 + \mathbf{e}_2\Big]\\
=&\mathsf{negl}(n) + \Pr_{\mathbf{A}\leftarrow\mathbb{Z}_q^{\lambda\times n}}\Big[\exists \mathbf{s} \in \mathbb{Z}_q^\lambda, \mathbf{e} \in [-q/4, q/4]^n \text{ s.t. } \mathbf{s} \neq \mathbf{0} \wedge \mathbf{A}^T\mathbf{s} = \mathbf{e}\Big]\\
<&\mathsf{negl}(n) + q^{-0.16\lambda} = \mathsf{negl}(n).
\end{aligned}$$

Here, the first "=" uses Theorem 11 ($ek = \mathbf{A}$ is statistically indistinguishable from uniform); the "<" follows from $\alpha q\sqrt{\log n} \leq q\sqrt{\log n}/(10\sqrt{k}) = \Theta(q \log n / \sqrt{\lambda \log \lambda}) = O(q/\sqrt{\log\log n}) < q/8$; the second "=" is because when $\mathbf{s}_1 = \mathbf{s}_2$ and $\mathbf{e}_1 \neq \mathbf{e}_2$, the equation $A^T\mathbf{s}_1 + \mathbf{e}_1 = \mathbf{A}^T\mathbf{s}_2 + \mathbf{e}_2$ does not hold; the third "=" results from replacing $\mathbf{s}_1 - \mathbf{s}_2$ by $\mathbf{s}$ and $\mathbf{e}_1 - \mathbf{e}_2$ by $\mathbf{e}$; and the "$\leq$" uses Lemma 6. □

Theorem 14 ($(\mathcal{U}_q^\lambda \times \tilde{\Psi}^n_{\alpha,q})$-invertibility). *Let $\lambda \in (\omega(\log n), O(n^{<1})]$, $q = q(\lambda) \in \mathsf{poly}(\lambda)$ such that $q > \omega(\lambda)$, $\ell = \omega(\log n)$, $\kappa = \lceil \log q \rceil$, $w = \lambda\kappa$, $\bar{n} = n - \ell w$, $k = \Theta(\lambda \log \lambda / \log n)$ such that $H_\infty(\tilde{\mathcal{B}}^{\bar{n}}_{k/\bar{n}}) > 2\lambda \log q$, $\alpha \leq \frac{1}{10\sqrt{k}}$. Let $(ek, ik) \leftarrow \mathsf{Sample}(1^n), \mathbf{s} \leftarrow \mathcal{U}_q^\lambda, \mathbf{e} \leftarrow \tilde{\Psi}^n_{\alpha,q}$. It holds that*

(i)

$$\Pr_{\substack{(ek,ik)\leftarrow \mathsf{Sample}(1^n) \\ \mathbf{s}\leftarrow \mathcal{U}_q^\lambda, \mathbf{e}\leftarrow \tilde{\Psi}_{\alpha,q}^n}}[\mathsf{Invert}(ik, \mathsf{Eval}(ek, (\mathbf{s}, \mathbf{e}))) = (\mathbf{s}, \mathbf{e})] = 1 - \mathsf{negl}(n).$$

(ii) if search $\mathsf{LWE}(\lambda, q, \alpha)$ *is hard, then for any PPT adversary* $\mathcal{A}$

$$\Pr_{\substack{(ek,ik)\leftarrow \mathsf{Sample}(1^n) \\ \mathbf{s}\leftarrow \mathcal{U}_q^\lambda, \mathbf{e}\leftarrow \tilde{\Psi}_{\alpha,q}^n}}[\mathcal{A}(ek, \mathsf{Eval}(ek, (\mathbf{s}, \mathbf{e}))) = (\mathbf{s}, \mathbf{e})] = \mathsf{negl}(n).$$

Proof. (i) Let $(\mathbf{A}, (\mathbf{A}, (\mathbf{R}_1, \ldots, \mathbf{R}_\ell), \mathbf{H})) = (ek, ik) \leftarrow \mathsf{Sample}(1^n)$. We have

$$\begin{aligned}
&\Pr_{\mathbf{s}\leftarrow \mathcal{U}_q^\lambda, \mathbf{e}\leftarrow \tilde{\Psi}_{\alpha,q}^n}[\mathsf{Invert}(ik, \mathsf{Eval}(ek, (\mathbf{s}, \mathbf{e}))) = (\mathbf{s}, \mathbf{e})] \\
\geq &\Pr_{\mathbf{s}\leftarrow \mathcal{U}_q^\lambda, \mathbf{e}\leftarrow \Psi_{\alpha,q}^n}[\mathsf{Invert}(ik, \mathsf{Eval}(ek, (\mathbf{s}, \mathbf{e}))) = (\mathbf{s}, \mathbf{e})] - \mathsf{negl}(n) \\
= &\Pr_{\mathbf{s}\leftarrow \mathcal{U}_q^\lambda, \mathbf{e}\leftarrow \Psi_{\alpha,q}^n}[\text{INVERTLWE}^{n,\lambda,\ell}(\mathbf{A}, (\mathbf{R}_1, \ldots, \mathbf{R}_\ell), \mathbf{H}, \mathbf{b}) = (\mathbf{s}, \mathbf{e})] - \mathsf{negl}(n) \\
= &1 - \mathsf{negl}(n),
\end{aligned}$$

where the first inequality is by definition of $\tilde{\Psi}_{\alpha,q}^n$, and the last equality is by Theorem 12.

(ii)

$$\begin{aligned}
&\Pr_{\substack{(ek,ik)\leftarrow \mathsf{Sample}(1^n) \\ \mathbf{s}\leftarrow \mathcal{U}_q^\lambda, \mathbf{e}\leftarrow \tilde{\Psi}_{\alpha,q}^n}}[\mathcal{A}(ek, \mathsf{Eval}(ek, (\mathbf{s}, \mathbf{e}))) = (\mathbf{s}, \mathbf{e})] \\
\leq &\Pr_{\substack{(ek,ik)\leftarrow \mathsf{Sample}(1^n) \\ \mathbf{s}\leftarrow \mathcal{U}_q^\lambda, \mathbf{e}\leftarrow \Psi_{\alpha,q}^n}}[\mathcal{A}(ek, \mathsf{Eval}(ek, (\mathbf{s}, \mathbf{e}))) = (\mathbf{s}, \mathbf{e})] + \mathsf{negl}(n) \\
\leq &\Pr_{\substack{\mathbf{A}\leftarrow \mathbb{Z}_q^{\lambda\times n} \\ \mathbf{s}\leftarrow \mathcal{U}_q^\lambda, \mathbf{e}\leftarrow \Psi_{\alpha,q}^n}}[\mathcal{A}(\mathbf{A}, \mathbf{A}^T\mathbf{s} + \mathbf{e}) = (\mathbf{s}, \mathbf{e})] + \mathsf{negl}(n) \leq \mathsf{negl}(n),
\end{aligned}$$

where the first inequality is by definition of $\tilde{\Psi}_{\alpha,q}^n$, the second inequality is by Theorem 11 ($\mathbf{A}$ is statistically close to random), and the last inequality is by hardness of search $\mathsf{LWE}(\lambda, q, \alpha)$.

□

6 Public-Key Encryption from LPN with Constant Noise

Yu, Zhang [YZ16] proposed a PKE scheme based on $(2^{\omega(n^{1/2})}, 2^{-\omega(n^{1/2})})$-hardness of $\mathsf{LPN}(n, \mu)$, where μ is a constant. In this section, we propose a simpler PKE scheme with equivalent security. This construction is very similar to that in Subsect. 3.1.

6.1 Single-Bit LPN-PKE Scheme with Weak Correctness

Construction. Let $\lambda = H_\infty(\Xi^{[n;k]})/2 = \Theta(\log^2 n)$, where $k = \log n$. Let $\mu \in (0, \frac{1}{2})$ be a constant.

- The message space is $\mathcal{M} = \{0, 1\}$.
- $\mathsf{KeyGen}(1^n)$: Given security parameter 1^n, it samples $\mathbf{A} \leftarrow \{0,1\}^{\lambda \times n}$, as well as $\mathbf{s} \leftarrow \{0,1\}^\lambda$, $\mathbf{e} \leftarrow \mathcal{B}_\mu^n$. Then it computes $\mathbf{b} := \mathbf{A}^T\mathbf{s} + \mathbf{e}$, and sets $(pk, sk) := ((\mathbf{A}, \mathbf{b}), \mathbf{s})$.
- $\mathsf{Enc}(pk, \mathfrak{m})$: Given the public key $pk = (\mathbf{A}, \mathbf{b})$ and the message $\mathfrak{m} \in \mathcal{M}$, it samples $\mathbf{r} \leftarrow \Xi^{[n;k]}$, and outputs $\mathfrak{c} := (\mathbf{c}_1, c_2)$ as ciphertext, where $\mathbf{c}_1 = \mathbf{Ar}$ and $c_2 = \mathbf{r}^T\mathbf{b} + \mathfrak{m}$.
- $\mathsf{Dec}(sk, \mathfrak{c})$: Given the secret key $sk = \mathbf{s}$ and the ciphertext $\mathfrak{c}$, parse $\mathfrak{c}$ into $(\mathbf{c}_1, c_2)$, output $d = c_2 - \mathbf{c}_1^T\mathbf{s}$.

Theorem 15 (Weak correctness). *Let $\lambda = \Theta(\log^2 n) = H_\infty(\Xi^{[n;k]})/2$, $\mu \in (0, 1/2)$ be a constant. Π^{LPN} has $(\frac{1}{2} + \frac{1}{\mathsf{poly}(n)})$-correctness.*

Remark 2. To make the scheme strongly correct, we cannot apply the method in Subsect. 3.2, i.e., generating a public key with ℓ secret keys, and encrypting the message for ℓ times. This is because the correctness of Π^{LPN} is only $\frac{1}{2} + \frac{1}{\mathsf{poly}(n)}$, which needs $\mathsf{poly}(n)$ times of repetition to reach $1 - \mathsf{negl}(n)$. However, we need $\ell \leq O(\lambda) = O(\log^2 n)$ to bound the min-entropy of $\Xi^{[n:k]}$. Therefore, to achieve strong correctness, we should apply a parallel repetition to not only the secret key but also the public key.

Proof. $d = c_2 - \mathbf{c}_1^T\mathbf{s} = \mathbf{r}^T\mathbf{e} + \mathfrak{m}$. Let $e' := \mathbf{r}^T\mathbf{e}$, then $e \sim (\mathcal{B}_\mu)^{\star k}$. By Lemma 8, $\Pr[e' = 1] = \frac{1}{2}(1 - (1 - 2\mu)^k) = \frac{1}{2} - \frac{1}{\mathsf{poly}(n)}$. So $\Pr[d = \mathfrak{m}] = \frac{1}{2} + \frac{1}{\mathsf{poly}(n)}$. □

Theorem 16 (CPA security). *Let $\lambda = \Theta(\log^2 n) = H_\infty(\Xi^{[n;k]})/2$, $\mu \in (0, 1/2)$ be a constant. Assume $\mathsf{LPN}(\lambda, \mu)$ is hard, then Π^{LPN} is IND-CPA secure.*

Remark 3. Similar to Lemma 2, we have the hardness of $\mathsf{LPN}(\lambda, \mu)$ can be implied by $(2^{\omega(n^{1/2})}, 2^{-\omega(n^{1/2})})$-hardness of $\mathsf{LPN}(n, \mu)$.

The proof of this theorem is almost the same as that of Theorem 6, and we postpone it to the full version.

Acknowledgments. We thank Yu Yu for discussions and anonymous reviewers for their valuable comments. L.J. and Y.C. are supported by Shanghai Qi Zhi Institute Innovation Program SQZ202405 and Tsinghua University start-up funding.

A Preliminary (Extended)

A.1 Linear Algebra and Lattices

For any ordered set $\mathbf{V} = \{\mathbf{v}_1, \ldots, \mathbf{v}_k\} \in \mathbb{R}^n$, denote its Gram-Schmidt orthogonalization as $\tilde{\mathbf{V}} = \{\tilde{\mathbf{v}}_1, \ldots, \tilde{\mathbf{v}}_k\}$, where $\tilde{\mathbf{v}}_i$ is the component of $\mathbf{v}_i$ orthogonal to $\mathsf{span}(\mathbf{v}_1, \ldots, \mathbf{v}_{i-1})$ for all $i = 1, \ldots, k$. For any basis $\mathbf{V} = \{\mathbf{v}_1, \ldots, \mathbf{v}_n\}$ of $\mathbb{R}^n$, its dual basis is defined as $\mathbf{V}^* = \mathbf{V}^{-T}$. If we orthogonalize $\mathbf{V}$ and $\mathbf{V}^*$ in forward and reverse order respectively, then we have $\tilde{\mathbf{v}}_i^* = \tilde{\mathbf{v}}_i / \|\tilde{\mathbf{v}}_i\|^2$. Particularly, $\|\tilde{\mathbf{v}}_i^*\| = 1/\|\tilde{\mathbf{v}}_i\|$.

An n-dimensional lattice L of rank $k \leq n$ is a discrete additive subgroup of $\mathbb{R}^n$. Given k linearly independent basis vectors $\mathbf{B} = \{\mathbf{b}_1, \ldots, \mathbf{b}_k \in \mathbb{R}^n\}$, the lattice generated by $\mathbf{B}$ is $L(\mathbf{B}) = L(\mathbf{b}_1, \ldots, \mathbf{b}_k) = \{\sum_{i=1}^k x_i \cdot \mathbf{b}_i : x_i \in \mathbb{Z}\}$. By default, we work with full-rank lattices unless explicitly mentioned. The dual of lattice $L \subseteq \mathbb{R}^n$ is defined as $L^* := \{\mathbf{y} \in \mathbb{R}^n : \langle \mathbf{y}, \mathbf{x} \rangle \in \mathbb{Z} \text{ for all } \mathbf{x} \in L\}$.

If $\mathbf{B}$ is a basis of a full-rank lattice L, then $\mathbf{B}^* = \mathbf{B}^{-T}$ is a basis of L^*. For an arbitrary matrix $\mathbf{A} \in \mathbb{Z}_q^{n \times m}$, define the following q-ary lattices

$$\begin{aligned} \Lambda^{\perp}(\mathbf{A}) &:= \{\mathbf{z} \in \mathbb{Z}^m : \mathbf{A}\mathbf{z} = 0 \bmod q\} \\ \Lambda(\mathbf{A}^T) &:= \{\mathbf{z} \in \mathbb{Z}^m : \exists \mathbf{s} \in \mathbb{Z}_q^n \text{ s.t. } \mathbf{z} = \mathbf{A}^T\mathbf{s} \bmod q\}. \end{aligned} \tag{2}$$

It is easy to check that $q \cdot \Lambda^{\perp}(\mathbf{A})^* = \Lambda(\mathbf{A}^T)$, that is, $\Lambda^{\perp}(\mathbf{A})^*$ and $\Lambda(\mathbf{A}^T)$ are dual lattices up to a scaling factor of q.

Lemma 6 ([CHL+25, Lemma 16]). *Let $q \geq 2, m \geq 2n \log q$, then for all but at most $q^{-0.16n}$ fraction of $\mathbf{A} \in \mathbb{Z}_q^{n \times m}$, we have $\lambda_1^{\infty}(\Lambda(\mathbf{A}^T)) \geq q/4$, where λ_1^{∞} is the first successive minimum in distance measured in the ℓ_∞-norm.*

A.2 Gaussians

In this paper, we focus on 1-dimensional Gaussians. For any real $r > 0$, define the Gaussian function on $\mathbb{R}$ with width parameter r as: $\forall x \in \mathbb{R},\ \rho_r(x) := e^{-\pi x^2/r^2}$. And we define the continuous Gaussian distribution D_r as: $\forall x \in \mathbb{R},\ D_r(x) := \rho_r(x)/r$. For any real $\alpha > 0$ and integer $q > 0$, we use the following version of discrete Gaussian distribution: $\forall i \in \mathbb{Z},\ \Psi_{\alpha,q}(i) := \int_{x=i-\frac{1}{2}}^{i+\frac{1}{2}} D_{\alpha q}(x) dx$. That is, $\Psi_{\alpha,q} \sim \lfloor D_{\alpha q} \rceil$.

A.3 Learning with Errors

In this paper, we focus on the following variant of LWE, which is put forward in [Reg05].

Definition 1 (Learning with errors). *Let $q = q(n)$ be a prime modulus. $m = m(n), \alpha = \alpha(n), t = t(n), \epsilon = \epsilon(n)$. We say the search $\mathsf{LWE}(n, q, \alpha)$ is (t, ϵ)-hard if for every inverter $\mathcal{A}$ of running time t,*

$$\Pr_{\mathbf{A} \leftarrow \mathbb{Z}_q^{n \times m}, \mathbf{s} \leftarrow \mathbb{Z}_q^n, \mathbf{e} \leftarrow \Psi_{\alpha,q}^m} [\mathcal{A}(\mathbf{A}, \mathbf{A}^T\mathbf{s} + \mathbf{e}) = \mathbf{s}] < \epsilon.$$

We say the decision $\mathsf{LWE}(n, q, \alpha)$ *is* (t, ϵ)*-hard if for every distinguisher* $\mathcal{D}$ *of running time* t,

$$\left| \Pr_{\mathbf{A} \leftarrow \mathbb{Z}_q^{n \times m}, \mathbf{s} \leftarrow \mathbb{Z}_q^n, \mathbf{e} \leftarrow \Psi_{\alpha,q}^m} [\mathcal{D}(\mathbf{A}, \mathbf{A}^T\mathbf{s} + \mathbf{e}) = 1] - \Pr_{\mathbf{A} \leftarrow \mathbb{Z}_q^{n \times m}} [\mathcal{D}(\mathbf{A}, \mathcal{U}_q^m) = 1] \right| < \epsilon.$$

When $t = n^{\omega(1)}$ *and* $\epsilon = n^{-\omega(1)}$, *we simply say the search (decision) LWE problem is hard.*

A.4 Learning Parity with Noise

The learning parity with noise (LPN) problem, which can be seen as an analog of LWE, is defined as follows.

Definition 2 (Learning parity with noise). *Let* $m = m(n), 0 < \mu < 1/2, t = t(n), \epsilon = \epsilon(n)$. *We say the search* $\mathsf{LPN}(n, \mu)$ *is* (t, ϵ)*-hard if for every inverter* $\mathcal{A}$ *of running time* t,

$$\Pr_{\mathbf{A} \leftarrow \{0,1\}^{n \times m}, \mathbf{s} \leftarrow \{0,1\}^n, \mathbf{e} \leftarrow \mathcal{B}_\mu^m} [\mathcal{A}(\mathbf{A}, \mathbf{A}^T\mathbf{s} + \mathbf{e}) = \mathbf{s}] < \epsilon.$$

We say the decision $\mathsf{LPN}(n, \mu)$ *is* (t, ϵ)*-hard if for every distinguisher* $\mathcal{D}$ *of running time* t,

$$\left| \Pr_{\mathbf{A} \leftarrow \{0,1\}^{n \times m}, \mathbf{s} \leftarrow \{0,1\}^n, \mathbf{e} \leftarrow \mathcal{B}_\mu^m} [\mathcal{D}(\mathbf{A}, \mathbf{A}^T\mathbf{s} + \mathbf{e}) = 1] - \Pr_{\mathbf{A} \leftarrow \{0,1\}^{n \times m}} [\mathcal{D}(\mathbf{A}, \mathcal{U}^m) = 1] \right| < \epsilon.$$

When $t = n^{\omega(1)}$ *and* $\epsilon = n^{-\omega(1)}$, *we simply say the search (decision) LPN problem is hard.*

A.5 Public-Key Encryption Schemes

Definition 3 (Public-key encryption schemes). *A public-key encryption scheme is a tuple of PPT algorithms* $(\mathsf{KeyGen}, \mathsf{Enc}, \mathsf{Dec})$ *with message space* $\mathcal{M}$ *such that*

- ***Key generation:*** $\mathsf{KeyGen}(1^n)$ *takes as input a security parameter* 1^n, *and outputs a pair of public and private keys* (pk, sk).
- ***Encryption:*** $\mathsf{Enc}(pk, \mathfrak{m})$ *takes a public key* pk *and a message* $\mathfrak{m} \in \mathcal{M}$ *as input, and outputs a ciphertext* $\mathfrak{c}$.
- ***Decryption:*** $\mathsf{Dec}(sk, \mathfrak{c})$ *takes as input a secret key* sk *and ciphertext* $\mathfrak{c}$, *and deterministically outputs a message* $\mathfrak{m}$.

Definition 4 (δ-correctness). *For* $0 < \delta \leq 1$, *we say that a public-key encryption scheme is* δ*-correct if for every* $\mathfrak{m} \in \mathcal{M}$, *it holds that*

$$\Pr_{(pk,sk) \leftarrow \mathsf{KeyGen}(1^n)} [\mathsf{Dec}(sk, \mathsf{Enc}(pk, \mathfrak{m})) = \mathfrak{m}] \geq \delta.$$

When $\delta > 1 - \mathsf{neg}(n)$, *we say the scheme is (strongly) correct. Otherwise, we say it is weakly correct if for any* $\mathfrak{m}' \in \mathcal{M}$ *such that* $\mathfrak{m}' \neq \mathfrak{m}$, *it holds that*

$$\Pr_{(pk,sk) \leftarrow \mathsf{KeyGen}(1^n)} [\mathsf{Dec}(sk, \mathsf{Enc}(pk, \mathfrak{m})) = \mathfrak{m}] - \Pr_{(pk,sk) \leftarrow \mathsf{KeyGen}(1^n)} [\mathsf{Dec}(sk, \mathsf{Enc}(pk, \mathfrak{m})) = \mathfrak{m}'] \geq \frac{1}{\mathsf{poly}(n)}.$$

Definition 5 (IND-CPA security). *A public-key encryption scheme Π is IND-CPA secure if for any PPT adversaries $\mathcal{A}$,*

$$\Pr[\mathsf{Exp}^{\mathsf{CPA}}_{\mathcal{A},\Pi}(1^n) = 1] = \frac{1}{2} + \mathsf{negl}(n),$$

where $\mathsf{Exp}^{\mathsf{CPA}}_{\mathcal{A},\Pi}(1^n)$ is the IND-CPA indistinguishability experiment defined as below:

- $\mathsf{KeyGen}(1^n)$ *is run to obtain* (pk, sk).
- *The adversary $\mathcal{A}$ takes 1^n and pk as input, and then outputs a pair of messages $\mathfrak{m}_0, \mathfrak{m}_1$ with the same length.*
- *A random bit $\beta \leftarrow \{0,1\}$ is chosen, and then a challenge ciphertext $\mathfrak{c} \leftarrow \mathsf{Enc}_{pk}(\mathfrak{m}_\beta)$ is computed and given to $\mathcal{A}$.*
- *$\mathcal{A}$ guesses a bit β'.*
- *The output of the experiment is defined to be 1 if $\beta' = \beta$ (indicating $\mathcal{A}$ succeeds), and 0 otherwise (indicating $\mathcal{A}$ fails).*

A.6 Injective Trapdoor Functions

Definition 6 (Trapdoor functions). *An (injective) trapdoor function family is a tuple of PPT algorithms* $(\mathsf{Sample}, \mathsf{Eval}, \mathsf{Invert})$ *with domain $\mathcal{D}$ and range $\mathcal{R}$ such that*

- $\mathsf{Sample}(1^n)$ *outputs (ek, ik), where ek is an evaluation key and ik is an inversion key (trapdoor).*
- $\mathsf{Eval}(ek, x)$ *takes as input a string $x \in \mathcal{D}$ and an evaluation key ek, and outputs a string $y \in \mathcal{R}$.*
- $\mathsf{Invert}(ik, y)$ *takes a string $y \in \mathcal{R}$ and an inversion key ik as inputs, outputting either a string $x \in \mathcal{D}$ or a special symbol $\perp$ to denote failure.*

Definition 7 (Injectivity). *For any injective trapdoor function (iTDF) family $\mathcal{T} : \mathcal{D} \to \mathcal{R}$ consisting of* $(\mathsf{Sample}, \mathsf{Eval}, \mathsf{Invert})$, *it holds that*

$$\Pr_{(ek,ik)\leftarrow\mathsf{Sample}(1^n)}[\exists x_1, x_2 \in \mathcal{D} \ s.t. \ (x_1 \neq x_2 \wedge \mathsf{Eval}(ek, x_1) = \mathsf{Eval}(ek, x_2))] = \mathsf{negl}(n).$$

Definition 8 (Φ-invertibility]). *For some distribution Φ on $\mathcal{D}$, an (injective) trapdoor function is easy to invert only with the trapdoor. More concretely, an iTDF family $\mathcal{T} : \mathcal{D} \to \mathcal{R}$ consisting of* $(\mathsf{Sample}, \mathsf{Eval}, \mathsf{Invert})$ *should be*

- *easy to invert with a trapdoor, i.e.,*

$$\Pr_{(ek,ik)\leftarrow\mathsf{Sample}(1^n), x\leftarrow\Phi}[\mathsf{Invert}(ik, \mathsf{Eval}(ek, x)) = x] = 1 - \mathsf{negl}(n).$$

- *hard to invert without a trapdoor, i.e., for any PPT adversary $\mathcal{A}$*

$$\Pr_{(ek,ik)\leftarrow\mathsf{Sample}(1^n), x\leftarrow\Phi}[\mathcal{A}(ek, \mathsf{Eval}(ek, x)) = x] = \mathsf{negl}(n).$$

A.7 Leftover Hash Lemma

We first present the definition of 2-universal hash function family as follows.

Definition 9. *A family of hash functions* $\mathcal{H} := \{h_k : \mathcal{X} \to \{0,1\}^l, k \in \mathcal{S}\}$ *is 2-universal if for any* $x_1, x_2 \in \mathcal{X}$ *such that* $x_1 \neq x_2$*, it holds that* $\Pr_{k \leftarrow \mathcal{S}}[h_k(x_1) = h_k(x_2)] \leq 2^{-l}$.

We present the leftover hash lemma [ILL89] as follows.

Lemma 7 (Leftover hash lemma). *Let* $X \in \mathcal{X}$ *be a random variable such that* $H_\infty(X) \geq k$*. Let* $h : \{0,1\}^s \times \mathcal{X} \to \{0,1\}^l$ *be any 2-universal hash function. If* $V \leftarrow \{0,1\}^s$*, then it holds that* $\mathsf{SD}((V, h(V,X)), (V, \mathcal{U}^l)) \leq 2^{\frac{l-k}{2}}$.

A.8 Probabilistic Bounds

In this subsection, we present some mathematical bounds.

Lemma 8 (Piling-up lemma). *For* $0 < \mu < 1/2$*, let* $X_1, \ldots, X_\ell$ *be independent random variables sampled from* $\mathcal{B}_\mu$*. Then,* $\bigoplus_{i=1}^{\ell} X_i \sim \mathcal{B}_\sigma$*, where* $\sigma = \frac{1}{2}(1-(1-2\mu)^\ell)$.

Lemma 9 (Laurent-Massart bounds [LM00, **Lemma 1]).** *The chi-squared distribution with k degrees of freedom, denoted as* $\chi^2(k)$*, is the distribution of a sum of k independent standard normal variables. Let* $X \sim \chi^2(k)$*. Then, for any* $x > 0$, $\Pr[X - k > 2\sqrt{kx} + 2x] \leq e^{-x}$.

Lemma 10. *When* $k = O(m^{<1})$, $H_\infty(\Xi^{[m;k]}) = \Theta(k \log m)$.

Proof. By the definition of min-entropy, we get

$$H_\infty(\Xi^{[m;k]}) = \log \binom{m}{k} = \sum_{i=1}^{k} \log \frac{i+m-k}{i} \in (k \log(m/k), k \log(m-k+1)).$$

Therefore, $H_\infty(\Xi^{[m;k]}) = \Theta(k \log m)$. □

Lemma 11. *For any* $a > 0$, $\Pr_{x \sim D_\alpha}[|x| \geq a] < \exp\left(-\frac{a^2\pi}{2\alpha^2}\right)$.

Proof. Consider

$$\Pr[x \geq a] = \int_{u=a}^{\infty} \frac{1}{\alpha} \exp\left(-\pi\left(\frac{u}{\alpha}\right)^2\right) \mathrm{d}u = \frac{1}{\alpha}\sqrt{\int_{u=a}^{\infty}\int_{v=a}^{\infty} \exp\left(-\pi\frac{u^2+v^2}{\alpha^2}\right) \mathrm{d}u\mathrm{d}v}.$$

Make a polar coordinate substitution, that is, let $u := \alpha\rho\cos\theta, v := \alpha\rho\sin\theta$, and we obtain

$$\Pr[x \geq a] < \frac{1}{\alpha}\sqrt{\int_{\rho=a/\alpha}^{\infty}\int_{\theta=0}^{\pi/2} \exp\left(-\pi\rho^2\right)\alpha^2\rho \mathrm{d}\rho\mathrm{d}\theta} = \sqrt{\frac{\pi}{2}\int_{\rho=a/\alpha}^{\infty} \exp\left(-\pi\rho^2\right)\rho \mathrm{d}\rho}.$$

Further let $t := \pi\rho^2$, and we get

$$\Pr[x \geq a] < \sqrt{\frac{\pi}{2}\int_{t=\pi a^2/\alpha^2}^{\infty} \frac{1}{2\pi}\exp(-t)\mathrm{d}t} = \sqrt{\frac{1}{4}\exp\left(-\frac{\pi a^2}{\alpha^2}\right)} = \frac{1}{2}\exp\left(-\frac{\pi a^2}{2\alpha^2}\right).$$

which implies $\Pr[|x| \geq a] < \exp\left(-\frac{\pi a^2}{2\alpha^2}\right)$. □

Lemma 12. *For $\alpha > 0$, let $e_1, e_2, \ldots, e_n \sim D_\alpha$, the following two inequalities hold with overwhelming probability.*

(i) $|\sum_{i=1}^n e_i| < 0.1\alpha\sqrt{n \log n}$.
(ii) $\sum_{i=1}^n e_i^2 < 0.16\alpha^2 n$.

Proof. (i) Since $\sum_{i=1}^n e_i \sim D_{\sqrt{n}\alpha}$, the conclusion can be directly deduced by applying Lemma 11.
(ii) By Lemma 9, we have $\Pr[\sum_{i=1}^n (\frac{\sqrt{2\pi}}{\alpha} e_i)^2 < 1.001n] = \mathsf{negl}(n)$, which implies $\sum_{i=1}^n e_i^2 < 0.16\alpha^2 n$ with overwhelming probability.

□

Lemma 13. *For any positive integers k, q, real constants α, let $\mathbf{e} \leftarrow \Psi_{\alpha,q}^k$, $\mathbf{t} \in \mathbb{R}^k$. If $\|\mathbf{t}\|_1 = o(q)$, then for any two constants γ, γ' such that $0 < \gamma < \gamma' < 1$, it holds that*

$$\Pr\left[|\langle \mathbf{e}, \mathbf{t}\rangle| < \gamma' q\right] > 1 - \exp\left(-\frac{\pi\gamma^2}{2\|\mathbf{t}\|_2^2\alpha^2}\right).$$

Proof. By definition, for every $1 \le i \le k$, $e(i)$ is obtained by sampling some $e_i' \sim D_\alpha$, and calculate $e(i) = \lfloor q e_i' \rceil$. Therefore, we may write $\langle \mathbf{e}, \mathbf{t}\rangle = \sum_{i=1}^k t(i) \lfloor q e_i' \rceil$. Since the bias introduced by the $\lfloor\cdot\rceil$ function does not exceed $1/2$, we have $|\langle \mathbf{e}, \mathbf{t}\rangle - \sum_{i=1}^k t(i) q e_i'| < \frac{\|\mathbf{t}\|_1}{2}$. Thus, it suffices to prove:

$$\Pr\left[\left|\sum_{i=1}^k t(i) q e_i'\right| < \gamma' q - \frac{\|\mathbf{t}\|_1}{2}\right] > 1 - \exp\left(-\frac{\pi\gamma^2}{2\|\mathbf{t}\|_2^2\alpha^2}\right).$$

Since $\|\mathbf{t}\|_1 = o(q)$, and γ, γ' are two constants such that $0 < \gamma < \gamma' < 1$, we have $\gamma' q - \frac{\|\mathbf{t}\|_1}{2} > \gamma q$. Therefore, we only need to prove

$$\Pr\left[\left|\sum_{i=1}^k t(i) e_i'\right| < \gamma\right] > 1 - \exp\left(-\frac{\pi\gamma^2}{2\|\mathbf{t}\|_2^2\alpha^2}\right).$$

Due to the properties of the normal distribution, $\sum_{i=1}^k t(i) e_i' \sim D_{\|\mathbf{t}\|_2\alpha}$. According to Lemma 11, the above statement holds. □

Corollary 2. *Let γ, γ' be two constant such that $0 < \gamma < \gamma' < 1$. If $k = o(q)$, then*

$$\Pr_{e \sim (\Psi_{\alpha,q})^{\star k}}\left[|e| < \gamma' q\right] > 1 - \exp\left(-\frac{\pi\gamma^2}{2k\alpha^2}\right).$$

Proof. Let $\mathbf{t} = (1, \ldots, 1) \in \mathbb{R}^k$, $\mathbf{x} \leftarrow \Psi_{\alpha,q}^k$. Then e and $\langle \mathbf{t}, \mathbf{x}\rangle$ have the same distribution. Using Lemma 13, we get the conclusion. □

A.9 Truncated Distributions

We first introduce the truncated Bernoulli distribution, which is put forward in [YZ16].

Definition 10. *For any $\mu \in (0,1)$, a sample $\mathbf{x} \sim \tilde{\mathcal{B}}_\mu^n$ is generated in the following procedure.*

(i) $\mathbf{x} \leftarrow \mathcal{B}_\mu^n$.
(ii) If $\mathsf{Ham}(\mathbf{x}) \notin [\frac{1}{2}\mu n, \frac{3}{2}\mu n]$, *discard* $\mathbf{x}$ *and go back to (i).*

When $\mu = \omega(1/n)$, we have $\tilde{\mathcal{B}}_\mu^n$ can be efficiently sampled, and $\mathsf{SD}(\tilde{\mathcal{B}}_\mu^n, \mathcal{B}_\mu^n) = \exp(-\Theta(\mu n))$, which can be proved using Chernoff Bound. What's more, for any positive integer $k = O(n^{<1})$, $\tilde{\mathcal{B}}_{k/n}^n$ can be viewed as a combination of $\Xi^{[n;k/2]}, \ldots, \Xi^{[n;3k/2]}$, so we have $H_\infty(\tilde{\mathcal{B}}_{k/n}^n) = \Theta(k \log n)$ by Lemma 10.

Then we define the truncated discrete gaussian distribution as follows.

Definition 11. *For any $\alpha > 0$, a sample $e \leftarrow \tilde{\Psi}_{\alpha,q}$ is generated in the following procedure.*

(i) $e \leftarrow \Psi_{\alpha,q}$.
(ii) If $e \notin [-q\alpha\sqrt{\log n}, q\alpha\sqrt{\log n}]$, *discard* e *and go back to (i).*

By Lemma 11, we know $\tilde{\Psi}_{\alpha q}$ can be efficiently sampled, and is statistically indistinguishable from $\Psi_{\alpha q}$.

B The IND-CPA Security of Π_λ^{LWE}

Proof of Theorem 6. Consider any adversary $\mathcal{A}$. We aim to demonstrate that $\mathcal{A}$'s probability of winning the IND-CPA security experiment is $\frac{1}{2} + \mathsf{negl}(n)$. We prove this by game hopping. To be precise, we define a sequence of games, where

(i) The first game is the same as $\mathsf{Exp}_{\mathcal{A},\Pi_\lambda^{LWE}}^{\mathsf{CPA}}(1^n)$
(ii) In the last game, $\mathcal{A}$ gains no advantage in correctly guessing the challenge bit.
(iii) Any two consecutive games are computationally indistinguishable.

Then the security of Π_λ^{LWE} will be established.

Game 0. In this game, the challenger $\mathcal{C}$ simulates exactly $\mathsf{Exp}_{\mathcal{A},\Pi_\lambda^{LWE}}^{\mathsf{CPA}}(1^n)$ for the adversary $\mathcal{A}$. Because this is a single-bit PKE, we can set $\mathfrak{m}_0 = 0$ and $\mathfrak{m}_1 = 1$ without loss of generality (thus there is no need for $\mathcal{A}$ to choose the message).

- The challenger $\mathcal{C}$ samples $\mathbf{A} \leftarrow \mathbb{Z}_q^{\lambda \times n}$, as well as $\mathbf{s} \leftarrow \mathbb{Z}_q^\lambda$, $\mathbf{e} \leftarrow \Psi_{\alpha,q}^n$, computes $\mathbf{b} := (\mathbf{A}^T\mathbf{s} + \mathbf{e}) \bmod q$, and sends $pk := (\mathbf{A}, \mathbf{b})$ to $\mathcal{A}$.
- $\mathcal{C}$ continues to choose a random bit $\beta \leftarrow \{0,1\}$, and compute $\mathbf{c}_1 = \mathbf{A}\mathbf{r}$, $c_2 = (\mathbf{r}^T\mathbf{b} + \lfloor q/2 \rceil \cdot \beta) \bmod q$. Then it gives the challenge ciphertext $\mathfrak{c} := (\mathbf{c}_1, c_2)$ to $\mathcal{A}$.
- After $\mathcal{A}$ guesses a bit β', $\mathcal{C}$ outputs 1 if $\beta' = \beta$, or outputs 0 otherwise.

Game 1. This game is identical to Game 0 except that the second element of the public key is sampled uniformly from $\mathbb{Z}_q^n$. In other words, the challenger samples $\mathbf{A} \leftarrow \mathbb{Z}_q^{\lambda \times n}$, $\mathbf{b}' \leftarrow \mathbb{Z}_q^n$, and sends $pk = (\mathbf{A}, \mathbf{b}')$ and ciphertext $\mathfrak{c} := (\mathbf{Ar}, (\mathbf{r}^T\mathbf{b}' + \lfloor q/2 \rceil \cdot \beta) \bmod q)$ to $\mathcal{A}$.

By hardness assumption of $\mathsf{LWE}(\lambda, q, \alpha)$, Game 1 is indistinguishable from Game 0.

Game 2. This game is identical to Game 1 except $\mathfrak{c}$ is chosen uniformly randomly. In other words, the challenger samples $\mathbf{A} \leftarrow \mathbb{Z}_q^{\lambda \times n}$, $\mathbf{b}' \leftarrow \mathbb{Z}_q^n$, and sends $pk = (\mathbf{A}, \mathbf{b}')$ and ciphertext $\mathfrak{c} \sim \mathcal{U}_q^n \times \mathcal{U}_q$.

By Lemma 7, $\mathsf{SD}((\mathbf{A}, \mathbf{b}, \mathbf{Ar}, \mathbf{r}^T\mathbf{b}), (\mathbf{A}, \mathbf{b}, \mathcal{U}^\lambda, \mathcal{U})) \leq 2^{((\lambda+1)\log q - H_\infty(\mathbf{r}))/2} = \mathsf{negl}(n)$. So Game 2 is indistinguishable from Game 1. What's more, in Game 2, $\mathcal{A}$ receives nothing about β. Thus we have $\Pr[\beta' = \beta] = \frac{1}{2}$. □

C Proof of Lemma 3

Proof. By following the Gram-Schmidt procedure directly, we work out the value of each $\tilde{\mathbf{t}}_i$ as follows. When $1 \leq i < \kappa$,

$$\tilde{\mathbf{t}}_i = (\frac{2^i}{\sum_{j=0}^{i-1} 4^j}, 2 \cdot \frac{2^i}{\sum_{j=0}^{i-1} 4^j}, \ldots, 2^{i-1} \cdot \frac{2^i}{\sum_{j=0}^{i-1} 4^j}, -1, 0, \ldots, 0)^T.$$

So we have

$$\|\tilde{\mathbf{t}}_i\|_1 = 1 + \sum_{j=0}^{i-1} 2^j \cdot \frac{2^i}{\sum_{j=0}^{i-1} 4^j} = 1 + (2^i - 1) \cdot \frac{2^i}{(4^i - 1)/3} = 1 + \frac{3 \cdot 2^i}{2^i + 1} = \frac{2^{i+2} + 1}{2^i + 1} \in [3, 4),$$

$$\|\tilde{\mathbf{t}}_i\|_2^2 = 1 + \sum_{j=0}^{i-1} 4^{j-1} \cdot (\frac{2^i}{\sum_{j=0}^{i-1} 4^j})^2 = 1 + \frac{4^i}{\sum_{j=0}^{i-1} 4^j} = \frac{4^{i+1} - 1}{4^i - 1} \in (4, 5].$$

When $i = \kappa$,

$$\tilde{\mathbf{t}}_\kappa = (\frac{q}{\sum_{j=0}^{\kappa-1} 4^j}, 2 \cdot \frac{q}{\sum_{j=0}^{\kappa-1} 4^j}, \ldots, 2^{\kappa-1} \cdot \frac{q}{\sum_{j=0}^{\kappa-1} 4^j})^T.$$

By $q \in [2^{\kappa-1} + 1, 2^\kappa - 1]$, we get

$$\|\tilde{\mathbf{t}}_\kappa\|_1 = \sum_{j=0}^{\kappa-1} 2^j \cdot \frac{q}{\sum_{j=0}^{\kappa-1} 4^j} = (2^\kappa - 1) \cdot \frac{q}{(4^\kappa - 1)/3} = \frac{3q}{2^\kappa + 1} \in (\frac{3}{2}, 3),$$

$$\|\tilde{\mathbf{t}}_\kappa\|_2^2 = \sum_{j=0}^{i-1} 4^j \cdot (\frac{q}{\sum_{j=0}^{\kappa-1} 4^j})^2 = \frac{q^2}{\sum_{j=0}^{\kappa-1} 4^j} = \frac{3q^2}{4^\kappa - 1} \in (\frac{3}{4}, 3).$$

□

D Proof of Lemma 5

Proof. Consider $\langle \mathbf{R}^T \bar{\mathbf{e}}, \tilde{\mathbf{t}}_j \rangle = \sum_{x=1}^{\kappa} \tilde{t}_j(x) \langle \mathbf{r}_x, \bar{\mathbf{e}} \rangle$. Define $\xi_x \sim \langle \mathcal{B}_{k/\bar{n}}^{\bar{n}}, \mathbf{e}' \rangle$ for all $1 \leq x \leq \kappa$.

$$|\mathbb{E}[\xi_x]| = \frac{k}{\bar{n}} |\sum_{i=1}^{\bar{n}} e'(i)| < 0.01 \sqrt{\frac{k \log \bar{n}}{\bar{n}}} < 0.01.$$

$$\mathbb{D}[\xi_x] = \frac{k}{\bar{n}} \cdot (1 - \frac{k}{\bar{n}}) \cdot \sum_{i=1}^{n} e'(i)^2 < \frac{0.16}{100}.$$

Let $\boldsymbol{\xi} = (\xi_1, \ldots, \xi_\kappa)^T$, and define $\zeta_j = \langle \boldsymbol{\xi}, \tilde{\mathbf{t}}_j \rangle = \sum_{x=1}^{\kappa} \tilde{t}_j(x) \xi_x$ for all $1 \leq j \leq \kappa$. By Lemma 3,

$$|\mathbb{E}[\zeta_j]| = |\sum_{x=1}^{\kappa} \tilde{t}_j(x) \mathbb{E}[\xi_x]| < 0.01 \|\tilde{\mathbf{t}}_j\|_1 < 0.04,$$

$$\mathbb{D}[\zeta_j] = \sum_{j=1}^{\kappa} \tilde{t}_j(x)^2 \mathbb{D}[\xi_x] < \frac{0.16}{100} \|\tilde{\mathbf{t}}_j\|_2^2 < 0.008.$$

By Chebyshev's inequality,

$$\Pr[|\zeta_j - \mathbb{E}[\zeta_j]| \geq 0.2] \leq \frac{\mathbb{D}[\xi]}{0.2^2} < 0.2,$$

so

$$\Pr[|\zeta_j| \geq 0.24] < 0.2.$$

Because for all $1 \leq x \leq \kappa$, $\mathbf{r}_x \sim \tilde{\mathcal{B}}_{k/\bar{n}}^{\bar{n}}$, by Chernoff bound we have

$$\mathsf{SD}(\mathbf{r}_x, \mathcal{B}_{k/\bar{n}}^{\bar{n}}) = \exp(-\Theta(k)).$$

Because the statistical distance will decrease after applying a function, we have

$$\mathsf{SD}(\langle \mathbf{r}_x, \mathbf{e}' \rangle, \xi_x) \leq \exp(-\Theta(k)),$$

and then it holds for all $1 \leq j \leq \kappa$ that

$$\mathsf{SD}(\langle \mathbf{R}^T \mathbf{e}', \tilde{\mathbf{t}}_j \rangle, \zeta_j) \leq \sum_{x=1}^{\kappa} \mathsf{SD}(\langle \mathbf{r}_x, \mathbf{e}' \rangle, \xi_x) \leq \kappa \exp(-\Theta(k)) = o(1).$$

Because the rounding error of $\lfloor \cdot \rceil$ is at most $\frac{1}{2}$, and $\mathsf{Ham}(\mathbf{r}_x) \leq \frac{3}{2}k$, we have

$$|\langle \mathbf{R}^T \cdot q\mathbf{e}', \tilde{\mathbf{t}}_j \rangle - \langle \mathbf{R}^T \bar{\mathbf{e}}, \tilde{\mathbf{t}}_j \rangle| = |\sum_{x=1}^{\kappa} \tilde{t}_j(x) \langle \mathbf{r}_x, q\mathbf{e}' - \lfloor q\mathbf{e}' \rceil \rangle| \leq \sum_{x=1}^{\kappa} \tilde{t}_j(x) \cdot \frac{3k}{4} = \frac{3k}{4} \|\tilde{\mathbf{t}}_j\|_1 = o(q).$$

Finally,

$$\begin{aligned}\Pr[|\langle \mathbf{R}^T\bar{\mathbf{e}}, \tilde{\mathbf{t}}_j\rangle| < \frac{q}{4}] > &\Pr[|\langle \mathbf{R}^T \cdot q\mathbf{e}', \tilde{\mathbf{t}}_j\rangle| + o(q) < \frac{q}{4}] \\ > &\Pr[|\langle \mathbf{R}^T\mathbf{e}', \tilde{\mathbf{t}}_j\rangle| < 0.24] \\ > &\Pr[|\zeta_j| < 0.24] \cdot (1 - o(1)) \\ > &0.79.\end{aligned}$$

□

E Proof of Theorem 12

Proof. Parse $\mathbf{e} = (\bar{\mathbf{e}}^T \| \underline{\mathbf{e}}_1^T \| \dots \| \underline{\mathbf{e}}_\ell^T)^T \in \mathbb{Z}^{\bar{n}} \times (\mathbb{Z}^w)^{\otimes \ell}$. By definition, there exists some $\mathbf{e}' \leftarrow D_\alpha^{\bar{n}}$ such that $\bar{\mathbf{e}} = \lfloor q\mathbf{e}' \rceil$. By Lemma 12, we have

(i) $|\sum_{i=1}^{\bar{n}} e'(i)| < 0.01\sqrt{\frac{\bar{n}\log\bar{n}}{k}}$,
(ii) $\sum_{i=1}^{\bar{n}} e'(i)^2 < \frac{0.16\bar{n}}{100k}$,

For every $1 \le i \le \ell$, parse $\mathbf{R}_i = (\mathbf{R}_{i,1} \| \dots \| \mathbf{R}_{i,\lambda}) \in (\mathbb{Z}_q^{\bar{n}\times\kappa})^{\otimes\lambda}$ and $\underline{\mathbf{e}}_i = (\underline{\mathbf{e}}_{i,1}^T \| \dots \| \underline{\mathbf{e}}_{i,\lambda}^T)^T \in (\mathbb{Z}^\kappa)^{\otimes\lambda}$. By Lemma 5, we have

$$\forall 1 \le h \le \lambda, \forall 1 \le j \le \kappa,\ \Pr[\langle \mathbf{R}_{i,h}^T\bar{\mathbf{e}}, \tilde{\mathbf{t}}_j\rangle < q/4] > 0.79$$

holds independently for every $1 \le i \le \ell$.

Besides, by Lemma 13, we have for every i, j, h that

$$\Pr[|\langle \underline{\mathbf{e}}_{i,h}, \tilde{\mathbf{t}}_j\rangle| < q/4] > 1 - \exp(-\frac{\pi \cdot (1/5)^2}{2\|\tilde{\mathbf{t}}_j\|_2^2 \cdot (1/10\sqrt{k})^2}) = 1 - \mathsf{negl}(n).$$

Let $\hat{\mathbf{e}}_i := (\hat{\mathbf{e}}_{i,1}^T \| \dots \| \hat{\mathbf{e}}_{i,\lambda})^T = \mathbf{R}_i^T\bar{\mathbf{e}} + \underline{\mathbf{e}}_i \in (\mathbb{Z}^\kappa)^{\otimes\lambda}$, then we have $\hat{\mathbf{e}}_{i,h} = \mathbf{R}_{i,h}^T\bar{\mathbf{e}} + \underline{\mathbf{e}}_{i,h}$ for every $1 \le h \le \lambda$. So

$$\Pr[|\langle \hat{\mathbf{e}}_{i,h}, \tilde{\mathbf{t}}_j\rangle| < q/2] > 0.79 \cdot (1 - \mathsf{negl}(n)) > 2/3$$

holds independently for every i, j, h.

Let $\hat{\mathbf{s}} = \mathbf{H}^T\mathbf{s}$, $\hat{\mathbf{b}}_i := \mathbf{R}_i^T\bar{\mathbf{b}} + \underline{\mathbf{b}}_i = \mathbf{G}_\lambda^T\hat{\mathbf{s}} + \hat{\mathbf{e}}_i$. By Lemma 4, we can use Algorithm 2 to get every entry of $\hat{\mathbf{s}}$ one by one. Because $\mathbf{H}$ is invertible, we can use the value of $\hat{\mathbf{s}}$ to compute $\mathbf{s}$, as well as $\mathbf{e} = \mathbf{b} - \mathbf{A}^T\mathbf{s}$. □

References

ABB+23. Aggarwal, D., et al.: Lattice problems beyond polynomial time. In: STOC, pp. 1516–1526. ACM (2023)

Bab86. Babai, L.: On lovász' lattice reduction and the nearest lattice point problem. Comb. **6**(1), 1–13 (1986)

BKP23. Bartusek, J., Khurana, D., Poremba, A.: Publicly-verifiable deletion via target-collapsing functions. In: CRYPTO (5), volume 14085 of Lecture Notes in Computer Science, pp. 99–128. Springer (2023)

BV11. Brakerski, Z., Vaikuntanathan, V.: Efficient fully homomorphic encryption from (standard) LWE. In: FOCS, pp. 97–106. IEEE Computer Society (2011)

CHL+25. Chen, Y., Zihan, H., Liu, Q., Luo, H., Tu, Y.: Algorithm, hardness, and oblivious sampling. In: CRYPTO, LWE with Quantum Amplitudes (2025)

GKM+00. Gertner, Y., Kannan, S., Malkin, T., Reingold, O., Viswanathan, M.: The relationship between public key encryption and oblivious transfer. In: FOCS, pp. 325–335. IEEE Computer Society (2000)

GPV08. Gentry, C., Peikert, C., Vaikuntanathan, V.: Trapdoors for hard lattices and new cryptographic constructions. In: STOC, pp. 197–206. ACM (2008)

GSW13. Gentry, C., Sahai, A., Waters, B.: Homomorphic encryption from learning with errors: conceptually-simpler, asymptotically-faster, attribute-based. In: CRYPTO (1), volume 8042 of Lecture Notes in Computer Science, pp. 75–92. Springer (2013)

GVW13. Gorbunov, S., Vaikuntanathan, V., Wee, H.: Attribute-based encryption for circuits. In: STOC, pp. 545–554. ACM (2013)

ILL89. Impagliazzo, R., Levin, L.A., Luby, M.: Pseudo-random generation from one-way functions (extended abstracts). In: STOC, pp. 12–24. ACM (1989)

Jus72. Justesen, J.: Class of constructive asymptotically good algebraic codes. IEEE Trans. Inf. Theory **18**(5), 652–656 (1972)

LM00. Laurent, B., Massart, P.: Adaptive estimation of a quadratic functional by model selection. Ann. Stat. 1302–1338 (2000)

MP12. Micciancio, D., Peikert, C.: Trapdoors for lattices: simpler, tighter, faster, smaller. In: EUROCRYPT, volume 7237 of Lecture Notes in Computer Science, pp. 700–718. Springer (2012)

PRS17. Peikert, C., Regev, O., Stephens-Davidowitz, N.: Pseudorandomness of ring-LWE for any ring and modulus. In: STOC, pp. 461–473. ACM (2017)

PVW08. Peikert, C., Vaikuntanathan, V., Waters, B.: A framework for efficient and composable oblivious transfer. In: CRYPTO, volume 5157 of Lecture Notes in Computer Science, pp. 554–571. Springer (2008)

Reg05. Regev, O.: On lattices, learning with errors, random linear codes, and cryptography. In: STOC, pp. 84–93. ACM (2005)

Vai20. Vaikuntanathan, V.: CS 294-168 Lattices, Learning with Errors and Post-Quantum Cryptography: Lecture 1 (2020). https://people.csail.mit.edu/vinodv/CS294/lecture1.pdf

YZ16. Yu, Y., Zhang, J.: Cryptography with auxiliary input and trapdoor from constant-noise LPN. In: CRYPTO (1), volume 9814 of Lecture Notes in Computer Science, pp. 214–243. Springer (2016)

Attacks on Public-Key Schemes

AI for Code-based Cryptography

Mohamed Malhou[1,2(✉)], Ludovic Perret[2,3], and Kristin Lauter[1]

[1] FAIR at Meta, Paris, France
{mmalhou,klauter}@meta.com
[2] CNRS, LIP6, Sorbonne Université, 75005 Paris, France
[3] EPITA Research Lab (LRE), EPITA, Le Kremlin-Bicêtre, France
ludovic.perret@epita.fr

Abstract. We introduce the use of machine learning in the cryptanalysis of code-based cryptography. Our focus is on distinguishing problems related to the security of NIST round-4 McEliece-like cryptosystems, particularly for Goppa codes used in `ClassicMcEliece` and Quasi-Cyclic Moderate Density Parity-Check (QC-MDPC) codes used in `BIKE`. We present `DeepDistinguisher`, a new algorithm that trains a transformer to distinguish structured codes from random linear codes. The results show that the new distinguisher achieves high accuracy in distinguishing Goppa codes, suggesting that their structure may be more recognizable by AI models. Our approach outperforms traditional attacks for distinguishing Goppa codes in certain settings and generalizes to longer code lengths without further training using a puncturing technique. We also present the first distinguishing results for MDPC and QC-MDPC codes.

Keywords: Classic McEliece · Goppa Codes · QC-MDPC · Code Distinguishability · Deep Learning · Transformers

1 Introduction

In recent years, the cryptographic community has been actively preparing for the cyber-security challenges arising from the impending advent of cryptographically relevant quantum computers. To address this quantum threat, the National Institute of Standards & Technology (NIST) started a multi-stage standardization effort [11] to replace current number-theoretic-based cryptographic standards with a new generation of quantum-resistant algorithms. In 2024, NIST standardized a first set of post-quantum cryptography (PQC) standards, including the Module-Lattice-Based Key-Encapsulation Mechanism (ML-KEM, [39]), the Module-Lattice-Based Digital Signature Algorithm (ML-DSA, [38]) and the Stateless Hash-Based Digital Signature Algorithm (SLH-DSA, [40]).

The standardization of post-quantum cryptography is still ongoing, with NIST currently conducting a fourth round of evaluations to identify additional key encapsulation mechanisms (KEMs) [41]. Candidates that remain in the fourth round all belong to code-based cryptography [8,18,42], a family based on the algorithmic and NP-hardness of decoding random linear codes [6,18]. In

C. Boura et al. (Eds.): SAC 2025, LNCS 16207, pp. 489–518, 2026.
https://doi.org/10.1007/978-3-032-10536-3_18

particular, two candidates follow the general framework of the McEliece cryptosystem [35]: `ClassicMcEliece` [1] that uses binary Goppa codes as initially proposed by Robert McEliece in 1978, and `BIKE` [2,37] a variant relying on Quasi-Cyclic Moderate Density Parity-Check (QC-MDPC) codes.

A fundamental question for these schemes, and post-quantum cryptography in general, is the hardness of the underlying algorithmic problems. This issue is both critical and highly challenging, as the security of standardized and candidate schemes for NIST has been intensively scrutinized in the past few years. Introducing any new cryptanalytic technique can be considered a notable achievement.

In this context, recent advances in Machine Learning (ML) provide a new paradigm to accelerate cryptanalysis. In particular, deep learning models – especially transformer-based architectures – have demonstrated remarkable success in pattern recognition, feature extraction, and automated discovery of hidden structures in high-dimensional data. In [32,33,49,50], the authors introduced the use of transformers to attack the Learning With Errors (LWE) problem [45], a central problem in post-quantum cryptography. The capability of these models to learn joint distributions of sequential data makes them a promising tool for identifying latent structures in algebraic constructions.

This paper presents a novel application of ML techniques to assess the security of code-based public-key cryptosystems. Specifically, we consider the problem of distinguishing structured public codes (e.g., Goppa or QC-MDPC) from random codes. To do so, we design a supervised learning framework on finite field data and introduce a transformer-based algorithm, `DeepDistinguisher`, designed to classify structured codes more effectively. Our work does not directly impact the security of Classic McEliece; however, we believe that our findings will inspire researchers to further explore this problem. To our knowledge, this is the first work that applies ML to a core hardness assumption in code-based cryptography rather than to side-channel leakage.

We validate our `DeepDistinguisher` via extensive experiments across a range of code parameters. For Goppa codes, we empirically demonstrate that `DeepDistinguisher` can classify structured codes from random with high accuracy, even outperforming the most recent approaches [13,20,43] for some specific parameters.

Organization of the Paper

The paper is organized as follows. We begin with a discussion of prior research relevant to our approach in 1 which appears as part of this introduction. Then, Sects. 2 and 3 provide the necessary background and definitions for understanding our work.

Our `DeepDistinguisher` is detailed in Sect. 4 where we describe the training framework, data generation process, and evaluation strategies. We highlight the importance of the choice of deep learning architecture and data representation.

Sect. 5 presents our experimental results, demonstrating that our model achieves high classification accuracy and outperforms traditional algebraic distinguishers such as FGOPT [20], CMT [13], and syzygy [43] on the toy parameter settings proposed in [43].

Additionally, we present distinguishing results on ternary Goppa codes, and certain binary alternant codes, but also the first specific distinguishing results on (QC) MDPC codes. Although our experimental results are limited, our findings suggest that distinguishing these codes is easier than finding low-weight codewords, the approach taken in [37].

Finally, in Sect. 6, we introduce a more challenging problem: given a public generator matrix of a Goppa code with missing entries, recover the missing values such that the outcome is a valid Goppa code. This is a harder problem than distinguishing and seems impossible without the knowledge of some information about the private key. Our model successfully recovers these missing values, demonstrating that the structure of Goppa codes can be learned and exploited by AI and that our `DeepDistinguisher` is not simply the statistical distinguisher described in Appendix A. The code has been open sourced for the community.[1]

Related Work

AI, and more specifically ML, is becoming a powerful approach in cryptanalysis, with a growing body of research demonstrating that neural networks can detect patterns. For instance, Gohr [23] showed that deep residual neural networks can serve as exceptionally strong differential distinguishers—outperforming classical methods on round-reduced Speck32/64 with very few chosen plaintexts.

In post-quantum cryptography, a first generation of ML techniques were used in [26] to attack group-based cryptosystems. More recently, the SALSA papers [32,33,49,50] leveraged recent advances in ML —- in particular the introduction of transformers [48] – to solve Learning with Errors (LWE) problems. Lastly, [29] considers learning-based information-theoretic metrics, leveraging mutual information estimation and binary classification to evaluate the security of cryptographic schemes under chosen-plaintext attacks (`IND-CPA`). The study demonstrates that neural networks can efficiently identify cryptosystems that are not `IND-CPA` secure by modeling the distinguishability of ciphertexts as a classification task.

In this paper, we present the first ML-based attack, `DeepDistinguisher`, on the distinguishing problem arising in the security of McEliece-like cryptosystems. In particular, we consider the *Goppa Code Distinguishing* (GD) problem [12]; probably the most famous example of code distinguishing problem.

*Problem 1 (Goppa Code Distinguishing (*GD*) problem).* Given a generator matrix $\mathbf{G} \in \mathcal{M}_{k\times n}(\mathbb{F}_q)$ of a $[n,k]_q$ linear code, the Goppa Code Distinguishing (GD) problem asks to decide if $\mathbf{G}$ is the generator matrix of a Goppa code or a randomly drawn matrix.

The GD problem was formally introduced in [12] and was initially believed to be hard. Thus, it served as an assumption for reducing the security of the

[1] Code is available at github.com/facebookresearch/ai4code-cryptanalysis.

McEliece cryptosystem to the problem of decoding random linear codes [17]. Our understanding of the hardness of GD has significantly shifted in the past ten years, culminating with the so-called *syzygy distinguisher* [43] that now solves GD for a broad range of parameters with a complexity asymptotically faster than the best generic decoding algorithms.

The syzygy distinguisher, as well as improved results on GD such as [13,14], is built on the polynomial-time distinguisher presented by Faugère, Gautier, Otmani, Perret, Tillich (FGOPT) [20]. The core idea behind the FGOPT distinguisher is to analyze the behavior of the Gröbner basis computation [9,10] of an algebraic system associated to McEliece's public key. This computation behaves differently if the algebraic system is generated from a McEliece public key or from a randomly generated matrix. FGOPT described specific linear relations occurring in such computations due to the Goppa (or alternant) structure, leading to a polynomial-time distinguisher solving GD for codes whose rate $R = \frac{k}{n}$ is close to 1. Since this result, a major open question has been how to extend the distinguishing rate.

At Asiacrypt'23, Couvreur, Mora and Tillich (CMT, [13]) finally demonstrated that the approach from [20] can be improved. CMT introduced a new algebraic modeling method and leveraged more general *algebraic relations*, known as syzygies, arising in the Gröbner basis computations. While FGOPT can distinguish codes with rates extremely close to 1, CMT pushed the boundaries of success to distinguishing rates in the range $[\frac{2}{3}, 1]$.

A central contribution of the latest distinguisher [43] is to precisely predict the syzygies arising at any step of the Gröbner computations. In particular, such a distinguisher can solve GD for a broad range of parameters with complexity which is sub-exponential in the error-correcting capacity. Asymptotically, this removes the limitation on the rate for the syzygy distinguisher. For fixed parameters, however, the situation is different. Remark that, unlike FGOPT, the CMT and syzygy distinguishers are not polynomial-time algorithms. The rate remains a limiting factor, and certain code parameters cannot be distinguished by either the syzygy or CMT distinguishers due to fundamental theoretical limitations and/or computational complexity constraints.

The code distinguishing problem for Quasi-Cyclic (QC) and general Moderate Density Parity-Check (MDPC) was formally introduced in [37]. To the best of our knowledge, no dedicated technique exists for distinguishing such codes. The only known approach, described in [37], relies on finding low-weight codewords in the public code – a problem equivalent to message recovery. This led the authors of [37] to introduce an assumption about the (exponential) hardness of distinguishing MDPC codes.

We emphasize that the hardness of GD has no direct impact on the security of McEliece yet. That is, there is currently no generic technique to mount an attack against McEliece using a distinguisher. However, recent results [5,13] demonstrated that techniques used for distinguishing alternant/Goppa codes can also be applied to attack a version of McEliece using generic alternant codes with high rates.

2 Preliminaries

2.1 Notations

Finite Fields. We consider the finite field $\mathbb{F}_q$ of order q with q a prime power. For some integer $m > 0, \mathbb{F}_{q^m}$ is a field extension of $\mathbb{F}_q$ of degree m: $\mathbb{F}_{q^m} \cong \mathbb{F}_q[x]/(g(x)) \cong \mathbb{F}_q[\alpha]$ with α a root of an irreducible polynomial $g(x)$ of degree m. Any element $\beta \in \mathbb{F}_{q^m}$ can be naturally associated with its vector form in $\mathbb{F}_q$ as $(c_0, \dots, c_{m-1}) \in \mathbb{F}_q^m$, where $\beta = \sum_{i=0}^{m-1} c_i \alpha^i$.

Vectors and Matrices. We use lowercase letters to represent integers, while integer intervals are expressed as $[\![a; b]\!]$. Matrices are denoted by bold uppercase letters, and vectors by bold lowercase letters. For a vector $\mathbf{v}$, the notation v_i refers to its i-th component, and $\mathbf{v}^\top$ denotes its transpose. $\mathcal{M}_{k\times n}(\mathbb{F})$ will denote the set of $k \times n$ matrices with coefficients over a finite field $\mathbb{F}$.

For a matrix $\mathbf{A} \in \mathcal{M}_{k\times n}(\mathbb{F})$, the element in the i-th row and j-th column is denoted by a_{ij}. A sub-matrix of $\mathbf{A}$, specified by a set of rows $\mathcal{I}$ and a set of columns $\mathcal{J}$, is written as $\mathbf{A}[\mathcal{I}, \mathcal{J}]$. Additionally, a specific row or column of a matrix $\mathbf{A}$ is indicated by $\mathbf{A}[i, :]$ and $\mathbf{A}[:, j]$, respectively.

2.2 Basics of Deep Learning

Before presenting our approach, we first introduce the fundamental concepts of deep learning to provide the necessary background for a clear understanding of our methodology [24].

A *deep neural network* is a parametric family of functions $F_\theta \colon \mathcal{X} \to \mathcal{Y}$, where $\theta \in \mathbb{R}^p$ represents all trainable parameters (i.e., the entries of weight matrices and bias vectors) [24] and $\mathcal{X}$ and $\mathcal{Y}$ are measurable spaces. Concretely, for an input $x \in \mathcal{X}$, one may write:

$$F_\theta \colon x \;\mapsto\; W_d\, \sigma\big(\cdots \sigma(W_1 x + b_1) \cdots\big) + b_d,$$

with each W_i a weight matrix, b_i a bias vector, and σ a fixed nonlinearity such as ReLU (Rectified Linear Unit $x \to \max(0, x)$) applied component-wise. In this case, the trainable parameters of F are $\theta = \{W_1, b_1, \dots, W_d, b_d\}$.

Training amounts to minimizing an empirical risk

$$\min_\theta \sum_i \ell\big(F_\theta;\, x_i,\, y_i\big),$$

where $\{(x_i, y_i)\}$ is a labeled dataset and ℓ is a chosen loss function. A common case is *binary classification*, where $\mathcal{Y} = \{0, 1\}$ and one trains F_θ to output probabilities in $[0, 1]$ by minimizing the *binary cross-entropy* loss [24]:

$$\sum_i \Big[-\, y_i \log\big(F_\theta(x_i)\big) \;-\; (1 - y_i) \log\big(1 - F_\theta(x_i)\big) \Big].$$

Parameters θ are typically updated via gradient-based algorithms (e.g., stochastic gradient descent) that converge to a θ^* that produces accurate predictions on new (held-out/validation) data. By the *universal approximation* theorem, sufficiently large networks can approximate wide classes of continuous functions on compact domains [16,28].

A *Transformer encoder* [48] is a deep sequence-to-sequence model that takes an ordered collection $\{x_1, \dots, x_n\} \subseteq \mathcal{X}$—which may be text tokens, image patches, matrix rows, etc.—and outputs a sequence of embeddings $H_L \in \mathbb{R}^{n\times d}$. Each x_i is first embedded (or projected) into $h_{0,i} \in \mathbb{R}^d$. Then, each of the L layers applies *multi-head self-attention* and a small *feed-forward* sub-network, with residual connections and normalization. Formally, for layer ℓ, we form affine queries, keys, and values from $H_{\ell-1}$, compute

$$\text{Att}(Q, K, V) = \text{softmax}\Big(\tfrac{QK^\top}{\sqrt{d_k}}\Big)\, V$$

for each attention head, concatenate the head outputs, and project them. We update

$$H'_\ell = \text{LayerNorm}\big(H_{\ell-1} + \text{MultiHeadAtt}(H_{\ell-1})\big)$$
$$H_\ell = \text{LayerNorm}\big(H'_\ell + \text{FFN}(H'_\ell)\big)$$

All parameters (in the attention and feed-forward blocks) are trained end-to-end via gradient descent to yield a final encoder representation H_L. If the task is a classification, then we project the hidden state H_L into the output space using a trainable linear layer [3,48].

3 Coding Theory

3.1 Linear Codes and the Bounded Distance Decoding Problem

A $[k, n]_q$ *linear code* $\mathcal{C} \subseteq \mathbb{F}_q^n$ is a k-dimensional subspace of $\mathbb{F}_q^n$. The rate of $\mathcal{C}$ is defined as k/n and elements of $\mathcal{C}$ are called codewords. $\mathcal{C}$ can be specified by a full rank *generator matrix* $\mathbf{G} \in \mathcal{M}_{k\times n}(\mathbb{F}_q)$ such that $\mathcal{C} = \{\mathbf{m}\cdot\mathbf{G} \mid \mathbf{m} \in \mathbb{F}_q^k\}$. The *standard form* of $\mathbf{G}$ is $\mathbf{G} = [\mathbf{I}_k \mid \mathbf{A}]$, with $\mathbf{I}_k$ being the $k \times k$ identity matrix. Equivalently, $\mathcal{C}$ can be represented by *parity-check matrix* $\mathbf{H} \in \mathcal{M}_{(n-k)\times n}(\mathbb{F}_q)$ that satisfies $\mathbf{H}\cdot\mathbf{c}^\top = \mathbf{0}_{(n-k)}, \forall \mathbf{c} \in \mathcal{C}$, and its row space is the dual of $\mathcal{C}$.

We introduce below a general operation on codes that will be used to extend the range of applicability of `DeepDistinguisher`.

Definition 1 (Punctured Code). *Given a code $\mathcal{C} \subseteq \mathbb{F}^n$, and a subset $\mathcal{I} \subset [\![1; n]\!]$, the punctured code over $\mathcal{I}$ is defined as:*

$$\mathcal{P}_{\mathcal{I}}(\mathcal{C}) = \Big\{ (c_i)_{i\in[\![1;n]\!]\setminus\mathcal{I}} \;\Big|\mathbf{c} \in \mathcal{C} \Big\}.$$

Code-based cryptography [8,18,42] is based on the intractability, i.e. NP-Hardness, of the Bounded Distance Decoding (BDD, [6]) problem:

*Problem 2 (Bounded Distance Decoding (*BDD*) problem).* Given the generator matrix $\mathbf{G} \in \mathcal{M}_{k\times n}(\mathbb{F}_q)$ of an $[n,k]_q$ linear code, a target $\mathbf{c} \in \mathbb{F}_q^n$, and an integer $t > 0$, the BDD problem asks to find – if any – $\mathbf{m} \in \mathbb{F}_q^k$ such that:

$$w_H(\mathbf{c} - \mathbf{m} \cdot \mathbf{G}) \leq t,$$

with w_H being the Hamming weight of the vector, i.e. the number of its non-zero coordinates.

Solving BDD for random codes, i.e. random generator matrices $\mathbf{G} \in \mathcal{M}_{k\times n}(\mathbb{F}_q)$, is a long-standing problem whose most effective algorithms are all computationally intractable [7,18,47].

3.2 McEliece Framework and Code Distinguishing Problem

The McEliece cryptosystem [35] is certainly the most popular code-based public-key cryptosystem. In particular, round-4 NIST candidates `ClassicMcEliece` [1] (which is based on the Niederreiter variant) and `BIKE` [2] follow the general framework described below.

- **Secret-Key.** A structured generator matrix $\mathbf{G}_s \in \mathcal{M}_{k\times n}(\mathbb{F}_q)$ of a $[n,k]_q$ linear code with a known decoding algorithm.
- **Public-Key.** A scrambled generator matrix $\mathbf{G} \in \mathcal{M}_{k\times n}(\mathbb{F}_q)$ derived from the secret-key $\mathbf{G}_s$.
- **Encryption.** Given a message $\mathbf{m} \in \mathbb{F}_q^k$, the ciphertext is computed as $\mathbf{c} = \mathbf{m} \cdot \mathbf{G} + \mathbf{e} \in \mathbb{F}_q^n$, where $\mathbf{e} \in \mathbb{F}_q^n$ is an error vector of small Hamming weight.
- **Decryption.** Given a ciphertext $\mathbf{c} \in \mathbb{F}_q^n$, the receiver applies the code's decoding algorithm to recover the message $\mathbf{m}$.

From this description, it is clear that the security of McEliece (message-recovery) relies on the hardness of BDD. In addition, it is natural to introduce a general distinguishability problem for a structured family of linear codes $\mathscr{F}$.

*Problem 3 (Code Distinguishability (*CD*) problem).* Given a generator matrix $\mathbf{G} \in \mathcal{M}_{k\times n}(\mathbb{F}_q)$ of an $[n,k]_q$ linear code, the CD problem asks to decide if $\mathbf{G}$ is the generator matrix of an $\mathscr{F}$-code or randomly drawn.

In this paper, $\mathscr{F}$ includes Goppa or alternant $(\mathscr{G}, \mathscr{A})$ codes as well as MDPC and QC-MDPC $(\mathscr{M}, \mathscr{Q} \cap \mathscr{M})$ codes.

3.3 Alternant and Goppa Codes

The family of codes used in `ClassicMcEliece` can be conveniently described by introducing Generalized Reed-Solomon codes.

Definition 2 (Generalized Reed-Solomon Code, [44]**).** *Let $\boldsymbol{\alpha} = (\alpha_1, \ldots, \alpha_n) \in \mathbb{F}_q^n$ be an n-tuple of distinct elements in $\mathbb{F}_q$, called a support, and $\boldsymbol{\beta} = (\beta_1, \ldots, \beta_n) \in (\mathbb{F}_q^*)^n$ an n-tuple of nonzero elements in $\mathbb{F}_q$, called multiplier. The Generalized Reed-Solomon code of length n and dimension t, denoted by $\mathrm{GRS}_{q,n,t}(\boldsymbol{\alpha}, \boldsymbol{\beta})$, is defined as:*

$$\mathrm{GRS}_{q,n,t}(\boldsymbol{\alpha}, \boldsymbol{\beta}) = \{(\beta_1 f(\alpha_1), \ldots, \beta_n f(\alpha_n)) \mid f \in \mathbb{F}_q[x], \deg(f) < t\}.$$

Remark that the following weighted Vandermonde matrix is a generator matrix of the GRS code.

$$\mathbf{V}_t[\boldsymbol{\alpha},\boldsymbol{\beta}] = \begin{pmatrix} \beta_1 & \beta_2 & \cdots & \beta_n \\ \beta_1\alpha_1 & \beta_2\alpha_2 & \cdots & \beta_n\alpha_n \\ \vdots & \vdots & \ddots & \vdots \\ \beta_1\alpha_1^{t-1} & \beta_2\alpha_2^{t-1} & \cdots & \beta_n\alpha_n^{t-1} \end{pmatrix}.$$

Alternant codes can be viewed as subfield subcodes of GRS codes.

Definition 3 (Alternant Code, [34]). *Let $\boldsymbol{\alpha} \in \mathbb{F}_{q^m}^n$ be a support and $\boldsymbol{\beta} \in (\mathbb{F}_{q^m}^*)^n$ be a multiplier as in Definition 2 such that $n \leq q^m$. The alternant code of degree t, denoted by $\mathcal{A}_{q,n,m,t}(\boldsymbol{\alpha},\boldsymbol{\beta})$, is given by:*

$$\mathcal{A}_{q,n,m,t}(\boldsymbol{\alpha},\boldsymbol{\beta}) = \mathrm{GRS}_{q^m,n,t}(\boldsymbol{\alpha},\boldsymbol{\beta})^\perp \cap \mathbb{F}_q^n.$$

$\mathcal{A}_{q,n,m,t}(\boldsymbol{\alpha},\boldsymbol{\beta})$ is $[n, k \geq n - mt]_q$ linear code.

Once the support and multiplier vectors are known, alternant codes of degree t can be decoded in polynomial-time up to errors with Hamming weight $t/2$ [34, Ch. 12]. McEliece cryptosystem relies on a sub-class of alternant codes.

Definition 4 (Goppa Code, [25]). *Let $\boldsymbol{\alpha} = (\alpha_1, \ldots, \alpha_n) \in \mathbb{F}_{q^m}^n$ be a support and $g(x) \in \mathbb{F}_{q^m}[x]$ be a degree t square-free polynomial, called a Goppa polynomial, such that $g(\alpha_i) \neq 0, \forall\, 1 \leq i \leq n$. The Goppa code, denoted $\mathcal{G}_{q,n,m,t}(\boldsymbol{\alpha}, g)$, is defined as follows:*

$$\mathcal{G}_{q,n,m,t}(\boldsymbol{\alpha}, g) = \mathcal{A}_{q,n,m,t}\left(\boldsymbol{\alpha}, \frac{1}{g(\boldsymbol{\alpha})}\right).$$

$\mathcal{G}_{q,n,m,t}(\boldsymbol{\alpha}, g)$ is an $[n, k \geq n - mt]_q$ linear code.

Goppa codes, viewed as alternant codes, naturally inherit a decoding algorithm that corrects up to $t/2$ errors. For binary Goppa codes ($q = 2$), we can improve this bound to correct twice as many errors in polynomial-time.

3.4 Codes with Sparse Parity-Check Matrices

BIKE [2,37] relies on linear codes described by compact and sparse matrices.

Definition 5 (Moderate Density Parity-Check codes, [37]). *An (n, k, w)-*MDPC *code is a linear code of length n, co-dimension k admitting a parity check matrix with constant row weight w which scales in $O(\sqrt{n \log n})$.*

BIKE adds a structure to MDPC codes allowing to decrease the size of the public-key.

Definition 6 (Quasi-cyclic codes, [37]). *An $[n, k]_q$-linear code is Quasi-Cyclic (*QC*) if there is some integer ℓ with $n = \ell n_0$ such that every cyclic shift of a codeword by ℓ places is again a codeword.*

3.5 Solving the Code Distinguishing Problem

A well-studied example of a code distinguishing problem occurs when the family $\mathscr{F}$ is restricted to Goppa or alternant codes (Sect. 3.3). This corresponds to the classical McEliece scheme and the Goppa Code Distinguishing (GD) problem.

The first efficient algorithm for solving this problem, FGOPT [20], relies critically on the code rate k/n. In [13, 20], the authors precisely characterize the range of parameters for which FGOPT can distinguish Goppa codes in polynomial time.

Definition 7 (Square–distinguishable Goppa code). *A Goppa code $\mathcal{G}(\boldsymbol{\alpha}, g)$, with $\boldsymbol{\alpha} = (\alpha_1, \ldots, \alpha_n) \in \mathbb{F}_{q^m}$ a support and $g(x) \in \mathbb{F}_{q^m}[x]$ a Goppa polynomial of degree t, is said to be square–distinguishable if:*

$$n > \binom{tm+1}{2} - \frac{m}{2}(t-1)(t-2), \qquad \textit{when } t < q-1 \tag{1}$$

$$n > \binom{tm+1}{2} - \frac{m}{2}t\left((2e_{\mathcal{G}}+1)t - 2(q-1)q^{e_{\mathcal{G}}-1} - 1\right), \textit{ otherwise,} \tag{2}$$

where $e_{\mathcal{G}} = \min\{i \in \mathbb{N} \mid t \leq (q-1)^2 q^i\} + 1 = \left\lceil \log_q\left(\frac{t}{(q-1)^2}\right)\right\rceil + 1.$

Note that similar results can be derived for alternant or binary Goppa codes.

In [13], Couvreur, Mora and Tillich (CMT) extended the concept of distinguishable codes by introducing a new class called d-distinguishable codes. This concept is based on invariants related to the Hilbert function, a fundamental tool from commutative algebra [15], commonly used to assess the complexity of Gröbner basis computations [9, 10]. In particular, it applies to Pfaffian ideals, i.e. ideals generated by symbolic minors of skew-matrices [19, 36], modeling specific relations of alternant and Goppa codes.

Definition 8 (d-distinguishable, simplified from [13]). *Let $\mathcal{C}$ be an $[n, tm]_{\mathbb{F}_{q^m}}$ linear code, $\mathcal{P}_2^+(\mathcal{C})$ be the Pfaffian ideal associated to $\mathcal{C}$ [13, Sec. 5.2] and $\mathrm{HF}_{\mathcal{P}_2^+(\mathcal{C})}$ be the corresponding Hilbert function. $\mathcal{C}$ is said to be d-distinguishable from a generic $[n, tm]$ linear code over $\mathbb{F}_{q^m}$ when the following holds:*

$$\mathrm{HF}_{\mathcal{P}_2^+(\mathcal{C})}(d) \neq \max\left(0, \sum_{i=0}^{d} \frac{(-1)^i}{tm+d-i-1}\binom{n-tm}{i}\binom{tm+d-i-1}{d-i+1}\binom{tm+d-i-1}{d-i}\right)$$

1-distinguishable codes correspond to square–distinguishable Goppa codes (Definition 7). In [13], the authors demonstrated that d-distinguishability, for $d > 1$, allows to distinguish a broader family of codes than FGOPT, albeit at a higher computational cost. In particular, the complexity of the CMT distinguisher is bounded from above by:

$$\mathcal{O}\left(\left(\binom{tm}{2} - k + 1\right)\binom{\binom{tm}{2} + d_{\mathrm{reg}} - 1}{d_{\mathrm{reg}}}^{\omega}\right), \tag{3}$$

where $2 \leq \omega < 3$ is a feasible linear algebra constant, and d_{reg} is the degree of regularity [4], i.e. the maximum degree reached in the computation of (degree-based) Gröbner basis of the Pfaffian ideal $\mathcal{P}_2^+(\mathcal{C})$. In [13], the authors conjecture that d_{reg} behaves asymptotically as $d_{\text{reg}} \sim c\frac{(tm)^2}{n-tm}$, where c is a constant close to $\frac{1}{4}$. These lead to a new algorithm that distinguishes codes with a rate in the range $[2/3, 1]$. Its complexity interpolates between polynomial-time (square–distinguishable Goppa codes) and super-exponential in the error-correcting capability of the code for constant rates.

The syzygy distinguisher [43] includes and extends previous results. It refines the algebraic modeling from CMT and conducts a more precise analysis of the syzygies occurring during a Gröbner computation. The dimension of these syzygies are related to so-called Betti numbers that depend on the structure of the code considered. These allow the author to present a new distinguisher that is asymptotically independent of the rate. Its complexity is bounded from above by

$$\kappa = q^{\left(\omega\frac{R^2}{1-R}+o(1)\right)\frac{(\log_q \log_q(n))^3}{(\log_q(n))^2}n},$$

where R is the rate of the dual code $R = mt/n$, and ω is the linear algebra exponent. The algorithm is not polynomial-time, but remains sub-exponential in the error-correcting capacity.

4 A Transformer-Based Algorithm for Code Distinguishing

In this section, we introduce a novel and natural method for code distinguishing based on deep learning. The motivation behind this approach is that a deep learning model, trained to classify samples from different families of codes, can potentially identify patterns revealed by a public generator matrix. Unlike classical approaches that rely on predefined heuristics or algebraic properties, a deep learning model can adaptively discover hidden structural differences between code families if any.

4.1 Deep Distinguisher

Let $\mathscr{F} \in \{\mathscr{G}, \mathscr{A}, \mathscr{M}, \mathscr{Q} \cap \mathscr{M}\}$ denote the code family of interest (Goppa, alternant, MDPC, and QC-MDPC codes), at a high level, we aim to learn a parametric classifier

$$D_{\boldsymbol{\theta}} : \mathbb{F}_q^{k\times n} \longrightarrow [0,1],$$

where $D_{\boldsymbol{\theta}}$ is a function parameterized by $\boldsymbol{\theta} \in \mathbb{R}^{d_{\text{model}}}$ and $D_{\boldsymbol{\theta}}(\mathbf{G})$ estimates the probability that the public generator matrix $\mathbf{G}$ spans a code in the target family $\mathscr{F}$. During training, we sample labeled pairs $\left(\mathbf{G}^{(i)}, y^{(i)}\right)$ with

$$y^{(i)} = \begin{cases} 1, & \text{if } \mathbf{G}^{(i)} \text{ generates a code in } \mathscr{F}, \\ 0, & \text{otherwise,} \end{cases}$$

and minimize the empirical cross-entropy loss

$$\mathcal{L}(\boldsymbol{\theta}) = -\frac{1}{N}\log\Big[\prod_{i=1}^{N} D_{\boldsymbol{\theta}}(\mathbf{G}^{(i)})^{y^{(i)}}\big(1 - D_{\boldsymbol{\theta}}(\mathbf{G}^{(i)})\big)^{1-y^{(i)}}\Big].$$

At inference time, we apply a threshold $\tau \in (0, 1)$ - usually $\frac{1}{2}$ - to obtain a binary decision rule:

$$\widehat{b}(\mathbf{G}_{\text{test}}) = \begin{cases} 1, & D_{\boldsymbol{\theta}}(\mathbf{G}_{\text{test}}) \geq \tau, \\ 0, & D_{\boldsymbol{\theta}}(\mathbf{G}_{\text{test}}) < \tau, \end{cases}$$

Model Architecture. Similarly to [46], our approach leverages an encoder-only Transformer model, which has demonstrated strong performance compared to other models we tried, namely, logistic regression, fully connected neural nets (FCN) and convolutional networks. Fully connected networks of the same size as our model do achieve some good accuracies after some period of training as shown in Table 8 in the appendix, but we find that they are very slow at learning and rarely find the best solution that yields 100% accuracy.

The model processes an input sequence of vectors through an embedding layer, followed by four layers consisting of *self-attention* and *feed-forward networks*. Each vector in the sequence has an embedding dimension of $d_{\text{emb}} = 1024$.

In the self-attention mechanism, the model employs multi-head attention mechanism with $h = 4$ heads, where each head operates on a subspace of dimension $d_{\text{head}} = \frac{d_{\text{emb}}}{h} = 256$. The input vectors are first projected into these lower-dimensional subspaces, processed independently by each head, and then recombined to restore the original embedding dimension.

The feed-forward network (FFN) in each block consists of two linear transformations with a *GELU* [27] non-linearity in between. It first expands the dimension to $4 \times d_{\text{emb}} = 4096$ using a fully connected layer, applies the activation function, and then projects the vectors back to the original embedding dimension d_{emb}.

After processing through these layers, the final sequence representation is obtained via *max-pooling* over the sequence length. The resulting pooled vector is then linearly projected into a scalar, which serves as the model's *logit* and is used in the loss function for optimization. We use Adam optimizer [30] with warmup ≈ 1000 steps and set the learning rate to $lr = 10^{-5}$ and weight decay to $\omega = 10^{-3}$. We use a binary cross-entropy loss function to optimize the model during training which is basically maximizing the likelihood of the training batches. To evaluate the model's performance, we measure accuracy and precision on a separate balanced test set.

Data Representation. This is a crucial factor in achieving our distinguishing results. In fact, given that the input is a standard form matrix over a finite field, multiple encoding strategies are possible, including a flat token stream, 2-D patches (Table 6), and column-sequence encodings, as explained in Appendix

C. Among these, the row-sequence strategy is the most effective: To reflect that **G** forms a row basis of a linear code, we treat the matrix as a sequence of row vectors. Each row is first cast into a numeric vector by lifting the finite field entries to $\mathbb{R}$ using the encoding guidelines described below, then linearly projected into the Transformer's embedding space. We add an absolute positional encoding on the sequence level.

When the base field is not $\mathbb{F}_2$, we encode the field elements differently based on the value of q. If q is prime, we use angular embedding as in [46], which doubles the dimension of the rows. Otherwise, if q is a prime power, we first represent the elements as vectors of polynomial coefficients, then apply the appropriate encoding based on the prime base field.

Example: The field $\mathbb{F}_9$ can be constructed as an extension of the base field $\mathbb{F}_3$ using the irreducible polynomial $x^2 + 1$. Let z be one of its roots. $\mathbb{F}_9$ elements are expressed as $a + bz$ with $a, b \in \mathbb{F}_3$. Therefore, we represent these elements as vectors (a, b). Now to encode $\mathbb{F}_3$ elements, we use angular embedding, resulting in a 4 dimensional vector $(\cos(2\pi\frac{a}{3}), \sin(2\pi\frac{a}{3}), \cos(2\pi i\frac{b}{3}), \sin(2\pi i\frac{b}{3})) \in \mathbb{R}^4$.

4.2 Datasets

We consider Goppa and Alternant codes with a fixed code length n. For a given set of parameters—extension degree m and degree $t \in \mathbb{N}$—we generate a dataset $\mathcal{D}_{\mathscr{F}}$ uniformly from the family $\mathscr{F}$ of codes, retaining only the codes of rank $k = n - mt$. Each generator matrix is computed in standard form. Additionally, we generate a dataset $\mathcal{D}_{\mathscr{R}}$ by uniformly sampling random linear codes with the same parameters and size, following the same procedure. We define $\mathcal{D} = \mathcal{D}_{\mathscr{F}} \cup \mathcal{D}_{\mathscr{R}}$, and use the notation $\mathcal{D}_{q,n,m,t}$ to explicitly specify the parameters when needed. It is important to note that $\mathscr{F} \subset \mathscr{R}$, meaning that, when generating the dataset for random linear codes, there is a non-zero probability that some samples might belong to $\mathscr{F}$ codes (e.g., Goppa or alternant codes). However, this probability is negligible due to the structure of the family $\mathscr{F}$ and the comparatively vast size of $\mathscr{R}$. As a result, its impact on the dataset is statistically insignificant for our analysis.

5 Experiments and Results

In this part, we present the experimental results of the `DeepDistinguisher` on alternant/Goppa codes (introduced in Sect. 3.3) and MDPC/QC-MDPC codes (Sect. 3.4). In the former case, we follow the methodology introduced in [43] to derive the parameters q, t, m and n (the code dimension is computed as $k = n - mt$). The approach is as follows:

- First, we fix the field size q and the extension degree m. We set the length as $n = q^m$ (full support) and find the largest t for which the code can be distinguished.

- Once such t is identified, we fix its value as well as the corresponding q and m. We then search for the smallest value of n that is still distinguishable.

Our experimental results for `DeepDistinguisher` are presented in two parts. In Sect. 5.1, we analyze a specific set of parameters introduced in [13,43]. The code considered is relatively small (length at most 64). However, this allows explicit comparison of different distinguishers on a common benchmark. In Sect. 5.2, we present more extensive results; pushing the practical experiments to code of length up to 1024. We conclude this part by providing experimental results for the codes underlying `BIKE`; demonstrating the flexibility of the `DeepDistinguisher` distinguisher (Sect. 5.3).

5.1 Comparing Distinguishers for Goppa on a Small Benchmark

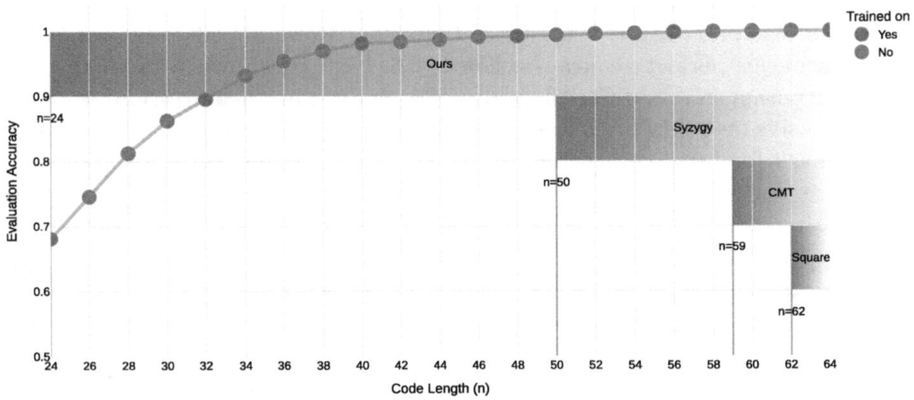

Fig. 1. Model accuracy as a function of code length. The model is trained on Binary Goppa Codes with extension degree $m = 6$ and irreducible polynomials of degree $t = 3$ as in [13,43]. The line and scatter points indicate the evaluation accuracy of our model on each tested value of code length. The scatter color indicates the range where the model was trained ($n = 24 + 8k$ for $k = 0, 1, ..$) showing that the model generalizes well to unseen input shapes. For attacks from the literature, we show the smallest code length reported in their respective papers, as no accuracy measures were provided.

In [13,43], the authors presented experimental results for their distinguishers on a Binary Goppa code with $q = 2, m = 6$ and $t = 3$. The maximal length is $n = 64$, the FGOPT distinguisher will be able to distinguish up to $n_{\text{square}} = 62$. The CMT distinguisher [13] reported $n_{\text{CMT}} = 59$ and [43] brings down to $n_{\text{syzygy}} = 50$. Below this length, the conditions for distinguishability from [43] are not verified anymore.

As highlighted in Figs. 1 and 2, our distinguisher works for any code length tested, with nearly 100% accuracy for most values of $n \geq 40$. We set a lower bound on the values of n such that the rate is no less than 0.20, which, for

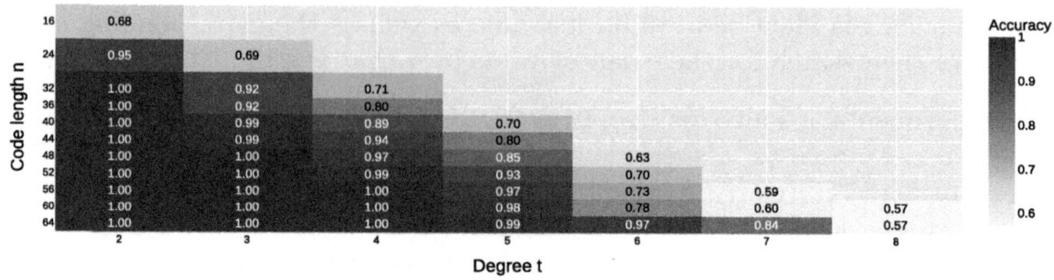

Fig. 2. Heatmap of the classification accuracy on test sets for $q = 2, m = 6$ as a function of code length n and degree parameter t. In this experiment, one model is trained per value of t only. Meaning the model is trained on codes with varying lengths n, allowing the model to interpolate well to unseen code lengths.

instance, corresponds to $n > 22$ when $t = 3$. The accuracy tends to drop for very small code rates.

In this case of $q = 2, m = 6$, our distinguisher works for all values of $t \in [\![2 : 9]\!]$, and achieves perfect accuracy when $t \leq 6$. Figure 2 shows a heatmap of our model's accuracy across different values of n and t. This visualization provides a comprehensive overview of how accuracy varies with these parameters, serving as a benchmark for further investigations and comparisons with other approaches and future works.

Inference Complexity. Since we are using a standard model size throughout our work, we can give an estimate of the time complexity of our distinguisher. In fact, the complexity of this distinguisher is determined by its inference time, which corresponds to performing a forward pass through the trained model times the number of calls to the model which is usually once. This cost is proportional to the model size (with at most $\leq 50M$ parameters) and scales polynomially with the input parameters k, n. In practice, calling our model takes about 10 milliseconds (ms) on CPU (or $100ms$ in one CPU thread) and less than $\approx 1ms$ on a GPU. While training requires several hours, it is a one-time, offline process whose cost will be amortized.

5.2 Distinguishing Goppa and Alternant Codes

Goppa codes demonstrate distinguishability across a range of parameters with some specific configurations that achieve perfect accuracy. Binary codes of length $n = 128$ and extension degree $m = 7$ can be distinguished up to polynomial degree $t = 8$, with 100% accuracy for $t \leq 4$ as shown in Table 2. For larger codes such as $n = 512, m = 9$, the model - of the same size as the 128-model - distinguishes codes up to $t = 4$. In general, we observe that the accuracy of the model is lower as the degree of the Goppa polynomial t and the extension degree m increase. Experiments show that alternant codes are harder to distinguish from random codes, achieving accuracy better than random only when $t \leq 3$, for codes of length $n = 64$ and extension degree $m = 6$, as demonstrated in Table 1.

Table 1. Distinguishing accuracy for Goppa/alternant codes with $n = 64$. In this experiment, for each parameter tuple (q, n, m, t), the model is trained on a dataset $\mathcal{D}_{q,n,m,t}$ of total size ≤ 40 million samples and evaluated on 10 k unseen samples. We use a batch size $b = 512$; the number of training steps (listed below) lets the reader compute the effective training-data budget ($\min\{40\,m, \text{steps} \times \text{batch size}\}$) and the number of epochs (steps $\times$ batch size $/40\,m$).

Code	(q, m)	**Degree** (t)	**Rate** (R)	**Accuracy (%)**	**Training Steps**
Goppa	(2,6)	2	0.81	99.12	1K
		3	0.72	98.88	8.5K
		4	0.63	98.52	22K
		5	0.53	98.24	48.5K
		6	0.44	96.68	243K
		7	0.34	84.60	848.5K
		8	0.25	57.42	90K
		9	0.16	75.92	296.5K
	(3,4)	2	0.88	98.25	9.8K
		3	0.81	98.02	82K
		4	0.75	90.34	154.2K
		5	0.69	54.71	113.8K
		6	0.63	52.52	44.8K
Alternant	(2,6)	2	0.81	57.82	15.6K
		3	0.72	53.06	14.4K
		4	0.63	51.80	18.8K

Goppa Codes with $q = 3, m = 4, n = 64$. When considering *ternary* Goppa codes with $m = 4$, we observe that the distinguishing task is more challenging compared to the binary case. Nevertheless, our distinguisher remains effective up to degree $t = 6$ (corresponding to a code rate of $R = 0.63$) as shown in Table 1. As the degree increases, accuracy drops considerably. For $t = 4$, the accuracy decreases to 90.34%, and for $t = 5$, it drops sharply to 54.71%, indicating that distinguishing becomes significantly harder.

Goppa Codes with $q = 2, m = 7$. We train the distinguisher on a 12M dataset of binary codes of extension degree $m = 7$ while varying the code lengths and degrees t. But first, we train on maximal code length $n = 128$ to figure out the highest distinguishable value of polynomial degree t. As illustrated in Table 2, the model perfectly distinguishes codes up to $t = 4$ which corresponds to a code rate of $R = 0.78$; a rate that is not square-distinguishable due to the condition in Equation (1). The accuracy starts to drop beyond that value of t but still does better than random. The highest degree t we can distinguish is $t = 8$ with a rate of $R = 0.56$ but only with a accuracy 0.52%. This rate is beyond the CMT [13] distinguishable range ($R \geq 2/3$). More details are provided in Table 2.

Next, we systematically vary the code length for each degree t to identify the point at which our distinguisher fails. Figure 3 presents a heatmap of accuracies for different pairs (n, t), illustrating the performance across various code lengths and degrees. These results serve as complementary benchmarks to the $m = 6$ case, where performance appears to be saturated, providing additional insights into our distinguisher's behavior. Notably, no public implementations of classical attacks are available for direct comparison, making our results a standalone reference for this setting.

Table 2. Distinguishing Results for Binary Goppa Codes with $n = 128$, $m = 7$. Balanced dataset $\mathcal{D}[q, n, m, t]$ of total size 40 million samples and evaluated on $10k$ unseen samples. We also show the time complexity of the classical attacks [13] $\mathbb{C}_{CMT}^{\text{sparse}} = 3\left(\binom{tm}{2} - k + 1\right)\left(\binom{\binom{tm}{2}+d_{\text{reg}}-1}{d_{\text{reg}}}\right)^2$. Our attack's cost is the inference cost which is less than 100 milliseconds on one CPU core for most experiments.

Goppa Degree (t)	**Rate (R)**	**Accuracy (%)**	**Training Steps**	$\mathbb{C}_{CMT}$
2	0.89	98.14	2K	–
3	0.84	99.48	91K	2^{24}
4	0.78	98.88	36K	2^{41}
5	0.73	64.52	579K	2^{65}
6	0.67	57.00	115K	2^{97}
7	0.62	54.42	411K	✗ 2^{139}
8	0.56	52.38	20K	✗ 2^{193}
9–17	0.51–0.07	≤ 51	600K	✗ $> 2^{264}$

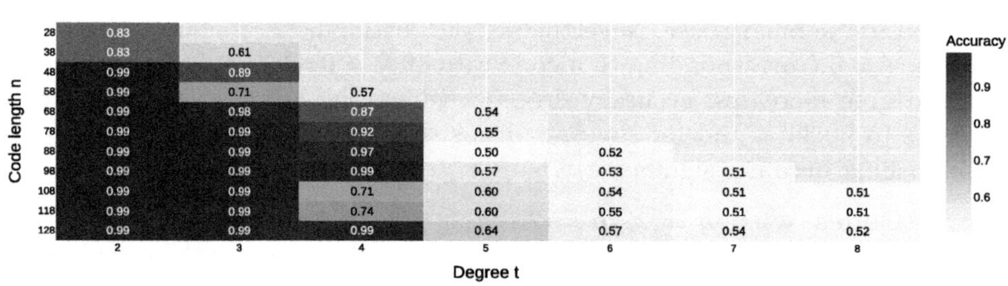

Fig. 3. Heatmap of model accuracy for classifying Goppa codes vs random codes $q = 2, m = 7$ as a function of code length n and degree parameter t.

Goppa Codes $n = 256$. To test the limits of our model on larger codes, we generate datasets of $8M$ samples ($4M$ for each class) for codes of length 256. We train the model of the same size on these datasets and report the accuracies obtained in Table 3. We notice the performance degrading fast with the degree t and only do better than random for $t \leq 5$. Further efforts and resources in terms of dataset generation, model size, and training compute are needed to figure out the scaling laws of our approach.

Table 3. Classification Accuracy (%) on balanced $10k$ eval datasets of binary irreducible Goppa codes of length $n = 256$. The model used is the same throughout the paper: a tokenizer-free encoder only transformer with 4 layers and $d = 1024$ embedding dimension.

Degree (t)	2	3	4	5	6
$n = 256, m = 8$	98.06	98.38	60.36	54.74	51.66

A notable pattern during training as shown in Fig. 4, is that the loss often almost stagnates for an extended period without the gradients vanishing before abruptly decreasing at a specific training step, denoted as $T_{q,m,t}$. This drop in loss tends to consistently occur much later for larger values of t, though the exact nature of the dependency between t and $T_{q,m,t}$ remains unclear. This raises a question about the applicability of gradient-based optimization on such tasks.

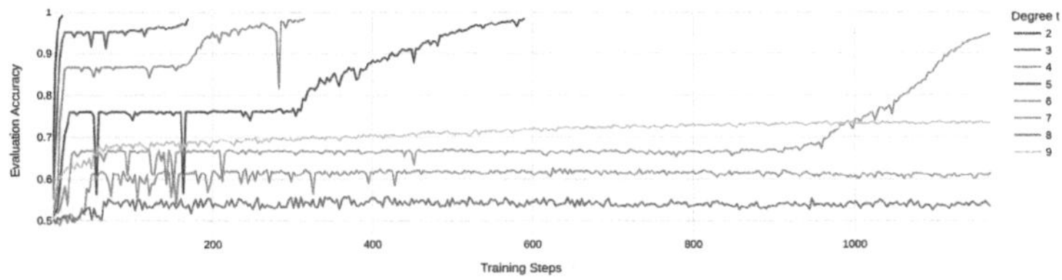

Fig. 4. Evolution of evaluation accuracy during training of the classifier over Goppa codes vs random codes with parameters $n = 64, q = 2, m = 6$. The color represents different values of the polynomial degree t.

Larger Codes with Code Puncturing. We applied the strategy discussed in Appendix B to evaluate the model trained on binary Goppa codes with $m = 7, n = 128$ on codes of parameters $n = 1024, m = 10, t = 2$ using algorithm 2 with 1000 trials. This experiment yields a 70% accuracy suggesting that there are probably unknown relationships between families of binary Goppa codes over different field extensions.

5.3 Distinguishing MDPC and QC-MDPC Codes

We adopt the same framework outlined in BIKE [2]. Specifically, we take $\ell = 2, n = \ell r$, implying that QC-MDPC code has rate $\frac{1}{2}$ and the corresponding parity-check matrix is composed of two circulant blocks. We train the model on codes of length $n = 158$ and vary the row weight w. Taking a block size $r = 79$ prime and odd values of $w/2$ ensures that the circulants are invertible in $\mathbb{F}_q$, which explains the values of w considered in Table 4. This table shows that we can distinguish MDPC codes up to $w = 14$ while for QC-MDPC, we could only distinguish codes with row weight $w = 6$.

This outcome is somewhat surprising, as one might expect the additional structure introduced in the Quasi-Cyclic case to make classification easier rather than harder. However, the circulant structure seems to introduce constraints that makes it more challenging for the model to extract distinguishing features. An avenue of improvement is to elaborate an effective representation of this structure in a way that helps the learning of the model.

Table 4. Maximum evaluation accuracy on Moderate-Density Parity-Check (MDPC) codes versus Quasi-Cyclic MDPC codes on the distinguishing task. The number of training steps needed to achieve these accuracies is also reported.

Code length & dim (n, r)	Code	Row weight (w)	Eval Accuracy	Train. Steps
158, 79	MDPC	10	97.14	445K
		11	74.36	265K
		12	65.39	200K
		13	58.28	145K
		14	54.90	220K
		16	51.73	335K
		18	51.05	220K
	QC-MDPC	6	98.02	78K
		10	51.31	738K
		14	51.36	1.08M
		18	51.21	905K

6 Hidden Goppa Code Problem

We introduce a new problem related to Goppa codes stronger than distinguishing but weaker than the key-recovery problem.

*Problem 4 (Hidden Goppa Code (*HGC*) problem).* Given a parameter $\zeta > 0$, and matrix $\widetilde{\mathbf{G}} \in \mathcal{M}_{k\times n}(\mathbb{F}_q \cup \{*\})$ with at most ζ placeholder symbols $*$, the HGC problem asks to find – if it exists – a completion $\widehat{\mathbf{G}} \in \mathcal{M}_{k\times n}(\mathbb{F}_q)$ of $\widetilde{\mathbf{G}}$ (i.e. obtained by replacing all placeholder symbols $*$ by field elements) such that $\widehat{\mathbf{G}}$ is a valid generator matrix for a Goppa code $\mathcal{G}(\boldsymbol{\alpha}, g)$ with $\boldsymbol{\alpha} \in \mathbb{F}_{q^m}^n$ a support and $g(x) \in \mathbb{F}_{q^m}[x]$ a Goppa polynomial of degree t.

This problem is trivial in the case of random linear codes, since any solution makes a valid code. However, for Goppa codes, the structure imposed by the algebraic properties of the code constrains the space of possible solutions. This structure is defined by the Goppa polynomial and the support set, which are not directly visible in the generator matrix. Therefore, any solution to the HGC problem must implicitly respect these hidden parameters, making it a non-trivial task.

It is known that revealing only $tm+1$ Goppa support points suffices to recover the McEliece secret key in polynomial time [31]. Thus, although HGC does not explicitly output any secret-key data, extracting a trained model's implicit knowledge—via interpretability or inversion techniques—could yield exactly the partial hints that classical algebraic attacks [21,22] lift to a complete key-recovery breach.

`DeepRecover`: Using the same transformer architecture as for the `DeepDistinguisher` with several hidden elements ranging between $\zeta = 1$ and $\zeta = 80$ out of $mt(n - mt)$ entries (e.g. 624 for $m = 6, t = 2, n = 64$), we were able to successfully train the model on this task achieving a component-wise accuracy as high as 80% for binary [64-52]-Goppa codes over extension degree $m = 6$ as shown in Table 5.

We find that larger values of ζ accelerate the model training but converge to a less optimal solution. Further investigations are required to understand better the limits of the feasibility of this problem. It is evident that there is a theoretical upper bound of ζ beyond which the number of possible solutions explodes and we think that our model works partially because, for the values we chose of ζ, the solution is either unique or there are not many solutions, allowing the model to recover the solution that we used to generate the given sample (generate a Goppa code, hide some entries, then ask the model to recover that exact solution instead of recovering any valid solution). It's worth noting that thanks to our `DeepDistinguisher`, we could also train the `DeepRecover` model to recover any valid solution since we can test in a gradient-friendly way whether a matrix is Goppa or not with high accuracy.

Table 5. Best component-wise accuracy for each polynomial degree t after training on Goppa codes with parameters $q = 2, n = 64, m = 6$. An accuracy of 50% is as good as random guessing.

Degree (t)	**Best Accuracy**
2	0.80
3	0.76
4	0.64
5	0.58
6	0.50

7 Conclusion

`DeepDistinguisher` achieves near-perfect classification on small parameters, however, its decisions cannot be explained by any linear function of the generator-matrix entries—indeed, training a logistic-regression (which would be able to find any affine hyperplane separating Goppa codes from non-Goppa codes) baseline recovers only the total-Hamming-weight test we described in Appendix A, which fails to approach 100 % accuracy and degrades rapidly as parameters grow.

Instead, our transformer must be exploiting non-linear correlations among the row-space basis vectors. In the small parameter regime, the algebraic structure of a Goppa generator matrix induces strong, low enough order correlations among its rows that our transformer's attention layers can easily pick up.

As the code rate $k/n = 1 - mt/n$ decreases by increasing t or m, the algebraic degree of the true invariants rises—forcing the model to learn ever more complex multilinear monomials—yet our fixed-size network and finite training set lack the capacity and coverage to generalize over that explosion of possibilities. Consequently, beyond a certain threshold in mt, `DeepDistinguisher`'s accuracy collapses to chance, mirroring the known intractability of distinguishing large-parameter Goppa codes from random codes.

Future explainability work should apply attention-map visualization and gradient-based saliency on the embeddings of Goppa code matrices to pinpoint exactly which combinations of row-interaction features carry the distinguishing signal.

This work is a first step in applying machine learning to code-based cryptography, opening up new possibilities for research. Future work could focus on improving these models, trying to distill a classical approach or algorithm that our model may be approximating, and figuring out the recurring behavior of the gradient descent when training on mathematical problems.

Appendices

A A Simple Statistical Hamming Weight Distinguisher

In this section, we present a simple statistical distinguisher based on an experimental observation about the distribution of generator matrices of Goppa codes. Computing the total Hamming weight of these matrices allows us to distinguish Goppa codes from *uniform* random codes, although with weaker performance compared to other methods.

We now fix the parameters under consideration, namely the code length n, extension degree m, Goppa degree t, and the dimension $k = n - mt$, and we consider random codes with the same dimension. Given a generator matrix $\mathbf{G} \in \mathcal{M}_{k \times n}(\mathbb{F}_q)$ from a code family $\mathscr{F} \in \{\mathscr{G}, \mathscr{R}\}$ (for Goppa versus random), we define its total Hamming weight as

$$w_H(\mathbf{G}) = \sum_{i=1}^{k} w_H(\mathbf{g}_i),$$

where $\mathbf{g}_i$ is the i-th row of $\mathbf{G}$. The variable $w_H(\mathbf{G})|_{\mathscr{F}}$ is a random variable that takes discrete values, with the distribution denoted as $p_{\mathscr{F}}$. To check for any differences in the behavior of $w_H(\mathbf{G})|_{\mathscr{F}}$ between the two distributions, we empirically estimate the total variation distance between $f_{\mathscr{G}}$ and $f_{\mathscr{R}}$ using $1M$ samples:

$$D_{TV}(\hat{f}_{\mathscr{G}}, \hat{f}_{\mathscr{R}}) = \frac{1}{2} \sum_{x \in \mathcal{X}} |\hat{f}_{\mathscr{G}}(x) - \hat{f}_{\mathscr{R}}(x)|.$$

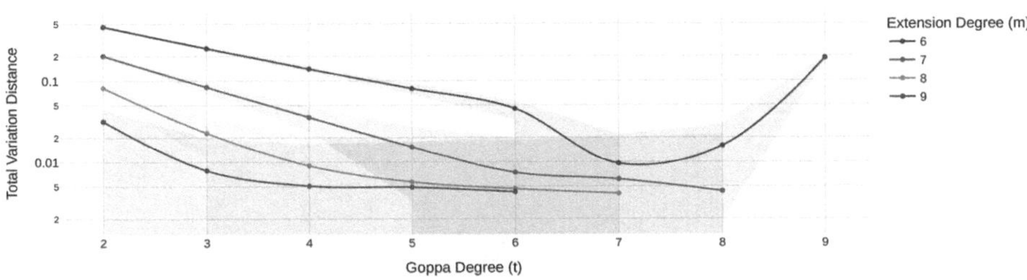

Fig. 5. Total variation distance of empirical distributions $p_{\mathscr{G}}$ (Goppa) and $p_{\mathscr{R}}$ (Random) of the total Hamming weight metric for binary codes of length $n = 64$ with varying extension degree m and polynomial degree t. The distance axis is in log scale showing the distance exponentially converging to 0. The plateauing might be because of the estimation error being high. 1M samples were used for probability estimation.

The empirical distributions $\hat{f}_{\mathscr{G}}$ and $\hat{f}_{\mathscr{R}}$ are shown as histogram plots in the appendix Fig. 6 for codes of length $n = 64$ and extension degree $m = 6$. We can see that the distributions don't match especially for small values of t and exceptionally for $t = 9$ when $n = 64$ and $m = 6$ which is not the case for larger codes. We show this by also varying the extension degree and plotting the empirical TV distance in Fig. 5 as a function of m and t. The distance is significant for small values of t but exponentially decreases.

To devise a statistical distinguisher, we can employ a hypothesis test based on the likelihood ratio. In the random case, the distribution of the total Hamming weight is known; a binomial distribution since it's a sum of independent Bernoulli variables with $p_{\mathscr{R}} = 0.5, N_{\mathscr{R}} = mt(n - mt)$ (only codes in standard form are considered). For the Goppa case, we make an assumption that the distribution is also a binomial and empirically estimate $\hat{p}_{\mathscr{G}}$ and $\hat{N}_{\mathscr{G}}$ using some training data.

Given a sample $x = w_H(\mathbf{G})$, we compute the likelihood ratio:

$$\log \Lambda(x) = \log \frac{\binom{\hat{N}_{\mathscr{G}}}{x}}{\binom{N_{\mathscr{R}}}{x}} + x \log \frac{\hat{p}_{\mathscr{G}}}{p_{\mathscr{R}}} + \log \frac{(1 - \hat{p}_{\mathscr{G}})^{\hat{N}_{\mathscr{G}} - x}}{(1 - p_{\mathscr{R}})^{N_{\mathscr{R}} - x}}$$

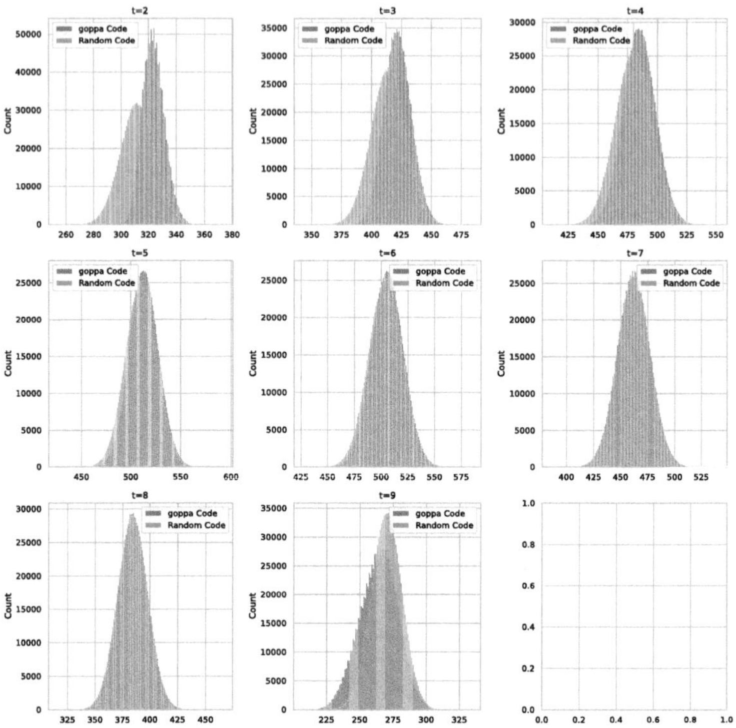

Fig. 6. Histograms of the total Hamming weight of the generator matrix of Goppa codes versus random linear codes: $w_{\mathscr{F}}(\mathbf{G}) = \sum_{i=1}^{k} w_H(g_i)$ for binary codes with parameters $n = 64, m = 6$ while varying polynomial degree t.

The distinguisher can therefore be expressed as follows:

$$\mathscr{D}(\mathbf{G}) = \mathbb{1}_{\{\log \Lambda(x) > \tau\}}(w_H(\mathbf{G}))$$

Using this simple distinguisher with $\tau = 0$, we can achieve a test accuracy of 73% on a balanced 1M dataset with the parameters of the first graph ($t = 2, n = 64, m = 6$) of Figure 6 and 62% accuracy on $t = 3$ and only 57% for $t = 4$.

It's worth noting that by changing the sampling distribution over random linear codes from uniformly random to $\mathcal{B}(p)^{k \times (n-k)}$ (independent Bernoulli entries) for p matching the experimental value for Goppa codes of the same parameters, this distinguisher will degrade.

B Out-of-Distribution Evaluation: Punctured Codes

To evaluate the distinguisher on instances of larger code lengths, we puncture the code by truncating the public generator matrix to fit into the training shape and assess the model on the resulting code. Initially, this approach does not yield satisfactory results when applied just once. However, by repeatedly truncating

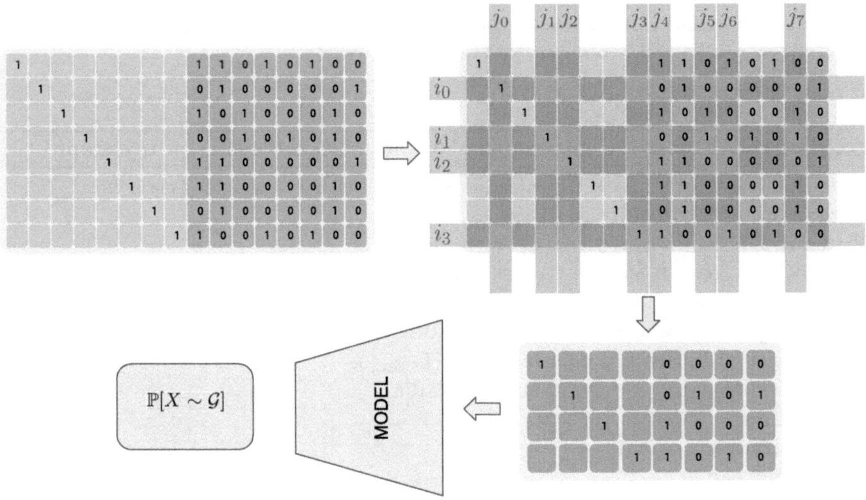

Fig. 7. To assess an [8, 4]-model (trained on codes of length $n = 8$ and dimension 4) on a [16, 8]-code, we puncture the input code by sampling $i_0 = j_0, \ldots, i_3 = j_3$ and $j_4, \ldots, j_7$ randomly to create a new [8, 4]-code in standard form.

the original matrix through subsampling of rows and columns, and evaluating the model on each of these subsampled matrices, we can improve performance. By aggregating the results, we determine an optimal decision threshold based on the number of positive classifications or vote counts on a validation set.

Algorithm 1. Sample Punctured SubCode

---

procedure SamplePuncturedSubCode($\mathbf{G}$)
  Input: Generator matrix $\mathbf{G} = \left(\mathbf{I}_{k_0} \mid \mathbf{A}\right) \in \mathbb{F}_q^{k_0 \times n_0}$
  Output: Punctured subcode matrix $\mathbf{G}[\mathcal{I}, \mathcal{J}]$
  Sample valid (n, k) such that $k \leq k_0$ and $n - k \leq n_0 - k_0$
  Sample k row indices $\mathcal{I}$ from $[\![0; k_0 - 1]\!]$ without replacement.
  Sample $n - k$ column indices $\mathcal{J}'$ from $[\![k_0; n_0 - 1]\!]$
  Form the set of column indices $\mathcal{J} = \mathcal{J}' \cup \mathcal{I}$
  return submatrix $\mathbf{G}[\mathcal{I}, \mathcal{J}]$
end procedure

More formally, given $\mathbf{G} = \left(\mathbf{I}_{k_0}\ \mathbf{A}\right) \in \mathbb{F}_q^{k_0 \times n_0}$ a standard form generator matrix of a linear code $\mathcal{C} \in \mathscr{F}$, to evaluate the model on punctured subcodes of $\mathcal{C}$, we first sample one of the training code parameters (k, n) such that $k \leq k_0$ and $n - k \leq n_0 - k_0$. Then sample k row indices $\mathcal{I}$ and $n - k$ column indices $\mathcal{J}'$ from the matrix $\mathbf{A}$ in addition to the k columns forming the identity matrix of shape k: $\mathcal{J} = \mathcal{J}' \cup \mathcal{I}$. This is important because during training, the model only sees standard form matrices so we don't expect it to generalize to unseen input in those first columns. Therefore, the identity matrix acts as a positional encoding of the sequence. Finally, we assess the model on $\mathbf{G}[\mathcal{I}, \mathcal{J}]$.

Algorithm 2. Evaluate distinguisher on larger codes using puncturing.

Require: Generator matrix $\mathbf{G} = \left(\mathbf{I}_{k_0} \mid \mathbf{A}\right) \in \mathbb{F}_q^{k_0 \times n_0}$, number of trials m
Ensure: Aggregated result of model evaluations

```
function EvaluateModel(G, k0, n0, m)
    Initialize result_sum ← 0
    for i = 1 to m do
        G_punc ← SamplePuncturedSubCode(G, k0, n0)
        result ← EvaluateDistinguisher(G_punc)
        result_sum ← result_sum + result
    end for
    return result_sum
end function
```

C Possible Data Representations

Among the key questions raised during the experiments is how to best represent numerically the input matrices $\mathbf{G}$ as sequences of numerical values/vectors which is the standard input to a transformer.

Flat Token Stream. A naïve language-model baseline flattens the generator matrix G row by row, inserting a special end-of-row separator after each row. Every finite-field symbol is then treated as a categorical token and embedded via a randomly-initialised lookup table. Although straightforward, this representation is inefficient: the resulting sequence length is kn (or $k(n-k)$ if the identity block of a systematic form is omitted), and the attention cost grows quadratically with that length. Moreover, the model must learn the algebraic relationships between field elements entirely from data, because none of that structure is provided *a priori*.

2-D patches in order to reduce the number of tokens, one can think of fragmenting the matrix $\mathbf{G}$ into patches and assign a token id to each distinct patch. The patch size is quantified by *height* h × *width* w. A large patch size would result in a shorter sequence but with a large vocabulary since patches become more distinct from each other. Some results are reported in Table 6.

A **column-sequence** representation is certainly feasible and experimented with; however, our experiments show that the row-sequence approach delivers the strongest results. The next-best option is a patch-embedding scheme with patch height $h = 1$, which essentially preserves the row-wise structure and therefore benefits from a similar inductive bias.

Table 6. Performance of the `DeepDistinguisher` distinguisher on classifying Goppa code generator matrices over $\mathbb{F}_q$ (here $q = 2$) when tokenizing the inputs by 2D patches, showing evaluation accuracy, recall, and specificity for different polynomial degrees and tokenization patch sizes. The data parameters are $q = 2, m = 8, n = 128$

Extension degree	Polynomial degree	Tokenization Patch	Eval Accuracy	Eval recall	Eval Specificity
8	2	1×4	0.711	0.771	0.649
		1×8	0.693	0.763	0.619
		4×1	0.601	0.762	0.446
		4×4	0.592	0.620	0.563
		8×1	0.585	0.710	0.458
8	3	1×4	0.529	0.725	0.334
		1×8	0.550	0.694	0.406
		4×1	0.534	0.545	0.524
		4×4	0.512	0.473	0.551
		8×1	0.529	0.640	0.417
8	4	1×4	0.530	0.323	0.732
		1×8	0.521	0.630	0.407
		4×1	0.526	0.608	0.444
		4×4	0.514	0.391	0.638
		8×1	0.516	0.610	0.425

D Implementation details

Datasets are generated using SageMath and saved in files for training. One noticeable artifact that occurs when standardizing non standard form binary codes in SageMath is that the resulting distribution of the generator matrix entries are not uniform due to the algorithm used to swap columns. Plotting the probabilities that an entry is 1 shows that some cells are less likely to be one. This occurs regardless of the code family. One way to avoid this is to simply discard non standard codes meaning we keep only about 29% of the codes. We use a small transformer of size ≈ 50 million trainable parameters with 4 layers and embedding dimension $d = 1024$. Our implementation is using torch and is based on the public implementation of SALSA [49].

E Model Architecture Ablations

We perform a detailed comparison of four neural architectures-Fully-Connected Network (FCN), LeftRight FCN, Attention FCN, and DeepDistinguisher—on binary Goppa codes with parameters $m = 6$, $n = 64$, across polynomial degrees $t \in \{2, 3, 4, 5, 6\}$. All models are matched to roughly 23–28 million parameters to ensure a fair comparison of efficiency and performance.

Table 7. Fixed experimental hyperparameters for $n = 64$

Parameter	**Value**
Model	encoder-only
Dataset	Goppa code dataset ($n = 64$), 6 M samples per class
Batch size (train/val)	512/2000
# training samples	12 000 000
# max epochs	30 or accuracy ≥ 0.99
Eval samples per validation	20 000
Validation interval	every 1000 steps
Optimizer	AdamW with linear warmup
• Learning rate	1×10^{-5}
• Warmup steps	1000
• Weight decay	1×10^{-3}
Gradient clipping norm	5.0
Encoder architecture	4 layers, 4 heads, 1024-d embeddings
Positional timescale	40
Precision	float16

`DeepDistinguisher` consistently achieves the highest evaluation accuracy and recall for every degree t, and does so with markedly fewer training steps than the competing architectures. At lower degrees ($t = 2, 3$), all models achieve high accuracy (≥ 0.965), but `DeepDistinguisher` converges in only 1000 and 24500 steps, respectively—an order of magnitude faster than Attention FCN and two orders faster than FCN variants. As t increases, the performance gap widens: for $t = 4, 5$, `DeepDistinguisher` maintains near-perfect accuracy (0.980–0.984) with moderate training times (133 000–569 500 steps), while the other models suffer substantial drops in recall and overall accuracy. Even at the highest complexity ($t = 6$), `DeepDistinguisher` attains 0.961 accuracy and perfect specificity in under one million steps, whereas the alternatives fall below 0.650 accuracy.

Table 8. Comparison of evaluation accuracy, recall, specificity, minimum training loss, and number of training steps for each model architecture across Goppa polynomial degrees t on data of binary Goppa codes with $m = 6, n = 64$. The considered models here are Fully-Connected Neural Network (FCN), `DeepDistinguisher` which the encoder only transformer, Left Right FCN which is a model that consists of applying an FCN on the left of the input matrix and on the right, operating on both rows and columns of the input matrices. Attention FCN is a custom encoder with self-attention layer and FCN only. Models are parameterized such that they have approximately the same size of 23 − 28 million parameters.

Polynomial degree	Architecture	Eval Accuracy	Eval Recall	Eval Specificity	Train Min Loss	Steps
2	Attention FCN	0.982	0.972	0.992	0.044	11500
2	DeepDistinguisher	**0.990**	0.980	1.000	0.060	1000
2	LeftRight FCN	0.981	0.966	0.996	0.077	65000
2	FCN	0.981	0.966	0.996	0.069	123000
3	Attention FCN	0.980	0.963	0.996	0.060	423000
3	DeepDistinguisher	**0.983**	0.971	0.995	0.054	24500
3	LeftRight FCN	0.971	0.955	0.986	0.057	1109000
3	FCN	0.965	0.934	0.995	0.080	826000
4	Attention FCN	0.865	0.747	0.980	0.281	1226500
4	DeepDistinguisher	**0.980**	0.965	0.995	0.048	569500
4	LeftRight FCN	0.887	0.788	0.988	0.254	1051500
4	FCN	0.866	0.747	0.980	0.229	577500
5	Attention FCN	0.765	0.536	0.988	0.443	1039500
5	DeepDistinguisher	**0.984**	0.973	0.995	0.066	133000
5	LeftRight FCN	0.765	0.538	0.985	0.409	567500
5	FCN	0.688	0.551	0.828	0.281	1149500
6	Attention FCN	0.620	0.454	0.790	0.265	319000
6	DeepDistinguisher	**0.961**	0.922	1.000	0.112	972000
6	LeftRight FCN	0.654	0.401	0.911	0.440	669000
6	FCN	0.543	0.387	0.696	0.419	291500

References

1. Albrecht, M.R., et al.: Classic McEliece: conservative code-based cryptography (2022). https://inria.hal.science/hal-04288769, round 4 submission to the NIST call for postquantum cryptographic primitives
2. Aragon, N., et al.: BIKE: bit flipping key encapsulation (2022)
3. Ba, J.L., Kiros, J., Hinton, G.E.: Layer normalization. arXiv preprint arXiv:1607.06450 (2016)
4. Bardet, M., Faugère, J.C., Salvy, B., Yang, B.Y.: Asymptotic behaviour of the degree of regularity of semi-regular polynomial systems. In: The Effective Methods in Algebraic Geometry Conference – MEGA 2005, pp. 1–14 (2005)
5. Bardet, M., Mora, R., Tillich, J.P.: Polynomial time key-recovery attack on high rate random alternant codes. IEEE Transactions on Information Theory (2023)
6. Berlekamp, E., McEliece, R., van Tilborg, H.: On the inherent intractability of certain coding problems. IEEE Trans. Inf. Theory **24**(3), 384–386 (1978)
7. Bernstein, D.J.: Grover vs. Mceliece. In: Sendrier, N. (ed.) Post-Quantum Cryptography, Third International Workshop, PQCrypto 2010, Darmstadt, Germany,

May 25-28, 2010. Proceedings. Lecture Notes in Computer Science, vol. 6061, pp. 73–80. Springer (2010). https://doi.org/10.1007/978-3-642-12929-2_6
8. Bernstein, D.J., Buchmann, J., Dahmen, E. (eds.): Post-quantum cryptography. Mathematics and Statistics Springer-11649; ZDB-2-SMA, Springer Berlin Heidelberg, Berlin, Heidelberg (2009). http://opac.inria.fr/record=b1128738
9. Buchberger, B.: Bruno Buchberger's PhD thesis 1965: an algorithm for finding the basis elements of the residue class ring of a zero dimensional polynomial ideal. J. Symbolic Comput. **41**(3-4), 475–511 (2006)
10. Buchberger, B., Collins, G.E., Loos, R.G.K., Albrecht, R.: Computer algebra symbolic and algebraic computation. SIGSAM Bull. **16**(4), 5–5 (1982)
11. Chen, L., et al.: Report on post-quantum cryptography. Reasearch report NISTIR 8105, NIST (2003). http://csrc.nist.gov/publications/drafts/nistir-8105/nistir_8105_draft.pdf
12. Courtois, N.T., Finiasz, M., Sendrier, N.: How to achieve a McEliece-based digital signature scheme. In: Boyd, C. (ed.) Advances in Cryptology - ASIACRYPT 2001, 7th International Conference on the Theory and Application of Cryptology and Information Security, Gold Coast, Australia, December 9-13, 2001, Proceedings. Lecture Notes in Computer Science, vol. 2248, pp. 157–174. Springer (2001). https://doi.org/10.1007/3-540-45682-1_10
13. Couvreur, A., Mora, R., Tillich, J.P.: A new approach based on quadratic forms to attack the McEliece cryptosystem. In: International Conference on the Theory and Application of Cryptology and Information Security, pp. 3–38. Springer (2023)
14. Couvreur, A., Otmani, A., Tillich, J.P.: Polynomial time attack on wild McEliece over quadratic extensions. IEEE Trans. Inf. Theory **63**(1), 404–427 (2016)
15. Cox, D.A., Little, J.B., O'Shea, D.: Ideals Varieties and Algorithms. Springer Verlag (2005)
16. Cybenko, G.: Approximation by superpositions of a sigmoidal function. Math. Control Signals Syst. **2**(4), 303–314 (1989)
17. Dallot, L.: Sécurité de protocoles cryptographiques fondés sur les codes correcteurs d'erreurs. (Security of cryptographic protocols based on error correcting codes). Ph.D. thesis, University of Caen Normandy, France (2010). https://tel.archives-ouvertes.fr/tel-01102440
18. Debris-Alazard, T.: Code-based cryptography: Lecture notes. CoRR abs/2304.03541 (2023). https://doi.org/10.48550/ARXIV.2304.03541
19. Faugère, J., Din, M.S.E., Spaenlehauer, P.: On the complexity of the generalized MinRank problem. J. Symb. Comput. **55**, 30–58 (2013). https://doi.org/10.1016/J.JSC.2013.03.004
20. Faugere, J.C., Gauthier-Umana, V., Otmani, A., Perret, L., Tillich, J.P.: A distinguisher for high-rate McEliece cryptosystems. IEEE Trans. Inf. Theory **59**(10), 6830–6844 (2013)
21. Faugère, J., Otmani, A., Perret, L., de Portzamparc, F., Tillich, J.: Structural cryptanalysis of McEliece schemes with compact keys. Des. Codes Cryptogr. **79**(1), 87–112 (2016). https://doi.org/10.1007/S10623-015-0036-Z
22. Faugère, J., Otmani, A., Perret, L., Tillich, J.: Algebraic cryptanalysis of McEliece variants with compact keys. In: Gilbert, H. (ed.) Advances in Cryptology - EUROCRYPT 2010, 29th Annual International Conference on the Theory and Applications of Cryptographic Techniques, Monaco / French Riviera, May 30 - June 3, 2010. Proceedings. Lecture Notes in Computer Science, vol. 6110, pp. 279–298. Springer (2010). https://doi.org/10.1007/978-3-642-13190-5_14

23. Gohr, A.: Improving attacks on round-reduced Speck32/64 using deep learning. In: Boldyreva, A., Micciancio, D. (eds.) Advances in Cryptology - CRYPTO 2019, pp. 150–179. Springer International Publishing, Cham (2019)
24. Goodfellow, I., Bengio, Y., Courville, A.: Deep Learning. MIT Press, Cambridge, MA (2016)
25. Goppa, V.D.: A new class of linear correcting codes. Problemy Peredachi Informatsii **6**(3), 24–30 (1970)
26. Gryak, J., Haralick, R.M., Kahrobaei, D.: Solving the conjugacy decision problem via machine learning. Exp. Math. **29**(1), 66–78 (2020). https://doi.org/10.1080/10586458.2018.1434704
27. Hendrycks, D., Gimpel, K.: Gaussian error linear units (GELUs). arXiv preprint arXiv:1606.08415 (2016)
28. Hornik, K.: Approximation capabilities of multilayer feedforward networks. Neural Netw. **4**(2), 251–257 (1991)
29. Kim, B.D., Vasudevan, V.A., D'Oliveira, R.G., Cohen, A., Stahlbuhk, T., Médard, M.: Cryptanalysis via machine learning based information theoretic metrics. arXiv preprint arXiv:2501.15076 (2025)
30. Kingma, D.P.: Adam: A method for stochastic optimization. arXiv preprint arXiv:1412.6980 (2014)
31. Kirshanova, E., May, A.: Breaking Goppa-based McEliece with hints. Inf. Comput. **293**, 105045 (2023)
32. Li, C., Wenger, E., Allen-Zhu, Z., Charton, F., Lauter, K.: SALSA VERDE: a machine learning attack on learning with errors with sparse small secrets. In: Proceedings of NeurIPS (2023)
33. Li, C.Y., et al.: SALSA PICANTE: a machine learning attack on LWE with binary secrets. In: Proceedings of ACM CCS (2023)
34. MacWilliams, F.J., Sloane, N.J.A.: The theory of error-correcting codes (1977). https://api.semanticscholar.org/CorpusID:118260868
35. McEliece, R.J.: A public-key cryptosystem based on algebraic. Coding Thv **4244**, 114–116 (1978)
36. Miller, E., Sturmfels, B.: Combinatorial Commutative Algebra, Graduate Texts in Mathematics, vol. 227. Springer-Verlag, New York (2005)
37. Misoczki, R., Tillich, J.P., Sendrier, N., Barreto, P.S.: MDPC-McEliece: new McEliece variants from moderate density parity-check codes. In: 2013 IEEE International Symposium on Information Theory, pp. 2069–2073. IEEE (2013)
38. National Institute of Standards and Technology: Module-Lattice-Based Digital Signature Standard. Federal Information Processing Standards Publication 204, U.S. Department of Commerce (2024). https://csrc.nist.gov/pubs/fips/204/final
39. National Institute of Standards and Technology: Module-Lattice-Based Key-Encapsulation Mechanism Standard. Federal Information Processing Standards Publication 203, U.S. Department of Commerce (2024). https://csrc.nist.gov/pubs/fips/203/final
40. National Institute of Standards and Technology: Stateless Hash-Based Digital Signature Standard. Federal Information Processing Standards Publication 205, U.S. Department of Commerce (2024). https://csrc.nist.gov/pubs/fips/205/final
41. National Institute of Standards and Technology (NIST): Post-Quantum Cryptography: Round 4 Submissions. https://csrc.nist.gov/projects/post-quantum-cryptography/round-4-submissions (2024). Accessed 31 Dec 2024
42. Overbeck, R., Sendrier, N.: Code-based cryptography, pp. 95–145. Springer Berlin Heidelberg, Berlin, Heidelberg (2009). https://doi.org/10.1007/978-3-540-88702-7_4

43. Randriambololona, H.: The syzygy distinguisher. In: Fehr, S., Fouque, P.A. (eds.) Advances in Cryptology - EUROCRYPT 2025, pp. 324–354. Springer Nature Switzerland, Cham (2025)
44. Reed, I.S., Solomon, G.: Polynomial codes over certain finite fields. J. Soc. Ind. Appl. Math. **8**(2), 300–304 (1960)
45. Regev, O.: On lattices, learning with errors, random linear codes, and cryptography. J. ACM (JACM) **56**(6), 1–40 (2009)
46. Stevens, S., et al.: SALSA FRESCA: Angular embeddings and pre-training for ml attacks on learning with errors. arXiv preprint arXiv:2402.01082 (2024)
47. Torres, R.C., Sendrier, N.: Analysis of information set decoding for a sub-linear error weight. In: Takagi, T. (ed.) Post-Quantum Cryptography - 7th International Workshop, PQCrypto 2016, Fukuoka, Japan, February 24-26, 2016, Proceedings. Lecture Notes in Computer Science, vol. 9606, pp. 144–161. Springer (2016). https://doi.org/10.1007/978-3-319-29360-8_10
48. Vaswani, A., et al.: Attention is all you need. In: Advances in Neural Information Processing Systems (NIPS), pp. 5998–6008 (2017)
49. Wenger, E., Chen, M., Charton, F., Lauter, K.E.: SALSA: attacking lattice cryptography with transformers. In: Proceedings of NeurIPS (2022)
50. Wenger, E., Saxena, E., Malhou, M., Thieu, E., Lauter, K.: Benchmarking attacks on learning with errors. Cryptology ePrint Archive, Paper 2024/1229 (2024). https://eprint.iacr.org/2024/1229

Practical Attack on All Parameters of the HPPC Signature Scheme

Pierre Briaud[1(✉)], Maxime Bros[2], Ray Perlner[3], and Daniel Smith-Tone[3,4]

[1] Simula UiB, Bergen, Norway
pierre@simula.no
[2] Associate, National Institute of Standards and Technology (NIST), Maryland, USA
maxime.bros@nist.gov
[3] National Institute of Standards and Technology (NIST), Maryland, USA
daniel.smith@nist.gov
[4] University of Louisville, Louisville, KY, USA

Abstract. HPPC is a multivariate signature scheme submitted to the NIST PQC standardization process in response to the recent call for additional signature schemes. We show that, despite some non-standard notational choices in the submission document, HPPC can be viewed as a special case of the well-studied, but broken for all practical parameters, HFE signature scheme. We further show that the HPPC construction introduces additional structure that further weakens the scheme. For instance, the central map has Q-rank 2 independently from the degree D of the central polynomial that is used.

Using these observations, we show that HPPC is weaker against the direct attack than claimed in the submission document and more crucially that all parameter sets can be practically broken using MinRank techniques. For instance, with a very naive implementation, we have been able to recover an equivalent key in approximately 8 min for security level 2, an hour and a half for security level 4, and slightly more than 7 h for security level 5.

1 Introduction

After selecting the first post-quantum standards for encryption and signature schemes, see [1], the National Institute of Standards and Technology (NIST) announced an expansion to their post-quantum cryptography standardization project and released a call for additional signature proposals [19].

The HPPC scheme [25,26] is one of the 10 multivariate submissions to this new call. It is in fact the only one that can be classified as a multivariate "big-field" scheme (other candidates such as SNOVA [29] use field extensions but in different ways or for different purposes). Its signature size is barely the smallest among all candidates, even though the public key is quite large compared to most of the other multivariate proposals. From a security point of view, HPPC was claimed to be as resistant as an HFE scheme [23] with a central polynomial

C. Boura et al. (Eds.): SAC 2025, LNCS 16207, pp. 519–538, 2026.
https://doi.org/10.1007/978-3-032-10536-3_19

of maximal degree. In the HFE case, it has been known for a long time that both the direct attack [10] and rank attacks [17] have a complexity which is essentially an increasing function of the degree of this central polynomial. This relationship, ultimately because the degree of an HFE map gives an upper bound on the Q-rank of its central map, has remained consistent, although rank attacks have progressed significantly at the end of NIST's previous call for encryption and signature schemes [2,28]. Finally, it must be noted that the description of HPPC uses the same tensor representation of quadratic forms as the one employed in the other candidate 3WISE [24], recently broken in [27].

Contributions. Although it is compared to an HFE scheme over $\mathbb{F}_2$ of maximal degree in the submission document, the HPPC scheme is actually constructed from a central polynomial of degree as small as $2^{10} + 1 = 1025$, in all parameter sets. Despite the unusual tensor representation, we show that all these parameter sets can be interpreted to have the structure of HFE over $\mathbb{F}_2$ with the same degree bound 1025. We further show that HPPC keys form an especially structured subclass of HFE keys, having Q-rank equal to 2 rather than 10, as would be expected for generic HFE keys with degree bound 1025.

As a result of this structure, we show that the polynomial system used in the direct attack exhibits degree fall polynomials of degree 3 and cannot be analyzed as a Boolean semi-regular system, as initially claimed. This analysis may be viewed as analogous to the results of [20–22] elucidating connections between properties of the extension field map and degree falls in the direct attack. Even though the study of degree falls in higher degrees seems more complicated, our tests suggest that the HPPC direct system is even easier to solve than a generic quadratic system with the same number of degree falls of degree 3 added.

More importantly, we show that all parameter sets can be practically broken with a key recovery attack based on a rank-2 MinRank problem. Our instance has matrices over $\mathbb{F}_2$ but solutions over $\mathbb{F}_{2^n}$, as in the rank attacks on HFE subsequent to [17], i.e., [6,28]. To solve this instance, we follow the strategy of [2], where an overdefined quadratic system in $n - 1$ variables is obtained from the Support-Minors modeling [4]. This method is slightly more efficient than relying on Kipnis-Shamir [17] or Minors, but the efficiency of our attack is mainly because the MinRank instance is not particularly hard. From the MinRank solutions, we finish the key recovery by solving linear equations. In that respect, the last step is much simpler than the one proposed by [6, §6.3.1] for even-rank HFE in characteristic 2. This is because our MinRank problem does not have the spurious solutions of [6, §6.3.1] (the same linear combinations produce matrices of rank 4 and not 2). For instance, our last step turns out to be much closer to that of [6] for HFE in odd characteristic, see [6, Theorem 9].

Navigation. The article is organized as follows. In Sect. 2, we establish notation for the paper, introduce the HPPC scheme, and discuss the relevant concepts for the attacks we develop. In Sect. 3, we present an analysis of a direct forgery attack on HPPC, proving that the claims of semi-regularity of the HPPC polynomial system are in error while extending the recent line of work on the direct attack in application to big-field multivariate schemes. In Sect. 4, we establish the Q-rank property of HPPC that forms the basis for a rank attack and illustrate how the solution of the MinRank instance can be used to perform a full key recovery. Our solving method based on Support-Minors is described in Sect. 5, where we briefly establish its complexity and present the performance of our implementation.

2 Preliminaries

2.1 Field Extension in HPPC

Let $\mathbb{F}_{2^n}$ be a degree-n extension of $\mathbb{F}_2$. The HPPC scheme constructs this extension explicitly as $\mathbb{F}_{2^n} = \mathbb{F}_2[x]/\langle f(x)\rangle$, where $f \in \mathbb{F}_2[x]$ is an irreducible polynomial of degree n. Let $\phi : \mathbb{F}_2[x]/\langle f(x)\rangle \to \mathbb{F}_2^n$ be the isomorphism that maps a polynomial residue class to its coefficient representation as a column vector, i.e.,

$$\phi : \sum_{i=0}^{n-1} g_i x^i \mapsto \boldsymbol{g} = (g_0, \ldots, g_{n-1})^{\mathsf{T}}.$$

The canonical basis of $\mathbb{F}_2^n$, denoted by $(\boldsymbol{e}_1, \ldots, \boldsymbol{e}_n)$, is such that $\boldsymbol{e}_i = \phi(x^{i-1})$ for all $i \in \{1..n\}$. Finally, let $\boldsymbol{C}_f \in \mathbb{F}_2^{n\times n}$ be the companion matrix of f. By definition, we have

$$\forall A \in \mathbb{F}_2[x]/\langle f(x)\rangle,\ \boldsymbol{C}_f \cdot \phi(A) = \phi(xA),$$

where the notation "$\cdot$" refers to a matrix-vector product.

For convenience, we will refer to elements of the quotient ring $\mathbb{F}_{2^n}[X]/\langle X^{2^n} - X\rangle$ as polynomials throughout this article. A linearized polynomial is a polynomial that induces an $\mathbb{F}_2$-linear map $\mathbb{F}_{2^n} \to \mathbb{F}_{2^n}$, i.e., all its monomials are of the form X^{2^j} for $j \in \{0..n-1\}$. A linearized permutation polynomial is a linearized polynomial that permutes $\mathbb{F}_{2^n}$, or equivalently, whose unique root in $\mathbb{F}_{2^n}$ is zero. The HPPC scheme heavily relies on matrix representations of linearized polynomials, as defined below.

Definition 1. *Let $\ell \in \mathbb{F}_{2^n}[X]/\langle X^{2^n} - X\rangle$ be a linearized polynomial and let ϕ be a fixed $\mathbb{F}_2$-isomorphism between $\mathbb{F}_{2^n}$ and $\mathbb{F}_2^n$. We define the matrix $\boldsymbol{M}_\ell \in \mathbb{F}_2^{n\times n}$ as the unique matrix such that*

$$\forall A \in \mathbb{F}_{2^n},\ \boldsymbol{M}_\ell \cdot \phi(A) = \phi(\ell(A)).$$

This matrix is explicitly given by

$$\boldsymbol{M}_\ell = \left[\phi(\ell(1)) \ldots \phi(\ell(x^{n-1}))\right].$$

Conversely, we will sometimes write $\ell_{\boldsymbol{N}}$ for the linearized polynomial associated to the matrix $\boldsymbol{N} \in \mathbb{F}_2^{n\times n}$ by the equation above.

The core operation in HPPC is to realize the product between two elements in $\mathbb{F}_{2^n}$. For that purpose, the scheme considers the matrix

$$\boldsymbol{M} = \left[\boldsymbol{I}_n\, \boldsymbol{C}_f \ldots \boldsymbol{C}_f^{n-1}\right] \in \mathbb{F}_2^{n\times n^2}. \tag{1}$$

Lemma 1. *Let* A, B *represent arbitrary elements in* $\mathbb{F}_{2^n} = \mathbb{F}_2[x]/\langle f(x)\rangle$ *and let* $\boldsymbol{M} \in \mathbb{F}_2^{n\times n^2}$ *be the matrix defined by Eq.* (1). *We have*

$$\boldsymbol{M} \cdot \phi(A) \otimes \phi(B) = \phi(AB).$$

Proof. By $\mathbb{F}_q$-linearity, it is sufficient to prove the statement for $A = x^{i-1}$, $i \in \{1..n\}$ and for an arbitrary element $B \in \mathbb{F}_2[x]/\langle f(x)\rangle$. In this case, we have just seen that $\phi(A) = \boldsymbol{e}_i$, so that the vector $\phi(A) \otimes \phi(B)$ is the column vector of length n^2 with a non-zero block at position i equal to $\phi(B)$. Thus

$$\boldsymbol{M} \cdot \phi(A) \otimes \phi(B) = \boldsymbol{C}_f^{i-1} \cdot \phi(B) = \phi(x^{i-1}B) = \phi(AB),$$

where the first equality comes from the definition of $\boldsymbol{M}$ and the second one is by definition of the companion matrix. □

2.2 Polynomials

In this paper, the total degree (also referred to as the standard degree) of a polynomial $P \in \mathbb{F}_{2^n}[X]$ will be denoted by $\deg(P)$. We will also make use of the notion of "$\mathbb{F}_2$-degree", as named in [10, §2.1], although the terminology is not standard. For instance, the same concept is referred to as the "q-degree" in [12].

Definition 2 ($\mathbb{F}_2$-degree). *The* $\mathbb{F}_2$*-degree of a polynomial* $P \in \mathbb{F}_{2^n}[X]/\langle X^{2^n} - X\rangle$*, denoted* $\deg_{\mathbb{F}_2}(P)$*, is defined as*

$$\deg_{\mathbb{F}_2}(P) = \max\{\mathrm{wt}_2(e) \mid X^e \textit{ appears in } P \textit{ with a non-zero coefficient}\},$$

where $\mathrm{wt}_2(e)$ *is the Hamming weight of the base-2 representation of* e.

In the context of big-field schemes, the public key or the secret key can be represented either as a univariate polynomial in $\mathbb{F}_{2^n}[X]/\langle X^{2^n} - X\rangle$ (the *univariate representation*), or as a set of Boolean multivariate polynomials (the *multivariate representation*). This latter view is enabled by the following isomorphism derived from ϕ:

$$\mathbb{F}_{2^n}[X]/\langle X^{2^n} - X\rangle \to (\mathbb{F}_2[x_1,\ldots,x_n]/\langle x_1^2 - x_1,\ldots,x_n^2 - x_n\rangle)^n. \qquad (2)$$

This map induces a bijection between univariate polynomials P over $\mathbb{F}_{2^n}$ of $\mathbb{F}_2$-degree d and n-tuples of multivariate polynomials p_i over $\mathbb{F}_2$ of degree d, and we refer to [12, §4] for more details.

We will consider polar forms of multivariate homogeneous quadratic polynomials in characteristic 2, either over $\mathbb{F}_2$ or over $\mathbb{F}_{2^n}$. The definition of the polar form in this case is recalled below.

Definition 3 (Polar form). *Let* q *be a homogeneous quadratic polynomial in characteristic* 2. *The polar form of* q *is the bilinear map* q' *defined by*

$$q'(\boldsymbol{x},\boldsymbol{y}) = q(\boldsymbol{x}+\boldsymbol{y}) + q(\boldsymbol{x}) + q(\boldsymbol{y}).$$

The main difference with the odd characteristic case is that there is no longer 1-to-1 correspondence between quadratic forms and symmetric bilinear forms in characteristic 2.

We will finally use the notion of Q-rank, whose relevance will become clearer when discussing rank attacks. An explicit definition of Q-rank can be found in [11, Definition 2], although this concept was already implicit in earlier works – for example, in [16] and [12, §4.4]. In this paper, we adopt the following formulation.

Definition 4 (Q-rank). *Let $P(X) \in \mathbb{F}_{2^n}[X]/\langle X^{2^n} - X\rangle$ be a polynomial whose monomials are all of $\mathbb{F}_2$-degree 2 and let $Q(P) \in \mathbb{F}_{2^n}[X_0, \ldots, X_{n-1}]$ be the quadratic form obtained by setting $X_0 = X, X_1 = X^2, \ldots, X_{n-1} = X^{2^{n-1}}$ in this polynomial. The Q-rank of P is defined as the rank of the skew-symmetric matrix representing the polar form of $Q(P)$.*

2.3 Description of HPPC

This section gives the multivariate and the univariate representation of the HPPC scheme, and we refer to [25,26] for a more detailed description. We also include a discussion on equivalent keys. This concept was not discussed in [25,26] but is common in the analysis of big-field multivariate schemes.

Multivariate Representation. The HPPC public key consists of n homogeneous quadratic polynomials $(p_1, \ldots, p_n)$, where each p_i belongs to $\mathbb{F}_2[\boldsymbol{x}] = \mathbb{F}_2[x_1, \ldots, x_n]$. In the following, we will write $\mathcal{P}(\boldsymbol{x})$ for the column vector in $\mathbb{F}_2[\boldsymbol{x}]^n$ whose entries correspond to these polynomials. In other words, there is a public matrix $\boldsymbol{A} \in \mathbb{F}_2^{n\times n^2}$ such that $\mathcal{P}(\boldsymbol{x}) = \boldsymbol{A}(\boldsymbol{x} \otimes \boldsymbol{x})$. The private key contains the following data:

- two invertible matrices $\boldsymbol{S}$ and $\boldsymbol{T}$ in $\mathbb{F}_2^{n\times n}$;
- two invertible matrices $\boldsymbol{L}_1$ and $\boldsymbol{L}_2$ in $\mathbb{F}_2^{n\times n}$ that represent linearized permutation polynomials. The matrix $\boldsymbol{L}_1 = \boldsymbol{M}_{\ell_1} \in \mathbb{F}_2^{n\times n}$ represents an arbitrary linearized permutation polynomial ℓ_1 while $\boldsymbol{L}_2 = \boldsymbol{M}_{\ell_2} \in \mathbb{F}_2^{n\times n}$ is picked as the representation of a monic linearized permutation polynomial ℓ_2 with maximal exponent 2^d;
- the matrix $\boldsymbol{M} \in \mathbb{F}_2^{n\times n^2}$ defined by Eq. (1).

The public key is obtained by the composition of these private components, namely

$$\mathcal{P}(\boldsymbol{x}) = \boldsymbol{T}\boldsymbol{M}(\boldsymbol{L}_1 \otimes \boldsymbol{L}_2\boldsymbol{L}_1)(\boldsymbol{S} \otimes \boldsymbol{S})(\boldsymbol{x} \otimes \boldsymbol{x}).$$

For all security levels, the value of d used in the definition of ℓ_2 is chosen as equal to 10. The provided parameter sets simply differ according to the value of n, i.e., $n = 128$ for HPPC128, $n = 192$ for HPPC192, and $n = 256$ for HPPC256.

Univariate Representation. To interpret all operations over $\mathbb{F}_{2^n}$, we fix $X = \phi^{-1}(\boldsymbol{x}) \in \mathbb{F}_{2^n}$. Using the above notation, there exists a linearized polynomial $\ell_{\boldsymbol{S}}$ such that $\boldsymbol{Sx} = \phi(\ell_{\boldsymbol{S}}(X))$. Then, we see that $\boldsymbol{L}_1\boldsymbol{Sx} = \phi(\ell_1 \circ \ell_{\boldsymbol{S}}(X))$ and $\boldsymbol{L}_2\boldsymbol{L}_1\boldsymbol{Sx} = \phi(\ell_2 \circ \ell_1 \circ \ell_{\boldsymbol{S}}(X))$. From there, Lemma 1 applied to $A = \ell_1 \circ \ell_{\boldsymbol{S}}(X)$ and $B = \ell_2 \circ \ell_1 \circ \ell_{\boldsymbol{S}}(X)$ shows that

$$\mathcal{P}(\boldsymbol{x}) = \boldsymbol{T} \circ \phi \circ (F \circ \ell_{\boldsymbol{S}}(X)) = \left(\boldsymbol{T} \circ \phi \circ F \circ \phi^{-1} \circ \boldsymbol{S}\right)(\boldsymbol{x}),$$

where $F(X) \in \mathbb{F}_{2^n}[X]/\langle X^{2^n} - X\rangle$ is the product $\ell_1 \times (\ell_2 \circ \ell_1)$.

Signing with the private key boils down to computing the roots of a polynomial of the form $G - Z$, where the scalar $Z \in \mathbb{F}_{2^n}$ is related to the message and where $G(X) = X \times \ell_2(X)$. This operation can be done efficiently because this polynomial is of small standard degree $2^d + 1$. In the following, the term "central polynomial" will mostly refer to the polynomial G. We have

$$\begin{aligned}\mathcal{P}(\boldsymbol{x}) &= \left(\boldsymbol{T} \circ \phi \circ G \circ \ell_1 \circ \phi^{-1} \circ \boldsymbol{S}\right)(\boldsymbol{x}) = \left(\boldsymbol{T} \circ \phi \circ G \circ \phi^{-1} \circ \boldsymbol{L}_1\boldsymbol{S}\right)(\boldsymbol{x}) \\ &= \left(\boldsymbol{T}' \circ \phi \circ G \circ \phi^{-1} \circ \boldsymbol{S}'\right)(\boldsymbol{x}), \qquad (3)\end{aligned}$$

where $\boldsymbol{S}' = \boldsymbol{L}_1\boldsymbol{S}$ and $\boldsymbol{T}' = \boldsymbol{T}$.

Equivalent Keys. Equivalent keys are a standard concept in the cryptanalysis of multivariate schemes. Two private keys are said to be equivalent if they correspond to the same public key. In the context of HPPC, equivalent keys will contain a univariate polynomial $\widetilde{G}$ that has the same "shape" – see [30] for the origin of this terminology – as the genuine central polynomial G, i.e., whose standard degree is as small as that of G. Since the construction of the scheme and the constraints on an equivalent central map are similar to those in HFE, we will estimate the number of HPPC equivalent keys by [30, Theorem 4.2] which we restate (adapted to our notation) here:

Theorem 1. *(Theorem 4.2 in [30]) For $(\boldsymbol{S}, F, \boldsymbol{T}) \in \mathbb{F}_2^{n\times n} \times \mathbb{F}_{2^n}[X] \times \mathbb{F}_2^{n\times n}$ an HFE private key, we have*

$$n \cdot 2^{2n}(2^n - 1)^2$$

equivalent private keys.

This result will allow us to keep the same degrees of freedom as in the HFE case for our key recovery attack.

2.4 Attacks on Big-Field Schemes

We study both the direct attack and rank attacks on HPPC. The direct attack is an algebraic attack that is generic to any multivariate scheme. In the context of digital signatures, the direct attack is used for forgery. In contrast, rank attacks are scheme-specific key recovery attacks. Both attacks employ Gröbner basis algorithms as a subroutine.

Direct Attack. Direct attacks attempt to solve the affine system $\mathcal{P}(\boldsymbol{x}) = \boldsymbol{t}$, where $\mathcal{P}$ is the public key and $\boldsymbol{t}$ is a public vector related to the message, by employing Gröbner basis algorithms. A critical concept in this context is that of degree fall polynomials, as this notion is often used to estimate the complexity of Gröbner basis methods.

Definition 5 (Degree fall, degree fall polynomial). *A degree fall on a set of polynomials* $\{f_1, \ldots, f_m\} \subset \mathbb{F}_q[x_1, \ldots, x_n]$ *is a relation of the form*

$$\sum_{i=1}^{n} g_i f_i = h,$$

for which $deg(h) < \max_i (deg(g_i f_i))$. *The polynomial* h *in such a relation will be called a degree fall polynomial and we will say that it is obtained as a degree fall from degree* $\max_i (deg(g_i f_i))$ *to degree* $deg(h)$.

It is easy to see that degree falls are the relations in $\mathbb{F}_q[x_1, \ldots, x_n]$ corresponding to syzygies in the graded module generated by the homogeneous components of the f_i's of highest degree. In particular, Definition 5 includes degree fall polynomials that correspond to trivial syzygies in this module. However, these degree falls play no role in the complexity analysis. In Proposition 1 below, the term "'non-trivial" will refer to degree falls that do not correspond to trivial syzygies. We caution the reader that, in certain exceptional cases, such degree falls may still be redundant for the computation.

Early attempts to estimate the complexity of solving the direct system $\mathcal{P}(\boldsymbol{x}) = \boldsymbol{t}$ in the case of HFE tried to grasp the behavior of the Gröbner basis algorithm from certain (univariate) polynomial combinations over the extension field with low $\mathbb{F}_2$-degree. This method was initiated in [16, §4] and formalized in [12, §4]. Since then, the same type of analysis has been applied to other big-field schemes [20–22]. The key observation is that, via the isomorphism defined in Eq. (2), two-powerings P^{2^j} correspond to n-tuples of linear combinations of the p_i's, and that any product $H(X)P(X)$ corresponds to n polynomial combinations (indexed by j) of the form $\sum_i h_{i,j} p_i$, where $\deg(h_{i,j}) = \deg_{\mathbb{F}_2}(H)$. In Sect. 3, we will use the following lemma.

Lemma 2 (Lemma 1 in [22]). *Let* $P(X) \in \mathbb{F}_{2^n}[X]/\langle X^{2^n} - X\rangle$ *be the univariate representation of the public key of a big-field scheme, and let* $H(X) \in \mathbb{F}_{2^n}[X]/\langle X^{2^n} - X\rangle$ *be such that*

$$\deg_{\mathbb{F}_2}(HP) < \deg_{\mathbb{F}_2}(H) + \deg_{\mathbb{F}_2}(P).$$

Then, in the public system $\phi(P) = (p_1, \ldots, p_n)$, *there are* n *degree falls from degree* $\deg_{\mathbb{F}_2}(H) + \deg_{\mathbb{F}_2}(P)$ *to degree* $\deg_{\mathbb{F}_2}(HP)$.

Rank Attacks. In these attacks, the main step is to solve an instance of the MinRank problem [8]. The MinRank problem consists in finding a linear combination, over a finite field, of a given collection of matrices such that the resulting matrix has rank at most r, the specified target rank. In the context of big-field schemes, this target rank is often related to the notion of Q-rank, as given in Definition 4. In the case of HFE without any modifiers, the central polynomial with standard degree D can be represented by a skew-symmetric matrix whose unique non-zero block lies in the top-left corner and has size $d \times d$, with $d \leq \lceil \log_2(D) \rceil$. As a result, the Q-rank is upper bounded by $\lceil \log_2(D) \rceil$, and this bound has been adopted as the target rank in rank attacks. In particular, in HPPC, the central polynomial is designed to mimic an HFE polynomial with maximal Q-rank, with the hope of resisting MinRank attacks.

3 Direct Attack

As been explained above, a sequence of recent results [20–22] has been able to tie algebraic relations among univariate polynomials over the extension field to degree fall relations in the Gröbner basis computation on the system over the small field that is used for forgery. This line of work can be viewed as the natural extension of the analysis of the direct attack on HFE of [12,16] in the context of lower Q-rank maps, see [9,18]. We found that these techniques may be directly applied to HPPC. Even though the direct attack still seems less efficient than the practical key recovery attack that we present afterward, it is important to note its existence, especially when considering the initial security claims.

The HPPC submission document [25] seems to indicate that the HPPC public key equations behave as a semi-regular system based on experiments in SageMath. Before moving on to our analysis, we want to point out some inaccuracies of [25, §7] regarding the notion of semi-regularity. A first issue is that the submission treats the field equations $x_i^2 + x_i = 0$ as an extra set of n equations added to the system $\mathcal{P}(\boldsymbol{x}) = \boldsymbol{t}$ and adopts the generating series $(1-t^2)^{2n}/(1-t)^n$ for the whole, see [25, §7.1.3]. This implicitly assumes that the field equations have a generic behavior, which is not true. For instance, the correct generating series for a Boolean semi-regular system with n quadratic equations in n variables is $(1+t)^n/(1+t^2)^n$ [5]. At this stage, we stress that the HPPC system has no reason to behave as such. A second issue is related to the SageMath experiments. To estimate the degree at which the system is solved, [25, §7.1.3] computes d_{reg}, the index of the first non-positive coefficient of the generating series. In [25, §7.2], this theoretical value is compared to an experimental degree d_{exp} obtained using the `degree_of_semi_regularity()` command. However, this command *assumes* that the input equations are semi-regular, which means that d_{exp} is not the result of an experiment. In particular, it is not a surprise that $d_{\text{exp}} = d_{\text{reg}}$, but this equality does not tell anything about the behavior of the equations.

It turns out that the public equations of HPPC cannot be analyzed as a semi-regular system, even a Boolean one. In the next subsection, we exhibit degree fall polynomials that tend to suggest that these public equations are much easier to solve than comparable semi-regular equations.

3.1 Degree Fall Polynomials

Our partial analysis of degree fall polynomials is presented in Propositions 1 and 2 below, which are stated with Faugère's F_4 algorithm [14] in mind. This algorithm proceeds through a sequence of steps, each processing a selected set of polynomial pairs. As F_4 follows the so-called normal strategy, which always selects pairs of minimal degree, degree fall polynomials are incorporated into the next step immediately upon discovery.

Proposition 1. *There are* $2n$ *non-trivial degree falls from degree* 3 *to degree* 2 *at the first step in degree* 3.

Proof. Without loss of generality, we can apply Lemma 2 to $F = \ell_1 \times (\ell_2 \circ \ell_1)$ instead of $P = \ell_T \circ F \circ \ell_S$ because the composition with ℓ_S and ℓ_T does not affect the degree of the polynomials. Then, in characteristic 2, both ℓ_1^2 and $(\ell_2 \circ \ell_1)^2$ are linearized polynomials. Therefore, we can use Lemma 2 twice with $H = \ell_1$ and $H = \ell_2 \circ \ell_1$ respectively, which yields $n + n = 2n$ degree fall polynomials from degree $3 = 1 + 2$ to degree 2. □

These initial degree falls trigger another set of $2n$ degree falls at the next step of the algorithm that we can still understand.

Proposition 2. *There are* $2n$ *degree falls from degree* 3 *to degree* 2 *at the second step in degree* 3.

Proof. We apply the same reasoning to $G_1 = \ell_1^2 \times (\ell_2 \circ \ell_1)$ and $G_2 = \ell_1 \times (\ell_2 \circ \ell_1)^2$ which are the result of the first step. Then, as above, the polynomials $\ell_1^2 G_1$ and $(\ell_2 \circ \ell_1)^2 G_2$ are products of one polynomial of $\mathbb{F}_2$-degree 1 and one of $\mathbb{F}_2$-degree 2 but they have $\mathbb{F}_2$-degree 2. Lemma 2 then gives $n + n = 2n$ degree falls. Finally, note that the polynomial $(\ell_2 \circ \ell_1) \times G_1 = \ell_1 \times G_2$ is also of $\mathbb{F}_2$-degree 2. However, as it is equal to F^2, it will trigger polynomials that are redundant to the computation[1]. □

Remark 1 (Dependency with respect to d). *The number of linearly independent degree falls at step 2° C 3 may differ from the number of degree falls predicted by Proposition 2 if the value of d is much smaller than* 10. *Intuitively, we cannot square the polynomial ℓ_1 endlessly because we will get redundancy, i.e., extra linear relations, coming from the polynomial $\ell_2 \circ \ell_1$.*

3.2 Experiments on the Direct System

We present the earliest steps of the F_4 algorithm and the associated degree fall polynomials on the direct system for several values of d and n in Appendix A. In our tests, we always ensure that the equations have a solution. The last step of

---

[1] Such polynomials would be counted as degree falls according to Lemma 2, since the definition used in [22], from which the lemma is taken, does not take into account their usefulness.

the algorithm that we give yields sufficiently many degree 1 polynomials so that Magma's default F_4 restarts from there and the subsequent steps are cheaper.

We note that Propositions 1 and 2 accurately predict the number of degree falls in degree 3 observed in our experiments. However, estimating the number of degree falls in higher degrees appears to be more complex. In particular, this quantity seems to depend not only on the degree d but also on the specific monomials present in ℓ_2. Our results correspond to a dense linearized polynomial ℓ_2 of standard degree 2^d, but different behavior was observed when using a sparser polynomial. We have not pursued this estimation further, as rank attacks seemed more efficient at this stage of our work. Still, we want to mention that a deeper analysis of such degree fall polynomials in higher degrees has already led to better attacks on other big-field schemes [20–22].

The rest of the paper presents our efficient rank attack to recover an equivalent key. In Sect. 4, we give the MinRank problem that we consider and we show how a solution to this problem can be used to complete the attack. In Sect. 5, we solve this MinRank problem using the Support-Minors modeling.

4 Rank Attack

The simple observation behind our rank attack is that the Q-rank of the HPPC polynomial $F = \ell_1 \times (\ell_2 \circ \ell_1)$ is equal to 2, regardless of the value of d. Indeed, both ℓ_1 and $\ell_2 \circ \ell_1$ are linear forms in $\mathbb{F}_{2^n}[X_0, \ldots, X_{n-1}]$ with the identification of Definition 4, and the quadratic form $Q(F)$ is the product of these two linear forms. This leads us to considering a rank-2 MinRank problem that is pretty similar to the one proposed by [6] to cryptanalyze HFE.

Our description will closely follow [6]. Let $(\theta_1, \ldots, \theta_n)$ be an $\mathbb{F}_2$-basis of $\mathbb{F}_{2^n}$ and let $\boldsymbol{M}_n \in \mathbb{F}_{2^n}^{n\times n}$ be the Moore matrix defined by

$$\boldsymbol{M}_n = \begin{bmatrix} \theta_1 & \theta_1^2 & \ldots & \theta_1^{2^{n-1}} \\ \theta_2 & \theta_2^2 & \ldots & \theta_2^{2^{n-1}} \\ \vdots & \vdots & \ddots & \vdots \\ \theta_n & \theta_n^2 & \ldots & \theta_n^{2^{n-1}} \end{bmatrix}. \tag{4}$$

We consider the more convenient isomorphism $\psi : \mathbb{F}_{2^n} \to \mathbb{F}_2^n$ given by this matrix, namely

$$\begin{array}{rcl} & \mathbb{F}_{2^n} \to & \mathbb{F}_2^n \\ \psi : & X \mapsto & (\boldsymbol{M}_n^{-1})^{\mathsf{T}} \begin{bmatrix} X \\ \vdots \\ X^{2^{n-1}} \end{bmatrix}. \end{array}$$

Its inverse is given by

$$\begin{array}{rcl} & \mathbb{F}_2^n \to & \mathbb{F}_{2^n} \\ \psi^{-1} : & \begin{bmatrix} x_1 \\ \vdots \\ x_n \end{bmatrix} \mapsto & \left((\boldsymbol{M}_n)^{\mathsf{T}} \begin{bmatrix} x_1 \\ \vdots \\ x_n \end{bmatrix} \right) [1], \end{array}$$

where $\boldsymbol{v}[1]$ refers to the top coordinate of the column vector $\boldsymbol{v}$ [6, Proposition 2]. Coming back to HPPC, there exists an invertible matrix $\boldsymbol{N} \in \mathbb{F}_2^{n\times n}$ such that the isomorphism ϕ used in the scheme is $\phi = \boldsymbol{N} \circ \psi$. The expression of $\boldsymbol{N}$ depends on the polynomial f appearing in the definition of ϕ but we will not need it in our attack. Moreover, we see in the univariate representation of the public key given by Eq. (3) that the $\boldsymbol{L}_1$ matrix can be "absorbed" into $\boldsymbol{S}'$. Therefore, we may proceed as if $\boldsymbol{S}'$ and $\boldsymbol{T}'$ were random invertible matrices and reason on the equation

$$\begin{aligned}\mathcal{P} &= \boldsymbol{T}'\boldsymbol{N} \circ \psi \circ G \circ \psi^{-1} \circ \boldsymbol{N}^{-1}\boldsymbol{S}' \\ &= \overline{\boldsymbol{T}} \circ \psi \circ G \circ \psi^{-1} \circ \overline{\boldsymbol{S}},\end{aligned}$$

where $\overline{\boldsymbol{S}} = \boldsymbol{N}^{-1}\boldsymbol{S}'$ and $\overline{\boldsymbol{T}} = \boldsymbol{T}'\boldsymbol{N}$. From this new equation, the rest follows as in [6]. We have

$$\begin{aligned}\begin{bmatrix} p_1(\boldsymbol{v}) \\ \vdots \\ p_n(\boldsymbol{v}) \end{bmatrix} &= \overline{\boldsymbol{T}}(\boldsymbol{M}_n^{-1})^\top \begin{bmatrix} G^{2^0}(\psi^{-1}(\overline{\boldsymbol{S}}\boldsymbol{v})) \\ \vdots \\ G^{2^{n-1}}(\psi^{-1}(\overline{\boldsymbol{S}}\boldsymbol{v})) \end{bmatrix} = \overline{\boldsymbol{T}}(\boldsymbol{M}_n^{-1})^\top \begin{bmatrix} \boldsymbol{v}^\top\overline{\boldsymbol{S}}^\top\boldsymbol{M}_n\boldsymbol{G}^{*0}\boldsymbol{M}_n^\top\overline{\boldsymbol{S}}\boldsymbol{v} \\ \vdots \\ \boldsymbol{v}^\top\overline{\boldsymbol{S}}^\top\boldsymbol{M}_n\boldsymbol{G}^{*n-1}\boldsymbol{M}_n^\top\overline{\boldsymbol{S}}\boldsymbol{v} \end{bmatrix} \\ &= \overline{\boldsymbol{T}}(\boldsymbol{M}_n^{-1})^\top \begin{bmatrix} \boldsymbol{v}^\top\overline{\boldsymbol{S}}^\top\boldsymbol{M}_n\boldsymbol{G}^{*0}\boldsymbol{M}_n^\top\overline{\boldsymbol{S}}\boldsymbol{v} \\ \vdots \\ \boldsymbol{v}^\top\overline{\boldsymbol{S}}^\top\boldsymbol{M}_n\boldsymbol{G}^{*n-1}\boldsymbol{M}_n^\top\overline{\boldsymbol{S}}\boldsymbol{v} \end{bmatrix},\end{aligned}$$

where $\boldsymbol{G}^{*i}$ is at this stage any matrix that represents the quadratic form $Q(G^{2^i})$ for $i \in \{0..n-1\}$. This matrix is not unique and to proceed further we need to consider symmetric representations (or equivalently skew-symmetric ones in the even characteristic case). As in [6,17], we take $\boldsymbol{A}+\boldsymbol{A}^\top$ instead of $\frac{\boldsymbol{A}+\boldsymbol{A}^\top}{2}$ since we are in characteristic 2 (this is basically the matrix representing the polar form of the quadratic form). Assuming such a representation, the relevant matrix $\boldsymbol{G}^{*0}$ is given in Lemma 3.

Lemma 3. *The skew-symmetric matrix* $\boldsymbol{G}^{*0}$ *such that* $Q(G)(X,\dots,X^{2^{n-1}}) = (X,\dots,X^{2^{n-1}})\boldsymbol{G}^{*0}(X,\dots,X^{2^{n-1}})^\top$ *can be defined from its first row, which contains non-zero entries only in position* $(1,j)$ *for* $j \in \{2..d+1\}$ *and such that the entry in position* $(1,d+1)$ *is equal to* 1.

Proof. Recall that $G(X) = X \times \ell_2(X)$, where $\ell_2 = \sum_{j=0}^{d-1} c_i X^{2^i} + X^{2^d}$ is a monic linearized polynomial of standard degree 2^d. Thus, the quadratic form

$$Q(G) = \textstyle\sum_{1\le i\le j\le n} b_{i,j} X^{2^{i-1}} X^{2^{j-1}}$$

is such that $b_{1,j} = c_{j-1}$ for $j \in \{1..d\}$, $b_{1,d+1} = 1$ and $b_{i,j} = 0$ if $i \ge 2$ and/or $j \ge d+2$. The expression of $\boldsymbol{G}^{*0}$ can be easily deduced from that of $Q(G)$. □

If we now let $\boldsymbol{G}^{*0} = (g_{i,j})_{i,j}$, where row and columns indexes range from 0 to $n-1$, we have $\boldsymbol{G}^{*k} = (g_{i-k,j-k}^{2^k})_{i,j}$ for any $k \in \{0..n-1\}$, where all differences

$i-k$ or $j-k$ must be understood modulo n (see for example [28, Proposition 1]). In the following, we will write Frob_k for the $\mathbb{F}_q$-linear map that maps the matrix with entries $m_{i,j}$ to the one with entries $m_{i-k,j-k}^{2^k}$, so that $\boldsymbol{G}^{*k} = \mathrm{Frob}_k(\boldsymbol{G}^{*0})$. Finally, we set $\boldsymbol{U} = (\overline{\boldsymbol{T}}^{\mathsf{T}})^{-1}\boldsymbol{M}_n$ and $\boldsymbol{W} = \overline{\boldsymbol{S}}^{\mathsf{T}}\boldsymbol{M}_n$. Overall, we obtain

$$\left[\boldsymbol{P}_1 \ldots \boldsymbol{P}_n\right](\boldsymbol{U} \otimes \boldsymbol{I}_n) = \left[\boldsymbol{W}\boldsymbol{G}^{*0}\boldsymbol{W}^{\mathsf{T}} \;\ldots\; \boldsymbol{W}\boldsymbol{G}^{*n-1}\boldsymbol{W}^{\mathsf{T}}\right]. \tag{5}$$

Here we use the fact that the matrices $\boldsymbol{W}\boldsymbol{G}^{*k}\boldsymbol{W}^{\mathsf{T}}$ all have rank 2. As in [6], we will retrieve one column of a matrix denoted by $\widetilde{\boldsymbol{U}}$ that plays the same role as $\boldsymbol{U}$ in Equation (5) but which is part of a possibly different equivalent key by solving a rank-2 MinRank problem with matrices over $\mathbb{F}_2$ but solutions over $\mathbb{F}_{2^n}$.

Our approach is to solve MinRank first to find such a $\widetilde{\boldsymbol{U}}$ and then to solve linear equations to recover the rest of the private key components. This method is similar to the ones proposed by [6,17] to attack HFE in odd characteristic. In particular, it highly differs from the key recovery technique devised in [6, §6.3.1] for HFE in characteristic 2. In [6, §6.3.1], the two attack steps could not be separated. There, MinRank was solved at the same time as retrieving the rest of the private key, which is both less natural and less efficient.

4.1 Recovering $\widetilde{U}$

From Eq. (5), we obtain

Proposition 3. *Let* $\boldsymbol{U} \in \mathbb{F}_{2^n}^{n\times n}$ *be the secret matrix* $(\overline{\boldsymbol{T}}^{\mathsf{T}})^{-1}\boldsymbol{M}_n$*. The columns of* $\boldsymbol{U}$ *are solutions (over* $\mathbb{F}_{2^n}$*) to the MinRank problem defined by the matrices* $\boldsymbol{P}_i \in \mathbb{F}_2^{n\times n}$ *for* $i \in \{1..n\}$*, with target rank* 2.

In Sect. 5, MinRank will be solved using the Support-Minors modeling. Before moving on, let us mention that the instance does not admit spurious solutions comparable to those of the form $\lambda\boldsymbol{G}^{*i} + \mu\boldsymbol{G}^{*i+1}$ for even rank HFE (we refer to [15] and [6, §6.3] for more details). Indeed, such matrices are here of expected rank 4 so that they are not problematic (this can be easily seen from the expression of $\boldsymbol{G}^{*i}$ that may be derived from Lemma 3). This is what explains that our attack method is close to the one employed for HFE in odd characteristic and deviates from the one of [6, §6.3.1] for HFE in characteristic 2.

The next subsection details how to finish the key recovery from an arbitrary rank 2 solution $\boldsymbol{Z} = \sum_{i=1}^{n} u_i\boldsymbol{P}_i \in \mathbb{F}_{2^n}^{n\times n}$. This solution is expected to correspond to a unique Frobenius power of G and thus to a column of a matrix $\widetilde{\boldsymbol{U}}$ equivalent to $\boldsymbol{U}$. Finally, it is standard how to reconstruct the full matrix $\widetilde{\boldsymbol{U}}$ from such a column, using [6, Proposition 6] or equivalently the special form of $\boldsymbol{M}_n$.

4.2 Recovering the Rest of the Equivalent Key

As announced above, we will recover the rest of the private key components by solving linear equations. We consider the permutation matrix $\boldsymbol{P} = \begin{bmatrix} \boldsymbol{0}_{n-1} & 1 \\ \boldsymbol{I}_{n-1} & 0 \end{bmatrix}$.

For an arbitrary matrix $\boldsymbol{A} \in \mathbb{F}_{2^n}^{n \times n}$ and for any index $k \in \{0..n-1\}$, we have

$$\text{Frob}_k(\boldsymbol{A}) = \boldsymbol{P}^k \boldsymbol{A}^{[k]} \boldsymbol{P}^{-k} = \boldsymbol{P}^k \boldsymbol{A}^{[k]} (\boldsymbol{P}^k)^\mathsf{T},$$

where the matrix $\boldsymbol{A}^{[k]}$ is obtained from $\boldsymbol{A}$ by raising each entry to the power 2^k.

Coming back to Eq. (5), we will assume without loss of generality and to clarify the description that our rank 2 matrix $\boldsymbol{Z}$ is equal to $\boldsymbol{W}\boldsymbol{G}^{*0}\boldsymbol{W}^\mathsf{T}$. For any index $k \in \{0..n-1\}$, we have $\boldsymbol{W}^{[k]} = \boldsymbol{W}\boldsymbol{P}^k$ by definition of $\boldsymbol{W}$ and by the special shape of $\boldsymbol{M}_n$. Therefore,

$$\begin{aligned} \boldsymbol{Z}^{[k]} &= \boldsymbol{W}^{[k]} \left(\boldsymbol{G}^{*0}\right)^{[k]} (\boldsymbol{W}^{-1})^{[k]} \\ &= \boldsymbol{W}\boldsymbol{P}^k \left(\boldsymbol{G}^{*0}\right)^{[k]} \boldsymbol{P}^{-k}\boldsymbol{W}^{-1} \\ &= \boldsymbol{W}\text{Frob}_k(\boldsymbol{G}^{*0})\boldsymbol{W}^{-1}. \end{aligned}$$

We will use this equality for $k \in \{1..n-d-1\}$ to derive a linear system in the n variables that constitute the first row $\boldsymbol{w}$ of $\boldsymbol{W}^{-1}$. Indeed, for such an index k, the first row of the matrix $\text{Frob}_k(\boldsymbol{G}^{*0})$ and thus the one of $\text{Frob}_k(\boldsymbol{G}^{*0})\boldsymbol{W}^{-1}$ is the zero vector. This follows once again from Lemma 3 and then from the expression of $\text{Frob}_k(\boldsymbol{G}^{*0}) = \boldsymbol{G}^{*k} = (g_{i-k,j-k}^{2^k})_{i,j}$ in function of $\boldsymbol{G}^{*0} = (g_{i,j})_{i,j}$. For each index k, the equality $\boldsymbol{w}\boldsymbol{Z}^{[k]} = \boldsymbol{0}_n$ gives n equations but only two of them are linearly independent since the rank of $\boldsymbol{Z}^{[k]}$ is 2. Overall, we get at most $2(n-d-1)$ linearly independent equations by using all the k indices.

Note that any vector proportional to the first row of $\boldsymbol{W}^{-1}$ will also yield solutions. If the parameters n and d satisfy $n \geq 2d+1$, which is the case in HPPC, these will be the only solutions. Thus, we solve the equations by fixing one variable to eventually recover a matrix $\widetilde{\boldsymbol{W}}$ equivalent to $\boldsymbol{W}$. Finally, we complete the key recovery by computing the matrix $\widetilde{\boldsymbol{G}^{*0}} = \widetilde{\boldsymbol{W}}^{-1}\boldsymbol{Z}\widetilde{\boldsymbol{W}}$. This matrix is necessarily associated with a central polynomial of HPPC shape.

5 Solving the MinRank Instance with Support-Minors

In this section, we solve the MinRank problem presented in Proposition 3. First, as in the HFE case, we are still able to recover an equivalent key by fixing one variable. For instance, we will fix the last variable to 1 and target a rank 2 matrix of the form

$$\boldsymbol{Z} = \textstyle\sum_{i=1}^{n-1} u_i \boldsymbol{P}_i + \boldsymbol{P}_n,$$

where the u_i's are the remaining variables. Since the $\boldsymbol{P}_i$'s have entries in $\mathbb{F}_2$, we expect essentially n solutions in $\mathbb{F}_{2^n}^{n-1}$ obtained from one another by applying the Frobenius map on each component.

Standard algebraic modelings to solve the MinRank problem are the Minors modeling, the Kipnis-Shamir modeling, and the Support-Minors (SM) modeling. We will present a solving method based on Support-Minors. We obtained similar results with Kipnis-Shamir, which should not be surprising given the proximity between the two modelings [3].

We will now briefly describe the SM system. The starting point is a factorization $\boldsymbol{Z} = \boldsymbol{DC}$ with unknown full-rank factors $\boldsymbol{D} \in \mathbb{F}_{2^n}^{n\times 2}$ and $\boldsymbol{C} \in \mathbb{F}_{2^n}^{2\times n}$. For $\ell \in \{1..n\}$, let $\boldsymbol{r}_\ell$ be the ℓ-th row of $\boldsymbol{Z}$ viewed as a vector of degree 1 forms in the u_i variables and let

$$\boldsymbol{C}_\ell = \begin{bmatrix} \boldsymbol{r}_\ell \\ \boldsymbol{C} \end{bmatrix}.$$

The SM modeling follows from the fact that the rank of $\boldsymbol{C}_\ell$ is at most 2 because the vector $\boldsymbol{r}_\ell$ belongs to the row space of $\boldsymbol{C}$. More precisely, the relevant system contains the set of all 3×3 minors of $\boldsymbol{C}_\ell$ for $\ell \in \{1..n\}$, i.e.,

$$\mathcal{F}_{\mathrm{SM}} = \{|\boldsymbol{C}_\ell|_{*,J},\ J \subset \{1..n\},\ \#J = 3,\ \ell \in \{1..n\}\}. \tag{6}$$

By Laplace expansion along the first row of $\boldsymbol{C}_\ell$, it is known that all the equations of $\mathcal{F}_{\mathrm{SM}}$ are bilinear in the u_i's and in the 2×2 minors of $\boldsymbol{C}$. The crux was in fact to consider the latter as new variables $c_T = |\boldsymbol{C}|_{*,T}$ for $T \subset \{1..n\}$, $\#T = 2$, called minor variables.

Modeling 1 (Support-Minors). *The Support-Minors modeling is the system obtained from Eq. (6) by Laplace expansion along the first row of the matrices and by setting as new unknowns $c_T = |\boldsymbol{C}|_{*,T}$ for $T \subset \{1..n\}$, $\#T = 2$. The system is affine bilinear in the u_i's and in these new minor variables.*

As in previous works, see [2,4,7,28], it will be convenient to restrict ourselves to SM subsystems. This is done by considering the minors constructed from only $\kappa \leq n$ columns of the $\boldsymbol{C}_\ell$ matrices. We still want the $\boldsymbol{C}_\ell$ submatrices to be of full-rank 2 so we include the 2 columns of the identity block $\boldsymbol{I}_2$ that is usually part of $\boldsymbol{C}$. In this way we obtain an SM subsystem containing $n\binom{\kappa}{3}$ affine bilinear equations in $n_u = n-1$ linear variables u_i but only $n_{c_T} = \binom{\kappa}{2} - 1$ minor variables (we fix to 1 the 2×2 minor which is the determinant of $\boldsymbol{I}_2$ exactly as in [2,4]).

5.1 "Big-Field" Support-Minors

Our method is to solve a simpler quadratic system in the u_i variables derived from the (affine) Support-Minors modeling, following the strategy presented in [2] for the big-field MinRank problem of Tao, Petzoldt and Ding [28]. Our description will entirely follow [2]. Here, the total number of monomials in SM is equal to

$$n_u n_{c_T} + n_u + n_{c_T} + 1 = (n_u + 1)(n_{c_T} + 1) = n\tbinom{\kappa}{2}.$$

We have more equations than the number of monomials if and only if $n\binom{\kappa}{3} \geq n\binom{\kappa}{2}$, say $\kappa \geq 5$. Under this condition, the rank of the system is necessarily smaller than $n\binom{\kappa}{2}$ because we have a solution. As we have seen, the solution set is stable by the action of the Frobenius map on each variable. Based on this observation, [2, Assumption 1] stated that this rank was equal to $n\binom{\kappa}{2} - n$ in the case of HFE. We will rely on the same assumption in the HPPC case.

The first step of the solving process is to perform linear combinations between the SM equations. Under the above assumption and by saturating the set of bilinear monomials, this will produce a total of

$$n\binom{\kappa}{2} - n - n_u n_{c_T} = n_{c_T} = \binom{\kappa}{2} - 1$$

linearly independent equations of degree 1 (recall that $n_u n_{c_T}$ refers to the number of monomials of exact degree 2). These equations necessarily involve one c_T variable from an argument similar to [2, Lemma 1], and we may use them to eliminate all the minor variables present in SM, by substitution. We can in fact directly apply [2, Lemma 1]. Indeed, the proof of this lemma simply exploits the special shape of the matrix $\boldsymbol{U}$ used in HFE, and we have the same matrix in HPPC. Overall, this step yields the announced quadratic system in the u_i's.

The second step is to solve the quadratic system using Gröbner bases. We note that this system can be made very overdefined by choosing a large value for κ. More precisely, it contains $(n-1)(\binom{\kappa}{2}-1)$ equations in $n-1$ unknowns. In the case of HFE, the argument of [2, Proposition 1] stated that a grevlex Gröbner basis could be obtained in degree 2 when $\binom{\kappa}{2} \geq n-1$.

In our experiments on HPPC, the very same assumption as [2, Assumption 1] on the rank of SM did not hold when the value κ was too small (for instance $\kappa = 5$), but it was satisfied for a larger value. In Sect. 5.3, we present our results for the least value of κ such that $\binom{\kappa}{2} \geq n-1$. For this number of columns, the number of linear polynomials produced at the first step was the expected one and the resulting quadratic system in the u_i's was already solved in degree 2.

5.2 Complexity Analysis

The cost of solving MinRank can be derived from the results of [2] as we use the same approach. For instance, the first step can be estimated by [2, Eq. (8)] or [2, Eq. (9)] and the second step by [2, Eq. (10)] if the resulting quadratic system is solved in degree 2, with $n_u = n-1$ and $n_{c_T} = \binom{\kappa}{2} - 1$. Noting that these two values are polynomial in n and using these estimates, we deduce that both steps have polynomial complexity in the case of HPPC.

The overall attack is, in fact, practical, and we have been able to complete a key recovery for all security levels. We could recover an equivalent key in a bit less than 8 min for security level 2 ($n = 128$), about 1 h and a half for security level 4 ($n = 192$), and a bit more than 7 h for security level 5 ($n = 256$). A more detailed breakdown of the running time is given in Table 1 of the next subsection.

5.3 Concrete Running Times

Table 1 presents the time spent on each of the steps of the key recovery. The time given in "Step 1" corresponds to the cost of generating the degree 1 polynomials by linear algebra on the SM system. The time given in "Step 2" is the cost of solving the final quadratic system. This includes the cost of computing the grevlex Gröbner basis (Gaussian elimination and checking that no new polynomials appear in degree 3) and the cost of the FGLM algorithm [13] to compute the variety of size n. For the sake of completeness, we also give the time spent to construct the SM system ("Build SM") and the one of the substitution of the degree 1 polynomials in SM to construct the final quadratic system ("Build quadratic"). These constructions were not detailed in Sect. 5.1, but they have no reason to be costly from a theoretical perspective (their rather high cost in Table 1 might be due to poor implementation).

For $n = 128$ and $n = 192$, we picked the least value of κ such that $\binom{\kappa}{2} \geq n-1$ to apply the above reasoning. For $n = 256$, the least value of κ satisfying this inequality is $\kappa = 24$. We have not been able to run Step 1 for this value of κ because we were limited by memory. Therefore, we give timings for $\kappa = 12$ columns. In particular, in this case, the time spent in Step 2 suggests that the quadratic system is solved in degree > 2.

Table 1. Attack running time on the HPPC security levels. All the numbers are in seconds and they correspond to one trial (they are not an average over several samples).

n	κ	Build SM	Step 1	Build quadratic	Step 2	Total
128	17	11.320	76.540	82.490	271.160	464.819 ($\approx 07'45''$)
192	21	49.570	655.700	627.130	4096.900	5552.319 ($\approx 1°32'32''$)
256	12	27.970	219.590	241.390	24405.100	25290.409 ($\approx 7°01'30''$)

Finally, we have not tried to find the value of κ for which Step 1 and Step 2 have roughly the same time complexity. This value will be larger than the one we give here, and thus the memory demand for Step 1 will be even more important.

6 Conclusion

This paper fully breaks HPPC because the time complexity of our rank attack is polynomial in n (we cannot simply increase the parameters). It is possible in principle to repair the scheme by modifying the central map to increase its Q-rank, but doing so would change the design and would not bring any advantage compared to older HFE-like schemes. Moreover, as with HFE, increasing the Q-rank enough to make the scheme secure (at least in any straightforward way) would make signing by the honest party unacceptably slow.

A Experiments for the Direct Attack

This appendix contains more details on the experiments of Sect. 3.2. The column "F_4 step degrees" gives the degree of the polynomials that are handled at each step of the F_4 algorithm as well as the possible degree fall polynomials. For example, "3 (2:80)" means that 80 quadratic degree fall polynomials are found at a step in degree 3. As stated in Sect. 3.2, the last step that is presented always produces linear equations (we do not give their number here).

Our results are consistent with Proposition 1 and Proposition 2, with the exception of the two underlined values in Table 2 (we refer to Remark 1 for a possible explanation of this discrepancy).

While it seems feasible to conjecture the number of degree falls in degree 4, we have not attempted to do it. In addition to experimental differences when

Table 2. HPPC direct system with $d = 5$.

n	F_4 step degrees
40	3 (2:80), 3 (2:80), 3
50	3 (2:100), 3 (2:100), 3
60	3 (2:120), 3 (2:120), 3
70	3 (2:140), 3 (2:280), 3
80	3 (2:160), 3 (2:240), 3

Table 3. HPPC direct system with $d = 7$

n	F_4 step degrees
40	3 (2:80), 3 (2:80), 3, 4
50	3 (2:100), 3 (2:100), 3, 4
60	3 (2:120), 3 (2:120), 3, 4
70	3 (2:140), 3 (2:140), 3, 4

Table 4. HPPC direct system with $d = 9$.

n	F_4 step degrees
46	3 (2:92), 3 (2:92), 3, 4 (3:3772), 4
47	3 (2:94), 3 (2:94), 3, 4 (3:3854), 4
48	3 (2:96), 3 (2:96), 3, 4 (3:3936), 4
49	3 (2:98), 3 (2:98), 3, 4 (3:4018), 4
50	3 (2:100), 3 (2:100), 3, 4 (3:4050), 4
51	3 (2:102), 3 (2:102), 3, 4 (3:4182), 4
52	3 (2:104), 3 (2:104), 3, 4 (3:4264), 4
54	3 (2:108), 3 (2:108), 3, 4 (3:4428), 4
55	3 (2:110), 3 (2:110), 3, 4 (3:4510), 4
56	3 (2:112), 3 (2:112), 3, 4 (3:4592), 4
58	3 (2:116), 3 (2:116), 3, 4 (3:4756), 4
60	3 (2:120), 3 (2:120), 3, 4 (3:4920), 4

the polynomial ℓ_2 was sparser pointed out in the main text, we also want to stress that our results are given for one trial on a given set of parameters. In some cases, two trials for the same parameter set have yielded different results for the number of degree falls in degree 4 (Tables 3, 4, 5, 6 and 7).

Table 5. HPPC direct system with $d = 10$.

n	F_4 step degrees
40	3 (2:80), 3 (2:80), 3, 4
45	3 (2:90), 3 (2:90), 3, 4 (3:2070), 4
46	3 (2:92), 3 (2:92), 3, 4 (3:736), 4
47	3 (2:94), 3 (2:94), 3, 4 (3:752), 4
48	3 (2:96), 3 (2:96), 3, 4 (3:768), 4
49	3 (2:98), 3 (2:98), 3, 4 (3:784), 4
50	3 (2:100), 3 (2:100), 3, 4 (3:800), 4
55	3 (2:110), 3 (2:110), 3, 4 (3:880), 4 (3:6050), 4
58	3 (2:116), 3 (2:116), 3, 4 (3:928), 4 (3:5859), 4
60	3 (2:120), 3 (2:120), 3, 4 (3:960), 4 (3:6061), 4
61	3 (2:122), 3 (2:122), 3, 4 (3:976), 4
65	3 (2:130), 3 (2:130), 3, 4 (3:2665), 4
70	3 (2:140), 3 (2:140), 3, 4 (3:2380), 4

Table 6. HPPC direct system with $d = 11$.

n	F_4 step degrees
40	3 (2:80), 3 (2:80), 3, 4
45	3 (2:90), 3 (2:90), 3, 4 (3:2070), 4
46	3 (2:92), 3 (2:92), 3, 4, 5
47	3 (2:94), 3 (2:94), 3, 4, 5
48	3 (2:96), 3 (2:96), 3, 4 (3:960), 4

Table 7. HPPC direct system with $d = 20$

n	F_4 step degrees
40	3 (2:80), 3 (2:80), 3, 4
50	3 (2:100), 3 (2:100), 3, 4, 5

References

1. Alagic, G., et al.: Status report on the third round of the NIST post-quantum cryptography standardization process. Tech. rep, National Institute of Standards and Technology, Gaithersburg, MD (July (2022)
2. Baena, J., Briaud, P., Cabarcas, D., Perlner, R., Smith-Tone, D., Verbel, J.: Improving support-minors rank attacks: applications to GeMSS and rainbow. In: Dodis, Y., Shrimpton, T. (eds.) Advances in Cryptology – CRYPTO 2022, pp. 376–405. Springer (2022)
3. Bardet, M., Bertin, M.: Improvement of algebraic attacks for solving superdetermined MinRank instances. In: Cheon, J.H., Johansson, T. (eds.) Post-Quantum Cryptography, pp. 107–123. Springer (2022)
4. Bardet, M., et al.: Improvements of algebraic attacks for solving the rank decoding and MinRank problems. In: Moriai, S., Wang, H. (eds.) ASIACRYPT 2020. LNCS, vol. 12491, pp. 507–536. Springer, Cham (2020). https://doi.org/10.1007/978-3-030-64837-4_17
5. Bardet, M., Faugère, J.C., Salvy, B., Yang, B.Y.: Asymptotic behaviour of the degree of regularity of semi-regular polynomial systems. https://api.semanticscholar.org/CorpusID:10699714
6. Bettale, L., Faugère, J.C., Perret, L.: Cryptanalysis of HFE, Multi-HFE and variants for odd and even characteristic. Des. Codes Crypt. **69**(1), 1–52 (2013)
7. Beullens, W.: Improved cryptanalysis of UOV and rainbow. In: Canteaut, A., Standaert, F.-X. (eds.) EUROCRYPT 2021. LNCS, vol. 12696, pp. 348–373. Springer, Cham (2021). https://doi.org/10.1007/978-3-030-77870-5_13
8. Buss, J.F., Frandsen, G.S., Shallit, J.O.: The computational complexity of some problems of linear algebra. J. Comput. Syst. Sci. **58**(3), 572–596 (1999)
9. Cartor, R., Smith-Tone, D.: EFLASH: a new multivariate encryption scheme. In: Cid, C., Jr., M.J.J. (eds.) Selected Areas in Cryptography – SAC 2018, pp. 281–299. Springer (2018)
10. Ding, J., Hodges, T.J.: Inverting HFE systems is quasi-polynomial for all fields. In: Rogaway, P. (ed.) CRYPTO 2011. LNCS, vol. 6841, pp. 724–742. Springer, Heidelberg (2011). https://doi.org/10.1007/978-3-642-22792-9_41
11. Ding, J., Perlner, R., Petzoldt, A., Smith-Tone, D.: Improved cryptanalysis of HFEv- via projection. In: Lange, T., Steinwandt, R. (eds.) Post-Quantum Cryptography, pp. 375–395. Springer (2018)
12. Dubois, V., Gama, N.: The degree of regularity of HFE systems. In: Abe, M. (ed.) ASIACRYPT 2010. LNCS, vol. 6477, pp. 557–576. Springer, Heidelberg (2010). https://doi.org/10.1007/978-3-642-17373-8_32
13. Faugère, J.C., Gianni, P.M., Lazard, D., Mora, T.: Efficient computation of zero-dimensional gröbner bases by change of ordering **16**(4), 329–344 (1993)
14. Faugère, J.C.: A new efficient algorithm for computing Gröbner bases (F4). J. Pure Appl. Algebra **139**(1), 61–88 (1999)
15. Jiang, X., Ding, J., Hu, L.: Kipnis-shamir attack on HFE revisited. In: Pei, D., Yung, M., Lin, D., Wu, C. (eds.) Information Security and Cryptology, pp. 399–411. Springer (2008)
16. Joux, A., Faugère, J.C.: Algebraic cryptanalysis of hidden field equation (HFE) cryptosystems using Grobner bases. In: Advances in Cryptology – CRYPTO 2003, pp. 44–60. Springer (2003)
17. Kipnis, A., Shamir, A.: Cryptanalysis of the HFE public key cryptosystem by relinearization. In: Wiener, M. (ed.) CRYPTO 1999. LNCS, vol. 1666, pp. 19–30. Springer, Heidelberg (1999). https://doi.org/10.1007/3-540-48405-1_2

18. Macario-Rat, G., Patarin, J.: Two-face: new public key multivariate schemes. In: Joux, A., Nitaj, A., Rachidi, T. (eds.) AFRICACRYPT 2018. LNCS, vol. 10831, pp. 252–265. Springer, Cham (2018). https://doi.org/10.1007/978-3-319-89339-6_14
19. NIST Cryptographic Technology Group: Call for Additional Digital Signature Schemes for the Post-Quantum Cryptography Standardization Process. NIST Computer Security Resource Center (2022). https://csrc.nist.gov/csrc/media/Projects/pqc-dig-sig/documents/call-for-proposals-dig-sig-sept-2022.pdf
20. Øygarden, M., Felke, P., Raddum, H.: Analysis of multivariate encryption schemes: application to Dob. In: Garay, J.A. (ed.) PKC 2021. LNCS, vol. 12710, pp. 155–183. Springer, Cham (2021). https://doi.org/10.1007/978-3-030-75245-3_7
21. Øygarden, M., Felke, P., Raddum, H., Cid, C.: Cryptanalysis of the multivariate encryption scheme EFLASH. In: Jarecki, S. (ed.) CT-RSA 2020. LNCS, vol. 12006, pp. 85–105. Springer, Cham (2020). https://doi.org/10.1007/978-3-030-40186-3_5
22. Øygarden, M., Felke, P., Raddum, H.: Analysis of multivariate encryption schemes: application to Dob and C*. Journal of Cryptology 2024 (to appear). https://eprint.iacr.org/2024/595
23. Patarin, J.: Hidden fields equations (HFE) and isomorphisms of polynomials (IP): two new families of asymmetric algorithms. In: Maurer, U. (ed.) EUROCRYPT 1996. LNCS, vol. 1070, pp. 33–48. Springer, Heidelberg (1996). https://doi.org/10.1007/3-540-68339-9_4
24. Rodriguez, B.G.: 3WISE: Cubic Element-Wise trapdoor based MPKC cryptosystem. NIST Round 1 submission to the Additional Call for Signature Schemes (2023). https://csrc.nist.gov/csrc/media/Projects/pqc-dig-sig/documents/round-1/spec-files/3wise-spec-web.pdf
25. Rodriguez, B.G.: HPPC: Hidden Product of Polynomial Composition. NIST Round 1 submission to the Additional Call for Signature Schemes (2023). https://csrc.nist.gov/csrc/media/Projects/pqc-dig-sig/documents/round-1/spec-files/hppc-spec-web.pdf
26. Rodriguez, B.G.: HPPC: Hidden Product of Polynomial Composition. Cryptology ePrint Archive, Paper 2023/830 (2023). https://eprint.iacr.org/2023/830
27. Smith-Tone, D.: A Total Break of the 3WISE Digital Signature Scheme. Cryptology ePrint Archive, Paper 2023/1535 (2023). https://eprint.iacr.org/2023/1535
28. Tao, C., Petzoldt, A., Ding, J.: Efficient key recovery for all HFE signature variants. In: Malkin, T., Peikert, C. (eds.) CRYPTO 2021. LNCS, vol. 12825, pp. 70–93. Springer, Cham (2021). https://doi.org/10.1007/978-3-030-84242-0_4
29. Wang, L.C., et al.: SNOVA. NIST Round 1 submission to the Additional Call for Signature Schemes (2023). https://csrc.nist.gov/csrc/media/Projects/pqc-dig-sig/documents/round-1/spec-files/snova-spec-web.pdf
30. Wolf, C., Preneel, B.: Equivalent Keys in HFE, C*, and Variations. In: Dawson, E., Vaudenay, S. (eds.) Progress in Cryptology – Mycrypt 2005, pp. 33–49. Springer (2005)

Algebraic Key-Recovery Side-Channel Attack on *Classic McEliece*

Michaël Bulois[1], Pierre-Louis Cayrel[2], Vlad-Florin Drăgoi[3,4(✉)], and Vincent Grosso[2]

[1] Université Jean Monnet, CNRS, Centrale Lyon, INSA Lyon, Université Claude Bernard Lyon 1, ICJ UMR 5208, 42023 Saint-Etienne, France
michael.bulois@univ-st-etienne.fr

[2] Université Jean Monnet Saint-Etienne, CNRS, Institut d'Optique Graduate School, Laboratoire Hubert Curien UMR 5516, 42023 Saint-Etienne, France
{pierre.louis.cayrel,vincent.grosso}@univ-st-etienne.fr

[3] Faculty of Exact Sciences, Aurel Vlaicu University, Arad, Romania
vlad.dragoi@uav.ro

[4] LITIS, University of Rouen Normandie, Saint-Etienne du Rouvray, France

Abstract. The ongoing standardization of post-quantum cryptography (PQC) by NIST has renewed attention to code-based cryptosystems, notably *Classic McEliece*, due to their long-standing resistance to cryptanalysis and strong security against quantum adversaries.

However, implementation-level vulnerabilities such as side-channel leakage remain a critical threat.

In this work, we present a novel algebraic side-channel attack targeting the decapsulation phase of *Classic McEliece*, specifically when implemented using the reference decoding algorithm based on BerlekampâĂŞMassey and matrix-vector multiplications. Our approach exploits Hamming weight leakage observed during syndrome computations and combines linear algebra techniques over finite fields with bit-level side-channel information. The proposed method significantly improves over previous attacks in terms of computational efficiency and robustness to noise, remaining effective even under realistic leakage inaccuracies. We provide both a theoretical analysis and a probabilistic model characterizing the success rate in noisy conditions.

Our results also contribute to the theoretical understanding of algebraic distinguishability of field elements from side-channel leakage, partially validating previously stated conjectures. Experimental simulations confirm the practicality of the attack, including for large parameter sets associated with high security levels.

Importantly, the attack specifically exploits leakage arising during the matrix–vector multiplication used to compute the double syndrome in the *Classic McEliece* reference implementation. The attack does not apply if the double syndrome is computed by other means (for example, using transposed additive FFTs), or if a different decoding algorithm is used that does not require computing the double syndrome at all. This highlights that informed algorithmic choices can serve as effective countermeasures and underscores the urgent need for rigorous side-channel

C. Boura et al. (Eds.): SAC 2025, LNCS 16207, pp. 539–566, 2026.
https://doi.org/10.1007/978-3-032-10536-3_20

evaluations and secure-by-design implementations of code-based cryptosystems.

Keywords: Post-quantum cryptography · Code-based cryptography · Classic McEliece · Side-channel attacks · Linear Algebra

1 Introduction

The NIST Post-Quantum Cryptography (PQC) standardization initiative, launched in 2017, has stimulated intense research into quantum-resistant public-key cryptosystems. In 2024, the lattice-based scheme CRYSTALS-Kyber [SAB+20], now standardized under the name ML-KEM, was selected as the primary algorithm for key encapsulation mechanisms (KEMs). For digital signatures, NIST retained Falcon and CRYSTALS-Dilithium—also lattice-based—alongside SPHINCS+, a hash-based scheme, to diversify cryptographic assumptions.

To further expand this diversity, NIST also evaluated code-based candidates. Among these, HQC [AAB+22] was selected for standardization. Conversely, *Classic McEliece* [ABC+22], despite its long-standing resistance to cryptanalysis, was excluded from immediate standardization by NIST. According to NIST, its ongoing parallel evaluation by the International Organization for Standardization (ISO) raised concerns about potential standard fragmentation. Its inclusion may be reconsidered following the conclusion of the ISO process. In the meantime, attention remains focused on practical concerns such as implementation efficiency and resistance to physical attacks.

In this work, we focus on *Classic McEliece*, a code-based KEM whose security relies on the hardness of decoding random linear codes—specifically, Goppa codes. Despite its name, *Classic McEliece* is built upon the Niederreiter cryptosystem [Nie86], and has withstood decades of cryptanalytic scrutiny.

However, as with many public-key schemes, *Classic McEliece* is vulnerable to side-channel attacks, which exploit physical information leaked during execution, such as timing, power consumption, or electromagnetic emissions. Code-based cryptosystems have been known to exhibit such leakage since well before the PQC standardization effort [HMP10,MSSS11,AHPT11,CEvMS16]. Over time, various countermeasures—e.g., masking, constant-time execution—have been proposed to mitigate these threats.

Following the PQC standardization efforts, software/hardware implementations of *Classic McEliece* have been developed [CC21,CCD+22,SKE+23, FLZG24]. These implementations aim to balance performance and security across diverse platforms, ranging from constrained embedded systems to high-throughput environments. Ensuring their resilience to physical attacks remains essential for secure deployment.

Scope and Limitations. This work targets a specific class of side-channel vulnerabilities in *Classic McEliece* implementations that rely on Berlekamp–Massey decoding, as found in the official reference software. In this setting, the attack exploits leakage arising during the matrix–vector multiplication used to compute the double syndrome. Consequently, the attack does not apply if the double syndrome is computed by other means (for example, using transposed additive FFTs [CC21], which is also used in the official optimized Classic McEliece implementations), or if a different decoding algorithm is used that does not require computing the double syndrome at all. For example the public syndrome could be decoded using Patterson algorithm, hence avoiding the re-computation of a double-syndrome. This underlines the critical role of implementation choices in achieving side-channel resistance.

1.1 Notations

We aim to remain as close as possible to the notations introduced in the Round-4 *Classic McEliece* design document [ABC+22].

Integers are denoted by lowercase letters. Sets are represented using calligraphic capital letters, e.g., $\mathcal{A}$, and we denote the cardinality of a set $\mathcal{A}$ by $\#\mathcal{A}$. A set of consecutive integers is denoted by $[\![n;m]\!] = \{i \in \mathbb{Z} \mid n \leq i \leq m\}$.

We denote by $\mathbb{F}_q$ the finite field of order q. Elements of $\mathbb{F}_q$ are represented by lowercase Greek letters, e.g., $\alpha \in \mathbb{F}_q$. Polynomials over $\mathbb{F}_q$ are denoted using bold Greek letters.

Bold lowercase letters are used to denote vectors, e.g., $\boldsymbol{v}$, while bold uppercase letters denote matrices, e.g., $\boldsymbol{H}$. For a matrix $\boldsymbol{H}$, we denote by h_{ij} the entry located in the ith row and j^{th} column. We denote the ith row and j^{th} column of $\boldsymbol{H}$ by $\boldsymbol{H}[i,:]$ and $\boldsymbol{H}[:,j]$, respectively. A submatrix of $\boldsymbol{H}$ indexed by a set of rows $\mathcal{I}$ and columns $\mathcal{J}$ is written $\boldsymbol{H}[\mathcal{I},\mathcal{J}]$.

The support of a vector $\boldsymbol{v}$ is defined as $\text{supp}(\boldsymbol{v}) = \{i \mid v_i \neq 0\}$. The notion of support can also be extended to lists of integers or other indexed, compatible data structures.

Definition 1 (Finite field representation). *Let m be an integer and $\boldsymbol{\zeta} \in \mathbb{F}_2[X]$ be an irreducible polynomial of degree m. An element $\alpha \in \mathbb{F}_{2^m}$ is represented as an element $\boldsymbol{\alpha} = (\alpha_0, \dots, \alpha_{m-1})$ of $\mathbb{F}_2^m$ via a fixed isomorphism $\mathbb{F}_{2^m} \cong \mathbb{F}_2[X]/(\boldsymbol{\zeta})$: $\alpha = \sum_{i=0}^{m-1} \alpha_i x^i$ where $x = \overline{X}$ is the class of X in $\mathbb{F}_2[X]/(\boldsymbol{\zeta})$ thus yielding an identification $\mathbb{F}_{2^m} \cong (\mathbb{F}_2)^m$.*

In particular, $\mathbb{F}_{2^m}$ is an $\mathbb{F}_2$-vector space with a distinguished basis $B_{can} = B_{can,\zeta} = (x^i)_{i \in [\![0,m-1]\!]}$.

Definition 2 (Hamming weight). *Let $\boldsymbol{c} \in \mathbb{F}_q^n$. Its Hamming weight is $\mathsf{wt}(\boldsymbol{c}) = \#\text{supp}(\boldsymbol{c})$. For $\alpha \in \mathbb{F}_{2^m}$ we define its Hamming weight by $\mathsf{wt}(\alpha) \overset{\text{def}}{=} \mathsf{wt}(\boldsymbol{\alpha})$, where $\boldsymbol{\alpha} \in (\mathbb{F}_2)^m$ is the binary extension of α.*

Definition 3 (Binary Hamming weight). *Let $\mathsf{wt}_2 : \mathbb{F}_{2^m} \to \mathbb{F}_2$ be defined by $\mathsf{wt}_2(\alpha_0, \dots, \alpha_{m-1}) = \sum_{i=0}^{m-1} \alpha_i$ where the sum is understood in $\mathbb{F}_2$. It is a linear form of $\mathbb{F}_{2^m}$, i.e. an element of the dual $\mathbb{F}_{2^m}^*$.*

The binary Hamming weight appears to be a natural candidate as a linear form that can be derived from side-channel information.

Definition 4 (Code). *A code $\mathscr{C}$ of length n is a subset of $\mathbb{F}_q^n$. An element $\mathbf{c} = (c_0, \ldots, c_{n-1}) \in \mathscr{C}$ is called a codeword. If $\mathscr{C}$ is a vector subspace of dimension k of the vector space $\mathbb{F}_q^n$, then $\mathscr{C}$ is a linear code of length n and dimension k. Such a linear code is referred to as an $[n,k]_q$ code.*

Definition 5 (Parity-check matrix). *Let $\mathscr{C}$ be an $[n,k]_q$ linear code, and let $\boldsymbol{H}$ be an $(n-k) \times n$ matrix such that*

$$\forall \mathbf{c} \in \mathscr{C}, \quad \boldsymbol{H}\boldsymbol{c}^T = 0.$$

Then, $\boldsymbol{H}$ is a parity-check matrix for $\mathscr{C}$. Let $\boldsymbol{v} \in \mathbb{F}_q^n$. The syndrome of the vector $\boldsymbol{v}$ with respect to $\boldsymbol{H}$ is defined as $\boldsymbol{s} = \boldsymbol{H}\boldsymbol{v}^T$.

Definition 6 (Goppa code). *Let $\mathcal{L} = \{\alpha_0, \ldots, \alpha_{n-1}\}$, where $\alpha_i \in \mathbb{F}_q$ and $\alpha_i \neq \alpha_j$ for $i \neq j$. Let $\gamma(x) \in \mathbb{F}_q[x]$ with $\deg(\gamma) = t$, such that $\forall \alpha \in \mathcal{L}, \gamma(\alpha) \neq 0$. The set*

$$\mathscr{G}(\gamma, \mathcal{L}) = \left\{ \mathbf{c} = (c_0, c_1, \ldots, c_{n-1}) \in \mathbb{F}_2^n : \sum_{i=0}^{n-1} \frac{c_i}{x - \alpha_i} \equiv 0 \text{ in } \mathbb{F}_q[x]/(\gamma(x)) \right\}$$

defines a Goppa code with parameters $\mathcal{L}$ and $\gamma(x)$. Additionally, let $\boldsymbol{H}$ be the $t \times n$ matrix defined as

$$\boldsymbol{H} = \begin{pmatrix} \gamma(\alpha_0)^{-1} & \cdots & \gamma(\alpha_{n-1})^{-1} \\ \vdots & \ddots & \vdots \\ \alpha_0^{t-1}\gamma(\alpha_0)^{-1} & \cdots & \alpha_{n-1}^{t-1}\gamma(\alpha_{n-1})^{-1} \end{pmatrix}.$$

Its expansion over $\mathbb{F}_2$, an $mt \times n$ matrix, serves as a parity-check matrix for $\mathscr{G}(\gamma, \mathcal{L})$.

1.2 The *Classic McEliece* KEM

Classic McEliece [ABC+22] is a Key Encapsulation Mechanism (KEM) based on the Niederreiter cryptosystem using Goppa codes.

In Table 1, we present the parameter sets for *Classic McEliece* and *toyeliece*, a smaller configuration intended for research and experimentation. In the ISO proposal,[1] the authors refined the parameter list and restricted it to the case $m = 13$. In particular, the irreducible polynomial ζ used to define the extension field $\mathbb{F}_{2^m}$ is given by

$$\zeta(x) = x^{13} + x^4 + x^3 + x + 1.$$

Classic McEliece [ABC+22] consists of three main algorithms:

[1] https://classic.mceliece.org/iso-mceliece-20230419.pdf.

Table 1. Classic McEliece [ABC+22] and `toyeliece` [BCM+25] parameter sets.

Parameter Set	toyeliece 51220	mceliece 348864	mceliece 460896	mceliece 6688128	mceliece 6960119	mceliece 8192128
m	9	12	13	13	13	13
n	512	3488	4608	6688	6960	8192
t	20	64	96	128	119	128

KeyGen : The key generation process selects a random permuted support $\mathcal{L}$, consisting of n distinct elements from $\mathbb{F}_{2^m}$, and an irreducible monic polynomial γ of degree t. Together, $(\gamma, \mathcal{L})$ form the secret key sk, which is used to compute the private parity-check matrix $\boldsymbol{H}_{\text{priv}}$. This matrix is then reduced to systematic form, yielding the public matrix $\boldsymbol{H}_{\text{pub}} = (\mathbf{I}_{mt} \,|\, \mathbf{T})$.

Encap : A random error vector $\boldsymbol{e} \in \mathbb{F}_2^n$ of Hamming weight t is sampled, and the ciphertext is computed as $\boldsymbol{z} = \boldsymbol{H}_{\text{pub}}\boldsymbol{e}^T$. The session key K is derived by hashing $\boldsymbol{e}$ and $\boldsymbol{z}$.

Decap : The error vector $\boldsymbol{e}$ is recovered from the ciphertext $\boldsymbol{z}$ using knowledge of γ and $\mathcal{L}$. The session key K is then derived by hashing $\boldsymbol{e}$ and $\boldsymbol{z}$.

In this article, we focus on the decapsulation algorithm, presented in Algorithm 1. In this step, the owner of the private key computes a syndrome polynomial using the Vandermonde structure of the Goppa code to decode the ciphertext $\boldsymbol{z}$ and derive the session key K.

Algorithm 1. The decapsulation algorithm of the *Classic McEliece* KEM

Input: Ciphertext $\boldsymbol{z}$ and private key $\mathsf{sk} = (\gamma, \mathcal{L})$
Output: Session key K

1: Compute the padded vector $\boldsymbol{v} = (\boldsymbol{z}, 0, \ldots, 0)$ of length n
2: Construct the matrix:

$$\boldsymbol{H}_{\text{priv}_{\gamma^2}} = \begin{pmatrix} \gamma(\alpha_0)^{-2} & \cdots & \gamma(\alpha_{n-1})^{-2} \\ \vdots & \ddots & \vdots \\ \alpha_0^{2t-1}\gamma(\alpha_0)^{-2} & \cdots & \alpha_{n-1}^{2t-1}\gamma(\alpha_{n-1})^{-2} \end{pmatrix}$$

3: Compute the syndrome: $\boldsymbol{s} = \boldsymbol{H}_{\text{priv}_{\gamma^2}}\boldsymbol{v}^T$
4: Use the Berlekamp-Massey algorithm to compute the error locator polynomial $\sigma(x)$
5: Evaluate $\sigma(\alpha_0), \ldots, \sigma(\alpha_{n-1})$ for $\alpha_i \in \mathcal{L}$ and recover the error vector $\boldsymbol{e}$
6: Compute $K = \mathsf{hash}(1\|e\|\boldsymbol{z})$
7: **return** K

In the remainder of this work, we focus on Step 3 of the above algorithm, namely the syndrome computation. To simplify notation, we define $\gamma(\alpha_i)^{-2} = \beta_i$ for $0 \leq i < n$.

1.3 Related Work

Side-Channel Scenario. Key-recovery side-channel attacks targeting both the reference and optimized implementations of *Classic McEliece* have been recently demonstrated [GJJ22, SCD+23, BCM+25, DCV+25]. Among these, several attacks focus on leakage during the syndrome computation step of the decapsulation process, each employing different strategies to address classifier accuracy and leakage modeling.

As shown in [DCV+25], the syndrome computation (see Step 3 of Algorithm 1) leaks side-channel information—specifically, power consumption traces—that enable an adversary to observe the following matrix:

$$\boldsymbol{H}_{\mathsf{wt}} = \begin{pmatrix} \mathsf{wt}(\beta_0) & \cdots & \mathsf{wt}(\beta_{n-1}) \\ \mathsf{wt}(\alpha_0\beta_0) & \cdots & \mathsf{wt}(\alpha_{n-1}\beta_{n-1}) \\ \vdots & \ddots & \vdots \\ \mathsf{wt}(\alpha_0^{2t-1}\beta_0) & \cdots & \mathsf{wt}(\alpha_{n-1}^{2t-1}\beta_{n-1}) \end{pmatrix}$$

Experimental results demonstrate that this leakage can be used to recover a sufficient number of pairs (α_i, β_i). The authors then formulate the following conjecture:

Conjecture 1 ([DCV+25]). For almost all degree-m monic irreducible polynomials $\boldsymbol{\zeta} \in \mathbb{F}_2[x]$, the extension field $\mathbb{F}_{2^m} \cong \mathbb{F}_2[X]/(\boldsymbol{\zeta})$ is such that almost all pairs $(\alpha, \beta) \in \mathbb{F}_{2^m}^* \times \mathbb{F}_{2^m}^*$ can be uniquely determined from $\boldsymbol{H}_{\mathsf{wt}}$, provided that t is sufficiently large.

In the same work [DCV+25], the conjecture was originally formulated based on a smaller subset of the information. Specifically, the authors claimed that fewer than $2t$ rows (denoted $d_{m,t} < 2t$) are sufficient to distinguish the pairs (α_i, β_i).

We also consider a noisy setting, in which several entries of $\boldsymbol{H}_{\mathsf{wt}}$ are incorrect—typically deviating from the correct value by either $+1$ or -1. The probability that a given value is correct is referred to as the *accuracy*, commonly denoted by a. In the experiments conducted in [DCV+25] using the ChipWhisperer platform [OC14], the observed accuracy for Hamming weight measurements exceeds 0.96.

Exploitation of the Leakage. In [DCV+25], a side-channel attack targets the syndrome computation step to recover both γ and $\mathcal{L}$. While the authors demonstrate that their method can tolerate some classifier inaccuracies, the attack still requires relatively high accuracy (≥ 0.945), i.e., low-noise measurement environments. In practice, such accuracy may not always be achievable in noisier setups.

In [VCC+25], the authors investigate the robustness of side-channel attacks on *Classic McEliece* in the presence of side-channel estimation errors. They propose a simple yet effective algorithm capable of recovering a list of Hamming weights from noisy measurements, where each Hamming weight is affected by an error of at most ± 1. Their algorithm achieves a high success rate in reconstructing the corresponding field elements, and notably, it requires only t out of n values (or equivalently mt values). However, the method is restricted to scenarios where the errors are bounded by ± 1.

In both studies, exhaustive search techniques are employed, resulting in high computational complexity. Table 2 summarizes the different attacks and the corresponding attack scenarios.

Table 2. Complexity comparison for the side-channel key-recovery attacks targeting the syndrome computation in the *Classic McEliece* KEM.

Article	**Scenario**	**Type of attack**	Accuracy
[DCV+25]	Erroneous Hamming weights $\Rightarrow (\alpha, \gamma(\alpha))$ not recovered	Exhaustive search precomputation	$a > 0.945$
[VCC+25]	Error ± 1 on Hamming weights $\Rightarrow (\alpha, \gamma(\alpha))$ recovered	Exhaustive search and decoding	$a > 0.81$
This article	Error ± 1 (or even higher[a]) on Hamming weights $\Rightarrow (\alpha, \gamma(\alpha))$ recovered	$\mathcal{O}(m^3 t)$ complexity and decoding	$a > 0.74$

[a] see Remark 5

1.4 The Berlekamp-Massey Algorithm

The Berlekamp-Massey algorithm [Mas69] is an efficient method for determining the shortest linear feedback shift register (LFSR) that generates a given binary sequence. Originally developed for decoding BCH and Reed-Solomon codes, it has found widespread applications in coding theory and cryptanalysis.

In the context of this work, we use the algorithm to recover the minimal polynomial $\chi(Y)$ that characterizes a sequence of Hamming weights modulo 2. This polynomial plays a central role in reconstructing secret key elements in our side-channel attacks on the *Classic McEliece* cryptosystem. By leveraging algebraic properties, the algorithm iteratively updates $\chi(Y)$ based on discrepancies observed in the sequence, ensuring an optimal reconstruction. For completeness, the Berlekamp-Massey algorithm is included in the Sect. A (Algorithm 5).

1.5 Contributions

In this work, we revisit side-channel key-recovery attacks targeting the reference implementation of *Classic McEliece* during the decapsulation phase. Building on the same threat model as in [VCC+25], we propose a novel attack that significantly improves upon previous approaches [VCC+25, DCV+25], both in terms of computational efficiency and resilience to estimation errors in the side-channel leakage.

Our contribution is threefold:

- **Improved robustness and efficiency.** We introduce a new algebraic attack that tolerates realistic noise levels in the leakage and exhibits much lower computational complexity, especially for high values of the extension degree m. Unlike prior approaches, our method scales well and remains practical for large parameter sets relevant to post-quantum security.
- **Algebraic framework for noisy leakage.** Our analysis offers a new perspective on the effectiveness of previous attacks by establishing an algebraic link between the Hamming weights of intermediate sensitive variables and the corresponding secret field elements. This connection holds even under noisy side-channel observations. The framework we develop generalizes to any $\mathbb{F}_2$-linear leakage function, although our results suggest that the parity of the Hamming weight is the most natural and realistic leakage function in practice.
- **Theoretical insights and generalization.** Our results deepen the understanding of Conjecture 1 from [DCV+25], showing that distinguishing field elements based on side-channel information remains feasible even when the exploited leakage is strictly less informative than in previous attacks. In particular, we explain why primitive elements of $\mathbb{F}_{2^m}$ can be efficiently distinguished in the noise-free case, and provide evidence supporting this behavior under realistic assumptions.

At the core of our approach is an efficient algorithm that operates on $\boldsymbol{H}_{\mathsf{wt}_2}$, the reduction modulo 2 of the matrix of Hamming weights observed during syndrome computation. This allows for accurate recovery of the pairs $(\alpha, \gamma(\alpha))$ with high probability, even in the presence of noise, and with complexity orders of magnitude lower than previous methods.

1.6 Organization

This article is organized as follows.

In Sect. 2, we study secret reconstruction from Hamming weight leakage in a noise-free setting, covering algebraic preliminaries, the reconstruction algorithm, theoretical justification, and complexity analysis.

Section 3 extends this to noisy environments, presenting decoding algorithms and analyzing success probabilities.

Section 4 discusses applications to other code-based cryptosystems.

Finally, Sect. 4.3 addresses implementation considerations and proposes countermeasures, highlighting decoding methods and general protections against side-channel leakage.

2 Recovering (α, β) from $\widetilde{\boldsymbol{H}}_{\mathsf{wt}}$: Algebraic Method

2.1 Algebraic Preliminaries

Let $\mathbb{K}$ be a field, V a vector space, and h a linear endomorphism of V (i.e., a $\mathbb{K}$-linear map $h : V \to V$). In the context of this paper, we have $\mathbb{K} = \mathbb{F}_2$ and $V = \mathbb{F}_{2^m}$ or its dual space $\mathbb{F}_{2^m}^* = \{\varphi : V \to \mathbb{F}_2 \mid \varphi \text{ linear}\}$.

The following hypothesis on the endomorphism h will be frequently used in what follows:

$$\text{The characteristic polynomial } \chi_h \text{ of } h \text{ is irreducible.} \qquad (H_1)$$

Lemma 1. *Assuming hypothesis* (H_1)*, there are no nontrivial* h*-stable subspaces of* V*. In other words, if* $W \subseteq V$ *satisfies* $h(W) \subseteq W$*, then either* $W = \{0\}$ *or* $W = V$*.*

Proof. Let $W \subseteq V$ be an h-stable subspace and choose a basis B of V obtained by extending a basis of W. The matrix of h relative to B then has a block upper-triangular form:

$$\begin{pmatrix} h_{|W} & * \\ 0 & h_{V/W} \end{pmatrix}.$$

Consequently, the characteristic polynomial factors as

$$\chi_h = \chi_{h_{|W}} \times \chi_{h_{V/W}}.$$

Since χ_h is irreducible by hypothesis, one of these factors must be trivial. Hence, either $\dim W = 0$ (i.e., $W = \{0\}$) or $\dim V/W = 0$ (i.e., $W = V$). □

In the following, the notation h^i denotes the i-th power of the endomorphism h, i.e., $h^2(\boldsymbol{v}) = h(h(\boldsymbol{v}))$.

Corollary 1. *Assume that* h *satisfies* (H_1)*. Then, for any nonzero vector* $\boldsymbol{v} \in V \setminus \{0\}$*, the family*

$$(\boldsymbol{v}, h(\boldsymbol{v}), h^2(\boldsymbol{v}), \ldots, h^{\dim V - 1}(\boldsymbol{v}))$$

forms a basis of V*.*

Moreover, if $\dim V \geq 2$*, then for any integer* $i \in \mathbb{Z}$*, the family*

$$(h^i(\boldsymbol{v}), h^{i+1}(\boldsymbol{v}), \ldots, h^{i+\dim V - 1}(\boldsymbol{v}))$$

is also a basis of V*.*

Proof. Consider the subspace

$$W = \langle h^i(\boldsymbol{v}) \mid i \in \mathbb{N} \rangle,$$

the smallest h-stable subspace of V containing $\boldsymbol{v}$. Since V is finite-dimensional, there exists a minimal integer n such that

$$h^n(\boldsymbol{v}) \in \langle \boldsymbol{v}, h(\boldsymbol{v}), \ldots, h^{n-1}(\boldsymbol{v}) \rangle.$$

Thus,

$$W = \langle \boldsymbol{v}, h(\boldsymbol{v}), \ldots, h^{n-1}(\boldsymbol{v}) \rangle.$$

By Lemma 1, the only h-stable subspaces of V are $\{0\}$ and V itself, and since $\boldsymbol{v} \neq 0$, it follows that $W = V$. Hence,

$$(\boldsymbol{v}, h(\boldsymbol{v}), \ldots, h^{n-1}(\boldsymbol{v}))$$

is a spanning set of V. By minimality of n, these vectors are linearly independent, so $n = \dim V$, proving the first assertion.

Now assume $\dim V \geq 2$. If $\ker(h)$ contains a nonzero vector $\mathbf{w}$, then $\mathbb{K}\mathbf{w}$ is a nontrivial h-stable subspace of dimension 1, contradicting Lemma 1. Hence, $\ker(h) = \{0\}$, so h is invertible. Therefore, $h^i(\boldsymbol{v})$ is well-defined and nonzero for all $i \in \mathbb{Z}$. The second assertion then follows directly from the first by applying powers of h or h^{-1}.

2.2 Linear Algebra Related to the Sequence $(\mathsf{wt}_2(\alpha^i\beta))_i$

Let $\alpha, \beta \in \mathbb{F}_{2^m}$. For any integer $i \in \mathbb{N}$, the element $\alpha^i\beta \in \mathbb{F}_{2^m}$ has a Hamming weight modulo 2 denoted by $\mathsf{wt}_2(\alpha^i\beta) \in \mathbb{F}_2$. In this subsection, we investigate the algebraic properties of the sequence

$$\mathcal{W}_{\alpha,\beta} := \left(\mathsf{wt}_2(\alpha^i\beta)\right)_{i\in\mathbb{N}},$$

which takes values in $\mathbb{F}_2$.

Our analysis relies on the following fundamental observations:

- The map $\mathsf{wt}_2 : \mathbb{F}_{2^m} \to \mathbb{F}_2$ is an $\mathbb{F}_2$-linear form,
- Multiplication by α defines a linear endomorphism $h_\alpha : \mathbb{F}_{2^m} \to \mathbb{F}_{2^m}$,
- This endomorphism induces a dual endomorphism $h_\alpha^* : \mathbb{F}_{2^m}^* \to \mathbb{F}_{2^m}^*$ on the dual space given by

$$h_\alpha^*(\varphi)(x) = \varphi(\alpha x), \quad \forall \varphi \in \mathbb{F}_{2^m}^*,\ x \in \mathbb{F}_{2^m}.$$

Remark 1. If B is a basis of $\mathbb{F}_{2^m}$ and B^* its dual basis, then the matrix representation of h_α^* in B^* satisfies

$$\mathrm{Mat}_{B^*}(h_\alpha^*) = \mathrm{Mat}_B(h_\alpha)^T.$$

In particular, the irreducibility condition (H_1) on h_α is equivalent to the same condition on h_α^*.

Lemma 2. *The hypothesis (H_1) on h_α is equivalent to the condition $\mathbb{F}_2[\alpha] = \mathbb{F}_{2^m}$.*

Proof. If $\mathbb{F}_2[\alpha] = \mathbb{F}_{2^m}$, then α is a root of an irreducible polynomial $\chi_\alpha \in \mathbb{F}_2[Y]$ of degree m. In the basis $(1, \alpha, \alpha^2, \ldots, \alpha^{m-1})$, the matrix of the endomorphism h_α is the companion matrix of χ_α. In particular, the characteristic polynomial χ_{h_α} of h_α coincides with χ_α, which is irreducible.

Conversely, if $\mathbb{F}_2[\alpha] \neq \mathbb{F}_{2^m}$, then the set $W := \mathbb{F}_2[\alpha]$ is a nontrivial h_α-stable subspace of $\mathbb{F}_{2^m}$. The result then follows from Lemma 1. □

From now on, we assume hypothesis (H_1) for α with $m \geq 2$, and denote by

$$\chi_\alpha = Y^m + \sum_{\ell=0}^{m-1} c_\ell Y^\ell \in \mathbb{F}_2[Y]$$

the irreducible monic polynomial of degree m with α as a root. As noted in the proof, it coincides with the characteristic polynomial of h_α (and of h_α^*).

Remark 2. The sequence $\mathcal{W}_{\alpha,\beta}$ can thus be viewed as the output of a linear feedback shift register (LFSR) over $\mathbb{F}_2$ with feedback polynomial χ_α (or $\chi_{\alpha^{-1}}$, depending on convention). This directly follows from the recurrence relation

$$\alpha^{i+m} = \sum_{\ell=0}^{m-1} c_\ell \alpha^{i+\ell}$$

and the linearity of wt_2.

We also introduce the family $\varphi_\alpha[i] := (h_\alpha^*)^i(\mathsf{wt}_2) \in \mathbb{F}_{2^m}^*$ for $i \in \mathbb{N}$, and note that by construction,

$$\varphi_\alpha[i](\beta) = \mathsf{wt}_2(\alpha^i \beta), \tag{1}$$

which corresponds to the i-th term of the sequence $\mathcal{W}_{\alpha,\beta}$.

From Corollary 1, we deduce that

$$B_\alpha^* := (\varphi_\alpha[0], \ldots, \varphi_\alpha[m-1])$$

is a basis of $\mathbb{F}_{2^m}^*$.

Let B_α be the basis of $\mathbb{F}_{2^m}$ dual to B_α^*. By definition, the coordinates of an element $\delta \in \mathbb{F}_{2^m}$ in this basis are given by

$$Mat_{B_\alpha}(\delta) = \left(\varphi_\alpha[0](\delta), \ldots, \varphi_\alpha[m-1](\delta)\right)^T. \tag{2}$$

When applied to $\delta = \beta$, equations (2) and (1) imply that the coordinates of β in the basis B_α form the initial state (seed) of the LFSR described in Remark 2.

To relate the coordinates of an element $\delta \in \mathbb{F}_{2^m}$ in the two bases B_α and B_{can} (see Definition 1), we use the change-of-basis formula:

$$Mat_{B_\alpha}(\delta) = Mat_{B_\alpha}(B_{can}) \times Mat_{B_{can}}(\delta). \tag{3}$$

2.3 Noise-Free Setting

Thanks to the results from Subsect. 2.2, we now have all the necessary tools to build an algorithm that reconstructs pairs (α_k, β_k) from the sequence of Hamming weights $\boldsymbol{H}_{\mathsf{wt}}[: k]$.

More precisely, let $\alpha, \beta \in \mathbb{F}_{2^m}$ such that $\mathbb{F}_2[\alpha] = \mathbb{F}_{2^m}$ and $\beta \neq 0$. For any $i \in [\![0, 2t]\!]$, define

$$w_i = \mathsf{wt}(\alpha^i \beta) \in [\![0, m]\!] \quad \text{and} \quad \bar{w}_i = \mathsf{wt}_2(\alpha^i \beta) \in \mathbb{F}_2,$$

so that $(\bar{w}_i)_i$ are the first $2t$ terms of the sequence $\mathcal{W}_{\alpha,\beta}$.

Then:

- algorithms, such as Berlekamp-Massey, allow us to recover the minimal polynomial generating a linearly recurrent sequence. By Remark 2, this lets us reconstruct the polynomial χ_α from the sequence $(\bar{w}_i)_{i\in[\![0,2\,m]\!]}$. The condition $\mathbb{F}_2[\alpha] = \mathbb{F}_{2^m}$ (equivalently (H_1) on h_α) corresponds to $\deg \chi_\alpha = m$, which can be tested. If this test fails (which occurs only for very few choices of α), we abandon the reconstruction for this specific pair α, β.
- Knowing that α is a root of χ_α leaves exactly m possible candidates for α. Denote the roots of χ_α by $\alpha^{(0)}, \ldots, \alpha^{(m-1)}$.
- For each $\alpha^{(\ell)}$, we can compute

$$C_\ell = Mat_{B_{\alpha^{(\ell)}}}(B_{can}).$$

Indeed, by Eq. (2), we have

$$C_\ell = \left(\mathsf{wt}_2((\alpha^{(\ell)})^i x^j)\right)_{i,j\in[\![0,m-1]\!]}.$$

Since $\chi_{\alpha^{(\ell)}} = \chi_\alpha$ is irreducible of degree m, we have $\mathbb{F}_2[\alpha^{(\ell)}] = \mathbb{F}_{2^m}$, so $B_{\alpha^{(\ell)}}$ forms a basis (as shown for B_α in Subsect. 2.2). Therefore, C_ℓ is invertible.
- Whenever $\alpha = \alpha^{(\ell)}$, combining Eqs. (3), (2) and (1) yields

$$Mat_{B_{can}}(\beta) = C_\ell^{-1} \times (\bar{w}_0, \ldots, \bar{w}_{m-1})^T.$$

For an arbitrary ℓ, we can always define and compute an element $\beta^{(\ell)} \in \mathbb{F}_{2^m}$ by setting

$$Mat_{B_{can}}(\beta^{(\ell)}) = C_\ell^{-1} \times (\bar{w}_0, \ldots, \bar{w}_{m-1})^T.$$

Note that the different pairs $(\alpha^{(\ell)}, \beta^{(\ell)})$ thus obtained generate identical sequences $\mathcal{W}_{\alpha^{(\ell)},\beta^{(\ell)}}$ since these are outputs of an LFSR with the same minimal polynomial χ_α and the same initial state (seed)

$$Mat_{B_{\alpha^{(\ell)}}}(\beta^{(\ell)})^T = \left(C_\ell Mat_{B_{can}}(\beta^{(\ell)})\right)^T = (\bar{w}_0, \ldots, \bar{w}_{m-1})^T.$$

- However, we claim that the original Hamming weight sequences $\left(\mathsf{wt}((\alpha^{(\ell)})^i \beta^{(\ell)})\right)_i$ very likely distinguish the m candidate pairs. This allows us to identify a unique matching pair, which must then be (α, β). Supporting evidence for this claim is provided in Lemma 3.

The central algorithm of this subsection can thus be summarized in the following pseudo-code.

Algorithm 2. Constructive algorithm to find pairs.

Input: The matrix $\boldsymbol{H}_{\mathsf{wt}}$

Output: t good pairs $(\alpha_k, \beta_k)_{k\in\mathcal{I}}$ with $\#\mathcal{I} = t$

1: $\mathcal{I} = \emptyset$, $k = -1$ ▷ $\mathcal{I}$ is the set of good pairs, k the index of a column

2: **while** $\#\mathcal{I} \neq t$ **do**

3: $k = k + 1$ ▷ browse $\boldsymbol{H}_{\mathsf{wt}_2} = \boldsymbol{H}_{\mathsf{wt}} \pmod 2$ column-wise

4: Construct $\mathcal{W} = (\mathsf{wt}_2(\alpha_k^i \beta_k))_{i\in[\![0,2m-1]\!]}$ from column k of $\boldsymbol{H}_{\mathsf{wt}_2}$

5: $\chi \leftarrow \mathrm{BM}(\mathcal{W})$ ▷ Apply Berlekamp-Massey's algorithm to $\mathcal{W}$ and store its generating polynomial

6: **if** $\deg(\chi) \neq m$ **then** ▷ α_k does not satisfy (H_1)

7: **go to** 3 ▷ go to line 3 to take the next column

8: **else**

9: Compute the roots of χ: $\alpha^{(0)}, \ldots, \alpha^{(m-1)}$

10: $\mathcal{J} = \emptyset$ ▷ $\mathcal{J}$ stores the $(\alpha^{(\ell)}, \beta^{(\ell)})$ compatible with $\boldsymbol{H}_{\mathsf{wt}}[:k]$

11: **for** $\ell \leftarrow 0$ to $m-1$ **do** ▷ browse the roots of χ

12: Compute

$$C_\ell = \begin{pmatrix} \mathsf{wt}_2((\alpha^{(\ell)})^0 x^0) & \ldots & \mathsf{wt}_2((\alpha^{(\ell)})^0 x^{m-1}) \\ \mathsf{wt}_2((\alpha^{(\ell)})^1 x^0) & \ldots & \mathsf{wt}_2((\alpha^{(\ell)})^1 x^{m-1}) \\ \vdots & \ddots & \vdots \\ \mathsf{wt}_2((\alpha^{(\ell)})^{m-1} x^0) & \ldots & \mathsf{wt}_2((\alpha^{(\ell)})^{m-1} x^{m-1}) \end{pmatrix}, \quad W = \begin{pmatrix} \mathsf{wt}_2(\alpha_k^0 \beta_k) \\ \mathsf{wt}_2(\alpha_k^1 \beta_k) \\ \vdots \\ \mathsf{wt}_2(\alpha_k^{m-1} \beta_k) \end{pmatrix}$$

13: Compute $\beta^{(\ell)} = C_\ell^{-1} \times W$

14: **if** $(\mathsf{wt}((\alpha_k^{(\ell)})^i (\beta_k^{(\ell)})))_i = (\mathsf{wt}(\alpha_k^i \beta_k))_i$ **then** ▷ use of $\boldsymbol{H}_{\mathsf{wt}}$

15: $\mathcal{J} \leftarrow$ Append $(\alpha^{(\ell)}, \beta^{(\ell)})$

16: **if** $\#\mathcal{J} = 1$ **then** ▷ a single match among the m pairs of candidates

17: $\alpha_k, \beta_k = \mathcal{J}[0]$

18: $\mathcal{I} \leftarrow$ Append (α_k, β_k, k) ▷ (α_k, β_k, k) indicates that (α_k, β_k) generates column k

Remark 3. The first part of the algorithm could also be applied to various linear leakages other than wt_2. For instance,

- The "trace" operator is also $\mathbb{F}_2$-linear, but it might be difficult to obtain via physical attacks.
- Taking every single coordinate in $(\mathbb{F}_2)^m$ is $\mathbb{F}_2$-linear. This is particularly true for least significant bit leakage, which in some devices can have a greater impact on power consumption than other bits.

Note that with such individual leakage (and without data on the full Hamming weight wt), we cannot distinguish the m roots of a given polynomial χ as done in line 14 and afterwards.

However, if one has access to two such leakages, each given wrong candidate $\alpha^{(\ell)}$ might give rise to different candidates $\beta^{(\ell)}$, $\beta^{(\ell)\prime}$ for each leakage, thus allowing to eliminate these candidates.

2.4 Theoretical Sufficiency of the Knowledge of $\mathsf{wt}(\alpha^i\beta)_i$

We now provide evidence of why the condition in line 16 should often be satisfied.

Given an irreducible $\mathbb{F}_2$-polynomial ζ of degree m (from which we construct $\mathbb{F}_{2^m}$ and its associated Hamming distance), we say that there is a *collision* between the distinct pairs (α, β) and (α', β') if the entire sequences $(\mathsf{wt}(\alpha^i\beta))_{i\in\mathbb{N}}$ and $(\mathsf{wt}((\alpha')^i\beta'))_{i\in\mathbb{N}}$ coincide. With the following lemma, we provide a proof for Conjecture 1.

Lemma 3. *Assume that ζ is primitive. Then there is no collision with a pair (α, β) such that α is primitive.*

Remark 4.
- The condition that ζ is primitive is necessary. Indeed, computations show that for some defining polynomials (such as $\sum_{i=0}^{12} X^i$ for $m = 12$) there are typically clusters of m collisions. From the discussion above Algorithm 2, these clusters must be made of the $(\alpha^{(\ell)}, \beta^{(\ell)})$ with $\ell \in [\![0, m-1]\!]$. However, for *Classic McEliece*, the primitivity condition on ζ is always satisfied.
- The condition that α is primitive is not too restrictive. In the worst case for *Classic McEliece*, $m = 12$, among the 4020 elements α such that $\mathbb{F}_2[\alpha] = \mathbb{F}_{2^m}$, 1728 are primitive. For the ISO parameters ($m = 13$), except for $\alpha = 0$ and $\alpha = 1$, all elements are primitive.
- The lemma only tells us that the Hamming weight sequences discriminate the candidates at some integer index which may be beyond $2t$, the length of the acquired sequence. But, since two different sequences necessarily differ at some point, there is no reason for the bifurcation not to occur early on.
- Effective computations show that the Hamming weight sequence indeed discriminates the candidates early on.

Proof. of Lemma 3 We can assume $m \geqslant 2$.

Note that if α is primitive, then α satisfies hypothesis (H_1). It follows from the discussion preceding Algorithm 2 that, whenever there is a collision with a pair (α', β') then $\alpha \neq \alpha'$ and $\chi_\alpha = \chi_{\alpha'}$. Since the different roots of a given irreducible polynomial are related by iterations of the Frobenius automorphism $Fr(\delta) = \delta^2$, there exists some $i_0 \in [\![1, m-1]\!]$ such that $\alpha' = \alpha^{2^{i_0}}$.

Since α is primitive and $\beta \neq 0$, we have $\mathbb{F}_{2^m} \setminus \{0\} = \{\alpha^i\beta | i \in [\![0, 2^m - 2]\!]\}$. We are interested in the indices $t_0, \ldots, t_{m-1}$ satisfying $\alpha^{t_\ell}\beta = x^\ell$ ($\ell \in [\![0, m-1]\!]$). Since α is primitive, those indices are well-defined modulo $2^m - 1$. Moreover, $x = \frac{x^\ell}{x^{\ell-1}} = \frac{\alpha^{t_\ell}\beta}{\alpha^{t_{\ell-1}}\beta} = \alpha^{t_\ell - t_{\ell-1}}$ so $t_0, \ldots, t_{m-1}$ forms an arithmetic progression in $\mathbb{Z}/(2^m-1)\mathbb{Z}$ with a common difference of $r := t_1 - t_0$. Since ζ is primitive, x is a generator of $(\mathbb{F}_{2^m} \setminus \{0\}, \times)$ so r is invertible in $\mathbb{Z}/(2^m-1)\mathbb{Z}$.

For (α', β'), the same holds, but we will only need to note that the indices $t'_0, \ldots, t'_{m-1}$ defined by $(\alpha')^{t'_\ell}\beta = x^\ell$ satisfy the equality $x = (\alpha')^{t'_\ell - t'_{\ell-1}}$.

We have chosen the indices t_ℓ since they are precisely the indices for which $\mathsf{wt}(\alpha^t\beta) = 1$. From the collision hypothesis, there exists a permutation σ of $[\![0, m-1]\!]$ such that for all ℓ, we have $t'_\ell = t_{\sigma(\ell)}$. From the relation between α and α', we deduce that $\alpha^{2^{i_0}(t_{\sigma(\ell)} - t_{\sigma(\ell-1)})} = (\alpha')^{t'_\ell - t'_{\ell-1}} = x$. In particular,

$(t_{\sigma(\ell)}2^{i_0})_\ell$ also forms an arithmetic progression in $\mathbb{Z}/(2^m-1)\mathbb{Z}$ with a common difference of r. This can also be reformulated as follows: $(t_{\sigma(\ell)})_\ell$ forms an arithmetic progression in $\mathbb{Z}/(2^m-1)\mathbb{Z}$ with a common difference of $r2^{m-i_0}$.

Let $c = \sigma(1) - \sigma(0) \in [\![-m+1, m-1]\!]$, then $rc = t_{\sigma(1)} - t_{\sigma(0)} = r2^{m-i_0}$. Similarly let $c' = \sigma^{-1}(1) - \sigma^{-1}(0) \in [\![-m+1, m-1]\!]$, then $rc' = 2^{i_0}(t_{\sigma(\sigma^{-1}(1))} - t_{\sigma(\sigma^{-1}(0))}) = 2^{i_0}r$. Combining these two equalities, we get the relation $rcc' = r2^{m-i_0}c' = 2^m r = r$. Since r is invertible, this yields $cc' = 1$ in $\mathbb{Z}/(2^m-1)\mathbb{Z}$.

In $\mathbb{Z}$, $-(m-1)^2 \leqslant cc' \leqslant (m-1)^2$. Since $(m-1)^2 < 2^m - 2$ $(m \geqslant 2)$, the only possibility to get $cc' = 1$ in $\mathbb{Z}/(2^m-1)\mathbb{Z}$ is that $cc' = 1$ in $\mathbb{Z}$. So $c, c' = \pm 1$. This contradicts the equality $c' = 2^{i_0}$ in $\mathbb{Z}/(2^m-1)\mathbb{Z}$ (deduced from $rc' = 2^{i_0}r$) since $i_0 \in [\![1, m-1]\!]$. □

2.5 Complexity

We analyze here the expected running time of Algorithm 2, which remains practical even for large values of m. The analysis assumes constant-time arithmetic over $\mathbb{F}_{2^m}$ and constant-time evaluation of $\mathsf{wt}_2(\cdot)$, which is a reasonable assumption given that m is relatively small (e.g., $m \leq 13$ in all *Classic McEliece* parameters).

The complexity analysis of our algorithm falls under the same hypothesis as [KM23, ABC+22] (Sect. 5 Selected parameter sets), more precisely, the code length $n \to \infty$ while $m = \mathcal{O}(\log_2(n))$ and $tm \approx \frac{n}{4}$.

Lemma 4. *The expected running time of Algorithm 2 is*

$$\mathcal{O}\left(\frac{(n\log_2(n))^2}{n_m}\right),$$

where n_m denotes the number of elements in the support $\mathcal{L}$ that satisfy the hypothesis (H_1). In particular, when $2^m - 1$ is a prime number, we have $n_m = n$ and the complexity simplifies to $\mathcal{O}(n(\log_2(n))^2)$.

Proof. Let us analyze the cost of a single iteration of the **while** loop in Algorithm 2, which attempts to recover a pair (α, β).

- **Berlekamp-Massey (Step 5):** Given a binary sequence of length $2m$, the Berlekamp-Massey algorithm runs in $\mathcal{O}(m^2)$ operations.
- **Root finding (Step 9):** We compute the m roots of a degree-m polynomial over $\mathbb{F}_{2^m}$. In characteristic 2, algorithms based on equal-degree factorization (e.g., via distinct-degree decomposition and root extraction) yield a cost of $\mathcal{O}(m^3)$ in practice.
- **Matrix construction (Step 12):** Computing the matrix $C_\ell \in \mathbb{F}_2^{m\times m}$ from the roots involves $\mathcal{O}(m^2)$ operations.
- **Linear system solving (Step 13):** Solving a linear system of size m over $\mathbb{F}_{2^m}$ has complexity $\mathcal{O}(m^c)$, where $c \leq 3$ is the exponent of matrix multiplication.

Overall, the complexity of a single iteration is dominated by the root-finding and linear system solving steps, and can be upper bounded by $\mathcal{O}(m^3)$.

Now, we estimate the expected number of iterations N_{it} needed to recover t valid (α, β) pairs. Let n_m be the number of support elements in $\mathcal{L}$ satisfying (H_1). At each iteration, an element from $\mathcal{L}$ is sampled uniformly at random. Assuming independence and no collisions (as suggested by Lemma 3), the probability that an iteration yields a useful pair is n_m/n.

To recover t correct pairs, the expected number of trials follows a geometric distribution with success probability n_m/n, giving:

$$N_{it} = t \cdot \frac{n}{n_m}.$$

Hence, the total complexity is $\mathcal{O}\left(\frac{(n \log_2(n))^2}{n_m}\right)$. In particular, if $2^m - 1$ is prime, then $\mathcal{L} = \mathbb{F}_{2^m}^*$, and $n = n_m$, so $N_{it} = t$ and the complexity simplifies to $\mathcal{O}(n(\log_2(n))^2)$.

□

Remark. The above estimate reflects practical costs under realistic parameters, with m fixed (typically $m \leq 13$). The asymptotic expression $\mathcal{O}\left(\frac{(n \log_2(n))^2}{n_m}\right)$ is therefore primarily indicative of behavior across increasing security levels. Our method remains efficient and usable even for extended variants of *Classic McEliece* with $m > 13$.

3 Improved Error-Correcting Algorithm

3.1 Noisy Setting

In [VCC+25], the authors proposed a more realistic model. Even in the noise-free scenario, such as the one in [DCV+25], the accuracy is not equal to 1.

As demonstrated by the DPA contest V3[2], the acquisition setting can drastically affect the success rate of an attack, or equivalently impact the accuracy of a distinguisher.

Indeed, in practice the accuracy of the Hamming weight distinguisher is less than 1, which is why they consider noisy estimations of the actual Hamming weight. The error on these estimations is defined by a categorical random variable. More precisely, an estimated weight sequence $\widetilde{\mathcal{W}}$ is a column vector of the noisy matrix $\widetilde{\boldsymbol{H}}_{\mathsf{wt}}$, defined as:

$$\widetilde{\boldsymbol{H}}_{\mathsf{wt}}[:, j] = \left(\mathsf{wt}(\alpha_j^i \beta_j) + \varepsilon_{i,j}\right)_{i \in [\![0; 2t-1]\!]},$$

with $\varepsilon_{i,j} \in \{0, 1, -1\}$. In other words, we can write $\widetilde{\mathcal{W}} = \mathcal{W} + \mathcal{E}$, where $\mathcal{W}$ is the correct Hamming weight sequence and $\mathcal{E}$ represents the error sequence. For

[2] https://dpacontest.telecom-paris.fr/v3/index.php.

a deeper understanding of the error model, we refer the reader to [GCCD23, VCC+25].

Notice that taking the mod 2 of the estimated weight sequence yields:

$$\widetilde{\mathcal{W}}_2 = \mathcal{W}_2 + \mathcal{E}_2,$$

where $\mathcal{W}_2$ is the correct mod 2 weight sequence and $\mathcal{E}_2$ is the mod 2 error sequence with $e_i \in \{0, 1\}$. Typically: - $e_i = 1$ indicates an error at position i in $\mathcal{W}_2$ (i.e., $\varepsilon_i \in \{1, -1\}$), - $e_i = 0$ indicates an error-free position (i.e., $\varepsilon_i = 0$).

This leads us to the central question:

Can we recover the BM polynomial generating the sequence $\mathcal{W}_2$ from a noisy sequence $\widetilde{\mathcal{W}}_2$?

To answer this, we propose two solutions: Algorithm 3 and Algorithm 4. Before analyzing these methods in detail, we outline the main steps of our error correction strategy.

1. **Mod 2 error correction:**
   - Use Algorithm 3 or Algorithm 4 to determine a BM polynomial that is likely to be the original polynomial generating the LFSR $\mathcal{W}_2$.
   - Recover $\mathcal{E}_2$ and hence $\mathcal{W}_2$ using this polynomial.
2. **Recover potential pairs:**
   - Apply Algorithm 2 (from line 6 to line 13) to recover a list of candidate pairs (α, β) satisfying $\mathcal{W}_2(\alpha, \beta) = \mathcal{W}_2$, where:

$$\mathcal{W}_2(\alpha, \beta) \stackrel{\mathsf{def}}{=} \left(\mathsf{wt}_2(\alpha_k^i \beta_k)\right)_{i \in [\![0; 2t-1]\!]}.$$

3. **Compute valid pairs:** For each candidate (α, β), compute the sequence:

$$\mathcal{W}(\alpha, \beta) \stackrel{\mathsf{def}}{=} \left(\mathsf{wt}(\alpha_k^i \beta_k)\right)_{i \in [\![0; 2t-1]\!]},$$

   and retain the pairs satisfying the following conditions:
   - On the error-free positions, the Hamming weight must match exactly:

$$\mathcal{W}(\alpha, \beta)_{[\![0; 2t-1]\!] \setminus \mathrm{supp}(\mathcal{E}_2)} = \widetilde{\mathcal{W}}_{\mathrm{supp}(\mathcal{E}_2)^c}.$$

   - On error positions, the difference must be ± 1:

$$\left(\mathcal{W}(\alpha, \beta) - \widetilde{\mathcal{W}}\right)_{\mathrm{supp}(\mathcal{E}_2)} \in \{-1, +1\}^{\#\mathrm{supp}(\mathcal{E}_2)}.$$

   If no pair satisfies these conditions, then the BM polynomial found in Step 1 was likely not the correct one.

Remark 5. These techniques can be extended to other error models, where errors e_i on the Hamming weights lie in $[\![-c, c]\!]$ for some $c > 1$, with high probability for $e_i = 0$ and low probability that $|e_i| > 1$ (e.g., a discrete Gaussian-like model). This can be handled either by keeping Step 3 unchanged (thus rejecting sequences where $|e_i| > 1$), or by allowing a small number of discrepancies below a defined threshold.

Algorithm 3. Majority rule

Input: $\widetilde{\mathcal{W}_2}$ — noisy mod 2 Hamming weight sequence obtained from SCA
Output: Most probable χ_k generating $\mathcal{W}_2$
1: $Polys \leftarrow [\,]$
2: **for** $i \leftarrow 0$ to $\lfloor \log_2(\frac{t}{m}) \rfloor$ **do**
3: $\quad s \leftarrow 2^i$
4: $\quad$ **for** $j \leftarrow 0$ to $2t - 2ms$ **do**
5: $\qquad w \leftarrow \widetilde{\mathcal{W}_2}[j : s : j + 2ms]$
6: $\qquad poly \leftarrow \mathrm{BM}(w)$
7: $\qquad$ **if** $\deg(poly) = m$ and $\mathrm{LSB}(poly) = 1$ **then**
8: $\qquad\quad Polys.\mathrm{append}(poly)$
return $\mathrm{argmax}_{p \in Polys} \#\{q \in Polys \mid q = p\}$ ▷ Most frequent polynomial

3.2 Algorithms for Error Correction

Algorithm 3 takes a noisy mod 2 Hamming weight sequence $\widetilde{\mathcal{W}_2}$ as input. It explores multiple sub-sequences of length $2m$ with various spacings (Line 2), applies the Berlekamp-Massey (BM) algorithm, and collects valid polynomials of degree m with least significant bit equal to 1 into the list *Polys*. The most frequent polynomial in this list is returned as the best candidate.

Algorithm 4. Sequence distance

Input: $\widetilde{\mathcal{W}_2}$ — noisy mod 2 Hamming weight sequence obtained from SCA
Output: Most probable BM polynomial χ_k and corresponding denoised sequence $\mathcal{W}_2$
$poly\_saved \leftarrow 0$, $min\_error \leftarrow 2t + 1$
for $i \leftarrow 0$ to $2t - 2m$ **do**
$\quad w \leftarrow \widetilde{\mathcal{W}_2}[i : i + 2m]$
$\quad poly \leftarrow \mathrm{BM}(w)$
$\quad Seq \leftarrow \mathrm{LFSR}(poly, w, \mathrm{length} = 2t)$
$\quad error \leftarrow \mathrm{dist}(Seq, \widetilde{\mathcal{W}_2})$
$\quad$ **if** $error < min\_error$ **then**
$\qquad min\_error \leftarrow error$
$\qquad poly\_saved \leftarrow poly$
$\qquad seq\_saved \leftarrow Seq$
return $poly\_saved$, seq_saved

Algorithm 4 takes a different approach: for each position in the sequence $\widetilde{\mathcal{W}_2}$, it considers a window of size $2m$, computes the corresponding BM polynomial, and reconstructs a candidate sequence for $\mathcal{W}_2$ by generating values both in the forward and backward directions using a Linear Feedback Shift Register (LFSR). The forward sequence is obtained by applying the LFSR from the initial window, and the backward sequence is built similarly by reversing both the window and the polynomial. The concatenation of these two partial sequences yields a full-length candidate sequence.

This candidate is then compared to the noisy sequence $\widetilde{\mathcal{W}_2}$ using the Hamming distance. The algorithm selects the polynomial that minimizes this distance, under the assumption that the correct polynomial will generate a sequence closer to the original, with fewer mismatches.

Importantly, as long as there exists at least one error-free sub-sequence of length $2m$ in the original sequence $\mathcal{W}_2$, the Berlekamp-Massey algorithm will recover the correct connection polynomial for that segment. In practice, we observe that wrong polynomials typically result in sequences with significantly more discrepancies, making this distance-based selection reliable when the overall noise level remains moderate.

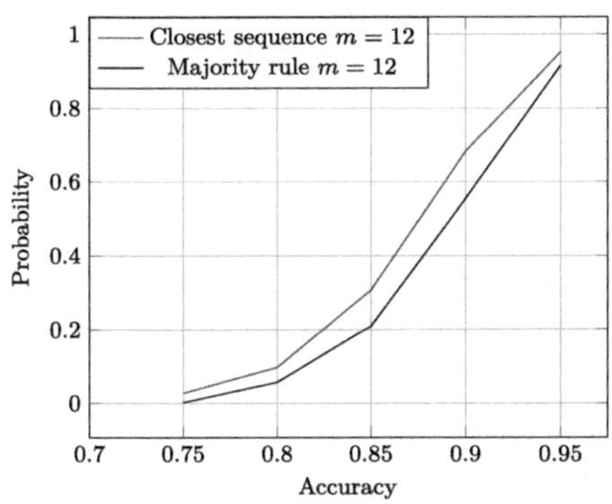

Fig. 1. Experimental success rate for polynomial recovery using majority vote rule and minimal distance.

Figure 1 shows the success rate of the two approaches in recovering the correct characteristic polynomial when the full-length sequence is affected by a number of random local bit flips. This noise model reflects typical side-channel measurement errors encountered when estimating the parity of Hamming weights. As illustrated in the figure, the distance-based approach (Algorithm 4) demonstrates greater resilience to noise. These empirical results can be compared with the theoretical predictions presented in Fig. 2b.

During our experiments with the majority rule method, we observed that feeding Berlekamp-Massey with faulty sequences of length $2m$ often led to repeated recovery of the same incorrect polynomial. This negatively impacts the success rate of the attack, as it shows that the presence of a single error within a $2m$-length window can result in a persistent incorrect output. In contrast, the distance-based method appears more robust: a sequence of length $2t$ affected by errors still allows recovery of the correct polynomial as long as it contains one error-free sub-sequence of length $2m$.

It is important to emphasize that both methods rely on the assumption that a correctly recovered characteristic polynomial—based on what is believed to be an uncorrupted sub-sequence can be used to reconstruct the full *guessed* sequence. This reconstructed sequence allows for the identification of error positions within the original noisy sequence. However, even when the error positions are known, determining the *direction* of the error (i.e., whether the Hamming weight was over- or underestimated) remains unresolved at this stage. This ambiguity is precisely addressed in Step 3 of the procedure described in the previous subsection.

A key empirical observation is the following: among 20,000 reconstruction attempts for (α, β) under a low accuracy scenario (0.74), only 392 yielded the correct pair. Crucially, among the remaining 19,608 incorrect predictions, **only one incorrect pair was not rejected** by Step 3. This highlights the effectiveness of the verification step: under reasonable accuracy conditions, the set $\mathcal{I}$ of candidate pairs (α, β) produced by Algorithm 2 contains the correct pair with high probability, and is extremely unlikely to contain false positives.

3.3 Success Probability

Since, an unerroneous $2m$ sequence allows one to reconstruct the correct sequence, we shall focus our analysis on this problem. Hence, the first step is to determine the probability that the error vector $\boldsymbol{e}$ of a given Hamming weight admits a zero sub-block of length $2m$.

The proofs of the results of this section are postponed to Appendix B

Lemma 5. *Let* $\boldsymbol{e} \in \mathbb{F}_2^{2t}$ *with* $\mathsf{wt}(\boldsymbol{e}) = l$. *The probability that* $\exists \mathcal{I} \subset [\![0; 2t-1]\!]$ *s.t.* $\boldsymbol{e}_{\mathcal{I}} = \boldsymbol{0}_{\#\mathcal{I}}$ *and* $\#\mathcal{I} \geq 2m$ *equals*

$$\sum_{j=1}^{\lfloor \frac{2t-l}{2m} \rfloor} \frac{(-1)^{j+1}\binom{l+1}{j}\binom{2t-2mj}{l}}{\binom{2t}{l}} \tag{4}$$

Now, let us see how the weight $\mathsf{wt}(\boldsymbol{e})$ depends on the accuracy of the classifier.

Remark 6. Recall that $\widetilde{\boldsymbol{H}}_{\mathsf{wt}}[, i] = (\mathsf{wt}(\beta_i) + \varepsilon_{0,i}, \ldots, \mathsf{wt}(\alpha_i^{2t-1}\beta_i) + \varepsilon_{2t-1,i})$ where $\varepsilon_{j,i}$ is a random variable that follows the categorical distribution, $Pr(\varepsilon_i = 0) = a$ and $Pr(\varepsilon_i = -1) = Pr(\varepsilon_i = 1) = \frac{1-a}{2}$. When moving down to $\mathbb{F}_2$ (where $1 = -1$) we obtain that $\boldsymbol{e}$ is a Bernoulli vector with $Pr(e_i = 0) = a$ and $Pr(e_i = 1) = 1 - a$. This implies that $\mathsf{wt}(\boldsymbol{e})$ is a discrete random variable that follows the Binomial distribution $\mathcal{B}(1 - a, 2t)$.

Proposition 1. *The probability that Algoeithm 4 output the correct sequence given* a, *the accuracy of the classifier, equals*

$$\sum_{l=0}^{2t}(1-a)^l a^{2t-l} \sum_{j=1}^{\lfloor \frac{2t-l}{2m} \rfloor} (-1)^{j+1}\binom{l+1}{j}\binom{2t-2mj}{l} \tag{5}$$

As demonstrated in Equation (2), the probability of successfully recovering a value of α is expressed as a function of both the distinguisher accuracy (see

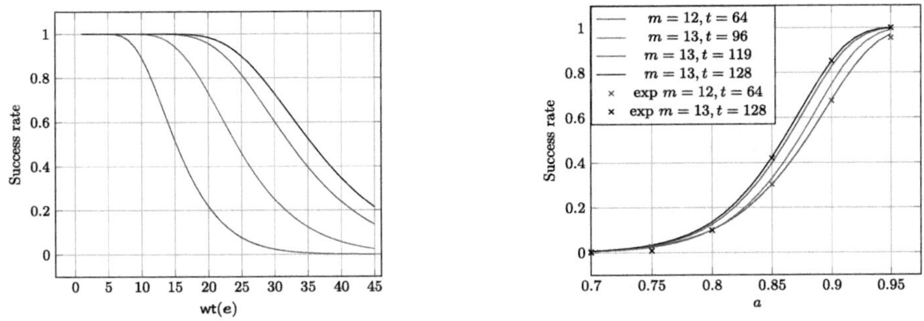

(a) $\Pr(success)$ in function of $\mathsf{wt}(\boldsymbol{e})$.

(b) $\Pr(success)$ in function of a.

Fig. 2. Theoretical probability of success of algorithm 4 for all *Classic McEliece* parameters in function of a) $\mathsf{wt}(\boldsymbol{e})$ and b) accuracy.

Fig. 2b) and the error weight (see Fig. 2a). The analysis reveals that the effectiveness of the attack is significantly influenced by the chosen security parameters. In particular, increasing these parameters tends to improve the success rate of the attack.

To assess the tightness and reliability of the theoretical bounds, extensive experiments were carried out. These confirmed that the theoretical predictions closely match the experimental outcomes. This correspondence is particularly valuable for evaluators: instead of performing full-scale attacks, one can estimate the distinguisher's accuracy and directly use the theoretical formula given in Equation (5) to predict the attack's success rate. This approach can substantially reduce evaluation time while maintaining meaningful security insights.

Bounding the Accuracy. Typically, it suffices to correctly recover t distinct pairs (α, β) in order to compute the polynomial $\gamma(x)$, which can then be used to reconstruct the full private key (see Sect. 4.1). Assume further that the extension field $\mathbb{F}_{2^m}$ is generated by a primitive polynomial—this is indeed the case for all ISO-specified parameter sets. As indicated by Lemma 3, this implies that no collisions are expected among the (α, β) pairs recovered via Algorithm 2. Consequently, we can lower bound the success probability of Algorithm 4 by t/n.

This observation allows us to derive a lower bound on the distinguisher accuracy a needed to ensure that $\Pr(\text{success}) \geq t/n$. For all *Classic McEliece* parameter sets (see Table 1), the ratio t/n is slightly below 0.021. Through numerical computation, we determined that this implies a lower bound of $a \geq 0.74$.

However, if one aims to employ more advanced techniques for key recovery—such as those described in [KM23, DCV+25]—then more than t correct α values are required. In particular, the method in [KM23] demands $mt+1$ correct values, leading to a stricter accuracy requirement of $a \geq 0.815$ for our algorithm. This same lower bound also applies in scenarios where $mt+\delta$ correct values are needed, as discussed in [DCV+25].

The source code for our experiments is available at https://github.com/vingrosso/keyRecoveryClassicMcEliece.

4 Applications

We now demonstrate two distinct contexts in which Algorithm 2 can serve as a foundational component for well-known key-recovery attacks.

4.1 Breaking Goppa Codes with Hints

Our approach fits within a broader framework—namely, the problem of breaking binary Goppa codes with additional side information (or *hints*). In this setting, the attacker is given the public binary Goppa code (i.e., a random basis for the private code, or equivalently, the matrix $\boldsymbol{H}_{\text{pub}}$), along with a set of helpful hints. The objective is to recover the private key, more specifically, the Goppa polynomial $\gamma(x)$ and the private support $\mathcal{L} \subseteq \mathbb{F}_{2^m}$.

Although it is always possible to define a canonical support $\mathcal{L}_{\text{can}} = \{\alpha^i \mid i \in [\![0, 2^m - 2]\!]\}$, where α is a generator of $\mathbb{F}_{2^m}^*$, two main challenges arise:

1. The exact positions (indices) of the elements α^i within the actual support $\mathcal{L}$ are unknown.
2. It is unclear which specific elements of $\mathbb{F}_{2^m}$ have been excluded during the construction of $\mathcal{L}$.

Except for the recent work in [DCV+25], existing solutions to this problem [Sen00, KM23] do not explicitly analyze how these hints are generated, nor do they quantify the amount of side information required to recover the private key.

In Table 3, we outline how the results of our method can be used to generate the necessary hints for input to these established Goppa code equivalence solvers.

Table 3. The hints provided by Algorithm 2 as input to existing solvers for Solving the Goppa code equivalence problem together with the minimum accuracy.

Algorithm 2 output	Hints	Complexity	Article
t pairs $(\alpha_i, \gamma(\alpha_i))$ $a \geq 0.74$	$\gamma(x)$	$\mathcal{O}(n^3 + 2^h n^2 \log n)$	[Sen00]
$mt+1$ pairs $(\alpha_i, \gamma(\alpha_i))$ $a \geq 0.815$	$mt+1$ elements α_i	$\mathcal{O}(n^5)$	[KM23]
	$t(m-2)+1$ elements α_i and $\gamma(x)$	$\mathcal{O}(n^4)$	
$mt+\delta$ pairs $(\alpha_i, \gamma(\alpha_i))$ $a \geq 0.815$	$mt+\delta$ correct pairs $(\alpha_i, g(\alpha_i))$	$\mathcal{O}\left(n(mt)^{c-1}\right)$, $c \leq 3$	[DCV+25]

4.2 Other McEliece Variants

Alternant codes and Generalized Reed-Solomon codes are both algebraic codes that were used in a McEliece type cryptosystem. We can show that our method can be applied to any of these codes in order to recover their structure. The underlying idea is that all these codes admit as parity-check matrix a Vandermonde type matrix. To define these code we require a support $\mathcal{L} \stackrel{\text{def}}{=} \{\alpha_0, \ldots, \alpha_{n-1}\} \subset \mathbb{F}_{2^m}$ of length $|\mathcal{L}| = n$ ($n \leq 2^m$) and a multiplier $\boldsymbol{u} \in \mathbb{F}_{2^m}^n$, with $u_i \neq 0$.

$$\boldsymbol{V}_k(\boldsymbol{v}, \mathcal{L}) \stackrel{\text{def}}{=} \begin{pmatrix} v_0 & \ldots & v_{n-1} \\ \alpha_0 v_0 & \ldots & \alpha_{n-1} v_{n-1} \\ \vdots & \ddots & \vdots \\ \alpha_0^{k-1} v_0 & \ldots & \alpha_{n-1}^{k-1} v_{n-1} \end{pmatrix}.$$

The Generalized-Solomon code of dimension k and length n can be defined as follows

$$\mathbf{GRS}_k(\boldsymbol{u}, \mathcal{L}) \stackrel{\text{def}}{=} \{(u_0 f(\alpha_0), \ldots, u_{n-1} f(\alpha_{n-1}) \mid f \in \mathbb{F}_{2^m}[x]\ ,\ \deg(f) < k\}.$$

The dual of a GRS code is still a GRS code, formally, we have $\mathbf{GRS}_k(\boldsymbol{u}, \mathcal{L})^\perp = \mathbf{GRS}_{n-k}(\boldsymbol{v}, \mathcal{L})$ where $v_i^{-1} = u_i \prod_{i \neq j}(\alpha_i - \alpha_j)$. This implies that $\boldsymbol{V}_{n-k}(\boldsymbol{v}, \mathcal{L})$ is a parity-check matrix of $\mathbf{GRS}_k(\boldsymbol{u}, \mathcal{L})$. A Reed-Solomon code is a GRS with multpiplier $\boldsymbol{u} = (1, \ldots, 1)$.

An alternate code of order r, denoted by $\mathbf{Alt}_r(\boldsymbol{u}, \mathcal{L})$, is a subfield-subcode, that can be defined using the parity-check matrix as follows

$$\mathbf{Alt}_r(\boldsymbol{u}, \mathcal{L}) = \{\boldsymbol{c} \in \mathbb{F}_2^n \mid \boldsymbol{V}_r(\boldsymbol{u}, \mathcal{L})\boldsymbol{c}^T = 0\}.$$

Its dimension is $k \geq n - rm$. Now we can see that $\mathscr{G}(\gamma, \mathcal{L}) = \mathbf{Alt}_t(\boldsymbol{u}, \mathcal{L})$ with $u_i = \gamma(\alpha_i)^{-1}$, where $\gamma(\alpha_i) \neq 0, \forall \alpha_i \in \mathcal{L}$.

Remark 7. Since Algorithm 2 recovers pairs (α_i, β_i) using the Hamming weight matrix of the Vandermonde matrix $\boldsymbol{V}(\boldsymbol{v}, \mathcal{L})$, we have

- for Goppa codes we recover $\beta_i = \boldsymbol{\gamma}^{-1}(\alpha_i)$;
- for alternant codes we recover $\beta_i \in \mathbb{F}_{2^m}$;
- for GRS code we recover $\beta_i = (u_i(\prod_{i \neq j}(\alpha_i - \alpha_j))^{-1}$ for $u_i \in \mathbb{F}_{2^m}$;
- for Reed-Solomon codes we can recover $\beta_i = (\prod_{i \neq j}(\alpha_i - \alpha_j))^{-1}$.

4.3 Countermeasures

While our attack shows that decoding implementations based on Berlekamp–Massey and matrix–vector multiplications are vulnerable to side-channel leakage through Hamming weight observations, several effective countermeasures are available.

First, high-performance embedded implementations such as [CC21] use transposed additive FFTs to compute the double syndrome. This design substantially modifies the leakage characteristics and greatly reduces the correlation with Hamming weight, making our attack ineffective in such environments.

Second, notice that removing the computation of the private syndrome completely eliminates side-channel attacks such as [DCV+25, VCC+25] and even our attack. Theoretical solutions exist, since the classical Niederreiter scheme does not require to re-compute the double syndrome vector. Indeed, the ciphertext $\boldsymbol{z}$ could be directly decrypted by the following well-known procedure: i) compute $\boldsymbol{z}^* = \boldsymbol{S}^{-1}\boldsymbol{z}$, where $\boldsymbol{S}$ is the non-singular matrix used to compute the systematic form of $\boldsymbol{H}_{\text{priv}}$, and ii) decode $\boldsymbol{z}^*$ using Patterson decoding algorithm. However, we want to stress that it is not yet clear how to implement Patterson's algorithm efficiently and securely in constant time [Ber24].

Beyond changing the decoding algorithm or syndrome computation method, standard side-channel countermeasures—including masking techniques [ISW03] and shuffling [VMKS12]—can be employed to further mitigate leakage during the decoding process.

We strongly recommend that any deployment of *Classic McEliece* or similar code-based cryptosystems combine algorithm-level protections with robust implementation-level countermeasures to ensure resilience against both classical and quantum-capable adversaries.

5 Conclusion

In this work, we introduced a novel algebraic key-recovery attack against the reference implementation of the *Classic McEliece* KEM in scenarios involving side-channel leakage. Our method advances the state of the art by offering improved computational efficiency and enhanced robustness to estimation errors arising from noisy side-channel observations.

By analyzing the structure of the leakage and employing linear-algebraic techniques over finite fields, we demonstrated that it is possible to recover the secret key even in the presence of realistic noise, with the success probability depending primarily on the accuracy of the underlying classifier. Importantly, our approach scales well to larger parameter sets, making it practical for attacking implementations targeting higher security levels.

We also provided theoretical justification for the feasibility of distinguishing field elements via side-channel measurements, thereby offering partial validation of conjectures previously proposed in the literature.

Furthermore, we discussed the broader relevance of our techniques to other code-based cryptosystems, including their application to generic Goppa and alternant code key-recovery scenarios. Our framework serves as a foundation for combining algebraic recovery strategies with other advanced cryptanalytic tools.

Future work will focus on extending our analysis to broader error models, improving recovery rates under lower measurement accuracy, and designing more effective countermeasures. In addition, we plan to evaluate our attack on actual power traces collected from hardware implementations, in order to assess its practical impact in real-world environments.

Acknowledgements. The authors would like to thank the reviewers for their constructive feedback and helpful suggestions, which were invaluable in refining this work. We would like to especially thank our shepherd, Prof. Ruben Niederhagen, for his detailed and constructive guidance during the revision process. V-F. Dragoi was financed by Aurel Vlaicu University of Arad through the research grant UAV-IRG-1-2025-12. P-L. Cayrel and V. Grosso received funding from the France 2030 program, managed by the French National Research Agency under grant agreement No. ANR-22-PETQ-0008 PQ-TLS.

A Berlekamp-Massey Algorithm

Algorithm 5. Berlekamp-Massey Algorithm

Input: A sequence $W = (w_0, w_1, \ldots, w_{2m-1})$ of Hamming weights modulo 2
Output: The minimal polynomial $\chi(Y)$ that generates the sequence

$L \leftarrow 0$ ▷ Current length of the characteristic polynomial
$\chi(Y) \leftarrow 1$ ▷ Initialize the polynomial as 1
$\chi_{\text{temp}}(Y) \leftarrow 1$
$\Delta \leftarrow 1$ ▷ Discrepancy value (initialized)
$l_{\text{old}} \leftarrow 0$ ▷ Index of last successful update
for $i = 0$ **to** $2m - 1$ **do** ▷ Iterate over the sequence
  Compute the discrepancy: $\Delta \leftarrow w_i + \sum_{j=1}^{L} \chi_j w_{i-j}$ ▷ If $\Delta = 0$, the sequence remains consistent with the current polynomial
  if $\Delta \neq 0$ **then** ▷ Update is needed if the discrepancy is nonzero
    $\chi_{\text{temp}}(Y) \leftarrow \chi(Y)$ ▷ Backup the current polynomial
    Update $\chi(Y) : \chi(Y) \leftarrow \chi(Y) - \Delta Y^{i-l_{\text{old}}} \chi_{\text{temp}}(Y)$
    if $2L \leq i$ **then** ▷ Check if the length of χ should be increased
      $L \leftarrow i + 1 - L$ ▷ Update the length of the polynomial
      $l_{\text{old}} \leftarrow i$
return $\chi(Y)$ ▷ Return the minimal polynomial

B Proofs of Results from Section 3.3

Let us begin with the proof of Lemma 5. We shall first recall some of the conventions needed here. $[x^l]P(x)$ will denote the extraction of the coefficient P_l from $P(x) = \sum_{i=0}^{n} P_i x^i$. Also we will denote the binary alphabet by $\mathcal{A} = \{0, 1\}$. Let $\mathcal{A}^* = \varepsilon, 0, 1, 00, \ldots$ denote the free monoid of finite length binary words where string concatenation is the monoid operation ($\varepsilon = 1_{\mathcal{A}^*}$ being the empty word). In terms of non-commutative formal series we can write

$$\left(\sum_{w \in \mathcal{A}^*} w\right)\left(1_{\mathcal{A}^*} - \sum_{a \in \mathcal{A}} a\right) = 1_{\mathcal{A}^*}. \tag{6}$$

Enumeration of binary words can now be done using the ordinary generating series. For example, when searching for all binary words of a given length, say l we are extracting $[x^l]\ \frac{1}{1-(x+x)} = \frac{1}{1-2x}$ since both letters from $\mathcal{A}$ count the same, which gives 2^l binary words. We can now proceed to the proof of our result.

Proof. To estimate the wanted probability we will determine its complement, i.e., the probability of having all blocks of consecutive zeros with length at most $2m-1$. Thus, we need to enumerate all binary words of length $2t$ with l occurrences of the letter 1 having less than $2m$ consecutive 0s. Such words are of the form $0^{<2m}(10^{<2m})^l$. If we map the letter 0 into the formal variable z and 1 into x we get that extracting $[z^{2t-l}]$ from $(1+z+\cdots+z^{2m-1})^{l+1}$ gives the wanted result. Indeed, in terms of (now commutative) formal series in z, we have

$$[x^l z^{2t-l}] \sum_{i \geq 0} (1+z+\cdots+z^{2m-1}) \left(x(1+z+\cdots+z^{2m-1})\right)^i$$

$$[x^l z^{2t-l}] \sum_{i \geq 0} x^i \left(\frac{1-z^{2m}}{1-z}\right)^{i+1}$$

$$[z^{2t-l}] \left(\frac{1-z^{2m}}{1-z}\right)^{l+1}.$$

The coefficient of z^{2t-l} in $(1+z+\cdots+z^{2m-1})^{l+1}$ also denoted in the literature by $\binom{l+1}{2t-l}_{2m-1}$ is a generalization of the binomial coefficient which admits the following combinatorial formula (see [BBK08])

$$\binom{l+1}{2t-l}_{2m-1} = \sum_{j=0}^{\lfloor \frac{2t-l}{2m} \rfloor} (-1)^j \binom{l+1}{j}\binom{2t-2mj}{l}.$$

The total number of binary words of length $2t$ having l occurrences of 1 equals $\binom{2t}{l}$ which yields the wanted result. □

Now, we can continue with the proof of Proposition 1

Proof. Using Lemma 5 and Remark 6 we deduce

$$Pr(succes) = \sum_{l=0}^{2t} Pr(succes \mid \mathsf{wt}(\boldsymbol{e}) = l) Pr(\mathsf{wt}(\boldsymbol{e}) = l) \tag{7}$$

$$= \sum_{l=0}^{2t} \binom{2t}{l} (1-a)^l a^{2t-l} \sum_{j=1}^{\lfloor \frac{2t-l}{2m} \rfloor} \frac{(-1)^{j+1} \binom{l+1}{j} \binom{2t-2mj}{l}}{\binom{2t}{l}} \tag{8}$$

$$= \sum_{l=0}^{2t} (1-a)^l a^{2t-l} \sum_{j=1}^{\lfloor \frac{2t-l}{2m} \rfloor} (-1)^{j+1} \binom{l+1}{j} \binom{2t-2mj}{l} \tag{9}$$

□

References

[AAB+22] Aguilar-Melchor, C., et al.: HQC. Technical report, National Institute of Standards and Technology (2022). https://csrc.nist.gov/Projects/post-quantum-cryptography/round-4-submissions

[ABC+22] Albrecht, M.R., et al.: Classic McEliece. Technical report, National Institute of Standards and Technology (2022). https://csrc.nist.gov/projects/post-quantum-cryptography/round-4-submissions

[AHPT11] Avanzi, R., Hoerder, S., Page, D., Tunstall, M.: Side-channel attacks on the McEliece and Niederreiter public-key cryptosystems. J. Cryptograhic Eng. **1**(4), 271–281 (2011)

[BBK08] Belbachir, H., Bouroubi, S., Khelladi, A.: Connection between ordinary multinomials, Fibonacci numbers, bell polynomials and discrete uniform distribution. In: Annales Mathematicae et Informaticae, volume 35, pp. 21–30. Eszterházy Károly College, Institute of Mathematics and Computer Science Eger (2008)

[BCM+25] Brinkmann, M., Chuengsatiansup, C., May, A., Nowakowski, J., Yarom, Y.: Leaky McEliece: secret key recovery from highly erroneous side-channel information. IACR Trans. Cryptographic Hardw. Embed. Syst. **2025**(2), 94–125 (2025)

[Ber24] Bernstein, D.J.: Understanding binary-Goppa decoding. IACR Commun. Cryptology **1**(1) (2024)

[CC21] Chen, M.-S., Chou, T.: Classic McEliece on the ARM Cortex-M4. IACR TCHES **2021**(3), 125–148 (2021)

[CCD+22] Chen, P.-J., et al.: Complete and improved FPGA implementation of classic McEliece. IACR TCHES **2022**(3), 71–113 (2022)

[CEvMS16] Chen, C., Eisenbarth, T., von Maurich, I., Steinwandt, R.: Horizontal and vertical side channel analysis of a McEliece cryptosystem. IEEE Trans. Inf. Forensics Secuity **11**(6), 1093–1105 (2016)

[DCV+25] Drăgoi, V.-F., Colombier, B., Vallet, N., Cayrel, P.-L., Grosso, V.: Full key-recovery cubic-time template attack on classic McEliece decapsulation. IACR TCHES **2025**(1), 367–391 (2025)

[FLZG24] Fallnich, D., Lanius, C., Zhang, S., Gemmeke, T.: Efficient ASIC architecture for low latency classic McEliece decoding. IACR TCHES **2024**(2), 403–425 (2024)

[GCCD23] Grosso, V., Cayrel, P.-L., Colombier, B., Dragoi, V.-F.: Punctured syndrome decoding problem - efficient side-channel attacks against classic McEliece. In: Kavun, E.B., Pehl, M. (eds.) COSADE 2023, volume 13979 of LNCS, pp. 170–192. Springer, Cham (2023)

[GJJ22] Guo, Q., Johansson, A., Johansson, T.: A key-recovery side-channel attack on classic McEliece implementations. IACR TCHES **2022**(4), 800–827 (2022)

[HMP10] Heyse, S., Moradi, A., Paar, C.: Practical power analysis attacks on software implementations of McEliece. In: Sendrier, N. (ed.) PQCrypto 2010. LNCS, vol. 6061, pp. 108–125. Springer, Heidelberg (2010). https://doi.org/10.1007/978-3-642-12929-2_9

[ISW03] Ishai, Y., Sahai, A., Wagner, D.: Private circuits: securing hardware against probing attacks. In: Boneh, D. (ed.) CRYPTO 2003. LNCS, vol. 2729, pp. 463–481. Springer, Berlin, Heidelberg (2003)

[KM23] Kirshanova, E., May, A.: Breaking Goppa-based McEliece with hints. Inf. Comput. **293**, 105045 (2023)

[Mas69] Massey, J.: Shift-register synthesis and BCH decoding. IEEE Trans. Inf. Theory **15**(1), 122–127 (1969)

[MSSS11] Molter, H.G., Stöttinger, M., Shoufan, A., Strenzke, F.: A simple power analysis attack on a McEliece cryptoprocessor. J. Cryptographic Eng. **1**(1), 29–36 (2011)

[Nie86] Niederreiter, H.: Knapsack-type cryptosystems and algebraic coding theory. Probl. Control Inf. Theory **15**(2), 159–166 (1986)

[OC14] O'Flynn, C., Chen, Z.D.: ChipWhisperer: an open-source platform for hardware embedded security research. In: Prouff, E. (ed.) COSADE 2014. LNCS, vol. 8622, pp. 243–260. Springer, Cham (2014). https://doi.org/10.1007/978-3-319-10175-0_17

[SAB+20] Schwabe, P., et al.: CRYSTALS-KYBER. Technical report, National Institute of Standards and Technology (2020). https://csrc.nist.gov/projects/post-quantum-cryptography/post-quantum-cryptography-standardization/round-3-submissions

[SCD+23] Seck, B., et al.: A side-channel attack against classic McEliece when loading the Goppa polynomial. In: El Mrabet, N., De Feo, L., Duquesne, S. (eds.) Progress in Cryptology - AFRICACRYPT 2023, pp. 105–125, Cham (2023). Springer Nature Switzerland

[Sen00] Sendrier, N.: Finding the permutation between equivalent linear codes: the support splitting algorithm. IEEE Trans. Inf. Theory **46**(4), 1193–1203 (2000)

[SKE+23] Sim, M., et al.: Efficient implementation of the classic McEliece on ARMv8 processors. In: Kim, H., Youn, J. (eds.) WISA 23. LNCS, vol. 14402, pp. 324–337. Springer, Singapore (2023)

[VCC+25] Vallet, N., Cayrel, P.-L., Colombier, B., Dragoi, V.-F., Grosso, V.: Optimizing key recovery in Classic McEliece: Advanced error correction for noisy side-channel measurements. Cryptology ePrint Archive, Paper 2025/802 (2025)

[VMKS12] Veyrat-Charvillon, N., Medwed, M., Kerckhof, S., Standaert, F.-X.: Shuffling against side-channel attacks: a comprehensive study with cautionary note. In: Wang, X., Sako, K. (eds.) ASIACRYPT 2012. LNCS, vol. 7658, pp. 740–757. Springer, Berlin, Heidelberg (2012)

An Attack on ML-DSA Using an Implicit Hint

Paco Azevedo-Oliveira[1,2(✉)], Jordan Beraud[2], and Louis Goubin[2]

[1] Thales DIS, Meudon, France
paco.azevedo-oliveira@thalesgroup.com
[2] Laboratoire de Mathématiques de Versailles, UVSQ, CNRS,
Université Paris-Saclay, 78035 Versailles, France
{jordan.beraud,louis.goubin}@uvsq.fr

Abstract. The security of ML-DSA, like most signature schemes, is partially based on the fact that the nonce used to generate the signature is unknown to any attacker. In this work, we exhibit a lattice-based attack that is possible if the nonces share implicit or explicit information. From a collection of signatures whose nonces share certain coefficients, it is indeed possible to build a collection of non full-rank lattices. Intersecting them, we show how to create a low-rank lattice that contains one of the polynomials of the secret key, which in turn can be recovered using lattice reduction techniques.

There are several interpretations of this result: firstly, it can be seen as a generalization of a fault-based attack on BLISS presented at SAC'16 by Thomas Espitau *et al.*. Alternatively, it can be understood as a side-channel attack on ML-DSA, in the case where an attacker is able to recover only one of the coefficients of the nonce used during the generation of the signature. For ML-DSA-II, we show that 4×160 signatures and few hours of computation are sufficient to recover the secret key on a desktop computer. Lastly, our result shows that simple countermeasures, such as permuting the generation of the nonce coefficients, are not sufficient.

Keywords: ML-DSA · side-channel attacks · lattice-based cryptanalysis

1 Introduction

After several years of competition, the NIST published in August 2023 the final version of the ML-DSA [NIS23] signature standard, previously known as Dilithium [BDK+21]. ML-DSA has been selected as the main signature standard to be used worldwide and in most cases. A proof of security, detailed in [BDK+21], provides a strong security guarantee for ML-DSA. In addition many papers [BVC+23, CKA+21, KLH+20, MUTS22, RJH+18, EAB+23] [RCDB22] have studied the security of ML-DSA in the event that the attacker has access to auxiliary information during signature generation. Other papers

C. Boura et al. (Eds.): SAC 2025, LNCS 16207, pp. 567–585, 2026.
https://doi.org/10.1007/978-3-032-10536-3_21

[BBK16, BP18, BAE+24, WNGD23, KPLG24] have studied its security under the condition that an attacker is able to inject one or more faults during signature generation.

In most signature schemes, the generation of a strong nonce – unknown to the attacker – is one of the keystones of the security, which collapses as soon as information on the nonce is revealed. For ECDSA, one of the pre-quantum signature standards, [FGR13] shows that it is sufficient for the attacker to obtain a set of signatures whose random values share a few bits, to find the secret key using lattice reduction techniques. Following these results, two papers [EFGT17, LZS+21] study the security of ML-DSA under the hypothesis of an attacker who would be able to recover (explicit or implicit) information about the nonce. In [EFGT17], the authors show that an attacker capable of introducing a fault at the time of nonce generation, a polynomial vector named $\mathbf{y}$ in ML-DSA, to obtain a polynomial $\mathbf{y}$ of abnormally low degree, can recover the secret key. Their attack is customized to BLISS, another signature algorithm based on structured lattices, but can be easily modified to be applied to ML-DSA. In [LZS+21] the authors prove that an attacker able to retrieve one precise bit of information on **each** coefficient of the nonce $\mathbf{y}$ will need 10 000 signatures to find the secret key.

In this paper, we extend the ML-DSA security analysis under the hypothesis of an attacker who is capable of learning information about the nonce $\mathbf{y}$. More specifically, we show that the ideas used in [EFGT17] give rise to a more general attack. We demonstrate that knowing one or more coefficients of the nonce used to generate a signature allows to reduce the rank of the lattice in which one of the polynomials of the secret key, namely $\mathbf{s}_1$, is contained. If one does not know sufficiently many coefficients, using a lattice reduction is not practical. On the other hand, with a collection of signatures, and by intersecting the different lattices obtained, we can create a lattice of low rank that contains $\mathbf{s}_1$ by construction, and thus retrieve $\mathbf{s}_1$. The main results of our article can be summarised as follows:

- Seen as a result of a fault attack, our attack generalizes that of [EFGT17], and becomes drastically more efficient if an attacker can recover at least two faulty signatures.
- Seen as a side-channel attack, if we assume that an attacker is able to find one of the coefficients of $\mathbf{y}$ thanks to the signature generation execution trace, he will need 4×160 signatures and few hours of computation to find the secret key, for ML-DSA-II.
- Seen as an exploitation of implicit information on the nonce, we obtain the same result as [FGR13] transposed to ML-DSA: assuming that the attacker knows a set of signatures whose nonces share an unknown coefficient in common, he can retrieve the position of the unknown coefficients and apply the method described in the previous point to find the secret key.

Outline. This paper is organized as follows. In Sect. 2, we review the necessary background about ML-DSA and lattice theory. In Sect. 3, we define an attack scenario, and show how it can be reformulated in terms of lattice reduction. In Sect. 4, we propose different variations of the result of Sect. 3. In addition to the theoretical results presented in Sect. 3, that apply regardless of the security level of ML-DSA, we present in Sect. 5 the practical results we obtained when attacking ML-DSA-II. Finally, in Sect. 6 we discuss the obtained results, their limitations and their implications.

2 Summary of ML-DSA and Lattices

In this section we begin by briefly introducing the notations and main functions used in ML-DSA. For a detailed description of ML-DSA, the reader is referred to [BDK+21]. We then review the main definitions and results on lattice theory, which will be used in the next section.

2.1 Notations

Definition 1. *Let α be an even (resp. odd) integer. We define $r' := r \bmod^{\pm}(\alpha)$ the unique $-\frac{\alpha}{2} < r' \leq \frac{\alpha}{2}$ (resp. $-\frac{\alpha-1}{2} \leq r' \leq \frac{\alpha-1}{2}$) such that $r' = r \mod (\alpha)$. We will speak of centered reduction modulo α. We define $r'' := r \bmod^{+}(\alpha)$ the unique $0 \leq r'' < \alpha$ such that $r'' = r \mod (\alpha)$.*

Definition 2. *We define $\phi_n = x^n + 1$ with n a power of 2 and q a prime, and introduce the following rings:*

$$\mathcal{R} := \mathbb{Z}[x]/(\phi_n) \text{ and } \mathcal{R}_q := \mathbb{Z}_q[x]/(\phi_n).$$

Definition 3. *For $w \in \mathbb{Z}_q$:*

$$||w||_\infty := |w \bmod^{\pm} (q)|.$$

For $\boldsymbol{w} = \sum_i w_i x^i \in \mathcal{R}$:

$$||\boldsymbol{w}||_\infty := \max_i ||w_i \bmod^{\pm}(q)||_\infty \text{ and } ||\boldsymbol{w}|| := \Big(\sum_i ||w_i||_\infty^2\Big)^{1/2}$$

and for $\mathbf{w} = (\mathbf{w}^{[1]}, ..., \mathbf{w}^{[l]}) \in \mathcal{R}^l$,

$$||\mathbf{w}||_\infty := \max_i ||\mathbf{w}^{[i]}||_\infty \text{ and } ||\mathbf{w}|| := \Big(\sum_i ||\mathbf{w}^{[i]}||^2\Big)^{1/2}.$$

Finally, we define two sets $S_\eta, \tilde{S_\eta} \subset \mathcal{R}$ as follows:

$$S_\eta := \{\boldsymbol{w} \in \mathcal{R} \mid ||\boldsymbol{w}||_\infty \leq \eta\} \text{ and } \tilde{S_\eta} := \{\boldsymbol{w} \bmod^{\pm} (2\eta) \mid \boldsymbol{w} \in \mathcal{R}\}.$$

Notation 1. *For an element $\mathbf{z}_1 \in \mathcal{R}^l$ we will note $\mathbf{z}_1 =(\mathbf{z}_1^{[1]}, ..., \mathbf{z}_1^{[l]}) \in \mathcal{R}^l$ and $\mathbf{z}_{1,i}^{[j]}$ will be the $i-th$ coefficient of the polynomial $\mathbf{z}_1^{[j]}$.*

2.2 Algorithm Description

ML-DSA is a signature scheme based on structured lattice, it uses matrices and vectors of $\mathcal{R}$ or $\mathcal{R}_q$, with the values of n and q fixed at $n = 256$ and $q = 2^{23} - 2^{13} + 1 = 8\,380\,417$ regardless of the security level. In addition, to reduce the size of the public key and to generate the signature ML-DSA uses algorithms that splits elements in $\mathbb{Z}_q$, namely $\texttt{Decompose}_q$, $\texttt{Power2Round}_q$, $\texttt{MakeHint}_q$ and $\texttt{UseHint}_q$. For a complete description of these algorithms, we refer to the ML-DSA specification [BDK+21].

Key Generation: The key generation algorithm is described in Algorithm 1. ML-DSA is based on the Module-LWE problem, a variant of the LWE problem introduced by Regev in [Reg05], which we will not recall here. From some seeds, $\mathbf{A} \in \mathcal{R}_q^{k \times l}$, $\mathbf{s}_1 \in S_\eta^l$ and $\mathbf{s}_2 \in S_\eta^k$ are generated and then $\mathbf{t} = \mathbf{A}\mathbf{s}_1 + \mathbf{s}_2$ is computed. Two optimisations are made to the public key, which is traditionally $(\mathbf{A}, \mathbf{t})$, to reduce its size. The first optimisation, the most natural, consists of transmitting only the seed used to generate the matrix $\mathbf{A}$. For the second optimisation, only $\mathbf{t}_1$ (the high part of $\mathbf{t}$ computed with $\texttt{Power2Round}_q$) is considered to be part of the public key.

Algorithm 1. KeyGen

Ensure: (pk, sk)
1: $\zeta \leftarrow \{0,1\}^{256}$
2: $(\rho, \rho', K) \in \{0,1\}^{256} \times \{0,1\}^{512} \times \{0,1\}^{256} := \mathrm{H}(\zeta)$
3: $\mathbf{A} \in \mathcal{R}_q^{k \times l} := \texttt{ExpandA}(\rho)$
4: $(\mathbf{s}_1, \mathbf{s}_2) \in S_\eta^l \times S_\eta^k := \texttt{ExpandS}(\rho')$
5: $\mathbf{t} := \mathbf{A}\,\mathbf{s}_1 + \mathbf{s}_2$
6: $(\mathbf{t}_1, \mathbf{t}_0) := \texttt{Power2Round}_q(\mathbf{t}, d)$
7: $tr \in \{0,1\}^{256} := \mathrm{H}(\rho \,||\, \mathbf{t}_1)$
8: **return** $pk = (\rho, \mathbf{t}_1)$, $sk = (\rho, K, tr, \mathbf{s}_1, \mathbf{s}_2, \mathbf{t}_0)$

Signature: The signature algorithm is described in Algorithm 2. The signer derives a masking vector $\mathbf{y} \in \mathcal{R}_q^l$, from which it calculates $\mathbf{w}_1$, the most significant bits of $\mathbf{w} := \mathbf{A}\,\mathbf{y}$ and then a challenge $c \in \mathcal{R}$ which is a sparse polynomial whose coefficients are in $\{-1, 0, 1\}$. It then calculates $\mathbf{z} := \mathbf{y} + c\,\mathbf{s}_1$, the main part of the signature, which verifies the following equation, used for verification:

$$\texttt{HighBits}_q(\mathbf{Az} - c\mathbf{t},\, 2\,\gamma_2) = \texttt{HighBits}_q(\mathbf{Ay} - c\mathbf{s}_2,\, 2\,\gamma_2).$$

The signer then checks that $\mathbf{z}$ does not give information about the secret key; if it does, it starts again by drawing another masking vector. Once $\mathbf{z}$ has passed the tests, we have the following equation:

$$\mathbf{w}_1 = \texttt{HighBits}_q(\mathbf{A}\mathbf{y} - c\mathbf{s}_2,\, 2\,\gamma_2) = \texttt{HighBits}_q(\mathbf{A}\mathbf{z} - c\mathbf{t},\, 2\,\gamma_2).$$

Since $\mathbf{t}_0$ is not known, anyone attempting to verify the signature cannot directly compute $\texttt{HighBits}_q(\mathbf{A}\mathbf{z} - c\mathbf{t}, 2\,\gamma_2)$. The signer adds $\mathbf{h} = \texttt{MakeHint}_q(-c\mathbf{t}_0, \mathbf{A}\mathbf{y} - c\mathbf{s}_2 + c\mathbf{t}_0, 2\gamma_2)$ to allow the verifier to calculate $\texttt{HighBits}_q(\mathbf{A}\mathbf{z} - c\mathbf{t}, 2\,\gamma_2)$, without the knowledge of $\mathbf{t}_0$. Finally, the signature is composed of the challenge c, $\mathbf{z}$, and the hint vector $\mathbf{h}$.

Algorithm 2. Sig

Require: sk, M
Ensure: $\sigma = (\tilde{c}, \mathbf{z}, \mathbf{h})$
$\mathbf{A} \in \mathcal{R}_q^{k\times l} := \texttt{ExpandA}(\rho)$
$\mu \in \{0,1\}^{512} := \mathrm{H}(tr \,||\, M)$
$\kappa := 0,\ (\mathbf{z}, \mathbf{h}) := \perp$
$\rho' \in \{0,1\}^{512} := \mathrm{H}(K \,||\, \mu)$
while $(\mathbf{z}, \mathbf{h}) = \perp$ **do**
    $\mathbf{y} \in \tilde{S}^{l}_{\gamma_1} := \texttt{ExpandMask}(\rho',\, \kappa)$
    $\mathbf{w} := \mathbf{A}\,\mathbf{y}$
    $\mathbf{w}_1 = \texttt{HighBits}_q(\mathbf{w},\, 2\,\gamma_2)$
    $\tilde{c} \in \{0,1\}^{256} := \mathrm{H}(\mu \,||\, \mathbf{w}_1)$
    $c \in B_\tau := \texttt{SampleInBall}(\tilde{c})$
    $\mathbf{z} := \mathbf{y} + c\,\mathbf{s}_1$
    $\mathbf{r}_0 := \texttt{LowBits}_q(\mathbf{w} - c\mathbf{s}_2,\, 2\,\gamma_2)$
    if $\|\mathbf{z}\|_\infty \geq \gamma_1 - \beta$ or $\|\mathbf{r}_0\|_\infty \geq \gamma_2 - \beta$ **then**
        $(\mathbf{z}, \mathbf{h}) := \perp$
    else
        $\mathbf{h} := \texttt{MakeHint}_q(-c\mathbf{t}_0, \mathbf{w} - c\mathbf{s}_2 + c\mathbf{t}_0, 2\gamma_2)$
        if $\|c\,\mathbf{t}_0\|_\infty \geq \gamma_2$ or $|\mathbf{h}|_{\mathbf{h}_j=1} > \omega$ **then**
            $(\mathbf{z}, \mathbf{h}) := \perp$
    $\kappa := \kappa + l$
return $\sigma = (\tilde{c}, \mathbf{z}, \mathbf{h})$

Verification: The verification algorithm is described in Algorithm 3. To verify the signature, it is sufficient to reconstruct the matrix $\mathbf{A}$ and the polynomial c on which the signer has commited. Using the vector $\mathbf{h}$ of the signature, we can recalculate $\mathbf{w}_1 = \texttt{HighBits}_q(\mathbf{A}\mathbf{z} - c\mathbf{t},\, 2\,\gamma_2)$, by using $\texttt{UseHint}_q$. Finally, the signature will be accepted if it is possible to reconstruct the correct c from $\mathbf{w}_1$ and if $\mathbf{z}$ meets the security conditions imposed during signature generation.

Algorithm 3. Ver

Require: pk, σ
1: $\mathbf{A} \in \mathcal{R}_q^{k \times l} :=$ `ExpandA`(ρ)
2: $\mu \in \{0,1\}^{512} := \mathrm{H}(\mathrm{H}(\rho \,||\, \mathbf{t}_1) \,||\, M)$
3: $c :=$ `SampleInBall`$(\tilde{c})$
4: $\mathbf{w}_1' :=$ `UseHint`$_q(\mathbf{h}, \mathbf{Az} - c\mathbf{t}_1 \cdot 2^d, 2\gamma_2)$
5: **return** $[\![||\mathbf{z}||_\infty < \gamma_1 - \beta]\!]$ and $[\![\tilde{c} = \mathrm{H}(\mu \,||\, \mathbf{w}_1')]\!]$ and $[\![|\mathbf{h}|_{\mathbf{h}_j=1} \leq \omega]\!]$

2.3 An Overview of Lattice Theory

The classic lattice definitions and unproven results from this Section are quoted from the book "The LLL Algorithm" [NV09].

Definition 4. *Let* $\mathbf{b}_1, \ldots, \mathbf{b}_d \in \mathbb{Q}^n$*. Denote by* $\mathcal{L}(\mathbf{b}_1, \ldots, \mathbf{b}_d)$ *the set of all integral linear combinations of the* $\mathbf{b}_i$*'s:*

$$\mathcal{L}(\mathbf{b}_1, \ldots, \mathbf{b}_d) = \{\sum_{i=1}^{d} n_i \mathbf{b}_i \mid n_1, \ldots, n_d \in \mathbb{Z}\}.$$

When $L = \mathcal{L}(\mathbf{b}_1, \ldots, \mathbf{b}_d)$*, we say that* L *is the lattice spanned by the* $\mathbf{b}_i$*'s, and that the* $\mathbf{b}_i$*'s are generators. When the* $\mathbf{b}_i$*'s are further linearly independent, we say that* $(\mathbf{b}_1, \ldots, \mathbf{b}_d)$ *is a basis of the lattice* L *in which case:*

$$\forall \mathbf{v} \in L,\ \exists!\, n_1, \ldots, n_d \in \mathbb{Z},\ \mathbf{v} = \sum_{i=1}^{d} n_i \mathbf{b}_i.$$

Definition 5. *We define the dimension or rank of a lattice* L *in* $\mathbb{R}^n$*, denoted by* $\dim(L)$*, as the dimension* d *of its linear span denoted by* $\mathrm{span}(L)$*. The lattice is said to be full-rank when* $d = n$*.*

Definition 6. *The dual of a lattice* L *is the set* L^* *define as:*

$$L^* = \{\mathbf{x} \in \mathrm{span}(L) \mid \forall \mathbf{y} \in L,\ \langle \mathbf{x}, \mathbf{y} \rangle \in \mathbb{Z}\}.$$

Proposition 1. *The dual of a lattice with basis* $\mathbf{B}$ *is a lattice with basis* $\mathbf{D} = \mathbf{B}(\mathbf{B}^\intercal\mathbf{B})^{-1}$.

Definition 7. *A non-singular matrix* $\mathbf{B} = (\mathbf{b}_1, \ldots, \mathbf{b}_n) \in \mathbb{Z}^{m \times n}$ *is in Hermite normal form (HNF) iff*

- *There exists* $1 \leq i_1 < \cdots < i_h \leq m$ *such that* $b_{i,j} \neq 0 \implies j < h$ *and* $i \geq i_j$*.*
- *For all* $k > j$*,* $0 \leq b_{i_j,k} < b_{i_j,j}$ *i.e. all elements at rows* i_j *are reduced modulo* $b_{i_j,j}$*.*

Proposition 2

1. *There exists a polynomial algorithm that transforms a matrix into HNF in a polynomial number of operations.*
2. *If* $\mathcal{L}(\mathbf{B}) = \mathcal{L}(\mathbf{H})$ *and* $\mathbf{B}, \mathbf{H}$ *are HNF then* $\mathbf{B} = \mathbf{H}$.
3. *Let* $\mathbf{B} \in \mathbb{Z}^{m \times n}$, *there exists an HNF matrix* $\mathbf{H}$ *such that* $\mathcal{L}(\mathbf{B}) = \mathcal{L}(\mathbf{H})$.

Proposition 3. *There exists a polynomial time algorithm that, on input a lattice basis* $\mathbf{B} \in \mathbb{Z}^{m \times n}$ *and an affine subspace* S, *outputs a new basis* $\tilde{\mathbf{B}} = (\tilde{\mathbf{b}}_1, \ldots, \tilde{\mathbf{b}}_n)$ *such that* $\mathcal{L}(\tilde{\mathbf{b}}_1, \ldots, \tilde{\mathbf{b}}_d) = S \cap \mathcal{L}(\mathbf{B})$, *where* d *is the dimension of* $S \cap \operatorname{span}(\mathbf{B})$.

Proposition 4. *There exists a polynomial time algorithm that, on input two lattice bases* $\mathbf{B}_1, \mathbf{B}_2 \in \mathbb{Z}^{n \times n}$, *outputs a new basis* $\mathbf{D}$ *such that* $\mathcal{L}(\mathbf{D}) = \mathcal{L}(\mathbf{B}_1) \cap \mathcal{L}(\mathbf{B}_2)$

Proof. See [Mic08] for proof.

We note that Proposition 4 can be generalized to the case of non-full-rank lattices. To the best of our knowledge, this generalization is not known in the literature, we state it below together with a proof.

Proposition 5. *There exists a polynomial time algorithm that, on input two lattices basis* $\mathbf{B}_1 \in \mathbb{Z}^{m_1 \times n}, \mathbf{B}_2 \in \mathbb{Z}^{m_2 \times n}$, *outputs a new basis* $\mathbf{D}$ *such that* $\mathcal{L}(\mathbf{D}) = \mathcal{L}(\mathbf{B}_1) \cap \mathcal{L}(\mathbf{B}_2)$.

Proof. Let $\mathbf{B}'$ a basis of $\operatorname{span}(\mathbf{B}_1) \cap \operatorname{span}(\mathbf{B}_2)$. We can easily compute a basis $\tilde{\mathbf{B}}_i$ of $\mathcal{L}(\mathbf{B}_i) \cap \operatorname{span}(\mathbf{B}')$ according to Proposition 3. We have

$$\mathcal{L}(\mathbf{B}_1) \cap \mathcal{L}(\mathbf{B}_2) = \mathcal{L}(\tilde{\mathbf{B}}_1) \cap \mathcal{L}(\tilde{\mathbf{B}}_2).$$

Moreover,

$$\operatorname{rank}(\operatorname{span}(\tilde{\mathbf{B}}_i)) = \operatorname{rank}(\operatorname{span}(\mathbf{B}_i) \cap \operatorname{span}(\mathbf{B}')) = \operatorname{rank}(\operatorname{span}(\mathbf{B}'))$$

and

$$\operatorname{span}(\tilde{\mathbf{B}}_1) = \operatorname{span}(\tilde{\mathbf{B}}_2).$$

So $\mathcal{L}(\tilde{\mathbf{B}}_1)$ and $\mathcal{L}(\tilde{\mathbf{B}}_2)$ are full rank lattices in $\mathcal{L}(\tilde{\mathbf{B}}_1, \tilde{\mathbf{B}}_2)$. We then use Propostion 2 to compute basis of $\mathcal{L}(\tilde{\mathbf{B}}_1, \tilde{\mathbf{B}}_2)$ and Propostion 4 to compute the intersection $\mathcal{L}(\tilde{\mathbf{B}}_1) \cap \mathcal{L}(\tilde{\mathbf{B}}_2)$ in $\mathcal{L}(\tilde{\mathbf{B}}_1, \tilde{\mathbf{B}}_2)$.

Remark 1. *The lattice intersection algorithm is based on the calculation of the HNF and the calculation of some dual basis. It is not difficult to implement an algorithm that calculates the HNF in a polynomial number of operations, however the resulting algorithm may run in super-polynomial time due to the explosion of the size of the coefficients during intermediate calculations.*

Worse still, for a lattice $L \subset \mathbb{Z}^n$, *it is not generally true that* $L^* \subset \mathbb{Z}^n$. *The HNF must therefore be calculated for matrices with coefficients in* $\mathbb{Q}$, *whose numerators and denominators explode. In the case of the lattices considered in practice in Sect. 5, this can lead to rounding errors when calculating the HNF and an explosion in calculation time. For this reason, in Sect. 3, we will take a different approach to intersect lattices from the state-of-the-art.*

Hard Lattices Problems:

Definition 8. *Let L be a lattice of $\mathbb{R}^n$. For all $1 \leq i \leq \dim(L)$, the $i-$th minimum $\lambda_i(L)$ is defined as the minimum of $\max_{1 \leq j \leq i}(||\mathbf{v}_j||)$ over all i linearly independent lattice vectors $\mathbf{v}_1, \ldots, \mathbf{v}_i \in L$.*

Problem 1. *Shortest Vector Problem (SVP): Given a lattice basis $\mathbf{B}$ find a nonzero lattice vector of lenght at most $\lambda_1(\mathcal{L}(\mathbf{B}))$.*

Problem 2. *Closest Vector Problem (CVP): Given a lattice basis $\mathbf{B}$ and a target vector $\mathbf{t}$ find a nonzero lattice vector within distance $\text{dist}(\mathbf{t}, \mathcal{L}(\mathbf{B}))$.*

Definition 9. *The Gram determinant of $\mathbf{b}_1, \ldots, \mathbf{b}_m \in \mathbb{R}^n$, denoted by $\Delta(\mathbf{b}_1, \ldots, \mathbf{b}_m)$ is the determinant of the $m \times m$ Gram matrix $(\langle \mathbf{b}_i, \mathbf{b}_j \rangle)_{1 \leq i,j \leq m}$. Furthermore, when the $\mathbf{b}_i$'s are linearly independent, $\sqrt{\Delta(\mathbf{b}_1, \ldots, \mathbf{b}_m)}$ is the $m-$dimensional volume of the parallelepiped spanned by the $\mathbf{b}_i$'s.*

Definition 10. *The volume of a lattice $L = \mathcal{L}(\mathbf{b}_1, \ldots, \mathbf{b}_d)$ is defined as:*

$$\text{vol}(L) = \sqrt{\Delta(\mathbf{b}_1, \ldots, \mathbf{b}_d)}$$

which is independent of the choice of the basis $(\mathbf{b}_1, \ldots, \mathbf{b}_d)$ of the lattice L.

Definition 11. *Let L be a sublattice in $\mathbb{R}^n$. A sublattice of L is a lattice M included in L: sublattices of L are the subgroups of L. If the rank of M is equal to the rank of L, we say that M is a full-rank sublattice of L. In which case the group index $[L : M]$ is finite and:*

$$\text{vol}(M) = \text{vol}(L) \times [L : M].$$

Theorem 1. *The `LLL` algorithm given as input a basis of a $d-$dimensional integer lattice $L \subset \mathbb{Z}^n$, outputs a basis $(\mathbf{b}_1, \ldots, \mathbf{b}_d)$ of L in time polynomial in the size of the basis such that:*

$$||\mathbf{b}_1|| \leq 2^{(d-1)/4} \text{vol}(L)^{1/d}.$$

More precisely, the complexity is $\mathcal{O}(d^5(d + log(B))log(B))$ where $B = \max_i(||\mathbf{b}_i||_2)$.

Theorem 2. *The `NearestPlane` algorithm given as input a basis of a integer lattice $L = \mathcal{L}(\mathbf{B}) \subset \mathbb{Z}^n$ and a target vector $\mathbf{t}$ output a lattice point $\mathbf{v}$ of L in time polynomial in the size of the basis such that:*

$$\forall i \in \{1, \ldots, n\}, \ \langle \mathbf{t} - \mathbf{v}, \mathbf{b}_i^* \rangle / ||\mathbf{b}_i^*|| \in [-1/2, 1/2),$$

where $\mathbf{B}^* = (\mathbf{b}_1^*, \ldots, \mathbf{b}_n^*)$ denote the Gram-Schmidt matrix of $\mathbf{B}$.

Assumption 1. *Let L be a $d-$dimensional lattice in $\mathbb{R}^n$. The Gaussian Heuristic "predicts" that $\lambda_1(L)$ would be close to:*

$$\left(\frac{\mathrm{vol}(L)}{\nu_d}\right)^{1/d} \approx \sqrt{\frac{d}{2\pi e}}\mathrm{vol}(L)^{1/d},$$

where ν_d denotes the volume of the closed unitary ball of $\mathbb{R}^d$.

Remark 2. *It is common to assume that if a vector $\mathbf{v} \in L$ is smaller than the Gaussian heuristic, then it is the smallest vector of L. It is then possible to solve the SVP, because a shortest vector of L can be found in its* `LLL`*-reduced basis, provided that the bound of Theorem 1 is sufficiently small. Similarly, the CVP can be solved by pre calculating the* `LLL`*-reduced basis and then applying the* `NearestPlane` *algorithm.*

3 Problem Definition and Attack Methodology

Following the same motivations as in [FGR13], we examine the security of ML-DSA in a scenario where an attacker obtains m messages signed under the same secret key and such that the nonces used during the generation of the signature share a certain number of coefficients. To simplify the presentation, in this section we assume that the common coefficients between the nonces are those of highest degree. Furthermore as $\mathbf{y} \in \mathcal{R}_q^l$ is a vector of polynomials, we present the reasoning only on $\mathbf{y}^{[1]}$, the first polynomial of $\mathbf{y}$. For the moment we assume we know m signatures $\sigma_1, \ldots, \sigma_m$ of `Sig` signed under the same secret key, such that:

$$\forall i \in \{1, \ldots, m\},\ \mathbf{y}_i^{[1]} = \sum_{j=0}^{d} \mathbf{y}_{i,j}^{[1]} x^j + \sum_{j=d+1}^{n-1} \mathbf{y}_{1,j}^{[1]} x^j$$

where $0 \leq d \leq n-2$ is unknown. By definition, $\mathbf{z} := \mathbf{y} + c\mathbf{s}_1$ so even if it means subtracting $\mathbf{z}_1$ from all the other $\mathbf{z}_i$, without loss of generality we can assume the last coefficients shared by the nonce to be zero, formally:

$$\forall i \in \{1, \ldots, m\},\ \mathbf{z}_i^{[1]} = \mathbf{y}_i^{[1]} + c_i\mathbf{s}_1^{[1]} \ \text{ with } \ \deg(\mathbf{y}_i^{[1]}) \leq d < n.$$

Lemma 1. *Assuming that for $i \in \{1, \ldots, m\}$ $c_i \in \mathcal{R}_q$ behaves like a random element of the ring $\mathcal{R}_q$, c_i is invertible in $\mathcal{R}_q$ with probability at least 99%.*

Proof. By the Chinese remainder theorem, $\mathcal{R}_q \cong \mathbb{Z}_q^n$, assuming that for $i \in \{1, \ldots, m\}$ c_i behaves like a random element of $\mathcal{R}_q$, the probability that c_i is invertible is $(1 - (1/q))^n \approx 0.999969$.

Therefore, in the rest of the article, the vectors c_i will be considered invertible without loss of generality. For each $i \in \{1, \ldots, m\}$, it exists a $P_i \in \mathcal{R}$ such that $c_i \times c_i^{-1} = 1 + qP_i$, where c_i^{-1} denotes the inverse of c_i seen as a element of $\mathcal{R}_q$. Therefore, $c_i^{-1}\mathbf{z}_i^{[1]} = c_i^{-1}\mathbf{y}_i^{[1]} + \mathbf{s}_1^{[1]} + qP_i\mathbf{s}_1^{[1]}$ and for all $i \in \{1, \ldots, m\}$:

$$\mathbf{s}_1^{[1]} \in L_i := \mathcal{L}\left(c_i^{-1}\mathbf{z}_i^{[1]}, \{c_i^{-1}x^j\}_{j\in\{0,\ldots,d\}}, \{qx^j\}_{j\in\{0,\ldots,n-1\}}\right).$$

This relation can be rewritten as:

$$\forall i \in \{1, \ldots, m\}, \quad \mathbf{s}_1^{[1]} \in \overline{L_i} := \mathrm{span}_{\mathbb{F}_q}\left(c_i^{-1}\mathbf{z}_i^{[1]}, \{c_i^{-1}x^j\}_{j\in\{0,\ldots,d\}}\right).$$

We have reformulated the problem of finding $\mathbf{s}_1^{[1]}$, as the calculation of a lattice intersection (or as an intersection of $\mathbb{F}_q$ vectorial spaces), indeed:

$$\mathbf{s}_1^{[1]} \in \bigcap_{1\leq i\leq m} L_i \quad \text{and} \quad \mathbf{s}_1^{[1]} \in \bigcap_{1\leq i\leq m} \overline{L_i}.$$

Switching between $\mathbb{F}_q$Subspaces and Lattices: One method would be to calculate the intersection of the lattices L_i using duality and the results of Sect. 2, although polynomial this method can be inefficient for large lattices, mainly due to rounding errors when calculating the HNF. The definition of $\overline{L_i}$'s simplifies this, allowing to calculate only intersections of vector spaces. Unfortunately, it is not possible to find a small element in a vector space directly. This is why we apply the following method:

1. Compute a basis $\mathbf{B} = (\mathbf{b}_1, \ldots, \mathbf{b}_\alpha)$ of the $\overline{L_i}$'s intersection, named $\overline{L}$.
2. View $\overline{L}$ as a integer lattice, by considering $L = \mathcal{L}(\mathbf{B}, \{qx^j\}_{j\in\{0,\ldots,n-1\}})$.
3. Retrieve $\mathbf{s}_1^{[1]}$ using LLL, according to the Gaussian heuristic, $\mathbf{s}_1^{[1]}$ will be the shortest vector of L.

This method allows to efficiently compute the intersection of L_i's because the lattice L calculated in steps 1 and 2 satisfies:

$$L = \bigcap_{1\leq i\leq m} L_i.$$

Remark 3. *Steps* 1 *and* 2 *provide a generic way of computing intersections of modular lattices. This method is more efficient than the classical one (which uses duality) described in Sect. 2.*

Since L is of full rank in $\mathbb{Z}^n$, LLL cannot be applied directly (as the approximation factor depends exponentially on the dimension). A classical way to overcome the problem, described in [EFGT17], consists in projecting L in lower dimension to recover $\mathbf{s}_1^{[1]}$ piece by piece.

Theorem 3. *Let $M_1, \ldots, M_m$ be m messages with the associated signatures $\sigma_1, \ldots, \sigma_m$ such that, for $i \in \{1, \ldots, m\}$, $\deg(\mathbf{y}_i^{[1]}) = d$. Under Assumption 1, $\mathbf{s}_1^{[1]}$ can be computed in polynomial time as soon as:*

$$d < n-2 \quad \text{and} \quad m \geq \frac{n-\alpha}{n-d-1}$$

where $\alpha \in \mathbb{N}$ denotes an integer where it is considered realistic to recover the shortest vector by applying LLL *or any other lattice reduction algorithm, on a lattice of dimension α.*

Proof.

$$\forall i \in \{1, \ldots, m\}, \quad \dim_{\mathbb{F}_q}\left(\overline{L_i}\right) = d+1 < n-1,$$

Let us consider, for $i \in \{1, \ldots, m\}$, $\phi_i : \mathbb{F}_q^n \to \mathbb{F}_q^{n-(d+1)}$ which verifies, $\overline{L_i} = \ker_{\mathbb{F}_q}(\phi_i)$. Therefore, by defining $\phi : x \to (\phi_1(x), \ldots, \phi_m(x))$:

$$\begin{aligned}\dim_{\mathbb{F}_q}\left(\bigcap_{1\leq i\leq m} \overline{L_i}\right) &= \dim(\ker_{\mathbb{F}_q}(\phi)) \\ &= n - \mathrm{rank}_{\mathbb{F}_q}(\phi).\end{aligned}$$

Assuming ϕ to be a random application, it has maximum rank and thus:

$$\dim_{\mathbb{F}_q}\left(\overline{L}\right) = \dim_{\mathbb{F}_q}\left(\bigcap_{1\leq i\leq m} \overline{L_i}\right) = n - m(n-(d+1)) \leq \alpha.$$

Let $L = \mathcal{L}(\mathbf{B}, \{qx^j\}_{j\in\{0,\ldots,n-1\}})$, where $\mathbf{B}$ is a basis of $\overline{L}$ and $I \subset \{0, \ldots, n-1\}$, with $|I| = l$ and $\varphi_I : \mathbb{Z}^n \to \mathbb{Z}^l$ the projection associated with I, then $L_I := \varphi_I(L)$ is an integer lattice in $\mathbb{Z}^l$ and $\varphi_I(\mathbf{s}_1^{[1]}) \in L_I$. According to the ML-DSA parameters, $||\mathbf{s}_1^{[1]}||_2 \leq \sqrt{n}\eta$ where $\eta \in \{2, 4\}$ depending on the security level, so $||\varphi_I(s_1^{[1]})||_2 \leq \sqrt{l}\eta$. Furthermore,

$$\mathrm{vol}(L_I) = \frac{\mathrm{vol}(q\mathbb{Z}^l)}{[L_I : q\mathbb{Z}^l]} = q^{l-\alpha}.$$

$\mathbf{s}_1^{[1]}$ will be the shortest vector of L_I, as soon as:

$$||\varphi(\mathbf{s}_1^{[1]})||_2 = \sqrt{l}\eta \ll \sqrt{\frac{n}{2\pi e}}\mathrm{vol}(L_I)^{1/l} = \sqrt{\frac{l}{2\pi e}}q^{1-m/l}.$$

In other words, with $C = \sqrt{2\pi e}\eta$:

$$l \geq \frac{\alpha}{1 - log(C)/log(q)} \approx \alpha(1 + \frac{log(C)}{log(q)}).$$

If it is considered realistic to solve the SVP in L_I of dimension l, then $\mathbf{s}_1^{[1]}$ can be found by applying LLL or any other lattice reduction algorithm.

3.1 Affine Space Optimisation

Even if Theorem 3 is sufficient to find $\mathbf{s}_1^{[1]}$ efficiently with a reasonable number of signatures, the $\overline{L_i}$'s are $\mathbb{F}_q$-subspaces of dimension $d+1$, and for their intersection to be non-trivial, it is necessary that $d < n-2$. In the following sub-section, we propose an affine optimisation which allow to intersect the $\overline{L_i}$'s in a non trivial way, even when the degree of the nonce is $n-2$ (*i.e.* when only the last coefficient of $\mathbf{y}$ is 0). More precisely, we had for all $i \in \{1, \ldots, m\}$:

$$\mathbf{s}_1^{[1]} \in L_i := \mathcal{L}\left(c_i^{-1}\mathbf{z}_i^{[1]}, \{c_i^{-1}x^j\}_{j\in\{0,\ldots,d\}}, \{qx^j\}_{j\in\{0,\ldots,n-1\}}\right).$$

But since $c_i^{-1}\mathbf{z}_i^{[1]} = c_i^{-1}\mathbf{y}_i^{[1]} + \mathbf{s}_1^{[1]} + qP_i\mathbf{s}_1^{[1]}$, the coordinate of $\mathbf{s}_1^{[1]}$ in $c_i^{-1}\mathbf{z}_i^{[1]}$ is always 1, it is possible to consider affine lattices, of dimension d. Formally for $i \in \{1, \ldots, m\}$:

$$\mathbf{s}_1^{[1]} \in L_{A_i} := c_i^{-1}\mathbf{z}_i^{[1]} + \mathcal{L}\left(\{c_i^{-1}x^j\}_{j\in\{0,\ldots,d\}}, \{qx^j\}_{j\in\{0,\ldots,n-1\}}\right).$$

As described previously, it is possible to write this intersection using $\mathbb{F}_q-$subspaces:

$$\forall i \in \{1, \ldots, m\}, \quad \mathbf{s}_1^{[1]} \in \overline{L_{A_i}} := c_i^{-1}\mathbf{z}_i^{[1]} + \mathrm{span}_{\mathbb{F}_q}\left(\{c_i^{-1}x^j\}_{j\in\{0,\ldots,d\}}\right).$$

So, finally:

$$\mathbf{s}_1^{[1]} \in L_A := \bigcap_{1\leq i\leq m} L_{A_i} \quad \text{and} \quad \mathbf{s}_1^{[1]} \in \overline{L_A} := \bigcap_{1\leq i\leq m} \overline{L_{A_i}}.$$

We cannot apply directly the results of Sect. 2, since the A_i's are affine spaces and not a vector spaces. The following strategy is proposed:

1. Compute a basis $\mathbf{B} = (\mathbf{b}_1, \ldots, \mathbf{b}_\alpha)$ and a vector $\mathbf{v}$ such that:
$$\overline{L_A} = \mathbf{v} + \mathrm{span}(\mathbf{B}).$$
2. View $\overline{L_A}$ as an affine lattice, by considering:
$$L_A = \mathbf{v} + \mathcal{L}\left(\mathbf{B}, \{qx^j\}_{j\in\{0,\ldots,n-1\}}\right).$$
3. Retrieve $\mathbf{s}_1^{[1]}$ using the `NearestPlane` algorithm, according to the Gaussian heuristic, $\mathbf{s}_1^{[1]} - \mathbf{v}$ will be the closest vector of $-\mathbf{v}$ in L_A.

Theorem 4. *Let m messages $M_1, \ldots, M_m$ with the associated signatures $(\mathbf{z}_i, c_i)_{i\in\{1,\ldots,m\}}$ such that for $i \in \{1, \ldots, m\}$, $\deg(\mathbf{y}_i^{[1]}) = d$. Under Assumption 1, $\mathbf{s}_1^{[1]}$ can be computed in polynomial time as soon as:*

$$d < n-1 \quad \text{and} \quad m \geq \frac{n-\alpha}{n-d}$$

where $\alpha \in \mathbb{N}$ denotes an integer where it is considered realistic to recover the shortest vector by apply `NearestPlane` *or any other CVP solver algorithm on a lattice of size α.*

Proof. Since the proof of Theorem 3 is similar, fewer details are provided.

$$\forall i \in \{1,\ldots,m\}, \quad \dim_{\mathbb{F}_q}\left(\overline{L_{A_i}}\right) = d < n-1,$$

and therefore:

$$\dim_{\mathbb{F}_q}\left(\overline{L_A}\right) = \dim_{\mathbb{F}_q}\left(\bigcap_{1\le i\le m} \overline{L_{A_i}}\right) = n - m(n-d) \le \alpha.$$

Let $L_A = \mathbf{v} + \mathcal{L}(\mathbf{B}, \{qx^j\}_{j\in\{0,\ldots,n-1\}})$, where $\mathbf{B}$ is a basis of the vectorial space $\overline{L_A}$ and $\mathbf{v} \in \overline{L_A}$. L_A is an affine lattice, and $\mathbf{s}_1^{[1]}$ will be the shortest vector on L_A, as in the proof of Theorem 3 we cannot use lattice reduction due to the dimension of L_A, but using an appropriate projection, one can retrieve $\mathbf{s}_1^{[1]}$ using the `NearestPlane` algorithm, according to the Gaussian heuristic, $\mathbf{s}_1^{[1]} - \mathbf{v}$ will be the closest vector of $-\mathbf{v}$ in $\mathcal{L}(\mathbf{B}, \{qx^j\}_{j\in\{0,\ldots,n-1\}})$.

4 Generalisation and Further Developments

In Sect. 3, it was assumed that the nonces had the same coefficients of higher degree. This section demonstrates that the two theorems of Sect. 3 continue to apply even when the positions of the common coefficients are unknown to the attacker.

In this section, we know m messages $M_1, \ldots, M_m$ with their associated signatures $\sigma_1, \ldots, \sigma_m$ such that the $\mathbf{y}_i$'s used during the signature share a block of ℓ coefficients in common[1], whose position is unknown. Again even if it means subtracting $\mathbf{z}_1$ from all the other $\mathbf{z}_i$'s, one can consider that the coefficients shared by $\mathbf{y}_1, \ldots, \mathbf{y}_m$ are zero. To simplify the calculations, we make the heuristic assumption that the coefficients of the $\mathbf{z}_i$'s are uniformly distributed in $\{-\gamma_1+1, \gamma_1\}$. According to the definition of c and $\mathbf{s}_1$, $||c\mathbf{s}_1||_\infty \le \beta$. So ℓ coefficients lie in $\{-\beta, \beta\}$. However, for any m signatures, the probability of this happening is:

$$\left(\frac{2\beta+1}{2\gamma_1}\right)^{\ell\times m}. \tag{1}$$

As soon as this probability is low enough, we can find the block of ℓ coefficients in common by looking at the family of coefficients of the $\mathbf{z}_i$'s. The same kind of reasoning can be applied if an attacker is able to retrieve a coefficient of $\mathbf{y}$ without knowing its exact position. Formally, we know a message M associated with its signature $\sigma = (\tilde{c}, \mathbf{z}, \mathbf{h})$ and α, for which there exists an unknown i in $\{1,\ldots,256\}$ such that $\mathbf{y}_i^{[1]} = \alpha$. It is possible to find i as soon as

$$\left|\{\mathbf{z}_i^{[1]}\}_{i\in\{1,\ldots,n\}} \bigcap \{\alpha-\beta,\ldots,\alpha+\beta\}\right| = 1.$$

[1] The case considered in Sect. 3 corresponds to a block of size $\ell = n - d$.

If not, the attacker cannot exploit the signature and proceeds with another one. Therefore, it will be possible to find i with probability:

$$\left(1-\frac{2\beta+1}{2\gamma_1}\right)^{n-1}. \tag{2}$$

We have chosen to present our result in the case where the nonce share a block of ℓ common coefficients, but in reality, due to the nature of $\mathcal{R}$, this result can be extended to many other contexts as we will discuss below.

Blocks of Hidden Shared Bits: The attack described previously can be generalized to the case where the nonces share multiple blocks of coefficients. According to the beginning of the present section, it is possible to statistically find the position of the common coefficients: We therefore assume that we know m messages $M_1, \ldots, M_m$ with their associated signatures $\sigma_1, \ldots, \sigma_m$ such that the $\mathbf{y}_i$'s used during the signature share a total of ℓ coefficients in common, divided into δ different blocks as shown in Fig. 1.

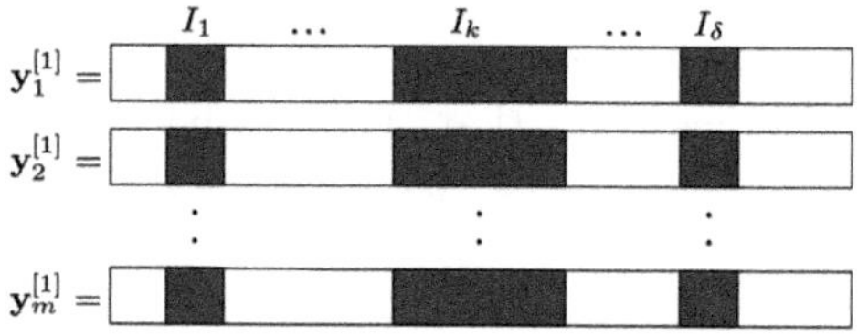

Fig. 1. Biased nonces.

Formally for all i in $\{1, \ldots, m\}$:

$$\mathbf{y}_i^{[1]} = \sum_{k=1}^{\delta} \sum_{j \in I_k} \mathbf{y}_{1,j}^{[1]} x^j + \sum_{j \notin \cup I_k} \mathbf{y}_{i,j}^{[1]} x^j$$

where $I_1, \ldots, I_\delta$ represent the coefficients of each block. If $\ell_1, \ldots, \ell_\delta$ denote the length of each block, by definition $\sum \ell_i = \ell$. Even if it means subtracting $\mathbf{z}_1$ from all the $\mathbf{z}_i$'s, it can be assumed that the shared coefficients of $(\mathbf{y}_i)_{i \in \{1,\ldots,m\}}$ are zero. Moreover by posing $P_k(x) = x^{n+1-b_k}$, where b_k denote the last element on the interval I_k for k in $\{1, \ldots, \delta\}$:

$$\deg(P_k \mathbf{y}_i^{[1]}) \leq n - 1 - b_k.$$

It is then sufficient to apply the attack described in Sect. 3 to the family $\{P_k \mathbf{z}_i\}_{(i,k) \in \{1,\ldots,m\} \times \{1,\ldots,\delta\}}$.

Applications to Fault Attacks: Our attack, inspired by the result in [EFGT17], can also be seen as a fault attack on the generation of $\mathbf{y}$, since an attacker who injects a fault to stop the generation of the coefficients of $\mathbf{y}^{[1]}$ prematurely will obtain a signature with a corresponding $\mathbf{y}^{[1]}$ of unusually low degree. In [EFGT17] the authors focus on the injection of a single fault on the BLISS signature scheme, we show that this attack works on ML-DSA and is drastically more effective when an attacker is able to retrieve more than one faulty signature. In particular, with sufficiently many faults injected, any part of the generation of $\mathbf{y}$ is vulnerable.

Applications to Side-Channel Attacks: This attack also applies to the case where, by analyzing the generation of the signature, an attacker is able to find one (one more) of the coefficients of the nonce used to generate the signature. To simplify the presentation, we assume that we know m messages $M_1, \ldots, M_m$ with their associated signatures $(\mathbf{z}_i, c_i)_{i \in \{1,\ldots,m\}}$ and $i_1, \ldots, i_m$ such that the attacker knows $\mathbf{y}^{[1]}_{1,i_1}, \ldots, \mathbf{y}^{[1]}_{m,i_m}$. To reduce the problem to the one described in Sect. 3, it is sufficient to pose the following .

$$\forall j \in \{1, \ldots, m\},\ P_j(x) = (\mathbf{y}^{[1]}_{j,i_j})^{-1} x^{n-1-i_j}.$$

Therefore, according to the definition of the P_j's, the last coefficient of each $P_j \mathbf{y}^{[1]}_j$ is 1, so this returns to the case of nonce which have their highest degree coefficients in common, as described in Sect. 3.

5 Experimental Results

To demonstrate our theoretical results in practice, we focused on finding the first polynomial of $\mathbf{s}_1$, $\mathbf{s}_1^{[1]}$. However, the reasoning for finding the other polynomials of $\mathbf{s}_1$ is strictly identical. Furthermore, the theory presented does not depend on the level of security, we have only tested the results on ML-DSA level 2 security. As the code is a proof of concept, the results are far from being optimized, all the tests and results presented in this section were carried out using `SageMath`, on a laptop computer equipped with an Intel(R) Core(TM) i7-10850H 2.70GHz CPU. The code used for the attack is available at https://github.com/AzevedoPaco/AttackML-DSA. The various constants for the three ML-DSA security levels are shown in Table 2. For Tables 3, 4 and 5, the success statistics are based on an average of 10 keys (Table 1).

Statistics for ML-DSA's Parameters: The probabilities formally described in Sect. 4 are calculated. One wants to find the position of ℓ coefficients in common for the nonces corresponding to m different messages, as the following paragraphs will show, the parameters useful in practical tests are typically: $(m, \ell) \approx (1, 150)$ (which was the case studied in the paper [EFGT17]), $(m, \ell) \approx (2, 75)$ and $(m, \ell) \approx (150, 1)$. For these values the quantity $m \times \ell$ is

Table 1. Settings for different security levels of ML-DSA

Security level	II	III	V
(k, l)	$(4, 4)$	$(6, 5)$	$(8, 7)$
γ_1	2^{17}	2^{19}	2^{19}
γ_2	$(q-1)/88$	$(q-1)/32$	$(q-1)/32$
η	2	4	2
τ	39	49	60
β	78	196	120

constant. Table 2 calculates the probabilities described in Sect. 4, for the three security level of ML-DSA.[2]

Table 2. Numeric application for probabilities in (1) and (2)

Security level	II	III	V
Numeric application in (1)	2^{-1605}	2^{-1707}	2^{-1813}
Numeric application in (2)	0.736	0.826	0.889

Retrieving $\mathbf{s}_1$ with a Single Faulty Signature: As mentioned in Sect. 4, the attack can be seen as a generalisation of the one described in [EFGT17], with a single signature, our results fall back to those against BLISS described in [EFGT17]. For a single signature and if we note d the degree of $\mathbf{y}^{[1]}$ at the time of its generation, l_{min} the minimum dimension in which the network can be projected, Table 3 summarizes the obtained results.

Table 3. Attack results with a single signature against ML-DSA-II

d	20	40	60	80	90
Theoretical l_{min}	27	53	79	105	118
l in practice	27	53	79	115	188
Probability of success	1	1	1	1	4/5
recover $\mathbf{s}_1^{[1]}$	0.272s	2.65s	13.69s	60.49s	866.9s
used algorithm	LLL	BKZ25	BKZ25	BKZ30	BKZ30

Retrieving $\mathbf{s}_1$ with Few Faulty Signatures: The main interest of our generalization is to show that the attack described in [EFGT17] becomes drastically

[2] for m and ℓ such that $m \times \ell \approx 150$.

more efficient when we assume the attacker is capable of injecting the same fault for at least two executions, Table 4 summarizes the results obtained for two faulty signatures (where the degree of each $\mathbf{y}^{[1]}$ is d).

Table 4. Attack results with two signatures against ML-DSA-II

d	90	110	130	150	170
$\dim_{\mathbb{F}_q}(L)$	1	1	6	46	86
Theoretical l_{min}	1	1	8	53	98
l in practice	50	50	50	60	110
Success for our l	1	1	1	1	1
recover $\mathbf{s}_1^{[1]}$	0.18s	0.198s	0.42s	2.44s	29.6s
used algorithm	LLL	LLL	LLL	LLL	BKZ25

With just one additional faulty signature, the attack is much more effective, when $m \leq 125$, using lattice reduction is useless since the intersection is trivial (it is a line directed by $\mathbf{s}_1^{[1]}$). By using 3 or more faulty signatures, it would be possible to find $\mathbf{s}_1^{[1]}$ with fewer $\mathbf{y}$ coefficients set to 0.

Retrieving $\mathbf{s}_1$ with a Single known Coefficient: This paragraph presents the results of the attack, as it was originally described in Sect. 3, Table 5 summarizes the attack results when the nonce of m signatures share the same last coefficient of highest degree.

Table 5. Attack results with m signatures against ML-DSA-II

m	220	200	180	160
$\dim_{\mathbb{F}_q}(L)$	36	56	76	96
Theoretical l_{min}	41	64	87	109
l in practice	50	65	90	120
Success for our l	1	1	1	1
recover $\mathbf{s}_1^{[1]}$	89.38s	84.27s	84.9s	1744.9s
used algorithm	LLL	BKZ25	BKZ25	BKZ30

6 Conclusion

This paper, built on [EFGT17]'s ideas, proposes an attack on ML-DSA under the assumption that an attacker has access to information (implicit or explicit) on the nonce. More precisely, our attacks assume redundancy of information on the nonces used during the generation of some signature, either in the form of unknown common coefficients or null coefficients or in the case where the attacker can know the value of one of the coefficients. In all these cases, we show that ML-DSA's secret key can be extracted from such a set of signatures, in a reasonable time and always with less than 4×160 signatures for ML-DSA-II.

Finding appropriate countermeasures against our new attacks is not obvious. For instance, a technique based on swapping the order of generation of the coefficients of $\mathbf{y}$ was suggested by the authors of [EFGT17] and seemed sufficient to thwart their attacks. However, this technique alone is not able to protect ML-DSA implementations against our improved fault attacks. This suggests the absence of a simple countermeasure and seems to indicate that it is necessary to mask the entire sampling algorithm.

Acknowledgments. This work received funding from the France 2030 program, managed by the French National Research Agency under grant agreements No. ANR-22-PETQ-0008 (PQ-TLS) and ANR-22-CMAS-0001 (QuanTEdu-France), and from ANRT (Association nationale de la recherche et de la technologie).

References

[BAE+24] Bronchain, O., Azouaoui, M., ElGhamrawy, M., Renes, J., Schneider, T.: Exploiting small-norm polynomial multiplication with physical attacks: application to CRYSTALS-Dilithium. IACR Trans. Cryptographic Hardw. Embedded Syst. **2024**(2), 359–383 (2024)

[BBK16] Bindel, N., Buchmann, J., Krämer, J.: Lattice-based signature schemes and their sensitivity to fault attacks. In: 2016 Workshop on Fault Diagnosis and Tolerance in Cryptography, FDTC 2016, Santa Barbara, CA, USA, August 16, 2016, pp. 63–77. IEEE Computer Society (2016)

[BDK+21] Bai, S., et al.: Algorithm specifications and supporting documentation (version 3.1) (2021). https://pq-crystals.org/dilithium/data/dilithium-specification-round3-20210208.pdf

[BP18] Bruinderink, L.G., Pessl, P.: Differential fault attacks on deterministic lattice signatures. IACR TCHES **2018**(3), 21–43 (2018). https://tches.iacr.org/index.php/TCHES/article/view/7267

[BVC+23] Berzati, A., Viera, A.C., Chartouny, M., Madec, S., Vergnaud, D., Vigilant, D.: Exploiting intermediate value leakage in Dilithium: a template-based approach. IACR TCHES **2023**(4), 188–210 (2023)

[CKA+21] Chen, Z., Karabulut, E., Aysu, A., Ma, Y., Jing, J.: An efficient non-profiled side-channel attack on the CRYSTALS-Dilithium post-quantum signature. In: 2021 IEEE 39th International Conference on Computer Design (ICCD), pp. 583–590 (2021)

[EAB+23] ElGhamrawy, M., et al.: From MLWE to RLWE: A differential fault attack on randomized & deterministic Dilithium. Cryptology ePrint Archive, Paper 2023/1074, 2023. https://eprint.iacr.org/2023/1074

[EFGT17] Espitau, T., Fouque, P.-A., Gérard, B., Tibouchi, M.: Side-channel attacks on BLISS lattice-based signatures: Exploiting branch tracing against strongSwan and electromagnetic emanations in microcontrollers. In: Thuraisingham, B.M., Evans, D., Malkin, T., Xu, D. (eds.) ACM CCS 2017, pp. 1857–1874. ACM Press (2017)

[FGR13] Faugère, J.-C., Goyet, C., Renault, G.: Attacking (EC)DSA given only an implicit hint. In: Knudsen, L.R., Huapeng, W. (eds.) SAC 2012. LNCS, vol. 7707, pp. 252–274. Springer, Heidelberg (2013)

[KLH+20] Kim, I.-J., Lee, T.-H., Han, J., Sim, B.-Y., Han, D.-G.: Novel single-trace ML profiling attacks on NIST 3 round candidate Dilithium. Cryptology ePrint Archive, Report 2020/1383 (2020). https://eprint.iacr.org/2020/1383

[KPLG24] Krahmer, E., Pessl, P., Land, G., Güneysu, T.: Correction fault attacks on randomized CRYSTALS-Dilithium. Cryptology ePrint Archive, Paper 2024/138 (2024). https://eprint.iacr.org/2024/138

[LZS+21] Liu, Y., et al.: On the security of lattice-based fiat-Shamir signatures in the presence of randomness leakage. IEEE Trans. Inf. Forensics Secur. **16**, 1868–1879 (2021)

[Mic08] Micciancio, D.: Efficient reductions among lattice problems. In: ACM-SIAM Symposium on Discrete Algorithms (2008)

[MUTS22] Marzougui, S., Ulitzsch, V., Tibouchi, M., Seifert, J.-P.: Profiling side-channel attacks on Dilithium: a small bit-fiddling leak breaks it all. Cryptology ePrint Archive, Report 2022/106 (2022). https://eprint.iacr.org/2022/106

[NIS23] NIST. Fips 204 (draft): Module-lattice-based digital signature standard. Federal Inf. Process. Stds. (NIST FIPS), National Institute of Standards and Technology, Gaithersburg, MD (2023). https://nvlpubs.nist.gov/nistpubs/FIPS/NIST.FIPS.204.ipd.pdf

[NV09] Phong, Q.N., Vallée, B.: The lll algorithm - survey and applications. In: Information Security and Cryptography (2009)

[RCDB22] Ravi, P., Chattopadhyay, A., D'Anvers, J.P., Baksi, A.: Side-channel and fault-injection attacks over lattice-based post-quantum schemes (kyber, Dilithium): Survey and new results. Cryptology ePrint Archive, Paper 2022/737 (2022). https://eprint.iacr.org/2022/737

[Reg05] Regev, O.: On lattices, learning with errors, random linear codes, and cryptography. In: Proceedings of the Thirty-Seventh Annual ACM Symposium on Theory of Computing, STOC '05, pp. 84–93, New York, NY, USA (2005). Association for Computing Machinery

[RJH+18] Ravi, P., Jhanwar, M.P., Howe, J., Chattopadhyay, A., Bhasin, S.: Side-channel assisted existential forgery attack on Dilithium - A NIST PQC candidate. Cryptology ePrint Archive, Report 2018/821 (2018). https://eprint.iacr.org/2018/821

[WNGD23] Wang, R., Ngo, K., Gärtner, J., Dubrova, E.: Single-trace side-channel attacks on CRYSTALS-Dilithium: Myth or reality? Cryptology ePrint Archive, Paper 2023/1931 (2023)

Isogeny-Based Cryptography

How (not) to Build Identity-Based Encryption from Isogenies

Elif Özbay Gürler[1](✉) and Patrick Struck[2]

[1] Technische Universität Darmstadt, Darmstadt, Germany
elif.oezbay@tu-darmstadt.de
[2] Universität Konstanz, Konstanz, Germany
patrick.struck@uni-konstanz.de

Abstract. In this work we show obstacles when constructing identity-based encryption (IBE) from isogenies. We first give a modular description for IBEs, what we call a canonical IBE, that consists of two components: an identity key derivation scheme and a public-key encryption scheme. This allows us to investigate the identity key derivation scheme (where the obstacles are rooted in) in isolation. We present several approaches, showing that they can either not be realized—extracting the secret keys would require to solve the underlying hardness assumption—or result in IBE schemes that are insecure—users can use their secret keys to compute secret keys of other users. Finally, we identify properties for isogeny-based trapdoor functions that one would need in order to overcome the identified obstacles.

1 Introduction

Encryption is one of the fundamental concepts of cryptography. Historically, encryption required the two communicating parties—Alice and Bob—to have some preshared key ahead of time, so-called symmetric encryption. In their seminal paper, Diffie and Hellman [25] introduced the concept of asymmetric or public-key encryption, where Alice has a key-pair consisting of a secret key, only known to her, and a public key, known by everyone. Using Alice's public key, Bob can encrypt messages that only Alice, using her secret key, can decrypt. The advantage of public-key encryption is that Alice and Bob no longer need a preshared key in order to securely communicate. Nevertheless, public-key encryption comes with the challenge that Bob needs an *authentic* copy of Alice's public key—something that is typically achieved via a public-key infrastructure.

A few years after Diffie and Hellman, Shamir [55] introduced the concept of identity-based encryption (IBE). Here, the identity of a user, say, Alice's email address, is used instead of a public key. While the concept of identity-based encryption was around for several years, the first efficient construction is due to Boneh and Franklin [10]. On a high-level, IBE relies on a trusted party holding a master key-pair (mpk, msk). Instead of using a public key of Alice, Bob can encrypt a message using the master public key mpk and Alice's identity id_A.

C. Boura et al. (Eds.): SAC 2025, LNCS 16207, pp. 589–615, 2026.
https://doi.org/10.1007/978-3-032-10536-3_22

When Alice joins the system—which might in fact take place after Bob has already encrypted messages under her identity—the trusted party will provide Alice with her secret key sk_{id_A} which it derives from its master secret key msk and Alice's identity id_A. The fact that Alice might join the system later, also reveals one of the main challenges for constructing IBE: the trusted party needs to be able to generate Alice's secret key *after* Bob computed her public key.[1]

Since the Boneh-Franklin IBE scheme is not based on quantum-hard assumptions, it will no longer be secure once large-scale quantum computers exist. A general question is therefore to construct IBE from quantum-hard assumptions. Clearly, hash-based cryptography does not work as it is limited to signature schemes. Multivariate cryptography seems less appealing as secure constructions tend to be signature schemes while proposed encryption schemes are often broken[2]. There are IBE constructions from lattices such as the one by Gentry et al. [37], which have also explicit security proofs against quantum adversaries [60]. Regarding code-based IBE constructions, we are only aware of the construction by Gaborit et al. [33], though this one was broken soon after [24]. The only isogeny-based IBE scheme was proposed by Fouotsa and Marco [32], which was also quickly shown to be insecure[3].

Isogeny-based IBE schemes, in particular, are appealing for another reason. Recently, Boneh et al. [11] gave a lower bound for the length of Fiat-Shamir signatures based on group actions. Although many compact isogeny-based signature schemes that are not based on group actions exist [3,5,20,23,28,49], the lower bound is restrictive. On the other hand, it is known that short signatures can be obtained from certain IBE schemes—as pointed out by Boneh and Franklin [10], and later treated formally in [19]. This transform can indeed be an alternative way of bypassing the aforementioned lower bound. Therefore, it remains an alluring open question whether secure IBE schemes can be constructed from isogenies.

1.1 Our Contribution

In this work, we explore different variants of constructing IBE from isogenies, showing several limitations yielding either insecure constructions or constructions that we cannot instantiate (yet). We focus on what we call a *canonical IBE* definition. This definition decomposes into a "normal" public-key encryption scheme and an identity key derivation (IKD) scheme. The latter is a primitive that we introduce—though it implicitly appears already in prior works—and

[1] Strictly speaking, there is no explicit public key of Alice in this setting. Looking ahead, though, we show in this work that the existing IBE constructions can actually be viewed as those where Bob can generate Alice's public key before her secret key is generated.

[2] An early example is the Matsumoto-Imai scheme [44] which got broken by Patarin [52]. In the recent NIST standardization process [50], all multivariate public-key encryption schemes were broken at the beginning of the first round.

[3] As declared in https://lauranemarco.github.io/research. Last accessed: 13th January 2025.

captures the gist of IBE: enabling the trusted party to extract the secret key of a user. The extraction requires the master secret key, where the public keys are derived from the master public key and the identity of a user. We claim that all IBE schemes can be put in the canonical form.

We then focus on constructing IKD schemes from isogenies. For the underlying PKE scheme, we first investigate the setting where the secret key *sk* is an isogeny between two elliptic curves which form the public key *pk*. The challenge for the IKD scheme is then to extract that secret isogeny from the two elliptic curves that are generated publicly based on the identity *id* and the master public key *mpk*. We cover various variants, depending on how the public key elliptic curves are computed. Looking at `CSIDH` (or also `FESTA`, `M-SIDH`, etc.), for instance, the starting curve would be the same for all users while the end curve would be different for each user. Unfortunately, we show that all these variants suffer from problems. Several constructions—for which the trusted party can extract the secret keys of users—turn out to be insecure: a malicious user Eve can leverage its own secret key sk_E to compute an isogeny equivalent to the secret key sk_A of another user Alice, allowing her to decrypt messages encrypted under Alice's public key. For constructions which do not suffer from the aforementioned insecurities, the problem lies in the construction of the IKD scheme. Extracting a secret key of the user essentially requires the trusted party to solve the underlying hardness assumption. Although this seems attainable with a trapdoor information included in *msk*—which will have the necessary power to invert the public key curve generated with *mpk* to compute the secret isogeny—the current state of isogeny-based trapdoor functions falls behind what is required. In addition to the limitations of isogeny-based trapdoor functions, another potential building block, i.e., random sampling of *Supersingular Elliptic Curves of Unknown Endomorphism Rings* (SECUER), is also missing in the literature. We further discuss the setting where the secret key is the knowledge of the endomorphism ring of the public key curve—which suffers from similar problems, and also covers the problem of the IBE proposal in [32].

Our results hold for all prominent isogeny settings (`CSIDH`, `SQISign`, etc.) since the obstacles and insecurities are indifferent to the setting. We only make the restriction that the secret key is an isogeny or the endomorphism ring of a supersingular elliptic curve which is prevalent in all the settings to the best of our knowledge. In light of these limitations, we conclude with a potential construction that requires a stronger trapdoor function than existing constructions and a SECUER generator.

1.2 Related Work

The concept of identity-based encryption was introduced by Shamir [55]. The first efficient constructions were given in [10,18]. Further constructions of IBE are given, e.g., in [1,46].

The first lattice-based instantiation is due to Gentry et al. [37], followed by more lattice-based constructions [2,14,31,41,58,59]. Ji et al. [39] give constructions based on NTRU lattices, as do Lu et al. [43] in concurrent work to ours.

The first code-based IBE scheme was given in [33], which was based on the code-based signature scheme RankSign [34], but broken in [24]. Tree-based approaches for IBE schemes were given in [13,26,27].

Quantum-resistant identity-based signatures are given in [40,53,56].

2 Preliminaries

We now recall the necessary background for this work. We start with the preliminaries on isogenies, and then continue with the definition of IBE schemes.

Throughout this work, we will be denoting random sampling with $\leftarrow_\$$, e.g., $x \leftarrow_\$ X$ will be interpreted as sampling an element x from a set X. A negligible function will be denoted as negl(λ), and an algorithm $\mathcal{A}$, with access to an oracle O, as $\mathcal{A}^{\mathsf{O}}$. Unless stated otherwise, all the algorithms take the security parameter λ as an implicit input. With double square brackets we will denote the boolean value of the statement, e.g., $[\![b = b']\!]$ is `true` (or 1) if and only if $b = b'$.

2.1 Isogeny-Based Cryptography

An elliptic curve E is an algebraic smooth curve defined by the equation $y^2 = x^3 + ax + b$ over a field $\mathbb{K}$. We denote the points defined on an elliptic curve E as a set $E(\mathbb{K})$, which contains all the (x, y) pairs over $\mathbb{K}$ that satisfy the equation, along with a special point $\mathcal{O}_E$, called point at infinity. This point set forms a group where the point at infinity is the identity of the group operation. This operation is called *point addition* denoted with $+$, and induces *scalar multiplication*, i.e., repetitive additions of points, e.g., $[k]P$ means P added to itself k times.

We denote the m-torsion subgroup with $E[m]$, which is the set of points over $\bar{\mathbb{K}}$ that give $\mathcal{O}_E$ when multiplied by m. If this subgroup is generated by two points P and Q, we denote it as $E_m = \langle P, Q \rangle$. For a field $\mathbb{K}$ with characteristic p, and a positive integer r, if $E[p^r](\bar{\mathbb{K}})$ is isomorphic to $\{0\}$, then we call E *supersingular*; if it is isomorphic to $\mathbb{Z}/p^r\mathbb{Z}$, then we call it *ordinary*. In the remainder of this work, we will always refer to supersingular elliptic curves, even if we omit the word *supersingular*.

An *isogeny* φ is a non-constant rational map between two elliptic curves, i.e., $\varphi\colon E \to E'$, with the condition that $\varphi(\mathcal{O}_E) = \mathcal{O}_{E'}$. The *degree* of an isogeny φ is denoted with $\mathtt{deg}(\varphi)$, and a degree l isogeny is often referred as an l-isogeny. For an isogeny $\varphi\colon E \to E'$, we call the set of points $P \in E$ such that $\varphi(P) = \mathcal{O}_{E'}$, the *kernel* of φ, i.e., $\mathtt{ker}(\varphi)$. An isogeny is *separable* if and only if the cardinality of its kernel is equal to its degree. We are only interested in separable isogenies, as they are determined by their kernels up to isomorphism.

The fundamental hardness assumption in isogeny-based cryptography is the isogeny path problem defined below.

Problem 1 (l-Isogeny Path Problem). *Given a prime p, and two supersingular elliptic curves E and E' defined over $\mathbb{F}_{p^2}$, compute an l-isogeny path for a prime $l \neq p$, i.e., a sequence of degree l isogenies, from E to E'.*

This problem is assumed to be hard, and has different variations [8,36] which are in use of well-known isogeny-based schemes.

An isogeny $\varphi : E \to E$ is called an *endomorphism* of E. All endomorphisms defined on E constitute a ring called *endomorphism ring*, denoted $\texttt{End}(E)$, with the operations being pointwise addition and composition. Computing the endomorphism ring of a supersingular elliptic curve is a hard problem that underlies a few isogeny-based cryptographic protocols, for instance [23,35]. Below we recall the definition of the problem.

Problem 2 (Endomorphism Ring Problem.) *Given a prime p, and a supersingular elliptic curve E defined over $\mathbb{F}_{p^2}$, compute four endomorphisms that generate the endomorphism ring $\texttt{End}(E)$ of E as a $\mathbb{Z}$-module.*

The endomorphism ring problem was thoroughly investigated in [45,51]—where Page and Wesolowski [51] showed that the problem is easy given access to a special oracle that reponds with independent non-scalar endomorphisms. Moreover, the endomorphism ring problem is also shown to be equivalent to the isogeny path problem [30,57].

We call the endomorphism ring of an elliptic curve *known* if it is efficiently computable, and *unknown* otherwise. Extending the nomenclature in [4], we will refer to *Supersingular Elliptic Curves of Unknown Endomorphism Ring* as SECUERs, and *Supersingular Elliptic Curves of Known Endomorphism Ring* as SECKERs.

It is often required in cryptographic protocols to generate supersingular elliptic curves, or hash into the supersingular isogeny graph on input a bit string. We now continue investigating such generators in the form of hash functions.

Random Supersingular Elliptic Curve Generation. We define supersingular elliptic curve generators in regard to the output being a SECUER, a SECKER, and a codomain of a random isogeny walk.

There is no efficient algorithm proposed in the literature that can efficiently generate SECUERs in the absence of a trusted party or a distributed protocol, as investigated in [4,12,42,47]. Nevertheless, we give a definition to use in our constructions for a comprehensive analysis.

Definition 3. *Let $\mathcal{E}ll$ be the set of supersingular elliptic curves defined over a field $\mathbb{K}$. A SECUER generator is a function $\texttt{H}^{\texttt{UE}}_{\mathcal{E}ll}\colon \{0,1\}^n \to \mathcal{E}ll$ such that, there exists no polynomial-time algorithm which, given $E \leftarrow \texttt{H}^{\texttt{UE}}_{\mathcal{E}ll}(x)$ for uniformly chosen $x \in \{0,1\}^n$, computes $\texttt{End}(E)$ with probability more than negligible.*

There are efficient SECKER generator constructions as mentioned in [12,47]. On the other hand, they have a vulnerability, namely the isogeny problem becomes easy when the domain and codomain curves are SECKERs. Nevertheless, we describe them as follows.

Definition 4. *Let $\mathcal{E}ll$ be the set of supersingular elliptic curves defined over a field $\mathbb{K}$, and $\mathcal{E}nd = \{\texttt{End}(E)\colon E \in \mathcal{E}ll\}$. A SECKER generator is a function $\texttt{H}^{\texttt{KE}}_{\mathcal{E}ll}\colon \{0,1\}^n \to \mathcal{E}ll \times \mathcal{E}nd$ such that the output is a pair in the form $(E, \texttt{End}(E))$ for an $E \in \mathcal{E}ll$.*

We often do not need the endomorphism ring explicitly, in which case we drop the second output, i.e., instead of $(E, \mathtt{End}(E)) \leftarrow \mathtt{H}^{\mathtt{KE}}_{\mathcal{E}ll}(x)$ we simply write $E \leftarrow \mathtt{H}^{\mathtt{KE}}_{\mathcal{E}ll}(x)$

One other way to generate random supersingular elliptic curves is to take a random walk on the isogeny graph, which was first observed by Pizer [54], and then found a use in cryptographic applications [17], i.e., CGL hash function. It can be formally described as follows.

Definition 5. *Let $\mathcal{E}ll$ be the set of supersingular elliptic curves defined over a field $\mathbb{K}$, and $\Phi_{E,D}$ be the set of all isogenies of degree*[4] *D starting from $E \in \mathcal{E}ll$. An* isogeny walk *(CGL) generator is an injective function $\mathtt{H}^{CGL}_{\mathcal{E}ll} : (E, x) \mapsto \varphi$ that on input a starting curve $E \in \mathcal{E}ll$, and a bit string $x \in \{0,1\}^n$, generates an isogeny walk $\varphi \in \Phi_{E,D}$ such that $\varphi : E \to E'$.*

The CGL generator can behave like a SECKER/SECUER generator depending on the domain curve E. If E has unknown endomorphism ring, then the codomain E' is conjecturally a SECUER. Similarly, if $\mathtt{End}(E)$ is known, then the codomain E' is again a SECKER, as $\mathtt{End}(E')$ is efficiently computable through the isogeny φ. However, this is not the case if the party that calls the CGL generator keeps the random walk secret, or if the walk is computed via a distributed protocol as described in [4]. Although we can treat the CGL generator as a SECUER in this case, there is a nuance here: the random walk can be a valuable information to the party that keeps it secret. This is especially relevant in an IBE construction since there exists a trusted party which can use the CGL as a SECUER and keep the random walk as a trapdoor. We will indeed investigate this approach in the following sections.

2.2 Identity-Based Encryption

Below we define identity-based encryption (IBE) schemes and its security.

Definition 6. *An identity-based encryption scheme consists of four efficient algorithms:*

- $\mathtt{KGen}(1^\lambda)$*: The key generation takes as input a security parameter 1^λ and outputs a master key-pair consisting of a master secret key msk and a master public key mpk,*
- $\mathtt{Enc}(mpk, id, m)$*: The encryption algorithm takes as input a master public key mpk, an identity id, and a message m, and it outputs a ciphertext c,*
- $\mathtt{Ext}(msk, id)$*: The extract algorithm takes as input a master secret key msk and an identity id, and outputs a secret key sk_{id},*
- $\mathtt{Dec}(sk, c)$*: The decryption algorithm takes as input a secret key sk and a ciphertext c, and it outputs a message m,*

[4] The degree is usually a power of a small prime.

where, by the correctness *of the scheme, the following holds*

$$\texttt{Dec}(sk_{id}, \texttt{Enc}(mpk, id, m)) = m\,,$$

such that $(msk, mpk) \leftarrow_{\$} \texttt{KGen}(1^\lambda)$*, and* $sk_{id} \leftarrow \texttt{Ext}(msk, id)$*.*

Similarly to PKE schemes, IND-CPA security is a standard security notion for IBE schemes, which ensures that an adversary learns nothing from the ciphertext, about the plaintext. The difference is that the adversary can choose the target identity under which one of the two messages is encrypted and can further obtain the secret keys from any identity *different* from the target identity. The IND-CPA security can be defined as follows.

Definition 7. *An IBE scheme* $\texttt{IBE} = (\texttt{KGen}, \texttt{Enc}, \texttt{Ext}, \texttt{Dec})$ *is* IND-CPA*-secure, if for any efficient adversary* $\mathcal{A} = (\mathcal{A}_0, \mathcal{A}_1)$ *(where* $\mathcal{A}_0$ *and* $\mathcal{A}_1$ *are assumed to share state),*

$$\left|\Pr\left[\text{IND-CPA}_{\texttt{IBE}}^{\mathcal{A},\mathsf{O}}(1^\lambda) = 1\right] - \frac{1}{2}\right| \le \text{negl}(\lambda),$$

where $\text{IND-CPA}_{\texttt{IBE}}^{\mathcal{A},\mathsf{O}}(\lambda)$ *is the game defined in Fig. 1.*

$\text{IND-CPA}_{\texttt{IBE}}^{\mathcal{A},\mathsf{O}}(1^\lambda)$	$\mathsf{O}(id_i)$
$\mathcal{C} \leftarrow \emptyset$	$\mathcal{C} \leftarrow \mathcal{C} \cup \{id_i\}$
$(msk, mpk) \leftarrow_{\$} \texttt{IBE.KGen}(1^\lambda)$	$sk_{id_i} \leftarrow \texttt{IBE.Ext}(msk, id_i)$
$(id, m_0, m_1) \leftarrow \mathcal{A}_0^{\mathsf{O}(\cdot)}(mpk)$	**return** sk_{id_i}
$b \leftarrow_{\$} \{0,1\}$	
$c \leftarrow \texttt{IBE.Enc}(mpk, id, m_b)$	
$b' \leftarrow \mathcal{A}_1^{\mathsf{O}(\cdot)}(c)$	
if $id \in \mathcal{C}$ **then return** $\perp$	
return $[\![b = b']\!]$	

Fig. 1. Definition of IND-CPA security for IBE schemes.

We note that, in the remainder of this work, we will be only focusing on key recovery attacks against IBE schemes, which trivially breaks IND-CPA security.

3 Isogeny-Based IBE: Pitfalls of a Seemingly Straightforward Approach

In this section, we present the potential ways of an isogeny-based IBE construction, along with the problems of each approach. First, in Sect. 3.1, we introduce the concept of *canonical IBE*—which relies on a PKE scheme as one of its underlying components, and additionally an *identity key derivation* (IKD), a primitive which we introduce. Section 3.2 and 3.3 discuss the problems of isogeny-based IKD constructions in two different settings; the former relies on Problem 1 where the secret key is an isogeny, and the latter relies on Problem 2 where the secret key is the knowledge of an endomorphism ring. Finally, Sect. 3.4 investigates the usage of trapdoor functions in IKD constructions. We defer the discussion on how to construct an IBE from isogenies—in light of our negative results in this section—to Appendix A.

3.1 Canonical Identity-Based Encryption

We now introduce a modular IBE definition, what we call a *canonical* IBE. What makes a difference here is that we isolate the key derivation operations—both for the keys of the trusted party, and the users—in a separate scheme, namely an IKD scheme. Below we first recall the definition of PKE schemes, followed by the definition of IKD schemes.

Definition 8. *A public-key encryption scheme (PKE) consists of three efficient algorithms:*

- $\texttt{KGen}(1^\lambda)$ *The probabilistic key generation algorithm takes as input a security parameter* λ *and outputs a key-pair consisting of a secret key* sk *and a public key* pk.
- $\texttt{Enc}(pk, m)$ *The probabilistic encryption algorithm takes as input a public key* pk *and a message* m, *and it outputs a ciphertext* c.
- $\texttt{Dec}(sk, c)$ *The deterministic decryption algorithm takes as input a secret key* sk *and a ciphertext* c, *and it outputs a message* m.

Definition 9. *An identity key derivation (IKD) scheme consists of three efficient algorithms:*

- $\texttt{KGen}(1^\lambda)$ *The probabilistic key generation algorithm takes as input a security parameter* 1^λ *and outputs a master key-pair consisting of a master secret key* msk *and a master public key* mpk.
- $\texttt{Ext-pk}(mpk, id)$ *The deterministic public key extraction algorithm takes as input a master public key* mpk *and an identity* id, *and outputs a public key* pk_{id}.
- $\texttt{Ext-sk}(msk, id)$ *The deterministic secret key extraction algorithm takes as input a master secret key* msk *and an identity* id, *and outputs a secret key* sk_{id}.

We introduce the IKD as a component of canonical IBEs for the sake of modularity, and easier analysis of the isogeny-based constructions. In particular, the security notions an IKD should satisfy—so that the canonical IBE is secure—is indeed an interesting question. However, it falls out of the scope of this work. Therefore, we will only mention its one-wayness, and compatibility with the PKE. The one-wayness is strictly necessary for the security against key-recovery attacks.

Definition 10. *Let* $\texttt{IKD} = (\texttt{KGen}, \texttt{Ext-pk}, \texttt{Ext-sk})$ *be an IKD scheme We call the* IKD one-way *if, for a master key-pair* $(msk, mpk) \leftarrow_\$ \texttt{IKD.KGen}(1^\lambda)$*, given* mpk*,* id*, and* $pk \leftarrow_\$ \texttt{IKD.Ext-pk}(mpk, id)$*, no polynomial-time adversary can find a* sk'*, such that* $sk' = sk \leftarrow_\$ \texttt{IKD.Ext-sk}(msk, id)$*, with probability more than negligible.*

Our definition of an IKD scheme captures the concept of preimage sampleable function (PSF) defined by Gentry *et al.* [37]—a PSF can be used to instantiate the trapdoor mechanism of our IKD definition.[5]

Furthermore, we need *compatibility* of the IKD and PKE as defined below. This property ensures that key pairs generated by the IKD are distributed like key pairs from the PKE scheme and is necessary to ensure the functionality of the (canonical) IBE scheme.

Definition 11. *Let* $\texttt{IKD} = (\texttt{KGen}, \texttt{Ext-pk}, \texttt{Ext-sk})$ *be an IKD scheme, and* $\texttt{PKE} = (\texttt{KGen}, \texttt{Enc}, \texttt{Dec})$ *be a PKE scheme. We call* IKD *and* PKE compatible*, if for all* id*, the key pairs* $(sk, pk) \leftarrow_\$ (\texttt{IKD.Ext-sk}(msk, id), \texttt{IKD.Ext-pk}(mpk, id))$ *are distributed identically to key pairs* $\texttt{PKE.KGen}(1^\lambda)$*, where* $(msk, mpk) \leftarrow_\$ \texttt{IKD.KGen}(1^\lambda)$*. The first distribution is taken over the random coins used to generate the master key-pair.*

Now, incorporating the components, i.e., PKE and IKD, the definition of a canonical IBE scheme can be given as follows.

Definition 12. *Let* $\texttt{IKD} = (\texttt{KGen}, \texttt{Ext-pk}, \texttt{Ext-sk})$ *be an IKD scheme and* $\texttt{PKE} = (\texttt{KGen}, \texttt{Enc}, \texttt{Dec})$ *be a PKE scheme, such that* IKD *and* PKE *are compatible. If* IKD *has a superpolynomial set of public keys, then we call* $\texttt{IBE} = (\texttt{KGen}, \texttt{Enc}, \texttt{Ext}, \texttt{Dec})$ *a* canonical IBE *scheme, where*

$$\begin{aligned}
\texttt{IBE.KGen}(1^\lambda) &:= \texttt{IKD.KGen}(1^\lambda)\\
\texttt{IBE.Enc}(mpk, id, m) &:= \texttt{PKE.Enc}(\texttt{IKD.Ext-pk}(mpk, id), m)\\
\texttt{IBE.Ext}(msk, id) &:= \texttt{IKD.Ext-sk}(msk, id)\\
\texttt{IBE.Dec}(sk, c) &:= \texttt{PKE.Dec}(sk, c).
\end{aligned}$$

We notice that the canonical IBE definition obviously matches with most of the constructions in the literature: in particular, the pairing-based scheme by Boneh and Franklin [10]; the lattice-based scheme by Gentry, Peikert, and Vaikuntanathan [37]; the code-based scheme by Gaborit *et al.* [33]; and the isogeny-based scheme by Fouotsa and Marco [32]. At first glance, the tree-based constructions by Döttling and Garg [27], and by Brakerski *et al.* [13] appear to be non-canonical because they are not constructed from a PKE scheme—like the aforementioned IBE schemes—but rely on more advanced primitives. It turns out, however, that every IBE scheme can generically be transformed into a canonical one by properly constructing a PKE along with a compatible IKD scheme out of it. With this observation, the focus on canonical IBE schemes is not a restriction but simplifies the exposition as we can focus on the IKD scheme

[5] Looking ahead, we discuss this at the end of the paper in Isogeny Construction 5.

in the following. This definition is useful in several ways; it provides an abstraction, it is modular, and it helps us reflect the obstacles of isogeny-based IBE construction through only one component in isolation—as the inherent problem reveals itself in the construction of the IKD scheme.

In the next three sections, we present the potential ways of a canonical isogeny-based IBE construction, along with the challenges of each approach. The challenges will appear in two ways:

1. there will be an efficient key-recovery attack,
2. the construction will require the trusted party to solve the underlying hardness assumption, i.e., Problem 1 (Isogeny Problem) and Problem 2 (Endomorphism Ring Problem).

We note that, the challenges occur regardless of the isogeny setting (`SIDH`, `CSIDH`, `SQISign`, etc.). The key-recovery attacks will make use of general techniques, and in all the settings, Problem 1 and Problem 2 are assumed to be hard.

To still be able to refer to the parameters of the PKE scheme, regardless of the setting, here we will define generic notations that will be used throughout this section. Assuming they align with the PKE scheme, we will denote the set of all supersingular elliptic curves as $\mathcal{E}ll$, the underlying prime as p, field as $\mathbb{K} = \mathbb{F}_{p^k}$ (for an unspecified degree k), the degree of the secret isogeny as D_{sk}, the set of all isogenies of degree D with domain E as $\Phi_{E,D}$.

3.2 Using Isogenies as Secret Keys

We now restrict ourselves to the prevalent structure where all elliptic curves are supersingular, the secret key is an isogeny, where the domain and codomain curves are included in the public key. This is the typical setup for isogeny-based key-exchange/encryption schemes, and we will not make any further restrictions regarding the PKE scheme to be used.

An isogeny-based IKD scheme involves two elliptic curves that are connected by a secret isogeny. Although the domain curve is usually fixed in the public parameter in most schemes, e.g., `SIDH` [38], `CSIDH` [15], and `SQISign` [23], we will not restrict ourselves in this sense, and put both curves in the public key. For the same reason, we will diverge from the common notation used in the literature where the domain and codomain curves are denoted E_0 and E_{pk} respectively. Throughout the text, the public domain and codomain curves of the user with identity id will be denoted as $E_{0,id}$, $E_{1,id}$, respectively. In some cases, the public key curves will happen to be fixed for all users, and we will denote this with id^*, e.g., E_{0,id^*}, and E_{1,id^*}. We will abuse notation by writing $E \in mpk$ to denote that elliptic curve E is part of the master public key mpk.

To cover all possible isogeny-based IKD constructions in a structured order, we will categorize the approaches with respect to the public curves being fixed or variable with respect to the identity. As subconstructions of these approaches, we will be investigating the ways the public curves can be generated. This can happen in 3 ways; via SECUER[6], SECKER, and CGL generators. A CGL generator can produce either a SECUER or a SECKER depending on the setting, but we opt to investigate it separately as it is the usual way of generating random curves.

Whether the endomorphism rings of the curves are known or not is crucial to be able to discuss the achievability of the constructions. Thus, we specify this information by using the superscripts; $\circ$, $\LEFTcircle$, $\bullet$, when denoting the curves, for unknown, unspecified, and known endomorphism rings, respectively. By unspecified we mean, the endomorphism ring can be known or unknown, and we consider both cases at once.

The constructions will be illustrated with isogeny diagrams in the remainder of this work. There, public isogenies that are known to all users will be shown with a black, solid arrow. A secret isogeny will be represented with red, and densely dashed arrows. In some cases, we will also illustrate the attacks against the constructions. Some attacks will involve isogenies which are not public by default, but computable by the attacker. These computable isogenies will be shown with blue and loosely dashed arrows.

Approach 0: Fixed Domain and Codomain Curves. We start with a naive IKD construction to illustrate the pattern one can follow comprehensively. We fix the public key curves and obtain a clearly insecure setting; however, it emphasizes the inherent problem of fixed curves that will be clearer as we progress.

Isogeny Construction 0 ($\texttt{IKD}_0$) *The* `IKD` *can be described with the following algorithms:*

- $\texttt{KGen}(1^\lambda)$ *On input a security parameter, choose two curves* $E^{\LEFTcircle}_{0,id^*}, E^{\LEFTcircle}_{1,id^*} \in \mathcal{E}ll$, *and output the key-pair* (msk, mpk), *such that* $E^{\LEFTcircle}_{0,id^*}, E^{\LEFTcircle}_{1,id^*} \in mpk$.
- $\texttt{Ext-pk}(mpk, id)$ *On input a master public key and an identity, output* $E^{\LEFTcircle}_{0,id^*}$ *and* $E^{\LEFTcircle}_{1,id^*}$.
- $\texttt{Ext-sk}(msk, id)$ *On input a master secret key and an identity, compute and output an isogeny* $\varphi_{sk} \colon E^{\LEFTcircle}_{0,id^*} \to E^{\LEFTcircle}_{0,id^*}$.

The construction is simply achievable, if `KGen` picks $E^{\LEFTcircle}_{0,id^*}$ and φ_{sk} first to compute $E^{\LEFTcircle}_{1,id^*}$, and puts φ_{sk} in msk. Therefore, `Ext-pk` simply outputs mpk, and the trusted party can extract the secret key which is already included in msk.

$$E^{\LEFTcircle}_{0,id^*} \xrightarrow{\varphi_{sk}} E^{\LEFTcircle}_{1,id^*}$$

Fig. 2. Illustration of the `Ext-pk` algorithm for $\texttt{IKD}_0$. Both curves are fixed by `Ext-pk`, so is the secret key isogeny.

[6] There is no efficient SECUER generator construction in the literature. Nonetheless, we take them into account for the sake of future advancements.

Problem of Isogeny Construction 0. Trivially, the secret and public keys are the same for every user, i.e., every user can use its own secret key to decrypt messages sent to other users. We will call this type of attack an *insider attack* from now on. It is important to note that if the endomorphism rings are known, i.e., $E^{\bullet}_{0,id^*}$ and $E^{\bullet}_{1,id}$, then even a party who is not involved in the system can compute the secret keys of the users and decrypt messages sent to the users in the system. This is possible due to the Deuring correspondence, which provides an efficient method to compute the isogeny connecting two curves with known endomorphism rings. However, in any variation where at least one of the curves has an unknown endomorphism ring, an outsider, i.e., an adversary that is not part of the system and therefore does not get a secret key from the trusted party, cannot attack the scheme as it needs to solve Problem 1 to compute the secret key.

Approach 1: Fixed Domain Curve, Variable Codomain Curve. The next approach keeps only the domain of the secret key isogeny fixed and allows the codomain to change regarding the identity. This is the general setting for isogeny-based schemes, e.g., `SIDH`, `CSIDH`, and `SQISign`.

Isogeny Construction 1 ($\mathtt{IKD}_1$**).** *The* `IKD` *can be described with the following algorithms:*

- `KGen`(1^λ) *On input a security parameter, choose a curve* $E^{\bullet}_{0,id^*} \in \mathcal{E}ll$, *and output the key-pair* (msk, mpk), *such that* $E^{\bullet}_{0,id^*} \in mpk$.
- `Ext-pk`(mpk, id) *On input a master public key and an identity, output* $E^{\bullet}_{0,id^*}$ *and a random*[7] $E^{\bullet}_{1,id}$ *depending on id and mpk.*
- `Ext-sk`(msk, id) *On input a master secret key and an identity, compute and output an isogeny* $\varphi_{sk}\colon E^{\bullet}_{0,id^*} \to E^{\bullet}_{1,id^*}$.

There are 3 variations[8] of this construction depending on how `Ext-pk` generates the public key curve, i.e. with a SECUER, SECKER, or CGL generator. Efficient SECUER generator constructions in the literature require either a trusted party setup, or a distributed protocol. Although, IBE schemes involve a trusted party, the `Ext-pk` algorithm is a publicly available algorithm by definition, and should not require an interaction with the trusted party. For the same reason, `Ext-pk` cannot be a distributed protocol either. However, taking into account possible future advancements on this problem, we will assume the existence of efficient SECUER generators, without trusted party interactions or distributed protocols.

Now, we describe the construction with a SECUER generator.

[7] Here and in the rest of the text, by "random", we mean deterministically computed by a random oracle. In particular, `Ext-pk` is deterministic in the sense that, for fixed *mpk* and *id*, it will produce the same output.

[8] The case of variable domain curve and fixed codomain curve is entirely symmetrical, which is why we do not consider it explicitly here.

Isogeny Construction 1.1 **($\mathtt{IKD}_{1.1}$).** *Let $\mathtt{H}^{\mathit{UE}}_{\mathcal{E}ll}$ be a SECUER generator. The* $\mathtt{IKD}$ *can be described with the following algorithms:*

- $\mathtt{KGen}(1^\lambda)$ *On input a security parameter, choose a curve $E^{\LEFTcircle}_{0,id^*} \in \mathcal{E}ll$, and output the key-pair (msk, mpk), such that $E^{\LEFTcircle}_{0,id^*} \in mpk$.*
- $\mathtt{Ext\text{-}pk}(mpk, id)$ *On input a master public key and an identity, output $E^{\LEFTcircle}_{0,id^*}$ and $E^{\circ}_{1,id} \leftarrow \mathtt{H}^{\mathit{UE}}_{\mathcal{E}ll}(mpk, id)$.*
- $\mathtt{Ext\text{-}sk}(msk, id)$ *On input a master secret key and an identity, compute and output an isogeny $\varphi_{sk} \colon E^{\LEFTcircle}_{0,id^*} \to E^{\circ}_{1,id}$.*

$$E^{\LEFTcircle}_{0,id^*} \overset{\varphi_{sk}}{\dashrightarrow} E^{\circ}_{1,id}$$

Fig. 3. Illustration of the $\mathtt{Ext\text{-}pk}$ algorithm of $\mathtt{IKD}_{1.1}$. The domain curve is fixed by the $\mathtt{KGen}$ algorithm. The codomain curve has unknown endomorphism ring, and is random with respect to the identity *id*.

Problem of Isogeny Construction 1.1. Here, assuming $E^{\circ}_{1,id}$ is random, the task of $\mathtt{Ext\text{-}sk}$ algorithm is to find an isogeny between two given curves, where one has unknown endomorphism ring. This requires solving Problem 1, which is assumed to be hard. However, the information included in msk cannot be overlooked. Assume msk includes a trapdoor information that recovers φ_{sk}. If $\mathtt{End}(E_{0,id^*})$ is known to the trusted party, then $\mathtt{End}(E_{1,id})$ is also known via φ_{sk}, which contradicts with $E_{1,id}$ being a SECUER. Conversely, if $\mathtt{End}(E_{0,id^*})$ is unknown to the trusted party, then the trapdoor information breaks Problem 1. There exists isogeny-based trapdoor functions that offer a similar functionality in a more restricted setting where the codomain curve does not fit in our SECUER definition but still provides security guarantees. We will investigate them in detail in Sect. 3.4, and explain why current isogeny trapdoors are not suitable for this task, and what can be done to overcome the difficulties. Delaying the discussion on trapdoors, we conclude that this construction is not possible to achieve.

The second approach is using a SECKER generator in the construction of $\mathtt{Ext\text{-}pk}$. This approach is insecure for trivial reasons, yet worth mentioning to better illustrate the pattern.

Isogeny Construction 1.2 **($\mathtt{IKD}_{1.2}$).** *Let $\mathtt{H}^{\mathit{KE}}_{\mathcal{E}ll}$ be a SECKER generator. The* $\mathtt{IKD}$ *can be described with the following algorithms:*

- $\mathtt{KGen}(1^\lambda)$ *On input a security parameter, choose a curve $E^{\LEFTcircle}_{0,id^*} \in \mathcal{E}ll$, and output the key-pair (msk, mpk), such that $E^{\LEFTcircle}_{0,id^*} \in mpk$.*
- $\mathtt{Ext\text{-}pk}(mpk, id)$ *On input a master public key and an identity, output $E^{\LEFTcircle}_{0,id^*}$ and $E^{\bullet} \leftarrow \mathtt{H}^{\mathit{KE}}_{\mathcal{E}ll}(mpk, id)$.*
- $\mathtt{Ext\text{-}sk}(msk, id)$ *On input a master secret key and an identity, compute and output an isogeny $\varphi_{sk} \colon E^{\LEFTcircle}_{0,id^*} \to E^{\bullet}$.*

As the public key curve $E^{\bullet}$ has known endomorphism ring, the `Ext-sk` algorithm is achievable if $\mathrm{End}(E^{\LEFTcircle}_{0,id^*}) \in msk$.

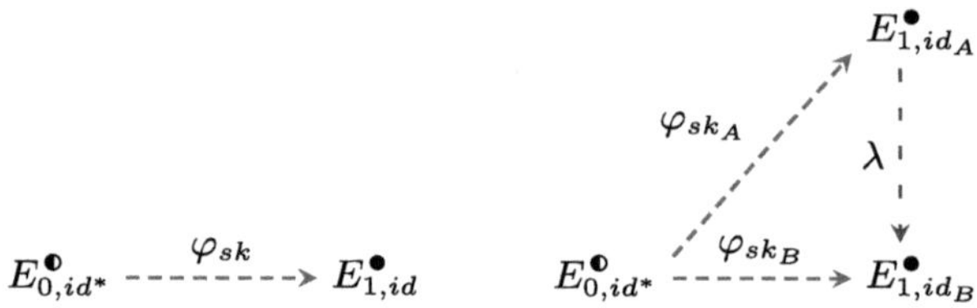

(a) The `Ext-pk` algorithm of $\texttt{IKD}_{1.2}$.

(b) The attack that reveals msk and/or the secret key of other parties via the computation of isogeny λ.

Fig. 4. Illustration of $\texttt{IKD}_{1.2}$ and the attack.

Problem of Isogeny Construction 1.2. The Deuring correspondence allowing the realization of `Ext-sk` also enables a trivial attack to the construction. Since all public key curves have known endomorphism rings, Bob can compute the isogeny λ connecting Alice's public key curve $E^{\bullet}$ to his public key curve $E^{\bullet}$. Then, once Bob learns his secret key isogeny φ_{pk_B}, the composition $\hat{\lambda} \circ \varphi_{sk_B}$ gives the secret key of Alice, as described in Fig. 4b. There is an even stronger attack leaking the msk. Bob can compute $\mathtt{End}(E^{\LEFTcircle}_{0,id^*})$ via Deuring correspondence with the knowledge of $\mathtt{End}(E^{\bullet})$ and φ_{sk_B}.

Last but not least, $E^{\LEFTcircle}_{1,id}$ can be generated via a CGL generator, i.e., $E^{\LEFTcircle}_{1,id}$ would be the codomain of a random walk on the isogeny graph. This approach is achievable and being used in isogeny-based schemes, but the IKD construction, described below, suffers from an insider attack.

Isogeny Construction 1.3 ($\texttt{IKD}_{1.3}$). *Let $\mathtt{H}^{CGL}_{\mathcal{E}ll}$ be a CGL generator. The* `IKD` *can be described with the following algorithms:*

- $\mathtt{KGen}(1^{\lambda})$ *On input a security parameter, choose two curves $E^{\LEFTcircle}_{0,id^*}, E^{\LEFTcircle}_{1} \in \mathcal{E}ll$, and output the key-pair (msk, mpk), such that $E^{\LEFTcircle}_{0,id^*}, E^{\LEFTcircle}_{1} \in mpk$*
- $\mathtt{Ext\text{-}pk}(mpk, id)$ *On input a master public key and an identity, compute an isogeny $\varphi_{id} \leftarrow \mathtt{H}^{CGL}_{\mathcal{E}ll}(E^{\LEFTcircle}_{1}, mpk, id)$, such that $\varphi_{id}\colon E^{\LEFTcircle}_{1} \to E^{\LEFTcircle}_{1,id}$. Output $E^{\LEFTcircle}_{0,id^*}$ and $E^{\LEFTcircle}_{1,id}$.*
- $\mathtt{Ext\text{-}sk}(msk, id)$ *On input a master secret key and an identity, compute and output an isogeny $\varphi_{sk}\colon E^{\LEFTcircle}_{0,id^*} \to E^{\LEFTcircle}_{1,id}$.*

To include the information of an isogeny $\lambda\colon E^{\LEFTcircle}_{0,id^*} \to E^{\LEFTcircle}_{1}$ in msk would easily allow trusted party to extract the secret keys. But as before, the problem appears as an insider attack.

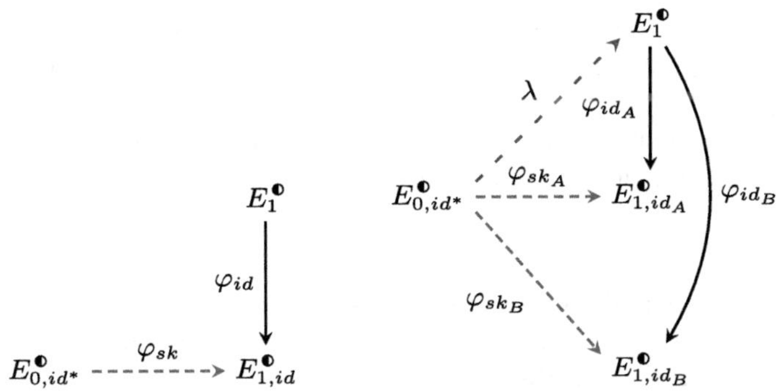

(a) The Ext-pk algorithm of $\mathtt{IKD}_{1.3}$.

(b) The attack that reveals the secret key of other parties via the computation of isogeny λ.

Fig. 5. Illustration of $\mathtt{IKD}_{1.3}$ and the attack.

Problem of the Isogeny Construction 1.3. In this construction, Bob, who enrolls with the system and learns his secret key φ_{sk_B} is able to find the isogeny $\lambda\colon E_{0,id^*}^{\bullet} \to E_1^{\bullet}$ through the composition $\hat{\varphi}_{id_B} \circ \varphi_{sk_B}$. With the knowledge of λ and publicly computable φ_{id_A}, he can compute the isogeny $\varphi'_{sk_A} = \varphi_{id_A} \circ \lambda$, as described in Fig. 5. This isogeny is not necessarily the secret key φ_{sk_A} of Alice, as we do not specify how the trusted party computes the secret key of Alice. Therefore, we need to make a case distinction to further analyze.

Now, consider two cases: (1) at least one of the endomorphism rings is known (2) none of the endomorphism rings are known. In the first case, any user can compute all the other endomorphism rings due to the known connections, which falls into the previous case in Construction 1.2. In the second case, the only way the trusted party can extract secret keys is via the knowledge of λ. Otherwise, i.e., $\varphi_{sk_A} \neq \varphi'_{sk_A}$, the trusted party could compute non-trivial[9] endomorphisms in the form $\hat{\varphi}_{sk_A} \circ \varphi'_{sk_A}$. Polynomially-many independent endomorphisms suffice to compute the whole endomorphism ring, which contradicts with the assumption that the trusted party does not know any endomorphim rings. Thus, either $\varphi_{sk_A} = \varphi_{id_A} \circ \lambda$, such that any party can compute $\lambda \in msk$, or the construction is insecure for the same reasoning as in Construction 1.2.

It is important to note that the random walks in CGL generators cannot be hidden to the one who generates, i.e., the users in the system. This would be possible in a setting where the Ext-pk algorithm involves an interaction with the trusted party. However, this is not the case in the definition of IBEs.

Therefore, Isogeny Construction 1, is either not possible to achieve or insecure. The construction appears to be impossible when the variable curve $E_{1,id}^{\bullet}$ that changes depending on the identity, is sampled via a SECUER generator.

[9] More specifically, non-scalar endomorphisms. In the CSIDH setting, however, the ones that are in the subring of a quadratic imaginary field $\mathbb{Q}(\sqrt{-D})$ are also considered trivial.

When $E^{\bullet}_{1,id}$ is sampled via a SECKER generator, the dangers of known endomorphism rings emerge inevitably. The plausible and straightforward approach is to sample $E^{\bullet}_{1,id}$ via a CGL generator; however this requires another fixed curve, $E^{\bullet}_1$ in Fig. 5, in the scheme. Similar to the situation in Approach 0, the existence of two fixed curves enables an attack, as the isogeny between them gets revealed unavoidably.

Approach 2: Variable Domain and Codomain Curves. To circumvent the pitfalls of fixed curves, we take the natural next step and make the domain curve of the secret key variable as well.

Isogeny Construction 2 ($\mathtt{IKD}_2$**).** *The* `IKD` *can be described with the following algorithms:*

`KGen`(1^λ) *On input a security parameter, output a key-pair* (msk, mpk)*.*
`Ext-pk`(mpk, id) *On input a master public key and an identity, output a random pair* $(E^{\bullet}_{0,id}, E^{\bullet}_{1,id})$ *depending on id and mpk.*
`Ext-sk`(msk, id) *On input a master secret key and an identity, compute and output an isogeny* $\varphi_{sk}\colon E^{\bullet}_{0,id} \to E^{\bullet}_{1,id}$*.*

Similar to Isogeny Construction 1, the random public key curves can be generated via a SECUER, SECKER, or CGL generator. This propagates to 6 variations[10]. We divide the variations into 2 categories, and investigate the variants within these categories as one, since the complications are either the same or alike.

We start with the first three variations, where at least one of the public key curves has unknown endomorphism ring. This results in the impossibility of achieving `Ext-sk`.

Isogeny Construction 2.1 ($\mathtt{IKD}_{2.1}$**).** *Let* $\mathtt{H}^{UE}_{\mathcal{E}ll}$*,* $\mathtt{H}^{KE}_{\mathcal{E}ll}$*, and* $\mathtt{H}^{CGL}_{\mathcal{E}ll}$ *be a SECUER generator, a SECKER generator, and a CGL generator, respectively. The* `IKD` *can be described with the following algorithms:*

`KGen`(1^λ) *On input a security parameter, output a key-pair* (msk, mpk)*.*
`Ext-pk`(mpk, id) *On input a master public key and an identity, output a random pair* $(E^{\circ}_{0,id}, E^{\bullet}_{1,id})$ *depending on id and mpk, where* $E^{\circ}_{0,id}$ *is generated via* $\mathtt{H}^{UE}_{\mathcal{E}ll}$*, and* $E^{\bullet}_{1,id}$ *is generated via* $\mathtt{H}^{UE}_{\mathcal{E}ll}$*,* $\mathtt{H}^{KE}_{\mathcal{E}ll}$*, or* $\mathtt{H}^{CGL}_{\mathcal{E}ll}$*. If* $E^{\bullet}_{1,id}$ *is generated via* $\mathtt{H}^{CGL}_{\mathcal{E}ll}$*, we assume there exists* $E^{\bullet}_1 \in mpk$ *s.t.* $\varphi_{id} \leftarrow \mathtt{H}^{CGL}_{\mathcal{E}ll}(E^{\bullet}_1)$*.*
`Ext-sk`(msk, id) *On input a master secret key and an identity, compute and output an isogeny* $\varphi_{sk}\colon E^{\circ}_{0,id} \to E^{\bullet}_{1,id}$*.*

Problem of Isogeny Construction 2.1. Similar to Isogeny Construction 1.1, one of the curves, i.e. $E^{\circ}_{0,id}$ have an unknown endomorphism ring, and the `Ext-sk` algorithm needs to find an isogeny between this curve and some other random

[10] As in Approach 1, we ignore the symmetric versions.

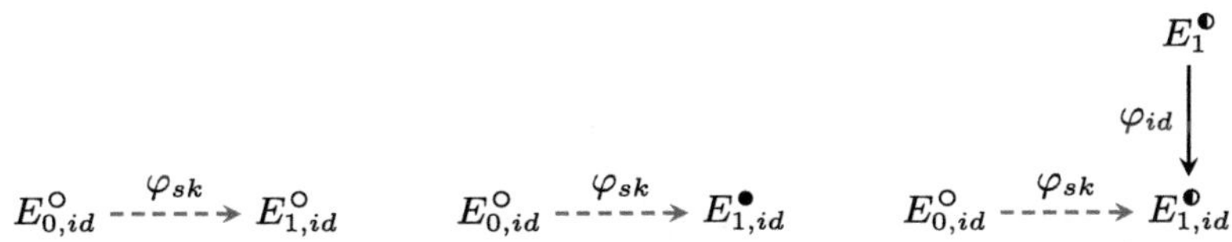

Fig. 6. Illustrations of the variations of $\texttt{IKD}_{2.1}$, which are impossible.

curve. This is again hard, due to Problem 1. Once more we postpone the discussion to Sect. 3.4 on the prospect of *msk* containing a trapdoor information that will ease this task. Besides that, we conclude all 3 variations of Isogeny Construction 2.1, as seen in Fig. 6, are not possible to achieve.

The other 3 variations include only the SECKER and CGL generators. This time, the constructions are all achievable but insecure. We wrap up the remaining in the following description, and continue with the attacks to the constructions.

Isogeny Construction 2.2 **($\texttt{IKD}_{2.2}$).** *Let* $\texttt{H}_{\mathcal{E}ll}^{KE}$ *be a SECKER generator, and* $\texttt{H}_{\mathcal{E}ll}^{CGL}$ *be a CGL generator. The* IKD *can be described with the following algorithms:*

$\texttt{KGen}(1^\lambda)$ *On input a security parameter, output a key-pair* (msk, mpk).
$\texttt{Ext-pk}(mpk, id)$ *On input a master public key and an identity, output a random pair* $(E_{0,id}^{\LEFTcircle}, E_{1,id}^{\LEFTcircle})$ *depending on the id and mpk, where the curves are either generated via* $\texttt{H}_{\mathcal{E}ll}^{KE}$ *or* $\texttt{H}_{\mathcal{E}ll}^{CGL}$.
$\texttt{Ext-sk}(msk, id)$ *On input a master secret key and an identity, compute and output an isogeny* $\varphi_{sk}\colon E_{0,id}^{\LEFTcircle} \to E_{1,id}^{\LEFTcircle}$.

Problem of Isogeny Construction 2.2. The complications of using SECKER and CGL generators appear once again in the remaining variations of the construction. When both domain and codomain have known endomorphism rings, as can be seen in Fig. 7a, an outsider attack exists which reveals φ_{sk} via the known endomorphism rings. In the variation shown in Fig. 7b, only the domain curves have known endomorphism rings, and codomain curves are generated via random walks from $E_1^{\LEFTcircle}$. The isogeny λ_0 can be computed with the information of known endomorphism rings of the domain curves. Moreover, the isogeny λ_1 is also computable as a composition of the random walks shown with black arrows. Therefore, Bob as a party in the system, can compute ${\varphi_{sk}}'_A = \hat{\lambda}_1 \circ \varphi_{sk\,B} \circ \lambda_0$. As in Construction 1.3, this isogeny is not necessarily the secret key of Alice, and a case distinction is required depending on whether the endomorphism rings of the codomain curves are known: If the endomorphism rings are known, then any party can compute all the endomorphism rings, resulting in the same setup as in Fig. 7a; Assuming the endomorphism rings are unknown, again leads to a contradiction. In the last variation shown in Fig. 7c, both domain and codomain curves are generated via random walks from $E_0^{\LEFTcircle}$ and $E_1^{\LEFTcircle}$, respectively. This enables the same attack as before, the mere difference is that Bob computes λ_0 differently. Namely, also as the composition of the random walks. Thus, all variations of Isogeny Construction 2.2 are insecure, where the first one suffers from an outsider attack while the other two suffer from an insider attack.

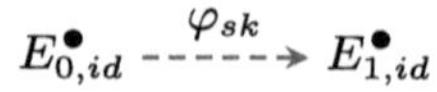

(a) Anyone can compute φ_{sk} as the endomorphism rings of both domain and codomain are known.

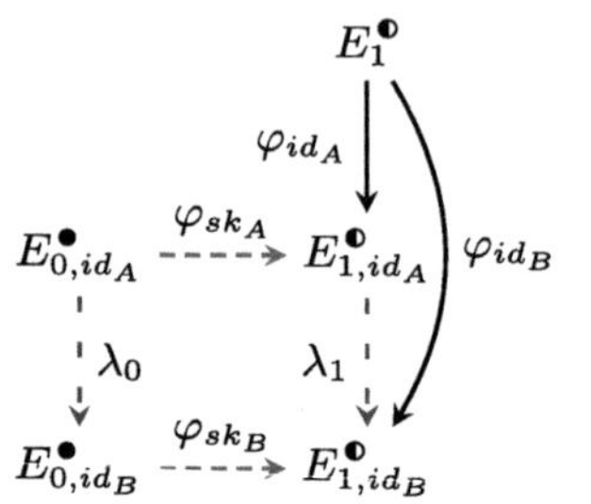

(b) One can compute λ_0 via the known endomorphism rings, and λ_1 via public random walks. Bob can learn $\varphi_{sk_A} = \hat{\lambda}_1 \circ \varphi_{sk_B} \circ \lambda_0$.

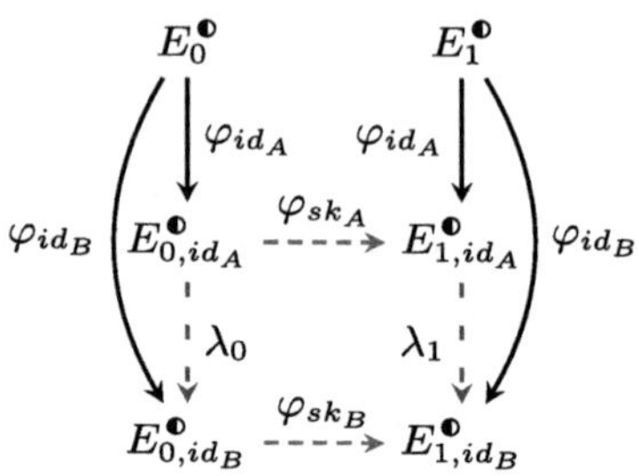

(c) Both λ_0 and λ_1 can be computed as the random walks are public. Bob can learn $\varphi_{sk_A} = \hat{\lambda}_1 \circ \varphi_{sk_B} \circ \lambda_0$.

Fig. 7. Illustrations of the variations of `Ext-pk` algorithms of $\mathtt{IKD}_{2.2}$, and the attacks to $\mathtt{IKD}_{2.2}$.

Approach 3: Larger Public Keys. To further broaden our scope, we discuss whether having larger public (and secret) keys helps circumvent the obstacles. We argue that increasing the number of curves in the user's public keys—therefore having multiple secret isogenies in the secret keys—does not mitigate the attacks. The public random walks, starting from a fixed curve in *mpk*, will nevertheless reveal all the secret isogenies to the other users, as before. However, it is reasonable to consider having multiple fixed curves in *mpk* to separate the public random walks. A similar structure can be seen in the signature schemes [9,22]. This approach would require a different curve in the master public key for each user—otherwise our attacks are still applicable, though restricted to users that share the same curve from the master public key. In this sense, the number of curves in the master public key scales with the number of users which would render it impractical. On top of that, the number of users would need to be fixed in advance when generating the master key-pair.

3.3 Using Endomorphism Rings as Secret Keys

Computing the endomorphism ring of a supersingular elliptic curve, i.e., Problem 2, is at heart of the security of several isogeny-based primitives, e.g., `SQISign` digital signature scheme [23] and its variants [6,20,23,48]. Therefore, the setting where the secret key is the knowledge of the endomorphism ring of the public key curve cannot be ignored when building an isogeny-based scheme. As proven by Page and Wesolowski [51], the endomorphism ring problem reduces to the one endomorphism problem, i.e., one can compute the whole endomorphism ring given access to an oracle OneEnd that repsonds with independent non-scalar endomorphisms on the curve. Benefiting from this result, when we talk about the security of the IKD construction, we will investigate whether the adversary can build this oracle—that implies it can compute the whole endomorphism ring which is the secret key.[11]

As before, the security of such construction boils down to how the public key curve is generated. Assuming the public key curve is sampled via a SECUER generator, the trusted party is required to solve Problem 2 to extract the secret key—which hinders the realization of the `Ext-sk` algorithm. Further, we immediately discard the option of using a SECKER generator as it contradicts the fact that the endomorphism ring is the secret, and should be unknown to other parties. Using a CGL generator seems to be the plausible approach; and in fact, it is what underlies the isogeny-based IBE scheme proposed by Fouotsa and Marco [32]. Unfortunately, the construction suffers from an attack which caused the proposal to be retracted afterwards. The construction, as we abstract via the `IKD` definition, is as follows.

Isogeny Construction 3 ($\mathtt{IKD}_3$). *Let* $\mathtt{H}^{CGL}_{\mathcal{E}ll}$ *be a CGL generator. The* `IKD` *can be described with the following algorithms:*

$\mathtt{KGen}(1^\lambda)$ *On input a security parameter, output a key-pair* (msk, mpk).
$\mathtt{Ext\text{-}pk}(mpk, id)$ *On input a master public key and an identity, output a random curve* E°_{id} *depending on the id and mpk, where the curve is generated via* $\mathtt{H}^{CGL}_{\mathcal{E}ll}$.
$\mathtt{Ext\text{-}sk}(msk, id)$ *On input a master secret key and an identity, compute and output the endomorphism ring* $\mathtt{End}(E^{\circ}_{id})$.

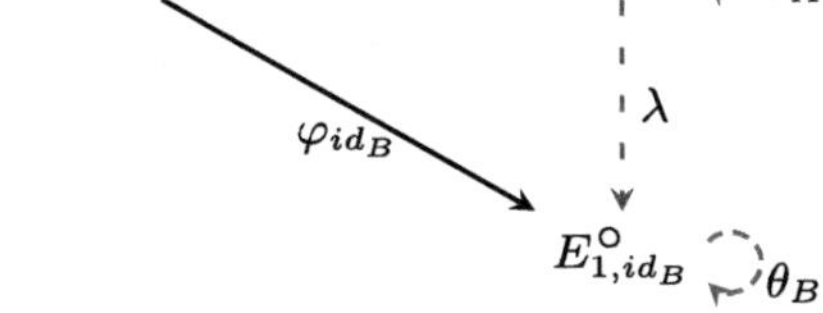

Fig. 8. Illustration of $\mathtt{IKD}_3$ and the attack.

Problem of Isogeny Construction 3. The attack is a combination of the generalized lollipop attack [16] and the reductions given in [51]. As can be seen in

[11] It is slightly easier to build this oracle in the `CSIDH` setting where the Frobenius endomorphism always exists. Nevertheless, we will present the generic attacks without using any setting-specific information.

Fig. 8, the public isogenies φ_{id_A} and φ_{id_B} allow one to compute the connecting isogeny $\lambda : E_{1,id_A} \to E_{1,id_B}$. Then, once Alice learns her secret endomorphism ring $\mathtt{End}(E^{\mathsf{O}}_{id})$, she can build the oracle OneEnd as follows: She samples an endomorphism θ_A, computes the endomorphism $\lambda \circ \theta_A \circ \hat{\lambda} = \theta_B \in \mathtt{End}(E^{\mathsf{O}}_{1,id_B})$. Alice then can compute the whole endomorphism ring $\mathtt{End}(E^{\mathsf{O}}_{1,id_B})$ using this oracle, and thus learn the secret key of Bob.

Thus, we conclude that the endomorphism ring approach similarly fails to give a secure IKD construction.

3.4 Trapdoors

In all constructions where the `Ext-sk` algorithm is needed to solve the underlying hardness assumption, it is only natural to ask if we can empower the trusted party with extra information. This information included in msk can allow the trusted party to solve the assumed to be hard problem. Especially since the `Ext-pk` algorithm that generates the public curves, takes mpk as input. This means the trusted party can make use of a trapdoor function family, so that the public key curves generated under mpk can be inverted via msk to compute the secret isogeny/endomorphism.

To the best of our knowledge, `FESTA` [7] and `SILBE` [29] are the only isogeny-based trapdoor functions proposed in the literature.[12] Now, we recall `FESTA`, and discuss the construction of `IKD` via trapdoor functions with it.

Definition 13 (`FESTA`). *Let E_0 be a supersingular elliptic curve defined over $\mathbb{F}_{p^2}$ for a prime p. Define $\langle P_b, Q_b\rangle = E_0[2^b]$ to be a fixed torsion basis, d_A, d_1, and d_2 be predefined degrees. The `FESTA` trapdoor function family $\mathtt{FESTA}(\mathtt{KGen}, f, f^{-1})$ can be described with the following algorithms:*

- $\mathtt{KGen}(1^\lambda)$ *On input a security parameter, set $pp = (E_0, p, P_b, Q_b, d_A, d_1, d_2)$. Choose an isogeny $\varphi_A\colon E_0 \to E_A$ of degree d_A, and an invertible diagonal matrix A. Compute the scaled image points $\begin{pmatrix} R_A \\ S_A \end{pmatrix} = A \begin{pmatrix} \varphi_A(P_b) \\ \varphi_A(Q_b) \end{pmatrix}$. Output $(sk, pk) = ((A, \varphi_A), (pp, E_A, R_A, S_A))$.*
- $f(1^\lambda, pk, x)$ *On input a security parameter, a public key pk, and an input x, parse $pk = (pp, E_A, R_A, S_A)$, and $x = (\langle K_1\rangle, \langle K_2\rangle, B)$. Compute two isogenies $\varphi_1\colon E_0 \to E_1$ and $\varphi_2\colon E_A \to E_2$ with kernels $\langle K_1\rangle, \langle K_2\rangle$ and of degree d_1 and d_2 respectively. Compute $\begin{pmatrix} R_1 \\ S_1 \end{pmatrix} = B \begin{pmatrix} \varphi_1(P_b) \\ \varphi_1(Q_b) \end{pmatrix}$ and $\begin{pmatrix} R_2 \\ S_2 \end{pmatrix} = B \begin{pmatrix} \varphi_2(R_A) \\ \varphi_2(S_A) \end{pmatrix}$. Output $y = (E_1, R_1, S_1, E_2, R_2, S_2)$.*
- $f^{-1}(1^\lambda, pk, sk, y)$ *On input a security parameter, a public key pk, a secret key sk, and an output y, parse $pk = (pp, E_A, R_A, S_A)$, $sk = (A, \varphi_A)$, and $y = (E_1, R_1, S_1, E_2, R_2, S_2)$. Compute the isogeny $\psi\colon \varphi_2 \circ \varphi_A \circ \hat{\varphi}_1\colon E_1 \to E_2$ via an `SIDH` attack. Recover the kernels $\langle K_1\rangle, \langle K_2\rangle$ of the isogenies φ_1, φ_2 respectively, and the matrix B. Output $x = (\langle K_1\rangle, \langle K_2\rangle, B)$.*

[12] Although the abbreviations `FESTA` and `SILBE` stand for the encryption schemes, we refer to the underlying trapdoor function for sake of conciseness.

It is crucial here to note that the inversion function f^{-1} is only guaranteed to invert valid output generated by f. This means, the trapdoor information (A, φ_A) is not enough by itself, to recover a secret isogeny connecting random public key curves [21]. In fact, this is a property of *preimage sampleable trapdoor functions* as defined in the lattice-based IBE paper [37]. In other words, for a uniformly chosen y, there exists an x such that $f(x) = y$, and the inversion function can efficiently find it via $f^{-1}(y) = x$. Since both FESTA and SILBE do not have this arbitrary output inversion property, it is not possible to randomly generate the public key curves, and extract the secret isogeny connecting them. Therefore, the only possible way is to generate the public key curves via the function f.

Isogeny Construction 4 ($\mathtt{IKD}_4$) *Let the parameters be the same as in the description of* FESTA. *The* IKD *can be described with the following algorithms:*

$\mathtt{KGen}(1^\lambda)$ *On input a security parameter* 1^λ*, compute*

$$(A_{msk}, \varphi_{msk}), (pp, E_{mpk}, R_{mpk}, S_{mpk}) \leftarrow_\$ \mathtt{FESTA.KGen}(1^\lambda).$$

Let H *be a random oracle that on input an id, outputs* $(\langle K_1\rangle, \langle K_2\rangle, B)$*, where* $\langle K_1\rangle, \langle K_2\rangle$ *are cyclic subgroups of* $E_0[d_1]$ *and* $E_{mpk}[d_2]$*, and* B *is an invertible diagonal matrix. Let* $(A_{msk}, \varphi_{msk}) \in msk$*, and* $(pp, E_{mpk}, R_{mpk}, S_{mpk}, \mathtt{H}) \in mpk$*, and output the key pair* (msk, mpk).

$\mathtt{Ext\text{-}pk}(mpk, id)$ *On input a master public key and an identity, output a public key* $pk = (E_{0,id}, R_{0,id}, S_{0,id}, E_{1,id}, R_{1,id}, S_{1,id}) \leftarrow f(1^\lambda, mpk, \mathtt{H}(id))$.

$\mathtt{Ext\text{-}sk}(msk, id)$ *On input a master secret key and an identity, compute* $pk \leftarrow f(1^\lambda, mpk, \mathtt{H}(id))$*. Invert the public key* $(\langle K_1\rangle, \langle K_2\rangle, B) \leftarrow f^{-1}(1^\lambda, mpk, msk, pk)$*. Recover and output* $\varphi_{sk}\colon E_{0,id} \to E_{1,id}$ *from the information of* msk *and* $(\langle K_1\rangle, \langle K_2\rangle, B)$.

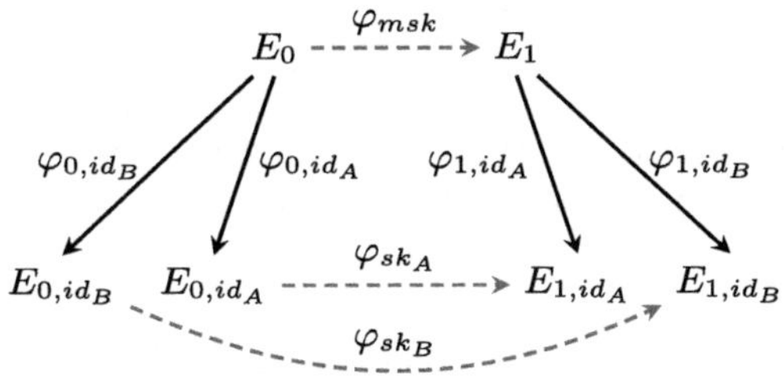

Fig. 9. Illustration of $\mathtt{IKD}_4$ and the attack that reveals the master secret key φ_{msk}.

Problem of Isogeny Construction 4. There is an insider attack to the scheme, as shown in Fig. 9, that works in the following way. Once Alice learns her secret isogeny φ_{sk_A}, she can compute the composition $\varphi_{msk} = \hat{\varphi}_{1,id_A} \circ \varphi_{sk_A} \circ \varphi_{0,id_A}$.

This partially reveals msk. Then, she can compute Bob's secret key via $\varphi_{sk_B} = \varphi_{1,id_B} \circ \varphi_{msk} \circ \hat{\varphi}_{0,id_B}$.

The instruments that enable the attack are reciprocal; either the fact that f runs a CGL generator revealing an isogeny path to the msk curves, or that f^{-1} cannot revert uniformly sampled outputs. The attack similarly applies when SILBE trapdoor function is used in place of FESTA, due to the same reasons.

4 How to Build IBE from Isogenies

It is apparent that the achievable constructions are insecure due to the vulnerabilities stemming from SECKER and CGL generators. On the other hand, when only SECUER generators are used, the trusted party is required to solve the underlying hardness assumption. Therefore, one needs a trapdoor function family—that provides the trusted party with the trapdoor information to solve the underlying hardness assumption. Admitting the difficulty of efficient SECUER generator instantiation, we claim it is still insufficient for an IBE construction, as we also require such trapdoor mechanism that we describe in Appendix A.

Acknowledgements. We thank Luca De Feo for very helpful comments and for pointing out that every IBE scheme can be transformed into a canonical one. This work was funded by the German Research Foundation (DFG) – SFB 1119 – 236615297, the German Federal Ministry of Research, Technology and Space (BMFTR) under the project QUDIS (16KIS2091) and PARFAIT (16KIS2145), and the Hector Foundation II.

A SECUER Trapdoors

To pinpoint what exactly is required for a secure isogeny-based IBE construction, we give the description of a strong primitive—as we call, a SECUER trapdoor function family.

Definition 14. *Let* $\mathtt{H}^{\mathit{UE}}_{\mathcal{E}ll}$ *be a SECUER generator. The SECUER trapdoor function family* $\Sigma = (\mathtt{KGen}, f, f^{-1})$ *consists of the following algorithms:*

$\mathtt{KGen}(1^\lambda)$ *On input a security parameter, output a key-pair* (pk, sk).
$f(pk, x)$ *On input* pk *and* x, *output* $E_x \leftarrow_\$ \mathtt{H}^{\mathit{UE}}_{\mathcal{E}ll}(pk, x)$.
$f^{-1}(sk, E_x)$ *On input* sk *and* E_x, *output* $\mathtt{End}(E_x)$.

This trapdoor function family is the analogue of preimage sampleable function families defined in [37]. The SECUER generator samples an element from the range of function f, and f^{-1} achieves to find its preimage. Nevertheless, we use the term SECUER to point out that it is strictly necessary for such construction to work.

We now give the description for an IKD construction that would work under the assumption that there exists an efficient SECUER trapdoor function instantiation.

Isogeny Construction 5 **($\mathtt{IKD}_5$).** *Let $\Sigma = (\mathtt{KGen}, f, f^{-1})$ be a SECUER trapdoor function family. The* IKD *can be described with the following algorithms:*

$\mathtt{KGen}(1^\lambda)$ *On input a security parameter, output a master key-pair* $(msk, mpk) \leftarrow \Sigma.\mathtt{KGen}(1^\lambda)$.

$\mathtt{Ext\text{-}pk}(mpk, id)$ *On input a master public key and an identity, output* $E_{id} \leftarrow f(mpk, id)$.

$\mathtt{Ext\text{-}sk}(msk, id)$ *On input a master secret key and an identity, compute and output a secret key* $\mathtt{End}(E_{id}) \leftarrow f^{-1}(msk, E_{id})$.

Since the public key curves are generated via a SECUER generator, the attacks that stem from the usage of SECKER and CGL generators no longer remain. Moreover, notice that due to the reductions between Problem 1 and Problem 2, the secret endomorphism ring $\mathtt{End}(E_{id})$ can be replaced with a secret isogeny $\varphi_{id} : E_0 \rightarrow E_{id}$, where $E_0 \in mpk$ is a supersingular elliptic curve with unknown endomorphism ring included in. Meaning, the instantiation of SECUER trapdoor function family implies an IBE scheme in both settings we discussed, i.e., secret key being either an isogeny or an endomorphism ring.

References

1. Agarwal, A., Fernando, R., Pinkas, B." Efficiently-thresholdizable batched identity based encryption, with applications. Cryptology ePrint Archive, Report 2024/1575 (2024)
2. Agrawal, S., Boneh, D., Boyen, X.: Efficient lattice (H)IBE in the standard model. In: Gilbert, H. (ed.) EUROCRYPT 2010. LNCS, vol. 6110, pp. 553–572. Springer, Heidelberg (2010). https://doi.org/10.1007/978-3-642-13190-5_28
3. Basso, A. et al. PRISM: simple and compact identification and signatures from large prime degree isogenies. In: Jager, T., Pan, J. (eds.) Public-Key Cryptography – PKC 2025. PKC 2025. LNCS, vol 15676. Springer, Cham (2025). https://doi.org/10.1007/978-3-031-91826-1_10
4. Basso, A. et al.: Supersingular curves you can trust. In: Hazay, C., Stam, M. (eds) Advances in Cryptology – EUROCRYPT 2023. EUROCRYPT 2023. LNCS, vol 14005. Springer, Cham (2023). https://doi.org/10.1007/978-3-031-30617-4_14
5. Basso, A., Dartois, P., De Feo, L., Leroux, A., Maino, L., Pope, G., Robert, D., Wesolowski, B.: SQIsign2D-West - the fast, the small, and the safer. In: Chung, K.-M., Sasaki, Yu. (eds.) ASIACRYPT 2024. Part III, volume 15486 of LNCS, pp. 339–370. Springer, Singapore (2024). https://doi.org/10.1007/978-981-96-0891-1_11
6. Andrea Basso, Luca De Feo, Pierrick Dartois, Antonin Leroux, Luciano Maino, Giacomo Pope, Damien Robert, and Benjamin Wesolowski. SQIsign2D-West: The fast, the small, and the safer. Cryptology ePrint Archive, Report 2024/760, 2024
7. Basso, A., Maino, L., Pope, G.: FESTA: Fast encryption from supersingular torsion attacks. In: Guo, J., Steinfeld, R. (eds.) ASIACRYPT 2023. Part VII, volume 14444 of LNCS, pp. 98–126. Springer, Singapore (2023)
8. Beullens, W., De Feo, L., Galbraith, S.D., Petit, C.: Proving knowledge of isogenies: a survey. DCC **91**(11), 3425–3456 (2023)

9. Beullens, W., Kleinjung, T., Vercauteren, F.: CSI-FiSh: efficient isogeny based signatures through class group computations. In: Galbraith, S.D., Moriai, S. (eds.) ASIACRYPT 2019. Part I, volume 11921 of LNCS, pp. 227–247. Springer, Cham (2019)
10. Boneh, D., Franklin, M.K.: Identity-based encryption from the Weil pairing. In: Kilian, J. (ed.) CRYPTO 2001. LNCS, vol. 2139, pp. 213–229. Springer, Berlin, Heidelberg (2001). https://doi.org/10.1007/3-540-44647-8_13
11. Boneh, D., Guan, J., Zhandry, M.: A lower bound on the length of signatures based on group actions and generic isogenies. In: Hazay, C., Stam, M. (eds.) EUROCRYPT 2023. Part V, volume 14008 of LNCS, pp. 507–531. Springer, Cham (2023). https://doi.org/10.1007/978-3-031-30589-4_18
12. Booher, J., et al.: Failing to hash into supersingular isogeny graphs. Cryptology ePrint Archive, Report 2022/518 (2022)
13. Brakerski, Z., Lombardi, A., Segev, G., Vaikuntanathan, V.: Anonymous IBE, leakage resilience and circular security from new assumptions. In: Nielsen, J.B., Rijmen, V. (eds.) EUROCRYPT 2018. LNCS, vol. 10820, pp. 535–564. Springer, Cham (2018). https://doi.org/10.1007/978-3-319-78381-9_20
14. Cash, D., Hofheinz, D., Kiltz, E., Peikert, C.: Bonsai trees, or how to delegate a lattice basis. In: Gilbert, H. (ed.) EUROCRYPT 2010. LNCS, vol. 6110, pp. 523–552. Springer, Heidelberg (2010). https://doi.org/10.1007/978-3-642-13190-5_27
15. Castryck, W., Lange, T., Martindale, C., Panny, L., Renes, J.: CSIDH: an efficient post-quantum commutative group action. In: Peyrin, T., Galbraith, S. (eds.) ASIACRYPT 2018. Part III, volume 11274 of LNCS, pp. 395–427. Springer, Cham (2018). https://doi.org/10.1007/978-3-030-03332-3_1
16. Castryck, W., Vercauteren, F.: A polynomial time attack on instances of M-SIDH and FESTA. In: Guo, J., Steinfeld, R. (eds.) ASIACRYPT 2023. Part VII, volume 14444 of LNCS, pp. 127–156. Springer, Singapore (2023)
17. Charles, D.X., Lauter, K.E., Goren, E.Z.: Cryptographic hash functions from expander graphs. J. Cryptol. **22**(1), 93–113 (2009)
18. Cocks, C.: An identity based encryption scheme based on quadratic residues. In: Honary, B. (ed.) 8th IMA International Conference on Cryptography and Coding. LNCS, vol. 2260, pp. 360–363. Springer, Berlin, Heidelberg (2001). https://doi.org/10.1007/3-540-45325-3_32
19. Cui, Y., Fujisaki, E., Hanaoka, G., Imai, H., Zhang, R.: Formal security treatments for signatures from identity-based encryption. In: Susilo, W., Liu, J.K., Mu, Y. (eds.) ProvSec 2007. LNCS, vol. 4784, pp. 218–227. Springer, Heidelberg (2007). https://doi.org/10.1007/978-3-540-75670-5_16
20. Dartois, P., Leroux, A., Robert, D., Wesolowski, B.: SQIsignHD: new dimensions in cryptography. In: Joye, M., Leander, G. (eds.) EUROCRYPT 2024. Part I, volume 14651 of LNCS, pp. 3–32. Springer, Cham (2024)
21. De Feo, L., Fouotsa, T.B., Panny, L.: Isogeny problems with level structure. In: Joye, M., Leander, G. (eds.) EUROCRYPT 2024. Part VII, vol. 14657. LNCS, pp. 181–204. Springer, Cham (2024). https://doi.org/10.1007/978-3-031-58754-2_7
22. De Feo, L., Galbraith, S.D.: SeaSign: Compact isogeny signatures from class group actions. In: Ishai, Y., Rijmen, V. (eds.) EUROCRYPT 2019. Part III, volume 11478 of LNCS, pp. 759–789. Springer, Cham (2019). https://doi.org/10.1007/978-3-030-17659-4_26
23. De Feo, L., Kohel, D., Leroux, A., Petit, C., Wesolowski, B.: SQISign: compact post-quantum signatures from quaternions and isogenies. In: Moriai, S., Wang, H. (eds.) ASIACRYPT 2020. Part I, volume 12491 of LNCS, pp. 64–93. Springer, Cham (2020). https://doi.org/10.1007/978-3-030-64837-4_3

24. Debris-Alazard, T., Tillich, J.-P.: Two attacks on rank metric code-based schemes: RankSign and an IBE scheme. In: Peyrin, T., Galbraith, S. (eds.) ASIACRYPT 2018. Part I, volume 11272 of LNCS, pp. 62–92. Springer, Cham (2018)
25. Diffie, W., Hellman, M.E.: New directions in cryptography. IEEE Trans. Inf. Theory **22**(6), 644–654 (1976)
26. Döttling, N., Garg, S.: From selective IBE to full IBE and selective HIBE. In: Kalai, Y., Reyzin, L. (eds.) TCC 2017. Part I, volume 10677 of LNCS, pp. 372–408. Springer, Cham (2017). https://doi.org/10.1007/978-3-319-70500-2_13
27. Döttling, N., Garg, S.: Identity-based encryption from the Diffie-Hellman assumption. In: Katz, J., Shacham, H. (eds.) CRYPTO 2017. Part I, volume 10401 of LNCS, pp. 537–569. Springer, Cham (2017). https://doi.org/10.1007/978-3-319-63688-7_18
28. Max Duparc and Tako Boris Fouotsa: SQIPrime: A dimension 2 variant of SQISignHD with non-smooth challenge isogenies. In: Chung, K.-M., Sasaki, Yu. (eds.) ASIACRYPT 2024. Part III, volume 15486 of LNCS, pp. 396–429. Springer, Singapore (2024). https://doi.org/10.1007/978-981-96-0891-1_13
29. Duparc, M., Fouotsa, T.B., Vaudenay, S.: SILBE: an updatable public key encryption scheme from lollipop attacks. In: Eichlseder, M., Gambs, S. (eds.) Selected Areas in Cryptography – SAC 2024. SAC 2024. LNCS, vol 15516. Springer, Cham (2025). https://doi.org/10.1007/978-3-031-82852-2_7
30. Eisenträger, K., Hallgren, S., Lauter, K., Morrison, T., Petit, C.: Supersingular isogeny graphs and endomorphism rings: reductions and solutions. In: Nielsen, J.B., Rijmen, V. (eds.) EUROCRYPT 2018. LNCS, vol. 10822, pp. 329–368. Springer, Cham (2018). https://doi.org/10.1007/978-3-319-78372-7_11
31. Emura, K., Katsumata, S., Watanabe, Y.: Identity-based encryption with security against the KGC: a formal model and its instantiation from lattices. In: Sako, K., Schneider, S., Ryan, P.Y.A. (eds.) ESORICS 2019. LNCS, vol. 11736, pp. 113–133. Springer, Cham (2019). https://doi.org/10.1007/978-3-030-29962-0_6
32. Fouotsa, T.B., Marco, L.: Towards identity based encryption from M-SIDH and the SIDH attacks. Presented at Leuven Isogeny Days 4, Leuven Belgium (2023). Accessed 13th January 2025
33. Gaborit, P., Hauteville, A., Phan, D.H., Tillich, J.-P.: Identity-based encryption from codes with rank metric. In: Katz, J., Shacham, H. (eds.) CRYPTO 2017. LNCS, vol. 10403, pp. 194–224. Springer, Cham (2017). https://doi.org/10.1007/978-3-319-63697-9_7
34. Gaborit, P., Ruatta, O., Schrek, J., Zémor, G.: RankSign: an efficient signature algorithm based on the rank metric. In: Mosca, M. (ed.) Post-Quantum Cryptography - 6th International Workshop. PQCrypto 2014, pp. 88–107. Springer, Cham (2014). https://doi.org/10.1007/978-3-319-11659-4_6
35. Galbraith, S.D., Petit, C., Silva, J.: Identification protocols and signature schemes based on supersingular isogeny problems. In: Takagi, T., Peyrin, T. (eds.) ASIACRYPT 2017. Part I, vol. 10624. LNCS, pp. 3–33. Springer, Cham (2017)
36. Galbraith, S.D., Vercauteren, F.: Computational problems in supersingular elliptic curve isogenies. Cryptology ePrint Archive, Report 2017/774 (2017)
37. Gentry, C., Peikert, C., Vaikuntanathan, V.: Trapdoors for hard lattices and new cryptographic constructions. In: Ladner, R.E., Dwork, C (eds.) 40th ACM STOC, pp.197–206. ACM Press (May 2008)
38. Jao, D., De Feo, L.: Towards Quantum-Resistant Cryptosystems from Supersingular Elliptic Curve Isogenies. In: Yang, B.-Y. (ed.) PQCrypto 2011. LNCS, vol. 7071, pp. 19–34. Springer, Heidelberg (2011). https://doi.org/10.1007/978-3-642-25405-5_2

39. Ji, W., et al.: Identity-based encryption from lattices with more compactness in the standard model. In: Eichlseder, M., Gambs, S. (eds.) SAC 2024. Part I, volume 15516 of LNCS, pp. 259–281. Springer, Cham (2024)
40. Jiang, Y., Zhu, Y., Wang, J., Zhang, Y.: Efficient online and non-interactive threshold signatures with identifiable aborts for identity-based signatures in the IEEE P1363 standard. Cryptology ePrint Archive, Report 2024/1333 (2024)
41. Katsumata, S., Yamada, S.: Partitioning via non-linear polynomial functions: more compact IBEs from ideal lattices and bilinear maps. In: Cheon, J.H., Takagi, T. (eds.) ASIACRYPT 2016. LNCS, vol. 10032, pp. 682–712. Springer, Heidelberg (2016). https://doi.org/10.1007/978-3-662-53890-6_23
42. Love, J., Boneh, D.: Supersingular curves with small non-integer endomorphisms (2020)
43. Lu, X., Fan, J., Au, M.H.: Relaxed lattice-based programmable hash functions: New efficient adaptively secure IBEs. Cryptology ePrint Archive, Report 2024/1535 (2024)
44. Matsumoto, T., Imai, H.: Public quadratic polynominal-tuples for efficient signature-verification and message-encryption. In: Günther, C.G. (ed.) EUROCRYPT'88. LNCS, vol. 330, pp. 419–453. Springer, Berlin, Heidelberg (1988). https://doi.org/10.1007/3-540-45961-8_39
45. Merdy, A.H.L., Wesolowski, B.: The supersingular endomorphism ring problem given one endomorphism. Cryptology ePrint Archive, Report 2023/1448 (2023)
46. Mitrokotsa, A., Mukherjee, S., Tomy, J.: Oblivious identity-based encryption - (IBE secure against an adversarial KGC). In: Eichlseder, M., Gambs, S. (eds.) SAC 2024. Part I, volume 15516 of LNCS, pp. 282–309. Springer, Cham (2024). https://doi.org/10.1007/978-3-031-82852-2_1
47. Mula, M., Murru, N., Pintore, F.: Random sampling of supersingular elliptic curves. Cryptology ePrint Archive, Report 2022/528 (2022)
48. Nakagawa, K., Onuki, H.: SQIsign2D-East: A new signature scheme using 2-dimensional isogenies. Cryptology ePrint Archive, Report 2024/771 (2024)
49. Nakagawa, K., et al.: SQIsign2D-East: A new signature scheme using 2-dimensional isogenies. In: Chung, K.-M., Sasaki, Yu. (eds.) ASIACRYPT 2024. Part III, volume 15486 of LNCS, pp. 272–303. Springer, Singapore (2024)
50. National Institute of Standards and Technology. Call for additional digital signature schemes for the post-quantum cryptography standardization process (2022). https://csrc.nist.gov/csrc/media/Projects/pqc-dig-sig/documents/call-for-proposals-dig-sig-sept-2022.pdf
51. Page, A., Wesolowski, B.: The supersingular endomorphism ring and one endomorphism problems are equivalent. In: Joye, M., Leander, G. (eds.) EUROCRYPT 2024. Part VI, volume 14656 of LNCS, pp. 388–417. Springer, Cham (2024). https://doi.org/10.1007/978-3-031-58751-1_14
52. Patarin, J.: Cryptanalysis of the matsumoto and imai public key scheme of Eurocrypt'88. In: Coppersmith, D. (ed.) CRYPTO 1995. LNCS, vol. 963, pp. 248–261. Springer, Heidelberg (1995). https://doi.org/10.1007/3-540-44750-4_20
53. Peng, C., Chen, J., Zhou, L., Choo, K.-K.R., He, D.: Csiibs: a post-quantum identity-based signature scheme based on isogenies. J. Inform. Sec. Appli. **54**, 102504 (2020)
54. Pizer, A.K.: Ramanujan graphs and hecke operators. Bull. Am. Math. Soc. **23**, 127–137 (1990)
55. Shamir, A.: Identity-based cryptosystems and signature schemes. In: Blakley, G.R., Chaum, D. (eds.) CRYPTO 1984. LNCS, vol. 196, pp. 47–53. Springer, Heidelberg (1985). https://doi.org/10.1007/3-540-39568-7_5

56. Shaw, S., Dutta, R.: Post-quantum secure identity-based signature achieving forward secrecy. J. Inform. Sec. Appli. **69**, 103275 (2022)
57. Wesolowski, B.: The supersingular isogeny path and endomorphism ring problems are equivalent. In: 62nd FOCS, pp. 1100–1111. IEEE Computer Society Press (February 2022)
58. Yamada, S.: Adaptively secure identity-based encryption from lattices with asymptotically shorter public parameters. In: Fischlin, M., Coron, J.-S. (eds.) EUROCRYPT 2016. Part II, volume 9666 of LNCS, pp. 32–62. Springer, Berlin, Heidelberg (2016). https://doi.org/10.1007/978-3-662-49896-5_2
59. Yamada, S.: Asymptotically compact adaptively secure lattice IBEs and verifiable random functions via generalized partitioning techniques. In: Katz, J., Shacham, H. (eds.) CRYPTO 2017. Part III, volume 10403 of LNCS, pp. 161–193. Springer, Cham (2017). https://doi.org/10.1007/978-3-319-63697-9_6
60. Zhandry, M.: Secure identity-based encryption in the quantum random oracle model. In: Safavi-Naini, R., Canetti, R. (eds.) CRYPTO 2012. LNCS, vol. 7417, pp. 758–775. Springer, Berlin, Heidelberg (2012). https://doi.org/10.1007/978-3-642-32009-5_44

PIsignHD: A New Structure for the SQIsign Family with Flexible Applicability

Kaizhan Lin[1], Weize Wang[1], Chang-An Zhao[2], and Yunlei Zhao[1,3](✉)

[1] College of Computer Science and Artificial Intelligence, Fudan University, Shanghai, China
{linkzh,ylzhao}@fudan.edu.cn, wzwang23@m.fudan.edu.cn
[2] School of Mathematics, Sun Yat-sen University, Guangzhou, China
zhaochan3@mail.sysu.edu.cn
[3] State Key Laboratory of Cryptology, Beijing, China

Abstract. In this paper, we propose a new structure for the SQIsign family: ***P****entagon* ***I****sogeny-based* ***Sign****ature in* ***H****igh* ***D****imension* (referred to as PIsignHD). The new structure separates the hash of the commitment and that of the message by employing two cryptographic hash functions. This feature is desirable in reality, particularly for applications based on mobile low-power devices or for those deployed interactively over the Internet or in the cloud computing setting.

This structure can be generally applied to all SQIsign variants. In this work, we focus on the instance based on SQIsignHD. Compared with SQIsignHD, PIsignHD has the same signature size (even smaller for some application scenarios). For the NIST-I security level, the signature size of PIsignHD can be reduced to 519 bits, while the SQIsignHD signature takes 870 bits. Additionally, PIsignHD has an efficient online signing process and enjoys much desirable application flexibility. In our experiments, the online signing process of PIsignHD runs in 4 ms.

Keywords: Digital signatures · SQIsign · SQIsignHD · Isogeny · Γ-protocol

1 Introduction

Isogeny-based cryptography is attractive for its compact keys in post-quantum cryptography, but the expensive computational cost limits the practical applications of isogeny-based cryptosystems. Various digital signatures under isogeny assumptions have been proposed in recent years, such as [4,13,19,23]. However, many of these schemes suffer from relatively large signature or public-key sizes.

Conversely, SQIsign [14] and SQIsignHD [12] fully highlight the compactness as isogeny-based signatures. SQIsign has a very efficient verification, but the signing phase is expensive due to the ideal-to-isogeny translation. Although the ideal-to-isogeny translation has been improved recently [15,25,29], it remains

C. Boura et al. (Eds.): SAC 2025, LNCS 16207, pp. 616–644, 2026.
https://doi.org/10.1007/978-3-032-10536-3_23

the main efficiency bottleneck in the signing phase. SQIsignHD applies the algorithms derived from SIDH attacks [6,27,33], and offers a remarkably smaller signature size and much faster response since the signer does not need to compute large degree isogenies. Conversely, the verification in SQIsignHD is inefficient as it involves isogeny computations in high dimension.

Motivation. Currently, both SQIsign and SQIsignHD are based on Σ-protocols. Therefore, the challenge is derived from the knowledge of the commitment and the message. However, this feature may result in inconvenient deployments or inefficient implementations, particularly for applications based on low-power devices or applications in the cloud computing setting. We present and discuss some motivating application scenarios below.

- **Application 1: Hardware wallet based on SIM card**. This is a typical application scenario based on mobile low-power devices. The SIM card acts as the signer who keeps the signing secret key and performs signing operations, while the message data to be signed is usually generated by applications in the mobile phone. When generating a signature based on a Σ-protocol, the SIM card has to compute the hash value of the concatenation of the commitment and the message data (note that when the message data is large, this would be unfriendly as the interaction cost is expensive), or transfer the commitment to the system on chip (SoC) to compute the hash value.
- **Application 2: Document online signing by enterprise**. When using the signature scheme in practice, particularly by enterprises, the signing server is usually deployed in the cloud or run by the enterprise. In the scenario of online signing, Σ-signatures require the signer to upload the entire document to the signature server. This may consume a significant amount of bandwidth and cause more computing burden on the signature server, resulting in a system bottleneck.

Remark 1. When sending the full message is problematic, one may consider signing a hash of the message instead of the full message. For signing the message m with Σ-signature, we need to consider the collision resistance of single-hashing $h(a||m)$, where a is the commitment and h is a hash function. But for signing $h(m)$, we need to consider the collision resistance of double-hashing $h(a||h(m))$. Double-hashing has much lower collision-resistance than single-hashing. That is the reason why Σ-signatures do not recommend to sign $h(m)$.

In 1989, Even, Goldreich and Micali [20] introduced online/offline signatures, which are desirable for low-power devices. The main idea of online/offline signatures is to divide the signature into the online phase and the offline phase. Generally, the online phase is required to be fast as possible, while the offline phase can be connected to the power. In 2013, Yao and Zhao [38] proposed Γ-protocols and a novel transformation method, known as Γ-transformation. Unlike Σ-signatures, the signatures via Γ-transformation separate the hash of the commitment a and that of the message m, by employing two secure hash functions h_1 and h_2 to compute the hash values $h_1(a)$ and $h_2(m)$, respectively.

From the target one-way property of h_1, the value $h_1(a)$ (or a set of values $\{h_1(a_1), h_1(a_2), \cdots, h_1(a_s)\}$ with commitments a_1, a_2, $\cdots$, a_s) can be public or stored on the verifier's side. Consequently, the verifier can precompute some intermediate values that are relevant to the hash values of the commitment to enhance the verification performance. Moreover, Γ-signatures allow the verifier to compute $h_2(m)$ in advance without the knowledge of the commitment a. When a trusted verifier would like to request the signer to sign a message m, it can transfer the hash value $h_2(m)$ instead of the whole message to the signer, thereby significantly reducing the communication cost and the computational cost of hashing for the signer in the response phase. The specific construction of Γ-signatures also benefits the online response of the signer, since all the intermediate values irrelevant to the message and used to generate the response can be computed offline. As a result, Γ-signatures offer an efficient online structure and enjoy the advantage of application flexibility.

Contribution. In this paper, we propose a new structure for the SQIsign family, which is illustrated in Fig. 1. The new structure is constructed via Γ-transformation. The main difference between the SQIsign family and our new structure is that the latter contains an additional isogeny $\varphi_{com} : E_1 \to E_2$, which is derived from the knowledge of the commitment. Besides, the challenge isogeny $\varphi_{chl} : E_A \to E_3$ is hashed from the knowledge of the message. Correspondingly, the response isogeny is from E_2 to E_3.

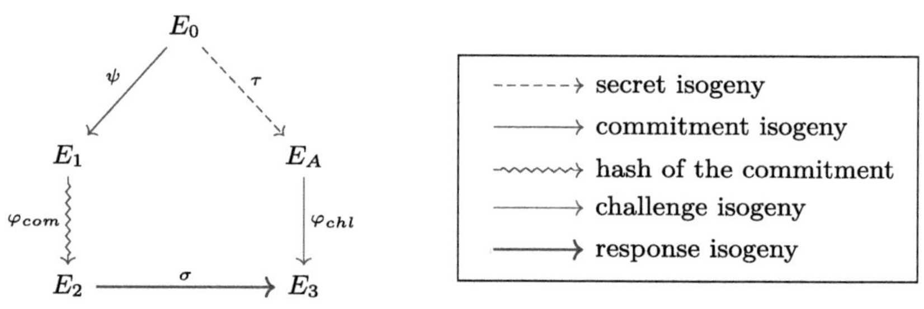

Fig. 1. A sketch of our new structure

Obviously, our new structure can be easily applied to the SQIsign family. To show the advantages of the new structure compared to the traditional structure, we take SQIsignHD as an instance and introduce ***P****entagon* ***I****sogeny-based* ***Sign****ature in* ***H****igh* ***D****imension* (referred to as PIsignHD or Π-signHD). At first glance, the efficiency of PIsignHD appears to be slightly inferior to SQIsignHD due to the additional isogeny involved. But in normal cases, SQIsignHD and PIsignHD have the same signature size. Furthermore, PIsignHD has the following additional advantages, which are attractive in applications.

- **Flexible challenge generation**: In SQIsignHD, the challenge isogeny is derived from the knowledge of the public key, the commitment and the message. Benefiting from Γ-transformation, the generation of the challenge isogeny in PIsignHD only requires the public key and the message. This feature tackles the applications as we mentioned above. In Applications 1 and 2, the signature requester can directly transmit the hash value of the message, which reduces transmission and computational requirements for the signer.

- **More compact signature in applications**: The signature of SQIsignHD involves the j-invariant of a supersingular curve. If the public storage is available, PIsignHD avoids storing it, and the signature size can be reduced from 6.5λ bits to around 3.5λ bits, where λ is the security parameter.
- **Fast online signing computations**: As previously mentioned, the verifier can transfer the kernel of the challenge isogeny instead of the whole message, saving the time for the signer to hash the message. Besides, the signer can precompute intermediate values that are irrelevant to the message. In our implementation, the online signature computations take only 4 ms.
- **Storage saving**: To adapt the online/offline technique in SQIsignHD, the signer has to store all the intermediate values that are used to sign the message. Conversely, PIsignHD allows some of the values to be public, or stored on the verifier's size. Therefore, PIsignHD reduces the storage requirements for the signer, which is preferred in applications.

Related Work. Recently, Renan and Kutas proposed a quantum-resistant adaptor signature called SQIAsignHD [32]. This scheme underlies SQIsignHD and utilizes the artificial orientation on SIDH [2]. We believe some techniques in this work could also be beneficial for SQIAsignHD with further research. Very Recently, several variants of SQIsignHD are proposed [1,17,28]. Our structure can also be applied to these schemes. More technical details are left as future work.

Organization. The remainder of our paper is organized as follows. Section 2 reviews the necessary preliminaries. In Sect. 3 we propose a high-level overview of PIsignHD and the underlying identification protocol. The security proofs are provided in Sect. 4. Section 5 introduces the concrete implementation of PIsignHD, and presents the experimental results. Finally we conclude in Sect. 6.

2 Preliminaries

In this section, we recall Γ-protocols and SQIsignHD. The necessary mathematical backgrounds are left in Appendix A, while the introductions of Σ-protocol and FiatShamir paradigm are left in Appendix B.

2.1 Γ-Protocol and Γ-Transformation

Assume that $\mathcal{P}$ and $\mathcal{V}$ are probabilistic polynomial time machines, and the advantage of $\mathcal{P}$ over $\mathcal{V}$ is that $\mathcal{P}$ knows w with $(x, w) \in \mathcal{R}$, where $\mathcal{R}$ is an $\mathcal{NP}$-relation. Then Γ-protocol proceeds as follows:

- $\mathcal{P}$ sends a commitment a and a random string d to $\mathcal{V}$;

- $\mathcal{V}$ sends a random string e to $\mathcal{P}$;
- $\mathcal{P}$ sends a reply z with respect to e, and $\mathcal{V}$ accepts or rejects based on (x, a, d, e, z).

Definition 1 ([38]). *Γ-protocol is a three-round public-coin protocol $\langle \mathcal{P}, \mathcal{V} \rangle$ for an $\mathcal{NP}$-relation $\mathcal{R}$ that proceeds as above. Besides, Γ-protocols should satisfy the following properties:*

- ***Completeness:*** *$\mathcal{V}$ always accepts if $\mathcal{P}$ and $\mathcal{V}$ follow the protocol.*
- ***Knowledge extraction:*** *Given two valid conversations (a, d, e, z) and (a, d', e', z') on any input x with $(d, e) \neq (d', e')$, one can recover the witness w such that $(x, w) \in \mathcal{R}$ in polynomial time with respect to an $\mathcal{NP}$-relation R_e, referred to as e-condition, that $R_e(d, d', e, e', z, z') = 1$. In particular, setting $d = d'$ implies that the protocol has the special soundness property*[1].
- ***Special honest verifier zero-knowledge (SHVZK):*** *There exists a probabilistic polynomial-time simulator $\mathcal{S}$, which takes as input x and outputs an accepting conversation (a', d', e', z'), with the same (or computationally indistinguishable) probability distribution as the conversation (a, d, e, z) of the real protocol.*

Γ-transformation can convey a Γ-protocol into a signature scheme. Different from Fiat-Shamir paradigm, Γ-transformation adapts two hash functions h_1, h_2 to compute $d = h_1(a)$ and $e = h_2(m)$, respectively. The verifier accepts if $d = h_1(a)$ and (a, d, e, z) is a valid conversation. To be precise, Γ-signatures are demonstrated as follows:

- **Key Generation**: The signer generates $x = F(w)$ such that $(x, w) \in \mathcal{R}$ where F is a one-way and polynomial-time computable function. The public key is x and the secret key is w.
- **Signature**: The signer randomly selects $r_P \in R_P$ and computes $a = f_a(r_P, x)$, where f_a is a polynomial-time computable function. Then, compute $d = h_1(a)$ where h_1 is a secure hash function. Given a message m, the signer computes $e = h_2(m)$, where h_2 is a secure hash function. From (w, a, d, e) the signer generates z, and finally outputs (a, d, z) as the signature[2].
- **Verification**: Given m, the verifier computes $e = h_2(m)$. The verifier accepts if $d = h_1(a)$ and (a, d, e, z) is a valid conversation, according to the polynomial-time computable verification procedure for the underlying Γ-protocol.

---

[1] The definition here is slightly different from that of [38]. They limit that the knowledge extracts when $\mathcal{R}_e(d, d', e, e') = 1$, where $\mathcal{R}_e$ is an $\mathcal{NP}$-condition. However, Γ-protocol only requires that the e-condition holds with overwhelming probability.

[2] In some specific signature schemes, such as Γ-signatures for DLP [38], the signature can be compressed by (d, z) since a can be computed according to (d, z).

2.2 SQIsignHD

SQIsignHD is a compact and post-quantum signature scheme introduced by Dartois, Leroux, Rebort and Wesolowski [11]. It is constructed from an identification protocol via Fiat-Shamir paradigm. Currently, there are two versions of SQIsignHD: FastSQIsignHD and RigorousSQIsignHD. We only focus on constructing a fast online signature scheme based on FastSQIsignHD for efficiency. The identification protocol underlying FastSQIsignHD proceeds as follows:

- **Setup**: Select a prime $p = c \cdot \ell^f \cdot \ell'^{f'} - 1$, where c is a small cofactor and $\ell^f \approx \ell'^{f'} \approx 2^\lambda$ with λ the security level. Define a supersingular elliptic curve E_0 whose endomorphism ring is known. Let g be an integer big enough but smaller than f.
- **Keygen**: The prover generates a random isogeny walk $\tau : E_0 \to E_A$ of degree $\ell'^\bullet \approx p$ and an equivalent isogeny $\tau' : E_0 \to E_A$ of degree $\ell^\bullet \approx p$. The public key is the elliptic curve E_A and the secret key is (τ, τ').
- **Commitment**: The prover generates a random (secret) isogeny walk $\psi : E_0 \to E_1$ of degree $\ell'^\bullet \approx p$. Afterwards, the prover sends E_1 to the verifier.
- **Challenge**: The verifier generates a random isogeny walk $\varphi : E_A \to E_2$ of degree $\ell'^{f'}$ and sends the description of φ to the prover.
- **Response**: From the knowledge of the secret key, the commitment and the challenge, the prover generates a new isogeny $\sigma : E_1 \to E_2$ of degree q such that q is ℓ^g-good, i.e., $\ell^g - q$ is a prime congruent to 1 modulo 4. Then the prover computes $\sigma(P_1)$ and $\sigma(Q_1)$ where $\{P_1, Q_1\}$ is the canonical basis of $E_1[\ell^f]$, and sends $(q, \sigma(P_1), \sigma(Q_1))$ to the verifier.
- **Verify**: the verifier generates the canonical basis $\{P_1, Q_1\}$ of $E_1[\ell^f]$. Then the verifier accepts if $(E_1, E_2, q, (P_1, Q_1), (\sigma(P_1), \sigma(Q_1)))$ correctly represents a q-isogeny σ from E_1 to E_2.

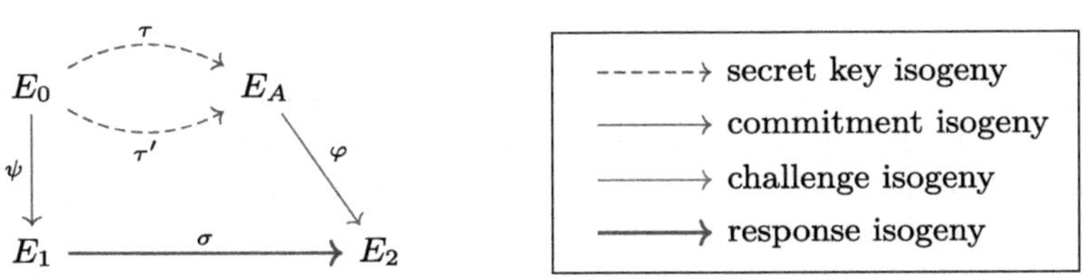

Fig. 2. A sketch of the SQIsignHD identification protocol

Compared with SQIsign, SQIsignHD avoids the complex ideal-to-isogeny translation. The main procedures are illustrated in Algorithm 1.

The following are the sub-algorithms applied in Algorithm 1:

- **IsogenyToIdeal**$(\ker(\varphi), \tau', I_{\tau'})$: Given the kernel of an isogeny φ: $E_A \to E_2$, an isogeny τ': $E_0 \to E_A$ of degree coprime to $\deg(\varphi)$ and the corresponding ideal $I_{\tau'} \subset \mathcal{O}$, outputs the ideal I_φ associated to φ;

Algorithm 1. FastRespond [11, Algorithm 2]

Require: The isogenies $\tau, \tau' : E_0 \rightarrow E_A$ of degree $\ell'^{\bullet}$ and $\ell^{\bullet}$ respectively, the ideals I_τ and $I_{\tau'}$ associated to τ and τ' respectively, the isogeny $\psi : E_0 \rightarrow E_1$ of degree $\ell'^{\bullet}$, the ideal I_ψ associated to ψ, the isogeny $\varphi : E_A \rightarrow E_2$ of degree $\ell'^{f'}$.

Ensure: $(\sigma(P_1), \sigma(Q_1), q)$ where (P_1, Q_1) is the canonically determined basis of $E_1[\ell^f]$ and $\sigma : E_1 \rightarrow E_2$ is an isogeny of ℓ^g-good degree q coprime to ℓ.

1: $I_\varphi \leftarrow$ **IsogenyToIdeal**$(\ker(\varphi), \tau', I_{\tau'})$, $J \leftarrow \overline{I_\psi} \cdot I_\tau \cdot I_\varphi$;
2: $I \leftarrow$ **RandomEquivalentIdeal**$_{\ell^g}(J)$ and compute the reduced norm q of I;
3: If q is not ℓ^g-good or $\gcd(q, \ell') \neq 1$, go back to Line 2;
4: Compute the canonical basis of $\{P_1, Q_1\}$ of $E_1[\ell^f]$;
5: $(\sigma(P_1), \sigma(Q_1)) \leftarrow$ **EvalTorsion**$_{\ell^f}(I, P_1, Q_1, \psi, \varphi \circ \tau, I_\psi, I_\tau \cdot I_\varphi)$;
6: **return** $(\sigma(P_1), \sigma(Q_1), q)$.

- **RandomEquivalentIdeal**$_{\ell^g}(J)$: Given an ideal J, outputs an equivalent ideal I that is uniformly random among ideals of norm $\leq \ell^g$;
- **EvalTorsion**$_{\ell^f}(I, P_1, Q_1, \rho_1, \rho_2, I_{\rho_1}, I_{\rho_2})$: Given an ideal I, a basis $\{P_1, Q_1\}$ of $E_1[\ell^f]$, and two isogenies $\rho_1 \colon E_0 \rightarrow E_1$ and $\rho_2 \colon E_0 \rightarrow E_2$ and the corresponding ideals I_{ρ_1}, I_{ρ_2}, outputs $\sigma(P_1)$ and $\sigma(Q_1)$, where σ is the isogeny associated to I.

In the response phase, the prover should evaluate the isogeny σ on the basis $\{P_1, Q_1\}$. Since the degree of σ is non-smooth in general, it is difficult to evaluate the isogeny directly with Vélu's formula [3,36]. However, note that the prover has the knowledge of the smooth degree isogenies from E_0 to E_1 and E_2, respectively, i.e., $\psi : E_0 \rightarrow E_1$ and $\varphi \circ \tau : E_0 \rightarrow E_2$. Furthermore, the endomorphism ring of E_0 is known. Assuming $\mathcal{O}\gamma = I_\psi \cdot I_\sigma \cdot \overline{I_\tau \cdot I_\varphi}$, it is easy to prove that

$$\sigma = \frac{\varphi \circ \tau \circ \gamma \circ \hat{\psi}}{[\deg(\varphi) \deg(\tau) \deg(\psi)]}. \tag{1}$$

Therefore, the prover can evaluate $\sigma(P_1)$ and $\sigma(Q_1)$ efficiently.

At first glance, the prover still has to evaluate several isogenies to generate the response. Fortunately, the current implementation of SQIsignHD applies a more elegant approach to eliminate almost all the isogeny computations. We provide a detailed review of the current implementation in Appendix C.

3 PIsignHD

In this section we propose the PIsignHD identification protocol, and the PIsignHD digital signature via Γ-transformation.

3.1 Identification Protocol

Let λ be a security parameter. The PIsignHD identification protocol goes as follows:

- **Setup**: Select a prime $p = c \cdot \ell^f \cdot \ell'^{f'} - 1$, where c is a small cofactor and $\ell^f \approx \ell'^{f'} \approx 2^\lambda$ with λ the security level. Define a supersingular elliptic curve E_0 whose endomorphism ring is known. Let g be an integer big enough but smaller than f.
- **Keygen**: The prover generates a random isogeny walk $\tau : E_0 \to E_A$ of degree $\ell'^\bullet \approx p$ and an equivalent isogeny $\tau' : E_0 \to E_A$ of degree $\ell^\bullet \approx p$. The public key is the elliptic curve E_A and the secret key is (τ, τ').
- **Commitment**: The prover generates a random isogeny walk $\psi : E_0 \to E_1$ of degree $\ell'^\bullet \approx p$ and an equivalent isogeny $\psi' : E_0 \to E_1$ of degree $\ell^\bullet \approx p$, and then selects a random cyclic isogeny walk $\varphi_{com} : E_1 \to E_2$ of degree $\ell'^{f'}$. Afterwards, the prover sends E_1 and the description of φ_{com} to the verifier.
- **Challenge**: The verifier generates a random isogeny walk $\varphi_{chl} : E_A \to E_3$ of degree $\ell'^{f'}$ and sends the description of φ_{chl} to the prover.
- **Response**: From the knowledge of the secret key, the commitment and the challenge, the prover generates a new isogeny $\sigma : E_2 \to E_3$ of degree q such that q is ℓ^g-good and coprime to ℓ', and computes $\sigma(P_2)$ and $\sigma(Q_2)$ where $\{P_2, Q_2\}$ is the canonical basis of $E_2[\ell^f]$. Then the prover sends $R = (q, \sigma(P_2), \sigma(Q_2))$ to the verifier.
- **Verify**: the verifier generates the canonical basis $\{P_2, Q_2\}$ of $E_2[\ell^f]$. Then the verifier accepts if $(E_2, E_3, q, (P_2, Q_2), (\sigma(P_2), \sigma(Q_2)))$ correctly represents a q-isogeny σ from E_2 to E_3.

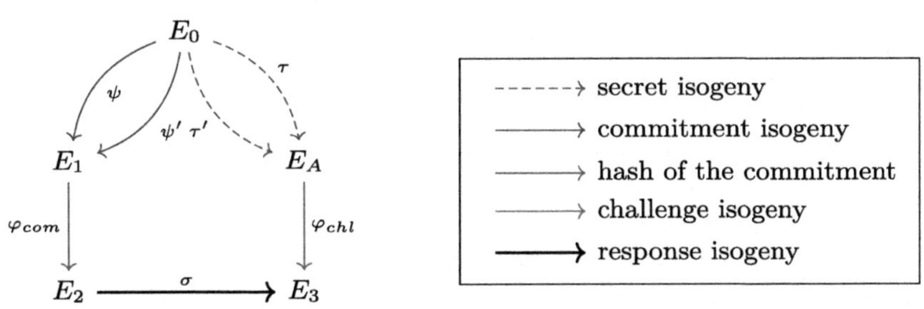

Fig. 3. A sketch of PIsignHD

The completeness property of our Γ-protocol is obvious. The security proofs of the knowledge extraction property and the zero-knowledge property are left in Sect. 4.

3.2 Digital Signature

Via Γ-transformation, PIsignHD is derived by the identification protocol in Sect. 3.1. The setup and the key generation phases are identical to those of the identification protocol. The signature and the verification proceed as follows:

- **Sign**: $(\text{sk}, m) \to \Sigma$ Pick a random (secret) isogeny $\psi : E_0 \to E_1$ of degree $\ell'^{\bullet} \approx p$ and an equivalent isogeny $\psi' : E_0 \to E_1$ of degree $\ell^{\bullet} \approx p$. Then, construct the cyclic isogeny $\varphi_{com} : E_1 \to E_2$ with respect to the hash of E_1. From the hash of m, construct the isogeny $\varphi_{chl} : E_A \to E_3$. Finally, generate a new isogeny $\sigma : E_2 \to E_3$ and compute the corresponding pairs $R = (\sigma(P_2), \sigma(Q_2), q)$ with $\{P_2, Q_2\}$ the canonical basis of $E_2[\ell^f]$ and q coprime to ℓ'. The signature is (E_1, R).
- **Verify**: $(\text{pk}, m, \Sigma) \to$ True or False Parse Σ as (E_1, R), where $R = (\sigma(P_2), \sigma(Q_2), q)$. Firstly, compute the isogeny $\varphi_{com} : E_1 \to E_2$ which is hashed from the knowledge of E_1. From the message m, construct the isogeny $\varphi_{chl} : E_A \to E_3$. Generate the determined canonical basis $\{P_2, Q_2\}$ of $E_2[\ell^f]$, and accept if $(E_2, E_3, q, (P_2, Q_2), (\sigma(P_2), \sigma(Q_2)))$ correctly represents a q-isogeny $\sigma : E_2 \to E_3$.

In the signing and verifying procedures, the isogenies φ_{com} and φ_{chl} are generated by hashing. To achieve this, we first define a secure hash function $\mathcal{H} : \{0,1\}^* \to [1, \mu]$, where $\mu = \ell'^{f'-1}(\ell' + 1)$. Same as SQIsign and SQIsignHD, we use the secure hash function $\mathcal{H}'$ defined in [16, Section 3.1], which is derived from [8]. Taking a supersingular curve E and an integer as inputs, the hash function $\mathcal{H}'$ outputs a cyclic $\ell'^{f'}$-isogeny with domain E. In practice, we set $\varphi_{com} = \mathcal{H}'(E_1, \mathcal{H}(j(E_1)))$ and $\varphi_{chl} = \mathcal{H}'(E_A, \mathcal{H}(m))$.

4 Security Proof

In this section we present the security proofs of PIsignHD. The proof of the completeness property is omitted as it is obvious. In the following, we focus on the proofs of the knowledge extraction property and the zero-knowledge property. The knowledge extraction proof is similar to the special soundness proof of the SQIsignHD identification protocol, but we need to prove that the e-condition holds with overwhelming probability as well. Several lemmas will be proposed to adequately illustrate this issue. The zero-knowledge proof parallels that of the SQIsignHD identification protocol, particularly we use the same oracle (Definition 2) to construct the simulator.

4.1 Knowledge Extraction

Recall the knowledge extraction property of Γ-protocols: Given two pairs of valid conversations (a, d, e, z) and (a, d', e', z') on any input x with $(d, e) \neq (d', e')$, one can recover the witness w such that $(x, w) \in \mathcal{R}$ in polynomial time with respect to an $\mathcal{NP}$-relation $\mathcal{R}_e$, referred to as the e-condition, that $\mathcal{R}_e(d, d', e, e', z, z') = 1$.

In the PIsignHD identification protocol, the commitment is E_1, while φ_{com} is a random isogeny starting from E_1. The challenge corresponds to $\varphi_{chl} : E_A \to E_3$, and the response is of form $R = (q, \sigma(P_2), \sigma(Q_2))$, where q is the degree of the response isogeny $\sigma : E_2 \to E_3$ and $(\sigma(P_2), \sigma(Q_2))$ are the images of the torsion basis $\{P_2, Q_2\}$ of $E_2[\ell^f]$ by σ. The hard problem underlying the knowledge extraction property is known as *Supersingular Endomorphism Problem*:

Problem 1 (Supersingular Endomorphism Problem). Given a prime p and a supersingular elliptic curve E over $\mathbb{F}_{p^2}$, find a non-trivial endomorphism of E that can be efficiently evaluated.

When φ_{com_1} and φ_{com_2} in the two pairs of valid conversations $(E_1, \varphi_{com_1}, \varphi_{chl_1}, R_1)$ and $(E_1, \varphi_{com_2}, \varphi_{chl_2}, R_2)$ are equivalent, the knowledge extraction property is reduced to the special soundness property. In this situation, the proof is almost consistent with the special soundness proofs of the SQIsignHD identification protocol. Similarly, it is easy to prove the knowledge extraction property when the challenges of the valid conversations are equivalent. When $\varphi_{com_1} \neq \varphi_{com_2}$ and $\varphi_{chl_1} \neq \varphi_{chl_2}$, one can also extract the knowledge under the e-condition that: $\mathcal{R}_e(\varphi_{com_1}, \varphi_{com_2}, \varphi_{chl_1}, \varphi_{chl_2}, \sigma_1, \sigma_2) = 1$ iff there does not exist $s \in \mathbb{Z}$ such that $[s] = \hat{\varphi}_{chl_2} \circ \sigma_2 \circ \varphi_{com_2} \circ \hat{\varphi}_{com_1} \circ \hat{\sigma}_1 \circ \varphi_{chl_1}$.

Proposition 1. *Let $(E_1, \varphi_{com_1}, \varphi_{chl_1}, R_1)$ and $(E_1, \varphi_{com_2}, \varphi_{chl_2}, R_2)$ be two pairs of accepting conversations, where $R_1 = (q_1, \sigma_1(P_2), \sigma_1(Q_2))$ and $R_2 = (q_2, \sigma_2(P_2'), \sigma_2(Q_2'))$ with $\langle P_2, Q_2 \rangle = E_2[\ell^f]$ and $\langle P_2', Q_2' \rangle = E_2'[\ell^f]$. If $(\varphi_{com_1}, \varphi_{chl_1}) \neq (\varphi_{com_2}, \varphi_{chl_2})$, then one can compute a non-trivial endomorphism of E_A that can be efficiently evaluated with respect to the e-condition that: $\mathcal{R}_e(\varphi_{com_1}, \varphi_{com_2}, \varphi_{chl_1}, \varphi_{chl_2}, \sigma_1, \sigma_2) = 1$ iff there does not exist $s \in \mathbb{Z}$ such that $[s] = \hat{\varphi}_{chl_2} \circ \sigma_2 \circ \varphi_{com_2} \circ \hat{\varphi}_{com_1} \circ \hat{\sigma}_1 \circ \varphi_{chl_1}$. If $\varphi_{com_1} = \varphi_{com_2}$ or $\varphi_{chl_1} = \varphi_{chl_2}$, then the e-condition always holds. Especially, the PIsignHD identification protocol has the special soundness property.*

Proof. Since the two conversations are valid, one can obtain the knowledge of the response isogenies $\sigma_1 : E_2 \to E_3$ and $\sigma_2 : E_2' \to E_3'$. Note that $\varphi_{com_1} : E_1 \to E_2$, $\varphi_{com_2} : E_1 \to E_2'$, $\varphi_{chl_1} : E_A \to E_3$ and $\varphi_{chl_2} : E_A \to E_3'$ are known. As illustrated in Fig. 4, $\alpha = \hat{\varphi}_{chl_2} \circ \sigma_2 \circ \varphi_{com_2} \circ \hat{\varphi}_{com_1} \circ \hat{\sigma}_1 \circ \varphi_{chl_1}$ is an endomorphism of E_A that can be efficiently evaluated.

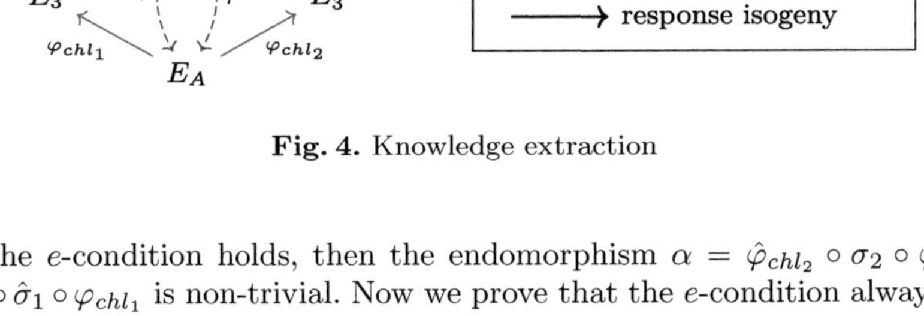

Fig. 4. Knowledge extraction

If the e-condition holds, then the endomorphism $\alpha = \hat{\varphi}_{chl_2} \circ \sigma_2 \circ \varphi_{com_2} \circ \hat{\varphi}_{com_1} \circ \hat{\sigma}_1 \circ \varphi_{chl_1}$ is non-trivial. Now we prove that the e-condition always holds if $\varphi_{com_1} = \varphi_{com_2}$ or $\varphi_{chl_1} = \varphi_{chl_2}$.

We first prove the endomorphism α is non-trivial if $\varphi_{com_1} = \varphi_{com_2}$. In this case $\alpha = [\ell'^{f'}]\hat{\varphi}_{chl_2} \circ \sigma_2 \circ \hat{\sigma}_1 \circ \varphi_{chl_1}$. Suppose for contradiction that $\alpha' = \hat{\varphi}_{chl_2} \circ \sigma_2 \circ \hat{\sigma}_1 \circ \varphi_{chl_1} = [s]$ with $s \in \mathbb{Z}$. Therefore, we have $q_1 q_2 \ell'^{2f'} = s^2$. Then

$$[\ell'^{f'} q_2] \circ \hat{\sigma}_1 \circ \varphi_{chl_1} = \hat{\sigma}_2 \circ \varphi_{chl_2} \circ \alpha' = [s] \circ \hat{\sigma}_2 \circ \varphi_{chl_2}.$$

Let $s = \ell'^{f'} \cdot s'$ with s' coprime to ℓ'. Then we have $[q_2] \circ \hat{\sigma}_1 \circ \varphi_{chl_1} = [s'] \circ \hat{\sigma}_2 \circ \varphi_{chl_2}$. Since q_1, q_2 and s' are coprime to ℓ', it follows that $\ker(\varphi_{chl_1}) = \ker(\varphi_{chl_2})$. This contradicts the fact that $(\varphi_{com_1}, \varphi_{chl_1}) \neq (\varphi_{com_2}, \varphi_{chl_2})$ and $\varphi_{com_1} = \varphi_{com_2}$. Therefore, the e-condition holds and the PIsignHD identification protocols has the special soundness property.

Assume that $\varphi_{chl_1} = \varphi_{chl_2}$. We would like to prove that α is also non-trivial. Clearly, the endomorphism $\beta = \hat{\varphi}_{com_2} \circ \hat{\sigma}_2 \circ \varphi_{chl_2} \circ \hat{\varphi}_{chl_1} \circ \sigma_1 \circ \varphi_{com_1} = [\ell'^{f'}]\hat{\varphi}_{com_2} \circ \hat{\sigma}_2 \circ \sigma_1 \circ \varphi_{com_1}$ of E_1 is trivial iff α is trivial. Suppose that β is trivial. Similar to the previous proof, one can deduce that $\ker(\varphi_{com_1}) = \ker(\varphi_{com_2})$. This is a contradiction because $(\varphi_{com_1}, \varphi_{chl_1}) \neq (\varphi_{com_2}, \varphi_{chl_2})$ and $\varphi_{chl_1} = \varphi_{chl_2}$. Therefore, when $\varphi_{chl_1} = \varphi_{chl_2}$ the endomorphism β must be non-trivial, i.e., the endomorphism α is non-trivial, which completes the proof. □

It remains to prove the e-condition holds with overwhelming probability, i.e.,

$$\Pr\left[\mathcal{R}_e(\varphi_{com_1}, \varphi_{com_2}, \varphi_{chl_1}, \varphi_{chl_2}, \sigma_1, \sigma_2) = 0\right] \leq \mathrm{negl}(\lambda),$$

where $\mathrm{negl}(\cdot)$ is a negligible function. This confirms that even if $\varphi_{com_1} \neq \varphi_{com_2}$ and $\varphi_{chl_1} \neq \varphi_{chl_2}$ (which is the common scenario in practice), the secret key can be extracted with overwhelming probability once the prover adapts the same commitment. In the following, we present Proposition 2 to tackle this problem. To prove Proposition 2, we first propose Lemmas 1, 2 and 3.

Lemma 1. *Let $\Phi_1 = [\ell'^{t_1}]\Phi'_1$, $\Phi_2 = [\ell'^{t_2}]\Phi'_2$ be two isogenies of degree $(\ell')^{2f'}$, where $\Phi'_1 : E_1 \to E_2$ and $\Phi'_2 : E_3 \to E_4$ are cyclic. Assume that $\sigma : E_2 \to E_3$ and $\sigma' : E_4 \to E_1$ are a q_1-isogeny and a q_2-isogeny with $\gcd(q_1, \ell') = 1$ and $\gcd(q_2, \ell') = 1$, respectively. If $\sigma' \circ \Phi_2 \circ \sigma \circ \Phi_1$ is a trivial endomorphism of E_1, i.e., there exists $s \in \mathbb{Z}$ such that $[s] = \sigma' \circ \Phi_2 \circ \sigma \circ \Phi_1$, then*

- *$t_1 = t_2$;*

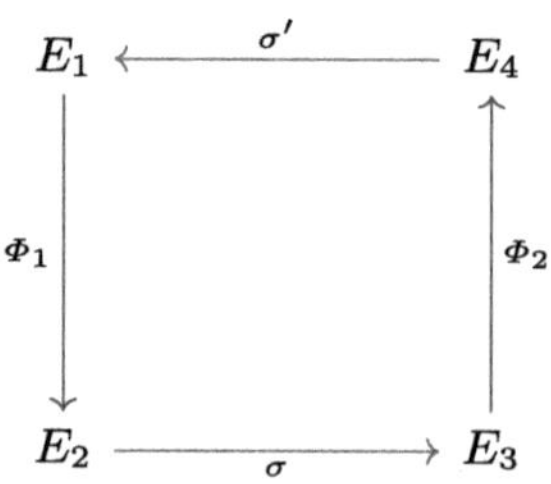

Fig. 5. A sketch of Lemma 1

– $[\sigma]_*\widehat{\Phi'_1} = \Phi'_2$, $[\sigma']_*\widehat{\Phi'_2} = \Phi'_1$;

Proof. From $\Phi_1 = [\ell'^{t_1}]\Phi'_1$, $\Phi_2 = [\ell'^{t_2}]\Phi'_2$, we have

$$[(\ell')^{2f'-t_1-t_2}s'] = \sigma' \circ \Phi'_2 \circ \sigma \circ \Phi'_1$$

for some $s' = \sqrt{q_1 q_2} \in \mathbb{Z}$ which is coprime to ℓ'.

We first prove $t_1 = t_2$. Without loss of generality, assume that $t_1 < t_2$. Since Φ'_1 is cyclic, suppose that $\ker(\Phi'_1) = \langle P \rangle$ where $P \in E_1[(\ell')^{2f'-2t_1}]$. Then, the endomorphism $[(\ell')^{2f'-t_1-t_2}s'] = \sigma' \circ \Phi'_2 \circ \sigma \circ \Phi'_1$ sends P to the point at infinity. It implies that $2f' - t_1 - t_2 \geq 2f' - 2t_1$, i.e., $t_1 \geq t_2$, which is a contradiction.

Now we prove the second claim. Suppose that $Q \in E_1[(\ell')^{2f'-2t_1}]$ such that $\langle P, Q \rangle = E_1[(\ell')^{2f'-2t_1}]$. Then $\ker(\widehat{\Phi'_1}) = \langle \Phi'_1(Q) \rangle$. From $t_1 = t_2$, we have $[(\ell')^{2f'-2t_1}s'] = \sigma' \circ \Phi'_2 \circ \sigma \circ \Phi'_1$ and thus $\sigma' \circ \Phi'_2 \circ \sigma \circ \Phi'_1(Q) = \infty_{E_1}$, i.e., $\ker(\widehat{\Phi'_1}) \subset \ker(\sigma' \circ \Phi'_2 \circ \sigma)$. Since σ and σ' have degrees coprime to ℓ', $\sigma(\ker(\widehat{\Phi'_1})) \subset \ker(\Phi'_2)$. It follows from $t_1 = t_2$ that $|\ker(\Phi'_2)| = |\sigma(\ker(\widehat{\Phi'_1}))|$. Therefore, $\ker(\Phi'_2) = \sigma(\ker(\widehat{\Phi'_1}))$, i.e., $[\sigma]_*\widehat{\Phi'_1} = \Phi'_2$. Analogously, one can imply the other deduction. This ends the proof. □

Remark 2. Lemma 1 shows that if the e-condition does not hold, then $\varphi_{chl_2} \circ \hat{\varphi}_{chl_1}$ is the pushforward isogeny of $\varphi_{com_2} \circ \hat{\varphi}_{com_1}$ through σ_1. Conversely, from $[\sigma_1]_*(\varphi_{com_2} \circ \hat{\varphi}_{com_1}) = \varphi_{chl_2} \circ \hat{\varphi}_{chl_1}$. we cannot deduce that the endomorphism $\alpha = \hat{\varphi}_{chl_2} \circ \sigma_2 \circ \varphi_{com_2} \circ \hat{\varphi}_{com_1} \circ \hat{\sigma}_1 \circ \varphi_{chl_1}$ is trivial. For example, if $q_1 = \deg(\sigma_1)$ and $q_2 = \deg(\sigma_2)$ are coprime, then in the proof of Lemma 1 the value $s' = \sqrt{q_1 q_2} \notin \mathbb{Z}$. In this case the e-condition always holds. Therefore, the probability that the e-condition does not hold is less than that of $[\sigma_1]_*(\varphi_{com_2} \circ \hat{\varphi}_{com_1}) = \varphi_{chl_2} \circ \hat{\varphi}_{chl_1}$.

Lemma 2. *Let ρ_1, ρ_2, ρ_3, ρ_4 be cyclic $\ell'^{f'}$-isogenies chosen uniformly at random, $\Phi_1 = \rho_2 \circ \rho_1$ and $\Phi_2 = \rho_4 \circ \rho_3$. If σ is a q-isogeny such that $\gcd(q, \ell') = 1$, then $Pr[[\sigma]_*\Phi_1 = \Phi_2] < (f'+1)(\ell')^{-2f'}$.*

Proof. Suppose that $\Phi_1 = \rho_2 \circ \rho_1 = [\ell^{t_1}]\Phi'_1$ and $\Phi_2 = \rho_4 \circ \rho_3 = [\ell^{t_2}]\Phi'_2$ with Φ'_1 and Φ'_2 cyclic. To satisfy $[\sigma]_*\Phi_1 = \Phi_2$, we have $t_1 = t_2$ and $\sigma(\ker(\Phi'_1)) = \ker(\Phi'_2)$. Since ρ_1, ρ_2, ρ_3, ρ_4 are chosen uniformly at random,

$$\Pr[t_i = u] = \begin{cases} \dfrac{\ell'}{\ell'+1}, \text{if } u = 0, \\ \dfrac{\ell'-1}{(\ell'+1)(\ell')^u}, \text{if } 0 < u < f', \\ \dfrac{(\ell')^{1-f'}}{\ell'+1}, \text{if } u = f'. \end{cases}$$

where $i = 1, 2$. On the other hand, we have

$$\Pr[[\sigma]_*\Phi'_1 = \Phi'_2 | t_1 = t_2 = u] = \begin{cases} \dfrac{(\ell')^{-2f'+2u+1}}{\ell'+1}, \text{if } 0 \leq u < f', \\ 1, \text{if } u = f'. \end{cases}$$

Therefore, the probability that $[\sigma]_*\Phi_1 = \Phi_2$ is

$$\begin{aligned}
\Pr[[\sigma]_*\Phi_1 = \Phi_2] =& \Sigma_{u=0}^{f'} \Pr[t_1 = u] \cdot \Pr[t_2 = u] \cdot \Pr\left[[\sigma]_*\Phi_1' = \Phi_2' \middle| t_1 = t_2 = u\right] \\
=& \Sigma_{u=0}^{f'} \Pr[t_1 = u]^2 \cdot \Pr\left[[\sigma]_*\Phi_1' = \Phi_2' \middle| t_1 = t_2 = u\right] \\
=& \frac{(\ell')^{-2f'+3}}{(\ell'+1)^3} + \Sigma_{u=1}^{f'-1} \frac{(\ell'-1)^2(\ell')^{-2f'+1}}{(\ell'+1)^3} + \frac{(\ell')^{-2f'+2}}{(\ell'+1)^2} \\
<& (\ell')^{-2f'} + (f'-1)(\ell')^{-2f'} + (\ell')^{-2f'} \\
=& (f'+1)(\ell')^{-2f'},
\end{aligned}$$

which completes the proof. □

Lemma 3. *Let P_1 and P_2 be points of order $\ell'^{f'}$ defined on E_1 and E_2, respectively. Assume that E_1, E_2 are supersingular and $\sigma' : E_1 \to E_2$ is an isogeny whose degree is coprime to ℓ'. If the endomorphism ring of E_2 is known, then one can generate an endomorphism ω of E_2 such that $\omega \circ \sigma'(P_1) = P_2$ in polynomial time.*

Proof. Let $\mathrm{End}(E_2)$ be the endomorphism ring of E_2. Suppose that $\{\theta_1, \theta_2, \theta_3, \theta_4\}$ is a basis of $\mathrm{End}(E_2)$ that can be evaluated at any point of E_2 in polynomial time. Since $\mathrm{End}(E_2) \otimes \mathbb{Z}/\ell'^{f'}\mathbb{Z}$ is isomorphic to $\mathbb{M}_2(\mathbb{Z}/\ell'^{f'}\mathbb{Z})$, there exist two endomorphisms in the basis $\{\theta_1, \theta_2, \theta_3, \theta_4\}$, mapping $\sigma'(P_1)$ to points that are linearly independent. For simplicity we assume that $\langle \theta_1(\sigma'(P_1)), \theta_2(\sigma'(P_1)) \rangle = E_2[\ell'^{f'}]$. This implies the existence of coefficients $s_1, s_2 \in \mathbb{Z}/\ell'^{f'}\mathbb{Z}$ satisfying that

$$P_2 = [s_1]\theta_1(\sigma'(P_1)) + [s_2]\theta_2(\sigma'(P_1)).$$

Let $\omega = s_1\theta_1 + s_2\theta_2$. Then $\omega \circ \sigma' : E_1 \to E_2$ is the desired isogeny that sends P_1 to P_2. □

Proposition 2. *Any prover $\mathcal{P}(\tau, c)$ (where τ is the secret key and c is the random coin) that can correctly execute the PIsignHD identification protocol and interact with the verifier ensures the knowledge extraction of the protocol.*

Proof. From Proposition 1, we only need to prove that the e-condition holds with overwhelming probability. Suppose that $\mathcal{P}(\tau, c)$ can break the e-condition with non-negligible probability for contradiction. Consider Algorithm 2 as follows:

Algorithm 2. Interaction

Require: The prover $\mathcal{P}(\tau; c)$ that correctly executes the PIsignHD identification protocol.

Ensure: Uniformly randomly selected $\ell'^{f'}$-isogenies $\hat{\phi}_1, \phi_2, \hat{\varphi}_1, \varphi_2$, and q-isogenies σ connecting the initial curves of $\hat{\phi}_1$ and $\hat{\varphi}_1$ such that $\gcd(q, \ell') = 1$.

1: Initialize a random coin c and a verifier $\mathcal{V}$ that correctly executes the PIsignHD identification protocol, and select a private key τ;

2: Run $\mathcal{P}(\tau; c)$ in interaction with $\mathcal{V}$, and record $(\psi, \phi_1, \varphi_1, \sigma_1)$;

3: Adjust the random coin to obtain c' such that $\mathcal{P}(\tau; c')$ uses the same commitment isogeny as $\mathcal{P}(\tau; c)$;

4: Run $\mathcal{P}(\tau; c')$ in interaction with $\mathcal{V}$, and record $(\psi, \phi_2, \varphi_2, \sigma_2)$;

5: **return** $(\hat{\phi}_1, \phi_2, \hat{\varphi}_1, \varphi_2, \sigma_1, \sigma_2)$.

From the assumption, the endomorphism $\alpha = \hat{\varphi}_{chl_2} \circ \sigma_2 \circ \varphi_{com_2} \circ \hat{\varphi}_{com_1} \circ \hat{\sigma}_1 \circ \varphi_{chl_1}$ is trivial with non-negligible probability. This deduces that $\Pr[[\sigma_1]_*(\phi_2 \circ \hat{\phi}_1) = \varphi_2 \circ \hat{\varphi}_1]$ is also non-negligible.

Take an honest prover as input in Algorithm 2. From Lemmas 1 and 2, we know that $\Pr[[\sigma_1]_*(\phi_2 \circ \hat{\phi}_1) = \varphi_2 \circ \hat{\varphi}_1] < (f' + 1)(\ell'^{-2f}) \approx 2^{-2\lambda}$, where ϕ_1, ϕ_2, φ_1 and φ_2 are chosen uniformly at random. This is a contradiction, as $\Pr[[\sigma_1]_*(\phi_2 \circ \hat{\phi}_1) = \varphi_2 \circ \hat{\varphi}_1]$ is non-negligible.

Take a malicious prover as input in Algorithm 2. Same as above, the malicious prover has to ensure $[\sigma_1]_*(\phi_2 \circ \hat{\phi}_1) = \varphi_2 \circ \hat{\varphi}_1$. Note that $[\sigma_1]_*(\hat{\phi}_1) = \hat{\varphi}_1$ is a necessary condition for $[\sigma_1]_*(\phi_2 \circ \hat{\phi}_1) = \varphi_2 \circ \hat{\varphi}_1$. Adapting Lemma 3, ensuring $[\sigma_1]_*(\hat{\phi}_1) = \hat{\varphi}_1$ is easy for the prover. However, since φ_2 and ϕ_2 are chosen uniformly at random after σ_1 is generated,

$$\Pr\left[[\sigma_1]_*(\phi_2 \circ \hat{\phi}_1) = \varphi_2 \circ \hat{\varphi}_1 \mid [\sigma_1]_*(\hat{\phi}_1) = \hat{\varphi}_1\right] = (\ell' + 1)^{-1}(\ell')^{-f'+1} \approx 2^{-\lambda},$$

which is still negligible. This contradicts with the assumption. □

4.2 Zero Knowledge

Same as the security proof for the SQIsignHD identification protocol, we use the following oracle to prove the PIsignHD identification protocol is special honest verifier zero-knowledge.

Definition 2 ([11, Definition 20]). *A random uniform good degree isogeny oracle (RUGDIO) is an oracle taking as input a supersingular curve $E/\mathbb{F}_{p^2}$ and returning an efficient representation $(\sigma(P_1), \sigma(Q_1), q)$ of a random isogeny $\sigma : E \to E'$, where $\{P_1, Q_1\}$ is a canonical basis of $E[\ell^f]$ and q is the degree of σ which is ℓ^g-good and coprime to ℓ'. Besides, the RUGDIO model satisfies that*

- *The distribution of E' is uniform in the supersingular isogeny graph.*
- *The conditional distribution of σ given E is uniform among isogenies from E to E' of ℓ^g-good degree coprime to ℓ'.*

With the help of the RUGDIO model, one can generate an efficient representation of an isogeny starting from a given supersingular elliptic curve E_1, whose degree is ℓ^g-good degree coprime to ℓ'. It has been argued in [11, Section 5.3] that access to the oracle does not offer any advantage in reducing the hardness of *Supersingular Endomorphism Ring Problem* (Problem 2), which can be reduced to *Supersingular Endomorphism Problem* (Problem 1) [18,30]. Same as the SQIsignHD identification protocol, we also have a heuristic assumption on the distribution of the commitment E_1.

Problem 2 (Supersingular Endomorphism Ring Problem). Given a prime p and a supersingular elliptic curve E defined over $\mathbb{F}_{p^2}$, find four endomorphisms of E that can be efficiently evaluated, to form a basis of the endomorphism ring of E.

Proposition 3. *Assume that the commitment E_1 is computationally indistinguishable from an elliptic curve chosen uniformly at random in the supersingular isogeny graph. Then the PIsignHD identification protocol is special honest verifier zero-knowledge in the RUGDIO model. In other words, there exists a simulator $\mathcal{S}$ with access to RUGDIO, satisfying that the distribution of the accepting conversation generated by $\mathcal{S}$ is computationally indistinguishable from the conversation of the PIsignHD identification protocol.*

Proof. We proceed similarly as the zero-knowledge proof of SQIsignHD [11, Theorem 21]. The simulator $\mathcal{S}$ is constructed as follows: Firstly, the simulator $\mathcal{S}$ selects an $\ell'^{f'}$-isogeny $\varphi'_{chl} : E_A \to E'_3$ uniformly at random. After that, the simulator adapts the RUGDIO model to generate an efficient representation R' of $\hat{\sigma'}$ from E'_3 to E'_2, which is also an efficient representation of σ from E'_2 to E'_3. Finally, the simulator $\mathcal{S}$ generates an $\ell'^{f'}$-isogeny $\hat{\varphi}'_{com} : E'_2 \to E'_1$ uniformly at random. The conversation of $\mathcal{S}$ is of form $(E'_1, \varphi'_{com}, R', \varphi'_{chl})$.

Assuming that the conversation of the PIsignHD identification protocol is of form $(E_1, \varphi_{com}, R, \varphi_{chl})$, we aim to prove that the distribution of $(E'_1, \varphi'_{com}, R', \varphi'_{chl})$ is computationally indistinguishable from that of $(E_1, \varphi_{com}, R, \varphi_{chl})$. Applying the RUGDIO model, the curve E'_2 is chosen uniformly at random in the supersingular isogeny graph. Since the isogeny $\hat{\varphi}'_{com} : E'_2 \to E'_1$ is also chosen uniformly at random, it follows that E'_1 is computationally indistinguishable from an elliptic curve chosen uniformly at random in the supersingular isogeny graph. Therefore, E_1 and E'_1 have the same distribution. Furthermore, the isogenies φ_{com} and φ'_{com} start from elliptic curves chosen uniformly at random in the supersingular isogeny graph and they are chosen uniformly at random, thus φ_{com} and φ'_{com} have the same distribution. Since $\varphi_{chl} : E_A \to E_3$ and $\varphi'_{chl} : E_A \to E'_3$ are chosen uniformly at random, thus they are indistinguishable.

Now we prove the efficient representations of σ and σ' are indistinguishable. From the second property of the RUGDIO model, the conditional distribution of $\hat{\sigma'}$ given E'_3 is uniform among isogeny from E'_3 to E'_2, i.e., the conditional distribution of σ' given E'_2 is uniform among isogeny from E'_2 to E'_3. From [11, Section 4.2], σ has the same distribution conditionally to E_2 and E_3. Notably, E_2,

E_2', E_3, E_3' are computationally indistinguishable from an elliptic curve chosen uniformly at random in the supersingular isogeny graph. This ends the proof. □

5 Implementation and Comparison

In this section, we show how to further reduce the signature size of PIsignHD thanks to the public storage (or the storage of the verifier's size). Besides, we explore how to implement PIsignHD with fast online signing via offline computations, and report the online/offline signature performance results of PIsignHD. Comparisons between SQIsignHD and PIsignHD are also discussed in detail.

5.1 Signature Compactness

Recall that the signature of PIsignHD is of the form (E_1, R) where $R = (\sigma(P_2), \sigma(Q_2), q)$: the domain E_1 of the isogeny φ_{com}, the evaluation on the canonical basis $\{P_2, Q_2\}$ of $E_2[\ell^f]$ through σ and the degree of σ. The size is the same as that of SQIsignHD.

Indeed, the signer can also transmit $(E_2, R, \ker(\hat{\varphi}_{com}))$ as the signature: the codomain E_2 of the isogeny φ_{com}, the evaluation on the canonical basis $\{P_2, Q_2\}$ of $E_2[\ell^f]$ through σ, the degree of σ and the kernel of $\hat{\varphi}_{com}$. In this scenario, the signature involves the additional information $\ker(\hat{\varphi}_{com})$. Therefore, the signature size is larger than that of SQIsignHD. In the following, we show how to compress $(E_2, R, \ker(\hat{\varphi}_{com}))$, making it more compact than the SQIsignHD signature.

Similar to SQIsignHD, one can also compress the torsion basis information utilizing the technique in Appendix C. Let $\{P_0, Q_0\}$, $\{P_1, Q_1\}$, $\{P_2, Q_2\}$ and $\{P_A, Q_A\}$ be the canonical bases of $E_0[\ell^f]$, $E_1[\ell^f]$, $E_2[\ell^f]$ and $E_A[\ell^f]$, respectively. Assume that

$$\begin{pmatrix} P_A \\ Q_A \end{pmatrix} = M_\tau \begin{pmatrix} \tau(P_0) \\ \tau(Q_0) \end{pmatrix}, \qquad \hat{\gamma} \begin{pmatrix} P_0 \\ Q_0 \end{pmatrix} = M_{\hat{\gamma}} \begin{pmatrix} P_0 \\ Q_0 \end{pmatrix},$$
$$\psi \begin{pmatrix} P_0 \\ Q_0 \end{pmatrix} = M_\psi \begin{pmatrix} P_1 \\ Q_1 \end{pmatrix}, \qquad \varphi_{com} \begin{pmatrix} P_1 \\ Q_1 \end{pmatrix} = M_{\varphi_{com}} \begin{pmatrix} P_2 \\ Q_2 \end{pmatrix}. \tag{2}$$

where $M_\tau, M_{\hat{\gamma}}, M_\psi, M_{\varphi_{com}} \in \mathbb{M}_2(\mathbb{Z}/\ell^f\mathbb{Z})$. Note that

$$\sigma = \frac{\varphi_{chl} \circ \tau \circ \gamma \circ \hat{\psi} \circ \hat{\varphi}_{com}}{[\deg(\varphi_{chl}) \deg(\tau) \deg(\psi) \deg(\varphi_{com})]}.$$

Then

$$\hat{\sigma} \circ \varphi_{chl} \circ \tau \begin{pmatrix} P_0 \\ Q_0 \end{pmatrix} = \frac{\varphi_{com} \circ \psi \circ \hat{\gamma} \circ \hat{\tau} \circ \hat{\varphi}_{chl} \circ \varphi_{chl} \circ \tau}{[\deg(\varphi_{chl}) \deg(\tau) \deg(\psi) \deg(\varphi_{com})]} \begin{pmatrix} P_0 \\ Q_0 \end{pmatrix}$$
$$= \frac{\varphi_{com} \circ \psi \circ \hat{\gamma}}{[\deg(\psi) \deg(\varphi_{com})]} \begin{pmatrix} P_0 \\ Q_0 \end{pmatrix}.$$

It follows from $\hat{\gamma}\begin{pmatrix} P_0 \\ Q_0 \end{pmatrix} = M_{\hat{\gamma}}\begin{pmatrix} P_0 \\ Q_0 \end{pmatrix}$ that

$$\hat{\sigma} \circ \varphi_{chl} \circ \tau \begin{pmatrix} P_0 \\ Q_0 \end{pmatrix} = \frac{M_{\hat{\gamma}}}{[\deg(\psi)\deg(\varphi_{com})]} \cdot \varphi_{com} \circ \psi \begin{pmatrix} P_0 \\ Q_0 \end{pmatrix}.$$

Further, from $\psi\begin{pmatrix} P_0 \\ Q_0 \end{pmatrix} = M_{\psi}\begin{pmatrix} P_1 \\ Q_1 \end{pmatrix}$ and $\varphi_{com}\begin{pmatrix} P_1 \\ Q_1 \end{pmatrix} = M_{\varphi_{com}}\begin{pmatrix} P_2 \\ Q_2 \end{pmatrix}$,

$$\hat{\sigma} \circ \varphi_{chl} \circ \tau \begin{pmatrix} P_0 \\ Q_0 \end{pmatrix} = \frac{M_{\hat{\gamma}} \cdot M_{\psi}}{[\deg(\psi)\deg(\varphi_{com})]} \cdot \varphi_{com} \begin{pmatrix} P_1 \\ Q_1 \end{pmatrix} = \frac{M_{\hat{\gamma}} \cdot M_{\psi} \cdot M_{\varphi_{com}}}{[\deg(\psi)\deg(\varphi_{com})]} \begin{pmatrix} P_2 \\ Q_2 \end{pmatrix}.$$

Same as the deduction in Equation (4):

$$M_{\tau} \cdot \begin{pmatrix} \hat{\sigma} \circ \varphi_{chl}(\tau(P_0)) \\ \hat{\sigma} \circ \varphi_{chl}(\tau(Q_0)) \end{pmatrix} = \hat{\sigma} \circ \varphi_{chl}\left(M_{\tau} \cdot \begin{pmatrix} \tau(P_0) \\ \tau(Q_0) \end{pmatrix}\right) = \hat{\sigma} \circ \varphi_{chl}\begin{pmatrix} P_A \\ Q_A \end{pmatrix}.$$

As a consequence,

$$\hat{\sigma} \circ \varphi_{chl}\begin{pmatrix} P_A \\ Q_A \end{pmatrix} = \frac{M_{\tau} \cdot M_{\hat{\gamma}} \cdot M_{\psi} \cdot M_{\varphi_{com}}}{[\deg(\psi)\deg(\varphi_{com})]} \begin{pmatrix} P_2 \\ Q_2 \end{pmatrix}.$$

Therefore, the signature can be compressed into $(E_2, M, q, \ker(\hat{\varphi}_{com}))$, where

$$M = \frac{M_{\tau} \cdot M_{\hat{\gamma}} \cdot M_{\psi} \cdot M_{\varphi_{com}}}{[\deg(\psi)\deg(\varphi_{com})]} = \frac{M_{\tau} \cdot M_{\hat{\gamma}} \cdot M_{\psi} \cdot M_{\varphi_{com}}}{[\deg(\psi)\ell'^{f'}]}.$$

To store $\ker(\hat{\varphi}_{com})$, we compress it by finding $k_{\hat{\varphi}_{com}} \in \mathbb{Z}/\ell'^{f'}\mathbb{Z}$ such that $\ker(\hat{\varphi}_{com})$ can be represented by $\langle P_2' + [k_{\hat{\varphi}_{com}}]Q_2'\rangle$ or $\langle Q_2' + [k_{\hat{\varphi}_{com}}]P_2'\rangle$ where $\{P_2', Q_2'\}$ is the canonical basis of $E_2[\ell'^{f'}]$. Note that $\{P_2', Q_2'\}$ can be recovered as E_2 is given. Therefore, one can transfer $(k_{\hat{\varphi}_{com}}, label_{\hat{\varphi}_{com}})$ instead of a generator of $\ker(\hat{\varphi}_{com})$, where $label_{\hat{\varphi}_{com}}$ is a bit used to distinguish the two cases mentioned above. This reduces the storage cost of $\ker(\hat{\varphi}_{com})$ to approximately λ bits.

As a Γ-signature, PIsignHD allows the signer to precompute all the intermediate values which are irrelevant to the message. In particular, the signer can precompute plenty of commitments, and store a list of codomains of the hash isogenies $D = \{E_2^{(1)}, E_2^{(2)}, \cdots, E_2^{(n)}\}$ in public, or on the verifier's side. Hence, the signer can transfer the index ind_E in D instead of the codomain of the hash isogeny. Generally, setting $n = 2^{32}$ is enough for practice.

With the help of the list D, the signature of PIsignHD can be compressed into $(ind_E, M, q, (k_{\hat{\varphi}_{com}}, label_{\hat{\varphi}_{com}}))$. From Remark 4, the entire action matrix M can be recovered once three entries of it are known, and its size can be further halved by revealing the actions of σ on a $2^{\lceil g/2 \rceil}$-torsion basis instead of $\{P_2, Q_2\}$. Therefore, the total storage cost is approximately $32+(3\cdot 0.5\lambda+1)+\lambda+(\lambda+1) = (3.5\lambda + 34)$ bits. For comparison, the signature size of SQIsignHD is about 6.5λ bits. For NIST-I security level ($\lambda = 128$), the signature size of PIsignHD is 519 bits, while the storage cost of SQIsignHD is 870 bits.

5.2 Offline/Online Signatures

As mentioned in Sect. 2.2, the isogeny φ_{chl} can be recovered by the verifier, and the signer can avoid isogeny computations relevant to φ_{chl}. Besides, the isogenies τ and τ' have been constructed in key generation. Therefore, the bottleneck of the response in SQIsignHD is the isogeny computations of the commitment.

In PIsignHD, the signer not only computes the codomain of ψ but an equivalent isogeny ψ' of coprime degree, due to the translation from the isogeny φ_{com} to the associated ideal $I_{\varphi_{com}}$. In addition, the signer has to construct and evaluate the isogeny φ_{com} to obtain the codomain E_2 and the action matrix M_ψ associated to ψ. Fortunately, by implementing online/offline computations, all the above parts can be computed offline and thus they do not affect the efficiency of the online response. Detailed descriptions of the offline/online signatures are presented in Algorithms 3 and 4.

Algorithm 3. Offlinesignature

Require: The initial curve E_0 with known Endomorphism ring.

Ensure: The curve E_2, the action matrix $M_{\varphi_{com}\circ\psi} = M_{\varphi_{com}} \cdot M_\psi$ with $M_{\varphi_{com}}$ and M_ψ defined in Equation (2), the ideal I associated to the isogeny $\varphi_{com} \circ \psi : E_0 \to E_2$, the integer $k_{\hat{\varphi}_{com}}$ and a bit $label_{\hat{\varphi}_{com}}$ used to determine $\ker(\hat{\varphi}_{com})$.

Generate a random isogeny walk $\psi : E_0 \to E_1$ of degree $\ell'^{\bullet} \approx p$ and an equivalent isogeny $\psi' : E_0 \to E_1$ of degree $\ell^{\bullet} \approx p$;
Compute the ideals I_ψ and $I_{\psi'}$ associated to ψ and ψ', respectively;
Compute the canonical bases $\{P_0, Q_0\}$ and $\{P_1, Q_1\}$of $E_0[\ell^f]$ and $E_1[\ell^f]$, respectively;
Compute the action matrix M_ψ as defined in Equation (2);
$\varphi_{com} \leftarrow \mathcal{H}'(E_1, \mathcal{H}(j(E_1)))$ and compute $\varphi_{com}(P_1)$ and $\varphi_{com}(Q_1)$;
Compute $\ker(\hat{\varphi}_{com})$, the kernel of $\hat{\varphi}_{com}$;
$I_{\varphi_{com}} \leftarrow$ **IsogenyToIdeal**$(\varphi_{com}, \psi', I_{\psi'})$;
Compute the canonical basis $\{P_2', Q_2'\}$ of $E_2[\ell'^{f'}]$;
Compute the action matrix $M_{\varphi_{com}}$ as defined in Equation (2);
$M_{\varphi_{com}\circ\psi} \leftarrow M_{\varphi_{com}} \cdot M_\psi$, $I \leftarrow I_{\varphi_{com}} \cdot I_\psi$;
Find $k_{\hat{\varphi}_{com}} \in \mathbb{Z}/\ell'^{f'}\mathbb{Z}$ such that $\ker(\hat{\varphi}_{com}) = \langle P_2' + [k_{\hat{\varphi}_{com}}]Q_2' \rangle$ or $\ker(\hat{\varphi}_{com}) = \langle [k_{\hat{\varphi}_{com}}]P_2' + Q_2' \rangle$;
$label_{\hat{\varphi}_{com}} \leftarrow 1$ if $\ker(\hat{\varphi}_{com}) = \langle P_2' + [k_{\hat{\varphi}_{com}}]Q_2' \rangle$, or $label_{\hat{\varphi}_{com}} \leftarrow 0$ otherwise;
$I \leftarrow$ **RandomEquivalentIdeal**$_{\ell^g}(I)$;
return E_2 and $(M_{\phi\circ\psi}, I, k_{\hat{\varphi}_{com}}, label_{\hat{\varphi}_{com}})$.

Remark 3. The signer can compute $\frac{M_{\varphi_{com}\circ\psi}}{\deg(\psi)\ell'^{f'}}$ offline and store it instead of $M_{\varphi_{com}\circ\psi}$ to further improve the online signing (Step 6 of Algorithm 4).

The constructions of ψ and ψ' are the efficiency bottlenecks of the offline computations. There are mainly two methods to achieve this: One is to generate ψ uniformly at random, then compute the associated ideal I_ψ and apply the KLPT

Algorithm 4. Onlinesignature

Require: The isogeny $\tau' : E_0 \to E_A$ of degree $\ell'^{\bullet} \approx p$, the ideals I_τ and $I_{\tau'}$ associated to τ and τ' respectively, the ideal $I_{\varphi_{com}\circ\psi}$ equivalent to $I_{\varphi_{com}} \cdot I_\psi$, the isogeny $\varphi_{chl} : E_A \to E_2$ of degree $\ell'^{f'}$, and the action matrices M_τ and $M_{\varphi_{com}\circ\psi}$ defined in Equation (2).

Ensure: The matrix M such that $(\hat{\sigma} \circ \varphi_{chl}(P_A), \hat{\sigma} \circ \varphi_{chl}(Q_A))^T = M \cdot (P_1, Q_1)^T$ and the degree q of the isogeny $\sigma : E_1 \to E_2$.

1: $I_{\varphi_{chl}} \leftarrow$ **IsogenyToIdeal**$(\varphi_{chl}, \tau', I_{\tau'})$, $J \leftarrow \overline{I_{\varphi_{com}\circ\psi} \cdot I_\tau \cdot I_{\varphi_{chl}}}$;
2: $I \leftarrow$ **RandomEquivalentIdeal**$_{\ell_1^g}(J)$ and compute the reduced norm q of I;
3: If q is not ℓ^g-good or $\gcd(q, \ell') \neq 1$, go back to Line 2;
4: Compute $\gamma \in \mathcal{O}$ such that $\mathcal{O}\gamma = I_\psi \cdot I \cdot \overline{I_\tau \cdot I_{\varphi_{chl}}}$;
5: Compute the action matrix $M_{\hat{\gamma}}$ as defined in Equation (2);
6: $M \leftarrow \frac{M_\tau \cdot M_{\hat{\gamma}} \cdot M_{\varphi_{com}\circ\psi}}{\deg(\psi)\ell'^{f'}}$;
7: **return** (M, q).

algorithm [24] to obtain an equivalent ideal, and finally translate it to the associated isogeny ψ' (note that in this case the degree of ψ' is approximately p^3); the other is to generate both of them simultaneously by the elegant techniques utilized in the key generation phase of SQIsignHD [11, Section 3.3]. Our implementation applies the latter one for efficiency. To reduce the storage cost for the ideal $I_{\varphi_{com}} \cdot I_\psi$, the signer can execute the algorithm **RandomEquivalentIdeal**$_{\ell^g}$ to generate an ideal $I \sim I_{\varphi_{com}} \cdot I_\psi$ with norm $\mathrm{Nrd}(I) \approx \sqrt{p}$. Note that the codomain E_2 can be public or stored on the verifier's size, while the tuple $(M_{\varphi_{com}\circ\psi}, I, k_{\hat{\varphi}_{com}}, label_{\hat{\varphi}_{com}})$ should be secret.

The online signature avoids the isogeny computations, thus all the operations are over the quaternions and linear algebra. Particularly, the efficiency bottleneck is the generation of the ideal associated to σ. Currently, the approach to obtain the target ideal is somewhat primitive. Finding a more efficient method for the ℓ^g-good equivalent ideal generation is essential to improve the performance of the online signature. We leave it as future work.

We note that the online signing phase of SQIsignHD can also be accelerated via precomputation. Precisely, the signer can precompute the isogeny ψ, the codomain E_1 and the action matrices such as M_ψ in Equation (3). This also avoids the isogeny computations in the online signing phase. However, SQIsignHD has several disadvantages in applications compared with PIsignHD when applying the offline/online computations:

- SQIsignHD requires larger storage requirements. To generate a signature with respect to the commitment E_1, the signer has to store I_ψ, M_ψ and E_1. Especially, since the commitment E_1 cannot be public, the signer has to store it before signing. For comparison, PIsignHD allows the list $D = \{E_2^{(1)}, E_2^{(2)}, \cdots, E_2^{(s)}\}$ to be public or be stored on the verifier's side. As a consequence, the signer only stores the information $I \sim I_{\varphi_{com}} \cdot I_\psi$, $M_{\varphi_{com}\circ\psi}$, $(k_{\hat{\varphi}_{com}}, label_{\hat{\varphi}_{com}})$ and a label ind_E instead when implementing PIsignHD, reducing the storage cost by approximately 3λ bits for each commitment.

- SQIsignHD has larger signature size. As discussed previously, PIsignHD allows the signer to further compress the signature thanks to the public list D. On the other hand, in SQIsignHD the knowledge of E_1 should be entirely transferred as it is not allowed to be public in advance. Although the signature of PIsignHD also involves the knowledge of the hash isogeny φ_{com}, it is still more compact than that of SQIsignHD due to the large storage requirement of the curve coefficient.
- The challenge isogeny in SQIsignHD is generated from the knowledge of both the commitment E_1 and the message m. Therefore, the online phase in SQIsignHD has to compute the hash of E_1 and m, i.e., $\mathcal{H}(E_1||m)$, and then generates the challenge isogeny $\varphi = \mathcal{H}'(E_A, \mathcal{H}(E_1||m))$. Conversely, in PIsignHD the challenge isogeny $\varphi_{chl} = \mathcal{H}'(E_A, \mathcal{H}(m))$. This is preferred in some specific applications. For example, the hash of the message m can be hashed by a trusted party. In this case, the signer is able to use a low-power device to generate the signature with respect to $\mathcal{H}(m)$, without handling the entire message. When applying SQIsignHD, the signer has to compute $\mathcal{H}(E_1||m)$ or transmit E_1 to the trusted party. The former enlarges the communication cost and the computational cost of online signing, while the latter requires an additional round of interaction.
- In PIsignHD, the verifier can precompute some intermediate values to fasten the verification. More details are left in the next subsection.

5.3 Experimental Results

Based on the SQIsignHD code[3], we implement the online/offline signatures of PIsignHD. We benchmark our code on Intel(R) Core(TM) i9-12900K 3.20 GHz with TurboBoost and hyperthreading features disabled. The code is available at

https://github.com/Kaizhan-Lin/PIsignHD.

As mentioned in this last subsection, SQIsignHD also benefits from the online/offline computations. In Table 1 we give an efficiency comparison between the offline/online responses of SQIsignHD and PIsignHD.

As excepted, the online response of SQIsignHD and PIsignHD is very fast and close. According to our experimental results, the online response takes only 4 ms. For comparison, the signature of SQIsignHD takes 22.4 ms on average. Therefore, the online response of SQIsignHD/PIsignHD is over 5 times faster than the entire signing procedure of SQIsignHD without offline precomputations.

While the implementation efficiency of online responses of PIsignHD remains unchanged regardless of whether the signature compression is employed, the offline computation is less efficient in the case when using the compression technique. The main reason is that the signer needs to compute the kernel of $\hat{\varphi}_{com}$ and compress it to $(k_{\hat{\varphi}_{com}}, label_{\hat{\varphi}_{com}})$ by computing discrete logarithms during the offline phase of compressed PIsignHD.

[3] https://github.com/Pierrick-Dartois/SQISignHD-lib.

Table 1. Comparison of the SQIsignHD and PIsignHD signing implementations targeting the NIST-I security level. For the performance results (expressed in millions of clock cycles), we execute 1000 times for a 256-bit message and record the average time.

Implementation		SQIsignHD	PIsignHD
Signature size (bits)	Original	870	870
	Compressed	-	519
Clock cycles (cc$\times 10^6$)	Original	70.1	89.8
	Offline (Uncompressed)	57.9	77.8
	Online (Uncompressed)	12.0	11.8
	Offline (Compressed)	-	89.6
	Online (Compressed)	-	11.8

In our implementation, we improve the performance of discrete logarithms in the signing phase by utilizing reduced Tate pairings [25]. Indeed, there are some other techniques in the literature which can be utilized to improve the implementation of the offline computations. For instance, one can employ interleaved modular multiplication algorithms [26] to reduce considerable memory loads and stores for multiplications in $\mathbb{F}_{p^2}$. Very recently, faster approaches for pairing computations in isogeny-based protocols are explored by [5,34], which are particularly beneficial for the acceleration of the action matrix computations. We note that in the real-world applications, the offline computations can be connected to the power. Hence, it is acceptable that the offline computations of PIsignHD are not as efficient as that of SQIsignHD.

In summary, the online response performance of both signatures is very close, while SQIsignHD has a faster implementation of the offline computations compared to PIsignHD. However, regarding various advantages as discussed in Sect. 5.2, PIsignHD appears more promising in practical applications.

Now we analyze the performance of other parts in PIsignHD.

The key generation phase of PIsignHD is identical to that of SQIsignHD, and thus the performance is the same.

When we do not apply the online/offline technique, the verification in PIsignHD needs to construct $\varphi_{com} : E_1 \to E_2$, which is the hash of E_1. Since φ_{com} is a power-smooth isogeny that can be efficiently constructed and evaluated, the overhead is negligible as the isogeny computations in high dimension dominate the computational cost. Therefore, the verification performance of PIsignHD is very close to that of SQIsignHD.

When adapting the online/offline technique, PIsignHD has the potential to achieve a better verification performance compared to SQIsignHD. In addition, some intermediate values can also be precomputed to fasten the verification. For example, the verifier can precompute the canonical basis of any supersingular curve in the list D. Besides, as the challenge isogeny can be generated without any interaction with the signer, the verifier can also compute the canonical basis of the codomain E_3 in advance. We are confident that the isogeny computation in high dimension can be accelerated via precomputation with further research.

6 Conclusion

In this paper we introduced a new structure for the SQIsign family, and proposed PIsignHD based on SQIsignHD. The flexible challenge generation benefits the implementation of PIsignHD in the real-world applications. Furthermore, PIsignHD has a shorter signature size compared with SQIsignHD. In addition, PIsignHD achieves a fast online response via offline computations with cheaper storage requirements.

In our future work, we aim to further enhance the performance of PIsignHD, including reducing the offline storage complexity for the prover, improving the efficiency of offline/online signing and verification, etc. We will also adapt the new structure to other efficient variants of SQIsign [1,10,17,28] to make them more competitive in applications. Additionally, it is interesting to develop practical Γ-signatures based on other isogeny-based protocols, such as CSIDH [7] and SIDH-like schemes [2,22].

Acknowledgment. We thank Yi-Fu Lai and all the anonymous reviewers for their constructive suggestions. Kaizhan Lin, Weize Wang and Yunlei Zhao are supported by The National Key Research and Development Program of China (No.2022YFB2701601), Shanghai Collaborative Innovation Fund (No.XTCX-KJ-2023-54) and Special Fund for Key Technologies in Blockchain of Shanghai Scientific and Technological Committee (No.23511100300). Chang-An Zhao is supported by the National Natural Science Foundation of China (No. 12441107), Guangdong Basic and Applied Basic Research Foundation (No. 2025A1515011764), Guangdong Major Project of Basic and Applied Basic Research (No. 2019B030302008) and Guangdong Provincial Key Laboratory of Information Security Technology (No. 2023B1212060026). 2019B030302008.

A Mathematical Background

This section provides the necessary mathematical preliminaries, including elliptic curves, isogenies, quaternion algebras, orders and ideals. We refer to [35,37] for more details.

Elliptic Curves. Elliptic curves are nonsingular projective curves with genus 1. For applications, elliptic curves defined in this paper are over a finite field $\mathbb{F}_q$, denoted by $E/\mathbb{F}_q$, where $q = p^n$ with prime $p > 3$ and $n \in \mathbb{N}^*$. An isomorphism class of elliptic curves can be entirely determined by its j-invariant. We use $j(E)$ to denote the j-invariant of E. All the rational points on the elliptic curve E and the point at infinity ∞_E[4] form an abelian group $E(\mathbb{F}_q)$ under point addition.

[4] The point at infinity of an elliptic curve is not necessarily the identity, but for simplicity we suppose that it is the identity point.

Let $\ell > 0$, the ℓ-torsion of E is defined as $E[\ell] = \{P \in E(\overline{\mathbb{F}_q}) | [\ell]P = \infty_E\}$, where $[\ell]$ is a multiplication-by-ℓ map. An elliptic curve E is supersingular if $E[p] = \{\infty_E\}$, otherwise E is said to be ordinary.

Isogenies. An isogeny $\varphi : E_1 \to E_2$ is a non-constant surjective morphism that sends ∞_{E_1} to ∞_{E_2}. Denote $\deg(\varphi)$ the degree of φ as a rational map. Two curves E_1 and E_2 are said to be isogenous over $\mathbb{F}_q$ if there exists an isogeny connecting them over $\mathbb{F}_q$. An isogeny φ is called cyclic if its kernel can be generated by one single point P, and separable if the cardinality of the kernel $\ker(\varphi) = \{P \in E_1(\overline{\mathbb{F}_q}) | \varphi(P) = \infty_{E_2}\}$ is equal to $\deg(\varphi)$. If $\deg(\varphi)$ is coprime to the characteristic of the finite field, then φ must be separable. We abbreviate a separable isogeny of degree ℓ as an ℓ-isogeny. Furthermore, for any isogeny $\varphi : E_1 \to E_2$, there exists a unique isogeny $\hat{\varphi} : E_2 \to E_1$ such that $\hat{\varphi} \circ \varphi = [\deg(\varphi)]$, i.e., the composition of the two isogenies is a multiplication-by-$\deg(\varphi)$ map. In this case, we call $\hat{\varphi}$ the dual isogeny of φ.

Let $\varphi_1 : E_0 \to E_1$ and $\varphi_2 : E_0 \to E_2$ be two separable isogenies with $\gcd(\deg(\varphi_1), \deg(\varphi_2)) = 1$. Then there exist two isogenies $\psi_1 : E_2 \to E_3$ and $\psi_2 : E_1 \to E_3$ such that $\ker(\psi_1) = \varphi_2(\ker(\varphi_1))$ and $\ker(\psi_2) = \varphi_1(\ker(\varphi_2))$, as illustrated in Fig. 6. We denote $\psi_1 = [\varphi_2]_*\varphi_1$ (resp. $\psi_2 = [\varphi_1]_*\varphi_2$) as the *pushforward* isogeny of φ_1 (resp. φ_2) through φ_2 (resp. φ_1). Conversely, the isogeny φ_1 (resp. φ_2) is called the *pullback* isogeny of ψ_1 (resp. ψ_2) through φ_2 (resp. φ_1), denoted by $\varphi_1 = [\varphi_2]^*\psi_1$ (resp. $\varphi_2 = [\varphi_1]^*\psi_2$). Note that ψ_1 and ψ_2 are also separable. In addition, there exists an isogeny $\Phi : E_0 \to E_3$ such that $\Phi = \psi_2 \circ \varphi_1 = \psi_1 \circ \varphi_2$.

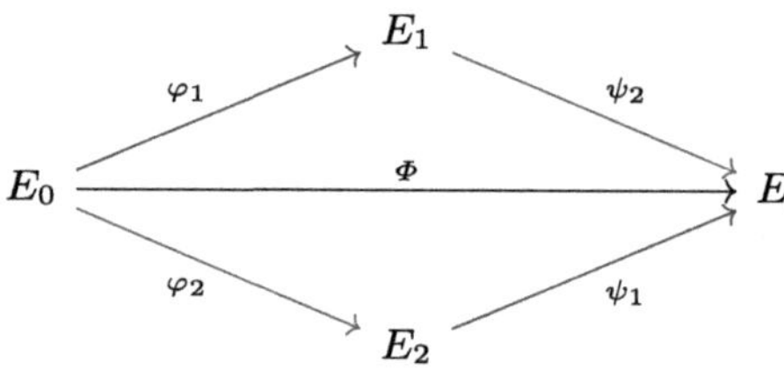

Fig. 6. A commutative isogeny diagram

The supersingular ℓ-isogeny graph is a graph whose vertices represent the supersingular $\overline{\mathbb{F}_p}$ classes and edges represent the equivalent classes of ℓ-isogenies connecting them. The graph is connected, essentially undirected and Ramanujan [31]. Moreover, the graph is $\ell + 1$-regular, meaning that there are exactly $\ell + 1$ equivalent classes of isogenies starting from a given supersingular $\overline{\mathbb{F}_p}$ class.

Endomorphism Rings. An endomorphism of E is either an isogeny from E to itself, or the constant morphism $[0]$. The set of all the endomorphisms forms a ring under addition and composition, denoted by $\text{End}(E)$. The endomorphism ring $\text{End}(E)$ is isomorphic to an order in a quaternion algebra if E is supersingular, or an order in a quadratic imaginary field if E is ordinary.

Quaternion Algebras, Orders and Ideals. A quaternion algebra over $\mathbb{Q}$ ramified at p and ∞ has the form $B_{p,\infty} = \mathbb{Q} + \mathbb{Q}i + \mathbb{Q}j + \mathbb{Q}k$, where $i^2 = -q$, $j^2 = -p$ and $k = ij = -ji$ with $q \in \mathbb{Z}$. The quaternion algebra has a canonical involution, mapping $\alpha = \alpha_1+\alpha_2 i+\alpha_3 j+\alpha_4 k$ to its conjugate $\overline{\alpha} = \alpha_1-\alpha_2 i-\alpha_3 j-\alpha_4 k$. The reduced trace and the reduced norm of α are defined as $\mathrm{Trd}(\alpha) = 2\alpha_1$ and $\mathrm{Nrd}(\alpha) = \alpha\overline{\alpha}$, respectively.

An order in $B_{p,\infty}$ is a full-rank lattice and also a subring. An order is called maximal if it is not contained in another order. A fractional ideal is a $\mathbb{Z}$-lattice of rank 4. Given an ideal I, its left order and right order are defined as

$$\mathcal{O}_L(I) = \{\alpha \in B_{p,\infty} | \alpha I \subset I\}, \mathcal{O}_R(I) = \{\alpha \in B_{p,\infty} | I\alpha \subset I\}.$$

A left (resp. right) $\mathcal{O}$-ideal I is a $\mathbb{Z}$-lattice of rank 4 satisfying that $\mathcal{O} \subset \mathcal{O}_L(I)$ (resp. $\mathcal{O} \subset \mathcal{O}_R I$) and $\mathcal{O}_L(I)$ and $\mathcal{O}_R(I)$ are maximal. An fractional ideal I is integral if $I \subset \mathcal{O}_L(I)$, which implies that $I \subset \mathcal{O}_R(I)$. Henceforth, we only focus on integral ideals and refer to them as ideals.

An ideal I is said to be invertible, if there exists an ideal I^{-1} such that $II^{-1} = \mathcal{O}_L(I)$ or $I^{-1}I = \mathcal{O}_R(I)$. Denote $\mathrm{Nrd}(I) = \gcd\{\mathrm{Nrd}(\alpha)|\alpha \in I\}$ the reduced norm of I, and $\overline{I} = \{\overline{\alpha}|\alpha \in I\}$ the conjugate of I. If I is invertible, then $I\overline{I} = \mathrm{Nrd}(I)\mathcal{O}_L(I)$ and $\overline{I}I = \mathrm{Nrd}(I)\mathcal{O}_R(I)$. An ideal I of integer reduced norm can be represented by $I = \mathcal{O}_L(I)\alpha + \mathcal{O}_L(I)\mathrm{Nrd}(I)$, where $\alpha \in \mathcal{O}_L(I)$. Two left $\mathcal{O}$-ideals I and J are equivalent if there exists $\beta \in B_{p,\infty}$ such that $I = J\beta$, denoted by $I \sim J$.

Deuring Correspondence. The Deuring correspondence provides a link between the world of supersingular elliptic curves and the world of quaternion algebras.

Let E be a supersingular curve, and suppose that the endomorphism ring $\mathrm{End}(E)$ is isomorphic to a maximal order $\mathcal{O}$ of $B_{p,\infty}$. Then an isogeny φ_I : $E \to E'$ corresponds to a kernel ideal $I = \{\alpha \in \mathcal{O}|\alpha(P) = \infty_E$ for all $P \in \ker(\varphi_I)\}$, and $\deg(\varphi_I) = \mathrm{Nrd}(I)$. Besides, the left order is isomorphic to $\mathcal{O}$, while the right order is isomorphic to $\mathrm{End}(E')$. In particular, an endomorphism of E corresponds to a principal ideal. Conversely, given a left $\mathcal{O}$-ideal I, the kernel $E[I] = \{P \in E(\overline{\mathbb{F}_p})|\alpha(P) = \infty_E$ for all $\alpha \in I\}$ determines an isogeny φ_I with $\ker(\varphi_I) = E[I]$ and $\deg(\varphi_I) = \mathrm{Nrd}(I)$. The conjugation $\overline{I}$ associates to the dual isogeny $\hat{\varphi}_I$. The multiplication of ideals $I \cdot J$ defines the composition $\varphi_J \circ \varphi_I$, where φ_I and φ_J are two isogenies associated to I and J, respectively. Note that in this case $\mathcal{O}_R(I) \cong \mathcal{O}_L(J)$. In addition, two left $\mathcal{O}$-ideals I and J are equivalent if and only if the isogenies φ_I and φ_J have the same domain and codomain up to isomorphism.

B Σ-Protocol and Fiat–Shamir Paradigm

Assume that $\mathcal{P}$ and $\mathcal{V}$ are probabilistic polynomial time machines, and the advantage of $\mathcal{P}$ over $\mathcal{V}$ is that $\mathcal{P}$ knows w with $(x, w) \in \mathcal{R}$, where $\mathcal{R}$ is an $\mathcal{NP}$-relation. Now concern the protocol that proceeds as follows:

- $\mathcal{P}$ sends a commitment a to $\mathcal{V}$;
- $\mathcal{V}$ sends a random string e to $\mathcal{P}$;
- $\mathcal{P}$ sends a reply z with respect to e, and $\mathcal{V}$ accepts or rejects based on (x, a, e, z).

Definition 3. *Σ-protocol is a three-round public-coin protocol $\langle \mathcal{P}, \mathcal{V} \rangle$ for an $\mathcal{NP}$-relation $\mathcal{R}$ that proceeds as above. Besides, Σ-protocols should satisfy the following properties:*

- ***Completeness:*** *$\mathcal{V}$ always accepts if $\mathcal{P}$ and $\mathcal{V}$ follow the protocol.*
- ***Special soundness:*** *Given two pairs of valid conversations (a, e, z) and (a, e', z') on any input x with $e \neq e'$, one can recover the witness w such that $(x, w) \in \mathcal{R}$ in polynomial time with overwhelming probability.*
- ***Special Honest Verifier Zero-Knowledge (SHVZK):*** *There exists a probabilistic polynomial-time simulator $\mathcal{S}$, which takes as input x, and outputs an accepting conversation (a', e', z'), with the same (or computationally indistinguishable) probability distribution as the conversation (a, e, z) of the real protocol.*

Given a Σ-protocol, Fiat-Shamir paradigm [21] can convert it to a signature scheme. The main idea is to set $e = h(a||m)$, where h is a hash function and m is the message. The modification allows the signer to sign the message without interacting with the verifier. The verifier accepts if (a, z) is a valid signature for m[5].

C Current Response Implementation of SQIsignHD

Suppose that $\{P_0, Q_0\}$, $\{P_1, Q_1\}$ and $\{P_A, Q_A\}$ are the canonical bases of $E_0[\ell^f]$, $E_1[\ell^f]$ and $E_A[\ell^f]$, respectively. Then assume

$$\begin{pmatrix} P_A \\ Q_A \end{pmatrix} = M_\tau \begin{pmatrix} \tau(P_0) \\ \tau(Q_0) \end{pmatrix}, \hat{\gamma} \begin{pmatrix} P_0 \\ Q_0 \end{pmatrix} = M_{\hat{\gamma}} \begin{pmatrix} P_0 \\ Q_0 \end{pmatrix}, \psi \begin{pmatrix} P_0 \\ Q_0 \end{pmatrix} = M_\psi \begin{pmatrix} P_1 \\ Q_1 \end{pmatrix}, \quad (3)$$

where $M_\tau, M_{\hat{\gamma}}, M_\psi \in \mathbb{M}_2(\mathbb{Z}/\ell^f\mathbb{Z})$. Recall from Equation (1) that $\sigma = \varphi \circ \tau \circ \gamma \circ \hat{\psi}/[\deg(\varphi)\deg(\tau)\deg(\psi)]$. Therefore, the prover can compute $\hat{\sigma} \circ \varphi \circ \tau(P_0)$ and $\hat{\sigma} \circ \varphi \circ \tau(Q_0)$ by the following:

$$\begin{aligned} \hat{\sigma} \circ \varphi \circ \tau \begin{pmatrix} P_0 \\ Q_0 \end{pmatrix} &= \frac{\psi \circ \hat{\gamma} \circ \hat{\tau} \circ \hat{\varphi} \circ \varphi \circ \tau}{[\deg(\varphi)\deg(\tau)\deg(\psi)]} \begin{pmatrix} P_0 \\ Q_0 \end{pmatrix} \\ &= \frac{\psi \circ \hat{\gamma} \circ \hat{\tau} \circ \tau}{[\deg(\tau)\deg(\psi)]} \begin{pmatrix} P_0 \\ Q_0 \end{pmatrix} \\ &= \frac{\psi \circ \hat{\gamma}}{[\deg(\psi)]} \begin{pmatrix} P_0 \\ Q_0 \end{pmatrix}. \end{aligned}$$

[5] In some specific signature schemes, such as SQIsign [9], the signature can be of form (e, z) since a can be recovered from (e, z).

Since $\hat{\gamma}\begin{pmatrix}P_0\\Q_0\end{pmatrix} = M_{\hat{\gamma}}\begin{pmatrix}P_0\\Q_0\end{pmatrix}$, one can deduce

$$\hat{\sigma}\circ\varphi\circ\tau\begin{pmatrix}P_0\\Q_0\end{pmatrix} = \frac{M_{\hat{\gamma}}}{[\deg(\psi)]}\cdot\psi\begin{pmatrix}P_0\\Q_0\end{pmatrix}.$$

It follows from $\psi\begin{pmatrix}P_0\\Q_0\end{pmatrix} = M_{\psi}\begin{pmatrix}P_1\\Q_1\end{pmatrix}$ that

$$\hat{\sigma}\circ\varphi\circ\tau\begin{pmatrix}P_0\\Q_0\end{pmatrix} = \frac{M_{\hat{\gamma}}\cdot M_{\psi}}{[\deg(\psi)]}\begin{pmatrix}P_1\\Q_1\end{pmatrix}.$$

Note that

$$M_\tau\cdot\begin{pmatrix}\hat{\sigma}\circ\varphi(\tau(P_0))\\\hat{\sigma}\circ\varphi(\tau(Q_0))\end{pmatrix} = \hat{\sigma}\circ\varphi\left(M_\tau\cdot\begin{pmatrix}\tau(P_0)\\\tau(Q_0)\end{pmatrix}\right) = \hat{\sigma}\circ\varphi\begin{pmatrix}P_A\\Q_A\end{pmatrix}. \qquad (4)$$

Therefore,

$$\hat{\sigma}\circ\varphi\begin{pmatrix}P_A\\Q_A\end{pmatrix} = \frac{M_\tau\cdot M_{\hat{\gamma}}\cdot M_{\psi}}{[\deg(\psi)]}\begin{pmatrix}P_1\\Q_1\end{pmatrix}.$$

Algorithm 5 summarizes the fast response using the above techniques. The signature is (E_1, q, M), where q is the degree of τ and $M = \frac{M_\tau\cdot M_{\hat{\gamma}}\cdot M_{\psi}}{[\deg(\psi)]}$. Since φ can be derived from E_1 and the message, the verifier has access to E_2, $\varphi(P_A)$ and $\varphi(Q_A)$. The verifier accepts if $(E_2, E_1, q, (\varphi(P_A), \varphi(Q_A)), (P_1^M, Q_1^M))$ correctly represents an isogeny from E_2 to E_1, where $(P_1^M, Q_1^M)^T = M\cdot(P_1, Q_1)^T$. This is equivalent to prove that σ is an isogeny from E_1 to E_2.

As shown above, the curve coefficient of E_2 is not required for the response generation. Therefore, the prover does not need to construct or evaluate the challenge isogeny φ. Furthermore, the information related to the secret isogeny τ (such as the action matrix M_τ) can be computed during key generation. As a result, the prover only needs to compute the commitment isogeny in the signing phase. All the other computations, such as the generation of the action matrix $M_{\hat{\gamma}}$, are executed over quaternions and linear algebra.

Remark 4. It should be noted that the signature size can be further compressed. For example, the verifier can recover the entire matrix M with only three entries of the action matrix M according to the techniques in [11, Section 6.1]. Furthermore, to verify the validity of the representation the prover can only reveal the actions of the response isogeny on an $\ell^{\lceil g/2\rceil}$-torsion basis. This halves the storage cost of M. In the meantime, one can set $g \leq 2f$ instead of $g \leq f$ when utilizing **RandomEquivalentIdeal**$_{\ell^g}$ to generate I_σ.[6]

[6] For efficiency, it is best to set $2f \geq g + 4$. See [11, Section 4.3, Sect. 4.4] for more details.

Algorithm 5. FasterRespond

Require: The isogeny $\tau' : E_0 \to E_A$ of degree $\ell'^{\bullet}$, the ideals I_τ and $I_{\tau'}$ associated to τ and τ' respectively, the ideal I_ψ associated to ψ, the isogeny $\varphi : E_A \to E_2$ of degree ℓ^f, and the action matrices M_τ and M_ψ defined in Equation (3).

Ensure: The matrix M such that $(\hat{\sigma} \circ \varphi(P_A), \hat{\sigma} \circ \varphi(Q_A))^T = M \cdot (P_1, Q_1)^T$ and the degree q of the isogeny $\sigma : E_1 \to E_2$.

1: $I_\varphi \leftarrow$ **IsogenyToIdeal**$(\ker(\varphi), \tau', I_{\tau'})$, $J \leftarrow \overline{I_\psi} \cdot I_\tau \cdot I_\varphi$;
2: $I \leftarrow$ **RandomEquivalentIdeal**$_{\ell_1^g}(J)$ and compute the reduced norm q of I;
3: If q is not ℓ^g-good or $\gcd(q, \ell') \neq 1$, go back to Line 2;
4: Compute $\gamma \in \mathcal{O}$ such that $\mathcal{O}\gamma = I_\psi \cdot I \cdot \overline{I_\tau \cdot I_\varphi}$;
5: Compute the action matrix $M_{\hat{\gamma}}$ as defined in Equation (3);
6: $M \leftarrow \frac{M_\tau \cdot M_{\hat{\gamma}} \cdot M_\psi}{[\deg(\psi)]}$;
7: **return** (M, q).

References

1. Basso, A., Dartois, P., Feo, L.D., Leroux, A., Maino, L., Pope, G., Robert, D., Wesolowski, B.: SQIsign2D-West. In: Chung, K.M., Sasaki, Y. (eds.) Advances in Cryptology - ASIACRYPT 2024, pp. 339–370. Springer Nature Singapore, Singapore (2025). https://doi.org/10.1007/978-981-96-0891-1_11
2. Basso, A., Fouotsa, T.B.: New SIDH countermeasures for a more efficient key exchange. In: Guo, J., Steinfeld, R. (eds.) Advances in Cryptology - ASIACRYPT 2023, pp. 208–233. Springer Nature Singapore, Singapore (2023). https://doi.org/10.1007/978-981-99-8742-9_7
3. Bernstein, D.J., de Feo, L., Leroux, A., Smith, B.: Faster computation of isogenies of large prime degree. In: Galbraith, S. (ed.) ANTS-XIV - 14th Algorithmic Number Theory Symposium. Proceedings of the Fourteenth Algorithmic Number Theory Symposium (ANTS-XIV), vol. 4, pp. 39–55. Mathematical Sciences Publishers, Auckland, New Zealand (2020)
4. Beullens, W., Kleinjung, T., Vercauteren, F.: CSI-FiSh: efficient isogeny based signatures through class group computations. In: Galbraith, S.D., Moriai, S. (eds.) ASIACRYPT 2019. LNCS, vol. 11921, pp. 227–247. Springer, Cham (2019). https://doi.org/10.1007/978-3-030-34578-5_9
5. Cai, S., Lin, K., Zhao, C.A.: Pairing optimizations for isogeny-based cryptosystems. IET Inf. Secur. **2024**(1), 9631360 (2024). https://doi.org/10.1049/2024/9631360
6. Castryck, W., Decru, T.: An efficient key recovery attack on SIDH. In: Advances in Cryptology–EUROCRYPT 2023: 42nd Annual International Conference on the Theory and Applications of Cryptographic Techniques, Lyon, France, 23-27 April 2023, Proceedings, Part V, pp. 423–447. Springer (2023). https://doi.org/10.1007/978-3-031-30589-4_15
7. Castryck, W., Lange, T., Martindale, C., Panny, L., Renes, J.: CSIDH: an efficient post-quantum commutative group action. In: Peyrin, T., Galbraith, S. (eds.) ASIACRYPT 2018. LNCS, vol. 11274, pp. 395–427. Springer, Cham (2018). https://doi.org/10.1007/978-3-030-03332-3_15
8. Charles, D.X., Lauter, K.E., Goren, E.Z.: Cryptographic hash functions from expander graphs. J. Cryptol. **22**(1), 93–113 (2009)
9. Chavez-Saab, J., et al.: SQIsign (2023). http://sqisign.org

10. Corte-Real Santos, M., Eriksen, J.K., Meyer, M., Reijnders, K.: ApresSQI: extra fast verification for sqisign using extension-field signing. In: Joye, M., Leander, G. (eds.) Advances in Cryptology - EUROCRYPT 2024, pp. 63–93. Springer Nature Switzerland, Cham (2024). https://doi.org/10.1007/978-3-031-58716-0_3
11. Dartois, P., Leroux, A., Robert, D., Wesolowski, B.: SQISignHD: New Dimensions in Cryptography. Cryptology ePrint Archive, Paper 2023/436 (2023). https://eprint.iacr.org/2023/436
12. Dartois, P., Leroux, A., Robert, D., Wesolowski, B.: SQIsignHD: new dimensions in cryptography. In: Joye, M., Leander, G. (eds.) Advances in Cryptology - EUROCRYPT 2024, pp. 3–32. Springer Nature Switzerland, Cham (2024). https://doi.org/10.1007/978-3-031-58716-0_1
13. De Feo, L., Galbraith, S.D.: SeaSign: compact isogeny signatures from class group actions. In: Ishai, Y., Rijmen, V. (eds.) EUROCRYPT 2019. LNCS, vol. 11478, pp. 759–789. Springer, Cham (2019). https://doi.org/10.1007/978-3-030-17659-4_26
14. De Feo, L., Kohel, D., Leroux, A., Petit, C., Wesolowski, B.: SQISign: compact post-quantum signatures from quaternions and isogenies. In: Moriai, S., Wang, H. (eds.) ASIACRYPT 2020. LNCS, vol. 12491, pp. 64–93. Springer, Cham (2020). https://doi.org/10.1007/978-3-030-64837-4_3
15. De Feo, L., Leroux, A., Longa, P., Wesolowski, B.: New Algorithms for the Deuring Correspondence: Towards Practical and Secure SQISign Signatures. In: Hazay, C., Stam, M. (eds.) Advances in Cryptology - EUROCRYPT 2023, pp. 659–690. Springer Nature Switzerland, Cham (2023)
16. De Feo, L., et alB.: Séta: Supersingular Encryption from Torsion Attacks. In: Tibouchi, M., Wang, H. (eds.) Advances in Cryptology – ASIACRYPT 2021, pp. 249–278. Springer International Publishing, Cham (2021)
17. Duparc, M., Fouotsa, T.B.: SQIPrime: a dimension 2 variant of SQISignHD with non-smooth challenge isogenies. In: Chung, K.M., Sasaki, Y. (eds.) Advances in Cryptology - ASIACRYPT 2024, pp. 396–429. Springer Nature Singapore, Singapore (2025). https://doi.org/10.1007/978-981-96-0891-1_13
18. Eisenträger, K., Hallgren, S., Lauter, K., Morrison, T., Petit, C.: Supersingular isogeny graphs and endomorphism rings: reductions and solutions. In: Nielsen, J.B., Rijmen, V. (eds.) EUROCRYPT 2018. LNCS, vol. 10822, pp. 329–368. Springer, Cham (2018). https://doi.org/10.1007/978-3-319-78372-7_11
19. El Kaafarani, A., Katsumata, S., Pintore, F.: Lossy CSI-FiSh: efficient signature scheme with tight reduction to decisional CSIDH-512. In: Kiayias, A., Kohlweiss, M., Wallden, P., Zikas, V. (eds.) PKC 2020. LNCS, vol. 12111, pp. 157–186. Springer, Cham (2020). https://doi.org/10.1007/978-3-030-45388-6_6
20. Even, S., Goldreich, O., Micali, S.: On-Line/off-line digital signatures. In: Brassard, G. (ed.) CRYPTO 1989. LNCS, vol. 435, pp. 263–275. Springer, New York (1990). https://doi.org/10.1007/0-387-34805-0_24
21. Fiat, A., Shamir, A.: How to prove yourself: practical solutions to identification and signature problems. In: Odlyzko, A.M. (ed.) CRYPTO 1986. LNCS, vol. 263, pp. 186–194. Springer, Heidelberg (1987). https://doi.org/10.1007/3-540-47721-7_12
22. Fouotsa, T.B., Moriya, T., Petit, C.: M-SIDH and MD-SIDH: countering SIDH attacks by masking information. In: Hazay, C., Stam, M. (eds.) Advances in Cryptology - EUROCRYPT 2023, pp. 282–309. Springer Nature Switzerland, Cham (2023). https://doi.org/10.1007/978-3-031-30589-4_10
23. Galbraith, S.D., Petit, C., Silva, J.: Identification protocols and signature schemes based on supersingular isogeny problems. J. Cryptol. **33**(1), 130–175 (2020)
24. Kohel, D., Lauter, K., Petit, C., Tignol, J.P.: On the quaternion ℓ-isogeny path problem. LMS J. Compu. Math. **17**(A), 418–432 (2014)

25. Lin, K., Wang, W., Xu, Z., Zhao, C.A.: A faster software implementation of SQIsign. IEEE Trans. Inf. Theory **70**(9), 6679–6689 (2024)
26. Longa, P.: Efficient algorithms for large prime characteristic fields and their application to bilinear pairings. IACR Trans. Cryptographic Hardware Embedded Syst. **2023**(3), 445–472 (2023)
27. Maino, L., Martindale, C., Panny, L., Pope, G., Wesolowski, B.: A direct key recovery attack on SIDH. In: Advances in Cryptology–EUROCRYPT 2023: 42nd Annual International Conference on the Theory and Applications of Cryptographic Techniques, Lyon, France, 23-27 April 2023, Proceedings, Part V, pp. 448–471. Springer (2023). https://doi.org/10.1007/978-3-031-30589-4_16
28. Nakagawa, K., et al.: SQIsign2D-East: a new signature scheme Using 2-dimensional isogenies. In: Chung, K.M., Sasaki, Y. (eds.) Advances in Cryptology - ASIACRYPT 2024, pp. 272–303. Springer Nature Singapore, Singapore (2025). https://doi.org/10.1007/978-981-96-0891-1_9
29. Onuki, H., Nakagawa, K.: Ideal-to-isogeny algorithm using 2-dimensional isogenies and its application to SQIsign. In: Chung, K.M., Sasaki, Y. (eds.) Advances in Cryptology - ASIACRYPT 2024, pp. 243–271. Springer Nature Singapore, Singapore (2025). https://doi.org/10.1007/978-981-96-0891-1_8
30. Page, A., Wesolowski, B.: The supersingular endomorphism ring and one endomorphism problems are equivalent. In: Joye, M., Leander, G. (eds.) Advances in Cryptology - EUROCRYPT 2024, pp. 388–417. Springer Nature Switzerland, Cham (2024)
31. Pizer, A.K.: Ramanujan graphs and Hecke operators. Bull. Am. Math. Soc. **23**(1), 127–137 (1990)
32. Renan, F., Kutas, P.: SQIAsignHD: SQIsignHD Adaptor Signature. Cryptology ePrint Archive, Paper 2024/561 (2024). https://eprint.iacr.org/2024/561
33. Robert, D.: Breaking SIDH in polynomial time. In: Advances in Cryptology–EUROCRYPT 2023: 42nd Annual International Conference on the Theory and Applications of Cryptographic Techniques, Lyon, France, 23-27 April 2023, Proceedings, Part V, pp. 472–503. Springer (2023). https://doi.org/10.1007/978-3-031-30589-4_17
34. Robert, D.: Fast pairings via biextensions and cubical arithmetic. Cryptology ePrint Archive, Paper 2024/517 (2024). https://eprint.iacr.org/2024/517
35. Silverman, J.H.: The Arithmetic of Elliptic Curves, 2nd Edition. Graduate Texts in Mathematics. Springer (2009)
36. Vélu, J.: Isogénies entre courbes elliptiques. C. R. Acad. Sci., Paris, Sér. A **273**, 238–241 (1971)
37. Voight, J.: Quaternion algebras. Springer Graduate Texts in Mathematics series. (2021)
38. Yao, A.C.C., Zhao, Y.: Online/offline signatures for low-power devices. IEEE Trans. Inf. Forensics Secur. **8**(2), 283–294 (2013)

Fully Homomorphic Encryption

Downlink (T)FHE Ciphertexts Compression

Antonina Bondarchuk[1(✉)], Olive Chakraborty[1(✉)], Geoffroy Couteau[2(✉)], and Renaud Sirdey[1(✉)]

[1] Université Paris-Saclay, CEA, List, Palaiseau, France
{antonina.bondarchuk,olive.chakraborty,renaud.sirdey}@cea.fr
[2] Université Paris Cité, CNRS, IRIF, Paris, France
couteau@irif.fr

Abstract. This paper focuses on the issue of reducing the bandwidth requirement for FHE ciphertext transmission. While this issue has been extensively studied from the *uplink* viewpoint (transmission of encrypted *inputs* towards an FHE calculation), where several approaches exist to essentially cancel FHE ciphertext expansion, the *downlink* case (transmission of encrypted *results* towards an end-user) has been the object of much less attention. In this paper, we address this latter issue with a particular focus on the TFHE scheme, for which we revisit a number of folklore methods, including several approaches for switching to more compact linearly homomorphic schemes, reducing the precision of T(R)LWE coefficients (while maintaining acceptable probabilities of decryption errors), and others. We also investigate how to use these methods in combination, depending on the number of encrypted results to transmit. We further perform extensive experiments demonstrating that the downlink TFHE ciphertext expansion factor can be practically reduced to values *below 10*, depending on the setup, with little additional computational burden.

1 Introduction

Since its inception more than ten years ago, Fully Homomorphic Encryption (FHE) has been the subject of a lot of research toward more efficiency and better practicality, with two main issues to be dealt with: the high computational cost of homomorphic operators and the large ciphertext expansion induced by FHE schemes. This paper focuses on the latter of these two issues, which leads to the following two problems, which are very different in nature depending on whether:

- Encrypted *inputs*, i.e. *freshly* encrypted ciphertexts, are transmitted towards an FHE calculation (which we refer to as the *uplink* case).
- Encrypted *results*, i.e. *evaluated* ciphertexts, obtained following some FHE calculation are transmitted towards an end-user for decryption (which we refer to as the *downlink* case).

This work was supported by the France 2030 ANR Projects ANR-22-PECY-003 Secure-Compute.

C. Boura et al. (Eds.): SAC 2025, LNCS 16207, pp. 647–678, 2026.
https://doi.org/10.1007/978-3-032-10536-3_24

Reducing the expansion factor for the uplink case has received a lot of attention over the last ten years or so. Indeed, FHE ciphertext expansion can be almost cancelled in this case by a technique usually referred to as transciphering, which simply consists in transmitting data encrypted by means of a symmetric scheme (say, AES) and homomorphically turning them into FHE-encrypted data by running the symmetric scheme decryption algorithm over the FHE scheme.

To do so, one has to pay the FHE expansion factor only to transmit an FHE encryption of the symmetric scheme key at setup time. As a result, many works focused on the issue of designing symmetric schemes amenable to practical homomorphic execution [2,3,18,29,33,36,37] or on optimizing the homomorphic execution of more standard ones [7,8,47]. Other approaches can also be applied to reduce that expansion factor. For instance, as all practical FHE schemes are based on (R)LWE, *in the symmetric setting* (where both encryption and decryption use the secret vector or polynomial $\mathbf{s}$), it is well known [1,44] that one can simply synchronize the sender and the receiver on a PRF to avoid sending the a term in the (R)LWE pairs. This results in an expansion factor of $\log_2 q / \log_2 t$, where q and t respectively denote the ciphertext and plaintext moduli of the scheme. For typical TFHE parameters, this approach leads to an expansion factor of "only" 8, almost for free.

Unfortunately, techniques such as the above are not applicable to the downlink case. Indeed, the dream of being able to convert FHE-encrypted results back to AES form is an ill-posed problem for several reasons, the first of which being that, as transciphering requires homomorphically executing the decryption function of the source scheme under the target scheme, the technique applies only towards a homomorphic scheme, which is of course not the case with AES. Likewise, the above synchronization technique does not apply to the downlink case, as the a term in evaluated (R)LWE pairs cannot be a priori chosen. As such, compressing FHE calculation results for downlink transmission requires completely different approaches. To the best of our knowledge, the study of this issue has been initiated in [15], which was the first paper to suggest switching from an FHE scheme to a more compact Linear Homomorphic Encryption (LHE) scheme. For example, considering an LWE ciphertext $(\mathbf{a}, b) \in \mathbb{Z}_q^n \times \mathbb{Z}_q$, the idea simply consists in executing the dot product $b - \langle \mathbf{a}, \mathbf{s} \rangle$ under the LHE given some form of encryption of $\mathbf{s}$ under the latter. Then one LHE ciphertext is transferred rather than $n+1$ elements in $\mathbb{Z}_q$, achieving some compression as soon as the size of an LHE ciphertext is smaller than $(n+1)\log_2 q$. Depending on the LHE at hand, several such dot products may be packed in a single LHE ciphertext in order to further enhance compression. Using this technique, they [15] further show that for GSW (with a binary plaintext domain and very specific parameters) and the Dåmgard-Jurik scheme as the LHE, it is possible to *asymptotically* achieve "rate 1" FHE (although this result is of theoretical interest as it relies on the fact that, for that latter scheme, the ratio between the plaintext modulus, N^k, and the ciphertext modulus, N^{k+1}, tends to 1 as k goes to infinity).

In essence, our paper builds on these ideas in a more practically minded fashion by focusing mainly on the non-asymptotic regime and considering several possible candidates for the LHE, depending on their plaintext/ciphertext size ratios, the amount of "partially decrypted" messages that can be packed in their plaintexts, and the conditions under which they admit an efficient decryption (as some LHE require solving a discrete log during decryption). We do so with an explicit focus on TFHE [25]. It stands out in the FHE landscape as an intrinsically LWE-based scheme compared to the other ones, which are based on RLWE. Because of all the above degrees of freedom, some LHE are more appropriate than others depending on the number of (T)FHE ciphertexts that need to be transmitted. We also investigate how this approach can be combined with other (lossy) compression techniques based on modulus switching, a simple folklore method already used in several works [20,34,35,48] for which we give rigorous bounds for the probability of erroneous decryption.

1.1 Summary of Contributions

The contributions of this paper can be summarized as follows:

- We address the issue of compressing *evaluated* (T)FHE ciphertexts to reduce the communication burden of transferring *results* from FHE computations prior to their decryption. Contrary to prior works, we do so in the non-asymptotic regime.
- We consider a simple, previously known (lossy) compression technique for TLWE and TRLWE ciphertexts, which consists in reducing the precision of their coefficients. Our contribution is then to carefully analyze the resulting noise increase and show how to choose the precision loss in order to comply with a preset probability of incorrect decryption. Then, we further demonstrate that this technique is a powerful tool when combined with other compression techniques.
- We propose a new "compressed" variant of the linearly homomorphic BCP03 cryptosystem with ciphertext size reduced to $\log \mu + |m|$, where μ is the modulus of the scheme and $|m|$ denotes the bitlength of the encrypted message m. This variant, which we refer to as *compressed Paillier-ElGamal* (CPG for short) in the sequel, may also be of independent interest.
- Building on the (known) idea of executing the linear part of the decryption function for a TLWE ciphertext over a more compact LHE scheme, we investigate several candidates for the LHE (including the above) in combination with other techniques from the state-of-the-art or the present paper to achieve a high compression rate of *evaluated* TFHE ciphertexts.
- We report extensive experimental results revealing the most appropriate regime for each technique (depending on parameters for TFHE as well as the number of FHE computation results that have to be transmitted).
- To the best of our knowledge, this paper is the first to demonstrate that expansion factors below 10 are practically achievable when transmitting results of FHE calculations, with limited additional computational burden.

1.2 Paper Organization

This paper is organized as follows: Sect. 2 surveys existing techniques to reduce FHE ciphertext transmission overhead. Section 3 reviews the basics of TFHE (needed for understanding the paper) and gives the necessary details on the LHE that we use in this paper. Then, in Sect. 4, we present the compression techniques for evaluated TFHE ciphertexts. In Sect. 5, we study several combinations of techniques in order to achieve high compression rates of TFHE evaluated ciphertexts. We then report our experimental results in Sect. 6 and conclude the paper in Sect. 7.

2 Related Work

In this section, we review existing techniques to reduce FHE ciphertext transmission overhead and analyze whether they are applicable for downlink ciphertext compression *under the TFHE scheme* (which is the focus of this paper). Table 1 summarizes the comparison of the various approaches.

Table 1. Related work comparison (✓- yes, – - no, ○ - can be naturally applied).

Paper	Uplink	Downlink	TFHE	BGV	BFV	CKKS	GSW
[21]	✓	✓	✓	✓	✓	✓	–
[6]	✓	–	–	✓	✓	✓	–
[5]	–	✓	✓	✓	✓	✓	–
[20]	✓	✓	✓	○	○	○	–
[34]	–	✓	○	✓	✓	○	–
[48]	–	✓	○	✓	✓	○	–
[15]	–	✓	○	○	○	○	✓
[35]	–	✓	✓	✓	✓	✓	–
Our	–	✓	✓	○	○	○	–

In [21], the authors provide a toolkit to transform (R)LWE-based ciphertexts by providing methods to perform a key-switching operation between LWE ciphertexts, to transform an LWE ciphertext into an RLWE-based ciphertext, and to merge multiple LWE ciphertexts into a single RLWE ciphertext. Although the proposed keyswitch and packing methods can be applied to the TFHE scheme [25], they do not achieve any ciphertext compression (the goal of [21] is to reduce the storage requirement for key-switching keys and the computational cost of the procedure). The authors claim that they achieve lightweight and low-latency communication from the client to the server (thus, on the uplink), but do not address the downlink case.

Paper [6] is focused on LWE to RLWE ring packing after uplink ciphertext transmission. The objective is to efficiently obtain a CRT-encoded RLWE ciphertext to support component-wise multiplications and not to achieve any compression. Although the authors focus on the CKKS scheme [23], the proposed techniques are also applicable to BGV [12] and BFV [10,31]. However, the approach cannot be easily applied for TFHE, as TRLWE samples use coefficient encoding. Moreover, their approach involves switching to larger ciphertext moduli (rather than smaller), which is both difficult to perform in the LWE setting of TFHE and does not achieve compression.

In [5], the authors focus on verifiable computation over HE data. As a side contribution, they also address the issue of minimizing the HE ciphertexts overhead for a verifier. Their main idea is to avoid transmitting RLWE ciphertexts with unused slots by means of a repacking procedure that also switches to a smaller plaintext modulus (hence also a smaller ciphertext modulus), at the expense of dropping the homomorphic properties before downlink transmission. The proposed approach is generic and can be adapted to TFHE, BGV, BFV, and CKKS.

In [20], the authors present a constant bandwidth TFHE-based ORAM scheme in a single server model. On the downlink, they use a ModSwitch operation [12] for TRLWE samples to reduce the communication cost. For the uplink scenario, [6,20,21] use the PRF-based synchronization technique, proposed in [1,44], to avoid sending (R)LWE $\mathbf{a}$ coefficients. As already discussed, this technique is not applicable for the downlink, as in this case $\mathbf{a}$ cannot be a priori known.

Papers [34,48] present HE-based protocols for neural networks. In both papers, to reduce FHE communication overhead, the authors use a technique similar to the one from [20]. Indeed, they achieve compression on the downlink by sending only some of the most significant bits in the components of the LWE ciphertexts. However, [20,34,48] provide only a very crude noise analysis and do not assess the impact of the technique on the probability of erroneous decryption.

Another approach attempting to reduce the downlink FHE communication burden consists in switching from an FHE scheme with linear decryption to an LHE scheme with a smaller expansion factor. This approach was first proposed in [15]. Like the present paper, that paper is focused on techniques to compress post-evaluation FHE ciphertexts (the downlink case) and does not discuss compression techniques for the uplink case. In that setting, it introduces a general approach to build a rate-1 FHE by switching from GSW-style schemes [4,14,32,39] to the Dåmgard-Jurik cryptosystem or to a "shrinked" RLWE scheme (ciphertext shrinking, Sect. B.2, is a technique introduced in that paper that has the nice property of not impacting the decryption error probability). The authors claim that a rate-1 expansion factor is achievable asymptotically (for very specific GSW parameters); as for the Dåmgard-Jurik cryptosystem, the rate $\frac{\log(\mu^y)}{\log(\mu^{y+1})} = 1 - \frac{1}{y+1}$ approaches 1 as y grows. In this case, however, the asymptotic growth of y also increases the computational cost of the latter scheme.

In [35], the authors put in an application for the idea from [15] of switching to the Paillier/Dåmgard-Jurik scheme. The authors also briefly mention the existence of different scheme switching/compression techniques (i.e. scheme switching as in [9], key/modulus switching, dimension reduction [13,40], transciphering, etc.), but do not compare their resulting expansion factors. They also use the idea from [15] to pack several LWE samples into a single LHE ciphertext and, interestingly, further improve this packing by first switching to a smaller ciphertext modulus. However, they do not formally assess the induced increase in decryption error probability beyond "just" stating that the smaller modulus q' should satisfy $q' \geq 2(n+1)t$ and investigate this technique only in the levelled BFV/BGV setting by then switching to the smaller modulus in the hierarchy. The authors experimentally conclude that this combined approach outperforms the other above LWE to RLWE packing approaches.

With respect to positioning, we revisit ideas from both [15] and [35] but adapt them to the specificities of the TFHE scheme, for which we provide a rigorous analysis of the induced decryption error probability, eventually leading to better compression ratios (4 to 5 times better than in [35]). We also consider a more exhaustive set of LHE depending on the number K of TFHE ciphertexts to transmit (including a new variant of the BPC03 scheme that allows us to achieve best-in-class compression in the regime where K is a few tens).

3 Preliminaries

3.1 General Notation

In the upcoming sections, we denote vectors by bold letters, so a vector $\mathbf{x}$ of n elements is $\mathbf{x} = (x_0, \ldots, x_{n-1})$. The inner product of two vectors $\mathbf{x}$ and $\mathbf{y}$ is $\langle \mathbf{x}, \mathbf{y} \rangle$. $x \xleftarrow{\$} \mathbb{D}$ denotes sampling uniformly x from $\mathbb{D}$, and $x \xleftarrow{\mathcal{N}(0,\sigma^2)} \mathbb{D}$ denotes sampling x from $\mathbb{D}$ following a Gaussian distribution of mean 0 and variance σ^2. We denote as $\mathbb{B}$ the set $\{0,1\}$ and by $\mathbb{T}$ the real $[0,1)$ torus, the set of real numbers modulo 1. $\mathbb{T}_N[X]$ denotes $\mathbb{R}[X]/(X^N+1) \mod 1$ and $\mathbb{B}_N[X]$ denotes polynomials in $\mathbb{Z}[X]/(X^N+1)$ with binary coefficients.

3.2 TFHE

The TFHE cryptosystem [25] was proposed by Chillotti et al. in 2016 and is notably implemented in the TFHE library [24]. It is intrinsically an LWE scheme working over the torus $\mathbb{T}$. TFHE relies on three types of ciphertexts: TLWE, TRLWE, and TRGSW. In this paper, we focus only on the issue of compressing TLWE and TRLWE ciphertexts, as only those have to be transmitted when performing homomorphic calculations. TRGSW ciphertexts are only used temporarily within the bootstrapping procedure and never transmitted (except, offline, for transferring the bootstrapping key).

- TLWE ciphertext: a pair $(\tilde{\mathbf{a}}, \tilde{b})$ is a valid TLWE encryption of $m \in \mathbb{Z}_t$ (for plaintext modulus t), with $\tilde{\mathbf{a}} \xleftarrow{\$} \mathbb{T}^n$ and $\tilde{b} \in \mathbb{T}$ if it verifies $\tilde{b} = \langle \tilde{\mathbf{a}}, \mathbf{s} \rangle + \frac{m}{t} + \tilde{e}$, where $\mathbf{s} \xleftarrow{\$} \mathbb{B}^n$ is a TLWE secret key, and $\tilde{e} \xleftarrow{\mathcal{N}(0,\sigma^2)} \mathbb{T}$ is a noise term.

– TRLWE ciphertext: a pair $(\tilde{\mathbf{a}}, \tilde{\mathbf{b}})$ is a valid TRLWE encryption of $\mathbf{m} \in \mathbb{Z}_t[X]/(X^N+1)$, with $\tilde{\mathbf{a}} \xleftarrow{\$} \mathbb{T}_N[X]$ and $\tilde{\mathbf{b}} \in \mathbb{T}_N[X]$ if it verifies $\tilde{\mathbf{b}} = \tilde{\mathbf{a}}\cdot\mathbf{s} + \frac{\mathbf{m}}{t} + \tilde{\mathbf{e}}$, where $\mathbf{s} \xleftarrow{\$} \mathbb{B}_N[X]$ is a TRLWE secret key, and $\tilde{\mathbf{e}} \xleftarrow{\mathcal{N}(0,\sigma^2)} \mathbb{T}_N[X]$ is a noise polynomial. Here polynomials are represented by vectors of their coefficients.

Please note that, as this paper focuses on the input/output of FHE calculations, only a high-level understanding of the inner workings of the TFHE scheme and, in particular, its bootstrapping procedure is required to understand this work. We refer the reader to [25] for further details.

Additionally, up to N TLWE ciphertexts can be packed to/unpacked from a single TRLWE ciphertext using standard techniques introduced in [11,25,43]. This may be useful for improving transmission efficiency (as we shall later discuss) or to perform batched homomorphic additions. As an LWE-based scheme, the TFHE decryption function is decomposed into a first linear part

$$\langle(\tilde{b}; -\tilde{\mathbf{a}}), (1; \mathbf{s})\rangle = \tilde{\varphi} = \frac{m}{t} + \tilde{\mathbf{e}} \tag{1}$$

followed by a scale (up) and round operation

$$\lceil t\tilde{\varphi} \rfloor = m. \tag{2}$$

In TFHE terminology, $\tilde{\varphi}$ is called the *phase* or the *partial decryption* of the ciphertext $(\tilde{\mathbf{a}}; \tilde{b})$. One key observation from [15] is that, given some encryption of $\mathbf{s}$ (with the appropriate form) over another LHE, (1) can be executed over the latter to get an encryption of φ under that LHE. How and when this is practically useful is investigated in the sequel. Equivalently, the scheme is always defined relative to a discretization of the torus by steps of $\frac{1}{q}$, where q is a power of two (typically either 2^{32} or 2^{64}). As such, TLWE or TRLWE ciphertexts are equivalently represented as LWE or RLWE ciphertexts over $\mathbb{Z}_q$ or $\mathbb{Z}_q[X]/(X^N + 1)$. When this representation is used, we will use the notations $(\mathbf{a}, b)$ and $(\mathbf{a}, \mathbf{b})$ instead of $(\tilde{\mathbf{a}}, \tilde{b})$ and $(\tilde{\mathbf{a}}, \tilde{\mathbf{b}})$ (with e.g., $\mathbf{a} = \lceil q\tilde{\mathbf{a}} \rfloor$ and similarly for the others). Note also that the phase computation (1) over $(\mathbf{a}, b)$ returns $\varphi = \Delta m + e$ with $\Delta = \frac{q}{t}$, and decryption is finalized by outputting

$$\left\lceil \frac{\varphi}{\Delta} \right\rfloor \tag{3}$$

instead of Eq. (2). We will use the illustrative parameters in Table 2 as a running example throughout the paper. This will allow us to provide illustrative numbers before the reader reaches Sect. 6 on experimental results, where several sets of TFHE parameters are investigated.

3.3 Linear Homomorphic Encryption Schemes

Table 3 provides the high-level characteristics of the LHE schemes that we consider in this paper (namely Paillier [42], Dåmgard-Jurik [30], Elliptic Curve

Table 2. Illustrative TFHE parameters used as a running example, σ_{TLWE} is the fresh LWE noise standard deviation, and σ_{BS} is the post-bootstrapping noise standard deviation. The parameters achieve 128-bit security according to the lattice-estimator and have been obtained following the methodology in [26].

λ	n	q	t	N	σ_{TLWE}	σ_{BS}
128	550	2^{32}	2	1024	$q \cdot 2.82 \times 10^{-4}$	$q \cdot 1.69 \times 10^{-2}$

ElGamal [38], and BCP03 [17]). As hinted in the previous section, we will consider using these schemes to evaluate the linear part of the TFHE decryption function, therefore converting one (or possibly more) ciphertext of size $(n+1)\log_2 q$ into a single ciphertext of the LHE scheme. For completeness, we briefly recall their definitions in Appendix Sect. A.

Table 3. Summary of main characteristics of the LHE schemes presented in Sect. A.

Cryptosystem	Plaintext domain	Ciphertext domain	Plaintext size (bits)	Ciphertext size (bits)	Expansion factor
Paillier	$\mathbb{Z}_\mu$	$\mathbb{Z}_{\mu^2}$	$\log_2 \mu$	$2\log_2 \mu$	2
Dåmgard-Jurik	$\mathbb{Z}_{\mu^y}$	$\mathbb{Z}_{\mu^{y+1}}$	$y\log_2 \mu$	$(y+1)\log_2 \mu$	$1+\frac{1}{y}$
EC ElGamal	$\mathbb{F}_\omega$	$\mathbb{F}_\omega^2$	$\mathfrak{p}$	$2\log_2 \omega$	$\frac{2\log_2 \omega}{\mathfrak{p}}$
BCP03	$\mathbb{Z}_\mu$	$\mathbb{Z}_{\mu^2}^2$	$\log_2 \mu$	$4\log_2 \mu$	4
CPG (Sect. 4.2)	$\mathbb{Z}_\mu$	$\mathbb{Z}_\mu \times \mathbb{Z}_{\mu^2}$	$\log_2 \mu$	$\log_2 \mu + \log_2 U$	$1+\frac{\log_2 U}{\log_2 \mu}$

4 Compression Building-Blocks for Evaluated TFHE Ciphertexts

4.1 ℓ-truncation

Now we turn our attention to the basic (folklore) compression technique, which consists in dropping least significant bits in LWE or RLWE pairs coefficients (we refer to it as ℓ-truncation rather than modulus switching to emphasize that we floor rather than round[1]). The main question is whether the additional noise that it finally induces may be small enough to allow significant compression without prohibitively increasing the probability for decryption errors to occur. The goal

[1] Indeed, the two techniques are different in intent: modulus switching is used to reduce the noise to allow further homomorphic computations, while ℓ-truncation increases it (preventing further computations) while still controlling the decryption error. It will be clear from Sect. 6.1 that rounding rather than flooring in ℓ-truncation does not significantly impact our results.

is then to carefully choose the number of discarded bits in order to comply with a preset probability of incorrect decryption, e.g., $\epsilon = 2^{-k}$ for $k = 40$, 64, or 128.

On one hand, TLWE ℓ-truncation can be combined with the LHE switching technique of Sect. 5 to increase the number of TLWE partial decryptions that can be packed into a single LHE ciphertext. On the other hand, its straightforward extension to TRLWE (Sect. C.2) is also useful as a stand-alone method: we can apply it after TLWE to TRLWE packing (Sect. B.1) to reduce the size of the coefficient of a TRLWE sample before transmission[2].

We study how ℓ-truncation may be applied to a TLWE ciphertext. Let $\mathbf{c} = (a_0, \ldots, a_{n-1}, b = a_n)$ denote a TLWE encryption of m. Given $\ell < \lceil \log_2(q) \rceil$, we define the following three operations:

- $\mathsf{PartialDec}(\mathbf{c}, \mathbf{s})$: return $a_n - \langle \mathbf{a}, \mathbf{s} \rangle = \Delta m + e$, with $\Delta = \frac{q}{t}$.
- $\mathsf{Trunc}(\mathbf{c}, \ell)$: set $a'_i = \lfloor \frac{a_i}{2^\ell} \rfloor$ for $i \in \{0, ..., n\}$ and return $\mathbf{c}' = (a'_0, \ldots, a'_n)$.
- $\mathsf{Rescale}(\mathbf{c}', \ell)$: set $a''_i = 2^\ell a'_i$ for $i \in \{0, ..., n\}$ and return $\mathbf{c}'' = (a''_0, \ldots, a''_n)$.

From these definitions, it follows that when $\mathbf{c}$ is a TLWE encryption of m with noise e (i.e. $\mathsf{PartialDec}(\mathbf{c}, \mathbf{s}) = \Delta m + e$), then $\mathbf{c}''$ is an encryption of m with noise

$$e'' = e - \sum_{i=0}^{n-1} e''_i s_i + e''_n \tag{4}$$

where $e''_i = -(a_i \mod 2^\ell)$. Indeed, let $a''_i = a_i + e''_i$ for $i \in \{0, ..., n\}$ (recall $b = a_n$), then decrypting $\mathbf{c}''$ yields

$$\begin{aligned} a''_n - \sum_{i=0}^{n-1} a''_i s_i &= b + e''_n - \sum_{i=0}^{n-1} a_i s_i - \sum_{i=0}^{n-1} e''_i \cdot s_i \\ &= \underbrace{\Delta m + e - \sum_{i=0}^{n-1} e''_i \cdot s_i + e''_n}_{e''} \end{aligned}$$

Now, given a preset probability of decryption error $\epsilon = 2^{-k}$ and a noise variance σ for e, we would like to be able to choose ℓ such that an ℓ-truncated ciphertext decrypts correctly with probability at least $1 - \epsilon$, i.e. following Eq. (4) $\Pr\left(|e''| < \frac{\Delta}{2}\right) \geq 1 - \epsilon$. We then have the following proposition, which provides us with a first lower bound for the choice of ℓ.

Proposition 1. *Let* $\mathbf{c}$ *denote a TLWE encryption of* m *subject to a centered Gaussian noise* e *with variance* σ^2*, and let* $\mathbf{c}' = \mathsf{Trunc}(\mathbf{c}, \ell_0)$ *with*

$$\ell_0 \leq \left\lfloor \log_2 \left(\frac{1}{n+1} \left(\frac{\Delta}{2} - \sigma\sqrt{2(k+1)\ln 2} \right) + 1 \right) \right\rfloor, \tag{5}$$

[2] It is worth mentioning that the RLWE ℓ-truncation technique can be applied to BGV [12], BFV [10,31], and CKKS [23] RLWE ciphertexts. As these FHE cryptosystems use composite ciphertext modulus, it is natural to think of reducing it via rescaling before applying ℓ-truncation and sending the final result to the client. We leave this idea as a perspective for future explorations.

and $\Delta = \frac{q}{t}$. *Then,* $\left\lceil \frac{1}{\Delta} \mathsf{PartialDec}(\mathsf{Rescale}(\mathbf{c}', \ell_0), \mathbf{s})) \right\rfloor = m$ *with probability at least* $1 - 2^{-k}$.

Proof. Let us start by bounding the probability that $\mathbf{c}'' = \mathsf{Rescale}(\mathbf{c}', \ell)$ incorrectly decrypts, i.e. following (4), that

$$\Pr\left(|e''| \geq \frac{\Delta}{2}\right) = \Pr\left(\left|e - \sum_{i=0}^{n-1} e_i'' s_i + e_n''\right| \geq \frac{\Delta}{2}\right),$$
$$\leq \Pr\left(|e| \geq \frac{\Delta}{2} - (n+1)(2^\ell - 1)\right),$$

as, by definition, $|e_i''| \leq 2^\ell - 1$. Assuming e follows a (centered) Gaussian distribution of variance σ^2, the Chernoff bound[3] tells us that $\Pr\left(|e''| \geq \frac{\Delta}{2}\right) \leq 2e^{-\frac{\left(\frac{\Delta}{2} - (n+1)(2^\ell - 1)\right)^2}{2\sigma^2}}$. Which, letting $2e^{-\frac{\left(\frac{\Delta}{2} - (n+1)(2^\ell - 1)\right)^2}{2\sigma^2}} = 2^{-k}$, leads to,

$$2^\ell = \frac{1}{n+1}\left(\frac{\Delta}{2} - \sigma\sqrt{2(k+1)\ln 2}\right) + 1,$$

hence the claim. □

Applying the ℓ-truncation technique, we focus on the probability of decryption error rather than the variance or infinite norm of the noise. It allows us to ensure correct decryption after truncation for a preset probability of decryption error. To do so, we based our noise analysis on the Chernoff bound rather than the erf function, as the former is more manageable for very low probabilities (e.g., 2^{-40}) and quite tight[4].

In general, we use Proposition 1 for evaluated ciphertexts, taking σ^2 as the post-bootstrapping variance σ^2_{BS}. To give an intuition, with our running TFHE parameter example (Table 2), for $\epsilon = 2^{-40}$, Proposition 1 leads to $\ell_0 = 19$, meaning a ciphertext size reduction of around 60%. Although it does not give us a closed-form formula for ℓ, we give a slightly more precise proposition in Sect. C.1.

4.2 Compressed Paillier-ElGamal (CPG)

In this section, we recall a standard variant of the BCP03 encryption scheme, which is commonly called Paillier-ElGamal [41,45] and features smaller ciphertext compared to the traditional BCP03 [17] (Sect. A.4) encryption scheme

---

[3] Recall that for a (centered) Gaussian deviate, the two-sided Chernoff bound is such that $P(|X| \geq \alpha) \leq 2e^{-\frac{\alpha^2}{2\sigma^2}}$.

[4] A bound for ℓ_0, obtained using the erf, differs from (5) by one term ($\sqrt{k \ln 2}$ vs $\mathrm{erf}^{-1}(1 - 2^{-k})$), which is more challenging to compute. Furthermore, $\mathrm{erf}^{-1}(1 - 2^{-k})$ is not defined for $k > 54$, while we want to determine ℓ_0 for $k = 64, 128$ as well.

($3 \log \mu$ bits versus $4 \log \mu$). Then, we show that this variants additionally supports an efficient *compression* procedure that allows to further reduce its ciphertext size down to $\log \mu + |m|$, where $|m|$ denotes the bitlength of the encrypted message m. This compression procedure is incompatible with the homomorphic features of the scheme but can be used once all homomorphic operations have been computed, before sending the final ciphertext to the owner of the secret key.

A Variant of BCP03 with Shorter Ciphertexts. The following variant of BCP03 is well-known and has roots in [27,28]:

- KeyGen: Let $\mu = pq$ be an RSA modulus. Choose a random $\alpha \in \mathbb{Z}_{\mu^2}^*$, a random value $d \in [1, \text{ord}(\mathbb{G})]$. Set $g = \alpha^2 \bmod \mu$ and $h = g^{\mu \cdot d} \bmod \mu^2$. Return a public key $pk = (\mu, g, h)$ and a secret key $sk = d$.
- Enc: For a given message $m \in \mathbb{Z}_\mu$, a random pad $r \xleftarrow{\$} \mathbb{Z}_{\mu^2}$ return a ciphertext $\mathbf{c} = (c_0, c_1)$ such that $c_0 = g^r \bmod \mu$, $c_1 = h^r(1+\mu)^m \bmod \mu^2$.[5]
- Dec: Compute $c = c_1(c_0)^{-\mu \cdot d} \bmod \mu^2$ and return $m = \frac{c-1}{\mu}$.

We make a few remarks on the above scheme. Compared with the traditional BCP03, h is now computed as a μ-th power. This implies that $c_1 = h^r(1+\mu)^m = (g^{rd})^\mu(1+\mu)^m \bmod \mu^2$ (without the component c_0) is actually a valid Paillier encryption of m. Second, the component c_0 is now given modulo μ, reducing the ciphertext size by 25%. This is without loss of security, as one can easily check that $[g^r \bmod \mu]^\mu = g^{\mu r} \bmod \mu^2$.

Eventually, security-wise, the scheme can be proven IND-CPA secure under the DCR assumption; hence, it achieves identical security guarantees compared to Paillier. This follows from a sequence of straightforward game hops. We believe this proof to be essentially folklore. However, to our knowledge it has not been explicitly described anywhere, and we include it for convenience:

- **Hybrid 1:** replace $h = g^{\mu d} \bmod \mu^2$ with a uniformly random $h \xleftarrow{\$} \mathbb{Z}_{\mu^2}^*$. Under the DCR assumption, this hybrid is indistinguishable from the real key generation algorithm.
- **Hybrid 2:** replace α with a random μ-th power $\alpha \leftarrow \beta^\mu \bmod \mu^2$ for $\beta \xleftarrow{\$} \mathbb{Z}_{\mu^2}$, and $g \leftarrow \alpha^2 \bmod \mu^2$. Under the DCR assumption, this hybrid is indistinguishable from the previous one.

Then, observe that in Hybrid 2, the message m is statistically hidden given a ciphertext (c_0, c_1). Indeed, the uniform distribution over $\mathbb{Z}_{\mu^2}$ is statistically close to the uniform distribution over $\mathbb{Z}_{\mu \cdot \phi(\mu)}$, because $\mu - \phi(\mu) = p + q - 1$ is of the order of $\sqrt{\mu}$. By the Chinese Remainder Theorem, as μ is coprime to $\phi(\mu)$, $\mathbb{Z}_{\mu \cdot \phi(\mu)}$ is isomorphic to $\mathbb{Z}_\mu \times \mathbb{Z}_{\phi(\mu)}$. Write $h = (1+n)^a g^b \bmod \mu^2$ for some (a, b) (all elements admit such a decomposition), where $a \neq 0$ and is coprime to μ

[5] Note that $(1+\mu)^m \equiv 1 + \mu m \mod \mu^2$ (from the Binomial Theorem applied to $(1+\mu)^m$).

with overwhelming probability. Then, observe that since g generates a subgroup of order $\phi(\mu)/4$, the ciphertext c_0 leaks only the value $r_0 = [r \bmod \phi(\mu)/4]$. In contrast, $c_1 = h^r(1+\mu)^m = (1+\mu)^{ar_1+m \bmod \mu} g^{br_0 \bmod \phi(\mu)/4} \bmod \mu^2$, where $r_1 = [r \bmod \mu]$ is statistically indistinguishable from random given r_0 (by coprimality of μ and $\phi(\mu)$). Hence, the value $ar_1 + m \bmod \mu$ statistically hides m. This concludes the proof. In the following, in line with previous works, we call the above scheme Paillier-ElGamal.

Distributed Discrete Logarithm. The scheme above enjoys shorter ciphertexts than the traditional BCP03, but still larger than Paillier ($3 \log \mu$ versus $2 \log \mu$). In this section, we recall the *distributed discrete logarithm* procedure introduced in [41,45]. At a high level, this procedure allows two parties, given divisive shares of $(1 + \mu)^m \bmod \mu^2$ over $\mathbb{Z}^*_{\mu^2}$, to non-interactively derive *subtractive shares* of m over $\mathbb{Z}_\mu$. We outline the procedure DDLog_μ below.

Input. An element $u \in \mathbb{Z}^*_{\mu^2}$.
Output. A value $v \in \mathbb{Z}_\mu$.
Procedure. Write $u = u_0 + \mu \cdot u_1$, where $u_0, u_1 \in \mathbb{Z}_\mu$ denote the base-μ decomposition of u. Return $v = u_1/u_0 \bmod \mu$.

We now explain why this procedure has the intended behavior. Let u, u' denote two divisive shares over $\mathbb{Z}^*_{\mu^2}$ of $(1 + \mu)^m \bmod \mu^2$; that is, $u'/u = (1 + \mu)^m = 1 + \mu m \bmod \mu^2$. Writing $u = u_0 + \mu \cdot u_1$ and $u' = u'_0 + \mu \cdot u'_1$, we obtain $u'_0 + \mu \cdot u'_1 = (u_0 + \mu \cdot u_1) \cdot (1 + \mu \cdot m) \bmod \mu^2$. The above equation yields $u_0 = u'_0 \bmod \mu$ and $u'_1 = u_1 + u_0 m \bmod \mu$. Therefore, $m = u'_1/u'_0 - u_1/u_0 \bmod \mu$: u'_1/u'_0 and u_1/u_0 form subtractive shares of m over $\mathbb{Z}_\mu$, as intended.

Compressing Ciphertexts via DDLog_μ. The distributed discrete logarithm procedure implies a simple and efficient compression mechanism for Paillier-ElGamal. The key observation is that given $c_0 = g^r \bmod \mu$, the holder of the secret key d can locally compute $u = c_0^{\mu \cdot d} = h^r \bmod \mu^2$. Then, u and c_1 form divisive shares of $c_1/u = (1+\mu m) \bmod \mu^2$. This immediately yields the following compression mechanism:

- $\mathsf{Compress}(c_0, c_1)$: run $v' \leftarrow \mathsf{DDLog}_\mu(c_1)$. Output (c_0, v').
- $\mathsf{Dec}'(c_0, v')$: compute $u \leftarrow c_0^{\mu \cdot d} \bmod \mu^2$ and $v \leftarrow \mathsf{DDLog}_\mu(u)$. Output $m = v' - v \bmod \mu$.

The resulting compressed ciphertext size is $2 \log \mu$, down from $3 \log \mu$, matching the size of a standard Paillier ciphertext. However, if m is known to be smaller than a bound $B < \mu/2^\lambda$ (where λ denotes a statistical security parameter), we can do better. The main observation (which is not new; the same observation was used in [41,45]) is that with overwhelming probability, v', v form subtractive shares of m *over the integers*. This stems from the following facts:

- Over the randomness of r, the value $v' = \mathsf{DDLog}_\mu(c_1) = \mathsf{DDLog}(h^r \cdot (1 + \mu m) \bmod \mu^2)$ is uniformly distributed over $\mathbb{Z}_\mu$.

- Then, if $m \leq B$, the probability that $v' - m$ causes a wraparound modulo μ is at most $B/\mu \leq 1/2^\lambda$, hence $v' - v = m$ over the integers.

This observation allows to further reduce the compressed ciphertext size by reducing v' modulo B:

- $\mathsf{Compress}(c_0, c_1)$: run $v' \leftarrow \mathsf{DDLog}_\mu(c_1)$ and set $v'' \leftarrow [v' \bmod B]$. Output (c_0, v'').
- $\mathsf{Dec}'(c_0, v')$: compute $u \leftarrow c_0^{\mu \cdot d} \bmod \mu^2$ and $v \leftarrow \mathsf{DDLog}_\mu(u)$. Output $m = v'' - v \bmod B$.

With this last optimization, the ciphertext size went down to $\log \mu + \log B$ bits. When B is small (e.g., $B \approx 2^{40}$ as in our application), this yields an almost twofold size improvement over a standard Paillier encryption. We note that a similar procedure has been previously described in the context of ElGamal encryption [16]. The Paillier-ElGamal variant, which we outline here, has the advantage of being extremely efficient, as compression amounts only to an inversion and a product modulo μ followed by a modular reduction.

5 Switching to LHE

In this section, we investigate several approaches to switch from TLWE homomorphic ciphertexts to (more compact) linearly homomorphic ones by executing the linear part of the (T)LWE decryption function, $b - \langle \mathbf{a}, \mathbf{s} \rangle$ (recall Eq. (1)), under the target linearly homomorphic scheme. As a result of this operation, we obtain encryptions of *partial decryptions* of TFHE ciphertexts under the target LHE. We consider several candidate LHE cryptosystems such as Paillier, Dåmgard-Jurik, EC ElGamal, and our compressed variant of BCP03 (Sect. 4.2). When the properties of the LHE allow it, we also consider packing the partial decryptions of *several* TFHE ciphertexts in a single LHE ciphertext in order to achieve better transmission efficiency when several evaluated TFHE ciphertexts have to be transmitted. To reduce the number of bits needed to encode a partial decryption (and hence be able to pack more partial decryptions per LHE ciphertext), we also investigate the use of this technique in conjunction with the ℓ-truncation technique, which we introduced in Sect. 4.1.

Overall, the most appropriate choice for the LHE depends on several factors, such as its plaintext/ciphertext ratio size, how many partial decryptions can be packed in its plaintexts, and the conditions under which it can decrypt efficiently (as some LHE require solving a discrete log in their decryption function). Because of all these degrees of freedom, some LHE are more appropriate than others for the purpose of transmitting a given number of evaluated TFHE ciphertexts.

5.1 A Generic Switching Algorithm

Let $\mathcal{E}_H$ denote an instance of TFHE and $\mathcal{E}_L$ a target LHE. Let μ denote the plaintext modulus of $\mathcal{E}_L$ and v denote the number of bits necessary to represent a partial decryption (because μ is generally much greater than q, the partial decryptions are *not* computed modulo q, and we have to account for the carries occurring in their computation). Then up to

$$M = \left\lfloor \frac{\lfloor \log_2 \mu \rfloor}{v} \right\rfloor \tag{6}$$

partial decryptions can be packed into a single LHE ciphertext. Switching then works as follows. Let $\mathbf{s} \in \mathbb{B}^n$ denote $\mathcal{E}_H$'s secret key, and let $c_s^{(i)} = \mathcal{E}_L.\mathsf{Enc}(s_i)$ for $i \in \{0, ..., n-1\}$ denote encryptions of its coefficients under $\mathcal{E}_L$. We further denote by $(\mathbf{a}^{(j)}, b^{(j)})$, $j \in \{0, ..., M-1\}$, the M TLWE pairs that we wish to convert. The conversion algorithm then starts with ciphertext $c = \mathcal{E}_L.\mathsf{Enc}(0)$. For $i = 0$ to $n-1$, we then perform, $c := c \oplus \left(-\sum_{j=0}^{M-1} 2^{jv} a_i^{(j)}\right) \odot c_s^{(i)}$, where $\oplus$ and $\odot$ respectively denote the addition and the multiplication-by-a-constant operator of $\mathcal{E}_L$ (remark that $-\sum_{j=0}^{M-1} 2^{jv} a_i^{(j)}$ lives in the clear domain of $\mathcal{E}_L$). Lastly, switching is finalized by doing[6]

$$c := c \oplus \mathcal{E}_L.\mathsf{Enc}\left(\sum_{j=0}^{M-1} 2^{jv} b^{(j)}\right). \tag{7}$$

Algorithm 1 summarizes the above. As such, the algorithm terminates with an encryption of $\sum_{j=0}^{M-1} 2^{jv} \left(b^{(j)} - \langle \mathbf{a}^{(j)}, \mathbf{s} \rangle\right)$ but *without the modulo q which is implicit in Eq.* (1). After LHE decryption, one may recover the j-th partial decryption by doing

$$\varphi^{(j)} = \left(\left\lfloor \frac{\mathcal{E}_L.\mathsf{Dec}(c)}{2^{jv}} \right\rfloor \mod 2^v\right) \mod q, \tag{8}$$

and decryption is finalized using Eq. (3). Lastly, (8) has to be slightly modified as follows when ℓ-truncation is applied,

$$\varphi^{(j)} = 2^{\ell} \left(\left\lfloor \frac{\mathcal{E}_L.\mathsf{Dec}(c)}{2^{jv'}} \right\rfloor \mod 2^{v'}\right) \mod q,$$

where $v' < v$ is used instead of v in Algorithm 1.

Considering our running TFHE parameters example of Table 2, with $q = 2^{32}$, we need $v = 42$ bits[7] to be able to represent a partial decryption prior to its reduction modulo q. This number goes down to 23 bits if we apply ℓ-truncation as proposed in Sect. 4.1 and drop 19 least significant bits in the coefficients of the LWE pairs prior to switching them (leading to a probability of erroneous decryption of 2^{-40}). We will use these numbers for illustration purposes in the next subsections.

[6] When the target LHE provides an addition-by-a-constant operator, the latter can be used in Eq. (7) instead of invoking the encryption function of the scheme.

[7] As we have to sum $n+1$ numbers (uniformly distributed) in $\{0, ..., q\}$, in the worst case, we get $(n+1)q$, which requires $\lceil \log_2(n+1) + \log_2 q \rceil$ bits. With n between 512 and 1024 and $q = 2^{32}$, 42 bits are conservatively required.

Algorithm 1. TLWEtoLHE

Input: Encryptions of $\mathcal{E}_H$'s secret key coefficients under $\mathcal{E}_L$, $c_s^{(i)} = \mathcal{E}_L.\mathsf{Enc}(s_i)$, M TLWE pairs $(\mathbf{a}^{(j)}, b^{(j)})$.

Output: $c \in \mathcal{E}_L.\mathcal{C}$ such that c is an encryption of $\sum_{j=0}^{M-1} 2^{jv}\left(b^j - \langle \mathbf{a}^j, \mathbf{s}\rangle\right)$.

1: $c = \mathcal{E}_L.\mathsf{Enc}(0)$
2: **for** $i = 0$, $i < n$, i++ **do**,
3: $\quad c := c \oplus \left(-\sum_{j=0}^{M-1} 2^{jv} a_i^{(j)}\right) \odot c_s^{(i)}$,
4: **end for**
5: **return** $c := c \oplus \mathcal{E}_L.\mathsf{Enc}\left(\sum_{j=0}^{M-1} 2^{jv} b^{(j)}\right)$.

5.2 Switching to Paillier

Recall Sect. 3.3, the Paillier scheme has respective plaintext and ciphertext domains $\mathbb{Z}_\mu$ and $\mathbb{Z}_{\mu^2}$, where μ is an RSA modulus. Following the previous section, we can pack up to $M = \left\lfloor \frac{\lfloor \log_2 \mu \rfloor}{v} \right\rfloor$ partial decryptions in a single Paillier ciphertext. Let K denote a number of partial decryptions that need to be transmitted, and let $r_1 = K \bmod M$ and $r_2 = \lfloor K/M \rfloor$; then we have to pack these partial decryptions M-by-M (from Algorithm 1) using r_2 Paillier ciphertexts when $r_1 = 0$ or $r_2 + 1$ such ciphertexts otherwise. When $r_1 = 0$, the expansion factor is then

$$\frac{\lceil 2\log_2 \mu \rceil}{M \log_2 t} \tag{9}$$

(this is also the asymptotic expansion factor when $K \to \infty$), and, otherwise, the expansion factor is given by $\frac{(r_2+1)\lceil 2\log_2 \mu \rceil}{K \log_2 t}$.

Considering an RSA modulus of 2048 bits (the usual recommendation to achieve 128 bits of security) and our running example of TFHE parameters (Table 2), we can pack around $2048/42 \approx 48$ TLWE partial decryptions per Paillier ciphertext. For $K \leq 48$ we then get an expansion factor of $4096/K$, i.e. 4096 for $K = 1$ and around 85 for $K = 48$ (which is also the asymptotic expansion factor). If we apply ℓ-truncation, then we can pack around $2048/23 \approx 89$ partial decryptions in a single Paillier ciphertext. For $K \leq 89$, we obtain an expansion factor between 4096 ($K = 1$) and 46 ($K = 89$), this latter also being the asymptotic expansion factor. *Keep in mind that these latter numbers must be compared with the raw expansion factor of 32800 induced by TLWE ciphertexts: for $K = 89$ (with ℓ-*truncation*)* the expansion thus becomes 713 times smaller. We explore more TFHE parameters in Sect. 6.

5.3 Switching to Dåmgard-Jurik

As an alternative to Paillier (and as initially considered in [15]), we may consider using the Damgård-Jurik scheme (recall the definition in Sect. 3.3), which generalizes the former scheme with $\mathbb{Z}_{\mu^y}$ and $\mathbb{Z}_{\mu^{y+1}}$ ($y > 1$) respectively as plaintext and ciphertext domains. Because the plaintext modulus is larger than for Paillier, it is possible to pack more TLWE partial decryptions into a single Dåmgard-Jurik ciphertext. Indeed, following Sect. 5.1, we can now pack up to $M = \left\lfloor \frac{\lfloor y \log_2 \mu \rfloor}{v} \right\rfloor$ partial decryptions in a single Dåmgard-Jurik ciphertext. As in the previous section, let K denote the number of partial decryptions that need to be transmitted, and let $r_1 = K \bmod M$ as well as $r_2 = \lfloor K/M \rfloor$, then we have to pack these partial decryptions M-by-M (Algorithm 1) using r_2 Dåmgard-Jurik ciphertexts when $r_1 = 0$, or $r_2 + 1$ such ciphertexts otherwise. When $r_1 = 0$, the expansion factor is then

$$\frac{\lceil (y+1) \log_2 \mu \rceil}{M \log_2 t} \tag{10}$$

(*for a fixed* y, this is also the asymptotic expansion factor when $K \to \infty$) and, otherwise, the expansion factor is given by $\frac{(r_2+1)\lceil (y+1)\log_2 \mu \rceil}{K \log_2 t}$. Interestingly, Dåmgard-Jurik asymptotically achieves the lowest expansion factor when both K and y increase to ∞. Indeed, (10) can be approximated by $\frac{v(y+1)\log_2 \mu}{y \log_2 \mu \log_2 t} = \frac{v(y+1)}{y \log_2 t}$ leading to $\lim_{y\to\infty} \frac{v(y+1)}{y \log_2 t} = \frac{v}{\log_2 t}$, which is the optimal rate achievable with the LHE switching technique.

Returning to our favorite running TFHE parameter example and considering, as for Paillier, a 2048-bit RSA modulus with $y = 2$, we can pack up to $M = 4096/42 \approx 97$ TLWE partial decryptions in a single Dåmgard-Jurik ciphertext. Then for $K = 97$ we illustratively obtain an expansion factor of around 63, this is also the asymptotic expansion factor (for fixed $y = 2$) which can then be compared with the value 85 obtained for Paillier. Lastly, putting ℓ-truncation into the picture leads to $M = 4096/23 \approx 178$ and an asymptotic expansion factor (again for fixed $y = 2$) of around 34. We compare the different methods and explore more TFHE parameters in Sect. 6.

5.4 Switching to Compressed Paillier-ElGamal

We now consider packing TLWE partial decryptions within ciphertexts of the compressed Paillier-ElGamal (CPG) scheme that we introduced in Sect. 4.2. As for Paillier (and Dåmgard-Jurik), this scheme has a plaintext modulus μ. However, the size of a ciphertext with an l-bit payload ($l \leq \log_2(\mu)$) is only $l + \lceil \log_2 \mu \rceil$. As a consequence, this scheme is best used when small numbers of TLWE partial decryptions have to be transmitted. As in the Paillier case, we can pack up to $M = \left\lfloor \frac{\lfloor \log_2 \mu \rfloor}{v} \right\rfloor$ partial decryptions in a single CPG ciphertext, and the two schemes achieve the same asymptotic expansion factor. However, when we wish to pack only $K \leq M$ partial decryptions in a CPG ciphertext, the resulting expansion factor is $\frac{Kv + \lceil \log_2 \mu \rceil}{K \log_2 t}$ compared to the Paillier case, which, recall Eq. (9), gives $\frac{2 \log_2 \mu}{K \log_2 t}$.

Returning again to our running TFHE parameters example of Table 2 (and reusing the numbers from the end of Sect. 5.2), we can pack up to 48 (w/o ℓ-truncation) or 89 (with ℓ-truncation) partial decryptions in a single CPG ciphertext. Without ℓ-truncation, for $K = 5$, 10, and 40 we then obtain respective expansion factors of 451, 247, and 93 (versus 819, 410, and 102 for Paillier). With ℓ-truncation into the picture, again for $K = 5$, 10, and 40, we respectively end up with 432, 228 and 74 (also versus 819, 410, and 102 for Paillier). More comparisons are provided in Sect. 6 on various parameter sets.

5.5 Switching to EC ElGamal

For completeness, we also briefly consider packing partial decryptions in EC ElGamal ciphertexts (recall the definition in Sect. 3.3). This scheme is the most compact that we consider in this work, but this compactness comes with the price of having to solve a discrete logarithm in the scheme decryption function. As such, we can only use it to encrypt small payloads (say, with a length of around or slightly above 40 bits). As a consequence, it is not possible to pack many TLWE partial decryptions in an EC ElGamal ciphertext, and this reduces its applicability to settings when no more than one or two evaluated TLWE ciphertexts have to be transmitted (using ℓ-truncation to decrease the number of bits needed to represent their partial decryptions). Still, in such cases, it is competitive with other approaches (transferring only one TLWE ciphertext always leads to the worst expansion factor, as the size of the LHE ciphertext is not amortized). Indeed, when a single TLWE ciphertext $(\mathbf{a}, b)$ has to be transmitted, switching to EC ElGamal by executing $b - \langle \mathbf{a}, \mathbf{s} \rangle$ over that cryptosystem will lead to a ciphertext of size around $\log_2 \omega$ bits, and an expansion factor will be $\frac{\lceil \log_2 \omega \rceil}{K \log_2(t)}$.

For our favorite running TFHE parameters example, with $t = 2$ and $K = 1$ we thus get 512 (which is the smallest expansion factor we obtain when transferring a single TLWE partial decryption, all the other LHEs being in the thousands in that case). If we apply ℓ-truncation, we can either accelerate the decryption function (only a discrete log with an upper bound of 23 bits then needs to be solved) or attempt to pack two partial decryptions (needing 46 bits in total) in a single ciphertext. In that latter case, the expansion factor gets down to 256.

6 Experimental Results and Comparisons

In our experimental analysis, we consider two TFHE parameter sets. The first set is identical to the running example we have used so far for illustrative purposes (Table 2) and our second parameter set is for $t = 16$ meaning that TFHE ciphertexts now have a 4-bit payload, rather than only 1 bit. We give the full parameter sets in Sect. D.

6.1 Relationship Between ℓ and k

Recall Eq. (5) on page 9, which tells the number of bits ℓ that we can drop in the coefficients of a TLWE pair in function of a target probability of decryption error 2^{-k}. Since ℓ is influenced by $\log_2 k$ and because a flooring occurs in the formula (as only an integer number of bits can be dropped), we can expect that a given choice for ℓ covers a wide range of decryption error probabilities.

We illustrate this in Table 4 for T(R)LWE ℓ-truncation. The table also shows that in both cases, ℓ-truncation does not prevent achieving a negl(λ) probability of decryption error, although of course fewer bits have to be dropped than for larger probabilities of error. Note that the probability of bootstrapping error has to be set consistently with the probability of erroneous decryption induced by ℓ-truncation. For example, since our parameter set for $t = 2$ induces a probability of bootstrapping error of 2^{-154}, Table 4 tells us that we can drop up to 18 bits per coefficient and still achieve an *overall* probability of decryption error less than 2^{-128}, i.e. FHE correctness with overwhelming probability[8]. For comparison, in Sect. E we provide a similar table (Table 8c) for ℓ values found using Proposition 2.

Table 4. Applying Proposition 1 for $t = 2, 16$ and several values for the probability of decryption error ϵ, the upper part represents a maximum value for ℓ when ℓ-truncating an evaluated (i.e. bootstrapped) TLWE ciphertext, and the bottom part – when ℓ-truncating a degree-N TRLWE ciphertext in which N n-dimensional evaluated TLWE ciphertexts have been packed.

t	ϵ		
	2^{-40}	2^{-64}	2^{-128}
2	19.863057	19.408270	17.486391
16	17.217345	17.151246	17.010226
2	19.747898	19.203378	15.716669
16	17.217326	17.151221	17.010187

6.2 Expansion Factors

We now turn our attention to the expansion factor metric, which, recall, is defined as the ratio between the ciphertext size and corresponding plaintext size. The expansion factor formulas for the T(R)LWE-based compression techniques and the LHE-based ones can be found in the respective sections describing these methods and in Sect. E. In Table 5 we then provide a comparison between the expansion factor obtained by the different methods for $t = 16$ as a function of K, the number of evaluated TLWE ciphertexts that have to be transmitted.

Overall, again for $t = 16$, when $K = 1$ or 2, EC ElGamal achieves the smallest expansion factors (128 and 64, respectively). In the range $2 < K \leq 81$, the lowest expansion factor is achieved by performing ℓ-truncation and then switching to CPG (achieving, for example, an expansion factor of around 16.5 for $K = 50$). Up to $K \leq 1000$, Dåmgard-Jurik (with $y = 2$) gives the best compression,

[8] This remark is important, as ensuring correctness is a natural countermeasure against the recent CPA^D attacks against TFHE and other schemes [19,22].

Table 5. Example expansion factors for each of the methods considered in this paper ($t = 16$). The rightmost column gives the asymptotic expansion factors when $K \to \infty$.

K	1	50	150	250	500	∞
TLWE	6008	6008	6008	6008	6008	6008
TLWE ℓ-truncation	2816.2	2816.2	2816.2	2816.2	2816.2	2816.2
Shrinking (Sect. B.2)	16393	328.8	110.2	66.5	33.7	9
TLWEtoTRLWE	16392	335.6	117.2	73.5	40.7	16
TLWEtoTRLWE + ℓ-truncation	7683.75	157.35	55	34.5	19.11	**7.5**
Paillier (w. packing)	1024	40.9	27.3	24.5	22.5	21.3
ℓ-truncation + Paillier (w. packing)	1024	20.4	13.6	16.3	14.3	12.6
DÃĕmgard-Jurik (w. packing)	1536	30.7	20.4	18.4	18.4	15.8
ℓ-truncation + D.-J. (w. packing)	1536	30.7	**10.2**	**12.2**	**12.2**	9.4
CPG (w. packing)	522.5	31	24.1	22.7	21.7	21.1
ℓ-truncation + CPG (w. packing)	518.25	**16.5**	13	14.4	13.4	12.5
EC ElGamal	**128**	–	–	–	–	–

achieving, for example, an expansion factor of around 12 for $K = 250$ and 500. For $K \geq 1000$, TRLWE packing followed by ℓ-truncation becomes the best option and leads to an expansion factor of around 7. This is summarized[9] in Table 6. As discussed in Sect. 5.3, if we forget practicality for a moment and let the y parameter of Dåmgard-Jurik increase and apply ℓ-truncation with $\ell = 17$ (Table 4), we will eventually achieve the smallest possible expansion factor of $\frac{32-17}{4} = 3.75$. As already emphasized, *all these expansion factors must be compared to the raw expansion factor of* 6008 *induced by TLWE ciphertexts for* $t = 16$.

6.3 Computational Costs

This section further investigates the computational cost of the methods described in this paper. For example, packing 1024 550-TLWE ciphertexts ($t = 2$) into a single TRLWE ciphertext takes 0.4 secs when implemented by means of TFHE-Lib. Then, switching 89 20-truncated partial decryptions ($t = 2$) to a Paillier ciphertext with a 2048-bit RSA modulus takes 3.41 secs[10] on a single-core, and this number gets down to 0.42 secs with mild parallelization on an average laptop. For Dåmgard-Jurik, we obtain (estimated) timings of 10.24 secs to switch

[9] We also give two illustrative plots (Figs. 1 and 2) of the expansion factors change in Sect. E.

[10] Note that it is faster to "decrypt-then-pack," which takes 2.83 secs (since computing the dot-product involves smaller numbers, hence leading to smaller exponent corresponding mult-by-const operations under Paillier) than to "pack-then-decrypt," which accounts for 3.41 secs.

Table 6. Most appropriate compression methods in function of K, the number of evaluated TLWE ciphertexts that have to be transmitted. The timings are given in seconds for the maximum value of K on the intervals: the first column corresponds to "pack-then-decrypt" switching, the second to "decrypt-then-pack," and the third to parallelized "decrypt-then-pack."

K	Most compressive method	Timing		
$1 \leq K \leq 2$	Switch. to EC ElGamal	0.02	0.01	0.001
$2 < K \leq 81$	ℓ-truncation + switch. to CPG (w.pack.)	6.93	5.66	0.86
$81 < K \leq 163$	ℓ-truncation + switch. to D.-J. (w.pack.)	13.87	11.32	1.73
$163 < K \leq 243$	ℓ-truncation + switch. to CPG (w.pack.)	20.79	16.89	2.58
$243 < K \leq 1141$	ℓ-truncation + switch. to D.-J. (w.pack.)	97.09	79.24	12.11
$1141 < K \leq 1228$	TLWEtoTRLWE + ℓ-truncation	0.4		
$1228 < K \leq 1304$	ℓ-truncation + switch. to D.-J. (w.pack.)	110.96	90.56	13.84
$K > 1304$	TLWEtoTRLWE + ℓ-truncation	0.4		

178 20-truncated partial ($t = 2$) with a 2048-bit RSA modulus. Lastly, the runtimes for CPG are very close to those of Paillier. Additional timings (for $t = 16$) are reported in Table 6.

All these numbers illustrate that our methods run quite fast in practice, especially when comparing to the cost and latency of a typical homomorphic computation, which is generally a matter of minutes, if not much more.

7 Conclusion

In this paper, we have proposed and experimentally studied a versatile and practical toolbox to address the issue of compressing evaluated (T)FHE ciphertexts, i.e. encrypted results obtained following the FHE evaluation of some useful function, to minimize their downlink transmission footprint towards decryption. To the best of our knowledge, while this issue is very important to FHE practice, it has so far been largely overshadowed in the literature by the issue of compressing input FHE ciphertexts, i.e. encrypted inputs towards the FHE evaluation of some useful function, to minimize their uplink transmission footprint from encryption. Still, the two issues are very different in nature, and their solutions require different corpora of techniques and tools. As key takeaways, we have revealed the regimes in which the techniques we have studied are best applicable, leading to the following concrete recommendations:

- Switching to EC ElGamal is the most compact option for transmitting a single evaluated TFHE ciphertext.
- Switching to our new compressed variant of BCP03 (with several partial decryptions packed in each ciphertext) is the most communication-efficient option for transmitting up to around 100 evaluated TFHE ciphertexts.

– Above this value, we recommend switching to Damgard-Jurik (also with several partial decryptions packed in each ciphertext) for compressing larger numbers of evaluated TFHE ciphertexts, although this approach may eventually become too computationally costly, and, in that case, TRLWE packing will provide relatively similar compression factors with a much lower computational cost.

Additionally, all these approaches can be combined with a simple precision reduction technique, which, we have shown, still allows to keep a manageable probability of erroneous decryption. This technique allows to pack more partial decryptions in each LHE ciphertext and thus further enhance compression. Compared to the previous works, which have essentially focused on asymptotic rates from a more theoretical viewpoint, all these approaches are practically applicable.

As a concluding remark, let us emphasize that the techniques developed in this paper are applicable and beneficial only to LWE-based schemes such as TFHE. This is so for several reasons: first, the LHEs that we are considering in this paper have a plaintext domain that is too small to absorb the large N typically used for RLWE schemes such as BFV or BGV (which then achieve relatively low expansion factors of $2\log_2 q/\log_2 t$ for both uplink and downlink[11] and by default fall in the large K regime in the terminology of Sect. 6) and similarly so for TRLWE ciphertexts. Likewise, the ℓ-truncation technique is not universally applicable. Indeed, as it significantly increases the ciphertext noise, it can be applied only to schemes with an efficient bootstrapping procedure (like TFHE), which then allows it to be applied to evaluated ciphertexts with a sufficient noise margin. Trying to apply this technique in the SHE setting for BFV or BGV would then require larger parameters and would most likely cancel the benefits of using ℓ-truncation in the first place. As a perspective, developing compression techniques practically applicable to partially filled evaluated RLWE ciphertexts is an interesting follow-up research question.

Acknowledgments. The authors would like to thank Pierre-Emmanuel Clet for lending his invaluable help and expertise during the discussions on TFHE.

A Linear Homomorphic Encryption Schemes

Here we briefly recall Paillier [42], Dåmgard-Jurik [30], Elliptic Curve ElGamal [38], and BCP03 [17] cryptosystems, which are used in the sequel.

A.1 Paillier

The Paillier cryptosystem [42] is a public key encryption scheme invented by Pascal Paillier in 1999. It is a partial homomorphic scheme that notably allows performing additions and multiplications-by-a-constant directly over its ciphertexts.

[11] Provided of course that these ciphertexts have no or only few unused slots.

- KeyGen: Choose two large prime numbers p and q randomly and independently such that $\gcd(pq,(p-1)(q-1)) = 1$. Compute $\mu = pq$, $\lambda = \varphi(\mu)$, and set $g = \mu + 1$, where $g \in \mathbb{Z}^*_{\mu^2}$, $\eta = \varphi(\mu)^{-1} \bmod \mu$. Return a public key $pk = (\mu, g)$ and a secret key $sk = (\lambda, \eta)$.
- Enc: Let m, $0 \leq m < \mu$, be a message to encrypt. Select a random $r : 0 < r < \mu$ and $\gcd(r, \mu) = 1$. Return a ciphertext $c \in \mathbb{Z}^*_{\mu^2}$ as $c = g^m \cdot r^\mu \bmod \mu^2$.
- Dec: Return $m = L(c^\lambda \bmod \mu^2) \cdot \eta \bmod \mu$, where $L(x) = \frac{x-1}{\mu}$.

In summary, for the Paillier scheme, a plaintext domain is $\mathbb{Z}_\mu$ and a ciphertext domain is $\mathbb{Z}_{\mu^2}$. A typical parameter choice to achieve 128-bit security or slightly above consists in taking a modulus μ on 2048 bits. A Paillier ciphertext is therefore of size 4096 bits with a 2048-bit payload (leading to an expansion factor of 2).

A.2 Dåmgard-Jurik

The Dåmgard-Jurik cryptosystem [30] is a generalization of the Paillier cryptosystem. It uses a plaintext modulus μ^y and a ciphertext modulus μ^{y+1}, where μ is an RSA modulus and $y \in \mathbb{Z}^+$. Then, Paillier is a special case with $y = 1$.

- KeyGen: Choose an admissible RSA modulus $\mu = pq$ and compute $\lambda = \mathrm{lcm}((p-1)(q-1))$. Return a public key $pk = (\mu)$ and a secret key $sk = (\lambda)$.
- Enc: Let an integer $m > 0$ be a message to encrypt. Choose $y : m < \mu^y$ and select a random $r \in \mathbb{Z}^*_\mu$. Return a ciphertext $c = r^{\mu^y}(1+\mu)^m \bmod \mu^{y+1}$.
- Dec: Compute $c^\lambda \bmod \mu^{y+1} = (1+\mu)^{m\lambda} \bmod \mu^{y+1}$. Compute $v = m\lambda \bmod n^y$ (apply an algorithm from Theorem 1 [30]). Return $m = v\lambda^{-1} \bmod n^y$.

In summary, for the Dåmgard-Jurik scheme, a plaintext domain is $\mathbb{Z}_{\mu^y}$ and a ciphertext domain is $\mathbb{Z}_{\mu^{y+1}}$. A typical parameter choice to achieve 128-bit security or slightly above consists in taking a modulus μ on 2048 bits. A Dåmgard-Jurik ciphertext is therefore of size $2048(y+1)$ bits with a $2048y$ bits payload. Note that a choice of y has no impact on security. Interestingly, an expansion factor for the Dåmgard-Jurik scheme is asymptotically such that $\lim_{y \to \infty} \frac{2048(y+1)}{2048y} = 1$.

A.3 Elliptic Curve ElGamal

Elliptic Curve ElGamal [38] is a public key additive homomorphic encryption scheme. It is a generalization of the ElGamal public key cryptosystem over an elliptic curve.

- KeyGen: Choose a large prime ω and an elliptic curve $E(\mathbb{F}_\omega)$. Choose a point $P \in E$, an integer $a < \mathrm{ord}(P)$ and compute $Q = aP$. Return a public key $pk = (E, P, Q)$ and a secret key $sk = (a)$.

- Enc: Let m, $0 \leq m < \omega$ be a message to encrypt. Express m as a point $X \in E$: $X = mP$. Choose random r and return the ciphertext $\mathbf{c} = (c_0, c_1)$ as $c_0 = rP$, $c_1 = X + rQ$.
- Dec: Compute $X = c_1 - ac_0$. Solve $X = mP$ and return m.

In summary, to set up the scheme, we choose an elliptic curve $y^2 = x^3 + ax + b \bmod \omega$ then a plaintext domain is $\mathbb{F}_\omega$ and a ciphertext domain is $\mathbb{F}_\omega^2$. A typical parameter choice to achieve 128-bit security or slightly above consists in taking an elliptic curve Curve25519. An EC-ElGamal ciphertext is therefore of size 510 bits with a 255-bit payload. However, let us also emphasize that the decryption function requires solving an elliptic curve discrete logarithm problem over Curve25519, which is practical only when a small upper bound is known for the decrypted message. This means that only $\mathfrak{p} \leq 50$ bits are truly usable from the plaintext domain.

A.4 BCP03

BCP03 [17] is another public key additive homomorphic cryptosystem that is an ElGamal-style variant of the Paillier scheme. The scheme is composed of three algorithms defined below.

- KeyGen: Let $\mu = pq$ be an RSA modulus. Choose a random $\alpha \in \mathbb{Z}_{\mu^2}^*$, a random value $d \in [1, \mathrm{ord}(\mathbb{G})]$. Set $g = \alpha^2 \bmod \mu^2$ and $h = g^d \bmod \mu^2$. Return a public key $pk = (\mu, g, h)$ and a secret key $sk = (d)$.
- Enc: For a given message $m \in \mathbb{Z}_\mu$, a random pad $r \xleftarrow{\$} \mathbb{Z}_{\mu^2}$ return a ciphertext $\mathbf{c} = (c_0, c_1)$ such that $c_0 = g^r \bmod \mu^2$, $c_1 = h^r(1+\mu)^m \bmod \mu^2$.
- Dec: Compute $c = c_1(c_0)^{-d} \bmod \mu^2$ and return $m = \frac{c-1}{\mu}$.

In summary, for a *vanilla* variant of this scheme, a plaintext domain is $\mathbb{Z}_\mu$ and a ciphertext domain is $\mathbb{Z}_{\mu^2}^2$. A typical parameter choice to achieve 128-bit security or slightly above consists in taking a modulus μ of around 2048 bits. A BCP03 ciphertext is therefore of size 8192 bits with a 2048-bit payload (leading to an expansion factor of 4). As such, this scheme might not appear competitive with the other LHE presented in this section; we, however, propose in Sect. 5.4 a more advanced variant, which we will refer to as *compressed Paillier-ElGamal* (CPG), in which c_0 is compressed onto 2048 bits and c_1 onto $\log_2 U$ bits (where U is an upper bound on the encrypted message). As such, this new variant will be much more competitive.

B Existing *downlink* Compression Techniques for FHE

B.1 TLWE Packing to One TRLWE

In this section, we discuss a *well-known* idea of packing (up to) $N > n$ TLWE samples into a single TRLWE sample in order to amortize the $\mathbf{a}$ vectors of TLWE samples. Doing that, we would need to transmit just one $\mathbf{a}$ vector for N TLWE samples rather than one $\mathbf{a}$ vector for each of N TLWE samples. This TLWE samples packing technique is called TFHE Public Functional Key Switching, which was introduced in [25]. We use TFHE Public Functional Key Switching with a function being an identity function, which allows to pack N TLWE samples by means of the $\mathbb{Z}-$module isomorphism into a single TRLWE sample whereby N TLWE messages $m_0, \ldots, m_{N-1} \in \mathbb{T} \mapsto m(X) = \sum_{i=0}^{N-1} m_i X^i \in \mathbb{T}_N[X]$.

Noise Analysis: Because additional noise increases a probability of erroneous decryption, it is important to characterize a noise variance σ^2_{pack} in a TRLWE sample obtained from TLWEtoTRLWE packing of N TLWE samples with *independent* noises of variance bounded by σ^2_{BS}. From [25], the error variance σ^2_{pack} satisfies:

$$\sigma^2_{\text{pack}} \leq R^2 \sigma^2_{\text{BS}} + nt_{\text{d}} N \sigma^2_{\text{TRLWE}} + \frac{n}{12} B_{\text{KS}}^{-2t_{\text{d}}}, \tag{11}$$

where $R = 1$ and σ^2_{TRLWE} is the variance[12] of the error in a keyswitch key (KS).

If $K < N$ TLWE samples have to be transmitted, it is possible to pack just $K < N$ TLWE samples into a single TRLWE sample assuming a *not-full packing* to avoid transmitting a part of the resulting TRLWE sample coefficients. It means that we "fill" the first K slots of TRLWE with TLWEs and keep $N - K$ slots empty. To transmit a not-fully packed TRLWE sample on the downlink, we transmit $\mathbf{a}$ and the first K coefficients of $\mathbf{b}$: $b_0, \ldots, b_{K-1}$. To decrypt this TRLWE sample, we perform a decryption of the first K slots of TRLWE.

Now, let's compute an expansion factor for TLWEtoTRLWE packing in the downlink case. Let a value $r_2 = \lfloor K/N \rfloor$ define how many fully packed TRLWE samples we get after packing K TLWE samples, and a value $r_1 = K \bmod N$ define how many TLWE samples are left to pack in a last not-fully packed TRLWE sample. It means that we need to transmit r_2 fully packed TRLWE samples and one not-fully packed TRLWE sample with r_1 (> 0) packed coefficients; then the size of the resulting ciphertexts is $2r_2 N \log_2 q + (N + r_1) \log_2 q$. At the same time, the resulting ciphertexts encrypt $r_2 N + r_1$ plaintext messages of size $\log_2 t$; thus, for $r_1 > 0$ the expansion factor is $\frac{(2r_2 N + N + r_1) \log_2 q}{(r_2 N + r_1) \log_2 t}$, and for $r_1 = 0 : \frac{2 \log_2 q}{\log_2 t}$. Then, for example, for $t = 2$ and $K = N = 1024$ the expansion factor is 64.

B.2 Shrinking

The so-called shrinking technique, first proposed in [15], allows for compressing ciphertexts from an FHE that supports linear decrypt-and-multiply, like the GSW scheme [32]. It can also be applied directly to compress BFV-style ciphertexts as well as TRLWE ones. In a nutshell, given a TRLWE sample $(\mathbf{a}, \mathbf{b})$, shrinking consists of computing two values, a 'helper' $r \in \mathbb{Z}_q$ and a value $w \in \mathbb{Z}_t$

[12] We use the identity function f as a public R-Lipschitz morphism; thus, $R = 1$; and note that the keyswitch key KS is a fresh TRLWE sample; hence, the variance of the error in KS is σ^2_{TRLWE}.

such that the decryption of the original ciphertext (which is not necessarily correct) can be recovered *exactly*[13] from r and w (as well as, of course, the knowledge of the secret key). Shrinking is interesting because a single helper value 'r' can be used to cover the N LWE samples assembled in an RLWE ciphertext.

In a nutshell, shrinking works as follows. Let $\mathbf{c} = (\mathbf{a}, \mathbf{b})$ be a TRLWE sample we need to compress, and let $\mathbf{s}$ be a TRLWE secret key. To shrink the TRLWE sample, we parse $\mathbf{b} = (b_0, \ldots, b_{N-1}) \in \mathbb{Z}_q^N$ and compute the union of intervals $U \subseteq \mathbb{Z}_q$, where $B = \sigma_{\text{TLWE}}$ is a TLWE noise bound.

$U = \bigcup_{i=0}^{N-1} \left(\left[\frac{\Delta}{2} - b_i - B, \frac{\Delta}{2} - b_i + B\right] \cup \left[-\frac{\Delta}{2} - b_i - B, -\frac{\Delta}{2} - b_i + B\right]\right)$, for $\Delta = q/t$. Then we pick any $r \in \mathbb{Z}_q \backslash U$ and for $i = [0, N-1]$ compute $w_i = \lceil b_i + r \rfloor_t$, where $\lceil x \rfloor_t = \left\lceil x \cdot \frac{t}{q} \right\rfloor \bmod t$ is a rounding function. The resulting shrunk sample is $\tilde{\mathbf{c}} = (r, \mathbf{a}, w_0, \ldots, w_{N-1})$. This therefore leads to an overhead of

$$\frac{(N+1)\log_2 q + N \log_2 t}{N \log_2 t} \tag{12}$$

i.e. for $N = 1024$ ($t = 2$) it is ≈ 33, or for $N = 2048$ ($t = 16$) ≈ 9. If only $K < N$ LWE samples are to be transmitted (we assume not-full packing for TRLWE), then, trivially from (12), the expansion factor is $\frac{(N+1)\log_2 q + K \log_2 t}{K \log_2 t}$.

To decrypt the shrunk TRLWE sample on the downlink, we do the following: we compute $\mathbf{v} = \mathbf{s} \cdot \mathbf{a}$ and parse $\mathbf{v} = (v_0, \ldots, v_{N-1})$. For $i \in [0, N-1]$ we then compute $m'_i = (w_i - \lceil v_i \rfloor_t) \bmod t$ and output $m' = (m'_0, \ldots, m'_{N-1})$. The equivalence between this decryption function and the original one then follows from Lemma 1 of [15]. Let us emphasize, however, that when used for compressing several TLWE ciphertexts, Shrinking affects the probability of erroneous decryption, as we can apply Shrinking only to TRLWE ciphertexts. As discussed in the previous section, packing several TLWE increases the noise deviation.

C Further Details on ℓ-truncation

C.1 Refined TLWE ℓ-truncation

Although it does not give us a closed-form formula for ℓ, the following proposition is a bit more precise than Proposition 1.

Proposition 2. *Let* $\mathbf{c}$ *denote a TLWE encryption of* m *subject to a centered Gaussian noise* e *with variance* σ^2, *and let* $\mathbf{c}' = \mathsf{Trunc}(\mathbf{c}, \ell)$, *then*

$$\left\lceil \frac{1}{\Delta} \mathsf{PartialDec}(\mathsf{Rescale}(\mathbf{c}', \ell_0), \mathbf{s})) \right\rfloor = m \text{ with probability at least}$$

$$1 - 2\exp\left(-\frac{\left(\frac{\Delta}{2} - \frac{1}{2}(n-1)(2^\ell - 1)\right)^2}{2\left(\sigma^2 + \frac{1}{12}(n+1)(2^{2\ell} - 1)\right)}\right).$$

[13] This is important for BFV-style schemes, which tend to induce large noise variances in evaluated ciphertexts.

Proof. Recall Eq. (4), we have $e'' = e + \sum_{i=0}^{n-1} \underbrace{(a_i \mod 2^\ell)}_{-e_i''} s_i - \underbrace{(a_n \mod 2^\ell)}_{-e_n''}$.

Under the assumption that q is a power of 2, $a_i \mod 2^\ell$ ($i \in \{0, ..., n-1\}$) is uniformly distributed over $\{0, ..., 2^\ell - 1\}$ as the associated a_i's are uniformly distributed in $\mathbb{Z}_q$. Additionally, $a_n \mod 2^\ell$ is also uniformly distributed over $\{0, ..., 2^\ell - 1\}$ as, following the LWE assumption, $b = a_n$ is indistinguishable from a uniform deviate over $\mathbb{Z}_q$. Let $n' = \sum_i s_i$; from the CLT, we can thus assume that e'' follows a Gaussian distribution with expectation $E[e''] = \frac{1}{2}(n' - 1)(2^\ell - 1) \leq \frac{1}{2}(n-1)(2^\ell - 1)$, and variance[14] $V[e''] = \sigma^2 + \frac{1}{12}(n'+1)(2^{2\ell} - 1) \leq \sigma^2 + \frac{1}{12}(n+1)(2^{2\ell} - 1)$. The claim follows from applying the Chernoff bound[15] to $\Pr\left(|e''| \geq \frac{\Delta}{2}\right)$. □

Using the latter Prop. in conjunction with Proposition 1 usually allows to slightly increase the number of bits that may be dropped off. For example, as discussed just above, with our running TFHE parameter set example, Proposition 1 tells that for $\epsilon = 2^{-40}$, $l_0 = 19$. Proposition 2, however, tells us that the probability of decryption error is bounded by $2^{-116.06}$ for that value (part of that gap is explained by the ceiling that occurs in (5), as we can only drop an integer number of bits). Then, if we choose $\ell = 20$, the bound drops to $2^{-81.78}$, still above our 2^{-40} target. As this is the cutoff value, we can finally settle on $\ell = 20$ meaning a ciphertext size reduction of 62.5%. Overall, the expansion factor goes from 8816 down to 3306, i.e. is reduced by a factor of 2.66.

C.2 TRLWE ℓ-truncation

ℓ-truncation can equally be applied to TRLWE ciphertext by dropping ℓ least bits on all the coefficients of the **b** polynomial. Because this is very similar to the TLWE case, we do not provide further details. For TRLWE, we also have the analogous of Proposition 1 with Eq. (5) replaced by (recall from Sect. B.1 that, by default, we pack N n-dimensional TLWE samples in a single degree-N TRLWE)

$$\ell_0 \leq \left\lfloor \log_2 \left(\frac{1}{n+1} \left(\frac{\Delta}{2} - \sqrt{-2\sigma^2 \ln(1 - \sqrt[N]{1 - 2^{-(k+1)}})} \right) + 1 \right) \right\rfloor,$$

which provides the guarantees that $\Pr\left(\|\mathbf{e}''\|_\infty \geq \frac{\Delta}{2}\right) \leq 2^{-k}$. However, let us emphasize that the above equation bounds the probability that an ℓ_0-truncated TRLWE ciphertext decrypts incorrectly, meaning that *a decryption error occurs in at least one slot of the message polynomial.* Since the present work is focusing on TFHE and is therefore TLWE-centric, we are only using TRLWE ciphertexts as a means to more efficiently transmit TLWE ciphertexts, and, in fine, it is

[14] Recall that the variance of the discrete uniform distribution over $\{a, ..., b\}$ is $\frac{1}{12}((b - a + 1)^2 - 1)$, leading to $\frac{1}{12}(2^{2l} - 1)$ when $a = 0$ and $b = 2^\ell - 1$.

[15] For a Gaussian deviate of expectation $\mu \geq 0$ and variance σ^2, it holds that $P(|X| \geq \alpha) \leq 2e^{-\frac{(\alpha-\mu)^2}{2\sigma^2}}$. Furthermore, for $\mu' \geq \mu$ and $\sigma' \geq \sigma$, $e^{-\frac{(\alpha-\mu)^2}{2\sigma^2}} \leq e^{-\frac{(\alpha-\mu')^2}{2\sigma'^2}}$.

the decryption error probability of these TLWE ciphertexts that is important to us. So despite the fact that we may use TRLWE ciphertexts for transmission, we stick to the tools provided in the previous section in the sequel. However, in using Proposition 1 and 2 to choose the number of bits that can be dropped from coefficients of a TLWE pair embedded in a TRLWE ciphertext, we have to take into account the extra variance induced by packing following Eq. (11).

Then, with our running TFHE parameter set example, Proposition 1 tells that for $\epsilon = 2^{-40}$, $l_0 = 19$. Proposition 2, however, tells us that the probability of decryption error is bounded by $2^{-100.55}$ for that value. Then, if we choose $\ell = 20$, the bound drops to $2^{-70.86}$, still above our 2^{-40} target. As this is the cutoff value, we can finally settle on $\ell = 20$ (as in the previous section, meaning that TRLWE packing does not affect how much we can truncate in the present setting). Assuming one fully packed TRLWE, we get a ciphertext size reduction of 56.25%. Overall, the expansion factor goes from 64 (Sect. B.1) down to 24, i.e. is reduced by a factor of 2.66.

D TFHE Parameters

In our experimental analysis, we consider the two TFHE parameter sets given in Table 7. The first set is identical to the running example we have used so far for illustrative purposes. This first parameter set is consistent with the "standard TFHE gate bootstrapping" approach, where TFHE is configured for performing operations over binary plaintexts (i.e. $t = 2$). This first parameter set achieves an error probability for bootstrapping of 2^{-154}. Our second parameter set is for $t = 16$, meaning that TFHE ciphertexts now have a 4-bit payload. This set is the most interesting because, as we shall see, the increased payload length will consistently lead to the smallest expansion factors in our experiments. Furthermore, several recent works, notably [46,47], hint that $t = 16$ may achieve an optimal tradeoff between the bootstrapping time (which increases with t) and the number of operations (which decreases with t) required when executing (useful) algorithms over TFHE. However, for $t = 16$, the bootstrapping error probability is increased to 2^{-46} and cannot be significantly lowered unless one is willing to increase q to 2^{64} (and also mechanically increase n). We do not consider this latter option, as it would result in a large performance hit for the FHE calculations themselves. Our two parameter sets achieve 128-bit security according to the lattice-estimator and have been obtained following the methodology in [26]. Note that, since we have used our parameter set for the case where $t = 2$ as a running example throughout the paper, the present section focuses essentially on the case where $t = 16$.

Table 7. Our TFHE parameter sets are for $t = 2$ (binary payloads) and 16 (4-bit payloads). The full set of parameters is provided for completion and reproducibility of our results, but we do not detail the meaning of them all. As of the second of the above tables, it provides the post-bootstrapping noise standard deviation σ_{BS} (which characterizes the noise present in evaluated ciphertexts) and the post-packing standard deviation (obtained after packing N, n-dimensional evaluated TLWE ciphertexts, hence with a noise deviation of σ_{BS}, in a *single* degree-N TRLWE ciphertext). The other two deviations are post-Blind Rotation (BR) and post-KeySwitch (KS), but we did not need to detail these operations in this paper.

t	q	n	N	l	t_{d}	B_{g}	B_{KS}	σ_{TLWE}	σ_{TRLWE}
2	2^{32}	550	1024	2	1	256	1024	$q \cdot 2.82 \times 10^{-4}$	$q \cdot 5.6 \times 10^{-8}$
16	2^{32}	750	2048	2	2	1024	1024	$q \cdot 7.7 \times 10^{-6}$	$q \cdot 9.6 \times 10^{-11}$

t	σ_{BR}	σ_{KS}	σ_{BS}	σ_{pack}
2	$q \cdot 1.12 \times 10^{-2}$	$q \cdot 1.27 \times 10^{-2}$	$q \cdot 1.69 \times 10^{-2}$	$q \cdot 1.81 \times 10^{-2}$
16	$q \cdot 3.62 \times 10^{-4}$	$q \cdot 4.92 \times 10^{-4}$	$q \cdot 6.1082 \times 10^{-4}$	$q \cdot 6.1087 \times 10^{-4}$

E Additional Tables and Plots

Method	Exp. factor
TLWE	$\frac{(n+1)\log_2 q}{\log_2 t}$
TLWE ℓ-truncation	$\frac{(n+1)(\log_2 q-\ell)}{\log_2 t}$
Shrinking	$\frac{(N+1)\log_2 q+K\log_2 t}{K\log_2 t}$
TLWEtoTRLWE	$\frac{(2r_2N+N+r_1)\log_2 q}{K\log_2 t}$
TLWEtoTRLWE + ℓ-truncation	$\frac{(2r_2N+N+r_1)(\log_2 q-\ell)}{K\log_2 t}$

(a) Expansion factor formula for the different methods based on TLWE/TRLWE when K evaluated TLWE ciphertexts have to be transmitted on the downlink. For RLWE-based methods, $r_1 = K \bmod N$ and $r_2 = \lfloor K/N \rfloor$ when the K n-dimensional TLWE are packed N-by-N in degree-N TRLWE ciphertexts.

Compression method	M	Exp. factor
Paillier (w. packing)	$\frac{\lfloor \log_2 \mu \rfloor}{v}$	$\frac{(r_2+1)\lceil 2 \log_2 \mu \rceil}{K \log_2 t}$
ℓ-truncation + Paillier (w. packing)	$\frac{\lfloor \log_2 \mu \rfloor}{v-\ell}$	
DÃČÂĕmgard-Jurik (w. packing)	$\frac{\lfloor y \log_2 \mu \rfloor}{v}$	$\frac{(r_2+1)\lceil (y+1) \log_2 \mu \rceil}{K \log_2 t}$
ℓ-truncation + D.-J. (w. packing)	$\frac{\lfloor y \log_2 \mu \rfloor}{v-\ell}$	
CPG (w. packing)	$\frac{\lfloor \log_2 \mu \rfloor}{v}$	$\frac{Kv+(r_2+1)\lceil \log_2 \mu \rceil}{K \log_2 t}$
ℓ-truncation + CPG (w. packing)	$\frac{\lfloor \log_2 \mu \rfloor}{v-\ell}$	$\frac{K(v-\ell)+(r_2+1)\lceil \log_2 \mu \rceil}{K \log_2 t}$
EC ElGamal	2	$\frac{\lceil \log_2 \omega \rceil}{K \log_2 t}$

(a) Expansion factor formula for the different LHE-based methods when K evaluated TLWE ciphertexts have to be transmitted on the downlink. Above, M is the number of TLWE partial decryptions that can be packed in a single LHE ciphertext (and v the number of bits required to represent one such partial decryption). Let $r_1 = K \bmod N$ and $r_2 = \lfloor K/N \rfloor$ when the K TLWE partial decryptions are packed M-by-M in LHE ciphertexts.

t	ϵ		
	2^{-40}	2^{-64}	2^{-128}
2	20	20	18
16	18	18	17
2	20	20	16
16	18	18	17

(b) Applying Prop. 2 for $t = 2, 16$ and several values for the probability of decryption error ϵ, the upper part represents a maximum value for ℓ when ℓ-truncating an evaluated (i.e. bootstrapped) TLWE ciphertext, and the bottom part – when ℓ-truncating a degree-N TRLWE ciphertext in which N n-dimensional evaluated TLWE ciphertexts have been packed.

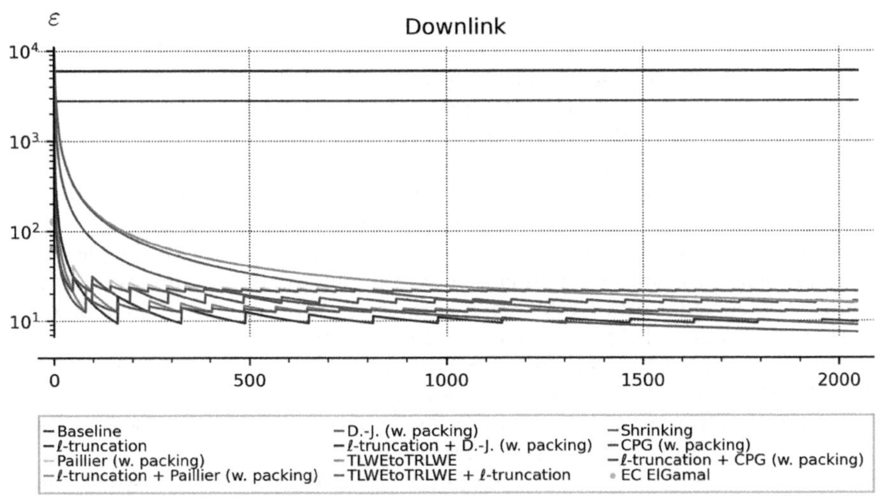

Fig. 1. Comparison of expansion factors for the downlink ciphertext compression methods studied in this paper and ℓ found using Proposition 1 ($t = 16$)

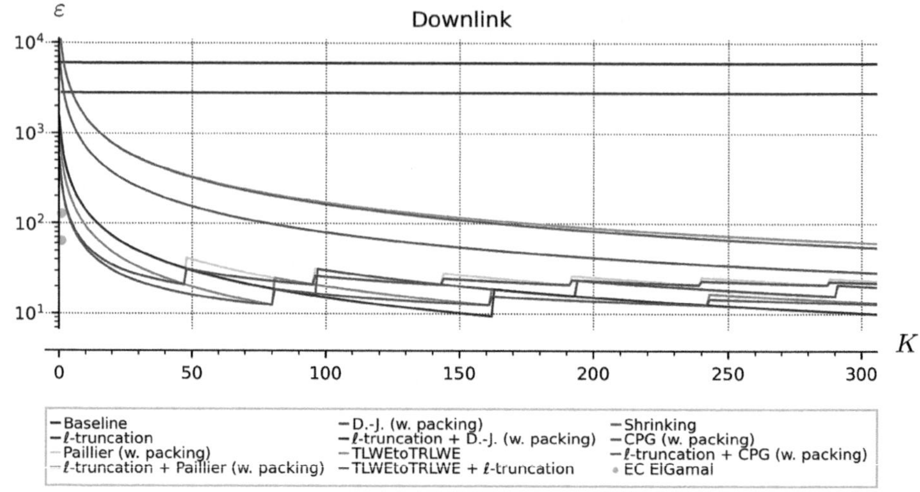

Fig. 2. Comparison of expansion factors for the downlink ciphertext compression methods studied in this paper for $K \leq 300$ and ℓ found using Proposition 1 ($t = 16$)

References

1. Ajtai, M.: Representing hard lattices with $o(n \log n)$ bits. In: STOC, pp. 94–103 (2005)
2. Albrecht, M.R., Rechberger, C., Schneider, T., Tiessen, T., Zohner, M.: Ciphers for MPC and FHE. In: EUROCRYPT, pp. 430–454 (2015)
3. Albrecht, M.R., et al.: Feistel structures for MPC, and more. In: ESORICS, pp. 151–171 (2019)
4. Alperin-Sheriff, J., Peikert, C.: Faster bootstrapping with polynomial error. In: CRYPTO, pp. 297–314 (2014)
5. Aranha, D.F., Costache, A., Guimarães, A., Soria-Vazquez, E.: HELIOPOLIS: verifiable computation over homomorphically encrypted data from interactive oracle proofs is practical. In: ASIACRYPT, pp. 302–334 (2024)
6. Bae, Y., et al.: HERMES: efficient ring packing using MLWE ciphertexts and application to transciphering. In: CRYPTO, pp. 37–69 (2023)
7. Bendoukha, A., Boudguiga, A., Sirdey, R.: Revisiting stream-cipher-based homomorphic transciphering in the TFHE era. In: FPS. pp. 19–33 (2021)
8. Bendoukha, A., Clet, P., Boudguiga, A., Sirdey, R.: Optimized stream-cipher-based transciphering by means of functional-bootstrapping. In: DBSec, pp. 91–109 (2023)
9. Boura, C., et al.: CHIMERA: combining ring-LWE-based fully homomorphic encryption schemes. J. Math. Cryptol., 316–338 (2020)
10. Brakerski, Z.: Fully homomorphic encryption without modulus switching from classical GapSVP. In: CRYPTO, pp. 868–886 (2012)
11. Brakerski, Z., Gentry, C., Halevi, S.: Packed ciphertexts in LWE-based homomorphic encryption. In: PKC, pp. 1–13 (2013)
12. Brakerski, Z., Gentry, C., Vaikuntanathan, V.: (leveled) fully homomorphic encryption without bootstrapping. In: ITCS, pp. 309–325 (2012)
13. Brakerski, Z., Vaikuntanathan, V.: Efficient fully homomorphic encryption from (standard) LWE. In: FOCS, pp. 97–106 (2011)

14. Brakerski, Z., Vaikuntanathan, V.: Lattice-based FHE as secure as PKE. In: ITCS, pp. 1–12 (2014)
15. Brakerski, Z., et al.: Leveraging linear decryption: rate-1 fully-homomorphic encryption and time-lock puzzles. In: TCC, pp. 407–437 (2019)
16. Brakerski, Z., et al.: Constant ciphertext-rate non-committing encryption from standard assumptions. In: TCC, pp. 58–87 (2020)
17. Bresson, E., et al.: A simple public-key cryptosystem with a double trapdoor decryption mechanism and its applications. In: ASIACRYPT, pp. 37–54 (2003)
18. Canteaut, A., et al.: Stream ciphers: a practical solution for efficient homomorphic-ciphertext compression. J. Cryptol., 885–916 (2018)
19. Checri, M., Sirdey, R., Boudguiga, A., Bultel, J.P.: On the practical CPAD security of "exact" and threshold FHE schemes. In: CRYPTO, pp. 3–33 (2024)
20. Chen, H., Chillotti, I., Ren, L.: Onion ring ORAM: efficient constant bandwidth oblivious RAM from (leveled) TFHE. In: CCS, pp. 345–360 (2019)
21. Chen, H., Dai, W., Kim, M., Song, Y.: Efficient homomorphic conversion between (ring) LWE ciphertexts. In: ACNS, pp. 460–479 (2021)
22. Cheon, J.H., Choe, H., Passelègue, A., Stehlé, D., Suvanto, E.: Attacks against the IND-CPAD security of exact FHE schemes. In: CCS, pp. 2505–2519 (2024)
23. Cheon, J.H., Kim, A., Kim, M., Song, Y.: Homomorphic encryption for arithmetic of approximate numbers. In: ASIACRYPT, pp. 409–437 (2017)
24. Chillotti, I., Gama, N., Georgieva, M., Izabachène, M.: TFHE: fast fully homomorphic encryption library, August 2016. https://tfhe.github.io/tfhe/
25. Chillotti, I., et al.: Faster fully homomorphic encryption: bootstrapping in less than 0.1 seconds. In: ASIACRYPT, pp. 3–33 (2016)
26. Clet, P.E., Boudguiga, A., Sirdey, R., Zuber, M.: ComBo: a novel functional bootstrapping method for efficient evaluation of nonlinear functions in the encrypted domain. In: AFRICACRYPT, pp. 317–343 (2023)
27. Cramer, R., Shoup, V.: Universal hash proofs and a paradigm for adaptive chosen ciphertext secure public-key encryption. In: EUROCRYPT, pp. 45–64 (2002)
28. Damgård, I., Groth, J., Salomonsen, G.: The theory and implementation of an electronic voting system. In: Secure Electronic Voting, pp. 77–98 (2003)
29. Dobraunig, C., et al.: Pasta: a case for hybrid homomorphic encryption. IACR Trans. Cryptogr. Hardw. Embed. Syst., 30–73 (2023)
30. Dåmgard, I., Jurik, M., Nielsen, J.B.: A generalization of Paillier's public-key system with applications to electronic voting. Int. J. Inf. Sec., 371–385 (2010)
31. Fan, J., Vercauteren, F.: Somewhat practical fully homomorphic encryption. In: IACR Cryptol. ePrint Arch., Paper 2012/144 (2012)
32. Gentry, C., Sahai, A., Waters, B.: Homomorphic encryption from learning with errors: conceptually-simpler, asymptotically-faster, attribute-based. In: CRYPTO, pp. 75–92 (2013)
33. Hoffmann, C., Méaux, P., Ricosset, T.: Transciphering, using FiLIP and TFHE for an efficient delegation of computation. In: INDOCRYPT, pp. 39–61 (2020)
34. Huang, Z., Lu, W., Hong, C., Ding, J.: Cheetah: lean and fast secure two-party deep neural network inference. In: USENIX, pp. 809–826 (2022)
35. Mahdavi, R.A., Diaa, A., Kerschbaum, F.: HE is all you need: compressing FHE ciphertexts using additive HE (2024). https://arxiv.org/abs/2303.09043
36. Méaux, P., Journault, A., Standaert, F., Carlet, C.: Towards stream ciphers for efficient FHE with low-noise ciphertexts. In: EUROCRYPT, pp. 311–343 (2016)
37. Méaux, P., et al.: Improved filter permutators for efficient FHE: better instances and implementations. In: INDOCRYPT, pp. 68–91 (2019)

38. Menezes, A.: Elliptic Curve Public Key Cryptosystems, vol. 234. Springer, New York (1993)
39. Mukherjee, P., Wichs, D.: Two round multiparty computation via multi-key FHE. In: EUROCRYPT, pp. 735–763 (2016)
40. Naehrig, M., Lauter, K.E., Vaikuntanathan, V.: Can homomorphic encryption be practical? In: CCSW, pp. 113–124 (2011)
41. Orlandi, C., Scholl, P., Yakoubov, S.: The rise of Paillier: homomorphic secret sharing and public-key silent OT. In: EUROCRYPT, pp. 678–708 (2021)
42. Paillier, P.: Public-key cryptosystems based on composite degree residuosity classes. In: EUROCRYPT, pp. 223–238 (1999)
43. Peikert, C., Vaikuntanathan, V., Waters, B.: A framework for efficient and composable oblivious transfer. In: CRYPTO, pp. 554–571 (2008)
44. Regev, O.: On lattices, learning with errors, random linear codes, and cryptography. In: STOC, pp. 84–93 (2005)
45. Roy, L., Singh, J.: Large message homomorphic secret sharing from DCR and applications. In: CRYPTO, pp. 687–717 (2021)
46. Trama, D., Clet, P.E., Boudguiga, A., Sirdey, R.: Designing a general-purpose 8-bit (T)FHE processor abstraction. Tr. Cr. Hardw. Emb. Syst., 535–578 (2025)
47. Trama, D., Clet, P., Boudguiga, A., Sirdey, R.: A homomorphic AES evaluation in less than 30 seconds by means of TFHE. In: WAHC, pp. 79–90 (2023)
48. Xu, T., Li, M., Wang, R.: Hequant: Marrying homomorphic encryption and quantization for communication-efficient private inference. CoRR (2024)

Efficient Full Domain Functional Bootstrapping from Recursive LUT Decomposition

Intak Hwang, Shinwon Lee, Seonhong Min, and Yongsoo Song(✉)

Seoul National University, Seoul, South Korea
{intak.hwang,chowon0708,minsh,y.song}@snu.ac.kr

Abstract. Fully Homomorphic Encryption over the Torus (TFHE) enables efficient evaluation of arbitrary lookup tables (LUT) over encrypted data, allowing complex functions to be computed without decryption. However, in TFHE, only lookup tables with a negacyclic structure can be homomorphically evaluated, which limits the range of functions that can be supported. To overcome this limitation and enable the evaluation of arbitrary functions, the notion of full-domain functional bootstrapping (FDFB) was introduced. However, existing FDFB methods require at least two consecutive bootstrapping operations to evaluate a single function, resulting in significant latency and overhead.

In this work, we present a novel FDFB scheme that supports arbitrary lookup tables by decomposing them into multiple small negacyclic LUTs and one compact full-domain LUT. This structure allows most computations to be handled by fast negacyclic bootstrapping, significantly reducing the computational cost. To address the need for maintaining distinct evaluation keys for each LUT length, we apply Extended Bootstrapping (PKC 2021), which enables all operations to run within a fixed ring dimension. Combined with Extended Bootstrapping, our method nearly halves the bootstrapping cost compared to prior FDFB approaches while maintaining a constant key size, negligible parameter overhead, and strong scalability.

Finally, we implement our algorithm using the TFHE-go library and evaluate its performance across various settings. Our method achieves up to a 3.41× speedup over previous FDFB schemes without increasing key size and retains up to a 1.91× advantage even when Extended Bootstrapping is applied to both.

Keywords: Homomorphic Encryption · Bootstrapping

1 Introduction

Homomorphic encryption(HE) is a cryptosystem that enables computation directly on encrypted data without requiring decryption. Since its first realization by Gentry [12], it has emerged as a powerful tool for enabling secure computation

C. Boura et al. (Eds.): SAC 2025, LNCS 16207, pp. 679–699, 2026.
https://doi.org/10.1007/978-3-032-10536-3_25

in various applications. In the past decade, there has been significant progress in performance for homomorphic encryptions. The current best-performing homomorphic encryption schemes are BGV [5], BFV [4,11], CKKS [7], TFHE [8], and FHEW [10], all of which derive their security from the hardness of the Learning With Errors (LWE) [25] and its variant over the ring of cyclotomic integers (RLWE) [23,26].

While most homomorphic encryption schemes primarily focus on supporting addition and multiplication over encrypted data, TFHE [8] and FHEW [10] distinguish themselves by enabling the direct evaluation of arbitrary Boolean gates with relatively low latency. This gate-by-gate computation model provides a practical foundation for applications that require fine-grained control over encrypted bits. Building on this capability, a series of follow-up works have further expanded the TFHE framework in meaningful directions. A particularly notable advancement is programmable bootstrapping [6,9,14], which builds upon prior support for multi-bit ciphertexts in TFHE by enabling the direct evaluation of complex lookup tables (LUT) during bootstrapping. This allows for expressive computation without introducing additional cost. Consequently, TFHE can efficiently evaluate functions that are difficult to represent using only additions and multiplications.

However, programmable bootstrapping is limited to evaluating LUTs with a negacyclic structure, which restricts the range of computable functions. To be specific, evaluated LUT $f_N : \mathbb{Z}_{2N} \to \mathbb{Z}_q$ should satisfy the negacyclic condition $f_N(i + N) = -f_N(i)$ for $i \in [0, N)$. To circumvent this limitation, a line of research on full-domain functional bootstrapping (FDFB) has emerged [18], aiming to support arbitrary LUT evaluation without such structural constraints. Various instantiations of FDFB have been proposed to improve the efficiency, but all existing approaches fundamentally require at least two bootstrapping operations, which makes the latency of FDFB roughly twice that of single bootstrapping.

1.1 Our Contribution

While full-domain functional bootstrapping (FDFB) significantly improves functional flexibility, this comes at the cost of increased computational overhead, as it typically requires multiple rounds of bootstrapping. In this work, we present a new FDFB algorithm that reduces the computational cost by up to half compared to the state-of-the-art FDFB, while incurring negligible parameter overhead and no increase in key size. Moreover, our FDFB algorithm is highly parallelizable, making it well-suited for practical deployment in large-scale secure computation settings.

Our algorithm is based on the key observation that any full-domain lookup table of length $N = 2^m$ can be decomposed into the sum of a negacyclic LUT of length 2^m and a full-domain LUT of length 2^{m-1}. More precisely, for any function f_{2^m} defined over $\mathbb{Z}_{2^m}$, we can write

$$f_{2^m}(i) = \bar{f}_{2^{m-1}}(i) + f_{2^{m-1}}(i),$$

where each component is given by

$$\bar{f}_{2^{m-1}}(i) = \frac{1}{2}\left(f_{2^m}(i) - f_{2^m}(i + 2^{m-1})\right), \quad f_{2^{m-1}}(i) = \frac{1}{2}\left(f_{2^m}(i) + f_{2^m}(i + 2^{m-1})\right).$$

Here, $\bar{f}_{2^{m-1}}$ corresponds to a function defined over $\mathbb{Z}_{2^m}$ with a negacyclic condition $\bar{f}_{2^{m-1}}(i + 2^{m-1}) = -\bar{f}_{2^{m-1}}(i)$ for $i \in [0, 2^{m-1})$, and $f_{2^{m-1}}$ is a function defined over $\mathbb{Z}_{2^{m-1}}$. By recursively applying the above decomposition μ times, an arbitrary full-domain lookup table can be expressed as the sum of μ negacyclic lookup tables of decreasing sizes and a single full-domain lookup table of length $2^{m-\mu}$, which can be written as $f_{2^m}(i) = f_{2^{m-\mu}}(i) + \sum_{k=1}^{\mu} \bar{f}_{2^{m-k}}(i)$.

This decomposition is particularly useful because FDFB is significantly slower than a single negacyclic functional bootstrapping, generally requiring at least twice the latency. Moreover, its computational cost increases proportionally with the LUT size. By breaking down a large full-domain LUT into several smaller negacyclic LUTs and a single small full-domain LUT, we can perform most of the computation using negacyclic bootstrapping, while only a small portion of the function needs to go through the costly FDFB. As a result, the overall evaluation time is substantially reduced compared to applying FDFB to the full lookup table.

For example, consider a full-domain LUT of length 2^m decomposed into three negacyclic LUTs of sizes 2^{m-1}, 2^{m-2}, and 2^{m-3}, along with a single full-domain LUT of size 2^{m-3}. Traditional FDFB evaluates the entire full-domain LUT using 2 bootstrapping operations over size 2^m. In contrast, our method evaluates the LUT at a total relative cost of $1/2+1/4+1/8$ with respect to a single negacyclic LUT evaluation, plus an additional $(1/8) \cdot 2$ for evaluating the small full-domain LUT twice, resulting in an overall relative cost of about $9/8$. Overall, this leads to nearly a $2\times$ improvement in bootstrapping efficiency in practice. In addition, our new bootstrapping algorithm is algorithmically parallelizable by evaluating each small lookup table in parallel. Then, essentially the latency will depend on the evaluation of the largest negacyclic lookup table, which leads to $4\times$ improvements in bootstrapping time when fully parallelized.

While this approach improves computational efficiency, it also requires evaluating LUTs of various lengths, which in turn necessitates maintaining distinct evaluation keys for each LUT size. This is because, to perform bootstrapping, the evaluator must access special public keys (referred to as evaluation keys) that enable operations such as KeySwitch and BlindRotate. These keys are designed to match the polynomial degree of the ciphertext, which is determined by the LUT size, so each LUT length typically requires a separate set of keys tailored to the corresponding ring dimension. To address this issue, we adopt the extended bootstrapping (EBS) [21], which leverages a ring isomorphism to rewrite polynomial operations in $\mathbb{Z}_q[X]/(X^{2^m} + 1)$ as 2^ν independent computations in $\mathbb{Z}_q[X]/(X^{2^{m-\nu}} + 1)$. This allows the evaluator to simulate higher degree bootstrapping using polynomials of lower degree, enabling all computations to remain within a fixed and compact ring dimension. As a result, LUTs of different lengths can be handled within a unified dimension, avoiding the need for multiple bootstrapping key sets.

Finally, we implement our algorithm using the TFHE-go library [15] and evaluate its performance and the required key size for bootstrapping. Our method achieves up to a 3.41× speedup over previous FDFB schemes without any increase in key size, and remains 1.91× faster even when EBS is applied to the previous FDFB. Another key advantage of our algorithm is its high parallelizability. Since the bootstrapping operations for the decomposed lookup tables are independent, they can be executed concurrently. As a result, our approach can achieve even greater performance gains when leveraging parallel execution.

1.2 Related Works

Several approaches for full-domain functional bootstrapping (FDFB) have been proposed in the literature:

- WoP-PBS [9] performs FDFB by extracting the most significant bit (MSB) of the encrypted message and using BFV multiplications to select the appropriate lookup table (LUT). This method requires more than two bootstrapping operations and incurs significant noise growth due to the BFV multiplication.
- Kluczniak and Shih [18] present an optimization that replaces BFV multiplications with multiple functional bootstrappings to select the LUT.
- Yang et al. [27] present an FDFB method that uses only two bootstrapping operations, improving efficiency while maintaining compact parameters.
- Kluczniak and Schild [19] and Ma et al. [24] propose several optimized FDFB schemes that improve efficiency over earlier approaches. For example, [24] introduces FDFB-Compress, which compresses the LWE message via a functional bootstrap and applies the target function on the compressed domain, significantly reducing parameter overhead and making it one of the most efficient FDFB schemes to date.
- Bon et al. [3] adopted an odd plaintext modulus to circumvent the negacyclic constraint. However, this approach is inherently restricted to odd plaintext settings.
- Bergerat et al. [1] and Li et al. [22] proposed FDFB schemes that support large-precision ciphertexts, overcoming the limitations of earlier methods whose bootstrapping could not efficiently scale to high-precision inputs.

Nevertheless, all existing approaches fundamentally require at least two bootstrapping operations, which remain a major bottleneck. Multi-value bootstrapping [6] is explored in [19,24] to evaluate multiple LUTs simultaneously in a single bootstrapping operation. This approach aims to reduce the number of bootstrapping steps by encoding multiple output values at once. However, this technique incurs significant noise growth and large parameter overhead, making it impractical for efficient implementations.

As an independent interest, Hwang et al. [16] recently proposed a new TFHE-like homomorphic encryption scheme which allows full-domain functional bootstrapping with only a single bootstrapping with slightly slower latency compared to the conventional TFHE bootstrapping.

2 Preliminaries

2.1 Notation

We denote the polynomial ring $\mathbb{Z}[X]/(X^N + 1)$ by R, where N is defined as 2^m for some integer m. The quotient ring R/qR is denoted by R_q. We also denote the set $\{0, 1\}$ by $\mathbb{B}$. For a distribution $\mathcal{X}$, we denote sampling a random variable x from $\mathcal{X}$ as $x \leftarrow \mathcal{X}$. A uniform distribution over a set S is denoted by $\mathcal{U}(S)$, and a Gaussian distribution with mean 0 and variance α^2 is denoted by ρ_α. The discrete Gaussian distribution over a lattice Λ with mean 0 and variance α^2, denoted by $\mathcal{D}_{\Lambda,\alpha}$, is defined as

$$\mathcal{D}_{\Lambda,\alpha}(\mathbf{x}) = \frac{\rho_\alpha(\mathbf{x})}{\sum_{\mathbf{v}\in\Lambda} \rho_\alpha(\mathbf{v})}.$$

We denote the infinity norm of polynomial p by $\|p\|_\infty$ which is defined as the maximum size of the coefficients. Throughout the paper, we use bold uppercase letters (e.g., $\mathbf{A}$) to denote matrices and bold lowercase letters (e.g., $\mathbf{b}$) to denote vectors. All vectors are treated as row matrices. For an integer vector $\mathbf{b}$, an integer a, and a positive integer q, we use the notation $[\mathbf{b}]_q$ and $[a]_q$ to denote the component-wise modular reduction of $\mathbf{b}$ and the modular reduction of a modulo q, respectively.

2.2 Learning With Errors

We describe the decisional learning with errors (LWE) assumption [25] and its variant over the ring of cyclotomic integers [23,26].

Definition 1 (Decisional LWE [25]). *For positive integers m, n, q, and distributions χ, ψ over $\mathbb{Z}$, the (decisional) LWE problem $\mathsf{LWE}_{m,n,q,\chi,\psi}$ is to distinguish the following distribution from the uniform distribution $\mathcal{U}(\mathbb{Z}_q^{m\times(n+1)})$:*

$$\{(\mathbf{A}\cdot\mathbf{s}+\mathbf{e} \pmod q, \mathbf{A}) \in \mathbb{Z}_q^{m\times(n+1)} \mid \mathbf{A} \leftarrow \mathcal{U}(\mathbb{Z}_q^{m\times n}), \mathbf{s} \leftarrow \chi^n, \mathbf{e} \leftarrow \psi^m\}.$$

Definition 2 (Decisional RLWE [23,26]). *For positive integers m, N, q, and distributions χ', ψ' over R, the (decisional) RLWE problem $\mathsf{RLWE}_{m,N,q,\chi',\psi'}$ is to distinguish the following distribution from the uniform distribution $\mathcal{U}(R_q^{m\times 2})$:*

$$\{(\mathbf{a}\cdot t+\mathbf{e} \pmod q, \mathbf{a}) \in R_q^2 \mid \mathbf{a} \leftarrow \mathcal{U}(R_q^m), t \leftarrow \chi', \mathbf{e} \leftarrow \psi'^m\}.$$

Based on these assumptions, LWE, RLWE cryptosystems can be defined. An LWE encryption of some plaintext $m \in \mathbb{Z}_q$ is given by $(b, \mathbf{a}) \in \mathbb{Z}_q^{n+1}$, where $b + \langle \mathbf{a}, \mathbf{s}\rangle = m + e \pmod q$ for the secret $\mathbf{s} \in \mathbb{Z}^n$ and some small noise $e \in \mathbb{Z}$. Similarly, an RLWE encryption of a plaintext $\mu \in R_q$ is given by $(b, a) \in R_q^2$, where $b + a \cdot t = \mu + e \pmod q$ for the secret $t \in R$, and some small noise $e \in R$.

2.3 Gadget Toolkit and RGSW

The gadget toolkit is a commonly used noise management technique for homomorphic encryption. For some integer $d > 0$, we call a vector $\mathbf{g} \in \mathbb{Z}^d$ and a function $h : \mathbb{Z}_q \to \mathbb{Z}^d$ a gadget vector and a decomposition function, respectively, if the following conditions hold for some small $\delta, \epsilon > 0$.

1. For any $a \in \mathbb{Z}_q$, $\|h(a)\|_\infty \leq \delta$.
2. For any $a \in \mathbb{Z}_q$, $\|a - \langle h(a), \mathbf{g}\rangle \pmod q\|_\infty \leq \epsilon$.

A typical example of the gadget vector and decomposition function is the digit decomposition. Assuming that the ciphertext modulus q is a multiple of B^d for some integer $B > 1$, the gadget vector $\mathbf{g}$ is given by $\left(\frac{q}{B^d}, \frac{q}{B^{d-1}}, \ldots, \frac{q}{B}\right)$ and the decomposition function h outputs each digit of $\lfloor \frac{B^d}{q} \cdot a \rceil$ in a balanced representation. Then, we can set $\delta = \frac{B}{2}$ and $\epsilon = \frac{q}{2B^d}$ for the inequalities above. It is worth noting that the gadget toolkit can be extended to the ring setting by applying the decomposition function on each coefficient of the input polynomial, so that it outputs a vector of ring elements over R. In this paper, we represent the gadget vector and decomposition function with these two parameters, B and d.

Established upon the gadget toolkit, the RGSW cryptosystem [13], which offers a level-free ciphertext-ciphertext multiplication, can be defined. Given a gadget vector $\mathbf{g} \in \mathbb{Z}^d$ and decomposition function $h : R_q \to R^d$, the RGSW encryption algorithm is described as follows.

- $\mathsf{RGSW.Enc}(t, \mu)$: Given the RLWE secret $t \in R$ and a message μ, sample $\mathbf{a} \leftarrow \mathcal{U}(R_q^{2d})$ and $\mathbf{e} \leftarrow \mathcal{D}^{2d}_{\mathbb{Z}^N,\beta}$. Compute and output

$$\begin{bmatrix} \mathbf{g} & \mathbf{0} \\ \mathbf{0} & \mathbf{g} \end{bmatrix} \cdot \mu + \left[-\mathbf{a} \cdot t + \mathbf{e} \pmod q \;\middle|\; \mathbf{a} \right] \in R_q^{2d \times 2}.$$

Now, we describe the *external product*, a multiplicative operation between RLWE and RGSW ciphertexts.

Definition 3 (External Product). *Let $c = (b, a) \in R_q^2$ be an RLWE ciphertext and $\mathbf{C} \in R_q^{2d\times 2}$ be an RGSW ciphertext associated with the gadget vector $\mathbf{g}$ and decomposition function h. The external product, denoted by $c \boxdot \mathbf{C}$ is defined as follows:*

$$c \boxdot \mathbf{C} = \begin{bmatrix} h(b) \\ h(a) \end{bmatrix}^\top \cdot \mathbf{C} \pmod q.$$

2.4 The TFHE Scheme

- $\mathsf{Setup}(1^\lambda)$: Given a security parameter λ, generate the following public parameters: LWE dimension n, RLWE dimension $N = 2^m$, error parameters $\alpha, \beta > 0$, plaintext and ciphertext modulus p, q, the gadget decomposition base and dimension B, d, and the key-switching base and dimension B', d' with corresponding gadget vector $\mathbf{g} \in \mathbb{Z}^d$, $\mathbf{g}' \in \mathbb{Z}^{d'}$ and decomposition function $h : \mathbb{Z}_q \to \mathbb{Z}^d$, $h' : \mathbb{Z}_q \to \mathbb{Z}^{d'}$. Define *scaling factor* Δ as $\frac{q}{p}$.

- $\mathsf{KeyGen}(1^\lambda)$:

- Sample $s_i \leftarrow \mathcal{U}(\mathbb{B})$ for $0 \le i < n$. Return the LWE secret key $\mathbf{s} = (s_0, s_1, \ldots, s_{n-1})$.
- Sample $t_i \leftarrow \mathcal{U}(\mathbb{B})$ for $0 \le i < N$. Return the RLWE secret key $\mathbf{t} = t_0 + t_1 X + \ldots + t_{N-1}X^{N-1}$. Write $\mathbf{t} = (t_0, t_1, \ldots, t_{N-1})$.
- Set $\mathsf{BRK}_i \leftarrow \mathsf{RGSW.Enc}(t, s_i)$ for $0 \le i < n$. Return the blind rotation key $\mathsf{BRK} = \{\mathsf{BRK}_i\}_{0 \le i < n}$, which is also referred to as the bootstrapping key.
- Sample $\mathbf{A}_{i,1} \leftarrow \mathcal{U}(\mathbb{Z}_q^{d' \times n})$ and $\mathbf{e}_i \leftarrow \mathcal{D}^{d'}_{\mathbb{Z},\alpha}$ for $0 \le i < N$. Set $\mathsf{KSK}_i \leftarrow (\mathbf{A}_{i,0} | \mathbf{A}_{i,1}) \in \mathbb{Z}_q^{d' \times (n+1)}$ where $\mathbf{A}_{i,0} = -\mathbf{A}_{i,1} \cdot s + \mathbf{g}' \cdot t_i + \mathbf{e}_i \pmod q$. Return the key switching key $\mathsf{KSK} = \{\mathsf{KSK}_i\}_{0 \le i < N}$

- $\mathsf{Enc}(\mathbf{s}, m)$: For a given secret key $\mathbf{s}$, and a message $m \in \mathbb{Z}_p$, sample $\mathbf{a} = (a_0, a_1, \ldots, a_{n-1}) \leftarrow \mathcal{U}(\mathbb{Z}_q^n)$ and $e \leftarrow \mathcal{D}_\alpha$. Return $\mathbf{c} = (b, \mathbf{a}) \in \mathbb{Z}_q^{n+1}$ where $b = -\langle \mathbf{a}, \mathbf{s} \rangle + \Delta m + e \pmod q$.

- $\mathsf{Dec}(\mathbf{s}, \mathbf{c})$: For a given secret key $\mathbf{s}$, and a LWE ciphertext $\mathbf{c} = (b, \mathbf{a}) \in \mathbb{Z}_q^{n+1}$, let $\mu = b + \langle \mathbf{a}, \mathbf{s} \rangle \pmod q$. Output $m = \lfloor \frac{1}{\Delta} \mu \rceil$.

- $\mathsf{ModSwitch}(\mathbf{c}, q')$: For a given LWE ciphertext $\mathbf{c} = (b, \mathbf{a}) \in \mathbb{Z}_q^{n+1}$, and a ciphertext modulus q', return $\bar{\mathbf{c}} = (\lfloor \frac{q'}{q} b \rceil, \lfloor \frac{q'}{q} \mathbf{a} \rceil) \in \mathbb{Z}_{q'}^{n+1}$.

- $\mathsf{BlindRotate}(\bar{\mathbf{c}}, \bar{f}_N, \mathsf{BRK})$: For a given LWE ciphertext $\bar{\mathbf{c}} = (\bar{b}, \bar{\mathbf{a}}) \in \mathbb{Z}_{2N}^{n+1}$, a negacyclic lookup table $\bar{f}_N : \mathbb{Z}_{2N} \to \mathbb{Z}_q$, and a blind rotation key BRK, run Algorithm 1. Here, $\bar{f}_N$ must satisfy the negacyclic condition

$$\bar{f}_N(x) = -\bar{f}_N(x+N) \quad \text{for all} \quad x \in [0, N).$$

Algorithm 1: BlindRotate

Input: A LWE ciphertext $(\bar{b}, \bar{\mathbf{a}}) \in \mathbb{Z}_{2N}^{n+1}$, a negacyclic lookup table $\bar{f}_N : \mathbb{Z}_{2N} \to \mathbb{Z}_q$, and the blind rotation key BRK

Output: A RLWE ciphertext $\in R_q^2$

Let $tv = \sum_{i=0}^{N-1} \bar{f}_N(i) \cdot X^i$

$\mathsf{ACC} \leftarrow (X^{-\bar{b}} \cdot tv, 0)$

for $i \leftarrow 0$ **to** $n-1$ **do**

  $\mathsf{ACC} \leftarrow \mathsf{ACC} + \left((X^{-\bar{a}_i} - 1) \cdot \mathsf{ACC}\right) \boxdot \mathsf{BRK_i}$

end

return ACC

• $\mathsf{SampleExtract}(\mathsf{ct})$: For a given RLWE ciphertext $\mathsf{ct} = (\sum_{i=0}^{N-1} b_i X^i, \sum_{i=0}^{N-1} a_i X^i) \in R_q^2$, return $(b_0, a_0, -a_{N-1}, \ldots, -a_1) \in \mathbb{Z}_q^{N+1}$. Note that $\mathsf{SampleExtract}$ does not introduce any additional noise.

• $\mathsf{KeySwitch}(\mathbf{c}, \mathsf{KSK})$: For a given LWE ciphertext $\mathbf{c} = (b, a_0, \ldots, a_{N-1}) \in \mathbb{Z}_q^{N+1}$, return $(b, \mathbf{0}) + \sum_{i=0}^{N-1} h'(a_i)^\top \cdot \mathsf{KSK}_i \pmod{q}$.

• $\mathsf{Bootstrap}(\mathbf{c}, \bar{f}_N, \mathsf{BRK}, \mathsf{KSK})$: For a LWE ciphertext $\mathbf{c}$, a given negacyclic lookup table $\bar{f}_N : \mathbb{Z}_{2N} \to \mathbb{Z}_q$, a blind rotation key BRK, and a key-switching key KSK, run Algorithm 2. $\bar{f}_N$ should satisfy the negacyclic condition.

Algorithm 2: TFHE Bootstrapping

Input: A LWE ciphertext $\mathbf{c} \in \mathbb{Z}_q^{N+1}$, a negacyclic lookup table $\bar{f}_N : \mathbb{Z}_{2N} \to \mathbb{Z}_q$, the blind rotation key BRK, and the key-switching key KSK
Output: A LWE ciphertext $\mathbf{c}_{out} \in \mathbb{Z}_q^{N+1}$
1 $\mathbf{c}_{ks} \leftarrow \mathsf{KeySwitch}(\mathsf{KSK}, \mathbf{c})$
2 $\bar{\mathbf{c}} \leftarrow \mathsf{ModSwitch}(\mathbf{c}_{ks}, 2N)$
3 $\mathsf{ACC} \leftarrow \mathsf{BlindRotate}(\bar{\mathbf{c}}, \bar{f}_N, \mathsf{BRK})$
4 $\mathbf{c}_{out} \leftarrow \mathsf{SampleExtract}(\mathsf{ACC})$
5 **return** $\mathbf{c}_{out}$

• $\mathsf{FDBlindRotate}(\bar{\mathbf{c}}, f_N, \mathsf{BRK})$: Given a ciphertext $\bar{\mathbf{c}} = (\bar{b}, \bar{\mathbf{a}}) \in \mathbb{Z}_N^{n+1}$ a full-domain lookup table $f_N : \mathbb{Z}_N \to \mathbb{Z}_q$, and a blind rotation key BRK, homomorphically evaluate the f_N.

$\mathsf{FDBlindRotate}$ generalizes $\mathsf{BlindRotate}$ by lifting the restriction to negacyclic lookup tables. Various instantiations of $\mathsf{FDBlindRotate}$ have been proposed in the literature [16,18,24]. Since $\mathsf{FDBlindRotate}$ generally requires two or more blind rotations, $\mathsf{FDBlindRotate}$ tends to be significantly more costly than negacyclic $\mathsf{BlindRotate}$.

3 Decomposition of Lookup Tables

In this section, we introduce a method to express a large full-domain lookup table into several smaller negacyclic lookup tables and a small full-domain lookup table. At the core of this method is a decomposition that expresses a lookup table $f_{2^m} : \mathbb{Z}_{2^m} \to \mathbb{Z}_q$ as the sum of a full-domain lookup table $f_{2^{m-1}} : \mathbb{Z}_{2^{m-1}} \to \mathbb{Z}_q$ and a negacyclic lookup table $\bar{f}_{2^{m-1}} : \mathbb{Z}_{2^m} \to \mathbb{Z}_q$. Here, a negacyclic lookup table $\bar{f}_{2^{m-1}}$ refers to a function satisfying the condition

$$\bar{f}_{2^{m-1}}(x) = -\bar{f}_{2^{m-1}}(x + 2^{m-1}) \quad \text{for all} \quad x \in [0, 2^{m-1}).$$

By recursively applying the decomposition to the smaller full-domain lookup tables for μ times, the original lookup table can be rewritten as the sum of μ

negacyclic lookup tables and one small full-domain lookup table. Figure 1 provides an intuitive visualization of the recursive decomposition with decomposition depth $\mu = 3$, illustrating how the full-domain lookup table $f_{2^m} : \mathbb{Z}_{2^m} \to \mathbb{Z}_q$ is expressed as the sum of 3 negacyclic components and a compact full-domain base table.

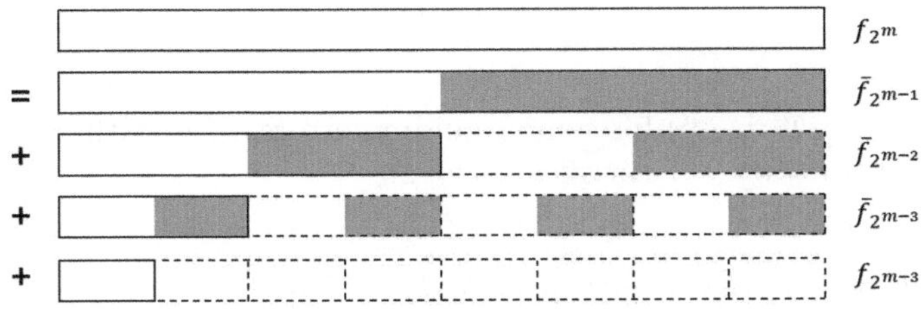

Fig. 1. Recursive decomposition of f_{2^m} with $\mu = 3$.

Following Lemma 1 and Theorem 1 formally state the decomposition structure.

Lemma 1. *Let f_{2^m} be a lookup table $f_{2^m} : \mathbb{Z}_{2^m} \to \mathbb{Z}_q$. Then there exists a lookup table $f_{2^{m-1}} : \mathbb{Z}_{2^{m-1}} \to \mathbb{Z}_q$ and a negacyclic lookup table $\bar{f}_{2^{m-1}} : \mathbb{Z}_{2^m} \to \mathbb{Z}_q$ such that for all $i \in \mathbb{Z}_{2^m}$, the value $f_{2^m}(i)$ can be reconstructed by the identity*

$$f_{2^m}(i) = \bar{f}_{2^{m-1}}(i) + f_{2^{m-1}}([i]_{2^{m-1}}) + e_i$$

where e_i is a small rounding error satisfying $|e_i| \leq 1$.

Proof. We define $f_{2^{m-1}}$ and $\bar{f}_{2^{m-1}}$ using the values of f_{2^m} as follows.

$$f_{2^{m-1}}(i) := \left\lfloor \frac{1}{2}\left(f_{2^m}(i) + f_{2^m}(i + 2^{m-1})\right) \right\rceil \quad (0 \leq i < 2^{m-1})$$

$$\bar{f}_{2^{m-1}}(i) := \begin{cases} \left\lfloor \frac{1}{2}\left(f_{2^m}(i) - f_{2^m}(i + 2^{m-1})\right) \right\rceil & (0 \leq i < 2^{m-1}) \\ -\bar{f}_{2^{m-1}}(i - 2^{m-1}) & (2^{m-1} \leq i < 2^m) \end{cases}$$

Where $f_{2^m}(i)$ is viewed as a real number, and the arithmetic is performed in $\mathbb{R}$. Then the identity

$$\begin{aligned} &\bar{f}_{2^{m-1}}(i) + f_{2^{m-1}}([i]_{2^{m-1}}) \\ &= \left\lfloor \frac{1}{2}\left(f_{2^m}(i) - f_{2^m}(i + 2^{m-1})\right) \right\rceil + \left\lfloor \frac{1}{2}\left(f_{2^m}(i) + f_{2^m}(i + 2^{m-1})\right) \right\rceil \\ &= \frac{1}{2}\left(f_{2^m}(i) - f_{2^m}(i + 2^{m-1})\right) + e'_i + \frac{1}{2}\left(f_{2^m}(i) + f_{2^m}(i + 2^{m-1})\right) + e''_i \\ &= f_{2^m}(i) + e_i \end{aligned}$$

holds for all $i \in [0, 2^{m-1})$ and

$$\begin{aligned}
&\bar{f}_{2^{m-1}}(i) + f_{2^{m-1}}([i]_{2^{m-1}}) \\
&= -\left\lfloor \frac{1}{2}\left(f_{2^m}(i - 2^{m-1}) - f_{2^m}(i)\right)\right\rceil + \left\lfloor \frac{1}{2}\left(f_{2^m}(i - 2^{m-1}) + f_{2^m}(i)\right)\right\rceil \\
&= -\frac{1}{2}\left(f_{2^m}(i - 2^{m-1}) - f_{2^m}(i)\right) + e_i' + \frac{1}{2}\left(f_{2^m}(i - 2^{m-1}) + f_{2^m}(i)\right) + e_i'' \\
&= f_{2^m}(i) + e_i
\end{aligned}$$

holds for all $i \in [2^{m-1}, 2^m)$ for some rounding errors e_i', e_i'' with $|e_i'|, |e_i''| \le \frac{1}{2}$, so that their sum $e_i = e_i' + e_i''$ satisfies $|e_i| \le 1$. □

Theorem 1. *Let f_{2^m} be a lookup table $f_{2^m} : \mathbb{Z}_{2^m} \to \mathbb{Z}_q$. For a given decomposition depth $1 \le \mu < m$, there exists a sequence of negacyclic lookup tables $\{\bar{f}_{2^k} : \mathbb{Z}_{2^{k+1}} \to \mathbb{Z}_q\}_{k=m-\mu}^{m-1}$ and a full-domain lookup table $f_{2^{m-\mu}} : \mathbb{Z}_{2^{m-\mu}} \to \mathbb{Z}_q$ such that, for all $i \in \mathbb{Z}_{2^m}$, the value $f_{2^m}(i)$ can be reconstructed by the identity*

$$f_{2^m}(i) = \sum_{k=m-\mu}^{m-1} \bar{f}_{2^k}([i]_{2^{k+1}}) + f_{2^{m-\mu}}([i]_{2^{m-\mu}}) + e_i.$$

where e_i is a small rounding error satisfying $|e_i| \le \mu$.

Proof. The proof follows by applying Lemma 1 recursively μ times. □

As $|e_i| \le \mu$ and $q \gg \mu$ in typical settings, the rounding error is negligible. We now present an algorithm that implements the decomposition described in Lemma 1 and Theorem 1.

- DecompLUT(f_{2^m}, μ): For a given full-domain lookup table $f_{2^m} : \mathbb{Z}_{2^m} \to \mathbb{Z}_q$ and decomposition depth μ, run Algorithm 3.

This algorithm recursively decomposes f_{2^m} by iteratively applying the decomposition described in Lemma 1. At each level, it computes the sum and difference of the first and second halves of the lookup table. The difference yields a negacyclic lookup table of size 2^k, and the sum becomes a smaller full-domain table of size 2^k used in the next iteration. After μ steps, the algorithm returns μ negacyclic lookup tables and a full-domain lookup table of size $2^{m-\mu}$, which can be used to reconstruct the original table.

4 A Faster Extended Full-Domain Bootstrapping

In this section, we present a new blind rotation algorithm for a faster full-domain functional bootstrapping, based on the recursive lookup table decomposition introduced in the previous section. Our method can utilize any existing FDFB method as a baseline without losing its efficiency and is also algorithmically parallelizable, unlike previous methods.

Algorithm 3: DecompLUT

Input: A full-domain lookup table $f_{2^m} : \mathbb{Z}_{2^m} \rightarrow \mathbb{Z}_q$, and a decomposition depth $1 \leq \mu < m$

Output: A sequence of negacyclic lookup table $\{\bar{f}_{2^k}\}_{k=m-\mu}^{m-1}$ where each $\bar{f}_{2^k} : \mathbb{Z}_{2^{k+1}} \rightarrow \mathbb{Z}_q$ and a full-domain lookup table $f_{2^{m-\mu}} : \mathbb{Z}_{2^{m-\mu}} \rightarrow \mathbb{Z}_q$

$current \leftarrow f_{2^m}$
for $k \leftarrow m-1$ ***down to*** $m-\mu$ **do**
  $n \leftarrow 2^k$
  for $i \leftarrow 0$ **to** $n-1$ **do**
    $new[i] \leftarrow \left\lfloor \frac{1}{2}(current[i] + current[n+i]) \right\rceil$
    $\bar{f}_{2^k}[i] \leftarrow \left\lfloor \frac{1}{2}(current[i] - current[n+i]) \right\rceil$
    $\bar{f}_{2^k}[n+i] \leftarrow -\bar{f}_{2^k}[i]$
  end
  $current \leftarrow new$
end
$f_{2^{m-\mu}} \leftarrow current$
return $\{\bar{f}_{2^{m-1}}, \ldots, \bar{f}_{2^{m-\mu}}\}$, $f_{2^{m-\mu}}$

In prior works, arbitrary lookup tables were evaluated with two or more consecutive negacyclic lookup table evaluations of double the size. Note that a single negacyclic lookup table can be evaluated via TFHE bootstrapping, and the latency of the bootstrapping is proportional to the size of the lookup table. Therefore, when evaluating a size N lookup table, the existing full-domain functional bootstrapping methods require the latency of at least two negacyclic functional bootstrapping of the size $2N$, ending up in roughly $4N$ unit time.

Instead, we propose to decompose the input size N lookup table into several negacyclic lookup tables and a compact lookup table with size $\leq N$, exploiting our novel recursive decomposition method. As a result, we can almost halve the latency of the full-domain functional bootstrapping without any compromise.

4.1 Bootstrapping with Recursive Lookup Table Decomposition

In Algorithm 4, the full-domain lookup table f_{2^m} is first decomposed using DecompLUT into a sequence of smaller negacyclic lookup tables $\{\bar{f}_{2^k}\}_{k=m-\mu}^{m-1}$ and a base full-domain table $f_{2^{m-\mu}}$. Each negacyclic lookup table $\bar{f}_{2^k} : \mathbb{Z}_{2^{k+1}} \rightarrow \mathbb{Z}_q$ satisfies the condition

$$\bar{f}_{2^k}(x) = -\bar{f}_{2^k}(x + 2^k) \quad \text{for all} \quad x \in [0, 2^k).$$

The algorithm then performs μ blind rotation on each $\{\bar{f}_{2^k}\}_{k=m-\mu}^{m-1}$, whose size decreases with k. After each blind rotation, sample extraction and key switching are applied to obtain an LWE ciphertext that is accumulated into the output. After processing all negacyclic components, a full-domain blind rotation is applied to the small-sized base lookup table $f_{2^{m-\mu}}$, along with a final sample extraction and key switching. The result is the sum of all partial ciphertexts, completing the evaluation. We provide the full algorithm in Algorithm 4.

Algorithm 4: Efficient Full Domain Functional Bootstrapping without EBS

Input: A LWE ciphertext $\mathbf{c} = (b, \mathbf{a}) \in \mathbb{Z}_q^{n+1}$, a full-domain lookup table $f_{2^m} : \mathbb{Z}_{2^m} \to \mathbb{Z}_q$, a decomposition depth $1 \le \mu < m$, a set of blind rotation key$\{\mathsf{BRK}_{2^k}\}_{k=m-\mu}^{m-1}$, and a set of key-switching key $\{\mathsf{KSK}_{2^k}\}_{k=m-\mu}^{m-1}$

Output: A LWE ciphertext $\mathbf{c}_{out} = (b, \mathbf{a}) \in \mathbb{Z}_q^{n+1}$

$\{\bar{f}_{2^k}\}_{k=m-\mu}^{m-1}$, $f_{2^{m-\mu}} \leftarrow \mathsf{DecompLUT}(f_{2^m}, \mu)$
$(\bar{b}, \bar{\mathbf{a}}) \leftarrow \mathsf{ModSwitch}((b, \mathbf{a}), 2^m)$
Let $\mathbf{c}_{out} = (0, \mathbf{0}) \in \mathbb{Z}_q^{n+1}$
for $k \leftarrow m - \mu$ **to** $m - 1$ **do**
  $\mathsf{ACC}_{\mathsf{res}} \leftarrow \mathsf{BlindRotate}(([\bar{b}]_{2^{k+1}}, [\bar{\mathbf{a}}]_{2^{k+1}}), \bar{f}_{2^k}, \mathsf{BRK}_{2^k})$
  $\mathbf{c}' \leftarrow \mathsf{SampleExtract}(\mathsf{ACC}_{\mathsf{res}})$
  $\mathbf{c}_{out} \leftarrow \mathbf{c}_{out} + \mathsf{KeySwitch}(\mathbf{c}', \mathsf{KSK}_{2^k})$
end
$\mathsf{ACC}_{\mathsf{res}} \leftarrow \mathsf{FDBlindRotate}(([\bar{b}]_{2^{m-\mu}}, [\bar{\mathbf{a}}]_{2^{m-\mu}}), f_{2^{m-\mu}}, \mathsf{BRK}_{2^{m-\mu}})$
$\mathbf{c}' \leftarrow \mathsf{SampleExtract}(\mathsf{ACC}_{\mathsf{res}})$
$\mathbf{c}_{out} \leftarrow \mathbf{c}_{out} + \mathsf{KeySwitch}(\mathbf{c}', \mathsf{KSK}_{2^{m-\mu}})$
return $\mathbf{c}_{out}$

Time Complexity. Our decomposition-based algorithm allows us to distribute the computation across smaller lookup tables. Since the cost of blind rotation grows almost linearly with the size of the lookup table, this decomposition leads to substantial savings. Our algorithm returns μ negacyclic lookup tables of size $N, \ldots, N/2^{\mu-1}$ and a regular lookup table of size $N/2^{\mu}$ where μ is the decomposition depth. Then, these lookup tables can be evaluated in a total of $N + \cdots + N/2^{\mu-1} + N/2^{\mu} \cdot 4 = 2N + N/2^{\mu-1}$ unit time without parallelization (N unit time with parallelization). In contrast, as mentioned earlier in this section, existing full-domain bootstrapping methods require a minimum of $4N$ unit time. Therefore, our decomposition-based algorithm provides substantial performance gains over conventional full-domain bootstrapping methods.

Key Size. Let n be the dimension of the input LWE ciphertext. Generally, to evaluate a negacyclic lookup table of size N, we require n RGSW ciphertexts with ring dimension N, and N key-switching keys, which roughly take $n \cdot N$ space complexity, up to a constant determined by the gadget parameters. Therefore, the existing full-domain bootstrapping methods require evaluation keys of the size $2nN$ unit size, as they leverage size $2N$ negacyclic lookup table evaluation. In contrast, our full domain functional bootstrapping algorithm consists of blind rotation over rings with different dimensions, namely $N, N/2, \ldots, N/2^{\mu-1}$ for the decomposition depth $\mu > 0$. To facilitate all the blind rotations over these ring degrees, we need evaluation keys of the size $n(N + N/2 + \cdots + N/2^{\mu-1}) = 2nN - nN/2^{\mu-1}$ unit size. To compare with the conventional method, our algorithm shows a slightly smaller key size overhead.

Our algorithm offers significant advantages over conventional full-domain functional bootstrapping, which typically requires two consecutive bootstrapping operations. By leveraging the negacyclic decomposition structure, our approach achieves the same functionality at a substantially reduced computational cost, cutting the overall cost by nearly half. Another important advantage of our method is that each blind rotation operates independently of the others, enabling highly parallelizable and scalable computation across all components. Furthermore, the FDBlindRotate algorithm for the base full-domain lookup table can be used as a black-box component, allowing any existing FDFB implementation such as [16,18,24] to be directly reused without modification. In addition, since our algorithm treats blind rotation as a black-box subroutine, it is compatible with a wide range of recent optimization techniques such as [2,20], all of which can be orthogonally integrated to further improve performance.

4.2 Optimization via Extended Bootstrapping

In this section, we discuss how to optimize the key size and noise growth for our novel functional bootstrapping method from lookup table decomposition without compromising the computational cost. As specified in the previous section, the evaluation key size of a vanilla TFHE scheme grows linearly to the size of the lookup table evaluated. This makes the evaluation of large lookup tables challenging, as the communication cost and the space complexity are increased. Therefore, we discuss how to make our approach truly scalable and practical by leveraging the *extended bootstrapping* (EBS) technique [21].

As a result, we can evaluate any size lookup table using a single shared blind rotation and key-switching key with a smaller unified ring dimension, by mapping high-dimensional polynomial rings to multiple copies of a lower-dimensional ring.

Extended Bootstrapping (EBS). Let us formally introduce the extended bootstrapping (EBS) proposed in [21]. The main idea of EBS is to rewrite polynomial operations in dimension $N = 2^m$ as 2^ν independent operations in dimension $2^{m-\nu}$ via a module isomorphism

$$\tau : \mathbb{Z}_q[X]/(X^{2^m}+1) \to \left(\mathbb{Z}_q[X]/(X^{2^{m-\nu}}+1)\right)^{2^\nu},$$

$$\tau\Big(\sum_{i=0}^{2^m} p_i X^i\Big) = \Big(\sum_{i=0}^{2^{m-\nu}} p_{2^\nu i} X^i, \cdots, \sum_{i=0}^{2^{m-\nu}} p_{2^\nu i+2^\nu-1} X^i\Big)$$

where ν is referred to as the extend factor. Then,

$$\tau\Big(\mathrm{RLWE}^{2^m}_{t_{\mathsf{ext}}}(pt)\Big) = \Big(\mathrm{RLWE}^{2^{m-\nu}}_t(pt_0), \cdots, \mathrm{RLWE}^{2^{m-\nu}}_t(pt_{2^\nu-1})\Big)$$

holds for $\tau(pt) = (pt_0, \cdots, pt_{2^\nu-1})$. Where the subscript denotes the secret key, the superscript specifies the RLWE ring degree, and the argument represents the encrypted plaintext. The extended key t_{ext} is constructed by copying the entries of t into the indices divisible by 2^ν and setting all other positions to zero.

Furthermore, under the assumption that $z \in \mathbb{Z}$, we can perform RGSW-RLWE external product in parallel by,

$$\begin{aligned} &\mathrm{RGSW}^{2^m}_{t_{\mathsf{ext}}}(z) \boxdot \mathrm{RLWE}^{2^m}_{t_{\mathsf{ext}}}(pt) \\ &\simeq \left(\mathrm{RGSW}^{2^{m-\nu}}_t(z) \boxdot \mathrm{RLWE}^{2^{m-\nu}}_t(pt_0), \cdots, \mathrm{RGSW}^{2^{m-\nu}}_t(z) \boxdot \mathrm{RLWE}^{2^{m-\nu}}_t(pt_{2^\nu-1})\right). \end{aligned}$$

Specifically, the decomposition enables each external product to be performed independently across 2^ν components. Because the RGSW ciphertext operates over a reduced dimension $2^{m-\nu}$, the entire procedure avoids additional key growth even when handling lookup tables of varying lengths.

- $\underline{\mathsf{ExtBlindRotate}_\nu(\bar{\mathbf{c}}, \bar{f}_{2^m}, \mathsf{BRK})}$: For a given LWE ciphertext $\bar{\mathbf{c}} = (\bar{b}, \bar{\mathbf{a}}) \in \mathbb{Z}^{n+1}_{2^{m+1}}$, a negacyclic lookup table $\bar{f}_{2^m} : \mathbb{Z}_{2^{m+1}} \to \mathbb{Z}_q$, an extend factor ν, and a blind rotation key BRK, run Algorithm 5.

Lines 3–8 in Algorithm 5 perform blind rotation in parallel across the 2^ν components of the decomposed accumulator $\overrightarrow{\mathsf{ACC}}$ using the module isomorphism τ.

Algorithm 5: $\mathsf{ExtBlindRotate}_\nu$

Input: A LWE ciphertext $(\bar{b}, \bar{\mathbf{a}}) \in \mathbb{Z}^{n+1}_{2^{m+1}}$, a negacyclic lookup table $\bar{f}_{2^m} : \mathbb{Z}_{2^{m+1}} \to \mathbb{Z}_q$, and the blind rotation key BRK

Output: A decomposed RLWE ciphertext $\overrightarrow{\mathsf{ACC}_0}$ with $\tau^{-1}\left(\overrightarrow{\mathsf{ACC}}\right) \in R_q^2$

1 Let $tv = \sum_{i=0}^{2^m-1} \bar{f}(i) \cdot X^i$
2 $\overrightarrow{\mathsf{ACC}} \leftarrow \tau\left((X^{-\bar{b}} \cdot tv, 0)\right)$
3 **for** $i \leftarrow 0$ **to** $n-1$ **do**
4     $\overrightarrow{\mathsf{RotACC}} \leftarrow \tau\left(X^{-\bar{\mathbf{a}}_i} \cdot \tau^{-1}\left(\overrightarrow{\mathsf{ACC}}\right)\right)$
5   **for** $j \leftarrow 0$ **to** $2^\nu - 1$ **do**
6         $\overrightarrow{\mathsf{ACC}_j} \leftarrow \mathsf{BRK}_i \boxdot \left(\overrightarrow{\mathsf{RotACC}_j} - \overrightarrow{\mathsf{ACC}_j}\right) + \overrightarrow{\mathsf{ACC}_j}$
7   **end**
8 **end**
9 **return** $\overrightarrow{\mathsf{ACC}_0}$

We now introduce an optimized version of Algorithm 4 that incorporates the extended bootstrapping (EBS) framework. By leveraging EBS, we can ensure that all RGSW operations are carried out over a unified reduced dimension $N' = 2^{m-\mu}$, thereby enabling the reuse of the same BRK across all components. Moreover, each $\mathsf{ExtBlindRotate}$ outputs a single accumulator $\overrightarrow{\mathsf{ACC}_0}$ of RLWE degree N', allowing all results to be key switched together using a single KSK.

This unified structure not only improves computational efficiency but also eliminates the key size overhead that arose in the original algorithm when handling lookup tables of varying lengths. Our optimized blind rotation algorithm with EBS is described in Algorithm 6. In the loop spanning Lines 5–8 of Algorithm 6, lookup tables of different lengths are processed using a common BRK with dimension N' by leveraging the EBS framework. To ensure that the reduced RLWE degree $2^{k-\nu}$ remains fixed at N' for each ExtBlindRotate, the extend factor ν is incremented by 1 in each iteration of the loop. Among the variants of FDBlindRotate, we adopt FDFB-Compress proposed in [21] as it introduces minimal parameter overhead and requires the fewest number of bootstrapping operations. Note that the input ciphertext for the call to FDBlindRotate at line Line 10 in Algorithm 6 is modulus switched to $\mathbb{Z}_{2^{m+1}}$, as FDFB-Compress requires a modulus twice the size of the full-domain lookup table.

Algorithm 6: Efficient Full Domain Functional Bootstrapping with EBS

Input: A LWE ciphertext $\mathbf{c} = (b, \mathbf{a}) \in \mathbb{Z}_q^{n+1}$, a full-domain lookup table $f_{2^m} : \mathbb{Z}_{2^m} \to \mathbb{Z}_q$, a decomposition depth $1 \le \mu < m$, the blind rotation key BRK and the key-switching key KSK

Output: A LWE ciphertext $\mathbf{c}_{out} = (b, \mathbf{a}) \in \mathbb{Z}_q^{n+1}$

1 $\{\bar{f}_{2^k}\}_{k=m-\mu}^{m-1}, f_{2^{m-\mu}} \leftarrow \mathsf{DecompLUT}(f_{2^m}, \mu)$
2 $(\bar{b}, \bar{\mathbf{a}}) \leftarrow \mathsf{ModSwitch}((b, \mathbf{a}), 2^m)$
3 Let $\mathsf{ACC}_{\mathsf{res}} = (0, 0) \in R_q^2$
4 $\nu \leftarrow 0$
5 **for** $k \leftarrow m - \mu$ **to** $m - 1$ **do**
6 $\quad \mathsf{ACC}_{\mathsf{res}} \leftarrow \mathsf{ACC}_{\mathsf{res}} + \mathsf{ExtBlindRotate}_\nu(([\bar{b}]_{2^{k+1}}, [\bar{\mathbf{a}}]_{2^{k+1}}), \bar{f}_{2^k}, \mathsf{BRK})$
7 $\quad \nu \leftarrow \nu + 1$
8 **end**
9 $(\tilde{b}, \tilde{\mathbf{a}}) \leftarrow \mathsf{ModSwitch}((b, \mathbf{a}), 2^{m+1})$
10 $\mathsf{ACC}_{\mathsf{res}} \leftarrow \mathsf{ACC}_{\mathsf{res}} + \mathsf{FDBlindRotate}(([\tilde{b}]_{2^{m-\mu+1}}, [\tilde{\mathbf{a}}]_{2^{m-\mu+1}}), f_{2^{m-\mu}}, \mathsf{BRK})$
11 $\mathbf{c}' \leftarrow \mathsf{SampleExtract}(\mathsf{ACC}_{\mathsf{res}})$
12 **return** $\mathbf{c}_{out} = \mathsf{KeySwitch}(\mathbf{c}', \mathsf{KSK})$

The exact description of our scheme is as follows. Enc and Dec, remain the same as in the original TFHE scheme.

• Setup(1^λ): Given a security parameter λ, generate the following public parameters: LWE dimension n, lookup table length N, decomposition depth μ where RLWE dimension is $N' = 2^{m-\mu}$, error parameters $\alpha, \beta > 0$, plaintext and ciphertext modulus p, q, the gadget decomposition base and dimension B, d, and the key-switching base and dimension B', d'. Define *scaling factor* Δ as $\frac{q}{p}$.

• KeyGen(1^λ):
- Sample $s_i \leftarrow \mathcal{U}(\mathbb{B})$ for $0 \le i < n$. Return the LWE secret key $\mathbf{s} = (s_0, s_1, \ldots, s_{n-1})$.

- Sample $t_i \leftarrow \mathcal{U}(\mathbb{B})$ for $0 \leq i < N'$. Return the RLWE secret key $t = t_0 + t_1 X + \ldots + t_{N'-1} X^{N'-1}$. Write $\mathbf{t} = (t_0, t_1, \ldots, t_{N'-1})$.
- Set $\mathsf{BRK}_i \leftarrow \mathsf{RGSW.Enc}(t, s_i)$ for $0 \leq i < n$. Return the blind rotation key $\mathsf{BRK} = \{\mathsf{BRK}_i\}_{0 \leq i < N'}$.
- Set $\mathsf{KSK} \leftarrow \mathsf{SwitchKeyGen}(\mathbf{s}, \mathbf{t})$. Return the key-switching key KSK.

• $\underline{\mathsf{OurFullDomainBootstrap}(\mathbf{c}, f_N, \mu, \mathsf{BRK}, \mathsf{KSK})}$: For a LWE ciphertext $\mathbf{c}$, a given full-domain lookup table $f_N : \mathbb{Z}_N \to \mathbb{Z}_q$, a decomposition depth μ, a blind rotation key BRK, and a key-switching key KSK, run Algorithm 6.

Even with the application of EBS, our method retains its performance advantage over conventional full-domain bootstrapping. Since the use of EBS is orthogonal to our decomposition-based optimization, the total computation time remains nearly halved compared to traditional methods, achieving up to a 2× speedup.

4.3 Error Analysis

In this section, we present a concrete error analysis of our new bootstrapping algorithm. We assume that each LWE and RLWE component is uniformly distributed over $\mathbb{Z}_q$ and R_q, respectively, under the (R)LWE assumption. As mentioned earlier, the gadget decomposition base and dimension are denoted by B and d, respectively, while the key-switching base and dimension are denoted by B' and d'.

Lemma 2 (ModSwitch and KeySwitch). *Let* $(\bar{b}, \bar{\mathbf{a}}) := \mathsf{ModSwitch}((b, \mathbf{a}), N)$, *and* $\mathbf{c}' := \mathsf{KeySwitch}(\mathbf{c}, \mathsf{KSK})$. *Then, the error variances after each operation satisfy:*

$$\mathsf{Var}\left(\mathsf{Err}\left(\frac{q}{N}\bar{b}, \frac{q}{N}\bar{\mathbf{a}}\right)\right) \leq \mathsf{Var}(\mathsf{Err}(b, \mathbf{a})) + V_{\mathsf{MS}},$$
$$\mathsf{Var}(\mathsf{Err}(\mathbf{c}')) \leq \mathsf{Var}(\mathsf{Err}(\mathbf{c})) + V_{\mathsf{KS}}.$$

where

$$V_{\mathsf{MS}} := \frac{n+1}{12N^2}, \quad V_{\mathsf{KS}} := \frac{1}{12B'^{2d'}} q^2 N^2 + \frac{1}{12}\alpha^2 d' N B'^2.$$

Proof. Follows from [17, Lemma 8,9]. □

Lemma 3 (Extended Bootstrapping). *Let* $\mathsf{ACC} := \mathsf{ExtBlindRotate}_\nu((\bar{b}, \bar{\mathbf{a}}), \bar{f}_N, \mathsf{BRK})$ *with extend factor* ν. *Then, the error variance after* $\mathsf{ExtBlindRotate}$ *satisfy:*

$$\mathsf{Var}(\mathsf{Err}(\mathsf{ACC})) \leq V_{\mathsf{EBR}} := n\Big(\frac{N}{2^\nu} + 1\Big)\frac{q^2}{6B^{2d}} + \frac{1}{3}dn\Big(\frac{N}{2^\nu}\Big)\beta^2 B^2.$$

In other words, error variance of extended blind rotation is determined by the reduced ring degree $N/2^\nu$, *and thus two instances with the same* $N/2^\nu$ *will have the same error variance.*

Proof. From [21, Proposition 2], we get that V_{EBR} corresponds to the error variance of a blind rotation with a reduced RLWE dimension of $N/2^{\nu}$ where ν is the extend factor. By substituting $N/2^{\nu}$ into the expression $n(N+1)\frac{q^2}{6B^{2d}} + \frac{1}{3}dnN\beta^2B^2$ from [17, Lemma 10], which gives the error variance for a blind rotation of RLWE dimension N, we obtain the result in lemma. □

Lemma 4 (Our Bootstrapping). *Input error variance of* ExtBlindRotate *and* FDBlindRotate *in Algorithm 6 is*

$$V_{\mathsf{MS}} + (\mu+1)V_{\mathsf{EBR}} + \mu^2 + V_{\mathsf{KS}}, \quad \frac{V_{\mathsf{MS}}}{4} + (\mu+1)V_{\mathsf{EBR}} + \mu^2 + V_{\mathsf{KS}}$$

respectively. Here, μ denotes the decomposition depth, and ν used in the definition of V_{EBR} is set equal to μ.

Proof. According to Lemma 3 the error variance introduced by ModSwitch is V_{MS} when the modulus is switched to $N = 2^m$, and $\frac{1}{4}V_{\mathsf{MS}}$ when switched to $2N = 2^{m+1}$.

During Algorithm 6, ExtBlindRotate and FDBlindRotate is invoked $(\mu+1)$ times—specifically in lines 5–7 and line 10. As stated in Lemma 3, each invocation of ExtBlindRotate and FDBlindRotate introduces an error term with the same variance V_{EBR}, since they all operate on the same reduced ring degree $N/2^{\mu} = 2^{m-\mu}$ with EBS. These errors accumulate over $\mu+1$ invocations, resulting in a total variance of $(\mu+1)V_{\mathsf{EBR}}$.

In addition, the rounding error introduced by the LUT decomposition in Theorem 1 contributes an error variance of at most μ^2. Since $\mu < \log N$, this contribution is negligible compared to other dominant terms.

Finally, the key switching step contributes an additional error variance of V_{KS}, which completes the total input variance as stated. □

Note that our blind rotation error is $\log(\mu+1)$ bits larger than the original EBS. However, this increase remains moderate in the overall error budget, as V_{MS} and V_{KS} are still the dominant contributors to the total variance.

5 Experimental Results

In this section, we present experimental results for our algorithm and compare them with previous works. The source code is available at https://github.com/SNUCP/fast-fdfb. Our implementation is written in Go, based on the TFHE-go library [15].

5.1 Parameter Selection

We provide benchmark results for both the non-EBS and EBS variants (corresponding to Algorithm 4 and Algorithm 6). The parameter sets for the non-EBS and EBS variants are provided in Table 1 and Table 2, respectively. For each plaintext modulus p ranging from 2^5 to 2^8, we specify distinct parameter sets.

In all parameter sets, we fix q, α, and β to 2^{64}, $2^{36.00}$, and $2^{12.65}$, respectively. All parameters are chosen to ensure 128-bit security while keeping the bootstrapping failure probability below 2^{-60}. The value of decomposition depth μ is chosen as large as possible to maximize performance, while ensuring that the reduced RLWE dimension $N' = N/2^{\mu}$ still achieves 128-bit security. Because the non-EBS variant incurs slightly larger errors during blind rotation and key switching, its gadget parameters are set to slightly larger values in certain cases.

Table 1. Parameter sets for the non-EBS variant

p	n	N	μ	B	d	B'	d'
2^5	1160	2^{12}	1	2^{22}	1	2^7	3
2^6		2^{13}	2		2		
2^7		2^{14}	3				
2^8		2^{15}	4				

Table 2. Parameter sets for the EBS variant

p	n	N	μ	B	d	B'	d'
2^5	1160	2^{12}	1	2^{22}	1	2^7	3
2^6		2^{13}	2				
2^7		2^{14}	3		2		
2^8		2^{15}	4				

5.2 Benchmark Results

Now we present the benchmark results of our full domain bootstrapping algorithm. The non-EBS and EBS variants were configured according to the parameter sets given in Table 1 and Table 2, respectively. All benchmarks were conducted on a single core of a desktop equipped with an Intel Core i7-12700F CPU and 32GB of RAM. Each benchmark was repeated 50 times, and the average runtime was reported. For comparison, we additionally implemented the FDFB-Compress scheme presented in [24], as it offers minimal parameter overhead and requires only two bootstrapping operations, which is the fewest among previously known full-domain bootstrapping schemes.

The resulting benchmark times are summarized in Table 3. We also provide the size of the public keys required for bootstrapping in Table 4.

As shown in Table 3 and Table 4, applying EBS to our new bootstrapping algorithm yields up to 1.50× speedup compared to the non-EBS version, while

Table 3. FDFB performance for each plaintext modulus p.

		$p = 2^5$	$p = 2^6$	$p = 2^7$	$p = 2^8$
Non-EBS	FDFB-Compress	79 ms	297 ms	655 ms	1470 ms
	Ours	59 ms	146 ms	300 ms	648 ms
EBS	FDFB-Compress	70 ms	134 ms	393 ms	823 ms
	Ours	57 ms	91 ms	234 ms	431 ms

Table 4. Bootstrapping key size for each plaintext modulus.

<table>
<tr><th></th><th></th><th>$p = 2^5$</th><th>$p = 2^6$</th><th>$p = 2^7$</th><th>$p = 2^8$</th></tr>
<tr><td>Non-EBS</td><td>FDFB-Compress</td><td>254 MB</td><td>798 MB</td><td>1.56 GB</td><td>3.12 GB</td></tr>
<tr><td></td><td>Ours</td><td>127 MB</td><td>598 MB</td><td>1.36 GB</td><td>2.98 GB</td></tr>
<tr><td rowspan="2">EBS</td><td>FDFB-Compress</td><td colspan="2" rowspan="2">127 MB</td><td colspan="2" rowspan="2">199 MB</td></tr>
<tr><td>Ours</td></tr>
</table>

significantly reducing the key size. In particular, without EBS, the key size can grow up to 25.1× larger, which is effectively mitigated by our EBS-based approach.

Moreover, our full-domain bootstrapping algorithm achieves substantially better performance than previous approaches without incurring any additional key size growth. For example, when the plaintext modulus is $p = 2^8$, our method is approximately 3.41× faster than FDFB-Compress without EBS, and 1.91× faster even when EBS is applied. Remarkably, our method is only 4.7% slower than a single instance of negacyclic bootstrapping, suggesting that it is nearly the most optimal full-domain bootstrapping algorithm.

Also, our algorithm can achieve even better performance thanks to its parallelizability. Unlike conventional blind rotation, which is inherently difficult to parallelize due to sequential dependencies, our method allows each blind rotation over decomposed LUTs to operate independently, enabling highly parallel and scalable computation across all components.

Acknowledgements. This work was partly supported by the National Research Foundation of Korea(NRF) grant funded by the Korea government(MSIT) (No. RS-2023-00211649) and Institute of Information & Communications Technology Planning & Evaluation (IITP) grant funded by the Korea government(MSIT) (No. RS-2024-00399491, Development of Privacy-Preserving Multiparty Computation Techniques for Secure Multiparty Data Integration).

References

1. Bergerat, L.: Parameter optimization and larger precision for (T)FHE. J. Cryptol. **36**(3), 28 (2023). https://doi.org/10.1007/S00145-023-09463-5
2. Bergerat, L., et al.: New secret keys for enhanced performance in (T)FHE. In: Luo, B., Liao, X., Xu, J., Kirda, E., Lie, D. (eds.) ACM CCS 2024: 31st Conference on Computer and Communications Security. pp. 2547–2561. ACM Press, Salt Lake City, UT, USA (October 14–18, 2024). https://doi.org/10.1145/3658644.3670376
3. Bon, N., Pointcheval, D., Rivain, M.: Optimized homomorphic evaluation of Boolean functions. IACR Trans. Cryptogr. Hardw. Embed. Syst. **2024**(3), 302–341 (2024). https://doi.org/10.46586/TCHES.V2024.I3.302-341
4. Brakerski, Z.: Fully homomorphic encryption without modulus switching from classical gapsvp. In: Annual cryptology conference, pp. 868–886. Springer (2012)
5. Brakerski, Z., Gentry, C., Vaikuntanathan, V.: (Leveled) fully homomorphic encryption without bootstrapping. ACM Trans. Comput. Theory (TOCT) **6**(3), 1–36 (2014)
6. Carpov, S., Izabachène, M., Mollimard, V.: New techniques for multi-value input homomorphic evaluation and applications. In: Cryptographers' Track at the RSA Conference, pp. 106–126. Springer (2019)
7. Cheon, J.H., Kim, A., Kim, M., Song, Y.: Homomorphic encryption for arithmetic of approximate numbers. In: Advances in cryptology–ASIACRYPT 2017: 23rd international conference on the theory and applications of cryptology and information security, Hong kong, China, December 3-7, 2017, proceedings, part I 23, pp. 409–437. Springer (2017)
8. Chillotti, I., Gama, N., Georgieva, M., Izabachène, M.: TFHE: fast fully homomorphic encryption over the torus. J. Cryptol. **33**(1), 34–91 (2020)
9. Chillotti, I., Ligier, D., Orfila, J.B., Tap, S.: Improved programmable bootstrapping with larger precision and efficient arithmetic circuits for TFHE. In: International Conference on the Theory and Application of Cryptology and Information Security, pp. 670–699. Springer (2021)
10. Ducas, L., Micciancio, D.: FHEW: bootstrapping homomorphic encryption in less than a second. In: Oswald, E., Fischlin, M. (eds.) Advances in Cryptology – EUROCRYPT 2015, Part I. Lecture Notes in Computer Science, vol. 9056, pp. 617–640. Springer Berlin Heidelberg, Germany, Sofia, Bulgaria (April 26–30, 2015). https://doi.org/10.1007/978-3-662-46800-5_24
11. Fan, J., Vercauteren, F.: Somewhat practical fully homomorphic encryption. Cryptology ePrint Archive (2012)
12. Gentry, C.: Fully homomorphic encryption using ideal lattices. In: Proceedings of the Forty-First Annual ACM Symposium on Theory of Computing, pp. 169–178. STOC '09, Association for Computing Machinery, New York, NY, USA (2009). https://doi.org/10.1145/1536414.1536440
13. Gentry, C., Sahai, A., Waters, B.: Homomorphic encryption from learning with errors: conceptually-simpler, asymptotically-faster, attribute-based. In: Advances in Cryptology–CRYPTO 2013: 33rd Annual Cryptology Conference, Santa Barbara, CA, USA, August 18-22, 2013. Proceedings, Part I, pp. 75–92. Springer (2013)
14. Guimarães, A., Borin, E., Aranha, D.F.: Revisiting the functional bootstrap in TFHE. IACR Trans. Cryptographic Hardware Embed. Syst. 229–253 (2021)
15. Hwang, I.: TFHE-go (2023). https://github.com/sp301415/tfhe-go

16. Hwang, I., Min, S., Song, Y.: Carousel: fully homomorphic encryption with bootstrapping over automorphism group. Cryptology ePrint Archive, Paper 2024/2032 (2024). https://eprint.iacr.org/2024/2032
17. Hwang, I., Min, S., Song, Y.: Practical circuit privacy/sanitization for TFHE. Cryptology ePrint Archive, Paper 2025/216 (2025). https://eprint.iacr.org/2025/216
18. Kluczniak, K., Schild, L.: FDFB: full domain functional bootstrapping towards practical fully homomorphic encryption. IACR Trans. Cryptogr. Hardw. Embed. Syst. **2023**(1), 501–537 (2023). https://doi.org/10.46586/TCHES.V2023.I1.501-537
19. Kluczniak, K., Schild, L.: FDFB^2: functional bootstrapping via sparse polynomial multiplication. Cryptology ePrint Archive, Paper 2024/1376 (2024). https://eprint.iacr.org/2024/1376
20. Lee, C., Min, S., Seo, J., Song, Y.: Faster TFHE bootstrapping with block binary keys. In: Liu, J.K., Xiang, Y., Nepal, S., Tsudik, G. (eds.) Proceedings of the 2023 ACM Asia Conference on Computer and Communications Security, ASIA CCS 2023, Melbourne, VIC, Australia, July 10-14, 2023, pp. 2–13. ACM (2023). https://doi.org/10.1145/3579856.3595804
21. Lee, K., Yoon, J.W.: Discretization error reduction for high precision torus fully homomorphic encryption. In: Boldyreva, A., Kolesnikov, V. (eds.) Public-Key Cryptography - PKC 2023 - 26th IACR International Conference on Practice and Theory of Public-Key Cryptography, Atlanta, GA, USA, May 7-10, 2023, Proceedings, Part II. Lecture Notes in Computer Science, vol. 13941, pp. 33–62. Springer (2023). https://doi.org/10.1007/978-3-031-31371-4_2
22. Liu, Z., Micciancio, D., Polyakov, Y.: Large-precision homomorphic sign evaluation using FHEW/TFHE bootstrapping. In: Agrawal, S., Lin, D. (eds.) Advances in Cryptology - ASIACRYPT 2022 - 28th International Conference on the Theory and Application of Cryptology and Information Security, Taipei, Taiwan, December 5-9, 2022, Proceedings, Part II. Lecture Notes in Computer Science, vol. 13792, pp. 130–160. Springer (2022). https://doi.org/10.1007/978-3-031-22966-4_5
23. Lyubashevsky, V., Peikert, C., Regev, O.: On ideal lattices and learning with errors over rings. In: Advances in Cryptology–EUROCRYPT 2010: 29th Annual International Conference on the Theory and Applications of Cryptographic Techniques, French Riviera, May 30–June 3, 2010. Proceedings 29, pp. 1–23. Springer (2010)
24. Ma, S., Huang, T., Wang, A., Zhou, Q., Wang, X.: Fast and accurate: efficient full-domain functional bootstrap and digit decomposition for homomorphic computation. IACR Trans. Cryptogr. Hardw. Embed. Syst. **2024**(1), 592–616 (2024). https://doi.org/10.46586/TCHES.V2024.I1.592-616
25. Regev, O.: On lattices, learning with errors, random linear codes, and cryptography. J. ACM (JACM) **56**(6), 1–40 (2009)
26. Stehlé, D., Steinfeld, R., Tanaka, K., Xagawa, K.: Efficient public key encryption based on ideal lattices. In: International Conference on the Theory and Application of Cryptology and Information Security, pp. 617–635. Springer (2009)
27. Yang, Z., Xie, X., Shen, H., Chen, S., Zhou, J.: TOTA: fully homomorphic encryption with smaller parameters and stronger security. Cryptology ePrint Archive, Paper 2021/1347 (2021). https://eprint.iacr.org/2021/1347

Side-Channel Analysis and Fault Attacks

Picking up the Fallen Mask: Breaking and Fixing the RS-Mask Countermeasure

Dilara Toprakhisar[1(✉)], Svetla Nikova[1], and Ventzislav Nikov[2]

[1] COSIC, KU Leuven, Leuven, Belgium
{dilara.toprakhisar,svetla.nikova}@esat.kuleuven.be
[2] NXP Semiconductors, Leuven, Belgium

Abstract. Physical attacks pose a major challenge to the secure implementation of cryptographic algorithms. Although significant progress has been made in countering passive attacks such as side-channel analysis (SCA), protection against fault attacks is still less developed. One reason for this is the broader and more complex nature of fault attacks, which makes it difficult to create standardized fault evaluation methodologies for countermeasures like those used for SCA. This makes it easier to overlook potential vulnerabilities that attackers could exploit. RS-Mask, published at HOST 2020, is such a countermeasure that has been affected by the absence of a systematic analysis method. The fundamental concept behind the countermeasure is to maintain a uniform distribution of variables, regardless of whether they are faulty or correct. This property is particularly effective against Statistical Ineffective Fault Attacks (SIFA), which exploit the dependency between fault propagation and the secret data.

In this work, we present several fault scenarios involving single fault injections on the AES implementation protected with RS-Mask, where the fault propagation depends on the secret data. This happens because the random space mapping used in RS-Mask countermeasure retains a dependency on the secret data, as it is derived based on the S-box input. To address this, we propose a new countermeasure based on the core concept of RS-Mask, implementing a single mapping for all S-box inputs, involving an intrinsic duplication. Next, we evaluate the effectiveness of the new countermeasure against fault attacks by comparing the fault detection rate across all possible fault locations and values for every input. Additionally, we examine the output differences between faulty and correct outputs for each input. Our results show that the detection rate is uniform for each input, which ensures security against statistical attacks utilizing both effective and ineffective faults. Moreover, the output differences being uniform for each input ensures security against differential fault attacks.

Keywords: Fault Attacks · SIFA · AES

C. Boura et al. (Eds.): SAC 2025, LNCS 16207, pp. 703–723, 2026.
https://doi.org/10.1007/978-3-032-10536-3_26

1 Introduction

Cryptographic algorithms are designed to be secure against cryptanalytic attacks; however, their physical implementations in embedded devices remain vulnerable to physical attacks. These attacks exploit the physical characteristics of the cryptographic implementations and can be broadly classified into two categories: passive attacks, which involve observing the device's behavior (*e.g.*, power consumption [22], timing [21], and electromagnetic emanation [15]), and active attacks, which induce errors in the computation through physical manipulations (*e.g.*, clock/voltage glitching [2], electromagnetic interference [9], and laser injections [17]).

Side-channel analysis (SCA), being a passive attack technique, leverages the information leakage arising from physical characteristics of the implementations such as timing and power consumption. To protect against SCA, masking [5,16,20,27] stands out as the most prominent countermeasure. Masking relies on splitting the secret input into a number of statistically independent shares, ensuring that even observing all but one share does not compromise the secret input. Notable approaches include, among others, Domain Oriented Masking (DOM) [16], which associates each share of the secret input with a distinct domain, and Threshold Implementations (TI) [24], which computes over coordinate functions operating on non-complete sets of secret input shares.

Differing from the passive observations exploited in SCA, fault attacks actively disrupt computations by injecting faults through physical fault injection mechanisms. Since Boneh *et al.* [3] first demonstrated fault attacks on RSA, numerous attack techniques have emerged to exploit injected faults in cryptographic implementations. These attacks exploit the data-dependent response to these injected faults. To protect against these attacks, redundancy is widely employed as a countermeasure, by employing temporal, spatial, or informational replication to detect whether a fault is injected or not. Upon a fault detection, redundancy-based techniques either suppress the output or infect it to prevent the adversary from extracting secret information. This approach has been further leveraged to enable error correction. Recent countermeasures combine redundancy with masking to provide simultaneous protection against both SCA and fault attacks, with masking also serving to enhance the protection against fault attacks. Such countermeasures were generally regarded as effective in protecting against fault attacks. However, Statistical Ineffective Fault Attacks (SIFA) [13], introduced in 2018, exploit data dependent fault propagation by collecting non-faulty ciphertexts, rendering redundancy vulnerable to such attacks. Building on this attack, Dobraunig *et al.* [12] utilized SIFA to overcome simple combination of masking with redundancy by faulting non-linear operations. Notable examples of such combined countermeasures include, but are not limited to, ParTI [31], CAPA [28], Private Circuits II [19], M&M [23], Impeccable Circuits [1,26,32], and Transform-and-Encode (TaE) [29], which were developed both before and after the introduction of SIFA. All these countermeasures employ redundancy in various forms (*e.g.,* linear codes, MAC tags) with different levels of error detection/correction granularity. Taking a different approach, Daemen *et al.* [8]

proposed the use of reversible operations, Toffoli gates, to ensure fault propagation independent of the secret data, with a single error check at the end of the encryption. Along the similar lines, the StaTI countermeasure [10] introduced the notion of "stability", a composable security property that ensures fault propagation independent of the secret data, enabling a single error check at the end of the encryption. Building on this concept, StaMAC [11] adopts the stability notion within MAC tags. Another countermeasure, Random Space Masking (RS-Mask) [25] that is published at HOST 2020, performs the S-box computations in a random space, eliminating any bias introduced by injected faults to the computations.

Despite these advancements in fault countermeasures, fault attacks still present a more complex and diverse attack surface compared to passive attacks, making the development of standardized fault evaluation methodologies challenging. The lack of systematic fault evaluation methodologies increases the risk of overlooking exploitable vulnerabilities in the countermeasures. Similarly, the RS-Mask countermeasure, while conceptually shows promise, particularly against statistical (ineffective) fault attacks, its fault evaluation is not comprehensive, leaving several attack scenarios unaddressed.

Contributions. In this work, we address existing gaps in the fault evaluation of RS-Mask and uncover previously overlooked vulnerabilities through specific fault scenarios involving single fault injections in the protected AES implementation. We demonstrate that RS-Mask's random space mapping retains a dependency on the secret data, therefore, failing to protect against statistical (ineffective) fault attacks, as well as differential fault attacks. These findings underscore the importance of thorough and systematic fault evaluations.

The identified vulnerabilities in RS-Mask stem from the use of distinct mappings derived for the S-box inputs (zero input vs. non-zero inputs), which are combined using an auxiliary variable. To address this issue, we propose an improved countermeasure that incorporates a single random space mapping for all S-box inputs. Our evaluation demonstrates that this approach achieves a uniform fault detection rate across all S-box inputs, ensuring robust protection against both statistical and differential fault attacks through intrinsic duplication. We additionally evaluate the side-channel security, and present hardware benchmark results.

Outline. In Sect. 2, we discuss the adversary and security models that are considered in this work, and provide an overview of the RS-Mask countermeasure. In Sect. 3, we discuss the fault security of the RS-Mask countermeasure, and outline the fault scenarios against the protected AES S-box implementation. Next, we describe our proposed countermeasure involving the random space masking specifically derived for the AES S-box in Sect. 4, and present its security and performance evaluation.

2 Preliminaries

In this section, we introduce the probing and the gate/register-faulting adversaries along with their respective security models assumed in this work. We then provide an overview of the RS-Mask countermeasure [25] and its hardware implementation details of the protected AES as described by the authors.

2.1 Adversary and Security Models

We consider an adversary with probing and faulting capabilities, assuming that these capabilities are not used in combination. The attack surface is considered as a Boolean circuit, a directed acyclic graph where the vertices correspond to Boolean gates, and the edges correspond to the wires. This circuit takes an input and calculates an output while having an internal state corresponding to the sharing of the secret data stored in the registers.

Probing capabilities. We assume the d-probing model introduced by Ishai *et al.* [20] to capture an attacker with probing capabilities. In this model, the adversary is restricted to observing at most d wires of the Boolean circuit, with the selected wires being specified before the circuit is executed. Additionally, we assume the glitch-extended robust probing model introduced by Faust *et al.* [14] to account for the physical effects of hardware glitches.

Faulting capabilities. We rely on the gate/register-faulting model [10] to capture an attacker with faulting capabilities. In this model, the adversary can replace an upper bounded number of gates or registers to output zero (through a reset fault), output one (through a set fault), or flip the output (through a bitflip fault). In this work, we consider a single gate/register-faulting adversary, where the adversary is capable of replacing one gate or register in the circuit throughout the whole computation, consistent with the single-fault attacks assumed in the RS-Mask countermeasure.

We adopt a more relaxed security model compared to the security guarantees associated with the gate/register-faulting model described in [10]. In our correctness model, we introduce a relaxation that allows the adversary to receive an incorrect output. However, this output remains *unexploitable* for all possible single fault injections. Specifically, the difference between the outputs of the faulty and correct circuits, given the same inputs, is uniformly distributed and independent of both the injected fault and the secret inputs. Moreover, the fault detection rate across all input values is also uniformly distributed. In our privacy model, we assume the same model described in [10]. Specifically, for every fixed injected fault, the probability of the abort signal is independent of the secret inputs of the circuit.

2.2 RS-Mask: Random Space Masking as an Integrated Countermeasure Against Power and Fault Analysis

The RS-Mask countermeasure [25] ensures that intermediate variables maintain a uniform distribution, even in the presence of fault injection. This uniformity protects implementations against statistical fault attack techniques such as SIFA, which exploit the bias in the distribution of intermediate variables. The core idea of the countermeasure is to map the intermediate variables into a random space, perform operations within this random space, and then transform the cipher output back to the original space. By employing uniform random mapping, the operations performed on the intermediate variables remain independent of the secret data.

The linear operations of the cipher are inherently protected through masking, requiring no additional protective measures. The S-box computations, however, are performed in a random space where intermediate variables maintain a uniform distribution. In the RS-Mask paper, the random space masking is designed such that the S-box outputs the correct value XORed with a uniform random value, neutralizing any bias induced by fault injection. The faults injected to the intermediate variables in the random space are influenced by the random values, ensuring that their propagation remains independent of the secret data.

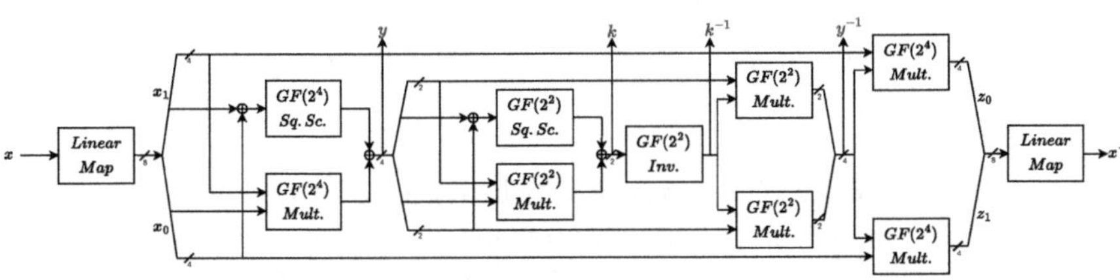

Fig. 1. Canright implementation of the $\mathbb{F}_{2^8}$ inverter in the AES S-box.

Derivation of RS mapping for AES. The mapping derived for the $\mathbb{F}_{2^8}$ inversion in the AES S-box ensures that, for a given input x, the output is $x^{-1} + r$, where r is a uniform random value. The mapping is specifically designed for the AES implementation based on the Canright construction [4], as depicted in Fig. 1. In this construction, the input to the $\mathbb{F}_{2^8}$ inversion is denoted by $x = x_1||x_0$, the input to the $\mathbb{F}_{2^4}$ inversion by y, the output of the $\mathbb{F}_{2^4}$ inversion by y^{-1}, and the output of the $\mathbb{F}_{2^8}$ inversion by $z = x^{-1} = z_1||z_0$.

For inputs where $x \neq 0$, the following output is computed:

$$\begin{aligned} z_1' &= z_1 + r_1 = (x_0 + yr_1)y^{-1} \\ z_0' &= z_0 + r_0 = (x_1 + yr_0)y^{-1}, \end{aligned} \tag{1}$$

where $r = r_1||r_0$ is the uniform random value masking the inversion output. To account for faults injected earlier in the inversion, the value y is derived along a separate data path from the input x, ensuring that y^{-1} does not correspond to the inverse of faulty y (or, conversely, that a faulty y^{-1} is not the inverse of correct y).

However, this approach does not apply to the case when $x = 0$, as both y and y^{-1} evaluate to zero. To handle the zero input case, the inverse of the random value r is XORed with the input x. This ensures that the output remains consistently masked with r, without relying on the calculations used for non-zero inputs (Eq. 1):

$$z' = (0 + r^{-1})^{-1} = 0 + r\,, \tag{2}$$

thereby aligning the behavior with that of non-zero inputs. To derive a unified mapping for all inputs, an auxiliary variable $f \in \mathbb{F}_{2^4}$ is introduced, along with its bitwise negation $\bar{f}$:

$$f = \begin{cases} (1,1,1,1), & x \neq 0 \quad (\bar{f} = (0,0,0,0)) \\ (0,0,0,0), & x = 0 \quad (\bar{f} = (1,1,1,1)) \end{cases}, \tag{3}$$

where $(1,1,1,1) = 15$ is the multiplicative unity in $\mathbb{F}_{2^4}$. Using this, the overall mapping is expressed as:

$$\begin{aligned} z_1' &= z_1 + r_1 = (x_0 + r_0^{-1}\bar{f} + yr_1 f)y^{-1} \\ z_0' &= z_0 + r_0 = (x_1 + r_1^{-1}\bar{f} + yr_0 f)y^{-1}\,, \end{aligned} \tag{4}$$

where $r^{-1} = r_1^{-1} || r_0^{-1}$.

Hardware implementation. The overall block diagram of the AES S-box implementation protected with RS-Mask countermeasure is presented in Fig. 2. In this implementation, the AES state is split into three shares, where one of the shares is the RS share, the random value r. The round keys are split into two shares, with the RS share set to zero. After the linear map is applied to the S-box input x, the RS share is added to one of the two data shares. All non-linear components in the design are implemented using threshold implementations (TI) [24] with three shares as the masking technique.

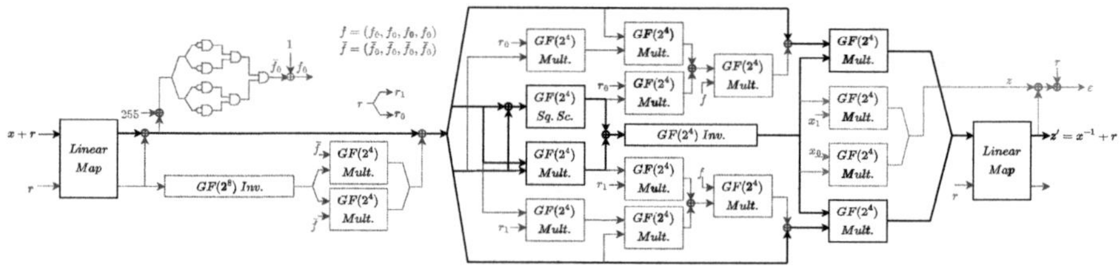

Fig. 2. AES S-box protected by RS-mask. Red components are the additional computations required for the RS mapping, green components are the additional components required for the infection mechanism. (Color figure online)

As the random value r is independent of all other shares, its inverse r^{-1} is computed in an unshared form. To protect against the effects of hardware glitches, the RS-Mask paper specifies that the non-linear components of this inversion circuit are registered. In parallel to the computation of r^{-1}, the auxiliary variable $f \in \mathbb{F}_{2^4}$ is computed using the Kronecker delta function. To maintain throughput, the whole design is implemented as a 10-stage pipeline.

Although RS-Mask maps intermediate variables to a random space, the authors acknowledge that the distribution of the output differences resulting from the injected faults may still be non-uniform. This non-uniformity makes the implementation vulnerable against differential fault attacks (DFA). To address this vulnerability, the authors propose an infection mechanism as an additional protection layer against DFA. As described above, the variables x_0, x_1 and y^{-1} are already available in the RS-Mask circuit. Using these, the output of the S-box inversion z can be recomputed with two additional $\mathbb{F}_{2^4}$ multipliers as shown in Fig. 2.

If no error occurs during the inversion, the expression $\varepsilon = z + r + z'$ evaluates to zero (see Eq. 4). Consequently, multiplying ε by a random value εr_1 (with r_1 being uniformly distributed) yields zero, and adding this to the S-box output has no effect. If an error occurs in the inversion circuit, then $\varepsilon \neq 0$, and the resulting product $\varepsilon r_1 \neq 0$ infects the S-box output.

However, this infection mechanism still does not protect against DFA, as an error in one byte propagates to the entire column with deterministic relations through the MixColumns operation. To mitigate this, the infection mechanism is extended by computing four random variables $\varepsilon_i = \varepsilon r_i$ for $i = 0, ..., 3$ using four uniformly random values r_i. ε_i is then added to the i-th byte of the respective column, randomizing all four bytes.

3 Security Analysis of RS-Mask

This section highlights the limitations of the AES S-box implementation protected using the RS-Mask countermeasure.

First of all, one notable consideration is the computation of r^{-1}, which includes additional register layers intended to mitigate the physical effects of hardware glitches. However, under the glitch-extended robust probing model introduced by Faust *et al.* [14], r, being a single share, can be directly provided to the simulator. As a result, these additional registers attempt to address an issue that is not relevant in this context, potentially introducing unnecessary implementation overhead.

Beyond the aforementioned overhead, another limitation of the RS-Mask countermeasure arises in its infection mechanism intended to protect against differential attacks. Specifically, the infection mechanism reuses the same S-box input x to recompute the expected output z, which is then compared with the actual output to generate the infection value εr_1. However, if a fault is injected to x, both the recomputed and actual outputs are affected similarly, causing ε, and thus the infection value, to evaluate to zero. As a result, the fault remains undetected and the state is uninfected. This allows DFA to still be successfully performed on the RS-Mask countermeasure by injecting a fault to the S-box input. We further explore this drawback in a fault scenario, which is elaborated upon later in this section.

Finally, in the rest of this section, we present several fault scenarios that demonstrate the vulnerability of the AES S-box implementation protected by RS-Mask countermeasure. Specifically, we identify and describe four groups of single fault locations that are vulnerable, as depicted in Fig. 3.

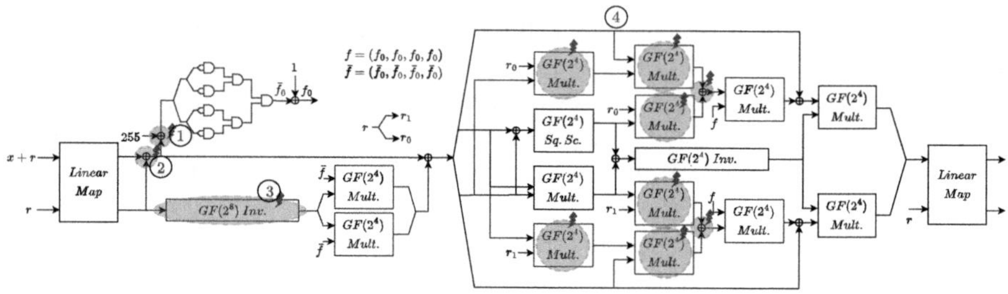

Fig. 3. Fault locations on AES S-box protected by RS-mask.

Fault location 1: Kronecker delta function. The Kronecker Delta function is evaluated at $x+255$ to compute f. In one fault scenario, an attacker injects an additive fault Δ at the XOR operation that computes $x + 255$ (indicated as number 1 in Fig. 3). As a result, the input to the Kronecker delta function becomes $x+255+\Delta$. The function then outputs $f = 0$ ($\bar{f} = 1$) if $x+\Delta = 0$ ($i.e.$, $x = \Delta$). Otherwise, if $x \neq \Delta$, the function outputs $f = 1$.

We analyze this fault scenario for three cases: $x = \Delta$, $x = 0$ and $x \neq \{0, \Delta\}$, where z' is the RS-Mask S-box output and z is the redundantly computed value used in the infection mechanism, as shown in Fig. 2 (if no fault is injected $z' = z + r$).

First, $x = \Delta$ implies $f = 0$. Then, using Eq. 4, we find:

$$
\begin{aligned}
z'_1 &= (\Delta_0 + r_0^{-1})y^{-1} \\
z'_0 &= (\Delta_1 + r_1^{-1})y^{-1},
\end{aligned}
$$

where $z' = (\Delta + r^{-1})^{-1}$, and

$$
\begin{aligned}
z_1 &= \Delta_0 y^{-1} \\
z_0 &= \Delta_1 y^{-1},
\end{aligned}
$$

where $z = \Delta^{-1}$. Then,

$$
\begin{aligned}
\varepsilon &= z + r + z' \\
&= \Delta^{-1} + r + (\Delta + r^{-1})^{-1}.
\end{aligned}
$$

If $r \neq 0$, then, $\varepsilon \neq 0$. Thus, the computation is infected.

Second, $x = 0$ implies $f = 1$ (and $y, y^{-1} = 0$). Then, using Eq. 4, we find $z' = 0$ ($z'_1 = 0$, $z'_0 = 0$), and $z = 0$ ($z_1 = 0$, $z_0 = 0$). Then,

$$\varepsilon = z + r + z' = r\,.$$

If $r \neq 0$, then, $\varepsilon \neq 0$. Thus, the computation is infected.

Third, $x \neq \{0, \Delta\}$ implies $f = 1$. Then, using Eq. 4, we find:

$$z'_1 = (x_0 + yr_1)y^{-1}$$
$$z'_0 = (x_1 + yr_0)y^{-1}\,,$$

where $z' = x^{-1} + r$, and

$$z_1 = x_0 y^{-1}$$
$$z_0 = x_1 y^{-1}\,,$$

where $z = x^{-1}$. Then,

$$\varepsilon = z + r + z' = 0\,.$$

Thus, the computation is not infected.

As a result, the computation is infected only when $x = \Delta$ or $x = 0$ (assuming $r \neq 0$). The attacker can then exploit this by performing the encryption twice: once with the fault injection and once without. If the outputs are different (indicating the encryption with a fault injected was infected), the attacker learns that $x = \Delta$ or $x = 0$. To distinguish between these two, the attacker can repeat the attack with a different Δ value. If the encryption with fault injection is again infected, it confirms that $x = 0$.

A potential fix involves replacing each AND gate in the Kronecker Delta function by a gate which outputs 1 only when both inputs are zero. Then, the Kronecker delta function can be computed directly on x, eliminating the need to first compute $x + 255$ as done in the original design.

Fault location 2: XOR of random r with the S-box input. The second fault scenario is that, an attacker injects an additive fault Δ at the XOR gate where the random value r is combined with the state after the linear map (indicated as number 2 in Fig. 3). This alters the S-box input to $x + \Delta$. Consequently, the $\mathbb{F}_{2^8}$ inversion output becomes $(x + \Delta)^{-1} + r$. However, as the infection mechanism is using the same faulty input $x + \Delta$, it fails to detect the injected fault, making the implementation susceptible to DFA. Specifically, the infection mechanism of the RS-Mask design only accounts for faults occurring within the $\mathbb{F}_{2^8}$ inversion circuit, and does not cover the faults injected at earlier stages.

A potential fix could involve introducing a full redundancy. This would mean replicating the entire circuit and including an error check mechanism at the end of the computation. Such a design ensures that effective faults injected at any point in the circuit are detected to protect against DFA.

Fault location 3: Inversion of r. The third fault scenario is that an attacker injects a fault within the inversion circuit that computes r^{-1} (indicated as number 3 in

Fig. 3) causing the output of that circuit to be $r^{-1} + \Delta$. We analyze this fault scenario in two cases, $x = 0$ and $x \neq 0$.

First, $x = 0$ implies $f = 0$. Then, using Eq. 4, we find:

$$\begin{aligned} z_1' &= (r^{-1} + \Delta_0)y^{-1} \\ z_0' &= (r^{-1} + \Delta_1)y^{-1}, \end{aligned}$$

where $z' = (r^{-1} + \Delta)^{-1}$, and $z = 0$ ($z_1 = 0$, $z_0 = 0$). Then,

$$\begin{aligned} \varepsilon &= z + r + z' \\ &= r + (r^{-1} + \Delta)^{-1}. \end{aligned}$$

Since $\Delta \neq 0$, $\varepsilon \neq 0$. Thus, the computation is infected.

Second, $x \neq 0$ implies $f = 1$. Then, using Eq. 4, we find:

$$\begin{aligned} z_1' &= (x_0 + yr_1)y^{-1} \\ z_0' &= (x_1 + yr_0)y^{-1}, \end{aligned}$$

where $z' = x^{-1} + r$, and

$$\begin{aligned} z_1 &= x_0 y^{-1} \\ z_0 &= x_1 y^{-1}, \end{aligned}$$

where $z = x^{-1}$. Then,

$$\varepsilon = z + r + z' = 0.$$

Thus, the computation is not infected.

As a result, the computation is infected only when $x = 0$ (if $r \neq 0$). Similar to the first fault scenario, the attacker can then exploit this by performing the encryption twice: once with the fault injection and once without. The outputs of both encryptions being different implies that the first encryption was infected, which also implies $x = 0$.

A potential fix could involve precomputing all (r, r^{-1}) pairs before the encryption. Then, the probability of selecting the faulty pair becomes $1/256$ considering a single fault injection. While this does not fully eliminate the vulnerability, it decreases the success probability of the attacker. A second potential fix could involve including r and r^{-1} in the infection mechanism, *i.e.*, infecting the computation by randomizing $(r^{-1})^{-1} + r$ which does not equal to zero if r^{-1} is faulty.

Fault location 4: Additional RS-Mask circuit inside the inversion. The fourth fault scenario is that an attacker injects an additive fault to one of the gates within the additional RS-Mask circuit, indicated as number 4 in Fig. 3. Any fault injected to these gates causes a faulty value at the input of the $\mathbb{F}_{2^4}$ multiplication with f. Then, the output of this multiplication is subsequently multiplied by y^{-1}, the $\mathbb{F}_{2^4}$ inversion output. We analyze this fault scenario in two cases, $x = 0$ and $x \neq 0$.

First, $x = 0$ implies $f = 0$, thereby nullifying the effect of the injected fault, as the faulty value is multiplied by zero. Then, using Eq. 4, we find $z' = r$, and $z = 0$. Then,

$$\varepsilon = z + r + z' = 0\,.$$

Thus, the computation is not infected.

Second, $x \neq 0$ implies $f = 1$. Then, using Eq. 4, we find:

$$\begin{aligned} z_1' &= (x_0 + (yr_1 + \Delta_1))y^{-1} \\ z_0' &= (x_1 + (yr_0 + \Delta_0))y^{-1}\,, \end{aligned}$$

where $z' = x^{-1} + r + \Delta'$, and

$$\begin{aligned} z_1 &= x_0 y^{-1} \\ z_0 &= x_1 y^{-1}\,, \end{aligned}$$

where $z = x^{-1}$. Then,

$$\varepsilon = z + r + z' = \Delta' \neq 0\,.$$

Thus, the computation is infected.

As a result, the infection applies when $x \neq 0$, due to the injected fault being propagated to the output when $f = 1$. As in the previous fault scenarios, the attacker can repeat the encryption and compare the outputs; if no difference between the outputs is observed, they infer that $x = 0$.

One potential fix against this fault scenario is to multiply r_0 and r_1 by f before the RS-Mask $\mathbb{F}_{2^8}$ inversion circuit. This ensures that any fault injected to the gates indicated as number 4 propagates to the output, regardless of the value of x. This is because, within the RS-Mask inversion circuit, the input to the inversion logic is never zero, even when $x = 0$. Only the propagation of the faults injected to r_0 or r_1 depends on f, however then, these faults are equivalent to register faults injected to the RS-Mask random r. These would have the same effect as using a different r value.

In the original paper, the security of RS-Mask countermeasure is evaluated against statistical (ineffective) fault attacks, focusing on a single location of fault injection. However, as the overall security of the countermeasure cannot be ensured by evaluating only this single scenario, such an evaluation remains incomplete. The fault scenarios discussed in this section highlight a critical observation: any additional circuit introduced to protect against fault attacks inherently expands the attack surface, and may introduce new points of vulnerability that could be exploited. Consequently, for countermeasures without provable security guarantees, it is essential to comprehensively evaluate any additional circuit introduced against fault attacks to identify potential vulnerabilities. Similarly, the proposed fixes for the fault scenarios presented in this section do not inherently ensure security. These fixes may further expand the attack surface, and therefore, they must undergo a rigorous evaluation to assess their security against fault attacks.

In the following section, we describe a random space mapping for Canright's AES S-box, where we systemically evaluate each gate in the resulting circuit.

4 An AES-Specific Countermeasure

In this section, we introduce an AES-specific countermeasure, based on the core idea of the RS-Mask countermeasure, protecting against single gate/register-faulting adversary. Unlike the RS mapping derived for the AES S-box implemented using the Canright construction, which is conditioned on the input value x, our proposed countermeasure derives a uniform mapping that is independent of the value of x.

Derivation of the random mapping for the AES S-box implemented using Canright construction. In Canright's AES S-box, as shown in Fig. 1, two inversion operations are performed in $\mathbb{F}_{2^8}$ and $\mathbb{F}_{2^4}$. Each involves multiplying the input of the inversion (x, y) by the corresponding outputs of the inner inversions (y^{-1}, k^{-1}). These multiplications are vulnerable to SIFA, as faults present in y^{-1} and k^{-1} are not propagated to the S-box output when the input x is zero (which also leads to y being zero).

The variables (x, y, k, k^{-1}, y^{-1}, and x^{-1}) referenced in this section correspond to those shown in Fig. 1.

Consider the following table, which summarizes the behavior of expressions derived from y and y^{-1} under different S-box input x conditions:

	y	y^{-1}	$yy^{-1}+1$	$y+yy^{-1}+1$	$y^{-1}+yy^{-1}+1$
$x=0$	0	0	1	1	1
$x \neq 0$	y	y^{-1}	0	y	y^{-1}

As observed in the above table, the following holds for all input values x:

$$(y+yy^{-1}+1)(y^{-1}+yy^{-1}+1)=1\,.$$

Similarly, the following expression also holds for all input values $x = x_1||x_0$:

$$x_0(yy^{-1}+1)=0$$
$$x_1(yy^{-1}+1)=0\,.$$

This behavior is in contrast to the original RS-Mask countermeasure, where the multiplication of y and y^{-1} introduces an input-dependent behavior.

We now describe the new mapping for the Canright's AES S-box as follows:

$$
\begin{aligned}
z'_1 &= z_1 + r_1 = (x_0 + (y + yy^{-1} + 1)r_1)(y^{-1} + yy^{-1} + 1) \\
z'_0 &= z_0 + r_0 = (x_1 + (y + yy^{-1} + 1)r_0)(y^{-1} + yy^{-1} + 1)\,,
\end{aligned} \tag{5}
$$

where $z' = z'_1 || z'_0 = x^{-1} + r$.

Similar to the RS-Mask countermeasure, analyzing the distribution of the output differences (between the faulty and correct S-box outputs) under faults present in y and y^{-1} reveals a non-uniform pattern. This non-uniformity exposes the design to differential fault attacks.

Rather than relying on an infection mechanism, which, when implemented correctly (*e.g.*, via full duplication), requires substantial area overhead, we propose a lightweight tweak to the random mapping. Specifically, we introduce an additional term, $(yy^{-1} + 1)r'y^{-1}$ to the S-box output. In the absence of faults, this term evaluates to zero, as shown in the table above. Here, r' is a uniform random value distinct from the one used in the main mapping described in Eq. 4. The modified mapping is given as follows, where $r = r_1 || r_0$ and $r' = r_3 || r_2$:

$$
\begin{aligned}
z'_1 &= z_1 + r_1 = (x_1 + (y + yy^{-1} + 1)r_1)(y^{-1} + yy^{-1} + 1) + (yy^{-1} + 1)r_3 y^{-1} \\
z'_0 &= z_0 + r_0 = (x_0 + (y + yy^{-1} + 1)r_0)(y^{-1} + yy^{-1} + 1) + (yy^{-1} + 1)r_2 y^{-1}\,.
\end{aligned} \tag{6}
$$

It is clear that this mapping is correct if no faults occur during the computation of y and y^{-1}.

We note that it is essential to compute y using a redundant datapath similar to the RS-Mask countermeasure in order to account for the faults that are injected earlier in the circuit.

As previously noted, the inversion in Canright's AES S-box involves two multiplications that are susceptible to SIFA. To ensure both multiplications are secure against SIFA, the mapping introduced in Eq. 5 is also applied to the $\mathbb{F}_{2^4}$ inversion. Furthermore, similar to the inversion in $\mathbb{F}_{2^8}$, k is also computed using a redundant datapath in order to account for the faults that are injected earlier in the circuit. We describe the mapping for the $\mathbb{F}_{2^4}$ inversion as follows:

$$
\begin{aligned}
y_1^{-1} &= (y_1 + (k + kk^{-1} + 1)r_5)(k^{-1} + kk^{-1} + 1) + r_5 \\
y_0^{-1} &= (y_0 + (k + kk^{-1} + 1)r_4)(k^{-1} + kk^{-1} + 1) + r_4\,,
\end{aligned} \tag{7}
$$

where $y^{-1} = y_1^{-1} || y_0^{-1}$.

Unlike the mapping derived for the inversion in $\mathbb{F}_{2^8}$ (Eq. 4), the corresponding mapping for the inversion in $\mathbb{F}_{2^4}$ naturally yields uniform output differences, eliminating the need for an additional random term.

To protect against differential fault attacks, we introduce an intrinsic redundancy by duplicating the S-box input. The random space mapping components computed from the first input are then used in the calculation of the second S-box output using the duplicated S-box input as shown in Fig. 4.

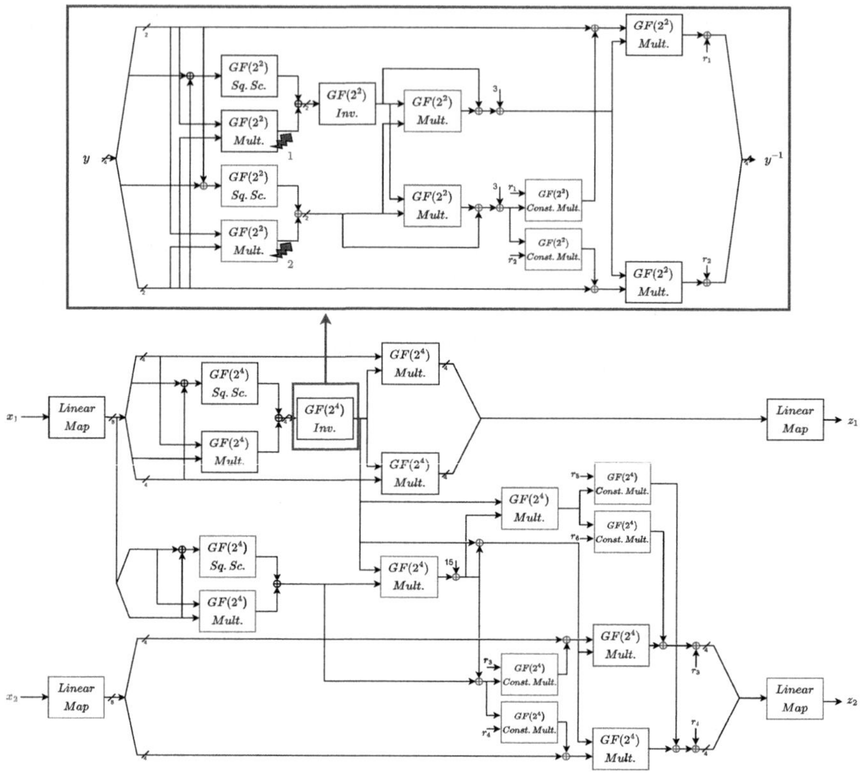

Fig. 4. $\mathbb{F}_{2^8}$ inversion of the AES S-box.

Hardware implementation. The overall block diagram of the AES S-box implementation protected using the proposed random space mapping is presented in Fig. 4. Similar to RS-Mask countermeasure, the state is split into three shares, however we do not keep the random mask values as part of the shared state. Meaning, all linear and non-linear components in the design operate over three shares.

The upper circuit in Fig. 4 depicts the mapping for the inversion in $\mathbb{F}_{2^4}$, and the lower circuit depicts the mapping for the whole AES S-box implemented using Canright's construction. The $\mathbb{F}_{2^4}$ inverter ($GF(2^4)$ $Inv.$) within the AES S-box uses the upper circuit. Components added beyond Canright's original AES S-box implementation are highlighted in red.

Our implementation builds on the $\mathbb{F}_{2^8}$ inversion circuit from [6] based on Consolidating Masking Schemes [27] with three shares to achieve second order security. In this construction, the inversion circuit consumes 162 bits of randomness. Building upon this foundation, we extend the circuit by integrating the additional components (shown as red in Fig. 4) required for the random space mapping. While extending the circuit, we adhere to the $d + 1$-share multipliers from the original inversion circuit. Together with the 20 bits of randomness required by the random space mapping and additional multiplications, our implementation consumes 344 bits of randomness. The design is implemented over 8 pipeline stages.

4.1 Side-Channel Security

In this section, we discuss the SCA security of the AES S-box implementation using the proposed random mapping. To evaluate the SCA security of our design, we perform TVLA (Test Vector Leakage Assessment) [7]. We perform the assessment for the S-box implemented with the proposed random space mapping by supplying it with fixed versus random inputs. The S-box is placed on a Xilinx Spartan-6 FPGA located on a SAKURA-G evaluation board [30], whereas masks generation is located on a separate control FPGA. The devices are supplied with a stable 6.144 MHz clock and an oscilloscope samples power consumption traces at a rate of 1GS/sec. The results of the first and second-order tests are depicted in Fig. 5. The results report no leakage regarding first and second-order probing security.

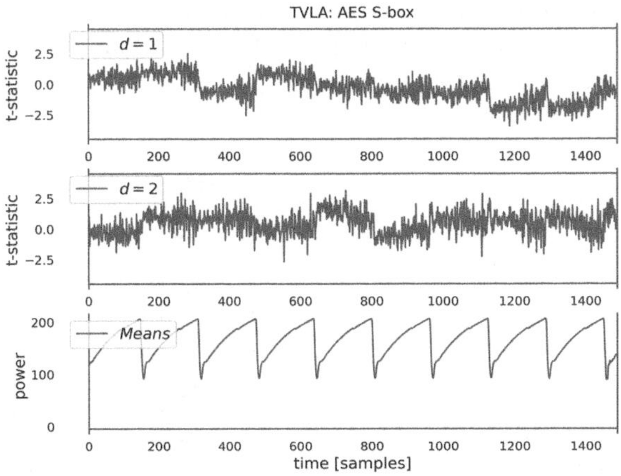

Fig. 5. TVLA result of the AES S-box implemented with the proposed random space mapping, first and second-order security, 100 million traces, and a sample trace.

4.2 Fault Security

We now discuss the fault security of the AES S-box implementation using the proposed random space mapping.

Existing provable methods for fault security evaluation, typically based on error detection or correction, are not applicable to our design. Rather than preventing the propagation of injected faults through detection or correction mechanisms, our countermeasure ensures that the injected faults are deliberately propagated to infect the circuit's state. As a result, the infected output that is not detected by the error detection circuit at the end of the encryption becomes unexploitable.

To evaluate the fault security of our AES-specific countermeasure, we analyze the detection rate of the injected faults. A uniform detection rate across all input values indicates resistance against statistical fault attacks. We performed an attack simulation on the C implementation of the AES S-box design to evaluate the security against a single gate/register-faulting adversary. Faults were modeled as XOR additions applied to the intermediate variables. To simulate this, we extended the C code of the design by XORing a fault variable with selected critical intermediate values. Specifically, faults were injected to each component of the S-box, namely XOR gates and all field operations as shown in Fig. 4). For each experiment, we marked the fault as detected if the outputs differed. For each input value, 500,000 experiments are conducted to account for wide range of fault values and random values introduced by the random mapping. The results demonstrated that the detection rate remains uniform across all input values for each fault location and fault value.

Figure 6a and 6b illustrate that the detection rate remains uniform across all S-box input values when a fault is injected to the output of the $\mathbb{F}_{2^2}$ multiplier (similar to the fault scenario used in the RS-Mask countermeasure). In our design, the multiplier is duplicated as part of the random mapping, corresponding to fault locations 1 and 2 in Fig. 4).

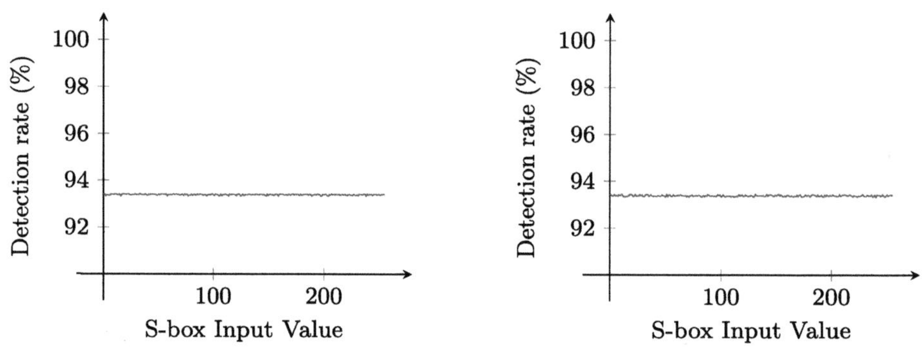

(a) Fault location 1 (b) Fault location 2

Fig. 6. Distribution of the detection rate across all S-box input values when a fault is injected to the output of the duplicated $\mathbb{F}_{2^2}$ multipliers denoted with fault location 1 and 2 in Fig. 4.

Figure 7 shows a uniform detection rate (%100 detection) across all S-box input values when simulating fault scenario 4, previously proposed against the RS-Mask countermeasure, by injecting a fault to the $\mathbb{F}_{2^4}$ constant multiplier as denoted with fault location 3 in Fig. 4.

We repeated the evaluation, this time focusing on the distribution of output differences. As before, for each experiment, the resulting output differences were

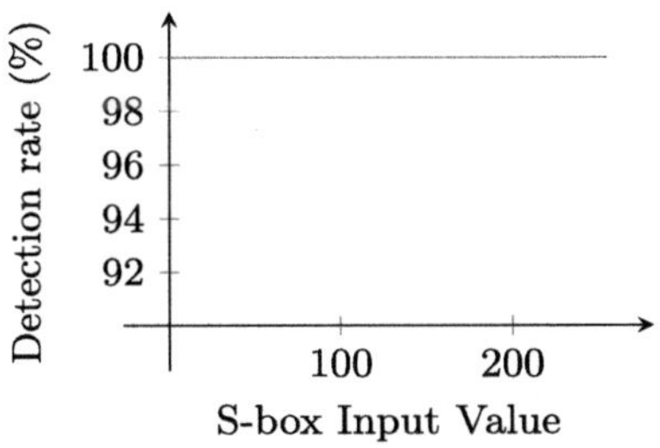

Fig. 7. Distribution of the detection rate across all S-box input values when a fault is injected to the output of the $\mathbb{F}_{2^4}$ constant multiplier (of the random mapping circuit) denoted with fault location 3 in Fig. 4.

recorded. The results show that the output differences are uniformly distributed across all S-box input values for every fault location and fault value tested. Together, these two evaluations demonstrates the correctness and the privacy of the protected AES S-box with the proposed random space mapping.

4.3 Hardware Benchmarks

In this section, we evaluate the hardware performance of our protected AES S-box implementation. We use the Synopsys Design Compiler (version S-2021.06-SP3) together with the open source NANGATE 45nm library. The hierarchical structure is preserved during the synthesis, and undesired optimizations are avoided.

We compare our protected AES S-box implementation secure against SCA and fault attacks with the AES S-box implementation from [6] based on Consolidated Masking Scheme secure against only SCA which we implemented ourselves. Both designs provide second-order SCA security. Compared to the implementation from [6], the number of masked field multiplications is doubled (one of which is duplicated using same randomness) in our implementation. Together with the extra randomness required by the random space mapping, our design requires 110 additional random bits. Regarding the area costs, our design introduces an area overhead of approximately 2.85.

We report only the overhead factors relative to their corresponding SCA-only designs for the RS-Mask countermeasure [25], λ-detection M&M [18] and StaMAC [11], rather than absolute area numbers. The selection of these countermeasures, in addition to RS-Mask, for comparison is motivated by the availability of area reports for their AES (S-box) implementations, as well as their protection against SCA and SIFA. While our design incurs a slightly higher area overhead compared to the original RS-Mask countermeasure, it offers stronger protection by additionally securing against SIFA and achieving second-order SCA security, features not offered by RS-Mask(Table 1).

Table 1. Hardware cost comparison of various designs.

Design	SCA Order	S-box Stages	Randomness [bit]	Area (kGE)	Overhead
SCA only [6]	2	6	162	4.5**	
RS-Mask [25]	1	10			2*
λ-detection M&M [18]	2	6	903		3.49*
StaMAC [11]	1	9	56		3.83*
This paper	2	8	344	12.84**	2.85

* overhead for the whole AES implementation
** only inversion

5 Conclusion

In this paper, we addressed the gaps in the fault evaluation of RS-Mask and identified several vulnerabilities through which a single fault injection in the protected AES implementation compromise its security. The attack scenarios we present demonstrate that the random space mapping proposed for the AES S-box in the RS-Mask countermeasure retains dependency on the secret data, allowing attackers to exploit this dependency under specific fault scenarios. Although RS-Mask includes a formal security proof, it only guarantees that the random space mapping produces uniformly distributed values, and it does not address the fault security of the additional circuit required to implement this mapping. Our analysis shows that this overlooked aspect introduces exploitable weaknesses. These findings highlight the critical need for more comprehensive fault evaluations in the design of fault countermeasures, as increasing area to protect against fault attacks may introduce new attack surface to the attackers.

Besides these attack scenarios, we proposed an AES-specific countermeasure involving a single random space mapping for all S-box input values without an auxiliary variable. With this unified mapping, we aimed to mitigate the vulnerabilities we identified in the RS-Mask countermeasure. Our evaluation of the proposed countermeasure confirms the improved robustness against statistical and differential fault attacks.

Acknowledgments. This work was supported by CyberSecurity Research Flanders with reference number VR20192203. This work has been partially supported by the National Science Fund of Bulgaria under Grant KP-06-N82/5.

References

1. Aghaie, A., Moradi, A., Rasoolzadeh, S., Shahmirzadi, A.R., Schellenberg, F., Schneider, T.: Impeccable circuits. IEEE Trans. Computers **69**(3), 361–376 (2020). https://doi.org/10.1109/TC.2019.2948617

2. Anderson, R.J., Kuhn, M.G.: Low cost attacks on tamper resistant devices. In: Christianson, B., Crispo, B., Lomas, T.M.A., Roe, M. (eds.) Security Protocols, 5th International Workshop, Paris, France, April 7-9, 1997, Proceedings. Lecture Notes in Computer Science, vol. 1361, pp. 125–136. Springer (1997https://doi.org/10.1007/BFb0028165
3. Boneh, D., DeMillo, R.A., Lipton, R.J.: On the Importance of Checking Cryptographic Protocols for Faults. In: Fumy, W. (ed.) EUROCRYPT 1997. LNCS, vol. 1233, pp. 37–51. Springer, Heidelberg (1997). https://doi.org/10.1007/3-540-69053-0_4
4. Canright, D.: A very compact s-box for AES. In: Rao, J.R., Sunar, B. (eds.) Cryptographic Hardware and Embedded Systems - CHES 2005, 7th International Workshop, Edinburgh, UK, August 29 - September 1, 2005, Proceedings. Lecture Notes in Computer Science, vol. 3659, pp. 441–455. Springer (2005).https://doi.org/10.1007/11545262_32
5. Chari, S., Jutla, C.S., Rao, J.R., Rohatgi, P.: Towards sound approaches to counteract power-analysis attacks. In: Wiener, M.J. (ed.) Advances in Cryptology - CRYPTO '99, 19th Annual International Cryptology Conference, Santa Barbara, California, USA, August 15-19, 1999, Proceedings. Lecture Notes in Computer Science, vol. 1666, pp. 398–412. Springer (1999). https://doi.org/10.1007/3-540-48405-1_26
6. Cnudde, T.D., Reparaz, O., Bilgin, B., Nikova, S., Nikov, V., Rijmen, V.: Masking AES with d+1 shares in hardware. In: Gierlichs, B., Poschmann, A.Y. (eds.) Cryptographic Hardware and Embedded Systems - CHES 2016 - 18th International Conference, Santa Barbara, CA, USA, August 17-19, 2016, Proceedings. Lecture Notes in Computer Science, vol. 9813, pp. 194–212. Springer (2016). https://doi.org/10.1007/978-3-662-53140-2_10
7. Cooper, J., et al.: Test vector leakage assessment (TVLA) methodology in practice. In: International Cryptographic Module Conference. vol. 20 (2013)
8. Daemen, J., Dobraunig, C., Eichlseder, M., Groß, H., Mendel, F., Primas, R.: Protecting against statistical ineffective fault attacks. IACR Trans. Cryptogr. Hardw. Embed. Syst. **2020**(3), 508–543 (2020). https://doi.org/10.13154/TCHES.V2020.I3.508-543
9. Dehbaoui, A., Dutertre, J., Robisson, B., Tria, A.: Electromagnetic transient faults injection on a hardware and a software implementations of AES. In: Bertoni, G., Gierlichs, B. (eds.) 2012 Workshop on Fault Diagnosis and Tolerance in Cryptography, Leuven, Belgium, September 9, 2012, pp. 7–15. IEEE Computer Society (2012). https://doi.org/10.1109/FDTC.2012.15
10. Dhooghe, S., Ovchinnikov, A., Toprakhisar, D.: Stati: protecting against fault attacks using stable threshold implementations. IACR Trans. Cryptographic Hardw. Embed. Syst. **2024**(1), 229–263 (2024)
11. Dhooghe, S., Ovchinnikov, A., Toprakhisar, D.: Stamac: fault protection via stable-mac tags. Cryptology ePrint Archive (2025)
12. Dobraunig, C., Eichlseder, M., Groß, H., Mangard, S., Mendel, F., Primas, R.: Statistical ineffective fault attacks on masked AES with fault countermeasures. In: Peyrin, T., Galbraith, S.D. (eds.) Advances in Cryptology - ASIACRYPT 2018 - 24th International Conference on the Theory and Application of Cryptology and Information Security, Brisbane, QLD, Australia, December 2-6, 2018, Proceedings, Part II. Lecture Notes in Computer Science, vol. 11273, pp. 315–342. Springer (2018). https://doi.org/10.1007/978-3-030-03329-3_11

13. Dobraunig, C., Eichlseder, M., Korak, T., Mangard, S., Mendel, F., Primas, R.: SIFA: exploiting ineffective fault inductions on symmetric cryptography. IACR Trans. Cryptogr. Hardw. Embed. Syst. **2018**(3), 547–572 (2018). https://doi.org/10.13154/tches.v2018.i3.547-572
14. Faust, S., Grosso, V., Pozo, S.M.D., Paglialonga, C., Standaert, F.: Composable masking schemes in the presence of physical defaults and the robust probing model. IACR Trans. Cryptogr. Hardw. Embed. Syst. **2018**(3), 89–120 (2018). https://doi.org/10.13154/TCHES.V2018.I3.89-120
15. Gandolfi, K., Mourtel, C., Olivier, F.: Electromagnetic analysis: Concrete results. In: Koç, Ç.K., Naccache, D., Paar, C. (eds.) Cryptographic Hardware and Embedded Systems - CHES 2001, Third International Workshop, Paris, France, May 14-16, 2001, Proceedings. Lecture Notes in Computer Science, vol. 2162, pp. 251–261. Springer (2001). https://doi.org/10.1007/3-540-44709-1_21
16. Groß, H., Mangard, S., Korak, T.: Domain-oriented masking: compact masked hardware implementations with arbitrary protection order. In: Bilgin, B., Nikova, S., Rijmen, V. (eds.) Proceedings of the ACM Workshop on Theory of Implementation Security, TIS@CCS 2016 Vienna, Austria, October, 2016, p. 3. ACM (2016). https://doi.org/10.1145/2996366.2996426
17. Habing, D.H.: The use of lasers to simulate radiation-induced transients in semiconductor devices and circuits. IEEE Trans. Nucl. Sci. **12**(5), 91–100 (1965)
18. Hirata, H., et al.: All you need is fault: Zero-value attacks on AES and a new λ-detection m&m. IACR Trans. Cryptogr. Hardw. Embed. Syst. **2024**(1), 133–156 (2024)
19. Ishai, Y., Prabhakaran, M., Sahai, A., Wagner, D.: Private Circuits II: Keeping Secrets in Tamperable Circuits. In: Vaudenay, S. (ed.) EUROCRYPT 2006. LNCS, vol. 4004, pp. 308–327. Springer, Heidelberg (2006). https://doi.org/10.1007/11761679_19
20. Ishai, Y., Sahai, A., Wagner, D.A.: Private circuits: securing hardware against probing attacks. In: Boneh, D. (ed.) Advances in Cryptology - CRYPTO 2003, 23rd Annual International Cryptology Conference, Santa Barbara, California, USA, August 17-21, 2003, Proceedings. Lecture Notes in Computer Science, vol. 2729, pp. 463–481. Springer (2003). https://doi.org/10.1007/978-3-540-45146-4_27
21. Kocher, P.C.: Timing attacks on implementations of diffie-hellman, rsa, dss, and other systems. In: Koblitz, N. (ed.) Advances in Cryptology - CRYPTO '96, 16th Annual International Cryptology Conference, Santa Barbara, California, USA, August 18-22, 1996, Proceedings. Lecture Notes in Computer Science, vol. 1109, pp. 104–113. Springer (1996). https://doi.org/10.1007/3-540-68697-5_9
22. Kocher, P., Jaffe, J., Jun, B.: Differential Power Analysis. In: Wiener, M. (ed.) CRYPTO 1999. LNCS, vol. 1666, pp. 388–397. Springer, Heidelberg (1999). https://doi.org/10.1007/3-540-48405-1_25
23. Meyer, L.D., Arribas, V., Nikova, S., Nikov, V., Rijmen, V.: M&m: masks and macs against physical attacks. IACR Trans. Cryptogr. Hardw. Embed. Syst. **2019**(1), 25–50 (2019). https://doi.org/10.13154/tches.v2019.i1.25-50
24. Nikova, S., Rechberger, C., Rijmen, V.: Threshold implementations against side-channel attacks and glitches. In: Ning, P., Qing, S., Li, N. (eds.) Information and Communications Security, 8th International Conference, ICICS 2006, Raleigh, NC, USA, December 4-7, 2006, Proceedings. Lecture Notes in Computer Science, vol. 4307, pp. 529–545. Springer (2006). https://doi.org/10.1007/11935308_38

25. Ramezanpour, K., Ampadu, P., Diehl, W.: Rs-mask: random space masking as an integrated countermeasure against power and fault analysis. In: 2020 IEEE International Symposium on Hardware Oriented Security and Trust, HOST 2020, San Jose, CA, USA, December 7-11, 2020, pp. 176–187. IEEE (2020). https://doi.org/10.1109/HOST45689.2020.9300266
26. Rasoolzadeh, S., Shahmirzadi, A.R., Moradi, A.: Impeccable circuits III. In: IEEE International Test Conference, ITC 2021, Anaheim, CA, USA, October 10-15, 2021, pp. 163–169. IEEE (2021). https://doi.org/10.1109/ITC50571.2021.00024
27. Reparaz, O., Bilgin, B., Nikova, S., Gierlichs, B., Verbauwhede, I.: Consolidating masking schemes. In: Gennaro, R., Robshaw, M. (eds.) Advances in Cryptology - CRYPTO 2015 - 35th Annual Cryptology Conference, Santa Barbara, CA, USA, August 16-20, 2015, Proceedings, Part I. Lecture Notes in Computer Science, vol. 9215, pp. 764–783. Springer (2015). https://doi.org/10.1007/978-3-662-47989-6_37
28. Reparaz, O., Meyer, L.D., Bilgin, B., Arribas, V., Nikova, S., Nikov, V., Smart, N.P.: CAPA: the spirit of beaver against physical attacks. In: Shacham, H., Boldyreva, A. (eds.) Advances in Cryptology - CRYPTO 2018 - 38th Annual International Cryptology Conference, Santa Barbara, CA, USA, August 19-23, 2018, Proceedings, Part I. Lecture Notes in Computer Science, vol. 10991, pp. 121–151. Springer (2018). https://doi.org/10.1007/978-3-319-96884-1_5
29. Saha, S., Jap, D., Roy, D.B., Chakraborti, A., Bhasin, S., Mukhopadhyay, D.: Transform-and-encode: A countermeasure framework for statistical ineffective fault attacks on block ciphers. IACR Cryptol. ePrint Arch. p. 545 (2019). https://eprint.iacr.org/2019/545
30. SAKURA: side-channel Attack User Reference Architecture. http://satoh.cs.uec.ac.jp/SAKURA/index.html
31. Schneider, T., Moradi, A., Güneysu, T.: Parti - towards combined hardware countermeasures against side-channel and fault-injection attacks. In: Robshaw, M., Katz, J. (eds.) Advances in Cryptology - CRYPTO 2016 - 36th Annual International Cryptology Conference, Santa Barbara, CA, USA, August 14-18, 2016, Proceedings, Part II. Lecture Notes in Computer Science, vol. 9815, pp. 302–332. Springer (2016). https://doi.org/10.1007/978-3-662-53008-5_11
32. Shahmirzadi, A.R., Rasoolzadeh, S., Moradi, A.: Impeccable circuits II. In: 57th ACM/IEEE Design Automation Conference, DAC 2020, San Francisco, CA, USA, July 20-24, 2020, pp. 1–6. IEEE (2020). https://doi.org/10.1109/DAC18072.2020.9218615

Diffuse Some Noise: Diffusion Models for Measurement Noise Removal in Side-Channel Analysis

Sengim Karayalçin[1(✉)], Guilherme Perin[1], and Stjepan Picek[2]

[1] Leiden University, Leiden, The Netherlands
s.karayalcin@liacs.leidenuniv.nl
[2] Radboud University, Nijmegen, The Netherlands
stjepan.picek@ru.nl

Abstract. Resilience against side-channel attacks is an important consideration for cryptographic implementations deployed in devices with physical access to the device. However, noise in side-channel measurements has a significant impact on the complexity of these attacks, especially when an implementation is protected with masking. Therefore, it is important to assess the ability of an attacker to deal with noise. While some previous works have considered approaches to remove (some) noise from measurements, these approaches generally require considerable expertise to be effectively employed or necessitate the ability of the attacker to capture a 'clean' set of traces without the noise. In this paper, we introduce a method for utilizing diffusion models to remove measurement noise from side-channel traces in a fully non-profiled setting. Denoising traces using our method considerably lowers the complexity of mounting attacks in both profiled and non-profiled settings. For instance, for a collision attack against the ASCADv2 dataset, we reduced the number of traces required to retrieve the key by 40%, and we showed similar improvements for ESHARD using a state-of-the-art MORE attack. Furthermore, we provide analyses of the scenarios where our method is useful and generate insights into how the diffusion networks denoise traces.

Keywords: Side-Channel Analysis · Deep Learning · Diffusion Models

1 Introduction

While standard cryptographic algorithms are generally considered (or, at least, believed after sufficient public analysis and scrutiny) theoretically secure, as retrieving the secret key from only inputs and outputs in a reasonable time is impossible, their real-world deployment poses additional attack surfaces. Deployments of these algorithms will unintentionally leak some information about their computation to the outside world through power consumption, timing, or electromagnetic emanation. These information leakages, or side channels, can allow

C. Boura et al. (Eds.): SAC 2025, LNCS 16207, pp. 724–752, 2026.
https://doi.org/10.1007/978-3-032-10536-3_27

an attacker to recover secret information from a device efficiently. Since being introduced by Kocher [19], significant research has been done into side-channel attacks (SCA) and their countermeasures. We can broadly categorize SCA into two categories: 1) non-profiled attacks, where an attacker collects side-channel leakages and uses statistical distinguishers to extract the secret key [4, 20] and 2) profiled attacks, where the attacker builds a model for the leakage using a copy (clone) device they have full control over [7]. From the machine learning perspective, we can divide the algorithms into generative and discriminative ones.[1]

While countermeasures for side-channel attacks exist, over recent years, a significant rise in deep learning-based SCA (DLSCA) has shown that these countermeasures can, in some cases, be circumvented, see, e.g., [24,36,37]. In the profiled setting, straightforward applications of discriminative models allow progressively more efficient attacks [17,26,45,53]. Similar approaches based on discriminative models have also been applied in the non-profiled setting [9,42]. To a lesser degree, there are approaches based on generative models that allow for pre-processing of side-channel traces to simplify/improve attacks [44,48,52].

While generative models can be a "natural" setting for SCA (for instance, the template attack [7] is generative), we see fewer developments with generative models-based SCA in the last years compared to the discriminative ones. A part of the reason for this is that discriminative models excel at distinguishing among classes, which is a common setup for SCA (since we commonly consider the classification task). On the other hand, generative models generate new data, which is a natural option for data augmentation, a direction already explored in SCA.

In this work, we propose a novel approach to denoise traces based on Denoising Diffusion Probabilistic Models (DDPMs). Using these models, we can effectively remove environmental (Gaussian) noise from side-channel traces without requiring a reference set of 'clean' traces or profiling labels (see Table 1 for an overview of comparable approaches). We experimentally validate our approach against several datasets and show improved attack performance for non-profiled collision attacks, non-profiled attacks using deep learning, higher order correlation power analysis (HO-CPA), and horizontal attacks. Additionally, when we consider profiling attacks, our technique can be used to improve the profiling complexity and ease the difficulty of finding good model architectures using hyperparameter search. Our main contributions are:

- We showcase the first use cases for DDPM models to pre-process traces in SCA.
- We provide an analysis of the trained DDPM models that explains how traces are denoised and gives insights into situations where denoising is (and is not) possible.

[1] A common division in machine learning-based SCA is into supervised and unsupervised machine learning, but that relates to the task and whether there are labels available and not how the algorithm works.

- We showcase improvements in attack performance for state-of-the-art non-profiled attacks after denoising using the proposed model. For collision attacks against ASCADv2, the required number of traces to retrieve the key is reduced by approximately 40%, and for MORE attacks against ESHARD, we show similar gains in performance.
- We show significantly decreased difficulty in finding model architectures and hyperparameter configurations for profiling attacks, especially in settings with low numbers of profiling traces.

Table 1. Comparing necessary assumptions for denoising traces.

	Denoising	No Countermeasure Disabling	No Profiling Labels
DAE [48]	✓	×	✓
DAE [15]	✓	✓	×
DDPMs [51]	×	✓	×
Ours	✓	✓	✓

The source code to reproduce the experiments is available in the following repository[2].

2 Background

2.1 Side-Channel Analysis

Side-channel attacks [19,20] are a class of attacks aiming at the implementation of cryptographic algorithms. The idea is that (physical) side-effects, e.g., timing [19], power [19], or the electromagnetic emanation [1] of the execution of the algorithm can leak information about secret internal values. An attacker then captures a (large) number of traces of the algorithm's execution by measuring one of these side channels and utilizes these to mount the attack.

We can broadly categorize side-channel attacks into two threat models. First, non-profiled attacks where an attacker utilizes statistical distinguishers to differentiate the correct (sub)key candidate from the wrong ones. Techniques here generally compute the hypothetical intermediate value for all possible (sub)key candidates and attempt to find a connection between these labels and the side-channel traces [4,20].

The second category includes profiled attacks. In this case, an attacker has access to (and full control of) an open copy of the device to be attacked. This allows the attacker to characterize the (physical) leakage using traces captured from the copy device, significantly improving the efficiency of attacks against the target [7,41].

[2] https://github.com/Sengim/diff_release.

Both of these categories of attacks rely on the fact that values that are operated on during the algorithm's execution are related to the measured traces. This relation is modeled by using a leakage model. A leakage model $f : Y \mapsto R$ mapping from an intermediate value $y \in Y$ to the leakage is generally composed of a part that relates to the hypothetical leakage of the value and a noise part. Common ways to model the leakage of this value are the Hamming Weight (HW) (the number of ones in the binary representation of y) or the Hamming Distance (HD) (the Hamming weight of the bitwise difference between y and the value it overwrites in a register).

To leverage this leakage model for key retrieval, the intermediate value an attacker targets needs to be related to the key and some known values. For AES implementations, the Sbox output in the first round is commonly used (for the Hamming weight and Identity leakage models). In this case, $y = \text{Sbox}(p_i \oplus k_i)$ where p_i and k_i are the i-th byte of the known plaintext and secret key. As these values are bytes, it is computationally feasible to calculate the hypothetical values for all 256 possible values of k_i and "match" those to the measured leakage. In this way, each key byte can be attacked separately, eventually leading to the recovery of the full key.

Signal-to-Noise Ratio (SNR). SNR is a leakage assessment metric that quantifies the amount of leakage that is present in a random value. For a set of traces X with intermediate values Y at sample index i, it is defined as:

$$\text{SNR}(X_i, Y) = \frac{\text{Var}_{y \in \mathcal{Y}}(E(X_i|y))}{E_{y \in \mathcal{Y}}(\text{Var}(X_i|y))}.$$

Here, E is the mean, Var is the variance of a random variable, and $\mathcal{Y}$ is the set of possible values in Y. We generally compute SNR for secret shares that leak directly (e.g., masks or masked sensitive values). In this work, we always compute SNR with 20 000 traces and the Identity leakage model.

2.2 Algorithmic Noise vs. Measurement Noise

We consider algorithmic noise to be the parts of the computation that are happening in parallel with the intermediate values we target. For example, an optimized hardware implementation of AES might execute several Sboxes in parallel, resulting in the Hamming weight of all output bits leaking together. If we want to target only one byte, the contribution to the leakage of the other bytes is considered noise. Measurement noise is then the part of the trace that is part of taking the physical measurements. This could be due to imperfections in the measurement setup or environmental factors. We generally assume this noise follows or is similar to, a Gaussian distribution [27].

The main difference between these types of noise for the purposes of unsupervised pre-processing of side-channel traces is that the algorithmic noise is part of the signal and is, therefore, not removed. An illustrative example is that if we take several measurements during the computation of a larger state, the algorithmic noise will stay the same for each of these samples, while the measurement noise will vary.

2.3 Datasets

ESHARD. The ESHARD dataset[3] contains EM measurements of an AES implementation protected with first-order Boolean masking. The dataset contains 1 400 sample points corresponding to the loading of the mask values and 100 000 traces with a fixed key. We target the Sbox output in the first round for all attacks. Note that we use the non-shuffled variant for all our analyses, as the shuffling was implemented by manipulating plaintexts a posteriori.

ASCADf. The ASCAD fixed key dataset (ASCADf)[4] contains EM measurements from an AES implementation protected with first-order Boolean masking. The dataset contains 60 000 traces with 100 000 samples each. We focus on a pre-selected window of 700 samples containing leakages for the masked Sbox computation in the first round for the 3rd key byte (which is the first masked byte). The dataset has a fixed key for all traces.

ASCADv2. The ASCADv2 dataset[5] contains power measurements of an AES implementation protected with an affine masking scheme and shuffling. The dataset contains 800 000 traces with 1 million sample points each. We take smaller part of the 15 000 sample extracted dataset used in [31], which contain 2 000 samples corresponding to a concatenation of indices 0-1 000 (loading masks), 6 040-6 540 (processing masked Sbox for third byte), and 11 250-11 750 (removing additive mask). Note that for this analysis, we disable shuffling by manipulating plaintexts a posteriori.

AES_HD. The AES_HD dataset[6] is an unprotected AES implementation on an FPGA board. The dataset contains 500 000 power traces using a fixed key. Each trace consists of 1 250 sample points. We target the Hamming Distance of register writing in the last round ($\text{Sbox}^{-1}[C_i \oplus k*] \oplus C_j$).

AES_HD_MM. The AES_HD_MM dataset[7] is an AES implementation on an FPGA board protected with first-order Boolean masking. The dataset contains 5 600 000 traces using a fixed key. The measurements contain 3 125 samples per trace. We target the same intermediate value as for AES_HD.

ASCON. The ASCON dataset[8] is an unprotected software implementation of the ASCON cipher in authenticated encryption mode [10]. The dataset consists of 200 000 traces where 100 000 traces use random keys for profiling and

---

[3] https://gitlab.com/eshard/nucleo_sw_aes_masked_shuffled.
[4] https://github.com/ANSSI-FR/ASCAD/tree/master/ATMEGA_AES_v1/ATM_AES_v1_fixed_key.
[5] https://github.com/ANSSI-FR/ASCAD/tree/master/STM32_AES_v2.
[6] https://github.com/AISyLab/AES_HD_Ext.
[7] https://chest.coe.neu.edu/?current_page=POWER_TRACE_LINK&software=ptmasked.
[8] https://zenodo.org/records/10229484.

100 000 traces use a fixed key. Each trace consists of 772 sample points corresponding to the first round of the initialization phase of the authenticated encryption protocol.

2.4 Discriminative vs. Generative Models

Machine learning algorithms can be divided into two categories: generative and discriminative. Discriminative algorithms are primarily concerned with simulating the conditional probability distribution of the output labels given the input features. The goal is to understand the decision boundary. On the other hand, generative algorithms are designed to simulate the joint probability distribution of the input features (possibly conditioned on labels). To create new samples, their goal is to learn the underlying data distribution.

2.5 Denoising Diffusion Probabilistic Models (DDPMs)

Denoising Diffusion Probabilistic Models were first introduced by Ho et al. [14]. Over the next few years, models based on the DDPM paradigm have outperformed state-of-the-art generative models on image generation and other tasks [50]. DDPM training is based on a relatively straightforward paradigm: during training, we iteratively add some noise to an image (or some other type of data) for T steps; this is referred to as the forward process (left direction in Fig. 1). Then, for an image x_t where noise has been added t times, we train the model to predict x_{t-1} and thereby remove noise. This is called the backward process (right direction in Fig. 1). The central idea here is that when we start from fully random noise and iteratively remove noise, we can generate realistic-looking images as the diffusion models try to 'amplify' patterns in the noise.

More formally, the forward process is defined using a Markov chain from x_0 (the original images) to x_T (Gaussian noise) and transitions $q(x_t|x_{t-1})$. We then have a noise schedule $\beta_0, \beta_1, \ldots, \beta_T$ and corresponding values $\alpha_0, \alpha_1 \ldots, \alpha_T$ (with $\alpha_0 = 0$ increasing to $\alpha_T = 1$). These α_i allow us to generate pairs x_t, x_{t-1} for arbitrary $1 < t \leq T$ using $x_t = (1-\alpha_t)x_0 + \alpha_t Z$ and $x_{t-1} = (1-\alpha_{t-1})x_0 + \alpha_{t-1} Z$ where $Z = \mathcal{N}(0,1)$. These pairs can then be used to minimize the squared error of our diffusion model parameterized with weights θ, i.e., $\arg\min_\theta (f_\theta(x_t, t-1) - x_{t-1})^2$ using uniformly sampled t from $[0, T]$ for each mini-batch. For a more detailed description of diffusion models, see [14].

3 Related Work

The profiling side-channel analysis started with the template attack [7]. A few years later, the stochastic attack was also introduced [41]. Interestingly, both of those attacks build generative models. With the introduction of "classical" machine learning in SCA, the community moved the attention to discriminative models. Still, deep learning-based generative models have been used in the last few years, with the primary goals to either pre-process the side-channel traces or generate synthetic traces.

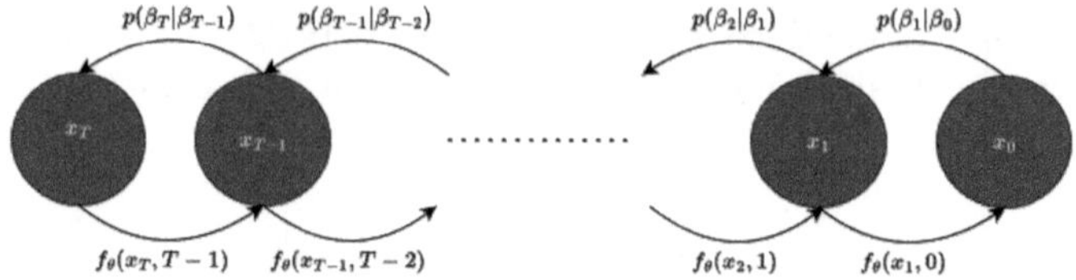

Fig. 1. Diagram illustrating the forward and backward process for training DDPMs, adapted from [14].

3.1 Pre-processing Using Neural Networks

While classical techniques for pre-processing side-channel traces have been explored, such techniques often require a significant domain expertise and error-prone manual intervention to achieve optimal results [23,27,34,38]. As such, the focus of the SCA community has recently moved to automated techniques utilizing deep learning. A first approach to using denoising autoencoders for removing noise from side-channel traces was proposed by Yang et al. [49]. There, the authors used trace averaging to imitate a 'clean' set of traces, which can then be used to train an autoencoder to remove noise from the original traces. Subsequently, Wu and Picek [48] extended the approach to cover more hiding countermeasures like desynchronization and random delays. Berg et al. [2] further investigated hyperparameter configurations for these networks. Finally, Hu et al. [15] included additional training objectives to improve the performance of autoencoders for removing noise from traces. Beyond autoencoders, Wu et al. [44] utilized triplet networks to extract representations from traces that can be used to mount template attacks.

More recently, several studies have explored generative approaches for pre-processing. Genevey-Metat et al. [11] utilized a GAN to translate traces between side-channel domains. Cao et al. [6] used a GAN approach to tackle portability challenges by transforming measurements from the attack device to the profiling device. Krček and Perin [21] use autoencoders to map traces to the same dimensions to reduce hyperparameter tuning efforts. Karayalçin et al. [16] investigated a Conditional Generative Adversarial Networks (CGANs)-based framework to emulate feature selection for masked implementations without access to mask values. Finally, Zaid et al. [52] used variational autoencoders to model the physical leakage and subsequently leverage these models for attacks.

The main limitation of these approaches for pre-processing is that they only work in settings with additional assumptions over the standard non-profiled setting. The approaches using autoencoders in [2,48,49] require a set of 'clean' traces that serve as a target for the networks. When considering Gaussian noise, this clean set can be emulated by averaging, but for masked implementations, this requires access to mask values [49] which is not always feasible even for evaluators [29]. For the methods in [6,15,16,44,52], a labeled profiling set (or access to masks values for [52]) is necessary for training the models. The trace translation in [11] requires paired measurements in different side-channel domains, and it necessitates that the target side-channel domain is easier to attack, essentially mimicking the 'clean' set of traces in [48]. None of these approaches can effectively pre-process traces in a fully non-profiled setting.

3.2 Other Approaches Using Generative Models in SCA

Several works have looked at applications of generative models for SCA. To generate additional traces, Wang et al. [43] considered CGANs to expand the size of the profiling set. Subsequently, Mukhtar et al. [33] improved upon the network architecture used in [43]. Yap and Jap [51] proposed the use of diffusion models to generate additional traces. Finally, Lu et al. [25] also use DDPMs to generate additional traces, but use a model architecture tailored for SCA. In all of these works, the authors relied on having access to a profiling device to label traces for training the networks. The resulting networks are then utilized to generate traces while providing label information to the network to control the trace generation. Note that while Transformers are often used in generative contexts in natural language processing, the Transformer architectures in [5,12,13,22] are used as classification models (i.e., in a discriminative setting).

4 Denoising Diffusion Probabilistic Models for Removing Noise in SCA

While utilizing DDPMs for data generation to improve side-channel attacks is a straightforward direction, the results from Yap and Jap [51] suggest that there do not seem to be any significant advantages to using DDPMs over previously used (C)GAN methods [33,43]. Additionally, using DDPMs for trace generation requires profiling labels (or even mask knowledge) to allow for useful trace generation, i.e., generating trace-label pairs, which limits the applicability to a profiled setting. On the other hand, we utilize unsupervised DDPMs to denoise traces. Notably, using unsupervised DDPMs means that our models cannot be used to generate new traces with corresponding labels. Conversely, utilizing the supervised DDPMs for denoising is possible, however, as these models require label information which means they cannot be used for unlabeled traces and have significant downsides for pre-processing (see Sect. 8.2).

The key idea here is to take a diffusion model parameterized with θ, $f_\theta : X^m \times T \mapsto X^m$, where X^m is a side-channel trace with m samples and $T = \mathbf{Z}_n$ that we train using standard diffusion model training (see Sect. 2.5) on our measured traces. After training, we then input actual traces (or x_0) and try to remove noise (or predict x_{-1}) from these traces. This then results in every original trace being transformed into a denoised version. We note that using diffusion models directly to take real samples as input and output a cleaner version has (to the best of our knowledge) not been done before. Image super-sampling using DDPMs has been done but generally requires specialized training setups and architectures [32].

The reasoning here is that we can consider the side-channel traces as a combination of signal S and environmental/measurement noise Z. If we then write

$x_i = q_i * x_i + (1 - q_i) * Z$, where q_i is some schedule for the forward process (note that $q_i < q_{i-1}$), the optimization objective becomes $min_\theta(f_\theta(x_i, i) - x_{i-1})^2$. As the trained model has been trained to remove Gaussian noise, the model should then be able to remove some of the actual noise Z present in the original trace. Notably, this assumes that the distribution of the environmental/measurement noise Z is (somewhat similar to) a Gaussian distribution, but this is a common assumption in the SCA domain, see, e.g., [7,27,48].

The main advantage of this approach is that the models are trained to be agnostic of implementation specifics. The only requirement is that the noise we are trying to remove follows a Gaussian distribution. As the diffusion model tries to reconstruct the trace, its output will also still follow the original trace's structure in terms of intermediate values. While this also holds for the denoising autoencoders in [48,49], the training procedure of the autoencoders necessitates access to a reference set of 'clean' traces, which requires the ability to disable countermeasures on a profiling device. Note that while in [48], the authors also emulate this reference set by averaging traces, this still requires a large number of additional measurements, complicating the process and making it only possible for unmasked implementations. Indeed, in masked implementations, an attacker cannot know in which traces the same intermediate values are processed (i.e., which traces to average) without access to masking randomness [49].

4.1 Network Architecture

To keep the focus of this work on the viability of DDPMs for denoising traces in an unsupervised context, we only use synchronized traces. This allows us to restrict our architecture to shallow MLPs as these have been shown to be effective for processing synchronized side-channel traces [37]. As such, the design choices for our architecture are relatively simple: we follow the general structure of a U-Net [39] where we first downsample for several layers, then keep the same dimensions for some layers to induce a compressed latent representation, and finally upsample again to the original trace dimensions. We utilize batch-normalization layers in the downsampling section of our network to stabilize training. The network architecture can be seen in Fig. 2.

4.2 Hyperparameter Setup

To train the DDPM models across all experiments, we use the Adam optimizer [18]. The learning rate is scheduled according to an exponential decay[9] schedule with an initial learning rate of 0.001, the decay rate of 0.96, and 10 000 decay steps. We train all models for 200 epochs using batch size 200. We use the *tanh* activation function for every intermediate layer and the linear activation for the output. We use $T = 16$ for all of the experiments with a linear noise-schedule [14]. These hyperparameters perform well and allow for reasonably effective denoising against the considered targets. We arrived at these values after

[9] https://www.tensorflow.org/api_docs/python/tf/keras/optimizers/schedules/ExponentialDecay.

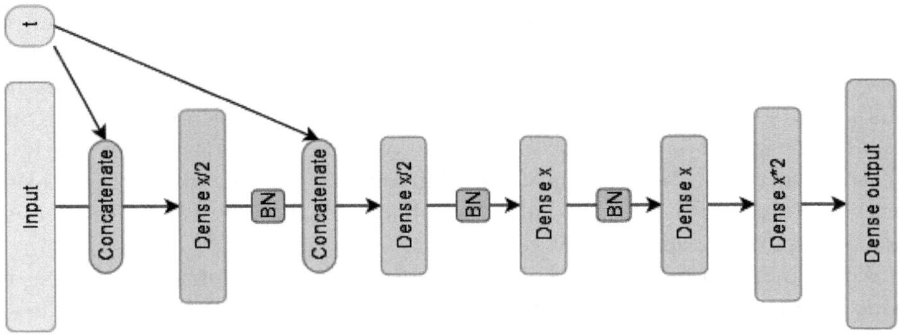

Fig. 2. General model architecture for the input of size X.

preliminary testing. Note that these are not optimal, but we refrain from further optimization. We consider finding optimal architectures/hyperparameters to be out of the scope of this work. We provide further experiments to show the effects of some hyperparameter variations in Appendix C, which indicate that hyperparameter optimization is not as difficult for these models as it is for conventional DLSCA.

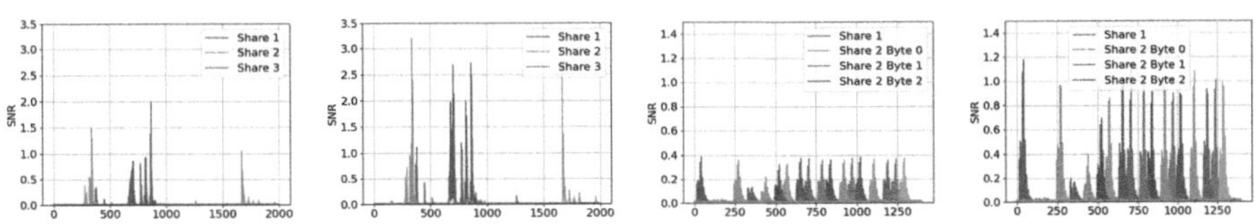

(a) Original (b) Diffused (c) Original (d) Diffused

Fig. 3. SNR values for secret shares for ASCADv2(left) and ESHARD(right).

For the denoising of the traces after training, we observe in the initial set of experiments that predicting traces with $t = T - 1 = 15$ ($f_\theta(x_0, 15)$) works significantly better than using $t = 0$ ($f_\theta(x_0, 0)$). As such, we use $t = 15$ for all experiments unless otherwise specified. Our intuition here is that for higher t, the model gets noisier inputs during training, which forces it to find patterns in its input data more aggressively, resulting in better denoising performance. However, we do not claim that this is always best, and further work exploring inference time uses/augmentations of diffusion models could result in further improvements.

4.3 Proof of Concept

To provide a proof of concept for our method, we first look at testing against (relatively) noisy trace sets from software targets. First, we consider the ASCADv2 target as this is currently the most difficult public software target. There, the leakage of the masked output is noisy (SNR around 0.08), which potentially allows for significant benefits. Second, the ESHARD target provides measurements of a software implementation where both the mask and masked Sbox output leak with relatively low SNRs (see original ESHARD SNRs in Fig. 3). Note that in this section, we only consider software targets where the measurements contain at least a moderate amount of measurement noise to highlight success cases of our method.

We train the models using all available traces and subsequently use the trained model to obtain denoised traces. We use the SNR of the secret shares in the traces (using the Identity leakage model) as a measure of how successful the noise removal was. In Fig. 3, we see the SNR results for a trimmed version of the ASCADv2 dataset. The results clearly show that the SNR peaks for all three shares are significantly improved. For ESHARD, we also see significant improvements in SNR in Fig. 3. These results show that our networks are effective at amplifying the side-channel signal. However, there are significant differences in the magnitude of the improvement for various secret shares and features. In Sect. 4.4, we aim to explain these differences using simulated traces.

In Fig. 4, we showcase histograms of the values in the highest SNR point for the secret shares. We can observe that, especially for share 1 of ASCADv2 and for ESHARD, the distributions are visibly much smoother, and the separation between classes is clearer for the diffused traces. These results indicate that the diffusion networks can effectively smooth out the noise from side-channel traces while maintaining the leakages.

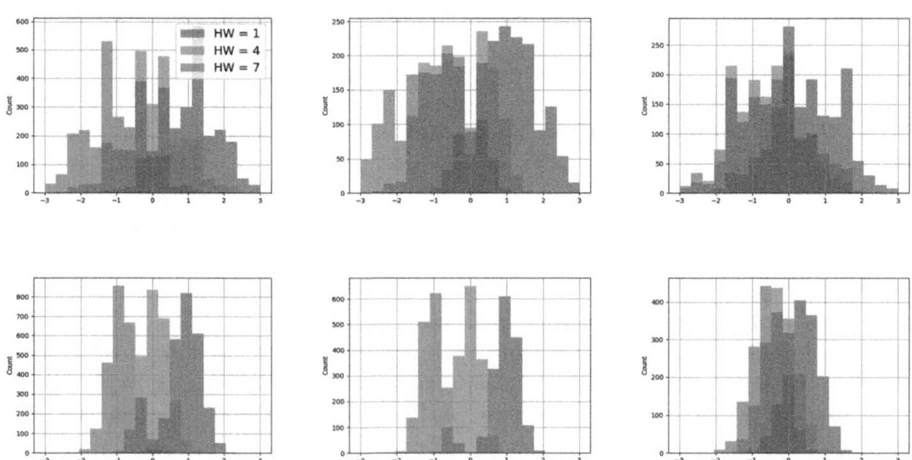

Fig. 4. Histogram for the HW values in the highest SNR samples for Original (top) and Diffused (bottom) traces for (left-right) ESHARD, ASCADv2 share 1, and ASCADv2 share 3.

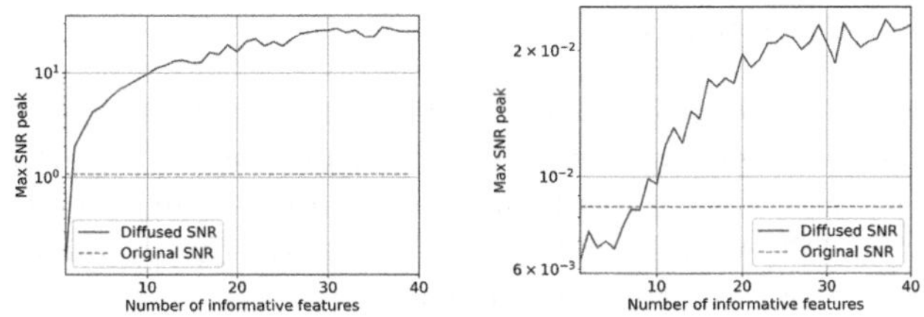

Fig. 5. Maximum SNR value for diffused traces simulations for varying numbers of informative points with low(left) and high(right) added noise.

4.4 Simulations

Next, we explore in what situations we can improve the SNR of side-channel measurements using our DDPMs. To accomplish this, we utilize simulations with varying noise levels and a varying number of informative points. We follow the procedure:

1. we generate traces of 100 points noise following a normal distribution, and then,
2. for $0 < n \leq 40$ of these points (to allow different settings), we include the Hamming weight of an 8-bit intermediate value y uniformly sampled from the range $[0, 255]$.

The main purpose of varying the number of leaky points is to determine how the DDPMs are amplifying the side-channel signal. While the results in Sect. 4.3 show clear improvements in terms of SNR for individual features, the networks cannot create more information than what is present in the original trace. As such, the increased SNR in individual features must come from other trace points. Intuitively, combining information from several points leaking the same value is a straightforward way to amplify the signal in each of these points. As can be seen in Fig. 5, there is a clear link between the number of leaky features and the level of SNR achieved. Notably, for both the high and low noise scenarios, the model does not increase the SNR if only one leaky feature is present. In the low-noise scenario, the model already shows significant improvement over baseline SNR when two leaky features are included, improving further with more leaky features. In the high-noise scenario, more leaky features are required before the SNR levels are improved over the baseline.

Overall, these results strongly suggest that diffusion models learn to differentiate the side-channel signal from noise by looking for correlated features in the trace. By finding and combining information from those related points, the model can decrease the error in its output. This is relevant for real-world side-channel traces when we take several measurements during an operation that leaks some sensitive value, e.g., the oscilloscope has a high sampling rate or some sensitive value is manipulated in several trace points.

4.5 Gradient Visualization

To validate that the DDPMs learn to combine information across correlated features in real-world settings, we visualize what features contribute to one of the output features. We use gradient visualization techniques that have been previously used in SCA [30]. In Fig. 6, we provide the gradient visualizations for the maximum SNR feature. We clearly see that sample points correlated with the most informative sample influence the model's output. Notably, these results explain the significant differences in the magnitude of the SNR increases for different secret shares of ASCADv2 we saw in Fig. 3. As can be seen in Fig. 6, the diffusion model can only utilize a small number of samples to combine information for share 3, while in the case of share 1, there are significantly more samples to learn from. These differences follow the demonstrated trends in Sect. 4.4. Note that the results for other targets are qualitatively the same using this analysis.

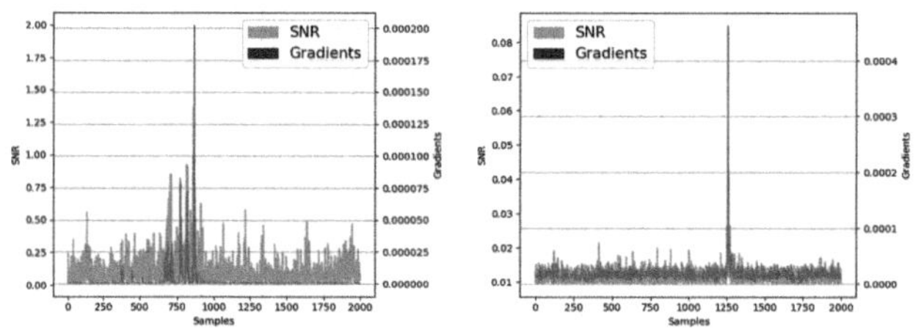

Fig. 6. Gradients vs. SNR values share 1 and 3 of ASCADv2.

5 Experimental Results

5.1 Non-profiled Attacks

Multi Output Regression Enhanced (MORE). This section provides results for state-of-the-art non-profiled attacks using DL [40]. The basic idea of this attack is to train one model labeled for every possible key and conduct the regression task. As the labels generated using the correct key are the only ones that are related to the trace, the model should then most accurately predict labels of the correct key. A ranking for key candidates can then be created by measuring the network error for each candidate. We only show results against ESHARD as breaking the ASCADv2 target is still infeasible using the MORE methodology, while for ASCADf and the hardware targets, diffusing traces does not make a difference in terms of attack performance. We generate a distribution of key ranks using 40 separate random models following the hyperparameter ranges used in [40]. We choose this method as it allows us to assess the impact of diffusing traces on the difficulty of defining an appropriate model configuration, and it reflects directly on the effectiveness of the ensemble-based attacks that use these random models. The diffusion model in this case is the same as in Appendix A using 10 000 traces. We use the HW leakage model and target the third key byte. The results in Fig. 7 showcase that diffusing the traces helps significantly. Attacks using diffused traces perform similarly at 20 000 traces to the attacks using 50 000 original traces. This indicates that diffusion models significantly help the consistency of training discriminative models, especially in more restricted settings.

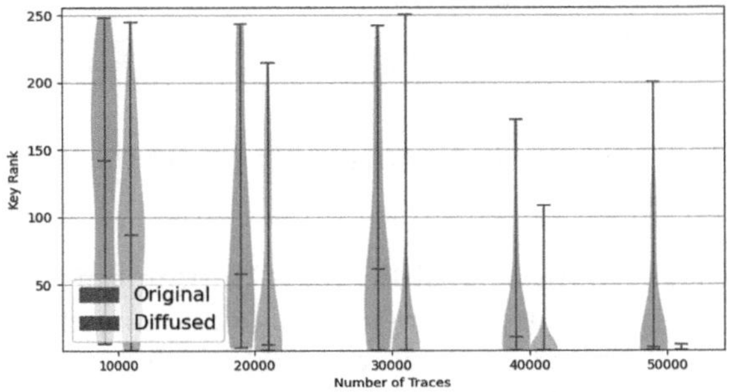

Fig. 7. MORE results for ESHARD.

Collision Attack Against ASCADv2. To demonstrate the practical relevance of our approach, we first showcase attacking results in a non-profiled context. We focus on the collision attacks as described by Wu et al. [46], which aim to recover the bitwise difference between sub-keys (key-deltas). These key-deltas can then be used to brute-force one key byte, leading to full key recovery (given correct key-deltas). We include this attack as it is the only attack that can break the ASCADv2 dataset in a non-profiled setting.[10] Note that Cristiani et al. [8] also showcased successful attacks against the same implementation, but they require a different acquisition campaign with significantly more traces.

For training the DDPM, we use the intervals given in [46]. Note that for these attacks, the shuffling countermeasure is disabled, and we simulate a fixed attack key for the profiling set (see [46] for details). To simplify the analysis, we concatenated the used 100 sample intervals into one 1 600 sample trace and trained the diffusion model on 20 000 such traces to limit computational overhead. We then executed 50 runs on randomly sampled traces from the 500 000 profiling traces and averaged key-delta ranks to achieve a Guessing Entropy(GE) estimate. The results in Fig. 8 clearly favor the diffused traces. In fact, using diffused traces can successfully reduce GE for all key-delta candidates below 1 using 60 000 traces, while three of the deltas are not fully recovered using 100 000 traces for the original traces.

[10] With shuffling disabled.

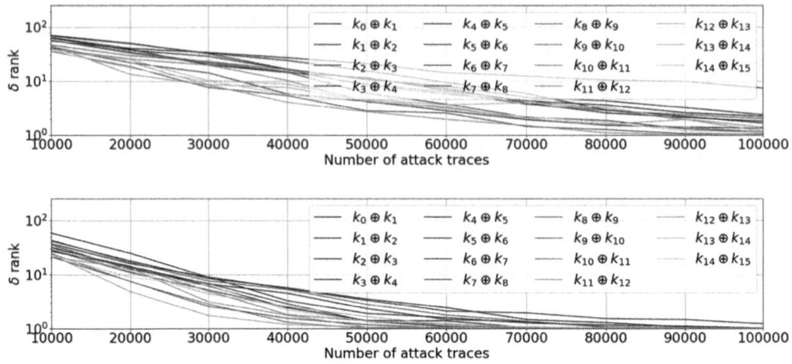

Fig. 8. ASCADv2 collision attacks for Original (top) and Diffused (bottom) traces.

Horizontal Attacks Against Public Key Implementation. To illustrate that our method is generally useful for analyzing side-channel traces, we showcase improvements to the horizontal attack from [35] which targets individual bits of the ECC key by classifying trace segments. In this attack, initial labeling that is only slightly better than random guessing (around 52%) is iteratively improved upon using CNNs. In this work, results are presented using both an optimized fixed CNN architecture and a new random CNN at each iteration (for more details, see [35]). Note that in subsequent work, it was shown that similar attack performance could be achieved in some cases using only one neuron instead of larger CNNs [3]. We only show results on the cswap_arith dataset as the cswap_pointer is significantly easier to attack, and almost every network setup achieves 100% accuracy on both the original and diffused traces. The diffusion model is trained in the standard way using the 63 750 traces. For this dataset, we use batch size 1 000 and obtain denoised traces with $t = 0$ instead of $t = 15$ as this achieved better results.

The results in Table 2 again show significant improvements to accuracies by using diffused traces. In all cases, the maximum accuracy using diffused traces is higher than using original traces. Especially in the case where only the simplest perceptron from [3] is used, we obtain 99.2% maximum accuracy using diffused traces while only 80% using the original traces. For CNNs, we see the fixed CNN improves between 10% and 15%, and using random CNNs, we find the only attack achieving 100% maximum accuracy uses diffused traces. Still, average accuracies are not always improved. This is mainly due to the number of iterations optimized for the original traces. For the diffused traces, the average accuracy is maximized in earlier iterations and subsequently decreases sooner.

6 Datasets with Algorithmic Noise

In previous sections, we have shown significantly improved attack performance against targets that have limited algorithmic noise. In these cases, it is clear

Table 2. Comparison of Average/Max single trace accuracy for key bits using the one neuron perceptron from [3] and CNN setups from [35].

	One neuron	CNN	CNN +Dropout	Random CNN	Random CNN + Dropout
Original	70.9/79.2%	63.6/73.7%	55.2/75.7%	71.7/80.0%	98.6/99.6%
Diffused	96.3/99.2%	70.8/87.1%	50.1/83.5%	62.6/81.1%	99.6/100%

from the results in Sect. 4.3 that the measurement noise is mitigated by using diffusion models. However, when we consider targets that process larger states, the denoising is less relevant.

In Fig. 9, we see that the DDPMs cannot improve the peak SNR for any of the targets without added noise. Only for AES_HD_MM, we see that the SNR of the other samples is increased by a marginal amount. Note that this does not seem to affect attack performance; for profiling attacks using 100 random MLP models using the ranges from Table 4, GE is 60.78 ± 23.95 and 59.85 ± 21.00 for original and diffused traces, respectively. Looking at traces with added Gaussian noise, we see improved SNR for ASCON and AES_HD_MM. For AES_HD, SNR does not improve, presumably, as the noise level is relatively high and the intermediate value is only leaked in a very small number of samples following the results on simulations in Sect. 4.4.

These results indicate that the diffusion models are not as useful for measurements with mostly algorithmic noise. However, even for hardware targets, we can see some improvements to SNR in specific samples, indicating that removing (some) measurement noise is still achievable in these cases. Additionally, when we add Gaussian noise, we see clear improvements in SNR for both the ASCON and the AES_HD_MM targets, reinforcing the usefulness of our diffusion models in scenarios with noisier measurements. Since noisier settings are more relevant from a practical perspective, and even the current results with deep learning perform well in scenarios with little noise, we consider our approach highly relevant and applicable in real-world settings.

7 Comparison with Denoising Autoencoders and Signal Processing

While several works have examined the use of techniques from the deep learning domain for pre-processing side-channel traces, almost none of these techniques are directly applicable in a non-profiled setting. As mentioned before, most either require profiling labels [15,16,44] or the ability to capture some 'clean' target traces [11,48,49]. However, as mentioned in Sect. 4.1 of [48], denoising autoencoders can be used for the same purpose.[11] We also include signal-processing

[11] Note that autoencoders trained in this way are equivalent to training DDPMs with one fixed noise step.

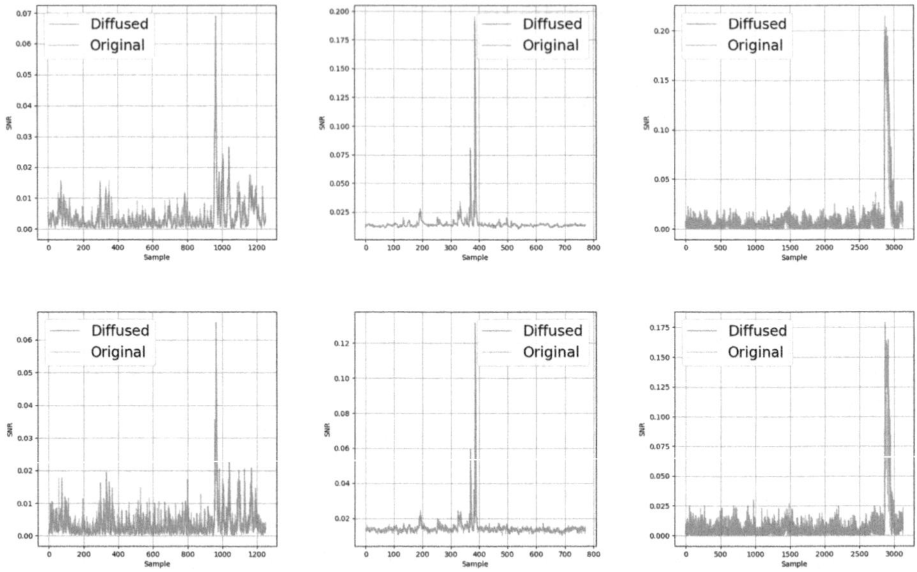

(d) AES_HD (e) ASCON (f) AES_HD_MM

Fig. 9. SNR values for intermediate values for various datasets for original traces (top) and traces with added noise (bottom).

techniques that can remove noise. We use moving averages and principal component analysis (PCA). For each of these, we try window sizes and number of components up to 100 and report the best results.

From the results in Table 3, we can see that autoencoders trained directly to reconstruct traces, i.e., without a 'clean' set, are not effective at removing measurement noise. Both the convolutional architecture from [48] and our DDPM architecture trained as autoencoders fail to increase SNR over the original traces. While tuning the architectures for each specific dataset could lead to improvements, we note that this is not necessary for our DDPMs. In addition, the autoencoders trained to reconstruct traces can easily overfit and memorize their training traces, increasing the difficulty of finding an appropriate architecture, especially in non-profiled contexts. Overall, it seems clear that in a scenario without a set of clean target traces (or label/mask knowledge), autoencoders are not appropriate for removing noise.

When we compare it to signal processing, we see that the performance is more competitive. In these cases, we mainly highlight that the optimal configuration differs for each setup. Notably, finding appropriate parameters depends on the physical leakage characteristics, and the appropriate parameters differ for different shares in the same traces (see ASCADv2 in Table 3). We note that it should generally be possible to use classical signal-processing techniques to achieve similar (or better) performance for individual shares but that doing this effectively in non-profiled settings (without access to masks/keys to verify the approach) is highly dependent on evaluator expertise.

Table 3. Comparison of max SNR peaks for denoising autoencoder (DAE) approach, moving averages (MA), and PCA. The (n) denotes the window size for MA and the number of components, respectively.

	Original	DDPM	DAE CNN from [48]	DEA using DDPM MLP network	MA(n)	PCA(n)
ASCADf	1.30	1.24	0.76	1.17	1.63(20)	**1.63(21)**
Eshard	0.39	1.06	0.20	0.03	1.40(7)	**1.63(40)**
ASCADv2 share 1	2.00	**8.90**	1.35	1.93	2.69(14)	2.35(41)
ASCADv2 share3	0.08	**0.19**	0.06	0.03	0.09(5)	0.03(99)

8 Discussion

Our results showcase that DDPM models can learn useful representations of side-channel traces in unsupervised contexts. Additionally, the analysis in Sect. 4.4 shows how the networks learn these representations and give an intuition for why the denoising can work. The mechanism is quite straightforward. To remove noise from a leaky sample point, the network needs more information about the leaking value. To accomplish this, it can find features that leak the same value and combine the information from these features to arrive at a less noisy version of the feature (see Sect. 4.5 for validation). In effect, we compress the information from several leaky samples into a singular sample.

The benefits of this for non-profiled attacks are clear. For these attacks, we often utilize only a single feature to represent each secret share [8]. In these contexts, our models allow for the implicit utilization of several leaky samples without having access to mask values. Additionally, for collision attacks, the stronger separation between classes can clearly reduce the number of traces necessary to detect key differences.

For profiled attacks, the benefits are less obvious. In principle, using LDA to reduce the dimension from a sufficiently large number of informative samples effectively compresses the information from all of those samples and thus eliminates the benefits of diffusing traces. Similarly, a well-trained neural network should implicitly combine the information available across a trace. However, in practice, we see significant benefits to denoising traces before training neural networks. Our results in Sect. 5.1(and in Appendix B) clearly indicate that the difficulty of finding appropriate hyperparameters for neural networks and the required number of traces for profiling is significantly reduced.

While our results show significant gains for the showcased attacks against some targets (specifically ESHARD and ASCADv2), it is clear that these benefits are not universal. Our method does not improve the SNR for datasets that contain mostly algorithmic noise. However, the SNR also does not seem to be harmed by pre-processing the traces using diffusion models, limiting the downside of using our method to the (limited) computational overhead required for training the diffusion model. The artificial addition of Gaussian noise in Sect. 6 also showcases that the method is still effective in more difficult scenarios when the measurements are more noisy.

The main takeaway from these results is that including diffusion models for pre-processing traces within the evaluation can significantly reduce the overhead caused by environmental noise while not requiring the same level of expertise to tune as other methods from the DL domain. The tuning of diffusion models in the SCA context seems relatively straightforward, and the pre-processing can be used to simplify any subsequent analysis. Especially in contexts where individual samples are used to represent the leakage from sensitive values, like (higher-order) CPA, our method allows for the combination of information from several samples without any additional access assumptions or alterations to the attack methodology. While the practical results presented in Sect. 5 showcase strong benefits in terms of attack performance, these are clearly influenced by our choice of datasets. Overall, the attack improvements are only present when the SNR of secret shares is similarly improved. For targets aside from ESHARD, ASCADv2, and cswap_arithmetic, utilizing our DDPMs does not seem to make a significant difference for practical attacks in our experiments unless we artificially inject Gaussian noise to simulate noisier measurement setups. Note that there may be some benefits (minor SNR improvements we see for AES_HD_MM and ASCON), but this did not make a difference for the considered attacks. Another consideration for interpreting our results is that the network and hyperparameter settings leave significant room for improvement. We aimed to present the denoising method using DDPMs, not to optimize the denoising performance for each specific scenario. In fact, even the results in Appendix C show that larger improvements than those presented in Sect. 5 are relatively straightforward to achieve by changing only one or two hyperparameters. Consequently, this suggests that future research looking into more complex network architectures and hyperparameter optimizations would still be beneficial in evaluating the full potential of our approach.

8.1 On Computational and Profiling Cost

While training generative models is often associated with significant computational and data requirements, our results showcase the opposite. We use relatively small models that require limited training data. The time required to train each of these models[12] requires between 10 min and 2 h, impacted quite heavily by the number of profiling traces used. Note that the time required to train these models is almost identical for autoencoders with the same model architectures.

Furthermore, we see that the requirement for large numbers of training data for reasonable performance is not that strong. In the success cases, training DDPMs for denoising using significantly fewer traces than are required to

[12] On a workstation equipped with an NVIDIA RTX 4080 and 64 GB of RAM.

successfully attack already improves the attack performance. Notably, this is because the models are not required to generate fully new traces and do not have to learn the relationship between traces and target values (see Sect. 8.2 for more discussion). In fact, as supported by simulation results in Sect. 4.4, what the models need to learn to denoise effectively is that certain values leak in several samples. This then means the models can combine the information in these points to amplify the leakage if the noise in these points is (somewhat) independent as we discuss in Sect. 6.

8.2 On the Relevance of Unsupervised Pre-processing

It may seem somewhat counter-intuitive to neglect using labels during pre-processing for profiled attacks given their availability. However, from our perspective, pre-processing methods that use label information suffer from the key limitation that they rely on learning the relation between traces and labels, which is the core challenge for conventional classification models. If the labels help the pre-processing, it is clearly possible for the pre-processing network, and probably a conventional classification network, to learn this relationship without the pre-processing.

Furthermore, any network that takes label information as its input to pre-process a trace cannot be used to pre-process traces from an attack set where the key is not known. Note that in non-profiled settings, it is potentially possible to use plaintext as a stand-in for the intermediate value to mitigate this issue [47]. However, this still does not mitigate the above downsides of such a label-based approach.

9 Conclusions and Future Works

We have presented an approach for utilizing DDPMs to remove noise from side-channel traces. As shown in Sect. 4.4, our approach is effective at increasing SNR levels of traces when several samples in the side-channel trace leak the same information. In these cases, DDPMs can combine information from several samples to remove noise from each of the individual samples. Notably, this is, to the best of our knowledge, the first approach that can effectively denoise traces in a fully non-profiled setting without a "clean" set of target traces. Furthermore, we showed significant improvements in attack performance for several state-of-the-art non-profiled attacks and similar improvements in the profiling complexity of deep learning models for profiled attacks. One of the main limitations of our work is that we focus on aligned traces. While directly training our models on misaligned traces does not pose any technical difficulties, achieving satisfactory performance in such a context is more difficult. In future work, we plan to investigate mechanisms for effectively applying our method to misaligned traces, as well as to investigate more complex network architectures. Besides this, there are a number of use cases within the SCA domain for our models, which could potentially be interesting. Some initial ideas include pre-training (parts of) classification models since diffusion models could aid in the training of profiling models and exploring whether the implicit compression of leakage from several features can be used to limit the computational overhead of subsequent attacks.

A Correlation Attacks

First, we investigate improvements to second-order CPA-based attacks. As these attacks utilize one sample for each secret share, the expectation is that we will see significant improvements as the diffusion models allow for the implicit utilization of information leaked across several correlated features. We showcase scenarios for ASCADf and ESHARD to show the effects of a diffusion model on the attack performance when SNR is improved (ESHARD) and when it is not (ASCADf). Note that as peak SNR is not improved for ASCADf, diffusing traces should have no impact on the performance of CPA-based attacks [28]. We select the highest SNR samples for each share in the original traces for these attacks and combine them using absolute difference as a shortcut to avoid testing all possible feature combinations.

The results in Fig. 10 indicate that clear improvements in attack performance are achieved. Note that for these attacks, the CPA results are not entirely representative of real-world attacks. In fact, we require more traces than are available in the attacks to train the diffusion models. Thus, to simulate representative attacks, we should train diffusion models for every subset of traces we attack in each of the attack simulations, which is impractical, especially when training diffusion models using low trace counts. However, for noisier targets where (very) large numbers of traces are necessary for key retrieval, this limitation is not an objection, as the diffusion model can be trained using the larger set. As such, the results in Fig. 10 indicate that trained diffusion models provide significant benefits for improving CPA attacks (or other attacks that represent the leakage of a secret share using a single sample point).

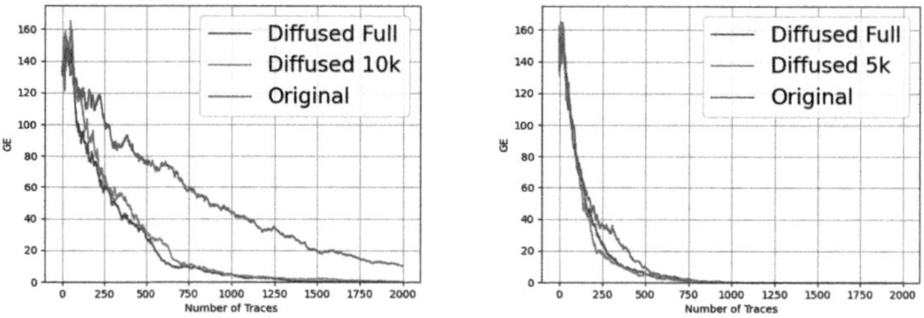

Fig. 10. CPA results for ESHARD(left) and ASCAD(right). Diffused 5k/10k refers to denoising with DDPMs trained with 5 000 or 10 000 traces, respectively

B Profiling Attacks

In this section, we explore the impact of using diffusion models to denoise traces in a profiled setting. We report the distribution of the attack performance of random models to assess the impact of using diffused traces on the difficulty of finding good model configurations.

B.1 Experimental Setup

To investigate the impact of using denoised traces for profiling attacks, we will examine the profiling complexity of attacks against several datasets. To do this, we randomly search small MLP models using the ranges in Table 4. This search is run using a varying number of profiling traces for original and diffused traces. We use two diffusion models, one trained with the maximum considered number of profiling traces and one with the minimum considered number of traces (5 000 and 25 000, and 10 000 and 70 000 for ASCADf and ESHARD, respectively).

Table 4. Hyperparameter search ranges for MLP architecture as a profiling attack model.

Hyperparameter	Options
Dense layers	1, 2, 3, 4
Neurons	10, 20, 50, 100, 200, 300, 400, 500
Activation Function	selu, relu,
Learning Rate	0.005, 0.001, 0.0005, 0.0001
Optimizer	Adam, RMSprop
Batch Size	100, 200, 300, 400, 500, 600, 700, 800, 900, 1000
Weight Initialization	random uniform, he uniform, glorot uniform

B.2 Results

Figure 11 shows the distribution of attacking results for the 100 random MLPs against ESHARD. The attack performance is significantly improved by utilizing diffused traces. For all the tested settings, we see that more of the models trained on diffused traces result in successful attacks. In fact, the distribution of attack performances at 30 000 diffused profiling traces is already better than the distribution using 70 000 original profiling traces. Additionally, in settings with lower numbers of profiling traces, only attacks using diffused traces can successfully recover the key in 2 000 traces.

In Fig. 11, the results for ASCADf are less impressive. In fact, in this case, there does not seem to be any difference between using diffused and original traces. These results indicate that for datasets where the diffusion models successfully improve SNR, it becomes significantly easier to define and train profiling

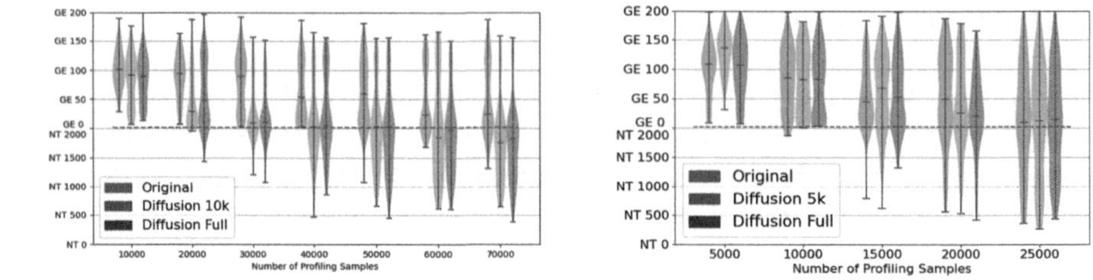

Fig. 11. Distribution of Guessing Entropy(GE)/number of traces to reach $GE = 0$ for 100 random MLPs for ESHARD(top) and ASCAD(bottom). Diffused 5k/10k refer to denoising with DDPMs trained with 5 000 or 10 000 traces respectively

Table 5. SNR peaks for varying noise schedules.

	quad	linear	cos	sig
ASCADv2	0.18	0.08	0.09	0.08
ESHARD	1.13	0.92	0.97	0.92

models that can retrieve the key, while for cases where the models do not improve SNR, the difficulty remains the same.

C Hyperparameter Evaluation

As we only utilize one architecture and hyperparameter configuration to achieve the results, we provide insights into the effects of varying this architecture/hyperparameter setup. All of these results are evaluated on the maximum SNR peaks of the first secret share of ESHARD (the mask) and the third share of ASCADv2 (the masked Sbox output). We chose these two secret shares as our standard architecture works well on these targets, and they are rather different in terms of the number of features that leak the secret shares (which can be seen in Sect. 4.3). Note that, we make the default values bold to improve readability.

C.1 Noise Schedules

The noise schedule is a key hyperparameter, and in Table 5, we see that switching to different schedules harms performance. However, for ESHARD, each schedule still significantly improves over the original SNR. For ASCADv2, none of the other schedules performed better than the original SNR, but the SNR is also not lowered. We note that other schedules may work better for different numbers of steps or other hyperparameter changes. Our results here do not mean the quadratic schedule is always best, and more specific work optimizing noise schedules for different side-channel setups could be an interesting direction for future work.

C.2 Architecture

The effects of varying the number of downsampling (and corresponding upsampling) layers are quite different for different targets. When only one downsampling layer is used, Table 6 shows that the difference from the original SNR is limited for both targets. When the number is increased, we see that for ESHARD, the SNR increases over our standard configuration, while for ASCADv2, the SNR decreases. In Table 7, varying the activation function results in somewhat decreased performance for ASCADv2, while for ESHARD, there does not seem to be much of an effect. Overall, defining an appropriate architecture is mainly the question of defining an appropriate depth. Using two blocks seems like a reasonable middle-ground for the network, not ignoring certain leakages that only contribute to a small number of features while still providing enough expressive power in the network to remove noise effectively.

Table 6. SNR peaks for varying numbers of downsampling blocks in the network.

	1	2	3	4
ASCADv2	0.08	0.18	0.08	0.02
ESHARD	0.63	1.13	1.61	1.48

Table 7. SNR peaks for varying activation functions.

	tanh	relu	selu	linear
ASCADv2	0.18	0.15	0.09	0.08
ESHARD	1.13	1.43	1.21	1.24

C.3 Training Time Hyperparameters

As can be seen in Table 8, the initial learning rate is quite an important factor. Only the standard 0.001 can effectively denoise ASCADv2. For ESHARD, it matters significantly less, and while the performance is best for our standard case, varying it still results in significant improvements over the original traces. Varying the number of steps T in Table 9 shows significant room for improvement over our baseline model. Especially for ASCADv2, we achieve another 50% improvement in peak SNR by optimizing T. Overall, this indicates that the specifying batch size and T are not too sensitive, and values in a broad range are effective. On the contrary, defining learning rates that are inappropriate can quickly result in models that do not learn anything for some targets.

Table 8. SNR peaks for varying initial learning rates.

	0.01	0.001	0.0001	0.0005	1e-05	5e-05
ASCADv2	0.02	0.18	0.05	0.08	0.02	0.04
ESHARD	0.02	1.13	0.98	0.99	0.98	0.97

Table 9. SNR peaks for varying number of steps T.

	4	8	16	32	128	512	1024
ASCADv2	0.10	0.18	0.18	0.20	0.27	0.09	0.02
ESHARD	1.27	1.28	1.13	1.15	1.16	1.53	1.56

Table 10. SNR peaks for varying numbers of epochs.

	10	25	50	100	200	400
ASCADv2	0.03	0.08	0.11	0.15	0.18	0.20
ESHARD	1.09	1.08	1.18	1.20	1.13	1.13

Table 11. SNR peaks for varying numbers of traces.

	10 000	20 000	30 000	40 000	50 000	60 000
ASCADv2	0.16	0.15	0.17	0.18	0.20	0.24
ESHARD	0.89	1.02	1.04	1.20	1.13	1.26

C.4 Epochs and Number of Traces

Table 11 shows that the models are surprisingly effective when given only a relatively small number of training traces. In fact, while using more traces obviously does not hurt, the benefits are only marginal, and for the fairly difficult case of ASCADv2's third share, we can already see a doubling of the SNR using only 10 000 traces. The number of epochs is somewhat more sensitive. In Table 10, for ESHARD, the model performance is already good with only 10 epochs, while for ASCADv2, good performance starts at 100 epochs.

References

1. Agrawal, D., Archambeault, B., Rao, J.R., Rohatgi, P.: The EM side—channel(s). In: Kaliski, B.S., Koç, K., Paar, C. (eds.) CHES 2002. LNCS, vol. 2523, pp. 29–45. Springer, Heidelberg (2003). https://doi.org/10.1007/3-540-36400-5_4
2. van den Berg, D., Slooff, T., Brohet, M., Papagiannopoulos, K., Regazzoni, F.: Data under siege: the quest for the optimal convolutional autoencoder in side-channel attacks. In: International Joint Conference on Neural Networks, IJCNN 2023, Gold Coast, Australia, 18-23 June 2023, pp. 1–9. IEEE (2023). https://doi.org/10.1109/IJCNN54540.2023.10191779

3. Boussam, S., Albillos, N.C.: Keep it unsupervised: horizontal attacks meet simple classifiers. In: Bhasin, S., Roche, T. (eds.) Smart Card Research and Advanced Applications - 22nd International Conference, CARDIS 2023, Amsterdam, The Netherlands, 14-16 November 2023, Revised Selected Papers. LNCS, vol. 14530, pp. 213–234. Springer (2023). https://doi.org/10.1007/978-3-031-54409-5_11
4. Brier, E., Clavier, C., Olivier, F.: Correlation power analysis with a leakage model. In: Joye, M., Quisquater, J.-J. (eds.) CHES 2004. LNCS, vol. 3156, pp. 16–29. Springer, Heidelberg (2004). https://doi.org/10.1007/978-3-540-28632-5_2
5. Bursztein, E., Invernizzi, L., Král, K., Moghimi, D., Picod, J.M., Zhang, M.: Generalized power attacks against crypto hardware using long-range deep learning. IACR Trans. Cryptographic Hardware Embedded Syst. **2024**(3), 472–499 (Jul 2024). https://doi.org/10.46586/tches.v2024.i3.472-499, https://tches.iacr.org/index.php/TCHES/article/view/11685
6. Cao, P., Zhang, H., Gu, D., Lu, Y., Yuan, Y.: AL-PA: cross-device profiled side-channel attack using adversarial learning. In: Oshana, R. (ed.) DAC '22: 59th ACM/IEEE Design Automation Conference, San Francisco, California, USA, 10 - 14 July 2022. pp. 691–696. ACM (2022). https://doi.org/10.1145/3489517.3530517
7. Chari, S., Rao, J.R., Rohatgi, P.: Template attacks. In: Kaliski, B.S., Koç, K., Paar, C. (eds.) CHES 2002. LNCS, vol. 2523, pp. 13–28. Springer, Heidelberg (2003). https://doi.org/10.1007/3-540-36400-5_3
8. Cristiani, V., Lecomte, M., Hiscock, T., Maurine, P.: Fit the joint moments: how to attack any masking scheme. IEEE Access **10**, 127412–127427 (2022). https://doi.org/10.1109/ACCESS.2022.3222760
9. Do, N.T., Le, P.C., Hoang, V.P., Doan, V.S., Nguyen, H.G., Pham, C.K.: Mo-dlsca: deep learning based non-profiled side channel analysis using multi-output neural networks. In: 2022 International Conference on Advanced Technologies for Communications (ATC), pp. 245–250 (2022). https://doi.org/10.1109/ATC55345.2022.9943024
10. Dobraunig, C., Eichlseder, M., Mendel, F., Schläffer, M.: Ascon v1.2: lightweight authenticated encryption and hashing. J. Cryptol. **34**(3), 33 (2021). https://doi.org/10.1007/S00145-021-09398-9
11. Genevey-Metat, C., Heuser, A., Gérard, B.: Trace-to-trace translation for SCA. In: Grosso, V., Pöppelmann, T. (eds.) Smart Card Research and Advanced Applications - 20th International Conference, CARDIS 2021, Lübeck, Germany, 11-12 November 2021, Revised Selected Papers. LNCS, vol. 13173, pp. 24–43. Springer (2021). https://doi.org/10.1007/978-3-030-97348-3_2
12. Hajra, S., Chowdhury, S., Mukhopadhyay, D.: Estranet: an efficient shift-invariant transformer network for side-channel analysis. IACR Trans. Cryptogr. Hardw. Embed. Syst. **2024**(1), 336–374 (2024). https://doi.org/10.46586/TCHES.V2024.I1.336-374
13. Hajra, S., Saha, S., Alam, M., Mukhopadhyay, D.: Transnet: shift invariant transformer network for side channel analysis. In: Batina, L., Daemen, J. (eds.) AFRICACRYPT 2022. LNCS, vol. 13503, pp. 371–396. Springer Nature Switzerland (2022). https://doi.org/10.1007/978-3-031-17433-9_16
14. Ho, J., Jain, A., Abbeel, P.: Denoising diffusion probabilistic models. In: Larochelle, H., Ranzato, M., Hadsell, R., Balcan, M., Lin, H. (eds.) Advances in Neural Information Processing Systems 33: Annual Conference on Neural Information Processing Systems 2020, NeurIPS 2020, 6-12 December 2020, virtual (2020), https://proceedings.neurips.cc/paper/2020/hash/4c5bcfec8584af0d967f1ab10179ca4b-Abstract.html

15. Hu, F., Shen, J., Vijayakumar, P.: Side-channel attacks based on multi-loss regularized denoising autoencoder. IEEE Trans. Inf. Forensics Secur. **19**, 2051–2065 (2024). https://doi.org/10.1109/TIFS.2023.3343947
16. Karayalçın, S., Krček, M., Wu, L., Picek, S., Perin, G.: It's a kind of magic: a novel conditional gan framework for efficient profiling side-channel analysis. In: Chung, K.M., Sasaki, Y. (eds.) Advances in Cryptology - ASIACRYPT 2024, pp. 99–131. Springer Nature Singapore, Singapore (2025). https://doi.org/10.1007/978-981-96-0944-4_4
17. Kim, J., Picek, S., Heuser, A., Bhasin, S., Hanjalic, A.: Make some noise. unleashing the power of convolutional neural networks for profiled side-channel analysis. IACR Trans. Cryptographic Hardware Embedded Syst., 148–179 (2019)
18. Kingma, D.P., Ba, J.: Adam: a method for stochastic optimization. In: Bengio, Y., LeCun, Y. (eds.) 3rd International Conference on Learning Representations, ICLR 2015, San Diego, CA, USA, 7-9 May 2015, Conference Track Proceedings (2015), http://arxiv.org/abs/1412.6980
19. Kocher, P.C.: Timing attacks on implementations of Diffie-Hellman, RSA, DSS, and other systems. In: Koblitz, N. (ed.) CRYPTO 1996. LNCS, vol. 1109, pp. 104–113. Springer, Heidelberg (1996). https://doi.org/10.1007/3-540-68697-5_9
20. Kocher, P., Jaffe, J., Jun, B.: Differential power analysis. In: Wiener, M. (ed.) CRYPTO 1999. LNCS, vol. 1666, pp. 388–397. Springer, Heidelberg (1999). https://doi.org/10.1007/3-540-48405-1_25
21. Krček, M., Perin, G.: Autoencoder-enabled model portability for reducing hyperparameter tuning efforts in side-channel analysis. J. Cryptogr. Eng. **14**(3), 475–497 (2024)
22. Kulkarni, P., Verneuil, V., Picek, S., Batina, L.: Order vs. chaos: a language model approach for side-channel attacks. IACR Cryptol. ePrint Arch. p. 1615 (2023). https://eprint.iacr.org/2023/1615
23. Le, T., Clédière, J., Servière, C., Lacoume, J.: Noise reduction in side channel attack using fourth-order cumulant. IEEE Trans. Inf. Forensics Secur. **2**(4), 710–720 (2007). https://doi.org/10.1109/TIFS.2007.910252
24. Lu, X., Zhang, C., Cao, P., Gu, D., Lu, H.: Pay attention to the raw traces: a deep learning architecture for end-to-end profiling attacks. IACR Trans. Cryptographic Hardware Embedded Syst. (2021)
25. Lu, Z., et al.: Scarefusion: side channel analysis data restoration with diffusion model. Microelectronics J.**156**, 106546 (2025). https://doi.org/10.1016/j.mejo.2024.106546, https://www.sciencedirect.com/science/article/pii/S1879239124002509
26. Maghrebi, H., Portigliatti, T., Prouff, E.: Breaking cryptographic implementations using deep learning techniques. In: Carlet, C., Hasan, M.A., Saraswat, V. (eds.) SPACE 2016. LNCS, vol. 10076, pp. 3–26. Springer, Cham (2016). https://doi.org/10.1007/978-3-319-49445-6_1
27. Maghrebi, H., Prouff, E.: On the use of independent component analysis to denoise side-channel measurements. In: Fan, J., Gierlichs, B. (eds.) COSADE 2018. LNCS, vol. 10815, pp. 61–81. Springer, Cham (2018). https://doi.org/10.1007/978-3-319-89641-0_4
28. Mangard, S.: Hardware Countermeasures against DPA – a statistical analysis of their effectiveness. In: Okamoto, T. (ed.) CT-RSA 2004. LNCS, vol. 2964, pp. 222–235. Springer, Heidelberg (2004). https://doi.org/10.1007/978-3-540-24660-2_18

29. Masure, L., Cristiani, V., Lecomte, M., Standaert, F.: Don't learn what you already know scheme-aware modeling for profiling side-channel analysis against masking. IACR Trans. Cryptogr. Hardw. Embed. Syst. **2023**(1), 32–59 (2023). https://doi.org/10.46586/tches.v2023.i1.32-59
30. Masure, L., Dumas, C., Prouff, E.: A comprehensive study of deep learning for side-channel analysis. IACR Trans. Cryptogr. Hardw. Embed. Syst. **2020**(1), 348–375 (2020). https://doi.org/10.13154/tches.v2020.i1.348-375
31. Masure, L., Strullu, R.: Side-channel analysis against anssi's protected AES implementation on ARM: end-to-end attacks with multi-task learning. J. Cryptogr. Eng. **13**(2), 129–147 (2023). https://doi.org/10.1007/S13389-023-00311-7
32. Moser, B.B., Shanbhag, A.S., Raue, F., Frolov, S., Palacio, S., Dengel, A.: Diffusion models, image super-resolution and everything: A survey. CoRR abs. arXiv:2401.00736 (2024). https://doi.org/10.48550/ARXIV.2401.00736
33. Mukhtar, N., Batina, L., Picek, S., Kong, Y.: Fake it till you make it: data augmentation using generative adversarial networks for all the crypto you need on small devices. In: Galbraith, S.D. (ed.) CT-RSA 2022. LNCS, vol. 13161, pp. 297–321. Springer, Cham (2022). https://doi.org/10.1007/978-3-030-95312-6_13
34. Oswald, D., Paar, C.: Improving side-channel analysis with optimal linear transforms. In: Mangard, S. (ed.) CARDIS 2012. LNCS, vol. 7771, pp. 219–233. Springer, Heidelberg (2013). https://doi.org/10.1007/978-3-642-37288-9_15
35. Perin, G., Chmielewski, L., Batina, L., Picek, S.: Keep it unsupervised: horizontal attacks meet deep learning. IACR Trans. Cryptogr. Hardw. Embed. Syst. **2021**(1), 343–372 (2021). https://doi.org/10.46586/TCHES.V2021.I1.343-372
36. Perin, G., Chmielewski, L., Picek, S.: Strength in numbers: improving generalization with ensembles in machine learning-based profiled side-channel analysis. IACR Trans. Cryptographic Hardware and Embedded Syst. **2020**(4), 337–364 (2020). https://doi.org/10.13154/tches.v2020.i4.337-364. https://tches.iacr.org/index.php/TCHES/article/view/8686
37. Perin, G., Wu, L., Picek, S.: Exploring feature selection scenarios for deep learning-based side-channel analysis. IACR Trans. Cryptographic Hardware Embedded Syst. **2022**(4), 828–861 (Aug 2022). https://doi.org/10.46586/tches.v2022.i4.828-861, https://tches.iacr.org/index.php/TCHES/article/view/9842
38. Merino Del Pozo, S., Standaert, F.-X.: Blind source separation from single measurements using singular spectrum analysis. In: Güneysu, T., Handschuh, H. (eds.) CHES 2015. LNCS, vol. 9293, pp. 42–59. Springer, Heidelberg (2015). https://doi.org/10.1007/978-3-662-48324-4_3
39. Ronneberger, O., Fischer, P., Brox, T.: U-Net: convolutional networks for biomedical image segmentation. In: Navab, N., Hornegger, J., Wells, W.M., Frangi, A.F. (eds.) MICCAI 2015. LNCS, vol. 9351, pp. 234–241. Springer, Cham (2015). https://doi.org/10.1007/978-3-319-24574-4_28
40. Savu, I., Krček, M., Perin, G., Wu, L., Picek, S.: The need for more: unsupervised side-channel analysis with single network training and multi-output regression. In: Wacquez, R., Homma, N. (eds.) Constructive Side-Channel Analysis and Secure Design, pp. 113–132. Springer Nature Switzerland, Cham (2024)
41. Schindler, W., Lemke, K., Paar, C.: A stochastic model for differential side channel cryptanalysis. In: Rao, J.R., Sunar, B. (eds.) CHES 2005. LNCS, vol. 3659, pp. 30–46. Springer, Heidelberg (2005). https://doi.org/10.1007/11545262_3
42. Timon, B.: Non-profiled deep learning-based side-channel attacks with sensitivity analysis. IACR Trans. Cryptogr. Hardw. Embed. Syst. **2019**(2), 107–131 (2019). https://doi.org/10.13154/tches.v2019.i2.107-131

43. Wang, P., et al.: Enhancing the performance of practical profiling side-channel attacks using conditional generative adversarial networks. CoRR abs arXiv:2007.05285 (2020)
44. Wu, L., Perin, G., Picek, S.: The best of two worlds: deep learning-assisted template attack. IACR Trans. Cryptogr. Hardw. Embed. Syst. **2022**(3), 413–437 (2022). https://doi.org/10.46586/TCHES.V2022.I3.413-437
45. Wu, L., Perin, G., Picek, S.: I choose you: automated hyperparameter tuning for deep learning-based side-channel analysis. IEEE Trans. Emerging Topics Comput., 1–12 (2022). https://doi.org/10.1109/TETC.2022.3218372
46. Wu, L., Perin, G., Picek, S.: Not so difficult in the end: Breaking the lookup table-based affine masking scheme. In: Carlet, C., Mandal, K., Rijmen, V. (eds.) Selected Areas in Cryptography - SAC 2023, pp. 82–96. Springer Nature Switzerland, Cham (2024). https://doi.org/10.1007/978-3-031-53368-6_5
47. Wu, L., Perin, G., Picek, S.: Weakly profiling side-channel analysis. IACR Trans. Cryptogr. Hardw. Embed. Syst. **2024**(3), 707–730 (2024). https://doi.org/10.46586/tches.v2024.i3.707-730, https://tches.iacr.org/index.php/TCHES/article/view/11901
48. Wu, L., Picek, S.: Remove some noise: On pre-processing of side-channel measurements with autoencoders. IACR Trans. Cryptogr. Hardw. Embed. Syst. **2020**(4), 389–415 (2020). https://doi.org/10.13154/tches.v2020.i4.389-415
49. Yang, G., Li, H., Ming, J., Zhou, Y.: CDAE: towards empowering denoising in side-channel analysis. In: Zhou, J., Luo, X., Shen, Q., Xu, Z. (eds.) ICICS 2019. LNCS, vol. 11999, pp. 269–286. Springer, Cham (2020). https://doi.org/10.1007/978-3-030-41579-2_16
50. Yang, L., et al.: Diffusion models: a comprehensive survey of methods and applications. ACM Comput. Surv. **56**(4), 105:1–105:39 (2024). https://doi.org/10.1145/3626235
51. Yap, T., Jap, D.: Creating from noise: Trace generations using diffusion model for side-channel attack. In: Andreoni, M. (ed.) Applied Cryptography and Network Security Workshops, pp. 102–120. Springer Nature Switzerland, Cham (2024). https://doi.org/10.1007/978-3-031-61486-6_7
52. Zaid, G., Bossuet, L., Carbone, M., Habrard, A., Venelli, A.: Conditional variational autoencoder based on stochastic attacks. IACR Trans. Cryptogr. Hardw. Embed. Syst. **2023**(2), 310–357 (2023). https://doi.org/10.46586/TCHES.V2023.I2.310-357
53. Zaid, G., Bossuet, L., Habrard, A., Venelli, A.: Methodology for efficient cnn architectures in profiling attacks. IACR Trans. Crypto. Hard. Embed. Syst. **2020**(1), 1–36 (Nov 2019). https://doi.org/10.13154/tches.v2020.i1.1-36, https://tches.iacr.org/index.php/TCHES/article/view/8391

Efficient SPA Countermeasures Using Redundant Number Representation with Application to ML-KEM

Rishub Nagpal[1(✉)], Vedad Hadžić[2], Robert Primas[2], and Stefan Mangard[1]

[1] Graz University of Technology, Graz, Austria
{rishub.nagpal,stefan.mangard}@tugraz.at
[2] Intel Labs, Portland, OR, USA
{vedad.hadzic,robert.primas}@intel.com

Abstract. Simple power analysis (SPA) attacks and their extensions, profiled and soft-analytical side-channel attacks (SASCA), represent a significant threat to the security of cryptographic devices and remain among the most powerful classes of passive side-channel attacks. In this work, we analyze how numeric representations of secrets can affect the amount of exploitable information leakage available to the adversary. We present an analysis of how mutual information changes as a result of the integer ring size relative to the machine word-size. Furthermore, we study the Redundant Number Representation (RNR) countermeasure and show that its application to ML-KEM can resist the most powerful SASCA attacks and provides a low-cost alternative to shuffling. We evaluate the performance of RNR-ML-KEM with both simulated and practical SASCA experiments on the ARM Cortex-M4 based on a worst-case attack methodology. We show that RNR-ML-KEM sufficiently renders these attacks ineffective. Finally, we evaluate the performance of the RNR-ML-KEM NTT and INTT and show that SPA security can be achieved with a 62.8% overhead for the NTT and 0% overhead for the INTT relative to the ARM Cortex-M4 reference implementation used.

Keywords: Power Analysis · Countermeasures · SASCA · ML-KEM

1 Introduction

In 2022, the National Institute of Standards and Technology (NIST) selected the CRYSTALS-Kyber [Ava+21] and CRYSTALS-Dilithium [Duc+18] to serve as the basis for new PQC standards and these algorithms were standardized as FIPS203 [ST24b] under the name ML-KEM and FIPS204 [ST24a] (ML-DSA) in August 2024.

Although these algorithms are thought to be resistant against quantum cryptanalysis, side-channel analysis (SCA) attacks still pose a threat to the security of their implementations. These attacks exploit information leakage

C. Boura et al. (Eds.): SAC 2025, LNCS 16207, pp. 753–780, 2026.
https://doi.org/10.1007/978-3-032-10536-3_28

about secret data from physical side-effects such as the power consumption, timing or electromagnetic radiation of a device computing a cryptographic algorithm [KJJ99,Koc96,QS01]. Power SCA attacks can be categorized as either simple power analysis (SPA), where an adversary inspects a small number of measurements of leaky functions ("traces"), or differential power analysis (DPA), where an adversary has access to a large number of traces. The discovery of SCA has motivated the design of countermeasures intended to minimize the amount of information leakage from these side-channels by e.g.,increasing the number of traces needed to extract secret information. Countermeasures against DPA such as masking, where sensitive variables are split into $t + 1$ randomized shares, are well-studied and proven effective [ISW03,DDF19,Cha+99]. In contrast, developing countermeasures against SPA attacks is still a challenging topic. Profiled or template attacks [CRR02] and their extensions [SLP05,CK13,CK14,Cas+23, SA08,Ren+11,Bro+19,VGS14,Mas+23] are a particularly strong class of SPA attacks which use powerful statistical models of device leakage to perform key-recovery. These attacks can circumvent masking [BS21] and can recover secrets with a single attack trace cf. [CRR02]. Countermeasures against SPA typically employ masking and randomize or shuffle the order of operations between executions to make it more difficult to perform profiling, but are costly in terms of performance [Vey+12]. SPA has been shown to be effective against several cryptographic algorithms such as the AES, RSA, ECC and post-quantum candidates including ML-KEM and Dilithium [Bol+19,KPP20,Ngo+21,Ham+21, Her+23a,Str+23,HME24,Qia+24,KPP20,Bro+24].

Lattice-based cryptography is particularly susceptible to a more optimal form of template attacks known as Soft-Analytical Side-Channel Attacks (SASCA) [VGS14]. These attacks exploit knowledge of device operations, combining leakages from multiple points in a trace into a factor graph encoding. An inference method like loopy belief propagation (BP) then computes posterior probabilities of secret-key variables based on these leakages. The Number Theoretic Transform (NTT) operation, which is essential to lattice-based cryptography efficiently, is susceptible to SASCA [PPM17,PP19,Her+23a] and shuffling countermeasures are particularly costly [Rav+20]. Hence, it is important to find SPA countermeasures for the NTT which are cheap to implement and effective against powerful attacks such as SASCA.

Related Works. Zijlstra et al. proposed applying Redundant Number Representation (RNR) to general RLWE public-key cryptographic schemes [ZBT19]. This technique randomizes secret-key coefficients with multiples of the group order to hide their values. Later, Heinz et al. showed that this technique is effective against DPA and fault attacks against ML-KEM [HP23] when using a large redundancy factor. Recently, Tosun et al. observed side-channel distinguishers in the distribution of Hamming weights due to the signed modular reduction arithmetic used in lattice-based cryptoschemes and utilized these distinguishers to enhance DPA attacks on both ML-KEM and ML-DSA [TMS24]. Although not studied by Tosun et al. , these distinguishers have huge implications on the effectiveness of SPA attacks. Previous SPA attacks on lattice cryptography in the literature may have unknowingly benefited from these distinguishers; therefore, it is essential to thoroughly study the impact these distinguishers have on SPA attacks.

Our Contributions. In this paper, we study the effectiveness of RNR against SPA attacks to better understand how this technique can reduce the amount of information leakage available to an adversary. In particular, we compare information leakage between different machine representations of data and show that there exists optimal numerical representations for storing secrets. We apply our findings to ML-KEM and show that the RNR-protected ML-KEM NTT^{-1} is resistant to state-of-the-art SASCA attacks in both simulation and practice. Our RNR-ML-KEM implementation incurs a 62.8% performance overhead to compute the NTT and 0% overhead to compute the INTT on the ARM Cortex-M4.

Concretely:

- We analyze the power side-channel leakage of arbitrary integer rings which are smaller than the machine-word size of a computing device and quantify the information leakage from this discrepancy.
- We analyze the Redundant Number Representation(RNR) countermeasure, which reduces the total information leakage by replacing a given integer ring with a larger, harmonic ring which contains multiples of the original.
- In particular, we create a RNRimplementation of ML-KEM and demonstrate its effectiveness against SASCAs in simulation and on a ARM Cortex-M4 embedded target.
- We then show that one of the best known SPA attack on ML-KEM, the k-trace attack of Hamburg et al. [Ham+21], is rendered ineffective on RNR-ML-KEM - without the need for additional countermeasures such as shuffling.
- We open-source our implementations, datasets and additional scripts for the broader SCA research community.[1]

2 Preliminaries

We provide a brief review of the ML-KEM algorithm and the Number Theoretic Transform. Following, we go into detail on modular arithmetic and the algorithms commonly implemented. Finally, we discuss Soft-Analytical Side-channel Attacks implemented with belief propagation and metrics to evaluate the attacks.

2.1 Lattice Cryptography

We briefly introduce the Module Learning with Errors (M-LWE) hard problem proposed by Langlois and Stehlé [LS15], which merges the LWE [Reg05] and Ring-LWE [LPR10] hard problems.

[1] https://github.com/rishubn/rnr-kyber-spa.

Algorithm 1. ML-KEM.PKE KeyGen [ST24b]

Output: pk, sk
1: $(\rho, \sigma) \leftarrow \texttt{SHA3-512}(\{0, 1, \ldots, 255\}^{32})$
2: $\hat{A} \leftarrow \texttt{SamplePolyMatrix}(\rho)$
3: $s \leftarrow \texttt{SamplePolyCBD}_{\eta_1}(\texttt{SHAKE-256}_{\eta_1}(\sigma, 0))$
4: $e \leftarrow \texttt{SamplePolyCBD}_{\eta_1}(\texttt{SHAKE-256}_{\eta_1}(\sigma, 1))$
5: $\hat{s} \leftarrow \mathsf{NTT}(s)$
6: $\hat{e} \leftarrow \mathsf{NTT}(e)$
7: $\hat{t} \leftarrow \hat{A} \circ \hat{s} + \hat{e}$
8: **return** $pk = (\hat{t}, \rho), sk = \hat{s}$

Algorithm 2. ML-KEM.PKE Encryption [ST24b]

Input: $pk = (\hat{t}, \rho)$, message $m \in \mathcal{R}_q$, seed $r \in \{0, 1, \ldots, 255\}^{32}$
Output: ciphertext $c = (c_1, c_2)$
1: $\hat{A} \leftarrow \texttt{SamplePolyMatrix}(\rho)$
2: $\hat{y} \leftarrow \mathsf{NTT}(\texttt{SamplePolyCBD}_{\eta_1}(\texttt{SHAKE-256}_{\eta_1}(r, 0)))$
3: $e_1 \leftarrow \texttt{SamplePolyCBD}_{\eta_1}(\texttt{SHAKE-256}_{\eta_1}(r, 1))$
4: $e_2 \leftarrow \texttt{SamplePolyCBD}_{\eta_2}(\texttt{SHAKE-256}_{\eta_2}(r, 2))$
5: $u \leftarrow \mathsf{NTT}^{-1}(\hat{A}^\mathsf{T} \circ \hat{y}) + e_1$
6: $v \leftarrow \mathsf{NTT}^{-1}(\hat{t}^\mathsf{T} \circ \hat{y}) + e_2 + m$
7: **return** $c = (\texttt{Compress}(u), \texttt{Compress}(v))$

Let $\mathbb{Z}_q$ be an integer ring modulo q and $\mathcal{R}_q = \mathbb{Z}_q[x]/(x^n + 1)$ be the polynomial ring of polynomials modulo $x^n + 1$ for some degree n. Further, let β_η denote the centered binomial distribution with parameter η, and $\mathcal{U}$ denote the uniform distribution over $\mathbb{Z}_q$. Then, the Module-LWE problem is formally defined as

$$(\boldsymbol{A}, \boldsymbol{b}) = \boldsymbol{A}^\mathsf{T}\boldsymbol{s} + \boldsymbol{e}, \tag{1}$$

with $\boldsymbol{s}$ being the secret-key, $\boldsymbol{A}$ the public matrix sampled from $\mathcal{U}$ and $\boldsymbol{e}$ an error vector sampled from β_η. The decisional M-LWE problem asserts that the tuple $(\boldsymbol{A}, \boldsymbol{b})$ is indistiguishable from a random sampling. The Kyber algorithm [Bos+18] is a public-key encryption (PKE) scheme which is now standardized as ML-KEM. Kyber is converted into a KEM via the Fujisaki-Okamoto (FO) transform [FO13, HHK17] and is conjectured to be IND-CCA2 secure. The polynomial ring in ML-KEM is parameterized with $q = 3329$ and $n = 256$ for all parameter sets. We give descriptions for the ML-KEM.PKE KeyGen (Algorithm 1), the ML-KEM.PKE Encryption (Algorithm 2) and the ML-KEM.PKE Decryption (Algorithm 3) algorithms and refer the reader to the ML-KEM specification [ST24b] for more details.

2.2 Number Theoretic Transform

The Number Theoretic Transform (NTT) is an algorithm analogous to the Discrete Fourier Transform (DFT) which allows to compute the product of two polynomials efficiently. We specify our description of the NTT on the polynomial ring of ML-KEM where the prime modulus $q = 3329$ and $n = 256$ and

Algorithm 3. ML-KEM.PKE Decryption [ST24b]

Input: ciphertext $c = (c_1, c_2)$, $sk = \hat{s}$
Output: message $m \in \mathcal{R}_q$
1: $(u, v) = (\texttt{Decompress}(c_1), \texttt{Decompress}(c_2))$
2: **return** $m = v - \mathsf{NTT}^{-1}(\hat{s}^{\mathsf{T}} \circ \mathsf{NTT}(u))$

use the explanation of [ST24b]. Since there are 128 256-th roots-of-unity but no 512-th root-of-unity, the NTT is considered partial. Therefore the polynomial $x^{256} + 1$ is factored with small polynomials of degree 2,

$$(x^{256} + 1) = \prod_{i=0}^{127} \left(x^2 - \zeta^{2i+1}\right).$$

We denote with ζ^n the n-th root-of-unity. The NTT of the polynomial a is:

$$\mathsf{NTT}(a) = \hat{a} = \hat{a}_0 + \hat{a}_1 x + \dots \hat{a}_{255} x^{255},$$

where

$$\hat{a}_i = \sum_{j=0}^{127} a_{2j} \zeta^{(2i+1)j} \qquad \text{and} \qquad \hat{a}_{2i+1} = \sum_{j=0}^{127} a_{2j+1} \zeta^{(2i+1)j}.$$

Multiplication of polynomials in the NTT domain is done by $\mathsf{NTT}^{-1}(\mathsf{NTT}(f) \circ \mathsf{NTT}(g))$. The basecase multiplication $\hat{h} = \hat{f} \circ \hat{g}$ is,

$$\hat{h}_{2i} + \hat{h}_{2i+1} x = (\hat{f}_{2i} + \hat{f}_{2i+1} x)(\hat{g}_{2i} + \hat{g}_{2i+1} x) \bmod \left(x^2 - \zeta^{2i+1}\right)$$

Implementing the NTT is similar to the DFT and common implementations utilize the Cooley-Tuckey (CT) butterfly [CT65] and the Gentleman-Sande (GS) butterfly [GS66] circuits. Hybrid designs utilize the CT butterfly on the forward pass and the GS butterfly on the inverse pass to avoid necessary bit-reversal steps. The incomplete ML-KEM NTT can be computed in seven butterfly layers.

2.3 Machine Representation of Integers

Computers natively work with integers in a finitely-sized domain $\mathbb{Z}_{2^l}$, in contrast to the infinitely large integer ring $\mathbb{Z}$ in mathematics. Here, l is usually referred to as the word size of a machine integer, and represents the number of bits needed to store the integer. Hence, an integer x is stored in a machine word as $\langle x \rangle_l = x - 2^l \left\lfloor \frac{x}{2^l} \right\rfloor$. Moreover, a stored integer can be interpreted either as *signed* or *unsigned.* The unsigned interpretation of $\langle x \rangle_l$ is $\langle x \rangle_l^+ = \langle x \rangle_l$, meaning that only integers $x \in \left[0, 2^l\right)$ have an unique representation and subsequent interpretation. The signed interpretation of $\langle x \rangle_l$ is given in two's complement, with $\langle x \rangle_l^\pm = \langle x \rangle_l - 2^l \left\lfloor \frac{\langle x \rangle_l}{2^{l-1}} \right\rfloor$, where only integers in the $x \in \left[-2^{l-1}, 2^{l-1}\right)$ have an unique representation and interpretation.

2.4 Modular Arithmetic

In this work, we are interested in addition and multiplication in modular integer rings $\mathbb{Z}_q$. More precisely, we are especially interested in rings $\mathbb{Z}_q$ where a canonical representation of each element fits into a machine word, e.g.,$\forall x \in \mathbb{Z}_q : \langle x \rangle_l^+ = x$. For more efficient computation, we often also impose the additional limitation $q \leq 2^{l-1}$ to ensure that additions do not overflow.

The results of an addition or multiplication are not necessarily the canonical representation of an element in $\mathbb{Z}_q$. In general, for $x, y \in [0, 2^{l-1})$, we have the (loose) result ranges $z = x + y \in [0, 2^l)$ and $w = x \cdot y \in [0, 2^{2l})$. While this preserves congruence, i.e.,$\langle z \rangle_l^+ = \langle x + y \rangle_l^+ \equiv x + y \mod q$ and $\langle w \rangle_{2l}^+ = \langle x \cdot y \rangle_{2l}^+ \equiv xy \mod q$, one must reduce the results back to the appropriate range $[0, 2^{l-1})$ in order to perform further operations. Commonly, due to the methods used for reduction, one goes a step further and reduces the results into their canonical represesentation, e.g.,the range $[0, q)$, or a representation with at most one redundant encoding e.g.,the range $[0, 2q)$. Effectively, such a reduction would compute z, respectively w as

$$z = (x + y) - q \left\lfloor \frac{x + y}{q} \right\rfloor \qquad \text{and} \qquad w = (xy) - q \left\lfloor \frac{xy}{q} \right\rfloor .$$

While we have illustrated these operations in modular arithmetic with the unsigned canonical representations, it is also possible to represent the elements of $\mathbb{Z}_q$ as signed numbers in the range $\left[-\left\lfloor \frac{q}{2} \right\rfloor, \left\lceil \frac{q}{2} \right\rceil\right)$, cf.Hua et al. [Hua+22, Hua+24]. Here, having $x, y \in [-2^{l-2}, 2^{l-2})$ is enough to prevent overflows or underflows in $z = x + y$ and $w = x \cdot y$. However, reductions are still necessary in order to establish these congruence invariants across multiple modular arithmetic operations.

In cryptographic implementations, the modular reduction is implemented using contant-time algorithms such as the ones of Barrett's [Bar86], Montgomery's [Mon85] and, most recently, Plantard's [Hua+22]. For lattice cryptography, the signed variants of these algorithms are perferred for computing the NTT for performance reasons. A detailed description of the Barrett and Montgomery reduction algorithms is given in Appendix A.

2.5 Soft-Analytical Side-Channel Attacks

Soft-Analytical Side-Channel Attacks (SASCAs) [VGS14] perform low-trace key-recovery attacks on cryptographic implementations. SASCAs improve upon template attacks by leveraging greater side-channel leakage using algorithmic knowledge and probabilistic modeling. In SASCAs, the algorithm is represented as a *factor graph*, encoding variables as circles and algorithmic operations as squares (called factors), connected by edges to illustrate their relationships. Side-channel leakage is incorporated through leakage factors which assign probability distributions to variables. An inference method, such as belief propagation [Pea82], computes marginal probabilities for secret-key variables which can then be used in a rank estimation. We formally describe the *loopy* belief propagation variant based on [VGS14, MM09, Nag+25] and refer readers there for additional details.

Let $\boldsymbol{x}$ be a set of n random variables, $\boldsymbol{x} \equiv \{x_i\}_{i=1,\ldots,n}$. The joint probability of the set can be expressed as the factorization,

$$P(\boldsymbol{x}) = \frac{1}{Z} \prod_{j=1}^{m} f_j(\boldsymbol{x}_I(j)).$$

Here, $\boldsymbol{x}_{I(j)}$ is the subset of variables in $\boldsymbol{x}$ which correspond to the factor f_j and Z is a normalization constant. The corresponding factor graph $\mathcal{G} = (\boldsymbol{x}, \boldsymbol{f}, \boldsymbol{e})$ is a bipartite graph which consists of the variable nodes $\boldsymbol{x}$, factor nodes $\boldsymbol{f}$ and edges $\boldsymbol{e}$ which connect subsets $\boldsymbol{x}_{I(j)}$ to f_j.

Marginal probability distributions of variable nodes are computed iteratively using belief propagation [Pea82]. Updates occur in two steps per iteration t: variables send messages to factors (Eq. 2), then factors send messages back to variables (Eq. 3), repeating until convergence.

$$\mu_{(t+1)}^{x_i \to f_j} = \prod_{j' \in I(i) \setminus j} \mu_{(t)}^{f_{j'} \to x_i}. \tag{2}$$

$$\mu_{(t)}^{f_j \to x_i} = \sum_{k \in I(j) \setminus i} f_j(\boldsymbol{x}_k) \prod_{i' \in I(j) \setminus i} \mu_{(t)}^{x_{i'} \to f_j}. \tag{3}$$

Finally, the marginal for a variable $\Pr[X_i = x_i]$ is computed as the product of all incoming messages:

$$\Pr[X_i = x_i] = \prod_{\{j | i \in I(j)\}} \mu^{f_j \to x_i}. \tag{4}$$

2.6 Information Theoretic Metrics

The Mutual Information (MI) metric relates the amount of information learned about a random variable X with its true leakage distribution $\mathcal{L}$.

$$\mathrm{I}[X; L] = \mathrm{H}[X] + \sum_{x \in \mathcal{X}} \Pr[x] \sum_{\ell \in \mathcal{L}} \Pr[\ell \mid x] \cdot \log_2 \Pr[x \mid \ell] \tag{5}$$

If the true leakage distribution is unknown, then a model of the leakage distribution may be used for the quantity $\Pr[\ell \mid x]$. If the leakage model differs from the true leakage, then the MI cannot be captured, instead the Perceived Information (PI) can be computed:

$$\mathrm{PI}[X; L] = \mathrm{H}[X] + \sum_{x \in \mathcal{X}} \Pr[x] \sum_{l \in \mathcal{L}_m} \Pr[l \mid x] \cdot \log_2 \Pr[x \mid l] \tag{6}$$

The PI is a lower bound of the MI [Bro+19] that converges to the MI if the model can match the true leakage distribution [Mas+23].

3 Redundant Number Representation(RNR)

In this section, we first analyze the connection between the integer ring $\mathbb{Z}_q$, its representation, and the information gain an adversary receives through Hamming weights. Afterwards, we discuss ways of reducing the information leaked through Hamming weight, and analyze the countermeasure called Redundant Number Representation(RNR), which significantly reduces the leakage, effectively eliminating it for ring sizes q far lower than the maximal representable integers in an l-bit machine word.

3.1 Information Gain from Hamming Weights

In the Hamming weight leakage model we assume that the sum of all machine-word bits are leaked to an adversary through the power side channel. In the past, this model, while crude, has proven to closely match the realities of physical observations. While noisy, observations of both power consumption and EM field perturbations strongly correlate with the number of '1' bits in the data processed by a CPU.

However, the information contained within the Hamming weight of a machine word is not constant and heavily depends on the actual data. For example, if we know that a cryptographic algorithm works with bits, and each bit is stored in a separate machine word, the information revealed through the Hamming weight, and thus power side channels, is perfect, i.e.,for $X \in \{0,1\}$, we have $\mathrm{W}(X) = X$ and thus $\mathrm{I}[X;\mathrm{W}(X)] = 1$. On the contrary, for cryptographic algorithms that work with large integer rings, e.g.,filling the whole machine word with $X \in \mathbb{Z}_{2^l}$, the Hamming weight $\mathrm{W}(X)$ leaks more information about X in an absolute sense, with $\mathrm{I}[X;\mathrm{W}(X)] \approx 3$ for $l = 16$, but this is due to the high starting entropy of X, with $\mathrm{H}[X] = l = 16$. Here, the relative information gain $\mathrm{I}[X;\mathrm{W}(X)]/\mathrm{H}[X]$ is much lower.

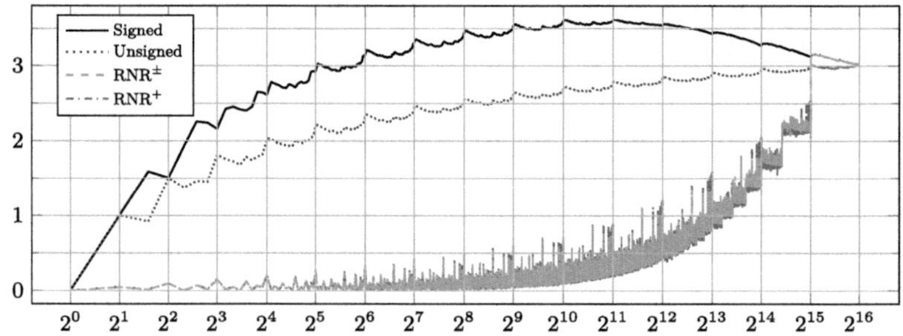

Fig. 1. Mutual information $\mathrm{I}[X;\mathrm{W}(X)]$ for an integer ring element $X \in \mathbb{Z}_q$ and its Hamming weight $\mathrm{W}(X)$ in 16-bit machine words, for different ring sizes $q \in [1, 2^{16})$.

Additionally, the representation of the integer ring $\mathbb{Z}_q$ matters, that is, whether we encode it in an unsigned manner as $X \in [0, q)$ or in a signed manner with $X \in \left[-\left\lfloor\frac{q}{2}\right\rfloor, \left\lceil\frac{q}{2}\right\rceil\right)$. Here, due to the nature of two's complement encoding for negative numbers, we expect that, for $q \ll 2^l$, the Hamming weight $\mathrm{W}(X)$ directly reveals whether $X < 0$ or $X \geq 0$, i.e.,about one additional bit of information about X. Figure 1 illustrates the amount of information that $\mathrm{W}(X)$ leaks about X for $q \in \left[1, 2^l\right)$ and a machine-word size of $l = 16$.

In almost all cases, the signed integer ring representation leaks more information through the Hamming weight. Prior work by Tosun et al. [TMS24] was the first to observe this discrepancy and use it to build better distinguishers for differential power analysis attacks on lattice-based post-quantum standardization candidates which perform computations in prime fields, i.e.,where q is a prime number.

3.2 Reducing the Mutual Information

From the identity $\mathrm{I}[X; \mathrm{W}(X)] = \mathrm{H}[\mathrm{W}(X)] - \mathrm{H}[\mathrm{W}(X) \mid X]$, it is apparent that in order to reduce $\mathrm{I}[X; \mathrm{W}(X)]$, one must either:

1. decrease the entropy $\mathrm{H}[\mathrm{W}(X)]$, i.e.,distribute the weights more evenly, or
2. increase the conditional entropy $\mathrm{H}[\mathrm{W}(X) \mid X]$, i.e.,make it less certain what the weight $\mathrm{W}(X)$ is for any $X \in \mathbb{Z}_q$.

Here, for the encoding range $[q_\mathrm{l}, q_\mathrm{h})$ representing $\mathbb{Z}_q$, the entropies $\mathrm{H}[\mathrm{W}(X)]$ and $\mathrm{H}[\mathrm{W}(X) \mid X]$ are defined as

$$\mathrm{H}[\mathrm{W}(X)] = -\sum_{w=0}^{l} \Pr[\mathrm{W}(X) = w] \log_2 (\Pr[\mathrm{W}(X) = w]) \quad \text{and}$$

$$\mathrm{H}[\mathrm{W}(X) \mid X] = \sum_{x \in [0,q)} \Pr[X \equiv x \bmod q]\, \mathrm{H}[\mathrm{W}(X) \mid X \equiv x \bmod q], \quad ;$$

$$\mathrm{H}[\mathrm{W}(X) \mid X \equiv x \bmod q] = -\sum_{w=0}^{l} \Pr[\mathrm{W}(X) = w \mid X \equiv x \bmod q] \cdot \log_2 (\Pr[\mathrm{W}(X) = w \mid X \equiv x \bmod q]).$$

Additionally, the probabilities, assuming X is uniformly distributed in $[q_\mathrm{l}, q_\mathrm{h})$, are

$$\Pr[\mathrm{W}(X) = w] = \frac{|\{x \mid q_\mathrm{l} \leq x < q_\mathrm{h}, \mathrm{W}(x) = w\}|}{q_\mathrm{h} - q_\mathrm{l}},$$

$$\Pr[X \equiv x \bmod q] = \frac{|\{x' \mid q_\mathrm{l} \leq x' < q_\mathrm{h}, x' \equiv x \bmod q\}|}{q_\mathrm{h} - q_\mathrm{l}}, \quad \text{and}$$

$$\Pr[\mathrm{W}(X) = w \mid X \equiv x \bmod q] = \frac{|\{x' \mid q_\mathrm{l} \leq x' < q_\mathrm{h}, \mathrm{W}(x') = w, x' \equiv x \bmod q\}|}{|\{x' \mid q_\mathrm{l} \leq x' < q_\mathrm{h}, x' \equiv x \bmod q\}|}.$$

From this perspective, we also see why both the unsigned encoding with $[q_\mathrm{l}, q_\mathrm{h}) = [0, q)$ and the signed encoding $[q_\mathrm{l}, q_\mathrm{h}) = \left[-\left\lfloor\frac{q}{2}\right\rfloor, \left\lceil\frac{q}{2}\right\rceil\right)$ lead to high mutual information $\mathrm{I}[X; \mathrm{W}(X)] = \mathrm{H}[\mathrm{W}(X)]$, since $\mathrm{H}[\mathrm{W}(X) \mid X] = 0$ because

$\mathrm{W}(X)$ is completely determined by X, with $\Pr[\mathrm{W}(X) = w \mid X \equiv x \bmod q] \in \{0, 1\}$. Moreover, it is apparent that the signed encoding reveals more information in most cases, as the probabilities $\Pr[\mathrm{W}(X) = w]$ are better distributed, i.e.,look more uniform, leading to a larger $\mathrm{H}[\mathrm{W}(X)]$.

In order to increase $\mathrm{H}[\mathrm{W}(X) \mid X]$, one must necessarily get rid of the constraint that $q_{\mathrm{h}} - q_{\mathrm{l}} = q$, i.e.,one must allow for redundant encodings of $\mathbb{Z}_q$, where each remainder class $x \in [0, q)$ has multiple $x' \in [q_{\mathrm{l}}, q_{\mathrm{h}})$ such that $x' \equiv x \bmod q$. More importantly, one must redefine the operations of addition and multiplication, with the associated modular reductions, such that the results remain in the full range $[q_{\mathrm{l}}, q_{\mathrm{h}})$.

3.3 The Redundant Number Representation(RNR) Countermeasure

As outlined in the previous section, one can reduce the information about elements of $X \in \mathbb{Z}_q$ that is leaked through Hamming weights $\mathrm{W}(X)$, by increasing the range domain $[q_{\mathrm{l}}, q_{\mathrm{h}})$ and thus also increasing the entropy $\mathrm{H}[\mathrm{W}(X) \mid X \equiv x \bmod q]$.

In the following, we describe an implementation of Redundant Number Representation(RNR), a countermeasure that achieves such an increased conditional entropy by computing in the integer ring $\mathbb{Z}_{\eta q}$ instead of $\mathbb{Z}_q$, where η is a positive integer. Here, the workflow of RNRis as follows:

1. Start with algorithm that works in integer ring $\mathbb{Z}_q$, with inputs $\mathbf{X} = (X_i)_{i=0}^{n}$ and outputs $\mathbf{Y} = (Y_i)_{i=0}^{m}$, where $X_i, Y_i \in \mathbb{Z}_q$.
2. Determine η as the largest positive integer such that the algorithm operations do not overflow or underflow and break the congruences if they were computed in $\mathbb{Z}_{\eta q}$.
3. Encode algorithm inputs X_i as $X_i' \in \mathbb{Z}_{\eta q}$, where $X_i' = X_i + Kq$ and K is sampled uniformly at random from $[0, \eta)$ for unsigned representations and from $\left[\left\lfloor -\frac{\eta}{2} \right\rfloor, \left\lceil \frac{\eta}{2} \right\rceil\right)$ for signed representations.
4. Compute the algorithm while all operations are over $\mathbb{Z}_{\eta q}$.
5. Decode the outputs Y_i' as $Y_i = Y_i' - q \left\lfloor \frac{Y_i'}{q} \right\rfloor$, and return them as the results of the algorithm.

Figure 1 shows the advantage of employing RNR, where we set $\eta = \left\lfloor \frac{2^l - 1}{q} \right\rfloor$ because there are no operations computed. Impressively, RNRmanages to virtually eliminate any information gained about X by knowing $\mathrm{W}(X)$ for $q \leq 2^{l/2}$, with $\mathrm{I}[X; \mathrm{W}(X)] < 0.5$. After that point, for larger ring sizes q, the mutual information increases, matching the non-RNRcase at $q = 2^{l-1}$.

In the rest of this work, we discuss an application of RNRto the ML-KEM algorithm and show that RNRcompletely mitigates SASCAs.

4 Case Study: Applying Redundant Number Representationto the ML-KEM NTT

In this section, we begin with an analysis of the information leakage present in the ML-KEM NTT^{-1}. Then, we compare between simulated SASCAs of the NTT^{-1} assuming signed and unsigned Hamming weight leakage using an attack similar to the worst-case k-trace attack of Hamburg et al. [Ham+21]. Finally, we describe how to implement RNR-protected ML-KEM and show that it sufficiently thwarts the attack.

Mutual Information Analysis of the ML-KEM NTT. As described in Subsect. 2.1, ML-KEM is parameterized on a polynomial ring parameterized by $n = 256$ and prime module $q = 3329$. The NTT function is an incomplete NTT which takes as input a vector of the 256 polynomial coefficients in $\boldsymbol{a} = (a_i)_{i=0}^{255}, a_i \in \mathbb{Z}_q$ and consists of seven butterfly layers. Furthermore, efficient implementations of the NTT store polynomial coefficients as signed 16-bit machine words e.g.,$\langle a_i \rangle_{16}^{\pm}$ for performance reasons (cf.Algorithm 5, Algorithm 7, [Hua+22]). Moreover, the NTT and its inverse directly operate on the secret-key and thus requires protections (cf.Algorithm 1, Algorithm 3).

The coefficients of an input polynomial can be modeled with a vector of 256 random variables, $\boldsymbol{X} = (X_i)_{i=0}^{255}$ where $X_i \in \mathbb{Z}_q$. The entropy of each X_i is, $\mathrm{H}[X_i] \approx 11.701$ bits, and the total entropy an adversary needs to eliminate is, $\mathrm{H}[\boldsymbol{X}] = \sum_{\boldsymbol{X}} \mathrm{H}[X_i] \approx 2995.4$ bits. The mutual information between a coefficient X_i and its Hamming weight $\mathrm{I}[X_i; \mathrm{W}(X_i)] \approx 3.561$ bits in a signed 16-bit machine word setting, $\langle a_i \rangle_{16}^{\pm}$. Thus, an adversary learns $\sum_{\boldsymbol{X}} \mathrm{I}[X_i; \mathrm{W}(X_i)] \approx 911.6$ bits of information from the Hamming weights of the coefficients alone, and the remaining entropy conditioned on this knowledge that must be eliminated is $\mathrm{H}[\boldsymbol{X}] - \sum_{\boldsymbol{X}} \mathrm{I}[X_i; \mathrm{W}(X_i)] \approx 2083.8$ bits. Following the analysis of Sect. 3, storing coefficient as unsigned words, $\langle a_i \rangle_{16}$ would reduce the amount of information learned from the Hamming weight to 2.756 bits and thus the total (conditional) entropy to eliminate is raised to $\approx$2289.9 bits. Thus, switching from signed to unsigned storage of polynomial coefficients would reduce the information leakage from Hamming weights by $\approx$206.092 bits in total.

The NTT butterfly operations further leak information jointly about the polynomial coefficient operands. Let $A, B \in \mathbb{Z}_q$ be random variables which represent butterfly inputs and $A', B' \in \mathbb{Z}_q$ represent butterfly outputs. The joint entropy of the inputs is, $\mathrm{H}[A, B] = \log_2 q^2 \approx 23.402$ bits. By enumerating the joint Hamming weight distribution of every possible input (A, B) and output (A', B') pairs, the information learned about A, B from knowing the Hamming weights $\mathrm{W}(A), \mathrm{W}(B), \mathrm{W}(A'), \mathrm{W}(B')$ is,

$$\mathrm{I}[A, B; \mathrm{W}(A), \mathrm{W}(B), \mathrm{W}(A'), \mathrm{W}(B')] \approx 13.879\, \mathit{bits}$$

for signed and $\approx$10.877 bits for unsigned representations of the integers. It holds that A and B are independent considering that the input polynomial coefficients are randomly sampled, then the adversary learns an additional $\approx$1.5 bits about each coefficient from signing after the first layer of butterflies from the Hamming weights.

4.1 Comparing SASCAs on Different Machine Representations

SASCAs on ML-KEM typically exploit the (inverse-)NTT steps and such attacks have been well-studied [PPM17,PP19,Ham+21,AER23]. The k-trace attack of Hamburg et al. [Ham+21] describes a methodology to perform private-key recovery efficiently using a decryption oracle. In the attack, ciphertexts are crafted such that a chosen number of polynomial coefficients will be equal to zero in the NTT domain. Hence, the input to the NTT^{-1} transformation will be a sparse vector that is the product of the secret-key and the ciphertext NTT-polynomials: $\mathsf{NTT}^{-1}(\hat{s} \circ \mathsf{NTT}(u))$. Then, combined with side-channel information, an adversary can perform an efficient attack e.g.,SASCA, to recover the NTT^{-1} sparse input coefficients and solve for the secret-key. In our experimental analysis, we adapt this attack under the simplified assumption that successfully recovering only a block of 32 non-zero contiguous coefficients is sufficient. This scenario, originally applicable only to Kyber1024 in Hamburg et al.'s work, was chosen for its effectiveness in high-noise cases, which better allows to interpolate the effectiveness of the RNR countermeasure. Furthermore, it assumes a more powerful adversary requiring less profiling and attack effort. In our setting, an adversary needs to eliminate ≈374.4 bits of entropy in total.

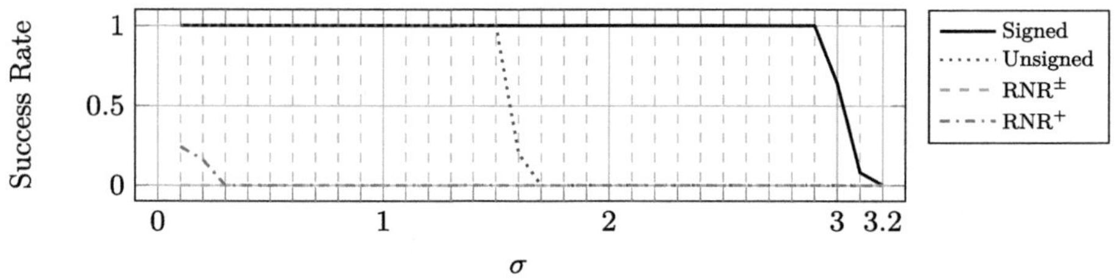

Fig. 2. SASCA on the signed, unsigned and the corresponding RNRvariants of the ML-KEM NTT^{-1} using simulated leakage traces.

Simulating SASCAs. As a starting point, we simulated SASCAs on the ML-KEM NTT^{-1} using leakages generated from a Hamming weight leakage model. In this model, a leakage trace, ℓ, is generated from the Hamming weight of an intermediate, x, plus the addition of normally distributed noise with mean zero and standard deviation parameterized by σ, i.e.,$\ell = \mathrm{HW}(x) + \mathcal{N}(0, \sigma)$. The factor graph model of the NTT^{-1} consists of variable nodes representing the input coefficients followed by the 7-layers GS-butterfly layers. We merge the arithmetic butterfly operations into a single butterfly factor based on the work Pessl et al. , who showed that this improves the outcome of the belief propagation by eliminating small loops [PP19].

Table 1. Parameter sets for implementing RNR-ML-KEM variants

Parameter	RNR^+	$RNR^\pm$
η	5	9
Barrett Radix R	2^{31}	2^{29}
Montgomery q^{-1}	39987	−22215

In total, the factor graph contains 1792 factors.

In our experiments, we compute the NTT^{-1} on a random sparse input vector with 32 contiguous non-zero values, $\boldsymbol{x} = \left(x_0, \dots x_{31}, \{0\}^{224}\right)$ with $x_i \in \mathbb{Z}_q$. We generate simulated Hamming weight leakages of the input vector and of the vector after each butterfly layer in the NTT^{-1} for a given machine representation. The leakages are assigned to the leakage factors in the factor graph and then we run belief propagation for 25 iterations and use no additional heuristics, as recommended by Nagpal et al. [Nag+25]. After BP, we compute the ranks of the marginal distributions for each of the non-zero input coefficients and the attack is considered successful if their sum is zero. In Fig. 2, we compare the impact of different machine representations on the SASCA. We report the average success rate of 25 SASCA experiments for noise levels $0.1 \leq \sigma \leq 3.2$ in increments of 0.1. The SASCA performs demonstrably better for signed storage: It achieves a 100% success rate until $\sigma \geq 3.0$. In contrast, the SASCA attacking unsigned storage does not fair so well: The performance of the attack degrades significantly when $\sigma \geq 1.6$. The implications of these results indicates that the faster performance of the NTT from using the signed machine storage comes at the cost of security. Overall, the total information available to the adversary is decreased by 25.7 bits by the change from signed to unsigned machine storage.

4.2 RNR-ML-KEM

From Sect. 3, it is clear that the ML-KEM integer field $\mathbb{Z}_q$ is an ideal candidate for protection with RNRsince the prime modulus is much smaller than the maximum representable integer in both signed and unsigned 16-bit machine word sizes. To do so, we define a larger integer ring whose module is the product of the ML-KEM prime and an odd integer, η, such that $\eta q < 2^l$. We propose signed and unsigned variants, denoted as $RNR^\pm$-ML-KEM and RNR^+-ML-KEM, with parameters $\eta^\pm$ and η^+ respectively. Here, according to the description of RNRin Subsect. 3.3 we must choose $\eta^\pm$ and η^+ in such a way that no overflows occur during the computation of the forward and inverse NTT, as well as other operations in ML-KEM. The butterfly operation in the forward NTT takes coefficients a and b, as well as a root of unity ζ, and produces the results $a' \equiv a + b\zeta \mod p$ and $b' \equiv a - b\zeta \mod p$.

Signed Case. For the signed case, assume that $a, b \in [-c, c]$ and $\zeta \in [-z, z]$, and that $b\zeta$ is reduced with the signed Montgomery reduction to get the term t.

According to the definition of Montgomery reduction, the result t is in the range $[-u, u]$, with $u = \frac{cz}{2^{16}} + \frac{\eta^{\pm}q}{2}$. The results a', b' of the butterfly operation are thus in the range $[-c-u, c+u]$. In the first layer of the forward NTT operation, we have $c = \frac{\eta^{\pm}q}{2}$ and $z = \frac{q}{2}$. We can then determine the upper bound for $\eta^{\pm}$ by enforcing that the computation of a' and b' does not overflow, i.e.,$c + u < 2^{15}$. Therefore,

$$\begin{aligned} \frac{\eta^{\pm}q}{2} + \left(\frac{\frac{\eta^{\pm}q}{2}\frac{q}{2}}{2^{16}} + \frac{\eta^{\pm}q}{2} \right) &< 2^{15} \\ \eta^{\pm} \cdot \left(q + \frac{q^2}{2^{18}} \right) &< 2^{15} \\ \eta^{\pm} &< \frac{2^{33}}{2^{18}q + q^2} < 10 \end{aligned} \quad (7)$$

Hence, one can pick any $\eta^{\pm} \in [1, 9]$. After performing a similar computation for the inverse NTT and getting the same positive integer range for $\eta^{\pm}$, we pick $\eta^{\pm} := 9$ for our implementation. Importantly, this forces us to perform a Barret reduction on a' and b' in the forward NTT butterfly operation to maintain the invariant $a, b \in [-c, c]$ for the next layer of the forward NTT. For the inverse NTT, one can perform fixpoint-based derivation to show that output b' produced via Montgomery reduction does not need to be additionally reduced via a Barrett reduction. For smaller choices of $\eta^{\pm}$, one may have to perform a Barret reduction only after a number forward or inverse NTT layers, e.g.,in the conventional implementation with $\eta^{\pm} = 1$, the forward NTT only performs a Barrett reduction after the last NTT layer.

Unsigned Case. For the unsigned case, the considerations are similar. Assume that $a, b \in [0, c]$ and $\zeta \in [0, z]$, and that t is the result of $b\zeta$ reduced with the unsigned Montgomery reduction. Consequently, t is in the range $[0, u]$, with $u = \frac{cz}{2^{16}} + \eta^{+}q$. We again determine the upper bound on η^{+} by enforcing that the computation of a' and b' does not overflow. We compute a' as usual, and therefore have the constraint $c+u < 2^{16}$, while b' must be cmoputed as $b' = a + \left(\left\lceil \frac{u}{q} \right\rceil q - t \right)$ to prevent underflows, and hence getting the constraint $c + \left(\left\lceil \frac{u}{q} \right\rceil q - t \right) < c + u + q < 2^{16}$. For the first layer, assuming $c = \eta^{+}q$ and $z = q$, we have

$$\begin{aligned} \eta^{+}q + \left(\frac{\eta^{+}q^2}{2^{16}} + \eta^{+}q \right) + q &< 2^{16} \\ \eta^{+} \cdot \left(2q + \frac{q^2}{2^{16}} \right) &< 2^{16} - q \\ \eta^{+} &< \frac{2^{32} - 2^{16}q}{2^{17}q + q^2} < 10 \end{aligned} \quad (8)$$

A similar analysis of the butterfly operation in the inverse NTT confirms that $\eta^{+} \in [1, 9]$, and thus we can choose $\eta^{+} := 9$ and perform necessary

Barrett reductions after additions and subtractions. Applying RNR to ML-KEM is straightforward, as it does not require additional randomness or operations: It requires changes only to the rejection sampling used in the functions `GeneratePolyMatrix`, `SamplePolyCBD` in Algorithm 1 and Algorithm 2 such that it outputs coefficients in $\mathbb{Z}_{\eta q}$ instead of $\mathbb{Z}_q$, and to modify the modular reduction parameters. As stated above, for larger η, it may be necessary to reduce intermediate additions and subtractions. We give pseudocode for implementing signed and unsigned RNR-variants of the $\mathsf{NTT}/\mathsf{NTT}^{-1}$ in Appendix B. With the above analysis, we use the parameter sets given in Table 1 for our RNR to ML-KEM implementations discussed in the rest of this work. Analyzing the information learned from Hamming weights similarly to the beginning of Sect. 4, RNRcoefficients have greater entropy: $\approx$14.871 bits for $X \in \mathbb{Z}_{\eta^{\pm}q}$ and 14.023 bits for $X \in \mathbb{Z}_{\eta^{+}q}$, respectively. On the other hand, RNRcoefficients exhibits far less information leakage: 0.888 bits for $X \in \mathbb{Z}_{\eta^{\pm}q}$ (1.219 bits in $\mathbb{Z}_{\eta^{+}q}$ resp.). The difference in leakage between RNRvariants is due to the smaller gap between storing integers integers in $\mathbb{Z}_{\eta^{\pm}q}$ with the signed storage,

$$2^{16} - \eta^{+}q > 2^{16-1} - \eta^{\pm}q.$$

Revisiting the NTT butterfly analysis, the joint entropy for two random variables representing integer coefficients in $\mathbb{Z}_{\eta^{\pm}q}$ is $\mathrm{H}[A, B]$ $\approx$29.741 bits ($\approx$28.046 bits for $\mathbb{Z}_{\eta^{+}q}$ resp.) and the information learned from knowing the Hamming weights of $A, B, A', B' \in \mathbb{Z}_{\eta q}$ is,

$$\mathrm{I}\left[A, B; \mathrm{W}(A), \mathrm{W}(B), \mathrm{W}(A')\, \mathrm{W}(B')\right] \approx 12.549\, bits$$

for coefficients in $\mathbb{Z}_{\eta^{\pm}q}$ ($\approx$11.744 bits in $\mathbb{Z}_{\eta^{+}q}$ resp.). The information learned from the first butterfly layer due to signed representations is reduced to 0.804 bits, while at the same time, the overall entropy is higher. We next evaluated both RNR-ML-KEM variants with the simulated SASCA experiments of Subsect. 4.1, also depected in Fig. 2. For all noise levels, the $RNR^{\pm}$variant renders the attack completely ineffective. When Hamming weights are known with certainty ($\sigma \leq 0.1$), attacks on RNR^{+}-ML-KEM succeed about 25% of the time. Compared to the experiments on the unprotected ML-KEM, the experiments show that RNRis effective at mitigating the attacks.

5 Experimental Analysis of RNR

In this section, we evaluate the effectiveness of the RNRcountermeasure against profiled SASCA attacks using both simulated and ARM Cortex-M4 traces of the reference ML-KEM NTT implementation. In both simulated and practical scenarios, we analyze the *signed*, *unsigned*,$RNR^{\pm}$ and RNR^{+} NTT implementations discussed in the previous sections. As in Subsect. 4.1, we perform the same chosen-ciphertext attack of Hamburg et al. [Ham+21] with the same assumptions.

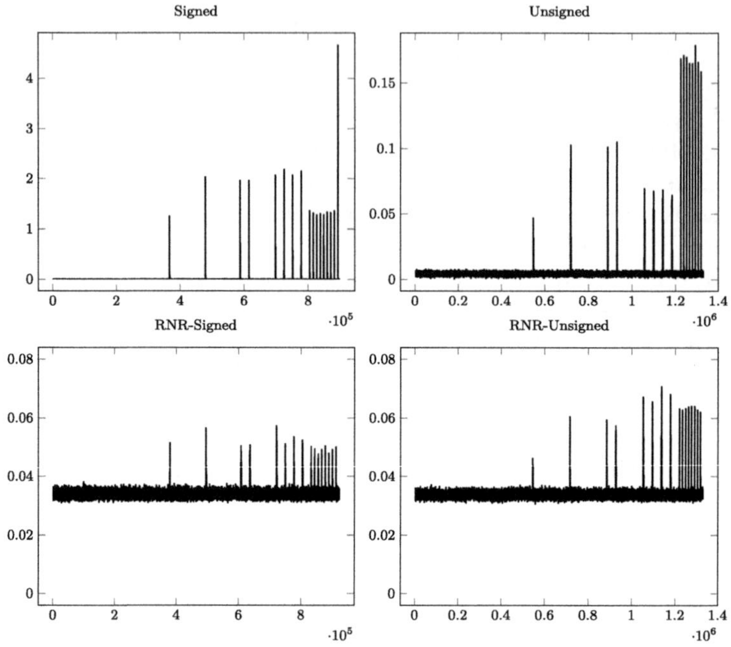

Fig. 3. The SNR of the first intermediate in the third layer of the NTT^{-1} computed from 100 000 profiling traces.

5.1 Attacking RNR-ML-KEM on the ARM Cortex-M4

To better understand how RNRperforms on real devices, we analyzed the four ML-KEM NTT implementations on the ARM Cortex-M4. Our experimental setup uses the Chipwhisperer CW308 UFO board [Inc24] with the STM32F303 target measured by the Picoscope 6404C oscilloscope. The measurement probe is amplified via a 20dB external LNA. The target is clocked at 10MHz and synchronized to the oscilloscope sampling frequency. We measure the full NTT^{-1} operation.

Profiling. The seven-layer NTT^{-1} used in ML-KEM, including the input vector, has 1792 intermediates which can be potentially profiled. We assume that only the first 32 intermediates in the input to the NTT^{-1} are non-zero. This leads to several interesting effects which benefit the profiling. First, the zeroed intermediates are known with absolute certainty and templates do not need to be constructed for those positions. Second, when a zeroed intermediate is an operand to a GS-butterfly, the result is either the unchanged or inverted input (prior to the ζ-multiplication). Thus the same value can appear in subsequent layers of the NTT^{-1} causing an "amplification" effect which can be exploited for a particular intermediate and results in a stronger template. Using both of these facts, we reduced the number of needed templates to 864 and the quality of templates in deeper layers of the NTT^{-1} is much better than shallow layers.

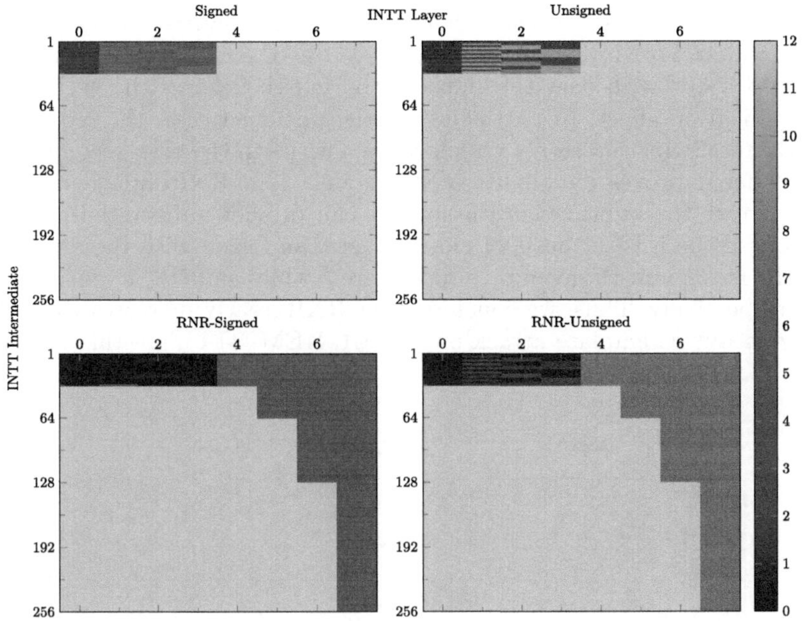

Fig. 4. The mean PI of the leakage models for all four cases as a result of profiling. We computed for nine levels of intermediates of the NTT^{-1}: The input, the seven layers of GS butterflies and the final finite-field multiplication. The quantities are given within $\pm$ 0.1 bits where possible with 95% confidence.

For each attack case, we built our templates as follows. We collected 100 000 profiling traces of the NTT^{-1} where the first 32 intermediate were random and the rest zeroed. Then, we computed the signal-to-noise ratio (SNR) to find points-of-interest to build the models. The SNR for the first intermediate in the fourth layer of the NTT^{-1} is shown in Fig. 3. This position in the NTT^{-1} shows the amplification effect: There are multiple peaks throughout the trace which can be used for template building. The signed attack case shows high SNR peaks, with several points above 1. To the right, the unsigned case already exhibits a strong reduction in SNR, reducing the maximum SNR by an order-of-magnitude. On the bottom row, both RNRimplementations reduce the SNR by two orders-of-magnitude compared to the signed case with the $RNR^{\pm}$implementation having the lowest SNR overall.

Next, after computing the SNR for every relevant intermediate, we selected points-of-interest (POIs) above an arbitrarily selected threshold, sorting them and selecting up to 1000 points per intermediate. We then constructed leakage models using an LDA classifier (using the implementation of SCALib [CB23]) individually. The number of subspace dimensions was tuned per model using a parameter sweep on a subset of intermediates. To assess the quality of the models, we computed the average perceived information computed using a fresh set of random traces, which we report in Fig. 4 within $\pm$ 0.1 bits with 95% confidence. In these plots, we show that RNRgreatly reduces the quality of the leakage models. For the signed and unsigned case, the models are able to predict the correct value with near certainty by the fourth layer of the NTT^{-1} due to the amplification effect. In particular for the unsigned case, the required additional Barrett reduction step with known quantities in the first, second and third layer further improves the quality of the models. The RNRimplementations are able to reduce the information the models can provide substantially. The shallow layers of the NTT^{-1} have PI close to zero, and even with the amplification effect, the maximum PI given by a model are 5.8 bits and 7.8 bits for $RNR^{\pm}$and RNR^{+}respectively. Thus, we conclude that RNRgreatly increases the difficulty of carrying out a template attack on the ML-KEM NTT^{-1} in this ideal adversarial scenario.

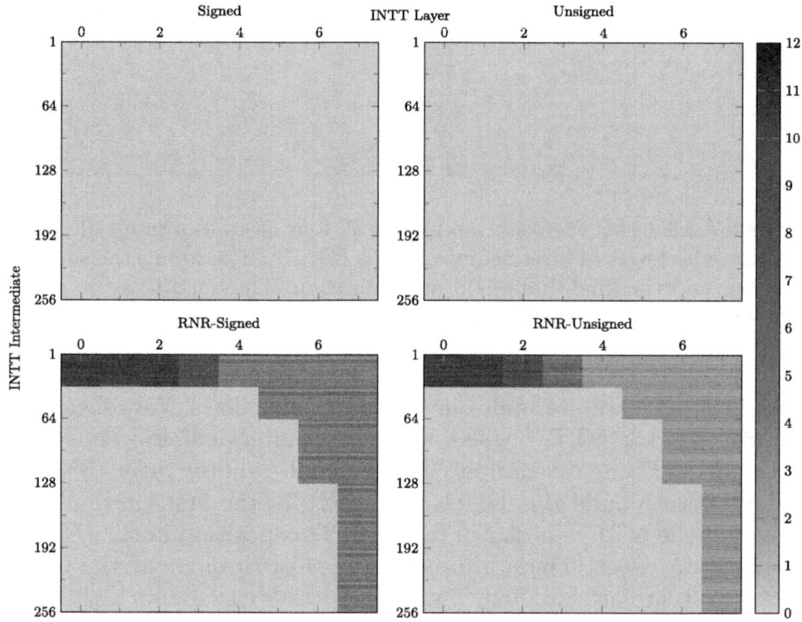

Fig. 5. Guessing entropy of each intermediate in the ML-KEM NTT^{-1} after a single-trace SASCA. 0 GE means the value is known without any uncertainty. Note, the colormap is inverted to make it easier to compare to Fig. 4.

Attack. We performed SASCAs on each implementation with our templates. In Fig. 5, we report the average guessing entropy of every intermediate in the eight layers of the NTT^{-1} over 25 independent experiments for each point. The attacks show that the inputs to both the signed and unsigned NTT^{-1} can be recovered after a single-trace, consistent with our results from the simulated SASCAs. Furthermore, the attack is rendered ineffective against both the $RNR^{\pm}$and

RNR^{+}implementations and the SASCA is unable to significantly improve the GE of the output of the templates. In the deeper layers, the belief propagation is able to reduce the GE of some intermediates due to the many known zeroed coordinates. However, it is unable to significantly reduce the GE in shallower layers due to the large uncertainty, which is a known problem with belief propagation on high entropy distributions [Nag+25].

Table 2. Performance evaluation of the four implementations of the ML-KEM-NTT^{-1} measured on the ARM Cortex-M4 compiled with `arm-none-eabi-gcc` version 10.3.1 for `-O0` and `-O3` with flags `-mcpu=cortex-m4 -mthumb -mfloat-abi=soft`. The results are reported in thousands ($\cdot 10^3$) of clock cycles.

Implementation	KCycles ($\cdot 10^3$)	
	-O0	-O3
Signed-NTT	127.02	26.48
Unsigned-NTT	158.00	36.75
$RNR^{\pm}$-NTT	196.01	50.70
RNR^{+}-NTT	260.52	84.74
Signed-NTT^{-1}	202.04	42.61
Unsigned-NTT^{-1}	270.39	64.91
$RNR^{\pm}$-NTT^{-1}	203.19	42.61
RNR^{+}-NTT^{-1}	305.59	91.15

Discussion. In our attacks, we utilized an adversarial setting highly favorable to the attacker in which they are able to craft ciphertexts to create many zeroed coefficients in the input polynomial to the NTT^{-1}, based on the k-trace attack of Hamburg et al. [Ham+21]. This attack is effective against masked implementations of the NTT^{-1} since shares can be attacked in a divide-and-conquer approach with SPA and the attack can be considered a worst-case scenario for evaluating the security of NTT^{-1} implementations against SPA.

The result of our simulated and experimental SASCAs show that the signed and unsigned implementation of the ML-KEM NTT^{-1} are highly vulnerable to SPA attacks. Based on the analysis of Sect. 3 and the PI estimation in Fig. 4, it is clear that the integer ring used in ML-KEM is small enough relative to the word-size to yield a large amount of information leakage that can be exploited. After applying RNR, the information leakage is reduced substantially – enough to render this worst-case attack ineffective.

Previous literature on SPA countermeasures on the ML-KEM NTT employ combinations of masking and shuffling [ZBT19, Rav+20]. Such countermeasures make it more difficult for an adversary to create templates and shuffling is a known to be effective against SASCA [VGS14]. Ravi et al. proposed several combinations of masking and shuffling to prevent SASCAs on ML-KEM and

Dilithium [Rav+20] between butterflies ("course-grained") or within butterflies ("fine-grained"). An evaluation by Hermelink et al. [Her+23b] showed that this countermeasure was effective against SASCAs on the ML-KEM-NTT and requires a more powerful adversary to execute an attack. However, the countermeasure of Ravi et al. comes with a significant performance overhead: They report between 7%-78% performance overhead across all ML-KEM operations on the ARM Cortex-M4 target. In contrast, RNR-ML-KEM achieves a similar margin of security against SPA with lower implementation effort: Only constants in the reduction algorithms and rejection sampling need to be adjusted. Furthermore, RNRcan be applied seamlessly on top of masking, if necessary. As masking is generally required to protect against DPA attacks, RNRoffers a low-cost yet effective alternative to shuffling. Heinz et al. suggested that RNRon ML-KEM may demask certain coefficients if a ζ is a multiple of the redundancy factor η [HP23]. Our experimental results show that this is not an issue in the context of SPA on the ML-KEM-NTT, even for the small η we chose. For further protections, one can mask the input ciphertexts with randomly sampled integers $r \in [0, \eta)$ to prevent any such demasking. In Table 2 we report the clock cycles needed to compute the ML-KEM-NTT and ML-KEM-NTT^{-1} on the ARM Cortex-M4 target for all four implementations we evaluate. With full optimizations (`-O3`), applying RNRto the signed NTT incurs a performance overhead of 62.8% (resp. 42.7% for `-O0`) and, for the unsigned NTT, RNRincurs a 79.0% overhead (resp. 49.0% for `-O0`). Both RNR/-variants require two additional barrett reductions to ensure that intermediate sums do not exceed the 16-bit (signed) integer range. In contrast, the baseline signed and the $RNR^{\pm}$NTT^{-1} implementations achieve the same performance since no additional changes are required to the NTT^{-1} other than changes to constants. On the otherhand, the RNR^{+}variant incurs a 27.7% penalty compared to the unsigned counterpart. This is due to a 64-bit multiplication in the Barrett reduction which is a costly operation on the ARM Cortex-M4. Since $RNR^{\pm}$suggests less information leakage from the analysis and PI measurements and does not compromise on performance, it is our primary recommendation for ML-KEM.

6 Conclusion

In this paper, we discuss the application of Redundant Number Representation(RNR) to counter SPA and SASCA. We analyzed how information can leak as a result of integer representations and reveal secrets more easily. We then applied these strategies to protect the ML-KEM NTT^{-1}, which deals directly with secrets, and showed that RNR-ML-KEM renders worst-case SASCA attacks ineffective in simulation and in practice on the ARM Cortex-M4. Finally, we show that our RNRimplementations achieve comparable performance to state-of-the-art masking/shuffling countermeasures. In particular, we highlight that the signed variant of the RNR-ML-KEM NTT^{-1} can compute with the same performance as an unprotected version. Applying RNRto optimized ML-KEM implementations as well as other schemes remain as directions for future works.

Acknowledgments. This research was funded in whole or in part by the Austrian Science Fund (FWF) (FWF SFB project SPyCoDe 10.55776/F85) and the Austrian Research Promotion Agency (FFG) via the AWARE project (FFG grant number 891092).

A Modular Reduction Algorithms

Algorithm 4. Unsigned Barrett Reduction

Input: $a \in [0, \beta), R = 2^k$
Output: $x \in [0, q), x \equiv a \bmod q$
1: $v \leftarrow \left\lfloor \frac{R}{q} \right\rceil / R$ ▷ *Pre-computed constant*
2: $t \leftarrow \left\lfloor \frac{a \cdot v}{R} \right\rfloor$
3: **return** $x = a - (t \cdot q)$

Algorithm 5. Signed Barrett Reduction [Sei18]

Input: $a \in [-\frac{\beta}{2}, \frac{\beta}{2}), R = 2^k$
Output: $x \in [-\frac{q}{2}, \frac{q}{2}), x \equiv a \bmod q$
1: $v \leftarrow \left\lfloor \frac{2^{\lfloor \log_2(q) \rfloor - 1}\beta}{q} \right\rceil$ ▷ *Pre-computed constant*
2: $t \leftarrow \left\lfloor \frac{av}{2^{\lfloor \log_2(q) \rfloor - 1}\beta} \right\rfloor$
3: $t \leftarrow tq \bmod \beta$
4: **return** $x = a - t$

Barrett Reduction [Bar86]. The Barrett reduction algorithm efficiently computes the modular reduction without the use of division by approximating the multiplicative inverse of q with a constant that is proportional to a power of two. Let $\beta = 2^l$ be the word-size large enough to fit the prime modulus q; if $q < 2^{16}$ then $\beta = 2^{16}$ and if $q < 2^{32}$ then $\beta = 2^{32}$. The original unsigned Barrett reduction computes $a \bmod q = a - q \cdot \lfloor a \cdot v \rceil$ with the quantity

$$v = \left\lfloor \frac{R}{q} \right\rceil / R,$$

where $R = 2^k$ and k is an arbitrary integer such that v approximates q^{-1}. The signed Barrett reduction [Sei18] computes the symmetric modulus $a \bmod {}^{\pm}q$ using a tighter approximation of q^{-1} when $0 < q < \frac{\beta}{2}$,

$$v = \left\lfloor \frac{2^{\lfloor \log_2 q \rfloor - 1}\beta}{q} \right\rceil.$$

Algorithm 6. Unsigned Montgomery Reduction

Input: $a \in [0, q\beta), q^{-1} \bmod \beta$ ▷ *$q^{-1} \bmod \beta$ is pre-computed.*
Output: $x \in [0, 2q), x \equiv a\beta^{-1} \bmod q$
1: $t \leftarrow a(-q^{-1}) \bmod \beta$
2: **return** $x \leftarrow (a + tq)/\beta$ ▷ *Division is implemented as right shift.*

Algorithm 7. Signed Montgomery Reduction [Sei18]

Input: $a \in [-\frac{q\beta}{2}, \frac{q\beta}{2})$
Output: $x \in [-q, q), x \equiv a\beta^{-1} \bmod q$
1: $v \leftarrow a(-q^{-1}) \bmod {}^{\pm}\beta$ ▷ *q^{-1} pre-computed*
2: $t \leftarrow \left\lfloor \frac{vq}{\beta} \right\rfloor$
3: **return** $x = \left\lfloor \frac{a}{\beta} \right\rfloor - t$

Montgomery Reduction [Mon85]. The Montgomery modular reduction algorithm is similar to the Barrett reduction in that it computes remainders via approximation, but for a larger domain $x \in [0, q\beta)$. Consider that x is the product of two integers $x = ab$ such that $0 \leq a < q$ and $0 \leq b < q$ and the goal is to compute $x \bmod q$. The algorithm requires the input $x = ab$ to be in the so-called *Montgomery domain* by multiplying the quantity $\beta \bmod q$ making the input to the algorithm $ab\beta \bmod q$. Since the CT and GS butterfly circuits are used to compute the NTT (and its inverse), the second multiplicand b is a power of the root-of-unity ζ and thus $b\beta \bmod q$ can be precomputed. Precomputing these constants in the Montgomery domain yields the output of the reduction in the normal domain, saving additional operations for the translation [Alk+16]. The signed variant(Algorithm 7) [Sei18] returns the signed result $x \in [-q, q)$ with slight modifications.

B NTT Algorithms

Algorithm 8. $RNR^{\pm}$-NTT

Input: $f \in \mathbb{Z}^{256}_{\eta^{\pm}q}$
Output: $\hat{f} \in \mathbb{Z}^{256}_{\eta^{\pm}q}$

$\hat{f} \leftarrow f$
$k \leftarrow 1; j \leftarrow 0$
for $\text{len} \leftarrow 128; \text{len} \geq 2; \text{len} \leftarrow \text{len}/2$ **do**
  for $\text{start} \leftarrow 0; \text{start} < 256; \text{start} \leftarrow j + \text{len}$ **do**
    for $j \leftarrow \text{start}; j < \text{start} + \text{len}; j{+}{+}$ **do**
      $t \leftarrow \mathsf{montgomery\_reduce}_{\eta^{\pm}}(\zeta^k \cdot \hat{f}_{j+\text{len}})$
      ▷ *The additional barrett reductions in the addition and subtraction below are only necessary for larger* $\eta^{\pm}$ ◁
      $\hat{f}_{j+\text{len}} \leftarrow \mathsf{barrett\_reduce}_{\eta^{\pm}}(\hat{f}_j - t)$
      $\hat{f}_j \leftarrow \mathsf{barrett\_reduce}_{\eta^{\pm}}(\hat{f}_j + t)$
    $k \leftarrow k + 1$

Algorithm 9. RNR^{+}-NTT

Input: $f \in \mathbb{Z}^{256}_{\eta^{+}q}$
Output: $\hat{f} \in \mathbb{Z}^{256}_{\eta^{+}q}$

$\hat{f} \leftarrow f$
$k \leftarrow 1; j \leftarrow 0$
for $\text{len} \leftarrow 128; \text{len} \geq 2; \text{len} \leftarrow \text{len}/2$ **do**
  for $\text{start} \leftarrow 0; \text{start} < 256; \text{start} \leftarrow j + \text{len}$ **do**
    for $j \leftarrow \text{start}; j < \text{start} + \text{len}; j{+}{+}$ **do**
      $t \leftarrow \mathsf{montgomery\_reduce}_{\eta^{+}}(\zeta^k \cdot \hat{f}_{j+\text{len}})$
      ▷ *The additional barrett reductions in the addition and subtraction below are only necessary for larger* η^{+} ◁
      $\hat{f}_{j+\text{len}} \leftarrow \mathsf{barrett\_reduce}_{\eta^{+}}((\eta^{+} + 1) \cdot q + \hat{f}_j - t)$
      $\hat{f}_j \leftarrow \mathsf{barrett\_reduce}_{\eta^{+}}(\hat{f}_j + t)$
    $k \leftarrow k + 1$

Algorithm 10. $RNR^{\pm}$-NTT^{-1}

Input: $\hat{f} \in \mathbb{Z}^{256}_{\eta^{\pm}q}$
Output: $f \in \mathbb{Z}^{256}_{\eta^{\pm}q}$

$f \leftarrow \hat{f}$
$k \leftarrow 127; j \leftarrow 0$
for $\text{len} \leftarrow 2; \text{len} \leq 128; \text{len} \leftarrow 2 \cdot \text{len}$ **do**
  for $\text{start} \leftarrow 0; \text{start} < 256; \text{start} \leftarrow j + \text{len}$ **do**
    for $j \leftarrow \text{start}; j < \text{start} + \text{len}; j{+}{+}$ **do**
      $t \leftarrow f_j$
      $f_j \leftarrow \mathsf{barrett\_reduce}_{\eta^{\pm}}(t + f_{j+\text{len}})$
      $f_{j+\text{len}} \leftarrow f_{j+\text{len}} - t$
      $f_{j+\text{len}} \leftarrow \mathsf{montgomery\_reduce}_{\eta^{\pm}}(\zeta^k \cdot f_{j+\text{len}})$
    $k \leftarrow k - 1$

Algorithm 11. RNR^{+}-NTT^{-1}

Input: $\hat{f} \in \mathbb{Z}_{\eta^{+}q}^{256}$
Output: $f \in \mathbb{Z}_{\eta^{+}q}^{256}$

$f \leftarrow \hat{f}$
$k \leftarrow 127; j \leftarrow 0$
for $\text{len} \leftarrow 2; \text{len} \leq 128; \text{len} \leftarrow 2 \cdot \text{len}$ **do**
  for $\text{start} \leftarrow 0; \text{start} < 256; \text{start} \leftarrow j + \text{len}$ **do**
    for $j \leftarrow \text{start}; j < \text{start} + \text{len}; j++$ **do**
      $t \leftarrow f_j$
      $f_j \leftarrow \mathsf{barrett\_reduce}_{\eta^{+}}(t + f_{j+\text{len}})$
      ▷ *The additional barrett reduction is only necessary for larger* η^{+} ◁
      $f_{j+\text{len}} \leftarrow \mathsf{barrett\_reduce}_{\eta^{+}}((\eta^{+} + 1) \cdot q + f_{j+\text{len}} - t)$
      $f_{j+\text{len}} \leftarrow \mathsf{montgomery\_reduce}_{\eta^{+}}(\zeta^{k} \cdot f_{j+\text{len}})$
    $k \leftarrow k - 1$

References

[AER23] Assael, G., Elbaz-Vincent, P., Reymond, G.: Improving single-trace attacks on the number-theoretic transform for cortex-M4. In: IEEE International Symposium on Hardware Oriented Security and Trust, HOST 2023, San Jose, CA, USA, 1–4 May 2023, pp. 111–121. IEEE (2023). https://doi.org/10.1109/HOST55118.2023.10133270

[Alk+16] Alkim, E., Ducas, L., Pöppelmann, T., Schwabe, P.: Post-quantum key exchange - a new hope. In: 25th USENIX Security Symposium, USENIX Security 16, Austin, TX, USA, 10–12 August 2016, pp. 327–343. USENIX Association (2016). https://www.usenix.org/conference/usenixsecurity16/technicalsessions/presentation/alkim

[Ava+21] Avanzi, R., et al.: CRYSTALS-Kyber algorithm specifications and supporting documentation (2021). https://pq-crystals.org/kyber/data/kyber-specification-round3-20210804.pdf

[Bar86] Barrett, P.: Implementing the rivest shamir and adleman public key encryption algorithm on a standard digital signal processor. In: Odlyzko, A.M. (ed.) CRYPTO 1986. LNCS, vol. 263, pp. 311–323. Springer, Heidelberg (1987). https://doi.org/10.1007/3-540-47721-7_24

[Bol+19] Bolboceanu, M., Brakerski, Z., Perlman, R., Sharma, D.: Order-LWE and the hardness of ring-LWE with entropic secrets. In: Galbraith, S.D., Moriai, S. (eds.) ASIACRYPT 2019. LNCS, vol. 11922, pp. 91–120. Springer, Cham (2019). https://doi.org/10.1007/978-3-030-34621-8_4

[Bos+18] Bos, J.W., et al.: CRYSTALS - Kyber: a CCA-secure module- lattice-based KEM. In,: IEEE European Symposium on Security and Privacy, EuroS&P 2018, London, United Kingdom, 24–26 April 2018, pp. 353–367. IEEE (2018). https://doi.org/10.1109/EUROSP.2018.00032

[Bro+19] Bronchain, O., Hendrickx, J.M., Massart, C., Olshevsky, A., Standaert, F.-X.: Leakage certification revisited: bounding model errors in side-channel security evaluations. In: Boldyreva, A., Micciancio, D. (eds.) CRYPTO 2019. LNCS, vol. 11692, pp. 713–737. Springer, Cham (2019). https://doi.org/10.1007/978-3-030-26948-7_25

[Bro+24] Bronchain, O., Azouaoui, M., ElGhamrawy, M., Renes, J., Schneider, T.: Exploiting small-norm polynomial multiplication with physical attacks application to CRYSTALSDilithium. IACR Trans. Cryptogr. Hardw. Embed. Syst. 359–383 (2024). https://doi.org/10.46586/TCHES.V2024.I2.359-383

[BS21] Bronchain, O., Standaert, F.X.: Breaking masked implementations with many shares on 32-bit software platforms or when the security order does not matter. IACR Trans. Cryptogr. Hardw. Embed. Syst. 202–234 (2021). https://doi.org/10.46586/TCHES.V2021.I3.202-234

[Cas+23] Cassiers, G., Devillez, H., Standaert, F.X., Udvarhelyi, B.: Efficient regression-based linear discriminant analysis for side-channel security evaluations towards analytical attacks against 32-bit implementations. IACR Trans. Cryptogr. Hardw. Embed. Syst. 270–293 (2023). https://doi.org/10.46586/TCHES.V2023.I3.270-293

[CB23] Cassiers, G., Bronchain, O.: SCALib: a side-channel analysis library. J. Open Source Softw. **8**, 5196 (2023). https://doi.org/10.21105/joss.05196

[Cha+99] Chari, S., Jutla, C.S., Rao, J.R., Rohatgi, P.: Towards sound approaches to counteract power-analysis attacks. In: Wiener, M. (ed.) CRYPTO 1999. LNCS, vol. 1666, pp. 398–412. Springer, Heidelberg (1999). https://doi.org/10.1007/3-540-48405-1_26

[CK13] Choudary, O., Kuhn, M.G.: Efficient template attacks. In: Francillon, A., Rohatgi, P. (eds.) CARDIS 2013. LNCS, vol. 8419, pp. 253–270. Springer, Cham (2014). https://doi.org/10.1007/978-3-319-08302-5_17

[CK14] Choudary, M.O., Kuhn, M.G.: Efficient stochastic methods: profiled attacks beyond 8 bits. In: Joye, M., Moradi, A. (eds.) CARDIS 2014. LNCS, vol. 8968, pp. 85–103. Springer, Cham (2015). https://doi.org/10.1007/978-3-319-16763-3_6

[CRR02] Chari, S., Rao, J.R., Rohatgi, P.: Template attacks. In: Kaliski, B.S., Koç, K., Paar, C. (eds.) CHES 2002. LNCS, vol. 2523, pp. 13–28. Springer, Heidelberg (2003). https://doi.org/10.1007/3-540-36400-5_3

[CT65] Cooley, J., Tukey, J.: An algorithm for the machine calculation of complex fourier series. Math. Comput. **19**, 297–301 (1965). http://dx.doi.org/10.1090/S0025-5718-1965-0178586-1

[DDF19] Duc, A., Dziembowski, S., Faust, S.: Unifying leakage models: from probing attacks to noisy leakage. J. Cryptol. **32**, 151–177 (2019). https://doi.org/10.1007/S00145-018-9284-1

[Duc+18] Ducas, L., et al.: CRYSTALSDilithium: a lattice-based digital signature scheme. IACR Trans. Cryptogr. Hardw. Embed. Syst. 238–268 (2018). https://doi.org/10.13154/TCHES.V2018.I1.238-268

[FO13] Fujisaki, E., Okamoto, T.: Secure integration of asymmetric and symmetric encryption schemes. J. Cryptol. **26**, 80–101 (2013). https://doi.org/10.1007/S00145-011-9114-1

[GS66] Gentleman, W.M., Sande, G.: Fast Fourier transforms: for fun and profit. In: Proceedings of the Fall Joint Computer Conference, 7–10 November 1966, pp. 53–578. Association for Computing Machinery (1966). https://doi.org/10.1145/1464291.1464352.

[Ham+21] Hamburg, M., et al.: Chosen ciphertext k-trace attacks on masked CCA2 secure kyber. IACR Trans. Cryptogr. Hardw. Embed. Syst. 88–113 (2021). https://doi.org/10.46586/TCHES.V2021.I4.88-113

[Her+23a] Hermelink, J., Mårtensson, E., Samardjiska, S., Pessl, P., Rodosek, G.D.: Belief propagation meets lattice reduction: security estimates for error-tolerant key recovery from decryption errors. IACR Cryptol. ePrint Arch. 98 (2023). https://eprint.iacr.org/2023/098

[Her+23b] Hermelink, J., Streit, S., Strieder, E., Thieme, K.: Adapting belief propagation to counter shuffling of NTTs. IACR Trans. Cryptogr. Hardw. Embed. Syst. 60–88 (2023). https://doi.org/10.46586/TCHES.V2023.I1.60-88.

[HHK17] Hofheinz, D., Hövelmanns, K., Kiltz, E.: A modular analysis of the fujisaki-okamoto transformation. In: Kalai, Y., Reyzin, L. (eds.) TCC 2017. LNCS, vol. 10677, pp. 341–371. Springer, Cham (2017). https://doi.org/10.1007/978-3-319-70500-2_12

[HME24] Xunyue, H., Meunier, Q.L., Encrenaz, E.: Blind- folded: simple power analysis attacks using data with a single trace and no training. IACR Trans. Cryptogr. Hardw. Embed. Syst. **2025**, 475–496 (2024). https://doi.org/10.46586/tches.v2025.i1.475-496

[HP23] Heinz, D., Pöppelmann, T.: Combined fault and DPA protection for lattice-based cryptography. IEEE Trans. Comput. **72**, 1055–1066 (2023). https://doi.org/10.1109/TC.2022.3197073

[Hua+22] Huang, J., et al.: Improved plantard arithmetic for lattice-based cryptography. IACR Trans. Cryptogr. Hardw. Embed. Syst. 614–636 (2022). https://doi.org/10.46586/TCHES.V2022.I4.614-636

[Hua+24] Huang, J., et al.: Yet another improvement of plantard arithmetic for faster kyber on low-end 32-bit IoT devices. IEEE Trans. Inf. Forensics Secur. **19**, 3800–3813 (2024). https://doi.org/10.1109/TIFS.2024.3371369

[Inc24] NewAE Technology Inc. Cw308 UFO Target Board (2024). https://www.newae.com/products/nae-cw308

[ISW03] Ishai, Y., Sahai, A., Wagner, D.: Private circuits: securing hardware against probing attacks. In: Boneh, D. (ed.) CRYPTO 2003. LNCS, vol. 2729, pp. 463–481. Springer, Heidelberg (2003). https://doi.org/10.1007/978-3-540-45146-4_27

[KJJ99] Kocher, P., Jaffe, J., Jun, B.: Differential power analysis. In: Wiener, M. (ed.) CRYPTO 1999. LNCS, vol. 1666, pp. 388–397. Springer, Heidelberg (1999). https://doi.org/10.1007/3-540-48405-1_25

[Koc96] Kocher, P.C.: Timing attacks on implementations of diffie-hellman, RSA, DSS, and other systems. In: Koblitz, N. (ed.) CRYPTO 1996. LNCS, vol. 1109, pp. 104–113. Springer, Heidelberg (1996). https://doi.org/10.1007/3-540-68697-5_9

[KPP20] Kannwischer, M.J., Pessl, P., Primas, R.: Single- trace attacks on keccak. IACR Trans. Cryptogr. Hardw. Embed. Syst. 243–268 (2020). https://doi.org/10.13154/TCHES.V2020.I3.243-268

[LPR10] Lyubashevsky, V., Peikert, C., Regev, O.: On ideal lattices and learning with errors over rings. In: Gilbert, H. (ed.) EUROCRYPT 2010. LNCS, vol. 6110, pp. 1–23. Springer, Heidelberg (2010). https://doi.org/10.1007/978-3-642-13190-5_1

[LS15] Langlois, A., Stehlé, D.: Worst-case to average-case reductions for module lattices. Des. Codes Cryptogr. **75**, 565–599 (2015). https://doi.org/10.1007/S10623-014-9938-4

[Mas+23] Masure, L., Cassiers, G., Hendrickx, J.M., Standaert, F.X.: Information bounds and convergence rates for side-channel security evaluators. IACR Trans. Cryptogr. Hardw. Embed. Syst. 522–569 (2023). https://doi.org/10.46586/TCHES.V2023. I3.522-569

[MM09] Mezard, M., Montanari, A.: Information, Physics, and Computation. Oxford University Press, Inc. (2009). isbn: 019857083X

[Mon85] Montgomery, P.L.: Modular multiplication without trial division. Math. Comput. **44**, 519–521 (1985)

[Nag+25] Nagpal, R., Cassiers, G., Primas, R., Knoll, C., Pernkopf, F., Mangard, S.: On loopy belief propagation for SASCAs. In: IACR Communications in Cryptology, vol. 1 (2025). https://doi.org/10.62056/ayl8ksdja

[Ngo+21] Ngo, K., Dubrova, E., Guo, Q., Johansson, T.: A side-channel attack on a masked IND-CCA secure saber KEM implementation. IACR Trans. Cryptogr. Hardw. Embed. Syst. 676–707 (2021). https://doi.org/10.46586/TCHES.V2021.I4.676-707

[Pea82] Pearl, J.: Reverend bayes on inference engines: a distributed hierarchical approach. In: Proceedings of the Second AAAI Conference on Artificial Intelligence, pp. 133–136. AAAI Press (1982). http://dl.acm.org/citation.cfm?id=2876686.2876719

[PP19] Pessl, P., Primas, R.: More practical single-trace attacks on the number theoretic transform. In: Schwabe, P., Thériault, N. (eds.) LATINCRYPT 2019. LNCS, vol. 11774, pp. 130–149. Springer, Cham (2019). https://doi.org/10.1007/978-3-030-30530-7_7

[PPM17] Primas, R., Pessl, P., Mangard, S.: Single-trace side-channel attacks on masked lattice-based encryption. In: Fischer, W., Homma, N. (eds.) CHES 2017. LNCS, vol. 10529, pp. 513–533. Springer, Cham (2017). https://doi.org/10.1007/978-3-319-66787-4_25

[Qia+24] Qiao, Z., Liu, Y., Zhou, Y., Zhao, Y., Chen, S.: Single Trace is all it takes: efficient side-channel attack on dilithium. IACR Cryptol. ePrint Arch. 512 (2024). https://eprint.iacr.org/2024/512

[QS01] Quisquater, J.-J., Samyde, D.: ElectroMagnetic Analysis (EMA): measures and counter-measures for smart cards. In: Attali, I., Jensen, T. (eds.) E-smart 2001. LNCS, vol. 2140, pp. 200–210. Springer, Heidelberg (2001). https://doi.org/10.1007/3-540-45418-7_17

[Rav+20] Ravi, P., Poussier, R., Bhasin, S., Chattopadhyay, A.: On configurable SCA countermeasures against single trace attacks for the NTT. In: Batina, L., Picek, S., Mondal, M. (eds.) SPACE 2020. LNCS, vol. 12586, pp. 123–146. Springer, Cham (2020). https://doi.org/10.1007/978-3-030-66626-2_7

[Reg05] Regev, O.: On lattices, learning with errors, random linear codes, and cryptography. In: Proceedings of the 37th Annual ACM Symposium on Theory of Computing, Baltimore, MD, USA, 22–24 May 2005, pp. 84–93. ACM (2005). https://doi.org/10.1145/1060590.1060603

[Ren+11] Renauld, M., Standaert, F.-X., Veyrat-Charvillon, N., Kamel, D., Flandre, D.: A formal study of power variability issues and side-channel attacks for nanoscale devices. In: Paterson, K.G. (ed.) EUROCRYPT 2011. LNCS, vol. 6632, pp. 109–128. Springer, Heidelberg (2011). https://doi.org/10.1007/978-3-642-20465-4_8

[SA08] Standaert, F.-X., Archambeau, C.: Using subspace-based template attacks to compare and combine power and electromagnetic information leakages. In: Oswald, E., Rohatgi, P. (eds.) CHES 2008. LNCS, vol. 5154, pp. 411–425. Springer, Heidelberg (2008). https://doi.org/10.1007/978-3-540-85053-3_26

[Sei18] Seiler, G.: Faster AVX2 optimized NTT multiplication for Ring- LWE lattice cryptography. IACR Cryptol. ePrint Arch. 39 (2018). http://eprint.iacr.org/2018/039

[SLP05] Schindler, W., Lemke, K., Paar, C.: A stochastic model for differential side channel cryptanalysis. In: Rao, J.R., Sunar, B. (eds.) CHES 2005. LNCS, vol. 3659, pp. 30–46. Springer, Heidelberg (2005). https://doi.org/10.1007/11545262_3

[ST24a] National Institute of Standards and Technology: Module-Lattice- Based Digital Signature Standard. Tech. rep. U.S, Department of Commerce (2024)

[ST24b] National Institute of Standards and Technology: Module-Lattice- Based Key-Encapsulation Mechanism Standard. Tech. rep. U.S, Department of Commerce (2024)

[Str+23] Strieder, E., Ilg, M., Heyszl, J., Unterstein, F., Streit, S.: ASCA vs. SASCA - a closer look at the AES key schedule. In: Constructive Side-Channel Analysis and Secure Design - 14th International Workshop, COSADE 2023, Munich, Germany, 3–4 April 2023, Proceedings, pp. 65–85. Springer, Heidelberg (2023). https://doi.org/10.1007/978-3-031-29497-6_4

[TMS24] Tosun, T., Moradi, A., Savas, E.: Exploiting the central reduction in lattice-based cryptography. IEEE Access **12**, 166814–166833 (2024). https://doi.org/10.1109/ACCESS.2024.3494593

[Vey+12] Veyrat-Charvillon, N., Medwed, M., Kerckhof, S., Standaert, F.-X.: Shuffling against side-channel attacks: a comprehensive study with cautionary note. In: Wang, X., Sako, K. (eds.) ASIACRYPT 2012. LNCS, vol. 7658, pp. 740–757. Springer, Heidelberg (2012). https://doi.org/10.1007/978-3-642-34961-4_44

[VGS14] Veyrat-Charvillon, N., Gérard, B., Standaert, F.-X.: Soft analytical side-channel attacks. In: Sarkar, P., Iwata, T. (eds.) ASIACRYPT 2014. LNCS, vol. 8873, pp. 282–296. Springer, Heidelberg (2014). https://doi.org/10.1007/978-3-662-45611-8_15

[ZBT19] Zijlstra, T., Bigou, K., Tisserand, A.: FPGA implementation and comparison of protections against SCAs for RLWE. In: Hao, F., Ruj, S., Sen Gupta, S. (eds.) INDOCRYPT 2019. LNCS, vol. 11898, pp. 535–555. Springer, Cham (2019). https://doi.org/10.1007/978-3-030-35423-7_27

Secret in OnePiece: Single-Bit Fault Attack on Kyber

Jian Wang[1,2], Weiqiong Cao[1,3,4](✉), Hua Chen[1], and Haoyuan Li[4]

[1] Trusted Computing and Information Assurance Laboratory, Institute of Software, Chinese Academy of Sciences, Beijing 100190, China
{wangjian2019,caoweiqiong,chenhua}@iscas.ac.cn
[2] University of Chinese Academy of Sciences, Beijing 100049, China
[3] Key Laboratory of Data and Intelligent System Security, Ministry of Education, China, Tianjin, China
[4] Zhongguancun Laboratory, Beijing, China
lihy@zgclab.edu.cn

Abstract. The post-quantum key encapsulation mechanism, Kyber, has recently been selected by the National Institution of Standards and Technology for standardization, making the study of its implementation security a critical concern. As a widely used countermeasure against implementation attacks, masking has been proven effective in protecting Kyber implementations from side-channel attacks. However, the masking process complicates the original scheme and introduces additional operations, raising the question of whether these changes open up new attack vectors.

In this paper, we propose a novel fault attack targeting the masked implementation of Kyber, focusing on the masked message decoder. Our generic single-bit fault attack is amplified by masked implementations of Kyber. Moreover, the randomness introduced by masking allows a stuck-at fault to behave as a bit-flip fault with a certain flip probability, thereby simplifying the complexity associated with fault injection. Based on a practical attacker model, we demonstrate that each faulted decapsulation reveals partial information about the secret key in the form of an inequality. By employing a solver based on statistical theory and two filtering techniques, the entire secret key can be efficiently recovered by solving the resulting system of inequalities. Only 36,000 (Kyber512), 54,000 (Kyber768), and 4,000,000 (Kyber1024) inequalities are required for key recovery.

We validated the effectiveness of our attack through experiments on an STM32F4 target board, with introducing the required faults by clock glitches. The experimental results demonstrate that the required number of faulted decapsualtion can be reduced from more than 540, 000 to 380, 000 when dealing with Kyber512. These findings highlight the risks brought by masking when considering fault attacks.

Keywords: Post-quantum cryptography · ML-KEM · CRYSTALS-Kyber · Fault attack · Masking

C. Boura et al. (Eds.): SAC 2025, LNCS 16207, pp. 781–804, 2026.
https://doi.org/10.1007/978-3-032-10536-3_29

1 Introduction

The National Institute of Standards and Technology (NIST) has recently made available for public a set of standards for post-quantum cryptography (PQC) algorithms. As these algorithms will be deployed in a multitude of embedded devices across the globe, it is of paramount importance to ensure their resilience against physical attacks. While the security of side-channel attacks has been extensively studied, that of fault attacks on PQC algorithms has received comparatively little attention. It is therefore imperative to evaluate the security of implementations of PQC algorithms to fault attacks.

In this study, we investigate the vulnerability of the CRYSTALS-Kyber (Kyber) algorithm, which serves as the foundation for the Module-Lattice Key-Encapsulation Mechanism Standard (ML-KEM), to fault attacks. To achieve chosen-ciphertext attack (CCA) security, the designers of Kyber applied the Fujisaki-Okamoto (FO) transform [11] to a chosen-plaintext attack (CPA) secure public key encryption (PKE) algorithm. During decapsulation, the ciphertext is first decrypted and then re-encrypted. In the event that the re-encrypted ciphertext does not match the original, the decapsulation process fails. From a fault attack perspective, the FO transform can be regarded as a redundancy countermeasure [1] designed to protect against malicious tampering. As a result, traditional fault attack techniques, such as the differential fault attack [3], are not directly applicable to Kyber.

Fault attacks targeting the key generation phase [10,21] or disrupting the FO transform [16,23] have proven effective. Several such attacks have been proposed [20], although they often involve high costs or are challenging to execute in practice. However, even observing whether an injected fault results in a decapsulation failure can benefit the attacker. Indeed, fault attacks have been devised that exploit this concept to achieve key recovery, including the safe-error attack [2,24] and the (statistical) ineffective fault attack [9]. Based on this concept, in 2020, Pessl *et al.* proposed a new fault attack on CCA-secure KEMs [19]. Following this, Hermelink *et al.* introduced a fault-enabled chosen-ciphertext attack on Kyber by combining fault injection with a chosen-ciphertext attack [13]. Their attack requires a single-bit flip and remains effective even with the presence of shuffling countermeasures. Later, Delvaux proposed a more general attack, known as the Roulette attack, along with an efficient solver [8]. Building on these advancements, Hermelink *et al.* [12] incorporated the solver with the lattice reduction framework from [7], reducing the number of inequalities required for successful key recovery.

Masking serves as a generic countermeasure to defend against side-channel attacks. It involves dividing a single intermediate value into multiple random shares, making it challenging to tamper with an intermediate value precisely using fault injection. Consequently, it can effectively defend against the majority of fault attacks. In lattice-based schemes, masking encompasses arithmetic masking, Boolean masking, and the conversion between arithmetic and Boolean masking (A2B and B2A). This increases the complexity of the algorithmic implementation. However, it remains unclear whether this added complexity introduces new vulnerabilities to fault attacks.

Delvaux's work [8] was among the first to explore this issue, focusing on the linear components of masked Kyber, such as polynomial multiplication and the number theoretic transform. He pointed out that the randomness inherent in masking could expedite the Roulette attack. However, more complex components, such as non-linear components like the message decoder were beyond the scope of this study. In 2024, Kundu *et al.* [14] identified an adder-carry leakage in the masked decoder proposed by Oder *et al.* [17], which enables a practical fault attack on masked Kyber. This highlights the need for increased scrutiny of non-linear components in masked implementations. Building on these findings, we aim to investigate one of the most advanced masked schemes of Kyber, which is proposed in [5]. Since attacks on the addition of offset [19] and A2B conversion [14] have been thoroughly investigated, this paper primarily focuses on the less-explored left part of the masked decoder. In essential, the principle contribution of this work can be summarized as follows:

- We conducted an analysis of the effectiveness of fault injection attacks on the masked Kyber scheme, identifying an exploitable fault attack vulnerability. Based on a practical attacker model, we demonstrate how an attacker can derive a system of inequalities that reveal information about the secret key. To the best of our knowledge, this is the first practical fault attack targeting the arbitrary-order masked message decoder in lattice-based schemes.
- By adapting a solver for the system of inequalities and employing two filtering techniques, we found that the secret keys can be recovered with no more than 36,000, 54,000, and 4,000,000 inequalities for Kyber512, Kyber768, and Kyber1024, respectively. As a side contribution, this is also the first evaluation of the cost of fault attack on the masked non-linear components of Kyber768 and Kyber1024.
- Leveraging the implementation characteristics of this masking scheme, we demonstrated that a simple instruction skip fault in the Bitslice process can achieve the desired bit-flipping effect. The feasibility of this fault injection method was validated through inducing clock glitches on a STM32F4 target board, resulting in successful key recovery. This approach demonstrates a significantly higher fault injection success rate compared to previous attacks, consequently necessitating fewer decapsulation attempts for successful key recovery. A detailed comparison is presented in Table 7.

Outline. This paper is organized as follows. In Sect. 2, we present the background knowledge utilized in this paper. Section 3 details our observations and introduces the basic attack method. In Sect. 4, we describe how to perform the attack on a practical masked implementation. In Sect. 5, we present practical evidence that supports our claims. Finally, we conclude this papaer and discuss potential countermeasures in Sect. 6.

2 Preliminaries

2.1 Notations

To simplify notation, we denote the ring of integers modulo q as $\mathbb{Z}_q$ and the ring of $\mathbb{Z}_q[X]/(X^n+1)$ as $\mathcal{R}_q$. Furthermore, we denote by $\mathbb{B}^k$ the set of byte arrays of length k. Regular font letters, such as v, denote elements in $\mathcal{R}_q$, with $v[i]$ representing the i-th coefficient in v. Specially, when we refer to a message $m \in \mathbb{B}^{32}$, we use $m[i]$ to denote the i-th bit in this message. Bold lower-case letters indicate vectors. By default, all vectors are column vectors, and we denote $\mathbf{v}[i]$ the i-th entry of a vector $\mathbf{v}$, and $\mathbf{v}[i,j]$ the j-th coefficient (bit) in its i-th entry when the entry is a polynomial (message), with the index starting at zero. For an element $z \in \mathbb{Q}$ we denote by $\lceil z \rfloor$ to the closest integer with ties being rounded up. z_i denotes the i-th bit in z, while $z^{(i)}$ denotes the i-th share of masked z. The notation $z^{(\cdot)}$ represents all shares of masked z. Additionally, the symbols $z^{(\cdot)A}$ and $z^{(\cdot)B}$ are used to denote arithmetic masking and Boolean masking, respectively. When dealing with polynoimials, the symbol $\circ$ represents vector multiplication between vectors (matrices and vectors).

2.2 Masked Kyber

The Kyber algorithm is constructed from a public-key encryption scheme (KyberPKE) and employs the Fujisaki-Okamoto (FO) transform [11] to convert the PKE into a CCA-secure key encapsulation mechanism (KyberKEM). A detailed specification is provided in Appendix A.

The secret-key-dependent operation in Kyber is the key decapsulation, in which the secret key and the ciphertext are first used to compute a noisy polynomial mp. Subsequently, the decoding function ($\mathrm{Compress}_q(z,1)$) maps each coefficient of the polynomial to a corresponding message bit. As illustrated in Fig. 1, a coefficient close to 0 is decoded as 0, while a coefficient close to $\lceil \frac{q}{2} \rceil$ is decoded as 1. Following decoding, the recovered message is re-encrypted. If the newly generated ciphertext does not match the original one, a decapsulation failure occurs, and a meaningless output is returned; Otherwise, the correct shared key is established and returned.

Bos *et al.* proposed the first comprehensive implementation of masked Kyber [5]. In their work, they introduced a new masked decoder for message decoding, which is based on a masked bit-sliced binary search. The core part of this decoder is the $\mathrm{Compress}_q^s$ function, as shown in Eq. 1.

$$\mathrm{Compress}_q^s(z) = \neg z_{11} \oplus (\neg z_{11} \cdot z_{10} \cdot z_9 \cdot (z_8 \oplus (\neg z_8 \cdot z_7))) \tag{1}$$

As illustrated in Algorithm 1, the whole decoding process starts with adding the offset $\lfloor \frac{3q}{4} \rfloor$ modulo q from the arithmetic shares with a subsequent A2B conversion to create $\lceil \log_2 q \rceil$-bit Boolean shares of the coefficient. Given these Boolean shares, it then suffices to securely compute whether the masked value

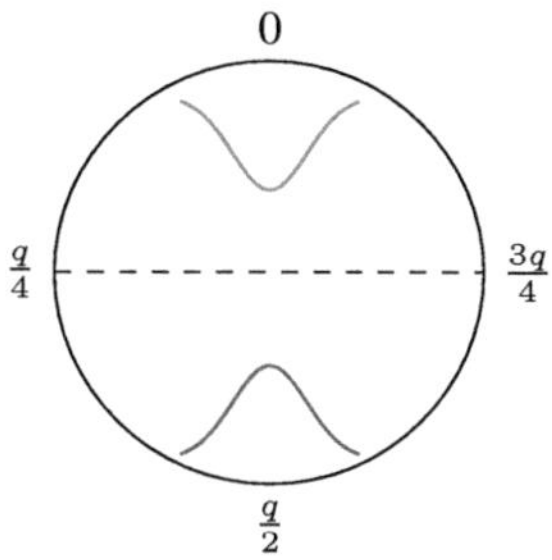

Fig. 1. The original decoding result. The red curve depicts the distribution of polynomial coefficients that are decoded as 1, whereas the green curve depicts the distribution of coefficients decoded as 0. (Color figure online)

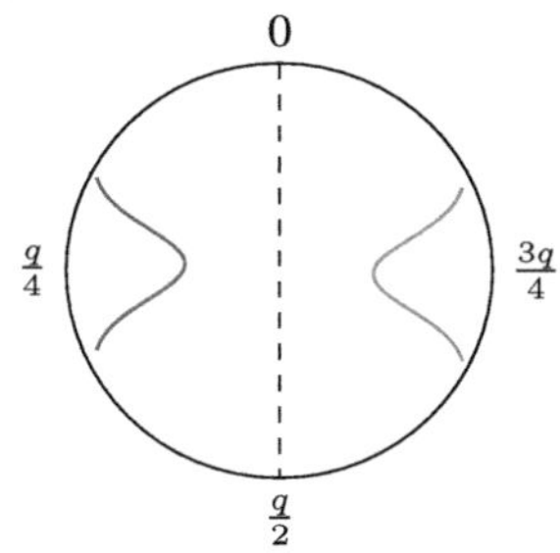

Fig. 2. The decoding result after $+3q/4$. The red curve depicts the distribution of polynomial coefficients decoded as 1, whereas the green curve depicts the distribution of coefficients decoded as 0. (Color figure online)

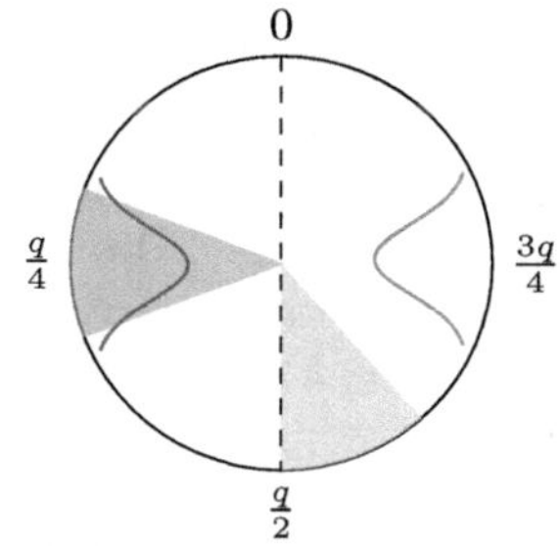

Fig. 3. The shaded regions depict intervals of coefficient that result in decapsulation failures after fault injection. Specifically, the blue regions denote interval containing coefficients exploitable in practical attacks. (Color figure online)

is smaller than $\frac{q}{2}$ using Eq. 1, where

$$\text{Compress}_q^s(z) = \begin{cases} 1, & \text{if } z < \dfrac{q}{2}; \\ 0, & \text{otherwise.} \end{cases}$$

The process correspond to the decoding results in Fig. 2. Following this, a masked binary search is performed, with the $\oplus$ and $\cdot$ operations replaced by their secure counterparts (SecXOR and SecAND). Additionally, the SecREF function is required for fulfilling security properties, which is beyond the scope of this paper. To enhance efficiency, the Boolean shares of the polynomial are converted into a bit-sliced representation, enabling the compress function to be executed in parallel. This bit slicing transformation is crucial to the performance of the masking decoder.

3 Generic Attack Description

In this section, we present our primary observation, which allows for a practical fault attack on the masking scheme proposed in [5]. The attack vulnerability arises from the intricate implementation of the masked message decoder, rather than from the original components of the plain Kyber. For the sake of simplicity, we will initially describe our attack in a non-masked manner, disregarding the obfuscation caused by masking and focus solely on the description provided in Eq. 1. Additionally, unless otherwise specified, all related parameter sets refer

Algorithm 1. Masked Decoder $\text{Compress}_q(z, 1) = \text{Compress}_q^s\left(z + \left\lfloor \frac{3q}{4} \right\rfloor \mod q\right)$

Input: $a^{(\cdot)A}$, $a \in \mathbb{Z}_q[X]$.
Output: $m'^{(\cdot)B}$, $m' = \text{Compress}_q(a, 1) \in \mathbb{Z}_{2^{256}}$.
1: **for** $i \leftarrow 0$ to $n-1$ **do**
2: $\quad a_i^{(0)A} = a_i^{(0)A} + \left\lfloor \frac{3q}{4} \right\rfloor \mod q$
3: $\quad a_i^{(\cdot)B} = \text{A2B}(a_i^{(\cdot)A})$
4: **end for**
5: $z^{(\cdot)B} = \text{Bitslice}(a^{(\cdot)B})$
6: $m'^{(\cdot)B} = \text{SecAND}(\text{SecREF}(\neg z_8^{(\cdot)B}), z_7^{(\cdot)B})$
7: $m'^{(\cdot)B} = \text{SecREF}(\text{SecXOR}(m'^{(\cdot)B}, z_8^{(\cdot)B}))$
8: $m'^{(\cdot)B} = \text{SecAND}(m'^{(\cdot)B}, z_9^{(\cdot)B})$
9: $m'^{(\cdot)B} = \text{SecAND}(m'^{(\cdot)B}, z_{10}^{(\cdot)B})$
10: $m'^{(\cdot)B} = \text{SecAND}(m'^{(\cdot)B}, \neg z_{11}^{(\cdot)B})$
11: $m'^{(\cdot)B} = \text{SecXOR}(m'^{(\cdot)B}, \neg z_{11}^{(\cdot)B})$
12: **return** $m'^{(\cdot)B}$

to Kyber512. The detailed attack on a specific masked implementation will be discussed in the following sections. Our attacker model is described as follows, which is a reasonable setting in a practical attack scenario.

Attacker Model. It is assumed that the attacker has access to the public key and is able to perform an arbitrary number of encapsulations using suitable messages. The attacker then transmits the resulting ciphertext from encapsulation to the target device and introduces a fault during the decapsulation process. The fault injection causes a bit flip in a decoded coefficient z, either before or during the decoding process. Ultimately, the attacker can observe whether a decapsulation failure occurs in accordance with the equality of the share keys derived from encapsulation and fault injected decapsulation.

Each faulted decapsulation result reveals partial information about the secret key, which is represented as an inequality involving the secret key as the unknown variable. By repeating this process and collecting sufficient inequalities, the attacker can solve the system of inequalities and thereby recover the full secret key.

3.1 Fault Effectiveness in Masked Decoder

Since the masked message decoder relies on bit-wise operations, introducing a bit fault may be easier compared to other fault types. Therefore, we first consider the impact of different bit flips. If a bit flip in z causes a flip in a decoded message bit d, an attacker will observe a decapsulation failure. Our primary objective is to determine whether flipping a specific bit in z will lead to a decapsulation failure and, more importantly, to assess what information the decapsulation result might reveal to the attacker.

Table 1. The possible intervals in which flipping z_{10} causes a decapsulation failure.

z_{10}	z_9	z_8	z_7	Interval of z	d
1	1	0	1	[1664, 2048)	$0 \to 1$
1	1	1	0	[1792, 2048)	
0	1	0	1	[640, 1024)	$1 \to 0$
0	1	1	0	[768, 1024)	

As previously stated in Eq. 1, the binary search-based decoding process only involves the five bits $z_7 \dots z_{11}$, and thus we will omit the analysis of the remain lower bits in z. Additionally, when $z_{11} = 1$, the decoding result is always fixed at 0, regardless of the values of the other bits, as shown in Eq. 2. Consequently, when focusing on the lower bits, we omit the interval $[2048, 3329)$, as it corresponds to $z_{11} = 1$.

$$d = 0 \oplus (0 \cdot z_{10} \cdot z_9 \cdot (z_8 \oplus (\neg z_8 \cdot z_7))) = 0 \tag{2}$$

We use z_{10} as an example to illustrate our analysis. Since we are only considering the case where $z_{11} = 0$, we can update Eq. 1 to reflect this in Eq. 3. The equation can be divided into two parts: one involving z_{10} only and the other consisting of the remaining bits. If either of the two parts equals to 0, the decoded message bit will be fixed to 0. This means that flipping z_{10} only becomes significant if the condition $z_9 \cdot (z_8 \oplus (\neg z_8 \cdot z_7)) \neq 0$ is satisfied. We recursively analyze the second part of the equation until all possible cases are considered. The results of this analysis are summarized in Table 1, where it is shown that flipping z_{10} will cause a flip in d and lead to decapsulation failure when $z \in [640, 1024) \cup [1664, 2048)$.

$$\text{Compress}_q^s(z) = \neg(z_{10} \cdot z_9 \cdot (z_8 \oplus (\neg z_8 \cdot z_7))), z < 2048 \tag{3}$$

We extend our recursive analysis to all five bits from z_7 to z_{11}, and the final results are presented in Table 2. The analysis reveals that if an attacker can flip any of the bits involved in the masked decoder, then observing the decapsulation result provides interval information about the decoded coefficient. This key insight allows the attacker to narrow down the possible values of the decoded coefficient, thereby facilitating the recovery of the secret key.

Nevertheless, determining whether this interval information can be exploited by an attacker requires further investigation. In accordance with the Kyber specification presented in Appendix A, the decoded polynomial, denoted as mp, is computed according to Eq. 4. Here, μ denotes the polynomial derived from the encoded message, and we define δ as the noise term to be eliminated during the decoding process. Let $\gamma = \Pr[\|\sigma\|_\infty \geq \lceil q/4 \rfloor]$. The design of Kyber [4] aims to achieve a security level of $1 - \gamma$ by ensuring elements of δ follow a specific probability distribution, thereby satisfying the necessary security properties. Additionally, the Kyber team has provided a Python script[1] for evaluating the

[1] https://github.com/pq-crystals/security-estimates.

Table 2. The interval information of z provided by the faulted decapsulation results.

	Decapsulation Failure	Decapsulation Success
z_{11}	$[0, 1792) \cup [2048, 3329)$	$[1792, 2048)$
z_{10}	$[640, 1024) \cup [1664, 2048)$	$[0, 640) \cup [1024, 1664)$
z_9	$[1152, 2048)$	$[0, 1152)$
z_8	$[1664, 1792)$	$[0, 1664) \cup [1792, 2048)$
z_7	$[1792, 1920)$	$[0, 1792) \cup [1920, 2048)$

probability distribution of δ.

$$\begin{aligned} mp &= v + \Delta v - (\mathbf{u} + \Delta \mathbf{u}) \circ \mathbf{s} \\ &= \mathbf{t} \circ \mathbf{r} + e_2 + \mu + \Delta v - (\mathbf{A} \circ \mathbf{r} + \mathbf{e}_1 + \Delta \mathbf{u}) \circ \mathbf{s} \\ &= \mathbf{r} \circ \mathbf{e} - (\mathbf{e}_1 + \Delta \mathbf{u}) \circ \mathbf{s} + e_2 + \Delta v + \mu \\ &= \delta + \mu \end{aligned} \tag{4}$$

Since the input coefficient z for Compress_q^s is equal to either $\lceil q/4 \rfloor + \delta$ or $\lceil 3q/4 \rfloor + \delta$, the script can also be used to evaluate the probability distribution of decoded coefficients. To illustrate, in the case of flipping z_8, a decapsulation failure occurs only if $z \in [1664, 1792)$. Accordingly, the probability of a noisy coefficient occurring within this interval is $2^{-103.9}$. This indicates that the probability of flipping z_8 and resulting in a decapsulation failure is essentially zero. Similarly, the same reasoning applies to other bits.

In accordance with the aforementioned guideline, selecting z_{10} for fault injection proves to be the optimal choice. When an attacker flips the z_{10} bit from 0 to 1, the probability that z falls into a interval resulting in decapsulation failure is $1 - 2^{-6.8}$ (approximately 99.1%), which is within an acceptable range for practical attacks. On the other hand, the opposite flip direction, corresponding to the interval $[1664, 2048)$, has a negligible probability of $2^{-39.8}$, making it impractical for exploitation in a real-world attack scenario. Consequently, when targeting the z_{10} bit for a fault attack, the entire interval of z can be divided into three distinct regions, as illustrated in Fig. 3.

If the value of z falls into the blank area in Fig. 3, a bit flip happened to z_{10} does not affect the decapsulation result, providing no useful information for the attack. However, when a decoded coefficient lies in the interval $[640, 1024)$ (the blue region) and z_{10} is flipped by fault injection, the attacker will observe a decapsulation failure. Similarly, the interval $[1664, 2048)$ (the gray region) has the same effect. Although a coefficient lies in $[1664, 2048)$ occurs with very low probability, it may still introduce some noise to the attack. Since the attacker has the ability to control the message bit corresponding to z during the encapsulation phase, they can ensure that $z < \frac{q}{2}$ by fixing the target message bit at 1. Furthermore, Kyber has an inherently low failure probability, as indicated in Table 8, which can be neglected in this attack due to its negligible occurrence. This leads to the following conclusion: during the decapsulation of a filtered ciphertext, if a bit flip occurs in z_{10} and the attacker observes a decapsulation failure, they can infer that $z \in [640, 1024)$. Otherwise, $z \in [0, 640) \cup [1024, 1664)$. The remainder of this section will demonstrate how key recovery can be achieved based on this observation.

3.2 Key Recovery Attack

In Eq. 4, $\Delta\mathbf{u}$ and Δv represent the losses introduced by the lossy compression of $\mathbf{u}$ and v, respectively. The value of Δv is computed as

$$\Delta v = \text{Decompress}(\text{Compress}(v, d_v), d_v) - v,$$

and $\Delta\mathbf{u}$ is determined analogously. Consequently, both Δv and $\Delta\mathbf{u}$ are publicly accessible. Furthermore, the variables $\mathbf{e}_1$, $\mathbf{r}$, e_2, and μ are involved in the encapsulation process and are therefore under the attacker's control. The only unknowns are $\mathbf{s}$ and $\mathbf{e}$, which are secret vectors generated during the key generation phase.

Following the description of the masked decoder, we set $z = mp[i] + \lfloor 3q/4 \rfloor \bmod q$ as the input to Compress_q^s. Thus, after a faulted decapsulation with a flip in z_{10}, if a decapsulation failure is observed, the attacker can infer that $z \in [640, 1024)$, which is equivalent to $\delta[i] \in [-192, 192)$. If a decapsulation success is observed, then $\delta[i] < -192$ or $\delta[i] \geq 192$. After performing ω faulted decapsultions, the attacker can obtain ω inequalities, represented as Eq. 5. Here, $\mathbf{M}$ and $\mathbf{b}$ represent the public information from the ω inequilities, while $\mathbf{x}$ represents the unknown vector of $\mathbf{s}$ and $\mathbf{e}$, which needs to be solved. This vector contains $2nk$ unknown coefficients, with each coefficient having $2\eta_1 + 1$ possible values. For simplicity, we refer to inequalities featuring the $\notin$ symbol as negative inequalities and those featuring the $\in$ symbol as positive inequalities. Throughout the remainder of this paper, we denote $\psi = 2nk$ and set $i = 0$.

$$\mathbf{Mx} + \mathbf{b} = \begin{pmatrix} (\mathbf{r})_{(0)}, -(\mathbf{e}_1 + \Delta\mathbf{u})_{(0)} \\ \cdots \\ (\mathbf{r})_{(\omega-1)}, -(\mathbf{e}_1 + \Delta\mathbf{u})_{(\omega-1)} \end{pmatrix} \begin{pmatrix} \mathbf{e} \\ \mathbf{s} \end{pmatrix} + e_2 + \Delta v \underset{\notin}{\in} [-192, 192) \quad (5)$$

Given the large number of inequalities and the inherent error rate in fault attacks, directly solving such a system of inequalities is impractical. To address this challenge, a series of solvers have been proposed, and the underlying approach is similar across these solvers. First, the distribution of all secret coefficients is initialized based on their sampling distribution. For instance, in Kyber, the coefficients in $\mathbf{s}$ and $\mathbf{e}$ follow a centered binomal distribution parameterized by η_1. Next, each coefficient iteratively updates its distribution based on the information provided by the system of inequalities. For the i-th inequality, which corresponds to a decryption failure, the probability that the k-th candidate of the j-th unknown coefficient is the correct guess is updated as shown in Eq. 6. This equation captures how the probability distribution evolves over iterations by factoring in contributions from the current inequality and other coefficients. The iterative process continues until a termination condition is satisfied. At that point, each coefficient selects the candidate with the highest probability as the final prediction for the secret key.

$$\mathsf{P}[i,j,k] = \Pr\left(-192 \leq \mathbf{M}[i,j](k-\eta_1) + \left(\sum_{j' \in [0,\psi-1]\setminus\{j\}} \mathbf{M}[i,j']\mathbf{x}[j']\right) + \mathbf{b}[i] < 192\right) \tag{6}$$

To implement such a solver, the belief propagation (BP)-based approach can be utilized, as demonstrated in [13]. The main bottleneck of this solver lies in the convolution operation, which involves computing all possible combinations of $x[j']$ for $j' \neq j$. To accelerate the process, previous work [19] proposed employing the Fast Fourier Transform (FFT) to optimize these convolutions, significantly reducing the time required to perform the updates. Additionally, a binary tree algorithm was introduced to avoid inefficient re-computations. More recently, a simplified method was presented in [8], which further reduces computational overhead. This method leverages the Central Limit Theorem (CLT) to approximate the sum of distributions using a normal distribution X. The mean of X is given by

$$\mu = \mathbf{M}[i,j](k-\eta_1) + \left(\sum_{j' \in [0,\psi-1]\setminus\{j\}} \mathbf{M}[i,j']\mathsf{E}[\mathbf{x}[j']]\right) + \mathbf{b}[i],$$

and the standard deviation is calculated as

$$\sigma = \sqrt{\sum_{j' \in [0,\psi-1]} \mathbf{M}[i,j']^2 \mathsf{Var}[\mathbf{x}[j']]}.$$

To convert it into a standard normal distribution, we perform the normalization and get the standard normal distribution Z. Therefore, by revisiting the solver, we can approximate Eq. 6 as Eq. 7.

$$\mathsf{P}[i,j,k] \approx \Pr\left(\frac{-192-\mu}{\sigma} \leq Z < \frac{192-\mu}{\sigma}\right) \tag{7}$$

This allows for rapid calculation of the probabilities using the cumulative distribution function (CDF) of the standard normal distribution, as shown in Eq. 8. By applying this approximation, the solving process is significantly accelerated, reducing the time required for hundreds times.

$$\mathsf{P}[i,j,k] \approx F_{norm}(\frac{192-\mu}{\sigma}) - F_{norm}(\frac{-192-\mu}{\sigma}) \tag{8}$$

In our attack, we adopt this simplified solver approach by adapting the probability calculation according to Eq. 7 and Eq. 8, thus tailoring it specifically to the inequalities derived in our attack. Moreover, by leveraging the CLT approximation and PMF calculations, this solver efficiently manages the substantial volume of inequalities generated throughout the attack, thereby enabling a feasible key recovery process even under constrained computational resources.

Table 3. The maximum and minimum values of Δv and e_2.

	Δv		e_2	
	#min	#max	#min	#max
Kyber512/768	−104	104	−2	2
Kyber1024	−52	52	−2	2

3.3 Boosting the Attack with Inequalities Filter

The attack proposed in [8] derives information from faulted decapsulations in the form of inequalities indicating either $\delta \geq 0$ or $\delta < 0$. Since the mean of the distribution of δ is 0, the proportions of positive and negative inequalities are balanced, approximately 50%:50%. In contrast, the inequalities obtained in our attack provide relatively imbalanced interval information. Specifically, for randomly generated ciphertexts, the obtained negative inequalities account for only $2^{-6.8} \approx 0.9\%$ in Kyber512, which presents a significant disadvantage for our solver. To address this, we adapt two filtering techniques to enhance the effectiveness of our attack. For comparison, the updated proportions after applying the filters are presented in Table 4.

Filter1: Removing Low-Contribution Inequalities Offline. In most cases, a noise coefficient $\delta[i] \in [-192, 192)$. Consequently, for many positive inequalities, most or all possible values of the secret coefficients satisfy the inequality. This renders these inequalities largely ineffective for distinguishing the correct candidates. We categorize such inequalities as low-contribution inequalities. To enhance the attack, it is crucial to identify high-contribution inequalities. According to the Central Limit Theorem, $\delta[i]$ is distributed approximately a normal distribution with mean $(\Delta_v + e_2)[i]$. Consequently, selecting ciphertexts where $(\Delta v + e_2)[i]$ approaches the boundary values ± 192 results in more incorrect secret coefficient candidates being excluded for the corresponding inequality.

The value of e_2 is sampled from a distribution parameterized by η_2, while the value of Δv are associated with the parameter d_v. The interval information for these two values is provided in Table 3. Without loss of generality, we choose to use the ciphertext of encapsulation where $|(\Delta v + e_2)[i]| \geq 94$ for Kyber512/768 and $|(\Delta v + e_2)[i]| \geq 42$ for Kyber1024.

This filtering technique allows the attacker to focus on ciphertexts more likely to produce high-contribution inequalities, significantly enhancing the effectiveness of our attack. Moreover, since suitable ciphertexts can be selected offline, this approach does not increase the overall attack cost.

We can infer that the required number of inequalities to solve the secret key for Kyber1024 will increase at a rate faster than what would be expected based solely on the increase in security level. This is due to the more biased values present in Kyber1024. A detailed analysis of this observation will be provided in the following subsection.

Table 4. The proportions of decapsulation success and failure.

	Without filter		With filter1		With filter1 and filter2	
	#fail	#success	#fail	#success	#fail	#success
Kyber512	99.1%	0.9%	95.5%	4.5%	$(95.5\% - \alpha)/(1 - \alpha)$	$4.5\%/(1 - \alpha)$
Kyber768	99.41%	0.59%	97%	3%	$(97\% - \alpha)/(1 - \alpha)$	$3\%/(1 - \alpha)$
Kyber1024	99.931%	0.069%	99.76%	0.24%	$(99.76\% - \alpha)/(1 - \alpha)$	$0.24\%/(1 - \alpha)$

Filter2: Increase the Proportion of Negative Inequalities. In our attack, we deal with a highly imbalanced system of inequalities, where the number of negative inequalities is significantly less than the positive ones. We have observed that this imbalance can cause the solver to converge prematurely. Initially, for Kyber512, the proportion of negative to positive inequalities was approx 0.9 : 99.1. With the filter1 applied, this proportion can be improved to some extend. There is no theoretical method to calculate the new proportion. We provide an experimental result in Table 4. However, this improvement is still insufficient for Kyber1024. To further address this issue, we revisit another filtering technique proposed in [14], called *rejection sampling*. In this approach, a random proportion α of the inequalities is rejected, but only from those generated in cases of positive inequalities. This selective rejection helps increase the proportion of negative inequalities, balancing the system and improving the performance of the solver, this improvement can be seen in Table 4. For example, with $\alpha = 94\%$, the proportion of inequalities from Kyber1024 can be brought to the same level as Kyber512 only using filter1.

4 Practical Attack on Masked Kyber

The attack described in Sect. 3 omits specific details of the masked implementation to provide a more intuitive understanding of our approach. In this section, we will delve into how the attack can be successfully executed in a practical masked implementation. Considering our attacker model, fault injections can be categorized into the following types:

- **Exact Fault**: The fault injection achieves the desired effect. Specifically, a noisy coefficient in the range $[640, 1024)$ results in a decapsulation failure; otherwise, decapsulation success is observed.
- **Invalid Fault**: The fault injection does not produce the expected outcome. For example, a noisy coefficient in the range $[640, 1024)$ does not lead to a decapsulation failure. This can be caused by either a failed fault injection or interference from the masking, which will be clarified later in this section.
- **Reset Fault**: The fault injection has an unintended consequence, disrupting the control flow and rendering the process unusable.
- **Unintended Fault**: The fault injection causes an unexpected result, such as a noisy coefficient outsides the range $[640, 1024)$ that still leads to a decapsulation failure.

4.1 Bit-Flip in Masking Implementation

First, considering the masking, an intermediate value is divided into $t+1$ shares. Before message decoding, these shares are transformed into Boolean masking using the A2B transformation, as outlined in Algorithm 1. For a Boolean-masked coefficient, if any share of a bit in z is flipped, such as $z_{10}^{(0)}$, the unmasked value of z_{10} will also be flipped.

This makes the bit-flip fault model ideal for our attack, which has already been applied in the attack proposed in [13]. However, executing precise bit flips in a practical setting is challenging. The stuck-at fault model used in [14] can also be applied to our attack. If $z_{10}^{(0)}$ is stuck at 0 or 1, due to the randomness of masking, on average, two decapsulations of the same ciphertext will yield a valid flip of the unmasked bit. By decapsulating a ciphertext β times, and with an appropriate choice of β, the effectiveness of a stuck-at fault approaches that of an ideal bit-flip fault, though it requires several times the number of additional decapsulation attempts.

The bit-flip and stuck-at faults can be injected over a relatively long time window, as shown in Table 5. Nonetheless, it is important to emphasize that inducing a single-bit fault remains highly challenging for an attacker.

4.2 Bit-Flip Based on Instruction Skip

The use of bitwise operations in the masked scheme has enabled the development of a more relaxed fault injection method for achieving the desired fault model. In [5], the authors stress the necessity of transforming the Boolean shares of the polynomial to a bit-sliced representation prior to compute the compression function. The bit-sliced representation allows parallel accelaration in an otherwise serial software implementation, offering a performance improvement concerned about the word size of the target platform. Given that only the five most significant bits will be used in subsequent operations, it is prudent to discard the lower seven bits in order to reduce the cost.

Although the implementation of BitSlice strongly depends on the capabilities of the target platform, the fundamental logic remains consistent. A basic description of the naive BitSlice process is provided in Algorithm 2, where the five most significant bits of l coefficients are stored in five registers in the bit-sliced representation. Notably, a critical step involves assigning a single bit of a coefficient to the target register. If an attacker manages to skip this step, the result bit will be fixed at 0, effectively creating a stuck-at-0 fault. Since the implementation is masked, the final outcome will appear as a random bit flip on the unmasked value with a probability of 50%. As we can perform β times fault injected decapsulations of the same ciphertext, once a decapsulation happens, then we can classify the inequality from this ciphertext as a positive inequality. Otherwise, all β decapsulations succeed, then a negative inequality generated. By selecting an appropriate β, we can minimize the influence of masking and invalid fault on our attack, and reduce the error rate of negative inequalities to nearly 0.

Algorithm 2. BitSlice

Input: a, a polynomial
Input: l, word size of target platform
Output: b, the bit-sliced representation of a

```
for i ← 0 to l − 1 do
    b[i] = 0
end for
for i ← 0 to 4 do
    for j ← 0 to l − 1 do
        bit = (a[j] ≫ (i + 7))&1
        bit = bit ≪ j
        b[i] = b[i] | bit
    end for
end for
```

Table 5. Available fault injection types for our attack.

Fault model	Injection Target
Bit-Flip	A2B
	Bitslice
Stuck-at 0/1	SecAND
	load/store
Instruction Skip	Bitslice

4.3 Other Feasible Fault Models

In addition to the exact instruction skip, other operations can also be leveraged for the attack. For instance, if the right operation ($\gg$) operation is skipped, then $z_0^{(0)}$ will replace $z_{10}^{(0)}$, resulting in a random bit fault. Similarly, if the left shift ($\ll$) operation is skipped, $a[j]_{10}^{(0)}$ will be set as 0 and $a[0]_{10}^{(0)}$ will incur a random fault.

Moreover, if the attacker have the capability to perform a single-bit fault injection, such as the stuck-at-0/1 fault used in [14], a more wide range of fault injection becomes available for our attack. Any operation involving z_{10} can serve as a target. A summary is provided in Table 5, demonstrating that key recovery can still be accomplished even without bit-sliced optimization. However, the use of bit slicing significantly weakens the requirements for the attacker.

5 Experiments

In this section, we first evaluate both the correctness and the performance of our attack based on the results of software simulation experiments. Subsequently, the feasibility of the attack was validated in a practical attack scenario by executing the attack on a STM32F405 target board, which utilizes clock glitches to induce instruction skip faults.

5.1 Experiments Setup

We employed the Chipwhisperer suite [18] to carry out our fault attack. The suite comprises an STM32F405 target board, which incorporates an ARM

Cortex-M4 core, in conjunction with a Chipwhisperer-Lite control board. The Chipwhisperer-Lite provides a 28MHz clock to the target board, thus it is also employed to generate clock glitches for fault injection.

The STM32F405 board serves as the victim device. The device receives ciphertext, performs decapsulation with the secret key, and subsequently returns a shared key. Since the implementation in [5] is not open-source and the fault attack only targets the message decoding process, the firmware running on the board is based on Kyber's reference implementation[2], equipped with the masked decoder described in [5]. In this implementation, the BitSlice process is a proof-of-concept implementation based on the naive approach described in Algorithm 2. The code was compiled using the *GNU Arm GCC Compiler 10.3.1* with *-O3* optimization.

When solving the obtained system of inequalities, we primarily used the simplified solver from [8]. Additionally, we also evaluated our attack using the BP-based solver from [12] for comparison. Both solvers were adapted from the source code provided in the respective original papers to suit our attack[3,4]. Empirically, we set the maximum number of iterations for the solvers to 8 and used the average number of recovered coefficients over 10 runs as the final result.

5.2 Evaluation of the Proposed Attack

First, we verify the correctness of our attack on Kyber512, which is expected to the easiest to break. The results, shown in Fig. 4, demonstrate that our attack is capable of recovering the secret coefficients, and the application of filter1 significantly reduces the required number of inequalities. With filter1 is applied, only 36, 000 inequalities are required for a full key recovery. When employing filter2 with $\alpha = 0.5$, we observe an improvement in the proportion of negative inequalities. However, this leads to a decrease in the success rate due to the reduced number of inequalities available for the solver.

Additionally, since there may be an error rate in fault attacks, we conducted another experiment to evaluate the error-tolerance ability of our attack. We observed that if β is not sufficiently large, some positive inequalities may be mistakenly identified as negative cases. To simulate this scenario, we intentionally corrupted a portion of the positive inequalities within the collected system of inequalities, thereby introducing an error rate in the negative inequalities. The results, shown in Fig. 5, indicate that our attack can tolerate an error rate of up to 30%, with only a reasonable increase in the required number of inequalities.

The results for all three security levels are provided in Fig. 6. The attack difficulty for Kyber768 is comparable to that of Kyber512, which aligns with our analysis. As expected, recovering the secret coefficients for Kyber1024 is significantly harder than for the previous two levels. Based on the analysis in Sect. 3, we identified that applying filter2 with $\alpha = 0.94$ yields a system of inequalities with

[2] https://github.com/pq-crystals/kyber.
[3] https://github.com/Crypto-TII/roulette.
[4] https://github.com/juliusjh/improved_decryption_error_recovery.

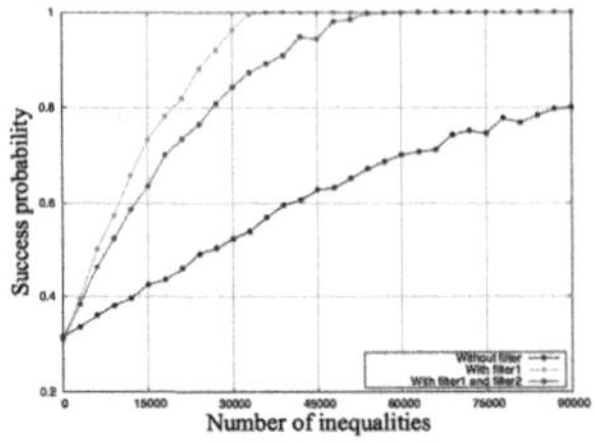

Fig. 4. Solving filtered and unfiltered inequalities for Kyber512.

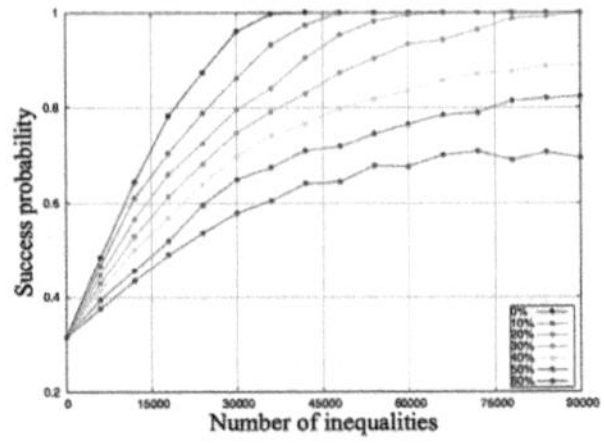

Fig. 5. Solving corrupted inequalities for Kyber512.

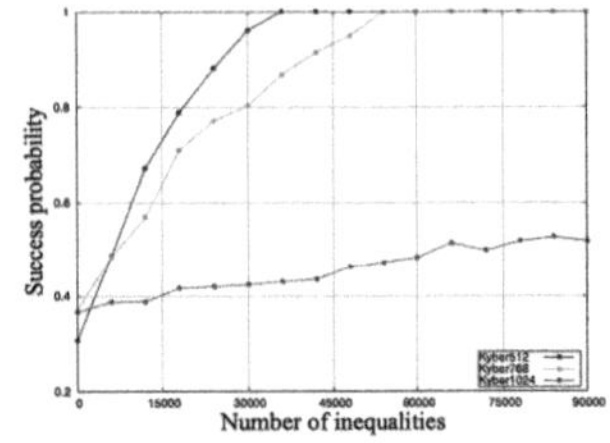

Fig. 6. Solving filtered inequalities for all three security levels.

a relatively acceptable ratio of negative to positive inequalities for Kyber1024. We conducted experiments to determine the number of inequalities required for full key recovery, and the results are shown in Fig. 7. The results indicate that 4,000,000 inequalities need to be collected, and the solver must solve a system of 240,000 inequalities for full key recovery.

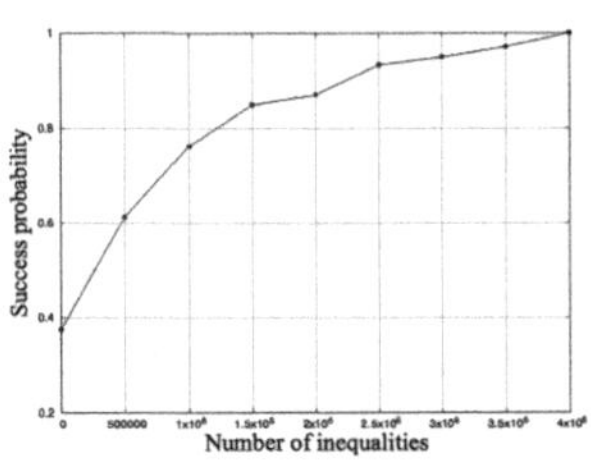

Fig. 7. Solving filtered inequalities for Kyber1024 with $\alpha = 0.94$.

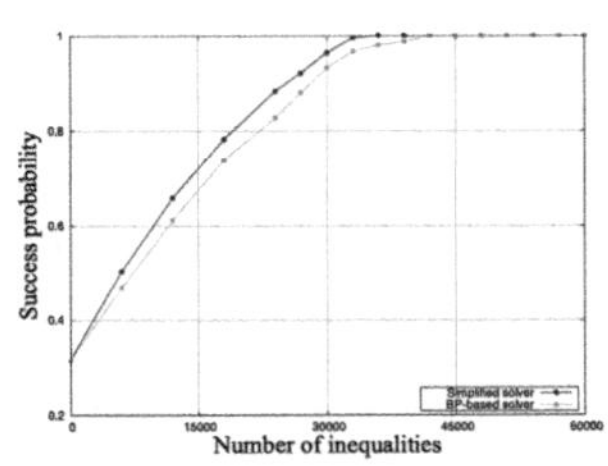

Fig. 8. Comparison between the simplified solver and BP-based solver.

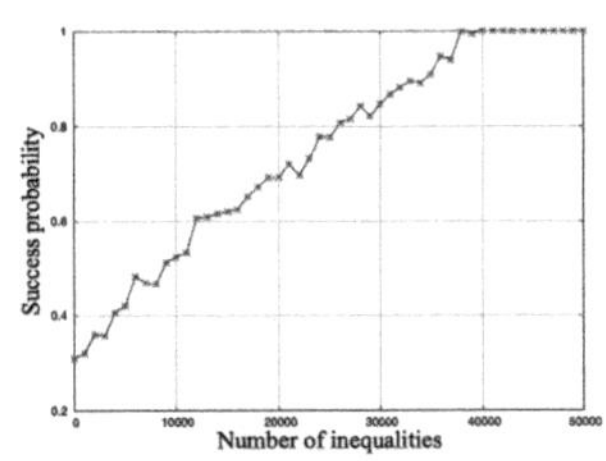

Fig. 9. The key-recovery results of practical attack experiments.

In [12], Hermelink *et al.* highlighted that the BP-based solver demonstrates an advantage in terms of the number of inequalities when applied to traditional attacks involving balanced inequalities. For comparison, we conducted an experiment to solve our system of inequalities using both solvers, with the results presented in Fig. 8. The findings indicate that, in our attack, the BP-based solver does not exhibit a discernible advantage. Given its higher requirements for runtime and memory, there is insufficient motivation to employ the BP-based solver in our attack.

5.3 Fault Profiling

To achieve an effective fault injection, selecting the correct fault injection parameter set is essential. For clock glitch-based fault injection, the main parameters involve determining when to insert the glitch (ext_offset) and what type of glitch to apply (offset and width). In this subsection, we detail the fault profiling process in our experiments.

A naive method to locate the target operation would be to scan through the entire decapsulation process from the beginning. However, this approach is highly time-consuming. Instead, we found that the start of the BitSlice process can be coarsely identified using power side-channel information. Since we are targeting the first coefficient, only a small portion of the process needs to be scanned. For simplicity, in our experiments, we placed a trigger signal at the beginning of the Bitslice process. It is worth noting, however, that the target operation remains identifiable solely through power trace analysis. This implies that the absence of a trigger signal would not impede attacks in real-world scenarios.

Even with precise identification of the target operation, there may still be a probability of fault injection failure, as the analysis in Sect. 4. Therefore, a critical aspect of the attack is how to handle error inequalities caused by imperfect fault injections.

Since the attacker can only observe whether decapsulation succeeds or fails, it is not possible to directly distinguish between an exact injection and an unintended injection in the case of a decapsulation failure. In the event of a destroyed injection, the attacker can simply retry the decapsulation with the same ciphertext. Similar to the strategy employed in [14], multiple faulted decapsulations can be performed on a single ciphertext to mitigate the issue of invalid injections. Fortunately, the solver used in our attack demonstrates a high tolerance for errors, minimizing concerns about destroyed-injection.

To determine suitable parameters for fault injection, we performed a scan across the intervals shown in Table 6. The offset and width represent the timing and duration of the glitch within a single clock cycle. Choosing smaller values for these parameters minimizes their impact on execution and reduces the likelihood of unintended faults. Similarly, the repeat parameter, which controls the number of glitches inserted during a single decapsulation, is fixed at 1 to further reduce unintended faults. As for the ext_offset, which determines how many clock cycles after the trigger signal the glitch is inserted, we empirically set the maximum scan value to 50 in our experiment. After the scanning process, the number of decapsulations that returned an unexpected share key from fault injection with varying ext_offset values is shown in Fig. 10. We observed that flips mainly occurred at ext_offset 28, 34, and 20. However, there is also the possiblility the some flips were caused by unintended faults. To filter this parameter, we propose the following method: for each candidate ext_offset, we use a parameter pair of offset and width that enables flips, then collect 500 inequalities through our fault attack. Next, we check whether the number of decapsulation successes aligns with or close to the theoretical proportion. Finally, we found that ext_offsets 28 and 34 did not result in any decapsulation successes, while ext_offset 20 showed the correct proportion. Thus, we selected ext_offset = 20 for our attack configuration.

Table 6. The intervals during parameters scanning.

offset	width	ext_offset	repeat
$[-20, 20]$	$[1, 20]$	$[1, 50]$	1

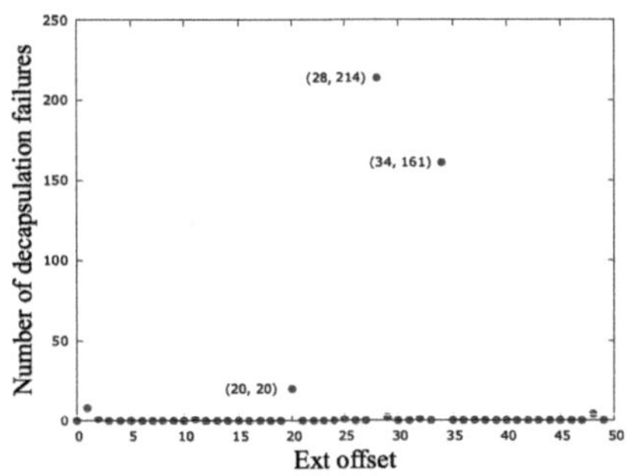

Fig. 10. The number of decapsulation failures with different ext_offset.

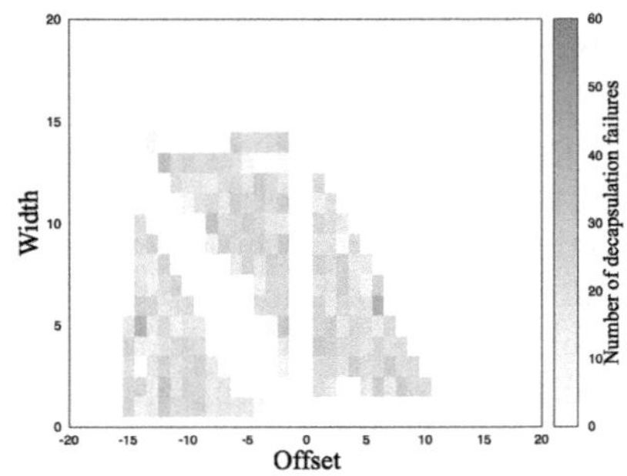

Fig. 11. The number of decapsulation failures with different (offset, width).

Additionally, to minimize the number of invalid injections and thereby lower the total number of decapsulations required for our attack, we fixed ext_offset at 20 and conducted 100 faulted decapsulations for each pair of offset and width. The resulting number of decapsulation failures is presented in Fig. 11.

5.4 Inequalities Acquirements and Key Recovery

Following the fault profiling phase, we conducted our attack using the predetermined parameters. Initially, we collected a total of 50,000 inequalities. To ensure the efficacy of the fault injections and minimize the occurrence of invalid injections, each decapsulation attempt was repeated 10 times. Among the inequalities, 28 negative inequalities are identified as error, indicating an error rate of 6.2%, while no erroneous positive inequalities were observed. We then applied our solver to recover the entire secret key. As illustrated in Fig. 9, we found that with at least 38,000 inequalities, we were able to recover the entire secret key for Kyber512. This result aligns with our simulation experiments, confirming the validity of our attack approach. This demonstrates that even with fewer attempts, our attack remains highly effective, significantly reducing the overall attack cost while maintaining high success rates.

5.5 Comparison

The simulation and practical experimental results indicate that the proposed attack is capable of successfully recovering the secret key of Kyber. A comprehensive analysis and comparison are presented in Table 7. The number of inequalities represents the results from simulation experiments under the assumption of perfect fault injection, while β indicates the required number of decapsulation attempts to perform a successful attack in the practical experiments.

In comparison to the attack described in [8], our attack targets the more complex part of the masked Kyber implementation, specifically the message decoder. The faulted decapsulation results produce an imbalanced system of inequalities, providing less information about the secret key compared to the approach in [8]. Consequently, our attack requires several times more inequalities theoretically. However, the attack in [8] relies on random faults in the polynomial coefficients, necessitating a larger number of decapsulation attempts of a ciphertext to generate an inequality (denoted by β) even with high-precision fault injection.

Specifically, to approach the error rate in our attack with $\beta = 10$ (approximately 6.2%), their attack would require $\beta > 100$ (see Fig. 7 in [8]). Thus, in practical scenarios, their attack requires significantly more faulted decapsulation attempts than ours. For instance, their practical experiments indicate that with $\beta \geq 20$, the error rate reaches approximately 50%. Under these conditions, successful key recovery requires 27,000 inequalities, corresponding to a total of 540,000 decapsulation attempts. In contrast, our attack with $\beta = 10$ requires only 38,000 inequalities to recover the secret key, corresponding to 380,000 decapsulation attempts, representing a reduction of approximately 30%.

Furthermore, the attack in [8] necessitates the manipulation of a compressed ciphertext coefficient of an otherwise correctly computed encapsulation. Therefore, the attack can be effectively mitigated by countermeasures such as the message polynomial sanity check proposed in [20]. In contrast, our attack does not rely on manipulated ciphertexts (MC), making it considerably harder to defend.

When compared to the attack described in [14], our approach requires slightly fewer inequalities. This is because a single faulted decapsulation in our attack provides boundary information on both sides, whereas the attack in [14] only obtains one boundary. Notably, our attack only requires a clock glitch to perform an instruction skip, while the attack in [14] requires a single-bit stuck-at fault using expensive electromagnetic pulse technique to inject fault with high precision for injection time and location. Moreover, our fault attack demonstrates a significantly higher success rate, allowing us to use a much smaller β, representing fewer faulted decapsulation attempts. Additionally, we are the first to evaluate the impact of this type of attack on Kyber768 and Kyber1024, discovering notable differences when handling Kyber1024 and providing an evaluation of the cost of recovering the full secret key for Kyber1024.

Table 7. Comparison between this work and previous attacks.

	Type of Inequalities	Security Level	No. Inequalities	β	Type of Faults	MC Req.
This work	$\delta \overset{\in}{\notin} [-192, 192)$	Kyber512	36,000	≥ 10	Clock glitch	✗
		Kyber768	54,000			
		Kyber1024	4,000,000			
[14]	$\delta \underset{<}{\geq} -192$	Kyber512	60,000	≥ 180	EM pulse	✗
[8]	$\delta \underset{<}{\geq} 0$	Kyber512	8,500	> 100	Clock glitch	✔
		Kyber768	9,400			
		Kyber1024	12,000			

6 Conclusion

In this paper, we propose a novel fault attack against masked Kyber. By employing an instruction skip fault, an attacker can successfully recover the full secret key of a practical masked Kyber implementation. The effectiveness of our attack stems from the structure of the masked message decoder introduced in [5], further enhanced by bit slicing-optimizated implementation of the decoder. These results underscore the vulnerability of masked implementations to fault attacks. The message decoder can also be extended to other lattice-based schemes, making our attack a broader threat to lattice-based cryptosystems. Notably, both the attacks on non-linear components of masked Kyber, this work and the one described in [14], are based on single-bit faults, demonstrating that the use of bit slicing can be advantageous for fault attackers.

To defend against this attack, several countermeasures can be considered. Mishra et al. [15] proposed a probabilistic method based on rejection sampling to mitigate this type of attack. However, integrating this approach into a masked implementation is challenging, as it requires two to three retries even for an unfaulted decapsulation. Coron et al. [6] introduced a new message decoder based on a table-based conversion algorithm. Our analysis has not identified similar vulnerabilities in this scheme. Nevertheless, this method incurs a higher probability of decryption failure; therefore, further investigation into its security is necessary. Finally, shuffling can serve as an effective countermeasure against our attack, since it obscures the index of the faulted coefficient. This uncertainty prevents the establishment of the inequality, thereby hindering the attack.

Acknowledgements. The authors appreciate the anonymous reviewers for their valuable feedback, and would like to especially thank our shepherd, Prof. Ruben Niederhagen, for his detailed and constructive guidance during the revision process. This work is supported by the National Natural Science Foundation of China under Grant U2336210, 62172395; and Beijing Natural Science Foundation under Grant L234085.

A Kyber

Kyber consists of three parts: key generation (Algorithm 3), encapsulation (Algorithm 4), and decapsulation (Algorithm 5) [22]. The KyberKEM is equipped with three parameter sets, corresponding to different security levels, which are defined by five individual parameters: k, η_1, η_2, d_u and d_v. Additionally, two constants n and q are used throughout the algorithm. The three parameter sets are given in Table 8. Also, Table 8 illustrates the negligible decapsulation failure probability inherent in Kyber.

Table 8. Parameter sets of Kyber.

	n	q	k	η_1	η_2	d_u	d_v	Decapsulation failure rate
Kyber512	256	3329	2	3	2	10	4	$2^{-138.8}$
Kyber768	256	3329	3	2	2	10	4	$2^{-164.8}$
Kyber1024	256	3329	4	2	2	11	5	$2^{-174.8}$

The decapsulation of Kyber comprises a decryption procedure (Algorithm 7), an encryption procedure (Algorithm 8) and the hash function-based symmetric primitives G, J. During the decapsulation process, the initial step is to perform decryption. The ciphertext is decrypted to an message $m \in \mathbb{B}^{32}$ using the secret key $\mathbf{s}$, whose coefficients belong to $[-\eta_1, \eta_1]$ and follow a centered binomial distribution. The message is subsequently re-encrypted to prevent outside exposure. The re-encrypted ciphertext is compared with the original ciphertext in the final step of the decapsulation process. If the two ciphertexts do not match, indicating a decryption error or tampering, the decapsulation procedure returns an error shared key derived from the original ciphertext.

Additionally, to reduce the ciphertext size, Kyber applies lossy compression to the coefficients in $\mathbf{u}$ and v, compressing each coefficient to d_u or d_v bits, respectively. The compression and decompression procedure can be found in Eq. 9 and Eq. 10. When $d = 1$, the Compress and Decompress functions are commonly referred to as message decoding and encoding in the general context of lattice-based schemes. Henceforth in this paper, the terms "encoding" and "decoding" will be utilized.

$$\text{Compress}_q(z, d) = \lceil (2^d/q) * z \rfloor \mod 2^d \tag{9}$$

$$\text{Decompress}_q(z, d) = \lceil (q/2^d) * z \rfloor \tag{10}$$

Algorithm 3. KyberKEM.KeyGen

Output: $pk \in \mathbb{B}^{384k+32}$
Output: $sk \in \mathbb{B}^{768k+96}$
$z \xleftarrow{\$} \mathbb{B}^{32}$
$(pk', sk') \leftarrow$ KyberPKE.KeyGen()
$pk \leftarrow pk'$
$sk \leftarrow (pk||sk'||\mathsf{H}(pk)||z)$
return (pk, sk)

Algorithm 4. KyberKEM.Encaps

Input: $pk \in \mathbb{B}^{384k+32}$
Output: shared key $K \in \mathbb{B}^{32}$
Output: ciphertext $c \in \mathbb{B}^{32d_u k+d_v}$
$m \xleftarrow{\$} \mathbb{B}^{32}$
$(K, r) \leftarrow G(m||H(pk))$
$c \leftarrow$ KyberPKE.Enc(pk, m, r)
return (K, c)

Algorithm 5. KyberKEM.Decaps

Input: ciphertext $c \in \mathbb{B}^{32d_u k+d_v}$
Input: $sk \in \mathbb{B}^{768k+96}$
Output: shared key $K \in \mathbb{B}^{32}$
$sk' \leftarrow sk[0 : 384k]$
$pk' \leftarrow sk[384k : 768k + 32]$
$h \leftarrow sk[768k + 32 : 768k + 64]$
$z \leftarrow sk[768k + 64 : 768k + 96]$
$m' \leftarrow$ KyberPKE.Dec(sk', c)
$(K', r') \leftarrow G(m', h)$
$\bar{K} \leftarrow J(z||c, 32)$
$c' \leftarrow$ KyberPKE.Enc(pk', m', r')
if $c \neq c'$ **then**
  $K' \leftarrow \bar{K}$
end if
return K'

Algorithm 6. KyberPKE.KeyGen

Output: $pk' \in \mathbb{B}^{384k+32}$
Output: $sk' \in \mathbb{B}^{384k}$
$d \xleftarrow{\$} \mathbb{B}^{32}$
$(\rho, \delta) \leftarrow G(d)$
$\mathbf{A} \leftarrow \mathcal{U}(\rho)$
$(\mathbf{s}, \mathbf{e}) \leftarrow \mathcal{X}(\delta)$
$\mathbf{t} \leftarrow \mathbf{A} \circ \mathbf{s} + \mathbf{e}$
$pk' \leftarrow \text{Pack}(\mathbf{t}||\rho)$
$sk' \leftarrow \text{Pack}(\mathbf{s})$
return (pk', sk')

Algorithm 7. KyberPKE.Dec

Input: $sk' \in \mathbb{B}^{384k}$
Input: ciphertext $c \in \mathbb{B}^{32(d_u k+d_v)}$
Output: message $m \in \mathbb{B}^{32}$
$c_1 \leftarrow c[0 : 32d_u k]$
$c_2 \leftarrow c[32d_u k : 32(d_u k + dv)]$
$\mathbf{u}_l \leftarrow \text{Decompress}_{d_u}(\text{Unpack}(c_1))$
$v_l \leftarrow \text{Decompress}_{d_v}(\text{Unpack}(c_2))$
$\hat{\mathbf{s}} \leftarrow \text{Unpack}_{12}(sk')$
$mp \leftarrow v_l - \mathbf{s} \circ \mathbf{u}_l$
$m \leftarrow \text{Pack}_1(\text{Compress}_1(mp))$
return m

Algorithm 8. KyberPKE.Enc

Input: $pk' \in \mathbb{B}^{384k+32}$
Input: message $m \in \mathbb{B}^{32}$
Input: randomness $r \in \mathbb{B}^{32}$
Output: ciphertext $c \in \mathbb{B}^{32(d_u k+d_v)}$
$\mathbf{t} \leftarrow \text{Unpack}(pk'[0 : 384k])$
$\rho \leftarrow pk'[384k : 384k + 32]$
$\mathbf{A} \leftarrow \mathcal{U}(\rho)$
$\mathbf{r}, \mathbf{e}_1, e_2 \leftarrow \mathcal{X}(r)$
$\mathbf{u} = \mathbf{A} \circ \mathbf{r} + \mathbf{e}_1$
$\mu \leftarrow \text{Decompress}_1(\text{Unpack}_1(m))$
$v \leftarrow \mathbf{t} \circ \mathbf{r} + e_2 + \mu$
$c_1 \leftarrow \text{Pack}_{d_u}(\text{Compress}_{d_u}(\mathbf{u}))$
$c_2 \leftarrow \text{Pack}_{d_v}(\text{Compress}_{d_v}(v))$
return $c \leftarrow (c_1||c_2)$

B Masked Decoder

The original masked decoder presented in [5] is shown in Eq. 11. During our analysis, we identified a potential issue at the boundary condition $x = \lfloor \frac{q}{4} \rfloor$, which can cause an error in the decryption result. The authors have clarified this issue, and the corrected version of the function, which resolves the edge case, is provided in Eq. 1.

$$\text{Compress}_q^s(z) = z_{11} \oplus (\neg z_{11} \cdot z_{10} \cdot z_9 \cdot (z_8 \oplus (\neg z_8 \cdot z_7))) \tag{11}$$

References

1. Bar-El, H., Choukri, H., Naccache, D., Tunstall, M., Whelan, C.: The sorcerer's apprentice guide to fault attacks. Cryptology ePrint Archive, Report 2004/100 (2004). https://eprint.iacr.org/2004/100
2. Bettale, L., Montoya, S., Renault, G.: Safe-error analysis of post-quantum cryptography mechanisms. Cryptology ePrint Archive, Report 2021/1339 (2021). https://eprint.iacr.org/2021/1339
3. Biham, E., Shamir, A.: Differential fault analysis of secret key cryptosystems. In: Kaliski, B.S. (ed.) CRYPTO 1997. LNCS, vol. 1294, pp. 513–525. Springer, Heidelberg (1997). https://doi.org/10.1007/BFb0052259
4. Bos, J., et al.: CRYSTALS – Kyber: a CCA-secure module-lattice-based KEM. Cryptology ePrint Archive, Report 2017/634 (2017). https://eprint.iacr.org/2017/634
5. Bos, J.W., Gourjon, M., Renes, J., Schneider, T., van Vredendaal, C.: Masking kyber: first- and higher-order implementations. IACR TCHES **2021**(4), 173–214 (2021). https://doi.org/10.46586/tches.v2021.i4.173-214, https://tches.iacr.org/index.php/TCHES/article/view/9064
6. Coron, J.S., Gérard, F., Montoya, S., Zeitoun, R.: High-order table-based conversion algorithms and masking lattice-based encryption. IACR TCHES **2022**(2), 1–40 (2022). https://doi.org/10.46586/tches.v2022.i2.1-40
7. Dachman-Soled, D., Ducas, L., Gong, H., Rossi, M.: LWE with side information: attacks and concrete security estimation. In: Micciancio, D., Ristenpart, T. (eds.) CRYPTO 2020. LNCS, vol. 12171, pp. 329–358. Springer, Cham (2020). https://doi.org/10.1007/978-3-030-56880-1_12
8. Delvaux, J.: Roulette: A diverse family of feasible fault attacks on masked Kyber. IACR TCHES **2022**(4), 637–660 (2022). https://doi.org/10.46586/tches.v2022.i4.637-660
9. Dobraunig, C., Eichlseder, M., Korak, T., Mangard, S., Mendel, F., Primas, R.: SIFA: exploiting ineffective fault inductions on symmetric cryptography. IACR TCHES **2018**(3), 547–572 (2018).https://doi.org/10.13154/tches.v2018.i3.547-572, https://tches.iacr.org/index.php/TCHES/article/view/7286
10. Fahr, M., ey al.: When frodo flips: end-to-end key recovery on FrodoKEM via rowhammer. In: Yin, H., Stavrou, A., Cremers, C., Shi, E. (eds.) ACM CCS 2022, pp. 979–993. ACM Press (2022).https://doi.org/10.1145/3548606.3560673
11. Fujisaki, E., Okamoto, T.: Secure integration of asymmetric and symmetric encryption schemes. In: Wiener, M. (ed.) CRYPTO 1999. LNCS, vol. 1666, pp. 537–554. Springer, Heidelberg (1999). https://doi.org/10.1007/3-540-48405-1_34

12. Hermelink, J., Mårtensson, E., Samardjiska, S., Pessl, P., Rodosek, G.D.: Belief propagation meets lattice reduction: security estimates for error-tolerant key recovery from decryption errors. IACR TCHES **2023**(4), 287–317 (2023).https://doi.org/10.46586/tches.v2023.i4.287-317
13. Hermelink, J., Pessl, P., Pöppelmann, T.: Fault-enabled chosen-ciphertext attacks on Kyber. In: Adhikari, A., Küsters, R., Preneel, B. (eds.) INDOCRYPT 2021. LNCS, vol. 13143, pp. 311–334. Springer, Cham (2021). https://doi.org/10.1007/978-3-030-92518-5_15
14. Kundu, S., Chowdhury, S., Saha, S., Karmakar, A., Mukhopadhyay, D., Verbauwhede, I.: Carry your fault: a fault propagation attack on side-channel protected LWE-based KEM. IACR TCHES **2024**(2), 844–869 (2024).https://doi.org/10.46586/tches.v2024.i2.844-869
15. Mishra, N., Mukhopadhyay, D.: Probabilistic algorithms with applications to countering fault attacks on lattice based post-quantum cryptography. Cryptology ePrint Archive, Paper 2024/551 (2024), https://eprint.iacr.org/2024/551, https://eprint.iacr.org/2024/551
16. Mondal, P., Kundu, S., Bhattacharya, S., Karmakar, A., Verbauwhede, I.: A practical key-recovery attack on LWE-based key-encapsulation mechanism schemes using rowhammer. In: Pöpper, C., Batina, L. (eds.) ACNS 24International Conference on Applied Cryptography and Network Security, Part III. LNCS, vol. 14585, pp. 271–300. Springer, Cham (2024). https://doi.org/10.1007/978-3-031-54776-8_11
17. Oder, T., Schneider, T., Pöppelmann, T., Güneysu, T.: Practical CCA2-secure masked Ring-LWE implementations. IACR TCHES **2018**(1), 142–174 (2018). https://doi.org/10.13154/tches.v2018.i1.142-174, https://tches.iacr.org/index.php/TCHES/article/view/836
18. O'Flynn, C., Chen, Z.D.: ChipWhisperer: an open-source platform for hardware embedded security research. In: Prouff, E. (ed.) COSADE 2014. LNCS, vol. 8622, pp. 243–260. Springer, Cham (2014). https://doi.org/10.1007/978-3-319-10175-0_17
19. Pessl, P., Prokop, L.: Fault attacks on CCA-secure lattice KEMs. IACR TCHES **2021**(2), 37–60 (2021).https://doi.org/10.46586/tches.v2021.i2.37-60, https://tches.iacr.org/index.php/TCHES/article/view/8787
20. Ravi, P., Chattopadhyay, A., Baksi, A.: Side-channel and fault-injection attacks over lattice-based post-quantum schemes (Kyber, Dilithium): survey and new results. Cryptology ePrint Archive, Report 2022/737 (2022). https://eprint.iacr.org/2022/737
21. Ravi, P., Roy, D.B., Bhasin, S., Chattopadhyay, A., Mukhopadhyay, D.: Number "Not Used" Once - practical fault attack on *pqm4* Implementations of nist candidates. In: Polian, I., Stöttinger, M. (eds.) COSADE 2019. LNCS, vol. 11421, pp. 232–250. Springer, Cham (2019). https://doi.org/10.1007/978-3-030-16350-1_13
22. Schwabe, P., et al.: CRYSTALS-KYBER. Tech. rep., National Institute of Standards and Technology (2022). https://csrc.nist.gov/Projects/post-quantum-cryptography/selected-algorithms-2022
23. Xagawa, K., Ito, A., Ueno, R., Takahashi, J., Homma, N.: Fault-injection attacks against NIST's post-quantum cryptography round 3 KEM candidates. In: Tibouchi, M., Wang, H. (eds.) ASIACRYPT 2021. LNCS, vol. 13091, pp. 33–61. Springer, Cham (2021). https://doi.org/10.1007/978-3-030-92075-3_2
24. Yen, S.M., Joye, M.: Checking before output may not be enough against fault-based cryptanalysis. IEEE Trans. Comput. **49**(9), 967–970 (2000).https://doi.org/10.1109/12.869328

Author Index

C. Boura et al. (Eds.): SAC 2025, LNCS 16207, pp. 805–806, 2026.
https://doi.org/10.1007/978-3-032-10536-3

GPSR Compliance

The European Union's (EU) General Product Safety Regulation (GPSR) is a set of rules that requires consumer products to be safe and our obligations to ensure this.

If you have any concerns about our products, you can contact us on ProductSafety@springernature.com

In case Publisher is established outside the EU, the EU authorized representative is:

Springer Nature Customer Service Center GmbH
Europaplatz 3
69115 Heidelberg, Germany

Batch number: 10704691

Printed by Printforce, the Netherlands